Alan Greenwood and his wife, Cleo, are the publishers of *Vintage Guitar* magazine, which they launched in 1986. *Vintage Guitar* is the largest monthly publication for guitar collectors, enthusiasts, and dealers. They also publish *Vintage Guitar*® Online at www.vintageguitar.com, and the fine line of Vintage Guitar Books. His collection includes several vintage instruments from the '50s, '60s and '70s, as well as newer production and custom-made guitars and amps. He lives in Bismarck, North Dakota.

Gil Hembree began collecting guitars in 1966 as a college student working at Kitt's Music on G Street in Washington, DC. He graduated from American University in '69 with a BSBA and two days after graduation he was hired by the General Motors Corporation. He held several assignments with GM including Financial Administrator of the Wichita Falls, Texas, plant (where he obtained his MBA from Midwestern State University), and Supervisor of Corporate Audit in Detroit. In January of 2000, after a 30-year career, he retired from GM and was contracted by Vintage Guitar as a market analyst for the Vintage Guitar Price Guide. Hembree maintains a diverse collection of guitars and amps including the 1955 Gibson Les Paul PAF Humbucker Test Guitar, a workhorse '48 Martin D-28, and an all-original near mint '59 Fender tweed Bandmaster. He lives with his wife, Jane, in a suburb near Flint, Michigan.

The Official Vintage Guitar® Magazine Price Guide
By Alan Greenwood and Gil Hembree

Vintage Guitar Books
An imprint of Vintage Guitar Inc., PO Box 7301, Bismarck, ND 58507, (701) 255-1197, Fax (701) 255-0250, publishers of *Vintage Guitar*® magazine and Vintage Guitar® Online at www.vintageguitar.com. Vintage Guitar is a registered trademark of Vintage Guitar, Inc.

ISBN 1-884883-14-1

Cover Photos: Michael Tamborrino/VG Archive.
Back Photos: '52 Fender P-Bass, Michael Tamborrino/VG Archive. '73 Univox Hi Flyer, Michael Wright. Stan Werbin: Steve Szilagyi/Elderly Instruments. Dave Amato: Rick Gould. Rick Nielsen: Mike Graham. Bob Page: Gil Hembree. Dave Rogers: Dave's Guitar Shop.

Cover Design: Doug Yellow Bird/Vintage Guitar, Inc.

Printed in the United States of America

www.texasguitarshows.com

www.solidbodyguitar.com
SOLIDBODYGUITAR.COM
THE BEST
HIGH-END
VINTAGE GUITARS
AND AMPS
2566 Hwy. 10
Mounds View, MN
55112
BUY-SELL-TRADE • 763-783-0080

mandolin bros. Ltd. TM
World's most complete & comfortable showroom of 1,000 fine new and vintage fretted Instruments.
REPAIR SHOP ON PREMISES
FENDER CUSTOM SHOP
GIBSON SUPER DEALER
Dream Fulfillment Center
629 Forest Ave., Staten Island, NY 10310
Tel: (718) 981-8585 ~ Fax: (718) 816-4416
mandolin@mandoweb.com
www.mandoweb.com

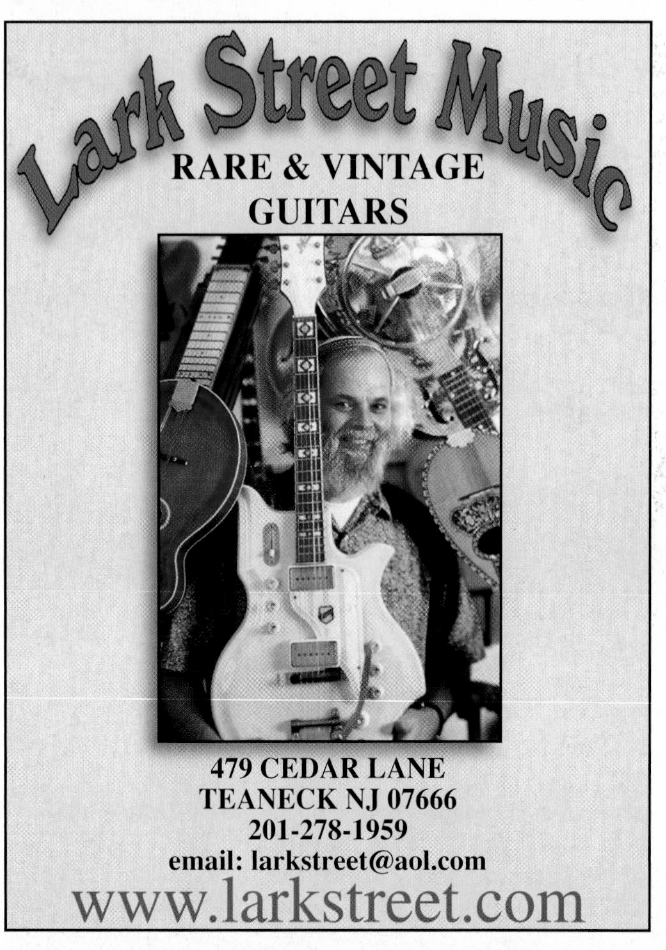
Lark Street Music
RARE & VINTAGE
GUITARS
479 CEDAR LANE
TEANECK NJ 07666
201-278-1959
email: larkstreet@aol.com
www.larkstreet.com

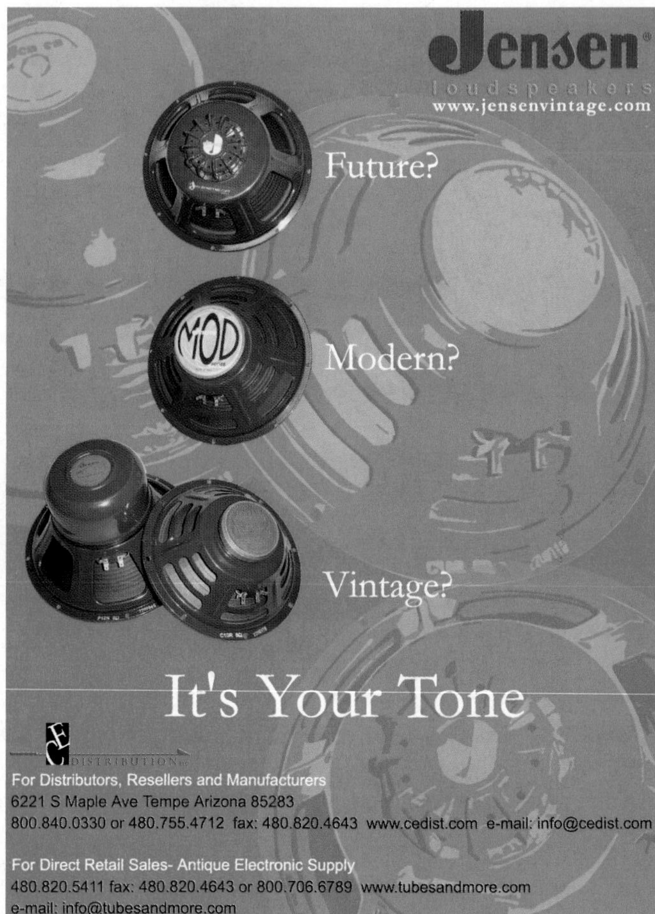
Jensen
loudspeakers
www.jensenvintage.com
Future?
Modern?
Vintage?
It's Your Tone
CE DISTRIBUTION
For Distributors, Resellers and Manufacturers
6221 S Maple Ave Tempe Arizona 85283
800.840.0330 or 480.755.4712 fax: 480.820.4643 www.cedist.com e-mail: info@cedist.com
For Direct Retail Sales- Antique Electronic Supply
480.820.5411 fax: 480.820.4643 or 800.706.6789 www.tubesandmore.com
e-mail: info@tubesandmore.com

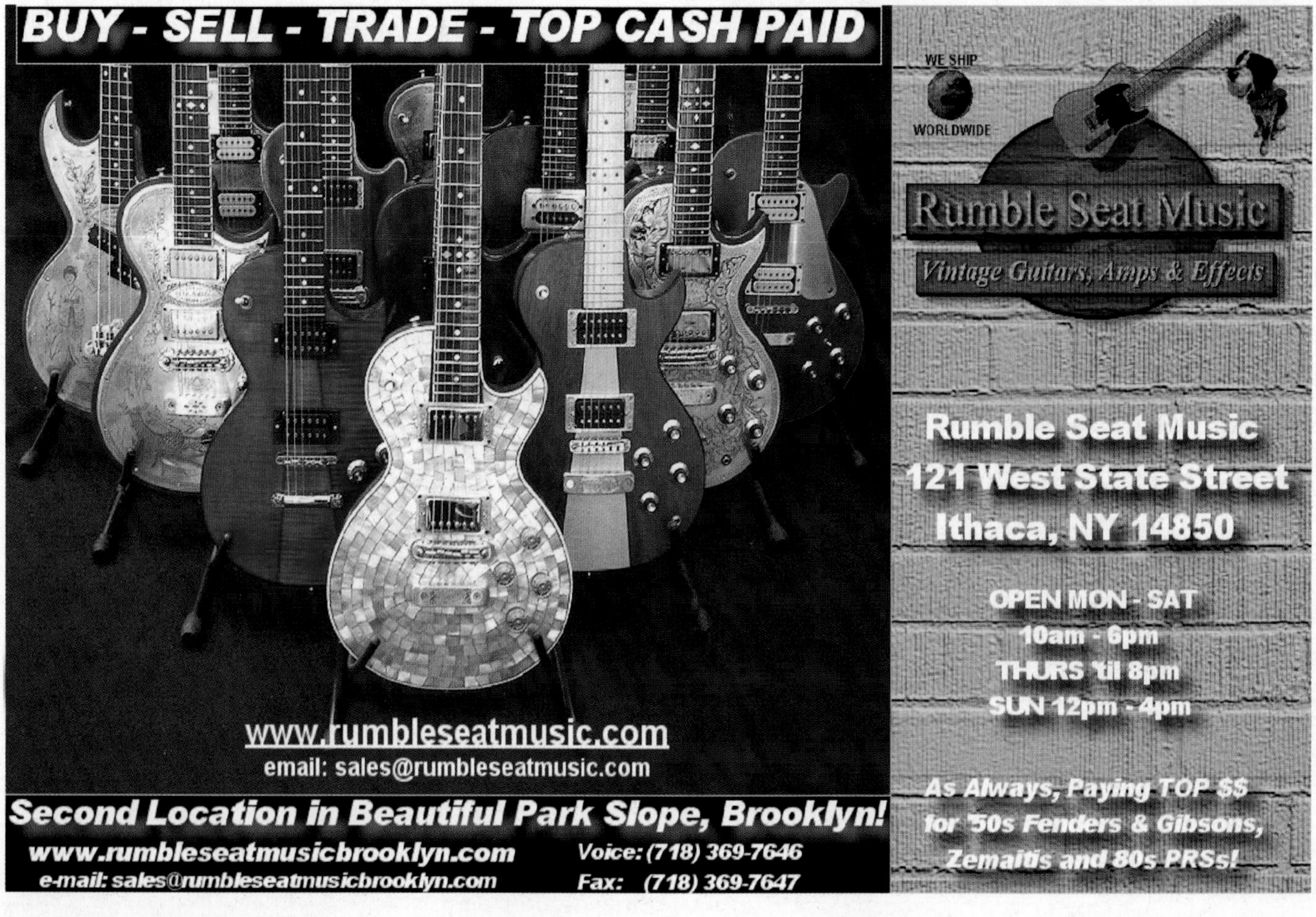

Table of Contents

Mid-'60s Vox Guitar-Organ and Vox Phantom XII with a Sears Silvertone Solid State 100 amplifier.

Introduction

Welcome Back

Many *Vintage Guitar Price Guide* users are repeat customers, so this year we say, "Welcome back." It is no secret that prices change every year, so we are committed to updating the *Price Guide* annually.

The first thing our customers do is find their favorite guitar and see how much it is worth. Perfect! That's what our book is all about. The next thing they do is check several other favorite models, comparing the current value to last year's. It's all great fun, and it's a big part of the market.

For those of you who are new to the Price Guide, we welcome you and we'd like to give you a little background information.

The *Price Guide* was originally created by Alan Greenwood in August of 1988. Greenwood founded *Vintage Guitar* magazine in '86 and he knew people wanted to know what their guitars

Using The Vintage Guitar Price Guide

The Official Vintage Guitar Price Guide deals with values for excellent condition, all-original instruments. Excellent condition suggests a beautifully cared for instrument that is pleasingly clean and contains no significant wear, blemishes, or damage.

The table of contents shows the major instrument sections used for this *Guide.* Each is organized in alphabetical order by brand name, then by model name. In a few instances we have separate sections for a company's most popular model names, especially when there has been a large variety of similar instruments issued and reissued. This has been done for Fender's Stratocasters, Telecasters, Precision and Jazz basses, and Gibson's Les Pauls, for example. The upper outside corner of each page of the *Guide* sports a dictionary-type heading showing the models or brands on that page. This is the quickest way to find your way around each section. The index at the back of the book shows the pages for each type of instrument by brand and is probably the best place to start when looking for a specific model or brand.

We have excellent brand and model historical information. Any changes within a model that affect values are also listed.

Much more information on many of the brands covered in this *Price Guide* is available in the "Brand Pages" section of the *Vintage Guitar* magazine website at www.vintageguitar.com.

If you'd like to be notified when the next *Vintage Guitar Price Guide* is available, send an email with your name, address and email address to vguitar@vguitar.com.

New Retail Pricing Information

We've added short listings for hundreds of individual luthiers and smaller shops. It is difficult to develop values on used instruments produced by these builders because much of their output is custom work, production is low, and/or they haven't been producing for long. In order to give you a better idea about the instruments they build, we have come up with five grades of retail values for new instruments. These grades convey only what prices the new builder charges, they are not indictitive of the quality of construction. We have applied this scale to all builders and manufacturers of new instruments.

The five retail price grades are:
Budget - up to $250 retail price,
Intermediate - $250 to $1,000,
Professional - $1,001 to $3,000,
Premium - $3,001 to $10,000,
Presentation - over $10,000.

We have also added the terms "production" and "custom" to indicate the work these builders do. Production means the company only offers specific models. Custom means they only do custom orders, and production/custom indicates they do both.

An example of one of these new listings would be:

Greenwood Guitars
1977-present. Luthier Alan Greenwood builds his intermediate grade, custom, solidbody guitars in Bismarck, North Dakota. He also builds mandolins.

This short bio tells you who the builder is, the types of instruments he builds, where he builds them, how long he has been operating under that brand, that he does only custom work, and that he asks between $1,000 and $3,000 for his guitars (intermediate grade).

Again, we have applied the retail price grades and production and/or custom labels to most new instrument manufacturers.

were worth, but there seemed to be no easy way to find out. Greenwood began surveying vintage guitar dealers and publishing the survey results each month in *Vintage Guitar*, and the results were first published in book form in '91. *Vintage Guitar* continues to offer guidance pricing each month in the magazine and in the annual *Vintage Guitar Price Guide.* Guitar dealers were happy to get the *VG Price Guide*, too, and *VG*'s early *Price Guide* motto described it as "The one the dealers use."

Volume 1 was very successful and people asked, "When will you publish another one?" So Greenwood set out to establish an 18-month cycle for updating the *Price Guide.* By late '99 the market was moving rapidly and a case could be made for publishing the *Guide* once a year.

Compiling *Price Guide* info grew to be more than person could handle, especially on an annual basis, so former General Motors financial administrator Gil Hembree was recruited to do the majority of the pricing research. Hembree still does most of the price research, including attending a half-dozen of the largest guitar shows each year. Greenwood does most of the builder and guitar model research, and is responsible for this year's added coverage of new builders.

Both authors are degreed accountants with extensive experience so their skills are perfect for the *Guide* in that they love guitars and are number crunchers.

Low to High Price Range

When surveying the market, Greenwood found that prices fell into a range of values. He also found that most guitars were generally rated as either very good, excellent, or near mint. He knew that for consistency any guitar in the survey must be all original and it's the "excellent condition" guitar that most people talk about. In 1991, Greenwood's vision was to provide a price guide that would provide a low-to-high price range for an all-original instrument in excellent condition. "Excellent condition" describes a well-cared-for instrument that is pleasingly clean and shows no significant wear, blemishes, or damage. An all-original instrument is one that has all the factory original parts, that is, the parts that came with the guitar when it left the builder's facility. The exception would be new strings for instruments and new tubes for amps.

An original instrument must have the original finish. A refinished guitar is generally worth about 50% or less of the values shown in the *Guide.* A repaired guitar, technically, is not all original. Repairs can make a guitar generally worth 5% to 50% less than the values shown. Any neck repairs or significant body repairs are considered serious repairs, and drop a guitar's value by up to 50%. A professional refret or very minor nearly-invisible body repair will reduce a guitars value by only 5%. But, the *Price Guide* is for crack-free, unrepaired instruments. Also, original finishes can fade, but the *Price Guide* is for unfaded examples. Slight fade only reduces the value by 5%, but heavily faded examples can reduce the value by as much as 25% to 50%.

Guidance Pricing

The *Price Guide* provides guidance pricing. Most excellent

Guitar Dealer Participants

The information refined on these pages comes from several sources, including the input of many knowledgeable guitar dealers. Without the help of these individuals, it would be very hard for us to provide the information here and in each issue of *Vintage Guitar* magazine. We deeply appreciate the time and effort they provide.

Andy Eder
Andy's Guitars

Tim Page & Bob Page
Buffalo Brothers

Norm Moren
Cold Springs Electrical Works

Stan Werbin
Elderly Instruments

Dave Hussong
Fretware Guitars

Charlie Dellavalle
Gothic City Guitars

Dave Belzer & Drew Berlin
Guitar Center

Dave Hinson
Killer Vintage

Timm Kummer
Kummer's Vintage Instruments

Buzzy Levine
Lark Street Music

Larry Wexer
Laurence Wexer, Ltd.

Stan Jay
Mandolin Brothers

Bob November
McKenzie River Music

Mike Reeder
Mike's Music

John Beeson
The Music Shoppe

Jay Jacus
New Jersey Guitar & Bass Center

Eliot Michael
Rumble Seat Music

Richard Friedman
Sam Ash & Manny's Music

David Davidson
Sam Ash Music - Carle Place

Eric Schoenberg
Schoenberg Guitars

Bruce Barnes & Kenny Rardin
Solidbodyguitar.com

Gil Southworth
Southworth Guitars

Scott Freilich
Top Shelf Music

John DeSilva
Toys From The Attic

Nate Westgor
Willie's American Guitars

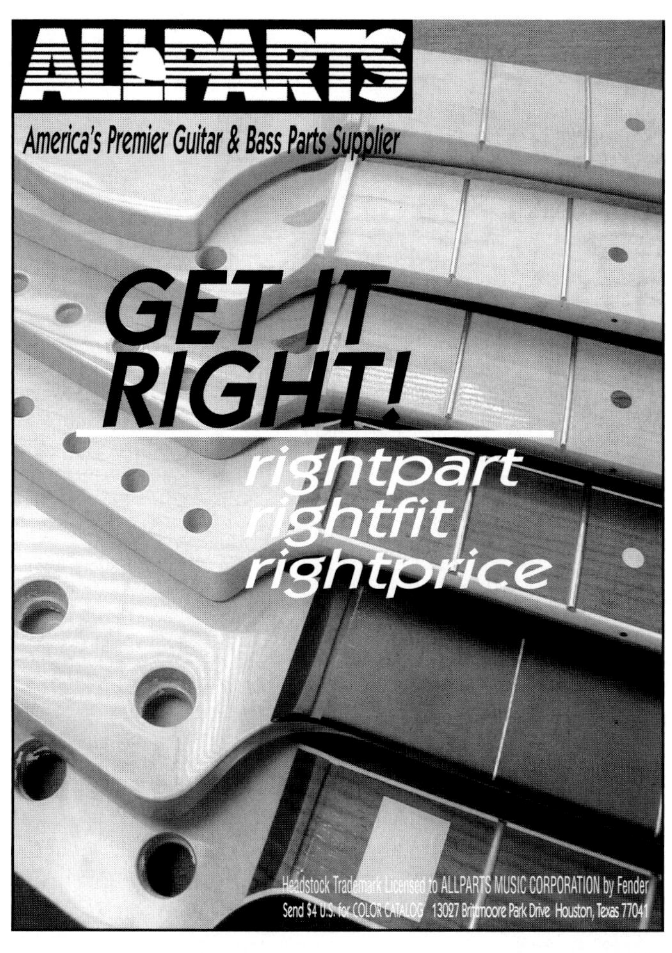
ALLPARTS
America's Premier Guitar & Bass Parts Supplier
GET IT RIGHT!
rightpart
rightfit
rightprice
Headstock Trademark Licensed to ALLPARTS MUSIC CORPORATION by Fender
Send $4 U.S. for COLOR CATALOG 13027 Brittmoore Park Drive Houston, Texas 77041

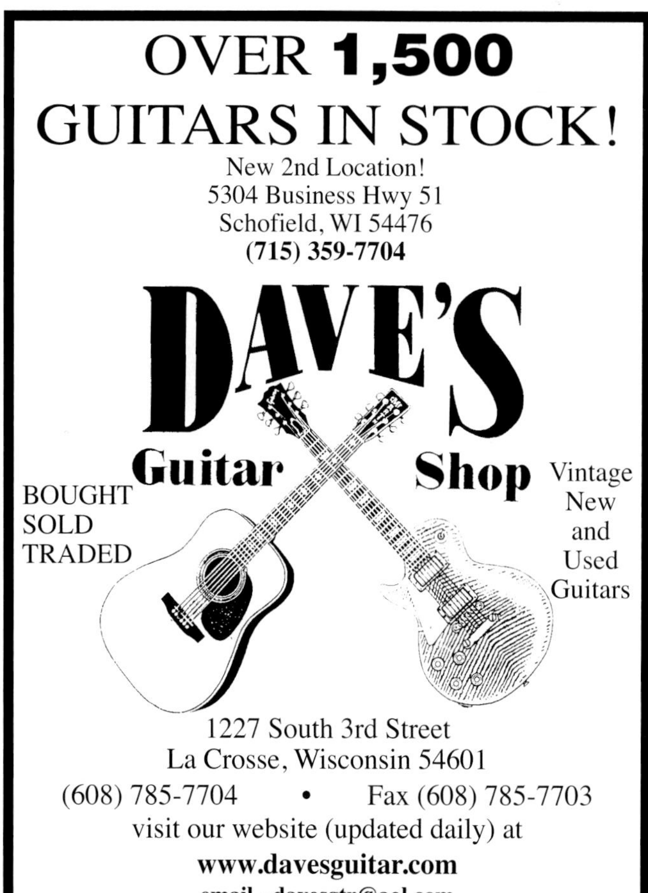
OVER 1,500
GUITARS IN STOCK!
New 2nd Location!
5304 Business Hwy 51
Schofield, WI 54476
(715) 359-7704
DAVE'S
Guitar Shop
BOUGHT
SOLD
TRADED
Vintage
New
and
Used
Guitars
1227 South 3rd Street
La Crosse, Wisconsin 54601
(608) 785-7704 • Fax (608) 785-7703
visit our website (updated daily) at
www.davesguitar.com
email - davesgtr@aol.com

Atlanta Vintage
Guitars

original instruments will fall within the price ranges found in this book, but every vintage guitar is different. No two will have the same amount of wear or color fade. Instruments that are less than excellent are considered to be in fair, good, or very good condition. That group of instruments is worth less than the values shown in this book. Conversely, an instrument may be nearly unplayed, which generally suggests near-mint to mint condition. Those mint instruments are worth more than the values listed here.

Gil Hembree (left) and Alan Greenwood at Vintage Guitar headquarters in Bismarck, ND with some of **VG's** ***guitar collection.***

Regarding excellent condition, some think the vintage guitar industry can be prone to "overgrading," the term used when a seller describes a guitar as being in better condition than it actually is. Each guitar should be evaluated on a case-by-case basis, and it is suggested that you know your seller well and that you deal with an established, well-known vintage guitar dealer.

For correctly graded instruments in excellent all-original condition, it is still possible for guitar dealers to sell nearly identical instruments for different prices. In New York City, the archtop market might be stronger than it is in California, and conversely something like the G&L market may be stronger in Leo Fender's home state versus the Big Apple. The stronger a market is, the more likely prices will be somewhat higher. Conversely, a weak market will have lower prices because there are fewer customers. The *Price Guide* works those regional differences into the low-to-high price ranges to represent the overall national (and international) market.

Information Sources

Where do we get our information? Initially, *Price Guide* founder Alan Greenwood relied heavily on vintage guitar dealer surveys. We still use dealer surveys and the survey group participants are particularly valuable because they deal with vintage instruments every day. Many of them deal with rare and highly soughtafter instruments, and without their help it would be difficult to establish the price ranges for those ultra-expensive pieces. Other survey participants deal with early-made G&L's, Deans, Paul Reed Smiths, Kramers, Jacksons, Charvels, etc., and early info on builders is not always easy to obtain.

Technology has come a long way since the first *Guide* was published in '91 and the authors now have a variety of sources. We get information from everywhere, including guitar shows and the Internet. And we do this full-time. It's our day job. We've done the work so you won't have to.

Precedent Value

The *Vintage Guitar Price Guide* is a precedent value guide. That means the values shown represent the value of guitars that have been recently sold. Precedent value suggests that the next guitar to be sold will be sold at a price equal to the most recently sold similar guitar (same model type, color, and condition). Buyers and sellers generally use prior selling prices - precedent value - when rationalizing a selling price. Precedent value develops over time (refer to Chart 1 which shows the smooth year-to-year changes in the precedent value of 27 vintage guitars). Precedent value is not strictly based upon the last guitar sold; rather it is based upon the last group of similar guitars sold with consistent pricing. Precedent value is not unlike valuation methods used in real estate. In real estate, a house is often listed for a value that is equal to the value of three equivalent houses that have recently sold.

In the case of extremely rare instruments, the *VG Price Guide* Dealer Survey team is particularly helpful. The team is asked to use all of its experience and knowledge to suggest the going rate for the rare instrument being surveyed. The thing about rare instruments is that the rumor mill acts fast within the vintage dealer network, and many know when a rare instrument has been sold.

The End User Price

The term "end user" appears more frequently than it did 10 years ago. In the vintage guitar industry "the end user" is the final purchaser. A typical end user is probably a collector or dedicated player.

The term is more popular now because it helps clarify pricing information. For example, someone might say, "The end user price for a 1971 Gibson Les Paul Deluxe goldtop is $1,900." The term helps avoid the confusion between a wholesale price and its retail price. The end user price is retail.

The term "wholesale price" is used less because owners selling guitars to dealers seem to have asking prices that are much closer to retail than wholesale. There's nothing wrong with that, because the vintage guitar market is based upon self-

interest. Sellers want to sell for as much as possible, and buyers want to pay the least amount possible.

Historically there has been a lot of confusion between the wholesale price a dealer wants to pay a seller, and the subsequent retail price that same dealer wants to garner from an end user. But in today's market, the 35% markup from vintage wholesale to vintage retail is almost gone.

In the past, some would say, "What is a vintage guitar really worth? Is it wholesale or retail?" The answer is that a guitar's value is based upon the end user's purchase price, which is the same as retail.

Dealer-to-dealer selling has always been something that creates confusion. Dealer-to-dealer selling, on a professional level, is an attempt to ultimately put a vintage guitar into the hands of an end user. In a dealer-to-dealer transaction, the selling dealer does not have an end-user customer, while the buying dealer thinks he does.

The selling prices shown in the *2004 Vintage Guitar Price Guide* are end-user prices. They reflect the fair price range that an end user should generally expect to pay. Remember that the *Price Guide* ranges are for instruments in all-original excellent condition. Instruments in very good condition will be worth less, and pieces that are near mint will be worth more. Also remember that there are regional differences, which may mean an end-user price in one part of the country may be different than the end-user price in another part of the country.

Conservative Pricing

Our methods assure that the *Price Guide* is conservative. We guard against "winner's curse," which suggests a buyer can so overvalue a collectible that he will win a bidding war, but he will then be "cursed" in the future because the overvalued guitar will eventually be sold at a significant loss. Winner's curse can occur in any collectibles' market. It can happen to anyone, but often it is a wealthy buyer who is cursed, because he has few financial boundaries. It is easy for him to overvalue a collectible. When the wealthy buyer subsequently becomes disinterested in the collectible, the item's value may drop. The *Price Guide* protects against winner's curse by requiring a number of buyers and sellers to set consistent selling prices over a reasonable period of time, thereby assuring their market price is valid and not just a one time or two-time buy.

Upward-Bias Valuation

Market sophistication and specialization tend to create an upward bias in valuation. *VG* has noted this trend for several years. We take upward bias into consideration when setting the price ranges on mid-level ($2,000 to $20,000) and high-end (over $20,000) vintage pieces. Market specialists tend to set market prices, and that is how it should be. The market specialist knows more about his segment. 1930s Martin D-45 specialists/collectors tend to have an upward pricing bias for D-45s versus '59 Gibson Les Paul Standards. Sophisticated buyers and sellers generally have an upward value bias that tends to establish the high end of a value range. These upward biases are not necessarily inaccurate. Historically, they have tended to be confirmed in the long-term market (a four-year period). Market specialization is not limited to pre-war Martins, maple-neck Stratocasters, 'Bursts, etc. More and more dealers are specializing in G&Ls, Deans, Paul Reed Smith, and other relatively new brands. As specialization continues, the value of those brands will probably increase (on an accumulative appreciation percentage basis) in line with the rest of the specialized market.

What Affects Value?

What affects value, and why do vintage guitar prices constantly go up? The common reply is supply and demand. There is a huge demand for excellent original vintage guitars, and there are not many around. Big demand, small supply! But there's more to it.

The value of a vintage guitar is not really based on supply and demand. It's based on *demand*. Demand is a function of a buyer's love and admiration of the vintage instrument. Love of the instrument is fundamental. The buyer must decide, "How much do I love this instrument; how much do I value this instrument?" Some philosopher said, "Love is irrational." So how *is* value rationalized? Rationalization begins with intrinsic value.

Basic Intrinsic Value

All guitars have a basic intrinsic value, which is the cost to build a near-duplicate model. For vintage instruments, it is nearly impossible to duplicate aged wood or aged pickups, but it is possible to build near copies. A well-made, detail-oriented reissue guitar establishes the intrinsic value of the vintage guitar being copied. But most vintage guitars have a value that is higher than their reissue equivalent. How, then, is value determined?

Beyond Basic Value

A simple explanation of value is, "A vintage guitar is worth whatever someone is willing to pay for it." But that really does not explain anything. To understand valuation you need to understand the history of the market and you have to get academic.

First, we'll look at the academic view. Valuation theory is a mix of the economic supply and demand theory and the sociologist's view of the social construction of demand. Someone once said that a new guitar still thinks it is a tree. It takes years for a soundboard of a new flat-top to loosen and "open up." It takes years for an electric guitar's neck to lose that "green feel" and get a played-in feel. Once a guitar ages and is broken in, it takes on the characteristic physical and tonal qualities of a vintage guitar.

Social Construction of Value

Since the 1970s, vintage guitar market bears and cynics have stated, "How can you justify these high selling prices?" When '59 Gibson Les Paul Standards sold for $1,500, then $2,500, then $10,000, etc., the same thing was heard; "How can this be? It is absurd!" Meanwhile from decade to decade, prices for the 1959

Mercury
Imperial
Slant 6V
Hammerhead
Rambler
Amped!
CARR
AMPLIFIERS
www.carramps.com 919.545.0747

Guitar
EMPORIUM
Since 1975

'Burst, and other vintage guitars, continued to rise.

As prices have risen, there has been a larger and larger gap between a guitar's intrinsic value and its current precedent value. This difference can be best explained using the sociologist's Social Construction of Value. Academic Dr. Thomas F. Brown, author of *Consumer Demand and the Social Construction of Industry,* breaks the social construction of value into two parts. The first is Symbolic Value, which is sensitive to cultural and social influences such as a guitar's "coolness" or "vibe." The second part is Rationalized Economic Value, which is a combination of precedent value and contingent value. A guitar's value is based upon its intrinsic value, then bolstered by symbolic value and rationalized economic value.

The more expensive a vintage guitar is, the more heavily influenced it is by symbolic value and rationalized economic value. On the other hand, cheap vintage guitars like an imported 1960s Zim-Gar actually have a negative symbolic value. A Zim-Gar's intrinsic value is equal to or higher than its actual vintage guitar market value, because a Zim-Gar has little or no symbolic or rationalized economic value.

Brown suggests that a guitar's value can be measured on four dimensions: 1. physical quality, 2. tonal quality, 3. symbolic value, and 4. rationalized economic value. Physical quality and tonal quality are basic - most people know the function and purpose of an old Les Paul, Stratocaster, or D-28. Symbolic value (a guitar's vibe or coolness), on the other hand, is more subjective, and it is sensitive to cultural and social influences.

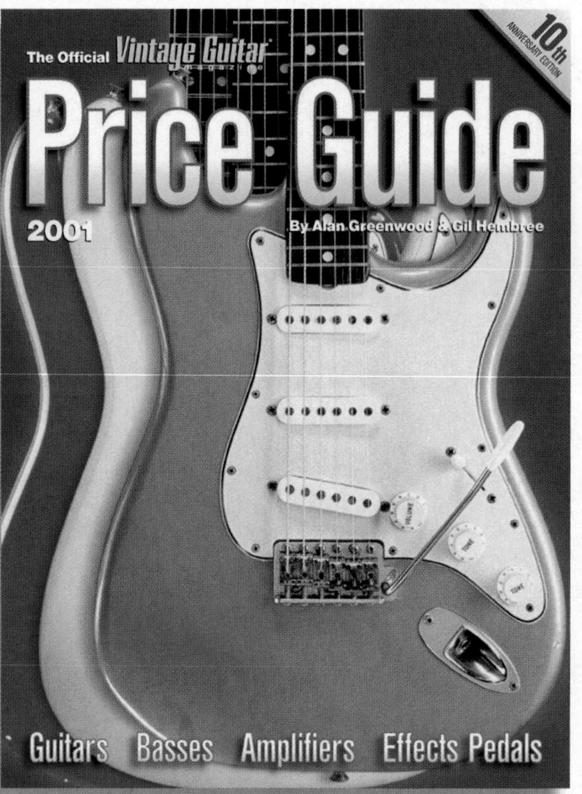

The 2001 Price Guide marked the début of the Greenwood-Hembree price guide team. Greenwood authored the Guide solo from 1991 – 2000.

The Buyer's View (Contingent Value)

Dr. Robert Schenk, author of *Economics: An Analysis of Unintended Consequences,* says, "The price of fine art, stamps, rare coins, and other collectibles seems in large part determined by what people expect others to be willing to pay. People are willing to spend $5,000 or more (often much more) for a collectible because, they are confident they can resell it at the same price or a price close to it."

This is called "contingent value." Today's savvy buyer purchases a vintage instrument contingent upon the fact that he expects that he can resell the instrument at a similar price. Contingent value is an important part of a buyer's economic rationalization. With the rising prices of vintage guitars, a prospective buyer can easily justify a purchase by saying, "I'll be able to sell it for more, but in the meantime I'll be able to enjoy owning and playing the guitar."

Contingent value is probably the most important facet of economic rationalization. Buyers say, "I can't lose." And it has been true, that over the long term (a four-year period), buyers of most vintage guitars have been able to sell their guitars for more (often much more) than what they paid for them. But as you will see later, contingent value has had a compounding effect on vintage guitar pricing, because when an owner sells his vintage guitar, he expects to get an amount equal to or more than he paid for it. When that seller sells to a guitar dealer (the most likely buyer), then the guitar dealer will have to mark up the guitar to cover expenses, and the price of the vintage guitar goes up.

Buyer's Preference

"Buyer's preference" is another term used by Dr. Schenk to more clearly define the vintage guitar market. In a specialty market, buyers demonstrate a preference towards certain qualities. The best example of this would be a highly-figured-top sunburst 1959 Gibson Les Paul Standard compared to a plaintop sunburst Les Paul Standard from the same year. An otherwise equal highly-flamed example can fetch much more than a guitar with a plain top. This variance is based upon buyer's preference.

Buyer's preference is not static. In the 'Burst (1958-1960 Gibson Les Paul Standard with sunburst finish) market of the early to mid '70s, playability and sunburst color were the key issues, with the vibe of the guitar, neck size, weight, and how it played more important than condition or originality. In the 2004 market, the high-end buyer stresses originality and figured maple tops (faded or unfaded). Even the slightest alteration to originality can mean tens of thousands of dollars.

Rule Of Thumb Pricing

Vintage retailers generally base their selling price on precedent value. The *Price Guide* is very helpful in this regard, because there are just too many guitars out there to keep tabs on, so a selling dealer will often check the *Price Guide* to confirm the current precedent value range. But if precedent values were always used, prices would never rise. Vintage guitar prices do rise.

Prices rise because sellers set prices based upon their rule-of-thumb pricing policy. Rule-of-thumb pricing policy takes

into consideration seller's profit expectation and overhead, and the guitar's precedent value, attributes, the purchase cost, and expected turnover rate (is it a hot seller, or is it a sitter?). The guitar will typically be valued near the price of the last similar guitar sold (its precedent value) if that value is justified by all of the rule-of-thumb factors.

The Guitar Dealer's View

The vintage dealer's implementation of rule-of-thumb pricing is a critical part of market mechanics. This is the supply side of the equation. There is a finite quantity of vintage guitars. But each year the number of people wanting vintage guitars seems to increase, and that puts pressure on the supply side. Dealers may have a difficult time obtaining salable inventory, and often have to pay more to obtain a nice guitar. Part of this goes back to the reverse effect of contingent value. For years, people have been buying vintage guitars contingent on the fact that they could sell them for an amount equal to what they paid. This has a compounding effect on vintage guitar pricing.

A vintage dealer's market function is distribution; buying and selling. In the mid 1960s, the early guitar dealers (mostly working part-time) would buy an old guitar in one part of town and sell it in another part of town. Circa 1970 some of these part-time dealers decided to become career vintage guitar dealers, and permanent brick and mortar vintage guitar stores were established. These dealers moved from a local market, to a regional market, to a national market, and finally to the international market. The main service the dealers provided was distribution. They would spend their time finding valuable guitars and offering their stock to customers who wanted them. This was an extremely valuable service because most of their customers did not have the expertise or, more importantly, the time to spend looking for their guitar of choice.

Early Market History

The closest thing to a price guide in the 1970s was dealer stock lists. Early participants would obtain dealer stock lists to see what the dealers were charging. This was probably the closest thing to consistent pricing.

By the late '70s, some dealers were so impressed with rising prices that they declared old guitars a good investment. So the term "investment" began to surface in the late '70s. In July of 1978, the first public guitar show was held in Dallas. But even then, attending dealers did not know what to charge, and really did not trust one another. Dealers at that show were primarily looking for better-playing guitars; that was the motivation, and it was more of a swap meet between dealers than anything else. For example, a Gretsch collector might get rid of a 1950s Strat so he could obtain the Gretsch of his dreams.

The early-1980s recession caused despair in the vintage market, and the future was somewhat uncertain. The babyboomers then re-entered the market. Babyboomers fueled the initial interest in vintage guitars, but faded in the late '70s and early '80s. They returned in the mid '80s, creating a vintage guitar bull market that has continued to this day.

The Current Market

We have prepared two charts to show some of what is going on in the vintage guitar market in 2004.

Chart 1 displays the pricing history of a typical vintage guitar. The chart shows that the value of the typical vintage guitar has been rising. Precedent values do rise over time, because of such things as seller's rule of thumb pricing policy. Chart 1 is called the Guitar Collector's Index, because it is an index of 27 guitar values. This group of guitars and basses includes models made between 1950 and '65 by Gibson (McCarty-era electrics), Fender (pre-CBS electrics), and Martin (folk-era flat tops). Each guitar had a unit value of less than $10,000 in 1991, the year the index was created. A high-end limit of $10,000 was used because mid-level vintage guitar values (defined as $1,000 to $10,000 in 1991, or defined as $2,000 to $20,000 in 2004) appreciate differently than ultra-expensive high-end vintage guitars (those with values above $20,000). The collection includes the following 27 instruments: from Fender, a '52 Esquire, '62 Jazz Bass, '64 LPB Jaguar, '58 Jazzmaster, '52 P-Bass, '64 P-Bass, '56 Stratocaster, '60 Stratocaster, '53 Telecaster, '58 Telecaster, and a '61 Jazz Bass; from Gibson, a '52 Les Paul Model, '58 Les Paul Custom, '54 Les Paul Jr., '61 SG Standard, '59 Les Paul Jr., '64 Thunderbird II, '61 ES-355, and a '65 EB-3; and from Martin (all from the Folk era), a '59 D-18, '62 D-28, '59 D-28 E, '58 000-18, and a '50 D-28.

This chart shows a relative flat rate of appreciation from '96 to 2000, with the total accumulative increase being only about 5%. Compare that to the 38% increase in the index from 2002 to 2004. Of course that's the beauty of a line graph, you can easily measure relative rate of growth by looking at the slope of the line from one year to the next, and the slope of the line from 2002 to 2004 defies gravity.

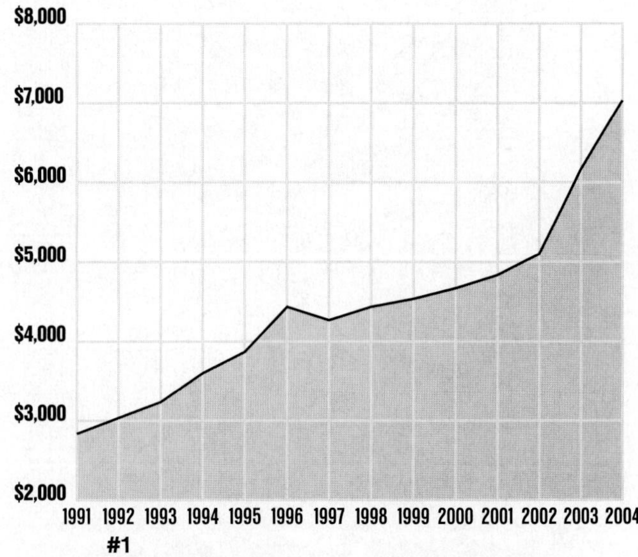

#1
Guitar Collectors Index Average Vintage Guitar Value

Chart 2 breaks out the three major vintage market brands – Fender, Gibson, and Martin. In dealer ads you often see Fenders, Gibsons, and Martins listed separately, and all other brands lumped together.

Gibson was the greatest guitar company of its era. Fender was a near-equal (but still smaller), because what it lacked in a variety of models it made up for with the era's finest amplifiers. Martin, while much smaller than Gibson and Fender, is a half-century older than Gibson and a century older than Fender.

The original idea behind Chart 2 was to determine if the vintage market phenomenon was broad or narrow. From 1991 to 2001 the answer seemed to be that the vintage market was a broad market, because Martin, Fender, and Gibson instruments were appreciating at a nearly equal rate. In 2003 and 2004, the group of Fenders in the index appreciated more rapidly than the Gibson group and the Gibson group appreciated more than the Martin group of instruments.

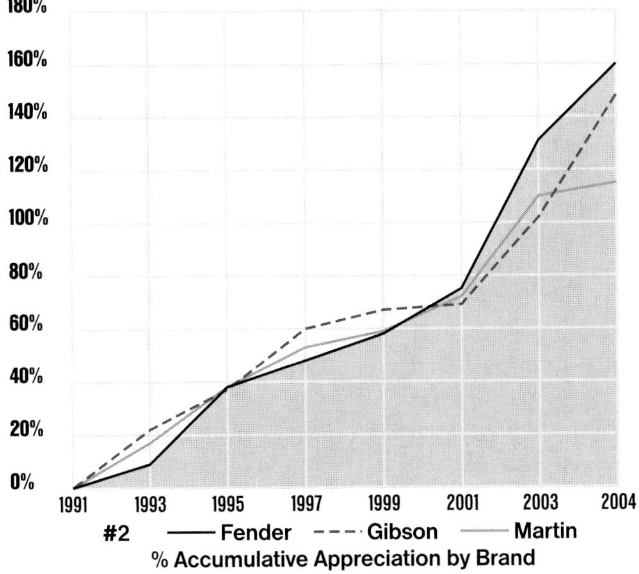

% Accumulative Appreciation by Brand

The chart suggests that in the early to mid 1990s, all classic vintage guitars were appreciating at a similar rate. Martins, Fenders, and Gibsons had near equal accumulative appreciation in 2001. From 2002-2004, that trend stopped, and the classic McCarty-era Gibsons and pre-CBS Fender electrics appreciated more than the 1950s folk-era Martins. This suggests a slightly narrower market where classic Fender and Gibson electrics out-performed the folk-era Martins. But this in not unexpected, and in fact it probably suggests a more advanced market where more highly soughtafter instruments appreciate more quickly.

Chart 3, entitled Martin Analysis, compares the Pre-War High-End 1930s Martin Flat-Top Index with the Post-War 1946-1950 Martin Flat-Top Index, the Martin Folk Index (1950s folk-era guitars), and the Fender Pre-CBS Electric Guitar Index. The chart shows the accumulative appreciation percent for each of these groups from 2001 to 2004. The hypothesis for this chart was that the High-End 1930s Martin Flat Top Index would out-perform (have a higher accumulative appreciation percentage increase) the Post-War Flat Top Index and the Folk-Era Index. And that is exactly what happened.

For the period, the Pre-War High-End Index appreciated by 41%, while the Fender Pre-CBS Electric Guitar Index appreciated 49%, and the Post-War 1946-1950 Index appreciated 36%, and the Folk-Era Index appreciated 25%.

This validates an assumption that the vintage market is a somewhat narrower market in 2004, meaning that the various market segments (flat-tops, electrics, archtops, etc.) are appreciating at different rates. In a broad market, the various indices would appreciate at about the same rate. But overall the market is still rather broad because most vintage guitars are appreciating in value.

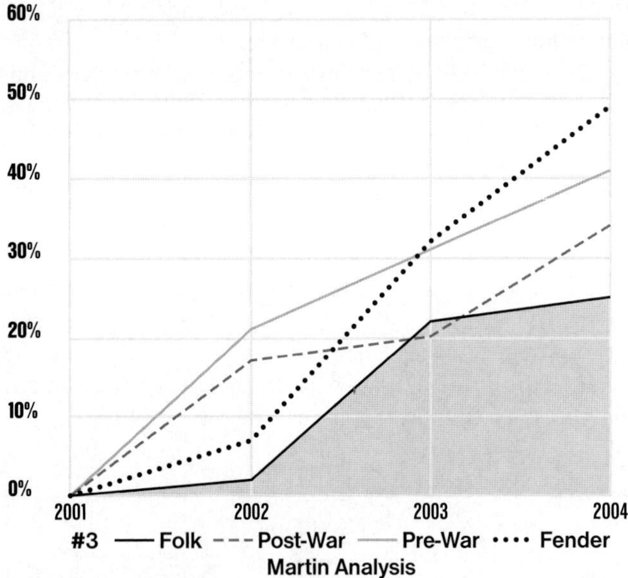

The Investor

The idea that vintage guitars are a good financial investment is nothing new. By the late '70s the vintage guitar market had established itself as more than just a fad. At least one well-known vintage guitar dealer began to promote vintage guitars as great investments. This dealer's initiative prompted a dialogue on the subject, and his intuition proved correct.

Academics would describe a typical guitar investor as being a "hedonistic investor," someone who considers the nonfinancial aspects of their investments as well as the anticipated return on investment. Put another way, this person loves his guitars, and loves their appreciating dollar value. Quite often, a hedonistic investor is in it for the long haul; they are typically not short-term investors.

Many investors in the financial stock market are strictly "economic investors," driven exclusively by financial goals. This person seeks the highest return, usually via straight equity investments for a relatively short time period.

The Dow Jones declined 16.8% in 2002, which was the worst percentage decline since 1977. The average vintage guitar increased 20% in value for 2002. The favorable variance between the loss in the Dow and gain in vintage guitars is 37%. It is important to remember that the selling expense for financial stocks is typically about 2%, whereas the selling expense for a vintage guitar can approximate 15% or more (consignment fees range from 10% to 20%). Even with a negative 13% selling expense variance, vintage guitars have a net favorable return of 24% (37% less 13%).

Vintage guitars have continued to appreciate during two completely different stock markets. They appreciated during America's longest bull market and during the recent perma-bear market. This fact suggests something powerful about vintage guitars as investments. To date, the guitar market has not demonstrated a tendency to be cyclical, with hills and valleys. Rather, it has shown a pattern of hills and plateaus, that is, a pattern of highly appreciating values followed by a period of slowly appreciating values, followed by a period of highly appreciating values, etc.

As noted earlier, the 2004 vintage guitar market continues to defy gravity, and many vintage guitars are continuing to increase in value. Each vintage guitar appreciates differently, and each vintage guitar is a separate investment. Of the 27 guitars in the Guitar Collectors Index (Chart 1), there were three that actually dropped in value. Based upon that limited study, 10% of the vintage guitar population probably dropped in value from 2003 to 2004.

Charts 1 and 2 are concerned with VG's Guitar Collector Index of 27 guitars. If you have a collection of guitars and you track those numbers, undoubtedly you'll notice that the value of your collection is increasing, but you may notice that the rate of appreciation may differ. It all depends upon the guitars that make up your collection.

Fairness In the Market

Most people think that rising vintage guitar values is a good thing. How do we know? Because most of the good

Builder Updates and Corrections

If you produce instruments for sale and would like to be included in the next *VG Price Guide*, send your infomation to al@vguitar.com. Include info on the types of instruments you build, model names and prices, yearly production, the year you started, where you are located and a short bio about yourself.

If any of you spot errors in the information about brands and models in this guide, or have information on a brand you'd like to see included, please contact us at the above email address. Your help is appreciated.

people we meet at guitar shows say that. When they find out their guitar has appreciated by 10%, they say, "Great!" Even though many of these people don't consider themselves true investors, they still think of their old guitar as a good investment. So, most people are happy to see values rise. But, there are some players who can't afford mid-level vintage instruments (valued at over $2,000), so rising values are a disappointment for them. In fact some say, "It's not fair that the world's great guitars are so expensive."

Vintage instruments have what academics call a "high elasticity of demand," which means the more income a guitar buyer has, the more likely he'll buy a pricey vintage guitar. This is an important factor in the market and it is yet another explanation of rising values. Rock stars, celebrities, professionals, industrialists, etc., with high incomes covet vintage guitars, and these people are willing to spend.

"People have different goals. One result of this difference is that people with identical incomes spend their money in different ways," says Robert Schenk. "Some enjoy frequent vacations, while others prefer to possess expensive items. Some people have goals which can be met only if they earn high incomes. Other people have goals which require less income but more leisure. If you look at a situation and decide that it's unfair because one person has too much and another has too little, you probably are making a judgment which compares goals."

Relics and Aged Instruments

In the 1990s, Gibson and Fender began to offer custom-built instruments that offered an aged, distressed, and played-in look. These well-built instruments were offered at prices that were often 10% to 20% of the price of the authentic vintage guitar counterpart. This idea was not at all a new one. Hundreds of years ago, violin manufacturers did the same thing when they offered aged and distressed violins that were made to look like the old masters. These Fender and Gibson instruments provide an important clue to valuation matters. The value of these new instruments reflect the Intrinsic Value of the vintage guitar that was being copied. A 2000 Fender '56 Relic Stratocaster established the intrinsic value for a real 1956 Fender "Mary Kaye" blond Stratocaster with gold hardware.

Relic and aged guitars instruments have been very popular and are often used on stage in place of the true vintage instrument. These guitars complement vintage instruments, and offer a genuine alternative to those who do not wish to pay high vintage guitar prices.

Summary

Most of the customers we meet at guitar shows say, "Wow, it must be a lot of work to put together this Price Guide?" We don't belabor the point, but it's true. That's why we say, "We've done the work so you won't have to." If a model is missing in the *Guide*, or if you'd like something clarified, please contact

gil@vguitar.com. If you are a builder and would like to be included, or want to correct mistakes in your info, please email al@vguitar.com.

More Information

Vintage Guitar's website, vintageguitar.com, is updated five times a week from the magazine's inventory of articles. This expanding resource includes interviews with many of your favorite guitarists, reviews of new gear and recordings, and historic information on many of the brands and models covered in this book.

Acknowledgments

Putting together a book of this size requires the talents of many people. Many vintage instrument dealers give their time and expertise to provide market information. We use many sources to determine the values, but the dealers who participate play an important part. Many of them provide additional info on certain brands and models and they are acknowledged throughout this *Guide*.

Randy Klimpert shares his love for ukes by providing the information and photos in that section. Several of the brand histories used in this edition are based on the work of Michael Wright, the longtime "Different Strummer" columnist for *VG*.

Several people at *VG* played an important role, as well. Sandi Stayton does the big job of compiling and cataloging information. Doug Yellow Bird designs the cover and the inside pages. Jeanine Shea assists with editing and, with James Jiskra, compiles the ads and dealer directory. Ward Meeker selects all the photos. We thank all of them for their usual fine work.

As always, we welcome suggestions, criticisms, and ideas to make future guides better. Contact us at Vintage Guitar, Inc., PO Box 7301, Bismarck, ND 58507, or by email at gil@vguitar.com.

Thank you,

Alan Greenwood and Gil Hembree

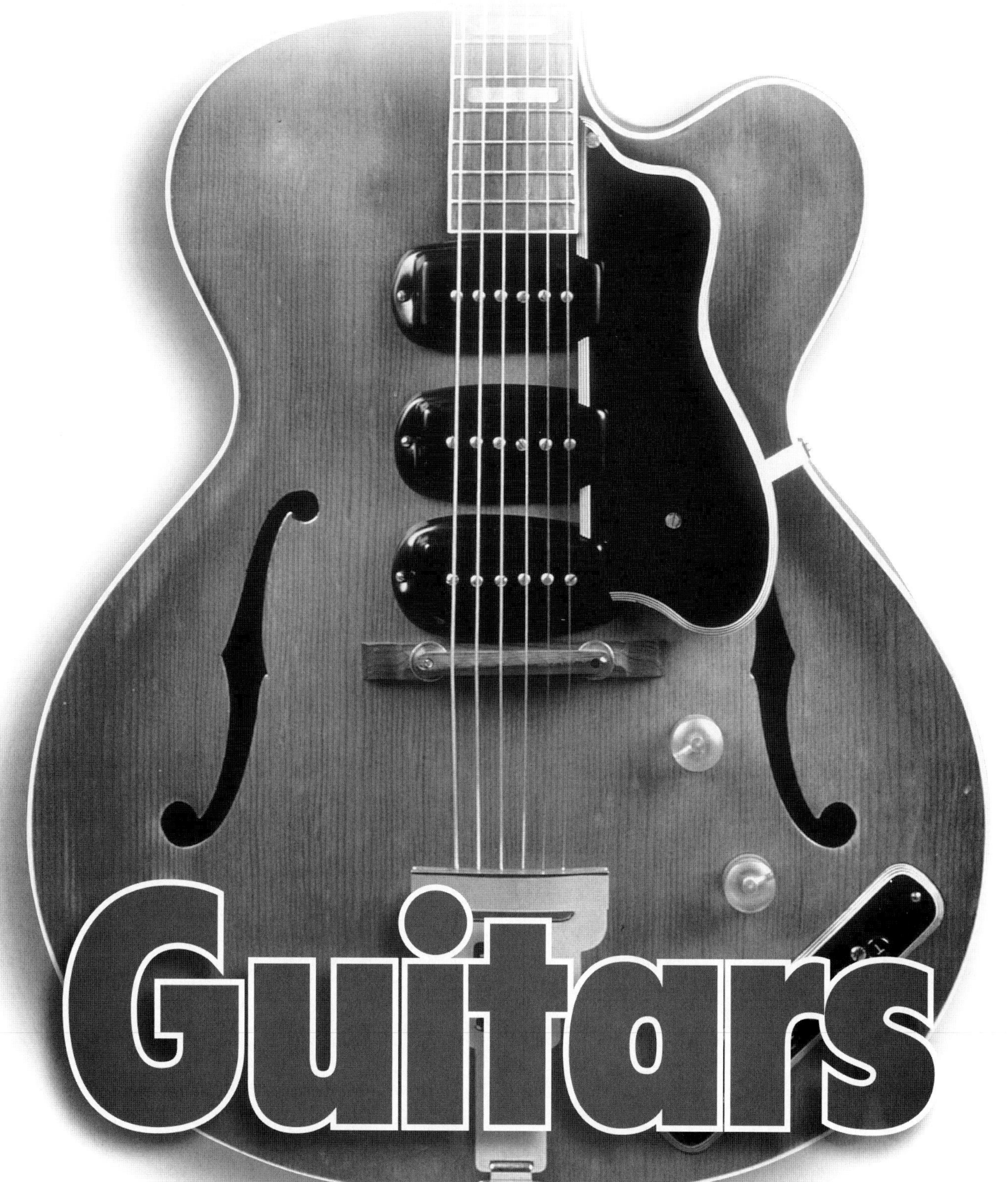
Guitars

GUITARS

Acoustic Black Widow

1963 Airline Super III

MODEL YEAR	FEATURES	EXC. COND. LOW	HIGH

A Fuller Sound

1998-present. Professional and premium grade, custom nylon and steel-string flat-tops built by Luthier Warren Fuller in Oakland, California.

Abel

1994-present. Custom aircraft-grade aluminum body, wood neck, guitars built by twins Jim and Jeff Abel in Evanston, Wyoming. They offered the Abel Axe from 1994-'96 and 2000-2001, and still do custom orders. They also made the Rogue Aluminator in the late '90s.

Axe

1994-1996. Offset double-cut aluminum body with dozens of holes in the body, wood neck, various colors by annodizing the aluminum body. Abel Axe logo on the headstock.

1994-1996	Non-trem model	$500	$700
1994-1996	Trem model	$400	$600

Abilene

Budget and intermediate grade, production, acoustic and electric guitars imported by Samick.

Acoustic Guitars

Recent import copies.

2000-2002		$75	$150

Electric Guitars

Solidbody and hollowbody electrics, designs often based on classic American models.

2000-2002		$75	$125

Abyss

1997-present. Luthier Kevin Pederson builds his premium grade, production/custom, hollowbody and solidbody guitars in Forest City, Iowa.

5th Anniversary Super Cut

2002. Limited edition model in honor of the firm's 5th anniversary. Single-cut Les Paul-style high end appointments.

2002	Flamed maple top	$2,300	$2,500

Acoustic

Ca. 1965-ca. 1987, present. Mainly known for solidstate amps, the Acoustic Control Corp. of Los Angeles, CA did offer guitars and basses from around '69 to late '74. The brandname was revived by Samick a few years ago on a line of amps.

Black Widow Guitar

1969-1970, 1972-1974. Both versions featured an unique Black equal double cutaway body with German carve, two pickups, a zero fret, and a protective "spider design" pad on back. The early version (called the AC500 Black Widow) had 22 frets, an "Ebonite" fingerboard, and pickups with one row of adjustable polepieces (described as "steel guitar dual pickups" in sales text). The later version was 24 frets, a rosewood 'board, and humbuckers with two rows of adjustable pole pieces (some '72s have the older style pickup). The jack and four control knobs were configured differently on the two versions. Acoustic outsourced the production of the guitars, possibly to Japan, but final 200 or so guitars produced by Semie Moseley. The AC700 Black Widow 12-string was also available for '69-'70.

1972-1974		$850	$1,000

Agile

1985-present. Budget grade, production, acoustic and electric guitars imported by Rondo Music of Union, New Jersey. They also offer mandolins.

LP4000

Import similar to Epiphone Les Paul.

2000s		$100	$150

Aims

Aims instruments were distributed by Randall Instruments in the mid-1970s.

Airline

Ca. 1958-1968. Airline was a brandname used by Montgomery Ward on acoustic, electric archtop and solidbody guitars and basses, amplifiers, steels, and possibly banjos and mandolins. Instruments manufactured by Kay, Harmony and Valco.

Acoustic Archtops (lower end)

1950s		$125	$300
1960s		$125	$300

Acoustic Archtops (higher end)

1950s		$300	$500
1960s		$300	$500

Acoustic Res-O-Glas Resonator

Res-o-glas, coverplate with M-shaped holes, asymmetrical peghead.

1964		$500	$650

Amp-In-Case Model

1960s. Double cutaway, single pickup, short-scale guitar with amplifier built into the case, Airline on grille.

1960s		$275	$350

Electric Hollowbodies

1950s	Barney Kessel copy	$550	$700
1960s	ES-175 copy	$300	$550
1960s	Harmony H-54 Rocket II copy	$250	$350
1960s	Harmony H-75 (335-style) copy	$400	$550

Electric Res-O-Glas

Res-o-glas is a form of fiberglass. The bodies and sometimes the necks were made of this material.

1960s		$600	$700

Electric Res-O-Glas Resonator

Res-o-glas is a form of fiberglass. These models have resonator cones in the body.

1960s		$600	$750

Electric Solidbodies (standard-lower end)

1960s		$250	$400

MODEL YEAR	FEATURES	EXC. COND. LOW	HIGH

Electric Solidbodies (deluxe-higher end)

Appointments may include multiple pickups, block inlays, additional logos, more binding.

1950s		$500	$625
1960s		$500	$575

Flat-Top (lower end, 13" body)

1960s		$50	$100

Alamo

1947-1982. Founded by Charles Eilenberg, Milton Fink, and Southern Music, San Antonio, TX, and distributed by Bruno & Sons. Alamo started out making radios, phonographs, and instrument cases. In 1949 they added amplifiers and lap steels. From '60 to '70, the company produced beginner-grade solidbody and hollow-core body electric Spanish guitars. The amps were all-tube until the '70s. Except for a few Valco-made examples, all instruments were built in San Antonio. See Guitar Stories Volume II, by Michael Wright, for a complete history of Alamo with detailed model listings.

Electric Hollowbodies

1960s		$125	$300

Electric Solidbodies

1960s		$125	$300

Alamo Guitars

2000-present. The Alamo brandname has been revived for a line of handcrafted, professional grade, production/custom, guitars by Alamo Music Products, which also offers Robin and Metropolitan brand guitars and Rio Grande pickups.

Alberico, Fabrizio

1998-present. Luthier Fabrizio Alberico builds his premium grade, custom, flat-top and classical guitars in Cheltenham, Ontario.

Alembic

1969-present. Premium and presentation grade, production/custom, guitars, baritones, and 12-strings built in Santa Rosa, California. They also build basses. Established in San Francisco by Ron and Susan Wickersham, Alembic started out as a studio working with the Grateful Dead and other bands on a variety of sound gear. By '70 they were building custom basses, later adding guitars and cabinets. By '73, standardized models were being offered.

California Special CSLG6

1990s-present. Double cut solidbody, six-on-a-side tuners, various colors.

1990s		$1,600	$1,800

Orion OLSB6

1990-present. Offset double cutaway, various colors.

1990s		$1,400	$1,600

MODEL YEAR	FEATURES	EXC. COND. LOW	HIGH

Pan-Alembic

1980s. Single cut body, maple fretboard, logo on pickguard, blade bridge pickup.

1980s	Cream	$250	$350

Series I

Early-1970s. Neck-through, double cutaway solidbody with bookmatched koa and black walnut core, three pickups in a single-coil and hum cancelling configuration, optional body styles available, Natural.

1970s		$2,500	$2,800

Allen Guitars

1982-present. Premium grade, production resonators, steel-string flat-tops, and mandolins built by Luthier Randy Allen, Colfax, CA.

Aloha

1935-1960s. Private branded by Aloha Publishing and Musical Instruments Company, Chicago, Illinois. Made by others.

Alray

1967. Electrics and acoustics built by the Holman-Woodell guitar factory in Neodesha, Kansas, who also marketed similar models under the Holman brand.

Alvarez

1965-present. Intermediate and professional grade, production, acoustic guitars imported by St. Louis Music. They also offer banjos and mandolins. Initially high-quality handmade Yairi guitars were exclusively distributed, followed by lower-priced Alvarez line. In 1990 the Westone brandname used on electric guitars and basses was replaced with the Alvarez name; these Alvarez electrics were offered until 2002. Many Alvarez electric models designed by luthier Dana Sutcliffe; several models designed by Dan Armstrong.

Classic I, II, III

1994-1999. Designs based on classic solidbody American models.

1994-1999		$150	$200

Flat-Top (lower end)

1966-present. Beginner-grade instruments, solid or laminate tops, laminate back and sides, little or no extra appointments. Some are acoustic/electric.

1970s		$50	$100
1980s		$75	$125
1990s		$100	$150

Flat-Top (mid-level)

1966-present. Solid tops, laminated back and sides, lower appointments such as bound fingerboards and headstocks, nickel hardware and pearl inlay.

1970s		$125	$225
1980s		$125	$225
1990s		$125	$225

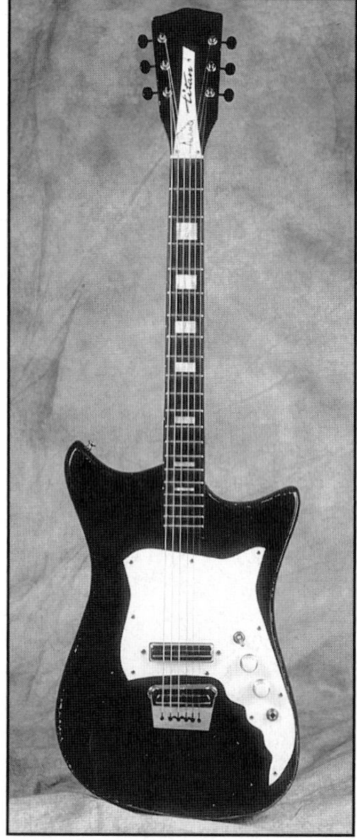

1964 Alamo Fiesta I

Allen resophonic

GUITARS

Alvarez-Yairi WY-1K

1969 Dan Armstrong lucite

MODEL YEAR	FEATURES	EXC. COND. LOW	HIGH

Flat-Top (mid-to-high-end)

1966-present. Solid spruce tops, solid mahogany or rosewood backs, laminated mahogany or rosewood sides, may have scalloped bracing, mid-level appointments like abalone headstock inlay, soundhole rosettes and herringbone body binding.

1970s		$250	$350
1980s		$250	$350
1990s		$250	$350

Flat-Top (high end)

1966-present. Solid rosewood and/or mahogany backs and sides, solid spruce tops, may have dovetail neck joint, highest appointments like abalone inlay and real maple binding.

1980s		$500	$600

Fusion Series (with piezo and EQ)

1981-present. Single cutaway, acoustic/electrics with EQ and transducer/piezo pickups. Earlier models had spruce tops with spruce or mahogany back and sides. More recent models have maple tops, backs and sides.

1980s		$300	$400
1990s		$300	$400

Alvarez Yairi

1966-present. Alvarez Yairi guitars are handcrafted and imported by St. Louis Music.

Flat-Top (mid-level)

Solid top of cedar or spruce, depending on model, mid-level appointments.

1970s		$400	$500
1980s		$400	$500
1990s		$400	$500

Flat-Top (higher-end)

Solid top of cedar or spruce, depending on model, higher-end appointments.

1970s		$600	$800
1980s		$600	$800
1990s		$600	$800

Fusion Series (with piezo and EQ)

1998-2002. Piezo bridge with volume and tone controls, higher-end appointments.

1990s		$700	$800

American Acoustech

1993-2001. Production steel string flat-tops made by Tom Lockwood (former plant manager for Guild) and Dave Stutzman (of Stutzman's Guitar Center) as ESVL Inc. in Rochester, New York.

American Archtop Guitars

1995-present. Premium and presentation grade, custom six- and seven-string archtops by luthier Dale Unger, in Stroudsburg, Pennsylvania.

American Conservatory (Lyon & Healy)

Late-1800s-early-1900s. Mainly catalog sales guitars and mandolins from the Chicago maker. Mid-level Lyon & Healy offering, above Lyon & Healy Lakeside brand, and generally under Lyon & Healy Washburn brand.

Harp Guitar Style G2210

Early-1900s. Two six-string necks with standard tuners, one neck fretless, rosewood back and sides, spruce top, fancy rope colored wood inlay around soundhole, sides and down the back center seam.

1917	Natural	$2,000	$3,000

American Showster

1986-present. Established by Bill Meeker and David Haines, Bayville, New Jersey. The Custom Series is made in the U.S.A., while the Standard Series (introduced in '97) is made in Czechoslovakia.

AS-57 Classic (original '57)

1987-present. Body styled like a 1957 Chevy tail fin, basswood body, bolt-on neck, one humbucker or three single-coil pickups, various colors.

1987		$1,100	$1,200

Ampeg

1949-present. Founded in '49 by Everett Hull as the Ampeg Bassamp Company in New York and has built amplifiers throughout its history. In '62 the company added instruments with the introduction of their Baby Bass and from '63 to '65, they carried a line of guitars and basses built by Burns of London and imported from England. In '66 the company introduced its own line of basses. In '67, Ampeg was acquired by Unimusic, Inc. From '69-'71 contracted with Dan Armstrong to produce lucite "see-through" guitars and basses with replaceable slide-in pickup design. In '71 the company merged with Magnavox. Beginning around '72 until '75, Ampeg imported the Stud Series copy guitars from Japan. Ampeg shut down production in the spring of '80. MTI bought the company and started importing amps. In '86 St. Louis Music purchased the company. In '97 Ampeg introduced new andreissue American-made guitar and bass models. They discontinued the guitar line in 2001.

AMG1

1999-2001. Dan Amstrong guitar features, but with mahogany body with quilted maple top, two P-90-style or humbucker-style pickups.

1999-2001	Humbuckers, gold hardware	$900	$1,000
1999-2001	Kent Armstrong pickups	$400	$600
1999-2001	P-90s, standard hardware	$400	$600

Dan Armstrong Lucite Guitar

1969-1971. Clear plexiglas solidbody, with interchangable pickups. Dan Armstrong reports that around 9,000 guitars were produced. Introduced in '69, but primary production was in '70-'71. Reissued in '98.

1969		$1,500	$1,600

MODEL YEAR	FEATURES	EXC. COND. LOW	HIGH
1970		$1,500	$1,600
1971		$1,500	$1,600

Dan Armstrong Lucite Guitar Reissue

1998-2001. Produced by pickup designer Kent Armstrong (son of Dan Armstrong). Offered in "smoked" (ADAG2) or "clear" (ADAG1).

1998-2001		$750	$850

Heavy Stud (GE-150/GEH-150)

1973-1975. Import from Japan. Single cut body, inexpensive materials, weight added for sustain.

1970s		$225	$275

Sonic Six (By Burns)

1964-1965. Solidbody, two pickups, tremolo, Cherry finish. Same as the Burns Nu-Sonic guitar.

1960s		$375	$475

Stud (GE-100/GET-100)

1973-1975. Import from Japan. SG body style, inexpensive materials, weight added for sustain. GET-100 included '70s-style SG tremolo assembly.

1970s		$200	$225

Super Stud (GE-500)

1973-1975. Import from Japan. SG body style, inexpensive materials, weight added for sustain. Top-of-the-line in the Stud Series.

1970s		$275	$300

Thinline (By Burns)

1963-1964. Semi-hollowbody, two F-holes, two pickups, double cutaway, tremolo. Import by Burns of London. Same as the Burns TR2 guitar.

1963-1964		$350	$450

Wild Dog (By Burns)

1963-1964. Solidbody, three pickups, shorter scale, tremolo, Sunburst finish. Import by Burns of London. Same as the Burns Split Sound.

1963-1964		$350	$450

Wild Dog De Luxe (By Burns)

1963-1964. Solidbody, three pickups, bound neck, tremolo, Sunburst finish. Import by Burns of London. Same as the Burns Split Sonic guitar.

1963-1964		$375	$500

Andersen Stringed Instruments

1978-present. Luthier Steve Andersen builds premium and presentation grade, production/custom flat-tops, archtops, and mandolins in Seattle, Washington.

Andreas

1995-present. Luthier Andreas Pichler builds his aluminium-necked, solidbody guitars and basses in Dollach, Austria.

Angelica

Ca. 1967-1972. Entry-level guitars imported from Japan.

Electric Solidbodies

Japanese import.

1970s		$100	$150

Angus

1976-present. Professional and premium grade, custom-made steel and nylon string flat-tops built by Mark Angus in Laguna Beach, California.

Antares

1990s. Korean-made budget acoustic guitars imported by Vega Music International of Brea, California.

Antique Acoustics

1970s-present. Luthier Rudolph Blazer builds production/custom flat-tops, 12-strings, and archtops in Tubingen, Germany.

Apollo

Ca. 1967-1972. Entry-level guitars imported by St. Louis Music.

Electric Guitars

Japanese imports.

1970s		$100	$125

Applause

1976-present. Budget and intermediate grade, production, acoustic and acoustic/electric guitars. They also offer basses, mandolins and ukes. Kaman Music's entry-level Ovation-styled brand. The instruments were made in the U.S. until around '82, when production was moved to Korea. On the U.S.-made guitars, the back of the neck was molded Urelite, with a cast aluminum neck combining an I-beam neck reinforcement, fingerboard, and frets in one unit. The Korea models have traditional wood necks.

AA Models (acoustic)

Imported. Laminate top, plastic or composition body. Specs and features can vary on AA Models.

1976-1981	U.S.-made	$100	$150
1980s		$75	$100

AE Models (acoustic/electric)

Imported. Laminate top, plastic or composition body. Specs and features can vary on AE Models.

1976-1981	U.S.-made	$200	$250
1980s		$150	$175
1990s		$150	$175

Arbor

Late-1980s imports by Midco International. Student level to mid-level near copies of classic and popular American models.

Electric Guitars

1980s.

1980s		$175	$300

Arch Kraft

1933-1934. Full-size acoustic archtop and flat-top guitars. Budget brand produced by the Kay Musical Instrument Company and sold through various distributors.

1963 Ampeg Wild Dog Deluxe

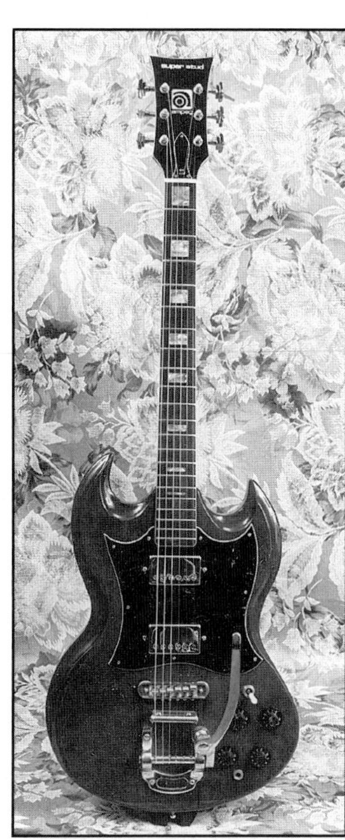

1973 Ampeg Super Stud

1986 Aria 1982T

1855 Ashborn Model 2

Acoustic Guitars (archtops or flat-tops)

MODEL YEAR	FEATURES	EXC. COND. LOW	HIGH
1930s		$175	$325

Aria Diamond

Aria established in Japan in 1953, Aria Diamonds were marketed in the 1960s.

Electric Guitars

Various models and appointments in the '60s.

MODEL YEAR	FEATURES	EXC. COND. LOW	HIGH
1960s		$300	$400

Aria Pro II

1960-present. Budget and intermediate grade, production, electric and acoustic guitars. They also make basses, mandolins, and banjos. Aria was established in Japan in '53 and started production of instruments in '60 using the Arai, Aria, Aria Diamond, and Diamond brandnames. The brand was renamed Aria Pro II in '75. Over the years, they have produced a variety of acoustic guitars, banjos, mandolins, electric solidbody guitars and basses, amplifiers, and effects. Around '87 Aria moved production of cheaper models to Korea, reserving Japanese manufacturing for more expensive models.

In around '95 some models were made in United States, though most contemporary guitars sold in U.S. are Korean. The name Aria Pro II is used mainly on electric guitars, with Aria used on others.

Models have been consolidated by sector unless specifically noted. Model series tend to run for several years and then discontinued.

Acoustic Solid Wood Top Guitars

1960s-1990s. Steel string models, various appointments, generally mid-level imports.

MODEL YEAR	FEATURES	EXC. COND. LOW	HIGH
1980s		$100	$150

Acoustic Veneer Wood Top Guitars

1960s-1990s. Steel string models, various appointments, generally entry-level imports.

MODEL YEAR	FEATURES	EXC. COND. LOW	HIGH
1980s		$75	$100

Classical Solid Wood Top Guitars

1960s-1990s. Various models, various appointments, generally entry-level imports.

MODEL YEAR	FEATURES	EXC. COND. LOW	HIGH
1980s		$100	$200

Classical Veneer Wood Top Guitars

1960s-1990s. Various models, various appointments, generally entry-level imports.

MODEL YEAR	FEATURES	EXC. COND. LOW	HIGH
1980s		$50	$100

Fullerton Series

1995-present. Various models with different appointments and configurations based on the classic offset double cut soldibody.

MODEL YEAR	FEATURES	EXC. COND. LOW	HIGH
1990s		$150	$200

Herb Ellis (PE-175/FA-DLX)

1978-1987 (Model PE-175) and 1988-1993 (Model FA-DLX). Archtop hollowbody, ebony fingerboard, two humbuckers.

MODEL YEAR	FEATURES	EXC. COND. LOW	HIGH
1977-1987		$400	$600

Solidbody Guitars

1960s-present. Various models, various appointments, generally mid-level imports.

MODEL YEAR	FEATURES	EXC. COND. LOW	HIGH
1960-1990		$200	$350

Titan Artist TA Series (335 copy)

1980-1990. Body styled like ES-335 with two humbucking pickups.

MODEL YEAR	FEATURES	EXC. COND. LOW	HIGH
1980s		$250	$325

Armstrong, Rob

1971-present. Custom steel- and nylon-string flat-tops, 12-strings, mandolins, basses, and parlor guitars made in Coventry, England by luthier Rob Armstrong.

Arpeggio Korina

1995-present. Professional, premium and presentation grade, production/custom, korina wood solidbody guitars built by luthier Ron Kayfield in Pennsylvania.

Artesano

Professional grade, production, classical guitars built in Valencia, Spain, and distributed by Juan Orozco. Orozco also made higher-end classical Orozco Models 8, 10 and 15.

Artinger Custom Guitars

1997-present. Luthier Matt Artinger builds his professional and premium grade, production/custom, hollow, semi-hollow, and chambered solidbody guitars and basses in Emmaus, Pennsylvania.

Ashborn

1848-1864. James Ashborn, of Wolcottville, Connecticut, operated one of the largest guitar making factories of the mid-1800s. Models were small parlor-sized instruments with ladder bracing and gut strings. Most of these guitars will need repair. Often of more interest as historical artifacts or museum pieces versus guitar collections.

Model 2

1848-1864. Flat-top, plain appointments, no position markers on the neck, identified by Model number.

MODEL YEAR	FEATURES	EXC. COND. LOW	HIGH
1855	Fully repaired	$400	$600

Model 5

1848-1864. Flat-top, higher appointments.

MODEL YEAR	FEATURES	EXC. COND. LOW	HIGH
1855	Fully repaired	$1,200	$1,500

Atkin Guitars

1993-present. Luthier Alister Atkin builds his production/custom steel and nylon string flat-tops and mandolins in Canterbury, England.

Austin

1999-present. Budget and intermediate grade, production, acoustic, acoustic/electric, resonator, and electric guitars imported by St. Louis Music. They also offer basses, mandolins and banjos.

MODEL YEAR	FEATURES	EXC. COND. LOW	HIGH

Era '62 Standard

2001-present. Tele-style body and configuration, solid hardware body, maple neck and rosewood fretboard.

2001 $125 $150

Austin Hatchet

Mid-1970s-mid-1980s. Trademark of distributor Targ and Dinner, Chicago, IL.

Hatchet

Travel guitar.

1981 $175 $200

Avanti

1960s. Import from Europe.

Electric Solidbody

1960s. Solidbody with triple single-coil pickups, dot markers, six-on-a-side tuners.

1960s $100 $150

Bacon & Day

Established in 1921 by David Day and Paul Bacon, primarily known for fine quality tenor and plectrum banjos in the '20s and '30s. Purchased by Gretsch circa '40.

Belmont

Gretsch era, two DeArmond pickups. Natural

1950s $900 $1,100

Ramona Archtop

1938 Sunburst $500 $800

1940 Sunburst $500 $800

Senorita Guitar

Sunburst, mahogany back and sides.

1940 $700 $1,000

Baker

1997-present. Established by Gene Baker, produced a line of professional and premium grade, production/custom, basses and solid and hollow body guitars in Santa Maria, California. Baker produced the Mean Gene brand of guitars from '88-'90. In September '03, the company's name and assets were sold; Gene Baker is no longer involved.

B1/B1 Chambered/B1 Hollow

1997-present. Double cut mahogany body, maple top, with a wide variety of options including chambered and hollowbody construction, set-neck.

1997-2003 $2,200 $2,400

BJ/BJ Hollow

1997-present. Double cut mahogany body, P-90-type pickups, several options available, set-neck.

1997-2003 $1,500 $2,000

BNT

1997-2000. Mahogany solidbody, maple top, with a wide variety of options, neck-through body.

1998 $2,000 $2,200

MODEL YEAR	FEATURES	EXC. COND. LOW	HIGH

Baldwin

1965-1970. The Baldwin company was founded in 1862, in Cincinnati, Ohio when reed organ and violin teacher named Dwight Hamilton Baldwin opened a music store that eventually became one of the largest piano retailers in the Midwest. In 1890, Baldwin began manufacturing upright pianos. In 1935, Baldwin pioneered electronic organs and developed the electronic church organ. By '65, the Baldwin Piano and Organ company was ready to buy into the guitar market but was outbid by CBS for the Fender company. Baldwin did procure Burns of London in September '65, and sold the guitars in the U.S. under the Baldwin name. Baldwin purchased the Gretsch guitar company in '67. English production of Baldwin guitars ends in '70, after which Baldwin concentrates on the Gretsch brand.

Baby Bison (Model 560 by mid-1966)

1966-1970. Double cutaway solidbody, scroll headstock, two pickups, shorter scale, tremolo. Black, Red or White finishes.

1960s $800 $950

Bison (Model 511 by mid-1966)

1965-1970. Double cutaway solidbody, scroll headstock, three pickups, tremolo. Black or White finishes.

1965-1969 $1,100 $1,300

Double Six (Model 525 by mid-1966)

1965-1970. Offset double cutaway solidbody, 12 strings, three pickups. Green or Red Sunburst.

1960s $1,100 $1,300

G.B. 66 De Luxe

1965-1966. Same as Standard with added "density control" on treble horn. Golden Sunburst.

1960s $600 $700

G.B. 66 Standard

1965-1970. Thinline Electric archtop, dual Ultra-Sonic pickups, offset cutaways. Red Sunburst.

1960s $550 $650

Jazz Split Sound/Split Sound (Model 503 mid-1966)

1965-1970. Offset double cutaway solidbody, scroll headstock, three pickups, tremolo. Red Sunburst or solid colors.

1960s $900 $1,000

Marvin (Model 524 by mid-1966)

1965-1970. Offset double cutaway solidbody, scroll headstock, three pickups, tremolo. White or Brown finish.

1960s $750 $850

Model 706

1967-1970. Double cutaway semi-hollowbody, scroll headstock, two pickups, two F-holes, 335 copy, no vibrato. Red or Golden Sunburst.

1960s $550 $650

Model 706 V

1967-1970. Model 706 with vibrato.

1960s $550 $650

Baker B1H

1967 Baldwin Baby Bison

Baldwin Double Six

1900 Bay State parlour guitar

MODEL YEAR	FEATURES	EXC. COND. LOW	HIGH

Model 712 R Electric XII

1967-1970. Model 712 with "regular" neck, 335-style body. Red or Gold Sunburst.

1960s		$550	$650

Model 712 T Electric XII

1967-1970. Model 712 with "thin" neck, 335-style body. Red or Gold Sunburst.

1960s		$550	$650

Nu-Sonic

1965-1970. Solidbody electric student model, six-on-a-side tuners. Black or Cherry finish.

1960s		$400	$500

Vibraslim (Model 548 by late-1966)

1965-1970. Double cutaway semi-hollowbody, two pickups, tremolo, two F-holes. Red or Golden Sunburst.

1960s		$700	$800

Virginian (Model 550 by mid-1966)

1965-1970. Single cut flat- top with 2 pickups, one on each side of soundhole, scroll headstock, tremolo, natural.

1960s		$900	$1,000

Baranik Guitars

1995-present. Premium grade, production/custom steel-string flat-tops made in Tempe, Arizona by luthier Mike Baranik.

Barclay

1960s. Thinline acoustic/electric archtops, solidbody electric guitars and basses imported from Japan. Generally shorter scale beginner guitars.

Electric Solidbody Guitars

Various models.

1960s	Various models	$125	$225

Barcus-Berry

1964-present. Founded by John Berry and Les Barcus introducing the first piezocrystal transducer. Martin guitar/Barcus-Berry products were offered in the mid-1980s. They also offered a line of amps from around '76 to ca. '80.

Model 2510

Steel strings, acoustic bridge pickups, active volume and tone controls, various colors.

1985		$250	$350

Model 2520 Two-Way

Semi-hollowbody cutaway, acoustic/electric, acoustic bridge pickup, neck magnetic pickup, active mixer, various colors.

1985		$250	$350

Model 2530 Three-Way

Semi-hollowbody acoustic/electric, acoustic bridge pickup, bridge and neck magnetic pickups, active mixer, various colors.

1985		$250	$350

MODEL YEAR	FEATURES	EXC. COND. LOW	HIGH

Barrington

1988-1991. Imports offered by Barrington Guitar Werks, of Barrington, Illinois. Models included solidbody guitars and basses, archtop electrics, and acoustic flat-tops. Barrington Music Products is still in the music biz, offering LA saxophones and other products.

BGW-800 (acoustic/electric)

1988-1991. Acoustic/electric, flat-top single cutaway with typical round soundhole, opaque White.

1988-1991		$400	$500

BRG-883 T (solidbody)

1988-ca 1991. Barrington's line of pointy headstock, double cut solidbodies.

1988-1991		$175	$225

Bartell of California

1964-1969. Founded by Paul Barth (Magnatone) and Ted Peckles. Mosrite-inspired designs.

Electric 12

Mosrite-style body.

1967		$1,100	$1,300

Bay State

1865-ca.1910. Bay State was a trademark for Boston's John C. Haynes Co.

BC Rich

Ca. 1966/67-present. Currently offering budget, intermediate, and premium grade, production/custom, import and U.S.-made, electric and acoustic guitars. They also offer basses. Founded by Bernardo Chavez Rico in Los Angeles, California. As a boy he worked for his guitar-maker father Bernardo Mason Rico (Valencian Guitar Shop, Casa Rico, Bernardo's Guitar Shop), building first koa ukes and later, guitars, steel guitars and Martin 12-string conversions. He started using the BC Rich name ca. '66-'67 and made about 300 acoustics until '68, when first solidbody electric made using a Fender neck.

Rich's early models were based on Gibson and Fender designs. First production instruments were in '69 with ten fancy Gibson EB-3 bass and ten matching Les Paul copies, all carved out of single block of mahogany. Early guitars with Gibson humbuckers, then Guild humbuckers, and, from '74-'86, DiMarzio humbuckers. Around 150 BC Rich Eagles were imported from Japan in '76. Ca. '76 or '77 some bolt-neck guitars with parts made by Wayne Charvel were offered. Acoustic production ended in '82 (acoustics were again offered in '95).

For '83-'86 the BC Rich N.J. Series ("N.J." Nagoya, Japan) was built by Masan Tarada. U.S. Production Series (U.S.-assembled Korean kits) in '84. From '86 on, the N.J. Series was made by Cort in Korea. Korean Rave and Platinum series begin around '86. In '87, Rich agrees to let Class

Axe of New Jersey market the Korean Rave, Platinum and N.J. Series. Class Axe (with Neil Moser) introduces Virgin in '87 and in '88 Rave and Platinum names are licensed to Class Axe. In '89, Rico licensed the BC Rich name to Class Axe. Both imported and American-made BC Riches are offered during Class Axe management. In 2000, BC Rich became a division of Hanser Holdings.

During '90-'91, Rico begins making his upscale Mason Bernard guitars (approx. 225 made). In '94, Rico resumes making BC Rich guitars in California.

First 340-360 U.S.-built guitars were numbered sequentially beginning in '72. Beginning in '74, serial numbers change to YYZZZ pattern (year plus consecutive production). As production increased in the late-'70s, the year number began getting ahead of itself. By '80 it was two years ahead; by '81 as much as four years ahead. No serial number codes on imports.

MODEL YEAR	FEATURES	EXC. COND. LOW	HIGH
Assassin			
1986-1998. Double cut body, two humbuckers, maple through-neck dot markers, various colors.			
1986-1989		$600	$700
1990-1998		$600	$700
Assassin (N.J. Series)			
1990s		$300	$350
B-28 Acoustic			
Ca.1967-1982. Acoustic flat-top, rosewood back and sides, herringbone trim.			
1970s		$500	$900
B-30 Acoustic			
Ca.1967-1982. Acoustic flat-top.			
1970s		$500	$900
B-38 Acoustic			
Ca.1967-1982. Acoustic flat-top, cocobolo back and sides, herringbone trim.			
1970s		$500	$900
B-45 Acoustic			
Hand-built, D-style rosewood body.			
1970		$2,400	$2,700
Bich (N.J. Series)			
Import.			
1980s		$250	$350
1990s		$250	$350
Bich (U.S.A. assembly)			
1976-1998. Four-point sleek body style. Assembly in U.S.A. Came in Standard top or Supreme with highly figured maple body.			
1970s	Supreme top	$1,300	$1,500
1980s	Standard top	$900	$1,100
1980s	Supreme top	$1,300	$1,500
1990s	Standard top	$900	$1,100
Bich 10-String			
1976-present. Doubles on four low strings.			
1979-1982		$1,600	$1,800
Bich Doubleneck			
Six/twelve doubleneck.			
1980s		$1,900	$2,400
Black Hole			
1988. Bolt-on neck, rosewood 'board, integrated pickup design, Floyd Rose.			
1988		$175	$275
Eagle Doubleneck			
Rosewood, cloud inlay.			
1975		$3,300	$3,900
Eagle Special			
1977-ca.1982. Koa.			
1981	Natural	$600	$900
Eagle Supreme			
1977-present.			
1977		$900	$1,300
Exclusive EM2			
1996-1998. Double cut solidbody, three-on-a-side tuners, dual humbuckers, various colors.			
1996-1998		$175	$225
G-String			
Kahler tremolo.			
1986		$250	$375
Gunslinger			
1987-1999. Inverted headstock, one (Gunslinger I) or two (Gunslinger II) humbuckers. Recessed cutout behind Floyd Rose allows player to pull notes up two full steps.			
1980s	Black, maple neck	$450	$600
1980s	Various graphic designs (e.g. Nagal)	$700	$800
1990s	Red Sparkle	$400	$550
Ironbird			
1981-present. Pointy body and headstock.			
1985		$500	$600
Ironbird Doubleneck			
Six/twelve doubleneck.			
1980s		$1,800	$2,300
Mockingbird			
1976-present. Maple or koa.			
1970s		$1,400	$1,800
1980s		$1,300	$1,400
1990s		$800	$1,200
Mockingbird (N.J. Series)			
1980s		$275	$375
Mockingbird Supreme			
1976-present. Offset rosewood body with sharp treble horn, cloud inlays, U.S.A.-made.			
1976-1979		$1,700	$2,000
1990s		$1,300	$1,600
Nighthawk			
1978-ca.1982. Bolt-on neck.			
1978-1982		$300	$500
Outlaw			
1987-ca. 1993. N.J. Series, like Gunslinger with reverse headstock.			
1990s		$1,000	$1,100
Phoenix			
1977-ca.1982. Bolt-on neck.			
1980		$300	$550

1982 BC Rich Bich

1980s BC Rich Mockingbird

BC Rich Stealth I Standard

Benedetto Fratello

MODEL YEAR	FEATURES	EXC. COND. LOW	HIGH

Seagull

1972-1976. Single cutaway solidbody, neck-through, two humbuckers.

1970s		$1,000	$1,300

Seagull Doubleneck

Koa.

1979		$3,200	$3,800

Seagull II

1976. Double cutaway solidbody, neck-through, two humbuckers.

1976		$800	$1,000

ST Platinum Series (import)

1986-1998. Import from Korea.

1986-1989		$250	$400

ST-III (U.S.A.-made)

Solidbody electric, bolt-on maple neck, two single-coils and one humbucker, Kahler tremolo, Black hardware. Variety of bold colors.

1980s		$400	$700
1990s		$400	$700

Stealth I Series II

1983-1989. Mahogany body and neck, dot inlays, 24-fret neck, two pickups.

1983-1989		$700	$900

Stealth I Standard

1983-1989. Maple body, two pickups, 24-fret neck, diamond-shaped inlays.

1983-1989		$700	$900

The Mag

U.S. Handcrafted Series Mockingbird Acoustic Supreme, with solid spruce top, quilted maple back and sides, pickup with preamp and EQ optional.

2000	Dark Sunburst	$950	$1,000

Virgin (N.J. Series)

1987-1993, 2000-present. Import from Japan and Korea.

1987-1993		$375	$400

Warlock

1981-present. Four-point sleek body style with widow headstock.

1980s		$775	$1,200
1990s		$775	$1,200

Warlock (N.J. Series)

1990s		$350	$500

Warlock (Platinum Series import)

1988-present. Lower-end import.

1988-2000		$300	$375

Bear Creek Guitars

1995-present. Luthier Bill Hardin worked for OMI Dobro and Santa Cruz Guitar before introducing his own line of professional and premium grade, custom-made Wessenborn-style guitars and ukuleles, made in Kula, Hawaii.

Beardsell Guitars

1996-present. Production/custom flat-tops, classical and electric solidbody guitars built by luthier Allan Beardsell in Toronto, Ontario.

MODEL YEAR	FEATURES	EXC. COND. LOW	HIGH

Beltona

1991-present. Production/custom metal body resonator guitars made in New Zealand by Steve Evans and Bill Johnson. Beltona was originally located in England.

Beltone

1930s-1940s. Lower-end models.

Resonator Copy

1930s-1940s. Resonator copy but without a real resonator, rather just an aluminum plate on a wooden top, body mahogany plywood.

1938		$250	$300

Benedetto

1968-present. Archtop guitars, violins and a few solidbodies hand-crafted by Robert Benedetto in East Stroudsburg, PA. He is especially known for refining the seven-string guitar. As of '99, Benedetto only makes special order instruments. He licensed the names of his standard models to Guild, which now makes them in their Custom Shop in Nashville, TN. (Refer to Benedetto FMIC for post-'99 instruments.)

Benny

Electric semi-hollow, 14 1/2" body, cutaway, chambered Sitka spruce top.

1990s	Natural	$4,000	$5,000

Benny Deluxe

Electric semi-hollow, chambered spruce top, abalone inlays, deluxe version of the Benny.

1990s	Sunburst	$5,000	$6,000

Cremona

Acoustic/electric archtop, single cutaway, 17" body, Natural.

1988		$16,000	$19,000

Fratello

Acoustic archtop, single cutaway, 17" body, Blond or Sunburst.

1980s		$13,000	$16,000
1990s		$13,000	$16,000

La Venezia

Acoustic archtop, single cutaway, 17" body.

1990s	Sunburst	$14,000	$17,000

Limelite Custom

1993. Single-cutaway, neck pickup, select aged wood, Blond.

1993		$20,000	$25,000

Manhattan

1989-1999. Archtop with 16" body, neck pickup, Blond.

1989-1999		$13,000	$15,000

Manhattan Custom

Carved 17" body, Blond.

1990s		$14,000	$16,000

Benedetto (FMIC)

1999-present. Premium and presentation, production/custom, acoustic and electric archtops. In '99, Bob Benedetto entered into an agreement

MODEL YEAR	FEATURES	EXC. COND. LOW	HIGH

with Fender (FMIC) to have the FMIC Guild Custom Shop, Nashville, TN, build Benedetto guitars under his guidance and supervision.

Manhattan

2000-present.

2000		$10,000	$12,000

Bently

ca.1985-1998. Student and intermediate grade copy style acoustic and electric guitars imported by St. Louis Music Supply. Includes the Series 10 electrics and the Songwriter acoustics (which have a double reversed B crown logo on the headstock). St. Louis Music replaced the Bently line with the Austin brand.

2230/2231/2232

Double cut solidbody, 3 pickups, dot markers, sunburst, red or black.

1980s		$75	$125

Songwriter Dreadnought 5111

Spruce top, mahogany, Natural.

1980s		$50	$100

Bertoncini Stringed Instruments

1995-present. Luthier Dave Bertoncini builds his premium grade, custom, flat-top guitars in Tacoma, Washington. He has also built solidbody electrics, archtops, mandolins and banjos.

Beyond The Trees

1976-present. Luthier Fred Carlson offers a variety of innovative designs for his professional and presentation grade, production/custom six- and 12-string flat-tops in Santa Cruz, California. He also produces the Sympitar (a six-string with added sympathetic strings) and the Dreadnautilus (a unique shaped headless acoustic).

Bigsby

1946-present. Pedal steel guitars, hollow-chambered electric Spanish guitars, electric mandolins, doublenecks, replacement necks on acoustic guitars, hand vibratos, all handmade by Paul Arthur Bigsby, machinist and motorcycle enthusiast (designer of '30s Crocker motorcycles), in Downey, California. Initially built for special orders. Bigsby was a pioneer in developing pedal steels. He designed a hand vibrato for Merle Travis. In '48, his neck-through hollow electrics (with Merle Travis) influenced Leo Fender, and Bigsby employed young Semie Moseley. In '56, he designed the Magnatone Mark series guitars and one Hawaiian lap steel.

He built less than 50 Spanish guitars, six mandolins, 125 to 150 pedal steels and 12 or so neck replacements. SN was stamped on the end of fingerboard: MMDDYY. In '65, the company was sold to Gibson president Ted McCarty who moved the tremolo/vibrato work to Kalamazoo. Bigsby died in '68.

Fred Gretsch purchased the Bigsby company from Ted McCarty in '99. A solidbody guitar and a pedal steel based upon the original Paul Bigsby designs were introduced January, 2002. Early Bigsby guitars command high value on the collectible market.

Solidbody Guitars

Late-1940s-early-1950s.

1948-1952	Natural	$18,000	$25,000

Bil Mitchell Guitars

1979-present. Luthier Bil Mitchell builds his professional and premium grade, production/custom, flat-top and archtop guitars in Wall, New Jersey.

Bischoff Guitars

1975-present. Professional and premium-grade, custom-made flat-tops built by luthier Gordy Bischoff in Eau Claire, Wisconsin.

Bishline Guitars

1985-present. Luthier Robert Bishline builds custom-made flat-tops, resonators, mandolins, and banjos in Tulsa, Oklahoma.

Black Jack

1960s. Violin-body hollowbody electric guitars and basses, possibly others. Imported from Japan by unidentified distributor. Manufacturers unknown, but some may be Arai.

Blackshear, Tom

1958-present. Premium and presentation grade, production, classical and flamenco guitars made by luthier Tom Blackshear in San Antonio, Texas.

Blade

1987-present. Gary Levinson started repairing guitars in '64 and started Levinson Music Products Ltd. in Switzerland in '87 to produce Blade solidbody guitars. Currently Blade produces intermediate and professional grade, production, solidbody guitars and basses.

California Custom CC

1994-present. Standard CS with maple top and high-end appointments.

1994-1999		$700	$1,000

California Deluxe

1994-1995. Standard CS with mahogany body and maple top.

1994-1995		$600	$700

California Hybrid

1998-2002. Standard CS with piezo bridge pickup.

1998-2002		$550	$650

California Standard CS

1994-present. Offset double cut, swamp ash body, bolt neck, five-way switch.

1994-1999		$350	$450

1985 Bently Series 10 graphite

1953 Bigsby

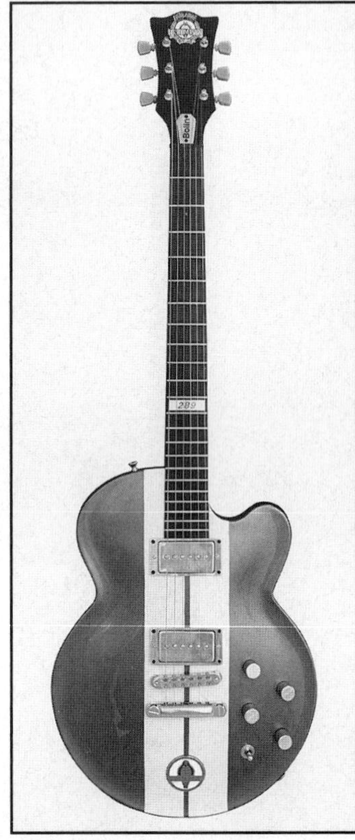

Bolin Cobra

Bourgeois D-150

MODEL YEAR	FEATURES	EXC. COND. LOW	HIGH

R 3

1988-1992. Offset double cut solidbody, bolt maple neck, six-on-a-side tuners, 3 single-coils.

1988-1992	$400	$500

R 4

1988-1992. Offset double cut solidbody, bolt maple neck, six-on-a-side tuners, 3 single-coils.

1988-1992	$500	$600

Blanchard Guitars

1994-present. Luthier Mark Blanchard builds premium grade, custom steel-string and classical guitars in Mammoth Lakes, California.

Blue Stars

1984-present. Luthier Bruce Herron builds his production/custom guitars in Fennville, Michigan. He also builds electric solidbody mandolins, lap steels, and ukes.

Travelmaster

Double cutaway, one humbucker, chip-resistant finish in various colors.

1990s	$200	$250

Bluebird

1930s. Private brand with Bluebird painted on headstock, probably made by Harmony or another Chicago mass-producer.

13" Flat-Top

1930s. Private brand with Bluebird painted on headstock.

1938	$50	$150

Boaz Elkayam Guitars

1985-present. Presentation grade, custom steel, nylon, and flamenco guitars made by luthier Boaz Elkayam in Chatsworth, California.

Bohmann

1878-ca. 1926. Acoustic flat top guitars, harp guitars, mandolins, banjos, violins made in Chicago, IL, by Joseph Bohmann (born 1848, Neumarkt, Bohemia, Czechoslovakia). Bohmann's American Musical Industry founded 1878. Guitar body widths are 12", 13", 14", 15". He had 13 grades of guitars by 1900 (Standard, Concert, Grand Concert sizes).

Early American use of plywood. Some painted wood finishes. Special amber-oil varnishes. Tuner bushings. Early ovalled fingerboards. Patented tuner plates and bridge design. Steel engraved label inside. Probably succeeded by son Joseph Frederick Bohmann.

Ca. 1896 12" body faux rosewood, 13", 14" and 15" body faux rosewood birch, 12", 13", 14" and 15" body Sunburst maple, 12", 13", 14" and 15" body rosewood.

By 1900 Styles 0, 1, 2 and 3 Standard, Concert and Grand Concert maple, Styles 1, 2, 3, 4, 5, 6, 7, 8, 9, 10, 11 and 12 in Standard, Concert, and Grand Concert rosewood.

MODEL YEAR	FEATURES	EXC. COND. LOW	HIGH

14 3/4" Flat-Top

Solid spruce top, veneered Brazilian rosewood back and sides, wood marquetry around top and soundhole, Natural. Each Bohmann should be valued on a case-by-case basis.

1900	$1,100	$1,400

Bolin

1978-present. Professional and premium grade, production/custom, solidbody guitars built by luthier John Bolin in Boise, Idaho. Bolin is well-known for his custom work. His Cobra guitars are promoted and distributed by Sanderson Sales and Marketing as part of the "Icons of America" Series.

Bond

1984-1985. Andrew Bond made around 1,400 Electraglide guitars in Scotland. Logo says "Bond Guitars, London."

ElectraGlide

1984-1985. Black carbon graphite one-piece body and neck, double cutaway, three single-coils (two humbuckers were also supposedly available), digital LED controls that required a separate transformer.

1984-1985	$1,000	$1,100

Bourgeois

1993-1999, 2000-present. Luthier Dana Bourgeois, Lewiston, Maine co-founded Schoenberg guitars building Schoenberg models from '86-'90. Bourgeois' 20th Anniversary model issued in '97. Bourgeois Guitars, per se, went of business at the end of '99. Patrick Theimer created Pantheon Guitars, which included seven luthiers (including Bourgeois) working in an old 1840s textile mill in Lewiston, Maine and Bourgeois models continued to be made as part of the Pantheon organization.

Serial Number List:

1993	1-70
1994	71-205
1995	206-350
1996	351-665
1997	666-1040
1998	1041-1450
1999	1451-1975

Country Boy

1990s-present. Pre-war D-style model designed for Ricky Skaggs with Sitka spruce top, select mahogany back and sides, Bourgeois script logo headstock inlay, individually labeled with a Ricky Skaggs label, Natural.

1990s	$1,800	$2,200

Custom OMS

1990s. Triple 0-size, 12-fret, Indian rosewood back and sides, Englemann spruce top.

1990s	$3,000	$3,300

MODEL YEAR	FEATURES	EXC. COND. LOW	HIGH

D - 20th Anniversary

1997. Special production of 20 instruments, "bearclaw" spruce top, select rosewood back and sides, luminescent mother-of-pearl fingerboard inlaid with ornate abalone floral pattern, fancy abalone rosette and border, Natural.

1997		$3,300	$3,500

JOM (Brazilian rosewood)

Jumbo Orchestra Model flat-top, 15 5/8", spruce top, Brazilian rosewood back and sides.

1990s		$2,800	$3,100

JOM (mahogany)

Jumbo Orchestra Model flat-top, 15 5/8", cedar top, mahogany back and sides.

1990s		$1,300	$1,600

JR-A

Artisan Series, 15 5/8", spruce top, rosewood back and sides.

1990s		$900	$1,100

Martin Simpson

1990s-present. Grand auditorium with unusual cutaway that removes one-half of the upper treble bout, Englemann spruce top, Indian rosewood back and sides, Natural.

1998		$2,600	$2,700

OMC (Brazilian rosewood)

1990s-present. Full-sized, soft cutaway flat-top, Adirondack spruce top, figured Brick Red Brazilian rosewood back and sides, Natural.

1990s		$5,000	$5,200

Slope D

D-size, 16", spruce top, mahogany back and sides.

1990s		$1,700	$2,000

Bown Guitars

1981-present. Luthier Ralph Bown builds custom steel-string, nylon-string, baritone, and harp guitars in Walmgate, England.

Bozo

1964-present. Bozo (pronounced Bo-zho) Padunovac learned instrument building in his Yugoslavian homeland. Since arriving in the United States in 1959, he has built a variety of high-end, handmade, acoustic instruments, many being one-of-a-kind. There are some Japanese-made models bearing his name dating from 1979-'80. He currently builds premium and presentation grade, production/custom guitars in Lindenhurst, Illinois.

Cutaway 12-String

Often old world Balkan ornamentation, generally Sitka spruce top, Indian rosewood back and sides, Widow-style headstock, ornamentation can vary.

1977	Standard ornamentation	$2,000	$2,500
1993	Elaborate ornamentation	$5,000	$6,000
1998	Elaborate custom ornamentation	$6,500	$7,500

Bradford

Mid-1960s. Brand name used by the W.T. Grant Company, one of the old "5 & 10" style retail stores similar to F.W. Woolworth and Kresge. Many of these instruments were made in Japan by Guyatone.

Acoustic Flat-Tops

Various colors.

1960s		$100	$200

Electric Solidbody Guitars

Various colors.

1960s		$100	$200

Breedlove

1990-present. Founded by Larry Breedlove and Steve Henderson. Professional, premium, and presentation grade, production/custom, steel and nylon string flat-tops built in Tumalo, Oregon. They also build mandolins. Several available custom options may add to the values listed here.

C1 (C10)

1990-present. Shallow concert-sized flat-top, non-cutaway, solid spruce top, mahogany back and sides, Natural.

1994-1995		$1,400	$1,600

C15/R

1990-present. Concert-size C1 with soft rounded cutaway, and optional cedar top and rosewood back and sides, gold tuners.

1997		$1,800	$2,000

RD20 X/R

(no longer made) Indian rosewood back and sides, sitka spruce top, winged bridge, abalone soundhole rosette.

1999		$1,800	$1,900

SJ20-12 W

Twelve strings, walnut (W) back and sides.

2000		$1,800	$2,000

Brian Moore

1992-present. Founded by Patrick Cummings, Brian Moore and Kevin Kalagher in Brewster, New York; they introduced their first guitars in '94. Initially expensive custom shop guitars with carbon-resin bodies with highly figured wood tops; later went to all wood bodies cut on CNC machines. The intermediate and professional grade, production, iGuitar/i2000series was introduced in 2000 and made in Korea, but set up in the U.S. Currently the premium grade, production/custom, Custom Shop Series guitars are handcrafted in La Grange, NY. They also build basses and electric mandolins.

C-45

Solidbody, mahogany body, bolt-on neck, two P-90-type pickups.

1990s		$900	$1,000

C-55

Solidbody, burl maple body, bolt-on neck.

1999		$900	$1,000

Breedlove AC-200

1990s Brian Moore MC/1

GUITARS

Brian Moore i2p

1965 Burns Jazz Split Sound

MODEL YEAR	FEATURES	EXC. COND. LOW	HIGH

C-90

Solidbody, figured maple top on mahogany body, bolt-on neck, hum-single-hum pickups.

1990s	Red Sunburst	$1,100	$1,300

DC1

High quality quilted maple top, double humbucker, single cutaway option, gold hardware.

1997-1998		$1,600	$1,900

iGuitar 2.13

2000-present. Solidbody Midi controller, dual humbuckers and piezo bridge pickup, figured maple top, gold hardware, made in Korea, sold in conjunction with a Roland processor.

2000		$450	$800

MC1

High-end model, quilted maple top, various pickup options including piezo and midi, gold hardware. Should be evaluated on a case-by-case basis.

1990s	Various options	$2,000	$4,000

Brian Stone Classical Guitars

Luthier Brian Stone builds his classical guitars in Corvallis, Oregon.

Brook Guitars

1993-present. Simon Smidmore and Andy Petherick build their production/custom Brook steel-string, nylon-strings, and archtops in Dartmoor, England.

Bruné, R. E.

1966-present. Luthier Richard Bruné builds his premium and presentation grade, custom, classical and flamenco guitars in Evanston, Illinois. He also offers his professional and premium grade Model 20 and Model 30, which are handmade in a leading guitar workshop in Japan. Bruné's "Guitars with Guts" column appears quarterly in *Vintage Guitar* magazine.

Bruno and Sons

1834-present. Established in 1834 by Charles Bruno, primarily as a distributor, Bruno and Sons marketed a variety of brandnames, including their own; currently part of Kaman.

Harp Guitar

1924		$1,500	$2,000

Parlor Guitar

Brazilian rosewood back and sides.

1880-1920		$750	$1,000

Bunker

1961-present. Founded by guitarist Dave Bunker, who started building custom guitars and basses while performing in Las Vegas in the '60s. Bunker began building guitars with his father and developed a number of innovations. Around '92 Bunker began PBC Guitar Technology in Allentown, PA, building American-made instruments for Ibanez. PBC closed in '97 and Bunker moved back to Washington State to start Bunker Guitar Technology and resumed production of several Bunker models. In early 2002, Bunker Guitars became part of Maple Valley Tone Woods of Port Angeles, WA.

Currently Bunker offers intermediate, professional, and premium grade, production/custom, guitars and basses built in Port Angeles. Most early Bunker guitars were pretty much custom-made in low quantities.

Electric Solidbody or Archtop Guitars

Various colors.

1960s		$750	$850
1970s		$750	$850
1980s		$750	$850
1990s		$750	$850

Burns

Jim Burns began building guitars in the late-1950s. Baldwin Organ (see Baldwin listing) purchased the company in '64 and offered the instruments until '70. The Burns name was revived by Burns London, with Jim Burns' involvement, offering reproductions of some of the classic Burns models of the '60s (distributed in the U.S. by Burns USA). Jim Burns passed away in August '98.

Bison

1964-1965. Double cutaway solidbody, three pickups, tremolo, Black or White.

1960s		$1,150	$1,350

Flyte

1974-1977. Fighter jet-shaped solidbody, pointed headstock, two humbucking pickups, Silver.

1970s		$700	$900

Jazz Split Sound

1962-1965. Offset double cutaway solidbody, three pickups, tremolo, Red Sunburst.

1960s		$950	$1,050

Marvin

1964-1965. Offset double cutaway solidbody, scroll headstock, three pickups, tremolo, White.

1960s		$800	$900

Nu-Sonic

1964-1965. Solidbody, two pickups, tremolo, White.

1960s		$350	$450

Split Sonic

1962-1964. Solidbody, three pickups, bound neck, tremolo. Sunburst finish.

1960s		$700	$800

TR-2

1960s		$300	$400

Burns (USA)

2000-present. Intermediate and professional grade, production, electric guitars and basses built in England. Reissue-style models include the Bison, Elite Custom, Marquee, Marquee Special.

MODEL YEAR	FEATURES	EXC. COND. LOW	HIGH

Burnside

1987-1988. Budget solidbody guitars imported by Guild.

Solidbody Electric/Blade

1987-1988. Kramer-style solidbody, fat pointy headstock.

1987-1988	Red-Orange Sunburst	$275	$375

Burton Guitars

1980-present. Custom classical guitars built by luthier Cynthia Burton in Portland, Oregon.

Buscarino Guitars

1981-present. Luthier John Buscarino builds his premium and presentation grade, custom archtops and steel-string and nylon-string flat-tops in Franklin, North Carolina.

Byers, Gregory

1984-present. Premium grade, custom classical and Flamenco guitars built by luthier Gregory Byers in Willits, California.

C. Fox

1997-2002. Luthier Charles Fox built his premium grade, production/custom flat-tops in Healdsburg, California. He has been building guitars since 1968 and has founded two schools of lutherie along the way. In 2002 Fox closed C. Fox Guitars with plans to later reopen as Charles Fox Guitars.

D (Napa Series)

1998-2002. D-style, sloped shoulders, solid Sitka spruce top, Indian rosewood back and sides, Natural.

1998		$1,700	$2,000

SJ (Napa Series)

1998-2002. SJ (small jumbo), solid Sitka spruce top, mahogany back and sides, Natural.

1998	Custom, higher-end appointments	$1,900	$2,400
1998	Standard appointments	$1,200	$1,500

CA (Composite Acoustics)

1999-present. Professional grade, production, carbon fiber composite guitars built in Lafayette, Louisiana.

Callaham

1989-present. Professional, production/custom, solidbody electric guitars built by luthier Bill Callaham in Winchester, Virginia. They also make tube amp heads.

Campellone

1978-present. Luthier Mark Campellone builds his premium grade, custom archtops in Smithfield, Rhode Island. He also made electrics and basses in the 1970s.

Deluxe

Seventeen inches, middle of the company product line, archtop, Blond or Sunburst.

1990-1995		$5,200	$6,000

Special

Sixteen to 18" archtop, carved spruce top, carved flamed maple back, flamed maple sides, Blond or Sunburst.

1994-1999		$6,200	$7,000

Campelloe Cameo

Carbonaro

1974-present. Luthier Robert Carbonaro builds his premium grade, production/custom, archtop and flat-top guitars in Santa Fe, New Mexico.

Carlos

ca.1976-late 1980s. Imported copies of classic American acoustics distributed by Coast Wholesale Music.

Model 240

1970s. D-18 copy with mahogany (laminate?) back and sides, spruce top, Natural.

1978		$150	$300

Model 275

1970s. D-35 copy with rosewood (laminate?) sides and three-piece back, spruce top, Natural.

1978		$175	$350

Carvin

1946-present. Intermediate and professional grade, production/custom, acoustic and electric guitars. They also offer basses and amps. Founded in Los Angeles by Hawaiian guitarist and recording artist Lowell C. Kiesel as the L.C. Kiesel Co. making pickups for guitars. Bakelite Kiesel-brand electric Hawaiian lap steels are introduced in early-'47. Small tube amps introduced ca. '47. By late-'49, the Carvin brandname is introduced, combining parts of names of sons Carson and Gavin. Carvin acoustic and electric Spanish archtops are introduced in '54. Instruments are sold by mail-order only. The company relocated to Covina, California in '49 and to Escondido, California in '68. Two retail stores opened in Hollywood and Santa Ana, California in '91.

Approx. 2,000-4,000 guitars made prior to '70 with no serial number. First serial number appeared in '70, stamped on end of fingerboard, beginning with #5000. All are consecutive. Later SN on neck plates.

Approximate SN ranges include:

- 1970: First serial number #5000.
- 1980-83: Serial numbers in 11000 range (approx. 1000/year) [koa DC200K #11815, 1981].
- 1983-84: #13000-15000.
- 1985-86: #17000-20000.
- 1988-89: #22000-25000.
- 1989-91: #26000-33000.
- 1992: #35000-ff.

Carvin C-850

GUITARS

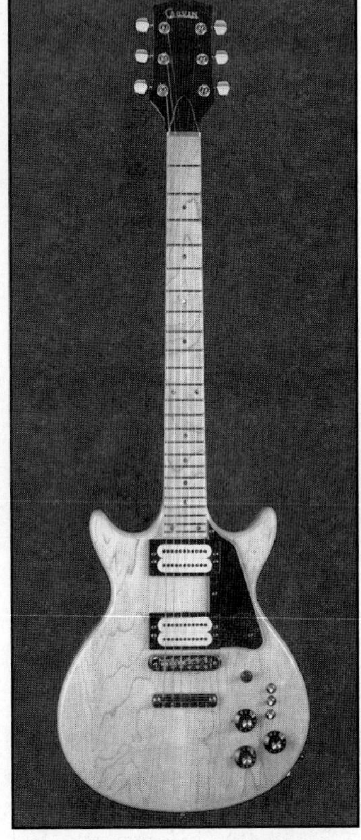
1992 Carvin DC-150

1992 Carvin DN612

MODEL YEAR	FEATURES	EXC. COND. LOW	HIGH

AE185

1994-present. Single cut acoustic/electric, F-hole.

1994		$600	$900

CM130

1976-early-1980s. Single cutaway solidbody, two humbucking pickups, phase and coil split switches.

1978		$500	$600

DB-630 Doubleneck

1970s. Six/four (bass) doubleneck.

1977		$700	$1,000

DBS-98 B Doubleneck

1970s. Three pickups, four/six strings. Natural.

1972		$700	$1,000

DC-100

1980s. Double cutaway solidbody.

1981		$350	$450

DC-125

1991-1996. Double cutaway solidbody, one humbucking pickup.

1990s		$500	$600

DC-127

1991-present.

1990s		$500	$600

DC-135

1991-present. Double cut, neck-through construction, single-single-hum pickups.

1990s		$500	$700

DC-150

1977-1991, 2002-present. Double cut soldibody, 2 humbuckers, stereo wiring.

1977-1991		$500	$700

DC-200

1980-present. Double cutaway solidbody, block inlays, two humbuckers.

1981		$500	$700

DC-400

1993-present. Double cut, koa body, flamed maple top, neck-through, and higher appointments.

1997		$600	$800

DN-612 Doubleneck

1981-1996. Twelve-string and six-string doubleneck, double cutaway.

1980s		$800	$1,000

DT-650 Doubleneck

Late-1970s. Doubleneck with 12/6 strings, maple body and necks, block inlays, two split-coil humbuckers for each neck.

1978		$800	$1,000

SGB

1955-1962. Single-cutaway slab body, two single-coil pickups (later humbuckers), TV Yellow finish, dot markers.

1950s	P-90-style pickups	$500	$600
1950s	Humbucker-style pickups	$500	$600

SH-225

Semi-hollowbody.

1981		$500	$600

TL-60 (T)

1993-present. Single cut, neck-thru solidbody, 2 single coils. The earlier T version had 1 humbucker, 1 single coil.

1993		$500	$600

Ultra V

1988-1993. V-shaped solidbody with bass wing shorter than treble side, block inlays, two humbucking pickups.

1986		$500	$600

Casa Montalvo

1987-present. Intermediate and professional grade, production/custom flamenco and classical guitars made in Mexico for George Katechis of Berkeley Musical Instrument Exchange.

Casio

1987-1988. Digital guitars imported from Japan, plastic body, synthesizer features.

DG10

1987. Self-contained digital guitar.

1987		$125	$175

DG20

Midi-capable digital guitar.

1987		$200	$275

Chandler

1984-present. Located in California, Paul Chandler started making pickguards and accessories in the '70s. In '84, he started to produce electric guitars, basses, and effects.

555 Model

1992-present. John Lennon Rickenbacker-style body, Firebird-style pickups, retro slotted headstock.

1992	TV Yellow	$500	$600

Austin Special

1991-1999. Resembles futuristic Danelectro, lipstick pickups, available in five-string version.

1991		$500	$650

Austin Special Baritone

1994-1999. Nicknamed "Elvis," Gold Metal-Flake finish, mother-of-toilet-seat binding, tremolo, baritone.

1994		$500	$700

Metro

1990s. Vague Strat-style slab body with P-90-style pickup in neck position and humbucker in the bridge position.

1990s		$500	$550

Telepathic

1994-2000. Classic single cut style, three models; Basic, Standard, Deluxe.

1990s	Basic	$400	$450
1990s	Deluxe	$600	$700
1990s	Standard	$500	$600

MODEL YEAR	FEATURES	EXC. COND. LOW	HIGH

Chapin

Professional and premium grade, production/custom, semi-hollow, solidbody, and acoustic electric guitars built by luthiers Bill Chapin and Fred Campbell in San Jose, California.

Chapman

1970-present. Made by Emmett Chapman, the Stick features 10 strings and is played by tapping both hands. The Grand Stick features 12 strings.

Stick

Ten or twelve strings, touch-tap hybrid electric instrument.

1970-1999	10 strings	$900	$950
1970-1999	12 strings	$1,100	$1,200

Charles Shifflett Acoustic Guitars

1990-present. Professional and premium grade, custom, classical and flamenco guitars built by luthier Charles Shifflett in High River, Alberta.

Charvel

1978-present. Founded by Wayne Charvel in California. U.S.-made '78-'85, a combination of imports and U.S.-made post-'85. Charvel also manufactured the Jackson brand. The earliest San Dimas Charvels were custom-built with wild graphics, locking trems, high-output pickups, and pointy headstocks. Charvel licensed its trademark to IMC in '85 and IMC moved the factory to Ontario, California in '86. On October 25, 2002, Fender Musical Instruments Corp. (FMIC) took ownership of Jackson/Charvel Manufacturing Inc. Currently Charvel offers intermediate and professional grade, production, solidbody electric guitars.

Electric guitar manufacturing info:

- 1986-1989 Japanese-made Models 1 through 8
- 1989-1991 Japanese-made 550 XL, 650 XL/Custom, 750 XL (XL=neck-through)
- 1989-1992 Japanese-made Models 275, 375, 475, 575
- 1990-1991 Korean-made Charvette models
- 1992-1994 Korean-made Models 325, 425

275 Deluxe Dinky

1989-1991. Made in Japan, offset double-cut solidbody, one single-coil and one humbucker ('89), three stacked humbuckers ('90-'91), trem.

1989	1 single, 1 humbucker	$350	$400
1990-1991	Stacked humbuckers	$350	$400

325SL

1992-1994. Dot inlays.

1992-1994		$325	$375

325SLX

1992-1994. Surfcaster-like thinline acoustic/electric, dual cutaways, F-hole, on-board chorus, shark inlays, made in Korea.

1992-1994		$350	$400

375 Deluxe

1989-1992. Maple or rosewood fingerboard, dot inlays, single-single-humbucker.

1989-1992		$375	$425

475

Humbucker-single-single configuration, bolt-on neck, dot markers.

1990s		$300	$350

475 Deluxe/Special

1989-1992. Introduced as Special, discontinued as Deluxe, bound rosewood fingerboard, shark fin markers, two oval stacked humbuckers and single bridge humbucker.

1989-1992		$300	$350

Avenger

1990-1991. Randy Rhoads-style batwing-shaped solidbody, 3 stacked humbuckers, trem, made in Japan.

1990-1991		$350	$400

Charvette

1990-1991. Charvette Series made in Korea, super-Strat-style, model number series 100 through 300.

1990-1991		$175	$275

Fusion Deluxe

1989-1991. Double cut solidbody, trem, one humbucker and one single-coil pickup, made in Japan.

1989-1991		$375	$425

Fusion Standard/AS FX 1

1993-1996. Double cut solidbody, trem, one regular and two mini humbuckers, made in Japan, also named AS FX1.

1993-1996		$325	$375

Model 1

1986-1989. Offset double cut solidbody, maple neck, dot inlays, 1 humbucker, tremolo, made in Japan.

1986-1989		$300	$350

Model 1A

1986-1989. As Model 1, but with 3 single-coils.

1986-1989		$300	$350

Model 1C

1986-1989. As Model 1, but with 1 humbucker, 2 single coils.

1986-1989		$325	$375

Model 2

1986-1989. As Model 1, but with rosewood 'board.

1986-1989		$325	$375

Model 3

1986-1989. As Model 2, but with 1 humbucker, 2 single coils.

1986-1989		$325	$375

1986 Charvel Model 2

1987 Charvel Model 3

GUITARS

Charvel Model 5

Collings D-2H

MODEL YEAR	FEATURES	EXC. COND. LOW	HIGH

Model 3A

1986-1988. As Model 3, but with 2 humbuckers.

1986-1988		$300	$350

Model 3DR

1988-1989. As Model 3, but with 1 humbucker and 1 single-coil.

1988-1989		$300	$350

Model 4

1986-1989. As Model 2, but with 1 regular humbucker and 2 stacked humbuckers mounted in the body (no pickguard), and with active electronics.

1986-1989		$350	$450

Model 4A

1986-1989. As Model 4, but with two regular humbuckers.

1986-1989		$325	$425

Model 5

1986-1989. As Model 4A, but is neck-thru construction, with JE1000TG active elctronics.

1986-1989		$375	$475

Model 5A

1988. Single humbucker and single knob version of Model 5, limited production, made in Japan.

1988		$350	$450

Model 6

1986-1989. As Model 4, but with shark's tooth fingerboard inlays.

1986-1989		$450	$550

Model 7

1988-1989. Single cut solidbody, bound top, reversed headstock, two single-coils, made in Japan.

1988-1989		$450	$600

Model 88 LTD

1988. Double cut solidbody, one slanted humbucker, shark fin inlay, 1000 built, made in Japan.

1988		$550	$700

ST Custom

1990-1992. Offset double cut ash solidbody, 2 single-coils and 1 humbucker, rosewood 'board, trem, made in Japan.

1990s		$350	$450

ST Deluxe

1990-1992. Same as ST Custom but with maple 'board.

1990s		$325	$375

Surfcaster

1991-1993. Offset double cut, F-hole, 2 single-coils, bound body, trem, made in Japan.

1992		$575	$775

Surfcaster 12

1991-1995. 12-string version of Surfcaster, no trem, made in Japan.

1992		$575	$775

Surfcaster HT (Model SC 1)

1994-1995. Offset double cut, F-hole, 2 single-coils, no trem, made in Japan.

1994		$475	$550

Chiquita

1979-present. Intermediate grade, production guitars made by Erlewine Guitars in Austin, Texas (see that listing). There was also a mini amp available.

Travel Guitar

1979-present. Developed by Mark Erlewine and ZZ Top's Billy Gibbons. 27" overall length solidbody.

1980s	Blond, Natural or Yellow	$200	$225
1980s	Red option	$250	$275

Chrysalis Guitars

1998-present. Luthier Tim White builds his premium grade, production/custom Chrysalis Guitar System, which includes interchangeable components that can be quickly assembled into a full-size electric/acoustic guitar, in New Boston, New Hampshire. A variety of instruments may be created, including 6- and 12- string electrics and acoustics, electric and acoustic mandocello and acoustic basses.

Cipher

1960s. Solidbody electric guitars and basses imported from Japan by Inter-Mark. Generally strange-shaped bodies.

Electric Solidbody Guitars

Student-level import.

1960s		$125	$175

Citron

1995-present. In 1975, Harvey Citron and Joe Veillette founded Veillette-Citron, which was best known for handcrafted, neck-thru guitars and basses. That company closed in 1983. Currently Citron builds professional and premium grade, production/custom solidbody guitars and basses in Woodstock, New York.

Collings

1986-present. Professional, premium, and presentation grade, production/custom, flat-top and archtop guitars built in Austin, Texas. They also build mandolins. Bill Collings started with guitar repair and began custom building guitars around '73. In '80, his relocated his shop from Houston to Austin and started Collings Guitars in '86.

000-2H (Indian rosewood)

1994-present. 15" 000-size, Indian rosewood back and sides, spruce top, slotted headstock, 12-fret neck, dot markers.

1994		$2,500	$3,700

C-10 (mahogany)

1994-present. 000-style, spruce top, mahogany back and sides, natural.

1995		$2,000	$2,500

GUITARS

MODEL YEAR	FEATURES	EXC. COND. LOW	HIGH

C-10 Deluxe (Indian rosewood)

Triple 0-size, spruce top, Indian rosewood back and sides, Natural.

1994-2002		$2,300	$3,000

C-100 (mahogany)

1986-1995. Quadruple 0-style, spruce top, mahogany back and sides, Natural. Replaced by CJ Jumbo.

1994		$2,000	$2,500

CJ Jumbo (Indian rosewood)

1995-present. Quadruple 0-style, spruce top, Indian rosewood back and sides, Natural.

1996		$2,500	$3,000

D-1

1994-present. D-style, 15 5/8", spruce top, mahogany back and sides, natural.

1995		$2,000	$2,500

D-1A Custom

Upgrade D-1 with Adirondack spruce top and higher appointments, Natural.

1999		$2,300	$3,000

D-1SB

Sunburst finish option for D-1 model.

2001		$2,300	$3,000

D-2 (Indian rosewood)

1986-1995. D-1 with Indian rosewood back and sides, Natural.

1986-1995		$2,500	$3,000

D-2H (Indian rosewood)

1986-present. Dreadnought. Same as D-2 with herringbone purfling around top edge.

1986-2001		$1,900	$2,300

D-2H/D-2HBZ (Brazilian rosewood)

Grade AA Brazilian rosewood, spruce top.

1994-2001		$4,500	$5,500

D-3 (Brazilian rosewood)

Similar to D-2H but with abalone purfling/rosette.

1994		$4,800	$5,300

OM-1 (mahogany)

1994-present. Grand concert, Sitka spruce top, mahogany back and sides, natural.

1994		$2,100	$2,300

OM-2HAV (Brazilian rosewood)

Adirondack spruce top, Brazilian rosewood back and sides, ivoroid-bound body.

1998		$4,500	$5,500

OM-3 (Brazilian rosewood)

Brazilian rosewood back and sides, Adirondack spruce top, fancy rosette.

1998		$6,000	$7,000

OM-3HC (Indian rosewood)

Single rounded cutaway, 15", spruce top, Indian rosewood back and sides, herringbone purfling.

1986		$2,800	$3,200

OM-42B (Brazilian rosewood)

Brazilian rosewood back and sides, Adirondack spruce top, fancy rosette and binding.

2000		$7,000	$8,000

MODEL YEAR	FEATURES	EXC. COND. LOW	HIGH

SJ (Indian rosewood)

Sitka spruce top, Indian rosewood or quilted maple back and sides.

1992		$2,800	$3,800

SJ-41 (Brazilian rosewood)

Cedar top, Brazilian rosewood back and sides.

1996		$7,000	$7,500

Comins

1992-present. Premium grade, custom archtops built by luthier Bill Comins in Willow Grove, Pennsylvania. He also has a line of amps built in collaboration with George Alessandro that were introduced in '03.

Chester Avenue

1994-present. Electric archtop, solid spruce top and back, 17" or 18" cutaway, options can vary.

1998		$5,500	$6,500

Classic

1995-present. Classic archtop jazz model, 17" cutaway, pickguard mounted neck pickup, block markers.

1997		$5,000	$5,500

Parlor

1995-present. 14" archtop with viola styling.

1995		$3,000	$3,500

Renaissance

1996-present. 17" archtop cutaway, carved European spruce top, solid curly maple back and sides, unique removable sound baffles, blond.

1998		$5,500	$6,000

Concertone

ca. 1914-1930s. Concertone was a brandname made by Chicago's Slingerland and distributed by Montgomery Ward. The brand was also used on other instruments such as ukuleles.

Conklin

1984-present. Intermediate, professional and premium grade, production/custom, 6, 7, 8, and 12 string solid and hollowbody electrics, and 4 to 9 string basses by luthier Bill Conklin. Originally located in Lebanon, Missouri, in '88 the company moved to Springfield, Missouri. Conklin instruments are made in the U.S. and overseas.

Conn

Ca. 1968-ca.1978. Student to mid-quality classical and acoustic guitars, some with bolt-on necks. Imported from Japan by band instrument manufacturer and distributor Conn/Continental Music Company, Elkhart, Indiana.

Acoustic Guitars

Japanese imports.

1970s		$150	$200
1980s		$150	$200

Classical Guitars

Student-level Japanese imports.

1970s		$150	$200

Collings CJ Jumbo

Collings OM2

1974 Conrad doubleneck

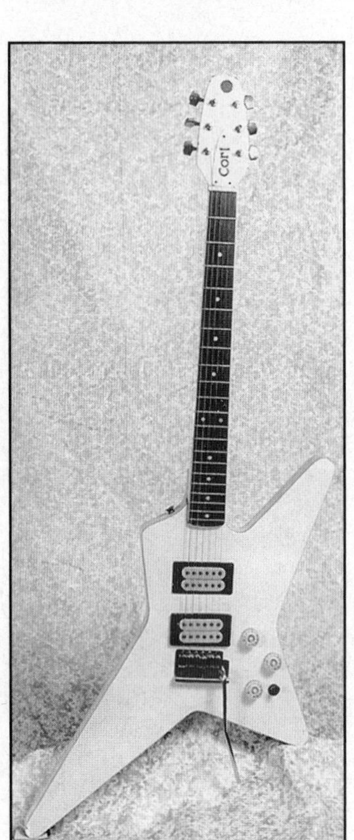

1984 Cort EX2T

MODEL YEAR | FEATURES | EXC. COND. LOW | HIGH

Connor, Stephan

1995-present. Luthier Stephan Connor builds his premium grade, custom nylon-string guitars in Waltham, Massachusetts.

Conrad

1972-1977. Mid- to better-quality copies of glued-neck Martin and Gibson acoustics and bolt-neck Gibson and Fender solidbodies. Also mandolins and banjos. Imported from Japan by David Wexler and Company, Chicago, Illinois.

Acoustical Slimline 12-String 40100

1970s. ES-335-style, 2 DeArmond-style pickups, rosewood board, 12 strings, dot markers.

1970s $100 $300

Acoustical Slimline 40080/40085

1970s. ES-335-style, 2 or 2 DeArmond-style pickups, rosewood board, block markers.

1970s $100 $300

Bison (40035/40030/40065/40005)

1970s. Bison copy, 1 to 4 pickups available, rosewood board, dot markers, 6-on-side headstock.

1970s $100 $200

Bumper (40223)

1970s. Armstrong Lucite copy, import.

1974 $225 $275

De Luxe Folk Guitar

1970s. Resonator acoustic, mahogany back, sides and neck, Japanese import.

1974 $175 $250

Master Size 40178

1972-1977. Byrdland copy.

1970s $350 $400

Violin-Shaped 12-String Electric 40176

1970s. Scroll headstock, 2 pickups, 500/1 control panel, bass side dot markers.

1970s $100 $300

Violin-Shaped Electric 40175

1970s. Scroll headstock, 2 pickups, 500/1 control panel, bass side dot markers, vibrato.

1970s $100 $300

White Styrene 1280 (solidbody)

1970s. Solid maple body covered with white styrene, 2 pickups, trem, bass side dot markers, white.

1970s $100 $300

Coral

Refer to Danelectro section.

Córdoba

Line of classical guitars handmade in Portugal and imported by Guitar Salon International.

Cordova

1960s. Classical nylon string guitars imported by David Wexler of Chicago.

Grand Concert Model WC-026

1960s. Highest model offered by Cordova, one-piece rosewood back, laminated rosewood sides, spruce top, Natural.

1963 $175 $300

Coriani, Paolo

1984-present. Production/custom nylon-string guitars and hurdy-gurdys built by luthier Paolo Coriani in Modeila, Italy.

Cort

1973-present. North Brook, Illinois-based Cort offers budget, intermediate and professional grade, production/custom, acoustic and solidbody, semi-hollow, hollow body electric guitars built in Korea. They also offer basses.

Doubleneck

Cherry, six/twelve necks, SG-style, Asian import.

1970s $250 $450

Electric Guitars

1973-present. A variety of models were offered, often copy guitars. These guitars were heavily distributed in the 1980s.

1973-1989 $175 $400

1990-1999 $55 $300

Crafter

2000-present. Line of intermediate and professional grade, production, acoustic and acoustic/electric guitars from Hohner. They also offer a bass.

Crafters of Tennessee

See listing under Tennessee.

Cranium

1996-present. Professional grade, production/custom, hollow, semi-hollow, and solidbody electrics built by luthier Wayne O'Connor in Peterborough, Ontario.

Crescent Moon

1999-present. Professional grade, production/custom, solidbody guitars and basses built by luthier Craig Muller in Baltimore, Maryland.

Crestwood

1970s. Copies of the popular classical guitars, flat-tops, electric solidbodies and basses of the era, imported by La Playa Distributing Company of Detroit.

Electric Guitars

1970s. Includes near copies of the 335 (Crestwood model 2043, 2045 and 2047), Les Paul Custom (2020), Strat (2073), Jazzmaster (2078), Tele (2082), and the SG Custom (2084).

1970s $100 $300

MODEL YEAR	FEATURES	EXC. COND. LOW	HIGH

Cromwell

1935-1939. Budget model brand built by Gibson and distributed by mail-order businesses like Grossman, Continental, and Richter & Phillips.

G-8

1935-1936. Archtop acoustic, F-holes, pressed mahogany back and sides, carved and bound top, bound back, pickguard and 'board, no truss rod.

1935		$350	$700

Crown

1960s. Violin-shaped hollowbody electrics, solidbody electric guitars and basses, possibly others. Imported from Japan.

Barney Kessel Copy

Double pointed cutaways, two humbucking pickups, laminated top, full-depth body.

1969		$400	$500

Electric Solidbody Guitars

Student-level Japanese import.

1960s		$100	$200

Crucianelli

Early 1960s. Italian guitars imported into the U.S. by Bennett Brothers of New York and Chicago around 1963 to '64. Crucianelli also made the Imperial brand guitars for the Imperial Accordion Company of Chicago.

Cumpiano

1974-present. Professional and premium grade, custom steel-string and nylon-string guitars, and acoustic basses built by luthier William Cumpiano in Northampton, Massachusetts.

Custom

1980s. Line of solidbody guitars and basses introduced in the early 1980s by Charles Lawing and Chris Lovell, owners of Strings & Things in Memphis.

D'Agostino

1976-early 1990s. Acoustic and electric solidbody guitars and basses imported by PMS Music, founded in New York City by former Maestro executive Pat D'Agostino, his brother Steven D'Agostino, and Mike Confortti. First dreadnought acoustic guitars imported from Japan in '76. First solidbodies manufactured by the EKO custom shop beginning in '77. In '82 solidbody production moved to Japan. Beginning in '84, D'Agostinos were made in Korea. Overall, about 60% of guitars were Japanese, 40% Korean.

Acoustic Flat-Tops

1976-1990. Early production in Japan, by mid-'80s, most production in Korea.

1970s		$150	$300

Electric Semi-Hollowbody Guitars

1981-early 1990s. Early production in Japan, later versions from Korea.

1980s		$250	$350

Electric Solidbody Guitars

1977-early 1990s. Early models made in Italy, later versions from Japan and Korea.

1970s		$250	$350

D'Angelico

John D'Angelico built his own line of archtop guitars, mandolins and violins from 1932 until his death in 1964. His instruments are some of the most sought-after by collectors. The following price ranges were developed after reviewing in-depth detail provided by the following contributors: Larry Wexer, Timm Kummer, Michael Katz, Charles Dellavalle, Dave Belzer, and Drew Berlin.

D'Angelico (L-5 Snakehead)

1932-1935. D'Angelico's L-5-style copy with snakehead headstock, his first model.

1932-1935	Sunburst	$14,000	$15,000

Excel/Exel (non-cutaway)

1936-1949. Non-cutaway, 17" width, one-three-ply bound F-hole. Natural finishes were typically not offered in the 1930s. Non-cut Excels were generally not offered after 1949 in deference to the Excel cutaway.

1936-1939	Sunburst, straight F-hole	$16,000	$18,000
1938-1939	Sunburst, standard F-hole	$16,000	$17,000
1940-1949	Natural	$18,000	$21,000
1940-1949	Sunburst, standard F-hole	$16,000	$17,000

Excel/Exel Cutaway

1947-1964. Cutaway, 17" width, one-three-ply bound F-hole. Larry Wexer noted from 1950-1957, D'Angelico guitars suffer from severe binding problems and many have replaced bindings. Replaced bindings make the guitar non-original and these repaired guitars have lower values.

1947-1949	Natural, non-original binding	$18,000	$25,000
1947-1949	Natural, original binding	$30,000	$40,000
1947-1949	Sunburst, non-original binding	$13,000	$20,000
1947-1949	Sunburst, original binding	$20,000	$35,000
1950-1959	Natural, non-original binding	$18,000	$25,000
1950-1959	Natural, original binding	$30,000	$40,000
1950-1959	Sunburst, non-original binding	$13,000	$20,000
1950-1959	Sunburst, original binding	$20,000	$35,000
1960-1964	Natural	$40,000	$45,000
1960-1964	Sunburst	$35,000	$40,000

1981 D'Agostino LP-500

1937 D'Angelico Excel

GUITARS

1960 D'Angelico New Yorker

D'Angelico II NYSD-9

MODEL YEAR	FEATURES	EXC. COND. LOW	HIGH

New Yorker (non-cutaway)

1936-1949. Non-cutaway, 18" width, five-ply-bound F-hole. New Yorker non-cutaway orders were overshadowed by the cutaway model orders starting in '47. All prices noted are for original bindings. Non-original (replaced) bindings will reduce the value by 33%-50%.

1936-1939	Sunburst	$20,000	$30,000
1940-1949	Natural	$20,000	$30,000
1940-1949	Sunburst	$20,000	$30,000

New Yorker Cutaway

1947-1964. Cutaway, 18" width, 5-ply-bound F-hole. New Yorker non-cutaway orders were overshadowed by the cutaway model orders starting in 1947. All prices noted are for original bindings. Non-original (replaced) bindings will reduce the value by 33%-50%.

1947-1949	Natural	$50,000	$70,000
1947-1949	Sunburst	$45,000	$60,000
1950-1959	Natural	$50,000	$70,000
1950-1959	Sunburst	$45,000	$60,000
1960-1964	Natural	$50,000	$70,000
1960-1964	Sunburst	$45,000	$60,000

New Yorker Special

1947-1964. Cutaway, 17" width, also called Excel New Yorker or Excel Cutaway New Yorker, has New Yorker styling. All prices noted are for original bindings. Non-original (replaced) bindings will reduce the value by 33%-50%.

1947-1949	Natural	$35,000	$45,000
1947-1949	Sunburst	$30,000	$40,000
1950-1959	Natural	$35,000	$45,000
1950-1959	Sunburst	$30,000	$40,000
1960-1964	Natural	$40,000	$55,000
1960-1964	Sunburst	$35,000	$45,000

Style A

1936-1945. Archtop, 17" width, unbound F-holes, block fingerboard inlays, multi-pointed headstock, nickel-plated metal parts.

1936-1939	Sunburst	$11,000	$13,000
1940-1945	Sunburst	$11,000	$13,000

Style A-1

1936-1945. Unbound F-holes, 17" width, arched headstock, nickel-plated metal parts.

1936-1939	Sunburst	$12,000	$14,000
1940-1945	Sunburst	$12,000	$14,000

Style B

1933-1948. Archtop 17" wide, unbound F-holes, block fingerboard inlays, gold-plated parts.

1936-1939	Sunburst	$14,000	$16,000
1940-1948	Sunburst	$14,000	$16,000

Style B Special

1933-1948. D'Angelico described variations from standard features with a 'Special' designation. Vintage dealers may also describe these instruments as 'Special'.

1936-1939	Sunburst	$14,000	$16,000
1940-1948	Sunburst	$14,000	$16,000

MODEL YEAR	FEATURES	EXC. COND. LOW	HIGH

D'Angelico (Vestax)

1988-present. Premium and presentation grade, production/custom, archtop, flat-top, and solidbody guitars built by luthier Hidesato Shino and Vestax near Tokyo, Japan. Distributed in the U.S. by D'Angelico Guitars of America, in Westfield, New Jersey.

D'Angelico II

Mid-1990s. Archtops built in the U.S. and distributed by Archtop Enterprises of Merrick, New York.

D'Aquisto

1965-1995. James D'Aquisto apprenticed under D'Angelico until the latter's death, at age 59, in 1964. He started making his own brand instruments in '65 and built archtop and flat top acoustic guitars, solidbody and hollowbody electric guitars. He also designed guitars for Hagstrom and Fender. He died in '95, at age 59.

Avant Garde

1987-1994. 18" wide, non-traditional futuristic model, approximately five or six instruments were reportedly made. Because of low production this pricing is for guidance only.

1990	Blond	$65,000	$110,000

Centura/Centura Deluxe

1994 only. 17" wide, non-traditional art deco futuristic archtop, approximately 10 made, the last guitars made by this luthier. Due to the low production this pricing is for guidance only.

1994	Blond	$65,000	$110,000

Excel (cutaway)

1965-1992. Archtop, 17" width, with modern thin-logo started in 1981.

1965-1969	Blond	$48,000	$50,000
1965-1969	Sunburst	$35,000	$40,000
1970-1979	Blond	$42,000	$47,000
1970-1979	Sunburst	$37,000	$39,000
1980-1992	Blond	$47,000	$52,000
1980-1992	Sunburst	$40,000	$42,000

HollowElectric

Early model with bar pickup, D'Aquisto headstock, 1970s model with humbuckers.

1965-1972	Sunburst	$13,000	$15,000

Jim Hall Model (hollow electric)

1965	Laminate top	$13,000	$14,000
1978	Solid top	$15,000	$16,000

New Yorker Classic (solidbody)

1980s. Only two were reported to be made, therefore this pricing is for guidance only.

1980s		$17,000	$19,000

New Yorker Deluxe (cutaway)

1965-1992. Most are 18" wide.

1965-1992	Blond	$50,000	$60,000
1965-1992	Sunburst	$45,000	$55,000

New Yorker Special (cutaway)

1966-1992. Most are 17" wide.

1966-1969	Sunburst	$32,000	$35,000

MODEL YEAR	FEATURES	EXC. COND. LOW	HIGH
1966-1979	Blond	$40,000	$45,000
1970-1979	Sunburst	$35,000	$37,000
1980-1992	Blond	$45,000	$50,000
1980-1992	Sunburst	$38,000	$40,000

New Yorker Special 7-String

1980s. Limited production 7-string, single cutaway, Sunburst.

1980s		$45,000	$48,000

Solo/Solo Deluxe

1992-1993. 18" wide, non-traditional non-cutaway art deco model, only two reported made. Because of low production this pricing is for guidance only.

1992-1993	Blond	$65,000	$110,000

D'Aquisto (Aria)

May 2002-present. Premium grade, production, D'Aquisto designs licensed to Aria of Japan by D'Aquisto Strings, Inc., Deer Park, New York.

Centura Electric

2002-present. Chambered solidbody.

2002	Blond option	$2,400	$2,600

D'Leco Guitars

1991-present. Luthier James W. Dale builds his premium grade, production/custom archtops in Oklahoma City, Oklahoma.

D'Pergo Custom Guitars

2002-present. Professional, premium, and presentation grade, production/custom, solidbody guitars built in Windham, New Hampshire. Every component of the guitars are built by D'Pergo.

Daily Guitars

1976-present. Luthier David Daily builds his premium grade, production/custom classical guitars in Sparks, Nevada.

Daion

1978-1985. Mid- to higher-quality copies imported from Japan. Original designs introduced in the '80s.

555 Headhunter

1980s. ES-335-style body.

1980-1985		$450	$900

Caribou

1980s. Acoustic/electric, cutaway body.

1980-1985		$350	$700

Mark I, II, III, IV

1978-1985. D-style, cedar or spruce top, various hardwood back and sides.

1978	Natural	$200	$400

Mark X

1980s.

1980-1985		$400	$800

Daisy Rock

2001-present. Budget and intermediate grade, production, full-scale and 3/4 scale, solidbody, semi-hollow, acoustic, and acoustic/electric guitars. Founded by Tish Ciravolo as a Division of Schecter Guitars, the Daisy line is focused on female customers. Initial offerings included daisy and heart-shaped electric guitars and basses.

Dan Armstrong

Dan Armstrong started playing jazz in Cleveland in the late-'50s. He moved to New York and also started doing repairs, eventually opening his own store on 48th Street in '65. By the late-'60s he was designing his Lucite guitars for Ampeg (see Ampeg for those listings). He moved to England in '71, where he developed his line of colored stomp boxes. Returning to the States in '75, he continues to be involved in the music industry.

Wood Body Guitar

1973-1975. Sliding pickup, wood body.

1973	White	$700	$800

Danelectro

1946-1969, 1996-present. Professional grade, production, electric guitars offered by the Evets Corporation, of San Clemente, California. They also offer effects and amps. The original Danelectro made amplifiers, solidbody, semi-hollow and hollowbody electric guitars and basses, electric sitar, and the Bellzouki under the Danelectro, Silvertone, Coral, Dane, Dan Armstrong Modified Danelectro brand names. Founded in Red Bank, New Jersey, by Nathan I. "Nate" or "Nat" Daniel, an electronics enthusiast with amplifier experience. In 1933, Daniel built amps for Thor's Bargain Basement in New York. In '34 he was recruited by Epiphone's Herb Sunshine to build earliest Electar amps and pickup-making equipment. From '35 to '42, he operated Daniel Electric Laboratories in Manhattan, supplying Epiphone.

He started Danelectro in '46 and made his first amps for Montgomery Ward in '47. In '48, began supplying Silvertone amps for Sears (various coverings), with his own brand (brown leatherette) distributed by Targ and Dinner as Danelectro and S.S. Maxwell. He developed an electronic vibrato in '48 on his Vibravox series amps. In '50 he developed a microphone with volume and tone controls and outboard "Echo Box" reverb unit. In the fall of '54, Danelectro replaced Harmony as provider of Silvertone solidbody guitars for Sears. Also in '54, the first Danelectro brand guitars appeared with tweed covering, bell headstock, and pickups under pickguard. The Coke bottle headstock debuts as Silvertone "Lightning Bolt" in '54, and is used on Danelectros for '56 to '66.

The company moved to Red Bank, New Jersey in '57, and in '58 relocated to Neptune, New Jersey. In '59, Harmony and Kay guitars replace all but three Danelectros in Sears catalog. In '66, MCA buys the company (Daniel remains with

1969 D'Aquisto New Yorker

Danelectro Convertible

GUITARS

Danelectro Doubleneck 6/4

1960 Danelectro U-1

MODEL YEAR	FEATURES	EXC. COND. LOW	HIGH

company), but by mid-'69, MCA halts production and closes the doors. Some leftover stock is sold to Dan Armstrong, who had a shop in New York at the time. Armstrong assembled several hundred Danelectro guitars as "Dan Armstrong Modified" with his own pickup design.

Rights to name acquired by Anthony Mark in late-'80s, who assembled a number of thinline hollowbody guitars, many with "Longhorn" shape, using Japanese-made bodies and original Danelectro necks and hardware. Since '96, Evets has offered a line of effects, amps, and guitars, many of which are reissues of the earlier instruments.

Bellzouki Double Pickup

1961-1969. 12-string electric, modified teardrop shape with two body points on both treble and bass bouts. Sunburst finish.

1960s		$900	$1,100

Bellzouki Single Pickup

1961-1969. 12-string electric, teardrop-shaped body. Sunburst finish.

1960s		$800	$900

Convertible

1959-1969. Acoustic/electric, double cutaway. Guitar was sold with or without the removable single pickup.

1950s	Pickup installed	$500	$600
1960s	Acoustic, no pickup	$300	$400
1960s	Pickup installed	$400	$500

Coral Firefly

1967-1969. ES-335-shaped body, F-holes, two pickups. Sold with or without vibrato.

1967		$400	$500

Coral Hornet 2

1967-1969. Jaguar-type body, two pickups. Sold with or without vibrato.

1967		$450	$600

Coral Sitar

1967-1969. Six-string guitar with 13 drone strings and three pickups (two under the six strings, one under the drones). Kind of a USA-shaped body.

1967		$1,800	$2,200

Deluxe Double Pickup (6028)

Double cutaway, two pointer knobs, two pickups, standard-size pickguard, master control knob. White (6026), Dark Walnut (6027), Honey Walnut (6028).

1960s		$650	$750

Deluxe Triple Pickup (6037)

Double cutaway, 3 pointer knobs, 3 pickups, standard-size pickguard, master control knob. White (6036), dark walnut (6037), honey walnut (6038).

1960s		$950	$1,100

Doubleneck (3923)

1959-1969. A "Shorthorn" double cutaway, bass and six-string necks, one pickup on each neck, Coke bottle headstocks.

1960s	White Sunburst	$1,300	$1,600

Electric Sitar

1967-1969. Traditional looking, oval-bodied sitar. No drone strings as on the Coral Sitar of the same period.

1967		$800	$1,000

Guitaralin (4123)

1963-1969. The "longhorn" guitar, with two huge cutaways, 32-fret neck, and two pickups.

1960s		$1,400	$1,500

Hand Vibrato Double Pickup (4021)

1960s. Two pickups, double cutaway, batwing headstock, simple design vibrato.

1960s	Black	$550	$650

Hand Vibrato Single Pickup (4011)

1960s. One pickup, double cutaway, batwing headstock, simple design vibrato.

1960s	Black	$350	$550

Model C

1955-ca.1958. Single cutaway, one pickup.

1956		$350	$450

Pro 1

1963-ca.1964. Odd-shaped double cutaway electric with squared off corners, one pickup.

1963		$350	$550

Standard Double Pickup

1959-1967. A "Shorthorn" double cutaway, two pickups, two stacked, concentric volume/tone controls, seal-shaped pickguard, Coke bottle headstock. The Black version of this guitar is often referred to as the Jimmy Page model because he occasionally used one.

1950s	Black	$1,000	$1,200
1960s		$650	$850

Standard Single Pickup

1958-1967. A "Shorthorn" double cutaway, one pickup, two regular control knobs, seal-shaped pickguard, Coke bottle headstock.

1960s		$450	$600

U-1

1956-ca.1960. Single cutaway, one pickup, Coke bottle headstock.

1950s	Custom color	$800	$900
1950s	Standard color	$400	$500

U-1 '56 Reissue

1998-1999. Single cutaway semi-hollow, masonite top and bottom, bolt-on neck, reissue of 1956 U-1, with single 'lipstick tube' pickup, various colors.

1998-1999		$75	$125

U-2

1956-1959. Single cutaway, two pickups, stacked concentric volume/tone controls, Coke bottle headstock.

1950s	Standard color	$500	$900

U-2 '56 Reissue

1998-present.

1990s		$100	$175

U-3 '56 Reissue

1999-present. Single cutaway reissue of 1956 U-3 with three 'lipstick tube' pickups, various colors.

1999		$150	$225

Dave Maize Acoustic Guitars

1991-present. Luthier Dave Maize builds his professional and premium grade, production/custom, flat-tops and acoustic basses in Cave Junction, Oregon.

David Thomas McNaught

1989-present. Professional, premium, and presentation grade, custom, solidbody guitars built by luthier David Thomas McNaught and finished by Dave Mansel in Locust, North Carolina. In '97, they added the production/custom DTM line of guitars.

Davis, J. Thomas

1975-present. Premium and presentation grade, custom, steel-string flattops, 12-strings, classicals, archtops, Irish citterns and flattop Irish bouzoukis made by luthier J. Thomas Davis in Columbus, Ohio.

de Jonge, Sergei

1972-present. Premium grade, production/custom classical and steel-string guitars built by luthier Sergei de Jonge in Oshawa, Ontario.

De Paule Stringed Instruments

1969-1980, 1993-present. Custom steel-string, nylon-string, archtop, resonator, and Hawaiian guitars built by luthier C. Andrew De Paule in Eugene, Oregon.

Dean

1976-present. Budget, intermediate and professional grade, production/custom, solidbody, hollowbody, acoustic, acoustic/electric, and resonator guitars made in the U.S. and overseas. They also offer basses, banjos, mandolins, and amps. Founded in Evanston, Illinois, by Dean Zelinsky. Original models were upscale versions of Gibson designs with glued necks, fancy tops, DiMarzio pickups and distinctive winged headstocks (V, Z and ML), with production beginning in '77. In '80 the factory was relocated to Chicago. Dean's American manufacturing ends in '86 when all production shifts to Korea. In '91 Zelinsky sold the company to Tropical Music in Miami, Florida. For '93-'94 there was again limited U.S. (California) production of the E'Lite, Cadillac and ML models under the supervision of Zelinksy and Cory Wadley. Korean versions were also produced. In '97 and '98, Dean offered higher-end USA Custom Shop models. In '98, they reintroduced acoustics.

Dating American models: first two digits is year of manufacture. Imports have no date codes.

MODEL YEAR	FEATURES	EXC. COND. LOW	HIGH
Baby ML			
	1982-1986. Downsized version of ML model.		
1980s		$400	$450
Baby V			
	1982-1986. Downsized version of the Flying V-shaped V model.		
1980s		$350	$400
Baby Z			
	1982-1986. Downsized version of the Explorer-shaped Z model.		
1980s		$350	$400
Bel Aire			
	1983-1984. Solidbody, possibly the first production guitar with humbucker/single/single pickup layout, U.S.A.-made. An import model from Asia was introduced in '87		
1983-1984		$550	$600
Bel Aire Import			
	1987-1990. Imported from Asia.		
1980s		$275	$325
Budweiser Guitar			
	Ca.1987. Shaped like Bud logo.		
1987		$400	$450
Cadillac (USA)			
	1979-1985. Single long treble horn on slab body.		
1979-1982		$650	$750
Cadillac Deluxe (USA)			
	1993-1994, 1996-1997. Single long-horn shape, American-made, various colors..		
1993-1994		$800	$1,000
1996-1997		$800	$1,000
Cadillac Reissue (import)			
	1992-1994. Single long-horn shape, two humbuckers, various colors.		
1994		$300	$350
Cadillac Standard			
	1996-1997. Slab body version.		
1996		$400	$450
E'Lite			
	1979-1985, 1994-1996. Single-horn shape.		
1980s		$800	$900
E'Lite Deluxe			
	Single-horn shape.		
1980s		$900	$1,000
Eighty-Eight			
	1987-1990. Offset double cut solidbody, import.		
1987		$200	$300
Golden E'Lite			
	Single pointy treble cutaway, fork headstock, Gold hardware, ebony fingerboard, Sunburst.		
1980		$900	$1,000
Hollywood Z (import)			
	1985-1986. Bolt-neck Japanese copy of Baby Z, Explorer shape.		
1985		$150	$250
Jammer (import)			
	1987-1989. Offset double cutaway body, bolt-on neck, dot markers, six-on-a-side tuners, various colors offered.		
1987-1989		$150	$200

Dean Baby ML

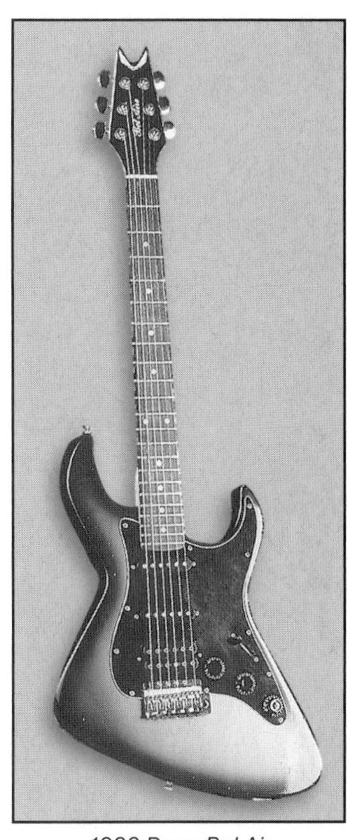

1983 Dean Bel Air

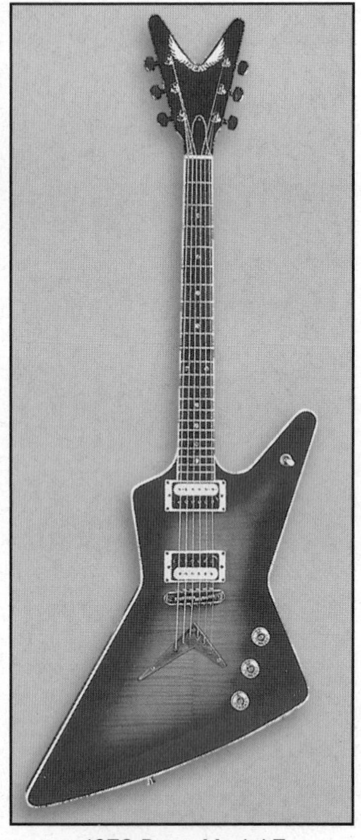

1978 Dean Model Z

Early-'80s Dean Z

MODEL YEAR	FEATURES	EXC. COND. LOW	HIGH

Mach I (import)

1985-1986. Limited run from Korea. Mach V with six-on-a-side tunes, various colors.

1985-1986		$150	$250

Mach V (import)

1985-1986. Pointed solidbody, two humbucking pickups, maple neck, ebony 'board, locking trem, various colors. Limited run from Korea.

1985-1986		$150	$250

Mach VII (USA)

1985-1986. Mach I styling, made in America, offered in unusual finishes.

1985		$700	$1,000

ML (import)

1983-1990. Korean-made.

1983-1990		$250	$300

ML (ML Standard/US-made)

1977-1986. There is a 'flame' model and a 'standard' model.

1977-1982		$1,000	$1,200

V (V flamed)

Flamed maple version of V Standard.

1977-1981		$700	$1,000

V (V Standard)

1977-1986. V copy, there is a 'standard' and a 'flame' model offered.

1977-1986		$1,000	$1,200

Z (Z Standard)

1977-1986. Explorer copy.

1970-1982	U.S.-made	$800	$1,200
1983-1986	Japanese import	$300	$500

Z Autograph (import)

1985-1987. The first Dean import from Korea offset double cutaway, bolt-on neck, dot markers, offered in several standard colors.

1985-1987		$150	$250

Z Coupe/Z Deluxe (USA Custom Shop)

1997-1998. Explore-style mahogany body offered in several standard colors, Z Deluxe with Floyd Rose tremolo.

1997-1998		$700	$1,100

Z Korina (USA Custom Shop)

1997-1998. Explorer Z Coupe with korina body, various standard colors.

1997-1998		$900	$1,000

Z LTD (USA Custom Shop)

1997-1998. Z Coupe with bound neck and headstock, offered in several standard colors.

1997-1998		$850	$950

Dean Markley

The string and pickup manufacturer offered a limited line of guitars and basses for a time in the late '80s.

Concert

1987. Solidbody, either 3 single-coils, 1 humbucker and 2 single-coils, or 1 humbucker.

1987		$225	$325

Custom Vintage

1987. Solidbody, dot or shark-tooth inlays, either 1 humbucker, 2 single-coils and 1 humbucker, 2 humbuckers, or 3 single-coils.

1987		$225	$325

Vintage

1987. Solidbody, vintage-style with either 3 single-coils or 1 humbucker and 2 single-coils.

1987		$225	$275

Dearstone

1993-present. Luthier Ray Dearstone builds his professional and premium grade, custom, mandolin-family instruments, archtop and acoustic/electric guitars, and violins in Blountville, Tennessee.

DeCava Guitars

1983-present. Professional and premium grade, production/custom, archtop and classical guitars built by luthier Jim DeCava in Stratford, Connecticut. He also builds ukes, banjos, and mandolins.

Dell'Arte

1997-present. Production/custom Maccaferri-style guitars from John Kinnard and Alain Cola. In '96, luthier John Kinnard opened a small shop called Finegold Guitars and Mandolins. In '98 he met Alain Cola, a long time jazz guitarist who was selling Mexican-made copies of Selmer/Maccaferri guitars under the Dell' Arte brandname. Cola wanted better workmanship for his guitars, and in October '98, Finegold and Dell' Arte merged. As of May '99 all production is in California.

Anouman Custom

1990s		$1,900	$2,000

Dennis Hill Guitars

1991-present. Premium and presentation grade, production/custom, classical and flamenco guitars and violins built by luthier Dennis Hill in Panama City, Florida. He has also built dulcimers and mandolins.

Desmond Guitars

1991-present. Luthier Robert B. Desmond builds his premium grade, production/custom classical guitars in Orlando, Florida.

DeTemple

1995-present. Premium grade, production/custom, solidbody electric guitars and basses built by luthier Michael DeTemple in Sherman Oaks, California.

DeVoe Guitars

1975-present. Luthier Lester DeVoe builds his premium grade, production/custom flamenco and classical guitars in Nipomo, California.

MODEL YEAR	FEATURES	EXC. COND. LOW	HIGH

Dick, Edward Victor

1975-present. Luthier Edward Dick currently builds his premium grade, custom, classical guitars in Denver, Colorado (he lived in Peterborough and Ottawa, Ontario until '95). He also operates the Colorado School of Luthrie.

Dickerson

1937-1947. Founded by the Dickerson brothers in 1937, primarily for electric lap steels and small amps. Instruments were also private branded for Cleveland's Oahu company, and for the Gourley brand. By '47, the company changed ownership and was renamed Magna Electronics (Magnatone).

Dillon

1975-present. Professional and premium grade, custom, flat-tops and acoustic basses built by luthier John Dillon originally in New Mexico, but currently in Bloomsburg, Pennsylvania.

DiPinto

1995-present. Intermediate grade, production retro-vibe guitars and basses from luthier Chris DiPinto of Philadelphia, Pennsylvania. Until late '99, all instruments built in the U.S., since then all built in Korea.

Ditson

1916-1930. Ditson guitars were made by Martin and sold by the Oliver Ditson Company of Boston. The majority of production was from 1916 to '22 with over 500 units sold in '21.

Concert Model Style 2

1916-1922. Similar in size to Martin Size 0.

1916-1922		$2,300	$2,500

Standard Model Style 1

1916-1922. Small body similar to Martin size 3, plain styling.

1916-1922		$1,200	$1,500

Standard Model Style 2

1916-1922. Small body similar to Martin size 3, plain styling.

1916-1922		$1,500	$1,800

Standard Model Style 3

1916-1922. Small body similar to Martin size 3, styling similar to D-28.

1916-1922		$2,300	$2,500

Dobro

1929-1942, ca. 1954-present. Currently, professional and premium grade, production, wood and metal body resophonic guitars offered by Gibson.

Founded 1929 in Los Angeles by John Dopyera, Rudy Dopyera, Ed Dopyera and Vic Smith (Dobro stands for "Dopyera Brothers"). Made instruments sold under the Dobro, Regal, Norwood Chimes, Angelus, Rex, Broman, Montgomery Ward, Penetro, Bruno, Alhambra, More Harmony, Orpheum, and Magn-o-tone brands.

Dobro instruments have a single cone facing outward with a "spider bridge" structure and competed with National products. Generally, model names are numbers referring to list price and therefore materials and workmanship (e.g., a No. 65 cost $65). Because of this, the same model number may apply to various different instruments. However, model numbers are never identified on instruments!

In '30, the company name was changed to Dobro Corporation, Ltd. In '32, Louis Dopyera buys Ted Kleinmeyer's share of National. Louis, Rudy and Ed now hold controlling interest in National, but in '32 John Dopyera left Dobro to pursue idea of metal resophonic violin. In December of '34 Ed Dopyera joins National's board of directors (he's also still on Dobro board), and by March of '35 Dobro and National have merged to become the National Dobro Corporation. Dobro moves into National's larger factory but continues to maintain separate production, sales and distribution until relocation to Chicago is complete. Beginning in early-'36 National Dobro starts relocating its offices to Chicago. L.A. production of Dobros continues until '37, after which some guitars continue to be assembled from parts until '39, when the L.A. operations were closed down. All resonator production ended in '42. Victor Smith, Al Frost and Louis Dopyera buy the company and change the name to the Valco Manufacturing Company. The Dobro name does not appear when production resumes after World War II.

In mid-'50s - some sources say as early as '54 - Rudy and Ed Dopyera began assembling wood-bodied "Dobros" from old parts using the name DB Original. In about '59, some 12-fret DB Originals were made for Standel, carrying both DB Original and Standel logos. In around '61, production was moved to Gardena, California, and Louis Dopyera and Valco transferred the Dobro name to Rudy and Ed, who produce the so-called Gardena Dobros. At this time, the "modern Dobro" logo appeared with a lyre that looks like two back-to-back "6s." Dobro Original debuts ca. '62. In late-'64 the Dobro name was licensed to Ed's son Emil (Ed, Jr.) Dopyera. Ed, Jr. designs a more rounded Dobro (very similar to later Mosrites) and has falling out with Rudy over it.

In '66 Semi Moseley acquires the rights to the Dobro brand, building some in Gardena, and later moving to Bakersfield, California. Moseley introduced Ed, Jr's design plus a thinline double-cutaway Dobro. Moseley Dobros use either Dobro or National cones. In '67 Ed, Sr., Rudy and Gabriella Lazar start the Original Music Instrument Company (OMI) and produce Hound Dog brand Dobros. In '68 Moseley goes bankrupt and in '70 OMI obtains the rights to the Dobro brand and begin production of OMI Dobros. In '75 Gabriella's son and daughter, Ron

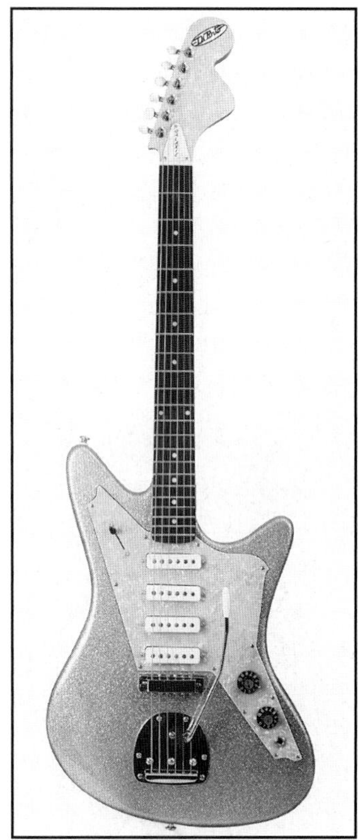

DiPinto Galaxie

1970s Dopyera Resonator

GUITARS

1937 Dobro Model 27 (squareneck)

1930s Dobro Model 45

MODEL YEAR	FEATURES	EXC. COND. LOW	HIGH

Lazar and Dee Garland, take over OMI. Rudy Dupyera makes and sells Safari brand resonator mandolins. Ed, Sr. dies in '77 and Rudy in '78. In '84 OMI was sold to Chester and Betty Lizak. Both wood and metal-bodied Dobros produced in Huntington Beach, California. Chester Lizak died in '92. Gibson purchased Dobro in '93 and now makes Dobros in Nashville, Tennessee.

Dobros generally feature a serial number which, combined with historical information, provides a clue to dating. For prewar L.A. guitars, see approximation chart below adapted from Gruhn and Carter's "Gruhn's Guide to Vintage Guitars" (Miller Freeman, 1991). No information exists on DB Originals.

Gardena Dobros had D prefix plus three digits beginning with 100 and going into the 500s (reportedly under 500 made). No information is available on Moseley Dobros.

OMI Dobros from '70-'79 have either D prefix for wood bodies or B prefix for metal bodies, plus three or four numbers for ranking, space, then a single digit for year (D XXXX Y or B XXX Y; e.g., "D 172 8" would be wood body #172 from '78). For '80-'87 OMI Dobros, start with first number of year (decade) plus three or four ranking numbers, space, then year and either D for wood or B for metal bodies (8 XXXX YD or 8 XXX YB; e.g., "8 2006 5B" would be metal body #2008 from '85). From '88-'92, at least, a letter and number indicate guitar style, plus three or four digits for ranking, letter for neck style, two digits for year, and letter for body style (AX XXXX NYYD or AX XXX NYYB).

L.A. Guitars (approx. number ranges, not actual production totals)

1928-30	900-2999
1930-31	3000-3999
1931-32	BXXX (Cyclops models only)
1932-33	5000-5599
1934-36	5700-7699
1937-42	8000-9999

Angelus
1933-1937. Wood body, round neck, two-tone Walnut finish. Continues as Model 19 in Regal-made guitars.

1930s		$900	$1,000

Cyclops 45
Square neck.

1931		$1,700	$1,800

DS33/Steel 33
1995-2000. Steel body with light Amber Sunburst finish, resonator with coverplate, biscuit bridge.

1995		$1,100	$1,300

Hula Blues
Brown, painted Hawaiian scenes, round neck.

1991		$700	$800

Model 1
Nickel.

1930s		$2,500	$3,000

MODEL YEAR	FEATURES	EXC. COND. LOW	HIGH

Model 27
1933-1937. Regal-made, wooden body.

1933-1937	Round neck	$1,500	$2,000

Model 27 (OMI)

1980s		$1,000	$1,200

Model 33

1980s		$1,000	$1,500

Model 33 D
1971-1987 (OMI), 1995-1997 (Gibson). Chrome-plated brass body, etched diamond, floral, and then lattice design on front. Available with round neck or square neck.

1970s		$1,000	$1,500

Model 33 H
1973-1997 (OMI & Gibson). Same as 33 D, but with etched Hawaiian scenes. Available as round or square neck.

1980s	Round neck	$1,200	$1,500

Model 36
1932-1934. Wood body with resonator.

1930s		$1,200	$2,000

Model 36 S
1980s. Chrome-plated brass body, square neck, slotted headstock, dot markers, engraved rose floral art.

1980s		$1,200	$1,400

Model 37
1933-1937. Regal-made wood body, bound body and fingerboard, 12-fret neck.

1930s	Sunburst, square neck	$1,600	$2,100

Model 37 G
1933-1937. California-made wood body, 12-fret round neck.

1930s		$1,500	$1,800

Model 37 Tenor
1933-1937 (Regal). Tenor version of No. 37.

1930s		$600	$800

Model 42

1930s		$1,500	$1,600

Model 45
1929-1933. California-made, wood body, round or square neck, dark stain.

1933	Natural, square neck	$1,700	$1,800

Model 55
1920-1930s. Unbound wood body, metal resonator, bound neck, Sunburst.

1928		$1,900	$2,000
1930		$1,900	$2,000

Model 60 Cyclops
1932-1933.

1932-1933		$2,500	$3,000

Model 60/Model 60 D (OMI)
1970-1993. Wood body (laminated maple) with Dobro resonator cone. Model 60 until '73 when renamed 60 D, and various 60 model features offered. Post-1993 was Gibson-owned production.

1970s		$950	$1,050
1980s		$850	$950
1990s		$800	$900

MODEL YEAR	FEATURES	EXC. COND. LOW	HIGH

Model 65

1920s-1930s. Wood body with sandblasted ornamental design top and back, metal resonator.

1928 Sunburst $3,100 $3,500

Model 66 (Cyclops)

1972-1995 (OMI & Gibson). Round neck and slotted peghead. Sunburst.

1978 Round neck $800 $1,000

Model 90 (Duolian) (OMI)

1972-1993. Chrome-plated, F-holes, etched Hawaiian scene.

1980s $1,300 $1,400

Model 125 De Luxe

1929-1934. Black walnut body, round or square neck, Dobro De Luxe engraved, triple-bound top, back and fingerboard, nickel-plated hardware. Natural.

1930s Round neck $3,000 $3,500

Regal Tenor 27-1/2

1933-1937. Tenor version of Model 27.

1930s $800 $900

Regal/Dobro 37

1933-1937. Regal-made wood body, bound body and fingerboard, 12-fret neck.

1930s Mahogany, round neck $1,500 $2,000

1930s Mahogany, square neck $2,000 $2,500

Regal/Dobro 46

1935-1942. Aluminum body, 14 frets, slotted peghead. Silver finish. Listed as No. 47 in 1939-1942.

1940 Round neck $1,100 $1,300

Regal/Dobro 47

1939-1942. Continuation of 46.

1940 Degraded finish (common problem) $900 $1,000

1940 Round neck, original finish $1,500 $2,000

Regal/Dobro 62

1935-1942. Nickel-plated brass body, Spanish dancer etching. Continued as No. 65 for 1939-'42.

1940 Round neck $3,000 $3,500

1940 Square neck $1,500 $2,000

Regal/Dobro Leader 14 M/14 H

1934-1935. Nickel-plated brass body, round or square neck, solid peghead.

1934 Round neck $2,000 $2,500

1934 Square neck $1,500 $1,800

Regal/Dobro Professional 15 M/15 H

1934-1935. Engraved nickel body, round or square neck, solid peghead.

1934 Round neck $3,000 $3,500

1934 Square neck $2,000 $2,500

Dodge

1996-present. Luthier Rick Dodge builds his intermediate and professional grade, production, solidbody guitars with changeable electronic modules in Tallahassee, Florida. He also builds basses.

MODEL YEAR	FEATURES	EXC. COND. LOW	HIGH

DC Classic/Convertible DC Classic

1996-present. Offset-style body, bolt-on neck, rear-mounted convertible electronic modules, various colors.

1996-1999 $575 $775

Domino

Ca. 1967-1968. Solidbody and hollowbody electric guitars and basses imported from Japan by Maurice Lipsky Music Co. of New York, New York, previously responsible for marketing the Orpheum brand. Models are primarily near-copies of EKO, Vox, and Fender designs, plus some originals. Models were made by Arai or Kawai. Earlier models may have been imported, but this is not yet documented.

Baron

1967-1968. Double cut body, three pickups, tremolo.

1967 $250 $500

Californian

1967-1968. Odd, squared body, copy of a Vox Phantom, two pickups, tremolo.

1967 $250 $500

Californian Rebel

1967-1968. Odd, squared-off, triangle-shaped body, one F-hole, two or three pickups, tremolo.

1967 $250 $500

Dawson

1967-1968. ES-335-style, two F-holes, two or three pickups.

1967 $250 $500

Don Musser Guitars

1976-present. Custom, classical and flat-top guitars built by luthier Don Musser in Cotopaxi, Colorado.

Doolin Guitars

1997-present. Luthier Mike Doolin builds his premium grade, production/custom acoutics featuring his unique double cutaway in Portland, Oregon.

Dorado

Ca. 1972-1973. Six- and twelve-string acoustic guitars, solidbody electrics and basses. Brandname used briefly by Baldwin/Gretsch on line of Japanese imports.

Acoustic 6-String Guitars

Japanese import.

1970s $200 $250

Dragge Guitars

1982-present. Luthier Peter Dragge builds his custom, steel-string and nylon-string guitars in Ojai, California.

1931 Dobro Model 66

1967 Domino Baron

GUITARS

1982 EKO CO-2 Cobra

1963 EKO CX-7 Artist

MODEL YEAR	FEATURES	EXC. COND. LOW	HIGH

Dragonfly Guitars

1994-present. Professional grade, production/custom, sloped cutaway flat-tops and acoustic basses, semi-hollow body electrics, and dulcitars built by luthier Dan Richter in Roberts Creek, British Columbia.

DTM

1997-present. See David Thomas McNaught listing.

Dunwell Guitars

1996-present. Professional and premium grade, custom, flat-tops built by luthier Alan Dunwell in Nederland, Colorado.

Dupont

Luthier Maurice Dupont builds his classical, archtop, Weissenborn-style and Selmer-style guitars in Cognac, France.

MD-50-E

Selmer-style cutaway flat-top, large bridge.

2001	$2,500	$2,700

Eaton, William

1976-present. Luthier William Eaton builds custom specialty instruments such as vihuelas, harp guitars, and lyres in Phoenix, Arizona. He is also the Director of the Robetto-Venn School of Luthiery.

Ed Claxton Guitars

1972-present. Premium grade, custom flat-tops made by luthier Ed Claxton, first in Austin, Texas, and currently in Santa Cruz, California.

Egmond

1960-1972. Entry-level import from Holland. Prices include original guitar case, and an example without the case is worth considerably less.

Electric Guitar

Solidbody or semi-hollow entry-level.

1960s	$250	$450

Ehlers

1985-present. Luthier Rob Ehlers builds his premium grade, production/custom, flat-top acoustic guitars in Oregon.

15 CRC

Cutaway, western red cedar top, Indian rosewood back and sides.

1996	$2,650	$2,850

15 SRC

Cutaway, European spruce top, Indian rosewood back and sides.

1998	$2,800	$3,000

16 BTM

European spruce top, mahogany back and sides, Troubadour peghead, Black lacquer finish.

1998	$2,800	$3,000

MODEL YEAR	FEATURES	EXC. COND. LOW	HIGH

16 SK Concert

Sixteen inch lower bout, relatively small upper bout, small waist, European spruce top, flamed Koa back and sides, diamond markers, Natural.

1993	$2,300	$2,500

16 SM

European spruce top, mahogany back and sides.

1999	$2,300	$2,400

16 SSC

Cutaway, European spruce top, English sycamore back and sides.

1996	$2,900	$3,100

25 C

Limited Edition Anniversary Model, European spruce top, Indian rosewood back and sides, abalone top border.

2001	$3,800	$4,000

Eichelbaum Guitars

1994-present. Luthier David Eichelbaum builds his premium grade, custom, flat-tops in Santa Barbara, California.

EKO

1959-1985, present. Acoustic, acoustic/electric, electric thinline and full-size archtop hollowbody, solidbody electric guitars and basses built by Oliviero Pigini and Company in Recanati, Italy, and imported by LoDuca Brothers, Milwaukee, Radio and Television Equipment Company in Santa Ana, California and others. First acoustic guitars followed by sparkle plastic-covered electrics by '62. Sparkle finishes are gone ca. '66. Pigini dies ca. '67. LoDuca Bros. phases out in early-'70s. By '75 EKO offers some copy guitars and they puchased a custom shop to make other brands by '78. Solidbody EKO guitars and basses are again being made in Recanati, Italy. Prices include the original guitar case, and instruments without the original case are worth less, often much less.

Barracuda

1966-ca.1978. ES-335 copy, two pickups.

1966-1978	$400	$450

Barracuda 12-String

1966-ca.1970. Twelve-string ES-335 copy, two pickups.

1966-1970	$350	$400

Cobra I

1966-1978. Double cut solidbody, single pickup, two knobs.

1966-1978	$275	$325

Cobra II

1966-1978. Double cut solidbody, dual pickups, two knobs.

1966-1978	$300	$350

MODEL YEAR	FEATURES	EXC. COND. LOW	HIGH

Cobra III

1966-1978. Double cut solidbody, three pickups, two knobs.

1966-1978		$325	$375

Cobra XII

1967-ca.1969. Double cut solidbody 12-string, two pickups.

1967-1969		$350	$475

Condor

1966-ca.1969. Double cut solidbody with three or four pickups.

1966-1969		$350	$400

Dragon

1967-ca.1969. Single cutaway archtop, two F-holes, three pickups, tremolo.

1967-1969		$425	$500

Florentine

1964-ca.1969. Double cutaway archtop, two pickups.

1964-1969		$475	$550

Kadett

1967-ca.1978. Double cutaway solidbody with point on lower bass side of body, three pickups, tremolo.

1967-1978		$400	$500

Kadett XII

1968-ca.1969. Double cutaway solidbody 12-string, with point on lower bass side of body.

1968-1969		$450	$500

Lancer

1967-ca.1969. Double cut solidbody, two pickups.

1967-1969		$300	$350

Lark I

Sunburst, thin hollow cutaway, one pickup.

1970		$375	$425

Lark II

Sunburst, thin hollow cutaway, two pickups.

1970		$375	$425

Model 500/1

1961-1964. Single pickup, plastic covered body.

1961-1964		$300	$400

Model 500/3V

1961-1964. Three pickups, vibrato, plastic covered body.

1961-1964	Plastic sparkle	$525	$625

Model 500/4

1961-1964. Four pickups, non-vibrato, plastic covered body.

1961-1964		$625	$725

Model 500/4V

1961-1964. Four pickups, vibrato, plastic covered body.

1961-1964	Blue Sparkle	$675	$775

Model 540 (Classical)

1960s. Nylon-string classical guitar.

1960s		$150	$200

Model 700/3V (Map-shape)

1961-1964. Three pickups, vibrato, map-shaped plastic body.

1961-1964	Woodgrain plastic	$925	$1,025

Model 700/4V (Map-shape)

1961-1967. Sort of map-shaped body, electric, with regular or sparkle top.

1960s	Standard finish	$925	$1,025
1961-1967	Red, Blue, Silver Sparkle	$1,125	$1,225

Ranger 12

1967-ca.1982. Flat-top 12-string, acoustic or with pickup with tone and volume control.

1967-1982		$350	$400

Rocket VI/Rokes

1967-ca.1969. Rocket-shape design, solidbody, six-string, says "Rokes" on the headstock. The Rokes were a popular English band that endorsed EKO guitars. Marketed as the Rocket VI in the U.S.; and as the Rokes in Europe. Often called the Rok.

1967-1969		$600	$800

Rocket XII

1967-ca.1969. Rocket-shape design, 12-string solidbody. Often called the Rok.

1967-1969		$600	$750

El Degas

Early-1970s. Japanese-made copies of classic America electrics and acoustics, imported by Buegeleisen & Jacobson of New York, New York.

Let's Play

Early-1970s. Les Paul single cut copy, black, block markers, 2 pickups.

1970s		$125	$175

Electar

See Epiphone listing.

Electra

1971-1984. Imported from Japan by St. Louis Music. Most instruments made by Matsumoku in Matsumoto, Japan. The Electra line replaced SLM's Japanese-made Apollo and U.S.-made Custom Kraft lines. First guitar, simply called The Electra, was a copy of the Ampeg Dan Armstrong lucite guitar and issued in '71, followed quickly by a variety of bolt-neck copies of other brands. In '75 the Tree of Life guitars debut with a leaf pattern carved into the top, and the Electra line expanded to 25 models. Gibson-style headstocks changed to wave or fan shape by '78. By around '81 ties with Matsumoku further solidified and decision eventually made to merge SLM's Electra brand with Matsumoku's Westone brand. Some Korean production begins in early-'80s. In the fall of '83, the Electra Brand becomes Electra Phoenix. By beginning of '84, the brandname becomes Electra-Westone and by the end of '84 just Westone. Matsumoku-made guitars have serial number in which first one or two digits represent the year of manufacture. Thus a guitar with a serial number beginning in 0 or 80 would be from 1980.

1962 EKO 500/4V

1971 The Electra

GUITARS

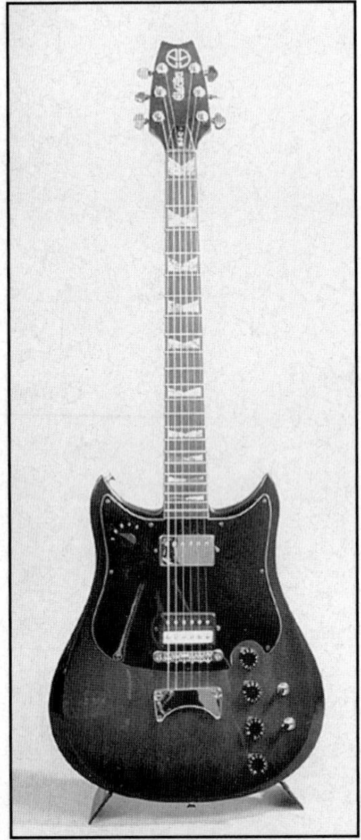
1981 Electra Outlaw

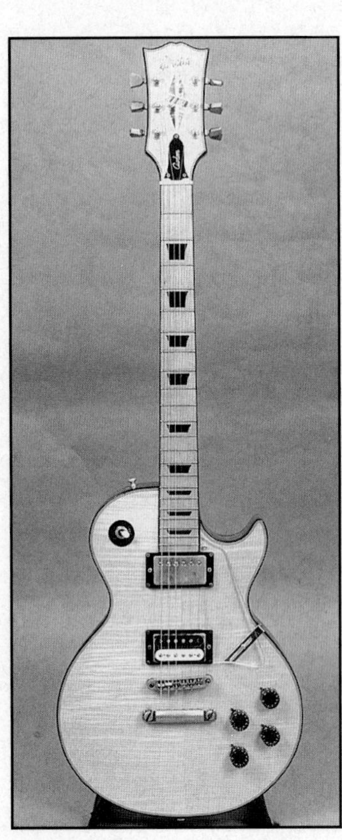
1976 Electra Super Rock

MODEL YEAR	FEATURES	EXC. COND. LOW	HIGH

Elvin Bishop

1976-ca.1980. ES-335 copy with tree-of-life inlay.

1977		$650	$750

MPC Outlaw

1976-1983. Has separate modules that plug in for different effects.

1976-1983		$400	$600

Phoenix

1980-1984. Double cut solidbody.

1982		$200	$350

Rock

1971-1973. Les Paul copy. Becomes the Super Rock in 1973.

1971-1973		$200	$300

Super Rock

1973-ca.1978. Les Paul copy. Renamed from Rock (1971-1973).

1973-1978		$300	$350

Electro

The Electro line was manufactured by Electro String Instruments and distributed by Radio-Tel. The Electro logo appeared on the headstock rather than Rickenbacker. Refer to the Rickenbacker section.

Elliott Guitars

1966-present. Premium and presentation grade, custom, nylon-string classical and steel-string guitars built by luthier Jeffrey Elliott in Portland, Oregon.

Emperador

1966-1992. Imported from Japan by Westheimer Musical Instruments. Early models appear to be made by either Teisco or Kawai; later models were made by Cort.

Acoustic Archtop Guitars

Japanese import.

1960s		$200	$300

Electric Solidbody Guitars

Japanese import.

1960s		$200	$300

Epiphone

Ca. 1873-present. Epiphone currently offers budget, intermediate and professional grade, production, solidbody, archtop, acoustic, acoustic/electric, resonator, and classical guitars made in the U.S. and overseas. They also offer basses, amps, mandolins and banjos. Founded in Smyrna, Turkey, by Anastasios Stathopoulos and early instruments had his label. He emigrated to the U.S. in 1903 and changed the name to Stathoupoulo. Anastasios died in 1915 and his son, Epaminondas ("Epi") took over. The name changed to House of Stathopoulo in '17 and the company incorporated in '23. In '24 the line of Epiphone Recording banjos debut and in '28 the company name was changed to the Epiphone Banjo Company. In '43 Epi Stathopoulo died and sons Orphie and Frixo took over. Labor trouble shut down the NYC factory in '51 and the company cut a deal with Conn/Continental and relocated to Philadelphia in '52. Frixo died in '57 and Gibson bought the company.

Kalamazoo-made Gibson Epiphones debut in '58. In '69 American production ceased and Japanese imports began. Some Taiwanese guitars imported from '79-'81. Limited U.S. production resumed in '82 but sourcing shifted to Korea in '83. In '85 Norlin sold Gibson to Henry Juszkiewicz, Dave Barryman and Gary Zebrowski. In '92 Jim Rosenberg became president of the new Epiphone division. Epiphone currently offers imports and U.S.-made models

1958 Korina Explorer

1997-present. Explorer with typical appointments, korina body.

1997-2000		$450	$500

1958 Korina Flying V

1997-present. Typical Flying V configuration, korina body.

1997-2000		$450	$550

1963 Firebird VII

2000-present. 3 mini-humbuckers, gold hardware, Maestro-style vibrato, block markers, Firebird Red, reverse body.

2000		$425	$500

Barcelone (classical)

1963-1968. Highest model of Epiphone 1960s classical guitars.

1963-1965		$600	$850
1966-1968		$550	$800

Bard 12-String

1962-1969. Flat-top, mahogany back and sides, Natural or Sunburst.

1962-1965		$1,000	$1,300
1966-1969		$900	$1,200

Blackstone

1931-1950. Acoustic archtop, Sunburst, F-holes.

1933-1934	Masterbuilt	$1,200	$1,500
1935-1937		$1,100	$1,300
1938-1939		$1,100	$1,200
1940-1941		$800	$1,100
1949		$700	$1,100

Broadway (Acoustic)

1931-1958. Non-cutaway acoustic archtop.

1931-1938	Sunburst, walnut body	$2,000	$3,200
1939-1942	Sunburst, maple body	$2,000	$3,200
1946-1949	Natural	$2,000	$2,900
1946-1949	Sunburst	$1,900	$2,600
1950-1958	Sunburst	$2,000	$2,500

Broadway (Electric)

1958-1969. Gibson-made electric archtop, single cutaway, two New York pickups (mini-humbucking pickups by '61), Frequensator tailpiece, block inlays. Sunburst or Natural finish with Cherry optional in '67 only.

1958-1964	Natural	$3,000	$4,000

MODEL YEAR	FEATURES	EXC. COND. LOW	HIGH
1958-1964	Sunburst	$2,900	$3,900
1965-1969	Sunburst	$2,000	$3,700
1966-1968	Natural	$2,300	$3,800
1967	Cherry option	$2,300	$3,800

Broadway Regent (Acoustic Cutaway)

1950-1958. Single cutaway acoustic archtop, Sunburst.

1950-1958		$2,500	$2,800

Broadway Tenor

1937-1953. Acoustic archtop, Sunburst.

1939		$900	$1,100
1950		$700	$900

Byron

1949-ca.1955. Acoustic archtop, mahogany back and sides, Sunburst.

1950		$400	$650
1955		$400	$650

Caiola Custom

1963-1970. Introduced as Caiola, renamed Caiola Custom in '66. Electric thinbody archtop, two mini-humbuckers, multi-bound top and back, block inlays. Walnut or Sunburst finish (Walnut only by '68).

1963-1964	Sunburst or Walnut	$2,300	$3,200
1965-1966	Sunburst or Walnut	$2,100	$3,000
1967-1968	Sunburst or Walnut	$1,900	$3,000
1969-1970	Walnut	$1,900	$2,800

Caiola Standard

1966-1970. Electric thinbody archtop, two P-90s, single-bound top and back, dot inlays. Sunburst or Cherry.

1966		$1,700	$2,600
1967-1968		$1,600	$2,500
1969-1970		$1,500	$2,400

Casino (one pickup)

1961-1970. Thinline hollowbody, double cutaway, one P-90 pickup, trapeze tailpiece, tune-o-matic bridge, vibrato optional by '62. Sunburst or Royal Tan finish (Cherry optional in '67).

1961-1964	Sunburst	$2,000	$2,200
1965-1966	Sunburst	$1,800	$2,000
1967-1968	Sunburst or optional cherry	$1,600	$1,800
1969-1970	Sunburst or optional cherry	$1,500	$1,700

Casino (two pickups)

1961-1970. Two pickup (P-90) version.

1961-1964	Royal Tan or sunburst	$3,300	$3,700
1965-1966	Sunburst	$3,100	$3,500
1967-1968	Sunburst or optional cherry	$3,000	$3,400
1969-1970	Sunburst or optional cherry	$2,900	$3,100

Casino Reissue

1995-present. Sunburst.

1990s		$650	$700

Century

1939-1970. Thinline archtop, non-cutaway, one pickup, trapeze tailpiece, Walnut finish. Sunburst finish available in '58, Royal Burgundy available '61 and only Sunburst finish available by '68.

1949	Large rectangular pickup	$900	$1,200
1950-1958	New York pickup	$900	$1,200
1959-1964	P-90 pickup	$900	$1,200
1965-1970		$800	$1,100

Coronet (Electric Archtop)

1939-1949. Electric archtop, laminated mahogany body, one pickup, trapeze tailpiece, Sunburst. Name continued as an electric solidbody in '58.

1939-1949		$800	$1,000

Coronet (Solidbody)

1958-1969. Solidbody electric, one New York pickup ('58-'59), one P-90 ('59-'69). Cherry or Black finish, Silver Fox finish available by '63. Reintroduced as Coronet USA '91-'94, Korean-made '95-'98.

1958	Cherry	$1,500	$2,100
1959	Cherry	$1,500	$2,000
1961	Cherry	$1,400	$1,900
1962	Cherry	$1,300	$1,800
1963	Cherry or Silver Fox	$1,200	$1,700
1964	Cherry or Silver Fox	$1,100	$1,600
1965	Cherry or Silver Fox	$1,000	$1,500
1966-1969	Cherry	$900	$1,400

Coronet (Import)

1970s. Import electric, Sunburst.

1970s		$250	$350

Crestwood Custom

1958-1970. Solidbody, two New York pickups ('58-'60), two mini-humbuckers ('61-'70), symmetrical body ('58-'62), asymmetrical ('63-'70), slab body with no Gibson equivalent model.

1958-1960	Cherry, New York pickups	$2,300	$2,700
1961-1964	Cherry, mini-humbuckers	$2,000	$2,400
1961-1964	White, mini-humbuckers	$2,400	$2,600
1964-1966	Pacific Blue	$2,400	$2,600
1965-1966	Cherry	$1,700	$2,000
1965-1966	White	$1,900	$2,200
1967-1968	Cherry	$1,500	$1,900
1967-1968	White	$1,700	$2,000
1969-1970	Cherry or White	$1,400	$1,900

Crestwood Deluxe

1963-1969. Solidbody with three mini-humbuckers, block inlay. Cherry or White finish.

1963-1964	Cherry	$2,200	$2,700
1963-1964	White	$2,400	$2,800
1965-1966	Cherry	$2,000	$2,500
1965-1966	White	$2,100	$2,700
1967-1968	Cherry	$1,800	$2,300

1966 Epiphone Casino

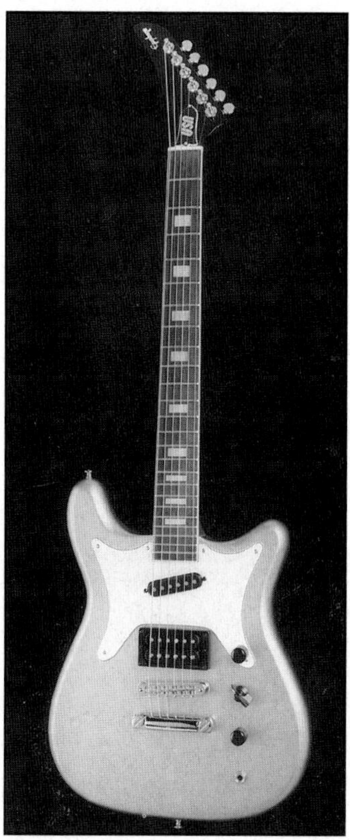

Epiphone Coronet

GUITARS

1959 Epiphone De Luxe Cutaway

1946 Epiphone Emperor

MODEL YEAR	FEATURES	EXC. COND. LOW	HIGH
1967-1968	White	$1,900	$2,400
1969	Cherry or White	$1,600	$2,100

De Luxe

1931-1957. Non-cutaway acoustic archtop, maple back and sides, trapeze tailpiece ('31-'37), frequensator tailpiece ('37-'57), gold-plated hardware. Sunburst or Natural finish.

1931-1934	Sunburst	$4,600	$5,600
1935-1939	Sunburst	$4,500	$5,500
1939	Natural, 1st year option	$5,500	$6,000
1940-1944	Natural	$5,300	$5,800
1940-1944	Sunburst	$4,300	$5,300
1945-1949	Natural	$4,600	$5,100
1945-1949	Sunburst	$3,600	$4,600
1950-1957	Natural	$3,200	$4,700
1950-1957	Sunburst	$2,700	$4,200

De Luxe Cutaway/Deluxe Cutaway

1953-1970. Renamed from De Luxe Regent, cataloged Deluxe Cutaway by Gibson in 1958. Special order by 1964 with limited production because acoustic archtops were pretty much replaced by electric archtops.

1953-1957	Epiphone NY-made	$3,500	$5,700
1958-1965	Gibson Kalamazoo, rounded cutaway	$3,800	$5,700
1965-1970	Special order only	$3,800	$7,000

De Luxe Electric (Archtop)

1954-1957. Single cutaway electric archtop, two pickups. Called the Zephyr De Luxe Regent from '48-'54.

1954-1957	Natural	$3,000	$4,600
1954-1957	Sunburst	$2,700	$4,400

De Luxe Regent (acoustic archtop)

1948-1952. Acoustic cutaway archtop, high-end appointments, rounded cutaway, renamed De Luxe Cutaway in 1953.

1948-1952		$3,900	$6,000

Del Ray

1995-2000. Offset double cut (vague PRS-style body), 2 blade humbuckers, dot markers, tune-o-matic, flamed maple top.

1995-2000		$325	$350

Devon

1949-1957. Acoustic archtop, non-cutaway, mahogany back and sides. Sunburst finish, optional Natural finish by '54.

1950-1953	Sunburst	$1,500	$1,700
1954-1957	Natural option	$1,700	$1,900
1954-1957	Sunburst	$1,400	$1,600

Dot (ES-335 Dot)

1997-present. Ephiphone's dot-neck 335 guitar.

1997-2000		$375	$450

Dwight

1963, 1967. Coronet labeled as "Dwight" for dealer. Seventy-five made in '63 and 36 in '67.

1963	Cherry	$1,000	$1,700

MODEL YEAR	FEATURES	EXC. COND. LOW	HIGH

El Diablo

1990s. Offset double cut acoustic/electric, onboard piezo and 3-band EQ, composite back and sides, spruce top, cherry sunburst.

1990s		$300	$325

El Dorado FT 90

1963-1970. Dreadnought flat-top acoustic, mahogany back and sides, multi-bound front and back, Natural.

1963-1964		$1,700	$2,200
1965-1970		$1,500	$2,100

Electar Model M

1935-1939. Epiphone's initial entry into the new electric guitar market of the mid-1930s. 14-3/4" laminate maple archtop, horseshoe pickup, trap door on back for installing electronics, Electra (not Epiphone) logo on headstock, oblong pickup replaces horseshoe pickup in late-1937.

1935-1936	Two control knobs	$1,200	$1,250
1937-1939	Three control knobs	$1,000	$1,200

Emperor (Acoustic Archtop)

1935-1957. Acoustic archtop, non-cutaway, maple back and sides, multi-bound body, gold-plated hardware. Sunburst, optional Natural finish by 1939.

1936-1938	Sunburst	$5,900	$6,900
1939-1949	Natural	$6,000	$7,000
1939-1949	Sunburst	$5,800	$6,800
1950-1954	Natural	$3,800	$6,500
1950-1954	Sunburst	$3,700	$6,300

Emperor (Thinline Electric)

1958-1969. Single cutaway, thinline archtop, three New York pickups in '58-'60, three mini-humbuckers '61 on, multi-bound, gold-plated hardware. Sunburst or Natural finish until '65 when only Sunburst was made.

1958-1959	Sunburst	$7,800	$9,300
1958-1960	Natural	$8,000	$9,500
1960	Sunburst	$7,700	$9,200
1961	Natural	$7,800	$9,300
1962-1969	Sunburst	$7,500	$9,000

Emperor Cutaway (formerly Emperor Regent)

1953-1970 (Gibson-made 1958 on). Renamed from Emperor Regent. Acoustic archtop, single cutaway, maple back and sides, multi-bound body, gold-plated hardware. Sunburst or Natural finish.

1953-1958	Natural	$7,700	$9,200
1953-1958	Sunburst	$6,300	$7,800

Emperor Electric

1953-1957. Archtop, single cutaway, three pickups, multi-bound body, Sunburst. Called the Zephyr Emperor Regent in '50-'53.

1953-1957		$4,500	$6,500

Emperor Regent

1948-1953. Acoustic archtop with rounded cutaway. Renamed Emperor Cutaway in 1953.

1948-1953	Sunburst	$6,500	$8,000
1948-1983	Natural	$7,700	$9,200

MODEL YEAR	FEATURES	EXC. COND. LOW	HIGH

Emperor Regent (reissued acoustic archtop cutaway)

1994-present. 17" archtop, spruce top, maple back and sides, floating pickup, sunburst.

1994-1999		$700	$900

Entrada (Classical)

1963-1968. Flat-top classical, Natural.

1963-1965		$450	$550
1966-1968		$400	$500

Espana (Classical)

1962-1968. Classical, maple back and sides, U.S.-made, natural. Imported in 1969 from Japan.

1962-1965		$550	$650
1966-1968		$500	$600

Firebird II/III

1995-2000. 2 mini-humbuckers, Firebird Red, dot markers.

1995-2000		$375	$400

Firebird 300

1986-1988. Korean import, Firebird Red.

1987		$250	$350

Firebird 500

1986-1988. Korean import, Firebird Red.

1987		$275	$375

Folkster FT 95

1966-1969. Fourteen inch small body, mahogany back and sides, double White pickguards.

1966-1969	Natural	$900	$1,000

FT 30

1941-1949. Acoustic flat-top, Brown stain, mahogany back and sides. Reintroduced as Gibson-made FT 30 Caballero in 1958.

1941-1949		$800	$1,000

FT 30 Caballero

1958-1970. Reintroduced from Epiphone-made FT 30. Gibson-made acoustic flat-top, Natural, all mahogany body, dot inlay. Tenor available 1963-1968.

1959-1960		$700	$900
1961-1964		$600	$800
1965-1970		$450	$650

FT 45

1941-1948. Acoustic flat-top, walnut back and sides, cherry neck, rosewood fingerboard. Natural top. Reintroduced as Gibson-made FT 45 Cortez in 1958.

1944		$1,400	$1,800

FT 45 Cortez

1958-1969. Reintroduced from Epiphone-made FT 45. Gibson-made acoustic flat-top, mahogany back and sides. Sunburst or Natural top (Sunburst only in '59-'62).

1958-1961	Sunburst	$1,000	$1,400
1962-1964	Sunburst	$900	$1,300
1965-1969	Sunburst	$800	$1,100

FT 79

1941-1958. Acoustic 16" flat-top, square shoulder D-style, walnut back and sides until '49 and laminated maple back and sides '49 on, Natural. Renamed FT 79 Texan by Gibson in '58.

1950-1958		$2,000	$2,500

FT 79 Texan

1958-1970, 1993-1995. Renamed from Epiphone FT 79. Gibson-made acoustic flat-top, mahogany back and sides. Sunburst or Natural top. Gibson Montana made 170 in '93-'95.

1958-1961		$2,500	$3,000
1962-1964		$2,300	$2,800
1965-1966		$1,900	$2,600
1967-1968		$1,600	$2,300
1969-1970		$1,300	$2,000

FT 110

1941-1958. Acoustic flat-top, Natural. Renamed the FT 110 Frontier by Gibson in 1958.

1944		$1,700	$2,200
1951		$1,600	$1,900

FT 110 Frontier

1958-1970, 1994. Renamed from FT 110. Acoustic flat-top, Natural or Sunburst. Gibson Montana made 30 in 1994.

1958-1966		$1,900	$2,700
1967-1969		$1,600	$2,500

G-310

1989-present. SG-style model with large pickguard.

1989-1999	With gig bag, not case	$225	$275

G-400 Deluxe

Mid-1990s. SG-style model with flamed maple top, 2 exposed humbuckers.

1996		$425	$450

Genesis

1979-1980 Double cutaway solidbody, two humbuckers with coil-taps, carved top, Red or Black. Available as Custom, Deluxe, and Standard models. Tawainese import.

1979-1980		$300	$400

Granada (Non-cutaway Thinbody)

1962-1969. Non-cutaway thinline archtop, one F-hole, one pickup, trapeze tailpiece. Sunburst finish.

1962-1966		$800	$900
1967-1969		$500	$700

Granada Cutaway

1965-1970. Single cutaway thinline archtop, one F-hole, one pickup, Sunburst.

1965-1966		$750	$950
1967-1970		$700	$900

Howard Roberts Custom

1965-1970. Single cutaway archtop, bound front and back, one pickup. Walnut finish (Natural offered 1966 only).

1965-1967		$2,800	$3,700
1968-1970		$2,200	$3,400

Howard Roberts III

1987-1991. Two pickups, various colors.

1987-1991		$600	$650

Howard Roberts Standard

1964-1970. Single cutaway acoustic archtop, bound front and back. Cherry or Sunburst finish. Listed in catalog as acoustic but built as electric.

1964-1965		$2,600	$3,500

1961 Epiphone Emperor

Epiphone Granada

GUITARS

1965 Epiphone Howard Roberts

1966 Epiphone Riviera

MODEL YEAR	FEATURES	EXC. COND. LOW	HIGH
1966-1967		$2,500	$3,400
1968-1970		$2,000	$3,200

Joe Pass Emperor II

1994-present. ES-175-style with rounded cutaway, block markers, 2 humbuckers.

1994-2000		$600	$650

Les Paul Custom

1988-present. Various colors.

1990s		$400	$500

Les Paul Special Double Cut

1995-2000. Bolt-on neck.

1995-2000		$200	$250

Les Paul Standard

1989-present. Solid mahogany body, carved maple top, two humbuckers.

1990s	Sunburst, foto-flame top	$350	$450

Les Paul XII

1998-2000. 12-string solidbody, trapeze tailpiece, flamed maple sunburst, standard configuration.

1998-2000		$550	$650

Madrid (Classical)

1962-1969. Classical, Natural.

1962-1965		$400	$500
1966-1969		$350	$450

Navarre

1931-1940. Flat-top, mahogany back and sides, bound top and back, dot inlay. Brown finish.

1936	Hawaiian, Masterbilt label	$1,000	$1,500

Nighthawk Standard

1995-2000. Epiphone's version of the Gibson Nighthawk, single cut, bolt neck, figured top.

1995-2000		$300	$350

Olympic (3/4 Scale Solidbody)

1960-1963. Twenty-two inch scale.

1960-1963	Sunburst	$625	$750

Olympic (Acoustic Archtop)

1931-1949. Mahogany back and sides.

1930s		$650	$800
1940s		$650	$800

Olympic Double (Solidbody)

1960-1969. Slab body, the same as the mid-1960s Coronet, Wilshire and Crestwood Series, single cut '60-'62, asymmetrical cut '63-'70, 2 Melody Maker single-coils, vibrato optional in '64 and standard by '65.

1960-1962	Sunburst, single cutaway	$800	$1,000
1963-1965	Sunburst, double cutaway	$800	$1,000
1966-1967	Cherry or Sunburst	$750	$900
1968-1969	Cherry or Sunburst	$725	$900

Olympic Single (Solidbody)

1960-1970. Slab body, the same as the mid-1960s Coronet, Wilshire and Crestwood Series, single cutaway 1960-1962, asymmetrical double cutaway 1963-1970, two Melody maker single-coil pickups, vibrato optional in 1964 and standard by 1965.

MODEL YEAR	FEATURES	EXC. COND. LOW	HIGH
1960-1962	Sunburst, single cutaway	$700	$900
1963-1965	Sunburst, double cutaway	$650	$900
1966-1970	Cherry or Sunburst	$625	$800

Olympic Special (Solidbody)

1962-1970. Short neck with neck body joint at the 16th fret (instead of the 22nd), single Melody Maker-style single-coil bridge pickup, small headstock, double cutaway slab body, dot markers, Maestro or Epiphone vibrato optional 1964-1965, slab body contour changes in 1965 from symmetrical to asymmetrical with slightly longer bass horn, Sunburst.

1964-1965		$625	$800
1966-1967		$600	$800
1968-1970		$575	$750

PR-200 (EA-20)

1992-present. Imported D-style, spruce top with satin finish, mahogany back and sides, Natural.

1992-1999		$150	$250

PR-350

1984-1999. Acoustic flat-top, mahogany D-style body. Also available with a pickup.

1984-1999		$175	$275

PR-350-CE

1989-1999. Acoustic flat-top, cutaway, mahogany D-style body. Also available with a pickup.

1989-1999		$250	$350

PR-600 ACS/ASB/N

1980s. Import 000-size flat-top, glued bridge, dot markers, Sunburst, from Japan.

1985-1988		$250	$400

Pro 1

1989-1996. Solidbody, double cutaway, one single-coil and one humbucking pickup, bolt-on neck, various colors.

1989-1996		$300	$400

Pro 2

1995-1998. Higher-end Pro I with Steinberger DB bridge, various colors.

1995-1998		$325	$400

Professional

1962-1967. Double cutaway, thinline archtop, one pickup. Mahogany finish.

1962-1967		$1,500	$1,800

Recording B

1928-1931. Asymmetrical body, cutaway bouts, flat-top, arched back, laminated maple back.

1928-1931		$1,500	$3,000

Riviera

1962-1970, 1993-1994. Double cut thinline archtop, 2 mini-humbuckers. Royal Tan standard finish changing to sunburst in '65, cherry optional by '66-'70. An additional 250 were made in Nashville in '93-'94. A Riviera import was available in '82 and for '94-present.

1962-1964	Tan or custom cherry	$2,500	$3,500
1965-1966	Sunburst or cherry	$2,500	$3,500
1966-1967	Burgundy Mist	$2,500	$3,500
1967-1968	Sunburst or cherry	$2,200	$3,500

MODEL YEAR	FEATURES	EXC. COND. LOW	HIGH
1967-1968	Walnut	$2,100	$3,400
1969	Sunburst or cherry	$2,000	$3,200

Riviera 12-String

1965-1970. Double cutaway, 12 strings, thinline archtop, two mini-humbuckers.

MODEL YEAR	FEATURES	LOW	HIGH
1965	Sunburst or cherry	$1,600	$1,900
1966	Sunburst or cherry	$1,500	$1,800
1967	Cherry	$1,400	$1,700
1967	Sunburst	$1,300	$1,600
1968-1970	Cherry	$1,300	$1,600

Riviera 12-String Reissue

1997-present. Korean-made reissue.

MODEL YEAR	FEATURES	LOW	HIGH
1997	Natural	$600	$800

Riviera Reissue

1994-present. Korean-made reissue.

MODEL YEAR	FEATURES	LOW	HIGH
1997	Natural	$550	$650

S-900

1986-1989. Neck-through-body, locking Bender tremolo system, two pickups with individual switching and a coil-tap control.

MODEL YEAR	FEATURES	LOW	HIGH
1986-1989		$350	$450

Serenader 12-String FT 85

1963-1969. Twelve strings, mahogany back and sides, dot inlay, Natural.

MODEL YEAR	FEATURES	LOW	HIGH
1963-1965		$1,000	$1,300
1966-1969		$900	$1,200

Seville (Classical)

1938-1941, 1961-1969 (Gibson-made). Classical guitar, mahogany back and sides, Natural. The '61-'63 version also available with a pickup.

MODEL YEAR	FEATURES	LOW	HIGH
1961-1965		$400	$600
1966-1969		$400	$550

Sheraton

1958-1970, 1993-1994. Double cut thinline archtop, 2 New York pickups '58-'60, 2 mini-humbuckers '61 on, frequensator tailpiece, multi-bound, gold-plated hardware. Sunburst or natural finish with cherry optional by '65. An additional 250 American-made Sheratons were built from '93-'94.

MODEL YEAR	FEATURES	LOW	HIGH
1958-1959	Natural, New York pickups	$8,000	$10,000
1960	Natural, New York pickups	$7,000	$9,000
1961-1963	Natural, mini-humbuckers	$6,500	$8,000
1961-1963	Sunburst, mini-humbuckers	$5,800	$7,000
1964-1965	Natural	$5,500	$6,500
1964-1965	Sunburst	$5,000	$6,000
1965	Cherry	$5,200	$6,200
1966	Sunburst or cherry	$4,500	$5,500
1967	Sunburst or cherry	$4,000	$5,300
1968	Sunburst or cherry	$3,800	$5,000
1969	Sunburst	$3,500	$4,500
1993-1994	Model reintroduced	$550	$650

Sheraton (Japan)

1978-1983. Early reissue, not to be confused with Sheraton II issued in late-1990s, Natural or Sunburst.

MODEL YEAR	FEATURES	LOW	HIGH
1978-1983		$500	$700

Sheraton II (reissue)

1997-present. Contemporary reissue, Natural or Sunburst.

MODEL YEAR	FEATURES	LOW	HIGH
1997-1999		$500	$575

Sorrento (one pickup)

1960-1970. Single cut thinline archtop, 1 pickup in neck position, tune-o-matic bridge, nickel-plated hardware, sunburst, natural or Royal Olive finish (cherry or sunburst by '68).

MODEL YEAR	FEATURES	LOW	HIGH
1960-1965		$1,400	$1,600
1966-1968		$1,200	$1,400
1969-1970		$1,000	$1,400

Sorrento (Reissue)

1997-2000.

MODEL YEAR	FEATURES	LOW	HIGH
1997-2000		$500	$550

Sorrento (two pickups)

1960-1970. Single cutaway thinline archtop, two pickups, tune-o-matic bridge, nickel-plated hardware. Sunburst, Natural or Royal Olive finish (Cherry or Sunburst by 1968).

MODEL YEAR	FEATURES	LOW	HIGH
1960-1965		$1,600	$2,000
1966-1968		$1,400	$1,900
1969-1970		$1,200	$1,900

Spartan

1934-1949. Acoustic archtop, multi-bound, trapeze tailpiece, Sunburst.

MODEL YEAR	FEATURES	LOW	HIGH
1930s		$800	$1,100
1940s		$650	$800

Spirit

1979-1983. American-made electric solidbody, double cutaway, carved top with two humbuckers, various colors.

MODEL YEAR	FEATURES	LOW	HIGH
1979-1983		$750	$850

Triumph

1931-1957. 15-1/4" '31-'33, 16-3/8" '33-'36, 17-3/8" '36-'57. Walnut back and sides until '33, laminated maple back and sides '33, solid maple back and sides '34, natural or sunburst.

MODEL YEAR	FEATURES	LOW	HIGH
1931-1932	Sunburst, laminated walnut body	$800	$1,400
1933	Sunburst, laminated maple body	$800	$1,400
1934-1935	Sunburst, solid maple body	$1,200	$1,500
1936-1940	Sunburst 17 3/8" body	$1,500	$2,000
1941-1949	Natural	$1,500	$2,000
1941-1949	Sunburst	$1,450	$1,950
1950-1957	Natural	$1,450	$1,950
1950-1957	Sunburst	$1,350	$1,750

1967 Epiphone Riviera

1963 Epiphone Sheraton

GUITARS

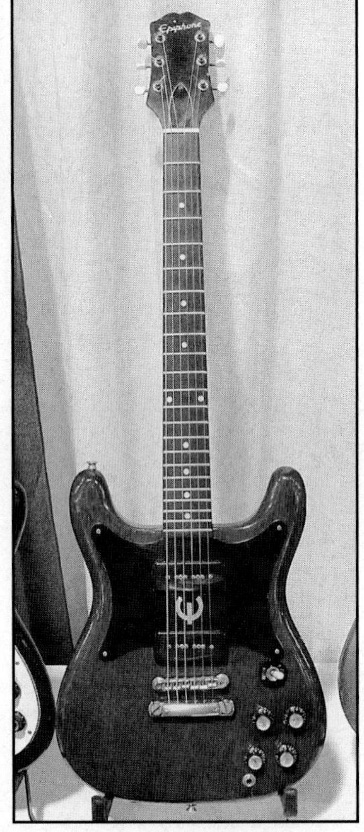
Epiphone Wilshire

1944 Epiphone Zenith

MODEL YEAR	FEATURES	EXC. COND. LOW	HIGH

Triumph Regent (Cutaway)

1948-1969. Acoustic archtop, single cutaway, F-holes. Renamed Triumph Cutaway in '53, then Gibson listed this model as just the Triumph from '58-'69.

1948-1958	Natural	$2,100	$2,700
1948-1958	Sunburst	$1,900	$2,500
1959-1965	Sunburst	$1,800	$2,400
1966-1968	Sunburst	$1,700	$2,300

Troubadour FT 98

1963-1969. 16" square shoulders, D-style, maple back and sides, gold-plated hardware, classical width fingerboard.

1963-1969		$1,300	$1,500

USA Map Guitar

1982-1983. Solidbody electric, mahogany body shaped like U.S. map, two pickups, American-made promotional model, Natural.

1982-1983		$1,400	$2,000

Wilshire

1959-1970. Double cutaway solidbody, two pickups, tune-o-matic bridge, Cherry.

1959	Symmetrical body	$2,300	$2,700
1960-1962	Thinner-style body, P-90s	$2,300	$2,700
1962	Mini-humbuckers	$2,300	$2,700
1963-1964	Asymmetrical body	$2,200	$2,600
1965-1966		$1,700	$2,000
1967-1968		$1,500	$1,900
1969-1970		$1,400	$1,900

Wilshire 12-String

1966-1968. Solidbody, two pickups, Cherry.

1966		$1,600	$1,900
1967-1968		$1,400	$1,800

Wilshire II

1984-1985. Solidbody, maple body, neck and fingerboard, two humbuckers, three-way switch, coil-tap, one tone and one volume control, various colors.

1984		$225	$275

Windsor

1959-1962. Archtop, one or two pickups, single cutaway thinline. Sunburst or Natural finish.

1959-1960	New York pickup	$1,400	$1,600
1961-1962	Mini-humbucker	$1,400	$1,600

X-1000

1986-1989. Electric solidbody, Korean-made, various colors.

1987		$225	$300

Zenith

1931-1969. Acoustic archtop, bound front and back, F-holes, Sunburst.

1931-1933		$700	$1,300
1934-1935	Larger 14 3/4" body	$800	$1,400
1936-1949	Still larger 16 3/8" body	$900	$1,500
1950-1958		$800	$1,400
1959-1961		$650	$1,150
1963-1964		$600	$1,100

MODEL YEAR	FEATURES	EXC. COND. LOW	HIGH

Zephyr

1939-1957. Non-cutaway electric archtop, one pickup, bound front and back, Blond or Sunburst. Name continued '58-'64 on thinline cutaway, two pickup model.

1939	Oblong pickup	$1,000	$1,700
1940-1943		$1,000	$1,700
1944-1946	Top mounted pickup	$1,000	$1,500
1947-1948	Metal covered pickup	$1,000	$1,400
1949-1957	New York pickup	$900	$1,400

Zephyr (Thinline Cutaway)

1958-1964. Gibson-made version, thinline archtop, single cutaway, two pickups. Natural or Sunburst finish.

1958-1959		$2,000	$2,700
1960-1964		$1,800	$2,500

Zephyr De Luxe (Non-cutaway)

1941-1954. Non-cutaway electric archtop, one or two pickups, multi-bound front and back, gold-plated hardware, Blond or Sunburst.

1941-1942		$2,500	$3,300
1945-1949		$2,500	$3,200
1951-1954		$2,000	$2,500

Zephyr De Luxe Regent (Cutaway)

1948-1954. Single cutaway electric archtop, one or two pickups until '50, then only two, gold-plated hardware. Sunburst or Natural finish. Renamed Deluxe Electric in '54.

1948-1949	Natural	$3,200	$3,800
1949	Sunburst	$3,000	$3,600
1950	Natural	$3,100	$3,700
1950	Sunburst	$2,900	$3,500
1951	Natural	$3,000	$3,600
1951	Sunburst	$2,800	$3,400
1952	Natural	$2,900	$3,500
1953	Natural	$2,800	$3,400
1953-1954	Sunburst	$2,600	$3,300

Zephyr Emperor Regent

1950-1954. Archtop, single rounded cutaway, multi-bound body, three pickups. Sunburst or Natural finish. Renamed Emperor Electric in 1954.

1950-1951	Natural	$4,400	$5,200
1950-1951	Sunburst	$4,200	$5,000
1952-1953	Natural	$4,200	$5,000
1952-1953	Sunburst	$4,000	$4,800
1954	Natural	$4,000	$4,800
1954	Sunburst	$3,700	$4,500

Zephyr Regent

1950-1958. Single cutaway electric archtop, one pickup, Natural or Sunburst. Called Zephyr Electric for '54-'58.

1950		$1,300	$2,700
1951		$1,200	$2,600
1953		$1,100	$2,500
1954		$1,000	$2,300
1955		$900	$2,200
1957		$800	$2,100

MODEL YEAR	FEATURES	EXC. COND. LOW	HIGH

Erlewine

1979-present. Professional and premium grade, production/custom guitars built by luthier Mark Erlewine in Austin, Texas. Erlewine also produces the Chiquita brand travel guitar.

ESP

1975-present. Intermediate, professional, and premium grade, production/custom, Japanese-made solidbody guitars and basses. Since '95, ESP has also offered the Korean-made LTD brand. ESP (Electric Sound Products) made inroads in the U.S. market with mainly copy styles in the early '80s, adding original designs over the years. In the '90s, ESP opened a California-based Custom Shop.

20th Anniversary

1995. Solidbody, double cut, ESP95 inlaid at 12th fret.

1995	Gold	$1,100	$1,200

Eclipse Custom (USA)

1998-2000. U.S. Custom Shop-built single cut mahogany body and maple top, various colors offered.

1998-2000		$900	$1,100

Eclipse Custom/Custom T (import)

1986-1988. Single cut mahogany solidbody, earliest model with bolt-on dot marker neck, 2nd version with neck-through design and block markers. The Custom T adds double locking tremolo.

1986-1987	Bolt-on neck, dot markers	$450	$550
1987-1988	Neck-through, block markers	$550	$650
1987-1988	Neck-through, Custom T	$550	$650

Eclipse Deluxe

1986-1988. Single cut solidbody, one single-coil and one humbucker pickups, vibrato.

1986-1988	Black	$400	$550

Horizon

1986, 1996-2001. Double cut neck-thru body, bound ebony 'board, one single-coil and one humbucker, buffer preamp circuit, various colors. Reintroduced 1996-2001with bolt-on neck, curved rounded point headstock.

1986		$350	$450
1996-2001		$250	$300

Horizon Classic (USA)

1993-1995. U.S.-made, carved mahogany body, set-neck, dot markers, various colors. Optional mahogany body with figured maple top also offered.

1993-1995	Figured maple top option	$1,200	$1,500
1993-1995	Standard mahogany body	$1,100	$1,300

Horizon Custom (USA)

1998-present. U.S. Custom Shop-made, mahogany body, figured maple top, bolt-on neck, mostly translucent finish in various colors.

1998		$1,100	$1,300

Horizon Deluxe (import)

1989-1992. Horizon Custom with bolt-on neck, various colors.

1989-1992		$550	$650

Hybrid I

1986 only. Offset double cutaway body, bolt-on maple neck, dot markers, six-on-a-side tuners, standard vibrato, various colors.

1986		$250	$350

Hybrid II

Offset double cutaway, rosewood board on maple bolt-on neck, lipstick neck pickup, humbucker bridge pickup, Hybrid II logo on headstock.

1980s		$300	$400

LTD EC-1000

2002-present. Deluxe appointments including abalone inlays and figured-top, 2 humbuckers, Korean-made.

2000s		$650	$750

LTD EC-300

2002-present. Single cut solidbody, 2 humbuckers, Korean-made.

2000s		$350	$400

LTD H-100

1998-present. Offset double-cut solidbody, 2 humbuckers, made in Korea.

1998-2003		$150	$175

LTD Viper

2000-present. Double cut SG style solidbody, 2 humbuckers.

2000s		$325	$425

M-I Custom

1987-1994. Offset double cutaway through-neck body, offset block markers, various colors.

1987-1994		$650	$750

M-I Deluxe

1987-1989. Double cut solidbody, rosewood 'board, two single-coils and one humbucker, various colors.

1987-1989		$550	$650

M-II

1989-1994, 1996-2000. Double cut solidbody, reverse headstock, bolt-on maple or rosewood cap neck, dot markers, various colors.

1989-1994		$700	$800

M-II Custom

1990-1994. Double cut solidbody, reverse headstock, neck-through maple neck, rosewood cap, dot markers, various colors.

1990-1994		$900	$1,000

ESP XTone PS-2V

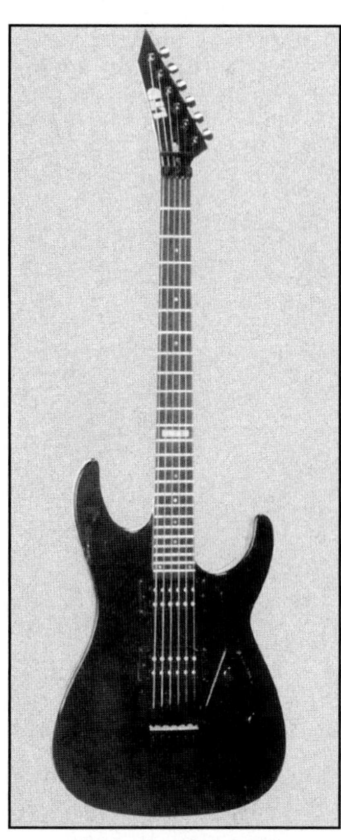

1998 ESP LTD M-200

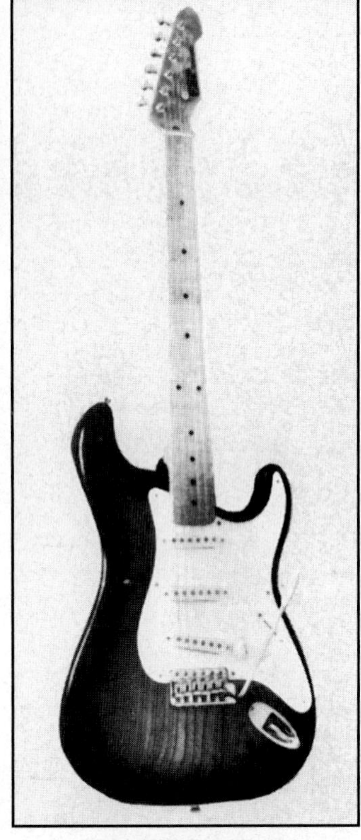
1986 ESP Traditional

Everett L Model

MODEL YEAR	FEATURES	EXC. COND. LOW	HIGH

M-II Deluxe

1990-1994. Double cut solidbody, reverse headstock, Custom with bolt-on neck, various colors.

1990-1994	$800	$900

Maverick/Maverick Deluxe

1989-1992. Offset double cutaway, bolt-on maple or rosewood cap neck, dot markers, double locking vibrola, six-on-a-side tuners, various colors.

1989	$250	$350

Metal I

1986 only. Offset double cutaway, bolt-on maple neck with rosewood cap, dot markers, various colors.

1986	$250	$350

Metal II

1986 only. Single horn V-style body, bolt on maple neck with rosewood cap, dot markers, various colors.

1986	$250	$350

Metal III

1986 only. Reverse offset body, bolt-on maple neck with maple cap, dot markers, Gold hardware, variou scolors.

1986	$300	$400

Mirage Custom

1986-1990. Double cut neck-thru solidbody, two-octave ebony fingerboard, block markers, one humbuck and two single-coil pickups, locking trem, various colors.

1980s	$500	$600

Mirage Standard

1986 only. Single pickup version of Mirage Custom, various colors.

1986	$275	$350

Phoenix

1987 only. Offset, narrow waist-style, through-neck mahogany body, Black hardware, dot markers, various colors.

1987	$450	$550

Phoenix Contemporary

Late-1990s. Firebird copy, three pickups vs. two on the earlier offering.

1998	$800	$850

S-454/S-456

1986-1987. Offset double cutaway, bolt-on maple or rosewood cap neck, dot markers, various colors.

1986-1987	$250	$500

S-500

1991-1993. Double cut figured ash body, bolt-on neck, six-on-a-side tuners, various colors.

1991-1993	$500	$700

Traditional

1989-1990. Double cutaway, three pickups, tremolo, various colors.

1989-1990	$500	$600

MODEL YEAR	FEATURES	EXC. COND. LOW	HIGH

Vintage/Vintage Plus S

1995-1998. Offset double cutaway, bolt-on maple or rosewood cap neck, dot markers, Floyd Rose locking vibrato or standard Strat-type vibrato, various colors.

1995-1998	$600	$900

Espana

Early-1960s-early-1970s. Distributed by catalog wholesalers. Built in Sweden.

Classical

Early-1960s-early-1970s. Guitars with white spruce fan-braced tops with either walnut, mahogany, or rosewood back and sides.

1970s	$125	$175

EL-36

1969-early-1970s. Thin hollow doublecut, two pickups, Natural.

1970s	$150	$200

Jumbo Folk

1969-early-1970s. Natural.

1970s	$125	$200

S-1 Classical

1969-early-1970s. Natural.

1970s	$125	$175

Essex (SX)

1985-present. Budget grade, production, electric and acoustic guitars imported by Rondo Music of Union, New Jersey. They also offer basses.

Euphonon

1934-1944. This Larson-made brand was intended to compete with the competition's new larger body, 14-fret, solid peghead (unslotted) models. Standard and D-style models were offered. Three models were offered ranging from the small 13-3/4" student model, to the top end 15" and 16" models. Euphonons with truss rods were marketed as Prairie State models.

Everett Guitars

1977-present. Luthier Kent Everett builds his premium grade, production/custom, steel-string and classical guitars in Atlanta, Georgia. He has also built archtops, semi-hollow and solidbody electrics, Dobro-styles, and mandolins.

Evergreen Mountain

1979-present. Professional grade, custom, flattops, tenor guitars, acoustic basses, and mandolins built by luthier Jerry Nolte ion Cove, Oregon. He also built over one hundred dulcimers in the 1970s.

Everly Guitars

1982-2001. Luthier Robert Steinegger built these premium grade, production/custom flattops in Portland, Oregon (also see Steinegger Guitars).

Falk

Custom archtop guitars built by luthier Dave Falk in Independence, Missouri.

Farnell

1989-present. Luthier Al Farnell builds his professional grade, production, solidbody guitars and basses in Ontario, California. He also offers his intermediate grade, production, "C" Series which is imported from China.

Favilla

1890-1973. Founded by the Favilla family in New York, the company began to import guitars in 1970, but folded in '73. American-made models have the Favilla family crest on the headstock. Import models used a script logo on the headstock.

Fender

1946 (1945)-present. Currently budget, intermediate, professional and premium grade, production/custom, electric, acoustic, acoustic/electric, classical, and resonator guitars built in the U.S. and overseas. They also build amps, basses, mandolins, banjos and violins.

Ca. 1939 Leo Fender opened a radio and record store called Fender Radio Service, where he met Clayton Orr "Doc" Kauffman, and in '45 they started KF Company to build lap steels and amps. In '46 Kauffman left and Fender started the Fender Electric Instrument Company. By '50 Fender's products were distributed by F.C. Hall's Radio & Television Electronics Company (Radio-Tel, later owners of Rickenbacker). In '53, Radio-Tel is replaced by the Fender Sales Company, which was run by Don Randall.

In January '65 CBS purchased the company for $13 million and renamed it Fender Musical Instruments Corporation. The CBS takeover is synonymous with a decline in quality - whether true or not is still debated, but the perception persists among musicians and collectors, and "Pre-CBS" Fenders are more valuable. Fender experienced some quality problems in the late-'60s. Small headstock is enlarged in '65 and the four-bolt neck is replaced by the three-bolt in '71. With high value and relative scarcity of Pre-CBS Fenders, even CBS-era instruments are now sought by collectors. Leo Fender kept on as consultant until '70. Fender went on to design guitars for Music Man and G&L. Bill Schultz and Dan Smith were hired from Yamaha in '81. In '82 Fender Japan is established to produce licensed Fender "copies" for sale in Japan. Also in '82, the Fender Squire brand debuts on Japanese-made instruments for the European market and by '83 they were imported into U.S.

In '84 CBS put Fender up for sale and it was purchased by investor group headed by Bill Schultz but the purchase does not include the Fullerton factory. While a new factory was being established at Corona, CA, all Fender Contemporary Stratocasters and Telecasters were made either by Fender Japan or in Seoul, Korea. U.S. production resumes in '86 with the American Standard Stratocaster. The Fender Custom Shop, run by Michael Stevens and John Page, opened in '87. The Mexican Fender factory is established in '90. In '95, Fender purchased the Guild guitar company. On January 3, 2002, Fender Musical Instruments Corporation (FMIC) announced the sale of holdings in the company. FMIC recapitalized a minority portion of the common stock. The recapitalization partners included Roland Corporation U.S. (Los Angeles) and Weston Presidio, a private equity firm (San Francisco). As of January 1, 2003, Fred Gretsch Enterprises, Ltd granted Fender the exclusive rights to develop, produce, market and distribute Gretsch guitars worldwide where FMIC is responsible for all aspects of the Gretsch product lines and brandnames, including development of new products. Fred Gretsch consulted during the changeover and will also consult on product development and quality control. Around the same time, Fender also acquired the Jackson/Charvel Guitar Company. As of 2003 FMIC also owned Fender, Guild, Squire, DeArmond, Benedetto, Rodriguez, and Floyd Rose.

Dating older Fender guitars is an imprecise art form at best. While serial numbers were used, they were frequently not in sequence, although a lower number will frequently be older than a substantially higher number. Often necks were dated, but only with the date the neck was finished, not when the guitar was assembled. Generally, dating requires triangulating between serial numbers, neck dates, pot dates, construction details and model histories.

From '50 through roughly '65, guitars had more-or-less sequential numbers in either four or five digits, though some higher numbers may have an initial 0 or - prefix. These can range from 0001 to 99XXX.

From '63 into '65, some instruments had serial numbers beginning with an L prefix plus 5 digits (LXXXXX). Beginning in '65 with the CBS takeover into '76, 6-digit serial numbers were stamped on F neckplates roughly sequentially from 10XXXX to 71XXXX. In '76 the serial number was shifted to the headstock decal. From '76-'77, the serial number began with a bold-face 76 or S6 plus 5 digits (76XXXXX).

From '77 on, serial numbers consisted of a two-place prefix plus 5 digits (sometimes 6 beginning in '91): '77 (S7, S8), '78 (S7, S8, S9), '79 (S9, E0), '80-'81 (S9, E0, E1), '82 (E1, E2, E3), '84-'85 (E4), '85-'86 (no U.S. production), '87 (E4), '88 (E4, E8), '89 (E8, E9), '90 (E9, N9, N0), '91 (N0), '92 (N2).

Serial numbers on guitars made by Fender Japan consist of either a two-place prefix plus 5 digits or a single prefix letter plus 6 digits: '82-'84 (JV), '83-'84 (SQ), '84-'87 (E), '85-'86+ (A, B, C), '86-'87 (F), '87-'88+ (G), '88-'89 (H), '89-'90 (I, J), '90-'91

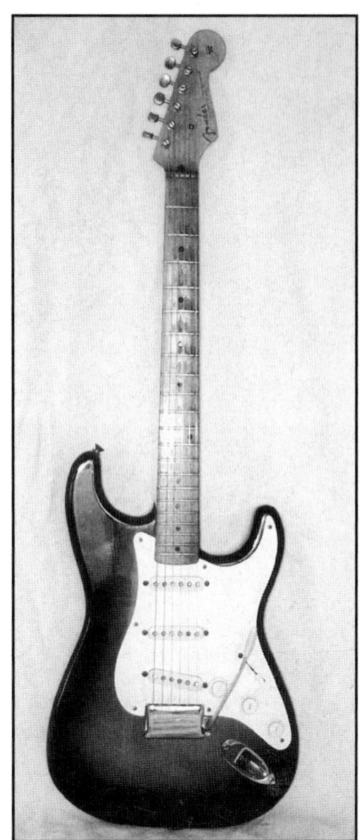

1957 Fender Stratocaster

1979 Fender Silver Anniversary Stratocaster

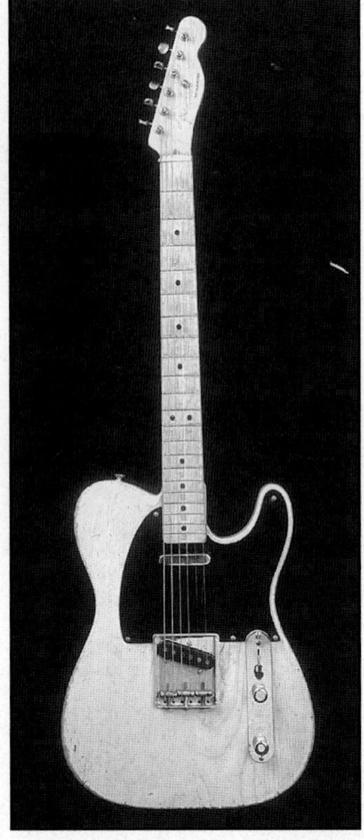

Fender Broadcaster

Fender Coronado II

MODEL YEAR	FEATURES	EXC. COND. LOW	HIGH

(K), '91-'92 (L), '92-'93 (M).

Factors affecting Fender values: The sale to CBS in '65 is a major point in Fender instrument values as CBS made many changes that collectors feel affected quality. The '70s introduced the three-bolt neck and other design changes that aren't that popular with guitarists. Custom color instruments, especially Strats from the '50s and early-'60s, can be valued much more than the standard Sunburst finishes. In '75 Fender dropped the optional custom colors and started issuing the guitars in a variety of standard colors.

The various Telecaster and Stratocaster models are grouped under those general headings.

'50s Relic/'51 No Caster Custom Shop

1996-present. Called the '50s Relic Nocaster for '96-'99, and '51 Nocaster in "NOS," "Relic," or "Closet Classic" versions at present, with the Relic Series being the highest offering.

1990s	Relic No Caster	$1,700	$1,900
2000s	Closet Classic	$1,200	$1,400

American Special Toronado

2002. Single cutaway alder body, bolt-on neck, 24 3/4" scale (unusual scale for Fender), medium jumbo frets, four control knobs, either DE-9000 single-coil pickups or two Atomic II humbucking pickups, Blond or Crimson Red.

2002		$700	$800

Avalon

1984-1995. Acoustic, mahogany neck, back and sides (nato after 1993), spruce top.

1984	Wine Red	$350	$450

Broadcaster

Mid-1950-early-1951. For a short time in early-1951, before being renamed the Telecaster, models had no Broadcaster decal; these are called "No-casters" by collectors. Renamed Telecaster.

1950	Blond	$22,000	$26,000
1951	Clipped decal, "No Caster"	$21,000	$25,000

Broadcaster Leo Fender Custom Shop

1999 only. Leo Fender script logo signature replaces Fender logo on headstock. Custom Shop Certificate signed by Phyllis Fender, Fred Gretsch, and William Schultz. Includes glass display case and poodle guitar case.

1999		$7,000	$8,000

Bronco

1967-1980. Slab solidbody, one pickup, tremolo, Red.

1967-1969		$600	$700
1970-1975		$500	$600
1976-1980		$450	$550

Bullet

1981-1983. Solidbody, came in 2- and 3-pickup versions (single-coil and humbucker), and single and double cutaway models. A later Squire version was also offered.

1981-1983	Three pickups	$350	$400
1981-1983	Two pickups	$300	$350

Squire Bullet

1985-1988. Fender Japan was established in 1982. Squire production began in 1983. Production was shifted to Korea in 1987.

1985-1988	Sunburst, humbuckers	$250	$400
1985-1988	White	$175	$300

Concert

1963-1970. Acoustic flat-top slightly shorter than King/Kingman, spruce body, mahogany back and sides (optional Brazilian or Indian rosewood, zebrawood or vermillion). Natural, Sunburst optional by 1968.

1963-1965	Natural	$600	$900
1966-1968	Natural or Sunburst	$500	$800
1979-1970	Natural or Sunburst	$500	$700

Coronado I

1966-1970. Thinline semi-hollowbody, double cutaway, tremolo, one pickup, single-bound, dot inlay.

1966-1967	Blue custom color	$1,100	$1,400
1966-1967	Cherry Red	$750	$850
1966-1967	Orange custom color	$950	$1,350
1966-1967	Sunburst	$750	$850
1966-1967	White (unfaded)	$1,000	$1,200
1968-1970	Sunburst	$600	$750

Coronado II

1966-1969 (Antigua finish offered until 1970). Thinline semi-hollowbody, double-cut, tremolo optional, 2 pickups, single-bound, block inlay. Available in standard finishes but special issues offered in Antigua and 6 different Wildwood finishes. Wildwood finishes were achieved by injecting dye into growing trees.

1966-1967	Blue, Silver, Orange custom colors	$1,200	$1,400
1966-1967	Cherry Red	$800	$1,000
1966-1967	Olympic White custom color	$1,100	$1,300
1966-1967	Sunburst	$800	$1,000
1966-1968	Wildwood (unfaded)	$1,200	$1,400
1968	Cherry Red	$700	$900
1968	Orange custom color	$1,100	$1,300
1968	Sunburst	$700	$900
1968	Wildwood	$1,100	$1,300
1969	Antigua	$1,000	$1,300
1969	Cherry Red	$600	$800
1969	Orange custom color	$1,000	$1,200
1969	Sunburst	$600	$800
1969	Wildwood	$1,000	$1,200
1970	Antigua	$900	$1,200

Coronado XII

1966-1969 (Antigua finish offered until 1970). Thinline semi-hollowbody, double cutaway, 12 strings, two pickups, block inlay. Standard, Antigua and Wildwood finishes available.

1966-1967	Cherry Red	$800	$1,000
1966-1967	Orange custom color	$1,200	$1,400

MODEL YEAR	FEATURES	EXC. COND. LOW	HIGH
1966-1967	Sunburst	$800	$1,000
1966-1967	Wildwood Green	$1,200	$1,400
1968	Cherry Red	$700	$900
1968	Orange custom color	$1,100	$1,300
1968	Sunburst	$700	$900
1968	Wildwood Rainbow Gold	$1,100	$1,300
1969	Antigua	$1,000	$1,300
1969	Cherry Red	$600	$800
1969	Orange custom color	$1,000	$1,200
1969	Sunburst	$600	$800
1969	Wildwood	$1,000	$1,200

Custom

1969-1971. Six-string solidbody that used up parts from discontinued Electric XII. Asymmetrical cutaway, long headstock, two split pickups. Also marketed as the Maverick.

1969-1970	Sunburst	$1,500	$1,800

Cyclone

1998-present. Mexican import, solidbody, contoured offset waist, poplar body. Various colors.

1998-2000		$325	$375

D'Aquisto Elite

1984, 1989-1995. Part of Fender's Master Series. Archtop, single cut, glued neck, one pickup, gold-plated hardware, made in Japan until '94. In '94 the Fender Custom Shop issued a version that retailed at $6,000. Various colors.

1989-1993	Japan made	$1,700	$2,000

D'Aquisto Standard

1984 (Serial numbers could range from 1983-1985). Part of Fender's Master Series. Archtop, single cutaway, glued neck, two pickups, made in Japan. Various colors.

1984		$1,500	$1,700

D'Aquisto Ultra

1994-2000, Custom Shop, made under the supervision of James D'Aquisto. Flamed maple back and sides, spruce top, ebony tailpiece, bridge and pickguard, all hand carved.

1994-2000		$6,000	$8,000

Duo-Sonic

1957-1969. Solidbody, 3/4-size, two pickups, short- and long-scale necks. Short-scale necks listed here (see Duo-Sonic II for long-scale). Reissued Mexican-made in 1994.

1957-1963	Blond	$1,100	$1,300
1964-1965	Blue, Red or White	$800	$1,000
1966-1969	Blue, Red or White	$700	$900

Duo-Sonic II

1965-1969. Solidbody, two pickups, long-scale neck. Though the long-scale neck Duo-Sonic was not known as the Duo-Sonic II until 1965, we have lumped all long-scales under the II for the purposes of this Guide.

1965-1969	Blue, Red, or White	$1,000	$1,200

Duo-Sonic Reissue

1994-1997. Made in Mexico.

1994-1997	Black, Red, or White	$150	$200

Electric Violin

1958-1976. Sunburst is the standard finish.

1958-1960	Natural, with bow	$1,400	$1,500
1960-1969	Natural, with bow	$1,300	$1,400
1970-1976	Natural, with bow	$1,200	$1,300

Electric XII

1965-1969. Solidbody, 12 strings, long headstock, two split pickups. Custom colors can fade or become darker; for example Lake Placid Blue changes to Green. The price ranges below are for instruments that are relatively unfaded. Many older guitars have some color fade and minor fade is factored into these values. Each custom color should be evaluated on a case-by-case basis.

Custom color Fenders can be forged and bogus finishes have been a problem. As the value of custom color Fenders has increased, so has the problem of bogus non-original finishes. The prices in the Guide are for factory original finishes in excellent condition. The prices noted do not take into account market factors such as fake instruments, which can have the effect of lowering a guitar's market value unless the guitar's provenance can be validated.

1965	Black	$2,200	$2,700
1965	Blue Ice	$2,500	$3,100
1965	Candy Apple Red	$2,200	$2,700
1965	Firemist Gold	$2,500	$2,900
1965	Lake Placid Blue	$2,200	$2,700
1965	Ocean Turquoise	$2,600	$3,600
1965	Olympic White	$2,200	$2,700
1965	Sherwood Green	$2,700	$3,200
1965	Shoreline Gold	$2,600	$3,100
1965	Sonic Blue	$2,600	$3,100
1965	Sunburst	$1,700	$2,200
1965	Surf Green	$2,700	$3,200
1966	Black	$2,100	$2,700
1966	Blue Ice	$2,400	$3,100
1966	Burgundy Mist	$2,400	$3,200
1966	Candy Apple Red	$2,100	$2,700
1966	Charcoal Frost	$2,400	$3,100
1966	Dakota Red	$2,200	$3,000
1966	Daphne Blue	$2,200	$3,000
1966	Fiesta Red	$2,200	$3,000
1966	Firemist Gold	$2,400	$3,100
1966	Firemist Silver	$2,400	$3,100
1966	Foam Green	$2,400	$3,100
1966	Inca Silver	$2,400	$3,100
1966	Lake Placid Blue	$2,100	$2,700
1966	Ocean Turquoise	$2,400	$3,100
1966	Olympic White	$2,100	$2,700
1966	Sherwood Green	$2,600	$3,200
1966	Shoreline Gold	$2,500	$3,100
1966	Sonic Blue	$2,500	$3,100
1966	Sunburst (late '66), block	$1,600	$1,900

1970s Fender Custom

1970s Fender Electric XII

GUITARS

1955 Fender Esquire

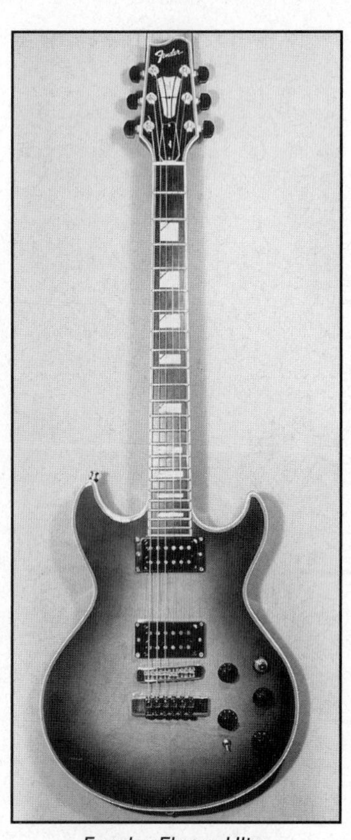
Fender Flame Ultra

MODEL YEAR	FEATURES	EXC. COND. LOW	HIGH
1966	Sunburst, dot inlay, unbound	$1,700	$2,100
1966	Surf Green	$2,600	$3,200
1966	Teal Green	$2,600	$3,200
1967	Lake Placid Blue	$2,000	$2,300
1967	Sunburst, block	$1,600	$1,800
1968	Sunburst	$1,500	$1,800
1969	Candy Apple Red	$1,900	$2,200
1969	Sunburst	$1,500	$1,700

Esprit Elite

1984. Part of the Master Series, made in Japan, double cut, semi-hollow, carved maple top, two humbuckers, bound rosewood 'board, snowflake inlays.

1984		$700	$900

Esprit Standard

1984. Part of the Master Series, made in Japan, double cut, semi-hollow, carved maple top, two humbuckers, bound rosewood 'board, dot inlays.

1984		$600	$800

Esprit Ultra

1984. Double cut, semi-hollow, carved spruce top, two humbuckers, bound rosewood 'board, split-block inlays, sunburst, gold hardware. Part of the Master Series, made in Japan.

1984		$900	$1,000

Esquire

1950-1970. Ash body, single cutaway, one pickup, maple neck, Black pickguard 1950-1954, White pickguard 1954 on.

1951	Blond, Black pickguard	$10,000	$11,000
1952-1954	Blond, Black pickguard	$9,000	$11,000
1954-1955	Blond, White pickguard	$7,000	$8,500
1956-1957	Blond	$6,400	$7,400
1958	Blond	$6,100	$6,700
1959	Blond, maple board	$5,600	$6,100
1959	Blond, slab board	$5,500	$6,000
1960	Blond	$5,300	$5,800
1960	Sunburst	$5,700	$6,200
1961	Blond	$5,200	$5,700
1961	Sunburst	$5,200	$5,700
1962	Blond	$5,000	$5,500
1963	Blond	$4,800	$5,100
1963	Candy Apple Red	$6,500	$7,500
1963	Sunburst	$4,800	$5,100
1963	White	$6,500	$7,500
1964	Blond	$4,700	$5,000
1964	Burgundy Mist	$7,000	$12,000
1965	Blond	$4,600	$4,900
1965	Lake Placid Blue	$5,000	$6,000
1966	Blond	$4,500	$4,800
1966	Olympic White	$4,800	$5,800
1967	Blond	$3,500	$4,300
1967	Blue Ice	$6,000	$8,000
1967	Lake Placid Blue	$4,800	$5,800
1967	Olympic White	$4,500	$5,500
1968	Blond	$3,100	$4,100
1968	Sunburst	$3,200	$4,200
1969	Blond	$3,000	$4,000
1969	Sunburst	$3,000	$4,000
1970	Blond	$2,800	$3,600

Esquire Custom

1959-1970. Same as Esquire, but with bound alder Sunburst body and rosewood fingerboard.

1959		$10,000	$13,000
1960		$9,500	$12,500
1961-1962	Slab board	$7,500	$10,000
1962-1964	Curve board	$6,500	$8,000
1965-1967		$5,500	$6,500
1968-1970		$5,000	$6,000

Esquire Custom Shop

Various colors.

1990s		$2,000	$2,250

F-Series Dreadnought Flat-Top

1969-1979. The F-Series were Japanese-made acoustics. Included were Concert- and Dreadnought-size instruments with features running from plain to bound necks and headstocks and fancy inlays. There was also a line of F-Series classical, nylon string guitars.

1969-1979		$175	$250

Flame Elite

1984. Part of the Master Series, made in Japan, neck-thru, double cut, solidbody, two humbuckers, rosewood 'board, snowflake inlays.

1984		$600	$800

Flame Standard

1984. Part of the Master Series, made in Japan, neck-thru, double cut, solidbody, two humbuckers, rosewood 'board, dot inlays.

1984		$600	$700

Flame Ultra

1984. Part of the Master Series, made in Japan, neck-thru, double cut, solidbody, two humbuckers, rosewood 'board, split block inlays (some with snowflakes), gold hardware.

1984		$750	$950

Gemini I

1984-ca.1989. Imported inexpensive classical nylon string acoustic.

1980s	Sunburst	$125	$175

Gemini II

1984-ca.1989. Imported Inexpensive dreadnought steel string acoustic.

1980s	Sunburst	$175	$225

Gemini III

1984-ca.1989. Imported acoustic.

1980s	Black	$200	$250

Harmony-Made Series

Early-1970s-mid-1970s. Harmony-made with white stencil Fender logo, mahogany. Natural or sunburst.

1970s		$75	$200

MODEL YEAR	FEATURES	EXC. COND. LOW	HIGH

Jag-Stang

1997-1999. Japanese-made, designed by Curt Cobain, body similar to Jaguar, tremolo, one pickup, oversize Strat peghead. Fiesta Red or Sonic Blue.

MODEL YEAR	FEATURES	LOW	HIGH
1997-1999		$400	$450

Jaguar

1962-1975. Reintroduced as Jaguar '62 in '95-'99. Custom colors can fade and often the faded color has very little similarity to the original color. The values below are for an instrument that is relatively unfaded. Each custom color should be evaluated on a case-by-case basis. Custom color Fenders can be forged and bogus finishes have been a problem. As the value of custom color Fenders has increased, so has the problem of bogus non-original finishes. The prices in the Guide are for factory original finishes in excellent condition. The prices noted do not take into account market factors such as fake instruments, which can have the effect of lowering a guitar's market value unless the guitar's provenance can be validated.

MODEL YEAR	FEATURES	LOW	HIGH
1962	Black	$2,400	$2,900
1962	Blond	$2,400	$2,900
1962	Burgundy Mist	$3,500	$4,500
1962	Dakota Red	$3,000	$3,500
1962	Daphne Blue	$3,000	$3,500
1962	Fiesta Red	$3,000	$3,500
1962	Foam Green	$3,500	$4,500
1962	Inca Silver	$3,500	$4,000
1962	Lake Pacid Blue	$2,500	$3,000
1962	Olympic White	$2,500	$2,800
1962	Shell Pink	$4,000	$4,500
1962	Sherwood Green	$3,000	$3,500
1962	Shoreline Gold	$3,000	$3,500
1962	Sonic Blue	$3,000	$3,500
1962	Sunburst	$2,000	$2,500
1962	Surf Green	$3,500	$4,500
1963	Black	$2,300	$2,800
1963	Candy Apple Red	$2,300	$2,800
1963	Fiesta Red	$2,800	$3,300
1963	Lake Placid Blue	$2,400	$2,900
1963	Lake Placid Blue, gold hardware	$3,000	$3,400
1963	Olympic White	$2,300	$2,800
1963	Shoreline Gold	$2,900	$3,400
1963	Sonic Blue	$2,900	$3,400
1963	Sunburst	$1,900	$2,100
1964	Black	$2,200	$2,800
1964	Burgundy Mist	$3,000	$3,500
1964	Candy Apple Red	$2,200	$2,800
1964	Fiesta Red	$2,500	$3,300
1964	Lake Placid Blue	$2,200	$2,800
1964	Olympic White	$2,200	$2,800
1964	Sonic Blue	$2,800	$3,400
1964	Sunburst	$1,800	$2,000
1965	Black	$1,800	$2,700
1965	Blue Ice	$2,500	$3,200
1965	Burgundy Mist	$2,700	$3,500
1965	Candy Apple Red	$1,900	$2,800
1965	Fiesta Red	$2,400	$3,300
1965	Firemist Gold	$2,400	$3,300
1965	Lake Placid Blue	$1,900	$2,800
1965	Ocean Turquoise	$2,400	$3,300
1965	Olympic White	$1,900	$2,800
1965	Shoreline Gold	$2,400	$3,300
1965	Sonic Blue	$2,400	$3,300
1965	Sunburst	$1,700	$1,900
1965	Teal Green	$2,400	$3,300
1966	Black	$1,700	$2,600
1966	Blond	$2,400	$3,500
1966	Blue Ice	$2,500	$3,200
1966	Candy Apple Red	$1,800	$2,700
1966	Fiesta Red	$2,200	$3,100
1966	Firemist Gold	$2,300	$3,300
1966	Lake Placid Blue	$1,800	$2,700
1966	Olympic White	$1,800	$2,700
1966	Sonic Blue	$2,200	$3,100
1966	Sunburst, block markers	$1,300	$1,700
1966	Sunburst, dot markers (early '66)	$1,500	$1,900
1967	Black	$1,600	$2,500
1967	Candy Apple Red	$1,800	$2,700
1967	Lake Placid Blue	$1,800	$2,700
1967	Sunburst	$1,300	$2,100
1968	Black	$1,500	$2,400
1968	Blue Ice	$1,800	$2,700
1968	Candy Apple Red	$1,600	$2,500
1968	Lake Placid Blue	$1,600	$2,500
1968	Olympic White	$1,600	$2,500
1968	Sunburst	$1,200	$1,650
1969	Black	$1,500	$2,300
1969	Blond	$1,500	$2,300
1969	Candy Apple Red	$1,500	$2,300
1969	Firemist Gold	$2,300	$2,800
1969	Firemist Silver	$2,300	$2,800
1969	Lake Placid Blue	$1,500	$2,300
1969	Ocean Turquoise	$2,500	$3,200
1969	Olympic White	$1,500	$2,300
1969	Sonic Blue	$2,300	$2,800
1969	Sunburst	$1,200	$1,600
1970	Sunburst	$1,200	$1,550
1971	Black	$1,500	$1,900
1971	Candy Apple Red	$1,600	$1,900
1971-1975	Sunburst	$1,200	$1,400

Jaguar '62

1995-present. Reintroduction of Jaguar, Japanese-made until 1999, then U.S.-made, basswood body, rosewood fingerboard. Various colors.

MODEL YEAR	FEATURES	LOW	HIGH
1995-1999	Import	$450	$550
1999-2003	U.S.A.-made	$950	$1,000

Jazzmaster

1958-1982. Contoured body, two pickups, rosewood fingerboard, clay dot inlay. Reintroduced as Japanese-made Jazzmaster '62 in 1995. Custom color Fenders can be forged and bogus finishes have been a problem. As the value of custom color Fenders has increased, so has the problem of bogus non-original finishes. The prices in the Guide are for factory original finishes in excellent condition. The

1965 Fender Jaguar

Fender Jaguar '62

GUITARS

1960 Fender Jazzmaster

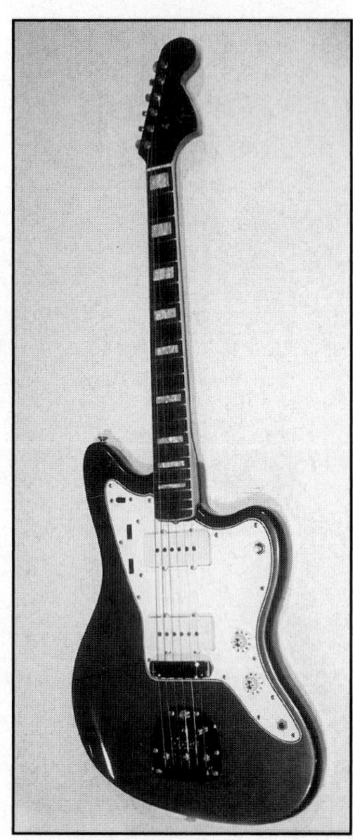
1966 Fender Jazzmaster

prices noted do not take intoaccount market factors such as fake instruments, which can have the effect of lowering a guitar's market value unless the guitar's provenance can be validated.

MODEL YEAR	FEATURES	EXC. COND. LOW	HIGH
1958	Sunburst	$3,500	$4,500
1958	Sunburst, rare maple fingerboard	$5,000	$6,000
1959	Olympic White	$4,000	$5,000
1959	Sonic Blue	$4,500	$5,800
1959	Sunburst	$3,500	$4,500
1960	Blond	$4,300	$5,300
1960	Olympic White	$3,900	$5,000
1960	Sunburst	$3,000	$4,000
1961	Blond	$4,500	$5,800
1961	Olympic White	$3,800	$5,000
1961	Shell Pink	$5,200	$6,700
1961	Sunburst	$2,900	$3,100
1962	Black, matching headstock	$4,000	$5,200
1962	Blond see-through over ash	$4,200	$5,700
1962	Burgundy Mist, slab board	$5,000	$6,500
1962	Fiesta Red, curve board	$4,000	$4,800
1962	Fiesta Red, slab board	$4,500	$5,800
1962	Lake Placid Blue, matching head stock, slab	$4,000	$5,300
1962	Lake Placid Blue, slab board	$3,900	$5,200
1962	Olympic White, slab board	$3,700	$5,000
1962	Shell Pink, slab board	$5,100	$6,600
1962	Shoreline Gold Metallic	$5,000	$6,500
1962	Sunburst, curve board	$2,600	$2,900
1962	Sunburst, slab board	$2,800	$3,100
1963	Blond	$4,000	$4,600
1963	Candy Apple Red	$3,800	$4,600
1963	Dakota Red	$4,000	$5,500
1963	Lake Placid Blue	$3,800	$4,600
1963	Olympic White	$3,600	$4,400
1963	Shoreline Gold	$4,700	$5,700
1963	Sunburst	$2,500	$2,800
1964	Blond	$3,500	$4,500
1964	Burgundy Mist	$3,900	$5,500
1964	Candy Apple Red	$3,700	$4,000
1964	Fiesta Red	$3,800	$5,500
1964	Ice Blue Metallic	$3,800	$5,500
1964	Lake Placid Blue	$3,700	$4,000
1964	Olympic White	$3,400	$3,800
1964	Sunburst	$2,400	$2,800
1965	Blond	$3,400	$4,500
1965	Candy Apple Red	$3,200	$3,700
1965	Dakota Red	$3,700	$5,500
1965	Fiesta Red	$3,700	$5,500
1965	Firemist Gold	$3,700	$5,500
1965	Ice Blue Metallic	$3,700	$5,500
1965	Lake Placid Blue	$3,300	$3,700
1965	Natural	$3,000	$3,500
1965	Olympic White	$3,000	$3,500
1965	Sonic Blue	$3,700	$5,500
1965	Sunburst	$1,800	$2,300
1966	Candy Apple Red	$2,900	$3,500
1966	Dakota Red	$3,500	$5,000
1966	Ice Blue Metallic	$3,500	$5,000
1966	Lake Placid Blue	$3,000	$3,500
1966	Olympic White	$2,900	$3,400
1966	Sunburst	$1,700	$2,100
1967	Lake Placid Blue	$2,800	$3,100
1967	Sunburst	$1,600	$2,100
1968	Sunburst	$1,600	$2,000
1969	Candy Apple Red	$2,300	$2,700
1969	Sunburst	$1,500	$2,000
1970-1972	Candy Apple Red	$1,700	$2,000
1970-1972	Sunburst	$1,300	$1,700
1973-1974	Natural	$1,000	$1,400
1973-1974	Sunburst	$1,200	$1,500
1975-1982	Sunburst	$1,000	$1,400

Jazzmaster '62

1996-present. Japanese-made reintroduction of Jazzmaster. Basswood body, rosewood fingerboard, U.S.-made from 1999. Various colors.

MODEL YEAR	FEATURES	LOW	HIGH
1995-1999	Import	$450	$550
1999-2003	U.S.A.-made	$950	$1,000

Jazzmaster The Ventures Limited Edition

1996. Japanese-made, ash body, two pickups, block inlay.

MODEL YEAR	FEATURES	LOW	HIGH
1996	Transparent Black	$800	$950

Katana

1985-1986. Import, wedge body style, glued neck, bound neck, two humbuckers, made in Japan. A one pickup Squire version was also available.

MODEL YEAR	FEATURES	LOW	HIGH
1985-1986	Black	$300	$400

Squire Katana

1985-1986. Import, wedge-shaped body, bridge pickup.

MODEL YEAR	FEATURES	LOW	HIGH
1985-1986	Black	$250	$350

King

1963-1965. Full-size 15 5/8" wide acoustic. Renamed Kingman in 1966.

MODEL YEAR	FEATURES	LOW	HIGH
1963-1965	Natural	$750	$1,000

Kingman

1966-1971. Full-size 15 5/8" wide acoustic. Slightly smaller by 1970. Offered in three Wildwood colors, referred to as the Wildwood acoustic which is a Kingman with dyed wood.

MODEL YEAR	FEATURES	LOW	HIGH
1966-1968		$750	$1,000
1969-1971		$750	$900

Lead I

1979-1982. Double cut solidbody with one humbucker. Black or Brown.

MODEL YEAR	FEATURES	LOW	HIGH
1979-1982		$400	$425

GUITARS

MODEL YEAR	FEATURES	EXC. COND. LOW	HIGH

Lead II

1979-1982. Double cut solidbody with two pickups. Black or Brown.

1979-1982		$425	$475

Lead III

1982. Double cut solidbody with two split-coil humbuckers, two three-way switches. Black or Brown.

1982		$475	$500

LTD

1969-1975. Archtop electric, single cutaway, gold-plated hardware, carved top and back, one pickup, multi-bound, bolt-on neck.

1969-1975	Sunburst	$3,500	$5,000

Malibu

1965-1970. Acoustic flat top, spruce top, mahogany back and sides. Black, Mahogany and Sunburst.

1965-1970		$500	$650

Marauder

1965 only. The Marauder has three pickups, and some have slanted frets. Only eight were made, thus it is very rare.

1965	Sunburst	$6,500	$8,000

Montego I

1968-1975. Electric archtop, single cut, bolt neck, 1 pickup, chrome-plated hardware.

1968-1975		$1,700	$2,500

Montego II

1968-1975. Electric archtop, single cut, bolt neck, 2 pickups, chrome-plated hardware.

1968-1975	Sunburst	$2,000	$2,700

Musiclander

1969-1972. Also called Swinger and Arrow. Solidbody, one pickup, arrow-shaped headstock, no model name on peghead. Red, white, and blue.

1969-1972		$1,200	$1,600

Musicmaster

1956-1980. Solidbody, one pickup, short-scale (3/4) neck, Blond. Restyled in '64 like Mustang with Red, White and Blue available that year. Regular-scale necks were optional and are called Musicmaster II from '64 to '69. After '69, II is dropped and Musicmaster continues with regular-scale neck.

1956-1959	Blond	$750	$950
1960-1964	Blond	$750	$800
1964-1969	Blue, Red, or White	$500	$650
1970-1974	Blue, Red, or White	$400	$500
1975-1980	Black or White	$350	$450

Musicmaster II

1964-1969. Solidbody, one pickup, long regular-scale neck version of Musicmaster. Red, White, and Blue.

1964-1969		$525	$675

Mustang

1964-1982, 1997-1998. Solidbody, two pickups. Reissued as '69 Mustang in 1996 and name changed back to Mustang 1997-1998. Dakota Red, Daphne Blue and Olympic White with Competition Red, Blue and Orange finishes added ca. 1969-1972. Competition finishes featured a racing stripe on the front of the body.

1964-1969	Various colors	$950	$1,300
1970-1979	Various colors	$850	$1,000
1980-1982	Various colors	$650	$800

Mustang '69 Reissue

1996-1999. Japanese-made reissue of Mustang. Name changed back to Mustang in 1997-1998.

1996-1999	Blue or White	$450	$550

Newporter

1965-1971. Acoustic flat-top, mahogany back and sides.

1965-1968	Spruce top	$400	$550
1968-1971	Mahogany top	$300	$400

Palomino

1965-1970. Acoustic flat-top, spruce top, mahogany back and sides, triple-bound. Black or Mahogany.

1965-1970		$500	$600

Performer

1985-1986. Imported Swinger-like body design, two slanted humbuckers.

1985-1986		$800	$900

Prodigy

1991-1995. Electric solidbody, double cutaway, chrome-plated hardware, two single-coil and one humbucker pickups. Blue or Black.

1991		$300	$400

Redondo

1969-1971. Mid-size flat-top, 14 3/8" wide. Replaces Newport spruce top model.

1969-1971		$400	$500

Robben Ford

1989-1994. Symmetrical double cutaway, two pickups, glued-in neck, solidbody with tone chambers, multi-bound, gold-plated hardware. After 1994 made in Fender Custom Shop.

1989-1994	Sunburst	$850	$1,300

Shenandoah 12-String

1965-1971. Acoustic flat-top, spruce top, mahogany back and sides.

1965-1968	Blond	$650	$800
1966-1968	Antigua	$900	$1,200
1969-1971	Antigua	$800	$1,100
1969-1971	Blond	$550	$750

Starcaster

1974-1980. Double cutaway, thinline semi-hollowbody, two humbuckers.

1974-1980	Most colors	$1,400	$1,700
1974-1980	Natural, mildly figured top	$1,600	$1,800

1969 Fender Mustang

Fender Newporter

1954 Fender Stratocaster

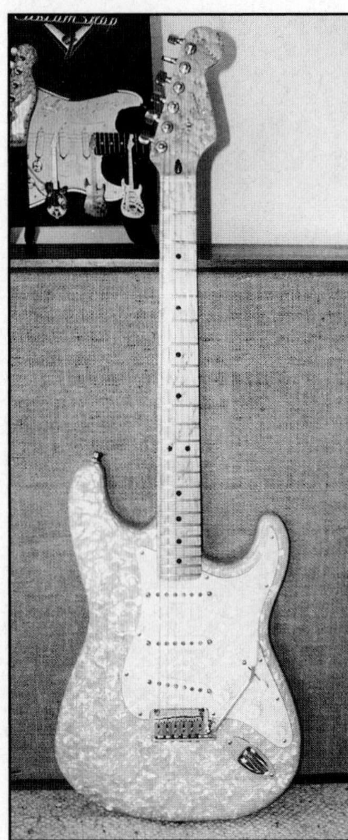

1995 Fender Moto Stratocaster

Stratocaster

The following are all variations of the Stratocaster. The first four listings are for the main U.S.-made models. All other Stratocaster models are listed alphabetically after that in the following order.

Stratocaster
Standard Stratocaster
American Standard Stratocaster
American Series Stratocaster
'50s Stratocaster (import)
'50s Relic Stratocaster
'54 Stratocaster
'54 Stratocaster FMT
'56 Closet Classic Stratocaster
'56 NOS Stratocaster
'56 Relic Stratocaster
'57 Stratocaster (U.S.-made)
'57 Special Stratocaster Custom Shop
'57 Stratocaster Custom Shop
'57 Vintage Stratocaster (Japan)
'58 Stratocaster Custom Shop
'58 Stratocaster (Dakota Red)
'60 Closet Classic Stratocaster
'60 NOS Stratocaster
'60 Relic Stratocaster
'60 Stratocaster Custom Shop
'60s Stratocaster (Japan)
'60s Relic Stratocaster
'62 Stratocaster
'62 Stratocaster (Japan)
'65 Stratocaster
'68 Stratocaster
'68 Stratocaster (Japan)
'72 Stratocaster
21st Century Limited Ed. Stratocaster
25th Anniversary Stratocaster
35th Anniversary Stratocaster
40th Anniversary Stratocaster
40th Ann. Diamond Ed. Stratocaster
50th Anniversary Stratocaster
50th Anniversary Stratocaster Relic
Aluminum Stratocaster
American Classic Stratocaster
American Deluxe Fat Stratocaster
American Deluxe Stratocaster
Big Apple Stratocaster
Bill Carson Stratocaster
Blue Flower Stratocaster
Bonnie Raitt Stratocaster
Bowling Ball/Marble Stratocaster
Buddy Guy Stratocaster
California Stratocaster
Collector's Edition Stratocaster ('62 reissue)
Contemporary Stratocaster (U.S.A.)
Contemporary Stratocaster (import)
Deluxe Strat Plus
Dick Dale Stratocaster
Elite Stratocaster
Eric Clapton Stratocaster
Floyd Rose Classic Stratocaster
Floyd Rose Relic Stratocaster
Foto Flame Stratocaster
Freddy Tavares Aloha Stratocaster
Gold Elite Stratocaster
Gold Stratocaster
Hank Marvin Stratocaster
Harley-Davidson 90th Anniversary Stratocaster
Hellecaster John Jorgenson Stratocaster
HLE Stratocaster
HM Stratocaster (import)
HM Stratocaster (U.S.-made)
Holoflake Stratocaster
Homer Haynes Ltd Ed Stratocaster
HRR Stratocaster
Jeff Beck Stratocaster
Jimi Hendrix Monterey Pop Stratocaster
Jimi Hendrix Tribute Stratocaster
Jimi Hendrix Voodoo Stratocaster
Jimmy Vaughan Tex-Mex Stratocaster
Lone Star Stratocaster
Moto Set Stratocaster
Paisley Stratocaster
Playboy 40th Anniversary Stratocaster
Powerhouse Deluxe Stratocaster
Richie Sambora Stratocaster
Roadhouse Stratocaster
Robert Cray Stratocaster
Set-Neck Stratocaster
Short-Scale (7/8) Stratocaster
Squier Stratocaster II
Squier Stratocaster Standard
Squier Stratocaster Standard (Affinity Series)
Squier Stratocaster Standard (Double Fat Strat)
Standard Stratocaster (Japan)
Standard Stratocaster (Mexico)
Stevie Ray Vaughan Stratocaster
Strat Plus
Stratocaster Special
Stratocaster XII
Sub Sonic Stratocaster
Super/Deluxe Super Stratocaster
Tanqurey Tonic Stratocaster
Texas Special Stratocaster
The Strat
U.S. Strat Ultra
Ventures Limited Edition Stratocaster
Walnut Elite Stratocaster
Walnut Stratocaster
Yngwie Malmsteen Stratocaster

Stratocaster

1954-1981. Two-tone Sunburst until '58, three-tone after. Custom color finishes were quite rare in the '50s and early-'60s and are much more valuable than the standard Sunburst finish. By the '70s, color finishes were much more common and do not affect the value near as much. In '75 Fender dropped the optional custom colors and started issuing the guitars in a variety of standard colors (sunburst, blond, white, natural, walnut and black). Three-bolt neck '72-'81, otherwise four-bolt.

Custom color Fenders can be forged and bogus finishes have been a problem. As the value of custom color Fenders has increased, so has the prob-

lem of bogus non-original finishes. The prices in the Guide are for factory original finishes in excellent condition. The prices noted do not take into account market factors such as fake instruments, which can have the effect of lowering a guitar's market value unless the guitar's provenance can be validated.

See Standard Stratocaster for 1982-1984 (following listing), and American Standard Stratocaster for 1986-2000. Currently called the American Series Stratocaster.

MODEL YEAR	FEATURES	EXC. COND. LOW	HIGH
1954	Sunburst 2-tone, ash body	$25,000	$30,000
1955	Sunburst 2-tone, ash body	$20,000	$25,000
1956	Blond, ash body, nickel hardware	$23,000	$31,000
1956	Mary Kaye Blond, ash body, gold hardware	$26,000	$36,000
1956	Sunburst, ash body	$15,000	$24,000
1957	Blond, nickel hardware	$22,000	$30,000
1957	Custom color, special order	$30,000	$35,000
1957	Mary Kaye Blond, Gold hardware, alder	$25,000	$35,000
1957	Sunburst, alder body	$15,000	$20,000
1958	Black	$18,000	$23,000
1958	Blond, nickel hardware	$22,000	$30,000
1958	Fiesta Red	$24,000	$29,000
1958	Mary Kaye Blond, gold hardware	$25,000	$35,000
1958	Sunburst 2-tone	$12,000	$15,000
1959	Blond, nickel hardware	$22,000	$30,000
1959	Mary Kaye Blond, gold hardware	$25,000	$35,000
1959	Sunburst 3-tone, maple board	$12,000	$14,000
1959	Sunburst, slab board	$11,000	$13,000
1960	Black	$20,000	$22,000
1960	Blond	$15,000	$17,000
1960	Burgundy Mist	$25,000	$28,000
1960	Dakota Red	$23,000	$27,000
1960	Daphne Blue	$18,000	$22,000
1960	Fiesta Red	$23,000	$27,000
1960	Foam Green	$26,000	$30,000
1960	Inca Silver	$20,000	$22,000
1960	Lake Placid Blue	$16,000	$17,000
1960	Olympic White	$15,000	$16,000
1960	Shell Pink	$29,000	$33,000
1960	Sherwood Green	$23,000	$27,000
1960	Shoreline Gold	$20,000	$22,000
1960	Sonic Blue	$18,000	$22,000
1960	Sunburst	$10,000	$12,000
1960	Surf Green	$26,000	$30,000
1961	Black	$18,000	$20,000
1961	Burgundy Mist	$23,000	$26,000
1961	Dakota Red	$21,000	$25,000
1961	Daphne Blue	$16,000	$20,000
1961	Lake Placid Blue	$14,000	$16,000
1961	Olympic White	$13,000	$15,000
1961	Sea Foam Green	$24,000	$28,000
1961	Sherwood Green Metallic	$21,000	$25,000
1961	Shoreline Gold	$18,000	$20,000
1961	Sonic Blue	$16,000	$20,000
1961	Sunburst	$12,000	$13,000
1962	Black, curved board	$13,000	$15,000
1962	Black, slab board	$16,000	$18,000
1962	Candy Apple Red, curved board	$12,000	$14,000
1962	Candy Apple Red, slab board	$14,000	$17,000
1962	Fiesta Red, curved board	$14,000	$16,000
1962	Fiesta Red, slab board	$16,000	$20,000
1962	Olympic White, curved board	$11,000	$13,000
1962	Olympic White, slab board	$13,000	$15,000
1962	Sonic Blue, curved board	$14,000	$18,000
1962	Sonic Blue, slab board	$16,000	$20,000
1962	Sunburst, curved board	$10,000	$11,000
1962	Sunburst, slab board	$12,000	$13,000
1963	Black	$12,000	$14,000
1963	Blond	$14,000	$16,000
1963	Candy Apple Red	$12,000	$14,000
1963	Dakota Red	$14,000	$16,000
1963	Fiesta Red	$14,000	$16,000
1963	Lake Placid Blue	$13,000	$15,000
1963	Olympic White	$11,000	$13,000
1963	Sea Foam Green	$17,000	$20,000
1963	Shoreline Gold	$16,000	$19,000
1963	Sonic Blue	$12,000	$16,000
1963	Sunburst	$8,500	$9,500
1964	Black	$11,000	$13,000
1964	Blond	$12,000	$14,000
1964	Burgundy Mist, faded	$17,000	$20,000
1964	Burgundy Mist, unfaded	$19,000	$22,000
1964	Candy Apple Red	$11,000	$13,000
1964	Daphne Blue	$15,000	$18,000
1964	Fiesta Red	$13,000	$15,000
1964	Inca Silver, faded	$16,000	$18,000

1958 Fender Stratocaster Mary Kaye

1956 Fender Stratocaster

1966 Fender Stratocaster (Charcoal Frost)

1966 Fender Stratocaster

MODEL YEAR	FEATURES	EXC. COND. LOW	HIGH
1964	Inca Silver, unfaded	$17,000	$20,000
1964	Lake Placid Blue	$13,000	$15,000
1964	Olympic White	$10,000	$12,000
1964	Shoreline Gold	$15,000	$18,000
1964	Sonic Blue	$12,000	$15,000
1964	Sunburst	$7,500	$8,500
1965	Black, L-Series	$9,000	$11,000
1965	Blond, "F" plate	$9,000	$11,000
1965	Burgundy Mist, mild fade	$18,000	$20,000
1965	Candy Apple Red	$9,000	$11,000
1965	Candy Apple Red, gold hardware	$10,000	$12,000
1965	Charcoal Frost	$11,000	$13,000
1965	Dakota Red, L-series	$10,000	$12,000
1965	Firemist Silver, faded	$12,000	$14,000
1965	Firemist Silver, unfaded	$14,000	$16,000
1965	Ice Blue Metallic	$12,000	$14,000
1965	Inca Silver	$13,000	$15,000
1965	Inca Silver, L-Series	$14,000	$16,000
1965	Lake Placid Blue	$9,000	$12,000
1965	Ocean Turquoise	$14,000	$16,000
1965	Olympic White	$8,000	$10,000
1965	Sea Foam Green	$14,000	$16,000
1965	Sonic Blue, "F" plate	$11,000	$14,000
1965	Sunburst, early '65 Green guard	$6,500	$7,000
1965	Sunburst, later '65 White guard	$5,800	$6,500
1966	Black	$8,000	$10,000
1966	Blond	$8,000	$10,000
1966	Candy Apple Red	$8,000	$10,000
1966	Ice Blue Metallic	$8,500	$11,000
1966	Inca Silver	$10,000	$12,000
1966	Lake Placid Blue	$8,500	$11,000
1966	Lake Placid Blue, gold hardware	$9,500	$12,000
1966	Sonic Blue	$10,000	$12,000
1966	Sunburst	$5,500	$6,500
1967	Fiesta Red	$9,000	$11,000
1967	Lake Placid Blue	$8,000	$10,500
1967	Sonic Blue	$9,000	$11,000
1967	Sunburst, maple cap	$5,500	$7,000
1967	Sunburst, rosewood neck	$4,500	$6,000
1968	Blond	$7,000	$9,000
1968	Candy Apple Red, maple cap	$8,500	$10,000
1968	Candy Apple Red, rosewood cap	$7,500	$9,000
1968	Dakota Red, maple cap	$10,000	$12,000
1968	Dakota Red, rosewood cap	$8,000	$10,000
1968	Fiesta Red, maple cap	$10,000	$12,000
1968	Fiesta Red, rosewood cap	$8,000	$10,000
1968	Lake Placid Blue, maple cap	$8,000	$10,000
1968	Lake Placid Blue, rosewood cap	$7,500	$9,500
1968	Olympic White, maple cap	$7,000	$9,000
1968	Olympic White, rosewood cap	$6,500	$8,500
1968	Sonic Blue, maple cap	$10,000	$12,000
1968	Sonic Blue, rosewood cap	$8,000	$10,000
1968	Sunburst, maple cap	$5,500	$7,000
1968	Sunburst, rosewood cap	$4,500	$6,000
1969	Candy Apple Red	$7,500	$9,500
1969	Firemist Gold	$8,000	$10,000
1969	Lake Placid Blue	$7,500	$9,500
1969	Natural	$5,500	$7,500
1969	Olympic White	$6,500	$8,500
1969	Sonic Blue, maple cap	$9,000	$11,000
1969	Sonic Blue, rosewood cap	$8,000	$10,000
1969	Sunburst	$4,500	$5,500
1970	Black, maple cap	$6,700	$7,700
1970	Black, rosewood cap	$5,500	$6,500
1970	Blond, maple cap	$6,200	$7,700
1970	Blond, rosewood cap	$5,000	$6,500
1970	Candy Apple Red, maple cap	$6,700	$7,700
1970	Candy Apple Red, rosewood cap	$5,500	$6,500
1970	Firemist Gold, maple cap	$7,700	$8,700
1970	Firemist Gold, rosewood cap	$6,500	$7,500
1970	Firemist Silver, maple cap	$7,700	$8,700
1970	Firemist Silver, rosewood cap	$6,500	$7,500
1970	Lake Placid Blue, maple cap	$6,700	$7,700
1970	Lake Placid Blue, rosewood cap	$5,500	$6,500
1970	Ocean Turquoise, maple cap	$7,700	$8,700
1970	Ocean Turquoise, rosewood cap	$6,500	$7,500
1970	Olympic White, maple cap	$6,700	$7,700

GUITARS

MODEL YEAR	FEATURES	EXC. COND. LOW	HIGH
1970	Olympic White, rosewood cap	$5,500	$6,500
1970	Sonic Blue, maple cap	$7,200	$8,200
1970	Sonic Blue, rosewood cap	$6,000	$7,000
1970	Sunburst, maple cap	$5,200	$6,200
1970	Sunburst, roswood cap	$4,000	$5,400
1971	Black, 4-bolt neck	$5,000	$6,000
1971	Candy Apple Red, 4-bolt neck	$5,000	$6,000
1971	Natural, 4-bolt neck	$4,500	$5,500
1971	Olympic White, 4-bolt neck, maple cap	$6,500	$7,500
1971	Olympic White, rosewood cap	$5,300	$6,300
1971	Sunburst, 4-bolt neck	$3,900	$4,900
1972	Black, 3-bolt neck	$2,100	$2,500
1972	Blond, 3-bolt neck	$2,100	$2,500
1972	Candy Apple Red, 3-bolt neck	$2,100	$2,500
1972	Lake Placid Blue, 3-bolt neck	$2,100	$2,500
1972	Olympic White, 3-bolt neck	$2,100	$2,500
1972	Sunburst, 3-bolt neck	$2,100	$2,300
1972	Transparent Blond	$2,100	$2,500
1973	Black	$2,000	$2,300
1973	Blond	$2,100	$2,300
1973	Candy Apple Red	$2,100	$2,400
1973	Lake Placid Blue	$2,100	$2,400
1973	Natural	$2,000	$2,300
1973	Olympic White	$2,000	$2,300
1973	Sunburst	$2,000	$2,300
1973	Walnut	$2,000	$2,300
1974	Black	$1,600	$2,200
1974	Blond	$1,700	$2,300
1974	Lake Placid Blue	$1,700	$2,300
1974	Natural	$1,500	$2,100
1974	Olympic White	$1,600	$2,200
1974	Sunburst, staggered poles	$1,700	$2,200
1974	Walnut	$1,700	$2,200
1974	Wine Red	$1,700	$2,200
1975	Various finishes	$1,500	$1,700
1976	Various finishes	$1,400	$1,600
1977	Various finishes	$1,200	$1,500
1978	Antigua	$1,300	$1,500
1978	Sunburst or walnut	$1,000	$1,300
1978	Various other finishes	$1,200	$1,400
1979	Antigua	$1,000	$1,500
1979	Sunburst	$1,000	$1,400
1979	Various other finishes	$1,000	$1,300
1980	Sunburst	$1,000	$1,400
1980	Various other finishes	$1,000	$1,300
1981	Capri Orange	$1,000	$1,400
1981	Cathay Ebony	$1,000	$1,400
1981	Maui Blue	$1,000	$1,400
1981	Monaco Yellow	$1,000	$1,400
1981	Morocco Red	$1,000	$1,400
1981	Various other finishes	$900	$1,200

Standard Stratocaster (includes 'Smith Strat')

1981-1984. Replaces the Stratocaster. Renamed the American Standard Stratocaster for '86-'00 (see next listing). Renamed American Series Stratocaster in '00. From '81/'82 to mid-'83, four knobs same as regular Strat but with four-bolt neck. In August '81, Dan Smith was hired by Bill Schultz and Fender produced an alder body, four-bolt neck, 21-fret, small headstock Standard Stratocaster that has been nicknamed the 'Smith Strat' (made from Dec. '81-'83). Mid-'83 to the end of '84 two knobs and pickguard mounted input jack. Not to be confused with current Standard Stratocaster, which is made in Mexico.

MODEL YEAR	FEATURES	LOW	HIGH
1981-1983	"Smith Strat", 4-bolt, 3 knobs	$950	$1,100
1983-1984	Various colors, 2 knobs	$650	$800

American Standard Stratocaster

1986-2000. See Stratocaster and Standard Stratocaster for earlier models. Renamed American Series Stratocaster in 2000.

MODEL YEAR	FEATURES	LOW	HIGH
1986-1989	Various colors	$700	$900
1989	Mary Kaye Limited Edition	$850	$950
1990-1999	Various colors	$600	$750
1995	Limited edition matching headstock	$700	$800

American Series Stratocaster

2000-present. Fender's updated standard production model, ash or alder body, rosewood fingerboard, dot markers, three staggered single-coil pickups, five-way switch, hand polished fret edges.

MODEL YEAR	FEATURES	LOW	HIGH
2001	Blond finish on ash body	$600	$700
2001	Various colors	$500	$600

'50s Relic Stratocaster Custom Shop

1996-1999. Relatively faithful reproduction of 1950s (ca. 1957) era Strat with 'played-in' feel, replaced by 1956 Strat.

MODEL YEAR	FEATURES	LOW	HIGH
1996-1999	Gold hardware	$1,600	$2,000
1996-1999	Mary Kaye Blond over ash	$1,600	$2,000
1996-1999	Various colors	$1,400	$1,800

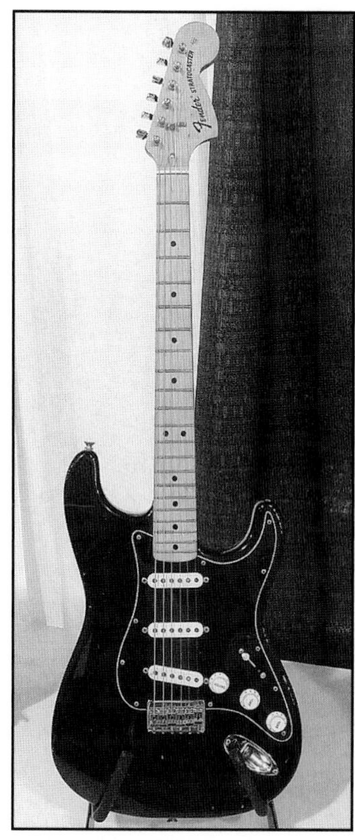

1973 Fender Stratocaster (hardtail)

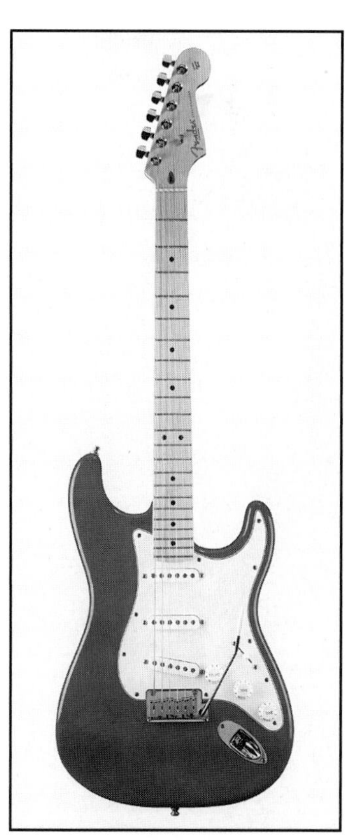

Fender American Series Stratocaster

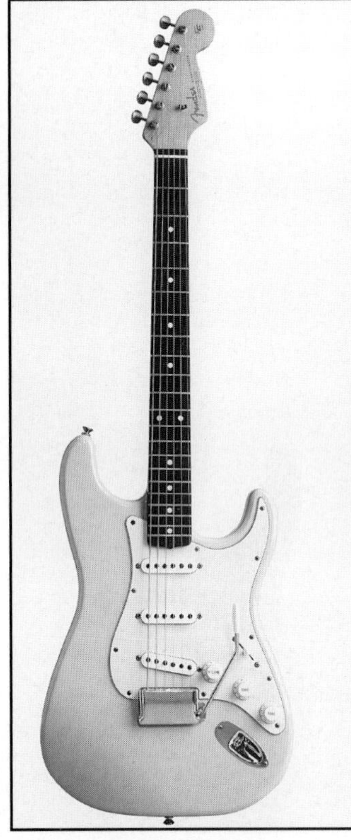

Fender '60s Closet Classic Stratocaster

1982 Fender '57 Stratocaster

MODEL YEAR	FEATURES	EXC. COND. LOW	HIGH

'50s Stratocaster (import)

1992-present. Part of Collectables Series, made in Japan, V-neck with skunk stripe, eight-screw single ply pickguard. Various colors.

1992-1999		$450	$600

'54 Stratocaster Custom Shop

1993-1998 (Custom Shop Classic reissue), 1997-present. Ash body, Custom '50s pickups, gold-plated hardware..

1993-1999	Various options	$1,400	$1,700

'54 Stratocaster FMT

1993-1998. Custom Classic reissue. FMT means Flame Maple Top. Also comes in Gold hardware edition.

1993-1998	Gold hardware option	$1,600	$1,800
1993-1998	Sunburst, highly figured	$1,500	$1,700

'56 Closet Classic Stratocaster Custom Shop

1999-present. Most detailed replica (and most expensive to date) of 1956 Strat, including electronics and pickups.

1999-2000		$1,700	$1,800

'56 NOS Stratocaster Custom Shop

1999-present. Most detailed replica (and most expensive to date) of 1956 Strat, including electronics and pickups.

1999-2000	Mary Kaye Blond, ash body	$1,500	$1,600
1999-2000	Sunburst, alder body	$1,400	$1,500

'56 Relic Stratocaster Custom Shop

1999-present. Most detailed replica (and most expensive to date) of 1956 Strat, including electronics and pickups.

1999-2000	Mary Kaye Blond, replica pickups	$1,900	$2,000
1999-2000	Sonic Blue custom color	$2,000	$2,100

'57 Stratocaster (U.S.-made)

1982-present. U.S.A.-made at the Fullerton, CA plant (1982-1985) and at the Corona, CA plant (1985-present).

1982-1999	Various colors	$900	$1,100
1986-1999	Blond, ash body	$1,000	$1,300

'57 Special Stratocaster Custom Shop

1992-1993. Flamed maple top, bird's-eye maple neck, run of 60 made. Sunburst.

1992-1993		$1,800	$1,900

'57 Stratocaster Custom Shop

Mid-1990s. Custom Shop, replaced by the more authentic, higher-detailed '56 Custom Shop Stratocaster by 1999. Custom Shop models can be distinguished by the original certificate that comes with the guitar.

1994-1996	Sunburst	$1,300	$1,400
1994-1997	Transparent Blond, ash body	$1,500	$1,600

MODEL YEAR	FEATURES	EXC. COND. LOW	HIGH

'57 Vintage Stratocaster (Japan)

1984-1985. Japanese-made. Various colors.

1984-1985		$450	$600

'58 Stratocaster Custom Shop

1996-present. Ash body, Fat '50s pickups, chrome or gold hardware. Custom Shop models can be distinguished by the original certificate that comes with the guitar.

1996-1999	Custom color, gold hardware	$1,600	$1,800
1996-1999	Sunburst, chrome hardware	$1,400	$1,500
1996-1999	Sunburst, gold hardware	$1,500	$1,600

'58 Stratocaster (Dakota Red) Custom Shop

1996. Run of 30 made in Dakota Red with matching headstock, maple neck, Texas special pickups, gold hardware.

1996		$1,600	$1,800

'60 Closet Classic Stratocaster Custom Shop

1999-present. Most detailed replica (and most expensive to date) of 1960 Strat, including electronics and pickups.

1999-2000		$1,700	$1,800

'60 NOS Stratocaster Custom Shop

1999-present. Most detailed replica (and most expensive to date) of 1960 Strat, including electronics and pickups.

1999-2000	Mary Kaye Blond, ash body	$1,500	$1,600
1999-2000	Various colors	$1,400	$1,500

'60 Relic Stratocaster Custom Shop

1999-present. Most detailed replica (and most expensive to date) of 1960 Strat, including electronics and pickups.

1999-2000	Mary Kaye Blond, replica pickups	$1,900	$2,000

'60 Stratocaster Custom Shop

Short-run production during the 1990s, permanent product line 1999-present. Various colors.

1994		$1,500	$1,700

'60s Relic Stratocaster Custom Shop

1996-1999. Relatively faithful reproduction of 1960s era Strat with 'played-in' feel, replaced by 1960 Relic.

1996-1999	Gold hardware	$1,600	$2,000
1996-1999	Various colors	$1,400	$1,800

'60s Stratocaster (Japan)

1992-present. Part of Collectables Series, made in Japan, U-neck slab board, various colors, some with foto flame.

1992-1999	Foto-flame option	$450	$600
1992-1999	Various colors	$450	$600

'62 Stratocaster

1982-present. U.S.A.-made at Fullerton, CA plant (1982-1985) then at Corona, CA plant (1985-present).

1982-1999	Various colors	$900	$1,100
1986-1989	Transparent Blond	$1,000	$1,300

MODEL YEAR	FEATURES	EXC. COND. LOW	HIGH

'62 Stratocaster (Japan)

1984-1985.

1984-1985	White	$450	$600

'65 Stratocaster Custom Shop

1998-1999. Built to 1965 small-headstock specs with rosewood or maple cap fingerboard, transition logo.

1998-1999	Maple cap board	$1,700	$1,800
1998-1999	Rosewood board	$1,700	$1,800

'68 Stratocaster Custom Shop

1990s. Jimi Hendrix-style, maple cap neck.

1990s		$1,700	$1,800

'68 Stratocaster (Japan)

1997-1999. Import from Japan, ash body, 1968 specs including large headstock, part of Collectables Series. Sunburst, Natural, Olympic White.

1997-1999		$450	$600

'72 Stratocaster

1988-1993. Made in Japan.

1988-1993	White	$450	$600

21st Century Limited Ed. Stratocaster Custom Shop

2000. One of first 100 to leave Fender in 2000, certificate with CEO William C. Schultz, 21st logo on headstock.

2000		$1,100	$1,200

25th Anniversary Stratocaster

1979-1980. Has "ANNIVERSARY" on upper body horn. Silver Metallic or White Pearlescent finish.

1979	White, 1st issue	$1,300	$1,400
1979-1980	Silver	$1,250	$1,350

35th Anniversary Stratocaster Custom Shop

1989-1991. Custom Shop model, figured maple top, Lace Sensor pickups, Eric Clapton preamp circuit.

1989-1991	Sunburst	$2,400	$2,700

40th Anniversary Stratocaster

1994 only. American Standard model (not Custom Shop model). Plain top, appearance similar to a 1954 maple-neck Stratocaster. Not to be confused with the Custom Shop 40th Anniversary Diamond Edition.

1994	Sunburst	$1,400	$1,700

40th Ann. Diamond Ed. Stratocaster Custom Shop

1994. Fortieth anniversary headstock inlay, flamed maple top on ash body, 1954-1994 inlay at 12th fret, Gold etched pickguard, Gold hardware.

1994	Sunburst	$4,500	$6,000

50th Anniversary Stratocaster Custom Shop

1995-1996. Flame maple top, three vintage-style pickups, Gold hardware, Gold 50th Anniversary coin on back of the headstock, 2500 made.

1995-1996	Sunburst	$1,500	$1,600

50th Anniversary Stratocaster Relic Custom Shop

1995-1996. Relic aged 'played-in' feel, diamond headstock inlay, 200 units planned.

1995-1996	Shoreline Gold	$2,600	$2,800

MODEL YEAR	FEATURES	EXC. COND. LOW	HIGH

Aluminum Stratocaster Custom Shop

1994-1995. Aluminum with anodized marble-variant finish.

1994-1995		$1,500	$2,000

American Classic Stratocaster

1993-present. Custom Shop version of American Standard, three pickups, tremolo, rosewood fingerboard, nickel or gold-plated hardware.

1993-1999	Transparent Blond finish on ash body	$1,600	$1,800
1993-1999	Various colors and options	$1,500	$1,700

American Deluxe Fat Stratocaster

1998-pre sent. Fender DH-1 bridge humbucker for 'fat sound', made in the U.S.A., premium alder or ash body.

1998-1999	Transparent finish on ash body	$950	$1,050
1998-1999	Various colors	$850	$950

American Deluxe Stratocaster (U.S.-made)

1998-present. Premium alder or ash body, made in the U.S.A.

1998-1999	Transparent finish on ash body	$950	$1,050
1998-1999	Various colors	$850	$950

Big Apple Stratocaster

1997-2000. Two humbucking pickups, five-way switch, rosewood fingerboard or maple neck, non-trem optional.

1997-2000	Various colors	$700	$800

Bill Carson Stratocaster

Ca. 1992. Based on the 1957 Strat, with bird's-eye maple neck and Cimarron Red finish. One left-handed and 100 right-handed guitars produced, serial numbers MT000-MT100. Made in Fender Custom Shop, the project was initiated by The Music Trader (MT) in Florida. Bill Carson was presented with MT007.

1992	Cimarron Red	$1,700	$2,000

Blue Flower Stratocaster

1988-1993. 1972 Strat reissue with a reissue 1968 Tele Blue Floral finish. Japanese-made.

1988-1993		$500	$800

Bonnie Raitt Stratocaster

1995-2000. Alder body, often in Blueburst, Bonnie Raitt's signature on headstock.

1995-2000		$900	$1,100

Bowling Ball/Marble Stratocaster

Ca.1983-1984. Standard Strat with one tone and one volume control, jack on pickguard. Called 'Bowling Ball Strat' due to the swirling, colored finish.

1984		$1,700	$2,200

Buddy Guy Stratocaster

1995-present. Maple neck, three Gold Lace Sensor pickups, ash body, signature model.

1995	Blond or Sunburst	$900	$1,100

California Stratocaster

1997-1999. Made in the U.S., painted in Mexico, two pickups.

1997-1999	Various colors	$450	$550

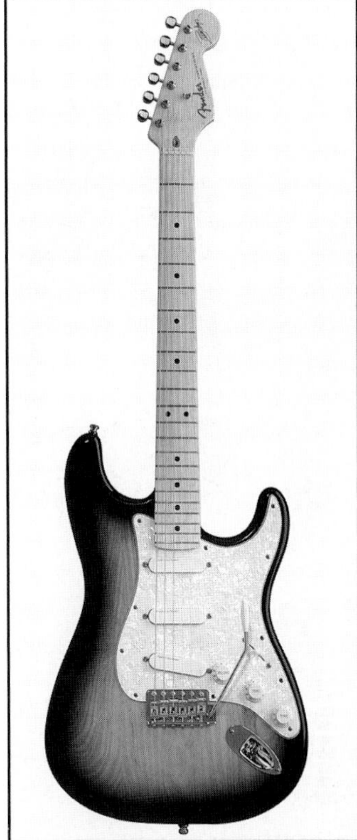

Fender Buddy Guy Stratocaster

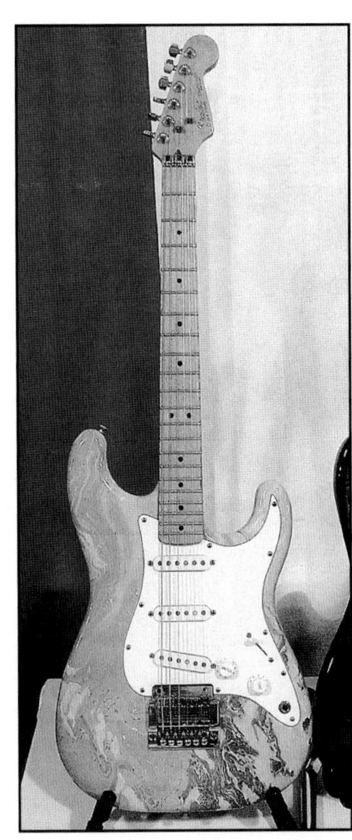

1983 Fender Bowling Ball/ Marble Stratocaster

GUITARS

1983 Fender Elite Stratocaster

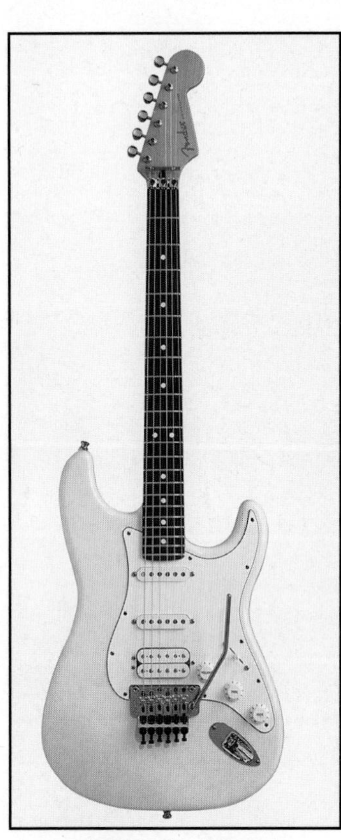

Fender Floyd Rose Classic Stratocaster

MODEL YEAR	FEATURES	EXC. COND. LOW	HIGH

Collector's Edition Stratocaster ('62 reissue)

1997. Pearl inlaid 1997 on 12th fret, rosewood fingerboard, alder body, Gold hardware, tortoise guard, nitro finish.

1997	Sunburst	$1,300	$1,500

Contemporary Stratocaster (U.S.A.) Custom Shop

1989-1998. U.S.A.-made, 7/8 scale body, hum/single/single pickups.

1989-1998	Various colors	$1,200	$1,500

Contemporary Stratocaster (import)

1985-1987. Import model used while the new Fender re-organized, Black headstock with Silver-White logo, Black or White 'guard, two humbucker pickups or single-coil and humbucker, two knobs and slider switch.

1985-1987	Gray Metallic, Black guard	$250	$300

Deluxe Strat Plus

1987-1998. Three Lace Sensor pickups, Floyd Rose, alder (poplar available earlier) body with ash veneer on front and back, various colors. Also see Strat Plus.

1987-1998		$600	$800

Dick Dale Stratocaster Custom Shop

1994-present. Alder body, reverse headstock, Chartreuse Sparkle finish.

1990s		$1,800	$2,000

Elite Stratocaster

1983-1984. The Elite Series feature active electronics and noise-cancelling pickups, push buttons instead of three-way switch, various colors. Also see Gold Elite Stratocaster and Walnut Elite Stratocaster.

1983-1984		$850	$1,000

Eric Clapton Stratocaster

1988-present. U.S.A.-made, 1957 reissue features, active electronics, three Lace Sensors, maple neck, various colors.

1988-1999		$750	$950

Floyd Rose Classic Stratocaster

1992-1997. 2 single-coils, bridge humbucker, Floyd Rose trem, various colors.

1992-1997		$700	$900

Floyd Rose Relic Stratocaster Custom Shop

1998-1999. Late '60s large headstock, one humbucker and two Strat pickups.

1999		$1,400	$1,600

Foto Flame Stratocaster

1995, 2000. Japanese-made Collectables model, alder and basswood body with Foto Flame (simulated woodgrain) finish on top cap and back of neck.

1995		$400	$550
2000		$400	$600

Freddy Tavares Aloha Stratocaster Custom Shop

1993-1994. Hollow aluminum body with hand engraved Hawaiian scenes, custom inlay on neck, 153 made.

1993-1994		$4,000	$4,500

Gold Elite Stratocaster

1983-1984. The Elite series feature active electronics and noise-cancelling pickups. The Gold Elite has gold hardware and pearloid tuner buttons. Also see Elite Stratocaster and Walnut Elite Stratocaster.

1983		$900	$1,200

Gold Stratocaster

1981-1983. Gold metallic finish and gold-plated brass hardware.

1981-1983		$1,100	$1,300

Hank Marvin Stratocaster

1995-1996. Feista Red.

1995		$1,400	$1,700

Harley-Davidson 90th Anniversary Stratocaster

1993. Custom Shop, 109 total made, Harley-Davidson and Custom Shop V logo on headstock (Diamond Edition, 40 units), nine units produced for the Harley-Davidson company without diamond logo, 60 units were not Diamond Edition, chrome-plated engraved metal body, engraved guard, Custom Shop Certificate important attribute.

1993		$10,000	$12,000

Hellecaster John Jorgenson Stratocaster

1997-99. Gold Sparkle 'guard, Gold hardware, split single-coils, rosewood 'board. Made in Japan.

1997		$900	$1,100

HLE Stratocaster Custom Shop

1988-1990.

1988-1990	Gold	$1,400	$1,600

HM Stratocaster (import)

1988-1992 (Imported 1988, U.S. and import production 1989-1990, U.S. only 1991-1992).

1988-1990	Bud Dry logo finish	$350	$450
1988-1990	Import	$200	$250

HM Stratocaster (U.S.-made)

1988-1992 ('88 Japanese-made, '89-'90 U.S.- and Japanese-made, '91-'92 U.S.-made). Heavy Metal Strat. Floyd Rose, regular or pointy headstock, black hardware, 1 or 2 humbuckers, 1 single-coil and 1 humbucker, or 2 single-coils and 1 humbucker. Later models have choice of 2 humbuckers and 1 single-coil or 2 single-coils and 1 humbucker.

1989-1992	U.S. production	$250	$350

Holoflake Stratocaster Custom Shop

1992-1993. Sparkle finish, maple neck, alder body.

1992-1993		$1,300	$1,500

Homer Haynes Ltd Ed Stratocaster Custom Shop

1988. 1959 Strat basics with Gold finish, Gold anodized guard, and Gold hardware.

1988		$1,500	$2,000

MODEL YEAR	FEATURES	EXC. COND. LOW	HIGH

HRR Stratocaster

1990-1995. Japanese-made, "hot-rodded" vintage-style Strat, Floyd Rose Tremolo system, three pickups, maple neck. Foto Flame, Black, Olympic White or Sunburst.

1990-1995		$300	$400

Jeff Beck Stratocaster

1994-present. Alder body, Lace Sensor pickups, special designed trem, various colors but mostly Surf Green.

1990s		$700	$900

Jimi Hendrix Monterey Pop Stratocaster Custom Shop

1997-1998. Near replica of Monterey Pop Festival "sacrifice" guitar.

1997	Red psychedelic-style finish	$6,500	$7,500

Jimi Hendrix Tribute Stratocaster

1997-2000. Left-handed guitar strung right-handed, maple cap neck, Olympic White finish.

1997-1999		$900	$1,100

Jimi Hendrix Voodoo Stratocaster

1998-2002. Right-handed body with reverse peghead, maple neck, sunburst, Olympic White, or black.

1998-1999		$1,100	$1,300

Jimmy Vaughan Tex-Mex Stratocaster

1997-present. Poplar body, maple 'board, Jimmy Vaughan signature on headstock, three Tex-Mex pickups. Various colors.

1997-1999		$350	$450

Lone Star Stratocaster

1996-2000. Alder body, one humbucker and two single-coil pickups, rosewood fingerboard or maple neck. Various colors.

1996-1999		$750	$775

Moto Set Stratocaster Custom Shop

1995-1996. Custom Shop set including guitar, case, amp and amp stand.

1995	White Pearloid	$4,500	$5,000

Paisley Stratocaster

Ca.1988-1994. Japanese-made 1972 Strat reissue with a reissue 1968 Tele Pink Paisley finish.

1988-1994		$800	$1,200

Playboy 40th Anniversary Stratocaster Custom Shop

1994. Nude Marilyn Monroe graphic on body.

1994		$5,500	$6,000

Powerhouse/Powerhouse Deluxe Stratocaster

1997-present. Import Standard Strat configuration with pearloid pickguard, various colors, some colors discontinued.

1997-1999		$400	$425

Richie Sambora Stratocaster

1993-2002. Alder body, Floyd Rose trem, maple neck.

1993-2002	Sunburst	$1,000	$1,200

MODEL YEAR	FEATURES	EXC. COND. LOW	HIGH

Roadhouse Stratocaster

1997-2000. U.S.-made, poplar body, tortoise shell pickguard, maple fingerboard, three Texas Special pickups. Various colors.

1997-2000		$650	$700

Robert Cray Stratocaster

1991-present. Custom Shop signature model, rosewood fingerboard, chunky neck, lighter weight, hard-tail non-tremolo, alder body, gold-plated hardware. Various colors.

1991-1999		$1,200	$1,400

Set-Neck Stratocaster Custom Shop

1992-1999. Mahogany body and figured maple top, four pickups, glued-in neck, active electronics. By 1996 ash body.

1992-1996		$1,200	$1,400

Short-Scale (7/8) Stratocaster

1989-1994. Similar to Standard Strat, but with two control knobs and switch, 24-inch scale vs. 25-inch scale, sometimes called a 'mini-Strat', Japanese import. Various colors.

1989-1994		$550	$600

Squier Stratocaster II

1989-1990. Import from India.

1989-1990		$80	$125

Squier Stratocaster Standard

1982-1998. Fender Japan was established in '82 with Squier production beginning in '83. Production was shifted to Korea in '87 and later allocated to China, India (Squier II '89-'90) and Mexico. This model is the low-cost Stratocaster Standard version of the Squier line. Various colors.

1982-1989		$200	$350
1990-1998		$150	$250

Squier Stratocaster Standard (Affinity Series)

Three single-coil pickups, made in China.

1999	Red	$75	$100

Squier Stratocaster Standard (Double Fat Strat)

Large headstock, two humbucker pickups, made in China.

1999	Red	$100	$150

Standard Stratocaster (Japan)

1985. Interim production in Japan while the new Fender reorganized, standard pickup configuration and tremolo system, three knobs with switch, traditional style input jack, traditional shaped headstock (Natural Maple color).

1985	Black or Red, White guard	$350	$550

Standard Stratocaster (Mexico)

Fender Mexico started production in 1990. Not to be confused with the American-made Standard Stratocaster of '81-'84. High end of range includes a hard guitar case, while the low end of the range includes only a gig bag. Various colors.

1990-1995		$225	$300
1996-1999		$250	$325

Fender Jeff Beck Stratocaster

Fender Richie Sambora Stratocaster

GUITARS

Fender Stevie Ray Vaughan Stratocaster

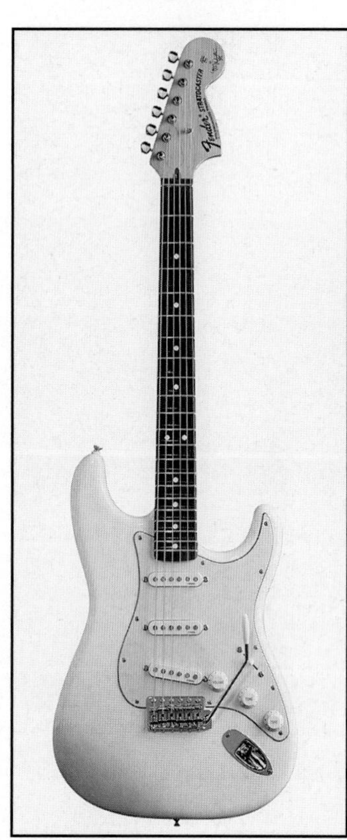
Fender Yngwie Malmsteen Stratocaster

MODEL YEAR	FEATURES	EXC. COND. LOW	HIGH

Stevie Ray Vaughan Stratocaster

1992-present. U.S.A.-made, alder body, Sunburst, gold hardware, SRV pickguard, lefty trem unit, Brazilian rosewood fingerboard (pau ferro by 1993).

1992-1999		$875	$1,000

Strat Plus

1987-1998. Three Lace Sensor pickups, alder (poplar available earlier) body, trem, rosewood fingerboard or maple neck, various colors. See Deluxe Strat Plus for ash veneer version.

1987-1989		$700	$800
1990-1998		$650	$750

Stratocaster Special (Mexico)

1993-1995. A humbucker and a single-coil pickup, 1 volume, 1 tone.

1993-1995		$300	$375

Stratocaster XII

1988-1995. Alder body, maple neck, 21-fret rosewood fingerboard, three vintage Strat pickups, Japanese-made. Various colors.

1988-1995		$600	$750

Sub Sonic Stratocaster

2000-present. Baritone model tuned B-E-A-D-G-B, single-single-hum pickup configuration, Strat-styling.

2000-2003		$900	$1,100

Super/Deluxe Super Stratocaster

1997-present. Import made in Mexico, part of Deluxe Series, Standard Strat features with maple neck.

1997-2003		$275	$300

Tanqurey Tonic Stratocaster

1988. Made for a Tanqurey Tonic liquor ad campaign giveaway in 1988; many were given to winners around the country. Ads said that they could also be purchased through Tanqurey, but that apparently didn't happen.

1988	Tanqurey Tonic Green	$950	$1,100

Texas Special Stratocaster Custom Shop

1991-1992. State of Texas map stamped on neck plate, Texas Special pickups, maple fretboard, 50 made.

1991-1992	Sunburst	$1,500	$2,000

The Strat

1980-1983. Alder body, four-bolt neck, large "Strat" on painted peghead, gold-plated brass hardware. Various colors.

1980-1983		$850	$1,100

U.S. Strat Ultra

1990-1997. Alder body with figured maple veneer on front and back, single Lace Sensor pickups in neck and middle, double Sensor at bridge, Ebony fingerboard.

1990-1997	Sunburst	$1,000	$1,100

Ventures Limited Edition Stratocaster

1996. Japanese-made tribute model, matches Jazzmaster equivalent.

1996	Black	$900	$1,000

MODEL YEAR	FEATURES	EXC. COND. LOW	HIGH

Walnut Elite Stratocaster

1983-1984. The Elite Series feature active electronics and noise-cancelling pickups. Walnut Elite has a walnut body and neck, gold-plated hardware and pearloid tuner buttons. Also see Elite Stratocaster and Gold Elite Stratocaster.

1983-1984	1 pickup	$1,700	$2,000
1983-1984	2 pickups	$1,800	$2,200

Walnut Stratocaster

1981-1983. American Black Walnut body and one-piece neck/fingerboard.

1981-1983		$1,900	$2,300

Yngwie Malmsteen Stratocaster

1988-present. U.S.-made, maple neck, scalloped fingerboard, three single-coil pickups. Blue, Red, White.

1988-1999		$900	$1,200

Telecaster

The following are all variations of the Telecaster. The first four listings are for the main U.S.-made models. All other Telecaster models are listed alphabetically after that in the following order.

Telecaster
Standard Telecaster
American Standard Telecaster
American Series Telecaster
'50s Telecaster (import)
'52 Telecaster
'60 Telecaster Custom
'62 Custom Telecaster
'63 Closet Classic Telecaster
'69 Blue Flower Telecaster
'69 Pink Paisley Telecaster
'69 Rosewood Telecaster
'69 Telecaster Thinline
'72 Custom Telecaster
'72 Telecaster Thinline
'90s Telecaster Thinline
40th Anniversary Telecaster
50th Anniversary Telecaster
Albert Collins Telecaster
Aluminum Telecaster
American Classic Telecaster
American Deluxe Telecaster
Black and Gold Telecaster
Buck Owens Ltd Edition Telecaster
California Fat Telecaster
California Telecaster
Contemporary Telecaster
Custom Classic Telecaster
Danny Gatton Telecaster
Deluxe Telecaster
Elite Telecaster
Foto Flame Telecaster
HMT Telecaster
James Burton Telecaster
Jerry Donahue Telecaster
John Jorgenson Telecaster
Rosewood Telecaster

MODEL YEAR	FEATURES	EXC. COND. LOW	HIGH
	Set-Neck Telecaster		
	Sparkle Telecaster		
	Squier Telecaster		
	Squier Telecaster Affinity		
	Standard Telecaster (Mexico)		
	Thinline Telecaster		
	Tele Jr./Set Neck Tele Jr.		
	Telecaster Custom		
	Telecaster Custom (II)		
	Telecaster Deluxe (import)		
	Telecaster Deluxe Nashville		
	Telecaster Plus Standard		
	Telecaster Thinline		

Telecaster

1951-1982. See Standard Telecaster (following listing) for 1982-1985, and American Standard Telecaster for 1988-2000. Currently called American Series Telecaster.

MODEL YEAR	FEATURES	EXC. COND. LOW	HIGH
1951	Blond, Black pickguard	$16,000	$22,000
1952	Blond, Black pickguard	$15,000	$21,000
1953	Blond, Black pickguard	$14,000	$20,000
1954	Blond, Black pickguard	$13,000	$19,000
1954	Blond, White pickguard	$11,000	$15,000
1955	Blond, White pickguard	$10,000	$15,000
1956	Blond	$9,000	$14,000
1957	Blond	$8,500	$13,000
1957	Custom color (various)	$25,000	$30,000
1958	Blond	$7,500	$10,000
1958	Sunburst	$10,000	$12,000
1959	Blond, maple neck	$7,000	$9,500
1960	Blond	$7,000	$9,000
1960	Sunburst	$9,500	$11,500
1961	Black	$9,000	$11,000
1961	Blond	$6,500	$9,000
1961	Dakota Red	$15,000	$17,000
1961	Fiesta Red	$15,000	$17,000
1961	Lake Placid Blue	$9,000	$11,000
1962	Blond, curved board	$6,000	$8,000
1962	Blond, slab board	$6,500	$8,500
1962	Fiesta Red, slab board	$14,000	$16,000
1962	Inca Silver, slab board	$13,000	$15,000
1962	Lake Placid Blue, curved board	$8,200	$10,200
1962	Lake Placid Blue, slab board	$9,000	$11,000
1962	Sea Foam Green, slab board	$14,000	$16,000
1962	Sherwood Green, slab board	$12,000	$15,000
1962	Shoreline Gold, slab board	$12,000	$15,000
1962	Sonic Blue, slab board	$11,000	$13,000
1962	Surf Green, slab board	$14,000	$16,000
1963	Black	$8,000	$10,000
1963	Blond	$6,000	$7,500
1963	Burgundy Mist	$12,000	$14,000
1963	Dakota Red	$12,000	$14,000
1963	Daphne Blue	$10,000	$12,000
1963	Fiesta Red	$13,000	$15,000
1963	Inca Silver	$12,000	$14,000
1963	Lake Placid Blue	$8,000	$10,000
1963	Olympic White	$8,000	$10,000
1963	Sea Foam Green	$13,000	$15,000
1963	Shell Pink	$15,000	$20,000
1963	Sherwood Green	$11,000	$13,000
1963	Shoreline Gold	$10,000	$12,000
1963	Sonic Blue	$10,000	$12,000
1963	Sunburst	$6,500	$8,000
1963	Surf Green	$13,000	$15,000
1964	Blond	$5,500	$7,200
1964	Sonic Blue	$10,000	$12,000
1965	Blond	$5,000	$6,500
1965	Candy Apple Red	$6,200	$7,200
1965	Lake Placid Blue	$6,000	$7,200
1966	Blond	$4,500	$5,500
1966	Candy Apple Red	$6,000	$7,000
1966	Firemist Gold	$6,500	$7,700
1966	Lake Placid Blue	$5,700	$6,700
1966	Olympic White	$5,500	$6,500
1966	Sunburst	$4,200	$5,200
1967	Black	$5,000	$6,000
1967	Blond	$3,700	$4,500
1967	Blond, Bigsby	$3,000	$3,900
1967	Candy Apple Red	$5,800	$6,800
1967	Ice Blue Metallic	$6,000	$7,000
1967	Lake Placid Blue	$5,800	$6,800
1967	Olympic White	$5,500	$6,500
1967	Sunburst	$4,000	$5,000
1968	Black	$4,500	$5,500
1968	Blond	$3,200	$4,000
1968	Blue floral	$6,300	$7,300
1968	Candy Apple Red	$5,800	$6,800
1968	Dakota Red	$6,200	$7,200
1968	Lake Placid Blue	$5,800	$6,800
1968	Pink Paisley	$6,600	$7,600
1968	Sunburst	$3,500	$4,500
1969	Blond	$2,800	$3,200
1969	Blue Floral	$6,300	$7,300
1969	Candy Apple Red	$4,800	$5,800
1969	Pink Paisley	$6,600	$7,600
1969	Sunburst	$3,000	$3,500
1969	White	$3,500	$4,500
1970	Blond	$2,700	$3,000
1970	Candy Apple Red	$3,800	$4,800
1970	Firemist Gold	$4,400	$5,400
1970	Sunburst	$2,600	$3,100
1971	Black, 3-bolt neck	$2,000	$2,400

1958 Fender Telecaster

1969 Fender Paisley Red Telecaster

GUITARS

'63 Closet Classic Telecaster

Fender Albert Collins Telecaster

MODEL YEAR	FEATURES	EXC. COND. LOW	HIGH
1971	Blond, 3-bolt neck	$2,000	$2,400
1971	Candy Apple Red, 3-bolt neck	$2,900	$3,500
1971	Sunburst, 3-bolt neck	$2,000	$2,400
1971	Transparent Brown, 3-bolt neck	$2,000	$2,400
1971	White, 3-bolt neck	$2,300	$2,900
1972	Black	$2,300	$2,900
1972	Blond	$1,900	$2,300
1972	Candy Apple Red	$2,600	$3,200
1972	Natural	$1,700	$2,200
1972	Sunburst	$1,700	$2,200
1973	Various colors	$1,600	$2,300
1974	Various colors	$1,500	$2,200
1975	Various colors	$1,500	$1,700
1976	Various colors	$1,400	$1,600
1977	Various colors	$1,200	$1,500
1978	Various colors	$1,000	$1,500
1979	Various colors	$1,000	$1,400
1980	Various colors	$1,000	$1,300
1981	Various colors	$900	$1,200
1982	Various colors	$800	$1,200

Standard Telecaster

1982-1985. See Telecaster for 1951-1983, and American Standard Telecaster (following listing) for 1988-2000. Not to be confused with the current Standard Telecaster, which is made in Mexico.

1982-1985	Blond	$550	$800

American Standard Telecaster

1988-2000. See Telecaster for 1951-1983, and Telecaster Standard for 1983-1985. All 1994 models have a metal 40th Anniversary pin on the headstock, but should not be confused with the actual 40th Anniversary Telecaster model (see separate listing). All standard colors. Renamed the American Series Telecaster in 2000.

1988-1989		$650	$850
1990-1999		$600	$725

American Series Telecaster

2000-present.

2000		$500	$600

'50s Telecaster (import)

1992-1999. Import from Japan, basswood body, Blond finish, Black guard.

1992-1999		$500	$600

'52 Telecaster

1982-present. 1952 Telecaster reissue, ash body, with maple neck or rosewood fingerboard.

1982-1999	Blond	$800	$1,000
1990-1999	Copper (limited number)	$800	$1,000

'60 Telecaster Custom (Custom Shop)

1997-present. U.S.A. custom shop, alder body, black or custom colors.

1999		$1,200	$1,400

'62 Custom Telecaster (import)

1985-1999. Made in Japan, bound top and back, rosewood fretboard.

1985-1999	Sunburst or Red	$500	$600

'63 Closet Classic Telecaster Custom Shop

1999-present. Alder body (or Blond on ash), original spec pickups, C-shaped neck, rosewood fingerboard.

1999	Blond on ash	$1,800	$1,900
1999	Candy Apple Red on alder	$1,600	$1,700

'69 Blue Flower Telecaster

Ca.1986-1994. Import. Blue Flower finish.

1986-1994		$700	$800

'69 Pink Paisley Telecaster

Ca.1986-1998. Import. Pink Paisley finish.

1986-1989		$700	$800
1990-1998		$500	$700

'69 Rosewood Telecaster

1986-1996. Japanese-made reissue, rosewood.

1986-1996		$1,000	$1,300

'69 Telecaster Thinline

1988-1998. Import, two Tele pickups.

1988-1998	Natural	$500	$600

'72 Custom Telecaster

1986-1999. Import.

1986-1999	Black or Red	$500	$600

'72 Telecaster Thinline

1988-1998. Import, two humbuckers.

1988-1998	Natural	$500	$600

'90s Telecaster Thinline

1998-2000. Ash body, single F-hole, natural Foto-Flame or transparent crimson.

1998-2000		$900	$1,100

40th Anniversary Telecaster Custom Shop

1988, 1999. Custom shop limited edition run of 300, two-piece flamed maple top, gold hardware (1988), flamed maple top over ash body, gold hardware (1999).

1988	1st run, high-end	$3,500	$4,000
1999	2nd run, plain top	$1,400	$1,600

50th Anniversary Telecaster Custom Shop

1995-1996. Flame maple top, two vintage-style pickups, Gold hardware, Gold 50th Anniversary coin on back of the headstock, 1250 made.

1996	Sunburst	$1,400	$1,500

Albert Collins Telecaster

1990-present. U.S.-made Custom Shop signature model, bound swamp ash body, humbucker pickup in neck position.

1990-1999	Blond	$1,100	$1,300
1995	Silver Sparkle	$1,200	$1,400

Aluminum Telecaster Custom Shop

1994-1995. Aluminum with anodized marble-variant finish.

1994-1995		$1,500	$2,000

GUITARS

MODEL YEAR	FEATURES	EXC. COND. LOW	HIGH

American Classic Telecaster Custom Shop

1993-2000. Handcrafted version of American Standard, thin lacquer-finished ash body, maple or rosewood 'board. Earlier versions had gold hardware and custom-color options.

1993-2000	Various colors and options	$1,300	$1,500

American Deluxe Telecaster

1998-present. Premium ash or alder body with see-through finishes.

1998-1999		$850	$950

Black and Gold Telecaster

1981-1982. Black finish, gold-plated brass hardware.

1981-1982		$1,150	$1,350

Buck Owens Ltd Edition Telecaster Custom Shop

1998-2002. Red, White and Blue Spparkle finish, gold hardware, gold 'guard, rosewood 'board, by Fender Japan.

1998-2002		$850	$950

California Fat Telecaster

1997-1998. Alder body, maple fretboard, Tex-Mex humbucker and Tele pickup configuration.

1997-1998		$450	$550

California Telecaster

1997-1998. Alder body, maple fretboard, Tex-Mex Strat and Tele pickup configuration.

1997-1998	Sunburst	$450	$550

Contemporary Telecaster (import)

1985-1987. Japanese-made used while the new Fender reorganized, two or three pickups, vibrato, Black chrome hardware, rosewood fingerboard.

1985-1987		$250	$300

Custom Classic Telecaster Custom Shop

2000-present. U.S.A. Custom Shop version of American Series, alder body, maple or rosewood 'board.

2000		$1,200	$1,400

Danny Gatton Telecaster

1990-present. Custom Shop signature model like 1953 Telecaster, maple neck, two humbucking pickups.

1990s	Frost Gold	$2,000	$2,100
1990s	Honey Blond	$2,000	$2,100

Deluxe Telecaster (U.S.A.-made)

1972-1981. Two humbucker pickups.

1972-1978	Brown	$1,400	$1,800
1972-1981	Blond	$1,500	$2,000
1978	Antigua	$1,500	$2,000

Elite Telecaster

1983-1985. Two active humbucker pickups, Les Paul-style three-way switch, two volume knobs, one presence and filter controls, chrome hardware, various colors.

1983-1985		$850	$1,000

Foto Flame Telecaster

1994-1995. Import. Sunburst or Transparent.

1994-1995		$450	$550

MODEL YEAR	FEATURES	EXC. COND. LOW	HIGH

HMT Telecaster

1990-1993. Japanese-made "Metal-rock" Tele, available with or without Floyd Rose tremolo, one Fender Lace Sensor pickup and one DiMarzio bridge humbucker pickup.

1990-1993	Black	$200	$250

James Burton Telecaster

1990-present. Ash body, three Fender Lace pickups. Available in black with gold paisley, black with candy red paisley, pearl white, and frost red.

1990-1999	Black and gold paisley, gold hardware	$800	$1,100
1990-1999	Frost red, black hardware	$500	$800
1990-1999	Pearl white, gold hardware	$500	$800
1990-2000	Black and red paisley, black hardware	$800	$1,000

Jerry Donahue Telecaster Custom Shop

1992-'01. Designed by Jerry Donahue, Tele bridge pickup and Strat neck pickup, three-saddle bridge, special passive circuitry, five-way switch.

1992-99	Sunburst	$1,200	$1,300

John Jorgenson Telecaster Custom Shop

1998-2001. Custom Shop, double-coil stacked pickups, Sparkle or Black finish. Early models had korina body.

1998-1999	Gold Sparkle	$1,300	$1,700

Rosewood Telecaster

1969-1972. Rosewood body and neck.

1969-1972		$5,000	$6,000

Set-Neck Telecaster

1990-1996. Glued-in neck, Custom Shop, two humbucking pickups. Set Neck CA "Country Artist" has one humbucker and one Tele pickup. Various colors.

1990-1996		$1,100	$1,300

Sparkle Telecaster Custom Shop

1993-1995. Poplar body, white pickguard, Sparkle finish: Champagne, Gold, Silver

1993-1995		$1,300	$1,500

Squier Telecaster

1983-1998. Fender Japan was established in '82 with Squier production beginning in '83. Production was shifted to Korea in '87 and later allocated to China, India (Squier II '89-'90) and Mexico. This model is the low-cost version of the Telecaster for Squier.

1983-1984	Blond, 1st year '70s-style logo	$250	$350
1985-1989	Black or Blond	$200	$300

Squier Telecaster Affinity (China)

Made in China, standard Telecaster styling. Various colors.

1999		$75	$100

Fender James Burton Telecaster

Fender Jerry Donahue Telecaster

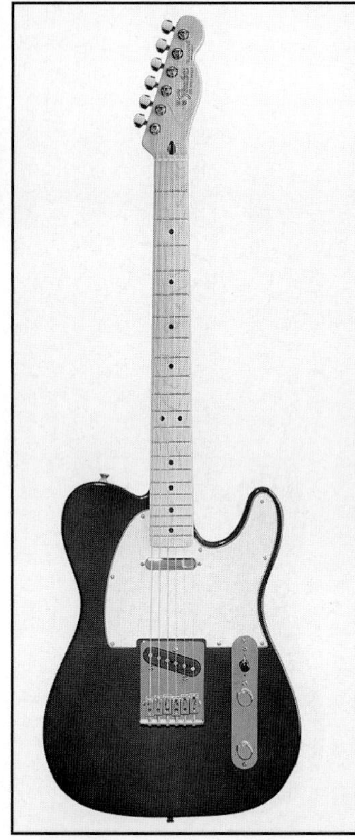

Fender Standard Telecaster

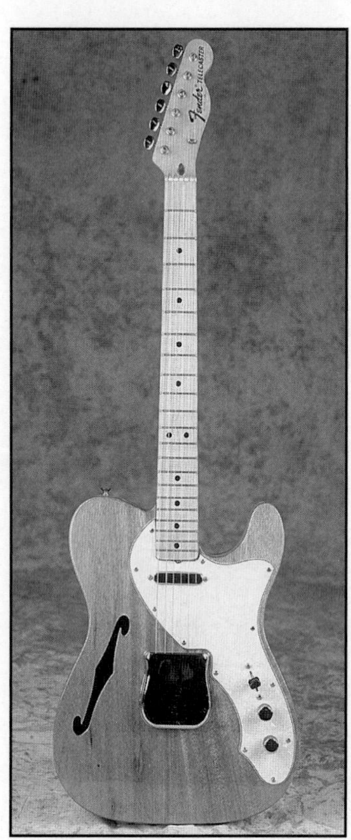

1968 Telecaster Thinline

Standard Telecaster (Mexico)

Production at the Mexico facility started in 1990. High end of range includes a hard guitar case, while the low end of the range includes only a gig bag. Various colors.

MODEL YEAR	FEATURES	EXC. COND. LOW	HIGH
1990-1999		$300	$350

Thinline Telecaster Custom Shop

MODEL YEAR	FEATURES	EXC. COND. LOW	HIGH
1990s	Gold Sparkle	$1,500	$1,700

Tele Jr./Set Neck Tele Jr. (Custom Shop)

1994, 1997-2000. Transparent Blond ash body, two P-90-style pickups, set neck, 11 tone chambers. 100 made in '94, reintroduced in '97.

MODEL YEAR	FEATURES	EXC. COND. LOW	HIGH
1994		$1,600	$1,800

Telecaster Custom

1959-1972. Body bound top and back, rosewood fingerboard, two Tele pickups. See Telecaster Custom (2nd Edition) for the one Tele/one humbucker version.

MODEL YEAR	FEATURES	EXC. COND. LOW	HIGH
1959	Sunburst	$12,000	$14,000
1960	Sunburst	$10,000	$12,000
1961	Black	$13,000	$16,000
1961	Dakota Red	$16,000	$19,000
1961	Fiesta Red	$16,000	$19,000
1961	Lake Placid Blue	$14,000	$16,000
1961	Sunburst	$12,000	$15,000
1962	Fiesta Red, slab board	$15,000	$18,000
1962	Inca Silver, slab board	$15,000	$18,000
1962	Lake Placid Blue, slab board	$13,000	$16,000
1962	Sea Foam Green, slab board	$17,000	$20,000
1962	Sherwood Green, slab board	$14,000	$17,000
1962	Shoreline Gold, slab board	$14,000	$17,000
1962	Sonic Blue, slab board	$15,000	$18,000
1962	Sunburst	$10,000	$11,000
1962	Surf Green, slab board	$17,000	$20,000
1963	Sunburst	$9,000	$10,000
1964	Sunburst	$8,000	$9,000
1965	Candy Apple Red	$9,000	$11,000
1965	Sunburst	$6,500	$7,500
1966	Sunburst	$5,500	$6,500
1967	Lake Placid Blue	$7,500	$9,000
1967	Sunburst	$5,000	$6,000
1968	Candy Apple Red, maple cap	$7,000	$8,500
1968	Sunburst, maple cap	$5,500	$6,500
1968	Sunburst, rosewood cap	$4,500	$6,000
1968	White	$6,500	$8,000
1969	Sunburst	$4,500	$5,500
1970	Sunburst	$4,000	$5,400
1971	Sunburst, 3-bolt neck	$2,900	$3,300
1971	Sunburst, 4-bolt neck	$3,600	$4,000
1972	Sunburst, 3-bolt neck	$2,800	$3,100

Telecaster Custom (II)

1972-1981. One humbucking and one Tele pickup, standard colors. See above for two Tele pickup version. Also called Custom Telecaster.

MODEL YEAR	FEATURES	EXC. COND. LOW	HIGH
1972-1975		$1,500	$2,000
1976-1981		$1,400	$1,800

Telecaster Deluxe (import)

1995-1998. Import, one Tele-style bridge pickup and two Strat-style pickups, rosewood fingerboard, Foto Flame '95-'97 and non-Foto Flame '97-'98.

MODEL YEAR	FEATURES	EXC. COND. LOW	HIGH
1995-1998	Sunburst	$450	$500

Telecaster Deluxe Nashville (Mexico)

1998-present. Tex-Mex Strat and Tele pickup configuration. Various colors.

MODEL YEAR	FEATURES	EXC. COND. LOW	HIGH
1998-1999		$450	$500

Telecaster Plus Standard

1990-1997. Two Lace Sensor pickups, one single-coil, one double. Different model, called Telecaster Plus (no standard) offered 1994-1997. Various colors.

MODEL YEAR	FEATURES	EXC. COND. LOW	HIGH
1990-1997		$650	$800

Telecaster Thinline

1968-1980. Semi-hollowbody, one F-hole, two Tele pickups, ash or mahogany body. In late-1971, the "tilt neck" was added and the two Tele pickups were switched to two humbuckers.

MODEL YEAR	FEATURES	EXC. COND. LOW	HIGH
1968	Natural	$3,000	$3,500
1968	Sunburst	$3,000	$3,500
1969	Black	$3,400	$3,700
1969	Burgundy Mist	$5,300	$5,700
1969	Natural	$3,000	$3,500
1969	Ocean Turquoise	$5,300	$5,700
1969	Sunburst	$3,000	$3,500
1970	Natural	$3,000	$3,300
1970	Sunburst	$3,000	$3,300
1971	Black, 3-bolt neck	$2,100	$3,300
1971	Mahogany, 3-bolt neck	$1,900	$2,700
1971	Natural, 3-bolt neck	$2,200	$2,700
1971	Sunburst, 3-bolt neck	$2,200	$2,700
1971	Walnut Brown, 3-bolt neck	$1,900	$2,700
1972	Black	$2,300	$3,100
1972	Candy Apple Red	$2,300	$3,100
1972	Lake Placid Blue	$2,300	$3,100
1972	Mahogany	$2,100	$2,600
1972	Natural	$2,100	$2,600
1972	Olympic White	$2,100	$2,600
1972	Sunburst	$2,100	$2,600
1973	Natural	$2,100	$2,600
1973	Sunburst	$2,100	$2,600
1974	Natural	$2,100	$2,600
1974	Olympic White	$2,300	$2,800
1974	Sunburst	$2,100	$2,600

MODEL YEAR	FEATURES	EXC. COND. LOW	HIGH
1974	Walnut	$2,100	$2,600
1975	Blond	$2,200	$2,800
1975	Natural	$1,900	$2,100
1976	Natural	$1,900	$2,100
1976	Walnut	$1,900	$2,100
1977	Natural	$1,800	$2,000
1978	Natural	$1,800	$2,000
1978	Sunburst	$1,900	$2,100
1978	Transparent Brown	$1,900	$2,100

Toronado

1999-present. Contoured offset-waist body with two Atomic Humbucker pickups. Offered in Black, Arctic White, Candy Apple Red, and Brown Sunburst.

1999-2001		$400	$500

Villager 12-String

1965-1971. Acoustic flat top, spruce top, mahogany back and sides, 12 strings. Natural.

1965-1968		$550	$750
1969-1971		$500	$700

Wildwood

1967-1969. Acoustic flat top with wildwood dyed top.

1967-1969	Various (faded)	$800	$1,000
1967-1969	Various (unfaded)	$1,200	$1,500

Fernandes

1969-present. Established in Tokyo. Early efforts were classical guitars, but they now offer a variety of guitars and basses.

AFR-120

1988-1998. Bolt-on neck, locking tremolo, graphic finishes, Natural.

1988		$300	$450

APG-100

1989-1996. Carved and bound maple top, mahogany back, maple neck, rosewood fingerboard, various pickup configurations, Sunburst.

1991-1996		$500	$600

FR-552

Introduced in 1987. One-piece maple neck, 24-fret fingerboard, deep cutaway, Fernandes Floyd Rose locking tremolo.

1988		$200	$275

LE-1

Introduced in 1987. Double cut alder body, maple or rosewood fingerboard, various colors.

1987		$200	$275

LE-2 G

1991-1998. LE-2 with Gold hardware.

1990s		$300	$400

LE-2/LE-2X

1991-1998. Double cut, hum-single-single non-pole pickups, Floyd-style vibrato (LE-2X double-locking), various colors.

1990s		$250	$350

TE-3

1993-1998. Natural.

1997		$450	$550

MODEL YEAR	FEATURES	EXC. COND. LOW	HIGH

TE-59/60

Introduced in 1987. Single cut alder body, Natural.

1987		$200	$300

Fina

Production classical and steel-string guitars built at the Kwo Hsiao Music Wooden Factory in Huiyang City, Guang Dong, mainland China. They also build acoustic basses.

Fine Resophonic

1988-present. Professional and premium grade, production/custom, wood and metal-bodied resophonic guitars (including reso-electrics), ukuleles, and mandolins built by luthiers Mike Lewis and Pierre Avocat in Vitry Sur Seine, France.

Fleishman Instruments

1974-present. Premium and presentation grade, custom flat-tops and acoustic and solidbody basses made by luthier Harry Fleishman in Sebastopol, California. He also offers electric uprights, designed by him and built in China. Fleishman also designs basses for others and is the director of Luthiers School International.

Fletcher Brock Stringed Instruments

1992-present. Custom flat-tops, archtops, and mandolin-family instruments made by luthier Fletcher Brock in Ketchum, Idaho.

Flowers Guitars

Premium grade, custom, archtop guitars built by luthier Gary Flowers in Baltimore, Maryland.

Fontanilla Guitars

1987-present. Luthier Allan Fontanilla builds his premium grade, production/custom, classical guitars in San Francisco, California.

Fouilleul

1978-present. Production/custom, classical guitars made by luthier Jean-Marie Fouilleul in Cuguen, France.

Frame Works

1995-present. Professional grade, production/custom, steel- and nylon-string guitars built by luthier Frank Krocker in Burghausen, Germany. The instruments feature a neck mounted on a guitar-shaped frame. Krocker has also built traditional archtops, flat-tops, and classicals.

Framus

1946-1975, 1996-present. "Frankische Musikindustrie" (Framus) founded in Erlangen, Germany by Fred Wilfer, relocated to Bubenreuth in '54, and to Pretzfeld in '67. Begun as an acoustic instrument manufacturer, Framus added

Fender Toronado

1972 Telecaster Thinline

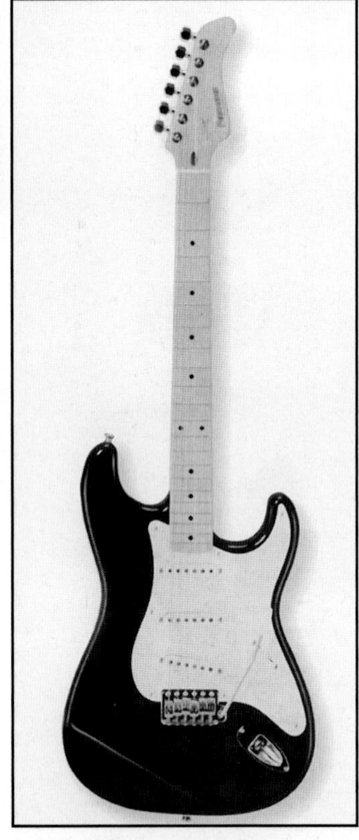
Fernandes LE-1

Framus Strato-Melodie 9-string

MODEL YEAR	FEATURES	EXC. COND. LOW	HIGH

electrics in the mid-'50s. Earliest electrics were mostly acoustics with pickups attached. Electric designs begin in early-'60s. Unique feature was a laminated maple neck with many thin plies. By around '64-'65 upscale models featured the "organtone," often called a "spigot," a spring-loaded volume control that allowed you to simulate a Leslie speaker effect. Better models often had mutes and lots of switches.

In the '60s, Framus instruments were imported into the U.S. by Philadelphia Music Company. Resurgence of interest in ca. '74 with the Jan Akkermann hollowbody followed by original mid-'70s design called the Nashville, the product of an alliance with some American financing. The brand was revived in '96, and distributed in the U.S. by Dana B. Goods (see following).

Atilla Zoller AZ 10

Early-1960s-late-1970s. Single cutaway archtop, two pickups, neck glued-in until the 1970s, bolt-on after. Model 5/65 30% lower in value than Model 5/67.

1969	Sunburst	$750	$900

Big 18 Solid Doubleneck 5/200

1968	Sunburst	$550	$700

Billy Lorento

Ca.1958-1977. Semi-hollowbody, single cutaway thinline, two pickups.

1962		$500	$800
1969		$500	$800

Caravelle 5/117

Ca.1965-1977. Double cutaway archtop, tremolo, two pickups, Cherry or Sunburst.

1960s		$400	$500

Golden Television 5/118

Ca. 1967-ca. 1970. Semi-hollowbody, natural light-colored solid spruce top, double cutaway, three pickups, Gold hardware, Cherry or Sunburst.

1967		$500	$700

Jan Akkerman

1974-1977. Single cutaway semi-hollowbody, two pickups, Gold hardware.

1975		$600	$800

King 5/98

Single cutaway flat-top.

1963		$400	$600

Missouri 5/60 (E Framus Missouri)

Ca.1960-1977. Non-cutaway acoustic archtop until 1965, single cutaway archtop with two pickups after, Natural or Sunburst.

1964		$400	$550

Nashville

1974-1977.

1974		$425	$575

Sorella 5/59

Ca.1955-1977. Single cutaway acoustic archtop.

1959-1964		$375	$475

MODEL YEAR	FEATURES	EXC. COND. LOW	HIGH

Strato de Luxe 12-String 5/068

Ca.1964-1972. Fender Jaguar-shaped solidbody, 12 strings, two pickups, tremolo.

1964	Sunburst	$400	$500

Strato de Luxe 5/168

Ca.1964-1972. Fender Jaguar-shaped solidbody, one, two, or three pickups, some models have Gold hardware.

1965	Sunburst	$400	$500

Strato Melodie 9-String

Ca.1963-1970. Solidbody, offset double cutaway, doubles on three high strings, two single-coil pickups, tremolo.

1965	Sunburst	$500	$700

Texan 12-String Flat-Top 5/296

1968	Natural or Sunburst	$200	$250

Framus (Warwick)

1996-present. The Framus brand name was re-introduced by Hans Peter Wilfer, the president of Warwick, with production in Warwick's factory in Germany. Currently offering professional and premium grade, production/custom, guitars and basses made in Germany.

Tennessee

1990s		$1,700	$1,750

Fresher

1973-1985. The Japanese-made Fresher brand was introduced in '73. The guitars were mainly copies of popular brands and were not imported into the U.S., but they do show up at guitar shows.

Solidbody Electrics

Japanese import.

1970s		$200	$350

Froggy Bottom Guitars

1970-present. Luthier Michael Millard builds his premium and presentation grade, production/custom flat-tops in Newfane, Vermont (until 1984 production was in Richmond, New Hampshire).

Fukuoka Musical Instruments

1993-present. Custom steel and nylon-string flat-tops and archtops built in Japan.

Futurama

1960s. Czechoslovakia company that supplied the European market. Student/budget level. Some hobbyists will recognize the brand name as Beatle George Harrison's first electric.

Fylde Guitars

1973-present. Luthier Roger Bucknall builds his professional and premium grade, production/custom acoustic guitars and basses in Penrith, Cumbria, United Kingdom. He also builds mandolins, mandolas, bouzoukis, and citterns.

MODEL YEAR	FEATURES	EXC. COND. LOW	HIGH

G & L

1980-present. Currently offering intermediate and professional grade, production/custom, solidbody and semi-hollowbody electric guitars made in the U.S. and overseas. They also make basses. Founded by Leo Fender and George Fullerton following the severance of ties between Fender's CLF Research and Music Man. The company was sold to John MacLaren and BBE Sound, when Leo Fender died in '91. In '98 they added their Custom Creations Department. In 2003 G & L introduced the Korean-made G & L Tribute Series. Several of the following price ranges were developed with help from Tim Page.

ASAT

1986-1998. Called the Broadcaster in 1985. 2 or 3 single-coil or 2 single-coil/one humbucker pickup configurations until early-'90s, 2 single-coils after.

1986		$700	$800
1987	Leo Fender sig. on headstock	$750	$850
1988-1991	Leo Fender sig. on body	$850	$950
1992-1998		$600	$800

ASAT III

1988-1991, 1996-1998. Single cutaway body, three single-coil pickups.

1988-1991	1st version, Leo era, 150 made	$950	$1,050
1996-1998	Post Leo era	$700	$800

ASAT '50

1999. Limited run of 10 instruments.

1999		$1,000	$1,250

ASAT 20th Anniversary

2000. Limited Edition of 50, ash body, tinted bird's-eye maple neck, two-tone Sunburst.

2000		$1,300	$1,500

ASAT Blues Boy Limited Edition

1999. Limited edition of 20.

1999		$1,000	$1,200

ASAT Blues Boy Semi-Hollow Limited Edition

1999. Limited edition, thin semi-hollow, limited edition of 12 units.

1999		$1,000	$1,400

ASAT Classic

1990-present. Two single-coil pickups, individually adjustable bridge saddles, neck-tilt adjustment and tapered string posts.

1990-1991	Signature on neck	$800	$1,000
1992-1997	3-bolt neck	$700	$850
1997-2003	4-bolt neck	$600	$800

ASAT Classic Blues Boy

2001-present. Humbucker neck pickup, single-coil at bridge.

2001-2003		$750	$900

ASAT Classic Blues Boy Semi-Hollow

1997-present. Chambered Classic with F-holes.

1997-1999		$800	$950

ASAT Classic Commemorative

1991-1992. Leo Fender signature and birth/death dating.

1991	Australian lacewood, 6 made	$4,000	$6,000
1991-1992	Cherryburst, 350 made	$2,400	$2,600

ASAT Classic Custom

1996-1997, 2002-present.

1996-1997	1st version	$850	$950
2002-2003	2nd version, 4-bolt neck	$700	$750

ASAT Classic Custom Semi-Hollow

2002-present.

2002-2003		$750	$850

ASAT Classic Semi-Hollow

1997-present.

1997-2003		$700	$800

ASAT Classic Three

1998. Limited Edition of 100 units.

1998		$1,000	$1,400

ASAT Custom

1996. No pickguard, 25 to 30 made.

1996		$800	$900

ASAT Deluxe

1997-present. Two humbuckers, flamed maple top, bound body.

1997	3-bolt neck, less than 100 made	$1,000	$1,400
1997-2003	4-bolt neck	$1,000	$1,100

ASAT Deluxe Semi-Hollow

1997-present. Two humbuckers.

1997-2003		$1,100	$1,300

ASAT Junior Limited Edition

1998-2002. Single cut semi-hollowbody, 2 single-coil pickups, short run of 250 units.

1998-2002		$900	$1,100

ASAT S-3

1998-2000. Three soap-bar single-coil pickups, limited production.

1998-2000		$700	$900

ASAT Semi-Hollow

1997-present. Semi-hollow version of ASAT Special.

1997-2003		$700	$800

ASAT Special

1992-present. Like ASAT, but with two larger P-90-type pickups, chrome hardware, various colors.

1992-1997	3-bolt neck	$600	$800
1997-2000	4-bolt neck	$600	$750

ASAT Special Deluxe

2001-present. No pickguard version of the Special with figured maple top.

2001-2003		$800	$850

ASAT Z-2 Limited Edition

1999. Limited edition of ten instruments, semi-hollow construction, natural ash, tortoise bound, engraved neckplate.

1999		$950	$1,050

G&L ASAT Classic Semi-Hollow

G&L ASAT 3

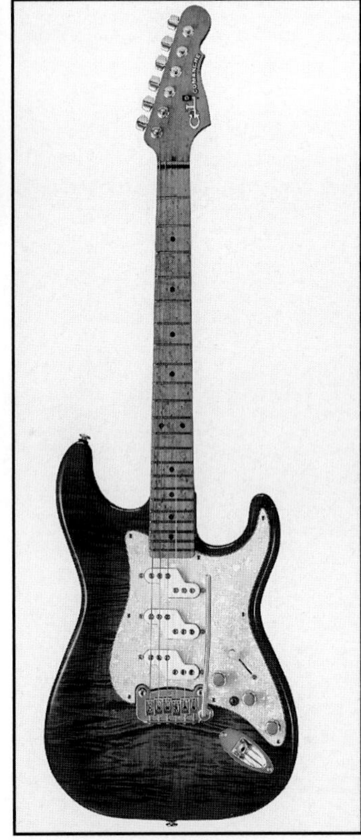

G&L Comanche

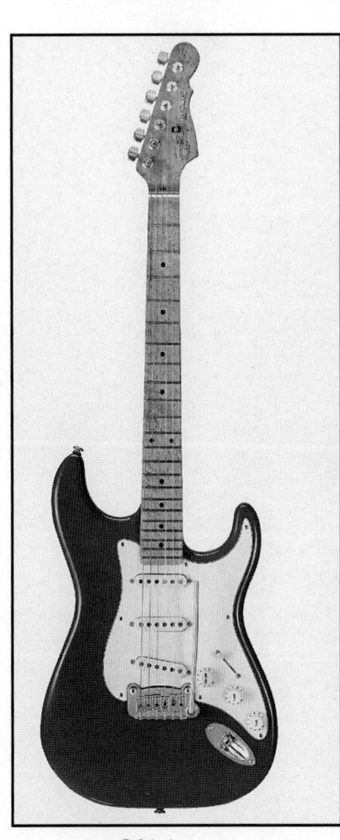

G&L Legacy

MODEL YEAR	FEATURES	EXC. COND. LOW	HIGH

ASAT Z-3

1998-present. Three offset-style Z-3 high output pickups.

1998-2003		$700	$800

ASAT Z-3 Semi-Hollow

1998-present. Semi-hollowbody-style, three offset-style Z-3 high output pickups.

1998-2003		$800	$900

John Jorgenson Signature Model ASAT

1995. About 190 made, Silver Metalflake finish.

1995		$1,000	$1,500

Broadcaster

1985-1986. Solidbody, two single-coil pickups with adjustable polepieces act in humbucking mode with selector switch in the center position. Black parts and finish. Name changed to ASAT in early-1986.

1985-1986	Signed by Leo, maple board	$1,800	$2,200
1985-1986	Signed by Leo, ebony board	$1,800	$2,100

Cavalier

1983-1986. Offset double cutaway, two humbuckers, 700 made.

1983-1986		$700	$1,000

Climax

1992-1996. Offset double cut, bolt maple neck, six-on-a-side tuners, double locking vibrato.

1992-1996	Blue	$750	$850

Climax Plus

1992-1996. Two humbuckers replace single-coils of the Climax, plus one single-coil.

1992-1996		$750	$850

Climax XL

1992-1996. Two humbuckers only.

1992-1996		$750	$850

Comanche V

1988-1991. Solidbody, three Z-shaped single-coil humbucking pickups, five-position selector switch, hard rock maple neck in choice of three radii, 22-fret rosewood fingerboard, vibrato, fine tuners, Leo Fender's signature on the body.

1988-1991	Sunburst	$850	$950

Comanche VI

1990-1991. Leo Fender's signature on the body, six mini-toggles.

1990-1991		$1,000	$1,300

F-100 (Model I and II)

1980-1986. Offset double cutaway solidbody, two humbuckers. Came in a I and II model - only difference is the radius of the fingerboard.

1980-1986	Natural	$700	$900

F-100 E (Model I and II)

1980-1982. Offset double cutaway solidbody, two humbuckers, active electronics, pre-amp. Came in a I and II model - only difference is the radius of the fingerboard.

1980-1982	Natural	$700	$900

MODEL YEAR	FEATURES	EXC. COND. LOW	HIGH

G-200

1981-1982. Mahogany solidbody, maple neck, ebony fingerboard, two humbucking pickups, coil-split switches, Natural or Sunburst, 209 made.

1981-1982		$1,000	$1,300

GBL-LE (Guitars by Leo Limited Edition)

1999. Limited edition of 25, semi-hollowbody, three pickups.

1999		$1,000	$1,300

George Fullerton Signature

1995-present. Double cut solidbody, sunburst.

1995-1997	3-bolt neck	$800	$1,000
1997-2003	4-bolt neck	$700	$800

HG-1

1982-1983. Five made.

1982-1983		$1,900	$2,100

HG-2

1982-1984.

1982-1983	Mustang-style body	$1,000	$1,500
1984	Strat-style body	$1,000	$1,500

Interceptor

1983-1991. Until 1986 it was sort of an X-shaped solidbody (1987-1989 was an offset double cutaway solidbody), either three single-coils, two humbuckers, or one humbucker and two single-coils.

1983-1985	1st X-body, about 70 made	$1,000	$1,200
1985-1986	2nd X-body, about 12 made	$1,300	$1,600
1988-1991	Strat-style body	$700	$900

Invader

1984-1991, 1998-present. Double cut solidbody, two single-coil and one humbucker pickups.

1984-1991	1st version	$500	$700
1998-2003	2nd version	$800	$900

Invader Plus

1998-present. Two humbuckers and single blade pickup in the middle position.

1998-2003		$800	$900

Invader XL

1998-present. Two humbuckers.

1998-2003		$750	$850

Legacy

1992-present. Classic double cut configuration, various colors.

1992-1994	3-bolt neck, Duncan SSLs	$650	$800
1995-1997	3-bolt neck, Alnicos	$600	$750
1997-2003	4-bolt neck, Alnicos	$550	$700

Legacy 2HB

2001-present. Two humbucker pickups.

2001-2003		$550	$700

Legacy Deluxe

2001-present. No pickguard, figured maple top.

2001-2003		$700	$850

Legacy HB

2001-present. One humbucker pickup at bridge position plus two single-coil pickups.

2001-2003		$600	$750

Legacy Special

1993-present. Legacy with 3 humbuckers, various colors.

MODEL YEAR	FEATURES	EXC. COND. LOW	HIGH
1992-1997	3-bolt neck	$600	$700
1998-2003	4-bolt neck	$550	$600

Nighthawk

1983. Offset double cutaway solidbody, three single-coil pickups, 269 made. Name changed to Skyhawk in 1984.

MODEL YEAR	FEATURES	EXC. COND. LOW	HIGH
1983	Sunburst	$650	$950

Rampage

1984-1991. Offset double cutaway solidbody, hard rock maple neck, ebony fingerboard, one bridge-position humbucker pickup.

MODEL YEAR	FEATURES	EXC. COND. LOW	HIGH
1984-1991	Sunburst	$600	$800

Rampage (reissue)

2000. Limited Edition of 70 units, supplied with gig bag and not hard case, Ivory finish.

MODEL YEAR	FEATURES	EXC. COND. LOW	HIGH
2000		$500	$700

S-500

1982-1995, 1997-present. Double cut mahogany or ash solidbody, maple neck, ebony or maple fingerboard, three single-coil pickups, vibrato.

MODEL YEAR	FEATURES	EXC. COND. LOW	HIGH
1982-1987	No mini-toggle	$600	$800
1988-1991	Mini-toggle, Leo's signature on body	$800	$1,000
1992-1995	3-bolt neck	$650	$800
1997-2003	4-bolt neck	$600	$700

S-500 Deluxe

2001-present. Deluxe Series features, including no pickguard and flamed maple top.

MODEL YEAR	FEATURES	EXC. COND. LOW	HIGH
2001-2003	Natural	$800	$900

SC-1

1982-1983. Offset double cutaway solidbody, one single-coil pickup, tremolo, 250 made.

MODEL YEAR	FEATURES	EXC. COND. LOW	HIGH
1982-1983	Sunburst	$600	$800

SC-2

1982-1983. Offset double cutaway solidbody, two MFD "soapbar" pickups, about 600 made.

MODEL YEAR	FEATURES	EXC. COND. LOW	HIGH
1982-1983	Mustang-style body	$500	$700
1983	Strat-style body	$500	$600

SC-3

1982-1991. Offset double cutaway solidbody, three single-coil pickups, tremolo.

MODEL YEAR	FEATURES	EXC. COND. LOW	HIGH
1982-1983	Mustang-style body	$550	$750
1984-1987	Strat-style body, no pickguard	$500	$700
1988-1991	Strat-style body with pickguard	$500	$600

Skyhawk

1984-1987. Renamed from Nighthawk. Offset double cutaway solidbody, three single-coil pickups with five-position switch, signature on headstock '84-'87, then on body '88-'91.

MODEL YEAR	FEATURES	EXC. COND. LOW	HIGH
1984-1987	Signature on headstock	$650	$750
1988-1991	Signature on body	$750	$850

Superhawk

1984-1987. Offset double cutaway solidbody, hard rock maple neck, ebony fingerboard, G&L or Kahler tremolos, two humbucker pickups, signature on the headstock.

MODEL YEAR	FEATURES	EXC. COND. LOW	HIGH
1984-1987		$550	$750

Will Ray Signature Model

2002-present. Will Ray signature on headstock, three Z-coil pickups, Hipshot B-Bender.

MODEL YEAR	FEATURES	EXC. COND. LOW	HIGH
2002-2003		$900	$1,000

G.L. Stiles

1960-1994. Built by Gilbert Lee Stiles (b. October 2, 1914, Independence, WV; d. 1994) primarily in the Miami, Florida area. First solidbody, including pickups and all hardware, built by hand in his garage. Stiles favored scrolls, fancy carving and walnut fingerboards. His later instruments were considerably more fancy and refined. He moved to Hialeah, Florida by '63 and began making acoustic guitars and other instruments. His acoustics featured double stressed (bent) backs for increased tension. He later taught for the Augusta Heritage Program and Davis and Elkins College in Elkins, WV. Only his solidbodies had consecutive serial numbers. Stiles made approximately 1000 solidbodies and 500 acoustics.

Gabriel's Guitar Workshop

1979-present. Production/custom steel- and nylon-stringed guitars built by luthier Gabriel Ochoteco in Germany until '84 and in Brisbane Australia since.

Gagnon

1998-present. Luthier Bill Gagnon builds his premium and presentation grade, production/custom, archtop guitars in Beaverton, Oregon.

Galanti

Ca.1962-ca.1967. Electric guitars offered by the longtime Italian accordion maker. They may have also offered acoustics.

Galiano

New Yorkers Antonio Cerrito and Raphael Ciani offered guitars under the Galiano brand during the early part of the last century. They used the brand both on guitars built by them and others, including The Oscar Schmidt Company.

Gallagher

1965-present. Professional and premium grade, production/custom, flat-top guitars built in Wartrace, Tennessee. J. W. Gallagher started building Shelby brand guitars in the Slingerland Drum factory in Shelbyville, Tennessee in 1963. In '65 he and his son Don made the first Gallagher guitar, the G-50. Doc Watson began using

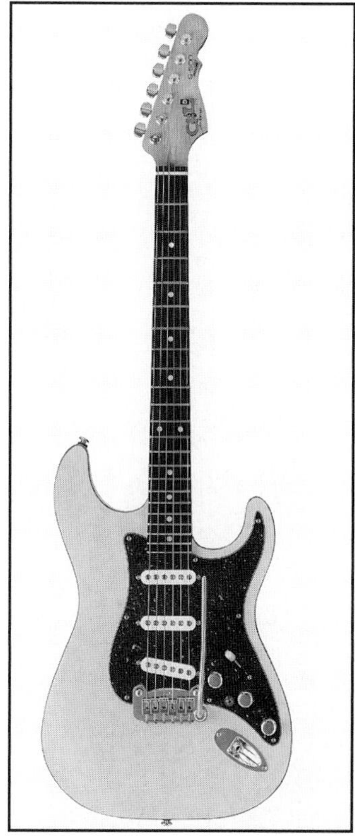

G&L S-500

Gallagher Doc Watson

GUITARS

Garrison G-4

Garrison G-25

MODEL YEAR	FEATURES	EXC. COND. LOW	HIGH

Gallagher guitars in 1968. In '76, Don assumed operation of the business when J. W. semi-retired. J. W. died in '79.

A-70 Ragtime Special

1978-present. Smaller (auditorium/00) body size, spruce top, mahogany back and sides, G logo, Natural.

1990-1999		$1,700	$1,800

Custom 12-String

Introduced in 1965. Mahogany, 12-fret neck, Natural.

1965		$1,000	$1,300

Doc Watson Model

1974-present. Spruce top, mahogany back and sides, scalloped bracing, ebony fingerboard, herringbone trim, Natural.

1974-1989		$1,400	$1,500

Doc Watson Model (cutaway)

1975-present. Spruce top, mahogany back and sides, scalloped bracing, ebony fingerboard, herringbone trim, Natural.

1985		$1,600	$1,700

Doc Watson 12-String

1995-2000		$1,400	$1,500

G-45

1970-present. Acoustic flat-top, mahogany back and sides, spruce top, rosewood fingerboard, Natural.

1980		$900	$1,100

G-70

1978-present. Flat-top, rosewood back and sides, herringbone trim on top and soundhole, mother-of-pearl diamond fingerboard inlays, bound headstock, natural.

1978-1998		$1,300	$1,600

G-71 Special

1970-present. Indian rosewood, herringbone trim, Natural.

1970-1979		$1,700	$1,800

Galloup Guitars

1994-present. Luthier Bryan Galloup builds his professional and premium grade, production/custom flat-tops in Big Rapids, Michigan. He also operates the Galloup School of Lutherie and The Guitar Hospital repair and restoration business.

Gamble & O'Toole

1978-present. Premium grade, custom classical and steel string guitars built by luthier Arnie Gamble in Sacramento, California, with design input and inlay work from his wife Erin O'Toole.

Ganz Guitars

1995-present. Luthier Steve Ganz builds his professional grade, production/custom classical guitars in Bellingham, Washington.

MODEL YEAR	FEATURES	EXC. COND. LOW	HIGH

Garcia

Made by luthier Federico Garcia in Spain until late-1960s or very early-'70s when production moved to Japan.

Classical (mahogany)

1960s. Made in Spain, mid-level, solid mahogany back and sides, solid spruce top.

1960s		$225	$275

Classical (rosewood)

1960s. Made in Spain, mid-level, solid rosewood back and sides, solid spruce top.

1960s		$450	$500

Classical (walnut/pine)

1970s. Made in Japan, mid-level, walnut back and sides, Spanish pine top.

1970s		$125	$150

Classical (walnut/spruce)

1960s. Made in Spain, mid-level, walnut back and sides, solid spruce top.

1970s		$400	$450

Garrison

2000-present. Intermediate and professional grade, production, acoustic and acoustic/electric guitars designed by luthier Chris Griffiths using the "Griffiths Active Bracing System" (a single integrated glass-fiber bracing system inside a solid wood body). He started Griffiths Guitar Works in 1993 in St. John's, Newfoundland, and introduced Garrison guitars in 2000.

G-20

2000-present. D-style, solid western red cedar top, solid birch back and sides.

2000		$300	$325

G-30

2000-present. D-style, solid spruce top, solid birch back and sides, dot markers.

2000		$350	$375

G-40 CE

2000-present. Single cut, D-size.

2002		$575	$650

Giannini

1900-present. Founded by guitar-builder Tranquill Giannini, this large Brazilian manufacturer was producing 30,000 instruments a year by 1930. Their acoustic instruments were being heavily imported into the U.S. by the late '50s. They added electric guitars in '60, but these weren't imported as much, if at all. Gianninis from this era used much Brazilian Rosewood. Currently Giannini offers a variety of stringed instruments.

Classical

Early-1970s. Nylon string import, small body.

1970s		$150	$300

CraViolia

1970s. Kidney bean-shaped rosewood body, acoustic. Line included a classical, a steel string, and a 12-string.

1972-1974	Natural	$200	$350

MODEL YEAR	FEATURES	EXC. COND. LOW	HIGH

CraViolia 12-String

Early-1970s. Kidney'bean shaped body, 12 strings.

1972-1974		$275	$350

Gibson

1880s (1902)-present. Intermediate, professional, and premium grade, production/custom, acoustic and electric guitars made in the U.S. They also build basses, mandolins, amps, and banjos under the Gibson name. Gibson also offers instruments under the Epiphone, Kramer, Steinberger, Dobro, Tobias, Valley Arts, Slingerland (drums), Baldwin (pianos), Trace Elliot, Electar (amps), Maestro, Gibson Labs, Oberheim, and Echoplex brandnames.

Founded in Kalamazoo, Michigan by Orville Gibson, a musician and luthier who developed instruments with tops, sides and backs carved out of solid pieces of wood. Early instruments included mandolins, archtop guitars and harp guitars. By 1896 Gibson had opened a shop. In 1902 Gibson was bought out by a group of investors who incorporated the business as Gibson Mandolin-Guitar Manufacturing Company, Limited. The company was purchased by Chicago Musical Instrument Company (CMI) in '44. In '57 CMI also purchased the Epiphone guitar company, transferring production from Philadelphia to the Gibson plant in Kalamazoo. Gibson was purchased by Norlin in late-'69 and a new factory was opened in Nashville, Tennessee in '74. The Kalamazoo factory ceased production in '84. In '85, Gibson was sold to a group headed by Henry Juskewiscz. Gibson purchased the Flatiron Company in '87 and built a new factory in '89, moving acoustic instrument production to Bozeman, Montana.

The various models of Firebirds, Les Pauls, and SGs are grouped together under those general headings. Custom Shop and Historic instruments are listed with their respective main model (for example, the '39 Super 400 Historical Collection model is listed with the Super 400s).

335 S Custom

1980-1981. Solidbody, 335-shaped, mahogany body, unbound rosewood 'board, 2 exposed Dirty Finger humbuckers, coil-tap, TP-6 tailpiece.

1980-1981	Sunburst	$700	$900

335 S Deluxe

1980-1982. Same as 335 S Custom but with bound ebony 'board, brass nut.

1980-1982	Cherry	$700	$900
1980-1982	Silverburst	$800	$1,100
1980-1982	Sunburst	$700	$900

335 S Standard

1980-1981. Solidbody, 335-shaped, maple body and neck, 2 exposed split-coil humbuckers, stop tailpiece, no coil-tap, unbound 'board.

1980-1981	Sunburst	$650	$750

Advanced Jumbo

1936-1940. Dreadnought, 16" wide, round shoulders, Brazilian rosewood back and sides, Sunburst. Reintroduced 1990-1997.

1936-1937		$35,000	$40,000
1938-1940		$32,000	$40,000

Advance Jumbo (reissue)

1990-1999, 2001-present. Issued as a standard production model, but soon available only as a special order for most of the '90s; currently offered as standard production. Renamed 1936 Advanced Jumbo for 1997-1998. There were also some limited-edition AJs offered during the '90s.

1990-1999		$1,600	$2,000
2001-2002	Reintroduced	$1,700	$1,900

B-15

1967-1971. Mahogany, spruce top, student model. Natural finish.

1967-1971		$500	$650

B-25

1962-1977. Flat-top, mahogany, bound body. Cherry Sunburst (Natural finish is the B-25 N).

1962-1969		$900	$1,000
1970-1977		$500	$800

B-25 3/4

1962-1968. Short-scale version, flat-top, mahogany body. Cherry Sunburst (Natural finish is the B-25 3/4 N).

1962-1968		$450	$550

B-25 N

1962-1977. Flat-top, mahogany, bound body. Natural (Cherry Sunburst finish is the B-25).

1962-1969		$900	$1,000
1970-1977		$500	$800

B-25 N 3/4

1966-1968. Short-scale version, flat-top, mahogany body. Natural (Cherry Sunburst finish is the B-25 3/4).

1966-1968		$450	$550

B-25-12

1962-1970. Flat-top 12-string version, mahogany, bound body. Cherry Sunburst (Natural finish is the B-25-12 N).

1962-1970		$600	$900

B-25-12 N

1962-1977. Flat-top 12-string version, mahogany, bound body. Natural (Cherry Sunburst is the B-25-12).

1962-1969		$800	$900
1970-1977		$450	$750

B-45-12

1961-1979. Flat-top 12-string, mahogany, round shoulders for 1961, square after. Sunburst (Natural finish is the B-45-12 N).

1961-1962	Round shoulders	$1,000	$1,300
1962-1969	Square shoulders	$800	$1,200
1970-1979	Square shoulders	$600	$1,000

Gibson Advanced Jumbo reissue

1981 Gibson 335-S Deluxe

GUITARS

1957 Gibson Barney Kessel

1957 Gibson Byrdland

MODEL YEAR	FEATURES	EXC. COND. LOW	HIGH

B-45-12 Limited Edition

1991-1992. Limited edition reissue with rosewood back and sides. Natural.

1991-1992		$1,200	$1,300

B-45-12 N

1963-1979. Flat-top 12-string, mahogany. Natural (Cherry Sunburst finish is the B-45-12).

1963-1969		$800	$1,200
1970-1979		$600	$1,000

B.B. King Custom

1980-1988. Lucille on peghead, two pickups, multi-bound, gold-plated parts, Vari-tone, Cherry or Ebony. Renamed B.B. King Lucille in 1988.

1980-1988		$1,400	$1,600

B.B. King Lucille

1988-present. Introduced as B.B. King Custom, renamed B.B. King Lucille. Lucille on peghead, two pickups, multi-bound, gold-plated parts, Varitone, Cherry or Ebony.

1988-2001		$1,400	$1,600

B.B. King Standard

1980-1985. Like B.B. King Custom, but with stereo electronics and chrome-plated parts, Cherry or Ebony.

1980-1985		$1,200	$1,400

Barney Kessel Custom

1961-1973. Double cutaway archtop, two humbuckers, Gold hardware. Cherry Sunburst.

1961-1964		$2,800	$3,200
1965-1966		$2,700	$3,100
1967-1969		$2,600	$3,000
1970-1973		$2,400	$2,800

Barney Kessel Regular

1961-1974. Double cutaway archtop, two humbuckers, nickel hardware. Cherry Sunburst.

1961-1964		$2,500	$3,000
1965-1966		$2,400	$2,900
1967-1969		$2,300	$2,800
1970-1973		$2,200	$2,700

Blue Ridge

1968-1979, 1989-1990. Flat-top, dreadnought, laminated rosewood back and sides. Natural finish. Reintroduced for 1989-1990.

1968-1979		$600	$1,000
1989-1990		$600	$1,000

Blue Ridge 12

1970-1978. Flat-top, 12 strings, laminated rosewood back and sides. Natural finish.

1970-1978		$500	$800

Blueshawk

1996-present. Small Les Paul single cutaway-type body with F-holes, two single-coil hum cancelling Blues 90 pickups, six-way Varitone rotary dial.

1996-2002		$500	$600

Byrdland

1955-1992. Thinline archtop, single cutaway (rounded until late-1960, pointed 1960-late-1969, rounded after 1969, rounded or pointed 1998-present), two pickups. Now part of the Historic Collection.

MODEL YEAR	FEATURES	EXC. COND. LOW	HIGH
1956-1957	Natural, P-90s	$9,200	$10,000
1956-1957	Sunburst, P-90s	$7,200	$8,000
1958-1959	Natural, PAFs	$8,500	$11,000
1958-1959	Sunburst, PAFs	$7,500	$9,000
1960-1962	Natural, PAFs	$8,000	$1,000
1960-1962	Sunburst, PAFs	$7,000	$8,000
1963-1964	Natural, Pat #	$7,000	$8,000
1963-1964	Sunburst, Pat #	$6,500	$7,500
1965-1969	Natural	$5,000	$5,500
1965-1969	Sunburst	$4,000	$5,000
1970-1979	Natural	$3,200	$4,800
1970-1979	Various other colors	$2,700	$4,300
1980-1992	Various colors	$3,500	$4,500

Byrdland Historic Collection

Various colors.

1993-2002		$3,500	$4,500

C-0 Classical

1962-1971. Spruce top, mahogany back and sides, bound top. Natural.

1962-1971		$350	$600

C-1 Classical

1957-1971. Spruce top, mahogany back and sides, bound body. Natural.

1957-1971		$400	$700

C-2 Classical

1960-1971. Maple back and sides, bound body. Natural.

1960-1971		$500	$800

C-4 Classical

1962-1968. Maple back and sides. Natural.

1962-1968		$500	$900

C-6 Classical

1958-1971. Rosewood back and sides, Gold hardware, Natural.

1958-1971		$600	$1,000

C-8 Classical

1962-1969. Rosewood back and sides. Natural.

1962-1969		$700	$1,000

CF-100

1950-1958. Flat-top, pointed cutaway, mahogany back and sides, bound body. Sunburst finish.

1950-1958		$1,900	$2,300

CF-100E

1951-1958. CF-100 with a single-coil pickup.

1950-1958		$2,000	$2,500

Challenger I

1983-1985. Single cutaway Les Paul-shaped solidbody, one humbucker pickup, bolt-on maple neck with rosewood fingerboard and dot markers. Silver finish standard.

1983-1985		$375	$400

Challenger II

1983-1985. Single cutaway Les Paul-shaped solidbody, two humbucker pickups, bolt-on maple neck with rosewood fingerboard and dot markers. Various colors.

1983-1985		$400	$425

MODEL YEAR	FEATURES	EXC. COND. LOW	HIGH

Chet Atkins CE

1981-1995. CE stands for 'Classical Electric'. Single cutaway, multi-bound body, rosewood board with standard width nut, Gold hardware, various colors. In 1995, the Atkins CE and CEC were consolidated into one model, the Chet Atkins CE/CEC, with an ebony fingerboard with a standard (CE) and classical (CEC) nut.

1981-1995		$900	$1,000

Chet Atkins CEC

1981-1995. Same as CE but with ebony board and 2" classical width nut, Black or Natural. In 1995, the Atkins CE and CEC were consolidated into one model, the Chet Atkins CE/CEC, with an ebony fingerboard with a standard (CE) and classical (CEC) nut.

1981-1995		$1,100	$1,300

Chet Atkins Country Gentleman

1986-present. Thinline archtop, single rounded cutaway, two humbuckers, multi-bound, Gold hardware, Bigsby. Brown or Red Wine.

1986-1995		$1,900	$2,200

Chet Atkins SST

1987-present. Steel string acoustic/electric solidbody, single cutaway, bridge transducer pickup, active bass and treble controls, gold hardware.

1986-2001		$1,100	$1,300

Chet Atkins SST-12

1990-1994. Similar to 6-string model, mahogany/spruce body, preamp circuit controls single transducer pickup. Natural or Ebony finish.

1990-1994		$1,600	$1,800

Chet Atkins Tennessean

1990-present. Single rounded cutaway archtop, two humbuckers, F-holes, bound body.

1990-1999		$1,500	$1,600

Chicago 35

1994-1995. Flat-top dreadnought, round shoulders, mahogany back and sides, prewar script logo.

1994-1995	Natural, factory electronics	$900	$1,000

Citation

1969-1971. 17" full-depth body, single cut archtop, 1 or 2 floating pickups, fancy inlay, natural or sunburst. Only 8 shipped for '69-'71. Reissued the first time '79-'83 and as part of the Historic Collection in '93.

1969-1971		$15,000	$24,000

Citation (1st reissue)

1979-1983. Reissue of 1969-'71 model. Reintroduced in '93 as part of Gibson's Historic Collection.

1979-1983		$15,000	$20,000

Citation (2nd reissue)

1993-present. Limited production via Gibson's Historic Collection. Natural or Sunburst.

1994-1999		$13,000	$14,000

MODEL YEAR	FEATURES	EXC. COND. LOW	HIGH

Corvus I

1982-1984. Odd-shaped solidbody with offset V-type cut, bolt maple neck, rosewood 'board, 1 humbucker. Standard finish was Silver Gloss, but others available at an additional cost.

1982-1984		$350	$450

Corvus II

1982-1984. Same as Corvus I, but with 2 humbuckers, 2 volume controls, 1 master tone control.

1982-1984		$400	$500

Corvus III

1982-1984. Same as Corvus I, but with 3 single-coil pickups, master volume and tone control, 5-way switch.

1982-1984		$450	$550

Country-Western

1956-1978. Flat-top, Natural finish version of SJ, round shoulders 1956-1962, square shoulders after that. Called the SJN in 1960 and 1961, the SJN Country Western after that.

1956-1959	Round shoulders	$2,400	$3,000
1960-1964	Round shoulders	$2,300	$2,800
1965	Square shoulders	$2,000	$2,400
1966-1969	Square shoulders	$1,800	$2,100
1970	Square shoulders	$1,500	$1,900

Crest Gold

1969-1971. Double cutaway thinline archtop, Brazilian rosewood body, two mini-humbuckers, bound top and headstock, bound F-holes, gold-plated parts.

1969-1971		$2,500	$3,000

Crest Silver

1969-1972. Double cutaway thinline archtop, Brazilian rosewood body, two mini-humbuckers, bound top and headstock, bound F-holes, silver-plated parts.

1969-1972		$2,000	$2,500

Dove

1962-1994. Flat-top acoustic, maple back and sides, square shoulders.

1962-1964	Natural	$3,000	$4,700
1962-1964	Sunburst	$2,700	$3,700
1965	Natural	$2,600	$4,300
1965	Sunburst	$2,200	$3,900
1966	Natural	$2,400	$4,100
1966	Sunburst	$2,000	$3,400
1967	Natural	$2,100	$3,500
1967	Sunburst	$1,900	$3,100
1968	Natural	$2,000	$3,100
1968	Sunburst	$1,800	$2,800
1969	Natural	$1,900	$2,800
1969	Sunburst	$1,700	$2,300
1970	Natural	$1,800	$2,700
1970	Sunburst	$1,700	$2,100
1971	Natural	$1,700	$2,500
1971	Sunburst	$1,600	$2,000
1972	Natural	$1,600	$2,300
1972	Sunburst	$1,500	$1,900
1973	Natural	$1,500	$1,900
1973	Sunburst	$1,400	$1,800

1957 Gibson C-2

1984 Gibson Corvus

1979 Gibson Dove

1960s Gibson EMS-1235

MODEL YEAR	FEATURES	EXC. COND. LOW	HIGH
1974-1979	Sunburst, black, nat	$1,400	$1,700
1980-1989	Sunburst, black, nat	$1,200	$1,500
1990-1999	Sunburst, natural	$1,100	$1,400

Dove "Dove In Flight" (Custom Shop)

1996-1998		$2,500	$2,900

Dove Commemorative

1994-1996. Natural.

1994		$1,500	$2,000

EAS Deluxe

1992-1994. Single cutaway flat-top acoustic/electric, solid flamed maple top, three-band EQ.

1993	Vintage Cherry Sunburst	$850	$950

EBS(F)-1250 Double Bass

1962-1970. Double cutaway SG-type solidbody, doubleneck with bass and six-string. Originally introduced as the EBSF-1250 because of a built-in fuzztone, which was later deleted. Only 22 made.

1962-1964		$7,000	$9,000
1965-1966		$5,000	$7,000
1967-1969		$4,500	$6,000
1970		$3,500	$5,000

EDS-1275 Double 12

1958-1968, 1977-1990. Double cut doubleneck with one 12- and one six-string. Thinline hollowbody until late-'62, SG-style solidbody '62 on.

1958-1959	Black, Cherry or White	$14,000	$18,000
1958-1959	Sunburst	$11,000	$13,000
1960-1962	Black, Cherry, or White	$13,000	$17,000
1960-1962	Sunburst	$10,000	$12,000
1968	Black, Sunburst, or White	$5,000	$6,000
1968	Jimmy Page exact specs	$6,000	$12,000
1977-1979	Sunburst, Walnut, or White	$1,600	$2,600
1980-1989	Sunburst, Walnut, or White	$1,500	$2,200
1990-1994	Sunburst, Walnut, or White	$1,500	$2,100
1995-2000	Various colors	$1,500	$2,000

EDS-1275 Double 12 (Historic Collection)

1991-1994. Historic Collection reissue.

1991-1994	White	$1,800	$2,100

EDS-1275 Double 12 Centennial

1994. Guitar of the Month (May), Gold medallion on back of headstock, Gold hardware.

1994	Cherry	$1,800	$2,100

EMS-1235 Double Mandolin

1958-1968. Double cutaway, doubleneck with one regular six-string and one short six-string (the mandolin neck). Thinline hollowbody until late-1962, SG-style solidbody 1962-1968. Black, Sunburst or White. Total of 61 shipped.

1958-1961		$10,000	$13,000
1962-1964		$6,000	$9,500
1965-1968		$4,500	$5,000

ES-5

1949-1955. Single cutaway archtop, three P-90 pickups. Renamed ES-5 Switchmaster in 1955.

1949-1955	Natural	$5,000	$7,000
1949-1955	Sunburst	$4,500	$6,500

ES-5 Switchmaster

1956-1962. Renamed from ES-5. Single cutaway (rounded until late-'60, pointed after) archtop, 3 P-90s until end of '57, humbuckers after, switchmaster control. The PAF pickups in this model are worth as much as the rest of the guitar. We have listed a non-original '58 with replaced pickups to demonstrate how value is reduced when the original PAFs are removed.

1956-1957	Natural, P-90s	$7,000	$8,000
1956-1957	Sunburst, P-90s	$6,000	$7,000
1957-1960	Natural, humbuckers	$10,000	$11,000
1957-1960	Sunburst, humbuckers	$9,000	$10,000
1957-1960	Sunburst, non-original pickups	$4,500	$5,500
1960-1962	Pointed Florentine cutaway	$9,000	$10,000

ES-5/ES-5 Switchmaster Custom Shop Historic

1995-2002.

1995-2002	ES-5, P-90s	$2,900	$3,000
1995-2002	Switchmaster, humbuckers	$2,900	$3,000

ES-100

1938-1941. Archtop, one pickup, bound body. Sunburst. Renamed ES-125 in 1941.

1938-1941		$900	$1,200

ES-120 T

1962-1970. Archtop, thinline, one F-hole, bound body, one pickup. Sunburst.

1962-1966		$800	$900
1967-1970		$500	$700

ES-125

1941-1943, 1946-1970. Archtop, non-cutaway, one pickup. Sunburst. Renamed from ES-100.

1941-1943	Renamed from ES-100	$900	$1,200
1946-1964		$900	$1,200
1965-1970		$800	$1,100

ES-125 C

1966-1970. Wide body archtop, single pointed cutaway, 1 pickup, sunburst.

1966-1970		$900	$1,200

ES-125 CD

1966-1970. Wide body archtop, single cutaway, two pickups. Sunburst.

1966-1970		$1,400	$1,600

ES-125 D

1957. Limited production (not mentioned in catalog), two pickup version of thick body ES-125. Sunburst.

1957		$1,300	$1,500

MODEL YEAR	FEATURES	EXC. COND. LOW	HIGH

ES-125 T

1956-1969. Archtop thinline, non-cutaway, one pickup, bound body. Sunburst.

1956-1964		$800	$1,000
1965-1969		$600	$900

ES-125 T 3/4

1957-1970. Archtop thinline, short-scale, non-cutaway, one pickup. Sunburst.

1957-1964		$700	$900
1965-1970		$500	$700

ES-125 TC

1960-1970. Archtop thinline, single pointed cutaway, bound body, one P-90 pickup. Sunburst.

1960-1964		$1,100	$1,500
1965-1970		$1,000	$1,400

ES-125 TD

1957-1963. Archtop thinline, non-cutaway, two pickups. Sunburst.

1957-1963		$1,300	$1,500

ES-125 TDC or ES-125 TCD

1960-1971. Archtop thinline, single pointed cutaway, two P-90 pickups. Sunburst.

1960-1964		$1,500	$1,700
1965-1966		$1,400	$1,600
1966-1971		$1,300	$1,500

ES-130

1954-1956. Archtop, non-cutaway, one pickup, bound body. Sunburst. Renamed ES-135 in 1956.

1954-1956		$1,100	$1,500

ES-135

1956-1958. Renamed from ES-130, non-cut archtop, 1 pickup, sunburst. Name reused on a thin body in the 1990s.

1956-1958		$1,100	$1,500

ES-135 (thinline)

1991-present. Single cut archtop thinline, laminated maple body, available with 2 humbuckers or 2 P-90s, chrome or gold hardware, sunburst.

1991-2002		$800	$1,200

ES-137 Custom (thinline)

2000s. Thinline, single cutaway, Ebony fretboard with split diamond markers, Varitone with two '57 Classic Humbuckers.

2002		$1,300	$1,400

ES-140 (3/4)

1950-1956. Archtop, single cutaway, one pickup, bound body, short-scale.

1950-1956	Natural option	$1,800	$2,500
1950-1956	Sunburst	$1,200	$1,600

ES-140 3/4 T

1957-1968. Archtop thinline, single cutaway, bound body, one pickup, short-scale. Sunburst.

1957-1968		$1,200	$1,600

ES-150

1936-1942, 1946-1956. Historically important archtop, non-cutaway, bound body, Charlie Christian bar pickup from 1936-1939, various metal covered pickups starting in 1940. Sunburst.

1936-1939	Charlie Christian pickup	$4,300	$5,000
1940-1942	Metal covered pickup	$3,000	$3,700
1946-1956	P-90 pickup	$1,500	$1,800

ES-150 DC

1969-1975. Archtop, double rounded cutaway, two humbuckers, multi-bound.

1969-1975	Cherry or Walnut	$1,900	$2,100
1969-1975	Natural	$2,100	$2,500

ES-165 Herb Ellis Model

1991-present. Single pointed cutaway hollowbody, one humbucker, gold hardware. Cherry, Ebony or Sunburst.

1991-1995		$1,500	$1,700

ES-175

1949-1971. Archtop, single pointed cutaway, one pickup (P-90 from 1949-early-1957, humbucker early-1957-1971), multi-bound.

1949-1953	Natural	$3,100	$3,600
1950-1952	Sunburst	$2,800	$3,300
1953	Sunburst	$2,600	$3,100
1954	Natural	$3,000	$3,500
1954	Sunburst	$2,500	$2,900
1955	Natural	$2,900	$3,400
1955-1956	Sunburst, P-90	$2,300	$2,700
1957-1959	Natural, humbucker	$4,700	$5,600
1957-1959	Sunburst, humbucker	$3,900	$4,700
1960	Sunburst	$3,700	$4,500
1961	Sunburst	$3,500	$4,300
1962	Sunburst	$3,400	$4,200
1963	Sunburst	$3,300	$4,100
1964	Sunburst	$3,200	$3,900
1965	Sunburst	$3,000	$3,700
1966	Natural	$3,200	$4,000
1966	Sunburst	$2,900	$3,500
1967	Natural	$3,000	$3,800
1967	Sunburst	$2,900	$3,400
1968-1969	Sunburst	$2,800	$3,300
1970	Sunburst	$2,400	$3,200
1971	Natural	$2,000	$3,000
1971	Sunburst	$2,000	$2,900

ES-175 CC

1978-1979. Archtop, single cutaway, one Charlie Christian pickup. Sunburst or Walnut.

1978-1979		$2,100	$2,500

ES-175 D

1951-present. Archtop, single cutaway, two pickups (P-90s from 1953-early-1957, humbuckers early-1957 on). Cataloged as the ES-175 Reissue since '91.

1952-1956	Natural	$4,000	$4,900
1952-1956	Sunburst	$3,000	$3,900
1957-1959	Natural, humbuckers	$5,100	$6,100
1957-1959	Sunburst, humbuckers	$4,400	$5,300
1960	Natural	$4,800	$5,800
1960	Sunburst	$4,100	$5,200
1961	Natural	$4,700	$5,700

Gibson ES-125

1959 Gibson ES-175

1958 Gibson ES-175N

1958 Gibson ES-295

MODEL YEAR	FEATURES	EXC. COND. LOW	HIGH
1961	Sunburst	$4,000	$5,100
1962	Natural	$4,600	$5,600
1962	Sunburst	$3,900	$5,000
1963	Sunburst	$3,800	$4,800
1964	Sunburst	$3,700	$4,700
1965	Sunburst	$3,500	$4,200
1966	Natural	$3,500	$4,400
1966	Sunburst	$3,500	$4,100
1967	Natural	$3,000	$3,800
1967	Sunburst	$3,100	$3,700
1967	Walnut	$3,100	$3,700
1967-1968	Sparkling Burgundy	$3,300	$3,800
1968	Black	$3,100	$3,700
1968	Natural	$3,100	$3,700
1968	Sunburst	$2,900	$3,500
1969	Sunburst	$2,900	$3,400
1969	Walnut	$2,800	$3,300
1970	Natural	$2,800	$3,300
1970	Sunburst	$2,600	$3,100
1971	Sunburst	$2,500	$3,000
1972	Natural	$2,600	$3,100
1972	Sunburst	$2,200	$2,900
1973	Natural, sunburst	$2,000	$2,500
1974-1976	Natural, sunburst	$1,900	$2,400
1977-1981	Natural, sunburst	$1,800	$2,400
1979	Wine Red	$1,800	$2,400
1980	Black	$1,800	$2,400
1980-1981	Walnut	$1,800	$2,400
1982-1984	Natural, sunburst	$1,700	$2,300
1985-1986	All finishes	$1,600	$2,200
1987-1988	All finishes	$1,500	$2,100
1988	White, Gold hardware	$1,700	$2,200
1989	Sunburst	$1,600	$2,100
1990	Natural	$1,600	$2,100
1990	Sunburst	$1,600	$2,000
1991	White, Gold hardware	$1,600	$2,200
1994-1996	Natural, sunburst	$1,600	$2,000
1998	Natural, flamed maple	$2,000	$2,500
1998	Sunburst, flamed maple	$1,800	$2,000
1999		$1,800	$2,300

ES-175 T

1976-1980. Archtop thinline, single pointed cutaway, two humbuckers. Various colors.

1976-1980		$1,800	$2,400

ES-225 T

1955-1959. Thinline, single pointed cutaway, one P-90 pickup, bound body and neck.

1955-1959	Natural	$1,800	$2,100
1955-1959	Sunburst	$1,600	$1,900

ES-225 TD

1956-1959. Thinline, single cutaway, two P-90s, bound body and neck.

1955-1959	Natural	$2,000	$2,300
1955-1959	Sunburst	$1,900	$2,100

ES-250

1939-1940. Archtop, carved top, special Christian pickup, multi-bound, high-end appointments.

1939-1940	Natural	$5,500	$6,500

ES-295

1952-1958. Single pointed cutaway archtop, 2 pickups (P-90s from 1952-late-1958, humbuckers after), gold finish, gold-plated hardware.

1952-1957	P-90 pickups	$4,300	$5,700
1957-1958	Humbuckers	$8,000	$10,000

ES-295 (reissue)

1990-1993. Reissue of ES-295, gold finish, 2 P-90 pickups, Bigsby.

1990-1993		$2,100	$2,300

ES-295 '52 Historic Collection

1993-2000. Higher end reissue of 1952 ES-295. Antique Gold finish, 2 P-90 pickups, Bigsby.

1994-1995		$2,200	$2,600

ES-300

1940-1942, 1945-1953. Archtop, non-cutaway, F-holes, had four pickup configurations during its run. Sunburst.

1940-1942	One pickup	$2,400	$2,600
1945-1948	One pickup	$2,400	$2,600
1949-1953	Two pickups	$2,500	$3,000

ES-320 TD

1971-1974. Thinline archtop, double cutaway, two single-coil pickups, bound body. Cherry, Natural, or Walnut finish.

1971-1974		$900	$1,100

ES-325 TD

1972-1978. Thinline archtop, double cutaway, two mini-humbuckers, one F-hole, bound body. Cherry or Walnut.

1972-1978		$1,000	$1,100

ES-330 T (single pickup)

1959-1963. Double rounded cutaway, thinline, 1 pickup, bound body and neck. In the '60s came with either an original semi-hard case (better than chip board) or a hardshell case. Prices quoted are for hardshell case; approximately $100 should be deducted for the semi-hard case.

1959-1961	Natural	$2,200	$2,800
1959-1961	Sunburst	$2,000	$2,600
1962-1963	Sunburst or cherry	$1,800	$2,100

ES-330 TD (two pickups)

1959-1972. Double rounded cutaway, thinline, 2 pickups, bound body and neck. In the '60s came with either an original semi-hard case (better than chip board) or a hardshell case. Prices noted for the hardshell case; approximately $100 should be deducted for the semi-hard case.

1959-1961	Natural	$3,000	$3,500
1959-1961	Sunburst	$2,800	$3,000
1962-1964	Sunburst or cherry	$2,300	$2,700
1965-1969	Sunburst or cherry	$1,800	$2,500
1967-1969	Burgundy Metallic	$2,200	$2,600
1969-1972	Walnut	$1,500	$2,100
1970-1972	Sunburst or cherry	$1,500	$1,800

GUITARS

MODEL YEAR	FEATURES	EXC. COND. LOW	HIGH

ES-335 TD

1958-1981. The original design ES-335 has dot fingerboard inlays and a stop tailpiece. In mid-1962, block inlays replaced the dots. In late-'64, the stop tailpiece was replaced with a trapeze tailpiece. The ES-335 TD was replaced by the ES-335 DOT in '81.

MODEL YEAR	FEATURES	EXC. COND. LOW	HIGH
1958	Natural, unbound neck	$30,000	$35,000
1958	Sunburst, bound neck	$20,000	$25,000
1958	Sunburst, unbound neck	$20,000	$30,000
1959	Natural, bound board	$30,000	$35,000
1959	Sunburst, bound board	$18,000	$25,000
1959	Sunburst, factory Bigsby	$14,000	$17,000
1960	Cherry, factory Bigsby	$13,000	$14,000
1960	Cherry, factory stop tail	$17,000	$19,000
1960	Natural	$28,000	$34,000
1960	Natural, factory Bigsby	$24,000	$29,000
1960	Sunburst, factory Bigsby	$13,000	$14,000
1960	Sunburst, factory stop tail	$16,000	$19,000
1961	Cherry, factory Bigsby	$12,500	$13,500
1961	Cherry, factory stop tail	$15,500	$18,500
1961	Sunburst, factory Bigsby	$12,500	$13,500
1961	Sunburst, factory stop tail	$15,500	$18,500
1962	Cherry, blocks, PAFs	$9,000	$10,000
1962	Cherry, blocks, pat. pickups	$8,000	$8,500
1962	Cherry, dots, PAFs	$9,500	$10,500
1962	Cherry, dots, pat. pickups	$8,250	$9,250
1962	Sunburst, blocks, PAFs	$9,000	$10,000
1962	Sunburst, blocks, pat. pickups	$8,000	$8,500
1962	Sunburst, dots, PAFs	$9,500	$10,500
1962	Sunburst, dots, pat. pickups	$8,250	$9,250
1963	Cherry or Sunburst	$8,000	$8,500
1963	Sunburst, factory Bigsby	$6,000	$6,500
1964	Cherry	$7,000	$8,000
1964	Cherry, factory Bigsby	$6,000	$7,000
1964	Cherry, with Maestro	$6,000	$7,000
1964	Sunburst	$8,000	$8,500
1964	Sunburst, factory bigsby	$7,000	$7,500
1964	Sunburst, with Maestro	$6,000	$7,000
1965	Cherry, trapeze tailpiece	$3,800	$4,800
1965	Cherry, with Maestro	$4,500	$5,000
1965	Sunburst, trapeze tailpiece	$4,000	$5,000
1966	Burgundy Metallic	$4,300	$5,000
1966	Cherry or Sunburst	$3,300	$4,000
1966	Pelham Blue (unfaded)	$4,500	$6,000
1967	Burgundy Metallic	$4,000	$4,700
1967	Cherry or Sunburst	$3,200	$3,800
1967	Walnut	$2,900	$3,400
1968	Black or Burgundy Metallic	$3,300	$3,800
1968	Cherry or Sunburst	$3,100	$3,500
1968	Walnut	$2,700	$3,100
1969	Cherry or Sunburst	$2,800	$3,200
1969	Walnut	$2,600	$2,800
1970	Cherry or Sunburst	$2,500	$2,700
1970	Walnut	$2,400	$2,600
1971	Various colors	$2,100	$2,500
1972-1973	Various colors	$2,000	$2,400
1974-1975	Various colors	$1,900	$2,300
1976	Various colors	$1,700	$2,200
1977	Various colors, coil tap	$1,600	$2,100
1978	Various colors	$1,500	$2,000
1979	Various colors	$1,400	$1,900
1980-1981	Various colors	$1,300	$1,800

ES-335 Dot

1981-1990. Reissue of 1960 ES-335 and replaces ES-335 TD. Now called the ES-335 Reissue.

MODEL YEAR	FEATURES	EXC. COND. LOW	HIGH
1982-1990	Black, Cherry, Sunburst, White	$1,700	$2,000
1982-1990	Natural Blond	$1,800	$2,100
1986-1990	Highly figured wood	$2,300	$2,500

ES-335 Dot CMT

1983-1985. Custom Shop ES-335 Dot with curly maple top and back, full-length center block, Gold hardware. Various colors.

MODEL YEAR	FEATURES	EXC. COND. LOW	HIGH
1983-1985		$2,000	$2,500

ES-335 Reissue

1991-present. Continuation of the ES-335 DOT and TD. A block inlay version, called the ES-335 Block, is also currently available. Black, Cherry, Natural Blond, Sunburst or White.

MODEL YEAR	FEATURES	EXC. COND. LOW	HIGH
1991-1999	Natural Blond	$1,700	$2,000
1991-2001	Other colors	$1,600	$1,900

1968 Gibson ES-330

1966 Gibson ES-335TD

GUITARS

1960s Gibson ES-335-12

1960 Gibson ES-345TD

MODEL YEAR	FEATURES	EXC. COND. LOW	HIGH

ES-335-12

1965-1971. Twelve-string version of the 335.

1965-1966	Cherry or Sunburst	$2,000	$2,300
1967-1969	Burgundy Metallic, Cherry or Sunburst	$1,700	$2,000

ES-335 '59 Historic Collection

Historical Series based upon 1959 ES-335 dot neck, figured maple top, nickel hardware, replica Orange label. Cherry.

1998		$2,500	$2,600

ES-335 '63 Historic Collection

Historical Series based upon 1962 ES-335 with small block markers, maple top, nickel hardware, replica Orange label. Cherry.

2000-2001		$2,000	$2,300

ES-335 Centennial

1994. Centennial edition, Gold medallion in headstock, diamond inlay in tailpiece. Cherry.

1994		$4,000	$4,500

ES-335 Custom Shop

1980s-1990s. Gibson Custom Shop logo on the back of the headstock.

1984	White, Gold hardware, 1984 only	$1,700	$1,900
1994	Blue Sparkle, dot neck	$2,200	$2,500

ES-335 TD CRR

1979. Country Rock Regular, a 335 with two stereo pickups, coil-tap. Sunburst.

1979		$1,400	$1,900

ES-335 Pro

1979-1981. Two humbucking pickups with exposed coils, bound fingerboard. Cherry or Sunburst.

1979-1981		$1,200	$1,400

ES-335 Showcase Edition

1988. Guitar of the Month series, limited production, Transparent White/Beige finish, Black gothic-style hardware, EMG pickups.

1988		$1,400	$1,500

ES-335 Studio

1986-1991. No F-holes, two Dirty Fingers humbucking pickups, bound body. Cherry or Ebony.

1986-1991		$1,200	$1,400

ES-340 TD

1968-1973. The 335 with a laminated maple neck, master volume and mixer controls.

1968	Natural	$2,400	$2,700
1969	Natural	$2,200	$2,500
1969	Walnut	$2,000	$2,300
1970	Natural	$1,900	$2,200
1970	Walnut	$1,800	$2,100
1971	Walnut	$1,700	$2,000
1972	Natural	$1,900	$2,200
1972	Walnut	$1,700	$2,000

ES-345 TD

1959-1983. The 335 with Vari-tone, stereo, two humbuckers, Gold hardware, double parallelogram inlays, stop tailpiece 1959-1964 and 1982-1983, trapeze tailpiece 1965-1982.

1959-1960	Natural	$18,000	$22,000
1959-1961	Cherry or sunburst	$8,000	$10,000
1962-1964	Cherry or sunburst	$5,500	$6,000
1962-1964	Sunburst, factory Bigsby	$4,500	$5,000
1965-1967	Burgundy Metallic	$3,200	$4,200
1965-1967	Sunburst or cherry	$3,000	$4,000
1968	Cherry	$2,600	$3,000
1968	Sunburst	$2,700	$3,100
1968	Walnut	$2,600	$2,900
1969	Sunburst	$2,500	$2,900
1969	Walnut	$2,300	$2,700
1970	Sunburst or cherry	$2,200	$2,700
1970	Walnut	$2,200	$2,500
1971	Sunburst or cherry	$2,100	$2,400
1972-1976	Various colors	$1,900	$2,200
1977	Various colors	$1,800	$2,100
1978	Various colors	$1,700	$2,100
1979-1981	Various colors	$1,600	$2,000

ES-347 TD/ES-347 S

1978-1993. A 335-style with Gold hardware, tune-o-matic bridge, two Spotlight double-coil pickups, coil-tap switch, bound body and neck. Name changed to ES-347S in 1987.

1978-1986		$1,500	$1,900
1987-1993	ES-347 S	$1,500	$1,900

ES-350

1947-1956. Originally the ES-350 Premier, full body archtop, single cutaway, one P-90 pickup until end of 1948, two afterwards.

1947-1956	Natural	$4,000	$5,500
1947-1956	Sunburst	$3,500	$5,000

ES-350 T

1955-1963. McCarty era, called the ES-350 TD in early-1960s. Thinline archtop, single cutaway (round 1955-1960 and 1977-1981, pointed 1961-1963), two P-90 pickups 1955-1956, humbuckers after, Gold hardware.

1956	Natural, two P-90s	$4,500	$5,500
1956	Sunburst, two P-90s	$4,000	$5,000
1957-1959	Natural, humbuckers	$6,000	$7,000
1957-1959	Sunburst, humbuckers	$5,500	$6,500
1960-1963	Natural	$5,000	$6,000
1960-1963	Sunburst	$4,500	$5,500

ES-350 T (2nd issue)

1977-1981. Norlin era, second issue of ES-350 T.

1977-1981	Natural	$3,000	$4,000
1977-1981	Sunburst	$2,700	$3,700

MODEL YEAR	FEATURES	EXC. COND. LOW	HIGH

ES-355 Centennial

1994. Custom Shop guitar of the month in June 1994, high-end custom appointments, gold-plated hardware. Sunburst.

1994	Sunburst	$4,000	$4,500

ES-355 TD

1958-1970. A 335-style with large block inlays, multi-bound body and headstock, two humbuckers. The 355 model was standard with a Bigsby, Sideways or Maestro vibrato. Non-vibrato models were an option. The prices shown assume a vibrato tailpiece. A factory stop tailpiece was considered an advantage and will fetch more. Early examples have factory Bigsby vibratos, early '60s have sideways vibratos, and late '60s have Maestro vibratos. Cherry finish was the standard finish.

1958-1962	Cherry, PAFs	$8,000	$10,000
1963-1964	Cherry, pat # pickups	$5,500	$6,000
1965-1967	Cherry	$4,000	$5,000
1965-1967	Sparkling Burgundy	$4,500	$5,500
1965-1967	Sunburst	$4,000	$5,000
1968-1969	Cherry	$3,500	$4,000
1969	Walnut	$3,300	$3,800

ES-355 TDSV

1959-1982. Stereo version of ES-335 with Vari-tone switch. A mono version was available but few were made. The 355 model was standard with a Bigsby, Sideways or Maestro vibrato. Non-vibrato models were an option. The prices shown assume a vibrato tailpiece. A factory stop tailpiece was considered an advantage and will fetch more. Early examples have factory Bigsby vibratos, early-'60s have Sideways vibratos and late-'60s have Maestro vibratos. Cherry finish was standard; Walnut became available in 1969.

1959-1960	Bigsby	$6,500	$9,000
1961-1962	Sideways, late PAFs	$6,000	$8,000
1963-1964	Maestro, pat # pickups	$5,000	$7,000
1965		$4,000	$6,000
1966		$3,000	$5,000
1967-1969	Maestro '67-'68, Bigsby '69	$2,500	$4,300
1970-1979	Bigsby	$2,300	$3,000

ES-369

1982. A 335-style with two exposed humbucker pickups, coil-tap. Sunburst.

1982		$1,300	$1,700

ES-775

1990-1993. Single cut hollowbody, 2 humbuckers, gold hardware. Ebony, natural or sunburst.

1990-1993		$2,600	$2,800

ES-Artist

1979-1985. A 335-style double cutaway thinline, semi-hollowbody, no F-holes, with two humbuckers, active electronics, Gold hardware. Ebony, Fireburst or Sunburst.

1979-1985		$1,400	$2,400

MODEL YEAR	FEATURES	EXC. COND. LOW	HIGH

EST-150

1937-1940. Tenor version of ES-150. Renamed ETG-150 in 1940. Sunburst.

1937-1940		$1,000	$1,400

ETG-150

1940-1942, 1947-1971. Renamed from EST-150. Tenor version of ES-150, one pickup. Sunburst.

1947-1971		$1,000	$1,400

Everly Brothers

1962-1972. Jumbo flat-top, huge double pickguard, star inlays. Natural is optional in 1963 and becomes the standard color in 1968. Reintroduced as the J-180 Everly Brothers in 1986.

1962-1964	Black	$8,000	$8,500
1963	Natural option	$8,000	$8,500
1965-1967	Black	$5,000	$5,500
1968-1969	Natural replaces Black	$3,000	$3,300
1970-1972	Natural	$2,800	$3,100

Explorer

1958-1959, 1963. Some 1958s shipped in 1963. Korina body, two humbuckers. The Explorer market is a very specialized and very small market, with few genuine examples available and a limited number of high-end buyers. The Explorer and Flying V markets are similar in that respect. The slightest change to the original specifications can mean a significant drop in value. The narrow price ranges noted are for all original, untouched examples that have the original guitar case and a strong verifiable provenance.

1958-1959		$120,000	$125,000
1963		$90,000	$100,000

Explorer (Mahogany body)

1976-1982. Mahogany body, two humbucking pickups.

1976-1982		$1,400	$1,600

Explorer (Alder body)

1983-1989. Alder body, two humbuckers, maple neck, ebony fingerboard, dot inlays, triangle knob pattern. Referred to as Explorer 83 in 1983.

1983-1989	Custom color limited runs	$1,000	$1,400
1983-1989	Standard finishes	$650	$1,000

Explorer '76/X-plorer

1990-present. Mahogany body and neck, rosewood fingerboard, dot inlays, two humbucking pickups. Name changed to X-plorer in 2002.

1990-1999	Standard finish	$850	$900
1998	Sunburst or Natural limited run	$900	$1,200

Explorer (Limited Edition Korina)

1976. Limited edition korina body replaces standard mahogany body. Natural.

1976		$1,900	$2,500

Explorer 90 Double

1989-1990. Mahogany body and neck, one single-coil and one humbucker, strings-through-body.

1989-1990		$800	$1,000

1963 Gibson Everly Brothers

1958 Gibson Explorer

1963 Gibson Firebird I

Gibson Firebird V

Explorer Centennial

1994 only. Les Paul Gold finish, 100 year banner inlay at 12th fret, diamonds in headstock and gold-plated knobs, Gibson coin in rear of headstock. Only 100 made.

MODEL YEAR	FEATURES	EXC. COND. LOW	HIGH
1994		$3,500	$3,800

Explorer CMT/The Explorer

1981-1984. Maple body, exposed-coil pickups, TP-6 tailpiece.

MODEL YEAR	FEATURES	EXC. COND. LOW	HIGH
1981-1984		$800	$1,300

Explorer Gothic

1998-2003. Gothic Series with black finish and hardware.

MODEL YEAR	FEATURES	EXC. COND. LOW	HIGH
1998-2003		$800	$950

Explorer Heritage

1983. Reissue of 1958 Explorer, Korina body, Gold hardware, inked serial number, only 100 made.

MODEL YEAR	FEATURES	EXC. COND. LOW	HIGH
1983	Black	$2,400	$2,600
1983	Gold	$2,400	$2,600
1983	Natural	$2,800	$3,000
1983	White	$2,400	$2,600

Explorer II (E/2)

1979-1983. Five-piece maple and walnut laminate body sculptured like V II, ebony fingerboard with dot inlays, two humbucking pickups, gold-plated hardware. Natural finish.

MODEL YEAR	FEATURES	EXC. COND. LOW	HIGH
1979-1983		$750	$1,000
1979-1983	Figured maple top option	$1,000	$1,200

Explorer III

1984-1985. Alder body, three P-90 pickups, two control knobs.

MODEL YEAR	FEATURES	EXC. COND. LOW	HIGH
1984-1985	Chrome hardware	$650	$950
1984-1985	Chrome hardware, locking trem	$600	$800
1985	Black hardware, Kahler	$650	$850

Explorer Korina

1982-1984. Korina body and neck, two humbucking pickups, gold hardware, standard eight-digit serial (versus the inked serial number on the Heritage Explorer of the same era).

MODEL YEAR	FEATURES	EXC. COND. LOW	HIGH
1982-1984		$2,500	$2,700

F-25 Folksinger

1963-1971. 14-1/2" flat-top, mahogany body, most have double white pickguard. Natural.

MODEL YEAR	FEATURES	EXC. COND. LOW	HIGH
1963-1964		$950	$1,100
1965-1969		$750	$950
1970-1971		$700	$950

Firebird I

1963-1969. Reverse body and one humbucking pickup 1963-mid-1965, non-reversed body and two P-90 pickups mid-1965-1969.

MODEL YEAR	FEATURES	EXC. COND. LOW	HIGH
1963	Sunburst, reverse	$4,000	$6,000
1964	Cardinal Red, reverse	$4,300	$6,500
1964	Sunburst, reverse	$3,000	$5,000
1965	Cardinal Red, reverse	$4,200	$6,400
1965	Golden Mist, non-reverse	$2,500	$4,000
1965	Sunburst, non-reverse	$1,900	$3,200
1965	Sunburst, reverse	$2,800	$4,700
1966	Sunburst, non-reverse	$1,800	$3,100
1967	Sunburst, non-reverse	$1,700	$3,000
1968	Sunburst, non-reverse	$1,600	$2,900
1969	Sunburst, non-reverse	$1,500	$2,800

Firebird I 1963 Reissue Historic Collection

1999-present. Neck-through, reverse body, Firebird logo on pickguard.

MODEL YEAR	FEATURES	EXC. COND. LOW	HIGH
1999	Sunburst	$1,500	$1,600
2002	Blue Swirl limited edition	$1,800	$2,200

Firebird I Custom Shop

1991-1992. Limited run from Custom Shop, reverse body, one pickup, gold-plated. Sunburst.

MODEL YEAR	FEATURES	EXC. COND. LOW	HIGH
1991		$1,400	$1,500

Firebird II/Firebird 2

1981-1982. Maple body with figured maple top, 2 full size active humbuckers, TP-6 tailpiece.

MODEL YEAR	FEATURES	EXC. COND. LOW	HIGH
1981-1982		$800	$1,300

Firebird III

1963-1969. Reverse body and two humbucking pickups 1963-mid-1965, non-reversed body and three P-90 pickups mid-1965-1969.

MODEL YEAR	FEATURES	EXC. COND. LOW	HIGH
1963	Cardinal Red	$6,500	$8,000
1963	Golden Mist	$6,500	$8,000
1963	Polaris White	$6,500	$8,000
1963	Sunburst	$4,500	$6,500
1964	Cardinal Red, reverse	$5,000	$8,500
1964	Polaris White, reverse	$5,000	$8,500
1964	Sunburst, reverse	$3,500	$6,000
1965	Frost Blue, reverse	$5,000	$8,500
1965	Inverness Green, non-reverse	$4,000	$6,500
1965	Sunburst, non-reverse	$2,500	$3,500
1965	Sunburst, reverse	$3,000	$5,000
1966	Sunburst, non-reverse	$2,300	$3,300
1967	Frost Blue	$2,900	$3,900
1967	Sunburst	$2,200	$3,200
1968	Pelham Blue	$2,800	$3,800

Firebird V

1963-1969,1994-present. Two humbucking pickups, reverse body 1963-mid-1965, non-reversed body mid-1965-1969.

MODEL YEAR	FEATURES	EXC. COND. LOW	HIGH
1963	Pelham Blue	$8,500	$10,000
1963	Sunburst	$6,000	$8,500
1964	Cardinal Red, reverse	$7,000	$9,500
1964	Sunburst, reverse	$5,000	$6,500

MODEL YEAR	FEATURES	EXC. COND. LOW	HIGH
1965	Cardinal Red, reverse	$6,000	$8,500
1965	Sunburst, non-reverse	$3,500	$4,000
1965	Sunburst, reverse	$4,500	$5,500
1966	Sunburst, non-reverse	$3,000	$3,600
1967	Sunburst	$2,500	$3,500
1968	Sunburst	$2,400	$3,400

Firebird V Celebrity Series

1990-1993. Reverse body, Gold hardware, two humbuckers. Various colors.

1990-1993		$1,000	$1,500

Firebird V Guitar Trader Reissue

1982. Guitar Trader commissioned Firebird reissue. Sunburst.

1982		$2,800	$3,200

Firebird V Medallion

1972-1973. Reverse body, 2 humbuckers, Limited Edition medallion mounted on body.

1972-1973		$3,200	$3,800

Firebird V Reissue/Firebird Reissue

1990-present. Based on Firebird V specs, reverse body, several colors available with Cardinal Red optional in 1991.

1990-2002	Various colors	$1,250	$1,300
1991-2002	Cardinal Red option	$1,350	$1,450

Firebird V-12

1966-1967. Non-reverse Firebird V-style body with standard six-on-a-side headstock and split diamond headstock inlay (like ES-335-12 inlay), dot markers, special twin humbucking pickups (like mini-humbuckers).

1966-1967	Custom color	$4,500	$6,000
1966-1967	Sunburst	$3,500	$4,700

Firebird VII

1963-1969. Three humbucking pickups, reverse body 1963-mid-1965, non-reversed body mid-1965-1969. Sunburst standard.

1963		$9,500	$12,500
1964		$9,000	$10,500
1965	Reverse	$8,500	$9,500
1966	Non-reverse	$4,500	$6,500
1967		$4,300	$6,300
1968		$4,200	$6,200
1968	Custom color	$6,000	$8,500

Firebird VII (Historic/Custom Shop)

1997-present. Standard color is Vintage Sunburst.

1997	Frost Blue	$2,400	$2,800
1997-1998	Various colors	$2,300	$2,500

Firebird VII Centennial

1994 only. Headstock medallion. Sunburst.

1994		$4,000	$5,000

Firebird 76

1976-1978. Reverse body, Gold hardware, two pickups.

1976-1978		$1,400	$2,000

Firebird 76/ Firebird I

1980-1982. Reintroduced Firebird 76 but renamed Firebird I.

1980-1982		$1,300	$2,000

FJ-N Jumbo Folk Singer

1963-1967. Square shoulders, jumbo flat-top. Natural finish with Deep Red on back and sides.

1963-1964		$1,100	$1,200
1965-1967		$950	$1,050

Flying V

1958-1959, 1962-1963. Only 81 shipped in '58 and 17 in '59. Guitars made from leftover parts and sold in '62-'63. Natural korina body, string-through-body design.

As with any ultra high-end instrument, each instrument should be evaluated on a case-by-case basis. The Flying V market is a very specialized market, with few untouched examples available, and a limited number of high-end buyers. The Explorer and Flying V markets are similar in that respect. The price ranges noted are for all-original, excellent condition guitars with the original Flying V case. The slightest change to the original specifications can mean a significant drop in value. The narrow price ranges noted are for all original, untouched examples that have the original guitar case and a strong provenance.

1958-1959		$80,000	$85,000

Flying V (Mahogany body)

1966-1967, 1969-1970, 1975-1980. Mahogany body, stud tailpiece.

1966-1967	Cherry or Sunburst	$5,000	$10,000
1969-1970	Cherry or Sunburst	$4,500	$9,000
1975	Various colors	$1,600	$2,400
1976	Various colors	$1,600	$2,300
1979	Silverburst	$2,000	$2,500
1979	Various colors	$1,500	$2,100
1980	Various colors	$1,500	$1,900

Flying V (Mahogany string-through-body)

1981-1982. Mahogany body, string-through-body design. Only 100 made, most in white, some red or black possible.

1981-1982	Black or Red	$1,400	$1,600
1981-1982	White	$1,300	$1,500

Flying V (Korina)/Flying v Heritage

1982-1984. Korina body, strings-through-body design, gold parts. The Heritage V had a letter and three digit serial number; the Flying V Korina had the standard eight-digit number.

1982-1984	Candy Apple Red	$2,000	$2,600
1982-1984	Natural	$2,500	$3,000
1982-1984	White or black	$1,900	$2,500

'67 Flying V/Flying V Reissue

1990-present. Called Flying V Reissue for first year. Mahogany body, stud tailpiece.

1990-1999	Various colors	$850	$900
1993	Cardinal Red custom color	$900	$1,200

1964 Gibson Firebird VII

1958 Gibson Flying V

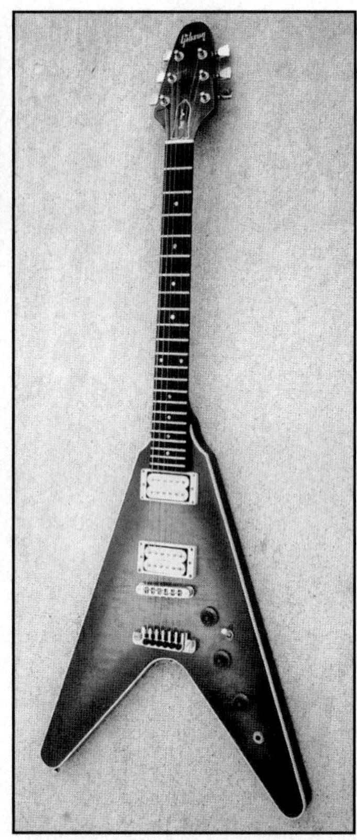

Gibson Flying V CMT

1970s Gibson Heritage

MODEL YEAR	FEATURES	EXC. COND. LOW	HIGH

Flying V 90 Double

1989-1990. Mahogany body, stud tailpiece, one single-coil and one double-coil humbucker, Floyd Rose tremolo. Ebony, Silver or White.

1989-1990		$800	$1,000

Flying V CMT/The V

1981-1985. Maple body with a curly maple top, two pickups, stud tailpiece. Natural or Sunburst.

1981-1985		$800	$1,300

Flying V Gothic

1998-2003. Satin black finish, black hardware, moon and star markers.

1998-2003		$800	$950

Flying V Historic Collection

1991-present. Recreation of the original 1958 Flying V, Gold hardware. Natural korina.

1991-1999		$4,500	$6,000

Flying V I/V 83/Flying V (no pickguard)

1981-1988. Introduced as Flying V I, then renamed Flying V '83 in 1983. Called Flying V from 1984 on. Alder body, two exposed humbuckers, maple neck, ebony fingerboard, dot inlays, Black rings, no pickguard, Ebony or Ivory finish, designed for lower-end market.

1981-1988		$650	$900

Flying V II

1979-1982. Five-piece maple and walnut laminate sculptured body, Ebony fingerboard with dot inlays, two V-shaped pickups (two Dirty Fingers humbuckers towards end of run), gold-plated hardware. Natural.

1979-1982		$1,000	$1,300

Hendrix Hall of Fame Flying V

Late-1991-1993. Limited Edition (400 made), numbered. Black.

1991-1993		$1,700	$1,900

Lonnie Mack Flying V

1993-1994. Mahogany body with Lonnie Mack-style Bigsby vibrato. Cherry.

1993-1994		$2,700	$2,900

Futura

1982-1984. Deep cutout solidbody, two humbucker pickups, Gold hardware. Black, White or Purple.

1982-1984		$500	$900

GB-1

1919-1923. Guitar-banjo, six-string neck, Walnut. Renamed GB-5 in 1923.

1919-1923		$800	$1,200

Gospel

1973-1979. Flat-top, square shoulders, laminated maple back and sides, arched back. Natural.

1973-1979		$800	$1,000

Gospel Reissue

1992-1997. Flat-top, cutaway with laminated mahogany back and sides and arched back. Natural or Sunburst.

1992-1997		$800	$1,000

MODEL YEAR	FEATURES	EXC. COND. LOW	HIGH

GY (Army-Navy)

1918-1921. Slightly arched top and back, low-end budget model.

1918	Sheraton Brown	$950	$1,050

Harley Davidson Limited Edition

1994-1995. Body 16" wide, flat-top, Harley Davidson in script and logo, 1500 sold through Harley dealers.

1994-1995	Black	$2,000	$2,500

Heritage

1965-1982. Flat-top dreadnought, square shoulders, rosewood back and sides (Brazilian until 1967, Indian 1968 on), bound top and back. Natural finish.

1966-1968	Brazilian rosewood	$1,700	$2,000
1968-1982	Indian rosewood	$1,400	$1,600

Heritage-12

1968-1970. Flat-top dreadnought, 12 strings, Indian rosewood back and sides, bound top and back. Natural finish.

1968-1970		$1,300	$1,500

HG-00 (Hawaiian)

1932-1942, 1991-present. Hawaiian version of L-00. 14-3/4" flat-top, mahogany back and sides, bound top, natural.

1937-1942		$1,500	$2,500

HG-20 (Hawaiian)

1929-1933. Hawaiian, 14-1/2" dreadnought-shaped, maple back and sides, round soundhole and 4 F-holes.

1929-1933		$2,000	$2,500

HG-22 (Hawaiian)

1929-1932. Dreadnought, 14 inches, Hawaiian, round soundhole and four F-holes, White paint logo, very small number produced.

1929-1932		$2,500	$2,700

HG-24 (Hawaiian)

1929-1932. 16" Hawaiian, rosewood back and sides, round soundhole plus 4 F-holes, small number produced.

1929-1932		$3,500	$4,500

HG-Century (Hawaiian)

1937-1938. Hawaiian, 14-3/4" L-C Century of Progress.

1937-1938		$2,400	$2,600

Howard Roberts Artist

1976-1980. Full body single cutaway archtop, soundhole, one humbucking pickup, Gold hardware, ebony fingerboard. Various colors.

1976-1980		$2,000	$2,100

Howard Roberts Artist Double Pickup

1979-1980. Two pickup version of HR Artist. Various colors.

1979-1980		$2,200	$2,300

Howard Roberts Custom

1974-1981. Full body single cutaway archtop, soundhole, one humbucking pickup, chrome hardware, rosewood fingerboard. Various colors.

1974-1981		$1,900	$2,000

GUITARS

MODEL YEAR	FEATURES	EXC. COND. LOW	HIGH

Howard Roberts Fusion

1979-1988. Single cutaway, semi-hollowbody, two humbucking pickups, chrome hardware, ebony fingerboard, TP-6 tailpiece, various colors. Renamed Howard Roberts Fusion IIL in 1988.

1979-1988		$1,300	$1,600

Howard Roberts Fusion III

1991-present. Renamed from Howard Roberts Fusion IIL. Same specs except for fingerstyle tailpiece and Gold hardware. Ebony or Sunburst.

1991-1999		$1,400	$1,700

Hummingbird

1960-present. Flat-top acoustic, square shoulders, mahogany back and sides, bound body and neck.

1960	Cherry Sunburst	$3,100	$4,200
1961	Cherry Sunburst	$3,000	$4,100
1962	Cherry Sunburst	$2,900	$4,000
1962	Cherry Sunburst, maple option	$3,000	$4,100
1963	Cherry Sunburst	$2,800	$3,900
1963	Cherry Sunburst, maple option	$2,900	$4,000
1964	Cherry Sunburst	$2,800	$3,800
1965	Cherry Sunburst	$2,700	$3,500
1966	Cherry Sunburst	$2,500	$3,300
1966	Natural	$2,500	$3,300
1967	Cherry Sunburst	$2,200	$3,100
1967	Natural	$2,400	$3,200
1968	Cherry Sunburst	$2,100	$2,700
1968	Natural	$2,200	$3,000
1969	Cherry Sunburst	$1,900	$2,400
1969	Natural	$2,000	$2,500
1970	Cherry Sunburst	$1,200	$2,000
1972	Cherry s/b or nat.	$1,500	$1,800
1973	Cherry s/b or nat.	$1,300	$1,700
1974	Cherry s/b or nat.	$1,000	$1,600
1975	Cherry s/b or nat.	$1,000	$1,500
1976	Cherry s/b or nat.	$900	$1,400
1978	Cherry Sunburst	$900	$1,300
1979	Cherry Sunburst	$900	$1,200
1980-1989	Cherry Sunburst	$1,000	$1,200
1990-2003	Cherry Sunburst	$1,000	$1,500

J-25

1983-1985. Flat-top, laminated spruce top, synthetic semi-round back, Ebony fingerboard. Natural or Sunburst.

1983-1985		$350	$450

J-30

1985-1993. Dreadnought-size flat-top acoustic, mahogany back and sides, Sunburst. Renamed J-30 Montana in 1994.

1985-1993		$1,000	$1,100

J-30 Montana

1994-1997. Renamed from J-30. Dreadnought-size flat-top acoustic, mahogany back and sides. Sunburst.

1994-1997		$1,100	$1,200

MODEL YEAR	FEATURES	EXC. COND. LOW	HIGH

J-40

1971-1982. Dreadnought flat-top, mahogany back and sides. Natural finish.

1971-1982		$1,100	$1,400

J-45

1942-1982, 1984-1993, 1999-present. Dreadnought flat-top, mahogany back and sides, round shoulders until 1968 and 1984 on, square shoulders 1969-1982. Sunburst finish (see J-50 for Natural version) then Natural finish also available in 1990s. Renamed J-45 Western in 1994, renamed Early J-45 in 1997 then renamed J-45 in 1999. The prices noted are for all-original crack free instruments. A single professionally repaired minor crack that is nearly invisible will reduce the value only slightly. Two or more, or unsightly repaired cracks will devalue an otherwise excellent original acoustic instrument. Repaired cracks should be evaluated on a case-by-case basis.

1942	Sunburst, banner logo	$4,200	$4,800
1943	Sunburst, banner logo	$4,100	$4,700
1944	Sunburst, banner logo	$4,000	$4,600
1945	Sunburst, banner logo	$4,000	$4,500
1946	Sunburst, banner logo	$3,800	$4,400
1947	Sunburst	$3,500	$4,300
1948	Sunburst	$3,400	$4,300
1949	Sunburst	$3,300	$4,300
1950	Sunburst	$3,200	$4,300
1951	Sunburst	$3,100	$4,300
1952	Sunburst	$3,000	$4,300
1953	Sunburst	$3,000	$4,100
1954	Sunburst	$2,900	$3,800
1955	Sunburst	$2,900	$3,500
1956	Sunburst	$2,800	$3,400
1957	Sunburst	$2,700	$3,300
1958	Sunburst	$2,600	$3,200
1959	Sunburst	$2,500	$3,100
1960-1962	Sunburst	$2,500	$3,000
1963	Sunburst	$2,400	$2,900
1964	Sunburst	$2,300	$2,800
1965	Sunburst	$2,000	$2,600
1966	Sunburst	$1,900	$2,300
1967	Sunburst	$1,700	$2,100
1968	Black, round shoulders	$1,900	$2,300
1968	Sunburst, round shoulders	$1,600	$2,000
1969	Sunburst, round shoulders	$1,500	$1,900
1969	Sunburst, square shoulders	$1,400	$1,800
1970	Sunburst, square shoulders	$1,300	$1,600
1971	Sunburst	$1,200	$1,600
1972	Sunburst	$1,100	$1,500
1973	Sunburst	$1,000	$1,400

1976 Gibson Howard Roberts

'40s Gibson J-45

GUITARS

1957 Gibson J-45

1973 Gibson J-50 Deluxe

MODEL YEAR	FEATURES	EXC. COND. LOW	HIGH
1974	Sunburst	$900	$1,300
1975-1982	Sunburst	$800	$1,200
1984-1993	Various colors	$800	$1,100

J-45 Buddy Holly Limited Edition

1995. Two hundred fifty made.

1995		$1,600	$1,800

J-45 Celebrity

1985. Acoustic introduced for Gibson's 90th anniversary, spruce top, rosewood back and sides, ebony fingerboard, binding on body and fingerboard. Only 90 made.

1985		$1,400	$1,800

J-45 Western

1994-1997. Previously called J-45. Name changed to Early J-45 in 1997.

1994-1997		$1,200	$1,500

J-45/Early J-45

1997-1999. J-45 model name for 1997 and 1998.

1997-1999		$1,200	$1,500

J-50

1945-1982, 1990-1995, 1998-present. Dreadnought flat-top, mahogany back and sides, round shoulders until 1968, square shoulders after. Natural finish (see J-45 for Sunburst version).

1945		$4,000	$4,500
1946		$3,800	$4,400
1947		$3,500	$4,300
1948		$3,400	$4,300
1949		$3,300	$4,300
1950		$3,200	$4,300
1951		$3,100	$4,300
1952		$3,000	$4,300
1953		$3,000	$4,100
1954		$2,900	$3,800
1955		$2,900	$3,500
1956		$2,800	$3,400
1957		$2,700	$3,300
1958		$2,600	$3,200
1959		$2,500	$3,100
1960-1962		$2,500	$3,000
1963		$2,400	$2,900
1964		$2,300	$2,800
1965		$2,000	$2,600
1966		$1,900	$2,300
1967		$1,700	$2,100
1968	Round shoulders	$1,600	$2,000
1969	Round shoulders	$1,500	$1,900
1969	Square shoulders	$1,400	$1,800
1970	Square shoulders	$1,300	$1,600
1971		$1,200	$1,600
1972		$1,100	$1,500
1973		$1,000	$1,400
1974		$900	$1,300
1975-1982		$800	$1,200
1990-1995		$800	$1,100
1998-2001		$1,200	$1,500

J-55 (Jumbo 55) Limited Edition

1994 only. Sixteen inch flat-top, spruce top, mahogany back and sides, 100 made. Sunburst.

1994		$1,700	$1,900

J-55 (reintroduced)

1973-1982. Flat-top, laminated mahogany back and sides, arched back, square shoulders, sunburst. See Jumbo 55 listing for '39-'43 version.

1973-1982		$600	$800

J-60

1992-1999. Solid spruce top dreadnought, square shoulders, Indian rosewood back and sides, multiple bindings, natural or sunburst.

1992-1999		$900	$1,100

J-60 Curly Maple

1993 and 1996. Curly maple back and sides, limited edition from Montana shop. Natural.

1993		$1,800	$2,000

J-100

1972-1974, 1985-1997, 2003-present. Flat-top jumbo, multi-bound top and back, black pickguard, dot inlays, mahogany back and sides. '80s version has maple back and sides, dot inlays and tortoise shell guard. Current model has maples back and sides, no pickguard, and J-200 style block fingerboard inlays.

1972-1974	Mahogany	$1,100	$1,200
1985-1997	Maple	$1,200	$1,300

J-100 Xtra

1991-1997, 1999-2003. Jumbo flat-top, mahogany back and sides, moustache bridge, dot inlays, various colors. J-100 Xtra Cutaway also available. Reintroduced in '99 with maple back and sides and single bound body.

1991-1997		$1,100	$1,300

J-160E

1954-1979. Flat-top jumbo acoustic, one bridge P-90 pickup, tone and volume controls on front. Sunburst finish. Reintroduced as J-160 in 1990.

1954-1961		$3,000	$4,000
1962	Beatles' vintage June '62	$3,200	$5,000
1963		$3,100	$4,100
1964	Lennon's 2nd model	$3,200	$4,500
1965		$3,100	$3,700
1966		$3,100	$3,500
1967		$2,800	$3,100
1968		$2,500	$2,800
1969		$1,800	$2,100
1970		$1,300	$1,600
1971-1979		$1,200	$1,500

J-160E (reissue)

1991-1997. Reintroduced J-160E with solid spruce top, solid mahogany back and sides.

1991-1997		$1,400	$1,700

J-180/Everly Brothers/The Everly Brothers

1986-present. Reissue of the '62-'72 Everly Brothers model. Renamed The Everly Brothers ('92-'94), then The Everly ('94-'96), then back to J-180. Black.

1986-1994		$1,000	$1,400
1994-1999		$1,400	$1,600

MODEL YEAR	FEATURES	EXC. COND. LOW	HIGH

J-185

1951-1959. Flat-top jumbo, figured maple back and sides, bound body and neck.

1951-1956	Natural	$7,000	$8,000
1951-1956	Sunburst	$6,500	$7,500
1957-1959	Natural	$6,800	$7,800
1957-1959	Sunburst	$6,300	$7,300

J-185 EC

1999-present. Acoustic/electric, rounded cutaway. Sunburst.

1999-2002		$1,400	$1,600

J-185 Reissue

1990-1995, 1999-present. Flat-top jumbo, figured maple back and sides, bound body and neck, Natural or Sunburst. Limited run of 100 between 1991-1992.

1990-1995		$1,800	$1,950

J-200/SJ-200

1947-1996. Labeled SJ-200 until ca.1954. Super Jumbo flat-top, maple back and sides. See SJ-200 for 1938-1942 rosewood back and sides model. Called J-200 Artist for a time in the mid-1970s. Renamed '50s Super Jumbo 200 in 1997 and again renamed SJ-200 Reissue in 1999. Standard finish is Sunburst.

1947-1949	Natural option	$9,000	$11,000
1947-1949	Sunburst	$8,000	$10,000
1950-1954	Natural option	$8,500	$10,000
1950-1954	Sunburst	$7,000	$9,000
1955-1959	Natural option	$7,000	$9,500
1955-1959	Sunburst	$6,500	$9,000
1960	Natural	$6,500	$9,000
1960	Sunburst	$6,000	$8,000
1961-1963	Natural option	$6,000	$8,000
1961-1963	Sunburst	$5,000	$7,000
1964	Natural	$5,000	$6,500
1964	Sunburst	$4,000	$6,000
1965	Natural or Sunburst	$4,000	$5,000
1966-1967	Natural or Sunburst	$3,500	$4,000
1968	Natural or Sunburst	$3,000	$3,500
1969	Natural or Sunburst	$2,700	$3,000
1970-1972	Natural or Sunburst	$2,600	$2,900
1973	Natural or Sunburst	$2,200	$2,600
1974-1992	Natural or Sunburst	$1,900	$2,100
1992-1996	Natural or Sunburst	$2,000	$2,200

J-200 Celebrity

1985-1987. Acoustic introduced for Gibson's 90th anniversary, spruce top, rosewood back, sides and fingerboard, binding on body and fingerboard. Sunburst. Only 90 made.

1985-1987		$2,800	$3,200

J-250 R

1972-1973, 1976-1978. A J-200 with rosewood back and sides, Sunburst. Only 20 shipped from Gibson.

1972-1973		$2,200	$2,600
1976-1978		$1,900	$2,100

Johnny Smith

1961-1989. Single cutaway archtop, one humbucking pickup, Gold hardware, multiple binding front and back.

1961-1962	Sunburst	$7,000	$8,000
1961-1963	Natural	$8,000	$9,000
1963-1964	Sunburst	$5,500	$6,500
1965-1967	Natural	$6,000	$7,000
1965-1967	Sunburst	$5,300	$6,000
1968-1969	Natural	$5,500	$6,500
1968-1969	Sunburst	$5,000	$5,500
1970-1973	Sunburst	$4,400	$5,200
1970-1973	Wine Red	$4,400	$4,700
1974-1989	Natural or sunburst	$4,000	$4,500

Johnny Smith Double

1963-1989. Single cutaway archtop, two humbucking pickups, Gold hardware, multiple binding front and back.

1963-1964	Sunburst	$6,500	$7,500
1965-1967	Natural	$6,500	$7,500
1965-1967	Sunburst	$5,500	$6,500
1968-1969	Sunburst	$5,200	$6,000
1970-1973	Sunburst	$5,000	$5,500
1974-1989	Natural	$4,700	$5,700
1974-1989	Sunburst	$4,500	$5,200

Jubilee

1969-1970. Flat-top, laminated mahogany back and sides, single bound body. Natural with Black back and sides.

1969-1970		$700	$800

Jubilee Deluxe

1970-1971. Flat-top, laminated rosewood back and sides, multi-bound body. Natural finish.

1970-1971		$800	$1,000

Jubilee-12

1969-1970. Flat-top, 12 strings, laminated mahogany back and sides, multi-bound. Natural.

1969-1970		$500	$700

Jumbo

1934-1936. Gibson's first Jumbo flat-top, mahogany back and sides, round shoulders, bound top and back, Sunburst. Becomes the 16" Jumbo 35 in late-1936.

1934-1936		$14,000	$16,000

Jumbo 35/J-35

1936-1942. Jumbo flat-top, mahogany back and sides, silkscreen logo, Sunburst. Reintroduced as J-35, square-shouldered dreadnought, in 1983.

1936		$8,500	$9,500
1937		$8,000	$9,000
1938-1939		$7,500	$8,500
1940-1942		$7,000	$8,000

1956 Gibson J-160E

1961 Gibson Johnny Smith

GUITARS

1931 Gibson L-00

1929 Gibson L-1

MODEL YEAR	FEATURES	EXC. COND. LOW	HIGH

Jumbo 55/J-55

1939-1943. Flat-top dreadnought, round shoulders, mahogany back and sides, pearl inlaid logo, Sunburst. Reintroduced in 1973 at J-55.

1939-1943		$13,000	$15,000

Jumbo Centennial Special

1994. Reissue of 1934 Jumbo, 100 made.

1994	Natural	$2,000	$2,200

Junior Pro

1987-1989. Single cutaway, mahogany body, KB-X tremolo system one humbucker pickup, Black chrome hardware, various colors.

1987-1989		$350	$450

Kalamazoo Award Model

1978-1981. Single cutaway archtop, bound F-holes, multi-bound top and back, one mini-humbucker, gold-plated hardware, woodgrain pickguard with bird and branch abalone inlay.

1978-1981	Natural, highly figured	$16,000	$18,000
1978-1981	Sunburst, highly figured	$14,000	$17,000

L-0

1926-1933, 1937-1942. Acoustic flat-top, maple back and sides 1926-1927, mahogany after.

1926-1933	Amber Brown	$1,500	$2,000
1937-1942	Various colors	$1,500	$2,000

L-00

1932-1946. Acoustic flat-top, mahogany back and sides, bound top to 1936 and bound top and back 1937 on.

1932-1936	Black or Sunburst	$2,000	$2,500
1937-1939	Black or Sunburst	$1,900	$2,400
1940-1946	Natural or Sunburst	$1,600	$2,200

L-00/Blues King

1991-1997. Mahogany back and sides, spruce top, Ebony or Sunburst.

1991-1997		$1,100	$1,400

L-1 (archtop)

1902-1925. Acoustic archtop, single-bound top, back and soundhole. Name continued on flat-top model in '26.

1902-1918	Natural Orange or Black	$1,300	$1,600
1917-1925	Sheraton Brown	$1,200	$1,400

L-1 (flat-top)

1926-1937. Acoustic flat-top, maple back and sides 1926-1927, mahogany after.

1926	Sheraton Brown	$2,000	$2,500
1930	Sunburst	$1,800	$2,300
1937	Sunburst	$1,700	$2,200

L-2 (archtop)

1902-1926. Round soundhole archtop, pearl inlay on peghead, 1902-1907 available in three body sizes: 12.5" to 16", 1924-1926 13.5" body width.

1926	Amber	$1,500	$1,800

L-2 (flat-top)

1929-1935. Acoustic flat-top, rosewood back and sides except for mahogany in 1931, triple-bound top and back. Limited edition model in 1994.

1931	Argentine Gray Sunburst	$2,000	$3,000
1932	Natural or Sunburst	$1,900	$2,700
1934	Natural	$1,800	$2,500

L-2 1929 Limited Edition

1994 only. Spruce top, Indian rosewood back and sides, raised pickguard.

1994		$1,400	$1,700

L-3 (archtop)

1903-1933. Acoustic archtop.

1903-1919		$1,600	$1,900
1920-1927	Round soundhole	$1,700	$2,000
1928-1933	Oval soundhole	$1,800	$2,100

L-4

1912-1956. Acoustic archtop.

1912-1919	Black	$1,700	$2,000
1920-1927	Red Sunburst, oval soundhole	$1,700	$2,000
1928-1934	Red Sunburst, round soundhole	$1,700	$2,200
1935-1942	Sunburst, F-holes	$1,700	$2,000
1940-1942	Natural option	$1,700	$2,000
1947-1956	Natural, crown peghead inlay	$1,700	$2,600
1947-1956	Sunburst, crown peghead inlay	$1,700	$2,600

L-4 C/L-4 CN

1949-1971. Single cutaway acoustic archtop.

1949-1959	Natural	$2,900	$3,100
1949-1959	Sunburst	$2,500	$2,700
1960-1965	Natural	$2,800	$3,000
1960-1965	Sunburst	$2,400	$2,600
1966-1969	Sunburst	$2,300	$2,500
1969-1971	Sunburst	$2,200	$2,400

L-4 CES

1958,1969, 1986-present. Single pointed cutaway archtop, two humbuckers, Gold parts, Natural or Sunburst. Now part of Gibson's Custom Collection.

1986-1999		$2,300	$2,800

L-5

1922-1958. Acoustic archtop, non-cutaway, multiple bindings, Lloyd Loar label until 1924, 17" body by 1935, Master Model label until 1927. Sunburst with Natural option later.

1922-1924	Lloyd Loar label	$40,000	$60,000
1925-1927	Master Model label	$18,000	$20,000
1928	Last dot markers	$10,000	$12,000
1929-1930	Block markers	$8,000	$10,000
1931-1932	Kaufman vibrola	$10,000	$11,000
1931-1932	Standard trapeze	$7,000	$9,000
1933-1934	16" body	$6,000	$8,000
1935-1940	17" body	$6,000	$7,000
1939-1940	Natural option	$7,000	$9,000
1946-1949	Natural option	$7,000	$8,000

MODEL YEAR	FEATURES	EXC. COND. LOW	HIGH
1946-1949	Sunburst	$5,000	$6,000
1950-1958	Natural	$5,000	$7,000
1950-1958	Sunburst	$4,000	$6,000

L-5 Premier/L-5 P

1939-1947. Introduced as L-5 Premier (L-5 P) and renamed L-5 C in 1948. Single rounded cutaway acoustic archtop.

1939-1940	Natural option	$17,000	$20,000
1939-1940	Sunburst	$16,000	$17,000

L-5 C

1948-1982. Renamed from L-5 Premier (L-5 P). Single rounded cutaway acoustic archtop. Sunburst.

1948		$12,500	$15,000
1949		$12,000	$14,500
1950-1959		$11,500	$12,500
1960-1962		$9,000	$10,000
1964-1965		$8,000	$9,000
1966-1967		$7,500	$8,500
1968		$6,000	$7,500
1969		$5,000	$6,500
1970-1972		$4,500	$6,000
1973-1975		$4,000	$5,000
1976-1982		$3,500	$5,000

L-5 CES

1951-present. Electric version of L-5 C, single round cutaway (pointed mid-1960-1969), archtop, two pickups (P-90s 1951-1953, Alnico Vs 1954-mid-1957, humbuckers after). Now part of Gibson's Historic Collection.

1951-1957	Natural, single coils	$15,000	$18,000
1951-1957	Sunburst, single coils	$12,000	$15,000
1958-1960	Natural, humbuckers	$17,000	$20,000
1958-1960	Sunburst, humbuckers	$14,000	$16,000
1961-1962	Natural, PAFs	$15,000	$18,000
1961-1962	Sunburst, PAFs	$12,000	$14,000
1963-1964	Natural, pat. #	$13,000	$15,000
1963-1964	Sunburst, pat. #	$10,000	$12,000
1965-1969	Natural	$7,000	$8,500
1965-1969	Sunburst	$6,000	$7,500
1970-1972	Natural or sunburst	$5,000	$6,000
1973-1992	Various colors	$4,500	$5,500

L-5 CES Custom Shop Historic Collection

1990s. Historic Collection Series. Sunburst.

1990s		$4,000	$6,000

L-5 CT (George Gobel)

1959-1961. Single cutaway, thinline archtop acoustic. Some were built with pickups, Cherry. Currently available in Gibson's Historic Collection.

1959-1961		$15,000	$20,000

L-5 CT (reissue)

1998-present. Natural.

1998		$5,000	$5,500

MODEL YEAR	FEATURES	EXC. COND. LOW	HIGH

L-5 S

1972-1985. Single cut solidbody, multi-bound body and neck, gold hardware, 2 pickups (low impedence '72-'74, humbuckers '75 on). Offered in natural, cherry sunburst or vintage sunburst.

1972-1974	Natural, gold hardware, low impedence	$3,100	$3,200
1972-1974	Sunburst, low impedence pickups	$2,400	$2,600
1975-1980	Natural, gold hardware, humbuckers	$3,400	$3,500
1975-1980	Sunburst, humbuckers	$2,700	$2,900

L-5 Studio

1996-2000. Normal L-5 dual pickup features, marble-style pickguard.

1996-2000	Translucent finish	$3,000	$3,500

L-5 Wes Montgomery Custom Shop

1993-present. Various colors.

1993-1999		$3,500	$4,500

L-6 S

1973-1975. Single cutaway solidbody, two humbucking pickups, stop tailpiece, Cherry or Natural. Renamed L-6 S Custom in 1975.

1973-1975		$475	$700

L-6 S Custom

1975-1980. Renamed from the L-6 S. Single cutaway solidbody, two humbucking pickups, stop tailpiece, Cherry or Natural.

1975-1980		$475	$700

L-6 S Deluxe

1975-1981. Single cutaway solidbody, two humbucking pickups, strings-through-body design, Cherry or Natural.

1975-1981		$475	$700

L-7

1932-1956. Acoustic archtop, bound body and neck, fleur-de-lis peghead inlay.

1932-1939	Sunburst	$2,500	$3,000
1940-1950	Natural or Sunburst	$2,200	$2,700
1951-1956	Natural or Sunburst	$2,000	$2,400

L-7 C

1948-1972. Single cutaway acoustic archtop, triple-bound top. Sunburst or Natural finish.

1948-1949	Natural	$3,600	$4,000
1948-1949	Sunburst	$3,100	$3,300
1950-1951	Natural	$3,400	$3,800
1950-1951	Sunburst	$3,100	$3,300
1952-1954	Natural	$3,300	$3,700
1952-1954	Sunburst	$2,600	$3,000
1955-1957	Natural	$3,100	$3,500
1955-1959	Sunburst	$2,600	$3,000
1960-1964	Sunburst	$2,500	$2,900
1965-1967	Sunburst	$2,400	$2,800
1968-1971	Sunburst	$2,200	$2,700

1915 Gibson L-4

1936 Gibson L-7

GUITARS

1962 Gibson L-5CN

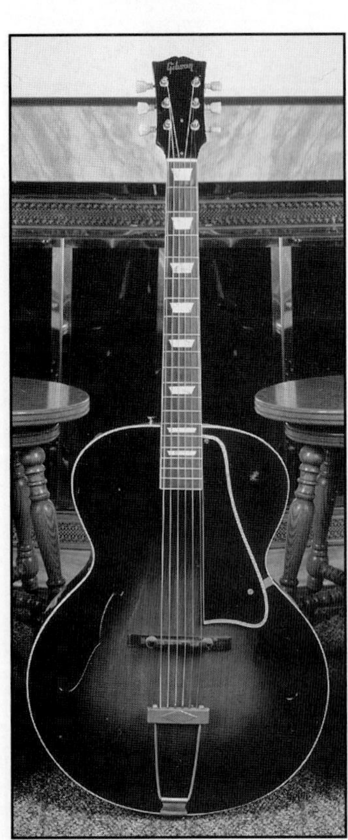
Gibson L-50

MODEL YEAR	FEATURES	EXC. COND. LOW	HIGH

L-10

1929-1939. Acoustic archtop, single-bound body and fingerboard.

1929-1933	Black, 16"	$1,600	$2,100
1934-1939	Black or Sunburst, 17", X-braced	$2,000	$2,500

L-12

1930-1955. Acoustic archtop, single-bound body, pickguard, neck and headstock, gold-plated hardware. Sunburst.

1930-1934	16" body	$2,400	$2,700
1935-1938	17" body, X-braced	$2,700	$2,900
1939-1941	Parallel top braced	$2,700	$2,900
1946-1955	Post-war production	$2,600	$2,800

L-12 Premier/L-12 P

1947-1950. L-12 with rounded cutaway. Sunburst.

1947-1950		$4,300	$4,600

L-30

1935-1943. Acoustic archtop, single-bound body. Black or Sunburst.

1935-1943		$700	$1,000

L-37

1937-1941. 14-3/4" acoustic archtop, flat back, single-bound body and pickguard, sunburst.

1937-1941		$750	$1,100

L-48

1946-1971. 16" acoustic archtop, single-bound body, sunburst.

1946-1965		$700	$900
1966-1971		$600	$750

L-50

1932-1971. 17-1/2" acoustic archtop, flat or arched back, round soundhole or F-holes, sunburst.

1933-1943		$900	$1,300
1946-1965	Trapezoid inlay	$1,000	$1,400
1966-1971		$800	$1,100

L-75

1932-1939. Fourteen and three/fourths inch archtop with round soundhole and flat back, size increased to 16" with arched back in 1935, small button tuners, dot markers, lower-end style trapeze tailpiece, pearl script logo. Sunburst.

1932-1934	14 3/4" body	$1,400	$1,900
1935-1939	16" body	$2,500	$3,000

L-C Reissue

Pearloid headstock and fingerboard.

1994		$2,100	$2,300

L-Century (L-C)

1933-1941. Curly maple back and sides, bound body, White pearloid fingerboard and peghead (all years) and headstock (until 1938). Sunburst.

1936	Sunburst	$3,000	$3,500

LC-1 Cascade

2002-present. Released November '02, LC-Series acoustic/electric, advanced L-00-style, solid quilted maple back and sides.

2002-2003		$900	$1,300

MODEL YEAR	FEATURES	EXC. COND. LOW	HIGH

Le Grande

1993-present. Electric archtop, 17", formerly called Johnny Smith.

1993-1999	Blond	$6,500	$7,000
1993-1999	Sunburst	$5,500	$6,000
2000-2003		$6,500	$7,000

Les Paul

Following are the various guitars bearing the Les Paul name, beginning with the one that started it all, the original Les Paul Model. All other versions are then listed alphabetically after that as follows:

Les Paul Model
'54 Les Paul Goldtop
'56 Les Paul Goldtop
'57 Les Paul Custom Black Beauty/three-pickup
'57 Les Paul Custom Black Beauty/two-pickup
'57 Les Paul Goldtop
'57 Les Paul Jr. Historic Collection
'58 Les Paul Flametop
'59 Les Paul Flametop
'60 Corvette (Custom shop)
'60 Les Paul Flametop
'60 Les Paul Jr. Historic Collection
Les Paul 25/50 Anniversary
Les Paul 25th Silver Anniversary (Guitar Center)
Les Paul 30th Anniversary
Les Paul 40th Anniversary (from 1952)
Les Paul 40th Anniversary (from 1959)
Les Paul 55
Les Paul (All Maple)
Les Paul Ace Frehley Signature
Les Paul Artisan
Les Paul Artist/L.P. Artist/Les Paul Active
Les Paul Bird's-Eye Standard
Les Paul Centennial ('59 Les Paul Special)
Les Paul Classic
Les Paul Classic Plus
Les Paul Classic Premium Plus
Les Paul Custom
Les Paul Custom '54
Les Paul Custom (Custom Shop)
Les Paul Custom 20th Anniversary
Les Paul Custom 35th Anniversary
Les Paul Custom Historic '54
Les Paul Custom Historic '68
Les Paul Custom Lite
Les Paul Custom Lite (Show Case Ed.)
Les Paul Custom Plus
Les Paul Custom SG 30th Anniversary
Les Paul DC Pro
Les Paul DC Standard
Les Paul DC Standard Plus
Les Paul DC Studio
Les Paul Deluxe
Les Paul Deluxe Hall of Fame
Les Paul Deluxe Limited Edition
Les Paul Elegant (Custom Shop)

MODEL YEAR	FEATURES	EXC. COND. LOW	HIGH

Les Paul Gary Moore Model
Les Paul Guitar Trader Reissue
Les Paul Heritage 80
Les Paul Heritage 80 Award
Les Paul Heritage 80 Elite
Les Paul Jimmy Page Model
Les Paul Jimmy Wallace Reissue
Les Paul Joe Perry Model
Les Paul Jr.
Les Paul Jr. 3/4
Les Paul Jr. Double Cutaway
Les Paul Jumbo
Les Paul KM (Kalamazoo Model)
Les Paul Leo's Reissue
Les Paul Limited Edition (3-tone)
Les Paul Old Hickory
Les Paul Personal
Les Paul Pro-Deluxe
Les Paul Professional
Les Paul Recording
Les Paul Reissue Flametop
Les Paul Reissue Goldtop
Les Paul Signature
Les Paul SmartWood Standard
Les Paul Special
Les Paul Special (reissue)
Les Paul Special 3/4
Les Paul Special Centennial
Les Paul Special Custom Shop
Les Paul Special Double Cutaway
Les Paul Spotlight Special
Les Paul Standard (Sunburst)
Les Paul Standard (SG body)
Les Paul Standard (reintroduced then renamed)
Les Paul Standard (reintroduced)
Les Paul Standard '58
Les Paul Standard Lite
Les Paul Strings and Things Standard
Les Paul Studio
Les Paul Studio Custom
Les Paul Studio Gem
Les Paul Studio Gothic
Les Paul Studio Lite
Les Paul TV
Les Paul TV 3/4
Les Paul Ultima
The Les Paul
The Paul
The Paul Firebrand Deluxe
The Paul II

Les Paul Model

1952-1958. The Goldtop, two P-90 pickups until mid-1957, humbuckers after, trapeze tailpiece until late-1953, stud tailpiece/bridge 1953-mid-1955, Tune-o-matic bridge 1955-1958. Renamed Les Paul Standard in 1958.

1952-1953	5/8" knobs	$6,000	$8,000
1952-1953	5/8" knobs, all Gold option, trapeze	$6,000	$8,000
1953	1/2" knobs, stop tail	$9,500	$11,500
1953	1/2" knobs, trapeze	$6,000	$7,000
1954-1955	All Gold option, stop tail	$11,000	$12,000
1954-1955	Stop tail	$10,000	$12,000
1955-1956	All Gold option, P-90s	$13,000	$18,000
1955-1957	Tune-o-matic, P-90s	$12,000	$18,000
1957-1958	Bigsby, humbuckers	$30,000	$35,000
1957-1958	Stud tail, humbuckers	$35,000	$40,000

'54 Les Paul Goldtop

1990s-present. Goldtop finish, two P-90s, '53-'54 stud tailpiece/bridge.

1997		$1,700	$1,800

'56 Les Paul Goldtop

1991-present. Renamed from Les Paul Reissue Goldtop. Goldtop finish, two P-90 pickups. Now part of Gibson's Historic Collection.

1991-1999		$1,800	$2,000
2000-2002		$2,000	$2,500

'57 Les Paul Custom Black Beauty/three-pickup

1991-present. Black finish, Gold hardware, three humbucker pickups. Part of Gibson's Historic Collection.

1991-1999		$2,000	$2,200

'57 Les Paul Custom Black Beauty/two-pickup

1991-present. Black finish, Gold hardware, two humbucker pickups. Part of Gibson's Historic Collection.

1991-1999		$1,900	$2,100

'57 Les Paul Goldtop

1993-present. Goldtop finish, two humbuckers. Now part of Gibson's Historic Collection.

1993-1999		$1,900	$2,100

'57 Les Paul Jr. Historic Collection

1998-present. High quality Historic reissue of '57 slab body, double cutaway Les Paul Jr.

1990s	TV Yellow	$1,400	$1,700

'58 Les Paul Flametop

Part of Gibson's Historic Collection. Sunburst.

2001		$2,300	$2,500

'59 Les Paul Flametop

1991-present. Renamed from Les Paul Reissue Flametop. Flame maple top, two humbuckers, thick 1959-style neck. Sunburst finish. Part of Gibson's Historic Collection. By 1998 Gibson guaranteed only AAA Premium grade maple tops would be used.

1991-2002		$3,400	$4,000

1953 Gibson Les Paul Model

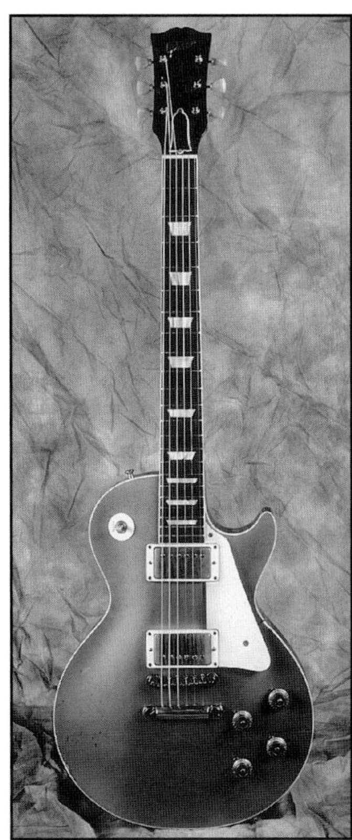

1957 Gibson Les Paul Model

GUITARS

1977 Gibson Les Paul Artisan

1956 Gibson Les Paul Custom

MODEL YEAR	FEATURES	EXC. COND. LOW	HIGH

'60 Corvette (Custom shop)

1995-1997. Custom Shop Les Paul, Chevrolet Corvette styling from 1960, distinctive styling, offered in six colors.

1995-1997		$5,000	$7,000

'60 Les Paul Flametop

1991-1999. Renamed from Les Paul Reissue Flametop. Flame maple top, two humbuckers, thinner neck. Sunburst finish. Part of Gibson's Historic Collection.

1991-1999		$3,400	$4,000

'60 Les Paul Jr. Historic Collection

Introduced in 1992. High quality Historic reissue of 1960 slab body, double cutaway Les Paul Jr. Cherry.

1995		$1,400	$1,700

Les Paul 25/50 Anniversary

1978-1979. Regular model with 25/50 inlay on headstock. Sunburst.

1978-1979	Moderate flame	$2,000	$2,500

Les Paul 25th Silver Anniversary (Guitar Center)

1978. Special order of 50 Les Paul Customs with Metallic Silver top, back, sides and neck. Commissioned by Guitar Center of California, most have 25th Anniversary etched in tailpiece.

1978		$2,000	$2,500

Les Paul 30th Anniversary

1982-1984. Features of a 1958 Les Paul Goldtop, two humbuckers, Thirtieth Anniversary inlay on 19th fret.

1982-1984		$2,000	$2,500

Les Paul 40th Anniversary (from 1952)

1991-1992. Black finish, two soapbar P-100 pickups, Gold hardware, stop tailpiece, 40th Anniversary inlay at 12th fret.

1991-1992		$1,600	$1,800

Les Paul 40th Anniversary (from 1959)

1999. Reissue Historic, highly figured.

1999		$3,600	$4,000

Les Paul 55

1974, 1976-1981. Single cutaway Special reissue, two pickups.

1974	Sunburst	$800	$1,000
1976-1981	Sunburst or Wine Red	$800	$1,000

Les Paul (All Maple)

1984. Limited run, all maple body, Super 400-style inlay, Gold hardware.

1984		$3,200	$3,400

Les Paul Ace Frehley Signature

1997-2001. Ace's signature inlay at 15th fret, three humbuckers. Sunburst.

1997-2001		$2,400	$2,800

Les Paul Artisan

1976-1982. Carved maple top, 2 or 3 humbuckers, gold hardware, hearts and flowers inlays on fingerboard and headstock, ebony, sunburst or walnut.

1976-1982		$1,600	$2,000

MODEL YEAR	FEATURES	EXC. COND. LOW	HIGH

Les Paul Artist/L.P. Artist/Les Paul Active

1979-1982. Two humbuckers (three optional), active electronics, Gold hardware, three mini-switches, multi-bound.

1979	Sunburst	$1,200	$1,500
1980-1982	Ebony or Sunburst	$1,200	$1,500

Les Paul Bird's-Eye Standard

Bird's-eye top, Gold hardware, two humbucking pickups.

1999	Transparent Amber	$1,800	$1,900

Les Paul Centennial ('59 Les Paul Special)

1994. Part of the Guitar of the Month program commemorating Gibson's 100th year, limited edition. Slab body Les Paul Special-style configuration, 100 made, Gold hardware, P-90 pickups, Gold medallion, commemorative engraving in pickguard. Cherry.

1994		$3,600	$4,000

Les Paul Classic

1990-1998, 2001. Has 1960 on pickguard (not on later models), two exposed humbucker pickups, Les Paul Model on peghead until 1993, Les Paul Classic afterwards.

1990-1996	Various colors, plain top	$1,000	$1,500
1990-1998	All Gold neck and body	$1,700	$1,900

Les Paul Classic Plus

1992-1996, 1999-2000. Les Paul Classic with fancier maple top, two exposed humbucker pickups.

1992-1996	Price depends on top figure	$1,700	$2,200

Les Paul Classic Premium Plus

1992-1996, 2000-2002. Les Paul Classic with AAA-grade flame maple top, two exposed humbucker pickups.

1992-1996	Price depends on top figure	$2,200	$2,800

Les Paul Custom

1953-1963 (renamed SG Custom late-1963), 1968-present. Les Paul body shape except for SG body 1961-1963, two pickups (three humbuckers mid-1957-1963 and 1968-1970, three pickups were optional various years after).

1954-1957	Single-coil plus	$7,500	$9,000
1954-1957	Single-coils with factory Bigsby	$7,000	$8,500
1957-1960	Humbuckers	$13,000	$16,000
1957-1960	Humbuckers with factory Bigsby	$11,000	$14,000
1961-1963	White, SG body	$7,000	$8,500
1968-1969	Black	$4,000	$4,800
1970-1973	2 pu, neck volute	$2,000	$2,400
1971-1973	Volute, 3 pu	$2,400	$2,700
1974	Volute, 2 pu	$1,800	$2,300
1975-1976	Black, volute, 2 pu	$1,600	$2,100
1975-1976	Others, volute, 2 pu	$1,500	$2,000
1977-1979	Black, volute, 2 pu	$1,400	$1,700

MODEL YEAR	FEATURES	EXC. COND. LOW	HIGH
1977-1979	Sunburst, volute, 2 pu	$1,500	$1,700
1977-1979	White, volute, 2 pu	$1,700	$1,900
1978	Black, 3 pickup option	$1,900	$2,200
1979	Silverburst, volute, 2 pus	$1,800	$2,200
1980-1983	Black, no volute, 2 pickups	$1,600	$1,800
1980-1983	Silverburst	$1,800	$2,000
1980-1983	Sunburst, no volute, 2 pus	$1,600	$1,800
1980-1983	White, no volute, 2 pus	$1,700	$1,900
1984-1985	2 pu	$1,500	$1,700
1985	Black, 3 pickup option	$1,700	$1,900
1985	Silverburst	$2,000	$2,400
1986-1989	Various colors	$1,400	$1,700
1990-1999	Various colors	$1,400	$1,700
2000-2002	Various colors	$1,400	$1,900

Les Paul Custom '54

1972-1973. Reissue of 1954 Custom, Black finish, Alnico V and P-90 pickups.

1972-1973	Black	$3,000	$3,500

Les Paul Custom (Custom Shop)

1997-present. Handbuilt Custom Shop quality, Gold hardware.

1997-1999		$1,700	$1,800

Les Paul Custom 20th Anniversary

1974. Regular two-pickup Custom, with Twentieth Anniversary inlay at 15th fret. Black or White.

1974		$2,000	$2,400

Les Paul Custom 35th Anniversary

1989. Gold hardware, three pickups, carved, solid mahogany body and neck, 35th Anniversary inlay on headstock. Black.

1989		$2,200	$2,600

Les Paul Custom Historic '54

1990s Historic Collection, 1954 appointments and pickup configuration. Black.

2000	Gold hardware	$2,000	$2,200

Les Paul Custom Historic '68

Historic Collection, Ebony block marked fretboard, Gold hardware, flamed maple top available, two pickups.

2000-2001	Flamed natural	$2,100	$2,400

Les Paul Custom Lite

1987-1990. Full-thickness carved maple top, ebony fingerboard, pearl block position markers, Gold hardware, PAF pickups, bound neck, headstock and body. Black.

1987-1990		$1,400	$1,800

Les Paul Custom Lite (Show Case Ed.)

1988. Showcase Edition, only 200 made, Gold top.

1988		$1,600	$2,000

Les Paul Custom Plus

1991-1998. Regular Custom with figured maple top. Sunburst finish or colors.

1991-1998		$2,300	$2,800

Les Paul Custom SG 30th Anniversary

1991. Thirtieth Anniversary edition of SG-style Les Paul Custom introduced in 1961, TV Yellow finish, 30th Anniversary logo.

1991		$2,100	$2,300

Les Paul DC Pro

1997-1998. Custom Shop, body like a 1959 Les Paul Junior, carved highly figured maple top, various options.

1997-1998		$1,800	$2,000

Les Paul DC Standard

1998-1999, 2001-present. Offset double cutaway, highly flamed maple top, mahogany set-neck, translucent lacquer finishes in various colors, typical Les Paul Model stencil logo on headstock and 'Standard' notation on truss rod cover. Reintroduced as Standard Lite in 1999 but without Les Paul designation on headstock or truss rod cover.

1998		$1,000	$1,250

Les Paul DC Standard Plus

2000s. Reintroduced as Plus Series with flamed top and Gold hardware.

2001	Cherry	$900	$1,100

Les Paul DC Studio

1997-1999. DC Series double cutaway like late '50s models, carved maple top, two humbucker pickups. Various colors.

1997-1999		$600	$700

Les Paul Deluxe

1969-1985. In 1969, the goldtop Les Paul Standard was renamed the Deluxe. Two mini-humbuckers (regular humbuckers optional in mid-'70s). Mid-'70s Sparkle tops are worth more than standard finishes. In '99, the Deluxe was reissued for its 30th anniversary.

1969	Goldtop	$2,500	$3,000
1970-1971	Goldtop	$1,500	$1,900
1970-1971	Sunburst	$1,400	$1,800
1971-1974	Cherry	$1,300	$1,900
1972-1975	Goldtop or s/b	$1,300	$1,700
1975-1977	Blue Sparkle	$2,900	$3,400
1975-1977	Natural	$1,400	$1,700
1975-1977	Red Sparkle	$2,900	$3,400
1976-1979	Goldtop, s/b, wine red	$1,300	$1,600
1980-1985	Black or wine red	$1,200	$1,500
1980-1985	Goldtop or s/b	$1,200	$1,600

Les Paul Deluxe Hall of Fame

1991. All Gold.

1991		$1,400	$1,600

Les Paul Deluxe Limited Edition

1999-2002. Limited edition reissue with Les Paul Standard features and Deluxe mini-humbuckers, Black.

1999-2002		$1,200	$1,500

Les Paul Elegant (Custom Shop)

1996-present. Custom Shop highly flamed maple top, abalone Custom Shop headstock inlay.

1996-1999		$2,100	$2,500

1960 Gibson Les Paul Custom

2001 Gibson Les Paul DC Standard

Gibson Les Paul Deluxe (blue sparkle)

1961 Gibson Les Paul Junior

MODEL YEAR	FEATURES	EXC. COND. LOW	HIGH

Les Paul Gary Moore Model

2000-2002. Signature Series model, Gary Moore script logo on truss rod cover, flamed maple top.

2000-2002		$1,600	$2,000

Les Paul Guitar Trader Reissue

1982-1983. Special order flametop Les Paul by the Guitar Trader Company, Redbank, NJ. Approximately 47 were built.

1982-1983	Std. humbuckers	$3,700	$4,000
1982-1983	Actual PAFs	$4,000	$6,000

Les Paul Heritage 80

1980-1982. Copy of 1959 Les Paul Standard. Curly maple top, mahogany body, rosewood fingerboard. Sunburst.

1980-1982		$2,500	$2,800

Les Paul Heritage 80 Award

1982. Ebony fingerboard, one-piece mahogany neck, gold-plated hardware. Sunburst.

1982		$2,600	$2,900

Les Paul Heritage 80 Elite

1980-1982. Copy of 1959 Les Paul Standard. Quilted maple top, mahogany body and neck, ebony fingerboard, chrome hardware. Sunburst.

1980-1982		$2,700	$3,000

Les Paul Jimmy Page Model

1995-1999. Jimmy Page signature on pickguard, mid-grade figured top, push-pull knobs for phasing and coil-tapping, Grover tuners, gold-plated hardware.

1995	Highly figured, 1st year	$3,500	$4,500
1995	Low to moderate figure, 1st year	$3,000	$3,700
1996-1999	Highly figured	$2,800	$3,700
1996-1999	Low to moderate figure	$2,500	$3,500

Les Paul Jimmy Wallace Reissue

1978-1997. Les Paul Standard '59 reissue with Jimmy Wallace on truss rod cover, special order by dealer Jimmy Wallace, figured maple top, Sunburst.

1982		$3,700	$4,000

Les Paul Joe Perry Model

1997-2001. Joe Perry signature on body.

1997-2001	Bone-Yard option with logo	$2,900	$3,000
1997-2001	Transparent Black, flamed	$1,900	$2,000

Les Paul Jr.

1954-1963, 1986-1992. One P-90 pickup, single cutaway solidbody '54-mid-'58, double cutaway '58-early-'61, SG body '61-'63. Renamed SG Jr. in '63. Reintroduced as single cut for '86-'92. Reissued as the 1957 Les Paul Jr. Single Cutaway in '98.

1954	Sunburst, single cut	$2,800	$3,800
1955-1958	Sunburst, single cut	$2,700	$3,500
1959-1961	Cherry, double cut, normal fade	$2,800	$3,200
1959-1961	Cherry, double cut, unfaded	$3,200	$3,800
1961-1963	Cherry, SG body	$1,500	$2,200
1986-1992	Cherry or Sunburst, single cut	$700	$850

Les Paul Jr. 3/4

1956-1961. One P-90 pickup, short-scale, single cutaway solidbody 1954-mid-1958, double cutaway 1958-early-1961.

1956-1958	Sunburst, single cut	$1,700	$2,500
1958-1959	Cherry, double cut	$1,500	$2,200
1960-1961	Cherry, double cut	$1,500	$2,100

Les Paul Jr. Double Cutaway

1986-1992, 1995-1996. Copy of 1950s double cutaway Jr., Cherry or Sunburst. Reissued as the 1957 Les Paul Jr. Double Cutaway in '98.

1986-1992		$750	$950

Les Paul Jumbo

1969-1970. Single rounded cutaway, flat-top dreadnought acoustic/electric, one pickup, rosewood back and sides. Natural.

1969-1970		$2,500	$2,800

Les Paul KM (Kalamazoo Model)

1979. Regular Les Paul Standard with two exposed humbuckers, made in Kalamazoo plant, KM on headstock. Sunburst.

1979		$1,500	$1,700

Les Paul Leo's Reissue

1980-1985. Special order from Gibson's Nashville facility for Leo's Music, Oakland, CA. Identified by L-Series serial number with L at the beginning of the number, flamed maple top.

1980-1985		$3,700	$4,000

Les Paul Limited Edition (3-tone)

1997. Limited Edition stamped on the back of the headstock, Les Paul Standard configuration with 'cloud' inlay markers, two-piece three-tone Sunburst finish over non-figured maple top.

1997		$2,400	$2,500

Les Paul Old Hickory

1998 only. Limited run of 200. Tulip poplar body from The Hermitage, Custom-style trim.

1998		$2,500	$3,000

Les Paul Personal

1969-1972. Two angled, low impedence pickups, phase switch, Gold parts. Walnut finish.

1970		$1,100	$1,350

Les Paul Pro-Deluxe

1978-1982. Two P-90 pickups, chrome-plated hardware. "Pro" engraved on truss rod cover, various colors.

1978-1982		$1,100	$1,350

Les Paul Professional

1969-1971, 1977-1979. Single cutaway, two angled, low impedence pickups, carved top. Walnut finish.

1969-1971		$1,100	$1,350

MODEL YEAR	FEATURES	EXC. COND. LOW	HIGH

Les Paul Recording

1971-1980. Two angled, low impedence pickups, high/low impedence selector switch. Various colors.

1971-1980		$1,100	$1,350

Les Paul Reissue Flametop

1983-1990. Flame maple top, two humbuckers, thicker 1959-style neck. Sunburst finish. Renamed '59 Les Paul Flametop in 1991.

1983-1990	Highly figured	$3,200	$3,700

Les Paul Reissue Goldtop

1983-1991. Goldtop finish, two P-100 pickups. Renamed '56 Les Paul Goldtop in 1991.

1983-1989		$1,500	$1,800
1990-1991		$1,600	$1,900

Les Paul Signature

1973-1978. Thin semi-hollowbody, double cutaway, two low impedence pickups, F-holes. Various colors.

1973-1978		$1,700	$2,200

Les Paul SmartWood Standard

1996-2002. Smartwood Series. Figured maple top, mahogany body, Smartwood on truss rod cover.

1998	Antique Natural	$1,000	$1,200

Les Paul Special

1955-1959. Slab solidbody, two pickups (P-90s in 1950s, P-100 stacked humbuckers on later version). Single cutaway until end of 1958, double in 1959. The 1989 reissue is a single cutaway. Renamed SG Special in late-1959.

1955-1959	TV Yellow	$5,500	$6,000
1959	Cherry (mid to late '59)	$5,000	$5,500

Les Paul Special (reissue)

1989-1998. Briefly introduced as Les Paul Junior II but name changed to Special in the first year. Single cutaway, two P-100 stacked humbucking pickups, tune-o-matic bridge, TV Yellow. In 1990 there was a run of 300 with LE serial number. Renamed Special SL in 1998.

1989-1998		$800	$1,000

Les Paul Special 3/4

1959. Slab solidbody, two P-90 pickups, double cutaway, short-scale. Cherry finish. Renamed SG Special 3/4 in late-1959.

1959		$3,800	$4,400

Les Paul Special Centennial

1994 only. One hundred made. Double cutaway, Cherry, 100 year banner at the 12th fret, diamonds in headstock and in gold-plated knobs, gold-plated Gibson coin in back of headstock.

1994		$3,700	$4,000

Les Paul Special Custom Shop

1999-present. Custom Shop decal on back of headstock. Black.

1999		$1,200	$1,300

Les Paul Special Double Cutaway

1976-1979, 1993-1998. Double cutaway, two pickups (P-90s in 1970s, P-100 stacked humbuckers in later version). Various colors.

1976-1979		$1,100	$1,500
1993-1998		$1,000	$1,200

Les Paul Spotlight Special

1983-1984. Curly maple and walnut top, two humbuckers, Gold hardware, multi-bound top, Custom Shop Edition logo. Natural or Sunburst.

1983-1984		$2,000	$2,200

Les Paul Standard (Sunburst)

1958-1960, special order 1972-1975. Les Paul Sunbursts from '58-'60 should be individually valued based on originality, color and the amount and type of figure in the maple top. Changed tuners or a Bigsby removal will drop the value. The noted price ranges are guidance valuations. Each '58-'60 Les Paul Standard should be evaluated on a case-by-case basis. As is always the case, the low and high range are for an all original, excellent condition, undamaged guitar. About 70% of the '58-'60 Les Paul Standards have relatively plain maple tops. Approximately 15% came with the Bigsby tailpiece. The majority of '58-'60 Les Paul Standards have moderate or extreme color fade.

Wider fret wire was introduced in early-'59. White bobbins were introduced in early- to mid-'59. Double ring Kluson Deluxe tuners were introduced in late-'60. It has been suggested that all '58-'60 models have two-piece centerseam tops. This implies that one-piece tops, three-piece tops and off-centerseam tops do not exist.

Sunburst language includes terms such as: arching medullary grain, swirling medullary grain, ribbon-curl, chevrons, Honey-Amber, receding red aniline, pinstripe, bookmatched, double-white bobbins, zebra bobbins, black bobbins, fiddleback maple, unburst finish, Honeyburst, lemon drop, quarter sawn, blistered figure, width of gradation, flat sawn, Teaburst, Bigsby-shadow, rift sawn, heel size, aged clear lacquer, three-dimensional figure, intense fine flame, tag-shadow, red pore filler, eastern maple fleck, medium-thick flame, shrunk tuners, wave and flame, flitch-matched, elbow discoloration, ambered top coat, natural gradation, grain orientation, script oxidation, asymmetrical figure Tangerineburst, Greenburst, and bird's-eye. As in any ultra high-end valuation, each instrument should be evaluated on a case-by-case basis. The 'burst market is heavily influenced by "buyer's preference" and "high-end bias."

1958	Highly flamed, good color	$120,000	$200,000
1958	Highly flamed, good color, Bigsby	$90,000	$175,000
1958	Highly flamed, good color, removed Bigsby	$80,000	$175,000
1958	Highly flamed, faded	$110,000	$180,000
1958	Highly flamed, faded, Bigsby	$80,000	$160,000

Gibson Les Paul Recording

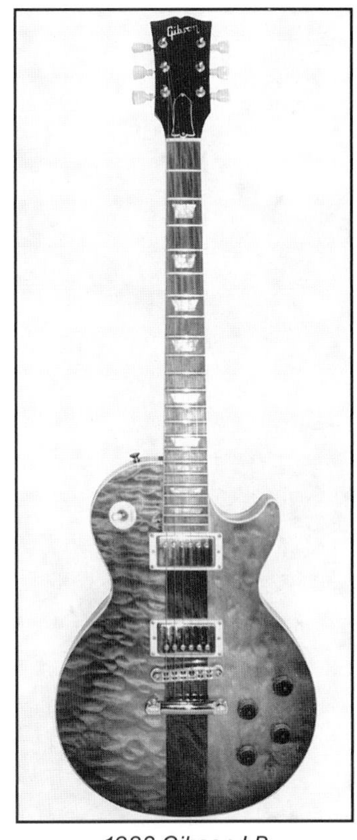

1983 Gibson LP Spotlight Special ASB

GUITARS

1959 Gibson Les Paul Standard

1960 Gibson Les Paul SG

MODEL YEAR	FEATURES	EXC. COND. LOW	HIGH
1958	Highly flamed, faded, removed Bigsby	$70,000	$160,000
1958	Medium flame, good color	$80,000	$160,000
1958	Medium flame, good color, Bigsby	$70,000	$150,000
1958	Medium flame, good color, removed Bigsby	$60,000	$140,000
1958	Medium flame, faded	$75,000	$150,000
1958	Medium flame, faded, Bigsby	$65,000	$140,000
1958	Medium flame, faded, removed Bigsby	$55,000	$130,000
1958	Plain top, good color	$65,000	$130,000
1958	Plain top, good color, Bigsby	$60,000	$110,000
1958	Plain top, good color, removed Bigsby	$50,000	$100,000
1958	Plain top, faded	$60,000	$100,000
1958	Plain top, faded, Bigsby	$55,000	$80,000
1958	Plain top, faded, removed Bigsby	$45,000	$70,000
1959	Highly flamed, good color	$120,000	$210,000
1959	Highly flamed, good color, Bigsby	$100,000	$185,000
1959	Highly flamed, good color, removed Bigsby	$85,000	$180,000
1959	Highly flamed, faded	$110,000	$190,000
1959	Highly flamed, faded, Bigsby	$90,000	$170,000
1959	Highly flamed, faded, removed Bigsby	$75,000	$165,000
1959	Medium flame, good color	$90,000	$170,000
1959	Medium flame, good color, Bigsby	$80,000	$160,000
1959	Medium flame, good color, removed Bigsby	$65,000	$145,000
1959	Medium flame, faded	$85,000	$160,000
1959	Medium flame, faded, Bigsby	$70,000	$150,000
1959	Medium flame, faded, removed Bigsby	$60,000	$135,000
1959	Plain top, good color	$75,000	$140,000
1959	Plain top, good color, Bigsby	$65,000	$120,000
1959	Plain top, good color, removed Bigsby	$55,000	$110,000
1959	Plain top, faded	$70,000	$110,000
1959	Plain top, faded, Bigsby	$60,000	$90,000
1959	Plain top, faded, removed Bigsby	$50,000	$80,000
1960	Highly flamed, good color	$120,000	$175,000
1960	Highly flamed, good color, Bigsby	$90,000	$160,000
1960	Highly flamed, good color, removed Bigsby	$80,000	$150,000
1960	Highly flamed, faded	$110,000	$160,000
1960	Highly flamed, faded, Bigsby	$80,000	$150,000
1960	Highly flamed, faded, removed Bigsby	$70,000	$140,000
1960	Medium flame, good color	$80,000	$150,000
1960	Medium flame, good color, Bigsby	$70,000	$135,000
1960	Medium flame, good color, removed Bigsby	$60,000	$120,000
1960	Medium flame, faded	$75,000	$140,000
1960	Medium flame, faded, Bigsby	$65,000	$120,000
1960	Medium flame, faded, removed Bigsby	$55,000	$110,000
1960	Plain top, good color	$65,000	$110,000
1960	Plain top, good color, Bigsby	$60,000	$100,000
1960	Plain top, good color, removed Bigsby	$50,000	$80,000
1960	Plain top, faded	$60,000	$90,000
1960	Plain top, faded, Bigsby	$55,000	$80,000
1960	Plain top, faded, removed Bigsby	$45,000	$70,000

Les Paul Standard (SG body)

1961-1963 (SG body those years). Renamed SG Standard in late-1963.

MODEL YEAR	FEATURES	EXC. COND. LOW	HIGH
1961-1962	Cherry, side vibrola, PAFs	$6,000	$7,000
1962	Ebony block tailpiece	$7,000	$7,500

MODEL YEAR	FEATURES	EXC. COND. LOW	HIGH
1963	Cherry	$5,500	$6,000

Les Paul Standard (reintroduced then renamed)

1968-1969. Comes back as a Goldtop with P-90s for 1968-1969 (renamed Les Paul Deluxe, 1969). Available as special order Deluxe 1972-1976.

MODEL YEAR	FEATURES	LOW	HIGH
1968	P-90s, small headstock	$5,500	$7,000
1968-1969	P-90s, large headstock	$5,000	$5,500

Les Paul Standard (reintroduced)

1976-present. Available as special order Deluxe 1972-1976. Reintroduced with two humbuckers 1976-present.

MODEL YEAR	FEATURES	LOW	HIGH
1972-1974	Goldtop or s/b, P-90s	$2,200	$2,500
1974-1975	Sunburst, humbuckers	$2,300	$2,600
1976	Sunburst	$1,700	$1,900
1976	Wine Red	$1,500	$1,700
1977	Sunburst	$1,600	$1,800
1978	Natural	$1,500	$1,700
1978	Sunburst	$1,500	$1,800
1979	Brown or cherry s/b	$1,400	$1,800
1979	Goldtop	$1,500	$1,900
1979	Natural or wine	$1,300	$1,700
1980	Sunburst	$1,300	$1,800
1980	Sunburst, mild flame	$1,700	$2,000
1980	Wine Red	$1,200	$1,700
1981	Sunburst	$1,300	$1,600
1981	Wine Red	$1,200	$1,500
1982	Black	$1,200	$1,400
1982	Brown Sunburst	$1,300	$1,500
1982	Cherry Sunburst	$1,400	$1,600
1982	Goldtop	$1,400	$1,600
1982	Wine Red	$1,200	$1,400
1983	Natural	$1,300	$1,500
1983-1986	Sunburst	$1,400	$1,600
1984	Sunburst	$1,400	$1,600
1985	Black	$1,200	$1,400
1985	Wine Red	$1,200	$1,400
1987-1989	Sunburst	$1,300	$1,600
1988-1989	White, gold hardware	$1,300	$1,600
1990-2002	Limited Edition colors	$1,600	$1,800
1990-2002	Various colors	$1,200	$1,600

Les Paul Standard '58

1971-1975. Goldtop, called the '58, but set up like a 1954 Goldtop with two soapbar pickups and stop tailpiece.

MODEL YEAR	FEATURES	LOW	HIGH
1971-1975		$3,000	$3,500

Les Paul Standard Lite

1999-2001. A member of DC body-style, renamed from DC Standard in 1999, reintroduced as Les Paul Standard DC Plus in 2001. Various translucent finishes.

MODEL YEAR	FEATURES	LOW	HIGH
1999-2001		$900	$1,000

Les Paul Strings and Things Standard

1975-1978. Special order flamed maple top Les Paul Standard model, built for Strings and Things, a Gibson dealer in Memphis. Valuation should be on a case-by-case basis. Sunburst.

MODEL YEAR	FEATURES	LOW	HIGH
1978	2-piece top	$4,000	$6,000
1978	3-piece top	$3,000	$3,500

Les Paul Studio

1983-present. Alder body, two humbuckers.

MODEL YEAR	FEATURES	LOW	HIGH
1983-1999	Various colors	$800	$1,000
2000-2002	Transparent Red	$800	$900

Les Paul Studio Custom

1984-1985. Alder body, two humbucking pickups, multi-bound top, gold-plated hardware. Various colors.

MODEL YEAR	FEATURES	LOW	HIGH
1984-1985		$900	$950

Les Paul Studio Gem

1996-1998. Limited edition with Les Paul Studio features, but using P-90 pickups instead of humbucker pickups, plus trapezoid markers and Gold hardware.

MODEL YEAR	FEATURES	LOW	HIGH
1996-1998		$750	$800

Les Paul Studio Gothic

2000s. Gothic Black.

MODEL YEAR	FEATURES	LOW	HIGH
2000-2001		$700	$750

Les Paul Studio Lite

1987-1998. Carved maple top, mahogany back and neck, two humbucker pickups. Various colors.

MODEL YEAR	FEATURES	LOW	HIGH
1987-1998		$800	$1,000

Les Paul TV

1954-1959. Les Paul Jr. with limed mahogany (TV Yellow) finish, single cutaway until mid-1958, double cutaway after. Renamed SG TV in late-1959.

MODEL YEAR	FEATURES	LOW	HIGH
1955-1958	Single cut	$5,000	$5,200
1958-1959	Double cut	$5,000	$5,200

Les Paul TV 3/4

1954-1957. Limed mahogany (TV Yellow) Les Paul Jr. 3/4. Short-scale, single cutaway.

MODEL YEAR	FEATURES	LOW	HIGH
1954-1957		$2,500	$3,500

Les Paul Ultima

1996-present. Custom Shop model, quilted Sunburst top, butterfly inlay, abalone trim.

MODEL YEAR	FEATURES	LOW	HIGH
1990s		$5,000	$6,500

The Les Paul

1976-1980. Figured maple top, two humbuckers, Gold hardware, rosewood binding, pickguard, fingerboard, knobs, cover plates, etc. Natural or rosewood finishing, Natural only by 1979.

MODEL YEAR	FEATURES	LOW	HIGH
1976-1980	Natural or Rosewood	$11,500	$12,500

The Paul

1978-1982. Walnut body, two exposed humbuckers.

MODEL YEAR	FEATURES	LOW	HIGH
1978-1982		$650	$700

The Paul Firebrand Deluxe

1980-1982. Single cutaway mahogany solidbody, rough Natural finish, Gibson branded in headstock, two exposed humbuckers.

MODEL YEAR	FEATURES	LOW	HIGH
1980-1982	Pelham Blue	$600	$700
1980-1982	Rough Natural	$400	$650

1950s Gibson Les Paul TV

Gibson Les Paul Ultima

GUITARS

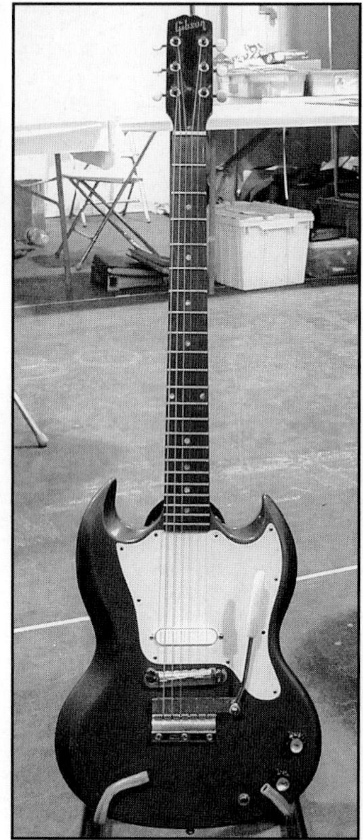
1970 Gibson Melody Maker

1964 Gibson Melody Maker 3/4

MODEL YEAR	FEATURES	EXC. COND. LOW	HIGH

The Paul II

1996-1998. Mahogany body, two humbucking pickups, rosewood dot neck. Renamed The Paul SL in 1998.

1996-1998		$550	$600

LG-0

1958-1974. Flat-top acoustic, mahogany, bound body, rosewood bridge 1958-1961 and 1968-1974, plastic bridge 1962-1967. Natural.

1958-1961	Rosewood bridge	$800	$1,200
1962-1964	Plastic bridge	$700	$950
1965-1967	Plastic bridge	$550	$850
1968-1969	Rosewood bridge	$500	$750

LG-1

1943-1968. Flat-top acoustic, spruce top, mahogany back and sides, bound body, rosewood bridge 1943-1961, plastic bridge after. Examples seen to 1974. Sunburst.

1943	Rosewood bridge	$1,500	$2,000
1944	Rosewood bridge	$1,400	$1,900
1945	Rosewood bridge	$1,400	$1,700
1946	Rosewood bridge	$1,300	$1,600
1947-1949	Rosewood bridge	$1,100	$1,600
1950-1961	Rosewood bridge	$1,000	$1,400
1962-1965	Adjustable plastic bridge	$900	$1,300
1966-1968	Adjustable plastic bridge	$800	$1,100

LG-2

1942-1962. Flat-top acoustic, spruce top, mahogany back and sides (some with maple 1943-1946), banner headstock 1942-1946, bound body, X-bracing. Sunburst finish. Replaced by B-25 in 1962.

1942		$2,300	$2,800
1943		$2,200	$2,700
1944		$2,100	$2,600
1945		$2,000	$2,500
1946		$1,900	$2,400
1947-1949		$1,800	$2,300
1950-1961		$1,600	$2,100
1962	Ajustable bridge	$1,300	$1,800

LG-2 H

1945-1955. Flat-top, Hawaiian. Natural or Sunburst.

1945-1955		$1,400	$1,900

LG-2 3/4

1949-1962. Short-scale version of LG-2 flat-top, wood bridge. Sunburst.

1949-1962		$1,200	$1,800

LG-3

1942-1963. Flat-top acoustic, spruce top, mahogany back and sides, bound body. Natural finish. Replaced by B-25 N.

1942		$2,500	$3,000
1943		$2,400	$2,900
1944		$2,300	$2,800
1945		$2,200	$2,700
1946		$2,100	$2,600
1947-1949		$2,000	$2,500

MODEL YEAR	FEATURES	EXC. COND. LOW	HIGH
1950-1962	Wood bridge	$1,500	$2,100
1962-1963	Plastic bridge	$1,400	$1,900

LG-12 (12-string)

1967-1973. 14-1/8" wide, mahogany back and sides, bound top, natural.

1967-1969	Adjustable saddle	$650	$850
1970-1974	Set saddle	$600	$800

Marauder

1975-1980. Single cutaway solidbody, pointed headstock, two pickups, bolt-on neck. Various colors.

1975-1980		$500	$700

Melody Maker

1959-1971. Slab solidbody, one pickup, single cutaway until 1961, double 1961-1966, SG body 1966-1971. Reintroduced as single cutaway in 1986-1993.

1959	Sunburst	$850	$1,250
1960	Sunburst	$800	$1,100
1961	Sunburst, single cut	$750	$1,000
1962	Cherry, double cut	$700	$950
1962	Sunburst, double cut	$700	$950
1963	Cherry, double cut	$650	$900
1964	Cherry	$650	$850
1964	Sunburst	$650	$850
1965	Cherry, double cut	$600	$800
1966	Blue or Red, SG body	$750	$1,050
1967-1969	Blue or Red	$700	$1,000
1968-1970	Walnut option	$700	$1,000

Melody Maker 3/4

1959-1970. Short-scale version.

1959-1965	Melody maker body	$625	$800
1966-1970	SG body	$600	$900

Melody Maker D

1960-1970. Two pickup version of Melody Maker. Reintroduced as Melody Maker Double in 1977.

1960	Sunburst, single cut	$900	$1,200
1961	Sunburst, single cut	$850	$1,150
1962	Sunburst, double cut	$800	$1,100
1963	Cherry, double cut	$750	$1,000
1964	Cherry, double cut	$700	$900
1965	Cherry, double cut	$650	$850
1966	Blue or Red, SG body	$950	$1,100
1966	Cherry, double cut	$650	$800
1967-1969	Blue, Red or White, SG body	$900	$1,150
1968-1970	Walnut option, SG body	$900	$1,150

Melody Maker III

1965-1971. SG-style double cutaway solidbody, three pickups. Various colors.

1967-1969		$1,100	$1,350
1970-1971		$1,000	$1,300

Melody Maker 12

1967-1971. SG-style solidbody, 12 strings, two pickups. Red, White or Pelham Blue.

1967-1971		$1,000	$1,150

MODEL YEAR	FEATURES	EXC. COND. LOW	HIGH

Melody Maker Double

1977-1983. Reintroduction of Melody maker D. Double cutaway solidbody, two pickups. Cherry or Sunburst.

1977		$550	$750

MK-35

1975-1978. Mark Series flat-top acoustic, mahogany back and sides, Black-bound body. Natural or Sunburst.

1975-1978		$650	$750

MK-53

1975-1978. Mark Series flat-top acoustic, maple back and sides, multi-bound body. Natural or Sunburst.

1975-1978		$750	$850

MK-72

1975-1978. Mark Series flat-top acoustic, rosewood back and sides, Black-bound body. Natural or Sunburst.

1975-1978		$850	$950

MK-81

1975-1978. Mark Series flat-top acoustic, rosewood back and sides, multi-bound body, Gold tuners, high-end appointments. Natural or Sunburst.

1975-1978		$900	$1,000

Moderne Heritage

1981-1983. Limited edition with approximately 143 made. Korina body, two humbucking pickups, Gold hardware.

1981-1983	Black or White	$2,400	$2,800
1981-1983	Natural	$2,800	$3,200

Nick Lucas

1928-1938. Flat-top acoustic, multi-bound body and neck, sunburst. Reintroduced in 1991 and '99.

1928	Mahogany, 12-fret, 13 1/3"	$5,000	$6,000
1928	Rosewood, 12-fret, 13 1/2"	$6,000	$7,000
1929-1933	Rosewood, 13-fret, 14 3/4"	$7,000	$8,000
1934-1938	Maple, 14-fret, 14 3/4"	$6,000	$7,000

Nick Lucas Reissue

1991-1992, 1999-present. Limited edition flat-top acoustic. Sunburst.

1991-1992		$1,500	$1,650

Nighthawk Custom

1993-1999. Flame maple top, Ebony fingerboard, Gold hardware, single/double/mini pickups.

1993-1999	Fireburst	$900	$1,000

Nighthawk Special

1993-1999. Single cut solidbody, figured maple top, double-coil and mini-pickup or with additional single-coil options, dot marker inlay. Cherry, ebony or sunburst.

1993-1999	.	$650	$750

Nighthawk Standard

1993-1999. Single cut solidbody, figured maple top, 2 or 3 pickups, double-parallelogram inlay. Amber, fireburst or sunburst.

1993-1999		$750	$950

MODEL YEAR	FEATURES	EXC. COND. LOW	HIGH

Nouveau NV6T-M

1986-1987. A line of Gibson flat-tops with imported parts assembled and finished in the U.S. Acoustic dreadnought, bound maple body, Natural.

1986-1987		$350	$450

RD Artist

1978-1982. Double cutaway solidbody, two humbuckers, TP-6 tailpiece, active electronics, ebony 'board, block inlays, gold-plated parts, various colors. Called just RD (no Artist) in '81 and '82.

1978-1982		$900	$1,000

RD Custom

1977-1979. Double cutaway solidbody, two humbuckers, stop tailpiece, active electronics, dot inlays, maple 'board, chrome parts. Natural or Walnut.

1977-1979		$1,100	$1,300

RD Standard

1977-1979. Double cutaway solidbody, two humbuckers, stop tailpiece, rosewood 'board, dot inlays, chrome parts. Natural, Sunburst or Walnut.

1977-1979		$1,000	$1,200

Roy Smeck Radio Grande Hawaiian

1934-1939. Dreadnought acoustic flat-top, rosewood back and sides, bound body and neck. Natural.

1934-1939		$6,500	$8,000

Roy Smeck Stage Deluxe Hawaiian

1934-1942. Dreadnought acoustic flat-top, mahogany back and sides, bound body. Natural.

1934-1942		$4,000	$6,000

S-1

1976-1980. Single cutaway solidbody, pointed headstock, three single-coil pickups, similar to the Marauder. Various colors.

1976-1980		$550	$600

SGs

Following are the various guitars, listed alphabetically, bearing the SG name:

'63 Corvette Sting Ray (Custom shop)

1996-1997. SG-style body carved to simulate split rear window on '63 Corvette, "Sting Ray" inlay, 150 instruments built. Offered in Black, White, Silver or Red.

1996-1997	Black	$3,000	$5,000

SG '61 Reissue

1993-present. Double cutaway SG body, two humbuckers, Cherry. See SG Reissue for 1986-1987, and SG '62 Reissue for 1988-1991.

1993-2002		$800	$1,100

SG '62 Reissue/SG Reissue

1986-1991. Called SG Reissue 1986-1987, SG '62 Reissue 1988-1991, and SG '61 Reissue 1993-present. Cherry.

1986-1987	SG reissue	$800	$1,100
1988-1991	'62 reissue	$800	$1,100

Gibson Nighthawk Custom

1963 Gibson SG Custom

GUITARS

Gibson SG Junior

Gibson SG Special

MODEL YEAR	FEATURES	EXC. COND. LOW	HIGH

SG 90 Double

1988-1990. SG body, updated electronics, graphite reinforced neck, two pickups. Cherry, Turquoise or White.

1988-1990		$500	$650

SG 90 Single

1988-1990. SG body, updated electronics, graphite reinforced neck, one humbucker pickup. Cherry, Turquoise or White.

1988-1990		$450	$600

SG Corvette Sting Ray L.E. (Custom Shop)

1996 only. SG-style body, Sting Ray inlay, 150 instruments built, offered in Black, Red or Silver.

1996		$1,900	$2,100

SG Custom

1963-1980. Renamed from Les Paul Custom, three humbuckers, vibrato. Made with Les Paul Custom plate from 1961-1963 (see Les Paul Custom). White finish until 1968, Walnut and others after.

1963	White	$5,500	$6,500
1964	White	$5,000	$6,000
1965	White	$4,500	$5,500
1966	White	$4,000	$5,000
1967	White	$3,500	$4,500
1968	White	$3,000	$4,000
1969	Walnut	$2,500	$3,500
1970-1973	Walnut	$2,000	$3,000
1970-1973	White option	$2,800	$3,500
1974-1976	Various colors	$2,000	$3,000
1977-1980	Various colors	$1,700	$2,500

SG Custom '67 Reissue/Les Paul SG '67 Custom

1991-1993. The SG Custom '67 Reissue has a Wine Red finish. The Les Paul SG '67 Custom (1992-1993) has a Wine Red or White finish.

1991-1993		$1,500	$2,000

SG Deluxe

1971-1974, 1981-1985, 1998-present. The 1970s models were offered in Natural, Cherry or Walnut finishes. Reintroduced in 1998 with three Firebird mini-humbucker-style pickups in Black, Ice Blue or Red finishes..

1971-1974	Cherry	$1,000	$1,400
1971-1974	Natural or Walnut	$900	$1,100
1981-1985	Various colors	$700	$900
1998-1999	Various colors	$700	$750

SG Exclusive

1979. SG with humbuckers, coil-tap and rotary control knob, block inlay, pearl logo (not decal), Black/Ebony finish.

1979		$900	$1,000

SG Firebrand

1980-1982. Double cut mahogany solidbody, rough Natural finish, Gibson branded in headstock, 2 exposed humbuckers.

1980-1982		$550	$700

SG Jr.

1963-1971, 1991-1994. One pickup, solidbody.

MODEL YEAR	FEATURES	EXC. COND. LOW	HIGH
1963	Alpine White	$2,200	$2,500
1963	Cherry	$1,500	$1,800
1964	Cherry	$1,400	$1,600
1964	White	$2,100	$2,400
1965	Cherry	$1,300	$1,500
1965	White	$2,000	$2,300
1966	Cherry	$1,200	$1,500
1967	Cherry	$1,100	$1,400
1968	Cherry	$1,000	$1,300
1968	White	$1,700	$2,000
1969	Cherry	$1,000	$1,200
1970	Cherry	$950	$1,150
1971	Cherry or Walnut	$950	$1,050
1991-1994	Various colors	$750	$900

SG Les Paul Custom

1987-1992. Three pickups. Called the SG '90 Les Paul Custom towards the end of its run.

1987-1989	Antique Ivory	$1,500	$1,800
1990-1992	White	$1,300	$1,600

SG Les Paul Custom 30th Anniversary

1991. SG body, three humbuckers, Gold hardware, TV Yellow finish, 30th Anniversary on peghead.

1991		$1,400	$1,700

SG Limited Edition Korina

1993. Limited edition SG specs using Natural korina (limba/mahogany from Africa).

1990s		$1,500	$1,800

SG Pete Townshend Signature (Historic/Custom Shop)

2000 only. SG Special with 1970 specs, large guard, two cases. Cherry Red.

2000		$2,200	$2,600

SG Pro

1971-1973. Two P-90 pickups, tune-o-matic bridge, vibrato. Cherry, Mahogany or Walnut.

1971-1973		$800	$1,000

SG Special

1959-1978, 1986-1996, 2000-2001. Rounded double cutaway for '59-'60, switched to SG body early-'61. Two P-90s '59-'71, two mini-humbuckers '72-'78, two regular size humbuckers on current version. Reintroduced variation to the SG line in '86-'99, then reintroduced again in '00.

1959	Cherry, slab, high neck pickup	$3,800	$4,500
1960	Cherry, slab, lower neck pickup	$4,000	$5,000
1961	Cherry, SG body	$2,800	$3,200
1962	Cherry	$2,600	$2,900
1962	White	$3,400	$3,600
1963	Cherry	$2,300	$2,600
1963	White	$3,300	$3,500
1964	Cherry	$2,200	$2,500
1964	White	$3,000	$3,300
1965	Cherry	$1,900	$2,100
1965	White	$2,500	$2,700
1966	Cherry	$1,800	$2,100
1966	White	$2,200	$2,400
1967	Cherry	$1,400	$1,900
1967	White	$1,700	$2,100
1968-1971	Cherry	$1,300	$1,600

MODEL YEAR	FEATURES	EXC. COND. LOW	HIGH
1972-1975	Cherry or Walnut	$1,000	$1,400
1976-1978	Cherry or Walnut	$1,000	$1,200

SG Special (reintroduced variation)

1986-1996. Reintroduced variation to the SG line.

1986-1996	Various color	$675	$700

SG Special (reintroduced again)

2000-2001. Second reintroduction of SG Special.

2000-2001	Cherry	$650	$700

SG Standard

1963-1981. Les Paul Standard changes to SG body, two humbuckers, some very early models have optional factory Bigsby.

1963	Cherry	$5,000	$6,000
1964	Cherry	$4,500	$5,500
1965	Cherry	$4,000	$5,000
1965	Pelham Blue (faded)	$4,000	$5,000
1965	Pelham Blue (not faded)	$6,500	$7,000
1966	Cherry	$3,800	$4,800
1967	Burgundy Metallic	$3,500	$4,500
1967	Cherry	$2,500	$3,500
1967	White	$3,200	$4,200
1968	Cherry	$2,300	$3,000
1969	Cherry, engraved lyre	$2,000	$2,800
1970	Cherry, engraved lyre	$1,800	$2,500
1970	Cherry, non-lyre tailpiece	$1,400	$1,700
1971	Cherry	$1,200	$1,500
1972-1975	New specs and colors	$1,000	$1,300
1976-1981	New color line-up	$1,000	$1,200

SG Standard (reintroduced)

1986-present. Reintroduced variation to SG Standard line, similar to 1962 version. Various colors.

1986-1999		$1,000	$1,200

SG Standard Korina

1993-1994. Korina version of SG Standard, limited run. Natural.

1993-1994		$1,300	$1,600

SG Tommy Iommi Signature (Historic/Custom Shop)

1999-present. SG body with signature humbucking pickups without poles, cross inlay markers. Ebony or Wine Red.

1999		$1,800	$2,200

SG TV

1959-1968. Les Paul TV changed to SG body. Double rounded cutaway solidbody for 1959-1960, SG body 1961-1968, one pickup, limed mahogany (TV yellow) finish.

1959-1961	TV Yellow, slab body	$4,000	$5,000
1961-1963	White, SG body	$2,200	$2,500

SG I

1972-1977. Double cutaway, mahogany body, one mini-humbucker pickup (some with SG Jr. P-90). Cherry or Walnut.

MODEL YEAR	FEATURES	EXC. COND. LOW	HIGH
1972-1977		$500	$600

SG II

1972-1976. Double cutaway, mahogany body, two mini-humbucker pickups (some SG IIs in 1975 had regular humbuckers). Cherry or Walnut.

1972-1976		$650	$700

SG III

1972-1974. Replaces SG-250. Double pointed cutaway, mahogany body, two mini-humbucker pickups. The SG III was the Sunburst version of the II. Some shipped as late as 1979.

1972-1974		$650	$700

SG-100

1971-1972. Double cutaway solidbody, one pickup. Cherry or Walnut.

1971-1972	Melody Maker pickup	$500	$900
1971-1972	P-90 pickup option	$1,000	$1,100

SG-200

1971-1972. Two pickup version of SG-100 in Black, Cherry or Walnut finish. Replaced by SG II.

1971-1972	Melody Maker pickups	$600	$1,000

SG-250

1971-1972. Two pickup version of SG-100 in Cherry Sunburst. Replaced by SG III.

1971-1972	Melody Maker pickups	$600	$1,000

SG-X (All American)

1998-1999. Named the SG-X in 1989, previously part of the all American series, SG body with single bridge humbucker. Various colors.

1998-1999		$400	$500

The SG

1979-1983. Normal SG specs, solid walnut body and neck, ebony 'board, 2 humbuckers, model name logo on truss rod.

1979-1983		$550	$750

The SG (Standard)

1983-1987. Normal SG specs, exposed humbuckers, model name logo on truss rod, walnut neck and walnut body, natural and other colors.

1983-1987		$600	$800

SJ (Southern Jumbo)

1942-1978,1991-1996. Flat-top, sunburst standard, natural optional starting in 1954 (natural finish version called Country-Western starting in '56), round shoulders (changed to square in '62).

1942-1944		$4,500	$5,500
1947-1948		$4,000	$5,000
1949-1950		$3,500	$4,500
1951-1953		$3,000	$4,000
1954-1956	Natural option, round shoulder	$3,200	$4,200
1954-1961	Round shoulder	$2,800	$3,800
1962-1964	Square shoulder	$2,000	$2,500
1965-1966		$1,700	$2,400
1967-1968		$1,500	$2,000
1969		$1,400	$1,700

1962 Gibson SG Standard

1983 Gibson The SG

GUITARS

1983 Gibson Sonex 180 Deluxe

1969 Gibson Super 400CES

MODEL YEAR	FEATURES	EXC. COND. LOW	HIGH
1970-1971		$1,200	$1,500
1972-1974		$1,100	$1,400

SJ Deluxe

1970-ca.1974. Flat-top acoustic, block inlays, mahogany back and sides.

1970-1974	Natural	$1,100	$1,300
1970-1974	Sunburst	$1,000	$1,200

SJ-100 1939 Centennial

1994. Acoustic flat-top, limited edition. Sunburst

1994		$1,500	$1,800

SJ-200 Ray Whitley/J-200 Custom Club

1994-1995. Based on Ray Whitley's late-1930s J-200, including engraved inlays and initials on the truss rod cover. Only 37 made. One of the limited edition models the Montana division released to celebrate Gibson's 100th anniversary.

1994-1995		$7,000	$9,000

Sonex-180 Custom

1980-1982. Two Super humbuckers, coil-tap, maple neck, Ebony board, single cut, body of "Multi-Phonic" synthetic material. Various colors.

1980-1982		$500	$600

Sonex-180 Deluxe

1980-1984. Hardwood neck, rosewood board, single cut, body of "Multi-Phonic" synthetic material, two pickups, no coil-tap. Various colors.

1980-1984		$450	$550

Spirit I

1982-1988. Double rounded cutaway, one pickup, chrome hardware, various colors.

1982-1988		$400	$550

Spirit II XPL

1985-1987. Double cutaway solidbody, Kahler trem, two pickups, various colors.

1985-1987		$450	$650

SR-71

1987-1989. Floyd Rose tremolo, one humbucker, two single-coil pickups, various colors. Wayne Charvel designed.

1987-1989		$450	$650

Style O

1902-1925. Acoustic archtop, oval soundhole, bound top, neck and headstock. Various colors.

1910-1925		$3,400	$4,400

Style U Harp Guitar

1902-1939. Acoustic six-string, with 10 or 12 sub-bass strings, maple back and sides, bound soundhole. Black.

1915-1919		$5,500	$6,000

Super 300 (non-cutaway)

1948-1955. Acoustic archtop, non-cutaway, bound body, neck and headstock. Sunburst.

1948-1955		$3,500	$5,000

Super 300 C (cutaway)

1954-1958. Acoustic archtop, rounded cutaway, bound body, neck and headstock. Sunburst with Natural option.

1954-1957	Natural option	$5,500	$7,200
1954-1957	Sunburst	$5,000	$6,800

MODEL YEAR	FEATURES	EXC. COND. LOW	HIGH

Super 400

1934-1941, 1947-1955. Acoustic archtop, non-cutaway, multi-bound, F-holes. Sunburst (see Super 400 N for Natural version).

1934		$8,000	$11,000
1935		$8,000	$10,000
1936-1941		$8,000	$9,500
1947-1955		$6,000	$8,500

Super 400 N

1940, 1948-1955. Natural finish version of Super 400, non-cutaway, acoustic archtop.

1940		$7,500	$9,000
1948-1950		$6,500	$8,500
1951-1952		$5,500	$7,500

Super 400 P (Premium)

1939-1941. Acoustic archtop, single rounded cutaway. Sunburst finish.

1939-1941		$15,000	$25,000

'39 Super 400 Historical Collection

1993-2000. Reissue of non-cutaway 1939 version. Part of Gibson's Historic Collection.

1993-1995	Sunburst	$5,500	$6,500
1993-1995	Wine Red Burgundy	$4,500	$5,000

Super 400 C

1948-1982. Introduced as Super 400 Premier. Acoustic archtop, single cutaway. Sunburst finish (Natural is called Super 400 CN).

1948-1957		$11,000	$15,000
1958-1959		$10,000	$13,000
1960-1963		$10,000	$12,000
1964-1965		$8,500	$11,000
1966-1969		$6,000	$9,000
1970-1974		$5,000	$7,000
1975-1982		$5,000	$6,000

Super 400 CN

1940-1941, 1950-1987. Natural finish version of Super 400 C.

1952-1959		$11,000	$15,000
1960-1964		$10,000	$13,000
1965-1969		$7,000	$10,000
1970-1977		$4,000	$6,000

Super 400 CES

1951-present. Electric version of Super 400 C. Archtop, single cutaway (round 1951-1960 and 1969-present, pointed 1960-1969), two pickups (P-90s 1951-1954, Alnico Vs 1954-1957, humbuckers 1957 on). Sunburst (Natural version called Super 400 CESN). Now part of Gibson's Historic Collection.

1951-1953	P-90 pickups	$13,000	$17,000
1954-1956	Alnico V pickups	$14,000	$18,000
1957-1959	Humbucker pickups	$15,000	$20,000
1960-1962		$13,000	$16,000
1963-1964		$12,000	$14,000
1965-1966		$7,500	$11,000
1967-1969		$7,000	$9,000
1970-1974		$6,500	$8,500
1975-1979		$6,500	$7,500
1980-1987		$4,500	$6,500

MODEL YEAR	FEATURES	EXC. COND. LOW	HIGH

Super 400 CESN

1952-present. Natural version of Super 400 CES. Now part of Gibson's Historic Collection.

1952		$20,000	$25,000
1953-1956	Single-coils	$18,500	$22,000
1957-1960	Humbuckers	$20,000	$30,000
1961	Sharp cut introduced	$18,000	$28,000
1962	PAFs	$13,000	$23,000
1963-1964	Pat. #	$11,000	$18,000
1965-1966		$10,000	$13,000
1967-1969		$8,000	$11,000
1970-1982		$5,000	$8,000

Super Jumbo 100

1939-1943. Jumbo flat-top, mahogany back and sides, bound body and neck, Sunburst. Reintroduced as J-100 with different specs in 1984.

1939-1943		$16,000	$22,000

Super Jumbo/Super Jumbo 200

1938-1947. Initially called Super Jumbo in 1938 and named Super Jumbo 200 in 1939. Name then changed to J-200 (see that listing) by '47 (with maple back and sides) and SJ-200 by the '50s. Named for super large jumbo 16 7/8" flat-top body, double braced with rosewood back and sides, sunburst finish.

1938-1939		$40,000	$55,000
1940-1942		$40,000	$50,000

Super V CES

1978-1993. Archtop, L-5 with a Super 400 neck. Natural or Sunburst.

1978-1993		$4,500	$5,500

Tal Farlow

1962-1971, 1993-present. Full body, single cut archtop, 2 humbuckers, triple-bound top. Reintroduced '93, now part of Gibson's Historic Collection.

1962-1964	Viceroy Brown	$7,500	$9,500
1965-1966	Viceroy Brown	$7,000	$8,000
1967-1969	Viceroy Brown	$6,000	$7,500
1970-1971	Viceroy Brown	$5,000	$6,000
1993-1999	Cherry or Viceroy Brown	$2,500	$3,000
1993-1999	Natural, figured wood	$2,800	$3,500

TG-0 (L-0 based)

1927-1933. Acoustic tenor based on L-0, mahogany body. Light Amber.

1927-1933		$1,200	$1,300

TG-0 (LG-0 based)

1960-1974. Acoustic tenor based on LG-0, mahogany body. Natural.

1960-1964		$650	$750
1965-1969		$550	$650
1970-1974		$450	$550

TG-1

1927-1937. Acoustic flat-top, tenor guitar based on L-1, mahogany back and sides, bound body. Sunburst.

1927-1937		$1,400	$1,500

MODEL YEAR	FEATURES	EXC. COND. LOW	HIGH

TG-25/TG-25 N

1962-1970. Acoustic flat-top, tenor guitar based on B-25, mahogany back and sides. Natural or Sunburst.

1962-1964		$700	$800
1965-1969		$600	$700
1970		$500	$600

TG-50

1934-1958. Acoustic archtop, tenor guitar based on L-50, mahogany back and sides. Sunburst.

1934-1940		$1,000	$1,200
1947-1949		$800	$1,100
1950-1958		$700	$900

Trini Lopez Deluxe

1964-1970. Double pointed cutaway, thinline archtop, two humbuckers, triple-bound. Sunburst.

1964-1970		$2,200	$2,500

Trini Lopez Standard

1964-1970. Double rounded cutaway, thinline archtop, two humbuckers, tune-o-matic bridge, trapeze tailpiece, single-bound. Cherry, Sparkling Burgundy and Pelham Blue finishes.

1964-1970	Cherry	$1,500	$2,000
1964-1970	Sparkling Burgundy option	$1,800	$2,200

U-2

1987-1991. Double cut, one humbucker and two single-coil pickups, Ebony or Red. Renamed Mach II in 1990.

1987-1991		$500	$600

US-1/US-3

1986-1991. Double cut maple top with mahogany back, 3 humbuckers (US-1), or three P-90s (US-3), standard production and Custom Shop.

1986-1991	US-3, P-90s	$500	$600

USA Map Guitar

1983. Mahogany body cutout like lower 48, two humbuckers, limited run promotion. Natural (nine made with American Flag finish).

1983	Natural	$1,800	$2,000
1983	Red, White and Blue	$2,500	$3,000

Victory MV II (MV 2)

1981-1984. Asymetrical double cutaway with long horn, three-way slider, maple body and neck, rosewood fingerboard, two pickups.

1981-1984		$550	$650

Victory MV X (MV 10)

1981-1984. Double cut solidbody, three humbucking pickups, five-way switch. Various colors.

1981-1984		$600	$700

XPL Custom

1985-1986. Explorer-like shape, exposed humbuckers, locking tremolo, bound maple top. Sunburst or White.

1985-1986		$550	$650

Gibson Tal Farlow

1967 Gibson Trini Lopez

GUITARS

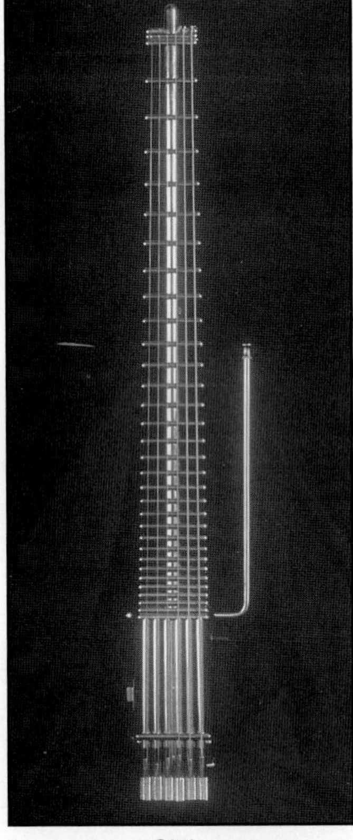
Gittler

Goodall Standard

MODEL YEAR	FEATURES	EXC. COND. LOW	HIGH

Giffin

1977-1988, 1997-present. Professional and premium grade, production/custom, hollow-, semi-hollow-, and solidbody guitars built by luthier Roger Giffin in West San Fernando Valley, California. For '77-'88, Giffin's shop was in London. From '88 to '93, he worked for the Gibson Custom Shop in California as a Master Luthier. In '97, Giffin set up shop in Sweden for a year, moving back to California in the Spring of '98. He also built small numbers of instruments during '67-'76 and '94-'96 (when he had a repair business).

Gila Eban Guitars

1979-present. Premium grade, custom, classical guitars built by luthier Gila Eban in Riverside, Connecticut.

Gilbert Guitars

1965-present. Custom classical guitars by luthiers John Gilbert and William Gilbert in Paso Robles, California. William has handled all production since 1991.

Gittler

1974-ca.1985. Minimalistic electric guitar designed by Allan Gittler, consisting basically of a thin rod with frets welded to it. A total of 560 were built, with Gittler making the first 60 in the U.S. from '74 to the early '80s. The remainder were made around '85 in Israel by the Astron corporation under a licensing agreement. Three Gittler basses were also built. Gittler emigrated to Israel in the early '80s and changed his name to Avraham Bar Rashi. He died in 2002. An U.S.-made Gittler is the only musical instrument in the Museum of Modern Art in New York.

Gittler (metal skeleton)

1971-1982		$2,500	$3,500
1982-1985		$1,500	$2,000

Godin

1987-present. Intermediate and professional grade, production, solidbody electrics and nylon and steel string acoustic/electrics from luthier Robert Godin. They also build basses and mandolins. Necks and bodies are made in La Patrie, Quebec with final assembly in Berlin, New Hampshire. Godin is also involved in the Seagull, Norman, and Patrick & Simon brand of guitars.

Acousticaster

1987-present. Various colors.

1987-1999		$450	$550

Acousticaster Deluxe

Spruce top, mahogany single cut body, rosewood fingerboard.

1990s		$500	$600

MODEL YEAR	FEATURES	EXC. COND. LOW	HIGH

G-1000

1990s. Double cut with long bass horn, Gold hardware, single-single-humbucker configuration.

1995	Sunburst	$400	$450

Glissentar

2000-present. Electric/acoustic nylon 11-string, solid cedar top, chambered maple body, fretless.

2000	Natural	$450	$500

Jeff Cook Signature

1994. Quilted maple top, light maple back, two twin rail and one humbucker pickups.

1994		$550	$600

LG

1995-present. Single cut carved slab mahogany body, 2 Tetrad Combo pickups ('95-'97) or 2 Duncan SP-90 pickups ('9-present), satin lacquer finish.

1997-2001	Cherry	$400	$450

LGXT

1997-present. Single cut silver leaf maple carved solidbody, 2 Duncan humbuckers. Various quality tops offered.

2000	AA top	$900	$1,000
2000	AAA top	$1,100	$1,300
2000	Standard top	$800	$900

Multiac Series

1994-present. Thinline electric with solid spruce top, RMC Sensor System electronics, available in either nylon string or steel string versions, built-in EQ, program up/down buttons.

1994-1999	Duet Nylon, classical	$800	$950
1994-1999	Steel string, single cut	$800	$950

Radiator

Late-1990s-present. Single cut, dual pickup, pearloid top, dot markers.

1999-2002		$275	$325

Golden Hawaiian

1920s-1930s. Private branded lap guitar most likely made by one of the many Chicago makers for a small retailer, publisher, cataloger, or teaching studio.

Guitars

1920s	Sunburst	$250	$450
1930s	Sunburst	$250	$450

Goodall

1972-present. Premium grade, custom flat-tops and nylon-strings, built by luthier James Goodall originally in California and, since 1992, in Kailua-Kona, Hawaii.

Gordon-Smith

1979-present. Intermediate and professional grade, production/custom, semi-hollow and solidbody guitars built by luthier John Smith in Partington, England.

MODEL YEAR	FEATURES	EXC. COND. LOW	HIGH

Gower

1955-1960s. Built in Nashville by Jay Gower, later joined by his son Randy. Gower is also associated with Billy Grammer and Grammer guitars.

G-55-2

1960s. J-50 square shoulder-style flat-top, triple abalone rosette, abalone fretboard trim, small block markers.

1960s	Natural	$1,000	$1,300

G-65 Flat-Top

1960s. J-45 square shoulder-style flat-top, lower belly bridge with pearl dots on bridge, dot markers.

1960s	Sunburst	$700	$1,100

Solidbody Electric

Mosrite influenced odd-shaped body, double pickup, bolt-onneck, Bigsby bridge, high output single-coil pickups.

1960s		$500	$800

Goya

1955-present. Brandname initially used by Hershman Musical Instrument Company of New York City, New York, in mid-'50s for acoustic guitars made in Sweden by Levin, particularly known for its classicals. By '63 the company had become the Goya Musical Instrument Corporation, marketing primarily Goya acoustics. Goya was purchased by Avnet, Inc., prior to '66, when Avnet purchased Guild Guitars. In '69, Goya was purchased by Kustom which offered the instruments until '71. Probably some '70s guitars were made in Japan. The brand name purchased by C.F. Martin in the late-'70s, with Japanese-made acoustic guitars, solidbody electric guitars and basses, banjos and mandolins imported in around '78 and continuing through the '80s. The brand is currently used on Korean-made acoustic and acoustic/electric guitars, banjos and mandolins.

Classical Guitars

1960s		$200	$300

Folk Guitars

1960s		$200	$300

Model 80/Model 90 Sparkle Top

1959-1962. Les Paul single cutaway-style body, replaceable modular pickup assembly. Sparkle top.

1961		$600	$700

Rangemaster

1967-1969. Double cutaway with two offset double-coil pickups and lots of buttons. Made by EKO.

1967	Sunburst	$500	$600

Graf, Oskar

1970-present. Luthier Oskar Graf builds his premium grade, production/custom flat-top, classical, and flamenco guitars, upright solidbody and acoustic basses, and lutes in Clarendon, Ontario.

Grammer

1965-1970. Founded by Bill Grammer then sold to Ampeg.

G-10

1965-1970. Solid Brazilian rosewood back and sides, solid spruce top, large crown-shaped bridge, pearl dot markers, Natural.

1965-1970		$1,250	$1,750

G-20

1965-1970. Natural.

1965-1970		$1,250	$1,750

G-30

1965-1970. Natural.

1965-1970		$1,250	$1,750

S-30

1965-1970. Solid spruce top, solid ribbon mahogany back and sides.

1965-1970		$1,000	$1,300

Granata Guitars

1989-present. Luthier Peter Granata builds his professional grade, custom, flat-top and resonator guitars in Oak Ridge, New Jersey.

Graveel

Production/custom, solidbody guitars built by luthier Dean Graveel in Indianapolis, Indiana.

Greco

1960s-present. Brandname used in Japan by Fuji Gen Gakki, maker of many Hoshino/Ibanez guitars; thus often Greco guitars are similar to Ibanez. Brand not actively marketed in U.S., but occasionally examples show up. During the '70s the company sold many high high-quality copies of American designs, though by '75 they offered many weird-shaped original designs, including the Iceman and carved people shapes. By the late-'70s they were offering neck-through-body guitars. The brand is still offered in Japan.

Electric Archtop Guitars

1960s		$200	$400

Electric Solidbody Guitars

1960s		$200	$400

Green, Aaron

1990-present. Premium and presentation grade, custom, classical and flamenco guitars built by luthier Aaron Green in Waltham, Massachusetts.

Greene

2000-2002. Professional grade, production/custom, electric solidbody guitars built by lutheir Jeffrey Greene in West Kingston, Rhode Island. He now works with Dean Campbell building the Greene & Campbell line of guitars.

Greene & Campbell

2002-present. Jeff Greene and Dean Campbell build their intermediate and professional grade, production/custom, solidbody guitars in Westwood, Massachusetts. Greene also built guitars under his own name.

60s Goya Rangemaster

1970s Grammer

1979 Gretsch BST 1000

1966 Gretsch Anniversary

MODEL YEAR	FEATURES	EXC. COND. LOW	HIGH

Greenfield Guitars

1997-present. Premium grade, production/custom, flat-top, classical, and electric archtop guitars built by luthier Michael Greenfield in Montreal, Quebec.

Gretsch

1883-present. Currently Gretsch offers intermediate, professional, and premium grade, production, acoustic, solidbody, hollowbody, double neck, resonator and Hawaiian guitars. They also offer basses and lap steels. Previous brands included Gretsch, Rex, 20th Century, Recording King (for Montgomery Ward), Dorado (Japanese imports).

Founded by Friedrich Gretsch in Brooklyn, NY, making drums, banjos, tambourines, and toy instruments which were sold to large distributors including C. Bruno and Wurlitzer. Upon early death of Friedrich, son Fred Gretsch Sr. took over business at age 15. By the turn of century the company was also making mandolins. In the '20s, they were distributing Rex and 20th Century brands, some made by Gretsch, some by others such as Kay. Charles "Duke" Kramer joins Gretsch in '35. In '40 Gretsch purchased Bacon & Day banjos. Fred Gretsch, Sr. retired in '42 and was replaced by sons Fred, Jr. and Bill. Fred departs for Navy and Bill runs company until his death in '48, when Fred resumes control. After the war the decision was made to promote the Gretsch brand rather than selling to distributors, though some jobbing continues. Kramer becomes Chicago branch manager in '48.

In '67 Baldwin of Cincinnati buys Gretsch. During '70-'72 the factory relocates from Brooklyn to Booneville, Arkansas and company headquarters moves to Cincinnati. A '72 factory fire drastically reduces production for next two years. In '78 Baldwin buys Kustom amps and sells Gretsch to Kustom's Charlie Roy, and headquarters are moved to Chanute, Kansas. Duke Kramer retires in '80. Guitar production ends '80-'81. Ca. '83 ownership reverts back to Baldwin and Kramer was asked to arrange the sale of the company. In '84 Fred Gretsch III was contacted and in '85 Gretsch guitars came back to the Gretsch family and Fred Gretsch Enterprises, Ltd (FGE). Initial Gretsch Enterprise models were imports made by Japan's Terada Company. In '95, some U.S.-made models were introduced. As of January 1, 2003, Fred Gretsch Enterprises, Ltd granted Fender Musical Instruments Corporation the exclusive rights to develop, produce, market and distribute Gretsch guitars worldwide where FMIC is responsible for all aspects of the Gretsch stringed instrument product lines and brandnames, including development of new products. Fred Gretsch will consult during the changeover and on product development and quality control.

MODEL YEAR	FEATURES	EXC. COND. LOW	HIGH

12-String Electric Archtop (6075/6076)

1967-1972. Sixteen inch double cutaway, two Super Tron pickups, 17 inch body option available. Sunburst (6075) or Natural (6076).

1967		$1,800	$2,100

Anniversary

1958-1972. Single cutaway hollowbody archtop, one pickup (Filtron 1958-1960, Hi-Lo Tron 1961 on), bound body. Named for Gretsch's 75th anniversary.

1958-1960	Green 2-tone, Filtron	$1,500	$1,700
1960	Sunburst, Filtron pickup	$1,200	$1,500
1961-1964	Green 2-tone, Hi-Lo Tron	$1,100	$1,400
1961-1964	Sunburst, Hi-Lo Tron	$1,000	$1,300
1965-1972	Green 2-tone	$1,000	$1,300
1965-1972	Sunburst	$900	$1,200

Astro-Jet (6126)

1965-1967. Solidbody electric, double cutaway, two pickups, vibrato, 4/2 tuner arrangement. Red top with Black back and sides.

1965-1967		$1,000	$1,500

Atkins Axe (7685/7686)

1976-1980. Solidbody electric, single pointed cutaway, two pickups. Ebony stain (7685) or red rosewood stain (7686). Called the Super Axe with added on-board effects.

1976-1980		$1,000	$1,250

Atkins Super Axe/Super Axe (7680/7681)

1976-1981. Single pointed cutaway solidbody with built-in phaser and sustain, five knobs, three switches. Red rosewood (7680) or ebony (7681) stains.

1976-1981	Ebony or red rosewood	$1,300	$1,700

Bikini Doubleneck

1961-1962. Solidbody electric. Separate six-string and bass neck-body units that slid into one of three body "butterflies" - one for the six-string only (6023), one for bass only (6024), one for double neck (six and bass - 6025). Components could be purchased separately. Prices here are for both necks and all three bodies.

1961		$1,500	$1,800

Black Hawk (6100/6101)

1967-1972. Hollowbody archtop, double cutaway, two pickups, G tailpiece or Bigsby vibrato, bound body and neck. Sunburst (6100) or Black (6101).

1967-1972		$1,600	$1,800

Bo Diddley (6138)

2000-present. Reproduction of rectangle-shaped, semi-hollow guitar originally made for Diddley by Gretsch.

2000	Firebird Red	$1,400	$1,600

Brian Setzer Signature (G6120-SSL)

1994-present. Hollowbody electric, double cutaway, two Alnico PAF Filtertron pickups, based on the classic Gretsch 6120. Formerly called the Brian

MODEL YEAR	FEATURES	EXC. COND. LOW	HIGH

Setzer Nashville and currently marked as the Brian Setzer Hot Rod in various colors.

1994-1999	Western Orange	$1,600	$1,800

Broadkaster (hollowbody)

1975-1980. Double cutaway archtop, hollowbody, two pickups. Natural or Sunburst.

1975-1980		$900	$1,200

Broadkaster (solidbody)

1975-1979. Double cutaway, maple body, two pickups, bolt-on neck. Natural (7600) or Sunburst (7601).

1975		$500	$550

BST 1000 Beast

1979-1980. Single cutaway solidbody, bolt-on neck, mahogany body. Available with one pickup in Walnut stain (8210) or Red stain (8216) or two pickups in Walnut (7617, 8215, 8217) or Red stain (8211).

1979-1980		$400	$450

BST 2000 Beast

1979. Symmetrical double cutaway solidbody of mahogany, two humbucking pickups, bolt-on neck, Walnut stain (7620 or 8220) or Red stain (8221).

1979		$450	$475

BST 5000 Beast

1979-1980. Asymmetrical double cutaway solidbody, neck-through, walnut and maple construction, two humbucking pickups, stud tailpiece. Natural walnut/maple (8250).

1979-1980		$475	$500

Burl Ives (6004)

1949-1955. Flat-top acoustic, mahogany back and sides, bound body. Natural top (6004).

1949-1955		$450	$600

Chet Atkins Country Gentleman (6122/7670)

1957-1981. Hollowbody, single cutaway to late-1962 and double after, two pickups, painted F-holes until 1972, real after. Mahogany finish (6122). Model number changes to 7670 in 1971.

1957-1960	Single cutaway	$5,000	$6,300
1961		$4,700	$6,200
1962	Single cutaway	$4,200	$4,900
1963	Double cutaway	$2,600	$3,400
1964		$2,500	$3,300
1965		$2,400	$3,200
1966		$2,300	$3,100
1967-1969		$2,300	$3,000
1970		$2,200	$2,900
1971-1981		$1,700	$2,300

Chet Atkins Hollowbody (6120)

1954-1964. Archtop electric, single cut to '61, double after, 2 pickups, vibrato, F-holes (real to '61 and fake after), G brand on top '54-'56. Orange finish (6120). Renamed Chet Atkins Nashville in '64.

1954-1956	G brand, single cut	$6,000	$7,300
1957-1959	No G brand	$5,500	$6,800
1960	Single cutaway	$5,000	$6,300
1961	Single cutaway	$4,700	$6,000
1961-1964	Double cutaway	$2,500	$3,000

MODEL YEAR	FEATURES	EXC. COND. LOW	HIGH

Chet Atkins Junior

1970. Archtop, single cutaway, one pickup, vibrato, open F-holes, double-bound body. Orange stain.

1970		$900	$1,150

Chet Atkins Nashville (6120)

1964-1970. Replaced Chet Atkins Hollowbody (6120). Electric archtop, double cut, 2 pickups, Amber Red (Orange). Renumbered 7660 in '71 (see below). Reissued in '90 as the Nashville.

1964		$2,500	$3,000
1965-1968		$2,400	$2,700
1969-1970		$2,300	$2,600

Chet Atkins Nashville (7660)

1971-1980. Previously numbered 6120. Electric archtop, double cutaway, two pickups, Amber Red (Orange). Reissued as Nashville in the 1990s.

1971		$2,200	$2,600
1972		$1,900	$2,300
1973-1977		$1,800	$2,200
1978-1980		$1,500	$1,900

Chet Atkins Solidbody (6121)

1955-1963. Solidbody electric, single cutaway, maple or knotty pine top, two pickups, Bigsby vibrato, G brand until 1957, multi-bound top, brown mahogany. Orange finish (6121).

1955-1957	G brand	$4,600	$5,600
1958	No G brand	$4,500	$5,500
1959	No G brand	$4,400	$5,300
1960-1963	No G brand	$4,300	$5,200

Chet Atkins Tennessean (6119)

1958-1970. Archtop electric, single cutaway, one pickup until 1961 and two after, vibrato. Renumbered as the 7655 in 1971 (see following).

1958		$2,600	$3,000
1959		$2,500	$2,900
1960	1 pickup	$2,400	$2,800
1961-1964	2 pickups	$2,300	$2,600
1965		$2,100	$2,400
1966-1967		$2,050	$2,250
1968-1970		$1,600	$1,900

Chet Atkins Tennessean (7655)

1971-1980. Renumbered from Tennesseean 6119 (see above). Archtop electric, single cutaway, two pickups, vibrato.

1971-1972		$1,600	$1,900
1973-1980		$1,400	$1,800

Clipper (6186)

1958-1975. Archtop electric, single cutaway, Sunburst, one pickup (6186) until 1972 and two pickups (6185) from 1972-1975. Also available in one pickup Natural (6187) from 1959-1961.

1958-1961	Natural or Sunburst	$900	$1,100
1962-1967	Sunburst	$900	$1,100
1968-1971	Sunburst, 1 pickup	$850	$950
1972-1975	Sunburst, 2 pickups	$875	$975

Committee (7628)

1975-1980. Neck-through electric solidbody, double cutaway, walnut and maple body, two pickups, four knobs. Natural.

1975-1980		$500	$650

Gretsch Burl Ives

1967 Gretsch Chet Atkins Nashville

GUITARS

1963 Gretsch Corvette

1956 Gretsch Duo-Jet

MODEL YEAR	FEATURES	EXC. COND. LOW	HIGH

Constellation

1955-1960. Renamed from Synchromatic 6030 and 6031. Archtop acoustic, single cutaway, G tailpiece, humped block inlay.

1955-1956		$1,800	$2,300
1957-1958		$1,700	$2,200
1959-1960		$1,500	$2,000

Convertible (6199)

1955-1958. Archtop electric, single cutaway, one pickup, multi-bound body, G tailpiece. Renamed Sal Salvadore in 1958.

1955-1958		$2,200	$2,400

Corsair

1955-1960. Renamed from Synchromatic 100. Archtop acoustic, bound body and headstock, G tailpiece. Available in Sunburst (6014), Natural (6015) or Burgundy (6016).

1955-1959		$1,000	$1,300
1960		$900	$1,200

Corvette (hollowbody)

1955-1959. Renamed from Electromatic Spanish. Archtop electric, one pickup, F-holes, bound body, 'Electromatic' on headstock. Sunburst.

1955-1959		$1,100	$1,400

Corvette (solidbody)

1961-1972, 1976-1978. Double cut slab solidbody, 1 pickup for '61-'68, and 2 pickups available by '63-'72 and '76-'78. From late-'61 through '63 a Twist option was offered featuring a Red candy stripe pickguard.

1961-1962		$700	$900
1961-1963	Twist pickguard	$900	$1,000
1963-1965	Custom color	$900	$1,200
1963-1965	Standard finish	$650	$850
1966-1972		$600	$800
1976-1978		$450	$550

Country Club

1954-1981. Renamed from Electro II Cutaway. Archtop electric, single cut, 2 pickups (Filter Trons after '57), G tailpiece, multi-bound.

1954-1956	Cadillac Green or nat.	$3,000	$4,300
1954-1956	Sunburst	$2,000	$3,300
1957-1958	Cadillac Green or nat.	$3,500	$4,800
1957-1958	Sunburst	$2,500	$3,800
1959	Cadillac Green or nat.	$3,500	$4,500
1959	Sunburst	$2,400	$3,500
1960	Cadillac Green	$3,300	$4,400
1960	Sunburst	$2,400	$3,500
1961	Sunburst	$2,300	$3,300
1961-1963	Cadillac Green or nat.	$3,000	$4,000
1962-1963	Sunburst	$2,200	$3,200
1964	Cadillac Green	$2,800	$4,000
1964	Sunburst	$2,200	$2,800
1965-1969	Sunburst or walnut	$1,900	$2,500
1970	Various colors	$1,900	$2,400
1971	Various colors	$1,900	$2,300
1972	Various colors	$1,900	$2,100
1974-1981	Various colors	$1,800	$2,000

Country Club 1955 (G6196-1955)(FGE)

1995-present. U.S-made reissue of Country Club, single cutaway, twin DeArmond pickups. Natural finish.

1990s		$2,500	$2,900

Country Roc (7620)

1974-1978. Single cutaway solidbody, two pickups, belt buckle tailpiece, western scene fretboard inlays, G brand, tooled leather side trim.

1974-1978		$1,400	$1,800

Deluxe Chet (7680/7681)

1973-1974. Electric archtop with rounded cutaway, Autumn Red (7680) or Brown Walnut (7681) finishes.

1973-1974		$2,500	$2,700

Double Anniversary

1958-1976. Archtop electric, single cut, 2 pickups, stereo optional until '63, green two-tone or sunburst.

1958-1959	Sunburst or green	$2,000	$2,500
1960-1961	Sunburst or green	$1,800	$2,300
1962-1964	Sunburst or green	$1,700	$2,200
1965-1968	Sunburst	$1,400	$1,900
1965-1969	Green 2-tone	$1,400	$1,900
1969-1973	Sunburst	$1,300	$1,800
1974-1975	Sunburst	$1,200	$1,700
1976	Sunburst	$1,100	$1,600

Duo-Jet

1953-1971. Solidbody electric, single cut until '61, double after, 2 pickups. Black (6128) with a few special ordered in green. Sparkle finishes were offered '63-'66. Reissued in '90.

1953-1957	Black	$3,800	$4,800
1956-1957	Cadillac Green	$6,000	$7,400
1958-1960	Black	$3,000	$4,000
1961-1962	Double cutaway	$2,500	$3,300
1963		$2,300	$3,100
1964		$2,100	$2,800
1965-1967		$2,000	$2,600
1968-1969	Super Trons	$1,800	$2,400
1970-1971	Super Trons	$1,600	$2,300

Duo-Jet Reissue

1990-present. Reissue of the 1950s solidbody, Black.

1990		$1,000	$1,300

Eldorado (6040/6041)

1955-1970, 1991-1997. Renamed from Synchromatic 400. Archtop acoustic, single cutaway, triple-bound fretboard and peghead.

1955-1959	Sunburst	$2,200	$2,600
1960	Natural	$2,500	$2,900
1960-1963	Sunburst	$2,000	$2,400
1964-1965	Sunburst	$1,900	$2,300
1966-1968	Sunburst	$1,800	$2,200
1969-1970	Sunburst	$1,700	$2,100

Electro II Cutaway (6192/6193)

1951-1953. Archtop electric, single cutaway, Melita bridge by 1953, two pickups, F-holes. Renamed Country Club in 1954.

1951-1953		$3,000	$3,500

MODEL YEAR	FEATURES	EXC. COND. LOW	HIGH

Electromatic Spanish (6185/6185N)

1940-1955. Hollowbody, 17" wide, one pickup. Renamed Corvette (hollowbody) in 1955.

1950-1955		$1,000	$1,300

Jet Fire Bird (6131)

1955-1971, 1990-present. Solidbody electric, single cutaway until 1961, double 1961-1971, two pickups. Black body with Red top. Reissued in 1990.

1955		$3,700	$4,500
1956-1958		$3,600	$4,500
1959-1960		$3,300	$4,200
1961	Double cutaway	$2,500	$3,500
1962		$2,400	$3,400
1963-1964		$2,300	$3,300
1967		$1,800	$2,150
1968-1971	Super Trons	$1,700	$2,050

Jimmie Rodgers (6003 flat-top)

1959-1962. Fourteen inch flat-top with round hold, mahogany back and sides. Renamed Folk Singing in 1963.

1959-1962		$400	$500

Jumbo Synchromatic 125F (flat-top)

1947-1955. 17" flat-top, triangular soundhole, bound top and back, metal bridge anchor plate, adjustable wood bridge. Natural top with sunburst back and sides or optional Translucent White-Blond top and sides.

1947-1955	Natural	$1,500	$2,000
1947-1955	White-Blond option	$1,500	$2,000

Model 25 (acoustic archtop)

1933-1939. 16" archtop, no binding on top or back, dot markers, sunburst.

1933-1939		$700	$900

Model 30 (acoustic archtop)

1939-1949. Sixteen-inch archtop, top binding, dot markers. Sunburst.

1939-1949		$800	$1,000

Model 35 (acoustic archtop)

1933-1949. Sixteen-inch archtop, single-bound top and back, dot markers. Sunburst.

1933-1949		$900	$1,100

Model 65 (acoustic archtop)

1933-1939. Archtop acoustic, bound body. Amber.

1933-1939		$1,000	$1,200

Model TW300T (Traveling Wilburys)

1988-1990. Promotional guitar, solidbody electric, single cutaway, one and two pickups, six variations, graphics.

1988-1990		$250	$300

Monkees

1966-1969. Hollowbody electric, double cutaway, two pickups, Monkees logo on pickguard, bound top, F-holes and neck, vibrato. Red.

1966-1968		$1,650	$1,850

New Yorker

Ca.1949-1970. Archtop acoustic, F-holes. Sunburst.

1949-1951		$650	$850
1952-1953		$600	$800
1954-1956		$550	$750
1957-1961		$525	$725
1962-1970		$500	$700

Princess (6106)

1963. Corvette-type solidbody double cut, 1 pickup, vibrato, gold parts. Colors available werewWhite/grape, blue/white, pink/white, or white/gold. Often sold with the Princess amp.

1963	White/Gold	$1,400	$1,600

Rally (6104/6105)

1967-1969. Archtop, double cutaway, two pickups, vibrato, racing strip on truss rod cover and pickguard. Green or Yellow.

1967-1969		$1,400	$1,700

Rambler (6115)

1957-1961. Small body electric archtop, single cutaway, one pickup, G tailpiece, bound body and headstock.

1957-1961		$1,100	$1,300

Rancher

1954-1980. Flat-top acoustic, triangle soundhole, western theme inlay, G brand until 1961 and 1975 and after, Golden Red (Orange). Reissued in 1990.

1954-1955	G brand	$4,000	$5,000
1956	G brand	$3,800	$4,900
1957-1961	G brand	$3,500	$4,700
1962-1963	No G brand	$3,100	$4,300
1964-1966	No G brand	$3,000	$4,200
1967	No G brand	$3,000	$4,000
1968-1969	No G brand	$2,900	$3,900
1975-1978	G brand	$3,700	$3,600
1979-1980	G brand	$2,600	$3,500

Roc I (7635)

1974-1976. Solidbody of mahogany, single cutaway, Duo-Jet-style body, one pickup, bound body and neck.

1974-1976		$650	$850

Roc II (7621)

1974-1977. Electric solidbody, single cutaway, two pickups, Duo-Jet-style body, bound body and neck.

1974-1977		$750	$950

Roc Jet

1969-1980. Electric solidbody, single cutaway, two pickups, adjustamatic bridge. Black or Pumpkin.

1969-1972		$1,050	$1,150
1973-1976		$950	$1,050
1977-1980		$900	$1,000

Round-Up (6130)

1954-1960. Electric solidbody, single cutaway, two pickups, G brand, belt buckle tailpiece. Orange.

1954-1956		$7,500	$9,000
1957-1960		$7,000	$8,500

Round-Up Reissue

1990-1995. Based on the 1950s model. Western Orange.

1990-1995		$1,300	$1,400

Sal Fabraio (cat's-eye) (6117)

1964-1968. Double cutaway thin electric archtop with distinctive cat's-eye F-holes, two pickups, order for resale by guitar teacher Sal Fabraio.

1964-1968	Sunburst	$1,800	$2,000

1973 Gretsch Roc Jet

1954 Gretsch Roundup (6130)

GUITARS

1955 Gretsch Silver Jet (6129)

1973 Gretsch Super Chet

MODEL YEAR	FEATURES	EXC. COND. LOW	HIGH

Sal Salvador (6199)

1958-1968. Renamed from Convertible. Electric archtop, single cutaway, one pickup, triple-bound neck and headstock. Sunburst (6199)

1958-1959		$2,100	$2,300
1960-1962		$2,000	$2,200
1963-1964		$1,900	$2,100
1965-1966		$1,600	$1,800
1967-1968		$1,500	$1,700

Sho Bro Hawaiian

1969-1978. Flat-top acoustic, non-cutaway, square neck, resonator, multi-bound, lucite fretboard.

1969-1978		$650	$700

Silver Jet (6129)

1954-1963. Solidbody electric, single cutaway until 1961, double 1961-1963, two pickups. Duo-Jet with Silver Sparkle top. Reissued in 1990.

1954-1960	Single cutaway	$4,300	$5,300
1961-1963	Double cutaway	$3,800	$4,300

Silver Jet 1957 Reissue (G6129-1957)

1990-present. Reissue of single cutaway 1950s Silver Jet, Silver Sparkle.

1990-1993		$1,200	$1,300
1994-1996		$1,300	$1,400
1997-2000		$1,400	$1,500

Southern Belle (7176)

1983. Electric archtop, Country Gentleman parts from the late-1970s assembled in Mexico and marketed as Southern Belle, based upon Belle (6122).

1983	Walnut	$1,000	$1,100

Sparkle Jet

1994-present . Electric solidbody, single cutaway, two pickups, Duo-Jet with Sparkle finish.

1990s		$1,000	$1,200

Streamliner Single Cutaway (6189/6190/6191)

1955-1959. Electric archtop, single cut, maple top, G tailpiece, 1 pickup, multi-bound. Bamboo Yellow (6189), sunburst (6190), or natural (6191). Name reintroduced as a double cutaway in '68.

1955-1959		$2,000	$2,200

Streamliner Double Cutaway

1968-1973. Reintroduced from single cut model. Electric archtop, double cut, 2 pickups, G tailpiece. Cherry or sunburst.

1968-1969		$1,100	$1,300
1970-1973		$900	$1,200

Sun Valley (6010/7515/7514)

1959-1977. Flat-top acoustic, laminated Brazilian rosewood back and sides, multi-bound top, Natural or Sunburst.

1959-1964		$650	$850
1965-1969		$550	$750
1970-1977		$500	$600

Super Chet (7690/7690-B/7691/7691-B)

1972-1980. Electric archtop, single rounded cutaway, two pickups, Gold hardware, mini control knobs along edge of pickguard, Autumn Red or Walnut.

1972-1975		$2,100	$2,900

MODEL YEAR	FEATURES	EXC. COND. LOW	HIGH
1976		$2,000	$2,800
1977-1979		$1,800	$2,400
1980		$1,700	$2,300

Synchromatic 75

1939-1949. Acoustic archtop, F-holes, multi-bound, large floral peghead inlay.

1939-1949		$1,000	$1,500

Synchromatic 100

1939-1955. Renamed from No. 100F. Acoustic archtop, double-bound body, Amber, Sunburst or Natural. Renamed Corsair in 1955.

1939-1949		$1,000	$1,500
1950-1955		$900	$1,200

Synchromatic 160

1939-1943, 1947-1951. Acoustic archtop, cat's-eye soundholes, maple back and sides, triple-bound, Natural or Sunburst.

1939-1949		$1,100	$1,600
1950-1951		$900	$1,300

Synchromatic 200

1939-1949. Acoustic archtop, cat's-eye soundholes, maple back and sides, multi-bound, gold-plated hardware, Amber or Natural.

1939-1949		$1,400	$1,900

Synchromatic 300

1939-1955. Acoustic archtop, cat's-eye soundholes until 1951and F-holes after, multi-bound, Natural or Sunburst.

1939-1949		$2,400	$3,000
1950-1955		$2,200	$2,400

Synchromatic 400

1940-1955. Acoustic archtop, cat's-eye soundholes until 1951and F-holes after, multi-bound, Gold hardware, Natural or Sunburst.

1940-1949		$5,300	$6,800
1950-1955		$5,000	$6,500

Synchromatic 6038

1951-1955. Acoustic archtop, single cutaway, G tailpiece, multi-bound bound, Sunburst. Natural version is 6039. Renamed Fleetwood in 1955.

1951-1955		$1,500	$1,900

Synchromatic Limited Model G450

1997. Acoustic archtop, hand carved spruce top, floating pickup, Sunburst, only 50 were to be made..

1997		$1,100	$1,400

Synchromatic Limited Model G450 M

1997. Maple top version of the G450, Sunburst.

1997		$1,200	$1,500

Synchromatic Sierra

1949-1955. Renamed from Synchromatic X75F (see below). Acoustic flat-top, maple back and sides, triangular soundhole. Sunburst.

1949-1955		$1,000	$1,500

Synchromatic X75F

1947-1949. Acoustic flat-top, maple back and sides, triangular soundhole. Sunburst. Renamed Synchromatic Sierra in 1949 (see above).

1947-1949		$1,000	$1,500

MODEL YEAR	FEATURES	EXC. COND. LOW	HIGH

TK 300 (7624/7625)

1977-1981. Double cutaway maple solidbody, one humbucker, bolt-on neck, six-on-a-side tuners, hockey stick headstock, Autumn Red or Natural.

1977-1981		$500	$700

Town and Country (6021)

1954-1959. Renamed from Jumbo Synchromatic 125 F. Flat-top acoustic, maple back and sides, triangular soundhole, multi-bound.

1954-1959		$1,500	$2,000

Van Eps 7-String (6079/6080)

1968-1978. Electric archtop, single cutaway, two pickups, seven strings, Sunburst or Walnut.

1968-1978		$2,500	$3,500

Viking (6187/6188/6189)

1964-1975. Electric archtop, double cutaway, two pickups, vibrato, Cadillac Green, Natural or Sunburst.

1964-1967		$1,500	$2,000
1968-1969		$1,400	$1,900
1970-1975		$1,000	$1,650

Wayfarer Jumbo (6008)

1969-1971. Flat-top acoustic dreadnought, non-cutaway, maple back and sides, multi-bound.

1969-1971		$450	$650

White Falcon 6136 Mono (single cutaway)

1955-1961. Single cutaway archtop, two pickups, non-stereo option (stereo is 6137), White. Continued 1974-1978 as 7593.

1955		$18,000	$25,000
1956-1957		$17,000	$23,000
1958		$15,000	$17,000
1959-1961		$13,000	$17,000

White Falcon (double cutaway)

1962-1981. Double cutaway archtop, two pickups, stereo or non-stereo. White.

1962		$6,000	$9,600
1963		$6,000	$9,500
1964		$5,400	$8,400
1965		$5,000	$7,800
1966		$5,000	$7,000
1968		$4,700	$6,500
1969		$4,700	$5,500
1970-1972		$3,900	$4,700
1974		$3,700	$4,600
1975		$3,600	$4,500
1976-1980		$3,500	$4,300
1981		$3,300	$4,200

White Falcon 7593 (single cutaway)

1974-1978. Single cutaway archtop, two pickups. White.

1974		$3,600	$4,600
1977		$3,300	$4,200

White Falcon 1955 Single Cutaway G6136

1990-present. Single and double cutaway versions of the White Falcon, issued under different model numbers and variations on the name. White, Silver or Black. Model numbers include 6136 (G tailpiece) and 7593 (Gretsch Bigsby tailpiece) (both initially called the I, '90 on), 7594 (initially called the II, '91 on), G6136 ('94 on), G6136BK (Black Falcon '95-'99), G6136SL (Silver Falcon single cutaway, 1955 reissue '96-'97), G7584SL (Silver Falcon double cutaway '96-'97).

1991	White	$1,700	$2,100

White Falcon 1955 Custom USA (G6136-1955)(FGE)

1995-1999. Single cutaway, DynaSonic pickups, Gold Sparkle appointments, rhinestone embedded knobs, solid spruce carved top, White.

1995-1999		$4,000	$4,700

White Falcon II G7594 (double cutaway)

1991-present. Import from Japan, double cutaway, standard Bigsby vibrato, White.

1994		$1,800	$2,100

White Penguin (6134)

1955-1964. Electric solidbody, single cut until '62, double '62-'64, 2 pickups, fewer than 100 made, white, gold sparkle bound, gold-plated parts. Some high-end guitar dealers make the following point about the White Penguin: "Find a real one!" This quote is not considered to be a casual or idle remark. More than any other model, there seems a higher concern regarding forgery vs. authentic.

1956-1958		$70,000	$80,000
1959-1964		$60,000	$70,000

White Penguin (reissue) (FGE)

1996-present. White finish, single cut, Metalflake Orange binding, Gold hardware including the DeArmond-style Dynasonic pickups, jeweled control knobs, space control bridge, ebony fingerboard with Grover Imperial stairstep Cadillac tailpiece.

1996		$2,800	$3,500

Griffin String Instruments

1976-present. Luthier Kim Griffin builds his professional and premium grade, production/custom, parlor, steel-string, and classical guitars in Greenwich, New York.

Grimes Guitars

1974-present. Premium and presentation grade, custom, flat-tops, nylon-strings, archtops, semi-hollow electrics made by luthier Steve Grimes originally in Port Townsend, Washington, and since 1982 in Kula, Hawaii.

Groove Tools

2002-present. Korean-made, production, intermediate grade, 7-string guitars offered by Conklin Guitars of Springfield, Missouri.

Grosh, Don

1993-present. Professional and premium grade, production/custom, solid and semi-hollow body guitars built by luthier Don Grosh in Santa Clarita, California. He also builds basses. Grosh worked in production for Valley Arts from '84-'92. Guitars generally with bolt necks until 2003 when set-necks were added to the line.

1940s Gretsch Synchromatic 400

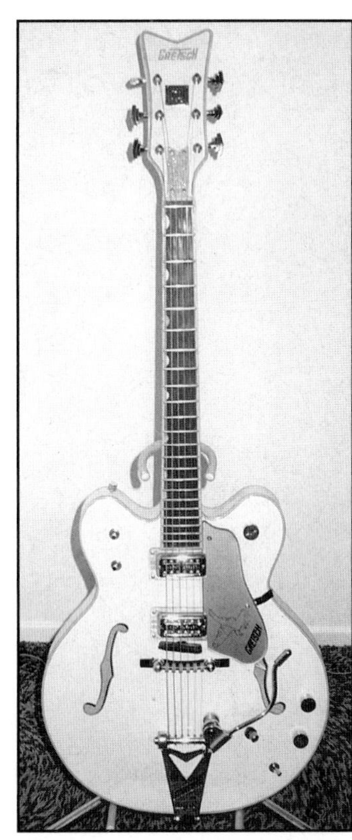

1967 Gretsch White Falcon

1999 Guild Artist Award

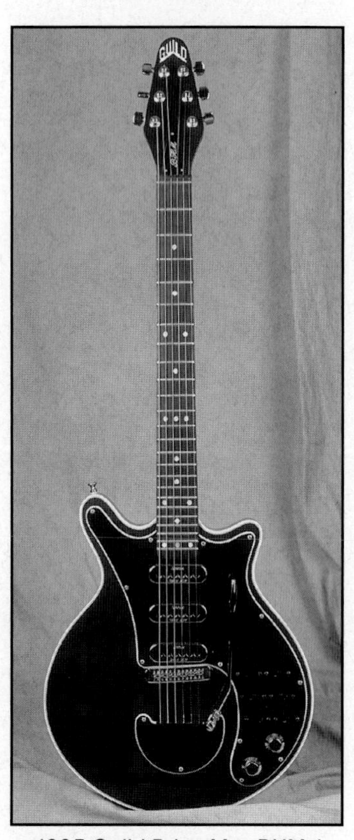

1995 Guild Brian May BHM-1

MODEL YEAR | FEATURES | EXC. COND. LOW | HIGH

Retro Classic

Classic offset double cut solidbody.

2001 $1,800 $2,000

Retro Vintage T

Classic sigle cut solidbody.

2001 $1,800 $2,000

Gruen Acoustic Guitars

1999-present. Luthier Paul Gruen builds his professional grade, custom steel-string guitars in Chapel Hill, North Carolina. His speciality is his E.Q. model, which features five soundholes, four of which can be plugged with wooden stoppers to give different tonal balances.

Guernsey Resophonic Guitars

1989-present. Production/custom, resonator guitars built by luthier Ivan Guernsey in Marysville, Indiana.

Guild

1952-present. Currently Guild offers professional and premium grade, production/custom, acoustic, acoustic/electric, hollowbody and semi-hollowbody guitars. Founded in New York City by jazz guitarist Alfred Dronge, employing many ex-Epiphone workers. The company was purchased by Avnet, Inc., in '66 and the Westerly, Rhode Island factory was opened in '68. Hoboken factory closed in '71 and headquarters moved to Elizabeth, New Jersey. Company was Guild Musical Instrument Corporation in '86 but was in bankruptcy in '88. Purchased by Faas Corporation, New Berlin, Wisconsin, which became the U.S. Musical Corporation. The brand was purchased by Fender Musical Instrument Corporation in '95. The Guild Custom Shop opened in Nashville, TN in '97. The Guild Custom Shop remains in Nashville, while all other Guild production has been moved to Corona, CA.

Aragon F-30

1954-1986. Acoustic flat-top, spruce top, laminated maple arched back (mahogany back and sides by 1959). Reintroduced as just F-30 in 1998.

1955-1965 $900 $1,200
1966-1970 $800 $1,000
1971-1986 $600 $800

Aragon F-30 NT

1959-1985. Natural finish version of F-30. Acoustic flat-top, spruce top, maple back and sides.

1959-1970 $900 $1,200
1971-1979 $700 $1,000
1980-1985 $600 $800

Aristocrat M-75

1955-1963, 1967-1968. Electric archtop, single cutaway, two pickups, Blond or Sunburst. Name changed to Bluesbird M-75 in 1968.

1955-1959 $2,300 $2,600
1960-1963 $2,100 $2,400

MODEL YEAR | FEATURES | EXC. COND. LOW | HIGH

Artist Award

1960-1999. Renamed from Johnny Smith Award. Electric archtop, single cutaway, floating DeArmond pickup (changed to humbucker in 1980), multi-bound, Gold hardware. Sunburst or Natural.

1961-1979 $3,900 $4,400
1980-1999 $3,500 $4,000

Bluegrass D-25

1968-1999. Flat-top, mahogany top until '76, spruce after, mahogany back and sides, various colors. Called Bluegrass D-25 M in late-'70s and '80s. Listed as D-25 in '90s.

1968-1989 $550 $750
1990-1999 $550 $700

Bluegrass D-25-12

1987-1992, 1996-1999. Renamed from D-212 12-String. 12-string version of D-25.

1987-1992 $650 $750

Bluegrass D-35

1966-1988. Acoustic flat-top, spruce top and mahogany back and sides, rosewood fingerboard and bridge, Natural.

1966-1969 $750 $950
1970-1988 $650 $850

Bluegrass Jubilee D-40

1963-1992. Acoustic flat-top, spruce top, mahogany back and sides, rosewood fingerboard and bridge, Natural.

1963-1979 $900 $1,000
1980-1992 $800 $950

Bluegrass Jubilee D-40 C

1975-1991. Acoustic flat-top, single Florentine cutaway, mahogany back and sides, rosewood fingerboard and bridge, Natural.

1975-1979 $825 $950
1980-1987 $800 $900
1988-1992 $800 $900

Bluegrass Jubilee D-44

1965-1972. Acoustic flat-top, spruce top, pearwood back and sides, ebony fingerboard, rosewood bridge.

1965-1968 $900 $1,000
1969-1972 $850 $950

Bluegrass Jubilee D-44M

1971-1985. Maple back and sides version.

1980s $700 $950

Bluegrass Special D-50

1963-1993. Acoustic flat-top, spruce top, rosewood back and sides, ebony fretboard, multi-bound.

1970-1973 $1,200 $1,300
1974 $1,150 $1,250
1975-1984 $1,100 $1,200
1985-1993 $1,050 $1,150

Bluesbird M-75 (hollowbody)

1968-1970. Reintroduced from Aristocrat M-75. Thinbody electric archtop of maple, spruce or mahogany, single cutaway, two pickups. Reintroduced as a solidbody in 1970.

1968-1970 $900 $1,200

MODEL YEAR	FEATURES	EXC. COND. LOW	HIGH

Bluesbird M-75 (solidbody)

1970-1978. Solidbody version of hollodbody Bluesbird M-75. Mahogany body, rounded cutaway, two pickups.

1970-1978		$900	$1,200

Bluesbird M-75 (solidbody reintroduced)

1984-1988. Brian Setzer design, poplar body, single cut, 2 pickups, vibrato. Reintroduced with different specs in '97.

1984-1988		$600	$700

Brian May BHM-1

1984-1987. Electric solidbody, double cutaway, vibrato, three pickups, bound top and back, Red or Green. Brian May Pro, Special and Standard introduced in 1994.

1984-1987		$2,000	$2,200

Brian May Pro

1994-1995. Electric solidbody, double cutaway, vibrato, three pickups, bound top and back, various colors.

1994-1995		$1,500	$1,700

Burnside HA-1

Solidbody, two pickups, non-locking tremolo.

1987		$250	$300

Burnside SO-1

Solidbody, three pickups, locking-nut tremolo.

1987		$250	$300

CA-100 Capri

1956-1973. Acoustic archtop version of CE-100, sharp Florentine cutaway, solid spruce top, laminated maple back and sides, rosewood 'board and bridge, nickel-plated metal parts, natural or sunburst.

1956-1973		$1,100	$1,400

Capri CE-100

1956-1985. Electric archtop, single Florentine cutaway, one pickup (two pickups by 1983), maple body, Waverly tailpiece. Sunburst. In 1959-1982 CE-100 D listed with two pickups.

1956-1957		$1,000	$1,300
1958		$1,000	$1,400
1959-1960		$1,050	$1,550
1961-1969		$1,000	$1,500
1970-1978		$900	$1,300
1979-1982		$800	$1,300
1982-1985	2 pickups	$1,200	$1,400

Capri CE-100 D

1956-1982. Electric archtop, single Florentine cutaway, two pickups, maple body, Waverly tailpiece (D dropped, became the Capri CE-100 in 1983).

1956-1965		$1,500	$1,700
1966-1968		$1,400	$1,600
1969		$1,300	$1,500
1970-1982		$1,200	$1,400

Citron X-92

1984. Electric solidbody, detachable body section, three pickups.

1984		$250	$300

Cordoba X-50

1961-1970. Electric archtop non-cutaway, laminated maple body, rosewood fingerboard, one pickup, nickel-plated parts, Sunburst. Also came as a slimline model called the Cordoba T-50 Slim.

1961-1964		$800	$950
1965-1970		$700	$850

Custom F-412 12-String

1968-1986. Special order only from 1968-1974, then regular production. Twelve-string version of F-50, acoustic flat-top, spruce top, maple back and sides, arched back, ebony fingerboard, bound neck, Gold hardware. Natural finish.

1974-1986		$1,000	$1,400

Custom F-512 12-String

1968-1986, 1990. Acoustic flat-top, 12 strings, spruce top, rosewood back and sides, bound neck, abalone inlays.

1968-1986		$1,100	$1,400

Custom Shop 45th Anniversary

1997 only. The Guild Custom Shop opened in Nashville, TN in 1997, two years after Fender Musical Instruments purchased Guild. The Guild Custom Shop remains in Nashville, while all other Guild production has been moved to Corona, CA. The 45th Anniversary features all solid wood, a spruce top and maple back and sides, with high-end appointments.

1997	Natural, Gold hardware	$2,000	$2,500

D-6 (D-6 E/D-6 HG/D-6 HE)

1992-1995. Flat-top, 15 3/4", mahogany back and sides, Natural satin non-gloss finish, options available.

1992-1995		$600	$650

D-15

1983-1988. Part of Mahogany Rush Series. Dreadnought, mahogany body and neck, rosewood fingerboard, dot inlay, peaked logo, unbound, Mahogany or Woodgrain Red satin finishes (gloss by 1987).

1983-1988		$500	$600

D-17

1983-1985. Part of the Mahogany Rush Series. Dreadnought, bound mahogany body. Natural Mahogany finish.

1983-1985		$500	$600

D-30

1987-1999. Acoustic flat top, spruce-top, laminated maple back and solid maple sides, rosewood fingerboard, multi-bound, various colors.

1987-1999		$750	$950

D-46

1980-1985. Dreadnought-size acoustic, ash back, sides, and neck, spruce top, ebony fingerboard, ivoroid binding top and back. Originally offered in Natural or Sunburst.

1980-1985		$800	$950

1970s Guild Bluesbird

Guild CE-100D

GUITARS

1997 Guild D-55

Guild Duane Eddy Deluxe DE-500

MODEL YEAR	FEATURES	EXC. COND. LOW	HIGH

D-55

1968-1987, 1990-present (Special Order 1968-1973, regular production after). Dreadnought-size acoustic, spruce top, rosewood back and sides, scalloped bracing, gold-plated tuners. Called the TV Model in earlier years, Sunburst or Natural.

YEAR	FEATURES	LOW	HIGH
1968		$1,800	$2,700
1969	13 made	$1,700	$2,200
1973		$1,500	$1,700
1974		$1,300	$1,600
1975-1990		$1,200	$1,600

D-60

1987-1990, 1998-2000. Renamed from D-66. Rosewood back and sides, 15 3/4", scalloped bracing, multi-bound top, slotted diamond inlay, G shield logo.

YEAR	FEATURES	LOW	HIGH
1987-1990		$1,500	$1,700

D-66

1984-1987. Rosewood back and sides, 15 3/4", scalloped bracing. Renamed D-60 in 1987.

YEAR	FEATURES	LOW	HIGH
1984-1987	Amber	$1,500	$1,700

D-70

1981-1985. Dreadnought acoustic, spruce top, Indian rosewood back and sides, multi-bound, ebony fingerboard with mother-of-pearl inlays.

YEAR	FEATURES	LOW	HIGH
1981-1985		$1,900	$2,100

D-212 12-String

1981-1983. Twelve-string version of D-25, laminated mahogany back and sides. Natural, Sunburst or Black. Renamed D-25-12 in 1987, reintroduced as D-212 1996-present.

YEAR	FEATURES	LOW	HIGH
1981-1983	Sunburst	$700	$900

D-412 12-String

1990-1997. Dreadnought, 12 strings, mahogany sides and arched back, satin finished, Natural.

YEAR	FEATURES	LOW	HIGH
1990-1997		$700	$900

DCE-1 True American

1993-1999. Acoustic/electric flat-top, single rounded cutaway, laminated mahogany back and sides. Natural satin finish (high gloss optional by 1998).

YEAR	FEATURES	LOW	HIGH
1993-1999		$750	$850

Del Rio M-30

1959-1964. Flat-top, 15", all mahogany body, satin non-gloss finish.

YEAR	FEATURES	LOW	HIGH
1959-1964		$1,100	$1,200

Detonator

1987-1988. Electric solidbody, double cutaway, three pickups, bolt-on neck, Guild/Mueller tremolo system, Black hardware.

YEAR	FEATURES	LOW	HIGH
1987-1988		$200	$250

Duane Eddy Deluxe DE-500

1962-1974, 1984-1987. Electric archtop, single rounded cutaway, two pickups (early years and 1980s version have DeArmonds), Bigsby, master volume, spruce top with maple back and sides. Available in Blond (BL) or Sunburst (SB).

YEAR	FEATURES	LOW	HIGH
1962		$4,000	$5,500
1963		$3,900	$5,400
1964-1965		$3,800	$5,300
1966-1974		$3,600	$5,100
1984-1987		$2,800	$3,500

Duane Eddy Standard DE-400

1963-1974. Electric archtop, single rounded cutaway, two pickups, vibrato, Natural or Sunburst. Less appointments than DE-500 Deluxe.

YEAR	FEATURES	LOW	HIGH
1963		$3,000	$4,000
1964	$2,900	$3,900	
1965		$2,800	$3,800
1966		$2,600	$2,800

Economy M-20

1958-1965, 1969-1973. Mahogany body, acoustic flat-top, Natural or Sunburst satin finish.

YEAR	FEATURES	LOW	HIGH
1958-1960		$800	$1,000
1961-1964		$550	$700
1965		$450	$600

F-5 CE

1992-2001. Acoustic/electric, single rounded cutaway, rosewood back and sides. Natural, Black or Sunburst finish.

YEAR	FEATURES	LOW	HIGH
1992-2001		$900	$1,100

F-45 CE

1983-1992. Acoustic/electric, single pointed cutaway, active EQ, preamp, spruce top, mahogany back and sides, rosewood fingerboard. Natural finish.

YEAR	FEATURES	LOW	HIGH
1983-1992		$800	$1,000

F-212 12-String

1968-1982. Acoustic flat-top jumbo, 12 strings, spruce top, mahogany back and sides.

YEAR	FEATURES	LOW	HIGH
1968-1979		$900	$1,000
1980-1982		$800	$900

F-212 XL 12-String

1966-1986. Acoustic flat-top, 12 strings, spruce top, mahogany back and sides, ebony fingerboard.

YEAR	FEATURES	LOW	HIGH
1966-1979		$950	$1,100
1980-1986		$850	$950

Freshman M-65

1958-1973. Electric archtop, single cutaway, mahogany back and sides, one single-coil pickup. Sunburst or Natural top.

YEAR	FEATURES	LOW	HIGH
1958		$900	$1,200

Freshman M-65 3/4

1958-1973. Short-scale version of M-65, electric archtop, single rounded cutaway, one pickup.

YEAR	FEATURES	LOW	HIGH
1958-1959	Natural or Sunburst	$900	$1,100
1960-1969	Cherry, Natural or Sunburst	$800	$1,000
1970-1973	Cherry or Sunburst	$700	$900

FS-46 CE

1983-1986. Flat-top acoustic/electric, pointed cutaway, Black, Natural or Sunburst.

YEAR	FEATURES	LOW	HIGH
1983-1986		$600	$700

G-5P

1988-ca.1989. Handmade in Spain, cedar top, gold-plated hardware.

YEAR	FEATURES	LOW	HIGH
1988-1989		$550	$600

GUITARS

MODEL YEAR	FEATURES	EXC. COND. LOW	HIGH

G-37

1973-1986. Acoustic flat-top, spruce top, laminated maple back and sides, rosewood fingerboard and bridge. Sunburst or Natural top.

1973-1986		$700	$900

G-41

1974-1978. Acoustic flat-top, spruce top, mahogany back and sides, rosewood fingerboard and bridge, 20 frets.

1974-1978		$800	$1,000

G-75

1975-1977. Acoustic flat-top, 3/4-size version of D-50, spruce top, rosewood back and sides, mahogany neck, ebony fingerboard and bridge.

1975-1977		$650	$850

G-212 12-String

1974-1983. Acoustic flat-top 12-string version of D-40, spruce top, mahogany back and sides. Natural or Sunburst.

1974-1980		$800	$900
1981-1983		$600	$1,000

G-212 XL 12-String

1974-1983. Acoustic flat-top, 12 strings, 17" version of G-212.

1974-1983		$900	$1,100

G-312 12-String

1974-1987. Acoustic flat-top 12-string version of the D-50, spruce top, rosewood back and sides.

1974-1987		$900	$1,100

George Barnes AcoustiLectric

1962-1972. Electric archtop, single cutaway, solid spruce top,curly maple back and sides, multi-bound, two humbuckers, gold-plated hardware. Sunburst or Natural finish.

1962-1972		$2,900	$3,200

GF-30

1987-1991. Acoustic flat-top, maple back, sides and neck, multi-bound..

1987-1991		$750	$950

GF-50

1987-1991. Acoustic flat-top, rosewood back and sides, mahogany neck, multi-bound.

1987-1991		$800	$1,100

Granada X-50

1954-1961. Electric archtop, non-cutaway, laminated all maple body, rosewood fingerboard and bridge, nickel-plated metal parts, one pickup, Sunburst. Renamed Cordoba X-50 in 1961.

1954-1958		$800	$900
1959		$775	$875
1960-1961		$750	$850

Jet Star S-50

1963-1970. Electric solidbody, double cutaway, mahogany or alder body, one pickup, vibrato optional by 1965, asymmetrical headstock until 1965. Reintroduced as S-50 in 1972-1978 with body redesigned to Gibson SG-style.

1963-1970	Red	$450	$600

JF-30

1987-present. Jumbo six-string acoustic, spruce top, laminated maple back, solid maple sides, multi-bound.

1987-1989		$800	$900
1990-1999		$750	$850

JF-30-12

1987-present. Twelve-string jumbo acoustic version of the JF-30, laminated maple back and solid maple sides; rosewood fingerboard, multi-bound.

1987		$950	$1,000

JF-50 R

1987-1988. Jumbo six-string acoustic, rosewood back and sides, multi-bound.

1987-1988		$800	$1,000

JF-65 R

1987. Renamed from Navarre F-50 R. Jumbo flat-top acoustic, spruce top, rosewood back and sides, multi-bound, gold-plated tuners. Reintroduced as JF-55 in 1989.

1987		$925	$1,200

JF-65-12

1987-2001. Jumbo flat-top 12-string, spruce top, laminated maple back and solid maple sides, multi-bound, gold tuners. Natural or Sunburst.

1987-1999		$1,050	$1,300

M-80 CS

1975-1984. Solidbody, double cutaway, two pickups, has M-80 on truss rod cover. Called just M-80 from 1980-1984.

1975-1984		$650	$700

Manhattan X-170 (Mini-Manhattan X-170)

1985-2002. Called Mini-Manhattan X-170 in '85-'86. Electric archtop hollowbody, single rounded cutaway, maple body, F-holes, two humbuckers, block inlays, gold hardware, Natural or Sunburst.

1985-1989		$1,200	$1,400
1990-1999		$1,250	$1,450

Manhattan X-175/X-175 B

1954-1985. Electric archtop, single rounded cutaway, laminated spruce top, laminated maple back and sides, two pickups, chrome hardware. Sunburst (X-175) or Natural (X-175B) finishes.

1954-1957	Sunburst	$2,050	$2,350
1958-1959	Sunburst	$2,000	$2,300
1960-1969	Sunburst	$1,900	$2,200
1970-1977	Sunburst	$1,600	$1,850
1978-1981	Sunburst	$1,400	$1,650
1982-1985	Natural	$1,300	$1,550

Mark I

1961-1973. Acoustic flat-top classical, Honduras mahogany body, rosewood fingerboard and bridge, satin finish, slotted headstock.

1961-1973		$300	$400

Mark II

1961-1986. Acoustic flat-top classical, spruce top, Honduras mahogany back and sides, rosewood fingerboard and bridge, satin finish, slotted headstock.

1970-1979		$350	$450

Guild F-212XL

1964 Guild
Jet Star S-50

GUITARS

Guild Nightbird

1999 Guild Polara S-100

MODEL YEAR	FEATURES	EXC. COND. LOW	HIGH

Mark III

1961-1986. Acoustic flat-top classical, spruce top, Peruvian mahogany back and sides, rosewood fingerboard and bridge, satin finish, slotted headstock, bound top and back.

1970-1979		$500	$600

Mark IV

1961-1986. Acoustic flat-top classical, rosewood or flamed pearwood back and sides, rosewood fingerboard and bridge, satin finish, slotted headstock.

1970-1979		$600	$700

Mark V

1961-1987. Rosewood or maple back and sides 1961-1978, rosewood only 1978 on.

1980-1987		$700	$900

Navarre F-50

1954-1986. Acoustic flat-top, spruce top, curly maple back and sides, rosewood fingerboard and bridge, 17" rounded lower bout, laminated arched maple back. Renamed JF-65 M in 1987.

1963-1975		$1,700	$2,000
1976		$1,550	$1,850
1977-1981		$1,450	$1,750
1982-1986		$1,400	$1,600

Navarre F-50 (reintroduced)

1994-1995.

1994-1995		$1,100	$1,300

Navarre F-50 R

1965-1986. Rosewood version of F-50, flat spruce top, rosewood back and sides, rosewood fingerboard and bridge. Renamed JF-65 R in 1987.

1965-1975		$1,700	$2,000
1976-1979		$1,450	$1,750
1980-1987		$1,450	$1,650

Nightbird

1985-1987. Electric solidbody, Les Paul-type body with single sharp cutaway, tone chambers, two pickups, multi-bound, Black or Gold hardware. Renamed Nightbird II in 1987.

1985-1987		$1,300	$1,400

Nightbird I

1987-1988. Like Nightbird but with chrome hardware, less binding and appointments, two pickups, coil-tap, phaser switch.

1987-1988		$1,100	$1,300

Nightbird II

1987-1992. Renamed from Nightbird. Electric solidbody, Les Paul-style body with single sharp cutaway, tone chambers, two pickups, multi-bound, Black hardware. Renamed Nightbird X-2000 in 1992.

1987-1992		$1,300	$1,400

Nightbird X-2000

1992-1996. Renamed from Nightbird II.

1992-1996		$1,300	$1,400

MODEL YEAR	FEATURES	EXC. COND. LOW	HIGH

Polara S-100

1963-1970. Electric solidbody, double cutaway, mahogany or alder body, rosewood fingerboard, two pickups, built-in stand until '70, asymmetrical headstock. In '70, Polara dropped from title (see S-100 Standard). Renamed back to Polara S-100 in '97.

1963-1970		$500	$700

Roy Buchanan T-200

1986. Single cutaway solidbody, two pickups, pointed six-on-a-side headstock, poplar body, bolt-on neck, gold and brass hardware.

1986		$550	$650

S-60

1976-1980. Electric solidbody, double cutaway, one pickup, all mahogany body, rosewood fingerboard.

1976-1980		$375	$400

S-60 D

1977-1981. Same as S-60 with two DiMarzio pickups.

1977-1981		$400	$500

S-65 D

1980-1981. Electric solidbody, double cutaway, three DiMarzio pickups, rosewood fingerboard.

1980-1981		$400	$500

S-90

1972-1977. Double cut SG-like body, 2 humbuckers, dot inlay, chrome hardware.

1972-1977		$600	$700

S-100 Standard

1970-1978. Redesigned Polara S-100 with offset double cutaway, two pickups, SG-style body. S-100 name is reissued in 1994-1997 then renamed Polara S-100 in 1997-present.

1970-1978		$700	$900

S-100 Reissue

1994-1997. Renamed Polara in 1997.

1994-1997		$600	$700

S-261

Ca.1985. Double cutaway, maple body, Black Kahler tremolo, one humbucker and two single-coil pickups, rosewood fingerboard.

1985		$350	$450

S-280 Flyer

1983-1984. Double cut poplar body, 2 humbuckers or 3 single-coils, maple or rosewood neck, dot markers.

1983-1984		$375	$450

S-281 Flyer

1983-1988. Double cut poplar body S-280 with locking vibrato, optional pickups available.

1983-1988		$375	$450

S-300 D

1977-1982. Same as S-300, but with a DiMarzio PAF and Super Distortion humbucker pickups.

1977-1982	Natural	$550	$600

MODEL YEAR	FEATURES	EXC. COND. LOW	HIGH

Savoy X-150

1954-1965, 1998-present. Electric archtop, single rounded cutaway, spruce top, maple back and sides, rosewood fingerboard and bridge, one single-coil pickup. Sunburst, Blond or Sparkling Gold finish. Reintroduced in 1998.

1954-1965		$1,400	$1,700

Slim Jim T-100

1958-1973. Electric archtop thinline, single cutaway, laminated all-maple body, rosewood fingerboard and bridge, Waverly tailpiece, one pickup, Natural or Sunburst.

1958-1960		$800	$1,100
1961-1963		$750	$1,050
1964-1973		$700	$950

Slim Jim T-100 D

1958-1973. Semi-hollowbody electric, single Florentine cutaway, thinline, two-pickup version of the T-100, Natural or Sunburst.

1958-1961		$900	$1,150
1962-1968		$850	$1,100
1969-1973		$800	$1,050

Songbird S-4

1987-1991. Designed by George Gruhn. Flat-top, mahogany back, spruce top, single pointed cutaway, pickup with preamp, multi-bound top, Black, Natural or White.

1987-1991		$550	$750

Standard F-112 12-String

1968-1982. Acoustic flat-top, 12 strings, spruce top, mahogany back, sides and neck.

1968-1973		$850	$1,000
1974-1982		$850	$900

Starfire I

1960-1964. Electric archtop, single cutaway thinline, laminated maple or mahogany body, bound body and neck, one pickup.

1960-1964	Starfire Red	$825	$950

Starfire II

1960-1976, 1997-2001. Electric archtop, single cutaway thinline, laminated maple or mahogany body, bound body and rosewood neck, two pickups. Reissued 1997-present.

1960-1965	Sunburst	$900	$1,100
1966-1975	Starfire Red	$800	$1,000

Starfire III

1960-1974, 1997-present. Electric archtop, single cut thinline, laminated maple or mahogany body, bound body and rosewood neck, 2 pickups, Guild or Bigsby vibrato, Starfire Red. Reissued 1997.

1960-1961		$1,000	$1,300
1962-1966		$1,000	$1,200
1967-1968		$900	$1,100
1969		$700	$1,100
1970-1974		$600	$900
1997	Reissue model	$800	$900

Starfire IV

1963-1987, 1991-present. Thinline, double cut semi-hollowbody, laminated maple or mahogany body, F-holes, 2 humbuckers, rosewood 'board, cherry or sunburst. Reissued in '91.

1963-1966		$1,500	$2,000
1967-1969		$1,400	$1,900
1970-1975		$1,300	$1,800
1976-1979		$1,100	$1,600
1980-1987		$900	$1,400
1991-1999		$900	$1,000

Starfire V

1963-1973, 1999-2002. Same as Starfire IV but with block markers, Bigsby and master volume. Natural or Sunburst finish. Reissued in '99.

1963-1967		$1,700	$2,000
1968-1969		$1,600	$1,900
1970		$1,500	$1,800
1971-1973		$1,400	$1,700

Starfire VI

1964-1979. Same as Starfire IV but with high appointments such as ebony fingerboard, pearl inlays, Guild/Bigsby vibrato, Natural or Sunburst.

1971-1979		$2,700	$3,200

Starfire XII

1966-1973. Electric archtop, 12 string, double cut, maple or mahogany body, set-in neck, 2 humbuckers, harp tailpiece.

1966-1967		$1,600	$1,800
1968-1969		$1,550	$1,700
1970-1971		$1,400	$1,550
1972-1973		$1,200	$1,400

Stratford A-350

1956-1973. Acoustic archtop, single rounded cutaway, solid spruce top with solid curly maple back and sides, rosewood fingerboard and bridge (changed to ebony by 1960). Sunburst.

1960-1962		$2,300	$2,700
1963-1965		$2,200	$2,600
1966-1973		$2,000	$2,400

Stratford X-350

1953-1965. Electric archtop, single rounded cutaway, laminated spruce top with laminated maple back and sides, rosewood fingerboard, the pickups, six push-button pickup selectors. Sunburst finish (Natural finish is X-375).

1953		$2,500	$2,900
1954-1956		$2,400	$2,800
1957-1959		$2,300	$2,700
1960-1965		$2,100	$2,500

Stratford X-375/X-350 B

1953-1965. Electric archtop, single cutaway, spruce top, curly maple back and sides, rosewood fingerboard and bridge, three pickups, one volume and one tone control, six push-button pickup selectors. Natural finish (Sunburst is X-350). Renamed X-350 B in 1958.

1953		$2,500	$2,900
1954-1956		$2,400	$2,800
1957-1959		$2,300	$2,700

Guild Starfire IV

Guild Stratford X-350

1966 Guild Thunderbird S-200

Guild X-88D Flying Star

MODEL YEAR	FEATURES	EXC. COND. LOW	HIGH
1960-1965		$2,100	$2,500

Stuart X-500/X-550/X-550 B

1953-1994. Electric archtop, single cutaway, laminated spruce top, laminated curly maple back and sides, two pickups, Sunburst. Blond version was called the X-550 until 1960, and the X-550 B afterwards, and are included here.

1953-1960		$2,700	$3,200
1961-1964		$2,500	$2,900
1965-1970		$2,300	$2,700
1971-1973		$2,200	$2,600
1974-1977		$2,100	$2,400
1978-1979		$2,000	$2,300
1980-1994		$2,000	$2,200

Studio 301

1968-1970. Thinline, semi-hollow archtop Starfire-style but with sharp horns, single pickup, Cherry or Sunburst.

1968-1970		$1,000	$1,200

Studio 302

1968-1970. Electric archtop thinline, double sharp cutaway, laminated maple body, rosewood fingerboard and bridge, two pickups, Cherry or Sunburst.

1968-1970		$1,300	$1,500

Studio 303

1968-1970. Thinline, semi-hollow archtop with sharp horns, 302 model with added Bigsby vibrato, Cherry or Sunburst.

1968-1970		$1,300	$1,500

T-250

1986-1988. Single cut body and pickup configuration with banana-style headstock.

1986-1988		$600	$650

Thunderbird S-200

1963-1968. Electric solidbody, offset double cutaway, built-in rear guitar stand, AdjustoMatic bridge and vibrato tailpiece, two humbucker pickups until changed to single-coils in 1966.

1963-1965	Humbuckers	$850	$1,100
1966-1967	Single-coils	$700	$850
1968		$650	$800

Troubador F-20

1956-1987. Acoustic flat-top, spruce top with maple back and sides (mahogany 1959 and after), rosewood fingerboard and bridge, Natural or Sunburst.

1956-1969		$700	$800
1970-1976		$600	$725
1977-1987		$550	$650

Valencia F-40

1954-1983. Acoustic flat-top, rounded lower bout, spruce top, maple back and sides, rosewood fingerboard and bridge. Sunburst finish.

1954-1980		$800	$900
1981-1983		$750	$850

MODEL YEAR	FEATURES	EXC. COND. LOW	HIGH

X-79 Skyhawk

1981-1986. Four-point solidbody, two pickups, coil-tap or phase switch, various colors.

1981-1986		$550	$650

X-88 Flying Star "Motley Crue"

1984-1986. Explorer meets Flying V pointy four-point star body, rocketship meets spearhead headstock on bolt-on neck, one pickup, optional vibrato.

1984-1986	Pearl White	$475	$600

X-700

1994-2000. Rounded cutaway, 17", solid spruce top, laminated maple back and sides, gold hardware, Natural or Sunburst.

1994-2000		$2,200	$2,300

Gurian

1965-1981. Luthier Michael Gurian started making classical guitars on a special order basis, in New York City. In 1969, he started building steel-string guitars as well. 1971 brought a move to Hinsdale, Vermont, and with it increased production.

JM

Mahogany, jumbo body with relatively wide waist (versus D-style or SJ-style), herringbone/rope trim.

1970s		$1,500	$1,700

JR3

Rosewood back and sides, U.S.A.- made

1970s		$1,900	$2,100

S-2-M

Mahogany, acoustic.

1970s		$800	$1,000

S-3-M

Mahogany.

1970s		$800	$1,000

S-3-R

Indian rosewood.

1970s		$1,200	$1,400

Guyatone

1933-present. Made in Tokyo by Matsuki Seisakujo, founded by Hawaiian guitarists Mitsuo Matsuki and Atsuo Kaneko (later of Teisco). Guya brand Rickenbacker lap copies in '30s. After a hiatus for the war ('40-'48), Seisakujo resumes production of laps and amps as Matsuki Denki Onkyo Kenkyujo. In '51 the Guyatone brand is first used on guitars, and in '52 they changed the company name to Tokyo Sound Company. Guyatones are among the earliest U.S. imports as Marco Polo, Winston, Kingston and Kent. Other brand names included LaFayette and Bradford. Production and exports slowed after '68.

Electric Hollowbody Archtops

Various models.

1950s		$250	$400

Electric Solidbody Guitars

Various models.

1950s		$250	$400
1960s		$200	$300

MODEL YEAR	FEATURES	EXC. COND. LOW	HIGH

Hagenlocher, Henner

1996-present. Luthier Henner Hagenlocher builds his premium grade, custom, nylon-string guitars in Granada, Spain.

Hagstrom

1921-1983. Founded by Albin Hagström (b. 1905-d. 1952) of Älvdalen, Sweden, who began importing accordions in 1921 and incorporated in '25. The name of the company was changed to A.B. Hagström, Inc. in '38, and a American sales office was established in '40. Electric guitar and bass production began in '58 with plastic-covered hollowbody De Luxe and Standard models, which were Les Paul-shaped guitars with a patented design. The guitars were imported into the U.S. by Hershman Music of New York as Goya 90 and 80 from '59-'61. Bass versions were imported in '61. Following a year in the U.S., Albin's son Karl-Erik Hagström took over the company as exclusive distributor of Fender in Scandinavia; he changed the U.S. importer to Merson Musical Instruments of New York (later Unicord in 1965), and redesigned the line. The company closed doors in 1983.

Corvette

Mid-1960s. Offset double cutaway solidbody, three single-coil pickups, multiple push-button switches, spring vibrato.

1965	Red	$800	$1,000

D'Aquisto (Jimmy D'Aquisto Model)

1969, 1976-1979. The Jimmy, designed by James D'Aquisto, electric archtop, F-holes, two pickups, Sunburst.

1976-1979		$700	$850

H-12 Electric 12-String

1965-1967. Double cutaway, two pickups, 12 strings.

1965-1967		$400	$550

Impala

1960s.

1965		$700	$800

Model I

1965-1971. Small double cut solidbody, two single-coil pickups. Early models have plastic top.

1965-1971		$300	$450

Model II

1965-1972. SG-type body with beveled edge, two pickups.

1965-1972		$300	$500

Model III

1965-1972, 1977. SG-type body with beveled edge, three pickups.

1965-1972		$300	$500
1977		$300	$500

Swede

1971-1982. Bolt-on neck, Les Paul-style, Black, Cherry or Natural.

1971-1982		$700	$850

Super Swede

1979-1983. Glued-in neck, Les Paul-style.

1979-1983		$800	$1,000

Viking

1965-1968, 1972-1975. Double cutaway 335-style thinline. Also advertised as the V-1.

1965-1968		$500	$600
1972-1975		$500	$600

Hallmark

1965. Founded by Joe Hall in Arvin, California, in '65. Hall had worked for Semie Moseley (before Mosrite) and had also designed guitars for Standel in the mid-'60s. Bill Grugget, the company's production manager (and who builds his own line of guitars) remembers that Hallmark didn't make a lot of guitars, estimating that approximately 40 were made before the money ran out.

Sweptwing

1965. Pointed body, sorta like a backwards flying V.

1965		$450	$550

Hamer

1974-present. Intermediate, professional and premium grade, production/custom, electric guitars made in the U.S. and overseas. Hamer also make basses and the Slammer line of instruments.

Founded in Arlington Heights, Illinois, by Paul Hamer and Jol Dantzig. Prototype guitars built in early-'70s were on Gibson lines, with first production guitar, the Standard (Explorer shape), introduced in '75. Hamer was puchased by Kaman Corporation (Ovation) in '88. The Illinois factory was closed and the operations were moved to the Ovation factory in Connecticut in '97.

Artist/Archtop Artist/Artist Custom

1995-present. Similar to Sunburst Archtop with semi-solid, F-hole design. Named Archtop Artist, then renamed Artist (with stop tailpiece)/Artist Custom in 1997.

1998	Artist, Sunburst	$1,200	$1,400

Blitz

1982-1984 (1st version), 1984-1990 (2nd version). Explorer-style body, two humbuckers, three-on-a-side peghead, dot inlays, choice of tremolo or fixed bridge. Second version same except has angled six-on-a-side peghead and Floyd Rose tremolo.

1982-1984	3-on-side peghead	$450	$900
1984-1990	6-on-a-side peghead	$450	$750

Californian

1987-1997. Solidbody double cut, bolt neck, 1 humbucker and 1 single-coil, Floyd Rose tremolo.

1987-1989		$450	$900
1990-1997		$450	$750

Californian Custom

1987-1997. Downsized contoured body, offset double cut, neck-through-body, optional figured maple body, Duncan Trembucker and Trem-single pickups.

1987-1989		$450	$900
1990-1997		$450	$750

1979 Hagstrom D'Aquisto

Hamer Artist Custom

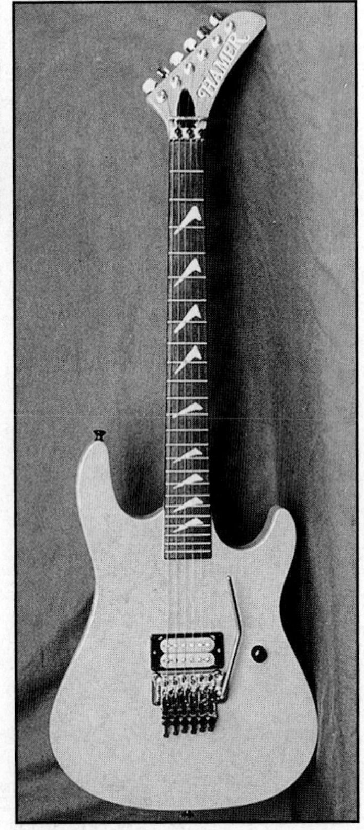

1987 Hamer Chaparrel

Hamer Diablo

MODEL YEAR	FEATURES	EXC. COND. LOW	HIGH

Californian Elite

1987-1997. Downsized contoured body, offset double cutaway, optional figured maple body, bolt-on neck, Duncan Trembucker and Trem-single pickups.

1987-1989		$400	$850
1990-1997		$400	$700

Centaura

1989-1995. Contoured body of alder or swamp ash, offset double cutaway, bolt-on neck, one humbucker and two single-coil pickups, Floyd Rose trem.

1989-1995	Sunburst	$450	$700

Chaparral

1985-1987 (1st version), 1987-1994 (2nd version). Contoured body, offset double cut, glued maple neck, angled peghead, 1 humbucker and 2 single-coils, trem. Second version has bolt neck with a modified peghead.

1985-1987	Set-neck	$375	$750
1987-1994	Bolt-on neck	$375	$600

Daytona

1993-1997. Contoured body, offset double cut, bolt maple neck, dot inlay, 3 single-coils, Wilkinson VSV trem.

1993-1997		$500	$600

Diablo

1992-1997. Contoured alder body, offset double cut, bolt maple neck, rosewood board, dot inlays, reversed peghead '92-'94, 2 pickups, tremolo.

1992-1997		$450	$550

Duo-Tone

1993-present. Acoustic/electric semi-hollowbody, double cutaway, bound top, glued-in neck, rosewood fingerboard, three pickups and EQ.

1993-1999		$500	$600

Eclipse

1994-1999. Asymmetrical double cut slab mahogany body, glued neck, 3-on-a-side peghead, rosewood board, dot inlays, 2 Duncan Mini-Humbuckers.

1994-1999	Cherry	$650	$750

FB I

1986-1987. Reverse Firebird-style body, glued-in neck, reverse headstock, one pickup, rosewood board with dot inlays. Also available in non-reverse body.

1986-1987		$350	$500

FB II

1986-1987. Reverse Firebird-style, glued-in neck, ebony fingerboard with boomerang inlays, angled headstock, two humbuckers, Floyd Rose trem. Also available as a 12-string.

1986-1987		$500	$550

Korina Standard

1995-1996. Limited run, Korina Explorer-type body, glued-in neck, angled peghead, two humbuckers.

1995-1996		$900	$1,200

MODEL YEAR	FEATURES	EXC. COND. LOW	HIGH

Maestro

1990. Offset double cutaway, seven strings, tremolo, bolt-on maple neck, three Seymour Duncan rail pickups.

1990		$650	$800

Miller Music Guitar

1985-1986. Miller Music graphic art (White letters on Red background), double cutaway.

1985-1986		$1,000	$1,500

Mirage

1994-1998. Double cutaway carved figured koa wood top. Initially with three single-coil pickups, dual humbucker option in 1995.

1994-1998	Transparent flamed top	$1,100	$1,200

Newport

1999-present. Double cutaway ES-330-style, thin archtop, dual single-coil pickups with metal covers.

1999	Black Cherry Sunburst	$1,300	$1,400

Phantom A5

1982-1884 (1st version), 1985-1986 (2nd version). Contoured offset double cutaway, glued-in neck, three-on-a-side peghead, one triple-coil and one single-coil pickups. Second version same but with six-on-a-side peghead and Kahler tremolo.

1982-1984		$475	$675

Phantom GT

1984-1986. Contoured body, offset double cutaway, glued-in fixed neck, six-on-a-side peghead, one humbucker, single volume control.

1984-1986		$375	$575

Prototype

1981-1985. Contoured mahogany body, double cutaway with one splitable triple-coil pickup, fixed bridge, three-on-a-side peghead. Prototype II has extra pickup and tremolo.

1981-1985		$650	$800

Scarab I

1984-1986. Multiple cutaway body, six-on-a-side peghead, one humbucker, tremolo, rosewood or ebony fingerboard, dot inlays.

1984-1986		$400	$600

Scarab II

1984-1986. Two humbucker version of the Scarab.

1984-1986		$400	$600

Scepter

1986-1990. Explorer-type body, ebony fingerboard with boomerang inlays, angled six-on-a-side peghead, Floyd Rose trem.

1986-1990		$350	$550

Special

1980-1983 (1st version), 1984-1985 (Floyd Rose version), 1992-1997 (2nd version). Double cut solidbody, flame maple top, glued neck, 3-on-a-side peghead, two humbuckers. Rose version has mahogany body with ebony board. The second version is all mahogany and has tune-o-matic bridge, stop tailpiece and Duncan P-90s.

1980-1983	1st version	$500	$800

MODEL YEAR	FEATURES	EXC. COND. LOW	HIGH
1984-1985	With Floyd Rose	$500	$800
1992-1997	2nd version	$400	$700

Special FM

1993-1997. Special with flamed maple top and dual humbuckers. Renamed the Special Custom in '97.

1993-1997		$700	$800

Standard

1974-1985, 1995-1999. Explorer-shaped body, maple top, bound or unbound body, glued neck, angled headstock, either unbound neck with dot inlays or bound neck with crown inlays, 2 humbuckers. Reissued in '94 with same specs but unbound mahogany body after '97. Higher dollar Standard Custom still available.

1974-1979		$1,500	$2,000
1980-1985		$900	$1,500
1995-1999		$500	$1,500

Steve Stevens I

1984-1992. Introduced as Prototype SS, changed to Steve Stevens I in 1986, contoured double cutaway, six-on-a-side headstock, dot or crown inlays, one humbucker and two single-coil pickups.

1984-1992		$650	$750

Steve Stevens II

1986-1987. One humbucker and one single-coil version.

1986-1987		$600	$700

Studio

1993-present. Double cutaway, flamed maple top on mahogany body, dual humbucker pickups, Cherry or Natural.

1993-1999		$700	$850

Sunburst

1977-1983, 1990-1992. Double cutaway bound solidbody, flamed maple top, glue-in neck, bound neck and crown inlays optional, three-on-a-side headstock, two humbuckers.

1977-1983		$800	$1,200
1990-1992		$800	$1,200

Sunburst Archtop

1991-present. Sunburst model with figured maple carved top, two humbuckers. Offered under various names:

Standard - unbound neck and dot inlays, tune-o-matic and stop tailpiece 1991-1993.

Custom - a Standard with bound neck and crown inlays 1991-1993.

Archtop - bound neck with crown inlays 1994-1997.

Studio Custom - bound neck with crown inlays 1997-present.

Studio - unbound body, by 1995 stud wrap-around tailpiece 1993-present.

Archtop GT - Gold top with P-90 soapbar-style pickups 1993-1997.

1991-1997		$800	$1,200

T-51

1993-1997. Classic single cut southern ash body, 2 single-coils.

1993-1997		$625	$700

T-62

1991-1995. Classic offset double cut solidbody, tremolo, pau ferro board, Lubritrak nut, locking tuners, 3-band active EQ.

1991-1995		$625	$700

TLE

1986-1992. Single cut mahogany body, maple top, glued neck, 6-on-a-side headstock, rosewood board, dot inlays, 3 pickups.

1986-1992		$600	$700

TLE Custom

1986-1992. Bound, single cutaway solidbody with maple top, glued-in neck, angled headstock, ebony fingerboard with boomerang inlays, three pickups.

1986-1992		$600	$700

Harmony

1892-1974, late 1970s-present. Huge, Chicago-based manufacturer of fretted instruments, mainly budget models under the Harmony name or for many other American brands and mass marketers. Harmony was at one time the largest guitar builder in the world. In its glory days, Harmony made over one-half of the guiltars built in the U.S. But by the early-'70s, the crash of '60s guitar boom and foreign manufacturers brought an end to the company. The company lasted from 1892 until 1974, with 1965 being Harmony's peak year.

The Harmony brand appeared on Asian-built intruments starting in the late '70s. In 2000, the Harmony name was reintroduced by MBT International. In '03, former MBT International marketing director Alison Gillette announced the launch of Harmony Classic Reissue Guitars and Basses.

Many Harmony guitars have a factory order number on the inside back of the guitar. The FON often contains the serial number.

Price includes original guitar case, hard sided or soft shell.

Archtone H1215

1950s. Lower-end archtop.

1950s	Sunburst	$100	$200

Blond H62

1950s-1960s. Thin body, dual pickup archtop, curly maple back and sides, spruce top. Blond.

1950s		$500	$800
1960s		$400	$700

Brilliant Cutaway H1310

1962-1965. Sixteen and one/half inch body (Grand Auditorium), acoustic archtop cutaway, block markers.

1962-1965	Sunburst	$450	$550

Broadway H954

1930s-1971. 15-3/4" body, acoustic archtop, dot markers, sunburst.

1960s	Sunburst	$250	$350

Buck Owens

Acoustic flat-top. Red, White and Blue.

1969		$500	$900

1985 Hamer Steve Stevens

Harmony Buck Owens

Harmony Hollywood

1930s Harmony Patrician

MODEL YEAR	FEATURES	EXC. COND. LOW	HIGH

Cremona

1930s-1952. Full-size archtop line, Harmony and Cremona logo on headstock, natural. Cutaways became available in '53.

1940s		$100	$250

Espanada H63/H64

1950s-1960s. Thick body, single cutaway, jazz-style double pickups. Black finish with White appointments.

1950s		$500	$800
1960s		$400	$700

Grand Concert H165

1960s. Flat-top, all mahogany body.

1960s		$200	$250

H72/H72V Double Cutaway Hollowbody

Late-1960s. Dual pickups, 335-style body, H72V includes vibrato tailpiece.

1969	Burgundy	$250	$450

H73 Double Cutaway Hollowbody

Double cutaway, two pickups.

1966		$250	$450

H75 Double Cutaway Hollowbody

Late-1960s. Triple pickups, 335-style body. Sunburst finish.

1960s		$500	$700

H76 Double Cutaway Hollowbody

Late-1960s. Triple pickups, 335-style body, Bigsby vibrato tailpiece. Sunburst.

1960s		$500	$700

H77 Double Cutaway Hollowbody

Late-1960s. Triple pickups, 335-style body. Cherry finish.

1960s		$500	$700

H78 Double Cutaway Hollowbody

Late-1960s. Triple pickups, 335-style body, Bigsby vibrato tailpiece. Cherry.

1960s		$500	$700

H79 Double Cutaway Hollowbody 12-String

Late-1960s. Unique slotted headstock, 335-12-style body. Cherry finish.

1960s		$600	$800

Hollywood H37/H39/H41

Auditorium-sized 15 3/4" non-cutaway electric archtop, H37 has a single pickup and Bronze finish, H39 has a single pickup and Brown Mahogany shaded finish, H41 has dual pickups and Brown finish.

1960		$175	$350

Master H945 (acoustic archtop)

1965-1966. Fifteen inch (Auditorium) acoustic archtop, block markers, music note painted logo on headstock.

1965-1966	Sunburst	$200	$300

Meteor H70/H71

1960s. Ultra thin, single cutaway, dual pickups, H70 Sunburst, H71 Natural.

1960s	H70	$300	$600
1960s	H71	$300	$600

Montclair

Archtop acoustic.

1960		$225	$300

Monterey H1456/H1457/H1325/H950/H952

1930s-1974. Line of Auditorium and Grand Auditorium acoustic archtop models. Not all Monterey models were made during the whole period.

1955	Model H952 Colorama	$300	$400
1963		$225	$300

Patrician F63

Archtop.

1940s		$250	$350

Rebel H81 (single pickup)

1970s. Single pickup version of Rebel H82.

1971		$175	$275

Rebel H82/H82G

Listed as a new model in 1971. Thin body, hollow tone chamber, double cutaway, H82 Sunburst, H82G Avacado shading, two pickups (H81 was a single pickup version).

1971	H82	$200	$300

Rocket H53/H54/H56/H59

Various models: Rocket I H53 has single pickup, Rocket II H54 has two pickups, Rocket VII H56 has two pickups and vibrato, Rocket III H59 has three pickups. Rockets were single cutaway, Brown Sunburst in the early-1960s and double cutaway Red Sunburst in the early-1970s.

1950s	1 pickup	$200	$350
1950s	2 pickups	$200	$450
1950s	3 pickups	$500	$650
1960s	1 pickup	$200	$350
1960s	2 pickups	$200	$450
1960s	3 pickups	$500	$650

Silhouette De Luxe Double H19

1964-1967. Double cut solidbody, deluxe pickups, block markers, advanced vibrato.

1965-1967	Sunburst	$325	$400

Silhouette H14/H15/H17

1964-1967. Double cut solidbody, H14 single pickup, H15 dual pickup, H17 dual with vibrato. The H17 was offered until '66.

1964-1966	H17	$225	$325
1964-1967	H14	$150	$200
1964-1967	H15	$200	$300

Singing Cowboys H1057

Western chuck-wagon scene stencil top, "Singing Cowboys" stenciled on either side of upper bouts. Brown background versus earlier Supertone version that had Black background.

1950s		$175	$300

Sovereign Jumbo Deluxe H1266

1960s-1970s. Jumbo nearly D-style, 16" wide body with out-size pickguard, Natural.

1960s		$500	$600
1970s		$450	$550

MODEL YEAR	FEATURES	EXC. COND. LOW	HIGH

Sovereign Jumbo H1260

1960s-1970s. Jumbo shape, 16" wide body, Natural.

1960s		$450	$550
1970s		$400	$500

Sovereign Western Special Jumbo H1203

1960s-1970s. Fifteen inch wide body, 000-style.

1960s		$500	$600

Stratotone Deluxe Jupiter H49

1958-1968. Single cut, tone chamber construction, 2 pickups, bound spruce top, curly maple back and 6 control knobs.

1950s		$300	$450

Stratotone Mars Electric H45/H46

1958-1968. Single cut, tone chamber construction, H45 with 1 pickup and sunburst finish, H46 with 2 pickups.

1950s		$200	$350

Stratotone Mercury Electric H47/H48

1958-1968. Single cut, tone chamber construction, H47 with 1 pickup, block inlay and curly maple sunburst top, H48 is the same with a blond top.

1950s		$250	$400

TG1201 Tenor

Spruce top, two-on-a-side tuners, Sovereign model tenor. Natural

1950s		$200	$300

Harptone

1893-ca. 1975. The Harptone Manufacturing Corporation was located in Newark, New Jersey. They made musical instrument cases and accessories and got into instrument production from 1934 to '42, making guitars, banjos, mandolins, and tiples. In '66 they got back into guitar production, making the Standel line from '67 to '69. Harptone offered flat-tops and archtops under their own brand until the mid-'70s when the name was sold to the Diamond S company, which owned Micro-Frets.

E-6N

D-style body, spruce top and mahogany back and sides, unique Harptone headstock, Natural.

1970		$850	$950

Hayes Guitars

1993-present. Professional and premium grade, production/custom, steel and nylon string guitars made by luthier Louis Hayes in Paonia, Colorado.

Haynes

1865-early 1900s. The John C. Haynes Co. of Boston, also made the Bay State brand.

Parlor Guitar

1900s-1920s. Small 12 1/2" parlor guitar with typical narrow bouts, spruce top, Brazilian rosewood back and sides, multicolored wood marquetry trim, Natural.

1910		$600	$800

MODEL YEAR	FEATURES	EXC. COND. LOW	HIGH

Heartfield

1989-1994. Founded as a joint venture between Fender Musical Instrument Corporation (U.S.A.) and Fender Japan (partnership between Fender and distributors Kanda Skokai and Yamano Music) to build and market more advanced designs (built by Fuji Gen-Gakki). First RR and EX guitar series and DR Bass series debut in '90. Talon and Elan guitar series and Prophecy bass series introduced in '91. The brand was dead by '94.

Elan

1989-1994. Carved-style bound double cut body, flamed top, dual humbuckers, offset PRS-style headstock.

1989-1994		$250	$300

EX

1990-1994. EX models have three single-coil pickups and Floyd Rose tremolo.

1990s		$150	$250

Talon

1989-1994. Strat-style body with wedge-triangle headstock, dot markers, hum/single/hum pickup configuration.

1989-1994	Blue	$150	$250

Heiden Stringed Instruments

1974-present. Luthier Michael Heiden builds his premium grade, production/custom, flat-top guitars and mandolins in Chilliwack, British Columbia.

Heit Deluxe

Ca. 1967-1970. Imported from Japan by unidentified New York distributor. Many were made by Teisco, the most famous being the Teisco V-2 Mosrite copy.

Acoustic Archtop Guitars

1967-1970. Various models.

1960s		$100	$200

Electric Solidbody Guitars

1967-1970. Various models.

1960s		$90	$150

Hemken, Michael

1993-present. Luthier Michael Hemken builds his premium grade, custom, archtops in St. Helena, California.

Heritage

1985-present. Professional, premium, and presentation grade, production/custom, hollow, semi-hollow, and solidbody guitars built in Kalamazoo, Michigan. They have also made banjos, mandolins, flat-tops, and basses in the past.

Founded by Jim Deurloo, Marvin Lamb, J.P. Moats, Bill Paige and Mike Korpak, all former Gibson employees who did not go to Nashville when Norlin closed the original Gibson factory in 1984.

1959 Harmony Sovereign

1968 Heit Deluxe solidbody

Heritage Johnny Smith

Heritage Sweet 16

MODEL YEAR	FEATURES	EXC. COND. LOW	HIGH

Eagle

1986-present. Single rounded cut semi-hollowbody, mahogany body and neck, one jazz pickup, F-holes.

1986-1999	Sunburst	$1,500	$2,000

Eagle Custom

Eagle with custom inlays.

2001		$2,300	$2,500

Gary Moore Model

1989-1991. Les Paul-style solidbody, two pickups, chrome hardware, Sunburst.

1989-1991		$2,000	$2,800

Golden Eagle

1985-present. Single cutaway hollowbody, back inlaid with mother-of-pearl eagle and registration number, multi-bound ebony board with mother-of-pearl cloud inlays, bound F-holes, gold-plated parts, ebony bridge inlaid with mother-of-pearl, mother-of-pearl truss rod cover engraved with owner's name, one Heritage jazz pickup, multi-bound curly maple pickguard.

1985-2000		$2,500	$3,000

H-140 CM

1985-present. Single pointed cutaway, solidbody with bound curly maple top, two humbucking pickups, chrome parts.

1985-1994	Curly maple top	$750	$850
1985-1994	Goldtop	$750	$850

H-147

1990-1991. Single cutaway Les Paul-shaped solidbody, two humbuckers, mahogany body, mother-of-pearl block inlays, Black or Gold hardware.

1990	Black	$650	$750

H-150 C/H-150 CM

1985-present. Single rounded cutaway solidbody, curly maple top, 2 pickups, chrome parts.

1985-1998	Cherry Sunburst	$800	$900

H-157 Ultra

Les Paul Custom-style, large block markers, figured maple top.

1993-1994		$1,200	$1,500

H-204 DD

1986-1989. Single cutaway solidbody of mahogany, curly maple top, one-piece mahogany neck, 22-fret rosewood fingerboard.

1986-1989		$500	$600

H-207 DD

1986-1989. Double cutaway solidbody of mahogany, curly maple top, one-piece mahogany neck, 22-fret rosewood fingerboard.

1986-1989		$500	$600

H-357

1989-1994. Firebird copy, neck-through-body.

1990s		$2,000	$2,200

H-535

1987-present. Double cutaway semi-hollowbody archtop, rosewood fingerboard, two humbucker pickups.

1987		$1,000	$1,100
1990		$1,000	$1,100
1996	Flamed maple top	$1,200	$1,300
2000-2002		$1,000	$1,300

MODEL YEAR	FEATURES	EXC. COND. LOW	HIGH

H-550

1990-present. Single cut hollow body, laminated maple top and back, multiple bound top, white bound pickguard, f-holes, 2 humbuckers.

1996-2000		$1,800	$2,200

H-575

1987-present. Single sharp cut hollow body, solid maple top and back, cream bound top and back, wood pickguard, f-holes, 2 humbuckers.

1990s		$1,000	$1,200

H-576

1990-present. Single rounded cut hollow body, laminated maple top and back, multiple bound top, single bound back and f-holes and wood pickguard, 2 humbuckers.

1990-1998		$1,000	$1,200

HFT-445

1987-2000. Flat-top acoustic, mahogany back and sides, spruce top, maple neck, rosewood board.

1987-2000		$500	$700

Johnny Smith

1989-2001. Custom hand-carved 17" hollowbody, single cutaway, F-holes, one pickup.

1989-1999	Optional colors	$2,900	$3,500
1989-1999	Sunburst	$2,700	$3,300

Parsons Street

1989-1992. Offset double cutaway, curly maple top on mahogany body, single/single/hum pickups, pearl block markers, Sunburst or Natural.

1990		$700	$800

Roy Clark

1992-present. Thinline, single cut semi-hollow archtop, gold hardware, 2 humbuckers, block markers.

1992-2002	Cherry Sunburst	$1,900	$2,000

Super Eagle

1988-present. Eighteen inch body, single cutaway electric archtop.

1989-1999	Optional colors	$2,850	$3,000
1989-1999	Sunburst	$2,650	$2,800

Sweet 16

1987-present. Single cut maple semi-hollowbody, spruce top, 2 pickups, pearl inlays.

1987-2000	Optional colors	$2,500	$3,000
1987-2000	Sunburst	$2,300	$2,800

Hill Guitar Company

1972-1980, 1990-present. Luthier Kenny Hill builds his professional and premium grade production/custom, classical and flamenco guitars in Felton, California and Michoacan, Mexico.

Hirade Classical

1968-present. Professional grade, production, classical guitars built in Japan by Takamine. The late Mass Hirade was the founder of the Takamine workshop. He learned his craft from master luthier Masare Kohno. Hirade "represents Takamine's finest craftsmanship and material." Solid tops.

MODEL YEAR	FEATURES	EXC. COND. LOW	HIGH

H-5

Solid cedar top, laminate rosewood body.

1980s		$900	$1,000

H-8

1989-1996. Solid spruce top, solid rosewood body.

1989-1996		$1,200	$1,400

HD-5C

Solid cedar top, rosewood laminate body, cutaway, pickup and preamp.

1980s		$900	$1,000

Hoffman Guitars

1971-present. Premium grade, custom flat-tops and harp guitars built by luthier Charles Hoffman in Minneapolis, Minnesota.

Höfner

1887-present. Budget, intermediate, and professional grade, production, archtop, acoustic, and classical guitars built in Germany and the Far East. They also produce basses and bowed-instruments.

Founded by Karl Höfner in Schonbach, Germany. Sons Josef and Walter joined the company in 1919 and 1921 and expanded the market worldwide. The company started producing guitars in 1925. They moved the company to Bavaria in '50 and are currently located in Hagenau.

Beatle Electric Model 459TZ

1960s. Violin-shaped 500/1 body, block-stripe position markers, transistor-powered flip-fuzz and treble boost.

1960s	Sunburst	$1,500	$1,700

Beatle Electric Model 459VTZ

1960s. Violin-shaped 500/1 body, same as Model 459TZ except with vibrato tailpiece.

1960s	Sunburst	$1,500	$1,700

Beatle Electric Model G459TZ Super

1960s. Violin-shaped 500/1 body, deluxe version of Model 459TZ, including flamed maple sides and narrow grain spruce top, Gold hardware, and elaborate inlays and binding.

1960s	Natural Blond	$1,700	$1,900

Beatle Electric Model G459VTZ Super

1960s. Violin-shaped 500/1 body, same as G459TZ Super but with vibrato tailpiece and narrow grain spruce top, Gold hardware.

1960s	Natural Blond	$1,700	$1,900

Club Model 126

1954-1970. Mid-sized single cutaway Guild Bluesbird or Les Paul-style body, dot markers, flamed maple back and sides, spruce top, listed with Hofner "Professional Electric Series."

1960s	Sunburst	$500	$700

Committee Model 4680 Thin Electric

1961-1968. Thinline archtop single cut Byrdland-style body, dual pickups, split-arrowhead markers, no vibrato, Sunburst.

1961-1968		$1,200	$1,400

MODEL YEAR	FEATURES	EXC. COND. LOW	HIGH

Deluxe Model 176

1964-1983. Double cut, 3 pickups, polyester varnished sunburst finish, vibrola tailpiece. Similar to Model 175 polyester varnished red and gold version.

1960s		$500	$700

Galaxy Model 175

1963-1966. Double cut, 3 pickups, red and gold vinyl covering, fancy red-patch pickguard, vibrola. Similar to Model 176 polyester varnished sunburst version.

1963-1966		$1,300	$1,600

Golden Hofner

Two pickups, F-holes.

1961		$1,100	$1,300

Model 172/172-R/172-S/172-I

1960s. Double cut body, polyester varnished wood (S suffix) or scruffproof vinyl (R or I suffix), 2 pickups, vibrato tailpiece.

1960s		$400	$500

Model 173/173-S/173-I

1960s. Double cut body, polyester varnished wood (S suffix) or scuffproof vinyl (I suffix), three pickups, vibrato tailpiece.

1960s	173-I	$400	$500
1960s	173-S	$500	$600

Model 180 Shorty Standard

1982. Small-bodied, single cut, solidbody, 1 pickup, travel guitar. The Shorty Super had a built-in amp and speaker.

1982		$250	$400

Model 471SE2 (electric archtop)

1969-1977. Large single pointed cutaway electric archtop, flamed maple back and sides, spruce top, black celluloid binding, ebony board, pearl inlays, blond finish.

1969-1977		$1,000	$1,200

Model 491 Flat-Top

1960s-1970s. J-45 slope shoulder body style, spruce top, mahogany back and sides, shaded Sunburst.

1970s		$300	$450

Model 496 Jumbo Flat-Top

1960s. J-185-style body with selected spruce top and highly flamed maple back and sides, gold-plated hardware, ornamented vine pattern pickguard.

1960s	Sunburst	$900	$1,100

Model 514-H Classical Concert

1960s. Concert model,lower-end of the Hofner classical line.

1960s	Natural	$200	$300

Model 4575VTZ (Professional, three pickups)

1960s. Extra-thinline acoustic, double cutaway with shallow rounded horns, three pickups, vibrato arm, Ruby-Red, includes treble boost and flip-fuzz, straight-line markers.

1960s	Ruby Red	$750	$1,150

1967 Höfner Committee

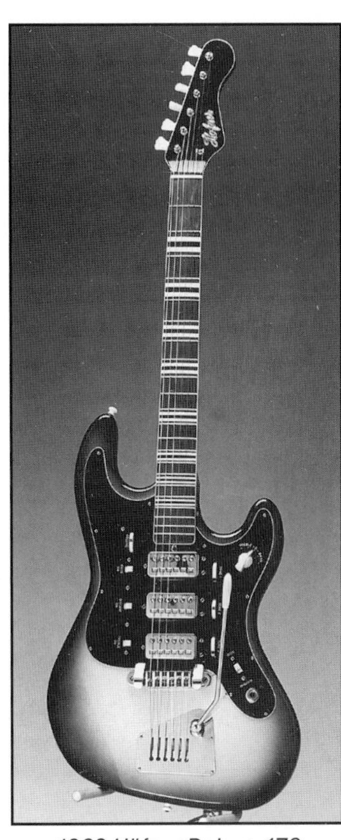

1963 Höfner Deluxe 176

GUITARS

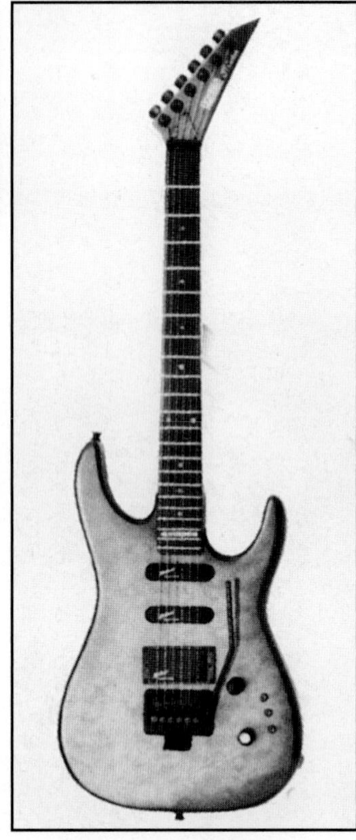
1989 Hohner ST Custom

Hondo H-2

MODEL YEAR	FEATURES	EXC. COND. LOW	HIGH

Model 4575VTZ (Professional, two pickups)

1960s. Extra-thinline acoustic, double cutaway with shallow rounded horns, two pickups, vibrato arm, Ruby-Red, includes treble boost and flip-fuzz, straight-line markers.

1960s	Ruby Red	$750	$950

Model 4600/V2 (Professional extra thin)

1960s. Thinline acoustic, double cutaway with shallow rounded horns, two pickups, vibrato arm, dot markers. Sunburst.

1960s	Sunburst	$600	$800

Model 470SE2 (electric archtop)

1961-1993. Large single rounded cutaway electric archtop on Hofner's higher-end they call "superbly flamed maple (back and sides), carved top of best spruce," 2 pickups, 3 control knobs, gold hardware, pearl inlay. Natural finish only.

1960s		$1,000	$1,200

President Model 4578TZ Dual Cutaway

Double pointed cutaway, thinline archtop, two pickups, non-vibrato.

1956-1965		$700	$1,000
1966-1970		$600	$900

Razorwood

Two pickups.

1980s	Natural	$400	$700

Hohner

1857-present. Budget and intermediate grade, production, acoustic and electric guitars. They also have basses, ukes and mandolins. Matthias Hohner, a clockmaker in Trossingen, Germany, founded Hohner in 1857, making harmonicas. Hohner has been offering guitars and basses at least since the early '70s. HSS was founded in 1986 as a distributor of guitars and other musical products. By 2000, Hohner was also offering the Crafter brands of guitars.

Alpha Standard

Designed by Klaus Scholler. Solidbody, stereo outputs, Flytune tremolo.

1987		$200	$300

Jacaranda Rosewood Dreadnought

Flat-top acoustic.

1978		$200	$350

Les Paul Custom Copy

Late-1970s-1980s. Single cutaway with all the typical Les Paul appointments, block markers.

1970s		$200	$300

Miller Beer Guitar

Solidbody, shaped like Miller beer logo.

1985		$300	$400

Professional

1980s. Single cut solidbody, maple neck, extra large pickguard.

1980s	Natural	$200	$300

SE-35

1989-mid-1990s. ES-335-style, 22 frets, graphite nut, two humbucker pickups.

1989	Natural	$200	$300

ST Victory

1987-mid-1990s. Part of the Professional Series. Double cut solid maple body, reverse headstock, tremolo, humbucker pickup.

1988	Blue	$200	$300

Hollenbeck Guitars

1970-present. Luthier Bill Hollenbeck builds his premium grade, production/custom, hollow and semi-hollow body acoustics and electric guitars in Lincoln, Illinois.

Holman

1966-1968. Built by the Holman-Woodell guitar factory in Neodesha, Kansas. The factory was started to build guitars for Wurlitzer, but that fell through by '67.

Hondo

1969-1987, 1991-present. Budget grade, production, Imported acoustic and electric guitars. They also offer basses. Originally imported by International Music Corporation (IMC) of Fort Worth, Texas, founded by Jerry Freed and Tommy Moore and named after a small town near San Antonio, Texas.

Early pioneers of Korean guitarmaking, primarily targeted at beginner market. Introduced their first electrics in '72. Changed brand to Hondo II in '74. Some better Hondos made in Japan '74-'82/'83. In '85 IMC purchases major interest in Jackson/Charvel, and the Hondo line was supplanted by Charvels. '87 was the last catalog before hiatus. In '88 IMC was sold and Freed began Jerry Freed International and in '91 he revived the Hondo name. Acquired by MBT International in '95, specializing in student-level instruments.

Acoustic Flat-Top Guitars

1969-1987, 1991-present.

1970s		$150	$250

Electric Hollowbody Guitars (misc.)

1969-1987, 1991-present.

1980s		$250	$400

Electric Solidbody Guitars (misc.)

1969-1987, 1991-present.

1969-1987		$250	$400
1991-1999		$100	$200

H 752 Fame

1990s. Single cut solidbody, Black single-ply pickguard, maple neck.

1990s	Blond	$150	$225

H 756 BTS Fame

1990s. Double cut solidbody, white pickguard, maple body, rosewood or maple fingerboard, Natural or Sunburst.

1990s		$150	$225

GUITARS

MODEL YEAR	FEATURES	EXC. COND. LOW	HIGH

Longhorn 6/12 Doubleneck copy

1970s-1980s. Copy of Danelectro Longhorn 6/12 Doubleneck guitar, Dano coke bottle-style headstock.

1980s	White Sunburst	$600	$800

Longhorn Copy

1970s. Copy of Danelectro Longhorn guitar, Dano Coke bottle-style headstock.

1970s	Brown	$350	$450

M 16 "Rambo-Machine Gun"

1970s-1980s. Machine gun body-style, matching machine gun-shaped guitar case, black or red.

1970s		$300	$600
1980s		$300	$600

Hopf

1906-present. Intermediate, professional, premium, and presentation grade, production/custom, classical guitars made in Germany. They also make basses, mandolins and flutes.

The Hopf family of Germany has a tradition of instrument building going back to 1669, but the modern company was founded in 1906. Hopf started making electric guitars in the mid-1950s. Some Hopf models were made by others for the company. By the late-1970s, Hopf had discontinued making electrics, concentrating on classicals.

Explorer Standard

1960s. Es-335-style body with sharp horns, center block, dual mini-humbucker-style pickups.

1960s		$350	$450

Saturn Archtop

1960s. Ofset cutaway, archtop-style soundholes, two pickups.

1960s	White	$600	$900

Super Deluxe Archtop

1960s. Archtop, 16 3/4", cat's-eye soundholes, carved spruce top, flamed maple back and sides.

1960s	Sunburst	$700	$900

Horabe

Classical and Espana models made in Japan.

Model 25 Classical

Solid top

1960s		$400	$500

Model 40 Classical

Solid cedar top, rosewood back and sides.

1960s		$500	$600

Hoyer

1874-present. Intermediate and professional grade, production, flat-top, classical, electric, and resonator guitars. They also build basses. Founded by Franz Hoyer, building classical guitars and other instruments. His son, Arnold, added archtops in the late-1940s, and solidbodies in the 1960s. In 1967, Arnold's son, Walter, took over, leaving the company in 1977. The company changed hands a few times over the following years. Walter started building guitars again in 1984 under the W.A. Hoyer brand, which is not associated with Hoyer.

MODEL YEAR	FEATURES	EXC. COND. LOW	HIGH

Junior

Early-1960s. Solidbody with unusual sharp horn cutaway, single neck pickup, bolt-on neck, dot markers, Arnold Hoyer logo on headstock, shaded Sunburst.

1962		$450	$550

Soloist Electric

Single cutaway archtop, two pickups, teardrop F-holes, Sunburst.

1960-1962		$500	$600

Humming Bird

1947-ca.1968. Japanese manufacturer. By 1968 making pointy Mosrite inspirations. Probably not imported into the U.S.

Electric Solidbody Guitars

1950s		$150	$300

Humphrey, Thomas

1970-present. Premium and presentation grade, custom, nylon-string guitars built by luthier Thomas Humphrey in Gardiner, New York. In 1996 Humphrey began collaborating with Martin Guitars, resulting in the Martin C-TSH and C-1R. Often the inside back label will indicate the year of manufacture.

Classical

Brazilian or Indian rosewood back and sides, spruce top, traditionally-based designs evolved over time with Millenium becoming a benchmark design in 1985, values can increase with new designs. Valuations depend on each specific instrument and year and type of construction. Price ranges are guidance only; each instrument should be evaluated on a case-by-case basis.

1976-1984		$4,000	$6,500

Millenium (classical)

1985-present. Professional performance-grade high-end classical guitar with innovative taper body design and elevated fingerboard. Tops are generally spruce (versus cedar) with rosewood back and sides.

1995-1996		$10,000	$13,000

Huss and Dalton Guitar Company

1995-present. Luthiers Jeff Huss and Mark Dalton build their professional and premium grade flat-tops and banjos in Staunton, Virginia.

Ibanez

1932-present. Budget, intermediate, and professional grade, production/custom, acoustic and electric guitars. They also make basses, amps, and effects.

Founded in Nagoya, Japan, by Matsujiro Hoshino as book and stationary supply, retailing musical instruments in 1909. He began importing instruments in 1921. His son Yoshitaro became president in '27 and began exporting. Manu-

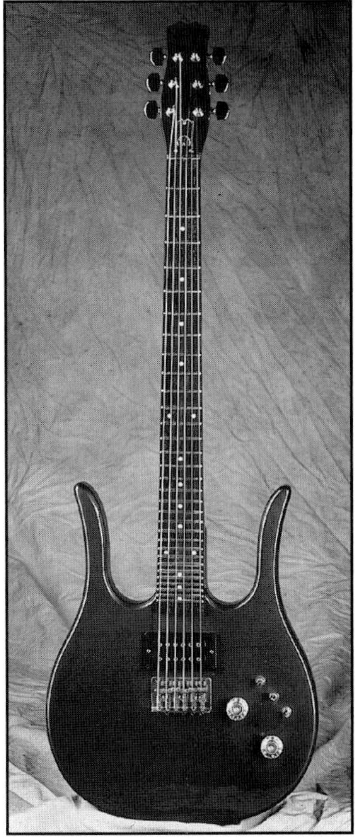

1978 Hondo II Longhorn

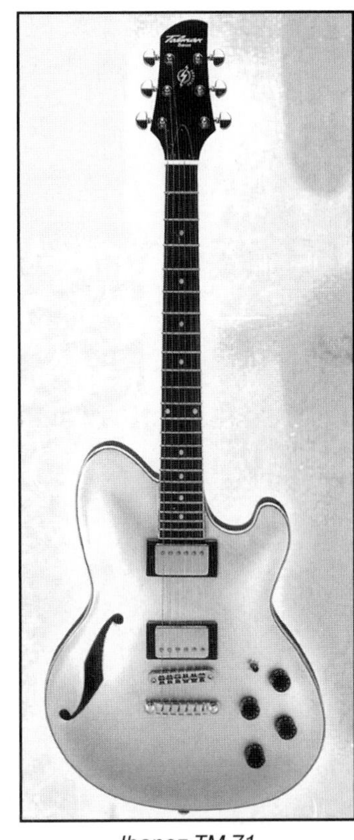

Ibanez TM-71

GUITARS

Ibanez AR-1200 Doubleneck Arist

1975 Ibanez Artist 2616

MODEL YEAR	FEATURES	EXC. COND. LOW	HIGH

facturing of Ibanez instruments began in '32. The company's factories were destroyed during World War II, but the business was revived in '50. Junpei Hoshino, grandson of founder, became president in '60; a new factory opened called Tama Seisakusho (Tama Industries). Brand names by '64 included Ibanez, Star, King's Stone, Jamboree and Goldentone, supplied by 85 factories serving global markets. Sold acoustic guitars to Harry Rosenblum of Elger Guitars ('59-ca.'65) in Ardmore, Pennsylvania, in early-'60s. Around '62 Hoshino purchased 50% interest in Elger Guitars, and ca. '65 changed the name to Ibanez.

Jeff Hasselberger headed the American guitar side beginning '73-'74, and the company headquarters are moved to Cornwells Heights, PA in '74. By '75 the instruments are being distributed by Chesbro Music Company in Idaho Falls, Idaho, and Harry Rosenblum sells his interest to Hoshino shortly thereafter. Ca. '81, the Elger Company becomes Hoshino U.S.A. An U.S. Custom Shop was opened in '88.

Most glued-neck guitars from 1970s are fairly rare.

Dating: copy guitars begin ca. 1971. Serial numbers begin 1975 with letter (A-L for month) followed by 6 digits, the first two indicating year, last four sequential (MYYXXXX). By 1988 the month letter drops off. Dating code stops early-1990s; by 1994 letter preface either F for Fuji or C for Cort (Korean) manufacturer followed by number for year and consecutive numbers (F4XXXX=Fuji, C4XXXX=Cort, 1994).

470 S/S470

1991-present. Offset double cut mahogany solidbody, single-single-hum pickups until about '95 (470 S), hum-single-hum (S470) afterwards.

1990s		$375	$425

540 S FM/S540FM

1992-1997. Mahogany solidbody, flame maple top, solid maple neck, rosewood board, single-single-hum pickups until '94 (540SFM), hum-single-hum (S540FM) afterwards.

1992-1997		$600	$800

540 S LTD/S540LTD

1990-1999. Offset double cut mahogany solidbody, solid maple neck, bound rosewood board, sharktooth inlays, hum-single-hum pickups. Model changed to S540LTD in '94.

1990s		$600	$800

AE400

1990s. Acoustic/electric, single cutaway with piezo, mahogany back and sides, spruce top.

1990s		$300	$350

AH-10 (Allan Holdsworth)

1985-1986. Offset double cut solidbody, bolt neck, single bridge humbucker, dot markers, various colors.

1985-1986		$300	$400

MODEL YEAR	FEATURES	EXC. COND. LOW	HIGH

Artist Doubleneck AR1200

1981-1984. Solid ash body, six/twelve strings, three-ply maple neck, Super 58 pickups, Gold hardware.

1981-1984		$1,000	$1,300

Artist Prestige AR2000

1998. Limited Edition, solidbody with symmetrical double cutaway, bound body, flame top, abalone dot inlay, gold hardware, tune-o-matic-style bridge.

1998		$800	$950

Artist Semi-Hollowbody AM Models

1979-1986. Small-size 335-style, semi-hollowbody, two pickups.

1979-1986		$800	$900

Artist Solidbody Models

There have been many Artist solidbodies since around 1974, but they are all similar in design. We have split the line, by level of features (hardware, tops, electronics), into regular and fancy.

1970s	Fancier features	$900	$1,100
1970s	Regular features	$600	$800
1980s	Fancier features	$900	$1,100
1980s	Regular features	$600	$800

AS80

1994-2002. ES-335-style body and layout, dot markers, chrome hardware.

2000s		$375	$400

AS100

1980s. ES-335 style, dot markers, toggle switch located in the normal spot near the control knobs.

1980s	Sunburst	$1,200	$1,300

AS200

1979-2001. ES-335 style, block markers, toggle switch located on upper treble bout. Replaced by the JSM100 in 2002.

1980s	Sunburst	$1,100	$1,300

AX125

2001-present. Double cut solidbody, 2 humbuckers, bolt neck.

2000s		$100	$200

Blazer

1980-1999. Offset double cut, 2 mini-switches for coil tap and phase, various colors.

1980s	Matching headstock	$300	$400

Bob Weir Model 2681

1975-1980. Double cut solidbody of carved solid ash, maple neck, ebony board with tree-of-life inlay, gold-plated Super 70 pickups. Only three to six of these were ever produced.

1975-1980		$1,500	$2,000

Bob Weir Standard Model 2680

1976-1980. Double cut solidbody of carved solid ash, maple neck, ebony board, dot markers, gold-plated Super 70 pickups, production model.

1976-1980		$700	$1,000

Concert CN-200

1978-1979. Carved maple top, mahogany body, seven layer Black/White binding, bolt-on neck, Super 80 pickups.

1978-1979		$300	$450

MODEL YEAR	FEATURES	EXC. COND. LOW	HIGH

Concert CN-250
1978-1979. Carved maple top, mahogany body, seven layer Black/White binding, bolt-on neck, rosewood board with vine inlay, Super 80 pickups.

1978		$325	$425

Concord 699
1970s. D-style flat-top, all maple including neck and fretboard.

1970s	Natural	$400	$500

Custom Agent 2405 (Scroll Les Paul)
1973-1977. Built as special order, known as scroll headstock Les Paul.

1973-1977		$1,000	$1,500

Custom Agent 2675
1975-1980. Carved maple top, fancy inlays, six strings, maple neck and ebony fretboard with pearl inlays, scroll peghead.

1977	Sunburst	$1,000	$1,100

Deluxe
Two pickups.

1976-1980		$300	$400

Deluxe 12-String
Two pickups.

1977		$425	$500

Destroyer II
1982-1986. Explorer-style large basswood body, some models had set-necks and some had bolt-on, two pickups. In 1984 smaller body hard rock version introduced.

1982-1986	Black	$525	$600

Destroyer Phil Colin
Mid-1980s. Explorer body style, three humbucking pickups.

1985		$525	$600

EX Series
1988-1994. Double cut solidbodies with long thin horns, various models, all models may not be included.

1988-1994		$150	$400

EX-1700
1993-1994. Offset double cut solidbody, 3 pickups, bound body.

1993-1994		$275	$325

EX-3700
1993-1994. Offset double cut solidbody, 3 pickups, bound maple top.

1993-1994		$275	$325

FA-100 NT
Late 1970s. Hollowbody ES-175-style, single cut, 2 pickups, F-holes, block inlays.

1978		$900	$1,100

FG-360S
Introduced in 1973. Les Paul Standard copy with bolt-on neck, trapezoid markers, maple top.

1973	Sunburst	$350	$375

GAX70
1997-present. Symmetrical double cut, 2 humbuckers, bolt-on neck, dot markers.

2000	Natural	$175	$200

GAX75
2001-present. GAX70 with Downshifter bridge.

2001	Black	$175	$200

George Benson GB-10
1977-present. Single cut, laminated spruce top, flame maple back and sides, 2 humbuckers, three-piece set-in maple neck, ebony board.

1970s	Blond	$1,900	$2,000
1970s	Sunburst	$1,600	$1,800
1980s	Blond	$1,800	$1,900
1980s	Sunburst	$1,500	$1,700
1990s	Blond	$1,700	$1,800
1990s	Sunburst	$1,400	$1,600

George Benson GB-20
1977-1983. Much larger than GB-10, laminated spruce top, flame maple back and sides, one pickup.

1977-1983		$1,700	$1,900

George Benson GB-100 Deluxe
1993-1996. GB-10 with high-end appointments including flamed maple top, pearl binding, sunburst finish pickguard, pearl vine inlay tailpiece, gold hardware, 2 mini-humbuckers.

1993-1996		$2,600	$2,800

Iceman IC-200
1978-1980. Set-neck, two humbuckers, four knobs, angled block inlays, 555 made.

1978-1980	Sunburst	$550	$750

Iceman IC-300
1995-present. Reintroduced line, made in Korea, standard model without tremolo.

1995-2001		$450	$500

Iceman IC-350
1995-1996. Reintroduced line, made in Korea, version with tremolo.

1995-1996		$400	$450

Iceman IC-500
1994. Limited production primarily for Japanese domestic market.

1994		$700	$900

Iceman Models Bolt-On Neck
1978-1983, 1994-present. Solidbody with single hooked cutaway. The Iceman was introduced in '75 with a glued neck; bolt necks were first offered in '78. Both were reintroduced to the U.S. in '94. The Iceman has been listed under various bolt-on and glued-neck model numbers over the years.

1978-1981		$500	$600

Iceman Models Set-Neck
1975-1983, 1994-present. Solidbody with single hooked cutaway. The Iceman was introduced in '75 with a glued neck; bolt necks were first offered in '78. Both were reintroduced to the U.S. in '94. The Iceman has been listed under various bolt-on and glued-neck model numbers over the years

1977-1981		$750	$1,000

1976 Ibanez 2405 Custom Agent

1978 ibanez Iceman

Ibanez PS-10

1970 Ibanez Model 20/20

MODEL YEAR	FEATURES	EXC. COND. LOW	HIGH

Iceman PS-10 (Paul Stanley)

1978-1979. Limited edition Paul Stanley model, abalone trim, Stanley's name engraved at 21st fret. Reintroduced in 1977 with upgraded model names.

1978-1979	Natural korina	$1,400	$1,600
1978-1979	Sunburst or black	$1,300	$1,500

IMG-2010 Guitar Controller MIDI

1985-1987. Similar to Roland GR-707, slim trianble-wedge body with treble horn.

1986		$350	$450

JEM 10th Anniversary

1996. Limited Edition signature Steve Vai model, bolt-on neck, vine metal pickguard, vine neck inlays, vine headstock art.

1996		$1,000	$1,600

JEM 777 VBK

1987-1996. Limited production variation of JEM 777.

1987-1996	Black, Green hardware	$1,700	$1,900

JEM 777 VSK

1987-1996. Basswood body with "Monkey Grip" through-body handle, maple neck, tilted headstock, two humbuckers and one single-coil pickups. Limited editions available in Loch Ness Green, signed and numbered by co-designer Steve Vai.

1987-1996		$1,200	$1,400

JEM 90th Anniversary

1997. Limited Edition signature Seve Vai model, textured Silver finish, chrome pickguard.

1997		$1,500	$2,000

JEM DNA (limited edition)

2000. Blood Red Swirl marble finish using Steve Vai's blood in the paint.

2000		$3,500	$4,000

Joe Pass Model JP-20

1982-1990. Full body, single cutaway, one pickup, abalone and pearl split block inlay, JP inlay on headstock.

1982-1990	Sunburst	$1,500	$1,700

JPM-100 John Petrucci

1998-1999. Offset double cut solidbody, 2 pickups, available in multi-color art finish.

1998-1999	Custom art finish	$1,300	$2,000

Lee Ritenour LR-10

1981-1987. Flame maple body, set-in neck bound in Cream, Quick Change tailpiece, twp pickups, Dark Red Sunburst. Body filled with foam to illuminate feedback.

1985		$700	$900

M340

1978-1980s. Flat-top, spruce top, flamed maple back and sides, maple board.

1978		$350	$450

Maxxas

1987-1988. Internal sound chambers, 2 pickups, neck-thru body, all-access neck joint system.

1987-1988		$700	$800

Model 600 Series

1970-1978. Copy era acoustic flat-tops with model numbers in the 600 Series, basically Gibson square shoulder dreadnought. Copies included Hummingbird (683 and 684) and Dove (693) pickguard reproductions. There were also copies of Martins with natural tops and Fender Kingmans with the six-on-a-side Kingman headstock (647). And there were 12-string copies as well. A Vintage Series of Martin copies were also offered.

1970-1978		$300	$600

Model 700 Series

1970-1978. Acoustic flat-tops, upgraded models such as the Brazilian Scent 750, with more original design content than 600 Series.

1970-1978		$300	$700

Model 1912

1974-1976. Has ES-355 styling and appointments but without varitone. Sunburst finish.

1974-1976		$900	$1,000

Model 2020

1970-1971. Initial offering of the copy era. Offset double cut, two unusual rectangular pickups, block markers, raised nailed-on headstock logo, sunburst.

1970-1971		$500	$700

Model 2335

1974-1977. Copy of the ES-175, Sunburst.

1974-1977		$600	$900

Model 2341

1974-1976. Part of "Oldies Series" of faithful reproductions, Les Paul Custom copy.

1974-1976		$500	$700

Model 2345/2345S/2345W

1974-1976. SG copy, Walnut finish, with Bigsby copy or stop tailpiece (2345S), version with three pickups.

1974		$400	$600

Model 2346

1974-1976. Part of "Oldies Series," SG Standard copy with Maestro vibrato copy.

1974		$400	$600

Model 2348

1974-1979. Mahogany body, bolt-on neck, two pickups, like Firebrand Firebird.

1976		$500	$700

Model 2350

1971-1977. Les Paul Custom copy, bolt-on neck, Black, gold hardware, a Cherry Sunburst finish (2350 Custom) was offered by '74.

1971-1977		$500	$600

Model 2355/2355M

1973-1977. ES-175 copy in Sunburst or M model in Natural maple.

1973-1977		$1,000	$1,200

Model 2359 Destroyer

1975-1977. Explorer copy, Korina body.

1975-1977		$700	$1,000

Model 2369 (Futura/Moderne)

1975-1977. Korina Moderne.

1975-1977		$900	$1,200

MODEL YEAR	FEATURES	EXC. COND. LOW	HIGH

Model 2370

1972. ES-345 Sunburst, the Cherry finish is the Model 2363R introduced in 1973.

1972		$750	$950

Model 2374 Crest

1974. ES-355-style, Walnut finish.

1974		$700	$900

Model 2375

1971-1978. Replaced earlier copy of Fender Strat, three traditional pickups.

1970s	Sunburst	$350	$550

Model 2377

1974. SG Pro copy, short production run, dot markers, Bigsby copy.

1974		$350	$400

Model 2383

1974-1975. SG Custom copy, White or Walnut finish, three humbucker-style pickups, gold hardware, Bigsby copy.

1974-1975	Walnut	$400	$800
1974-1975	White	$450	$850

Model 2384

1974-1975. Fender Telecaster Thinline copy variant with dual humbuckers, ash body.

1974-1975		$400	$500

Model 2387 (Rocket Roll/Rocket Roll Sr.)

1975-1977. Nearer-copy of Flying V, set-neck, dot markers, gold-covered pickups.

1975-1977		$900	$1,100

Model 2390

1974-1975. ES-345 copy, Walnut finish.

1974		$700	$900

Model 2395

1974-1975. ES-345 copy variant with maple fingerboard and Natural finish.

1974		$700	$900

Model 2397

1974-1975. Variant with ES-335-style body, low impedance electronics, trapezoid markers, Goldtop.

1974		$700	$900

Model 2401

1974-1975. Goldtop hollowbody Les Paul Signature copy with bolt-on neck.

1974-1975		$700	$900

Model 2402/2402DX

1974-1975. SG-style 6/12 doubleneck, DX model has gold hardware.

1974-1975		$600	$900

Model 2404

1974-1975. SG guitar and bass doubleneck copy. Walnut in '74, white finish available in '75.

1974-1975		$600	$1,100

Model 2406

1975-1976. SG doubleneck copy with two six-string necks. Cherry finish.

1975		$600	$1,100

Model 2407

1975-1978. Fender Stratocaster doubleneck copy.

1975-1978		$700	$800

Model 2451

1975-1976. L-6 S copy with maple fingerboard, in Black or Natural finish.

1975		$350	$500

Model 2453

1975-1979. Copy of the Howard Roberts Custom, round soundhole, arched curly maple top, maple back and sides, maple laminate set-neck, rosewood 'board, pearl block markers, one pickup, fancy tailpiece, gold hardware. Burgundy or Sunburst.

1975-1979		$800	$1,100

Model 2454

1974-1975. ES-335 TD copy, set-neck, small block markers, Byrdland-style tailpiece. Cherry finish over ash.

1974		$500	$1,000

Model 2455

1974-1975. L-5 CES copy.

1974		$1,100	$1,800

Model 2460

1971-1977. L-5 copy.

1971-1977		$800	$1,200

Model 2461

1976-1979. Johnny Smith copy, laminated spruce top, curly maple back and sides, set-in neck, ebony 'board, pearl blocks, two pickups, gold hardware, Sunburst or Natural.

1976-1979		$1,500	$1,900

Model 2630

1976-1979. ES-335 copy, Sunburst. Reintroduced as AS200 in 1980.

1976-1979		$500	$1,000

Musician MC-400

1978-1980. Ash top with maple and mahogany back, seven-piece laminated maple/walnut neck-through-body, ebony fretboard, Gold plating.

1978-1980		$500	$700

Performer PG-400AV

1978-1979. Maple top and mahogany back, set-in (high end) or bolt-on (low end) bound neck, rosewood or ebony fingerboard, Super 70 pickup.

1979	Set-neck	$300	$400

PF-12

1990s. D-style flat-top with stylized rosette, Natural finish, rosewood board with dot markers, glued bridge.

1990s		$350	$375

PF-100

1978-1979. Les Paul copy, mahogany back/maple top, bolt-on bound maple neck, two humbucker pickups, Black.

1978-1979		$300	$500

PF-200

1978-1979. Mahogany back and maple top, 22-fret bound maple bolt-on neck, Super 70 pickup, Sunburst.

1978-1979		$300	$450

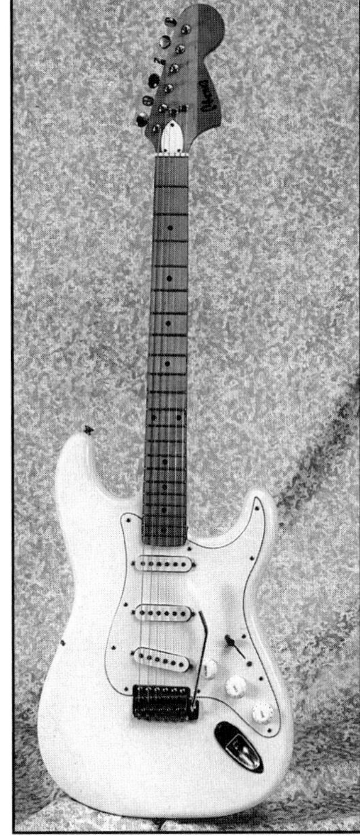

Ibanez Model 2375

Ibanez Model 2384

1984 Ibanez Roadstar

1978 Ibanez Studio ST-300

MODEL YEAR	FEATURES	EXC. COND. LOW	HIGH

PF-300

1978-1980. Les Paul copy, mahogany back and maple top, maple bolt-on or set-in bound neck, Super 70 pickup.

1978	Bolt-on neck	$350	$550
1978	Set-neck	$450	$650

PL-1770

Part of Pro Line series.

1985	Red/Orange Metallick	$400	$500

PL-2550

Part of the Pro Line series. Pushbuttons allow user to present two separate sounds, two single-coil and one humbucker pickups.

1986		$250	$350

PM-20 Pat Metheny

1997-1999. Double cut semi-hollow body, f-holes, 1 pickup, rosewood board.

1997-1999		$900	$1,000

PR-1660PW

Mid-1980s. Randy Rhodes-style body, dual humbucking pickups, White.

1985		$250	$275

RG220B

1994-1999. Offset double cut solidbody, 2 humbuckers.

1994-1999		$350	$400

RG270

1994-present. Offset double cut solidbody, pointy headstock, 2 humbuckers, dot markers, various colors.

1994-2000		$250	$300

RG470

1993-2002. Double long thin pointy horn cutaway solidbody, 3 pickups, dot markers.

1993-2000		$300	$350

RG550/RG550DX

1991-2001. Pointy headstock, long thin pointy horn double cutaway solidbody, hum-single-hum. Black (RG550) or Purple (RG550DX–'91-'94 only).

1991-1994	Purple DX	$500	$600
1991-2001	Black	$500	$600

RG570

1992-2002. Double long pointy cut, 3 pickups, black hardware.

1992-2002		$300	$350

RG1200

1992. Offset double cut solidbody, 3 pickups, flame maple top.

1992		$450	$500

RGT42

2001-present. Double long thin pointy horn cutaway solidbody, 2 humbuckers, dot markers, locking tremolo.

2001		$400	$450

Roadstar/Roadstar II

1983-1989. Offset double cut, split into several different model series in late-'80s to early-'90s.

1983-1989		$250	$350

Roadster

1979-1983. Offset double cut, maple fretboard, bolt-on neck, satin finish body. Replaced by Roadstar series in '83.

1979-1983		$250	$350

Rocket Roll II RR440

1982-1986. Flying V body but with six-on-a-side headstock, pearloid block markers.

1982	Sunburst	$275	$325

RT650

1993. RT Series, offset double cutaway with long slim horns, bolt-on maple neck with rosewood fretboard, dot markers, flamed top.

1993		$400	$500

RX20/GRX20

1994-present. Offset double cut maple or agatis solidbody, 2 humbuckers, trem, became the alder-bodied GRX in '99.

1990s		$175	$200

Studio ST300

1978-1980. Maple/ash body, active tone system, tri-sound switch, natural, gold hardware, 2 pickups.

1978-1980		$400	$600

Studio ST50

1979-1980. Set-neck, small offset SG-style mahogany solidbody, 2 pickups.

1979-1980		$400	$500

Talman TC420

1994-1999. Offset double cut solidbody, bolt-on neck, three-on-a-side tuners, two humbuckers, dot markers.

1994-1999	Black or Green	$350	$425

Talman TC620

1994-1997. Two stacked P-90 looking humbucker version of the Talman series solidbodies. The BP version was black with pearloid guard.

1994-1997		$275	$375

Talman TC630

1994-1998. Offset double cut solidbody, three-on-a-side tuners, three lipstick pickups, dot markers.

1994-1998	Black or Ivory	$400	$475

Universe 7-String UV7/UV77

1990-1998. Several UV seven-string guitar models with different appointments, long slim pointed horns.

1990-1998	UV7 and UV77, various colors	$1,000	$1,200
1990-1998	UV7 P, White	$900	$1,000

Universe UV-777LNG

1990s. Universe model in Lockness Green (LNG), offset double cut solidbody with long slim horns.

1991		$1,800	$2,000

USGR-1 Custom Shop (U.S.A.)

1992 only. Snakeskin finish.

1992		$700	$800

V-300BS

1978-1980s. Part of the Vintage Series. Acoustic dreadnought, spruce top, mahogany back and sides. Sunburst finish.

1978		$200	$300

GUITARS

MODEL YEAR	FEATURES	EXC. COND. LOW	HIGH

Y2K Joe Satriani

2000. Clear see-through plexi-style body.

2000		$1,800	$2,200

Imperial

Ca.1963-ca.1970. Imported by the Imperial Accordion Company of Chicago, Illinois. Early guitars made in Italy. By ca. 1966 switched to Japanese guitars.

Electric Solidbody Guitars

1963-1968. Italian-made until 1966, then Japanese-made, includes the Tonemaster line.

1963-1968		$100	$250

J Burda Guitars

Flat-top guitars built by luthier Jan Burda in Berrien Springs, Michigan.

Jan Burda Flat-Top

1990s. Solid spruce top, figured walnut back and sides, flamed maple peghead, no logo, U.S.-made.

1990s	Natural	$850	$900

J. Pena Fernandez

Classical

Brazilian rosewood back and sides, cedar top, full-size classical guitar, higher-end luthier.

1977		$5,000	$5,500

J.B. Player

1980s-present. Budget and intermediate grade, production, imported acoustic, acoustic/electric, and solidbody guitars. They also offer basses, banjos and mandolins. Founded in United States. Moved production of guitars to Korea but maintained a U.S. Custom Shop. MBT International/ Musicorp took over manufacture and distribution in '89.

JBA-2000

1994-1997. Solid-top acoustic, herringbone binding, abalone inlays, Gold hardware.

1994-1997		$125	$250

PG-121

1992-1996. Offset double cut solidbody, 3 pickups, various colors.

1992-1996	Various colors	$125	$250

J.R. Zeidler Guitars

1977-present. Luthier John Zeidler builds his premium and presentation grade, custom, flat-top, 12-string, and archtop guitars and mandolins in Wallingford, Pennsylvania.

Auditorium Cutaway

Introduced in 1982. Sitka or Adirondack spruce top, Indian rosewood sides, gold hardware.

1990s		$4,800	$5,200

Concert

1990s. Spruce top, Indian rosewood back and sides. The name does not denote the size, which approximates 00 Grand Concert.

1992		$5,800	$6,200

MODEL YEAR	FEATURES	EXC. COND. LOW	HIGH

J. T. Hargreaves Basses And Guitars

1995-present. Luthier Jay Hargreaves builds his premium grade, production/custom, acoustic basses, classical, and steel-string guitars in Seattle, Washington.

Jackson

1980-present. Currently Jackson offers intermediate, professional, and premium grade, production, electric guitars. They also offer basses. Founded as Charvel by Wayne Charvel in Azusa, California in '76. In '78 Grover Jackson bought out Charvel and moved it to San Dimas. Jackson made custom-built bolt-on Charvels. In '82 the pointy, tilt-back Jackson headstock became standard. The Jackson logo was born in '80 and used on a guitar designed as Randy Rhoad's first flying 'V'. Jacksons were neck-through construction. The Charvel trademark was licensed to IMC in '85. IMC moved the Jackson factory to Ontario, CA in '86. Grover Jackson stayed with Jackson/Charvel until '89 (see Charvel in the Guitar section). On October 25, 2002, Fender Musical Instruments Corp (FMIC) took ownership of Jackson/Charvel Manufacturing Inc.

DR3

1996-2001. Dinky Reverse. Double cut solidbody, reverse headstock, triangle markers, dual humbuckers, locking vibrato, various colors, made in Japan. Flamed maple top available.

1998		$300	$400

DR5

1996 only. Offset double cut solidbody, 2 Kent Armstrong humbuckers, rosewood board, dot markers.

1996		$300	$400

JSX94

1994-1995. Offset double cut solidbody, single/single/hum, rosewood board, dot markers.

1994-1995		$250	$350

Kelly Custom

1984-early 1990s. Neck-through solidbody, Kahler tremolo, 2 humbuckers, ebony fingerboard with shark's tooth inlays, bound neck and headstock.

1986		$500	$800

Kelly Pro

1994-1995. Pointy-cut solidbody, neck-thru, 2 humbuckers, bound ebony 'board, sharkfin inlays.

1994-1995		$500	$800

Kelly Standard

1993-1995. Pointy-cut solidbody, bolt neck, 2 humbuckers, dot markers.

1993-1995		$350	$450

Kelly XL

1994-1995. Pointy-cut solidbody, bolt neck, 2 humbuckers, bound rosewood 'board, sharkfin inlays.

1994-1995		$400	$600

Imperial Tonmaster Elite

Jackson Soloist

Jackson Phil Collen

Jay Turser JT-LT Custom

MODEL YEAR	FEATURES	EXC. COND. LOW	HIGH

King V Pro

1993-1995. Soft V-style neck-thru solidbody, sharkfin markers, 2 humbuckers.

1993-1995		$500	$700

King V STD

1993-1995. Bolt neck version of King V.

1993-1995		$350	$450

Phil Collen

1989-1991, 1993-1995. Offset double-cut maple neck-thru solidbody, six-on-a-side tuners, one volume, bound ebony 'board, U.S.-made. Early version has poplar body, 1 humbucker; later version with basswood body, 1 single-coil and 1 humbucker.

1993-1995		$900	$1,100

Phil Collen PC1

1996-present. Quilt maple top, bolt-on maple neck, maple board, koa body '96-'00, mahogany body '01-present, 1 humbucker and 1 single coil '96-'97, humbucker, stacked humbucker, and single coil '98-present.

1996-2000		$900	$1,200

PS2

1994-2000. Offset double cut solidbody, single/single/hum, rosewood fingerboard, dot markers.

1994-2000		$150	$250

PS3

1994-2000. Rhoads wedge-style body, two humbuckers, rosewood fingerboard, dot markers.

1994-2000		$150	$250

Randy Rhoads

1983-present. V-shaped neck-thru solidbody, two humbuckers.

1983-1986	Kahler trem	$1,400	$1,500
1983-1986	Rose trem or string-through	$1,900	$2,000

Randy Rhoads Limited Edition

1992 only. Sharkfin-style maple neck-through body, gold hardware, White with Black pinstriping, block inlays, six-on-a-side tuners, U.S.-made. Only 200 built.

1992		$1,200	$1,500

Soloist

1986-1990. Double-cut, neck-thru, string-thru solidbody, two humbuckers, bound rosewood 'board U.S.-made. Replaced by the Soloist USA in '90.

1984-1986	San Dimas build	$1,000	$1,600
1987-1990		$800	$1,000

Soloist Custom

1993-1995. Double cut, neck-thru solidbody, one humbucker and two single-coils, bound ebony 'board, shark's tooth inlays, U.S.-made.

1993-1995		$700	$900

Warrior USA

1990-1992. Four point neck-thru solidbody, 1 humbucker and 1single-coil, triangle markers, active electronics, U.S.-made. The Warrior Pro was Japanese version.

1990s	Red	$1,300	$1,500

James R. Baker Guitars

1996-present. Luthier James R. Baker builds his premium grade, custom, archtops in Shoreham, New York.

Janofsky Guitars

1978-present. Production classical and flamenco guitars built by luthier Stephen Janofsky in Amherst, Massachusetts.

Jaros

1995-present. Professional and premium grade, production/custom, solidbody and acoustic/electric guitars built by father and son luthiers Harry and Jim Jaros in Rochester, Pennsylvania.

Jay Turser

1997-present. Budget and intermediate grade, production, imported acoustic, acoustic/electric, electric and resonator guitars. They also offer basses and amps. Designed and developed by Tommy Rizzi for Music Industries Corp.

JT-134

2001-present. Single cut semi-solidbody, 2 humbuckers.

2001		$175	$200

JT-134DC

2001-present. Double cut semi-solidbody, 2 humbuckers.

2001		$225	$250

JT-200 Serpent

2001-present. Single cut solidbody, bookmatched flamed maple top, multi-piece abalone and mother-of-pearl serpent inlay on fretboard.

2001		$300	$350

Jeff Traugott Guitars

1991-present. Premium and presentation grade, custom, flat-top, nylon-string, and acoustic/electric guitars built by luthier Jeff Traugott, in Santa Cruz, California.

Jeremy Locke Guitars

1985-present. Premium grade, production/custom, classical and flamenco guitars built by luthier Jeremy Locke in Coomera, South East Queensland, Australia.

Jerry Jones

1981-present. Intermediate grade, production, semi-hollow body electric guitars and sitars from luthier Jerry Jones, built in Nashville, Tennessee. They also build basses.

Electric Sitar

1991-present. Buzz-bar sitar bridge, individual pickup for sympathetic strings. Custom color gator finish.

1990s		$500	$550

Longhorn Guitarlin

1994-present. Large cutaway Guitarlin-style body.

1990s	Sunburst	$450	$550

MODEL YEAR	FEATURES	EXC. COND. LOW	HIGH

Jim Redgate Guitars

1992-present. Luthier Jim Redgate builds his premium grade, custom, nylon-string classical guitars in Belair, Adelaide, South Australia.

John Le Voi Guitars

1970-present. Production/custom, gypsy jazz guitars, flat-tops, archtops, and mandolin family instruments built by luthier John Le Voi in Lincolnshire, United Kingdom.

John Price Guitars

1984-present. Custom classical and flamenco guitars built by luthier John Price in Australia.

Johnson

Mid-1990s-present. Budget, intermediate and professional grade, production, acoustic, classical, acoustic/electric, resonator and solidbody guitars imported by Music Link, Brisbane, California. Johnson also offers basses, amps, mandolins, ukuleles and effects.

Jon Kammerer

1995-present. Luthier Jon Kammerer builds his professional grade, custom, acoustic and electric guitars in Keokuk, Iowa.

Jordan

1981-present. Professional and premium grade, custom, flat-top and archtop guitars and electric violins and cellos built by luthier John Jordan in Concord, California.

K & S

1992-1998. Hawaiian-style and classical guitars distributed by George Katechis and Marc Silber and handmade in Paracho, Mexico. A few 16" wide “Leadbelly” Model 12-strings were made in Oakland, California by luthier Stewart Port. K & S also offered mandolins, mandolas and ukes. In ’98, Silber started marketing guitars under the Marc Silber Guitar Company brand and Katechis continued to offer instruments under the Casa Montalvo brand.

Kakos, Stephen

1975-present. Luthier Stephen Kakos builds his premium grade, production/custom, classical guitars in Mound, Minnesota.

Kalamazoo

1933-1942, 1965-1970. Budget brand built by Gibson. Made flat-tops, solidbodies, mandolins, lap steels, banjos and amps. Amps and solidbodies were built ’65-’67.

KG-1/KG-1 A

1965-1969. Offset double cut (initial issue) or SG-shape (second issue), one pickup, Model 1 A with spring vibrato, Red, Blue or White.

1965-1969	$100	$250

MODEL YEAR	FEATURES	EXC. COND. LOW	HIGH

KG-2/KG-2 A

1965-1970. Offset double cut (initial shape) or SG-shape, two pickups, Model 2 A with spring vibrato. Red, Blue or White.

1965-1970	$200	$350

KG-11

1933-1941. Flat-top, all mahogany, 14" with no pickguard. Sunburst.

1933-1941	$400	$600

KG-14

1936-1940. Flat-top L-0-size, mahogany back and sides, with pickguard. Sunburst.

1936-1940	$650	$800

KG-21

1936-1941. Fifteen inch archtop (bent, not curved), dot markers, bound top. Sunburst.

1936-1941	$500	$700

KG-31

1935-1940. Archtop L-50-size, 16" body, non-carved spruce top, mahogany back and sides.

1936	$600	$750

KTG-14 Senior

1936-1940. Flat-top L-0-size tenor, mahogany back and sides, bound top. Sunburst.

1938	$250	$400

Kamico

Brand started in 1947. Flat-top acoustic guitars. Low-end budget brand made by Kay Musical Instrument Company and sold through various distributors.

Acoustic Flat-Tops

1940s. Made by Kay.

1940s	$150	$250

Kapa

Ca. 1962-1970. Begun by Dutch immigrant and music store owner Kope Veneman in Hyattsville, Maryland whose father had made Amka guitars in Holland. Kapa is from K for Kope, A for son Albert, P for daughter Patricia, and A for wife Adeline. Crown shield logo from Amka guitars. The brand included some Hofner and Italian imports in ’60. Ca. ’66 Kapa started offering thinner bodies. Some German Pix pickups ca. ’66. Thinlines and Japanese bodies in ’69. Kapa closed shop in ’70 and the parts and equipment were sold to Micro-Frets and Mosrite. Later Veneman was involved with Bradley copy guitars imported from Japan. Approximately 120,000 Kapas were made.

Challenger

1962-1970. Had a three way toggle from 1962-1966/67 and two on/off switches from 1966/67-1970.

1963	$250	$400

Cobra

1962-1970. One pickup.

1968	$250	$400

Jerry Jones Electric Sitar

Kalamazoo KG-14

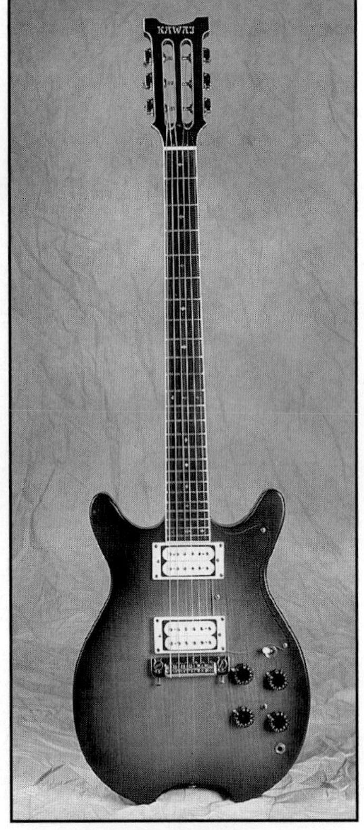

Kawai KS-700

1957 Kay Barney Kessel

MODEL YEAR	FEATURES	EXC. COND. LOW	HIGH

Continental

1966-1970. Offset double cutaway.

1966	$250	$400

Continental 12-String

1966-1970.

1966	$250	$400

Minstrel

1968-1970. Teardrop-shaped, three pickups.

1970	$250	$400

Minstrel 12-String

1968-1970. Teardrop-shaped, 12 strings.

1968	$250	$400

Wildcat

1962-1970. Mini offset double cut, three pickups, mute.

1965	$250	$400

Kathy Wingert Guitars

1996-present. Luthier Kathy Wingert builds her premium grade, production/custom, flat-tops in Rancho Palos Verdes, California.

Kawai

1927-present. Kawai is a Japanese piano and guitar maker. They started offering guitars around '56 and they were imported into the U.S. carrying many different brand names, including Kimberly and Teisco. In '67 Kawai purchased Teisco. Odd-shaped guitars were offered from late-'60s through the mid-'70s. Few imports carrying the Kawai brand until the late-'70s; best known for high quality basses. By '90s they were making plexiglass replicas of Teisco Spectrum 5 and Kawai moon-shaped guitar. Kawai recently quit offering guitars and basses.

Acoustic Hollowbody Archtops

1956-1990s.

1960s	$200	$250

Electric Archtop Guitars

1956-1990s.

1960s	$250	$300
1970s	$250	$300

Kay

Ca. 1931 (1890)-1969. Originally founded in Chicago, Illinois as Groehsl Company (or Groehsel) in 1890, making bowl-backed mandolins. Offered Groehsl, Stromberg, Kay Kraft, Kay, Arch Kraft brand names, plus made guitars for S.S.Maxwell, Old Kraftsman (Spiegel), Recording King (Wards), Supertone (Sears), Silvertone (Sears), National, Dobro, Custom Kraft (St.Louis Music), Hollywood (Shireson Bros.), Oahu and others. In 1921 the name was changed to Stromberg-Voisinet Company. Henry Kay "Hank" Kuhrmeyer joined the company in '23 and was secretary by '25. By the mid-'20s the company was making many better Montgomery Ward guitars, banjos and mandolins, often with lots of pearloid.

First production electric guitars and amps are introduced with big fanfare in '28; perhaps only 200 or so made. Last "Stromberg" instruments seen in '32. Kuhrmeyer becomes president and the Kay Kraft brand was introduced in '31, probably named for Kuhrmeyer's middle name, though S-V had used Kay brand on German Kreuzinger violins '28-'36. By '34, if not earlier, the company is changed to the Kay Musical Instrument Company. A new factory was built at 1640 West Walnut Street in '35. The Kay Kraft brand ends in '37 and the Kay brand is introduced in late-'36 or '37. Violin Style Guitars and upright acoustic basses debut in '38. In '40 the first guitars for Sears, carrying the new Silvertone brandname, are offered.

Kamico budget line introduced in '47 and Rex flat-tops and archtops sold through Gretsch in late-'40s. Kuhrmeyer retires in '55 dies a year later. Sidney M. Katz becomes president, Bob Keyworth vice-president in '55. New gigantic factory in Elk Grove Village, Illinois opens in '64. Seeburg purchased Kay in '66 and sold it to Valco in '67. Valco/Kay went out of business in '68 and its assets were auctioned in '69. The Kay name went to Sol Weindling and Barry Hornstein of W.M.I. (Teisco Del Rey) who began putting Kay name on Teisco guitars. By '73 most Teisco guitars are called Kay. Tony Blair of A.R. Musical Enterprises purchased the Kay name in '80. See *Guitar Stories Volume II*, by Michael Wright, for a complete history of Kay with detailed model listings.

Artist K48 (archtop)

1947-1951. Non-cutaway archtop, 17" solid spruce top with figured maple back and sides, split block inlays, sunburst or black.

1947-1951	$900	$1,400

Barney Kessel Artist

1957-1960. Single cutaway, 15 1/2" body, one (K6701) or two (K6700) pickups, Kelvinator headstock, sunburst or blond.

1957-1960	$1,000	$2,000

K11/K8911 Rhythm Special

1952-1960. Single cut acoustic archtop, curly maple back and sides, bound board, sunburst or blonde. K11 for '52-'56, K8911 '57-'60.

1952-1960	$300	$500

K20 (archtop)

1939-1942. 16" archtop, solid spruce top, maple back and sides, sunburst.

1939-1942	$250	$300

K26

1955-1959. J-200 copy, block markers, natural.

1955-1959	$500	$700

K44 (archtop)

1947-1951. Non-cut archtop, solid spruce top, 17" curly maple veneered body, block markers, sunburst.

1947-1951	$400	$500

GUITARS

MODEL YEAR	FEATURES	EXC. COND. LOW	HIGH

K45 (archtop)

1952-1954. Non-cut archtop, 17" body, engraved tortoiseshell-celluloid headstock, large block markers, natural.

1952-1954		$450	$550

K46 (archtop)

1947-1951. Non-cut archtop, solid spruce top, 17" curly maple-veneered body, double-eighth note headstock inlay, sunburst.

1947-1951		$500	$600

K48/K21 Jazz Special (solidbody)

Late-1960s. Slim solidbody with three reflective pickups, garden spade headstock, fancy position Circle K headstock logo.

1968	White	$400	$500

K100 Vanguard (slab solidbody)

1961-1966. Offset double cut slab body, genuine maple veneered top and back over hardwood body, sunburst.

1961-1966		$125	$175

K102 Vanguard (slab solidbody)

1961-1966. Double pickup version of the K100, sunburst.

1961-1966		$150	$200

K300 Double Cutaway Solid Electric

1962-1966. 2 single-coils, block inlays, some with curly maple top and some with plain maple top, natural.

1962-1966		$500	$600

K535 (thinline double cutaway)

1961-1965. Double cut, 2 pickups, vibrato, sunburst.

1960	Sunburst	$350	$400

K592 (thinline electric)

1962-1966. Thinline semi-acoustic/electric, double Florentine cut, 2 or 3 pickups, Bigsby vibrato, pie-slice inlays.

1962-1966	Cherry	$450	$500

K1961 (solidbody thinline)

1960-1965. Part of the Value Leader line, thinline single cut, hollowbody, identified by the single chrome-plated checkered body length guardplate on the treble side of the strings, laminated maple body, hard rock maple neck, dot markers, 1 neck pickup.

1960-1965	Sunburst	$300	$450

K1962 (solidbody thinline)

1960-1965. Dual pickup version of K1961.

1960-1965	Sunburst	$400	$500

K1963 (solidbody thinline)

1960-1965. Triple pickup version of K1961.

1960-1965	Sunburst	$400	$600

K1982 Style Leader/Jimmy Reed

1960-1965. Part of the Style Leader mid-level Kay line. Sometimes dubbed Jimmy Reed of 1960s. Easily identified by the long brushed copper dual guardplates on either side of the strings. Brown or gleaming Golden Blond (Natural) finish, laminated curly maple body, 2 pickups, simple script Kay logo.

1960-1965		$400	$500

K1983 Style Leader/Jimmy Reed

1960-1965. 3 pickup version of the K1982, brown or natural.

1960-1965		$400	$600

K6533 (Value Leader single arched)

1961-1965. Value Leader was the budget line of Kay, full body, 1 pickup, archtop, sunburst.

1961-1965		$200	$300

K6535 (Value Leader double arched)

1961-1965. Value Leader was the budget line of Kay, full body, 2 pickups, archtop, sunburst.

1961-1965		$200	$300

Speed Demon K571

1961-1965. Thinline semi-acoustic/electric, single pointed cutaway, 1 pickup, some with Bigsby vibrato. There was also a Speed Demon solidbody.

1961-1965		$300	$500

Speed Demon K572

1961-1965. 2 pickup version of the Speed Demon thinline.

1961-1965		$350	$450

Speed Demon K573

1961-1965. 3 pickup version of the Speed Demon.

1961-1965		$400	$600

Swingmaster K671/K672

1961-1965. Single rounded cutaway semi-hollowbody, 1 (K671) or 2 (K672) pickups.

1961-1965		$700	$1,100

Thin Twin K161 "Jimmy Reed"

1952-1958. Cutaway semi-hollow, 2 pickups, bird's-eye maple, often called the Jimmy Reed, sunburst.

1952-1958		$500	$700

Upbeat K8995

1958-1960. Less expensive alternative to Barney Kessel Jazz Special, 2 pickups, sunburst.

1958-1960		$800	$1,200

Kay (Asian-American Mfg. Co.)

1980-present. Tony Blair, president of Asian-American Mfg. Co., purchased the Kay nameplate in 1980, with a market focus on first-time buyers.

Kay Kraft

Ca. 1931-1937. First brand name of the Kay Musical Instrument Company as it began its transition from Stromberg-Voisinet Company to Kay (see Kay for more info).

Kay Kraft Recording King

1930s		$300	$500

Keller Custom Guitars

1994-present. Professional grade, production/custom, solidbody guitars built by luthier Randall Keller in Mandan, North Dakota.

Keller Guitars

1975-present. Premium grade, production/custom, flat-tops made by luthier Michael L. Keller in Rochester, Minnesota.

1950s Kay Upbeat

Kay 573 Speed Demon

1995 Kendrick Townhouse

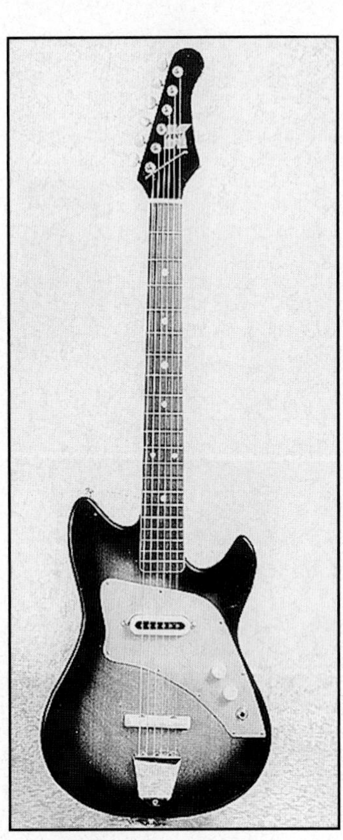

1964 Kent No. 540

MODEL YEAR	FEATURES	EXC. COND. LOW	HIGH

Kendrick

1989-present. Premium grade, production/custom, solidbody guitars built in Texas. Founded by Gerald Weber in Pflugerville, Texas and currently located in Kempner, Texas. Mainly known for their handmade tube amps, Kendrick also offers speakers and effects.

Kent

Ca. 1962-1969. Imported from Japan by Buegeleisen and Jacobson of New York, NY. Manufacturers unknown but many early guitars were made by Guyatone and Teisco.

Acoustic Flat-Tops

1962-1969.

1960s		$100	$150

Acoustic/Electric Guitars

1962-1969.

1960s		$150	$250

Electric 12-String

1960s. Thinline 335-type electric with double pointy cutaways, 12 strings, slanted dual pickup

1960s	Sunburst	$250	$450

Semi-Hollow Electric

1960s. Thinline 335-type electric with offset double pointy cutaways, slanted dual pickups, various colors.

1960s		$250	$450

Solidbody Electrics

1962-1969. Models include Polaris I, II and III, Lido, Copa and Videocaster.

1960s	Century Red	$100	$200

Kevin Ryan Guitars

1989-present. Premium grade, custom, flat-tops built by luthier Kevin Ryan in Westminster, California.

Kimberly

Late-1960s-early-1970s. Private branded import made in the same Japanese factory as Teisco.

May Queen

1960s. Same as Teisco May Queen with Kimberly script logo on headstock and May Queen Teisco on the pickguard.

1960s		$300	$600

Kingston

Ca. 1958-1967. Imported from Japan by Jack Westheimer and Westheimer Importing Corporation of Chicago, IL. Early examples made by Guyatone and Teisco.

Electric Hollowbodies

1958-1967. Imported from Japan.

1960s		$100	$175

Kinscherff Guitars

1990-present. Luthier Jamie Kinscherff builds his premium grade, production/custom, flat-top guitars in Austin, Texas.

MODEL YEAR	FEATURES	EXC. COND. LOW	HIGH

Klein Acoustic Guitars

1972-present. Luthiers Steve Klein and Steven Kauffman build their production/custom, premium and presentation grade flat-tops and acoustic basses in Sonoma, California.

Klein Electric Guitars

1988-present. Steve Klein added electrics to his line in 1988. In 1995, he sold the electric part of his business to Lorenzo German, who continues to produce professional and premium grade, production/custom, solidbody guitars and basses in Linden, California.

Knutsen

1890s-1920s. Luthier Chris J. Knutsen of Tacoma and Seattle, Washington, experimented with and perfected Hawaiian and harp guitar models.

Convertible

1909-1914. Flat-top model with adjustable neck angle that allowed for a convertible Hawaiian or Spanish setup.

1909-1914		$1,800	$2,000

Harp Guitar

1900s. Normally 11 strings with fancy purfling and trim.

1900-1910		$4,500	$6,500

Knutson Luthiery

1981-present. Professional and premium grade, custom, archtops, flat-tops, acoustic and electric mandolins, and electric upright basses built by luthier John Knutson in Forestville, California.

Kona

1920s. Acoustic Hawaiian guitars sold by C.S. Delano, and thought to be made by Herman Weissenborn. Weissenborn appointments in line with style number, with thicker body and solid neck construction.

Style 3

Koa.

1920s		$2,000	$3,000

Style 4

Brown koa.

1920s		$2,000	$3,000

Koontz

1970-late 1980s. Luthier Sam Koontz started building custom guitars in the late '50s. Starting in '66 Koontz, who was associated with Harptone guitars, built guitars for Standel. In '70, he opened his own shop in Linden, New Jersey, building a variety of custom guitars. Koontz died in the late '80s. His guitars varied greatly and should be valued on a case-by-case basis.

GUITARS

MODEL YEAR	FEATURES	EXC. COND. LOW	HIGH

Kramer

1976-1990, 1997-present. Currently Kramer offers budget and intermediate grade, production, imported acoustic, acoustic/electric, semi-hollow and solidbody guitars. They also offer basses, amps and effects.

Founded by New York music retailer Dennis Berardi, ex-Travis Bean sales rep Gary Kramer and ex-Norlin executive Peter LaPlaca. Initial financing provided by real estate developer Henry Vaccaro. Parent company named BKL Corporation (Berardi, Kramer, LaPlaca), located in Neptune City, New Jersey. The first guitars were designed by Berardi and luthier Phil Petillo and featured aluminum necks with wooden inserts on back to give them a "wooden" feel. Guitar production commenced in late-'76.

Control passed to Guitar Centers of Los Angeles for '79-'82, which recommended switch to more economical wood necks. Aluminum necks were phased out during the early-'80s, and were last produced in '85. In '89, a new investment group was brought in with James Liati as president, hoping for access to Russian market, but the company went of business in late-'90.

In '95 Henry Vaccaro and new partners revived the company and designed a number of new guitars in conjunction with Phil Petillo. However, in '97 the Kramer brandname was sold to Gibson. In '98, Henry Vaccaro released his new line of aluminum-core neck, split headstock guitars under the Vacarro brand name.

Non-U.S.A.-made models include the following lines: Aerostar, Ferrington, Focus, Hundred (post-'85 made with three digits in the 100-900), Showster, Striker, Thousand (post-'85 made with four digits in the 1000-9000), XL (except XL-5 made in '80s). Seral numbers for import models include:

Two alpha followed by four numbers: for example AA2341 with any assortment of letters and numbers.

One alpha followed by five numbers: for example B23412.

Five numbers: for example 23412.

Model number preceeding numbers: for example XL1-03205.

The notation "Kramer, Neptune, NJ" does indicate U.S.A.-made production.

Most post-'85 Kramers were ESP Japanese-made guitars. American Series were ESP Japanese components that were assembled in the U.S.

The vintage/used marked makes value distinctions between U.S.-made and import models. Headstock and logo shape can help identify U.S. versus imports as follows:

Traditional or Classic headstock with capital K as Kramer: U.S.A. '81-'84.

Banana (soft edges) headstock with all caps KRAMER: U.S.A. American Series '84-'86.

Pointy (sharp cut) headstock with all caps KRAMER: U.S.A. American Series '86-'87.

Pointy (sharp cut) headstock with downsized letters Kramer plus American decal: U.S.A. American Series '87-'94.

Pointy (sharp cut) headstock with downsized letters Kramer but without American decal, is an import.

250-G Aluminum Neck

1977-1979. Offset double cut, tropical woods, aluminum neck, dot markers, 2 pickups.

1977		$350	$500

300-HST (import)

1988-1991. Strat-style body, pointy-style headstock with large Kramer logo.

1988-1991		$200	$300

650-G Artist Aluminum Neck

1977-1980. Aluminum neck, ebonol fingerboard, double cutaway solidbody, two humbuckers.

1977-1980		$450	$550

Aerostar ZX Series (import)

1986-1989. Offset double cut solidbodies, pointy six-on-a-side headstock. Models include the 1 humbucker ZX10, 2 humbucker ZX20, 3 single coil ZX30, and hum/single/single ZX30H.

1986-1989	ZX10	$100	$150
1986-1989	ZX20 and ZX30	$110	$160
1986-1989	ZX30H	$120	$170

Baretta

1984-1986. Offset double cutaway, banana six-on-a-side headstock, one pickup, Floyd Rose trem, Black hardware, U.S.A.-made.

1984-1986		$550	$650

DMZ 1000 Custom

1978-1981. Double cutaway with larger upper horn, aluminum neck, two pickups. Changed to thin-horned double cutaway by mid-1980.

1978		$400	$500

DMZ 2000 Custom

1978-1981. Solidbody double cutaway with larger upper horn, bolt-on aluminum T-neck, slot headstock, two splitable pickups.

1978	Black	$450	$550

DMZ 3000 Custom

1978-1981. Solidbody double cutaway with larger upper horn, aluminum neck, slot headstock, three single-coil pickups, stop tailpiece.

1978		$450	$550

DMZ 6000G Custom

1979-1981. Offset double cutaway, bird's-eye maple/burled walnut, aluminum neck, two humbuckers, active preamp, stop tailpiece.

1979		$450	$550

Duke Custom/Standard (headless)

1981-1982. Headless aluminum neck, 22-fret neck, one pickup, Floyd Rose trem.

1981		$400	$450

Duke Special (headless)

1982-1985. Headless aluminum neck, two pickups, tuners on body.

1983		$425	$475

1979 Kramer DMZ-2000

1977 Kramer 650G

2000 Kramer Focus

Kustom K-200

MODEL YEAR	FEATURES	EXC. COND. LOW	HIGH

E.E. Pro I

1987-1988. Designed by Elliot Easton. Offset double cut, six-on-a-side headstock, Floyd Rose trem, 2 single-coils and 1 humbucker

1987-1988		$400	$450

E.E. Pro II

1987-1988. Same as E.E. Pro I, but with fixed-bridge tailpiece, three pickups, five-position switching and master volume.

1987-1988		$400	$450

Ferrington

1985-1990. Acoustic-electric, offered in single and double cutaway, bolt-on electric-style neck, transducers, made in Korea.

1980s		$400	$450

Focus 1000 (import)

1984-1988. Offset double cut, banana six-on-a-side headstock (pointy droopy headstock in '87), 1 humbucker, Rose trem. Import from Japan.

1984-1988		$200	$300

Focus 2000 (import)

1984-1988. Same as Focus 1000, but with classic six-on-a-side headstock and 2 humbuckers. Banana headstock in '85, pointy droopy headstock in '87.

1984-1988		$250	$400

Focus 3000 (import)

1984-1988. Same as Focus 2000, but with hum/single/single pickups. Banana headstock in '85, pointy droopy headstock in '87.

1984-1988		$275	$450

Focus 4000 (import)

1984-1986. Offset double cut with 3 single coils for '84; Vanguard V shape with 2 humbuckers for '85-'86.

1984-1986		$275	$450

Focus 6000 (import)

1986-1988. Same as Focus 3000, but with hum/single/single pickups and 5-way switch. Pointy droopy headstock in '87.

1986-1988		$275	$450

Focus Classic (import)

1986-1989. Offset double cut, six-on-a-side headstock, 3 single-coils, Floyd Rose trem.

1986-1989		$250	$400

Gene Simmons Axe

1980-1981. Axe-shaped guitar, aluminum neck, 1 humbucker, slot headstock, stop tailpiece.

1980-1981		$1,000	$2,500

Gorky Park (import)

1986-1989. Triangular balalaika, bolt-on maple neck, pointy droopy six-on-a-side headstock, one pickup, Floyd Rose trem. Red with iron sickle graphics, tribute to Russian rock. Reissued in late-1990s.

1986-1989		$500	$700

Pacer

1982-1984. Offset double cut, six-on-a-side headstock, 3 single coils, bolt-on maple neck and 'board.

1982-1984		$450	$550

Pacer Deluxe

1983-1986. Pacer with hum/single/single pickups.

1981-1986		$450	$600

Pacer Imperial

1981-1986. Offset double cut, bolt-on maple neck with maple cap, 2 humbuckers.

1981-1986		$450	$600

ProAxe (U.S.A.-made)

1989-1990. Offset double cut, sharp pointy headstock, dot markers, 2 or 3 pickups.

1989-1990		$450	$600

Striker (import)

1984-1989. Korean imports, offset doube cut, single-single-double pickup layout, various colors. Series included Striker 100, 200, 300, 400, 600 and 700 Bass.

1984-1989	Striker 100	$200	$250
1984-1989	Striker 200	$210	$260
1984-1989	Striker 300	$220	$270
1985-1989	Striker 400	$240	$290
1986-1989	Striker 600	$250	$300

Vanguard Series

1981-1986, 1999-present. U.S.A.-made or American Series (assembled in U.S.). Flying V shape, 1 humbucker, aluminum (Special '81-'83) or wood (Custom '81-'83) neck. Added for '83-'84 were the Imperial (wood neck, 2 humbuckers) and the Headless (alum neck, 1 humbucker). For '85-'86, the body was modified to a Jackson Randy Rhoads style V body, with a banana headstock and 2 humbuckers. In '99 this last design was revived as an import.

1980s		$500	$600

XL-5 Custom

1980-1981. Asymmetrical double cutaway, aluminum neck, 2 pickups, three-way switch, coil-tap, phase, BadAss.

1980-1981		$1,100	$1,400

Kramer-Harrison, William

1977-present. Luthier William Kramer-Harrison builds his premium grade, custom, classical and flat-top guitars in Kingston, New York.

Kubicki

1973-present. Kubicki is best known for their Factor basses, but did offer a few guitar models in the early '80s. See Bass section for more company info.

Kustom

1968-present. Founded by Bud Ross in Chanute, Kansas, and best known for the tuck-and-roll amps, Kustom also offered guitars from '68 to '69. See Amp section for more company info.

Electric Hollowbody Guitars

1968-1969. Hollowed-out two-part bodies; includes the K200A (humbucker, Bigsby), the K200B (single-coils, trapeze tailpiece), and the K200C (less fancy tuners), various colors.

1960s		$700	$800

MODEL YEAR	FEATURES	EXC. COND. LOW	HIGH

Kyle, Doug

1990-present. Premium grade, custom, Selmer-style guitars made by luthier Doug Kyle in England.

La Baye

1967. Designed by Dan Helland in Green Bay, Wisconsin and built by the Holman-Woodell factory in Neodesha, Kansas. Introduced at NAMM and folded when no orders came in. Only 45 prototypes made. A few may have been sold later as 21st Century.

2x4 6-String

1967. Narrow plank body, controls on top, two pickups, trem. A 12-string version was also made.

1967		$650	$800

LA Guitar Factory

1997-present. Founded by Ari Lehtela and Luke Lukuer in Charlotte, North Carolina. Lehtela became the sole owner in 2000. From '97 to '03, LA offered production and custom models. Currently, Lehtela uses the LA Guitar Factory brand on his professional and premium grade, production, solidbody and tone chambered guitars and basses. He markets his premium grade, custom guitars - mainly jazz body carved tops - under Lehtela guitarCraft.

La Scala

Ca. 1920s-1930s. La Scala was another brand of the Oscar Schmidt Company of New Jersery, and was used on guitars, banjos, and mandolins.

Lace Music Products

1979-present. Intermediate and professional, production, electric guitars from Lace Music Products, a division of Actodyne General Inc. which was founded by Don Lace Sr., inventor of the Lace Sensor Pickup. In '96 Lace added amplifiers and in 2001 they added guitars. In '02, they also started offering the Rat Fink brand of guitars.

Lado

1973-present. Founded by Joe Kovacic, Lado builds professional and premium grade, production/custom, solidbody guitars and basses in Lindsay, Ontario. Some model lines are branded "J. K. Lado."

Lafayette

Ca. 1963-1967. Sold through Lafayette Electronics catalogs. Early Japanese-made guitars from pre-copy era, generally shorter scale beginner guitars. Many made by Guyatone, some possibly by Teisco.

Acoustic Thinline Archtop Guitars

1963-1967. Various models.

1960s		$100	$200

MODEL YEAR	FEATURES	EXC. COND. LOW	HIGH

Lakeside (Lyon & Healy)

Late-1800s-early-1900s. Mainly catalog sales of guitars and mandolins from the Chicago maker. Marketed as a less expensive alternative to the Lyon & Healy Washburn product line.

Harp Guitar - Jumbo Style G3740

Early-1900s. Spruce top, rosewood finished birch back and sides, two six-string necks with standard tuners, one neck is fretless without dot markers, rectangular bridge.

1917	Natural	$1,500	$2,500

Langejans Guitars

1971-present. Premium grade, production/custom, flat-top, 12-string, and classical guitars built by luthier Delwyn Langejans in Holland, Michigan.

Larrivee

1968-present. Professional and premium grade, production/custom, acoustic and acoustic/electric guitars built in Vancouver, British Columbia. Founded by Jean Larrivee, who apprenticed under Edgar Monch in Toronto. He built classic guitars in his home from '68-'70 and built his first steel string guitar in '71. Moved company to Victoria, BC in '77 and to Vancouver in '82. In '83, he began building solidbody electric guitars until '89, when focus again returned to acoustics.

Larrivee uses the following model designations: 05 Mahogany Standard, 09 Rosewood Standard, 10 Deluxe, 19 Special, 50 & 60 Standard (unique inlay), 70 Deluxe, and 72 Presentation.

C-10 Deluxe

Late-1980s-1990s. Sitka spruce top, Indian rosewood back and sides, sharp cutaway, fancy binding.

1989		$1,500	$1,700

C-72 Cutaway Presentation

Spruce top, Indian rosewood back and sides, sharp cutaway, ultra-fancy abalone and pearl hand-engraved headstock.

1990s	Mermaid headstock	$2,500	$3,000

C-72 Presentation

Spruce top, Indian rosewood back and sides, non-cut Style D, ultra-fancy abalone and pearl hand-engraved headstock.

1990s	Jester headstock	$2,000	$2,500

D-70 Dreadnought Standard

1992		$1,500	$2,000

L-09 Rosewood Standard

All solid wood construction, East Indian rosewood back and sides, African ebony board and bridge, wood binding and rosette mosaic, fiine grain Sitka spruce top.

1983		$1,000	$1,100

RS-4 CM Carved Top

Introduced in 1987. Carved Top Series. Electric, Sunburst or translucent finishes.

1987		$900	$1,200

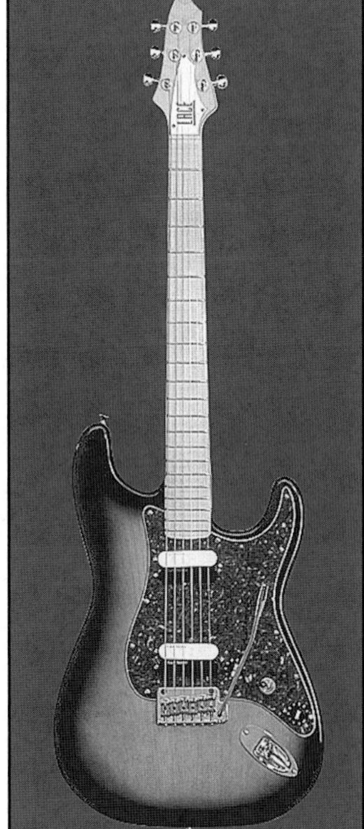

Lace California Twister

1995 Larrivee C-72 Presentation

GUITARS

Larson Brothers Euphanon

1912 Larson Bros./Dyer harp guitar

MODEL YEAR	FEATURES	EXC. COND. LOW	HIGH

Larson Brothers (Chicago)

1900-1944. Carl and August Larson built guitars under a variety of names, (refer to Stetson, Maurer and Prairie State listings).

Laskin

1971-present. Luthier William "Grit" Laskin builds his premium and presentation grade, custom, steel-string, classical, and flamenco guitars in Toronto, Ontario. Many of his instruments feature extensive inlay work.

Classical

All solid wood, German spruce top, Indian rosewood back and sides, portrait headstock inlay.

1980s		$3,000	$4,000

Flamenco

All solid wood, spruce top, cypress back and sides, ebony friction pegs.

1980s		$2,500	$3,000

Jumbo Brazilian

All solid wood, bear claw sitka spruce top, Brazilian rosewood back and sides, double loon headstock inlay.

1980s		$2,500	$3,000

Jumbo Cutaway

Indian rosewood back and sides, spruce top, double abalone rosette, woman and candle deluxe headstock inlay.

1992	Natural	$7,000	$8,000

Leach Guitars

1980-present. Luthier Harvey Leach builds his professional and premium grade, custom, flat-tops, archtops, acoustic basses, and solidbody electrics in Cedar Ridge, California.

Lehmann Stringed Instruments

1971-present. Luthier Bernard Lehmann builds his professional and premium grade, production/custom, flat-top, archtop, classical and Gypsy guitars in Rochester, New York. He also builds lutes, Vielles and Rebecs.

Lehtela guitarCraft

2003-present. Premium grade, custom, guitars - mainly jazz body carved tops - built by luthier Ari Lehtela in Charlotte, North Carolina. He markets his non-custom production models under LA Guitar Factory.

Les Stansell Guitars

1980-present. Luthier Les Stansell builds his premium grade, custom, nylon-string guitars in Pistol River, Oregon.

Lindert

1986-present. Luthier Chuck Lindert makes his intermediate and professional grade, production/custom, Art Deco-vibe electric guitars in Chelan, Washington.

MODEL YEAR	FEATURES	EXC. COND. LOW	HIGH

Lopez, Abel Garcia

1985-present. Luthier Abel Garcia Lopez builds his premium grade, custom, classical guitars in Mexico.

Loprinzi

1972-present. Professional and premium grade, production/custom, classical and steel-string guitars built in Clearwater, Florida. They also build ukes. Founded by Augustino LoPrinzi and his brother Thomas in New Jersey. The guitar operations were taken over by AMF/Maark Corp. in '73. LoPrinzi left the company and again started producing his own Augustino Guitars, moving his operations to Florida in '78. AMF ceased production in '80, and a few years later, LoPrinzi got his trademarked name back.

LM-15

Mahogany back and sides.

1970s		$600	$750

LR-15

Rosewood.

1973		$900	$1,200

LR-15-12

1975		$900	$1,200

Lord

Mid-1960s. Acoustic and solidbody electric guitars imported by Halifax.

Acoustic Guitars

Various models.

1960s		$75	$175

LTD

1995-present. Intermediate grade, production, Korean-made solidbody guitars and basses offered by ESP. See ESP for models.

Lucas Custom Instruments

1989-present. Premium and presentation grade, production/custom, flat-tops built by luthier Randy Lucas in Columbus, Indiana.

Lucas, A. J.

1990-present. Luthier A. J. Lucas builds his production/custom, classical and steel string guitars in Lincolnshire, England.

Lyle

Ca. 1969-1980. Imported by distributor L.D. Heater in Portland, OR. Generally higher quality Japanese-made copies of American designs. Manufacturers unknown, but some early ones, at least, made by Arai and Company.

Acoustics

1969-1980. Various models.

1970s		$100	$175

Electric Thinline Archtop Guitars

1969-1980. Various models.

1970s		$125	$200

MODEL YEAR	FEATURES	EXC. COND. LOW	HIGH

Lyon & Healy

In the 1930s, Lyon & Healy was an industry giant. It operated a chain of music stores, and manufactured harps (their only remaining product), pianos, Washburn guitars and a line of brass and wind instruments. (See Washburn, American Conservatory, Lakeside, and College brands.)

Lyric

1996-present. Luthier John Southern builds his professional and premium grade, custom, semi-hollow and solidbody guitars in Tulsa, Oklahoma. He also builds basses.

M. Campellone Guitars

See listing under Campellone Guitars

Maccaferri

1923-1990. Built by luthier and classical guitarist Mario Maccaferri (b. May 20, 1900, Cento, Italy; d. 1993, New York) in Cento, Italy; Paris, France; New York, New York; and Mount Vernon, New York. Maccaferri was a student of Luigi Mozzani from 1911 to 1928. His first catalog was in '23, and included a cutaway guitar. He designed Selmer guitars in '31. Maccaferri Invented the plastic clothespin during World War II and used that technology to produce plastic ukes starting in '49 and Dow Styron plastic guitars in '53. He made several experimental plastic electrics in the '60s and plastic violins in the late-'80s.

See *Guitar Stories Volume II*, by Michael Wright, for a complete history of Maccaferri with detailed model listings.

G40 Deluxe Arched Top

1953-1958. Plastic construction.

1950s		$200	$400

Showtime Classical

1959-1969. Plastic construction, no decoration by 1965.

1959		$175	$225

Magnatone

Ca. 1937-1971. Founded as Dickerson Brothers in Los Angeles, California and known as Magna Electronics from '47, with Art Duhamell president. Brands include Dickerson, Oahu (not all), Gourley, Natural Music Guild, Magnatone. In '59 Magna and Estey merged and in '66 the company relocated to Pennsylvania. In '71, the brand was taken over by a toy company.

Cyclops

1930s. Dobro-made resonator guitar.

1930s		$500	$650

Tornado

1965-1966. Offset double cut body, 3 DeArmond pickups, vibrato.

1965-1966		$400	$600

Typhoon

1965-1966. Double cut solidbody, three DeArmond pickups, vibrato.

1965-1966		$400	$600

Zephyr

1965-1966. Double cut with two DeArmond single-coil pickups, metallic finish, vibrato.

1965-1966		$400	$550

Mako

1985-1989. Line of solidbody guitars and basses and solidstate amps from Kaman (Ovation, Hamer).

Various Solidbody Guitars

1980s. Imports with bolt-on necks.

1985-1989		$150	$250

Manuel Rodriguez and Sons, S.L.

1905-present. Professional, premium, and presentation grade, custom flat-top and nylon-string guitars from Madrid, Spain.

Manzanita Guitars

1993-present. Custom, steel-string, Hawaiian, and resonator guitars built by luthiers Manfred Pietrzok and Moritz Sattler in Rosdorf, Germany.

Manzer Guitars

1976-present. Luthier Linda Manzer builds her premium and presentation grade, custom, steel-string, nylon-string, and archtop guitars in Toronto, Ontario.

Mapson

1995-present. Luthier James L. Mapson builds his premium and presentation grade, production/custom, archtops in Santa Anna, California.

Marc Silber Guitar Company

1998-present. Intermediate and professional grade, production, flat-top, nylon-string, and Hawaiian guitars designed by Marc Silber and made in Mexico. These were offered under the K & S Guitars and/or Silber brands for 1992-'98. Silber also has ukuleles.

Marchione Guitars

1993-present. Premium and presentation grade, custom, archtops and solidbodies built by Stephen Marchione originally in New York City, but currently in Houston, Texas.

Marco Polo

1960- ca.1964. Imported from Japan by Harry Stewart and the Marco Polo Company of Santa Ana, CA. One of the first American distributors to advertise inexpensive Japanese guitars. Manufacturers unknown, but some acoustics by Suzuki, some electrics by Guyatone.

Maccaferri G-40

Marchione Whitfield

GUITARS

1936 Martin 0-17

1930 Martin 0-18

MODEL YEAR	FEATURES	EXC. COND. LOW	HIGH

Acoustic Hollowbody Guitars

1960-1964. Various models.

1960s		$100	$200

Mark Lacey Guitars

1974-present. Luthier Mark Lacey builds his premium and presentation archtops and flat-tops in Nashville, Tennessee.

Mark Wescott Guitars

1980-present. Premium grade, custom, flat-tops, built by luthier Mark Wescott in Marmora, New Jersey.

Marling

Ca. 1975. Budget line instruments marketed by EKO of Recanati, Italy; probably made by them, although possibly imported.

Acoustic Guitars

1975. Includes the steel-string S.110, and the dreadnoughts W.354 Western, and W.356 Western.

1975		$75	$100

Electric Guitars

1975. Includes the E.400 (semi-acoustic/electric), E.490 (LP-style), E.480 (single cut-style), and the 460 (Manta-style).

1970s		$75	$150

Martin

1833-present. Intermediate, professional, premium, and presentation grade, production/custom, acoustic, acoustic/electric, and resonator guitars. Founded in New York City by Christian Frederick Martin, former employee of J. Staufer in Vienna, Austria. Moved to Nazareth, Pennsylvania in 1839. Early guitars were made in the European style, many made with partners John Coupa, Charles Bruno and Henry Schatz. Scalloped X-bracing was introduced in the late-1840s. The dreadnought was introduced in 1916 for the Oliver Ditson Company, Boston; and Martin introduced their own versions in 1931.

Martin model size and shape are indicated by the letter prefix (e.g., 0, 00, 000, D, etc.); materials and ornamentation are indicated by number, with the higher the number, the fancier the instrument (e.g., 18, 8, 35, etc.). Martin offered electric thinline guitars from '61-'68 and electric solidbodies from '78-'82. The Martin Shenandoah was made in Asia and assembled in U.S. Japanese Martin Sigma ('72-'73) and Korean Martin Stinger ('85 on) imported solidbodies. See Michael Wright's Guitar Stories Vol. II for more information on Martin's electric guitars.

0-15

1935, 1940-1943, 1948-1961. All mahogany, unbound rosewood fingerboard, slotted peghead and 12-fret neck until 1934, solid peghead and 14-fret neck thereafter. Natural Mahogany.

MODEL YEAR	FEATURES	EXC. COND. LOW	HIGH
1935	2 made, maple/birch	$2,300	$2,500
1940-1943		$1,600	$1,900
1948-1949		$1,500	$1,800
1950-1959		$1,400	$1,600
1960-1961		$1,300	$1,400

0-15 T

1960-1963. Tenor with Style 15 appointments. Natural mahogany.

1960-1963		$900	$1,000

0-16 NY

1961-1995. Mahogany back and sides, 12 frets, slotted peghead, unbound extra-wide rosewood fingerboard. Natural.

1961-1969		$1,400	$1,500
1970-1979		$1,200	$1,400
1980-1989		$1,100	$1,300
1990-1995		$1,000	$1,250

0-17

1906-1917, 1929-1948, 1966-1968. First version has mahogany back and sides, three Black soundhole rings, rosewood bound back, unbound ebony fingerboard, 12 frets, slotted peghead. Second version (1929 and on) is all mahogany, three White-Black-White soundhole rings, top bound until 1930, thin Black backstripe, 12 frets and slotted peghead until 1934, solid peghead and 14 frets thereafter. Natural Mahogany.

1929-1934	Bar frets, 12 fret-style	$1,700	$2,000
1934-1939	T-frets, 14 fret-style	$1,900	$2,200
1940-1945		$1,700	$2,000
1946-1948		$1,600	$1,800
1966-1968		$1,200	$1,600

0-17 H

1930-1939. Hawaiian, mahogany back and sides, 12 frets clear of body. Natural.

1930-1939		$1,700	$2,200

0-17 T

1932-1960. Mahogany back and sides, tenor. Natural.

1932-1942		$800	$1,000
1942-1945	Ebony rod	$700	$900
1946-1949	Sitka spruce	$750	$950
1950-1960	Mahogany	$700	$900

0-18

1898-1996. Rosewood back and sides until 1917, mahogany back and sides after, Adirondack spruce top until 1946. Slotted peghead and 12 frets until 1934, solid peghead and 14 frets after 1934. Braced for steel strings in 1923, improved neck in late-1934, non-scalloped braces appear late-1944. Natural.

1898-1922	Gut string bracing	$2,300	$2,800
1923-1939	Braced for steel in 1923	$2,700	$3,200
1940-1944	Scalloped braces	$2,500	$3,000
1945-1949		$2,000	$2,600
1950-1959		$1,700	$2,300
1960-1969		$1,000	$2,200
1970-1979		$900	$1,300

GUITARS

MODEL YEAR	FEATURES	EXC. COND. LOW	HIGH

0-18 G (Classical)

1960s. Special order classical nylon string model. Natural.

1961		$1,000	$2,200

0-18 K

1918-1935. Hawaiian, all koa wood, braced for steel strings in 1923, T-frets and steel T-bar neck in late-1934. Natural.

1920-1922		$2,200	$2,400
1923-1927	Steel string bracing	$2,400	$2,600
1928-1935		$2,500	$2,800

0-18 T

1929-1995. Mahogany body, spruce top, tenor. Natural.

1929-1939		$1,400	$1,600
1940-1959		$1,300	$1,500
1960-1964		$1,250	$1,450
1965-1969		$1,200	$1,400
1970-1979		$1,100	$1,300

0-21

1898-1948. Rosewood back and sides, Adirondack spruce top until 1946, 12 frets, braced for steel strings in 1923, T-frets and steel T-bar neck in late-1934, non-scalloped braces in late-1944. Natural.

1898-1926		$2,600	$3,000
1927-1946	Steel string bracing	$2,700	$3,500

0-26

1850-1890. Rosewood back and sides, ivory-bound top, rope-style purfling.

1850-1890		$2,700	$3,200

0-28

1870s-1931, 1937 (six made), 1969 (one made). Brazilian rosewood back and sides, braced for steel strings in 1923, herringbone binding until 1937. Natural.

1890-1927		$4,500	$5,500
1928-1931		$5,000	$6,000

0-28 K

1917-1931, 1935. Hawaiian, all koa wood, braced for steel strings in 1923. Natural.

1917	Spruce top option	$4,500	$5,500
1917-1924	Figured koa	$4,500	$5,500
1925-1931	Steel string bracing	$5,000	$6,000

0-28 T

1930-1931. Tenor neck.

1930-1931		$2,800	$3,500

0-30

1899-1921. Brazilian rosewood back and sides, ivory-bound body, neck and headstock.

1899-1921		$4,500	$5,500

0-42

1870s-1942. Brazilian rosewood back and sides, 12 frets. Natural.

1890-1926	Braced for gut strings	$10,000	$11,000
1927-1929	Steel string bracing	$11,000	$12,000

0-45

1904-1939. Brazilian rosewood back and sides. Natural.

1904-1927		$18,000	$24,000

MODEL YEAR	FEATURES	EXC. COND. LOW	HIGH

00-16 C

1962-1977, 1980-1983. Classical, mahogany back and sides, five-ply bound top, satin finish, 12 frets, slotted peghead. Natural.

1962-1969		$1,000	$1,200
1970-1977		$800	$1,100

00-17

1908-1917, 1930-1960, 1982-1988. Mahogany back and sides, 12 frets and slotted headstock until 1934, solid headstock and 14 frets after 1934, Natural Mahogany. Reissued in 2002 with a high gloss finish.

1930-1939		$2,000	$2,300
1940-1944		$1,900	$2,200
1945-1949		$1,800	$2,100
1950-1960		$1,700	$1,900
2002	Reissue model	$1,000	$1,100

00-17 H

1934-1936. Hawaiian set-up, mahogany body, no binding.

1934-1936		$1,900	$2,200

00-18

1898-1995. Rosewood back and sides until 1917, mahogany after, braced for steel strings in 1923, improved neck in late-1934, war-time design changes 1942-1946, non-scalloped braces in late-1944, Adirondack spruce top until 1946. Natural.

1898-1922		$3,500	$4,500
1923-1939	Braced for steel in '23	$4,000	$5,500
1936-1939	Sunburst option	$5,500	$7,500
1940-1941		$4,000	$5,500
1942-1943	Ebony rod	$4,000	$4,800
1944	Scalloped braces early '44	$3,500	$4,500
1944-1946	Non-scalloped braces	$2,600	$3,200
1946	Steel bar neck	$3,000	$3,400
1947-1949		$2,700	$3,100
1950-1952		$2,400	$3,000
1953-1958	Last of Kluson early '58	$2,200	$2,800
1958-1959	Grover tuners late '58	$2,100	$2,700
1960-1962		$2,000	$2,600
1963-1965		$1,800	$2,200
1966	Black guard late '66	$1,500	$2,000
1966	Tortoise guard early '66	$1,600	$2,100
1967		$1,400	$1,900
1968		$1,300	$1,750
1969		$1,300	$1,600
1970-1979		$1,200	$1,400
1980-1989		$1,100	$1,300
1990-1995		$1,000	$1,200

00-18 C

1962-1995. Renamed from 00-18 G in 1962. Mahogany back and sides, classical, 12 frets, slotted headstock. Natural.

1962-1969		$1,300	$1,600
1970-1979		$1,000	$1,200

1927 Martin 0-21

1957 Martin 00-18

Martin 00-21GE

1927 Martin 00-45

MODEL YEAR — FEATURES — EXC. COND. LOW — HIGH

00-18 E
1959-1964. Flat top Style 18, single neck pickup and two knobs, heavier bracing. Natural.

1959-1964 — $2,300 — $2,600

00-18 G
1936-1962. Mahogany back and sides, classical, Natural. Renamed 00-18 C in 1962.

1936-1949 — $1,600 — $2,500
1950-1962 — $1,100 — $1,500

00-18 Gruhn Limited Edition
1995. Sitka spruce top, C-shaped neck profile, 25 made.

1995 — $1,400 — $1,600

00-18 H
1935-1941. Hawaiian, mahogany back amd sides, 12 frets clear of body, Natural. The Price Guide is generally for all original instruments. The H conversion is an exception, because converting from H (Hawaiian-style) to 00-18 specs is considered by some to be a favorable improvement and something that adds value.

1935-1941 — $3,500 — $4,000
1935-1941 Converted to Spanish — $4,000 — $5,500

00-18 SH (Steve Howe)
1999-2000. Limited edition run of 250.

1999-2000 — $2,400 — $2,600

00-21
1898-1996. Brazilian rosewood back and sides, changed to Indian rosewood in 1970, dark outer binding, unbound ebony fingerboard until 1947, rosewood from 1947, slotted diamond inlays until 1944, dot after. Natural.

1898-1926 Braced for gut strings — $4,500 — $6,000
1927-1931 Braced for steel in '27 — $6,000 — $7,500
1932-1939 — $6,500 — $7,800
1940-1943 Scalloped braces — $6,200 — $7,500
1944-1949 Non-scalloped braces — $5,000 — $5,500
1950-1959 — $4,000 — $4,500
1960-1969 Brazilian rosewood — $2,500 — $4,000
1970-1979 Indian rosewood — $1,200 — $1,500
1980-1989 — $1,000 — $1,200

00-21 NY
1961-1965. Brazilian rosewood back and sides, no inlay. Natural.

1961-1965 — $2,800 — $3,300

00-28
1898-1941, 1958 (one made), 1977 (one made), 1984 (two made). Brazilian rosewood back and sides, changed to Indian rosewood in 1977, herringbone purfling through 1941, White binding and unbound fingerboard after 1941, no inlays before 1901, diamond inlays from 1901 to 1941, dot after. Natural.

1898-1924 Gut strings — $6,500 — $8,500
1925-1931 Braced for steel in '25 — $7,500 — $9,000
1932-1941 Special order — $8,000 — $9,500

MODEL YEAR — FEATURES — EXC. COND. LOW — HIGH

00-28 C
1966-1995. Renamed from 00-28 G. Brazilian rosewood back and sides, changed to Indian rosewood in 1970, classical, 12 frets. Natural.

1966-1969 — $2,100 — $3,000
1970-1979 — $1,400 — $1,800

00-28 G
1936-1962. Brazilian rosewood back and sides, classical, Natural. Only 17 made. Reintroduced as 00-28 C in 1966.

1936-1939 — $4,400 — $5,500
1940-1949 — $4,000 — $5,000
1951-1962 — $3,200 — $4,000

00-40 H
1928-1939. Hawaiian, Brazilian rosewood back and sides, 12 frets clear of body, Natural. H models are sometimes converted to standard Spanish setup. In higher-end models this can make the instrument more valuable to some people.

1928-1939 — $7,000 — $13,000
1928-1939 Converted to Spanish — $10,000 — $16,000

00-40 K
Few were made (only 6). Figured koa, Natural.

1930 — $19,000 — $21,000

00-42
1898-1942, 1973 (one made), 1994-1996. Brazilian rosewood back and sides, Indian rosewood in 1973, pearl top borders, 12 frets, ivory bound peghead until 1918, ivoroid binding after 1918. Natural.

1898-1926 Gut strings — $13,000 — $16,000
1927-1942 Steel strings — $15,000 — $20,000

00-44 Soloist/Olcott-Bickford Artist Model
1913-1939. Custom-made in small quantities, Brazilian rosewood, ivory or faux-ivory-bound ebony fingerboard.

1913-1939 — $32,000 — $40,000

00-45
1904-1938, 1970-1995. Brazilian rosewood back and sides, changed to Indian rosewood in 1970, 12 frets and slotted headstock until 1934 and from 1970 on 14 frets, and solid headstock from 1934-1970. Natural.

1904-1927 — $25,000 — $35,000
1928-1938 — $35,000 — $45,000

000-1R
1996-present. Acoustic, solid spruce top with laminated Indian rosewood sides. Natural satin finish.

1996-1999 — $650 — $900

000-15 Auditorium
1997-present. All solid wood mahogany body, dot markers, Natural.

1997-1999 — $650 — $700

000-16
1989-1995. Acoustic, mahogany back and sides, diamonds and squares inlaid. Name changed to 000-16 T Auditorium in 1996. Sunburst.

1989-1995 — $1,200 — $1,400

MODEL YEAR	FEATURES	EXC. COND. LOW	HIGH

000-16 T

1996-1997. All solid wood mahogany back and sides, higher appointments than 000-15.

MODEL YEAR	FEATURES	LOW	HIGH
1996-1999		$800	$1,000

000-18

1911-present (none in 1932-1933). Rosewood back and sides until 1917, mahogany back and sides from 1917, longer scale in 1924-1934, 12 frets clear of body until 1933, changed to 14 frets in 1934. Improved neck late-1934, war-time changes 1941-1946, non-scalloped braces in late-1944, switched to from Adirondack spruce to Sitka spruce top in 1946 (though some Adirondack tops in 1950s and 1960s), Natural. Now called the 000-18 Auditorium.

MODEL YEAR	FEATURES	LOW	HIGH
1924-1931	25.5" scale, 12-fret clear	$6,000	$8,000
1934-1939	24.5" scale, 14-fret clear	$7,000	$9,000
1939	Sunburst option	$8,000	$10,000
1940-1941		$6,000	$8,000
1942-1943	Ebony rod	$4,000	$5,700
1943	Sunburst option	$5,500	$6,200
1944	Scalloped braces early '44	$5,000	$5,900
1944-1946	Non-scalloped braces	$3,000	$4,000
1946	Steel bar neck	$3,500	$4,500
1947-1949		$3,200	$4,000
1950-1952		$3,000	$3,500
1953-1958	Last of Kluson early '58	$2,700	$3,200
1958-1959	Grover tuners late '58	$2,600	$3,100
1960-1962		$2,500	$3,000
1963-1965		$2,200	$2,600
1966	Black guard late '66	$1,800	$2,150
1966	Tortoise guard early '66	$2,000	$2,400
1967	Last of Maple bridgeplate	$1,800	$2,150
1968		$1,700	$2,000
1969		$1,600	$1,800
1970-1979		$1,400	$1,500
1980-1989		$1,300	$1,400
1990-1999		$1,200	$1,300
2000-2002		$1,200	$1,300

000-21

1902-1924 (22 made over that time), 1931(2), 1938-1959, 1965 (1), 1979 (12). Brazilian rosewood back and sides, changed to Indian rosewood in 1970. Natural.

MODEL YEAR	FEATURES	LOW	HIGH
1938-1941	Pre-war specs	$10,000	$13,000
1942-1944	Ebony rod, scalloped	$9,000	$12,000
1944-1946	Ebony rod, non-scalloped	$6,000	$9,500
1946-1949	Steel bar neck	$5,000	$7,500
1950-1959		$4,000	$6,000

000-28

1902-present. Brazilian rosewood back and sides, changed to Indian rosewood in 1970, herringbone purfling through 1941, White binding and unbound fingerboard after 1941, no inlays before 1901, slotted diamond inlays from 1901-1944, dot after, 12 frets until 1932, 14 frets 1931 on (both 12 and 14 frets were made during 1931-1932). Natural.

MODEL YEAR	FEATURES	LOW	HIGH
1928-1931	12 frets	$19,000	$26,000
1931-1936	14 frets	$20,000	$27,000
1937-1939		$18,000	$25,000
1940-1941		$17,000	$20,000
1942-1943	Ebony rod	$13,000	$16,000
1944	Scalloped braces early '44	$12,000	$15,000
1944-1946	Herringbone, ebony bar neck	$8,000	$10,000
1946	Herringbone, steel bar neck	$9,000	$11,000
1947-1949	Start of non-herringbone '47	$7,000	$9,000
1950-1952		$6,000	$7,000
1953-1958	Last of Kluson early '58	$5,000	$6,000
1958-1959	Grover tuners late '58	$4,800	$5,800
1960-1962		$4,500	$5,500
1963-1965		$4,000	$5,000
1966	Black guard late '66	$3,300	$4,300
1966	Tortoise guard early '66	$3,500	$4,500
1967	Last of maple bridgeplate	$3,300	$4,300
1968	Rosewood bridgeplate	$3,000	$4,000
1969	Last of Brazilian rosewood	$3,000	$4,000
1970-1979	Indian rosewood	$1,400	$1,700
1980-1989	Indian rosewood	$1,400	$1,600
1990-1999	Indian rosewood	$1,300	$1,500
2000-2002		$1,300	$1,500

000-28 C

1962-1969. Brazilian rosewood back and sides, classical, slotted peghead. Natural.

MODEL YEAR	FEATURES	LOW	HIGH
1962-1968		$2,200	$2,300

000-28 EC Eric Clapton Signature

1996-present. Sitka spruce top, Indian rosewood back and sides, herringbone trim. Natural.

MODEL YEAR	FEATURES	LOW	HIGH
1996-1999		$1,900	$2,400

000-28 Golden Era

1996 only. Sitka spruce top, rosewood back and sides, scalloped braces, herringbone trim, 12-fret model. Natural.

MODEL YEAR	FEATURES	LOW	HIGH
1996		$2,800	$3,200

000-41

1996. Customshop style 000-41.

MODEL YEAR	FEATURES	LOW	HIGH
1996		$2,600	$2,700

1947 Martin 000-18

1943 Martin 000-28

Martin 000-45 JR

1993 Martin D-1

MODEL YEAR	FEATURES	EXC. COND. LOW	HIGH
000-42			
1918, 1921-1922, 1925, 1930, 1934, 1938-1943. Brazilian rosewood back and sides. Natural.			
1938-1943		$29,000	$32,000
000-42 EC Eric Clapton			
1995. Style 45 pearl-inlaid headplate, ivoroid bindings, Eric Clapton signature, 24.9" scale, flat top, Sunburst top price is $8320 (1995 price). Only 461 made.			
1995		$7,000	$8,500
000-45			
1906, 1911-1914, 1917-1919, 1921-1942, 1971-1993. Brazilian rosewood back and sides, changed to Indian rosewood in 1970, 12-fret neck and slotted headstock until 1934 (but seven were made in 1970 and one in 1975), 14-fret neck and solid headstock after 1934. Natural.			
1921-1927	Braced for gut strings	$35,000	$50,000
1928-1929	Braced for steel string	$45,000	$55,000
1930-1933		$55,000	$65,000
1934-1936	14 frets, C.F.M. inlaid	$65,000	$75,000
1937-1939		$63,000	$73,000
1940-1942		$60,000	$70,000
000-45 JR (Jimmie Rodgers) Golden Era			
1997. Adirondack spruce top, Brazilian rosewood back and sides, scalloped high X-braces, abalone trim, Natural, 100 made.			
1997		$11,000	$12,000
000-C16			
1990-1995. Cutaway acoustic, mahogany back and sides, diamonds and squares inlay. Name changed to 000-C16T Auditorium in 1996.			
1990-1995		$1,000	$1,200
0000-28 Custom			
1998. Jumbo-size 0000 cutaway body, Indian rosewood, sitka spruce top.			
1998		$2,900	$3,000
0000-28 H			
1997-present. Jumbo-size 0000 body, 28 herringbone trim.			
1997-1999		$2,200	$2,400
1-17			
1906-1917 (1st version), 1931-1934 (2nd version). First version has spruce top, mahogany back and sides. Second version has all mahogany with flat Natural finish.			
1930s		$1,500	$1,800
1-21			
1860-1926. Initially offered in size 1 in the 1860s, ornate soundhole rings.			
1880-1910		$2,500	$2,800
1-26			
1950-1890. Rosewood back and sides, ivory-bound top, rope-style purfling.			
1850-1890		$2,400	$3,000
1-28			
1880-1923. Style 28 appointments including Brazilian rosewood back and sides.			
1902		$4,000	$5,000
1-45			
1904-1919. Only six made, slotted headstock and Style 45 appointments.			
1904		$16,000	$20,000
2 1/2-17			
1856-1897. The first Style 17s were small size 2 1/2 and 3, these early models use Brazilian rosewood.			
1890-1897		$1,500	$1,800
2 1/2-18			
1865-1898. Parlor-size body with Style 18 appointments.			
1865-1898		$2,200	$2,700
2-15			
1939-1964. All mahogany body, dot markers.			
1939		$1,200	$1,300
2-17			
1910, 1922-1938. 1910 version has spruce top, mahogany back and sides. 1922 on, all mahogany body. No body binding after 1930.			
1922-1930		$1,400	$1,700
2-17 H			
1927-1931. Hawaiian, all mahogany, 12 frets clear of body.			
1927-1931		$1,400	$1,700
2-27			
1857-1907. Brazilian rosewood back and sides, pearl ring, zigzag back stripe, ivory bound ebony fingerboard and peghead.			
1888		$3,200	$4,000
2-28 T			
1929-1930. Tenor neck, Brazilian rosewood back and sides, herringbone top purfling.			
1929-1930		$2,000	$2,500
3-17			
1856-1897. The first Style 17s were small size 2 1/2 and 3. The early models use Brazilian rosewood, spruce top, bound back, unbound ebony fingerboard.			
1890-1897		$1,280	$1,600
5-15 T			
1949-1963. All mahogany, non-gloss finish, tenor neck.			
1950-1959		$800	$1,000
5-18			
1898-1989. Rosewood back and sides (changed to mahogany from 1917 on), 12 frets, slotted headstock.			
1923-1939	Braced for steel in '23	$2,200	$2,800
1940-1944		$2,000	$2,600
1945-1949		$1,900	$2,300
1950-1959		$1,800	$2,000
1960-1969		$1,400	$1,800
1970-1989		$800	$1,200
7-28			
1980-1995, 1997-present. Seven/eighths body size of a D-model, Style 28 appointments.			
1980		$2,000	$2,500

MODEL YEAR	FEATURES	EXC. COND. LOW	HIGH

C-1

1931-1942. Acoustic archtop, mahogany back and sides, spruce top, round hole until 1933, F-holes appear in 1932, bound body. Sunburst.

1931-1942		$1,100	$1,500

C-2

1931-1942. Acoustic archtop, Brazilian rosewood back and sides, carved spruce top, round hole until 1933, F-holes appear in 1932, zigzag back stripe, multi-bound body, slotted-diamond inlay. Sunburst.

1931-1942		$1,700	$2,500

C-2 Conversion

1931-1942. The Vintage Guitar Price Guide lists original, excellent condition instruments. A C-2 Conversion is an exception. The C-2 archtop was not and continues to be generally less popular than a flat top with similar appointments. C series archtops and H series Hawaiians converted to Spanish setup flat tops have more appeal to some players and collectors. The C-2 Conversion requires removal of the arched top and installation of a high quality spruce top. Appointments may vary.

1931-1942	High-end appointments	$4,000	$8,000

Custom OM-45 Deluxe (custom shop)

1998-1999. Limited custom shop run of 14, Adirondack spruce and typical Style 45 appointments.

1998-1999		$14,000	$14,500

D-1

1992-present. Name first used for the prototype of the D-18, made in 1931. Name revived for current model with mahogany body, "A-frame" bracing, available as an acoustic/electric.

1992-1999		$550	$600

D12-18

1973-1995. Mahogany back and sides, 12 strings, 14 frets clear of body, solid headstock.

1973-1979		$1,300	$1,400
1980-1989		$1,200	$1,300
1990-1995		$1,100	$1,300

D12-20

1964-1991. Mahogany back and sides, 12 strings, 12 frets clear of body, slotted headstock.

1964-1969		$1,500	$1,900
1970-1979		$1,400	$1,500
1980-1991		$1,300	$1,400

D12-28

1970-present. Indian rosewood back and sides, 12 strings, 14 frets clear of body, solid headstock.

1970-1979		$1,500	$1,800
1980-1989		$1,500	$1,700
1990-1999		$1,400	$1,600

D12-35

1965-1995. Brazilian rosewood back and sides, changed to Indian rosewood in 1970, 12 strings, 12 frets clear of body, slotted headstock.

1965-1969	Brazilian rosewood	$2,300	$3,000
1970-1979	Indian rosewood	$1,500	$1,800
1980-1989		$1,400	$1,600
1990-1995		$1,300	$1,500

MODEL YEAR	FEATURES	EXC. COND. LOW	HIGH

D12-45 (special order)

1970s. Special order instrument, not a standard catalog item, with D-45 appointments, Indian rosewood.

1970-1979		$4,500	$5,500

D12XM

2001-present. Wood composite mahogany laminate D body, solid wood neck, decal rosette, screened headstock logo, unique DX bracing, built in Nazareth, PA.

2001		$350	$450

D-15

1997-present. All mahogany body.

1997-2002		$475	$550

D-16 A

1987-1990. North American ash back and sides, solid spruce top, scalloped bracing, rosewood fingerboard and bridge, solid mahogany neck.

1987-1990		$1,000	$1,200

D-16 GT

1999-present. D-16 T specs with mahogany back and sides, but with glossy top instead of satin.

1999		$650	$800

D-16 H

1991-1994. Full-size dreadnought, mahogany back and sides with satin finish, herringbone marquetry, vintage X-bracing, scalloped braces, optional acoustic pickup or active preamp system. Replaced by D-16 T in 1996.

1991-1995		$1,000	$1,200

D-16 M

1986, 1988-1990. Mahogany back and sides, non-gloss satin finish.

1988-1990		$800	$900

D-16 T

1996-present. Solid spruce top, solid mahogany back and sides, scalloped braces, satin finish.

1996-1999		$850	$950

D-16 TR

1996-present. Solid spruce top, solid rosewood back and sides, scalloped braces, satin finish.

1996-1999		$1,100	$1,300

D-18

1932-present. Mahogany back and sides, spruce top, Black back stripe, 12-fret neck, changed to 14 frets in 1934.

1932-1933	12-fret neck	$25,000	$28,000
1934-1936	14-fret neck	$20,000	$23,000
1937-1938		$17,000	$20,000
1939		$15,000	$18,000
1940-1941		$13,000	$16,000
1942-1943	Ebony rod	$12,000	$14,000
1944	Non-scalloped braces late '44	$5,500	$6,500
1944	Scalloped braces early '44	$11,000	$13,000
1945	Ebony rod	$5,500	$6,500
1946	Steel bar neck	$6,000	$7,000
1947-1949		$5,000	$6,250
1950-1952		$3,500	$4,500

Martin 12-28

1990s Martin D-16H

1970 Martin D-18

Martin D-18 S

MODEL YEAR	FEATURES	EXC. COND. LOW	HIGH
1953-1958	Klusons to early '58	$3,500	$4,000
1958-1959	Grover tuners late '58	$3,200	$3,600
1960-1962		$2,900	$3,400
1963-1965		$2,800	$3,200
1966	Black guard late '66	$2,300	$2,700
1966	Tortoise guard early '66	$2,500	$2,800
1967	Last of maple bridgeplate	$2,100	$2,500
1968	Rosewood bridgeplate	$1,900	$2,300
1969		$1,600	$1,900
1970-1979		$1,300	$1,400
1980-1989		$1,200	$1,300
1990-1999		$1,100	$1,300
2000-2002		$1,100	$1,300

D-18 E

1958-1959. D-18 factory built with DeArmond pickups which required ladder bracing (reducing acoustic volume and quality).

1958-1959		$2,800	$3,200

D-18 GE (Golden Era)

1995. Part of the Golde Era Series which cipied a 1937 D-18, 272 made.

1995		$1,800	$2,400

D-18 LE

1986-1987. Limited Edition, quilted or flamed mahogany back and sides, scalloped braces, Gold tuners with ebony buttons.

1986-1987		$1,700	$1,900

D-18 MB

1990. Limited Edition Guitar of the Month, flame maple binding, Engelmann spruce top signed by shop foremen, X-brace. Total of 99 sold.

1990		$1,600	$1,800

D-18 S

1967-1993. Mahogany back and sides, 12-fret neck, slotted headstock. Majority of production before 1977, infrequent after that.

1967-1969		$1,600	$2,400
1970-1979		$1,000	$2,100

D-18 V (Vintage)

1992. Guitar of the month, low-profile neck, scalloped braces, bound. Total of 218 sold.

1992		$1,700	$1,800

D-18 VM

1996-present.

1996-1999		$1,400	$1,500

D-18 VMS

1996-present. Same as VM except X-brace placement.

1996-1999		$1,500	$1,750

D-19

1977-1988. Deluxe mahogany dreadnought, optional mahogany top, multi-bound but unbound rosewood fingerboard.

1977-1988		$1,200	$1,400

MODEL YEAR	FEATURES	EXC. COND. LOW	HIGH

D-21

1955-1969. Brazilian rosewood back and sides, rosewood fingerboard, chrome tuners.

1955-1958	Klusons to early '58	$4,500	$5,000
1958-1959	Grover tuners late '58	$4,100	$4,850
1960-1962		$3,900	$4,650
1963-1965		$3,500	$4,500
1966-1967		$2,800	$4,000
1968-1969		$2,500	$3,500

D-25 K

1980-1989. Dreadnought-size with koa back and sides and spruce top.

1980-1989		$1,500	$1,700

D-25 K2

1980-1989. Same as D-25K, but with koa top and Black pickguard.

1980-1989		$1,600	$1,800

D-28

1931-present. Brazilian rosewood back and sides (changed to Indian rosewood in 1970), 1936 was the last year for the 12-fret model, 1944 was the last year for scalloped bracing, 1947 was the last year herringbone trim was offered, Natural. Ultra high-end D-28 Martin guitar (pre-1947) valuations are very sensitive to structural and cosmetic condition. Finish wear and body cracks for ultra high-end Martin flat tops should be evaluated on a case-by-case basis. Small variances within the 'excellent condition' category can lead to notable valuation differences.

1931-1932		$55,000	$65,000
1933		$50,000	$60,000
1934-1936	14-fret neck	$35,000	$45,000
1937-1939		$33,000	$41,000
1940-1941		$32,000	$35,000
1942-1943	Ebony rod	$25,000	$27,000
1944	Scalloped braces early '44	$23,000	$25,000
1944	Non-scalloped late '44	$15,000	$18,000
1945-1946	Herringbone, ebony bar neck	$15,000	$18,000
1946	Herringtone, steel bar neck	$16,000	$19,000
1947-1949	Non-herringbone starting '47	$9,000	$11,000
1950-1952		$7,000	$9,000
1953-1958	Klusons to early '58	$6,000	$7,000
1958-1959	Grover tuners late '58	$5,500	$6,500
1960-1962		$5,000	$6,000
1963-1965		$4,500	$5,500
1966	Black guard late '66	$3,800	$4,800
1966	Tortoise guard early '66	$4,000	$5,000
1967	Last of maple bridgeplate	$3,800	$4,800
1968	Rosewood bridgeplate	$3,500	$4,500

MODEL YEAR	FEATURES	EXC. COND. LOW	HIGH
1969	Last of Brazilian rosewood	$3,500	$4,500
1970-1979	Indian rosewood	$1,500	$1,800
1980-1989		$1,500	$1,700
1990-1999		$1,400	$1,600
2000-2002		$1,400	$1,600

D-28 (1935 Special)

1993. Guitar of the Month, 1935 features, Indian rosewood back and sides, peghead with Brazilian rosewood veneer.

1993		$1,600	$2,200

D-28 E

1959-1964. Electric, Brazilian rosewood back and sides, two DeArmond pickups, Natural.

1959-1964		$3,200	$3,500

D-28 LSH

1991. Guitar of the Month, Indian rosewood back and sides, herringbone trim, snowflake inlay, zig-zag back stripe.

1991		$1,600	$1,800

D-28 P

1988-1990. P stands for low-profile neck, Indian rosewood back and sides.

1988-1990		$1,200	$1,500

D-28 S

1966-1993. Rosewood back and sides, 12-fret neck.

1966-1969	Brazilian rosewood	$3,200	$4,200
1970-1979	Indian rosewood	$1,400	$1,700
1980-1993		$1,300	$1,600

D-28 V

1983-1985. Brazilian rosewood back and sides, Limited Edition, herringbone trim, slotted diamond inlay.

1983-1985		$4,000	$5,000

D-2832 Shenandoah

1984-1993. Dreadnought acoustic, spruce top, V-neck, laminated rosewood sides, three-piece rosewood back.

1984-1993		$500	$800

D-35

1965-present. Brazilian rosewood back and sides, changed to Indian rosewood in 1970, three-piece back, Natural with Sunburst option.

1965-1969	Brazilian rosewood	$3,100	$3,900
1970-1979	Indian rosewood	$1,500	$1,800
1970-1979	Sunburst option	$1,700	$2,100
1980-1989		$1,400	$1,600
1980-1989	Sunburst optioin	$1,600	$1,900
1990-2000		$1,300	$1,500
2000-2002		$1,300	$1,500

D-35 S

1966-1993. Brazilian rosewood back and sides, changed to Indian rosewood in 1970, 12-fret neck, slotted peghead.

1967-1969	Brazilian rosewood	$3,100	$3,900
1970-1979	Indian rosewood	$1,500	$1,800
1980-1989		$1,600	$1,900
1990-1993		$1,300	$1,500

MODEL YEAR	FEATURES	EXC. COND. LOW	HIGH

D-3532 Shenandoah

1984-1993. Dreadnought acoustic, spruce top, V-neck, laminated rosewood sides, three-piece rosewood back.

1984-1993		$600	$900

D-37 K

1980-1995. Dreadnought-size, koa back and sides, spruce top.

1980-1995		$2,000	$2,200

D-37 K2

1980-1995. Same as D-37 K, but has a koa top and Black pickguard.

1980-1995		$2,000	$2,200

D-41

1969-present. Brazilian rosewood back and sides for the first ones in 1969 then Indian rosewood, bound body, scalloped braces, Natural.

1969	Brazilian rosewood	$8,000	$14,000
1970-1979	Indian rosewood	$2,640	$3,300
1980-1989		$2,300	$2,500
1990-1999		$2,200	$2,400
1990-1999	Sunburst option	$2,300	$2,500
2000-2002		$2,100	$2,300

D-41 BLE

1989. Guitar of the Month, Brazilian rosewood back and sides, inlaid abalone binding on top, soundhole, fingerboard and headstock, hexagon fingerboard inlays, abalone C.F. Martin headstock logo. Total of 58 sold.

1989		$2,800	$3,800

D-42

1996-present. Dreadnought, Indian rosewood back and sides, spruce top, pearl rosette and inlays, snowflake fingerboard inlays, Gold tuners, gloss finish.

1996-2002		$2,600	$2,800

D-42 LE

1988 only. D-42-style, limited edition (75 sold), scalloped braces, low profile neck.

1988		$2,000	$2,500

D-42 V

1985. Vintage Series, 12 made, Brazilian rosewood, scalloped braces.

1985		$7,000	$9,000

D-45

1933-1942 (96 made), 1968-present. Brazilian rosewood back and sides, changed to Indian rosewood during 1969. The pre-World War II Martin D-45 is one of the "holy grails." The noted price ranges are guidance pricing only. A pre-war D-45, or any ultra-expensive vintage guitar, should be evaluated on a case-by-case basis. The price ranges are for all-original guitars in excellent condition. These ranges are for a crack-free guitar. Unfortunately, many older acoustics have a crack or two. Because of these cracks, ultra-expensive acoustics are generally more difficult to evaluate than ultra-expensive solidbody electrics. Technically, a repaired body crack makes a guitar non-original, but the vintage market generally considers a professionally repaired crack to be original.

1963 Martin D-28

1966 Martin D-35

GUITARS

1997 Martin D-45

2002 Martin D-45 V

MODEL YEAR — FEATURES — EXC. COND. LOW — HIGH

Crack width, length and depth can vary, therefore extra attention to detail is suggested.

1936 Only 2 made $190,000 $240,000
1937 Only 2 made $175,000 $220,000
1938 Only 9 made $170,000 $210,000
1939 Only 14 made $160,000 $175,000
1940 Only 19 made $150,000 $170,000
1941 Only 24 made $140,000 $160,000
1942 Only 19 made $130,000 $150,000
1968-1969 Brazilian rosewood $25,000 $27,000
1970-1974 Indian rosewood $5,500 $6,500
1975-1979 $5,000 $6,000
1980-1987 $4,500 $5,000
1988-1989 Scalloped braces, low profile $4,300 $5,000
1990-1999 $3,800 $4,500
2000-2002 $3,800 $4,300

D-45 (1939 Reissue)

High-grade spruce top, figured Brazilian rosewood back and sides, high X and scalloped braces, abalone trim, Natural, Gold tuners.

1992 $11,000 $14,000

D-45 200th Anniversary (C.F. Martin Sr. Deluxe)

1996 only. Commemorative model for C.F. Martin Sr.'s birth in 1796, Brazilian Deluxe Edition, Natural.

1996 $13,000 $15,000

D-45 Custom

Brazilian rosewood back and sides.

1991-1992 $5,000 $10,000

D-45 Deluxe

1993 only. Guitar of the Month, Brazilian rosewood back and sides, figured spruce top, inlay in bridge and pickguard, "Tree of Life" inlay on fingerboard, pearl borders and back stripe, Gold tuners with large Gold buttons. Total of 60 sold.

1993 $15,000 $17,000

D-45 Gene Autry

1994 only. Gene Autry inlay (two options available), Natural.

1994 $10,000 $15,000

D-45 S

1969-1993. Brazilian rosewood back and sides, 12-fret neck, S means slotted peghead, only 50 made.

1988-1993 $7,000 $9,000

D-45 Steven Stills Signature

2002. Limited edition of 91.

2002 $12,000 $14,000

D-45 V

1983-1985. Brazilian rosewood back and sides, scallopred braces, snowflake inlay, Natural. Name revived in '99.

1983-1985 $12,000 $13,000

MODEL YEAR — FEATURES — EXC. COND. LOW — HIGH

D-45 VR

1997-1999. Scalloped braces, high X-bracing, vintage aging toner, snowflake inlay. Name changed to D-45 V in '99.

1997-1999 $5,000 $6,000

D-62

1989-1995. Dreadnought, flamed maple back and sides, spruce top, chrome-plated enclosed Schaller tuners.

1989-1995 $1,600 $2,000

D-62 LE

1986. Flamed maple back and sides, spruce top, snowflake inlays, Natural, Guitar of the Month October 1986.

1986 $1,760 $2,200

D-76

1975-1976. Limited Edition, Indian rosewood back and sides, three-piece back, herringbone back stripe, pearl stars on fingerboard, eagle on peghead. Only 200 made in 1975 and 1,976 made in 1976.

1976 $2,700 $3,000

DC-1 E/DC-1 M (cutaway)

1995-present. Cutaway design, all solid wood, mahogany back and sides, spruce top, transducer pickup.

1995-1999 $800 $900

DM

1990-present. Solid sitka spruce top, laminated mahogany back and sides, dot markers, Natural satin.

1990-1999 $500 $600

DXM

2001-present. Wood composite mahogany laminate D body, solid wood neck, decal rosette, screened headstock logo, unique DX bracing, built in Nazareth, PA.

2001 $375 $425

E-18

1979-1982. Offset double cutaway, maple and rosewood laminate solidbody, two DiMarzio pickups, phase switch, Natural.

1979-1982 $600 $800

EM-18

1979-1982. Offset double cutaway, maple and rosewood laminate solidbody, two exposed-coil humbucking pickups, coil split switch.

1979-1982 $600 $800

EMP-1

1998-1999. Employee series designed by Martin employee team, cutaway solid spruce top, ovangkol wood back and sides with rosewood middle insert (D-35-style insert), on-board pickup.

1998-1999 $1,900 $2,200

F-1

1940-1942. Mahogany back and sides, carved spruce top, multi-bound, F-holes. Sunburst.

1940 $1,900 $2,200

GUITARS

MODEL YEAR	FEATURES	EXC. COND. LOW	HIGH

F-7

1935-1942. Brazilian rosewood back and sides, F-holes, carved top, back arched by braces, multi-bound. Sunburst top finish.

1935-1942	$6,000	$7,500

F-9

1935-1941. Highest-end archtop, Brazilian rosewood, Martin inlaid vertically on headstock, seven-ply top binding, 45-style back strip. Sunburst.

1935-1941	$11,000	$15,000

F-50

1961-1965. Single cutaway thinline archtop with laminated maple body, one pickup.

1961-1965	$1,100	$1,200

F-55

1961-1965. Single cutaway thinline archtop with laminated maple body, two pickups.

1961-1965	$1,100	$1,400

F-65

1961-1965. Electric archtop, double cutaway, F-holes, two pickups, square-cornered peghead, Bigsby. Sunburst.

1961-1965	$1,200	$1,700

GT-70

1966-1968. Electric archtop, bound body, F-holes, single cutaway, two pickups, tremolo. Burgundy or Black finish.

1966-1968	$1,000	$1,300

GT-75

1966-1968. Electric archtop, bound body, F-holes, double cutaway, two pickups, tremolo. Burgundy or Black finish.

1966-1968	$1,100	$1,600

Hawaiian Guitar

2002-present. Hawaiian scene, similar to the Cowboy guitar model.

2002	$800	$1,000

HD-28 (Standard Series)

1976-present. Indian rosewood back and sides, scalloped bracing, herringbone purfling.

1976-1979	$1,600	$1,900
1980-2002	$1,500	$1,800

HD-28 BLE

1990. Guitar of the Month, Brazilian rosewood back and sides, herringbone soundhole ring, low profile neck (LE), chrome tuners.

1990	$4,000	$5,000

HD-28 GM LSH

1994. "Grand Marquis" Guitar of the Month, rosewood back and sides, large soundhole with double herringbone rings, snowflake inlay in bridge.

1994	$2,500	$3,000

HD-28 LE

1985. Guitar of the Month, rosewood back and sides, scalloped bracing, herringbone top purfling, diamonds and squares fingerboard inlay, V-neck.

1985	$2,500	$2,800

HD-28 MP

1990. Bolivian rosewood back and sides, scalloped braces, herringbone top purfling, zipper back stripe, low profile neck.

1990	$1,500	$1,800

HD-28 P

1987-1989. Rosewood back and sides, scalloped braces, herringbone, low profile neck (P), zigzag back stripe.

1987-1989	$1,500	$1,800

HD-28 V

1930s herringbone styling with advanced bracing.

1999	$1,700	$1,800

HD-282 R

1994 only.

1994	$1,360	$1,700

HD-2832 Shenandoah

1980s.

1984	$500	$700

HD-35

1978-present. Indian rosewood back and sides, herringbone top trim, zipper back stripe.

1978-1979	$1,700	$1,800
1980-1989	$1,600	$1,700
1990-1999	$1,600	$1,700

HOM-35

1989. Herringbone Orchestra Model Guitar of the Month, scalloped braces, three-piece Brazilian rosewood back, bookmatched sides, 14-fret neck. Only 60 built.

1989	$4,500	$5,000

J-1 Jumbo

1997-present. Jumbo body with mahogany back and sides.

1997-1999	$850	$900

J12-40

1985-1996. Called J12-40 M from '85-'90. Rosewood back and sides, 12 strings, 16" jumbo size, 14-fret neck, solid peghead, gold tuners.

1985-1996	$1,500	$1,800

J12-65

1985-1995. Called J12-65m for '84-'90. Jumbo-style 65 12-string, spruce top, figured maple back and sides, gold-plated tuning machines, scalloped bracing, ebony board, tortoiseshell-style binding. Natural.

1985-1995	$1,500	$1,800

J-18/J-18M

1987-1996. J-size body with Style 18 appointments, natural. Called J-18M for '87-'89.

1987-1996	$1,200	$1,300

J-40

1990-present. Called J-40 M from 1985-1989. Jumbo, Indian rosewood back and sides, triple-bound fingerboard, hexagonal inlays.

1990-1999	$1,800	$2,200

1963 Martin F-65

1966 Martin GT-75

GUITARS

1927 Martin OM-28

2002 Martin OM-18 V

MODEL YEAR	FEATURES	EXC. COND. LOW	HIGH

J-40 M

1985-1989. Jumbo, Indian rosewood back and sides, triple-bound fingerboard, hexagonal inlays. Name changed to J-40 in 1990.

1985-1989		$1,800	$2,200

J-65/J-65 M

1985-1995. Jumbo acoustic featuring maple back and sides, gold-plated tuners, scalloped bracing, ebony fingerboard, tortoiseshell-style binding.

1985-1995		$1,800	$2,200

M-36

1978-1997. Indian rosewood back and sides, bound fingerboard, low profile neck, multi-bound, White-Black-White back stripes.

1978-1997		$1,400	$1,500

M-38

1977-1996. Indian rosewood back and sides, multi-bound, low profile neck, gold-plated tuners, stained top.

1977-1996		$2,000	$2,200

MC-28

1981-1996. Rosewood back and sides, single cutaway acoustic, oval soundhole, scalloped braces. Natural.

1981-1996		$1,500	$1,600
1990s	Natural	$1,500	$1,600

MC-68

1985-1995. Auditorium-size acoustic, rounded cutaway, maple back and sides, Gold tuners, scalloped bracing, ebony fingerboard, tortoiseshell-style binding. Natural or Sunburst.

1985-1995		$1,600	$1,700

MTV-1 Unplugged

1996. Body is 1/2 rosewood and 1/2 mahogany, scalloped bracing, MTV logo on headstock.

1996		$1,600	$1,700

N-20

1968-1995. Classical, Brazilian rosewood back and sides (changed to Indian rosewood in 1969), multi-bound, 12-fret neck, solid headstock (changed to slotted in 1970). Natural.

1968-1970	Brazilian rosewood	$1,840	$2,300
1971-1995	Indian rosewood	$1,200	$1,500

OM-18

1930-1934. Orchestra Model, mahogany back and sides, 14-fret neck, solid peghead, banjo tuners (changed to right-angle in 1931).

1930-1933	Natural	$12,000	$15,000
1934	Sunburst	$13,000	$16,000

OM-18 V

1999-present. Vintage features.

1999-2002		$1,500	$1,800

OM-21 (Standard Series)

1992-1997. Triple 0-size, 15 1/8", spruce top, rosewood back and sides. Natural.

1992-1997		$1,200	$1,300

OM-28

1929-1933. Orchestra Model, Brazilian rosewood back and sides, 14-fret neck, solid peghead, banjo tuners (changed to right-angle in 1931). Reintroduced with Indian rosewood in 1990.

1929-1930	Small guard, banjo tuners	$32,000	$35,000
1931-1933	Large guard	$25,000	$28,000

OM-28 (reissue)

1990-1996. Indian rosewood back and sides.

1990-1996		$1,800	$2,200

OM-28 PB (Perry Bechtel)

1993. Guitar of the Month, signed by Perry Bechtel's widow Ina, spruce top, Indian rosewood back and sides, zigzag back stripe, chrome tuners, V-neck, only 50 made.

1993		$5,000	$5,300

OM-28 VR

1990-1996. Orchestra Model, reintroduced OM-28 with rosewood back and sides.

1990-1996		$1,800	$2,100

OM-42

1999-present. Indian rosewood back and sides, Style 45 snowflake markes, rounded neck profile.

1999-2002		$2,500	$2,600

OM-42 PS (Paul Simon)

1997. Bookmatched sitka spruce top, Indian rosewood back and sides, 42 and 45-style features, low profile PS neck, 500 made.

1997		$4,000	$4,300

OM-45 Deluxe Reissue

1994.

1994		$4,000	$4,200

OM-45 Deluxe/OM-45

1930-1933. OM-style, 45 level appointments with pearl inlay in pickguard and bridge. Only 14 OM-45 Deluxe instruments made. Regular OM-45 with normal 45-style appointments. Condition is critically important on this or any ultra high-end instrument, minor flaws are critical to value.

1930	OM-45 Deluxe	$90,000	$120,000
1930-1933	OM-45	$75,000	$90,000

OMC-28

1990. Guitar of the Month with rounded cutaway, Gold tuners, low profile neck, pearl Martin script logo in headstock, label signed by C.F. Martin IV.

1990		$1,700	$2,100

R-18

1933-1942. Spruce arched top (carved top by 1937), mahogany back and sides, 14-fret neck, bound top. Sunburst.

1933-1942		$1,000	$1,800

SPD-16 TR

Special Edition D-body cutaway, all solid wood with spruce top, rosewood back and sides, abalone snowflake markers.

1996		$1,200	$1,300

MODEL YEAR	FEATURES	EXC. COND. LOW	HIGH

Stauffer-Style

1830s-ca.1850s. One of C.F. Martin's earliest models, distinguished by the scrolled, six-on-a-side headstock. Ornamentation varies from guitar to guitar.

1830s	Plain, no ivory	$3,000	$7,000
1830s	Very fancy, ivory board and bridge	$5,000	$12,000

Marvel

Ca. 1950s- ca. 1960s. Brand name used for budget instruments marketed by Peter Sorkin Company in New York, New York. Sorkin manufactured and distributed Premier guitars and amplifiers made by its Multivox subsidiary.

Marvel instruments were primarily beginner-grade. Brand disappears by mid-1960s.

Electric Solidbody Guitars

1950s-mid-1960s. Various models.

1950s		$125	$225

Mason

1936-1939. Henry L. Mason on headstock, wholesale distribution, similar to Gibson/Cromwell, pressed wood back and sides.

Student/Intermediate Student Guitars

1936-1939. Various flat-top and archtop student/budget models.

1936-1939		$300	$700

Maton

1946-present. Intermediate and professional grade, production/custom, acoustic, acoustic/electric, hollow body and solidbody guitars built in Box Hill, Victoria, Australia. Founded by Bill May and his brother Reg and still run by the family. Only available in USA since '82.

Mauel Guitars

1995-present. Luthier Hank Mauel builds his premium grade, custom, flat-tops in Auburn, California.

Maurer

1900-1944. Robert Maurer's Chicago-based woodworking shop was bought by Larson Brothers in 1900, but the Maurer name was retained. Low-end and high quality models were offered.

13" Acoustic Flat-Top (Standard)

Early-1900s. Rosewood back and sides, spruce top, 12 3/4", made by Larson Brothers of Chicago.

1910		$2,000	$3,000

13" Higher-End Flat-Top (Brazilian)

Early-1900s. Spruce top, 13 5/8", Brazilian rosewood back and sides, high-end pearl appointments, slotted headstock.

1910	Natural	$4,000	$5,000

14" Flat-Top (Brazilian)

1920s-1930s. Mid-sized (about 14") with Brazilian rosewood back and sides, attractive appointments.

1920s	Abalone trim	$6,000	$8,500
1930s		$6,000	$8,500

14" Flat-Top (Mahogany)

1920s-1930s. Mid-sized (about 14") with mahogany back and sides, standard appointments.

1930s		$3,000	$4,000

15" High-end Flat-Top (Brazilian)

Early-1900s. Brazilian rosewood back and sides, tree of life inlay, 15", pearl-bound.

1920s		$9,000	$11,500

McAlister Guitars

1997-present. Premium grade, custom, flat-tops built by luthier Roy McAlister in Watsonville, California.

McCollum Guitars

1994-present. Luthier Lance McCollum builds his premium grade, custom, flat-top and harp guitars in Colfax, California.

McCurdy Guitars

1983-present. Premium grade, production/custom, archtops built by luthier Ric McCurdy originally in Santa Barbara, California and, since 1991, New York, New York.

McGill Guitars

1976-present. Luthier Paul McGill builds his premium grade, production/custom, classical, resonator, and acoustic/electric guitars in Nashville, Tennessee.

MCI, Inc

Ca. 1976-1990s. Musiconics International (MCI), Waco, Texas, introduced the world to the Guitorgan, invented by Bob Murrell. Later, they also offered effects and a steel guitar. In the '90s, a MIDI version was offered.

GuitOrgan B-35

1970s (ca. 1976-1978?). Duplicated the sounds of an organ and more. MCI bought ES-335-style guitars from others (Univox) and outfitted them with lots of switches and buttons. Each fret has six segments that correspond to an organ tone. There was also a B-300 version.

1976		$1,000	$1,500

McInturff

1996-present. Professional and premium grade, production/custom, solidbody guitars built by luthier Terry C. McInturff in Holly Springs, North Carolina. McInturff spent 17 years doing guitar repair and custom work before starting his own guitar line.

Taurus Standard

Single cutaway, carved flamed maple top on chambered mahogany body, dual humbucker pickups, Gold hardware.

1996-2001	Sunburst	$1,900	$2,100

1830s Martin Stauffer

Mcinturff Sportster

GUITARS

Metropolitan Glendale Deluxe

Metropolitan Westport Custom

MODEL YEAR	FEATURES	EXC. COND. LOW	HIGH

McPherson Guitars

1981-present. Premium grade, production, flattops built by luthier Mander McPherson in Sparta, Wisconsin.

Mean Gene

1988-1990. Heavy metal style solidbodies made by Gene Baker, of Baker U.S.A. fame, and Eric Zoellner in Santa Maria, California. They built around 30 custom guitars.

Megas Guitars

1989-present. Luthier Ted Megas builds his premium grade, custom, archtop and solidbody guitars, originally in San Franciso, and currently in Portland, Oregon.

Mello, John F.

1973-present. Premium grade, production/custom, classical and ftat-top guitars built by luthier John Mello in Kensington, California.

Melphonic

1960s. Brand built by the Valco Company of Chicago.

Resonator Guitar

Valco-made.

1965		$500	$700

Melville Guitars

1988-present. Luthier Christopher Melville builds his premium grade, custom, flat-tops in Milton, Queensland, Australia.

Menkevich Guitars

1970-present. Professional and premium grade, production/custom, classical and flamenco guitars built by luthier Michael Menkevich in Elkins Park, Pennsylvania.

Mermer Guitars

1983-present. Luthier Richard Mermer builds his premium grade, production/custom, steel-string, nylon-string, and Hawaiian guitars in Sebastian, Florida.

Merrill Brothers

1998-present. Premium grade, production/custom, steel-string and harp guitars built by luthiers Jim and Dave Merrill in Williamsburg, Virginia.

Mesrobian

1995-present. Luthier Carl Mesrobian builds his professional and premium grade, custom, archtop guitars in Salem, Massachusetts.

MODEL YEAR	FEATURES	EXC. COND. LOW	HIGH

Messenger

1967-1968. Built by Musicraft, Inc., originally of 156 Montgomery Street, San Francisco, California. The distinguishing feature of the Messengers is a metal alloy neck which extended through the body to the tailblock, plus mono or stereo outputs. Sometime before March '68 the company had relocated to Astoria, Oregon. Press touted "improved" magnesium neck, though it's not clear if this constituted a change from '67. Brand disappears after '68.

Electric Hollowbody Archtop Guitar

1967-1968. Symmetrical vague ES-330 body shape, metal neck with rosewood fingerboards, stereo.

1967-1968	Rojo Red	$2,000	$2,400

Metropolitan

1995-present. Professional and premium grade, production/custom, retro-styled solidbodies designed by David Wintz reminiscent of the '50s National Res-o-glas and wood body guitars. They feature full-scale set-neck construction and a wood body instead of Res-o-glas. Wintz also makes Robin and Alamo brand instruments.

Glendale Custom

1997-present. Single cut, African fakimba body, set-neck, two pickups, various colors.

1997		$1,500	$1,700

Glendale Custom Acoustic

1997-present. Single cut, African fakimba body, set-neck, three pickups including piezo.

1997		$2,000	$2,300

Glendale Deluxe

1997-present. Single cut, African fakimba body, set-neck, two pickups, dot markers.

1997		$900	$1,100

Glendale Super Acoustic

1997-present. Single cut, flamed maple top, three pickups including piezo, Gold hardware.

1997		$3,000	$3,500

Tanglewood Custom

1996-present. Map-shape body, National Glenwood 98 copy with dual humbucking pickups, solid basswood body (versus Res-o-glas) but with high quality, highly buffed finish in various colors. Does not include piezo bridge that is offered on the Tanglewood Custom Acoustic.

1996-1997		$1,500	$1,700

Tanglewood Custom Acoustic

1996-present. Map-shape body, Custom model with added piezo bridge pickup, various colors.

1996-1997		$2,000	$2,300

MODEL YEAR	FEATURES	EXC. COND. LOW	HIGH

Tanglewood Deluxe

1996-present. Map-shape, set-neck, two pickups, dot markers.

1996	$900	$1,100

Westport Custom

1997-present. Single cut, three pickups, art deco design, African fakimba body, set-neck, various colors.

1997	$1,500	$1,700

Westport Custom Acoustic

1997-present. Single cut, three pickups, art deco design, African fakimba body, set-neck.

1997	$2,000	$2,300

Westport Deluxe

1997-present. Single cut, two humbuckers.

1997	$900	$1,000

Westport Super Acoustic

1997-present. Single cut, three pickups with piezo, art deco design, Africa fakimba body, set-neck.

1997	$3,200	$3,500

Michael Dunn Guitars

1968-present. Luthier Michael Dunn builds his production/custom Maccaferri-style guitars in New Westminster, British Columbia. He also offers a harp uke and a Weissenborn- or Knutsen-style Hawaiian guitar, and has built archtops.

Michael Lewis Instruments

1992-present. Luthier Michael Lewis builds his premium and presentation grade, custom, archtop guitars and mandolins in Grass Valley, California.

Michael Silvey Custom Guitars

2003-present. Production/custom solidbody electric guitars built by Michael Silvey in North Canton, Ohio.

Microfrets

1967-1975. Manufactured in Frederick, Maryland, the over 20 models of Microfrets guitars sported innovative designs and features.

Baritone Signature

1971. Baritone version of Signature Guitar, sharply pointed double cutaway, with or without F-holes, single or double dot inlays.

1971	$400	$700

Baritone Stage II

1971-ca. 1975. Double cutaway, two pickups.

1971-1975	$400	$700

Calibra I

1969-1975. Double cutaway, two pickups, F-hole.

1969-1975	$500	$600

Covington

1967-1969. Offset double cutaway, two pickups, F-hole.

1967-1969	$650	$900

MODEL YEAR	FEATURES	EXC. COND. LOW	HIGH

Golden Comet

1969-1971. Double cutaway, two pickups, F-hole.

1969-1971	$450	$700

Golden Melody

1969-1971. Offset double cutaway, two pickups, F-hole, M-shaped metal design behind tailpiece.

1969-1971	$600	$900

Huntington

1969-1975. Double cutaway, two pickups.

1969-1975	$600	$900

Orbiter

1967-1969. Odd triple cutaway body, thumbwheel controls on bottom edge of pickguard.

1967-1969	$600	$900

Plainsman

1967-1969. Offset double cutaway, two pickups, F-hole, thumbwheel controls on bottom edge of pickguard.

1967-1969	$750	$1,000

Signature

1967-1969. Double cutaway, two pickups.

1967-1969	$350	$700

Spacetone

1969-1971. Double cutaway, two pickups.

1969-1971	$500	$800

Stage II

1969-1975. Offset double cutaway, two pickups.

1969-1975	$400	$700

Swinger

1971-1975. Offset double cutaway, two pickups.

1971-1975	$500	$800

Wanderer

1969. Double cutaway, two pickups.

1969	$400	$700

Mike Lull Custom Guitars

1995-present. Professional and premium grade, production/custom, guitars and basses built by luthier Mike Lull in Bellevue, Washington.

Milburn Guitars

1990-present. Luthiers Orville and Robert Milburn build their premium grade, custom, classical guitars in Sweet Home, Oregon.

Mirabella

1997-present. Professional and premium grade, custom archtops, flat-tops, hollowbody, and solidbody guitars built by luthier Cristian Mirabella in Babylon, New York. He also builds mandolins and ukes.

MJ Guitar Engineering

1993-present. Professional, premium, and presentation grade, production/custom, hollow-body and solidbody guitars and basses built by luthier Mark Johnson in Rohnert Park, California.

1972 Microfrets Calibra I

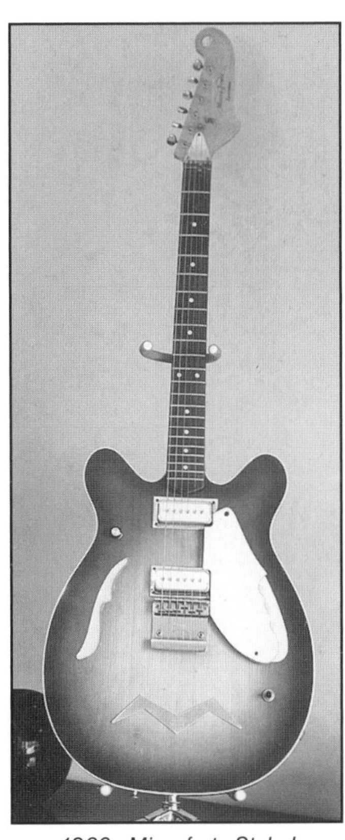

1960s Microfrets Style I

GUITARS

Moonstone M-80

Morgaine Mintage '61

MODEL YEAR	FEATURES	EXC. COND. LOW	HIGH

Modulus

1978-present. Founded by Geoff Gould in the San Francisco area, currently built in Novato, California. Modulus currently offers professional grade, production/custom, solidbody electric guitars. They also build electric basses.

Genesis 2/2T

1996-present. Double cutaway, long extended bass horn alder body, bolt-on carbon fiber/red cedar neck, hum-single-single pickups, locking vibrato (2T model), various colors.

1999		$1,000	$1,100

Moll Custom Instruments

1996-present. Luthier Bill Moll builds his professional and premium grade, archtops and solidbody basses in Springfield, Missouri. He also builds violins, violas and cellos.

Monrad, Eric

1993-present. Premium, custom, flamenco and classical guitars built by luthier Eric Monrad in Healdsburg, California.

Montalvo

See listing under Casa Montalvo.

Monteleone

1976-present. Presentation grade, production/custom, archtop guitars built by Luthier John Monteleone in Islip, New York.

Eclipse

17" electric archtop, natural orange.

1991		$15,000	$16,000

Radio City

18" acoustic archtop cutaway, art deco fretboard inlays, golden blond.

1996	Golden Blond	$19,000	$21,000

Moon (Scotland)

1979-present. Intermediate and premium grade, production/custom, acoustics and electrics from luthier Jimmy Moon and built Glasgow, Scotland. They also build mandolin family instruments.

Moonstone

1972-present. Professional, premium, and presentation grade production/custom flat-tops, acoustic and electric basses, and solid and semi-hollow electric guitars, built by luthier Steve Helgeson in Eureka, California. Higher unit sales in the early-1980s. Some models have an optional graphite composite neck built by Modulus.

Eclipse Standard

1979-1983. Figured wood body, offset double cutaway, neck-through, dot markers, standard maple neck. Natural finish.

1979-1983		$1,500	$1,700

MODEL YEAR	FEATURES	EXC. COND. LOW	HIGH

Explorer

1980-1983. Figured wood body, Explorer-style, neck-through, standard maple neck. Natural finish.

1980-1983		$1,500	$1,700

Flaming V

1980-1984. Figured wood body, Flying V-style, neck-through, standard maple neck. Natural finish.

1980-1984		$1,500	$1,700

M-80

1980-1984. Figured wood 335-style body, standard maple or optional graphite neck. Natural finish.

1980s	Optional graphite neck	$2,000	$3,000
1980s	Standard maple neck	$1,500	$1,900

Vulcan Deluxe

1979-1983. Figured maple carved-top body, offset double cutaway, diamond markers, standard maple neck. Natural finish.

1979-1983		$1,600	$2,200

Vulcan Standard

1979-1983. Mahogany carved-top body, offset double cutaway, dot markers, standard maple neck. Natural finish.

1979-1983		$1,500	$2,100

Morales

Ca.1967-1968. Made in Japan by Zen-On. Not heavily imported into the U.S., if at all.

Acoustic Hollowbody Guitars

1967-1968. Various models.

1967		$125	$200

More Harmony

1930s. Private branded by Dobro for Dailey's More Harmony Music Studio. Private branding was common in the 1930s for the Chicago makers, who branded for catalog companies, teaching studios, publishers, and music stores. More Harmony silk-screen logo on the headstock.

More Harmony Dobro

1930s. Fourteen inch wood body with upper bout F-holes and metal resonator.

1930s	Sunburst	$600	$700

Morgaine Guitars

1994-present. Luthier Jorg Tandler builds his professional and premium grade, production/custom electrics in Germany.

Morris

1970s-present. Intermediate, professional and premium grade, production, acoustic guitars imported by Moridaira of Japan. Morris guitars were first imported into the U.S. from the early '70s to around '90. They are again being imported into the U.S. starting in 2001.

MODEL YEAR	FEATURES	EXC. COND. LOW	HIGH

000 Copy

1970s. Brazilian rosewood laminate body, import.

1970s		$300	$400

D-45 Copy

Brazilian laminate body.

1970s		$450	$550

Mortoro Guitars

1992-present. Luthier Gary Mortoro builds his premium grade, custom, archtop guitars in Miami, Florida.

Mosrite

The history of Mosrite has more ups and downs than just about any other guitar company. Founder Semie Moseley had several innovative designs and had his first success, at age 19, building doubleneck guitars for super picker Joe Maphis and protégé Larry Collins. Next came the Ventures, who launched the brand nationally by playing Mosrites and featuring them on album covers. At its '60s peak, the company was turning out around 1,000 guitars a month. The company ceased production in '69, and Moseley went back to playing gospel concerts and built a few custom instruments during the '70s.

In the early-'80s, Mosrite again set up shop in Jonas Ridge, North Carolina, but the plant burned down in November, '83, taking about 300 guitars with it. In early-'92, Mosrite relocated to Booneville, Arkansas, producing a new line of Mosrites, of which 96% were exported to Japan, where the Ventures and Mosrite have always been popular. Semie Moseley died, at age 57, on August 7, '92 and the business carried on until finally closing its doors in '93. The Mosrite line has again been revived by Mosrite of California which offers many reissues.

Throughout much of the history of Mosrite, production numbers were small and model features often changed. As a result, exact production dates are difficult to determine.

Brass Rail

1970s. Double cutaway solidbody, has a brass plate running the length of the fingerboard.

1970s		$800	$950

Celebrity 1

Late-1960s-1970s. Thick hollowbody, two pickups.

1970s	Sunburst	$700	$1,000

Celebrity 2 Standard

Late-1960s-1970s. Thin hollowbody, two pickups. In the 1970s, it came in a Standard and a Deluxe version.

1970s		$700	$1,000

MODEL YEAR	FEATURES	EXC. COND. LOW	HIGH

Celebrity 3

Late-1960s. Thin hollowbody, double cutaway, two pickups, F-holes.

1960s		$700	$1,000

Combo Mark 1

1966-1968. Bound body, one F-hole.

1967		$1,300	$1,700

D-100 Californian

1960s. Double cutaway, resonator guitar with two pickups.

1967		$800	$1,200

D-40 Resonator Guitar

1960s.

1960s		$700	$1,000

Joe Maphis Mark 1

1960s. Double cutaway solidbody, two pickups.

1960s	Natural	$1,000	$1,500

Joe Maphis Mark XVIII

1960s. Six/twelve doubleneck solidbody, double cutaway, two pickups on each neck, Moseley tremolo on six-string.

1960s		$2,000	$3,000

Mosrite 1988

1988-early-1990s. Has traditional Mosrite body styling, Mosrite pickps and bridge.

1988		$500	$800

Ventures 12-String

1966-1968. Double cutaway solidbody, 12 strings.

1967		$1,500	$2,000

Ventures Mark V

1963-1968. Double cutaway solidbody.

1960s		$2,000	$2,500

Ventures Model

1963-1968. Double cutaway solidbody, triple-bound body 1963, no binding after, Vibramute for 1963-1964, Moseley tailpiece 1965-1968.

1963	Blue, bound	$5,000	$7,000
1963	Red, bound	$5,000	$7,000
1963	Sunburst, bound	$4,500	$6,500
1964	Blue, Vibramute	$4,000	$6,500
1964	Red, Vibramute	$4,000	$6,500
1964	Sunburst, Vibramute	$4,000	$6,000
1965	Blue, Moseley tailpiece	$3,000	$4,500
1965	Blue, Vibramute	$4,000	$6,500
1965	Red, Moseley tailpiece	$3,000	$4,500
1965	Red, Vibramute	$4,000	$6,500
1965	Sunburst, Moseley tailpiece	$3,000	$4,000
1965	Sunburst, Vibramute	$4,000	$6,000
1966	Moseley tailpiece	$2,800	$3,800
1967	Moseley tailpiece	$2,500	$3,500
1968	Moseley tailpiece	$2,000	$3,000

'60s Mosrite Celebrity

1960s Mosrite Ventures 12-string

1976 Mossman Southwind

1995 Music Man
Edward Van Halen

MODEL YEAR	FEATURES	EXC. COND. LOW	HIGH

Mossman

1965-present. Professional and premium grade, production/custom, flat-top guitars built in Sulphur Springs, Texas. They have also built acoustic basses. Founded by Stuart L. Mossman in Winfield, Kansas. In '75, fire destroyed one company building, including the complete supply of Brazilian rosewood. They entered into an agreement with C.G. Conn Co. to distribute guitars by '77. 1200 Mossman guitars in a Conn warehouse in Nevada were ruined by being heated during the day and frozen during the night. A disagreement about who was responsible resulted in cash flow problems for Mossman. Production fell to a few guitars per month until the company was sold in '86 to Scott Baxendale. Baxendale sold the company to John Kinsey and Bob Casey in Sulphur Springs in '89.

Flint Hills

1970-mid-1980s. Flat-top acoustic, rosewood back and sides.

1970-1979	$1,400	$1,600

Great Plains

1970-mid-1980s. Flat-top, Indian rosewood, herringbone trim.

1970-1979	$1,400	$1,600

Southwind

1976-ca. 1986, mid-1990s-2002. Flat-top, abalone trim top.

1976-1979	$1,500	$1,700

Tennessee

1975-1979. D-style, spruce top, mahogany back and sides, rope marquetry purfling, rope binding.

1975-1979	$1,200	$1,500

Tennessee 12-String

1975-1979.

1975-1979	$1,200	$1,500

Winter Wheat

1976-1979, mid-1990s-present. Flat-top, abalone trim. Natural finish.

1976-1979	$1,600	$1,800

Winter Wheat 12-String

1976-1979. Twelve-string version of Winter Wheat, Natural.

1976-1979	$1,600	$1,800

Mozzani

Built in shops of Luigi Mozzani (b. March 9, 1869, Faenza, Italy; d. 1943) who opened lutherie schools in Bologna, Cento and Rovereto in 1890s. By 1926 No. 1 and 2 Original Mozzani Model Mandolin (flat back), No. 3 Mandola (flat back), No. 4 6-String Guitar, No. 5 7-, 8-, and 9-String Guitars, No. 6 Lyre-Guitar.

Acoustic Flat-Top Guitars

1920s	$250	$400

Murph

1965-1966. Mid-level electric semi-hollow and solidbody guitars built by Pat Murphy in San Fernado, California. Murph logo on headstock.

Electric Solidbody Guitars

1965-1966	$600	$850

Electric XII

1965-1966	$650	$850

Music Man

1972-present. Professional grade, production, solidbody guitars built in San Luis Obispo, California. They also build basses. Founded by ex-Fender executives Forrest White and Tom Walker in Orange County, California. Music Man originally produced guitar and bass amps based on early Fender ideas using many former Fender employees. They contracted with Leo Fender's CLF Research to design and produce a line of solidbody guitars and basses. Leo Fender began G & L Guitars with George Fullerton in '82. In '84, Music Man was purchased by Ernie Ball and production was moved to San Luis Obispo.

Edward Van Halen

1990-1995. Basswood solidbody, figured maple top, bolt-on maple neck, maple fingerboard, binding, two humbuckers. Named changed to Axis.

1991-1995	$1,800	$2,200

Sabre I

1978-1982. Offset double cutaway solidbody, maple neck, two pickups. Sabre I comes with a flat fingerboard with jumbo frets.

1978-1982	$600	$700

Sabre II

1978-1982. Same as Sabre I, but with an oval 7 1/2" radius fingerboard.

1978-1982	$600	$700

Silhouette

1986-present. Offset double cutaway, contoured beveled solidbody, various pickup configurations.

1987-1995	$750	$850

Steve Morse Model

1987-present. Solidbody, 4 pickups, humbuckers in the neck and bridge positions, 2 single-coils in the middle, special pickup switching, six-bolt neck mounting, maple neck.

1987-1995	$800	$900

Stingray I

1976-1982. Offset double cutaway solidbody, flat fingerboard radius.

1976-1979	$600	$800
1980-1982	$600	$700

Stingray II

1976-1982. Offset double cutaway solidbody, rounder fingerboard radius.

1976-1979	$700	$800
1980-1982	$600	$700

Musicvox

1996-present. Intermediate grade, production, Korean-made retro-vibe guitars and basses from Matt Eichen of Cherry Hill, New Jersey.

GUITARS

MODEL YEAR	FEATURES	EXC. COND. LOW	HIGH

Napolitano Guitars

1993-present. Luthier Arthur Napolitano builds his professional and premium grade, custom, archtop guitars in Allentown, New Jersey.

Nashville Guitar Company

1985-present. Professional and premium grade, custom, flat-top guitars built by luthier Marty Lanham in Nashville, Tennessee. He has also built banjos.

Custom Slide

Weissenborn Hawaiian copy with hollow neck, Natural koa.

1997		$3,000	$3,500

National

Ca. 1927-present. The company was founded in Los Angeles as the National String Instrument Corporation by John Dopyera, George Beauchamp, Ted Kleinmeyer and Paul Barth. In '29 Dopyera left to start the Dobro Manufacturing Company with Rudy and Ed Dopyera and Vic Smith. The Dobro company competed with National until the companies reunited. Beauchamp and Barth then left National to found Ro-Pat-In with Adolph Rickenbacker and C.L. Farr (later becoming Electro String Instrument Corporation, then Rickenbacher). In '32 Dopyera returns to National and National and Dobro start their merger in late-'33, finalizing it by mid-'34. Throughout the '30s, National and Dobro maintained separate production, sales and distribution. National Dobro moved to Chicago '36. In Chicago, archtop and flat top bodies are built primarily by Regal and Kay; after '37 all National resonator guitar bodies made by Kay. L.A. production is maintained until around '37, although some assembly of Dobros continued in L.A. (primarily for export) until '39 when the L.A. offices are finally closed. By ca. '39 the Dobro brand disappears.

In '42, the company's resonator production ceased and Victor Smith, Al Frost and Louis Dopyera buy the company and change name to Valco Manufacturing Company. Post-war production resumes in '46. Valco is purchased by treasurer Robert Engelhardt in '64. In '67, Valco bought Kay, but in '68 the new Valco/Kay company went out of business. In the Summer of '69 the assets, including brandnames, were auctioned off. The National and Supro names were purchased by Chicago-area distributor/importer Strum 'N' Drum (Noble, Norma brands). The National brand is used on copies in early- to mid-'70s, and the brandname went into hiatus by the '80s.

In '88 National Resophonic Guitars is founded in San Luis Obispo, California, by Don Young, with production of National-style resonator guitars beginning in '89 (see following). In the '90s, the National brand also resurfaces on inexpensive Asian imports.

National Resonator guitars are categorized by materials and decoration (from plain to fancy): Duolian, Triolian, Style 0, Style 1, Style 2, Style 3, Style 4, Don #1, Style 97, Don #2, Don #3, Style 35.

National guitars all have serial numbers, which provide clues to date of production. This is a complex issue. This list combines information included in George Gruhn and Walter Carter's *Gruhn's Guide to Vintage Guitars* (Miller Freeman, 1993), which was originally provided by Bob Brozman and Mike Newton, with new information provided by Mike Newton.

Serial	Date
Pre "Chicago" numbers	
A101-A450	1935-1936
"Chicago" numbers	
A prefix (some may not have the prefix)	1936-mid-1997
B prefix	Mid-1937-1938
C prefix	Late-1938-1940
G prefix up to 200	Ea. 1941-ea. 1942
G suffix under 2000	Ea. 1941-ea. 1942
G suffix 2000-3000s (probably old parts)	1943-1945
G suffix 4000s (old parts)	Late 1945-mid-1947
V100-V7500	1947
V7500-V15000	1948
V15000-V25000	1949
V25000-V35000	1950
V35000-V38000	1951
X100-X7000	1951
X7000-X17000	1952
X17000-X30000	1953
X30000-X43000	1954
X43000-X57000	1955
X57000-X71000	1956
X71000-X85000	1957
X85000-X99000	1958
T100-T5000	1958
T5000-T25000	1959
T25000-T50000	1960
T50000-T75000	1961
T75000-T90000	1962
G100-G5000	1962
T90000-T99000	1963
G5000-G15000	1963
G15000-G40000	1964
1 prefix	1965-ea. 1968
2 prefix	Mid-1968

Aragon De Luxe

1939-1942. Archtop with resonator (the only archtop resonator offered), spruce top and maple back and sides.

1939-1942	Light Brown	$4,700	$6,200

Bel-Aire

1953-1961. Single pointed cut archtop, 2 pickups until '57, 3 after, master tone knob and jack, bound body, sunburst.

1953-1961		$700	$900

National Bel-Aire

1955 National Debonaire

GUITARS

1960 National Glenwood

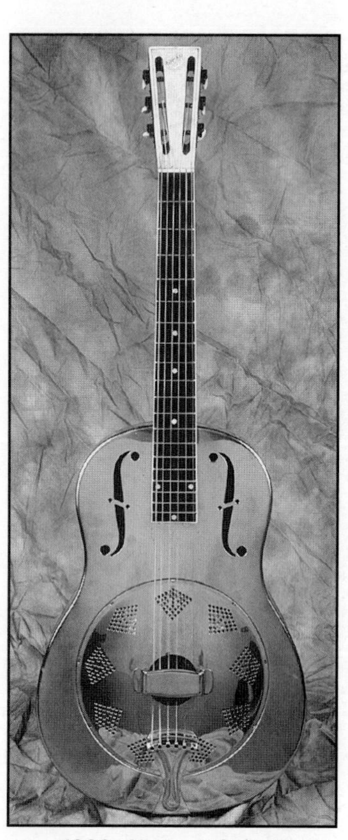
1930s National Style N

MODEL YEAR	FEATURES	EXC. COND. LOW	HIGH

Bluegrass 35

1963-1965. Acoustic, non-cutaway single-cone resonator, Res-O-Glas body in Arctic White.

1963-1965		$600	$800

Bobbie Thomas

Ca.1967-1968. Double cutaway thinline hollowbody, bat-shaped F-holes, two pickups, Bobbie Thomas on pickguard, vibrato.

1967-1968		$300	$550

Bolero

1956-1957. Les Paul-shape, control knobs mounted on pickguard, single pickup, trapeze tailpiece.

1956-1957	Sunburst	$550	$650

California

1949-1955. Electric hollowbody archtop, multi-bound, F-holes, trapeze tailpiece, one pickup. Natural.

1949-1955		$650	$900

Club Combo

1952-1955, 1959-1961. Electric hollowbody archtop, two pickups, rounded cutaway.

1952-1955		$700	$950
1959-1961		$950	$1,000

Don Style 1

1934-1936. Plain body with engraved borders, pearl dot inlay, 14 frets, single-cone.

1934-1936	Silver (nickel-plated)	$2,300	$4,000

Don Style 2

1934-1936. Geometric Art Deco body engraving, 14 frets, single-cone, fancy square pearl inlays and pearloid headstock overlay.

1934-1936	Silver (nickel-plated)	$2,800	$5,000

Don Style 3

1934-1936. Same as Style 2 but more elaborate floral engravings, fancy pearl diamond inlays, 14 frets, single-cone.

1934-1936	Silver (nickel-plated)	$3,500	$6,500

Duolian

1930-1939. Acoustic steel body, frosted paint finish until '36, mahogany-grain paint finish '37-'39, round neck, square neck available in '33, 12-fret neck until 1934 then 14-fret.

1930-1934	Round neck, 12 frets	$2,000	$2,300
1935-1939	Round neck, 14 frets	$1,900	$2,200

Estralita

1934-1942. Acoustic with single-cone resonator, mahogany top and back, F-holes, multi-bound.

1934-1942	Shaded Brown	$800	$1,100

Glenwood

1954-1958. Les Paul-shaped solidbody, wood body, not fiberglass, single cutaway, multi-bound, two pickups. Renamed Glenwood Deluxe with Bigsby in 1959.

1954-1958	Natural	$1,200	$1,300

Glenwood 98

1962-1965. USA map-shaped solidbody of molded Res-O-Glas, 2 regular and 1 bridge pickups, vibrato. Pearl white finish.

1962-1965		$1,800	$2,400

Glenwood 99

1962-1965. USA map-shaped solidbody of molded Res-O-Glas, two regular and one bridge pickups, butterfly inlay. Snow white.

1962-1965		$2,000	$2,900

Glenwood Deluxe

1959-1961. Renamed from Glenwood. Les Paul-shaped solidbody, wood body, not fiberglass, multi-bound, two pickups, vibrato.

1959-1961	Factory Bigsby	$1,200	$1,300

Model 1155

1948-1961. Flat top acoustic with Gibson body, mahogany back and sides, bolt-on neck.

1948-1961		$700	$1,000

Newport 82

1963-1965. Renamed from Val-Pro 82. USA map-shaped Res-O-Glas, one pickup. Red finish.

1963-1965		$1,000	$1,300

Newport 84

1963-1965. Renamed from Val-Pro 84. USA map-shaped Res-O-Glas, one regular and one bridge pickups. Sea Foam Green finish.

1963-1965		$1,100	$1,400

Newport 88

1963-1965. Renamed from Val-Pro 88. USA map-shaped Res-O-Glas, two regular and one bridge pickups. Black finish.

1963-1965		$1,600	$1,900

Reso-phonic

1956-1964. Pearloid-covered, single cut semi-solidbody acoustic, single resonator, maroon or white. Also a non-cut, square neck version was offered, which is included in these values.

1956-1959	White pearloid	$900	$1,000
1960-1964	White pearloid	$800	$950

Silvo (electric Hawaiian)

1937-1941. Nickel-plated metal body, flat-top with small upper bout, F-holes, square neck, two knobs on either side of rectangular pickup, multiple straight line art over dark background on body, Roman numeral parallelogram markers, National badge logo on headstock, Silvo name on coverplate.

1937-1941	Silver	$2,300	$3,500

Studio 66

1961-1964. Electric solidbody of Res-O-Glas, single cutaway, one pickup. Renamed Varsity 66 in 1964.

1961-1964	Beige	$1,100	$1,400

Style O

1930-1942. Acoustic single-cone brass body (early models had a steel body), Hawaiian scene etching, 12-fret neck 1930-1934, 14-fret neck 1935 on, round (all years) or square (1933 on) neck.

1930-1942	Round neck	$3,000	$3,500
1933-1942	Square neck	$2,000	$2,500

MODEL YEAR	FEATURES	EXC. COND. LOW	HIGH

Style 1 Tricone

1927-1943. German silver body tricone resonator, ebony fingerboard, mahogany square (Hawaiian) or round (Spanish) neck, plain body, 12-fret neck until 1934, 14-fret after.

1927-1932	Round neck	$4,000	$6,000
1928-1932	Square neck	$2,500	$3,000

Style 1 Tricone Plectrum

1928-1935. Twenty-six inch scale versus the 23" scale of the tenor.

1928-1935		$2,400	$2,800

Style 1 Tricone Tenor

1928-1935. Tenor, four strings, 23" scale, square neck is Hawaiian, round neck is Spanish.

1928-1935		$2,200	$2,600

Style 2 Tricone

1927-1942. German silver body tricone resonator, Wild Rose engraving, square (Hawaiian) or round (Spanish) neck, 12-fret neck until 1934, 14-fret after.

1930s	Round neck	$9,000	$12,000
1930s	Square neck	$3,000	$4,000

Style 2 Tricone Plectrum

1928-1935. Twenty-six inch scale versus the 23" scale of the tenor.

1928-1935		$4,500	$5,500

Style 2 Tricone Tenor

1928-1935. Tenor.

1928-1935		$4,000	$5,000

Style 3 Tricone

1928-1941. German silver body tricone resonator, Lily-of-the-Valley engraving, square (Hawaiian) or round (Spanish) neck, 12-fret neck until 1934, 14-fret after. Reintroduced with a nickel-plated brass body in 1994.

1930s	Round neck	$14,000	$16,000
1930s	Square neck	$4,000	$6,000

Style 3 Tricone Plectrum

1928-1935. Twenty-six inch scale versus the 23" scale of the tenor.

1928-1935		$6,000	$7,000

Style 3 Tricone Tenor

1928-1939.

1928-1939		$5,500	$6,500

Style 4 Tricone

1928-1940. German silver body tricone resonator, chrysanthemum etching. 12-fret neck until 1934, 14-fret after. Reissued in 1995 with same specs.

1930s	Round neck	$23,000	$25,000
1930s	Square neck	$6,500	$8,000

Style 35

1936-1942. Brass body tricone resonator, sandblasted minstrel and trees scene, 12 frets, square (Hawaiian) or round (Spanish) neck.

1936-1942	Round neck	$6,000	$7,000
1936-1942	Square neck	$3,400	$3,600

Style 97

1936-1940. Nickel-plated brass body tricone resonator, sandblasted scene of female surfrider and palm trees, 12 frets, slotted peghead.

1930s	Square neck	$4,500	$6,000

Style N

1930-1931. Nickel-plated brass body single-cone resonator, plain finish, 12 frets.

1930-1931		$3,000	$3,500

Triolian

1928-1941. Single-cone resonator, wood body replaced by metal body in 1929, 12-fret neck and slotted headstock 1928-1934, changed to 14-fret neck in 1935 and solid headstock in 1936, round or square (1933 on) neck available.

1928-1936	Various colors	$2,500	$2,700
1937	Fake rosewood grain finish	$2,000	$2,400

Trojan

1934-1942. Single-cone resonator wood body, F-holes, bound top, 14-fret neck.

1934-1942	Round neck	$1,100	$1,300

Val-Pro 82

1962-1963. USA map-shaped Res-O-Glas, one pickup, Red finish. Renamed Newport 82 in 1963.

1962-1963	Red	$1,000	$1,400

Val-Pro 84

1962-1963. USA map-shaped Res-O-Glas, one regular and one bridge pickups, Snow White finish. Renamed Newport 84 in 1963.

1962-1963		$1,000	$1,400

Val-Pro 88

1962-1963. USA map-shaped Res-O-Glas, two regular and one bridge pickups, Black finish. Renamed Newport 88 in 1963.

1962-1963		$1,500	$2,000

Varsity 66

1964-1965. Renamed from Studio 66 in 1964. Molded Res-O-Glas, one pickup, two knobs.

1964-1965	Beige	$1,100	$1,400

Westwood 72

1962-1964. USA map-shaped solid hardwood body (not fiberglas), one pickup.

1962-1964	Sunburst	$600	$900

Westwood 75

1962-1964. USA map-shaped solid hardwood body (not fiberglas), one regular and one bridge pickups. Cherry-to-Black Sunburst finish.

1962-1964		$700	$900

Westwood 77

1962-1965. USA map-shaped solid hardwood body (not fiberglas), two regular and one bridge pickups. Cherry finish.

1962-1965		$800	$1,000

National Reso-Phonic

1988-present. Professional and premium grade, production/custom, single cones, basses, acoustic-electrics, tricones, and ukuleles (all with resonators), built in San Luis Obispo, California. McGregor Gaines and Don Young formed the National Reso-Phonic Guitar Company with the objective of building instruments based upon the original National designs.

1962 National Val-Pro 82

National Westwood 75

GUITARS

O'Hagan Twenty Two

Novax Expression Classic

MODEL YEAR	FEATURES	EXC. COND. LOW	HIGH

Reso-Lectric R-2

1993-1996. Thin single-cutaway body with single-cone resonator, maple veneer top, lipstick neck pickup, pearloid or tortoiseshell celluloid pickguard.

1993-1996		$600	$800

Nickerson Guitars

1983-present. Luthier Brad Nickerson builds his professional and premium grade, production/custom, archtop and flat-top guitars in Northampton, Massachusetts.

Noble

Ca. 1950-ca. 1969. Instruments made by others and distributed by Don Noble and Company of Chicago. Plastic-covered guitars made by EKO debut in '62. Aluminum-necked Wandré guitars added to the line in early-'63. By ca. '65-'66 the brandname is owned by Chicago-area importer and distributor Strum 'N' Drum and used mainly on Japanese-made solidbodies. Strum 'N' Drum bought the National brand name in '69 and imported Japanese copies of American designs under the National brand and Japanese original designs under Norma through the early '70s. The Noble brand disappears at least by the advent of the Japanese National brand, if not before.

Acoustic Archtop Guitars

1940-1969. Various models.

1960s		$175	$275

Norma

Ca.1965-1970. Imported from Japan by Strum 'N Drum, Inc. of Chicago (see Noble brand info). Early examples were built by Tombo, most notably sparkle plastic covered guitars and basses.

Electric Solidbodies

1965-1970. Type of finish has affect on value.

1960s	Non-sparkle finish	$150	$350

Sparkle Solidbody

1965-1970.

1960s	Blue, Red or Gold Sparkle	$400	$500

Norman

1972-present. Intermediate grade, production, acoustic and acoustic/electric guitars built in LaPatrie, Quebec. Norman was the first guitar production venture luthier Robert Godin was involved with. He as since added the Seagull, Godin, and Patrick & Simon brands of instruments.

Northworthy Guitars

1987-present. Professional and premium grade, production/custom, flat-tops, electric guitars, basses, and mandolin-family instruments built by luthier Alan Marshall in Ashbourne, Derbyshire, England.

MODEL YEAR	FEATURES	EXC. COND. LOW	HIGH

Norwood

1960s budget imports.

Electric Solidbodies

1960s. Offset double cut body, three soapbar-style pickups, Norwood label on headstock.

1960s		$125	$175

Novax Guitars

1989-present. Luthier Ralph Novak builds his fanned-fret professional and premium grade, production/custom, solidbody and acoustic guitars and basses in San Leandro, California.

Nyberg Instruments

1993-present. Professional grade, custom flat-top and Maccaferri-style guitars, mandolas, bouzoukis, and citterns built by luthier Lawrence Nyberg in Hornby Island, British Columbia.

O'Hagan

1979-1983. Designed by clarinetist and importer Jerol O'Hagan in St. Louis Park, Minnesota. Primarily neck-through construction, most with German-carved bodies. In '81 became Jemar Corporation and in '83 it was closed by the I.R.S., a victim of recession.

SN=YYM(M)NN (e.g., 80905, September '80, 5th guitar); or MYMNNN (e.g., A34006, April 1983, 6th guitar). Approximately 3000 total instruments were made with the majority being NightWatches (approx. 200 Twenty Twos, 100-150 Sharks, 100 Lasers; about 25 with bird's-eye maple bodies).

Laser

1981-1983. Solidbody, double cutaway, maple or walnut body, set-thru neck, three single-coil Schaller pickups.

1981-1983		$350	$550

Shark

1979-1983. Explorer-looking solidbody.

1979-1983		$350	$500

Twenty Two

1980-1983. Flying V copy, two humbuckers.

1980-1983		$350	$500

Oahu

1926-1985, present. The Oahu Publishing Company and Honolulu Conservatory, based in Cleveland, Ohio was active in the sheet music and student instrument business in the '30s. An instrument, set of instructional sheet music, and lessons were offered as a complete package. Lessons were often given to large groups of students. Instruments, lessons, and sheet music could also be purchased by mail order. The Oahu Publishing Co. advertised itself as "The World's Largest Guitar Dealers." Most '30s Oahu guitars were made by Kay.

Guitar Models from the Mid-'30s include: 71K (jumbo square neck), 72K (jumbo roundneck),

MODEL YEAR	FEATURES	EXC. COND. LOW	HIGH

68B (jumbo, vine body decoration), 68K (deluxe jumbo square neck), 69K (deluxe jumbo roundneck), 65K and 66K (mahogany, square neck), 64K and 67K (mahogany, roundneck), 65M (standard-size, checker binding, mahogany), 53K (roundneck, mahogany), 51 (black, Hawaiian scene, pearlette fingerboard), 51K (black, pond scene decoration), 52K (black, Hawaiian scene decoration), 50 and 50K (student guitar, brown). The brand has been revived on a line of tube amps.

Round Neck 14" Flat-Top

1930s. Spruce top, figured maple back and sides, thin logo.

1932		$1,000	$1,400

Style 50K Student Guitar

Student-size guitar, Brown finish.

1935		$200	$250

Style 65M

Standard-size mahogany body, checker binding, Natural Brown.

1933		$250	$350

Style 68K De Luxe Jumbo (square neck)

Hawaiian, 15.5" wide, Brazilian back and sides, spruce top, fancy pearl vine inlay, abalone trim on top and soundhole, rosewood pyramid bridge, fancy pearl headstock inlay, butterbean tuners, ladder-braced, Natural. High-end model made for Oahu by Kay.

1935		$3,500	$4,000

Odessa

1981-1990s. Budget guitars imported by Davitt & Hanser (BC Rich). Mainly acoustics in the '90s, but some electrics early on.

Iceman Copy

1981-mid-1980s. Iceman body, dual humbuckers, checker rope-style top binding, block markers, Sunburst.

1980s		$150	$175

Ohio

Mid-1960s. European solidbodies, most likely made in France or Italy around 1964-'66. Sparkle finish, bolt-on aluminum necks, strings-thru-body design.

Old Kraftsman

Ca. 1930s-ca. 1960s. Brandname used by the Spiegel catalog company for instruments made by other American manufacturers, including Kay and even Gibson. The instruments were of mixed quality, but some better grade instruments were comparable to those offered by Wards.

Archtops

1930s-1960s. Various models.

1930s	17", Stauffer-style headstock	$550	$650
1950s		$275	$375
1960s		$250	$350

MODEL YEAR	FEATURES	EXC. COND. LOW	HIGH

Thin Twin Jimmy Reed Model

1950s		$450	$600

Olson Guitars

1977-present. Luthier James A. Olson builds his presentation grade, custom, flat-tops in Circle Pines, Minnesota.

D Custom

1977-present. D-style, Sitka spruce top, Indian rosewood back and sides, fancy pearl appointments, Natural.

1980		$7,000	$8,000

D Cutaway

1977-present. D-style with sharp cutaway, Sitka spruce top, Indian rosewood back and sides.

1987		$7,000	$8,000

Orpheum

1897-1942, 1944-ca.1967. Orpheum originally was a brandname of Rettberg and Lange, who made instruments for other companies as well. William Rettberg and William Lange bought the facilities of New York banjo maker James H. Buckbee in 1897. Lange went out on his own in '21 to start the Paramount brand. He apparently continued using the Orpheum brand as well. He went out of business in '42. In '44 the brand was acquired by New York's Maurice Lipsky Music Co. who used it primarily on beginner to medium grade instruments, which were manufactured by Regal, Kay, and United Guitar (and maybe others). In the early '60s Lipsky applied the brandname to Japanese imports. Lipsky dropped the name around '67.

Cutaway Thin Electric (Kay Thin Twin K-161)

Introduced 1952-1953 by Kay and also sold as the Orpheum Cutaway Thin Electric. Two tube/bar pickups, four knobs, block markers, curly maple top and back, mahogany sides.

1953	Natural	$550	$600

Orpheum Special (Regal-made)

1930s slot head, Dobro-style wood body, metal resonator.

1930s	Sunburst	$900	$1,100

Ultra Deluxe Professional Cutaway Model 899

1950s. 17" cutaway, two pickups, 2 knobs, maple back and sides, top material varies, dot markers, finishes as follows: E-C copper, E-G gold, E-G-B gold-black sunburst, E-B blond curly maple, E-S golden orange sunburst.

1953	All finishes	$1,200	$2,500

Oscar Schmidt

1879-ca. 1939, 1979-present. Budget and intermediate grade, production, acoustic, acoustic/electric, and electric guitars distributed by Washburn. They also offer mandolins, banjos, and the famous Oscar Schmidt autoharp.

1960 Old Kraftsman

1999 Olson SJ

1978 Ovation Adamas 1687

Ovation Breadwinner

MODEL YEAR	FEATURES	EXC. COND. LOW	HIGH

The original Oscar Schmidt Company, Jersey City, NJ, offered banjo mandolins, tenor banjos, guitar banjos, ukuleles, mandolins and guitars under their own brand and others (including Sovereign and Stella). By the early 1900s, the company had factories in the U.S. and Europe producing instruments. Oscar Schmidt was also an early contributor to innovative mandolin designs and the company participated in the 1900-1930 mandolin boom. The company hit hard times during the Depression and was sold to Harmony by the end of the '30s. In '79, Washburn acquired the brandname.

Stella Model No. 501D

Decalmania top.

1921		$150	$250

Outbound Instruments

1990-2002. Intermediate grade, production, travel-size acoustics from the Boulder, Colorado-based company.

Ovation

1966-present. Intermediate and professional grade, production, acoustic and acoustic/electric guitars built in the U.S. They also build basses and mandolins.

Ovation's parent company, helicopter manufacturer Kaman Corporation, was founded in 1945 by jazz guitarist and aeronautical engineer Charles Huron Kaman in Bloomfield, Connecticut. In the '60s, after losing a government contract, Kaman began looking to diversify. When offers to buy Martin and Harmony were rejected, Kaman decided to use their helicopter expertise (working with synthetic materials, spruce, high tolerances) and designed, with the help of employee and violin restorer John Ringso, the first fiberglass-backed ("Lyracord") acoustic guitars in '65. Production began in '66 and the music factory moved to New Hartford, Connecticut, in '67. Early input was provided by fingerstyle jazz guitarist Charlie Byrd, who gave Kaman the idea for the name "ovation." C. William Kaman II became president of the company in '85. Kaman Music purchased Hamer Guitars in '88, and Trace Elliot amplifiers (U.K.) in '90.

Adamas 1587

1979-1998. Carbon top, walnut, single cutaway, bowl back, binding, mini-soundholes.

1985	Black Sparkle	$1,500	$2,000

Adamas 1687

1977-1998. Acoustic/electric, carbon top, non-cutaway, bowl back, mini-soundholes.

1990	Sunburst	$1,600	$1,700

Adamas II 1881 NB-2

1993-1998. Acoustic/electric, single cutaway, shallow bowl.

1990s	Brown	$1,100	$1,300

MODEL YEAR	FEATURES	EXC. COND. LOW	HIGH

Anniversary Electric 1657

1978. Deep bowl, acoustic/electric, abalone inlays, gold-plated parts, carved bridge, for Ovation's 10th anniversary. They also offered an acoustic Anniversary.

1978		$600	$800

Balladeer Artist 1121 (shallow bowl)

1968-1990. Acoustic, non-cutaway with shallow bowl, bound body.

1972	Natural	$350	$450

Balladeer Custom 1112 (deep bowl)

1976-1990. Acoustic, deep bowl, diamond inlays.

1976-1990	Natural	$400	$500

Balladeer Custom 12-String Electric 1655/1755

1982-1994. Twelve-string version of Balladeer Custom Electric.

1982-1994	Sunburst	$400	$500

Balladeer Custom Electric 1612/1712

1976-1990. Acoustic/electric version of Balladeer Custom, deep bowl.

1976-1990	Natural	$400	$500

Breadwinner 1251

1971-1983. Axe-like shaped single cutaway solidbody, two pickups, textured finish, Black, Blue, Tan or White.

1970s		$450	$650

Celebrity CC-57

1990-1996. Laminated spruce top, shallow bowl, mahogany neck.

1990-1996	Black	$250	$300

Classic 1613/1713

1971-1993. Acoustic/electric, non-cutaway, deep bowl, no inlay, slotted headstock, Gold tuners.

1971-1993	Natural	$500	$600

Classic 1663/1763 (deep bowl)

1982-1998. Acoustic/electric, single cutaway, deep bowl, cedar top, EQ, no inlay, slotted headstock, Gold tuners.

1982-1998		$500	$600

Classic 1863 (shallow bowl)

1989-1998. Acoustic/electric, single cutaway, shallow bowl, no inlay, cedar top, EQ, slotted headstock, Gold tuners.

1989-1998		$550	$650

Contemporary Folk Classic Electric 1616

1974-1990. Acoustic/electric, no inlay, slotted headstock. Natural or Sunburst.

1974-1990	Natural	$300	$400

Country Artist Electric 1624

Introduced in 1971. Acoustic/electric, non-cutaway, shallow bowl, slotted headstock, no inlay, chrome tuners.

1971-1975	Natural	$500	$600

Custom Legend 1659/1759

1980-present. Acoustic/electric, 12 strings, abalone top border, fingerboard binding, abalone floral inlay, Gold tuners. Natural or Sunburst.

1980s		$600	$800

GUITARS

MODEL YEAR	FEATURES	EXC. COND. LOW	HIGH

Deacon 12-String 1253
1975. Axe-shaped solidbody, diamond inlay, two pickups. Only a few made.

1975		$450	$550

Deacon 1252
1973-1980. Axe-shaped solidbody electric, active electronics, diamond fret markers.

1973-1980	Sunburst	$450	$550

Elite 1718 (deep bowl)
1982-1997. Acoustic/electric, non-cutaway, deep bowl, solid spruce top, Adamas-type soundhole, volume and tone controls, stereo output.

1990s	Sunburst	$700	$800

Elite 1768 (deep bowl)
1990-1998. Deep bowl cutaway acoustic/electric.

1990s	Natural	$700	$800

Elite 1868 (shallow bowl)
1983-present. Acoustic/electric, cutaway, shallow bowl.

1990s	Sunburst	$700	$800

Elite Doubleneck
1989-1990s. Six- and twelve-string necks, can be ordered with a variety of custom options.

1989		$700	$900

Glen Campbell 12-String 1118 (K-1118)
1968-1982. Acoustic, 12 strings, shallow bowl version of Legend, Gold tuners, diamond inlay.

1968-1982		$600	$700

Glen Campbell Artist Balladeer 1127
1968-1990. Acoustic, shallow bowl, diamond inlay, Gold tuners.

1970s	Natural	$450	$500

Hurricane 12-String K-1120
1968-1969. ES-335-style electric semi-hollowbody, double cutaway, 12 strings, F-holes, two pickups.

1968-1969		$400	$500

Josh White 1114
1967-1970, 1972-1983. Designed by and for folk and blues singer Josh White, has wide 12-fret to the body neck, dot markers, classical-style tuners.

1967-1970		$500	$700
1972-1983		$400	$600

Legend 1117
1967-1999. Deep bowl acoustic, five-ply top binding, Gold tuners, various colors (most Natural).

1976-1999		$400	$500

Legend 12-String 1866

1989-present. Acoustic/electric, cutaway, 12 strings, shallow bowl, five-ply top binding.

1990	Black	$600	$700

Legend 1869

1990s	Natural	$600	$800

Legend Cutaway 1667
1982-1996. Acoustic/electric, cutaway, deep bowl, abalone, Gold tuners.

1982-1989		$500	$700
1990-1996		$500	$700

MODEL YEAR	FEATURES	EXC. COND. LOW	HIGH

Legend Electric 1617
1972-1998. Acoustic/electric, deep bowl, abalone, Gold tuners, various colors.

1972-1998		$400	$500

Pacemaker 12-String Electric 1615
1972-late-1970s.

1972-1977		$600	$700

Patriot Bicentennial
*1976. Limited run of 1776 guitars, Legend Custom model with drum and flag decal and "1776*1976" decal on lower bout.*

1976		$700	$900

Pinnacle
1990-1992. Spruce or sycamore top, broad leaf pattern rosette, mahogany neck, piezo bridge pickup.

1990-1992	Sunburst	$400	$500

Pinnacle Shallow Cutaway
1990-1994. Pinnacle with shallow bowl body and single cutaway.

1990-1994	Sunburst	$450	$550

Preacher 12-String 1285
1975-1983. Double cutaway solidbody, 12 strings, two pickups.

1975-1983		$400	$500

Preacher 1281
1975-1982. Solidbody, mahogany body, double cutaway, two pickups.

1975-1982		$400	$500

Preacher Deluxe 1282
1975-1982. Double cutaway solidbody, two pickups with series/parallel pickup switch and mid-range control.

1975-1982		$450	$550

Thunderhead 1460
1968-1972. Double cutaway, two pickups, Gold hardware, phase switch, master volume, separate tone controls, pickup balance/blend control, vibrato.

1968-1972		$350	$450

Tornado 1260
1968-1973. Same as Thunderhead without phase switch, with chrome hardware.

1968-1973		$400	$500

UK II 1291
1980-1982. Single cutaway solidbody, two pickups, body made of Urelite on aluminum frame.

1980-1982		$600	$800

Ultra GS
Various colors.

1985		$175	$225

Viper 1271
1975-1982. Single cutaway, two single-coil pickups.

1975-1982		$350	$450

Viper EA 68
1994-present. Thin acoustic/electric, single cutaway mahogany body, spruce top over sound chamber with multiple upper bout soundholes.

1990s	Black	$600	$700

Ovation Deacon 12-string

Ovation Tornado

1996 Parker Fly

1996 P-44

MODEL YEAR	FEATURES	EXC. COND. LOW	HIGH

Viper III 1273

1975-1982. Single cutaway, three single-coil pickups.

1975-1982		$400	$500

P. W. Crump Company

1975-present. Luthier Phil Crump builds his custom flat-tops and mandolin-family instruments in Arcata, California.

Palen

1998-present. Premium grade, production/custom, archtop guitars built by luthier Nelson Palen in Beloit, Kansas.

Pantheon Guitars

2000-present. Patrick Theimer created Pantheon which offers premium grade, production/custom, flat-tops built by seven luthiers (including Dana Bourgeois) working in an old 1840s textile mill in Lewiston, Maine.

Paramount

1930s. Private brand made by Martin for the banjo company.

Style L

1930s. Small body with resonator added, limited production to about 36 instruments.

1930s		$3,000	$3,500

Parker

1992-present. Intermediate, professional, and premium grade, production/custom, solidbody guitars featuring a thin skin of carbon and glass fibers bonded to a wooden guitar body. They also build basses. Located northwest of Boston, Parker was founded by Ken Parker and Larry Fishman. Korg USA committed money to get the Fly Deluxe model into production. Production started July '93. The Parker Custom Shop opended January 1, 2003.

Concert

1997 only. Solid Sitka spruce top, only piezo system pickup, no magnetic pickups. Transparent Butterscotch.

1997		$1,300	$1,400

Fly Artist

1998-1999. Solid Sitka spruce top, vibrato, Deluxe-style electronics. Transparent Blond finish.

1998-1999		$1,600	$1,800

Fly Classic

1996-1998, 2000-present. One-piece Honduras mahogany body, basswood neck, electronics same as Fly Deluxe.

1996-1998	Transparent Cherry	$1,000	$1,200
2000-2002	Transparent Cherry	$1,100	$1,300

Fly Deluxe

1993-present. Ultra-thin poplar body, basswood neck, two pickups a Fishman transducer in bridge, various colors. The guitar weighs only five pounds. Early models, '93-'96, were offered with or without vibrato, then the non-vibrato model was discontinued. The Deluxe normally came with a quality gig bag, but also offered with a hardshell case, which would add about $50 to the values listed.

1993-1999		$800	$1,000

Fly Supreme

1996-1999. One-piece flame maple body, electronics same as the Fly Deluxe, includes hard molded case.

1996-1999	Highly flamed Butterscotch	$2,000	$2,500

NiteFly/NiteFly NFV1/NFV3/NFV5

1996-1999. Three single-coil pickups NiteFly, Fishman piezo system, bolt-on neck, maple body for '96-'98, ash for '99, various colors. Called the NiteFly in '96, NiteFly NFV1 ('97-'98), NiteFly NFV3 ('98), NiteFly NFV5 ('99).

1996-1999		$500	$600

NiteFly/NiteFly NFV2/NFV4/NFV6/SA

1996-present. Two single-coil and one humbucker pickup NiteFly, Fishman piezo system, bolt-on neck, maple body for '96-'98, ash for '99-present, various colors. Called the NiteFly in '96, NiteFly NFV2 ('97-'98), NiteFly NFV4 ('98), NiteFly NFV6 ('99), NiteFly SA (2000-present).

1990s		$600	$700

P-38

2000-present. NiteFly-style ash body, bolt-on maple neck, rosewood board, vibrato, piezo bridge pickup and active Parker Alnico humbucker and two single-coils, gig bag, various colors.

2000		$400	$450

P-44

2002-present. NiteFly-style mahogany body, flamed maple top, bolt-on maple neck, rosewood board, vibrato, piezo bridge pickup and two special Parker humbucker pickups, various colors.

2002	Sunburst	$450	$550

Tulipwood Limited Edition

1998. Limited build of 35 guitars, standard Deluxe features with tulipwood body.

1998		$1,300	$1,400

Paul Reed Smith

1985-present. Intermediate, professional and premium grade, production/custom, solid and semi-hollow body guitars made in the U.S. and imported. They also build basses. Paul Reed Smith built his first guitar in '75 as an independent study project in college and refined his design over the next 10 years. After building two prototypes and getting several orders from east coast guitar dealers, Smith was able to secure the support necessary to start PRS. The initial PRS models retailed around the $2,000 price point, which was an untapped market in the mid-'80s. This market plan worked extremely well as PRS soon became a significant player in the OEM guitar market. In 2001 PRS introduced the Korean-made SE Series.

MODEL YEAR	FEATURES	EXC. COND. LOW	HIGH

10th Anniversary

1995. Only 200 made, offset double cut, carved maple figured top, mahogany body, ebony board, mother-of-pearl inlays, abalone purfling, gold McCarty pickups, either 22-fret wide-fat or wide-thin mahogany neck, 10th Anniversary logo.

1995		$3,500	$4,500

Artist II/Artist 22

1993-1995. Curly maple top, mahogany body and neck, maple purfling on rosewood 'board, inlaid maple bound headstock, abalone birds, 22 frets, gold hardware. Short run of less than 500 instruments.

1993-1995		$3,000	$3,500

Artist Limited

1994-1995. Like the Artist II with 14-Carat gold bird inlays, abalone purfling on neck, headstock and truss rod cover, Brazilian rosewood 'board. 165 made.

1994-1995		$4,500	$5,000

Artist/Artist I/Artist 24

1991-1994. Carved maple top, offset double cut mahogany body, 24-fret neck, bird markers, less than 500 made. A different Custom 24 Artist package was subsequently offered in the 2000s.

1991-1994		$3,500	$4,000

CE 22

1994-2000. Double cut carved alder (1995) or mahogany (post 1995) body, bolt-on maple neck with rosewood 'board, dot inlays, two humbuckers, chrome hardware, translucent colors. Options include vibrato and gold hardware and custom colors.

1994-2000	Standard features	$1,100	$1,400
1994-2000	Upgrade options	$1,400	$1,600

CE 22 Maple Top

1994-present. CE 22 with figured maple top, upgrade options included gold hardware, custom colors or 10 top.

1994-1999	Standard features	$1,400	$1,700
1994-1999	Upgrade options	$1,700	$2,000

CE 24 (Classic Electric, CE)

1988-2000. Double cut alder body, carved top, 24-fret bolt-on maple neck, two humbuckers, dot inlays. Upgrade options included gold hardware, custom colors or 10 top.

1988-1989	Standard features	$1,100	$1,400
1988-2000	Upgrade options	$1,400	$1,600
1990-1999	Standard features	$1,200	$1,400

CE 24 Maple Top (CE Maple Top)

1989-present. CE 24 with figured maple top, 24-fret fingerboard, upgrade options may include any or all the following: Gold hardware, custom colors or 10 top.

1989-2000	Standard features	$1,400	$1,700
1989-2000	Upgrade options	$1,700	$2,000

Custom (Custom 24/PRS Custom)

1985-present. Double cut solidbody, curly maple top, mahogany back and neck, pearl and abalone moon inlays, 24 frets, two humbuckers, trem. Options include quilted or 10 Top, bird inlays, and gold hardware.

MODEL YEAR	FEATURES	EXC. COND. LOW	HIGH
1985	Standard features	$4,000	$5,500
1985	Upgrade options	$4,500	$6,000
1986	Standard features	$3,700	$5,000
1986	Upgrade options	$4,200	$5,500
1987	Standard features	$3,500	$4,500
1987	Upgrade options	$4,000	$5,000
1988	Standard features	$3,000	$3,500
1988	Upgrade options	$4,000	$4,500
1989	Standard features	$2,500	$3,000
1989	Upgrade options	$3,500	$4,000
1990	Upgrade options	$3,000	$3,500
1991	Upgrade options	$2,900	$3,400
1992	Upgrade options	$2,000	$2,500
1993	Upgrade options	$2,000	$2,400
1994	Upgrade options	$1,900	$2,400
1995	Upgrade options	$1,900	$2,300
1996	Standard features	$1,500	$2,000
1996-1999	Upgrade options	$1,800	$2,300
2000-2001	Upgrade options	$1,900	$2,300

Custom 22 (mahogany)

1993-present. Offset double cut solid mahogany body, 22-fret set-neck, opaque finish, chrome hardware, upgrade options include gold hardware and/or custom color.

1993-1999		$1,400	$1,800

Custom 22 (maple top)

1993-present. Custom 22 with flamed or quilted maple top on mahogany body, 22-fret set-neck, upgrade option is gold hardware. Normally the quilt top is higher than flamed top.

1993-1999	Standard features	$1,600	$2,000
1993-1999	Upgrade options	$1,900	$2,400

Custom 24 (walnut)

1992. Two made, seamless matched walnut over mahogany.

1992		$4,500	$5,500

Dragon I

1992. 22 frets, PRS Dragon pickups, wide-fat neck, gold hardware, board inlay of a dragon made of 201 pieces of abalone, turquoise and mother-of-pearl. Limited production of 50 guitars.

1992		$18,000	$21,000

Dragon II

1993. 22 frets, PRS Dragon pickups, wide-fat neck, gold hardware, fingerboard inlay of a dragon made of 218 pieces of gold, coral, abalone, malachite, onyx and mother-of-pearl. Limited production of 100 guitars.

1993		$15,000	$18,000

Dragon III

1994. Carved maple top, mahogany back, 22 frets, PRS Dragon pickups, wide-fat neck, gold hardware, fingerboard inlay of a dragon made of 438 pieces of gold, red and green abalone, mother-of-pearl, mammoth ivory, and stone. Limited production of 100 guitars.

1994		$15,000	$18,000

PRS Custom 22

PRS Custom 24

1993 PRS Dragon II

2002 PRS Single Cut

MODEL YEAR	FEATURES	EXC. COND. LOW	HIGH

EG 3

1990-1991. Double cut solidbody, bolt-on 22-fret neck, three single-coil pickups.

1990-1991	Flamed 10 top	$1,300	$1,500
1990-1991	Opaque finish	$900	$1,100

EG 4

1990-1991. Similar to EG 3 with single/single/hum pickup configuration.

1990-1991		$1,100	$1,300

EG II

1991-1995. Double cut solidbody, bolt-on neck, 3 single-coils, single/single/humbucker, or hum/single/hum pickup options.

1991-1995		$1,100	$1,250

EG II Maple Top

1991-1995. EG II with figured maple top, chrome hardware.

1993		$1,500	$1,700

Golden Eagle

1997-1998. Very limited production, eagle head and shoulders carved into lower bouts, varied high-end appointments.

1997-1998		$18,000	$26,000

Limited Edition

1989-1991, 2000. Double cut, semi-hollow mahogany body, figured cedar top, gold hardware, less than 300 made. In 2000, single cut, short run of five Antique White and five Black offered via Garrett Park Guitars.

2000	White, single cutaway	$2,200	$2,400

McCarty Archtop (spruce)

1998-2000. Deep mahogany body, archtop, spruce top, 22-fret set-neck.

1998-2000	Chrome hardware	$1,800	$2,400
1998-2000	Gold hardware	$1,900	$2,500

McCarty Archtop Artist

1998-2002. Highest grade figured maple top and highest appointments.

1998	Gold hardware	$4,500	$5,500

McCarty Hollowbody (spruce)

2000-present. Similar to Hollowbody I.

2000	Standard features	$1,700	$2,100
2000	Upgrade options	$2,000	$2,300

McCarty Hollowbody II

1998-present. Medium deep mahogany hollowbody, figured maple top, 22-fret set-neck, chrome hardware.

1998-2001		$2,500	$3,500

McCarty Hollowbody/Hollowbody I

1998-present. Medium deep mahogany hollowbody, spruce top, 22-fret set-neck, chrome hardware.

1998-1999	Standard features	$1,700	$2,300
1998-1999	Upgrade options	$2,000	$2,600

McCarty Model

1994-present. Mahogany body with figured maple top, upgrade options may include a 10 top, Gold hardware, bird inlays.

1994-1999	Standard features	$1,600	$2,000
1994-1999	Upgrade options	$2,000	$2,300

MODEL YEAR	FEATURES	EXC. COND. LOW	HIGH

McCarty Soapbar (maple)

1998-present. Soapbar with figured maple top option, nickel hardware.

1998		$1,900	$1,700

McCarty Soapbar/Soapbar Standard

1998-present. Solid mahogany body, P-90-style 'soapbar' pickups, 22-fret set-neck, nickel-plated hardware, upgrade options may include gold hardware and bird inlays.

1994-1999	Standard features	$1,500	$1,700
1994-1999	Upgrade options	$1,700	$1,900

PRS Guitar

1985-1986. Set-neck, solid mahogany body, 24-fret 'board, two humbuckers, chrome hardware, renamed Standard from '87-'98 then Standard 24 from '98. PRS with opaque finish and matching headstock.

1985-1986	Sunburst	$4,000	$5,000

Rosewood Ltd.

1996. Mahogany body with figured maple top, one-piece rosewood neck with ultra-deluxe tree-of-life neck inlay, Gold hardware.

1996	Tree-of-life inlay	$9,000	$10,000

Santana

1995-1998. Solid-mahogany body, slightly wider lower bout than other models, figured maple top, 24-fret set-neck, symmetric Santana headstock versus usual PRS offset headstock design, unique body purfling at bookmatch glue joint and between pickup mounts, chrome and nickel-plated hardware, limited production special order.

1995-1998	Yellow	$5,000	$8,000

Santana II

1998-present. Three-way toggle replaces former dual mini-switches, special order only.

1998-1999	Yellow	$4,000	$4,300

Santana SE

2001-present. Solid mahogany body, set mahogany neck, 2 humbuckers, thin diagonal line position markers.

2001-2002		$375	$400

Signature/PRS Signature

1987-1991. PRS-shape solid mahogany body with figured maple top, set-neck, 24 frets. Hand-signed signature on headstock. Limited run of 1,000 guitars.

1987-1991		$4,500	$5,500

Single Cut

2000-present. Single cutaway design, mahogany body, maple top, 22-fret fingerboard, upgrade options include 10 top flamed maple, gold hardware, bird inlays.

2000-2001	Standard features	$1,600	$1,800
2000-2001	Upgrade options	$1,900	$2,100

Standard

1987-1998. Set-neck model, solid mahogany body, 24-fret fingerboard, dual humbucker pickups, chrome hardware. Originally called PRS Guitar from 1985-1986 (see that listing). Renamed Standard 24 from 1998.

MODEL YEAR	FEATURES	EXC. COND. LOW	HIGH
1987-1989		$1,500	$2,000
1987-1989	Limited custom color	$2,000	$2,500
1990-1998		$1,200	$1,500

Standard 22

1994-present. Solid mahogany body, 22-fret set-neck.

1994-1999		$1,400	$1,600

Standard 24

1998-present. Renamed from Standard, solid mahogany body, 24-fret set-neck.

1998-1999		$1,400	$1,600

Studio Maple Top

1990-1991. Mahogany solidbody, bird fingerboard inlays, two single-coil and one humbucking pickups, tremolo, transparent finish.

1990-1991		$2,000	$2,300

Swamp Ash Special

1996-present. Solid swamp ash body, 22-fret bolt-on maple neck, three pickups, upgrade options available.

1996-1999	Figured maple neck option	$1,300	$1,600

Tremonti SE (import)

2002-present. Single cut, contoured mahogany body, 2 humbuckers, stop tailpiece.

2002-2003		$375	$425

Pawar

1999-present. Founded by Jay Pawar, Jeff Johnston and Kevin Johnston in Willoughby Hills, Ohio, Pawar builds professional and premium grade, production/custom, solidbody guitars that feature the Pawar Positive Tone System with over 20 single coil and humbucker tones.

Stage Turn of the Century

1999-present. Chambered swamp ash double cut solidbody, figured maple top, bass-side scroll horn, set-neck.

2000		$1,400	$1,500

Peavey

1965-present. Headquartered in Meridan, Mississippi, Peavey builds budget, intermediate, professional, and premium grade, production/custom, electric guitars. They also build basses, amps, PA gear, effects and drums. Hartley Peavey's first products were guitar amps. He added guitars to the mix in '78.

Axcelerator/AX

1994-1998. Offset double cutaway swamp ash or poplar body, bolt-on maple neck, dot markers, AX with locking vibrato, various colors.

1994-1998		$300	$350

Defender

1994-1995. Double cutaway, solid poplar body, two humbuckers and one single-coil pickup, locking Floyd Rose tremolo, metallic or pearl finish.

1994-1995		$125	$175

Destiny

1989-1992. Double cutaway, mahogany body, maple top, neck-through-bridge, maple neck, three integrated pickups, double locking tremolo.

1989-1992		$250	$325

Destiny Custom

1989-1992. Destiny with figured wood and higher-end appointments, various colors.

1989-1992		$375	$475

Detonator AX

1995-1998. Double cut, maple neck, rosewood board, dot markers, hum/single/hum pickups.

1995-1998	Black	$300	$350

EVH Wolfgang

1996-present. Offset double cutaway arched top body, bolt-on neck, offered with stop tailpiece or Floyd Rose vibrato. Also offered with quilted or flamed maple top upgrade option.

1996-1999	Flamed maple	$600	$800
1996-1999	Standard top	$500	$700

EVH Wolfgang Special

1997-present. Offset double cutaway lower-end Wolfgang model, various opaque finishes, flamed top optional.

1997-1999	Flamed maple top	$500	$600
1997-1999	Standard finish	$400	$500

Falcon/Falcon Active/Falcon Custom

1987-1992. Double cut, three pickups, passive or active electronics, Kahler locking vibrato.

1987-1992	Custom color	$200	$250
1987-1992	Standard color	$150	$200

Firenza

1994-1999. Offset double cutaway, bolt-on neck, single-coil pickups.

1994-1999		$200	$300

Firenza AX

1994-1999. Upscale Firenza Impact with humbucking pickups.

1994-1999		$300	$400

Generation S-1/S-2

1988-1994. Single cutaway, maple cap on mahogany body, bolt-on maple neck, six-on-a-side tuners, active single/hum pickups, S-2 with locking vibrato system.

1988-1994		$250	$300

Horizon/Horizon II

1983-1985. Extended pointy horns, angled lower bout, maple body, rear routing for electronics, two humbucking pickups. Horizon II has added 'blade' pickup.

1983-1985		$150	$200

Hydra Doubleneck

1985-1989. Available as a custom order, 12/6-string necks each with two humbuckers, three-way pickup select.

1985-1989		$350	$450

Impact 1/Impact 2

1985-1987. Offset double cutaway, Impact 1 has higher-end synthetic fingerboard, Impact 2 with conventional rosewood fingerboard.

1985-1987		$200	$250

Pawar Stage

1999 Peavey Wolfgang Special

GUITARS

Peavey Razer

1978 Peavey T-60

MODEL YEAR	FEATURES	EXC. COND. LOW	HIGH

Mantis

1984-1989. Hybrid X-shaped solidbody, one humbucking pickup, trem, laminated maple neck.

1984-1989		$175	$225

Milestone 12-String

1985-1986. Double offset cutaway, 12 strings.

1985-1986		$175	$225

Milestone/Milestone Custom

1983-1986. Offset double cutaway.

1983-1986		$150	$200

Mystic

1983-1989. Double cutaway, two pickups, stop tailpiece initially, later Power Bend vibrato, maple body and neck.

1983-1989		$150	$200

Nitro I Active

1988-1990. Active electronics.

1988-1990		$250	$300

Nitro I/II/III

1986-1989. Offset double cutaway, banana-style headstock, one humbucker (I), two humbuckers (II), or single/single/hum pickups (III).

1986-1989	Nitro I	$150	$200
1986-1989	Nitro II	$175	$225
1986-1989	Nitro III	$200	$250

Odyssey

1990-1994. Single cutaway, figured carved maple top on mahogany body, humbuckers.

1990-1994		$500	$600

Patriot

1983-1987. Double cut, single bridge humbucker.

1983-1987		$100	$150

Patriot Plus

1983-1987. Double cut, two humbucker pickups, bi-laminated maple neck.

1983-1987		$150	$175

Patriot Tremolo

1986-1990. Double cut, single bridge humbucker, tremolo, replaced the standard Patriot.

1986-1990		$100	$175

Predator/Predator AX/Predator DX

1985-1988, 1990-2000. Double cut poplar body, two pickups until '87, three after, vibrato.

1985-1988		$150	$200
1990-2000		$150	$225

Raptor

1997-present. Offset double cut solidbody, 3 single-coils, 2 knobs and toggle.

1997-2002		$120	$130

Razer

1983-1989. Double cutaway with arrowhead point for lower bout, two pickups, one volume and two tone controls, stop tailpiece or vibrato.

1983-1989		$200	$250

T-15

1981-1983. Offset double cutaway, bolt-on neck, dual ferrite blade single-coil pickups.

1981-1983	Natural	$150	$200

MODEL YEAR	FEATURES	EXC. COND. LOW	HIGH

T-15 Amp-In-Case

1981-1983. Amplifier built into guitar case and T-15 guitar.

1981-1983		$200	$300

T-25

1979-1985. Synthetic polymer body, two pickups, Cream pickguard. Sunburst finish.

1979-1985		$150	$200

T-25 Special

1979-1985. Same as T-25, but with super high output pickups, phenolic fingerboard, Black/White/Black pickguard. Ebony Black finish.

1982		$150	$200

T-26

1982-1986. Same as T-25, but with three single-coil pickups and five-way switch.

1982-1986		$175	$225

T-27

1981-1983. Offset double cutaway, bolt-on neck, dual ferrite blade single-coil pickups.

1981-1983		$175	$225

T-30

1982-1985. Short-scale, three single-coil pickups, five-way select. By 1983 amp-in-case available.

1982-1985		$150	$175

T-60

1978-1988. Contoured offset double cutaway, ash body, six-in-line tuners, two humbuckers, through-body strings. By 1987 maple bodies. Finishes include Natural, Sunburst and some Black.

1978-1988		$175	$200

T-1000 LT

1992-1994. Double cutaway, two single-coils and humbucker with coil-tap.

1992-1994		$175	$225

Tracer Custom

1989-1990. Tracer with two single/hum pickups and extras.

1989-1990		$150	$200

Tracer/Tracer II

1987-1994. Offset scooped double cutaway with extended pointy horns, poplar body, one pickup, Floyd Rose.

1987-1994		$125	$175

Vandenberg Quilt Top

1989-1994. Designed by Whitesnake's Adrian Vandenberg, two humbuckers, glued-in neck, quilted maple top, mahogany body and neck.

1989-1994		$600	$800

Vandenberg Signature

1988-1994. Double cut, reverse headstock, bolt-on neck, locking vibrato, various colors.

1988-1994		$500	$700

Vortex I/Vortex II

1986. Streamlined Mantis with two pickups, three-way, Kahler locking vibrato. Vortex II has Randy Rhoads Sharkfin V.

1986		$200	$250

MODEL YEAR	FEATURES	EXC. COND. LOW	HIGH

Pegasus Guitars and Ukuleles

1977-present. Premium grade, custom steel-string guitars built by luthier Bob Gleason in Kurtistown, Hawaii, who also builds ukulele family instruments.

Pennco

Ca. 1974-1978. Generally high quality Japanese-made copies of American acoustic, electric and bass guitars. Probably (though not certainly) imported into Philadelphia during the copy era. Includes Martin- and Gibson-style dreadnoughts with laminated woods, bolt-neck copies of the Gibson Les Paul, Fender Stratocaster, Telecaster and Rickenbacker 4001 bass, mandolins and banjos.

Acoustic Flat-Tops

1974-1978. Various models.

1974-1978		$150	$200

Electric Solidbodies

1970s. Japanese copy, SG body.

1970s		$200	$250

Pensa (Pensa-Suhr)

1982-present. Premium grade, production/custom, solidbody guitars built in the U.S. They also build basses. Rudy Pensa, of Rudy's Music Shop, New York City, started building Pensa guitars in '82. In '85 he teamed up with John Suhr to build Pensa-Suhr instruments. Name changed back to Pensa in '96.

MK 1 (Mark Knopfler)

1985-present. Offset double cut solidbody, carved flamed maple bound top, 2 single-coils and 1 humbucker, gold hardware, dot markers, bolt-on neck.

1985-1992		$1,800	$2,200

Suhr Custom

1985-1989. Two-piece maple body, bolt-on maple neck with rosewood fingerboard. Custom order basis with a variety of woods and options available.

1985-1989	Flamed maple top	$1,600	$2,000

Suhr Standard

1985-1989. Double cut, single/single/hum pickup configuration, opaque solid finish normally, dot markers.

1985-1989		$1,200	$1,400

Perry Guitars

1982-present. Premium grade, production/custom, classical guitars and lutes built by luthier Daryl Perry in Winnipeg, Manitoba.

Petillo Masterpiece Guitars

1965-present. Luthiers Phillip J. and David Petillo build their intermediate, professional and premium grade, custom, steel-string, nylon-string, 12-string, resonator, archtop, and Hawaiian guitars in Ocean, New Jersey.

Petros Guitars

1992-present. Premium grade, production/custom, flattop, 12-string, and nylon-string guitars built by luthier Bruce Petros in Kaukauna, Wisconsin.

Phantom Guitar Works

1992-present. Intermediate grade, production/custom, classic Phantom, Teardrop and Mandoguitar shaped solid and hollowbody guitars and basses assembled in Clatskanie, Oregon. Phantom was established by Jack Charles, former lead guitarist of the band Quarterflash.

Pimentel and Sons

1951-present. Luthiers Lorenzo Pimentel and sons build their professional, premium and presentation grade, flattop, jazz, cutaway electric, and classical guitars in Albuquerque, New Mexico.

Pleasant

Late 1940s-ca.1966. Solidbody electric guitars, obviously others. Japanese manufacturer. Probably not imported into the U.S.

Electric Solidbodies

1940s-1966. Various models.

1950s		$125	$200

Prairie State

Mid-1920s. Larson Brothers brand, basically a derivative of Maurer & Company, but advertised as "a new method of guitar construction." The Prairie State equivalent models were slightly more expensive than the Maurer models (on average 5% to 10% more). Prairie State guitars were also promoted "reinforced with steel" and "the tube or support near the top withstands the strain of the strings, leaving the top or sound-board free and resilient." One or more steel tubes are noticable running from the neck block to the tail block, when looking through the round soundhole. These guitars were advertised as being suitable for playing steel (high nut and steel strings). Steel strings were the rage in the 1920s (re: Martin finally converting all guitar models to steel strings by 1928).

1932 Prairie State Catalog Models - description and prices:

Style 225 Concert $65.00
Style 425 Auditorium $70.00
Style 426 Style 425 Steel $70.00
Style 427 Reinforced Neck $75.00
Style 428 Style 427 Steel $75.00
Style 235 Concert with trim $80.00
Style 335 Grand Concert + trim $83.00
Style 435 Auditorium with trim $85.00
Style 340 Grand Concert fancy $90.00
Style 350 Grand Concert fancy $97.00
Style 440 Auditorium fancy trim $93.00
Style 450 Auditorium fancy trim $100.00

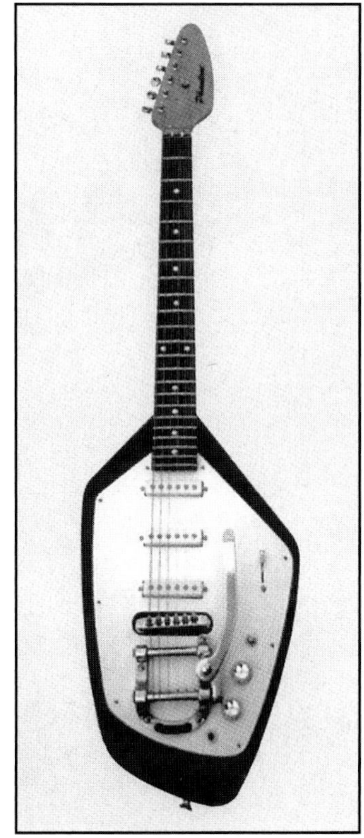

Phantom Guitar

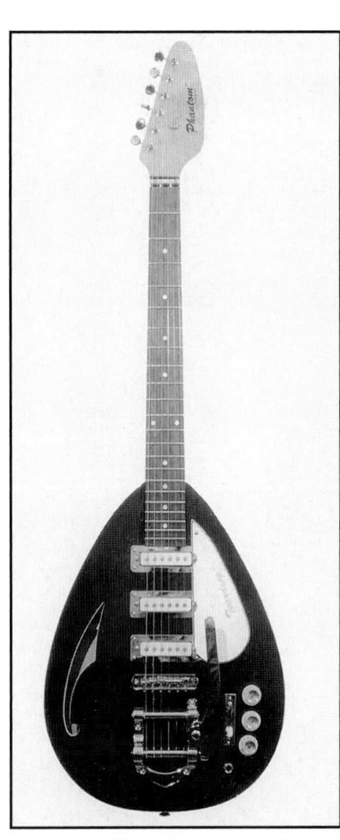

Phantom Teardrop Hollowbody

GUITARS

1959 Premier Custom

Premier Deluxe E-621

MODEL YEAR	FEATURES	EXC. COND. LOW	HIGH

Small Higher-End Flat-Top
Mid-1920s. Spruce top, 13 5/8" scale, Brazilian rosewood back and sides, high-end pearl appointments, slotted headstock.

1925	Natural	$4,000	$5,000

Premier
Ca.1938-ca.1975, 1990s-present. Currently budget and intermediate grade, production, import guitars and basses.

Brands originally offered by Premier include Premier, Multivox, Marvel, Belltone and Strad-O-Lin. Produced by Peter Sorkin Music Company in Manhattan, New York City, NY, who began in Philadelphia, relocating to NYC in '35. First radio-sized amplifiers and stick-on pickups for acoustic archtops were introduced by '38. After World War II, they set up the Multivox subsidiary to manufacture amplifiers ca. '46. First flat-top with pickup appeared in '46.

Most acoustic instruments made by United Guitar Corporation in Jersey City, NJ. Ca. 1957 Multivox acquires Strad-O-Lin. Ca.'64-'65 their Custom line guitars are assembled with probably Italian bodies and hardware, Japanese electronics, possibly Egmond necks from Holland. By ca. '74-'75, there were a few Japanese-made guitars, then Premier brand goes into hiatus.

The rights to the Premier brandname are held by Entertainment Music Marketing Corporation in New York. The Premier brand reappears on some Asian-made solidbody guitars and basses beginning in the '90s. In-depth model details are provided by John Brinkmann.

Bantam Custom
1950s-1960s. Model below Special, single cutaway archtop, dot markers, early models with White potted pickups, then metal-covered pickups, and finally Japanese-made pickups (least valued).

1950s		$550	$650
1960s		$550	$650

Bantam Deluxe
1950s-1960s. Single cutaway archtop, fully bound, sparkle knobs, early models with white potted pickups, then metal-covered pickups, and finally Japanese-made pickups (least valued), block markers, single or double pickups (deduct $100 for single pickup instrument).

1950s	Blond	$1,000	$1,200
1950s	Sunburst	$900	$1,000
1960s	Blond	$1,000	$1,200
1960s	Sunburst	$900	$1,000

Bantam Special
1950s-1960s. Model below Deluxe, single cutaway archtop, dot markers, early models with White potted pickups, then metal-covered pickups, and finally Japanese-made pickups (least valued), single or double pickup models offered (deduct $100 for single pickup instrument).

1950s		$650	$750
1960s		$650	$750

Custom (solidbody scroll models)
1958-1970. Notable bass scroll cutaway, various models with various components used, finally import components only.

1958-1970	1 pickup	$350	$500
1958-1970	2 pickups	$450	$600
1958-1970	3 pickups	$550	$700

Deluxe Archtop (L-5-style)
1950s-1960s. Full body 17 1/4" archtop, square block markers, single cutaway, early models with White potted pickups, later into the 1960s metal pickups.

1950s	Blond	$1,000	$1,600
1950s	Sunburst	$1,000	$1,400
1960s	Blond	$1,000	$1,600
1960s	Sunburst	$1,000	$1,400

Semi-Pro 16" Archtop
1950s-early-1960s. Thinline electric 16" archtop with 2 1/4" deep body, acoustic or electric.

1950s	Acoustic non-electric	$650	$750
1950s	Electric	$750	$850
1960s	Acoustic non-electric	$650	$750
1960s	Electric	$750	$850

Semi-Pro Bantam Series (thinline)
1960s. Thinline electric archtop with 2 3/4" deep body, offered in cutaway and non-cutaway models.

1960s		$250	$350

Special Archtop (L-5-style)
1950s-1960s. Full body 17 1/4" archtop, less fancy than Deluxe, single cutaway, early models with White potted pickups, later into the 1960s metal pickups.

1950s		$800	$1,000
1960s		$800	$1,000

Studio Six Archtop
1950s-early-1960s. Sixteen inch wide archtop, single pickup, early pickups White potted, changed later to metal top.

1950s		$500	$600
1960s		$500	$600

Queen Shoals Stringed Instruments
1972-present. Luthier Larry Cadle builds his production/custom, flattop, 12-string, and nylon-string guitars in Clendenin, West Virginia.

Queguiner, Alain
1982-present. Custom flattops, 12-strings, and nylon-strings built by luthier Alain Quiguiner in Paris, France.

R.C. Allen
1972-present. Luthier R. C. "Dick" Allen builds professional and premium grade, custom, hollowbody and semi-hollowbody guitars in El Monte, California. He has also built solidbody guitars.

MODEL YEAR	FEATURES	EXC. COND. LOW	HIGH

Rahbek Guitars

2000-present. Professional and premium grade, production/custom, solidbody electrics built by luthier Peter Rahbek in Copenhagen, Denmark.

RainSong

1995-present. Professional grade, prodution, all-graphite acoustic guitars built in Woodinville, Washington. The guitars were developed after years of research by luthier engineer John Decker with help from luthier Lorenzo Pimentel, engineer Chris Halford, and sailboard builder George Clayton. The company was started in Maui, but moved to Woodinville.

WS-1000/Windsong Cutaway

1999-present. Jumbo cutaway body, onboard electronics.

1999		$1,200	$1,300

Ramirez

1882-present. Founded by José Ramírez, the company is now in its fourth generation of family ownership in Madrid, Spain.

Flamenco

European spruce top, cyprus back and sides.

1964-1965		$3,000	$4,000

R4 Classical

1995-1997. All solid wood, western red cedar top, rosewood back and sides.

1995-1997		$1,000	$1,500

Randy Reynolds Guitars

1996-present. Luthier Randy Reynolds builds his premium grade, production/custom classical and flamenco guitars in Colorado Springs, Colorado.

Rarebird Guitars

1978-present. Luthier Bruce Clay builds his professional and premium grade, production/custom, acoustic, electric solidbody and hollowbody guitars and mini guitars in Arvada, Colorado. He also builds basses.

Rat Fink

2002-present. Intermediate grade, production, guitars and basses from Lace Music Products, the makers of the Lace Sensor pickup. The instruments feature the artwork of Ed "Big Daddy" Roth.

Recording King

1936-1941. Brand name used by Montgomery Ward for instruments made by various American manufacturers, including Kay, Gibson and Gretsch. Generally mid-grade instruments. M Series are Gibson-made archtops.

M-2

1936-1941. Gibson-made archtop with carved top and F-holes, maple back and sides.

1940		$500	$700

MODEL YEAR	FEATURES	EXC. COND. LOW	HIGH

M-3

1936-1941. Gibson-made archtop, F-holes, maple back and sides, carved top.

1939		$800	$1,100

M-5

1936-1941. Gibson-made archtop with F-holes, maple back and sides, trapeze tailpiece, checkered top binding.

1939		$1,000	$1,400

Regal

Ca. 1884-1966, 1987-present. Intermediate and professional grade, production, acoustic and wood and metal body resonator guitars. They also build basses.

Originally a mass manufacturer founded in Indianapolis, Indiana, the Regal brandname was first used by Emil Wulschner & Son. In 1901 new owners changed the company name to The Regal Manufacturing Company. The company was moved to Chicago in 1908 and renamed the Regal Musical Instrument Company. Regal made brands for distributors and mass merchandisers as well as marketing its own Regal brandname. Regal purchased the Lyon & Healy factory in '28. Regal was licensed to co-manufacture Dobros in '32 and became the sole manufacturer of them in '37 (see Dobro for those instruments). Most Regal instruments were beginner-grade; however, some very fancy archtops were made during the '30s. The company was purchased by Harmony in '54 and absorbed. From '59 to '66, Harmony made acoustics under the Regal name for Fender. In '87 the Regal name was revived on a line of resonator instruments by Saga.

Concert Folk H6382

1960s. Regal by Harmony, solid spruce top, mahogany back and sides, dot markers.

1960s	Natural	$250	$300

Deluxe Dreadnought H6600

1960s. Regal by Harmony. Solid spruce top, mahogany back and sides, bound top and back, rosewood fingerboard, dot markers.

1960s	Natural	$250	$350

Dreadnought 12-String H1269

1960s. Regal by Harmony. Solid spruce top, 12-string version of Deluxe.

1960s	Natural	$250	$350

Model 27

1933-1942. Birch wood body, mahogany or maple, two-tone Walnut finish, single-bound top.

1930s		$600	$1,000

Model 45

1933-1937. Spruce top and mahogany back and sides, bound body.

1930s	Square neck	$900	$1,300

Model 75

1939-1940. Metal body.

1939	Square neck	$1,000	$1,500

Rahbek Standard

Rat Fink RF 2

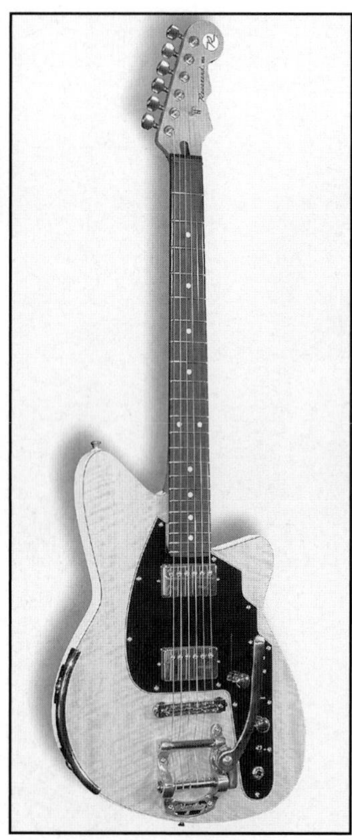

Reverend Rocco

Rick Turner Model One

MODEL YEAR | FEATURES | EXC. COND. LOW | HIGH

Renaissance

1978-1980. Plexiglass solidbody electric guitars and basses. Founded in Malvern, Pennsylvania, by John Marshall (designer), Phil Goldberg and Daniel Lamb. Original partners gradually leave and John Dragonetti takes over by late-1979. The line is redesigned with passive electronics on guitars, exotic shapes, but when deal with Sunn amplifiers falls through, company closes.

Fewer than 300 of first series made, plus a few prototypes and several wooden versions; six or so prototypes of second series made. SN=M(M)YYXXXX: month, year, consecutive number. Brandname currently used on a line of guitars and basses made by Rick Turner in Santa Cruz, CA.

Electric Plexiglass Solidbody Guitar

1978-1980. Models include the SPG (1978-79, DiMarzio pickups, active electronics), T-200G (1980, "Bich-style" with two passive DiMarzio pickups), and the S-200G (1980, double cutaway, two DiMarzio pickups, passive electronics).

1970s $400 $600

Renaissance Guitars

1994-present. Professional grade, custom, semi-acoustic flat-top and nylon-string guitars and basses and solidbody guitars and basses built by luthier Rick Turner in Santa Cruz, California.

Reuter Guitars

1984-present. Professional and premium grade, custom, flat-top, 12-string, resonator, and Hawaiian guitars built by luthier John Reuter, the Director of Training at the Roberto-Venn School of Luthiery, in Tempe, Arizona.

Reverend

1996-present. Intermediate grade, production, guitars and basses built in Warren, Michigan, by luthier Joe Naylor, who also founded Naylor Amps. They also build amps and effects.

Semi-Hollow Electric

1997-present. Offset double cutaway semi-hollowbody, bolt-on maple neck, with various pickup options, various colors. Models include Avenger, Commando, Hitman, Rocco, Slingshot and Spy, variations of a similar theme.

1997-1999 $500 $600

Rex

1930s-1940s. Generally beginner-grade guitars made by Harmony and Kay and sold through Fred Gretsch distributors.

Acoustic Flat-Top Guitars

1940s. Various models.

1940s $250 $350

MODEL YEAR | FEATURES | EXC. COND. LOW | HIGH

Ribbecke Guitars

1972-present. Premium and presentation grade, custom thinline, flat-top, and archtop guitars built by luthier Tom Ribbecke in Healdsburg, California.

Richter Mfg.

1930s. One of many Chicago makers of the era.

Small 13" Guitar

1930s. Typical small 13" lower bout body, slotted headstock, decalmania art over Black finish, single dot markers.

1930s $350 $450

Rick Turner

1979-1981, 1990-present. Rick Turner has a long career as a luthier, electronics designer and innovator. He also makes the Renaissance line of guitars in his shop in Santa Cruz, California.

Rickenbacker

1931-present. Professional and premium grade, production/custom, acoustic and electric guitars built in California. They also build basses. Founded in Los Angeles as Ro-Pat-In by ex-National executives George Beauchamp, Paul Barth and National's resonator cone supplier Adolph Rickenbacher. Rickenbacher was born in Basel, Switzerland in 1886, emigrated to the U.S. and moved to Los Angeles in 1918, opening a tool and die business in 1920.

In the mid-'20s, Rickenbacher began providing resonator cones and other metal parts to George Beauchamp and Louis Dopyera of National String Instrument Corporation and became a shareholder in National. Beauchamp, Barth and Harry Watson came up with wooden "frying pan" electric Hawaiian lap steel for National in '31; National was not interested, so Beauchamp and Barth joined with Rickenbacher as Ro-Pat-In (probably for ElectRO-PATent-INstruments) to produce Electro guitars. Cast aluminum frying pans were introduced in '32. Some Spanish guitars (flat top, F-holes) with Electro pickups were produced beginning in '32.

Ro-Pat-In changes their name to Electro String Instrument Corporation in '34, and brand becomes Rickenbacher Electro, soon changed to Rickenbacker, with a "k." Beauchamp retires in '40. There was a production hiatus during World War II. In '53, Electro was purchased by Francis Cary Hall (born 1908), owner of Radio and Television Equipment Company (Radio-Tel) in Santa Ana, CA (founded in '20s as Hall's Radio Service, which began distributing Fender instruments in '46). The factory was relocated to Santa Ana in '62 and the sales/distribution company's name is changed from Radio-Tel to Rickenbacker Inc. in '65.

1950s serial numbers have from four to seven letters and numbers, with the number following

MODEL YEAR	FEATURES	EXC. COND. LOW	HIGH

the letter indicating the '50s year (e.g., NNL8NN would be from 1958). From '61 to '86 serial numbers indicate month and year of production with initial letter A-Z for the year A=1961, Z=1986) followed by letter for the month A-M (A=January) plus numbers as before followed by a number 0-9 for the year (0=1987; 9=1996).

Combo 400

1956-1958. Double cutaway, neck-through-body, one pickup, Gold anodized pickguard, 21 frets. Replaced by Model 425 in 1958.

1956-1958		$1,000	$1,500

Combo 800

1954-1959. Offset double cut, 1 horseshoe pickup until late-1957, second bar type after. Called the Model 800 in the 1960s.

1957-1959		$1,000	$1,500

Combo 850

1957-1959. Extreme double cutaway, one pickup until 1958, two after, Maple or Turquoise. Called Model 850 in the 1960s.

1957		$1,400	$1,800

Electro ES-17

1964-1975. The Electro line was manufactured by Electro String Instruments and distributed by Radio-Tel. The Electro logo rather than Rickenbacker appeared on the headstock. The Electro line included the short-scale ES-16 and standard-scale ES-17. The ES-17 has a glued-in neck, cutaway, one pickup.

1964-1969	Fireglo	$800	$1,000

Electro Spanish (Model B Spanish)

1935-1943. Small guitar with a lap steel appearance played Spanish-style. Hollow bakelite body augmented with five chrome plates. Called the Model B circa 1940.

1935-1936		$4,000	$4,800
1938-1939		$3,800	$4,600
1940-1943	Model B	$3,600	$4,400

Model 230 Hamburg

1983-1991. Offset double cutaway, two pickups, dot inlay, rosewood fingerboard, chrome-plated hardware.

1983		$500	$600

Model 325 JL

1989-1993. John Lennon Limited Edition, three vintage Ric pickups, vintage vibrato, maple body; 3/4-size rosewood neck. A 12-string and a full-scale version are also available.

1989-1993		$1,200	$1,400

Model 325C58

2002. Designed as near-copy of the 1958-made model that John Lennon saw in Germany.

2002		$1,400	$1,600

Model 330

1958-present. Thinline hollowbody, two pickups, slash soundhole. Natural or Sunburst.

1958-1960		$2,000	$2,500
1965-1968		$1,600	$2,000
1984-1999		$800	$1,000

MODEL YEAR	FEATURES	EXC. COND. LOW	HIGH

Model 330/12

1965-present. Thinline, two pickups, 12-string version of Model 300.

1964-1965		$1,500	$2,300
1966		$1,500	$2,300
1968		$1,500	$2,300
1969		$1,500	$2,300
1989		$1,100	$1,400
1990-1997		$1,100	$1,200

Model 331 Light Show

1970-1975. Model 330 with translucent top with lights in body that lit up when played.

1970-1975		$6,000	$8,000

Model 335 Capri

1958-1978. Thinline, two pickups, vibrato. Called the 330VB from 1985-1997. The Capri Model name is technically reserved for the 1958 to mid-1960s vintage, these models had a two inch depth. Ca. Mid-1960 the body depth was reduced to 1 1/2". Rickenbacker dropped the Capri name in 1960.

1958	Fireglo	$3,500	$4,300
1958	Natural	$3,500	$4,300
1959	Fireglo	$2,800	$3,900
1960	Fireglo	$2,700	$3,800
1966-1967	Fireglo	$1,400	$2,300

Model 345 Capri

1958-1974. Thinline 330-345 series, version with three pickups and vibrato tailpiece. The Capri Model name is technically reserved for the 1958 to mid-1960s vintage, these models had a two inch depth. Body depth was reduced to 1 1/2" circa mid-1960 and Capri name was dropped.

1958		$3,500	$4,600
1961		$3,000	$3,500
1966	Jetglo Black	$2,000	$2,500

Model 350 VB Liverpool

1983-1997. Thinline, three pickups, vibrato, no soundhole.

1983-1989		$800	$900

Model 360

1958-present. Deluxe thinline, two pickups, slash soundhole.

1958-1959		$2,100	$2,600
1960-1963		$1,800	$2,400
1964-1969	New style body, rounded horns	$1,600	$2,000
1970-1972		$1,450	$1,800
1973-1977		$1,100	$1,400
1978-1979		$1,000	$1,300
1980-1989		$950	$1,200
1990-1999		$950	$1,100

Model 360 VB

1984-1991. Two pickups, bound body, vibrato. Renamed Model 360 WB in 1991.

1984-1991		$1,000	$1,300

Model 360 WB

1991-1998. Renamed from Model 360 VB. Two pickups, bound body, vibrato.

1991-1998	Jetglo	$1,000	$1,300

Rickenbacker 331 Light Show

Rickenbacker 325

1968 Rickenbacker 375

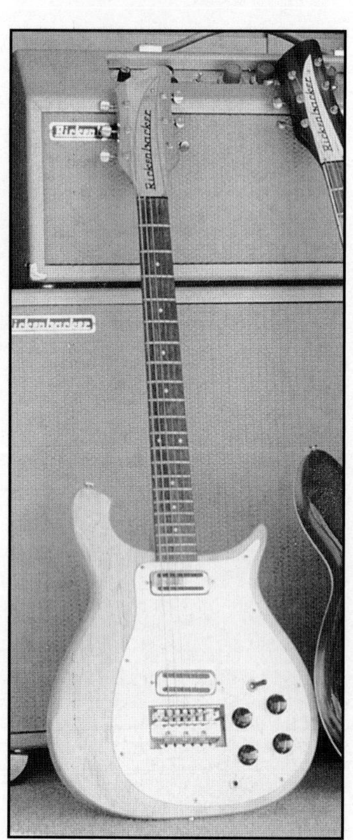

1961 Rickenbacker Model 450

MODEL YEAR	FEATURES	EXC. COND. LOW	HIGH

Model 360/12

1964-present. Deluxe thinline, two pickups, 12-string version of Model 360, Rick-O-Sound stereo.

1964	36 made	$2,600	$3,100
1965	480 made	$2,600	$3,100
1966	1164 made	$2,300	$2,800
1967		$2,200	$2,600
1968		$2,100	$2,400
1969		$1,800	$2,100
1970-1979		$1,200	$1,700
1980-1989		$900	$1,500
1990-1999		$1,000	$1,500
2000-2001		$1,000	$1,300

Model 360/12V64

1985-2001. Deluxe thinline with 1964 features, two pickups, 12 strings, slanted plate tailpiece.

1985-2001		$1,300	$1,600

Model 365

1958-1974. Deluxe thinline, two pickups, vibrato. Called Model 360 VB from 1984-1997.

1958-1989	Late	$2,700	$3,300
1960-1964		$2,300	$2,900
1965-1969		$2,100	$2,700
1970-1974		$2,000	$2,500

Model 365 F

1960 and 1962. Thin full-body (F designation) with recorded production only in 1960.

1960	10 made	$2,400	$3,100
1962	2 made	$2,400	$3,100

Model 366/12 Convertible

1966-1974. Two pickups, 12 strings, comb-like device that converts it to a six-string. Production only noted in 1968, perhaps available on custom order basis.

1966	7 made	$2,400	$3,100
1968	125 made	$2,400	$3,100

Model 370

1958-1990, 1994-present. Deluxe thinline, three pickups. Could be considered to be a dealer special order item from 1958-1967 with limited production (1958=0, 1959=4, 1960=0, 1961=3, 1962-1967=0, then started more regularly in 1968).

1959	4 made	$3,400	$4,500
1961	3 made	$3,000	$4,000
1968		$1,700	$2,400
1973		$1,400	$1,900
1985-1990		$1,200	$1,400
1994-2002		$1,200	$1,400

Model 370/12

1965-1990, 1994-present. Not regular production until 1980, deluxe thinline, three pickups, 12 strings. Could be considered to be a dealer special order item in the 1960s and 1970s with limited production.

1985-1990		$1,000	$1,200
1994-2002		$1,200	$1,400

Model 370/12 Limited Edition (Roger McGuinn)

1988. Roger McGuinn model, 1000 made, higher-quality appointments.

1988		$3,300	$3,700

Model 375

1958-1974. Deluxe thinline, three pickups, vibrato.

1958-1959		$3,200	$3,900
1960-1964		$2,900	$3,700
1965-1970	Sporadic limited production	$2,500	$3,500

Model 381

1958-1963,1969-1974. Double cutaway archtop, two pickups, slash soundhole, solid pickguard. Reintroduced in 1969 with double split-level pickguard.

1969-1974		$1,800	$2,300

Model 381 JK

1988-1997. John Kay model, two humbucking pickups, active electronics, stereo and mono outputs.

1988-1997		$1,400	$1,700

Model 381/12V69

1987-present. Reissue of 381/12, deep double cutaway carved body from single piece of maple, sound cavity is carved inside body, cat's-eye soundhole, 21-fret rosewood fingerboard; triangle inlays, vintage-style pickups, bridge with 12 individually ajustable saddles. Finishes include Fireglo, Mapleglo and Jetglo.

1987-1999		$1,600	$1,800

Model 381V69

1987-1991. Reissue of the 1968 Model 381. Renamed Model 381V68 in 1991.

1987-1991		$1,600	$1,800

Model 4080 6/4 Doubleneck

1975-1992. Six- and four-string bolt-on necks, cresting wave body and headstock, stereo, two pickups for each neck, R tailpiece.

1970s	Mapleglo	$2,000	$2,500

Model 420

1965-1983. Non-vibrato version of Model 425, single pickup.

1958-1964	Light sporadic production	$1,000	$1,300
1965-1969		$900	$1,300
1970-1983		$800	$1,100

Model 425

1958-1973. Double cutaway solidbody, one pickup. Sunburst.

1958-1959		$1,100	$1,300
1960-1965		$1,050	$1,300
1966-1969		$1,000	$1,200
1970-1973		$900	$1,150

Model 450

1958-1984. Replaces Combo 450. 2 pickups (3 optional '62-'77), cresting wave body shape.

1965-1967		$1,200	$1,700
1984		$600	$1,000

Model 450/12

1964-1985. Double cutaway solidbody, 12-string version of Model 450, two pickups.

1964-1967		$1,300	$1,700

Model 456/12 Convertible

1968-1978. Double cutaway solidbody, two pickups, comb-like device to convert it to six-string.

1968-1970		$1,400	$1,700

MODEL YEAR	FEATURES	EXC. COND. LOW	HIGH

Model 460

1961-1985. Double cutaway solidbody, two pickups, neck-through-body, deluxe trim.

1961-1966	Small consistent production	$1,300	$1,600
1974		$1,000	$1,300

Model 480

1973-1984. Double cutaway solidbody with long thin bass horn in 4001 bass series style, two pickups, cresting wave body and headstock, bolt-on neck.

1973-1979		$800	$950
1980-1984		$750	$850

Model 615

1962-1977. Double cutaway solidbody, two pickups, vibrato.

1962-1965		$1,300	$1,800
1966-1969		$1,200	$1,700

Model 620

1974-present. Double cutaway solidbody, deluxe binding, two pickups, neck-through-body.

1974-1979		$950	$1,050
1980-1989		$900	$1,000
1990-1999		$700	$800

Model 620/12

1981-present. Double cutaway solidbody, two pickups, 12 strings, standard trim.

1981-1989		$1,000	$1,300
1990-1999		$900	$1,300

Model 625

1962-1977. Double cutaway solidbody, deluxe trim, two pickups, vibrato.

1962-1965		$1,900	$2,100
1966-1969		$1,800	$2,000

Model 650D Dakota

1993-present. Tulip-shaped neck-through solidbody, single pickup, chrome hardware, oil-satin finish.

1993-1999		$600	$650

Model 650S Sierra

1993-present. Tulip-shaped neck-through solidbody, single pickup, Gold hardware, oil-satin finish.

1993-1999		$650	$750

Model 660/12 TP

1991-1997. Tom Petty model, 12 strings, cresting wave body, two pickups, deluxe trim. Limited run of 1000.

1991-1997		$1,400	$1,800

Robert Guitars

1981-present. Luthier Mikhail Robert builds his premium grade, production/custom, classical guitars in Summerland, British Columbia.

Robertson Guitars

1995-present. Luthier Jeff Robertson builds his premium grade, production/custom flat-top guitars in South New Berlin, New York.

MODEL YEAR	FEATURES	EXC. COND. LOW	HIGH

Robin

1982-present. Professional and premium grade, production/custom, guitars from David Wintz and located in Houston, Texas. They also make Metropolitan (since 1996) and Alamo (since 2000) brandname guitars.

Artisan

1985-late 1980s. Double cut bound mahogany solidbody, 2 humbuckers, bound rosewood board.

1980s	Sunburst, flame top	$600	$700

Avalon Classic

1994-present. Les Paul copy, figured maple top, exposed humbucking pickups, two knobs, upper bass bout toggle.

1994		$1,200	$1,400

Medley Special

1986-1995. Ash body, maple neck, rosewood board, 24 frets, various pickup options.

1986-1995		$350	$450

Medley Standard

1986-present. Upgrade version of Medley Special with swamp ash or basswood body, bolt-on neck.

1986-1992	Swamp ash	$450	$550

Octave

Early 1990s. Tuned an octave above standard tuning, bolt maple neckFull body size with 15 1/2" short-scale bolt maple neck.

1990s	White	$500	$800

Raider I

1985-1991. Double cut solidbody, 1 humbucker, maple neck, either maple or rosewood board.

1985-1991	Sunburst	$350	$450

Raider II

1985-1991. Same as Raider I but with two humbuckers.

1985-1991	Sunburst	$400	$500

Raider III

1985-1991. Same as Raider I but with 3 humbuckers.

1985-1992	Sunburst	$450	$500

Ranger

1983-present. Swamp ash body, figured maple neck, rosewood or maple board, three pickups.

1986	Orange	$500	$700

RDN-Doubleneck Octave/Six

1983. Six-string standard-scale neck with three pickups, six-string octave neck with one pickup, double cutaway, solidbody.

1983	Black	$400	$600

Soloist

1983-late 1980s. Mahogany solidbody, carved maple top, two pickups.

1980s		$400	$500

Roland

Best known for keyboards, effects, and amps, Roland offered synthesizer-based guitars and basses from 1977 to '86.

Rickenbacker Model 650

Robin Ranger Custom

Rowan Cimarron

1976 S.D. Curlee Standard

MODEL YEAR	FEATURES	EXC. COND. LOW	HIGH

GR-707 Synth Guitar

1983-1986. Slab-wedge asymmetrical body, bass bout to headstock support arm, two humbucker pickups, multi-controls.

1983-1986	Silver	$900	$1,100

GS-500 Synth Guitar/Module

1977-1986. Three pickups.

1977-1980	Sunburst	$500	$900

Rono

1967-present. Luthier Ron Oates builds his professional and premium grade, production/custom, flat-top, jazz, Wiesenborn-style, and resonator guitars in Boulder, Colorado. He also builds basses and mandolins.

Rowan

1997-present. Professional and premium grade, production/custom, solidbody and acoustic/electric guitars built by luthier Michael Rowan in Garland, Texas.

Royden Guitars

1996-present. Professional grade, production/custom, flat-tops and solidbody electrics built by luthier Royden Moran in Peterborough, Ontario.

Rubio, German Vasquez

1993-present. Luthier German Vasquez Rubio builds his professional and premium grade, production/custom classical and flamenco guitars in Los Angeles, California.

Ruck, Robert

1966-present. Premium grade, custom classical and flamenco guitars built by luthier Robert Ruck in Kalaheo, Hawaii.

Running Dog Guitars

1994-present. Luthier Rick Davis builds his professional and premium grade, custom flat-tops in Richmond, Vermont.

Rustler

1993-mid 1990s. Solidbody electrics with hand-tooled leather bound and studded sides and a "R" branded into the top, built by luthier Charles Caponi in Mason City, Iowa.

RWK

1991-present. Luthier Bob Karger builds his intermediate grade, production/custom, solidbody electrics and travel guitars in Highland Park, Illinois.

S. B. Brown Guitars

1994-present. Custom flat-tops made by luthier Steve Brown in Fullerton, California.

MODEL YEAR	FEATURES	EXC. COND. LOW	HIGH

S. B. MacDonald Custom Instruments

1988-present. Professional and premium grade, custom, flat-top, resonator, and solidbody guitars built by luthier Scott B. MacDonald in Huntington, New York.

S.D. Curlee

1975-1982. Founded in Matteson, Illinois by music store owner Randy Curlee, after an unsuccessful attempt to recruit builder Dan Armstrong. S.D. Curlee gutiars were made in Illinois, while S.D. Curlee International instruments were made by Matsumoku in Japan. The guitars featured mostly Watco oil finishes, often with exotic hardwoods, and unique neck-through-bridge construction on American and Japanese instruments. These were the first production guitars to use a single-coil pickup at the bridge with a humbucker at the neck, and a square brass nut. DiMarzio pickups. Offered in a variety of shapes, later some copies. Approximately 12,000 American-made basses and 3,000 guitars were made, most of which were sold overseas. Two hundred were made in '75-'76; first production guitar numbered 518.

Electric Solidbody Guitars

1975-1982. Models include the '75-'81Standard I, II and III, '76-'81? International C-10 and C-11, '80-'81 Yanke, Liberty, Butcher, Curbeck, Summit, Special, and the '81-'82 "Destroyer", "Flying V."

1970s		$400	$550

Sadowsky

1980-present. Professional and premium grade, production/custom, solidbody, archtop, and electric nylon-string guitars and basses built by luthier Roger Sadowsky in Brooklyn, New York.

Vintage Style

Swamp ash body, Barden pickups, vintage-style gears, bridge, control plate and pickguard.

1982	Sunburst	$800	$1,000

Sahlin Guitars

1975-present. Luthier Eric Sahlin builds his premium grade, custom, classical and flamenco guitars in Spokane, Washington.

Samick

1958-2001, 2002-present. Budget, intermediate and professional grade, production, acoustic and electric guitars. They also build basses, mandolins, ukes, and banjos. Samick also distributes Abilene and Silvertone brand instruments.

Samick started out producing pianos, adding guitars in '65 under other brandnames. In '88 Samick greatly increased their guitar production. The Samick line of 350 models was totally closed out in 2001. A totally new line of 250 models was introduced January 2002 at NAMM. All 2002

MODEL YEAR	FEATURES	EXC. COND. LOW	HIGH

models have the new compact smaller headstock and highly styled S logo. 2002 model production in Korea and Indonesia.

FV-450

1996-2001. Flying V style solidbody, 2 humbuckers.

1990s		$275	$325

HF-650

1994-2001. L-5 style jazz archtop, 2 humbuckers, gold hardware, maple body.

1994-2001		$500	$600

SW-218 CE (acoustic cutaway)

1996-2001. Cutaway D-style, piezo bridge pickup, unusual laser cut soundhole cover.

1996-2001	Natural	$250	$300

Sand Guitars

1979-present. Luthier Kirk Sand opened the Guitar Shoppe in Laguna Beach, California in 1972 with James Matthews. By 1979, he started producing his own line of premium grade, production/custom-made flat-tops.

Santa Cruz

1976-present. Professional, premium and presentation grade, production/custom, flat-top, 12-string, and archtop guitars from luthier Richard Hoover in Santa Cruz, California. Founded by Hoover, Bruce Ross and William Davis. Hoover became sole owner in 1989. Custom ordered instruments with special upgrades may have higher values than the ranges listed here.

D 12-Fret

Fifteen and one-half inch scale, 12-fret neck, slotted headstock, round shoulders, spruce top, mahogany back and sides, notch diamond markers, herringbone trim and rosette. Special order models will vary in value and could exceed the posted range.

1990s	Natural	$1,600	$2,600

F

1994-present. Fifteen and seven-eighths inch scale with narrow waist, Sitka spruce top, Indian rosewood back and sides.

1990s	Natural	$2,100	$2,300

FJZ17 (17" cutaway archtop)

1990s. Seventeen inch scale cutaway archtop, spruce top, curly maple body, with floating pickups.

1990s	Sunburst	$6,000	$7,000

OM (Orchestra Model)

1987-present. Orchestra model acoustic, Sitka spruce top, Indian rosewood (Brazilian optional) back and sides, herringbone rosette, scalloped braces.

1987-1989	Brazilian rosewood	$4,200	$5,000
1987-1989	Indian rosewood	$2,200	$2,500
1990s	Brazilian rosewood	$4,000	$4,800
1990s	Indian rosewood	$2,200	$2,500

MODEL YEAR	FEATURES	EXC. COND. LOW	HIGH

Tony Rice

Dreadnought-size, Indian rosewood body, Sitka spruce top, solid peghead, zigzag back stripe, pickup optional.

1980s	Indian rosewood	$2,500	$3,000
1991		$2,300	$2,900

Tony Rice Professional

Brazilian rosewood back and sides, carved German spruce top, zigzag back stripe, solid peghead.

1980s	Brazilian rosewood	$4,500	$5,500
1990s	Brazilian rosewood	$4,300	$5,300

Vintage Jumbo

Sixteen inch scale, round shouldered J-50-style body, Sitka spruce, figured mahogany back and sides.

1990s	Natural	$2,300	$2,500

Sawchyn Guitars

1972-present. Professional and premium grade, production/custom, flat-top and flamenco guitars and mandolins built by luthier Peter Sawchyn in Regina, Saskatchewan.

Schaefer

1997-present. Premium grade, production/custom electric archtops handcrafted by luthier Edward A. Schaefer in Fort Worth, Texas.

Schecter

1976-present. Intermediate, professional and premium grade, production/custom, acoustic and electric guitars. They also offer basses. Guitar component manufacturer originally founded by David Schecter, later offering complete instruments with new management and innovations by 1994. Schecter guitars are made in the U.S. and their Diamond Series is made in Korea.

Avenger

1997-present. Offset double cutaway with long pointed bass horn, arched mahogany body, bolt-on neck, six-on-a-side tuners, dual humbucker pickups.

1997	Custom color	$700	$900
1997	Sunburst	$500	$700

Avenger 7

1997-present. Offset double cutaway with long pointed bass horn, arched mahogany body, bolt-on neck, six-on-a-side tuners, dual humbucker pickups, seven-string option.

1998	Custom color	$950	$1,050

Diamond A1

1997-2000. Offset double cutaway with long pointed bass horn, arched mahogany body, bolt-on neck, various colors.

1998		$325	$375

Diamond A7

1997-2000. Seven strings, offset double cutaway with long pointed bass horn, arched mahogany body, bolt-on neck, various colors.

1998		$300	$400

Santa Cruz Tony Rice Professional

2001 Schaefer Rhythmmaster

GUITARS

1986 Schon Standard

Sekova Les Paul copy

MODEL YEAR	FEATURES	EXC. COND. LOW	HIGH

Scheerhorn

1989-present. Professional and premium grade, custom, resonator and Hawaiian guitars built by luthier Tim Scheerhorn in Kentwood, Michigan.

Acoustic/Electric (Resophonic)

Small body resophonic, solid flamed maple body, resonator with spider bridge, mini-humbucker and transducer pickups.

1997	Red Sunburst	$2,500	$2,750

Schoenberg

1986-present. Premium grade, production/custom, flat-tops offered by Eric Schoenberg of Tiburon, California. From 1986-'94 guitars made to Schoenberg's specifications by Martin. From 1986-'90 constructed by Schoenberg's luthier and from 1990-1994 assembled by Martin but voiced and inlaid in the Schoenberg shop. Current models made to Schoenberg specs by various smaller shops.

000-30

1990-1994. Martin-assembled, 12 frets to the body, Brazilian rosewood back and sides, six made.

1990-1994		$10,000	$11,000

OM Model

1990s. Specifications can vary, specific valuation on a case-by-case basis. The value noted is Style 28.

1990s	Brazilian rosewood	$7,000	$8,000
1990s	Indian rosewood	$4,000	$5,000

Soloist

1986-1994. Adirondack spruce top, Brazilian rosewood back and sides.

1989	Brazilian rosewood	$7,000	$8,000

Schon

1986-1991. Designed by guitarist Neal Schon, early production by Charvel/Jackson building about 200 in the San Dimas factory. The final 500 were built by Larivee in Canada. Leo Knapp also built custom Schon guitars from '85-'87, and '90s custom-made Schon guitars were also available.

Standard (U.S.A.-made)

1986 only. San Dimas/Jackson model, single cutaway, pointy headstock shape, "Made in U.S.A." on headstock.

1986		$1,000	$1,500

Standard (Canadian-made)

1987-1991. "Made in Canada" on headstock.

1987-1988	Single cutaway	$300	$400
1989-1991	Reverse double cutaway	$300	$400

Schramm Guitars

1990-present. Premium grade, production/custom, classical and flamenco guitars built by luthier David Schramm in Clovis, California.

Schroder Guitars

1993-present. Luthier Timothy Schroder builds his premium grade, production/custom, archtops in Northbrook, Illinois.

Schwartz Guitars

1992-present: Premium grade, custom, flat-top guitars built by luthier Sheldon Schwartz in Concord, Ontario.

ScoGo

2001-present. Professional and premium grade, production/custom, solidbody guitars built by luthier Scott Gordon in Parkesburg, Pennsylvania.

Seagull

1980-present. Intermediate grade, production, acoustic and acoustic/electric guitars built in Canada. Seagull was founded by luthier Robert Godin, who also has the Norman, Godin, and Patrick & Simon brands of instruments.

Sebring

1980s-present. Entry level Korean imports distributed by V.M.I. Industries.

L-5 Copy

1980s. Large body, dual pickup, copy of L-5 archtop.

1980s		$300	$400

Semi-hollowbody Guitars

1990s		$300	$400

Seiwa

1980s. Entry-level to mid-level Japanese imports, logo may indicate "since 1956."

Century Crown

1980s. Classic offset double cut copy.

1980s		$200	$250

Sekova

Mid-1960s-mid-1970s. Entry level instruments imported by the U.S. Musical Merchandise Corporation of New York.

Grecian

1968		$200	$300

Serge Guitars

1995-present. Luthier Serge Michaud builds his production/custom, classical, steel string, resophonic and archtop guitars in Breakeyville, Quebec.

Sexauer Guitars

1967-present. Premium and presentation grade, custom, steel-string, 12-string, nylon-string, and archtop guitars built by luthier Bruce Sexauer in Petaluma, California.

Shanti Guitars

1985-present. Premium and presentation grade, custom, steel-string, 12-string, nylon-string and archtop guitars built by luthier Michael Hornick in Avery, California.

MODEL YEAR	FEATURES	EXC. COND. LOW	HIGH

Shelley D. Park Guitars

1991-present. Luthier Shelley D. Park builds her professional grade, custom, nylon- and steel-string guitars, in Vancouver, British Columbia.

Sheppard Guitars

1993-present. Luthier Gerald Sheppard builds his professional and premium grade steel-string guitars in Kingsport, Tennessee.

Shifflett

Luthier Charles Shifflett builds his premium grade, production/custom, flat-top, classical, flamenco, resophonic, and harp guitars, acoustic basses, and banjos in High River, Alberta.

Sho-Bro

1969-1978. Brandname distributed by Gretsch.

Grand Slam

1978. Acoustic, spruce top, mahogany neck, Jacaranda sides and back, and mother-of-pearl inlays, abalone soundhole purfling.

1978		$350	$450

Sigma

1970-present. Budget and intermediate grade, production, import acoustic guitars distributed by C.F. Martin Company.

DR-28 H

1970-1996. Dreadnaught, laminated rosewood back and sides, herringbone binding.

1980s		$400	$550

DR-35 H

1970-1996. D-35 copy, imported.

1970s		$400	$550

GCS-6

Grand concert semi-narrow waist body, laminated spruce top, mahogany back and sides.

1994	Natural	$150	$200

Signet

Ca.1973. Acoustic flat-top guitars, imported from Japan by Ampeg/Selmer.

Acoustic Flat-Tops

1973. Various models.

1973		$75	$150

Silber

1992-1998. Solid wood, steel-string guitars designed by Marc Silber, made in Paracho, Mexico, and distributed by K & S Music. Silber continues to offer the same models under the Marc Silber Guitar Company brand.

Silvertone

1941-ca. 1970, present. Brandname of Sears instruments which replaced their Supertone brand name in 1941. The Silvertone name was used on Sears phonographs, records and radios as early as the 'teens, and on occasional guitar models. When Sears divested itself of the Harmony guitar subsidiary in '40 it turned to other suppliers including Kay. In '40 Kay-made archtops and Hawaiian electric lap steels appeared in the catalog bearing the Silvertone brand, and after 1941-1942, all guitars, regardless of manufacturer, were called Silvertone.

Sears offered Danelectro-made solidbodies in the fall of '54. Danelectro hollowbodies appeared in '56. By '65, the Silvertones were Teisco-made guitars from W.M.I., but never sold through the catalog. First imports shown in catalog were in '69. By '70, most guitars sold by Sears were imports and did not carry the Silvertone name. Currently, Samick offers a line of amps under the Silvertone name.

Amp-In-Case

The one pickup guitar, introduced in 1962, came with a smaller wattage amp without tremolo. The two pickup model, introduced in 1963, came with a higher-watt amp with tremolo and better quality Jensen speaker. Gray Tolex covered the guitar-amp case.

1960s	1 pickup	$250	$350
1960s	2 pickups	$350	$450

Belmont

1950s. Single cutaway solidbody, double pickup.

1958	Black	$300	$350

Espanada

Bigsby, two pickups.

1960s	Black	$325	$375

Estrelita

Semi-hollowbody archtop, two pickups, Harmony-made.

1960s	Black	$325	$375

Meteor

Single cutaway, one pickup.

1955	Sunburst	$200	$300

Student-level 13" Flat-Top

Harmony-made, 13" lower bout.

1960s		$60	$80

Simon & Patrick

1985-present. Intermediate and professional grade, production, acoustic and acoustic/electric guitars built in Canada. S&P was founded by luthier Robert Godin and named after his sons. He also produces the Seagull, Godin, and Norman brands of instruments.

Skylark

Skylark was the house brand of the JC Penney company.

Electric Solidbodies

Various models.

1980s		$125	$225

1962 Silvertone Amp-in-Case

'60s Silvertone semi-hollowbody

1939 Slingerland Songster

Stahl Style 4

MODEL YEAR	FEATURES	EXC. COND. LOW	HIGH

Slammer

1990-present. Budget and intermediate grade, production, guitars and basses imported by Hamer. Originally Slammers were upscale copies of Hamer models made in Korea. In '96, production of a more budget line was switched to Indonesia.

Slingerland

1930s-mid-1940s. The parent company was Slingerland Banjo and Drums, Chicago. The company offered other stringed instruments into the 1940s. They also marketed the May Bell brand. The guitars were made by other companies. Slingerland Drums is now owned by Gibson.

Nitehawk

1930s. Sixteen inch arch top, 'Nitehawk" logo on headstock, fancy position neck markers.

1930s		$500	$750

Songster Archtop

1930s.

1938		$400	$600

Smart Musical Instruments

1986-present. Luthier A. Lawrence Smart builds his premium grade, custom, flat-top guitars and mandolin family instruments in McCall, Idaho.

Smith, George

1959-present. Custom classical and flamenco guitars built by luthier George Smith in Portland, Oregon.

Smith, Lawrence K.

1989-present. Luthier Lawrence Smith builds his professional and premium grade, production/custom, flat-top, nylon-string, and archtop guitars in Thirrow, New South Wales, Australia.

Somogyi, Ervin

1971-present. Luthier Ervin Somogyi builds his presentation grade, production/custom, flat-top, flamenco, and classical guitars in Oakland, California.

SonFather Guitars

1994-present. Luthier David A. Cassotta builds his production/custom, flattop, 12-string, nylon-string and electric guitars in Rocklin, California.

Southwell Guitars

1983-present. Premium grade, custom, nylon-string guitars built by luthier Gary Southwell in Nottingham, England.

Sovereign

ca.1920-ca.1938. Sovereign was originally a brandname of The Oscar Schmidt Company of Jersey City, NJ, and used on guitars, banjos and mandolins. In the late 1930s, Harmony purchased several trade names from the Schmidt Company, including Sovereign and Stella. Sovereign then ceased as a brandname, but Harmony continued using it on a model line of Harmony guitars.

Specimen Products

1984-present. Luthier Ian Schneller builds his professional and premium grade, production/custom, aluminum and wood body guitar and basses in Chicago, Illinois. He added tube amps and speaker cabinets in '86. He also builds basses and ukes.

Spector/SSD

1975-1990 (Spector), 1991-1998 (SSD), 1998-present (Spector SSD). Known mainly for basses, Spector offered U.S.-made guitars during 1975-'90 and '96-'99, and imports for '87-'90 and '96-'99. Since 2003, they again offer U.S.-professional grade, production, solidbody guitars. See Bass Section for more company info.

St. George

1960s. Early Japanese import.

Electric Solidbody

1960s. Early Japanese import duplicate of Zim Gar model, top mounted controls, three pickups, bolt-on neck.

1960s	Sunburst	$60	$150

St. Moritz

1960s. Imported from Japan by unidentified distributor. Manufacturers unknown, but some appear to be either Teisco or Kawai. Generally shorter scale beginner guitars, some with interesting pickup configurations.

Electric Thinline Archtop Guitars

Various models.

1960s		$75	$175

Stahl

1900-1944. Made in association with Larson Brothers. Valuation based on style number.

Style 4 Flat-Top

1930s. Mahogany body.

1930s		$3,000	$3,500

Style 5 Flat-Top

1930s. Mahogany body.

1930s		$3,000	$3,500

Style 6 Orchestra Special Flat-Top

1930s. Rosewood body.

1929-1930		$6,500	$7,500

Style 7 Special Solo Flat-Top

1930s. Thirteen and one-half inch scale, choice rosewood body, White spruce top, fancy appointments.

1930s		$7,000	$8,000

Style 8 Special Solo Flat-Top

1930s. Choicest rosewood body, finest White spruce top, fancy appointments.

1930s		$8,000	$8,500

MODEL YEAR	FEATURES	EXC. COND. LOW	HIGH

Style 9 Artist Special Flat-Top

1930s. Choicest rosewood body, finest White spruce top, fancy appointments.

1930s		$9,000	$9,500

Standel

1952-1974, 1997-present. Amp builder Bob Crooks offered instruments under his Standel brandname three different times during the '60s. In '61 Semie Moseley, later of Mosrite fame, made two models of guitar and one bass for Standel, in limited numbers. Also in '61, Standel began distributing Sierra steels and Dobro resonators, sometimes under the Standel name. In '65 and '66 Standel offered a guitar and a bass designed by Joe Hall, who would later make the Hallmark guitars (it is not clear who made them). In '66 Standel connected with Sam Koontz, who designed and produced the most numerous Standel models (but still in reatively small numbers) in Newark, NJ. These models hit the market in '67 and were handled by Harptone, which was associated with Koontz. By '70 Standel was out of the guitar biz. See Amp section for more company info.

Custom Deluxe Solidbody 101/101X

1967-1968. Custom with better electronics, 101X has no vibrato. Sunburst, Black, Pearl White and Metallic Red.

1967-1968		$1,000	$1,200

Custom Deluxe Thin Body 102/102X

1967-1968. Custom with better electronics, 102X has no vibrato. Offered in Sunburst and five solid color options.

1967-1968		$1,000	$1,200

Custom Solidbody 201/201X

1967-1968. Solidbody, two pickups, vibrola, two pointed cutaways, headstock similar to that on Fender XII, 201X has no vibrato. Sunburst, black, pearl white and metallic red.

1967-1968		$800	$900

Custom Thin Body 202/202X

1967-1968. Thin body 335-style, headstock similar to that on Fender XII, 202X has no vibrato. Offered in Sunburst and five solid color options.

1967-1968		$800	$900

Stauffer

1800s. Old World violin and guitar maker, Georg Stauffer.

Guitar

1830	Fancy model, pearl trim	$12,000	$13,000

Stefan Sobell Musical Instruments

1982-present. Premium grade, production/custom, flattop, 12-string, and archtop guitars, mandolins, citterns and bouzoukis built by luthier Stefan Sobell in Hetham, Northumberland, England.

MODEL YEAR	FEATURES	EXC. COND. LOW	HIGH

Steinberger

1979-present. Currently Steinberger offers budget, intermediate, and professional grade, production, electric guitars. They also offer basses. Founded by Ned Steinberger, who started designing NS Models for Stuart Spector in '76. In '79, he designed the L-2 headless bass. In '80, the Steinberger Sound Corp. was founded. Steinberger Sound was purchased by the Gibson Guitar Corp. in '87, and in '92, Steinberger relocated to Nashville.

GL-4S

Has two single-coil pickups and one double-coil pickup, headless, tremolo.

1980s		$650	$950

GP-3T

Headless, three single-coil pickups, available with S-Trem or Trans-trem.

1980s		$500	$650

S-Trem

Bridge can lock tremolo unit in place to give a non-tremolo fixed bridge, EMG high-impedance pickups.

1980s		$550	$700

Steinegger

1976-present. Premium grade, custom steel-string flat-top guitars built by luthier Robert Steinegger in Portland, Oregon.

Style D-28

Brazilian rosewood, herringbone trim.

1990s		$5,000	$5,500

Stella

Founded in 1879, Stella was a brand name of the Oscar Schmidt Company and was used on low-mid to mid-level instruments. Oscar Schmidt produced all types of stringed instruments and was very successful in the 1920s. Company salesmen reached many rural areas and Stella instruments were available in general stores, furniture stores, and dry goods stores, ending up in the hands of musicians such as Leadbelly and Charlie Patton. Harmony acquired the Stella brandname in '39 and built thousands of instruments with that name in the '50s and '60s. Harmony dissolved in '74. The Stella brand has been reintroduced by MBT International.

00 Style

Early-1900s. Oak body flat-top.

1908		$800	$1,100

Harp Guitar

Early-1900s.

1915		$1,500	$1,900

Singing Cowboy

Late-1990s. Copy of Supertone (Black background)/Silvertone/Harmony Singing Cowboy, import with laminated wood construction and ladder bracing.

2000	Stencil over Black	$50	$75

1968 Standel 510

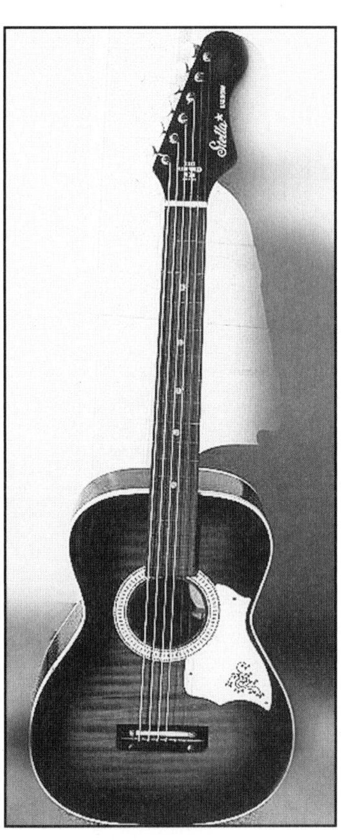

Stella/Harmony

1952 Stromberg Master 400

1930 Stromberg Deluxe

MODEL YEAR	FEATURES	EXC. COND. LOW	HIGH

Stetson & Co.

Early-1900s. Larson Brothers brand (similar to Maurer or Prairie State).

Small Higher-End Flat-Top

Early-1900s. Thirteen and five-eighths inch lower bout, spruce top, Brazilian rosewood back and sides, high-end pearl appointments, slotted headstock.

1910	Natural	$3,000	$4,000

Strad-O-Lin

Ca.1920s-ca.1960s. The Strad-O-Lin company was operated by the Hominic brothers in New York, primarily making mandolins for wholesalers. Around '57 Multivox/Premier bought the company and also used the name on guitars, making both electrics and acoustics. Premier also marketed student level guitars under the U.S. Strad brand.

Stromberg

1906-1955, 2001-present. Intermediate and professional grade, production, archtop guitars inported by Larry Davis.

Founded in Boston by master luthier Charles Stromberg, a Swedish immigrant. Sons Harry and Elmer apprenticed at the Stromberg shop. The shop was well-known for tenor banjos, but when the banjo's popularity declined, Elmer began building archtop orchestra model guitars. The shop moved to Hanover Streen in Boston in 1927 and began producing custom order archtop guitars, in particular the 16" G-series and the Deluxe. As styles changed the G-series was increased to 17 3/8" and the 19" Master 400 model was introduced in '37.

Larry Davis of WD Music Products revived the lapsed Stromberg trademark and introduced a series of moderately priced jazz guitars in June, 2001. The models are crafted by a small Korean shop with component parts supplied by WD.

Deluxe

1927-1955. Non-cutaway, 16" body from 1927-1934, 17 3/8" body after 1935.

1927-1930		$8,500	$11,500

G-1

1927-1955. Non-cutaway, 16" body from 1927-1935, 17 3/8" body after 1935.

1927-1935	Sunburst, 16" body	$8,000	$10,000
1936-1955	Sunburst, 17 3/8" body	$9,000	$11,000

G-3

Early 1930s. Archtop, 16 3/8", three segment F-holes, ladder bracing, Gold hardware, engraved tailpiece, eight-ply pickguard, five-ply body binding, laminate maple back, fancy engraved headstock with Stromberg name, less total refinement than higher-end Stromberg models.

1927-1935		$8,500	$11,500

MODEL YEAR	FEATURES	EXC. COND. LOW	HIGH

Master 300

1937-1955. Nineteen inch non-cutaway.

1937-1955		$25,000	$40,000

Master 400

1937-1955. Nineteen inch top-of-the-line non-cutaway.

1937-1955		$40,000	$70,000

Master 400 Cutaway

1949. Only seven cutaway Strombergs are known to exist.

1949	Natural	$75,000	$85,000

Stromberg-Voisinet

1921-ca.1932. Marketed Stromberg (not to be confused with Charles Stromberg of Boston) and Kay Kraft brand names, plus guitars of other distributors and retailers. Stromberg was the successor to the Groehsl Company (or Groehsel) founded in Chicago, Illinois in 1890; and the predecessor to the Kay Musical Instrument Company. In 1921, the name was changed to Stromberg-Voisinet Company. Henry Kay "Hank" Kuhrmeyer joined the company in '23 and was secretary by '25. By the mid-'20s, the company was making many better Montgomery Ward guitars, banjos and mandolins, often with lots of pearloid.

Joseph Zorzi, Philip Gabriel and John Abbott left Lyon & Healy for S-V in '26 or '27, developing two-point Venetian shape, which was offered in '27. The first production of electric guitars and amps was introduced with big fanfare in 1928; perhaps only 200 or so made. The last "Stromberg" acoustic instruments were seen in '32. The Kay Kraft brand was introduced by Kuhrmeyer in '31 as the company made its transition to Kay (see Kay). See Guitar Stories Volume II, by Michael Wright, for a complete history of Stromberg-Voisinet/Kay with detailed model listings.

Archtop Deluxe

1920s-1930s. Venetian cutaways, oval soundhole, decalomania art on top, trapeze tailpiece. Later offered under the Kay-Kraft brand.

1930s	Light Sunburst	$500	$600

Archtop Standard

1920s-1930s. Venetian cutaways, oval soundhole, no decalomania art, plain top, trapeze tailpiece. Later offered under the Kay-Kraft brand.

1930s	Light Sunburst	$450	$550

Superior Guitars

1987-present. Intermediate grade, production/custom Hawaiian, flamenco and classical guitars and mandolin-family instruments made in Mexico for George Katechis Montalvo of Berkeley Musical Instrument Exchange.

MODEL YEAR	FEATURES	EXC. COND. LOW	HIGH

Supertone

1914-1941. Brandname used by Sears, Roebuck and Company for instruments made by various American manufacturers, including especially its own subsidiary Harmony (which it purchased in 1916). When Sears divested itself of Harmony in 1940, instruments began making a transition to the Silvertone brandname. By 1941 the Supertone name was gone.

Acoustic Flat-Top (high-end appointments)

1920s	Pearl trim 00-42 likeness	$1,200	$2,300
1920s	Pearl trim, Lindbergh model	$1,200	$1,900

Acoustic Flat-Tops (13" wide, non-stencil)

1930s		$150	$300

Gene Autrey Melody Ranch

Thirteen inches wide with stencil.

1930s		$250	$450

Lone Ranger (stencil)

Introduced in 1936. Black with Lone Ranger stencil, Silver-painted fretboard, 13" wide, glued bridge.

1936		$200	$300

Singing Cowboys

Mid- to late-1930s-1941. Supertone Singing Cowboy guitars featured a Black background vs. the later Harmony models with a Brown background. Supertone name was returned in 1941 and replaced by the Silvertone name.

1930s		$250	$300

Supertone 'Wedge'

1930s. Triangle-shaped 'wedge' body, laminate construction, Blue-Silver Supertone label inside sound chamber, art decals on body.

1930s		$200	$250

Supro

1935-1968. Budget brand of National Dobro Company. Some Supro models also sold under the Airline brand for Montgomery Ward. In 1942 Victor Smith, Al Frost and Louis Dopyera bought National and changed the name to Valco Manufacturing Company. Valco Manufacturing Company name changed to Valco Guitars, Inc., in '62. Company treasurer Robert Engelhardt bought Valco in '64. In '67 Valco bought Kay and in '68 Valco/Kay went out of business. In the summer of '69, Valco/Kay brand names and assets were sold at auction and the Supro and National names purchased by Chicago-area importer and distributor Strum N" Drum (Norma, Noble). The Supro name was never used on imports. In the early-'80s, ownership of the Supro name was transferred to Archer's Music, Fresno, California. Some Supros assembled from new-old-stock parts.

Belmont

1955-1964. For '55-'60, 12" wide, single cut, one neck pickup, two knobs treble side in pickguard, reverse-stairs tailpiece, No-Mar plastic Maroon-colored covering. For '60, size nicreased to 13 1/2" wide. For '62-'64, Res-o-glas fiberglass was used for the body, a slight cutaway on bass side, one bridge pickup, two knobs on opposite sides. Polar White.

1955-1959	Black or White No-Mar	$600	$800
1960-1962	Black or White No-Mar	$500	$700
1961-1964	Polar White Res-o-glas	$700	$900

Bermuda

1962 only. Slab body (not beveled), double pickups, dot markers, Cherry glass-fiber finish.

1962		$600	$800

Collegian Spanish

1939-1942. Metal body, 12 frets. Moved to National line in 1942.

1939-1942	Maple	$1,000	$1,200

Coronado/Coronado II

1961-1967. Listed as II in 1962. Fifteen and one-half inch scale, single cutaway Gibson thinline-style, two pickups with four knobs and slider. Natural Blond spruce top. Changed to slight cutaway on bass side in 1962 when renamed II.

1961-1967	Natural	$700	$900

Dual-Tone

1954-1966. The Dual Tone had several body style changes, all instruments had dual pickups. '54, 11 1/4" body, No Mar Arctic White plastic body ('54-'62). '55, 12" body. '58, 13" body. '60, 13 1/2" body. '62, Res-o-glas Ermine White body, light cutaway on bass side.

1954-1961	Arctic White No-Mar	$700	$900
1962-1966	Ermine White Res-o-glas	$800	$1,000

Folk Star

1964-1967. Molded Res-o-glas body, single-cone resonator, dot inlays.

1964-1967	Fire Engine Red	$750	$900

Jazzmaster-style Solidbody (import)

1970s. Student-level vague Jazzmaster-style body, single pickup, large Supro logo on headstock, import by Strum 'N Drum.

1970s	Sunburst	$150	$250

Kingston

1962-1963. Double cutaway slab body, bridge pickup, glass-fiber Sand finish, similar to same vintage Ozark.

1962-1963		$400	$600

Martinique

1962-1967. Single cutaway, 13 1/2" wide, two standard and one bridge pickups, six knobs on bass side, one knob and slider on treble side, block markers, cataloged as "Supro's finest electric," Val-Trol script on pickguard, Bigsby vibrato tailpiece. Ermine White Polyester Glas.

1962-1967	Blue	$1,000	$1,200
1962-1967	Ermine White Polyester Glas	$1,000	$1,200

1936 Supertone Lone Ranger

1965 Supro S-555

1963 Supro Thermoelectric

1994 Takamine PSF-94

MODEL YEAR	FEATURES	EXC. COND. LOW	HIGH

Ozark

1952-1954, 1958-1967. Non-cutaway, one pickup, dot inlay, White pearloid body. Name reintroduced in 1958 as a continuation of model Sixty with single cutaway, Dobro tailpiece.

1952-1954	White pearloid	$400	$600
1958-1967	Poppy Red, double cutaway	$400	$600

Ranchero

1948-1960. Full body electric archtop, neck pickup, dot markers, bound body.

1948-1960	Sunburst	$600	$700

Sahara

1960-1964. Thirteen and 1/2" body-style similar to Dual-Tone, single pickup, two knobs.

1960-1964		$800	$1,000

Silverwood/Val-Trol

1960-1962. Single cutaway, 13 1/2" wide, two standard and one bridge pickups, six knobs on bass side, one knob and slider on treble side, block markers, cataloged as "Supro's finest electric." Natural Blond. Val-Trol script on pickguard. Renamed Martinique in 1962.

1960-1962		$1,000	$1,200

Sixty

1955-1958. Single cutaway, single pickup, becomes Ozark in 1958.

1955-1958	White No-Mar plastic	$400	$600

Special 12

1958-1960. Single cutaway, replaces Supro Sixty, neck pickup pickguard mounted.

1958-1960		$400	$600

Super

1958-1964. Twelve inch wide single cutaway body style like mid-1950s models, single bridge pickup, short-scale. Ivory.

1958-1964	Ivory	$450	$550

SX

See listing for Essex.

Tacoma

1995-present. Intermediate, professional, and premium grade, production, acoustic guitars produced in Tacoma, Washington. They also build acoustic basses and mandolins.

Chief

1997-present. Full-sized flat-top with upper bass bout soundhole.

1997-1999	Natural	$450	$500
1997-2000	On-board electronics	$600	$700

DM9

2000-present. D-style, solid spruce top, mahogany back and sides, satin finish.

2000	Natural	$375	$400

DR20

1997-present. D-style, solid Sitka spruce top, solid rosewood back and sides, herringbone trim, abalone rosette.

1997-1999	Natural	$500	$600

MODEL YEAR	FEATURES	EXC. COND. LOW	HIGH

Papoose

1995-present. Travel-size mini-flat-top, all solid wood, mahogany back and sides, cedar top, Natural satin finish.

1995-1999		$250	$300

PM15

Grand Concert, solid spruce top, solid mahogany back and sides.

1995		$550	$575

Takamine

1962-present. Intermediate, professional, and premium grade, production, steel and nylon string guitars. Takamine is named after a mountain near its factory in Sakashita, Japan. Mass Hirade joined Takamine in '68 and revamped the brand's designs and improved quality. In '75, Takamine began exporting to other countries, including U.S. distribution by Kaman Music (Ovation). In '78, Takamine introduced acoustic/electric guitars. They offered solidbody electrics for '83-'84.

Acoustic Electric Cutaways (laminate)

All laminate (plywood) construction, cutaway, standard features, pickup and preamp.

1980s		$150	$300
1990s		$150	$300

Acoustic Electrics (laminate construction)

All laminate (plywood) construction, non-cutaway, standard features, pickup and preamp.

1980s		$300	$400
1990s		$300	$400

Acoustic Electrics (solid top)

Solid wood top, sides and back can vary, cutaway, standard features, preamp and pickup.

1980s		$400	$900
1990s		$400	$900

Classical Guitars (solid top)

Solid wood (often cedar) top, classical, sides and back can vary.

1980s		$400	$600
1990s		$400	$600

Collectors (limited edition)

Each year a different limited edition collector's guitar is issued.

1997 - solid top, koa body, cutaway, Natural finish, preamp and pickup.

1998 - solid top, rosewood body, cutaway, Natural finish, preamp and pickup.

1999 - solid top, rosewood body, cutaway, Natural finish, preamp and pickup.

2000 - solid top, rosewood body, cutaway, Natural finish, preamp and pickup.

2001 - solid top, rosewood body, cutaway, Natural finish, preamp and pickup.

1990s		$900	$1,100

Taku Sakashta Guitars

1994-present. Premium and presentation grade, production/custom, archtop, flat-top, 12-sting, and nylon-string guitars, built by luthier Taku Sakashta

MODEL YEAR	FEATURES	EXC. COND. LOW	HIGH

in Sebastopol, California.

Taylor

1974-present. Intermediate, professional, premium, and presentation grade, production/custom, acoustic and acoustic/electric guitars built in El Cajon, California. Founded by Bob Taylor, Steve Schemmer and Kurt Listug in Lemon Grove, California, the company was originally named the Westland Music Company, but was soon changed to Taylor (Bob designed the guitars and it fit on the logo). Taylor and Listug bought out Schemmer in '83.

Baby Mahogany

1997-present. All mahogany, 3/4 dreadnought, not the same as Baby Mahogany (M).

1997-1999 $150 $250

Baby Mahogany (M)

1998-present. The 3/4-size dreadnought, spruce top Baby became available in '96; this solid mahogany top version was an option starting in '98, sapele-laminate back and sides.

1998-1999 $250 $350

Baby Rosewood

2000-present. Three-fourth dreadnought, solid Sitka spruce top, laminated Indian rosewood back and sides.

2000 $200 $350

Big Baby

2000-present. Fifteen-sixteenths-size dreadnought, solid Sitka spruce top, sapele-mahogany laminated back and sides, satin finish, gig bag.

2000-2001 $350 $450

Model 310 Dreadnought

1998-present. D-style solid spruce top, sapele-mahogany back and sides.

1998 $700 $800

Model 310ce Dreadnought

1998-present. D-style Venetian cutaway, solid spruce top, sapele-mahogany back and sides, onboard electronics.

1998 $800 $900

Model 312ce Grand Concert

1998-present. Grand Concert Venetian cutaway, solid spruce top, sapele-mahogany back and sides, onboard electronics.

1998 $700 $800

Model 314 Grand Auditorium

1998-present. Mid-size Grand Auditorium-style, solid spruce top, sapele-mahogany back and sides.

1998 $700 $900

Model 314ce Grand Auditorium

1998-present. Grand Auditorium Venetian cutaway, solid spruce top, sapele-mahogany back and sides, onboard electronics.

1998 $800 $900

Model 315ce Jumbo

1998-present. Jumbo-style Venetian cutaway, solid spruce top, sapele-mahogany back and sides, onboard electronics.

1998 $900 $1,000

MODEL YEAR	FEATURES	EXC. COND. LOW	HIGH

Model 355 Jumbo 12-String

1998-present. Jumbo 12-string, solid spruce top, sapele-mahogany back and sides.

1998-1999 $900 $1,000

Model 355ce Jumbo 12-String

1998-present. Jumbo 12-string cutaway, solid spruce top, sapele-mahogany back and sides, onboard electrics.

1998 $950 $1,050

Model 410 Dreadnought

1991-present. D-style, solid spruce top, mahogany back and sides until 1998, African ovangkol back and sides after 1998.

1990s $800 $900

Model 410ce Dreadnought

1991-present. Cutaway, solid spruce top, mahogany back and sides until 1998, African ovangkol back and sides after 1998.

1991-1999 Satin $900 $1,000

Model 412 Grand Concert

1991-1998. Solid spruce top, mahogany back and sides until 1998, African ovangkol back and sides after 1998.

1991-1998 $700 $800

Model 412ce Grand Concert

1998-present. Cutaway electric version replaced the 412 in '98.

1998 $800 $900

Model 414 Grand Auditorium

1998-present. Solid Sitka spruce top, ovangkol back and sides, pearl dot inlays.

1998 Natural $900 $1,000

Model 414ce Grand Auditorium

1998-present. Cutaway version, solid Sitka spruce top, ovangkol back and sides, pearl dot inlays.

1998 Natural $1,000 $1,100

Model 415 Jumbo

1998-present. Solid Sitka spruce top, ovangkol back and sides, pearl dot inlays.

1998 $800 $900

Model 420

1990-1997. D-style, Sitka spruce top, maple back and sides.

1990-1997 Natural $800 $900

Model 455 12-String

2001-present. Solid Sitka spruce top, ovangkol back and sides, dot markers.

2001 $900 $1,000

Model 455ce 12-String

2001-present. Cutaway electric version, solid Sitka spruce top, ovangkol back and sides, dot markers, onboard electronics.

2001 $1,000 $1,100

Model 510 Dreadnought

1978-present. All solid wood, spruce top, mahogany back and sides.

1978-1979 $1,000 $1,250

1980-1999 $1,000 $1,100

Taylor Big Baby

Taylor 310ce

Taylor 712

Taylor 955

MODEL YEAR	FEATURES	EXC. COND. LOW	HIGH

Model 510c Dreadnought
1978-1998. Cutaway version of Model 510.

1978-1998		$1,250	$1,350

Model 512 Grand Concert
1978-2000. Solid Engelmann spruce top, solid American mahogany back and sides, dot markers.

1978-1999		$1,100	$1,300

Model 512c Grand Concert
1978-1998. Solid Engelmann spruce top, solid American mahogany back and sides, dot markers.

1995		$1,200	$1,400

Model 514c Grand Auditorium
1990-1998. Venetian cutaway, solid spruce or solid red cedar top, mahogany back and sides, no electronics.

1990-1998	Natural	$1,300	$1,500

Model 514ce Grand Auditorium
1998-present. Venetian cutaway, solid red cedar top, mahogany back and sides, onboard electronics.

1998		$1,400	$1,600

Model 555 Jumbo 12-String
1994-present. Solid Sitka spruce top, solid mahogany back and sides, higher-end appointments.

1994-1999		$1,300	$1,500

Model 555ce Jumbo 12-String
1994-present. Cutaway, solid Sitka spruce top, solid mahogany back and sides, higher-end appointments, onboard electronics.

1994-1999		$1,400	$1,600

Model 610 Dreadnought
1978-1998. Solid spruce top, solid maple back and sides, generally with Amber stained finishes.

1997		$1,200	$1,300

Model 610ce Dreadnought
1998-present. Solid spruce top, solid maple back and sides, generally with opaque finishes, onboard electronics.

1998		$1,300	$1,500

Model 612ce Grand Concert
1998-present. Solid spruce top, solid maple back and sides, generally with opaque finish, onboard electronics.

1998		$1,500	$1,600

Model 614 Grand Auditorium
1978-1998. Solid spruce top, solid maple back and sides, generally with Amber stained finishes.

1997-1998		$1,400	$1,500

Model 614ce Grand Auditorium
1998-present. Solid spruce top, solid maple back and sides, generally with opaque finish, onboard electronics.

1998		$1,500	$1,600

Model 655 Jumbo
1978-1998. Solid spruce top, solid maple back and sides, generally with Amber stained finishes.

1987-1997		$1,500	$1,600

Model 655-12 20th Anniversary

1990s		$1,500	$1,700

MODEL YEAR	FEATURES	EXC. COND. LOW	HIGH

Model 655ce Jumbo
1998-present. Solid spruce top, solid maple back and sides, generally with opaque finish, onboard electronics.

1998		$1,600	$1,800

Model 710
1977-present. Dreadnought-size, rosewood back and sides, spruce top.

1995		$1,400	$1,500

Model 712 Grand Concert
1984-present. Grand Concert small body, solid wood, non-cutaway, rosewood back and sides, spruce top, cedar soundboard.

1984-1989		$1,400	$1,500
1990-1999		$1,400	$1,500

Model 712ce Grand Concert
2000-present. Cutaway, Engelmann spruce top, rosewood back and sides, onboard electronics.

2000		$1,400	$1,600

Model 755 12-String
1990-1998. D-style, 12 strings, solid spruce top, rosewood back and sides.

1990-1998	Natural	$1,400	$1,600

Model 810 Dreadnought
1975-present. Classic original Taylor design - early model.

1975-1999		$1,300	$1,800

Model 810ce Dreadnought
1998-present. Cutaway, solid Sitka spruce top, Indian rosewood back and sides, onboard electronics.

1998-1999		$1,400	$1,900

Model 815c Jumbo
1993-1998. Cutaway, no electronics, solid Sitka spruce top, Indian rosewood back and sides.

1993-1998		$1,300	$1,500

Model 815ce Jumbo
1998-present. Cutaway, solid Sitka spruce top, Indian rosewood back and sides, onboard electronics.

1998		$1,400	$1,600

Model 855 Jumbo 12-String
1993-present. Jumbo (J-200-style) 12-string, solid Sitka spruce top, rosewood back and sides.

1993-1998	Natural	$1,500	$1,700

Model 912c Grand Concert
1993-2002. Rosewood back and sides, abalone.

1993-1999		$2,200	$2,400

Model K10 Koa Dreadnought
1983-present. Acoustic dreadnought, koa back and sides, spruce top, distinctive binding.

1990s		$1,800	$2,100

Model K20 Koa Dreadnought
1983-1992. Non-cutaway D-style, koa body, abalone rosette.

1983		$1,300	$1,500

Model K20c Koa Dreadnought
1998-2002. Cutaway, koa body, Engelmann spruce top optional.

1998-1999		$1,800	$2,000

MODEL YEAR	FEATURES	EXC. COND. LOW	HIGH

Model LKSM6 12-String

1997-present. Jumbo 12-string, spruce top, American mahogany back and sides.

1998		$1,400	$1,600

Model PS15 Jumbo

1996-present. Solid Engelmann spruce top, Brazilian rosewood back and sides, scalloped X-bracing, high-end appointments.

1998		$4,000	$5,000

Model W10 Dreadnought

1998-present. Claro walnut back and sides, optional tops include Sitka spruce, western red cedar, or claro walnut.

1998		$1,200	$1,400

Teisco

1946-1974, 1994-present. Founded in Tokyo, Japan by Hawaiian and Spanish guitarist Atswo Kaneko and electrical engineer Doryu Matsuda, the original company name was Aoi Onpa Kenkyujo; Teisco was the instrument name. Most imported into U.S. by Chicago's W.M.I. Corporation and Jack Westheimer beginning ca. '63-'64, some early ones for New York's Bugeleisen and Jacobson. Brandnames made by the company include Teisco, Teisco Del Rey, Kingston, World Teisco, Silvertone, Kent, Kimberly and Heit Deluxe.

In '56, the company's name was changed to Nippon Onpa Kogyo Co., Ltd., and in '64 the changed again to Teisco Co., Ltd. In January '67, the company was purchased by Kawai. After '73, the brandname was converted to Kay in U.S.; Teisco went into hiatus in Japan until being revived in the early-'90s with plexiglass reproductions of the Spectrum 5 (not available in U.S.). Some older Teisco Del Rey stock continued to be sold in U.S. through the '70s.

EG-27

Two pickups.

1960s		$100	$200

K-4L/ET-460 Super Deluxe

1966-1969. Solidbody electric.

1966-1969		$200	$400

May Queen

1968-1969. Cutaway teardrop with F-hole body, two pickups, tremolo tailpiece.

1960s		$300	$600

Spectrum II

1968-1969. Solidbody electric, two pickups.

1968-1969		$200	$300

Spectrum V

1966-1969. Solidbody Electric.

1966-1969		$300	$500

Tele-Star

1965-ca.1972. Imported from Japan by Tele-Star Musical Instrument Corporation of New York, NY. Primarily made by Kawai, many inspired by Burns designs, some in cool sparkle finishes.

Electric Hollowbody Archtop Guitars

1967-1970.

1968	Various models	$100	$200

Tennessee

1970-1993, 1996-present. Luthier Mark Taylor builds his professional and premium grade, production/custom, acoustic guitars in Old Hickory, Tennessee. He also builds mandolins, banjos and the Tut Taylor brand of resophonic guitars. Mark and his father Robert "Tut" Taylor started making the Tennessee brand of acoustic and resophonic guitars, banjos, and mandolins in 1971. In '77, Tut left the company and Mark continued on as Crafters of Tennessee. In '93, Mark and Greg Rich started building instruments as Rich and Taylor. In '96, Mark resumed production under the Tennessee brand.

Thompson Guitars

1980-present. Luthier Ted Thompson builds his professional and premium grade, production/custom, flat-top, 12-string, and nylon-string guitars in Vernon, British Columbia.

Threet Guitars

1990-present. Premium grade, production/custom, flat-tops built by luthier Judy Threet in Calgary, Alberta.

Timeless Instruments

1980-present. Luthier David Freeman builds his professional, premium and presentation grade, custom, flattop, 12-string, nylon-string, and resonator guitars, mandolins and dulcimers in Tugaske, Saskatchewan.

Timm Guitars

1997-present. Professional grade, custom, flat-top, resonator and travel guitars built by luthier Jerry Timm in Auburn, Washington.

Timtone Custom Guitars

1993-present. Luthier Tim Diebert builds his premium grade, custom solidbody, chambered-body, acoustic, and lap steel guitars in Grand Forks, British Columbia.

Tippin Guitar Co.

1978-present. Professional, premium and presentation grade, production/custom, flattop guitars built by luthier Bill Tippin in Marblehead, Massachusetts.

Tokai

1947-present. Japan's Tokai Company started out making a keyboard harmonica that was widely used in Japanese schools. In the late '60s, Tokai hooked up with Tommy Moore, a successful instrument merchandiser from Fort Worth, Texas,

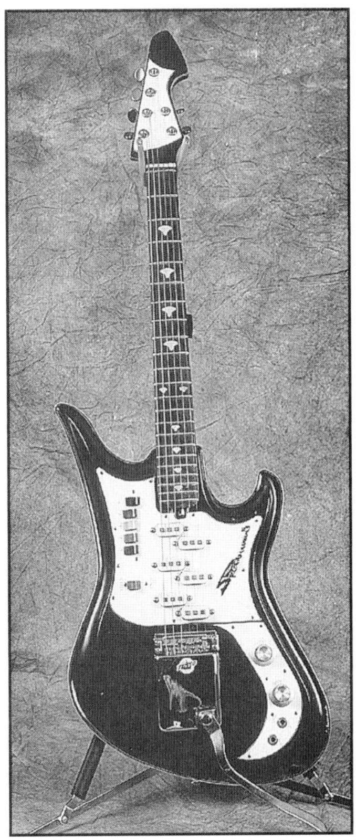

Teisco Spectrum 5

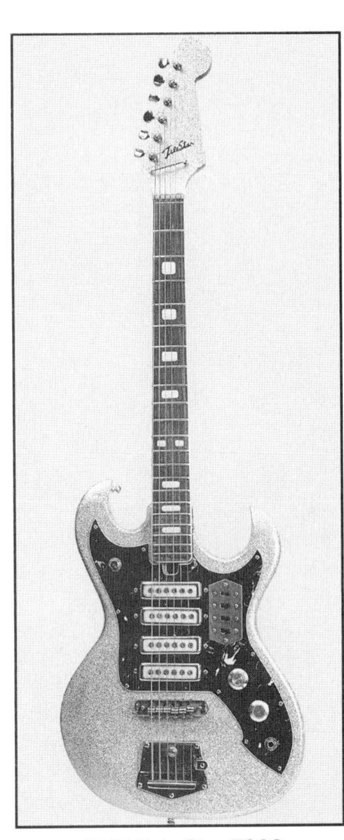

1967 Tele Star 5003

GUITARS

1982 Tokai AST-56

1970s Travis Bean

MODEL YEAR	FEATURES	EXC. COND. LOW	HIGH

and by '70 they were producing private label and OEM guitars. The guitars were sold in the U.S. under the brandnames of various importers. By the '70s, the Tokai name was being used on the instruments. Today Tokai continues to offer electrics, acoustics, and electric basses.

ASD 403 Custom Edition

Double cut solidbody, two single-coil/one humbucker pickups, locking tremolo.

1980s		$350	$450

ASD 56

Maple neck, three pickups, various colors.

1980s	Various colors	$350	$450

Tom Anderson Guitarworks

1984-present. Professional and premium grade, production/custom, solid and semi-solidbody guitars built by luthier Tom Anderson in Newbury Park, California.

Classic

1984-present. Double cut solidbody, classic 3 pickup configuration. Colors and appointments can vary.

1984-1999		$1,200	$1,600

Cobra

1993-present. Single cut solid mahogany body with figured maple top.

1993-2002		$1,500	$1,800

Drop Top

1992-present. Double cut solidbody, single/single/humbucker pickups, various specs.

1992-1999		$1,500	$1,800

Hollow Classic

1996-present. Ash double cut with tone chambers, 3 pickups.

1996-1999		$1,400	$1,700

Toyota

1972-?. Imported from Japan by Hershman of New York, NY. At least one high-end acoustic designed by T. Kurosawa was ambitiously priced at $650.

Electric Hollowbody Archtop Guitars

1970s. Various models.

1970s		$100	$200

Traphagen, Dake

1972-present. Luthier Dake Traphagen builds his premium grade, custom, nylon-string guitars in Bellingham, Washington.

Traugott Guitars

1991-present. Premium grade, production/custom, flat-tops and acoustic/electrics built by luthier Jeff Traugott in Santa Cruz, California.

Travis Bean

1974-1979, 1999. Aluminum-necked solidbody electric guitars and basses. The company was founded by motorcycle and metal-sculpture enthusiast Travis Bean and guitar repairman Marc McElwee in Southern California; soon joined by Gary Kramer (see Kramer guitars). Kramer left Travis Bean in '75 and founded Kramer guitars with other partners. Guitar production began in mid-'76. The guitars featured carved aluminum necks with three-and-three heads with a "T" cutout in the center and wooden fingerboards. Some necks had bare aluminum backs, some were painted Black. A total of about 3,650 instruments were produced. Travis Bean guitar production was stopped in the summer of '79.

Serial numbers were stamped on headstock and were more-or-less consecutive. These can be dated using production records published by Bill Kaman in Vintage Guitar magazine. Original retail prices were $895 to $1195.

The company started production again in '99 with updated versions of original designs and new models.

TB-1000 Artist

Aluminum neck with T-slotted headstock, double cutaway 335-size archtop body, two humbucking pickups, four controls, block markers on fingerboard.

1970s		$1,200	$1,600

TB-1000 Standard

Aluminum neck with T-slotted headstock, double cutaway body, two humbucking pickups, four controls, small pickguard, dot markers on fingerboard.

1970s		$1,200	$1,600

TB-3000 Wedge Guitar

Aluminum neck with T-slotted headstock, triangle-shaped body, two humbucking pickups, four controls, block markers on fingerboard.

1970s		$1,400	$1,800

Triggs

1992-present. Luthiers Jim Triggs and his son Ryan build their professional and premium grade, production/custom, archtop, flat-top, and solidbody guitars originally in Nashville, and, since '98, in Kansas City, Kansas. They also build mandolins.

Byrdland

Seventeen inch Byrdland-style, single cutaway, dual humbuckers, flamed maple top, back and sides.

1997	Natural	$2,800	$3,200

Excel

Seventeen inch archtop cutaway, carved spruce top, flamed maple back and sides, Excel logo.

1999	Sunburst	$5,700	$6,000

New Yorker

Eighteen inch archtop cutaway, carved spruce top, figured maple back and sides, Empire State New Yorker logo. Blond or Sunburst.

1992-2000		$6,000	$7,500

True North Guitars

1994-present. Luthier Dennis Scannell builds his premium grade, custom, flat-tops in Waterbury, Vermont.

GUITARS

MODEL YEAR	FEATURES	EXC. COND. LOW	HIGH

True Tone

1960s. Guitars and amps retailed by Western Auto, manufactured by Chicago guitar makers like Kay. The brand was most likely gone by '68.

Double Cutaway Electric Archtop (K592)

1960s. Made by Kay and similar to their K592 double cutaway thinline acoustic, two pickups, Bigsby tailpiece. Burgundy Red.

1964		$350	$450

Jazz King (K573 Speed Demon)

1960s. Kay's K573 Speed Demon, three pickups, thinline archtop electric with F-hole, eighth note art on pickguard.

1964	Sunburst	$350	$550

Rock 'n Roll Electric (K100)

1960s. Kay's K100, slab body, single pickup, but with a bright Red multiple lacquer finish.

1964	Red	$175	$225

Solidbody (K300 Kay)

1960s. Made by Kay and similar to their K300, double cut, dual pickups and vibrola arm.

1966	Red	$400	$550

Speed Master (K6533 Value Leader Archtop)

1960s. Made by Kay and similar to their K6533 full-body electric archtop Value Leader line, eighth note art pickguard.

1964	Sunburst	$150	$250

Tut Taylor

Line of professional and premium grade, production/custom, resophonic guitars built by luthier Mark Taylor of Crafters of Tennessee in Old Hickory, Tennessee. Brand named for his father, dobro artist Tut Taylor. Taylor also builds the Tennessee line of guitars, mandolins and banjos and was part of Rich and Taylor guitars for 1993-'96.

TV Jones

1993-present. Professional and premium grade, production/custom, hollow, chambered, and solid body guitars built by luthier Thomas Vincent Jones originally in California, now in Poulsbo, Washington. The instruments have either Jones or TV Jones inlaid on the headstock. He also builds pickups.

Unique Guitars

2003-present. Professional and premium grade, production/custom, solidbody guitars and basses built by Joey Rico in California. Joey is the son of Bernie Rico, the founder of BC Rich guitars.

Univox

1964-1978. Univox started out as an amp line and added guitars around '68. Guitars were imported from Japan by the Merson Musical Supply Company, later Unicord, Westbury, NY. Many if not all supplied by Arai and Company (Aria, Aria Pro II), some made by Matsumoku. Univox Lucy ('69) first copy of lucite Ampeg Dan Armstrong. Generally mid-level copies of American designs.

MODEL YEAR	FEATURES	EXC. COND. LOW	HIGH

Acoustic Flat-Tops

1969-1978. Various models.

1970s		$100	$250

Bi-Centennial

1976. Offset double cut, heavily carved body, brown stain, 3 humbucker-style pickups.

1976		$500	$800

Electric Hollowbodies

Various models.

1970s		$300	$500

Electric Solidbodies

Includes Flying V, Mosrite and Hofner violin-guitar copies.

1970s		$300	$500

Vaccaro

1997-present. Founded by Henry Vaccaro, Sr., one of the founders of Kramer Guitars. Intermediate and professional grade, production/custom, aluminum-necked guitars and basses designed by Vaccaro, former Kramer designer Phil Petillo, and Henry Vaccaro, Jr., and made in Asbury Park, New Jersey.

Valco

Valco, from Chicago, was a big player in the guitar and amplifier business. Their products were private branded for other companies like National, Supro, Airline, Oahu, and Gretsch.

Valencia

1985-present. Budget grade, production, classical guitars imported by Rondo Music of Union, New Jersey.

Valley Arts

Ca. 1977-present. Production/custom, semi-hollow and solidbody guitars built in Nashville. Valley Arts originally was a Southern California music store where partner Mike McGuire taught and did most of the repairs. Around '77, McGuire and Valley Arts started making custom instruments on a large scale. By '83, they opened a separate manufacturing facility to build the guitars. In '92 Samick acquired half of the company with McGuire staying on for a year as a consultant. Samick offered made-in-the-U.S. production and custom models under the Valley Arts name. As of 2002, Valley Arts is a division of Gibson Guitar Corp., which builds the guitars in Nashville. They reintroduced the line in January, '02.

California Pro (U.S.-made)

1983-2002. Double cut body, six-on-a-side tuners, single/single/humbucker, two knobs and switch, serial number begins with CAL.

1995	Green Opaque	$500	$550

1970 Univox Lucy

Tut Taylor resophonic

GUITARS

1940s Vega Duo-Tron

Veleno Original

MODEL YEAR	FEATURES	EXC. COND. LOW	HIGH

Optek Fretlight (U.S.-made)

Double cut body, about 126 LED lights in fretboard controlled by a scale/chord selector.

1990	Black Opaque	$500	$1,500

Standard Pro (U.S.-made)

1990-1993. Double cut body, six-on-a-side tuners, single/single/humbucker, two knobs and switch, serial number begins with VA.

1990-1993		$500	$550

Vantage

1977-present. Intermediate grade, production, acoustic and electric guitars imported by Samick. They also build basses. Instruments from Japan from '77-'90 and from Korea from '90-present.

Electric Solidbodies

Student- to mid-level instruments, various models.

1980s		$150	$250

L-5 copy

1980s. L-5 copy, rounded cutaway, block markers, humbucking-style pickups, upper bass bout toggle.

1980s	Sunburst	$400	$500

Vega

1903-present. The original Boston-based company was purchased by C.F. Martin in 1970. In 1980, the Vega trademark was sold to a Korean company. The original name 'Vega' means 'star' and a star logo is often seen on the original Vega guitars.

C-series Archtops

1930-1950s. Several different C-model numbers, mid-level archtops including carved solid tops with bookmatched figured maple backs, Natural or Sunburst.

1930s		$1,000	$1,400
1940s		$1,000	$1,400
1950s	Cutaway	$1,000	$1,400

Duo-Tron Electric Archtop

1940s-1950s. Mid-level large body non-cutaway archtop, single pickup, block markers, Natural or Sunburst.

1940s		$1,000	$1,400
1950s		$700	$1,000

FT-90 (flat-top)

1960s. Fifteen inch body with narrow waist, dot markers, Vega logo.

1960s	Natural	$450	$550

Parlor Guitar

Early-1900s. Small parlor-sized instrument, Brazilian rosewood back and sides. Styles vary, fancy appointments associated with higher-end models, including binding, purfling and inlays.

1900	Mid-level	$1,200	$2,000
1914	Higher-end	$1,700	$2,700

Profundo Flat-Top

1940s. Flat top D-style body, spruce top, mahogany back and sides.

1940s	Natural	$1,300	$1,600

MODEL YEAR	FEATURES	EXC. COND. LOW	HIGH

Vega, Charles

1993-present. Luthier Charles Vega builds his premium, production/custom, nylon-string guitars in Baltimore, Maryland.

Veillette

1991-present. Luthier Joe Veillette (of Veillette-Citron fame) builds his professional grade, production/custom, electric guitars and baritone guitars in Woodstock, New York. He also builds basses and mandolins.

Gryphon MK IV (12-string)

Twelve strings, 18 1/2"-scale solidbody (like 1960s Vox Phantom 12) using under-saddle piezo technology vs. magnetic pickups.

2002		$1,000	$1,200

Veillette-Citron

1975-1983. Founded by Joe Veillette and Harvey Citron who met at the NY College School of Architecture in the late '60s. Joe took a guitar building course from Michael Gurian and by the Summer of '76, he and Harvey started producing neck-thru solidbody guitars and basses. Veillette and Citron both are back building instruments.

Veleno

1967, 1970-1976, 2003-present. All-aluminum electric solidbody guitars, travel guitars, and bass. Built by John Veleno in St. Petersburg, Florida. First prototype in '67. Later production begins in late-'70 and lasts until '75 or '76. He is again producing guitars. The guitars were chrome or gold-plated, with various anodized colors. In 2003, John Veleno reintroduced his brand.

The Traveler Guitar was the idea of B.B. King; only ten were made. Two ankh guitars were made for Todd Rundgren in '77. Only one bass was made. Only approximately 185 instruments were made, sequentially numbered. See *Guitar Stories Volume II*, by Michael Wright, for a complete history of Veleno guitars.

Original (Aluminum Solidbody)

1973-1976. V-headstock, chrome and aluminum.

1973		$7,000	$9,000

Traveler Guitar

1973-1976. Limited production of about a dozen instruments, drop-anchor-style metal body.

1973-1976		$9,000	$10,000

Ventura

1970s. Import copies distributed by C. Bruno (Kaman). Copy models include Howard Roberts, ES-335, SG, Flying V, Les Paul Special slab body, L-5, Barney Kessel, ES-175, and various Les Pauls. Acoustic copies include Dove, J-200, D-style, and Classical.

MODEL YEAR	FEATURES	EXC. COND. LOW	HIGH

Barney Kessel copy

1970s. Sharp-pointed double cutaway electric archtop.

1970s	Sunburst	$350	$450

ES-175 copy (V-1007)

1970s. Sharp-pointed single cutaway, double pickups, block markers, ES-175 copy.

1970s	Natural or Sunburst	$350	$450

L-5 copy

1970s	Sunburst	$350	$450

Les Paul copy

Various colors.

1970s		$250	$350

Versoul, LTD

1989-present. Production/custom steel-string flat-top, acoustic/electric, nylon-string, resonator, solidbody, baritone guitars, basses, and sitars built by luthier Kari Nieminen in Helsinki, Finland.

Victor Baker Guitars

1998-present. Professional and premium grade, custom, carved archtop, flattop and solidbody electric guitars built by luthier Victor Baker in Philadelphia, Pennsylvania.

Vivi-Tone

Early- to mid-1930s. Designed and promoted by former Gibson designer Lloyd Loar.

Guitar

1930s. Deep archtop-style body with F-holes on the backside and magnetic bridge pickup.

1936	Sunburst	$1,800	$2,100

Vox

1957-1972, 1982-present. Name introduced by Jennings Musical Instruments (JMI) of England. First Vox products were amplifiers brought to the market in 1958 by Tom Jennings and Dick Denny. Guitars were introduced in '61, with an Echo Unit starting the Vox line of effects in '63.

Guitars and basses bearing the Vox name were offered from 1961-'69 (England, Italy), '82-'88 (Asia), and for '98-2001 (U.S.). Vox products are currently distributed in the U.S. by Korg USA. Special thanks to Jim Rhoads of Rhoads Music in Elizabethtown, PA, for help on production years of these models.

Apollo

1967-1968. Single sharp cutaway, 1 pickup, distortion, treble and bass booster. Available in Sunburst or Cherry.

1967-1968		$500	$700

Bobcat

1965-1968. Double cut ES-335 body style, block markers, 3 pickups, vibrato, 2 volume and 2 tone controls.

1965-1968		$550	$800

Bossman

1967-1968. Single rounded cutaway, 1 pickup, distortion, treble and bass booster. Available in Sunburst or Cherry.

1967-1968		$400	$500

Bulldog

1966. Solidbody double cutaway.

1966		$400	$600

Delta

1967-1968. Solidbody, 2 pickups, distortion, treble and bass boosters, vibrato, 1 volume and 2 tone controls. Available in White only.

1967-1968		$700	$1,000

Folk XII

1966-1969. D-style 12-string flat-top, large three point pickguard, block markers.

1967-1968	Natural	$450	$550

Guitar-Organ

1966. Standard Phantom with oscillators from a Continental organ installed inside. Plays either organ sounds, guitar sounds, or both. Weighs over 20 pounds.

1966		$1,500	$2,000

Mando Guitar

1966. Made in Italy, 12-string mandolin thing.

1966		$1,400	$1,600

Mark III

1998-2001. Teardrop reissue.

1998-2001		$700	$800

Mark IX

1966. Solidbody teardrop-shaped, 9 strings, 3 pickups, vibrato, 1 volume and 2 tone controls.

1966	Sunburst	$800	$950

Mark VI

1965-1967. Teardrop-shaped solidbody, three pickups, vibrato, one volume and two tone controls.

1965-1967	Sunburst	$700	$1,100

Mark VI Reissue

1998-2001.

1998-2001		$700	$800

Mark XII

1965-1967. Teardrop-shaped solidbody, 12 strings, 3 pickups, vibrato, 1 volume and 2 tone controls.

1965-1967	Sunburst	$900	$1,000

Phantom VI

1962-1967. Five-sided body, 6 strings, 3 pickups, vibrato, 1 volume and 2 tone controls.

1962-1964	English-made	$1,800	$2,000
1965-1967	Italian-made	$1,100	$1,300

Phantom XII

1964-1967. Five-sided body, 12 strings, 3 pickups, vibrato, 1 volume and 2 tone controls.

1964	English-made	$1,800	$2,000
1965-1967	Italian-made	$1,100	$1,300

Spitfire

1965-1967. Solidbody double cut, 3 pickups, vibrato tailpiece.

1965-1967		$400	$500

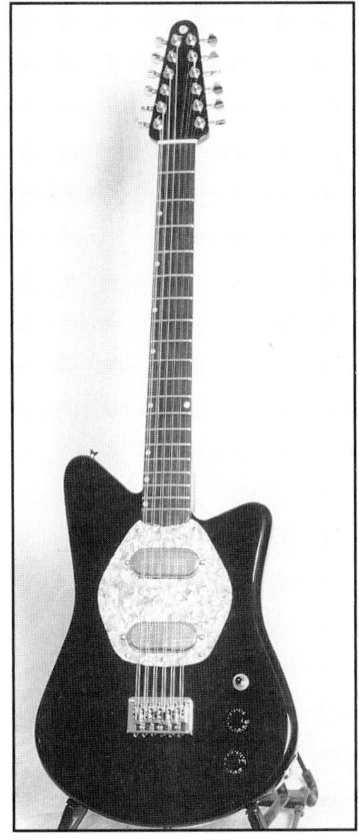

Versoul Roya

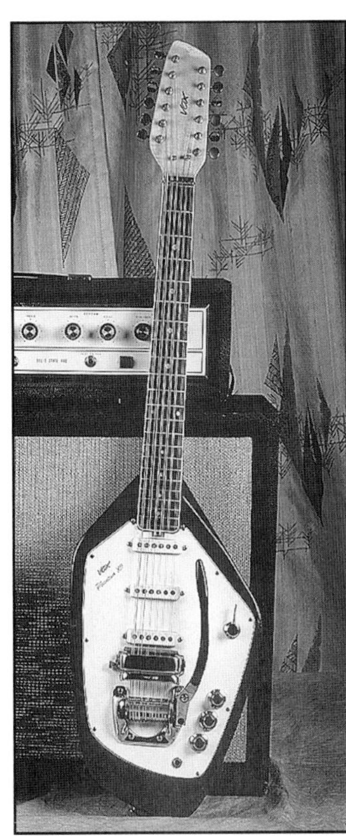

Vox Phantom XII

1966 Vox Tempest

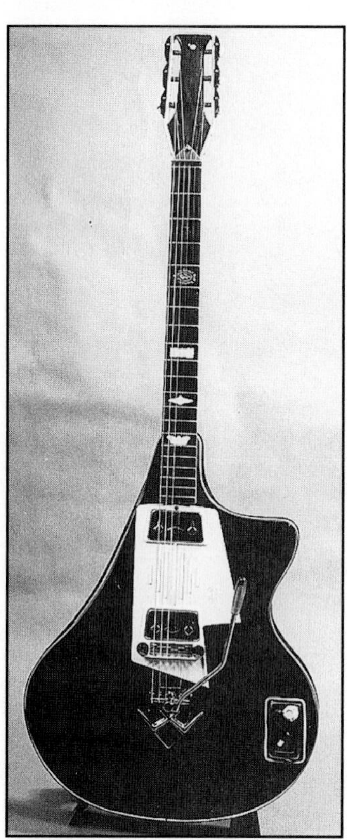

1965 Wandré Model Karak

MODEL YEAR	FEATURES	EXC. COND. LOW	HIGH

Starstream

1967-1968. Teardrop-shaped hollowbody, 2 pickups, distortion, treble and bass boosters, wah-wah, vibrato, 1 volume and 2 tone controls, three-way pickup selector. Available in Cherry or Sandburst.

1967-1968		$900	$1,000

Starstream XII

1967-1968. Teardrop-shaped hollowbody, 12 strings, 2 pickups, distortion, treble and bass boosters, wah-wah, vibrato, 1 volume and 2 tone controls, three-way pickup selector. Available in Cherry or Sandburst.

1967-1968		$900	$1,000

Stroller

1961-1966. Made in England, solidbody, single bridge pickup, Hurricane-style contoured body, dot markers.

1961-1966	Red	$300	$400

Student Prince

1965-1967. Mahogany body thinline archtop electric, 2 knobs, dot markers, made in Italy.

1965-1967		$300	$400

Super Ace

1963-1965. Solidbody double cutaway.

1963-1965		$300	$350

Super Lynx

1965-1967. Similar to Bobcat but with 2 pickups and no vibrola, double cut, 2 pickups, adjustable truss rod, 2 bass and 2 volume controls.

1965-1967		$450	$800

Super Lynx Deluxe

1965-1967. Super Lynx with added vibrato tailpiece.

1965-1967		$550	$800

Super Meteor

1965-1967. Solidbody double cutaway.

1965-1967		$250	$300

Tempest XII

1965-1967. Solidbody double cut, 12 strings, 3 pickups.

1965-1967		$450	$550

Tornado

1965-1967. Thinline archtop, single pickup, dot markers.

1965-1967	Sunburst	$300	$350

Typhoon

1965-1967. Hollowbody single cut, 2 pickups, three-piece laminated neck.

1965-1967		$350	$450

Ultrasonic

1967-1968. Hollowbody double cut, 2 pickups, distortion, treble and bass boosters, wah-wah, vibrato, 1 volume and 2 tone controls, three-way pickup selector. Available in Sunburst or Cherry.

1967-1968		$650	$850

Walker

1994-present. Premium and presentation grade, production/custom, flat-top and archtop guitars built by luthier Kim Walker in North Stonington, Connecticut.

Wandre (Davoli)

Ca. 1956/57-1969. Solidbody and thinline hollowbody electric guitars and basses created by German-descended Italian motorcycle and guitar enthusiast, artist, and sculptor from Milan, Italy, Wandre Pelotti. Brandnames include Wandre (pronounced "Vahn-dray"), Davoli, Framez, JMI, Noble, Dallas, Avalon, Avanti I and others. Until '60, they were built by Pelotti himself; from '60-'63 built in Milan by Framez; '63-'65 built by Davoli; '66-'69 built in Pelotti's own factory.

The guitars originally used Framez pickups, but from '63 on (or earlier) they used Davoli pickups. Mostly strange shapes characterized by neck-through-tailpiece alunimum neck with plastic back and rosewood fingerboard. Often multi-color and sparkle finishes, using unusual materials like linoleum, fiberglass and laminates, metal bindings. Often the instruments will have numerous identifying names but usually somewhere there is a Wandre "blob" logo.

Distributed early on in the U.K. by Jennings Musical Industries, Ltd. (JMI) and in the U.S. by Don Noble and Company. Model B.B. dedicated to Brigitte Bardot. Among more exotic instruments were the minimalist Krundaal Bikini guitar with a built-in amplifier and attached speaker, and the "pogo stick" Swedenbass. These guitars are relatively rare and highly collectible.

Warrior

1995-present. Professional, premium, and presentation grade, production/custom, acoustic and solidbody electric guitars built by luthier J.D. Lewis in Roseville, Georgia. Warrior also builds basses.

Washburn

1974-present. Budget, intermediate, professional, and premium grade, production/custom, acoustic and electric guitars made in the U.S., Japan, and Korea. They also make basses, amps, banjos and mandolins.

Originally a Lyon & Healy brandname, the Washburn line was revived in '74, promoted by Beckman Musical Instruments. Beckman sold the rights to the Washburn name to Fretted Instruments, Inc. in '76. Guitars originally made in Japan and Korea, but production moved back to U.S. in '91.

AF-40V Ace Frehley

1985-1988. Four-pointed solidbody, pointy headstock, one pickup, locking trem, Red lightning bolt starting on body and going half way up neck.

1985-1988		$500	$800

D-42 SW Harvest

1983-1989. Flat-top, spruce top, rosewood back, sides and pickguard, maple binding, purfling. Name currently used on similar model.

1983-1989		$400	$450

MODEL YEAR	FEATURES	EXC. COND. LOW	HIGH

D-42 SW Harvest Deluxe

1983-1989. Same as Harvest, but with abalone trim and cat's-eye board inlays, Gold tuners. Name currently used on similar model.

1983-1989		$450	$600

D-50S

1978-ca. 1985. Dreadnought, herringbone trim, rosewood back and sides, pearl inlays.

1978-1985		$350	$450

DC-80E

1988-1992. Extended cutaway, dreadnought, cedar top, on-board preamp.

1988-1992		$450	$550

Mirage

1983-1985. Single cut acoustic/electric classical.

1983-1985		$250	$300

Monterey 12-String

Early 1980s. Thin body, 12 strings.

1981		$250	$350

Spirit DL

1983-1985. Single cut acoustic/electric folk/classical.

1983-1985		$250	$300

Washburn (Lyon & Healy)

1880s-ca.1949. Washburn was founded in Chicago as one of the lines for Lyon & Healy to promote high quality stringed instruments, circa 1880s. The rights to manufacture Washburns were sold to J.R. Stewart Co. in '28, but rights to Washburn name were sold to Tonk Brothers Of Chicago. In the Great depression (about 1930), J.R. Stewart Co. was hit hard and declared bankruptcy. Tonk Brothers bought at auction all Stewart trade names, then sold them to Regal Musical Instrument Co. Regal built Washburns by the mid-'30s. The Tonk Brothers still licensed the name. These Washburn models lasted until ca. '49. In '74 the brand resurfaced.

Model 1897

High-end appointments, plentiful pearl, 18 frets, slightly larger than parlor size.

1910	Natural	$2,500	$3,500

Model 1915

Brazilian rosewood back and sides.

1928		$1,800	$2,200

Style 188

Rosewood back and sides with full pearl fingerboard inlaid with contrasting colored pearl. Pearl on edges and around soundhole.

1890s		$4,000	$4,500

Watkins/WEM

1957-present. Watkins Electric Music (WEM) was founded by Charlie Watkins. Their first commercial product was the Watkins Dominator (wedge Gibson stereo amp shape) in '57. They made the Rapier line of guitars and basses from the beginning. Watkins offered guitars and basses up to 1982.

MODEL YEAR	FEATURES	EXC. COND. LOW	HIGH

Wayne

1998-present. Professional and premium grade, production/custom, solidbody guitars built by luthiers Wayne and Michael (son) Charvel in Paradise, California.

Webber

1988-present. Professional grade, production/custom flat-top guitars built by luthier David Webber in North Vancouver, British Columbia.

000 12-Fret

1990s. Fifteen 1/4" lower bout 000-style, 12-fret to the body slot-head neck, Sitka spruce top, Indian rosewood back and sides, W logo on headstock.

1990s		$1,300	$1,600

D

1990s. Fifteen and one-half inch D-style, spruce top, rosewood back and sides, W logo on headstock.

1990s	Natural	$1,300	$1,600

Wechter

1984-present. Intermediate and professional grade, production/custom, flat-top, 12-string, and nylon string guitars and acoustic basses from luthier Abe Wechter in Paw Paw, Michigan. Until 1994 he built guitars on a custom basis. In '95, he set up a manufacturing facility in Paw Paw to produce his new line. Wechter was associated with Gibson Kalamazoo from the mid-'70s to '84.

Pathmaker 12

1994-present. Double cutaway, acoustic flat-top, 12 strings with onboard electronics.

1990s	Natural gloss	$800	$1,000

Pathmaker Elite

1994-present. Double cutaway, acoustic/electric flat-top, cedar top, walnut back and sides.

1994-1999	Sunburst	$800	$1,000

Pathmaker Standard

1994-present. Double cutaway, acoustic flat-top, solid Sitka spruce top, solid mahogany back and sides or optional rosewood back and sides.

1994-1999	Natural gloss	$800	$1,000

Weissenborn

1910s-1937. Hermann Weissenborn was well-established as a luthier in Los Angeles by the early 1910s. Most of his production was in the '20s and '30s until his death in 1937. He made parlour guitars and ukes, but is best remembered for his Hawiian guitars that caught the wave of Hawiian music popularity. That music captivated America after being introduced to the masses at San Francisco's Panama Pacific International Exposition which was thrown in 1915 to celebrate the opening of the Panama Canal and attended by more than 13 million people.

Style #1 Hawaiian

Koa.

1926		$2,500	$3,000

1910 Washburn Style 1897

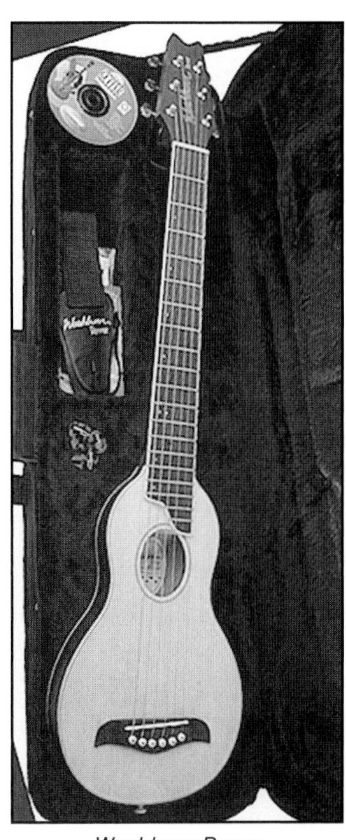

Washburn Rover

GUITARS

1930 Weissenborn Style 1

1986 Westone
Pantera Deluxe X350

MODEL YEAR	FEATURES	EXC. COND. LOW	HIGH

Style #2 Hawaiian

1926		$3,000	$3,300

Style #3 Hawaiian

Natural koa.

1926		$3,500	$3,700

Style #4 Hawaiian

Koa.

1927		$4,000	$4,500

Style A Spanish

1924		$1,800	$3,000

Style B Spanish

1924		$2,300	$3,500

Style C Spanish

1924		$2,800	$4,000

Style D Spanish

1924		$3,800	$5,000

Wendler

1999-present. Intermediate and professional grade, production/custom, solidbody, electro-acoustic guitars from luthier Dave Wendler of Ozark Instrument Building in Branson, Missouri. In '91, Wendler patented a pickup system that became the Taylor ES system.

Westbury-Unicord

1978-ca. 1983. Imported from Japan by Unicord of Westbury, New York. High quality original designs, generally with two humbuckers, some with varitone and glued-in necks.

Deluxe

1978-1981. Double cutaway solidbody, two exposed humbucker pickups.

1978-1981	White	$350	$450

Standard

1978-1981. Double cutaway solidbody, two exposed humbucker pickups, dot markers, Westbury logo on headstock.

1978-1981	Sunburst	$275	$350

Westone

1970s-1990. Made by Matsumoku in Matsumoto, Japan and imported by St. Louis Music. Around '81, St. Louis Music purchased an interest in Matsumoku and began to make a transition from its own Electra brandname to the Westone brandname previously used by Matsumoku. In the beginning of '84, the brandname became Electra-Westone with a phoenix bird head surrounded by circular wings and flames. By the end of '84 the Electra name was dropped, leaving only Westone and a squared-off bird with W-shaped wings logo. Electra, Electra-Westone and Westone instruments from this period are virtually identical except for the brand and logo treatment. Many of these guitars were made in very limited runs and are relatively rare.

Matsumoku-made guitars feature a serial number in which the first one or two digits represent the year of manufacture. Electra-Westone guitars should begin with either a 4 or 84.

MODEL YEAR	FEATURES	EXC. COND. LOW	HIGH

Corsair

1989-1991. Endorsed by Steve Lynch. Built-in DSR-5 Harmonic Enhancer.

1989		$175	$250

Pantera II

1990-1991. Like the Trevor Rabin III, but with two humbuckers and finer features.

1990		$250	$350

Rabin III

1989		$200	$250

Thunder I

Early-mid-1980s. Solidbody electric.

1982		$200	$250

Weymann

Incorporated in 1904 to market stringed instruments, but mainly known for banjos. Early guitar models made by Regal and Vega.

Parlor Guitar

1904-ca. 1920. Small 14 5/8" body parlor-style, fancy pearl and abalone trim, fancy fretboard markers.

1910	Natural	$3,000	$4,000

Wilkins

1984-present. Custom guitars built by luthier Pat Wilkins in Van Nuys, California. Wilkins also does finish work for individuals and a variety of other builders.

Windsor

Ca. 1890s-ca. 1914. Brandname used by Montgomery Ward for flat top guitars and mandolins made by various American manufacturers, including Lyon & Healy and, possibly, Harmony. Generally beginner-grade instruments.

Acoustic Flat-Top Guitars

1890s-1914.

1900s		$200	$300

Winston

Ca. 1963-1967. Imported from Japan by Buegeleisen and Jacobson of New York. Manufacturers unknown, but some are by Guyatone. Generally shorter scale beginner guitars.

Electric Thinline Archtop Guitars

Ca.1963-1967.

1960s		$150	$250

Worland Guitars

1997-present. Professional grade, production/custom, flat-top, 12-string, and harp guitars built by luthier Jim Worland in Rockford, Illinois.

WRC Music International

1989-mid-1990s. WRC Music International by Wayne Richard Charvel, who was the original founder of Charvel Guitars.

MODEL YEAR	FEATURES	EXC. COND. LOW	HIGH

Wright Guitar Technology

1993-present. Luthier Rossco Wright builds his unique intermediate grade, production, travel/practice steel-string and nylon-string guitars in Eugene, Oregon.

Wurlitzer

Wurlitzer marketed a line of American- and foreign-made guitars starting in 1965. The American ones were built from '65-'66 by the Holman-Woodell guitar factory in Neodesha, Kansas. In '67, Wurlitzer switched to Italian-made Welson guitars.

Model 2077 (Martin 0-K)

1920s. Made by Martin for Wurlitzer who had full-line music stores in most major cities. Size 0 with top, back and sides made from koa wood, limited production of about 28 instruments.

1922	Natural	$5,000	$5,500

Model 2090 (Martin 0-28)

1920s. Made by Martin for Wurlitzer who had full-line music stores in most major cities. Size 0 with appointments similar to a similar period Martin 0-28. Limited production of about 11 instruments. Wurlitzer branded on the back of the headstock and on the inside back seam. Martin name also branded on inside seam.

1922	Natural	$7,000	$8,000

Wild One "Stereo"

1960s. Two pickups, blond.

1967		$400	$550

Yamaha

1946-present. Budget, intermediate, professional, and presentation grade, production/custom, acoustic, acoustic/electric, and electric guitars. They also build basses, amps, and effects.

Japanese instrument maker founded in 1887. Began acoustic guitar production in 1946. Solidbody electric production began in '66. Production shifted from Japan to Taiwan (Yamaha's special-built plant) in '84, though some high-end guitars still made in Japan. Some Korean production began in '90s.

AE-11

1966-1974. Single cut, arched top, glued neck, 2 pickups.

1966-1974	Natural	$500	$700

AE-12

1973-1977. ES-350T-style model.

1973-1977		$500	$800

AE-18

1973-1977. AE-12 with upgrade inlays and gold hardware.

1973-1977		$550	$850

AE-500

1998-2000. Vague Les Paul-style body with rounded cutaway horn, 2 humbuckers, pearloid guard, dot markers.

1998-2000		$275	$375

MODEL YEAR	FEATURES	EXC. COND. LOW	HIGH

APX-4

1992-1995. Acoustic/electric cutaway flat-top.

1992-1995		$400	$500

APX-10

1987-1994. Acoustic/electric flat-top cutaway, 2 pickups, stereo two-way. Called APX-10T if ordered with rosewood back and sides.

1987-1994		$450	$550

DW-8 VRS

1990s. D-style flat-top, sunburst, solid spruce top, higher-end appointments like abalone rosette and top purfling.

1990s		$475	$575

Eterna Acoustic

1983-1994. Folk style acoustics, there were 4 models.

1983-1994		$200	$250

FG-345

1983-1994. Bound top flat-top.

1983-1994		$300	$350

FG-410

1984-1994. Flat-top acoustic; the 410E had a pickup.

1984-1994		$300	$350

FG-412SB II 12-String

1983-1994. 12-string flat top.

1983-1994	Sunburst	$300	$400

FG-430A

1984-1994. D-style flat-top.

1984-1994		$350	$400

G-245S

1981-1985. Classical, solid spruce top, rosewood back and sides.

1981-1985		$200	$350

G-255S

1981-1985. Classical, spruce top, Indian rosewood back and sides.

1981-1985		$300	$450

Image Custom

1989-1992. Electric double cut, flamed maple top, active circuitry, LED position markers.

1989-1992		$300	$400

L-8 Acoustic

1984-1996. Solid top D-style acoustic.

1984-1996		$300	$350

Pacifica (standard features)

1980s-1990s. Strat-style body with longer horns, dot markers.

1990s		$200	$350

Pacifica 921

1986-1992. Offset double cut solid body, 2 humbuckers, 1 stacked single coil. The first of many Yamaha Pacifica PAC models.

1986-1992		$200	$350

RGX Standard

1988-1992. Electric, carved maple top, bolt-on neck, 3 pickups, bypass switch.

1988-1992		$200	$250

Yamaha FG Jr.

1989 Yamaha RGX Standard

Yamaha SA-2000

Yamaha SG-1500

MODEL YEAR	FEATURES	EXC. COND. LOW	HIGH

RGX-610M

1987-1992. Electric, basswood body, maple board, one high-output Alnico II humbucker.

1987-1992 $200 $300

RGZ-312

1989-1992. Offset double cut solid body, bolt neck, 2 single-coils and 1 humbucker, dot markers.

1989-1992 $300 $350

RGZ-820R

1993-1994. Blues Saraceno Signature Model, bolt neck, 2 humbuckers, dot markers.

1993-1994 $400 $500

SA-700

1980s. ES-335-style with stud mounted tailpiece (vs. trapeze), dot markers, dual humbuckers, SA (Super Axe) Series, Super Axe script logo on headstock, SA700 logo on bell cap truss rod cover.

1980s $800 $950

SA-2000

1979-1984. ES-335-style electric archtop, stud mounted tailpiece (vs. trapeze), block markers, 2 humbuckers, SA (Super Axe) Series, gold hardware. Sunburst or burgundy finish.

1979-1984 $850 $1,000

SBG-200

1983-1992. Solidbody, glued neck, unbound, dot inlays on rosewood 'board, gold hardware, white top.

1983-1992 $200 $350

SBG-2000

1983-1992. Electric, double cut beveled body, set-neck, 2 pickups.

1983-1992 $250 $350

SBG-2100

1984-1992. Double cut solidbody, set-neck.

1984-1992 $200 $350

SE-250

1986-1992. Electric, offset double cut, 2 pickups.

1986-1992 $200 $350

SE-350 H

1986-1992. Solidbody, offset double cut, two humbuckers.

1986-1992 $200 $350

SG-3

1965-1966. Early double cut solidbody with sharp horns, bolt-, 3 hum-single pickup layout, large white guard, rotor controls, tremolo.

1965-1966 $850 $950

SG-30

1973-1976. Slab Katsura wood solidbody, bolt neck, two humbuckers, dot inlays.

1973-1976 $350 $450

SG-30A

1973-1976. Slab maple solidbody, bolt neck, two humbuckers, dot inlays.

1973-1976 $350 $450

SG-35

1973-1976. Slab mahogany solidbody, bolt neck, two humbuckers, parallelogram inlays.

1973-1976 $350 $500

MODEL YEAR	FEATURES	EXC. COND. LOW	HIGH

SG-35A

1974-1976. Slab maple solidbody, bolt neck, two humbuckers, parallelogram inlays.

1973-1976 $350 $500

SG-40

1972-1973. Bolt-on neck, carved body, single cutaway.

1972-1973 $350 $500

SG-45

1972-1976. Glued neck, single cutaway, bound flat-top.

1972-1976 $400 $600

SG-60

1972 only. Bolt-on neck, carved body, single cutaway.

1972 $300 $500

SG-60T

1973 only. SG-60 with large cast vibrato system.

1973 $300 $500

SG-65

1972-1976. Glued neck, single cutaway, bound flat-top.

1972-1976 Set-neck $400 $600

SG-70

1974-1976. Slab maple solidbody, glued neck, two humbuckers, dot inlays, large pickguard.

1974-1976 $400 $600

SG-80

1972 only. Bolt-on neck, carved body, single cutaway.

1972 $400 $600

SG-80T

1973 only. SG-68 with large cast vibrato system.

1973 $400 $600

SG-85

1972-1976. Glued neck, single cutaway, bound flat-top.

1972-1976 $400 $600

SG-90

1974-1976. Carved top mahogany solidbody, glued neck, elevated pickguard, bound top, dot inlays, chrome hardware.

1974-1976 $450 $600

SG-175

1974-1976. Carved top mahogany solidbody, glued neck, elevated pickguard, abalone bound top, abalone split wing or pyramid inlays, gold hardware.

1974-1976 $600 $800

SG-500/SBG-500

1976-1978, 1981-1983. Carved unbound maple top, double pointed cutaways, glued neck, two exposed humbuckers, three-ply bound headstock, bound neck with clay split wing inlays, chrome hardware. Reissued as the SBG-500 (800S in Japan) in '81.

1976-1978 SG-500 $600 $700

1981-1983 SBG-500 $600 $700

MODEL YEAR	FEATURES	EXC. COND. LOW	HIGH

SG-700

1976-1978. Carved unbound maple top, double pointed cutaways, glued neck, two humbuckers, three-ply bound headstock, bound neck with clay split wing inlays, chrome hardware.

1976-1978		$700	$900

SG-700S

1999-2001. Set neck, mahogany body, two humbuckers with coil tap.

1999-2001		$600	$800

SG-800

1977-ca.1980. Same as SG-700, but with White binding. Probably not exported to the U.S.

1977-1980		$700	$900

SG-1000/SBG-1000

1976-1983 ('84 in Japan). Carved maple top, double pointed cutaways, glued neck, 2 humbuckers, 3-ply bound headstock, unbound body, bound neck with clay split wing inlays, gold hardware. Export model name changed to SBG-1000 in '80.

1976-1983		$700	$900

SG-1500

1976-1979. Carved maple top, double pointed cutaways, laminated neck-thru-body neck, laminated mahogany body wings, 2 humbuckers, 5-play bound headstock and body, bound neck with dot inlays, chrome hardware. Name used on Japan-only model in the 1980s.

1976-1979		$900	$1,000

SG-2000/SBG-2000/SG-2000S

1976-1984 (1988 in Japan). Carved maple top, double pointed cutaways, laminated neck-thru-body neck, laminated mahogany body wings, 2 humbuckers, 5-ply bound headstock and body, bound neck with abalone split wing inlays, gold hardware. In '80, the model was changed to the SBG-2000 in the U.S., and the SG-2000S everywhere else except Japan (where it remained the SG-2000). Export model renamed SBG-2100 in 1984.

1976-1984		$800	$950

SG/SBG-3000/SG-3000 Custom/Professional

1982-1985. Similar to SG-2000, but with solid mahogany body wings, higher output humbuckers, and abalone purfling on top.

1982-1985		$900	$1,000

SHB-400

1981-1985. Solidbody electric, set-in neck, two pickups.

1981-1985		$250	$350

SSC-500

1983-1992. Solidbody electric, three pickups, set-in neck.

1983		$250	$350

Weddington Classic

1989-1992. Electric solidbody, redesigned set-in neck/body joint for increased access to the higher frets.

1989-1992		$300	$450

Yanuziello Stringed Instruments

1980-present. Production/custom resonator and Hawaiian guitars built by luthier Joseph Yanuziello, in Toronto, Ontario.

Zeiler Guitars

1992-present. Custom flat-top, 12-string, and nylon-string guitars built by luthier Jamon Zeiler in Cincinnati, Ohio.

Zemaitis

1960-1999. Tony Zemaitis (born Antanus Casimere Zemaitis) began selling his guitars in 1960. He emphasized simple light-weight construction and was known for hand engraved metal front guitars. Each hand-built guitar was a unique instrument. Ron Wood was an early customer and his use of a

Zemaitis created a demand for the custom-built guitars. Approximately six to ten instruments were built each year. Tony retired in 1999, and passed away in 2002 at the age of 67.

Acoustic Models

1965	Acoustic 12-string, 1st year	$23,000	$27,000
1980s	Acoustic 12-String D-hole	$11,000	$13,000
1980s	Acoustic 12-string heart-hole	$20,000	$25,000
1980s	Acoustic 6-string D-hole	$9,000	$11,000
1980s	Acoustic 6-string heart-hole	$11,000	$13,000

Electric Models

1980s	Disc-front	$20,000	$25,000
1980s	Metal-front	$12,000	$20,000
1980s	Pearl-front	$20,000	$25,000
1994	"Black Pearl"	$30,000	$36,000
1995	Disc-front 40th Anniversary	$28,000	$36,000

Zen-On

1946-ca.1968. Japanese manufacturer. By 1967 using the Morales brand name. Not heavily imported into the U.S., if at all (see Morales).

Acoustic Hollowbody Guitars

1946-1968. Various models.

1950s		$100	$175

Zeta

1982-present. Professional and premium grade, production/custom, semi-hollow and resonator guitars, many with electronic and MIDI options, made in Oakland, California. They also make basses, amps and mandolins.

1965 Zemaitis acoustic 12-string

1983 Zemaitis Metal-Front

Zion Classic

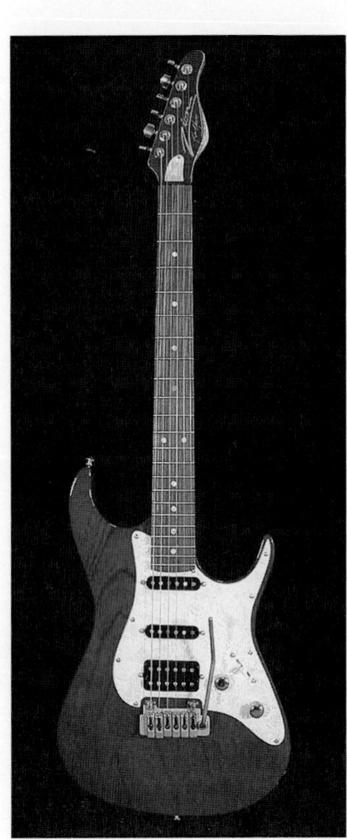
Zion Radicaster

MODEL YEAR	FEATURES	EXC. COND. LOW	HIGH

Zim-Gar

1960s. Imported from Japan by Gar-Zim Musical Instrument Corporation of Brooklyn, New York. Manufacturers unknown. Generally shorter scale beginner guitars.

Electric Solidbody Guitars

1960s.

1960s	Sunburst	$120	$175

Zimnicki, Gary

1980-present. Luthier Gary Zimnicki builds his professional and premium grade, custom, flat-top, 12-string, nylon-string, and archtop guitars in Allen Park, Michigan.

Zion

1980-present. Professional and premium grade, production/custom, semi-hollow and solidbody guitars built by luthier Ken Hoover, originally in Greensboro, North Carolina, currently in Raleigh.

Classic

1989-present. Double cut solidbody, six-on-a-side headstock, opaque finish, various pickup options, dot markers.

1990s	Custom quilted top	$650	$750
1995	Opaque finish	$400	$500

Graphic

1980s-1994. Double cut basswood body, custom airbrushed body design, bolt-on neck.

1990	Green Frost Marble	$800	$900

Radicaster

1987-1990s. Double cut basswood body, graphic finish, bolt-on neck, various pickup configurations.

1990s	Marble finish	$600	$700

The Fifty

1994-present. Single cut ash solidbody, two single coils, bolt-on neck.

1990s	Custom figured top	$650	$750
1990s	Natural, plain top	$500	$600

Zolla

1979-present. Professional grade, production/custom, electric guitars built by luthier Bill Zolla in San Diego, California. Zolla also builds basses, necks and bodies.

Zon

1981-present. Currently luthier Joe Zon only offers basses, but he did also build guitars from '85-'91. See Bass Section for more company info.

Basses

BASSES

Acoustic Black Widow

Alamo Titan

Acoustic

Ca. 1965-ca. 1987. Mainly known for solidstate amps, the Acoustic Control Corp. of Los Angeles, CA did offer guitars and basses from around '69 to late '74. The brandname was revived a few years ago by Samick for a line of amps.

Black Widow Bass

1969-1970, 1972-1974. Around '69 Acoustic offered the AC600 Black Widow Bass (in both a fretted and fretless version) which featured an unique black equal double cutaway body with German carve, an "Ebonite" fingerboard, two pickups, each with one row of adjustable polepieces, a zero fret, and a protective "spider design" pad on back. Also available was the AC650 short-scale. The '72-'74 version had the same body design, but had a rosewood 'board and only one pickup with two rows of adjustable pole pieces (the '72s had a different split-coil pickup with four polepieces, two front and two back). Acoustic outsourced the production of the basses, possibly to Japan, but at least part of the final production was by Semie Moseley.

MODEL YEAR	FEATURES	EXC. COND. LOW	HIGH
1972-1974		$600	$800

Airline

1958-1968. Brandname for Montgomery Ward. Built by Kay, Harmony and Valco.

Electric Solidbody Basses

MODEL YEAR	FEATURES	EXC. COND. LOW	HIGH
1960s	Various models	$150	$300

Pocket 3/4 Bass (Valco/National)

1962-1966. Airline brand of double cut 'Pocket Bass,' short-scale, 2 pickups, 1 acoustic bridge and 1 neck humbucker. Sunburst and other colors.

MODEL YEAR	FEATURES	EXC. COND. LOW	HIGH
1962-1968		$250	$650

Alamo

1947-1982. Founded by Charles Eilenberg, Milton Fink, and Southern Music, San Antonio, TX. Distributed by Bruno & Sons. See Guitar section for more company info or *Guitar Stories Volume II*, by Michael Wright, for a complete history of Alamo with detailed model listings.

Eldorado Bass (Model 2600)

1965-1966. Solidbody, 1 pickup, angular offset shape, double cut.

MODEL YEAR	FEATURES	EXC. COND. LOW	HIGH
1965-1966		$200	$250

Titan Bass

1963-1970. Hollowbody, 1 pickup, angular offset shape.

MODEL YEAR	FEATURES	EXC. COND. LOW	HIGH
1963-1970		$200	$250

Alembic

1969-present. Professional, premium, and presentation grade, production/custom, 4-, 5-, and 6-string basses built in Santa Rosa, California. They also build guitars. Established in San Francisco as one of the first handmade bass builders. Alembic basses come with many options concerning woods (examples are maple, bubinga, walnut, vermilion, wenge, zebrawood), finishes, inlays, etc., all of which affect the values listed here. These dollar amounts should be used as a baseline guide to values for Alembic.

Anniversary Bass

1989. 20th Anniversary limited edition, walnut and vermillion with a walnut core, 5-piece body, 5-piece neck-through. Only 200 built.

MODEL YEAR	FEATURES	EXC. COND. LOW	HIGH
1989		$1,900	$2,100

Custom Shop Built Basses

1969-present. Various one-off and/or custom built instruments. Each instrument should be evaluated individually. Prices are somewhat speculative due to the one-off custom characteristics and values can vary greatly.

MODEL YEAR	FEATURES	EXC. COND. LOW	HIGH
1978	Dragon Double-neck	$5,000	$15,000
2000	Stanley Clarke Custom	$3,000	$5,000

Distillate 4 Bass

MODEL YEAR	FEATURES	EXC. COND. LOW	HIGH
1980s		$900	$1,500

Distillate 5 Bass

1979-1991. Exotic woods, active electronics.

MODEL YEAR	FEATURES	EXC. COND. LOW	HIGH
1980s		$1,000	$1,600

Elan 4 Bass

1985-1996. Available in 4-, 5-, 6- and 8-string models, 3-piece through-body laminated maple neck, solid maple body, active electronics, solid brass hardware. Offered in a variety of hardwood tops and custom finishes.

MODEL YEAR	FEATURES	EXC. COND. LOW	HIGH
1985-1996	Light Brown quilted maple	$800	$1,300

Elan 5 Bass

1985-1996. Available in 4-, 5-, 6- and 8-string models, 3-piece through-body laminated maple neck, solid maple body, active electronics, solid brass hardware. Offered in a variety of hardwood tops and custom finishes.

MODEL YEAR	FEATURES	EXC. COND. LOW	HIGH
1985-1996	Coco bolo upgrade	$1,500	$2,400
1985-1996	Light Brown quilted maple	$900	$1,400

Epic 5-String Bass

Five-string version, large pointed bass horn.

MODEL YEAR	FEATURES	EXC. COND. LOW	HIGH
1997		$1,000	$1,400

Epic Bass

1993-present. Special edition mahogany body with various tops, extra large pointed bass horn, maple/walnut veneer set-neck. Available in 4-, 5-, and 6-string versions.

MODEL YEAR	FEATURES	EXC. COND. LOW	HIGH
1997-1998	Natural highly flamed maple	$900	$1,100

Essence 4 Bass

1991-present. Mahogany body with various tops, extra large pointed bass horn, walnut/maple laminate neck-through.

MODEL YEAR	FEATURES	EXC. COND. LOW	HIGH
1995	Natural highly flamed maple	$1,500	$1,600

MODEL YEAR	FEATURES	EXC. COND. LOW	HIGH

Essence 5 Bass

1991-present. Mahogany body with various tops, extra large pointed bass horn, walnut/maple laminate neck-through.

1990s	Natural highly flamed maple	$1,600	$1,900

Essence 6 Bass

1991-present. Mahogany body with various tops, extra large pointed bass horn, walnut/maple laminate neck-through.

1992		$1,400	$1,700

Exploiter Bass

1980s. Explorer-style 4-string body, figured wood, neck-through design.

1984-1988	Transparent, figured maple	$1,400	$2,000

Persuader Bass

1983-1991.

1987		$700	$900

Series I Bass

1971-present. Mahogany body with various tops, maple/purpleheart laminate neck-through, active electronics. Available in 3 scale lengths and with 4, 5 or 6 strings.

1970s	Medium- or long-scale	$2,200	$2,800
1970s	Short-scale	$2,000	$2,600
1980s	Medium- or long-scale	$2,200	$2,800
1980s	Short-scale	$2,000	$2,700

Series II Bass

Generally custom-made option, each instrument valued on a case-by-case basis, guidance pricing only.

1990s		$4,000	$7,000

Spoiler Bass

1981-1999. Solid mahogany body, maple neck-through, 4 strings, active electronics.

1980s	Various high-end wood options	$1,300	$1,500
1990s	Various high-end wood options	$1,300	$1,500

Alvarez

1965-present. Imported by St. Louis Music. See Guitar section for more company info.

Electric Solidbody Basses (mid-level)

1990s. Import copies of Tobias and other high-end brands, many with long cutaway horns.

1990s		$350	$450

American Conservatory (Lyon & Healy)

Late-1800s-early-1900s. Mainly catalog sales guitars and mandolins from the Chicago maker. Mid-level Lyon & Healy offering, above their Lakeside brand, and generally under their Washburn brand.

Monster Bass G2740

Early-mid-1900s. 6-string acoustic flat-top, spruce top, birch back and sides with rosewood stain, Natural. Their catalog claimed it was "Indespensable to the up-to-date mandolin and guitar club."

1917		$3,000	$5,000

Ampeg

1949-present. Ampeg was founded on a vision of an amplified bass peg, which evolved into the Baby Bass. Ampeg has sold basses on and off throughout its history. See Guitar section for more company info.

AEB-1 Bass

1966-1967. F-holes through-body, fretted, scroll headstock, pickup in body, sunburst. Reissued as the AEB-2 for 1997-1999.

1966-1967		$1,500	$1,700

ASB-1 Devil Bass

1966-1967. Long-horn body, fretted, triangular F-holes through the body, Fireburst.

1966-1967		$2,000	$3,000

AUB-1 Bass

1966-1967. Same as AEB-1, but fretless, sunburst. Reissued as the AUB-2 for 1997-1999.

1966-1967		$1,500	$1,800

BB-4 Baby Bass

1962-1971. Electric upright slim-looking bass that is smaller than a cello. Available in sunburst, white, red, black, and a few turquoise. Reissued as the ABB-1 Baby Bass for 1997-'99.

1960s	Solid color	$2,500	$3,000
1960s	Sunburst	$2,000	$2,500

BB-5 Baby Bass

1964-1971. Five-string version.

1960s	Sunburst	$2,500	$3,000

Dan Armstrong Lucite Bass

1969-1971. Clear solid lucite body, did not have switchable pickups like the Lucite guitar.

1969-1971		$1,100	$1,300

Dan Armstrong Lucite Bass Reissue

1990s. Reissue lucite body, Dan Armstrong Ampeg block lettering on pickguard.

1990s		$750	$850

GEB-101 Little Stud Bass

1973-1975. Import from Japan, '60s Precision Bass-style body and controls, two-on-a-side tuners.

1973-1975		$300	$400

GEB-750 Big Stud Bass

1973-1975. Import from Japan. Offset double cut solidbody, two-on-a-side tuners.

1973-1975		$300	$400

Angelica

1967-1975. Student and entry-level imports from Japan.

Electric Solidbody Basses

Japanese imports.

1970s	Various models	$100	$175

Alvarez AE4PB

Ampeg AEB-1

1976 Aria Mach 1

1967 Baldwin Bison

MODEL YEAR	FEATURES	EXC. COND. LOW	HIGH

Apollo

Ca. 1967-1972. Entry-level instruments imported from Japan by St. Louis Music. See Guitar section for more company info.

Electric Hollowbody Basses

Japanese imports.

1970s	$100	$175

Applause

1976-present. Kaman Music's entry-level Ovation-styled brand. The instruments were made in the U.S. until around 1982, when production was moved to Korea. See Guitar section for more company info.

Acoustic/Electric AE-40 Bass

Cutaway, flat-top acoustic/electric bass. Natural.

1980s	$250	$300

Arbor

Late-1980s. Student to mid-level near copy imports by Midco International.

Electric Basses

1980s. Various models.

1980s	$200	$300

Aria Pro II

1960-present. Originally branded as Aria; renamed Aria Pro II in '75. Original designs until the '70s when the copy era began. See Guitar section for more company info.

Electric Basses

Various styles and appointments.

1980s	$200	$375

Baldwin

1965-1970. The giant organ company got into guitars and basses in '65 when it bought Burns Guitars of England and sold those models in the U.S. under the Baldwin name. See Guitar section for more company info.

Baby Bison Bass

1966-1970. Scroll head, 2 pickups, black, red or white finishes.

1960s	$600	$1,000

Bison Bass

1965-1970. Scroll headstock, 3 pickups, black or white finishes.

1960s	$700	$1,500

G.B. 66 Bass

1965-1970. Bass equivalent of G.B. 66 guitar, covered bridge tailpiece.

1960s	$400	$600

Vibraslim Bass

1965-1970. Thin body, scroll head, 2 pickups, sunburst.

1960s	$400	$600

Barclay

1960s. Generally shorter-scale, student-level imports from Japan.

MODEL YEAR	FEATURES	EXC. COND. LOW	HIGH

Electric Solidbody Basses

Various colors.

1960s	$125	$175

Bass Collection

1985-1992. Mid-level imports from Japan, distributed by Meisel Music of Springfield, New Jersey. Sam Ash Music, New York, sold the remaining inventory from '92 to '94.

SB301 Bass

1985-1992. Offset double cut, bolt neck, ash or alder body, various colors.

1980s	$250	$350

SB302 Bass

1985-1992. Offset double cut, bolt fretless neck, ash or alder body, various colors.

1980s	$250	$350

SB305 5-String Bass

1985-1992. Offset double cut, bolt neck, ash or alder body, various colors.

1980s	$300	$425

SB401 Bass

1985-1992. Offset double cut, bolt neck, basswood body, active electronics, various colors.

1980s	$400	$525

SB402 Bass

1985-1992. Offset double cut, bolt fretless neck, basswood body, active electronics, various colors.

1980s	$400	$525

SB405 5-String Bass

1985-1992. Offset double cut, bolt neck, basswood body, active electronics, various colors.

1980s	$500	$625

SB501 Bass

1985-1992. Offset double cut, bolt neck, alder body, active electronics, various colors.

1988	$500	$625

SB601 Bass

1985-1992. Offset double cut, bolt neck, maple/walnut body, active electronics, various colors.

1980s	$600	$725

BC Rich

1966-present. B.C. Rico has offered American and import basses since '69. See Guitar section for more company info and production details.

Bich Bass

1976-1998. Solidbody, neck-through, 2 pickups.

1980s	$650	$800

Eagle Bass (import)

B.C. Rico and NJ Series imports.

1980s	$250	$300

Eagle Bass (U.S.A. assembly)

1977-1996. Curved double cut solidbody, natural.

1977-1979	$1,050	$1,350
1980-1989	$1,000	$1,300

MODEL YEAR	FEATURES	EXC. COND. LOW	HIGH

Ironbird Bass

1984-1998. Kinda star-shaped, neck-through, solidbody, 2 pickups, active electronics, diamond inlays.

1980s		$600	$800

Mockingbird Bass

1976-present.

1980s		$950	$1,250

Nighthawk Bass

Introduced ca. 1979.

1980s		$600	$800

Seagull Bass

1972-1998.

1972-1979		$900	$1,100
1980-1989		$800	$1,000
1990-1998		$700	$900

Son Of A Rich Bass

1980s		$750	$900

Warlock Bass

1981-present.

1980s		$700	$900

Black Jack

1960s. Entry-level and mid-level imports from Japan.

Electric Solidbody Basses

Various colors.

1960s		$100	$200

Bradford

1960s. House brand of W.T. Grant department store, often imported. See Guitar section for more company info.

Electric Solidbody Basses

Various colors.

1960s		$100	$200

Burns

Baldwin purchased Burns in the mid-'60s and sold some of the Burns models under the Baldwin name. See Guitar section for more company info.

Nu-Sonic Bass

1968		$500	$600

Carvin

1946-present. Founded by Lowell C. Kiesel and named after sons Carson and Galvin. See Guitar section for more company info.

LB-20 Bass

1991-present.

1990s		$350	$450

LB-40 Bass

Polyurethane finished maple, fretless.

1982		$350	$450

LB-50 Bass

Offset double cut solidbody, 2 humbuckers, ebony board standard, maple optional, with dot markers.

1980		$400	$500

V-220 Bass

1980s		$350	$450

MODEL YEAR	FEATURES	EXC. COND. LOW	HIGH

Charvel

1978-present. U.S.-made from '78 to '85 and a combination of imports and U.S.-made post-'85. See Guitar section for more company info.

850 XL Bass

1988-1991. 4-string, neck-through-body, active electronics.

1988-1991		$300	$400

CX-490 Bass

1991-1994. Double cut, 4-string, bolt neck.

1991-1994		$175	$225

Eliminator Bass

1990-1991. Offset double cut, active electronics, bolt neck.

1990-1991		$200	$250

Fusion V Bass

1989-1991. 5-string, offset double cut with extreme bass horn.

1989-1991	Pearl White	$500	$700

Model 1 Bass

1986-1989. Double cut, bolt neck, one pickup.

1986-1989		$175	$225

Model 2 Bass

1986-1989. Double cut, bolt neck, two pickups.

1986-1989		$250	$350

Model 3 Bass

1986-1989. Neck-through-body, 2 single-coil pickups, active circuitry, master volume, bass and treble knobs.

1986-1989		$300	$350

Model 5 Bass

1986-1989. Double cut, P/J pickups.

1986-1989		$350	$400

Star Bass

Early 1980s. Four-point solidbody, one pickup, brass hardware, one piece maple neck.

1980s		$350	$400

Surfcaster Bass

1991-1994. Semi-hollow, lipstick tube pickups.

1991-1994		$600	$950

Cipher

1960s. Student market import from Japan.

Electric Solidbody Basses

1960s. Japanese imports.

1960s		$100	$175

Citron

1995-present. Luthier Harvey Citron (of Veillette-Citron fame) builds his professional and premium grade, production/custom basses and solidbody guitars in Woodstock, New York.

Clevinger

1982-present. Established by Martin Clevinger, Oakland, California. Mainly specializing in electric upright basses, but has offered bass guitars as well.

1988 BC Rich Bich Bass

Charvel Model 3

BASSES

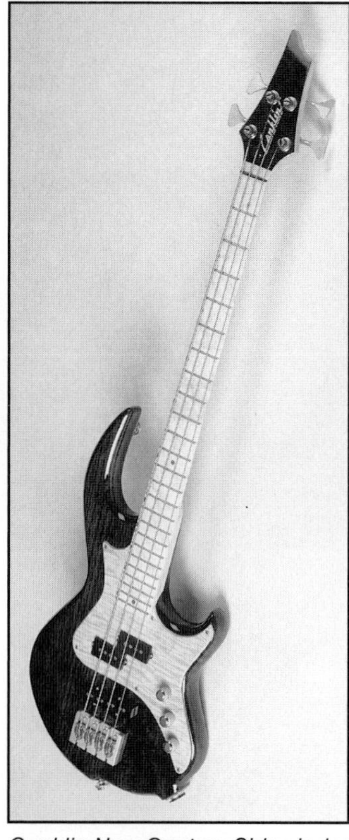
Conklin New Century Sidewinder

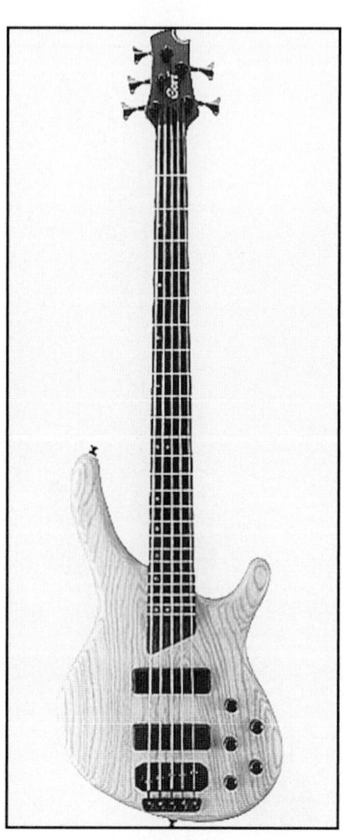
Cort C5

MODEL YEAR	FEATURES	EXC. COND. LOW	HIGH

Upright Solidbody Electric Bass

1982-present. Straight vertical-shaped compact body. Several options available that can increase values. Black.

1980s		$2,300	$2,500

College Line

One of many Lyon & Healy brands, made during the era of extreme design experimentation.

Monster Bass (Style 2089)

Early-1900s. 22" lower bout, flat-top guitar/bass, natural.

1915		$3,200	$4,000

Conklin

1984-present. Intermediate, professional, and premium grade, production/custom basses and guitars from luthier Bill Conklin, originally in Lebanon, Missouri, and since '88 in Springfield, Missouri. Conklin instruments are made in the U.S. and overseas.

GT-4 (Groove Tools) Bass

2001-present. Offset double cut with large bass horn, bolt neck, clear hard finish.

2001		$500	$550

GT-7 (Groove Tools) Bass

2001-present. Offset double cut with large bass horn, bolt neck, clear hard finish.

2001		$800	$850

M.E.U. (Mobile Electric Upright) Bass

1995-present. Cello-style hollowbody, played in an upright position, 4- or 5-string.

1995	Four strings	$1,200	$1,300

Conrad

Ca. 1968-1978. Student and mid-level import copies by David Wexler, Chicago, IL.

Model 40096 Acoustical Slimline Bass

EB-2 copy, import, 2 pickups.

1970s		$175	$300

Model 40177 Violin-Shaped Bass

Scroll headstock, import, 2 pickups.

1970s		$125	$225

Model 40224 Bumper Bass

Ampeg Dan Armstrong lucite copy, import.

1970s		$225	$275

Professional Bass

Copy of Fender Jazz Bass, import.

1970s		$150	$250

Professional Bison Bass

EB-3 copy, import, 2 pickups.

1970s		$150	$250

Cort

1973-present. North Brook, Illinois-based Cort offers intermediate and professional grade, production, acoustic and solidbody electric basses built in Korea. They also offer guitars.

Electric Solidbody Bass

Various models.

1973-1999		$100	$300

Crafter

2000-present. Intermediate grade, production, acoustic/electric bass from Hohner. They also offer guitars.

Crestwood

1970s. Copy models imported by La Playa Distributing Company of Detroit. Product line includes copies of the popular classical guitars, flat-tops, electric solidbodies and basses of the era.

Electric Basses

1970s. Includes near copies of the EB-2 (Crestwood model 2048), Beatle Bass (2049), Telecaster Bass (2079), Les Paul Bass (2090), SG EB-3 Bass (2092), Solidbody Bass (2093), and the Jazz Bass (2098).

1970s		$100	$300

Crown

1960s. Violin-shaped hollowbody electrics, solidbody electric guitars and basses, possibly others. Imported from Japan.

Electric Solidbody Basses

Japanese imports.

1960s		$100	$300

Cumpiano

1974-present. Professional and premium grade, custom steel-string and nylon-string guitars, and acoustic basses built by luthier William Cumpiano in Northampton, Massachusetts.

Custom

1980s. Line of solidbody guitars and basses introduced in the early-1980s by Charles Lawing and Chris Lovell, owners of Strings & Things in Memphis.

D'Agostino

1976-early 1990s. Import company established by Pat D'Agostino. Solidbodies imported from EKO Italy '77-'82, Japan '82-'84, and in Korea for '84 on. Overall, about 60% of guitars were Japanese, 40% Korean. See Guitar section for more company info.

Electric Solidbody Basses

Various models.

1970s		$150	$350

Daion

1978-1985. Higher quality copy imports from Japan. Original designs introduced in '80s.

Savage Bass

1980-1985. Maple neck, rosewood board, 22 nickel-silver frets.

1980-1985		$300	$600

MODEL YEAR	FEATURES	EXC. COND. LOW	HIGH

Danelectro

1946-1969, 1997-present. Danelectro has offered basses throughout most of its history. See Guitar section for more company info.

Model 1444L Bass

Ca.1958-ca.1964. Two pickups, masonite body, single cut. Copper.

1958-1959	$600	$800
1960-1962	$550	$750
1963-1964	$500	$700

Model 3412 Shorthorn Bass

1958-ca.1966. Coke bottle headstock, 1 pickup. Copper finish.

1958-1959	$600	$700
1960-1962	$550	$650
1963-1964	$500	$600
1965-1966	$450	$550

Model 3612 Shorthorn 6-string Bass

1958-ca.1966. Coke bottle headstock, 1 pickup. Copper finish.

1958-1959	$850	$1,050
1960-1962	$800	$1,000
1963-1964	$700	$900
1965-1966	$600	$800

Model 4423 Longhorn Bass

1958-ca.1966. Coke bottle headstock, 2 pickups. Copper finish.

1958-1959	$1,350	$1,450
1960-1962	$1,300	$1,400
1963-1964	$1,100	$1,200
1965-1966	$1,000	$1,100

Model 4423 Longhorn Bass Reissue

1997-present. New Danelectro company longhorn reissue.

1997-1999	$200	$250

UB-2 6-String Bass

Ca.1956-ca.1959. Single cutaway, 2 pickups.

1956-1959	$850	$1,050

Dave Maize Acoustic

1991-present. Luthier Dave Maize builds his premium grade, production/custom, acoustic basses in Cave Junction, Oregon. He also builds flat-tops.

Dean

1976-present. Founded by Dean Zelinsky, Dean has offered a variety of American and import bass models. See Guitar section for more company info.

Baby ML Bass

1982-1986. Downsized version of ML. U.S.-made.

1982-1986	$250	$550

Mach V Bass

1985-1986. U.S.-made pointed solidbody, 2 pickups, rosewood 'board.

1985-1986	$300	$500

ML Bass

1977-1986. Flying V/Explorer combo body style, fork headstock, U.S.-made.

1977-1983 U.S.A.-made	$900	$1,000
1984-1986 Import	$250	$300

Dean Markley

The string and pickup manufacturer offered a limited line of guitars and basses for a time in the late '80s.

Vintage Bass

1987. Maple neck, maple or ash body, maple or rosewood 'board, solidbody, either split P-type or a P-J combination pickups.

1987	$250	$375

Dillon

1975-present. Professional and premium grade, custom, acoustic basses and flat-tops built by luthier John Dillon originally in New Mexico, but currently in Bloomsburg, Pennsylvania.

Dingwall

1988-present. Luthier Sheldon Dingwall, Saskatoon, Canada, started out producing guitar bodies and necks, eventually offering complete guitars and basses. Currently Dingwall offers professional to premium grade, production/custom 4, 5, and 6-string basses featuring the Novax Fanned-Fret System.

DiPinto

1995-present. Intermediate grade, production retro-vibe guitars and basses from luthier Chris DiPinto of Philadelphia, Pennsylvania. Until late '99, all instruments built in the U.S., since then all built in Korea.

Domino

Ca. 1967-1968. Imported from Japan by Maurice Lipsky Music of New York, mainly copies, but some original designs. See Guitar section for more company info.

Beatle Bass

1967-1968. Beatle Bass-style.

1960s	$100	$300

Fireball Bass

1967-1968. Vox Phantom IV copy.

1960s	$100	$300

Dorado

Ca. 1972-1973. Name used briefly by Baldwin/Gretsch on line of Japanese imports.

Electric Solidbody Basses

Japanese imports.

1970s	$100	$250

Dragonfly

1994-present. Professional grade, production/custom, sloped cutaway flat-tops and acoustic

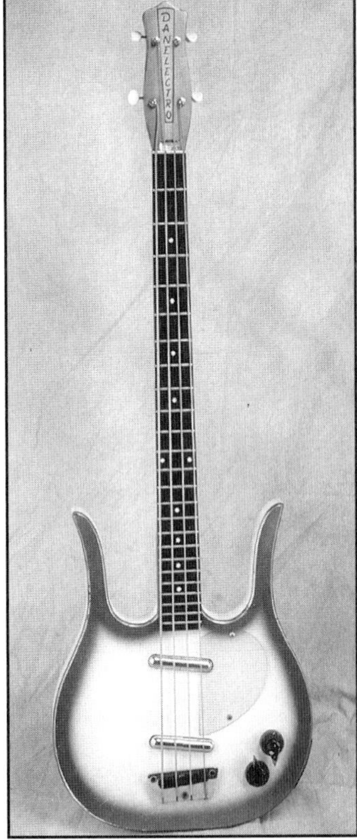

Danelectro 4423 Longhorn Bass

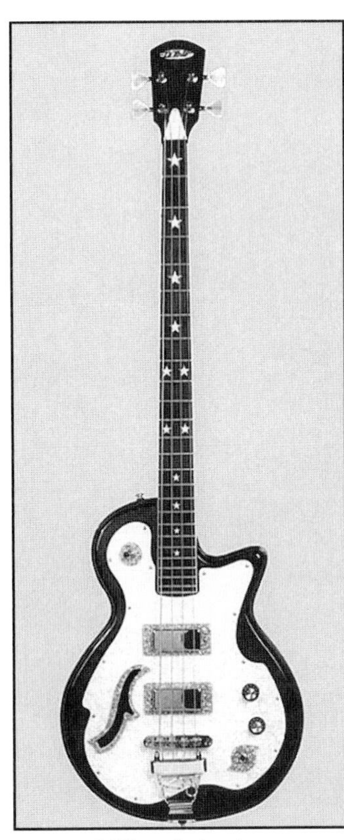
DiPinto Belvedere

BASSES

BASSES

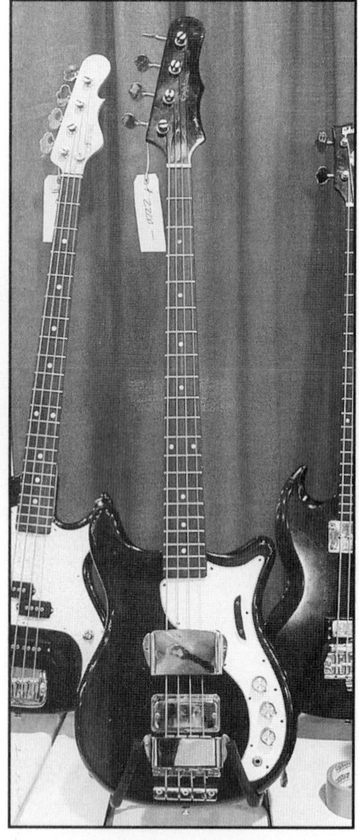

1967 Epiphone Embassy

Epiphone Jack Casady

MODEL YEAR	FEATURES	EXC. COND. LOW	HIGH

basses, semi-hollowbody electrics, and dulcitars built by luthier Dan Richter in Roberts Creek, British Columbia.

Earthwood

1972-1985. Acoustic designs by Ernie Ball with input from George Fullerton. One of the first to offer acoustic basses.

Acoustic Bass

1972-1985. Big bodied acoustic bass alternative between Kay double bass and solidbody Fender bass.

1978		$900	$1,200

EKO

1959-1985. Built by the Oliviero Pigini Company, Italy. Importers included LoDuca Brothers, Milwaukee, Wisconsin. See Guitar section for more company info.

Cobra Bass II

1967-ca.1969. Offset double cutaway solidbody, 2 pickups.

1967-1969		$300	$350

Kadett Bass

1967-1978. Red or sunburst.

1967-1978		$275	$325

Model 1100/2 Bass

1961-1966. Jaguar-style plastic covered solidbody, 2 pickups. Sparkle finish.

1961-1966		$450	$550

Model 995/2 Violin Bass

1966-ca.1969.

1966-1969		$400	$500

Rocket IV/Rokes Bass

1967-early-1970s. Rocket-shape design, solidbody, says "Rokes" on the headstock. The Rokes were a popular English band that endorsed EKO guitars. Marketed as the Rocket IV in the U.S. and as the Rokes in Europe. Often called the Rok. Sunburst, 1 pickup.

1967-1971		$450	$850

Electra

1971-1984. Imported from Japan by St. Louis Music. See Guitar section for more company info.

MPC Outlaw Bass

1970s. Has 2 separate modules that plug in for different effects. Neck-through-body.

1970s		$200	$500

Other Electric Solidbody Basses

Japanese imports, various models.

1970s		$150	$500

Emperador

1966-1992. Student-level imports of Westheimer Musical Instruments. Early models appear to be made by either Teisco or Kawai; later models were made by Cort.

Electric Solidbody Basses

Japanese imports. Various models.

1960s		$100	$250

MODEL YEAR	FEATURES	EXC. COND. LOW	HIGH

Engelhardt

Engelhardt specializes in student acoustic basses and cellos and is located in Elk Grove Village, Illinois.

EM-1 Maestro Bass

A popular school model upright acoustic bass, spruce top, curly maple back, rosewood trimmings, 3/4 size, sunburst.

1970s		$400	$600

Supreme Bass

Professional quality 3/4 size upright bass, spruce top, curly maple back, ebony trimmings.

1970s		$1,000	$1,600

Epiphone

1928-present. Epiphone didn't add basses until 1959, after Gibson acquired the brandname. The Gibson Epiphones were American-made until '69, then all imports until into the '80s, when some models were again made in the U.S. See Guitar section for more company info. Currently Epiphone offers intermediate and professional grade, production, acoustic and electric basses.

B-5 Acoustic Bass Viol

1950s. Three-fourths size laminate construction.

1950s		$3,500	$3,700

EB-0 Bass

1998-present. SG body style, single pickup, bolt-on neck.

1998-1999		$200	$350

EB-3 Bass

1999-present. SG body style, two pickups.

1999		$300	$400

EBM-4 Bass

1991-1998. Alder body, maple neck, split humbucker. White.

1990s		$300	$400

Embassy Deluxe Bass

1963-1969. Solidbody, double cut, 2 pickups, tune-o-matic bridge, cherry finish.

1963-1964		$1,000	$1,300
1965-1969		$900	$1,200

Newport Bass (one pickup model)

1961-1970. Double cut cherry solidbody, 1 pickup (2 pickups optional until '63), two-on-a-side tuners until '63, four-on-a-side after that.

1961-1965		$600	$900
1966-1970		$550	$850

Newport Bass (two pickup model)

1961-1970. Double cut solidbody, 2 pickups, two-on-a-side tuners, cherry.

1961-1965		$800	$1,100
1966-1970		$750	$1,000

Rivoli Bass (double pickup)

1970 only. Double pickup Epiphone version of Gibson EB-2D.

1970	Sunburst	$1,000	$1,600

MODEL YEAR	FEATURES	EXC. COND. LOW	HIGH

Rivoli Bass (single pickup)

1959-1970. ES-335-style semi-hollowbody bass, two-on-a-side tuners, 1 pickup (2 in '70). Reissued in 1994 as the Rivoli II.

1965-1966		$900	$1,100
1967-1968		$850	$1,100
1969-1970		$850	$1,050

Thunderbird IV Bass

1997-present. Reverse-style mahogany body, 2 pickups, sunburst.

1990s		$350	$550

Viola Bass

1990s-present. Beatle Bass 500/1 copy, sunburst.

1990s		$450	$500

ESP

1975-present. Japanese-made electric guitars and basses. ESP (Electric Sound Products) made inroads in the U.S. market with mainly copy styles in the early days, mixing in original designs over the years. In the '90s, ESP opened a California-based Custom Shop. Currently they offer intermediate, professional, and premium grade, production/custom, electric basses.

B-1 Bass

1990s. Vague DC-style slab solidbody with bolt-on neck, ESP and B-1 on headstock.

1990s		$500	$550

Horizon Bass

Available in 4- and 5-strings, active electronics, 34" scale, ebony board, small headstock, heavily contoured body is flamed jasperwood.

1980s	4 Strings	$400	$500

Evergreen Mountain

1979-present. Professional grade, custom, flat-tops, tenor guitars, acoustic basses, and mandolins built by luthier Jerry Nolte in Cove, Oregon. He also built over a hundred dulcimers in the 1970s.

Fender

1946-present. Leo Fender is the father of the electric bass. The introduction of his Precision Bass in late 1951 changed forever how music was performed, recorded and heard. Leo followed with other popular models of basses that continue to make up a large part of Fender's production. Please note that all the variations of the Jazz and Precision Basses are grouped under those general headings. See the Guitar section for more company info. Currently Fender offers intermediate, professional, and premium grade, production/custom, electric and acoustic basses made in the U.S. and overseas.

Bass V

1965-1970. Five strings, double cut, 1 pickup, dot inlay '65-'66, block inlay '66-'70.

MODEL YEAR	FEATURES	EXC. COND. LOW	HIGH
1965	Lake Placid Blue	$2,500	$2,800
1965	Olympic White	$2,500	$2,700
1965	Sunburst	$2,000	$2,200
1966	Candy Apple Red	$2,400	$2,500
1966	Ice Blue Metallic	$2,600	$2,900
1966	Ocean Turquoise	$2,600	$2,900
1966	Olympic White	$2,200	$2,500
1966	Sunburst	$1,700	$2,200
1967	Lake Placid Blue	$2,200	$2,500
1967-1969	Sunburst	$1,700	$2,100
1970	Sunburst	$1,700	$2,000

Bass VI

1961-1975. Six strings, Jazzmaster-like body, 3 pickups, dot inlay until '66, block inlay '66-'75. Reintroduced as Japanese-made Collectable model '95-'98.

1961	Blond	$5,000	$6,000
1961-1962	Sunburst	$3,500	$4,500
1962	Black	$5,000	$6,000
1962	Burgundy Mist	$6,000	$7,000
1962	Dakota Red	$5,500	$6,500
1962	Daphne Blue	$5,000	$6,000
1962	Fiesta Red	$5,500	$6,500
1962	Inca Silver	$5,500	$6,500
1962	Olympic White	$4,500	$5,500
1962	Sea Foam Green	$6,500	$7,500
1962	Shell Pink	$6,500	$7,500
1962	Sherwood Green	$6,000	$7,000
1962	Shoreline Gold	$5,500	$6,500
1962	Sonic Blue	$5,000	$6,000
1962	Surf Green	$6,500	$7,500
1962-1963	Blond	$4,500	$5,500
1962-1963	Lake Placid Blue	$4,500	$5,500
1963	Black	$4,500	$5,500
1963	Candy Apple Red	$4,500	$5,500
1963	Sunburst	$3,300	$4,300
1964	Lake Placid Blue	$3,500	$4,500
1964	Sunburst	$3,300	$3,900
1965	Candy Apple Red	$3,300	$3,700
1965	Lake Placid Blue	$3,300	$3,700
1965	Sunburst	$3,200	$3,500
1966	Sunburst, block inlay	$3,000	$3,400
1966	Sunburst, dot inlay	$2,900	$3,300
1967-1968	Sunburst, block inlay	$2,700	$3,200
1969	Sunburst	$2,600	$3,000
1970	Sunburst	$2,500	$2,800
1971	Sunburst	$2,400	$2,700
1972	Olympic White	$2,900	$3,300
1972	Sunburst	$2,300	$2,700
1973	Sunburst	$2,200	$2,600
1974-1975	Sunburst	$2,000	$2,400

Bass VI Reissue

1995-1998. Reintroduced import. Sunburst.

1995-1998		$650	$750

BG-29 Bass

1990s. Acoustic flat-top bass with single cutaway, two-on-a-side tuners, Fishman on-board comtrols. Black.

1990s		$350	$400

Epiphone Rivoli

1963 Fender Bass VI

BASSES

1963 Fender Jazz Bass

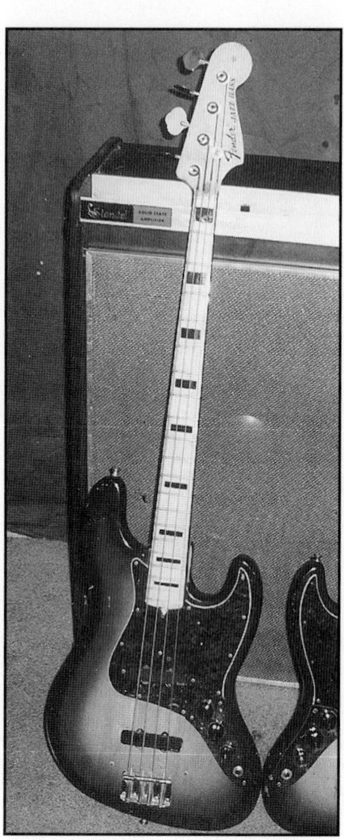
1972 Fender Jazz Bass

MODEL YEAR	FEATURES	EXC. COND. LOW	HIGH

Bullet Bass (B30, B34, B40)

1982-1983. Alder body, 1 pickup, offered in short- and long-scale, U.S.-made, but replaced with the Japanese-made Squire Bullet Bass. Red or walnut.

1982-1983		$350	$500

Coronado I Bass

1966-1970. Thinline, double cutaway, one pickup, dot inlay. Sunburst and Cherry Red were the standard colors, but custom colors could be ordered.

1966-1970	Cherry Red	$800	$1,100
1966-1970	Other custom colors	$1,000	$1,300
1966-1970	Sunburst	$800	$1,100
1966-1970	White custom color	$850	$1,150

Coronado II Bass

1967-1972. Thinline, double cutaway, two pickups, block inlay. Sunburst and Cherry Red were the standard colors, but custom colors could be ordered. Antigua available on Coronado II, Coronado Antigua and Electric XII only in the late '60s.

1967-1972	Cherry Red	$900	$1,200
1967-1972	Coronado Antigua	$1,100	$1,400
1967-1972	Other custom colors	$1,100	$1,400
1967-1972	Sunburst	$900	$1,200
1967-1972	White custom color	$950	$1,250

HM Bass IV

1989-1991. Japanese-made, 4-string, basswood body, no pickguard, 3 Jazz Bass pickups, master TBX, sunburst.

1989-1991		$400	$425

HM Bass V

1989-1991. Japanese-made, 5-string version of HM.

1989-1991		$450	$475

Jazz Bass

The following are the various Jazz Bass models. The main American-made models are listed first, with the others alphabetically as follows:

- Jazz Bass
- Standard Jazz Bass
- American Standard Jazz Bass
- '62 Jazz Bass
- American Deluxe Jazz Bass
- American Deluxe Jazz V Bass
- Deluxe Jazz Bass (active)
- Deluxe V Jazz Bass (active)
- Foto Flame Jazz Bass
- Geddy Lee Signature Jazz Bass
- Gold Jazz Bass
- Jazz Bass 50th Anniversary 5-String Bass
- Jazz Bass Special (import)
- Jazz Plus Bass
- Jazz Plus V Bass
- Noel Redding Signature Jazz Bass
- Standard Jazz Bass (later model)

Jazz Bass

1960-1981. Two stack knobs '60-'62, three regular controls '62 on. Dot markers '60-'66, block markers from '66 on. Rosewood fingerboard standard, but maple available from '68 on. With the introduction of vintage reissue models in '81, Fender started calling the American-made version the Standard Jazz Bass. That became the American Standard Jazz Bass in '88 and then became the American Series Jazz Bass in 2000.

The custom colors listing are for unfaded or very slightly faded examples. Moderately faded examples will approximate values somewhat below the low end of the value range. A heavily faded example will be worth much less than the ranges shown, even if the heavily faded example is otherwise . in excellent, original condition. A heavily faded example will have a tint that is unlike an unfaded example. Fade does not always mean 'lighter tint'. For example, a heavily faded Lake Placid Blue can turn dark green. A heavily faded instrument will fetch a value that is slightly higher than a standard Sunburst example.

Post 1971 Jazz Bass values are affected more by condition than color or neck option. The Jazz Bass was fitted with a three-bolt neck or bullet rod in late-1974. Prices assume a three-bolt neck starting in 1975.

Custom color Fenders can be forged and bogus finishes have been a problem. As the value of custom color Fenders has increased, so has the problem of bogus non-original finishes. The prices in the Guide are for factory original finishes in excellent condition. The prices noted do not take into account market factors such as fake instruments, which can have the effect of lowering a guitar's market value unless the guitar's provenance can be validated.

1960	Sonic Blue	$16,000	$19,000
1960	Sunburst, stack knobs	$13,000	$16,000
1960	Surf Green	$18,000	$20,000
1960	White	$14,000	$17,000
1961	Dakota Red, stack knobs	$16,000	$18,000
1961	Daphne Blue, stack knobs	$14,000	$17,000
1961	Fiesta Red, stack knobs	$16,000	$18,000
1961	Lake Placid Blue, stack knobs	$12,000	$15,000
1961	Sonic Blue, stack knobs	$14,000	$17,000
1961	Sunburst, stack knobs	$12,000	$14,000
1962	Black, 3 knobs	$9,000	$12,000
1962	Black, stack knobs	$11,000	$14,000
1962	Blond, 3 knobs	$9,000	$12,000
1962	Blond, stack knobs	$11,000	$14,000
1962	Burgundy Mist, 3 knobs	$13,000	$16,000

MODEL YEAR	FEATURES	EXC. COND. LOW	HIGH
1962	Burgundy Mist, stack knobs	$16,000	$18,000
1962	Dakota Red, 3 knobs	$12,000	$15,000
1962	Dakota Red, stack knobs	$15,000	$17,000
1962	Daphne Blue, 3 knobs.	$11,000	$14,000
1962	Daphne Blue, stack knobs	$13,000	$16,000
1962	Fiesta Red, 3 knobs	$12,000	$15,000
1962	Fiesta Red, stack knobs	$15,000	$17,000
1962	Inca Silver, 3 knobs	$12,000	$15,000
1962	Inca Silver, stack knobs	$15,000	$17,000
1962	Lake Placid Blue, 3 knobs	$9,000	$12,000
1962	Lake Placid Blue, stack knobs	$11,000	$14,000
1962	Olympic White, 3 knobs	$9,000	$12,000
1962	Olympic White, stack knobs	$11,000	$14,000
1962	Sea Foam Green, 3 knobs	$14,000	$17,000
1962	Sea Foam Green, stack knobs	$17,000	$19,000
1962	Shell Pink, 3 knobs	$16,000	$19,000
1962	Shell Pink, stack knobs	$19,000	$21,000
1962	Sherwood Green, 3 knobs	$13,000	$16,000
1962	Sherwood Green, stack knobs	$16,000	$18,000
1962	Shoreline Gold, 3 knobs	$12,000	$15,000
1962	Shoreline Gold, stack knobs	$15,000	$17,000
1962	Sonic Blue, 3 knobs	$11,000	$14,000
1962	Sonic Blue, stack knobs	$13,000	$16,000
1962	Sunburst, 3 knobs	$8,000	$10,000
1962	Sunburst, stack knobs	$11,000	$13,000
1962	Surf Green, 3 knobs	$14,000	$17,000
1962	Surf Green, stack knobs	$17,000	$19,000
1963	Blond	$8,000	$10,000
1963	Coral Pink, matching headstock	$17,000	$19,000
1963	Dakota Red, matching headstock	$11,000	$13,000
1963	Lake Placid Blue	$8,000	$10,000
1963	Olympic White, matching headstock	$8,000	$10,000
1963	Sonic Blue	$10,000	$12,000
1963	Sunburst	$7,000	$9,000
1964	Black	$8,000	$10,000
1964	Blond	$8,000	$10,000
1964	Burgundy Mist	$11,000	$14,000
1964	Candy Apple Red, matching headstock	$8,000	$10,000
1964	Dakota Red, matching headstock	$10,000	$12,000
1964	Fiesta Red	$10,000	$12,000
1964	Lake Placid Blue, matching headstock	$8,000	$10,000
1964	Olympic White (unfaded)	$8,000	$10,000
1964	Sherwood Green	$12,000	$14,000
1964	Sonic Blue	$9,000	$11,000
1964	Sunburst	$6,000	$8,000
1965	Black	$6,500	$8,000
1965	Burgundy Mist	$8,000	$12,000
1965	Candy Apple Red, matching headstock	$7,000	$8,000
1965	Dakota Red	$7,500	$8,500
1965	Fiesta Red	$7,500	$8,500
1965	Firemist Gold, matching headstock	$8,000	$11,000
1965	Ice Blue Metallic	$8,000	$10,000
1965	Lake Placid Blue, matching headstock	$7,000	$8,000
1965	Olympic White	$6,500	$7,500
1965	Sonic Blue, matching headstock	$7,500	$10,000
1965	Sunburst	$5,500	$6,000
1966	Black, dot markers	$5,500	$7,500
1966	Candy Apple Red, block markers	$5,500	$7,500
1966	Candy Apple Red, dot markers	$6,000	$7,700
1966	Ice Blue Metallic, dot markers	$6,500	$8,000
1966	Lake Placid Blue, matching headstock	$6,000	$7,600
1966	Olympic White, dot markers	$5,500	$7,500
1966	Sea Foam Green, dot markers	$7,000	$8,500
1966	Shoreline Gold, dot markers	$7,500	$8,500

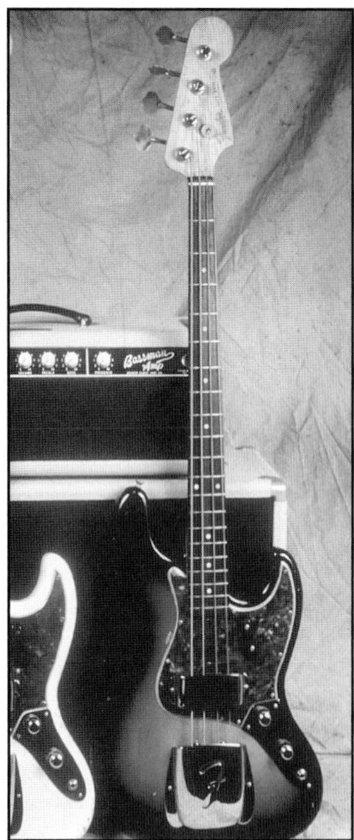
1961Fender Jazz Bass

Fender '62 Jazz Bass

BASSES

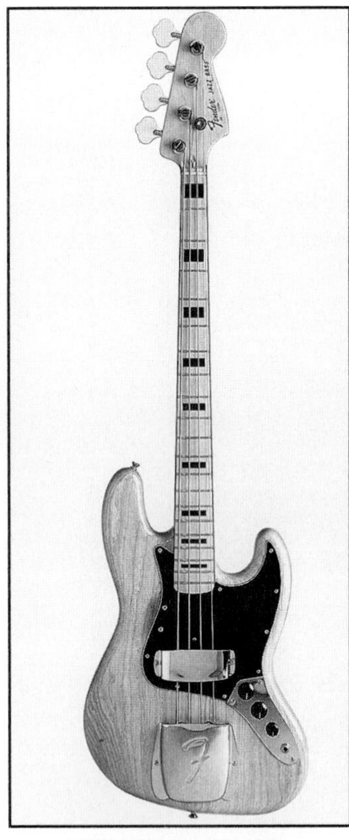
1975 Fender Jazz Bass

Fender American Series Jazz Bass

MODEL YEAR	FEATURES	EXC. COND. LOW	HIGH
1966	Sonic Blue, block markers	$6,500	$8,000
1966	Sonic Blue, dot markers	$7,000	$8,500
1966	Sunburst, block markers	$4,000	$4,500
1966	Sunburst, dot markers	$4,400	$5,000
1967	Candy Apple Red, block markers	$4,000	$6,500
1967	Olympic White, block markers	$4,000	$6,500
1967	Sonic Blue	$5,500	$7,000
1967	Sunburst, block markers	$3,500	$4,000
1968	Black, matching headstock	$4,000	$6,000
1968	Blond	$3,100	$3,600
1968	Candy Apple Red	$4,000	$6,000
1968	Cream	$3,000	$4,000
1968	Firemist Silver	$4,400	$6,200
1968	Lake Placid Blue	$4,000	$6,000
1968	Sonic Blue	$4,000	$6,000
1968	Sunburst	$3,100	$3,600
1969	Blond	$2,900	$3,400
1969	Candy Apple Red	$3,700	$5,700
1969	Cream	$2,800	$3,800
1969	Lake Placid Blue	$3,700	$5,700
1969	Olympic White, matching headstock	$3,700	$5,700
1969	Sherwood Green	$4,000	$6,000
1969	Sonic Blue	$4,000	$6,000
1969	Sunburst	$2,900	$3,400
1970	Black	$2,800	$3,300
1970	Blond	$2,800	$3,300
1970	Olympic White	$2,800	$3,300
1970	Sunburst	$2,400	$2,900
1971	Black	$2,700	$2,900
1971	Candy Apple Red	$3,000	$3,300
1971	Sunburst	$2,200	$2,700
1972	Black	$2,300	$2,700
1972	Blond	$2,000	$2,500
1972	Candy Apple Red	$2,300	$2,700
1972	Lake Placid Blue	$2,300	$2,800
1972	Olympic White	$2,300	$2,700
1972	Sunburst	$2,000	$2,500
1973	Black	$2,300	$2,400
1973	Blond	$2,000	$2,300
1973	Blond, fretless	$2,000	$2,300
1973	Olympic White	$2,200	$2,400
1973	Sunburst	$1,800	$2,300
1973	Walnut Brown	$2,100	$2,200
1974	Black, maple board	$2,000	$2,200
1974	Blond	$2,000	$2,200
1974	Blond, maple board	$2,000	$2,300
1974	Brown, maple board	$1,900	$2,100
1974	Olympic White	$2,100	$2,300
1974	Olympic White, maple neck, Black markers	$2,100	$2,300
1974	Sunburst, 4-bolt neck	$1,700	$2,200
1974	Walnut	$1,500	$2,000
1975	Black	$1,800	$2,000
1975	Blond	$1,700	$1,800
1975	Olympic White	$1,800	$2,000
1975	Sunburst, 3-bolt neck	$1,600	$1,900
1975	Walnut	$1,500	$1,800
1976	Black	$1,600	$1,800
1976	Blond, maple neck	$1,500	$1,700
1976	Sunburst	$1,600	$1,900
1976	Sunburst, maple neck	$1,700	$2,000
1977	Black, maple neck	$1,600	$1,800
1977	Blond, maple neck	$1,500	$1,700
1977	Brown, maple neck	$1,600	$1,800
1977	Sunburst	$1,600	$2,000
1977	White	$1,600	$1,800
1978	Antigua	$1,600	$2,000
1978	Black	$1,600	$1,800
1978	Blond, maple neck	$1,500	$1,700
1978	Brown	$1,600	$1,800
1978	Sunburst	$1,600	$2,000
1978	White	$1,600	$1,800
1978	Wine Red	$1,500	$1,700
1979	Blond	$1,400	$1,800
1979	Sunburst	$1,300	$1,700
1979	Transparent Red	$1,300	$1,700
1980	Antigua	$1,500	$1,800
1980	Black	$1,400	$1,700
1980	Blond	$1,300	$1,600
1980	Sunburst	$1,300	$1,600
1981	Black	$1,100	$1,500
1981	Black and Gold Collector's Edition	$1,300	$1,600
1981	International Capri Orange	$1,000	$1,400
1981	International Maui Blue	$1,000	$1,400
1981	International Monaco Yellow	$1,000	$1,400
1981	International Morocco Red	$1,000	$1,400
1981	Sahara Taupe (Light Brown)	$1,000	$1,400
1981	Sunburst	$1,000	$1,400

Standard Jazz Bass

1981-1988. Replaced Jazz Bass ('60-'81) and was then replaced by the American Standard Jazz Bass in '88. Name now used on import version.

MODEL YEAR	FEATURES	EXC. COND. LOW	HIGH
1981-1988	Mary Kaye Blond option, gold trim	$1,000	$1,300
1981-1988	Various colors	$800	$1,100

American Standard Jazz Bass

1988-2000. Replaced the Standard Jazz Bass (1981-1988) and was replaced by the American Series Jazz Bass in 2000. Various colors.

MODEL YEAR	FEATURES	EXC. COND. LOW	HIGH
1988-2000		$600	$800

MODEL YEAR	FEATURES	EXC. COND. LOW	HIGH

'62 Jazz Bass

1982-present. U.S.A.-made, reissue of 1962 Jazz Bass.

1982-1985	Standard colors	$1,000	$1,200
1986-1989	Standard colors	$950	$1,100
1990-1999	Rare colors	$1,100	$1,300
1990-2003	Standard colors	$950	$1,050

American Deluxe Jazz Bass

1998-present. U.S.-made, active electronics, alder or ash body. Alder body colors are sunburst or transparent Red, ash body colors are white blond, transparent teal green or transparent purple.

1998-1999	Various colors	$750	$850

American Deluxe Jazz V Bass

1998-present. Made in the U.S.A., active electronics, alder or ash body, 5-string model, various colors.

1998-1999		$800	$900

Deluxe Jazz Bass (active)

1995-present. Made in Mexico, active electronics, various colors.

1995-1999		$350	$400

Deluxe V Jazz Bass (active)

1995-present. Made in Mexico, various colors.

1995-1999		$400	$450

Foto Flame Jazz Bass

1995. Japanese import. Alder and basswood body with Foto Flame figured wood image.

1995		$600	$700

Geddy Lee Signature Jazz Bass

1998 only. Limited run import.

1998		$550	$650

Gold Jazz Bass

1981-1984. Gold finish and gold-plated hardware.

1981-1984		$1,000	$1,200

Jazz Bass 50th Anniversary 5-String Bass

1995-1996. Sunburst, rosewood.

1995-1996		$700	$1,000

Jazz Bass Special (import)

1984-1991. Japanese-made, Jazz/Precision hybrid, Precision-shaped basswood body, Jazz neck (fretless available), 2 P/J pickups, black hardware. Black, blond, white, sunburst.

1984-1991		$450	$550

Jazz Plus Bass

1990-1994. Alder body, 2 Fender-Lace Jazz Bass Sensors, active electronics, rotary circuit selector, master volume, balance, bass boost, bass cut, treble boost, treble cut. Various colors.

1990-1994		$600	$700

Jazz Plus V Bass

1990-1994. 5-string version.

1990-1994		$650	$750

Noel Redding Signature Jazz Bass

1997. Limited Edition, import, artist signature on pickguard.

1997		$600	$650

MODEL YEAR	FEATURES	EXC. COND. LOW	HIGH

Standard Jazz Bass (later model)

1988-present. Imported from various countries. Not to be confused with '81-'88 American-made model with the same name.

1990s		$200	$250

JP-90 Bass

1990-1994. Two P/J pickups, rosewood board, poplar body, black or red.

1990-1994		$550	$600

Marcus Miller Signature Jazz Bass

1998-present. Japanese import, sunburst.

1998-1999		$600	$650

Musicmaster Bass

1970-1983. Shorter scale, solidbody, 1 pickup, various colors.

1970-1983		$450	$500

Mustang Bass

1966-1982. Shorter scale, solidbody, 1 pickup. Offered in standard and competition colors. "Competition" colors refer to racing stripes on the body. Various colors.

1966-1969		$1,000	$1,200
1970-1979		$900	$1,100
1980-1982		$800	$1,000

Performer Bass

1985-1986. Swinger-like body style, active electronics. Various colors.

1985-1986		$900	$950

Precision Bass

The following are the various Precision Bass models. The main American-made models are listed first, with the others alphabetically as follows:

- Precision Bass
- Standard Precision Bass
- American Standard Precision Bass
- American Series Precision Bass
- '51 Precision Bass
- '55 Custom Shop Precision Bass
- '57 Precision Bass
- '57 Precision Bass (import)
- '62 Precision Bass
- '62 Precision Bass (import)
- 40th Anniversary Custom Shop Precision Bass
- American Deluxe Precision Bass
- Elite I Precision Bass
- Elite II Precision Bass
- Foto Flame Precision Bass
- Gold Elite I Precision Bass
- Gold Elite II Precision Bass
- Precision Bass (import - Japan)
- Precision Bass Lyte
- Precision Bass Special
- Precision U.S. Plus/Plus Bass
- Standard Precision Bass (later model)
- Walnut Elite I Precision Bass
- Walnut Elite II Precision Bass
- Walnut Precision Bass Special

1978 Fender Musicmaster Bass

1971 Fender Mustang Bass

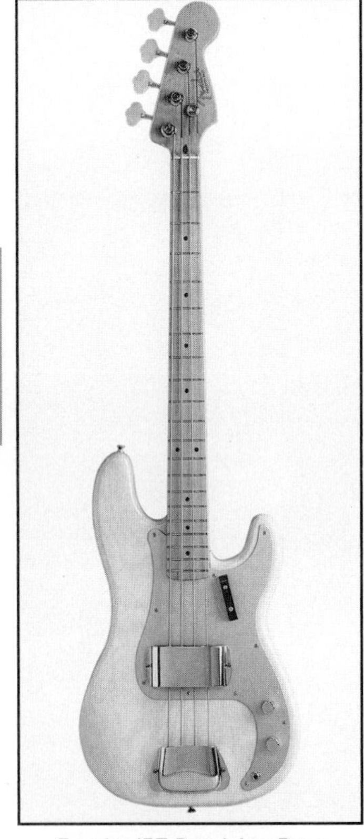

Fender '57 Precision Bass

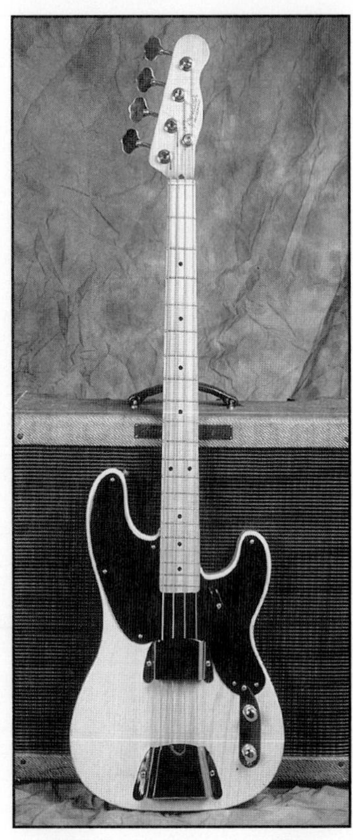

1953 Fender Precision Bass

Precision Bass

1951-1981. Slab body until '54. One-piece maple neck standard until '59, optional after '69. Rosewood fingerboard standard '59 on (slab until mid-'62, curved after). Blond finish standard until '54, Sunburst standard after that (two-tone '54-'58, three-tone after '58). Replaced by the Standard Precision Bass in '81-'85, then the American Standard Precision in '88-2000. Renamed American Series Precision Bass in 2000.

The custom colors listings are for unfaded or very slightly faded examples. Moderately faded examples will approximate values somewhat below the low end of the value range. A heavily faded example will be worth much less than the ranges shown, even if the heavily faded example is otherwise in excellent, original condition. A heavily faded example will have a tint that is unlike an unfaded example. Fade does not always mean 'lighter tint'. For example, a heavily faded Lake Placid Blue can turn dark Green. A heavily faded instrument will fetch a value that is slightly higher than a standard Sunburst example.

Custom color Fenders can be forged and bogus finishes have been a problem. As the value of custom color Fenders has increased, so has the problem of bogus non-original finishes. The prices in the Guide are for factory original finishes in excellent condition. The prices noted do not take into account market factors such as fake instruments, which can have the effect of lowering a guitar's market value unless the guitar's provenance can be validated.

Unlike the Jazz and Telecaster Basses, the Precision Bass was never fitted with a three-bolt neck or bullet rod.

MODEL YEAR	FEATURES	EXC. COND. LOW	HIGH
1951	Butterscotch Blond, slab body	$6,500	$9,500
1952	Butterscotch Blond, slab body	$6,500	$9,000
1953	Butterscotch Blond, slab body	$6,500	$8,800
1954	Blond, contour body	$6,500	$7,000
1954	Butterscotch Blond, slab body	$6,000	$8,500
1955	Blond, contour body	$6,000	$6,500
1956	Blond, contour body	$5,900	$6,300
1956	Sunburst	$5,800	$6,100
1957	Sunburst, anodized guard late '57	$5,700	$5,900
1957	Sunburst, White guard early '57	$5,700	$5,900
1958	Blond option	$5,800	$6,000
1958	Sunburst, anodized guard	$5,700	$5,900
1959	Sunburst, maple neck, tortoise guard	$5,700	$5,900
1959	Sunburst, slab rosewood, tortoise guard	$5,600	$5,800
1960	Sunburst, slab rosewood	$5,500	$5,700
1961	Dakota Red	$8,500	$9,500
1961	Daphne Blue	$7,500	$8,500
1961	Lake Placid Blue	$5,800	$6,700
1961	Olympic White	$5,800	$6,700
1961	Sunburst, slab rosewood	$4,600	$5,600
1961	Transparent Blond	$5,500	$5,700
1962	Black, curved board	$4,675	$5,525
1962	Black, slab board	$5,500	$6,500
1962	Blond, curved board	$4,675	$5,525
1962	Blond, slab board	$5,500	$6,500
1962	Burgundy Mist, curved board	$8,100	$8,900
1962	Burgundy Mist, slab board	$9,500	$10,500
1962	Dakota Red, curved board	$7,200	$8,100
1962	Dakota Red, slab board	$8,500	$9,500
1962	Daphne Blue, curved board	$6,375	$7,225
1962	Daphne Blue, slab board	$7,500	$8,500
1962	Fiesta Red, curved board	$7,200	$8,100
1962	Fiesta Red, slab board	$8,500	$9,500
1962	Foam Green, curved board	$8,925	$9,775
1962	Foam Green, slab board	$10,500	$11,500
1962	Inca Silver, curved board	$7,225	$8,075
1962	Inca Silver, slab board	$8,500	$9,500
1962	Lake Placid Blue, curved board	$4,700	$5,500
1962	Lake Placid Blue, slab board	$5,500	$6,500
1962	Olympic White, curved board	$4,700	$5,500
1962	Olympic White, slab board	$5,500	$6,500
1962	Shell Pink, curved board	$10,625	$11,475
1962	Shell Pink, slab board	$12,500	$13,500
1962	Sherwood Green, curved board	$8,075	$8,925

MODEL YEAR	FEATURES	EXC. COND. LOW	HIGH
1962	Sherwood Green, slab board	$9,500	$10,500
1962	Shoreline Gold, curved board	$7,225	$8,075
1962	Shoreline Gold, slab board	$8,500	$9,500
1962	Sonic Blue, curved board	$6,375	$7,225
1962	Sonic Blue, slab board	$7,500	$8,500
1962	Sunburst, curved board	$4,200	$4,675
1962	Sunburst, slab board	$4,500	$5,500
1962	Surf Green, curved board	$8,925	$9,775
1962	Surf Green, slab board	$10,500	$11,500
1963	Blond, curved board	$4,500	$5,400
1963	Candy Apple Red, curved board	$4,600	$6,400
1963	Dakota Red, curved board	$7,100	$8,000
1963	Fiesta Red, curved board	$7,100	$8,000
1963	Lake Placid Blue, curved board	$4,600	$5,400
1963	Olympic White, curved board	$4,600	$5,400
1963	Sunburst, curved board	$4,000	$4,500
1964	Burgundy Mist	$6,600	$7,700
1964	Candy Apple Red	$4,500	$5,300
1964	Fiesta Red	$6,500	$7,500
1964	Lake Placid Blue	$4,600	$5,400
1964	Olympic White	$4,300	$5,100
1964	Sherwood Green	$6,600	$7,600
1964	Shoreline Gold	$6,600	$7,600
1964	Sunburst	$3,500	$4,500
1965	Black	$4,500	$5,500
1965	Blond	$3,900	$4,300
1965	Burgundy Mist	$5,100	$6,500
1965	Candy Apple Red	$4,300	$5,000
1965	Charcoal Frost	$4,800	$5,800
1965	Fiesta Red	$4,600	$6,000
1965	Lake Placid Blue	$4,300	$5,000
1965	Olympic White	$3,900	$5,000
1965	Sherwood Green	$4,600	$6,000
1965	Sunburst	$3,400	$3,800
1966	Candy Apple Red	$3,300	$4,000
1966	Firemist Gold	$4,600	$5,500
1966	Ice Blue Metallic	$4,600	$5,500
1966	Lake Placid Blue	$3,800	$4,500
1966	Olympic White	$3,600	$4,300
1966	Sherwood Green	$4,600	$5,500
1966	Sunburst	$3,100	$3,500
1967	Candy Apple Red	$3,200	$3,700
1967	Sunburst	$2,700	$3,000
1968	Black	$2,600	$3,100
1968	Candy Apple Red	$2,700	$3,300
1968	Sunburst	$2,500	$2,900
1969	Black, maple neck	$2,200	$2,600
1969	Black, rosewood neck	$2,200	$2,600
1969	Candy Apple Red	$2,300	$2,700
1969	Firemist Gold	$3,000	$4,000
1969	Lake Placid Blue	$2,300	$2,700
1969	Olympic White	$2,200	$2,500
1969	Sunburst	$2,200	$2,500
1970	Olympic White	$2,000	$2,500
1970	Sonic Blue	$2,600	$3,600
1970	Sunburst, maple cap on maple	$2,000	$2,900
1970	Sunburst, rosewood	$1,900	$2,300
1970	Sunburst, rosewood, fretless	$1,700	$2,300
1971	Black	$1,700	$2,200
1971	Blond	$1,200	$2,000
1971	Firemist Gold, maple neck	$2,400	$3,000
1971	Lake Placid Blue	$2,000	$2,400
1971	Olympic White	$1,700	$2,000
1971	Sonic Blue	$2,400	$3,000
1971	Sunburst, rosewood	$1,600	$2,100
1972	Black, all necks	$1,300	$1,900
1972	Blond, all necks	$1,500	$2,000
1972	Candy Apple Red, all necks	$1,500	$2,100
1972	Lake Placid Blue, all necks	$1,500	$2,100
1972	Olympic White, all necks	$1,400	$1,900
1972	Sonic Blue, all necks (last year)	$2,400	$3,000
1972	Sunburst, all necks	$1,500	$2,000
1972	Walnut, all necks	$1,400	$1,900
1973-1974	Black, all necks	$1,300	$1,800
1973-1974	Blond, all necks	$1,400	$1,900
1973-1974	Candy Apple Red, all necks	$1,500	$2,000
1973-1974	Lake Placid Blue, all necks	$1,500	$2,000
1973-1974	Natural, all necks	$1,300	$1,800
1973-1974	Olympic White, all necks	$1,500	$1,800
1973-1974	Sunburst, all necks	$1,400	$1,900
1973-1974	Walnut, all necks	$1,300	$1,800
1975-1976	Black, all necks	$1,200	$1,500
1975-1976	Blond, all necks	$1,200	$1,500
1975-1976	Natural, all necks	$1,100	$1,400
1975-1976	Olympic White, all necks	$1,200	$1,500
1975-1976	Sunburst, all necks	$1,200	$1,500
1975-1976	Walnut, all necks	$1,100	$1,400
1977-1979	Antigua, all necks	$1,300	$1,600
1977-1979	Black, all necks	$1,000	$1,500
1977-1979	Blond, all necks	$1,000	$1,500

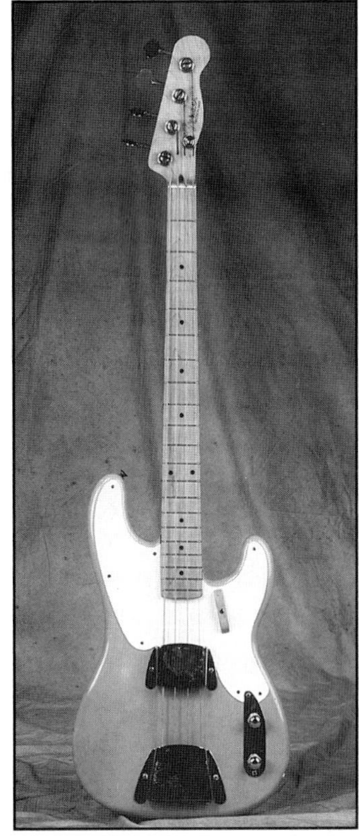
1955 Fender Precision Bass

1978 Fender Precision Bass (Antigua)

BASSES

Fender Squire Bullet Bass

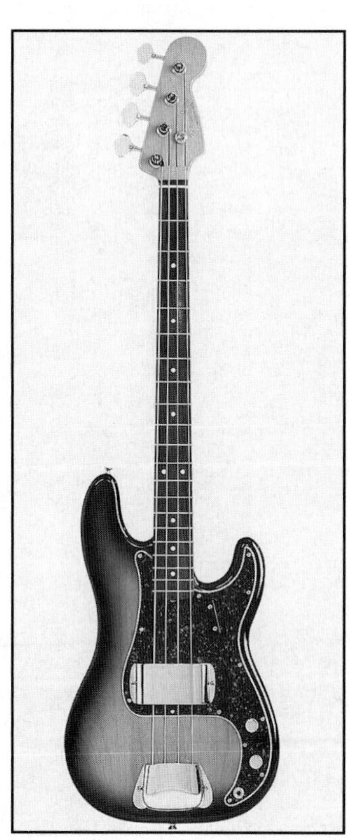

Fender '62 Precision Bass

MODEL YEAR	FEATURES	EXC. COND. LOW	HIGH
1977-1979	Natural, all necks	$1,000	$1,400
1977-1979	Olympic White, all necks	$1,100	$1,400
1977-1979	Sunburst, all necks	$1,200	$1,500
1977-1979	Walnut, all necks	$1,000	$1,400
1977-1979	Wine, all necks	$1,100	$1,400
1980-1981	Antigua, all necks	$1,200	$1,500
1980-1981	Arctic White, all necks	$800	$1,200
1980-1981	Black, all necks	$800	$1,400
1980-1981	International Capri Orange	$800	$1,200
1980-1981	International Maui Blue	$800	$1,200
1980-1981	International Monaco Yellow	$800	$1,200
1980-1981	International Morocco Red	$800	$1,200
1980-1981	Natural, all necks	$700	$1,100
1980-1981	Sunburst, all necks	$800	$1,000
1980-1981	Wine, all necks	$700	$1,100

Standard Precision Bass

1981-1985. Replaces Precision Bass, various colors. Replaced by American Standard Precision 1988-2000. The Standard name is used on import Precision model for 1988-present.

1981-1985		$800	$1,000

American Standard Precision Bass

1988-2000. Replaces Standard Precision Bass. Replaced by American Series Precision in 2000.

1988-1989	Blond, gold hardware	$1,000	$1,100
1988-1989	Various colors	$900	$1,000
1990-2000	Various colors	$700	$900

American Series Precision Bass

2000-present. Replaces American Standard Precision Bass. Various colors.

2000-2002		$650	$800

'51 Precision Bass

2003-present. Import from Japan, does not include pickup or bridge covers as part of the package. Blond or Sunburst.

2003		$275	$225

'55 Custom Shop Precision Bass

2003-present. Custom Shop built with '55 specs including oversized pickguard, one-piece maple neck/fretboard, preproduction bridge and pickup covers, single-coil pickup. Offered in N.O.S., Closet Classic or highest-end Relic.

2003	Closet Classic option	$1,700	$1,800
2003	N.O.S. optioin	$1,500	$1,600
2003	Relic option	$1,900	$2,000

'57 Precision Bass

1982 - present. U.S.A.-made, reissue of 1957 Precision. Various colors.

1982-1989		$1,000	$1,200
1990-1999		$1,000	$1,200

'57 Precision Bass (import)

1984-1986. Foreign-made. Black.

1984-1986		$450	$600

'62 Precision Bass

1982-present. U.S.A.-made reissue of 1962 Precision, alder body.

1982-1989	Mary Kaye Blond, gold hardware	$1,100	$1,300
1982-1989	Standard colors	$1,000	$1,200
1990-1999	Rare colors	$1,100	$1,300
1990-1999	Standard colors	$950	$1,050
1999	Mars Music custom color	$1,100	$1,300
2000-2003	Standard colors	$950	$1,050

'62 Precision Bass (import)

1984-1986. Foreign-made. Black.

1984-1986		$450	$600

40th Anniversary Custom Shop Precision Bass

1991. Four hundred made, quilted Amber maple top, Gold hardware.

1991		$1,400	$1,700

American Deluxe Precision Bass

1998-present. Made in U.S.A., active electronics, alder or ash body. Alder body colors - Sunburst or Transparent Red. Ash body colors - White Blond, Transparent Teal Green or Transparent Purple.

1998-1999		$700	$875

Elite I Precision Bass

1983-1985. The Elite Series feature active electronics and noise-cancelling pickups. Ash body, two pickups, various colors.

1983-1985		$700	$900

Elite II Precision Bass

1983-1985. The Elite Series feature active electronics and noise-cancelling pickups. Ash body, two pickups, various colors.

1983-1985		$750	$950

Foto Flame Precision Bass

1995. Made in Japan. Simulated woodgrain finish on top of the body. Natural or Sunburst.

1995		$500	$575

Gold Elite I Precision Bass

1983-1985. The Elite Series feature active electronics and noise-cancelling pickups. Gold-plated hardware version of the Elite Precision I, 1 pickup.

1983-1985		$700	$900

Gold Elite II Precision Bass

1983-1985. Two pickup vesrion.

1983-1985		$750	$950

Precision Bass (import - Japan)

1984-1986. Traditional styling, various colors.

1984-1986		$300	$450

Precision Bass Lyte

1992-2001. Japanese-made, smaller, lighter basswood body, 2 pickups, sunburst.

1992-2001		$500	$575

Precision Bass Special

1980-1983, 1997-present. Active electronics, gold-plated brass hardware, one split-coil pickup. '90s version similar, but with chrome hardware and is made in Mexico.

1980-1983	Candy Apple Red or Lake Placid Blue	$800	$1,000

MODEL YEAR	FEATURES	EXC. COND. LOW	HIGH
1997-1999	Various colors (Mexico)	$350	$500

Precision U.S. Plus/Plus Bass

1989-1992. P-style bass with P-bass and Jazz bass pickup, various model variations. Black.

1989-1992		$850	$900

Standard Precision Bass (later model)

1988-present. Traditional style, import. Currently made in Mexico. Not to be confused with 1981-1985 American-made model with the same name.

1988-1999		$300	$350

Walnut Elite I Precision Bass

1983-1985. The Elite Series feature active electronics and noise-cancelling pickups. Walnut body, 1 pickup, rosewood fingerboard. Natural.

1983-1985		$650	$850

Walnut Elite II Precision Bass

1983-1985. Two pickup version.

1983-1985		$700	$900

Walnut Precision Bass Special

1980-1983. Precision Bass Special with a walnut body. Natural.

1980-1983		$900	$1,200

Squire Bullet Bass

Japanese-made, Squire-branded, replaces Bullet Bass. Black.

1980s		$200	$250

Squire Jazz Bass

1990s-present. Jazz bass import, without cover plates. Various colors.

1990s		$175	$200
2000s		$150	$180

Stu Hamm Urge Bass (U.S.A.)

1992-present. Contoured Precision-style body with smaller wide treble cutaway, J and P pickups, various colors.

1992-1999		$750	$850

Telecaster Bass

1968-1979. Slab solidbody, one pickup, fretless option '70. Blond and custom colors available (Pink Paisley or Blue Floral '68-'69).

1968	Black	$2,200	$2,600
1968	Blond	$2,000	$2,400
1968	Blue Floral	$5,500	$6,000
1968	Pink Paisley	$5,500	$6,000
1969	4-bolt, single-coil	$2,000	$2,400
1970	4-bolt, single-coil	$1,900	$2,200
1971	4-bolt, single-coil	$1,800	$2,000
1972	4-bolt, single-coil	$1,500	$1,800
1973-1974	3-bolt, humbucker	$1,400	$1,800
1975-1976	3-bolt, humbucker	$1,250	$1,600
1977-1978	3-bolt, humbucker	$1,050	$1,500

Fernandes

1969-present. Intermediate and professional grade, production, solidbody basses. Established 1969 in Tokyo. Early efforts were classical guitars, but they now offer a variety of guitars and basses.

APB-40 Bass

1990s. High-end-style copy with opaque finish, extended long bass horn, P-Bass and J-Bass dual pickups.

1990s		$350	$450

FRB-80 Bass

FRB Series basses have active electronics. The FRB-80 has slotted neck joint construction.

1988		$250	$350

TEB-1 Bass

1993-1996.

1993	Black	$300	$400
1994	Cream	$300	$400

Fleishman Instruments

1974-present. Premium and presentation grade, acoustic and solidbody basses and custom flattops made by luthier Harry Fleishman in Sebastopol, California. He also offers electric uprights, designed by him and built in China. Fleishman also designs basses for others and is the director of Luthiers School International.

Framus

1946-1975, 1996-present. Founded by Fred Wilfer, Erlangen, Germany in '46. Relocated to Bubenreuth in '54, and to Pretzfeld in '67. Imported into the U.S. by Philadelphia Music Company in the '60s.

Brand revived in '96 by Fred's son Hans Peter Wilfer, who also founded Warwick basses. Brand is distributed in the U.S. by Dana B. Goods, and currently offers professional and premium grade, production/custom, guitars and basses made in Germany.

Electric Upright Bass

1950s. Full-scale neck, triangular body. Black.

1958		$1,400	$1,600

Star Bass 5/150 (Bill Wyman)

1959-1968. Early flyer says, "Bill Wyman of the Rolling Stones prefers the Star Bass." The model name was later changed to Framus "Stone" Bass.

1959-1964		$550	$700
1965-1968		$450	$600

Strato Starbass 5/156

1960s. Beige, cherry or sunburst.

1960s		$250	$350

Upright Bass Viol

Carved top.

1940s		$3,000	$5,000

Fylde

1973-present. Luthier Roger Bucknall builds his professional and premium grade, production/custom acoustic guitars and basses in Penrith, Cumbria, United Kingdom. He also builds mandolins, mandolas, bouzoukis, and citterns.

Fender Stu Hamm Urge

1968 Fender Telecaster Bass

BASSES

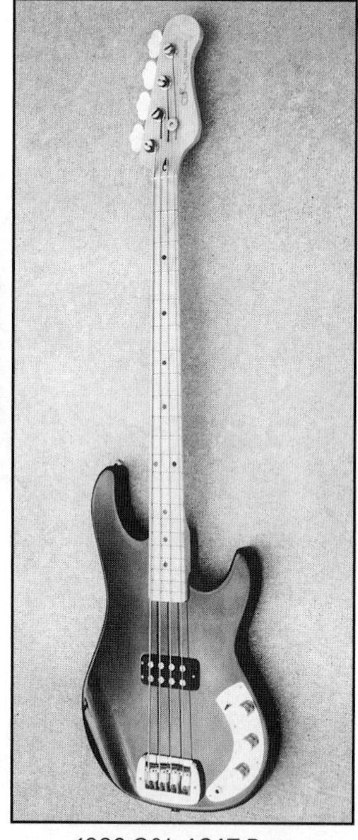

1980 G&L ASAT Bass

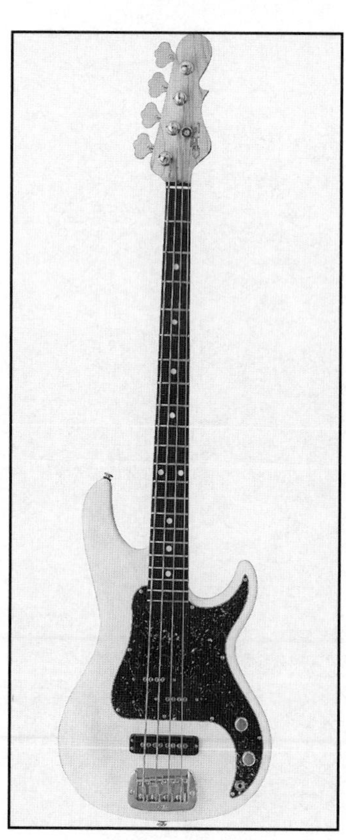

G&L SB-2

MODEL YEAR	FEATURES	EXC. COND. LOW	HIGH

G & L

1980-present. Founded by Leo Fender and George Fullerton. See Guitar section for more company info. Currently offering intermediate and professional grade, production/custom, electric basses made in the U.S. In 2003, G & L introduced the Korean-made G & L Tribute Series. A Tribute logo is clearly identified on the headstock.

ASAT Bass

1989-present. Single cut solidbody, active and passive modes, 2 humbuckers, various colors.

1989-1991	About 400 made	$600	$700
1992-2003		$500	$600

ASAT Commemorative Bass

1991-1992. About 150 made, 4-string ASAT commemorating Leo Fender's life.

1991-1992		$1,400	$1,600

ASAT Semi-Hollow Bass

2001-present. Semi-hollowbody style on ASAT bass.

2001-2003		$650	$800

Climax Bass

1992-1996. Single active humbucker MFD pickup.

1992-1996		$450	$550

El Toro Bass

1983-1991. Double cut solidbody, 2 active, smaller, humbucker, sunburst.

1983-1991		$600	$900

Interceptor Bass

1984-1991. Sharp pointed double cut solidbody, 2 active, smaller humbuckers, sunburst.

1984-1991		$600	$700

JB-2 Bass

2001-present. Jazz Bass-styled body, 2 Alnico pickups.

2001-2003		$550	$650

L-1000 Bass

1980-1994. Offset double cut solidbody, 1 pickup, various colors.

1980-1994		$500	$700

L-1500 Bass/L-1500 Custom Bass

1997-present.

1997-2003		$500	$600

L-1505 Bass

1998-present. 5-string version, single MFD humbucker.

1998-2003		$600	$650

L-2000 Bass

1980-present. Offset double cut solidbody, 2 pickups, active electronics. Originally, the L-2000 was available with active (L-2000E) or passive (L-2000) electronics.

1980-1982		$700	$850
1983-1991		$700	$800
1992-2003		$600	$650

L-2000 Custom Bass

1997 only.

1997		$700	$800

L-2000 Fretless Bass

1980-1981.

1980-1981		$800	$900

L-2000(E) Bass

1980-1982. Offset double cut solidbody, 2 pickups, active electronics. Originally, the L-2000 was available with active (L-2000E) or passive (L-2000) electronics.

1980-1982		$750	$850

L-2500 Bass

1997-present. 5-string, dual MFD humbuckers.

1997-2003		$600	$800

L-2500 Custom Bass

1997 only.

1997		$700	$850

L-5000 Bass

1988-1992. Offset double cut solidbody, G & L Z-shaped split-humbucking pickup, 5 string. Approximately 400 made.

1988-1992		$500	$600

L-5500 Bass

1993-1997.

1993-1997		$600	$700

L-5500 Custom Bass

1997 only.

1997		$550	$650

LB-100 Bass

1993-2000. Follow-up to earlier Legacy Bass.

1993-2000		$450	$550

Legacy Bass

1992-1993. Offset double cut solidbody, 1 split-coil pickup. Renamed LB-100 in '93.

1992-1993		$450	$550

Lynx Bass

1984-1991. Offset double cut solidbody, 2 single-coils, black.

1984-1991		$650	$750

SB-1 Bass

1982-2000. Solidbody, maple neck, body and board, split-humbucker pickup.

1982-1984	Single J-Bass style pickup	$450	$600
1985-2000	Single P-Bass style pickup	$400	$550

SB-2 Bass

1982-present. Maple neck with tilt adjustment, 1 split-coil humbucker and 1 single-coil bridge pickup.

1982-1984	2 P style pickups	$450	$600
1988-2003	One P and one J style PU	$500	$550

G.L. Stiles

1960-1994. Built by Gilbert Lee Stiles primarily in the Miami, Florida area. See Guitar section for more company info.

Electric Solidbody Basses

Various models.

1970s		$300	$400

BASSES

Gibson

1902-present. Gibson got into the electric bass market with the introduction of their Gibson Electric Bass in '53 (that model was renamed the EB-1 in '58 and reintroduced under that name in '69). Many more bass models followed. Currently Gibson offers professional grade, production, U.S.-made electric basses. See the Guitar section for more company info.

Gibson's Custom Colors can greatly increase the value of older instruments. Here are the Custom Colors offered from '63 to '69: Cardinal Red, Ember Red, Frost Blue, Golden Mist Metallic, Heather Metallic, Inverness Green, Kerry Green, Pelham Blue Metallic, Polaris White, Silver Mist Metallic.

EB-0 Bass

1959-1979. Double cutaway slab body with banjo-type tuners in '59 and '60, double cutaway SG-type body with conventional tuners from '61 on, one pickup. Faded Custom Colors are of less value.

MODEL YEAR	FEATURES	EXC. COND. LOW	HIGH
1959-1960	Cherry, banjo tuners, slab body	$2,300	$2,500
1961	Cherry, right-angle tuners, SG body	$1,000	$1,700
1962	Cherry	$1,000	$1,500
1963-1964	Cherry	$1,000	$1,300
1965	Cherry	$900	$1,200
1966-1968	Cherry	$900	$1,100
1968	Black	$1,000	$1,200
1968	Burgundy Metallic (faded)	$1,500	$1,800
1968	Burgundy Metallic (unfaded)	$1,800	$2,200
1968	Pelham Blue (faded)	$1,500	$1,800
1968	Pelham Blue (unfaded)	$1,800	$2,200
1969	Pelham Blue Metallic	$1,500	$1,800
1969-1970	Cherry	$800	$1,000
1972-1973	Cherry	$700	$900
1973	Walnut	$700	$900
1975-1976	Cherry	$500	$700

EB-0 F Bass

1962-1965. EB-0 with added built-in fuzz. Cherry.

MODEL YEAR	FEATURES	EXC. COND. LOW	HIGH
1962		$1,000	$1,500
1963-1964		$1,000	$1,300
1965		$900	$1,200

EB-0 L Bass

1969-1979. 34.5 inch scale version of the EB-0.

MODEL YEAR	FEATURES	EXC. COND. LOW	HIGH
1969-1970	Cherry	$700	$850
1971	Cherry	$650	$800
1971	Walnut	$650	$800

EB-1 Bass

1969-1972. The Gibson Electric Bass ('53-'58) is often also called the EB-1 (see Electric Bass). Violin-shaped mahogany body, one pickup, standard tuners.

MODEL YEAR	FEATURES	EXC. COND. LOW	HIGH
1969-1972		$1,500	$1,700

EB-2 Bass

1958-1961, 1964-1972. ES-335-type semi-hollowbody, double cut, 1 pickup, banjo tuners '58-'60 and conventional tuners '60 on.

MODEL YEAR	FEATURES	EXC. COND. LOW	HIGH
1958	Sunburst, banjo tuners	$2,200	$2,600
1959	Natural, banjo tuners	$2,300	$2,700
1959	Sunburst, banjo tuners	$2,100	$2,500
1960	Sunburst, banjo tuners	$2,000	$2,500
1961	Sunburst, conventional tuners	$1,600	$2,200
1964-1966	Sunburst	$1,200	$1,500
1966-1967	Sparkling Burgundy	$1,300	$1,900
1967-1968	Sunburst, cherry or walnut	$1,200	$1,400
1969	Cherry	$1,000	$1,300
1969	Sunburst	$1,000	$1,300
1970	Sunburst	$800	$1,100

EB-2 D Bass

1966-1972. 2 pickup version of EB-2, cherry, sunburst, or walnut.

MODEL YEAR	FEATURES	EXC. COND. LOW	HIGH
1966-1967		$1,500	$1,800
1968		$1,400	$1,600
1969		$1,200	$1,500
1970-1972		$1,100	$1,200

EB-3 Bass

1961-1979. SG-style solidbody, 2 humbuckers, solid peghead '61-'68 and '72-'79, slotted peghead '69-'71, cherry or walnut.

MODEL YEAR	FEATURES	EXC. COND. LOW	HIGH
1961-1965		$1,700	$1,900
1966-1969		$1,600	$1,800
1970		$1,300	$1,500
1971-1972		$1,200	$1,400
1973-1974		$1,100	$1,300
1975-1979		$1,000	$1,200

EB-3 L Bass

1969-1972. 34.5" scale version of EB-3, cherry, natural, or walnut.

MODEL YEAR	FEATURES	EXC. COND. LOW	HIGH
1969-1971		$1,100	$1,300
1972		$1,000	$1,200

EB-4 L Bass

1972-1975. SG-style, one humbucker, 34.5" scale, Cherry or Walnut.

MODEL YEAR	FEATURES	EXC. COND. LOW	HIGH
1972-1975		$800	$1,100

EB-6 Bass

1960-1966. Introduced as semi-hollowbody 335-style six-string with one humbucker, changed to SG-style with two pickups in '62.

MODEL YEAR	FEATURES	EXC. COND. LOW	HIGH
1960	Sunburst, 335-style	$4,200	$4,500
1961	Sunburst, 335-style	$4,300	$4,400
1962-1966	Cherry, SG-style	$3,500	$4,200

Gibson EB-0

Gibson EB-4L

Gibson RD Artist

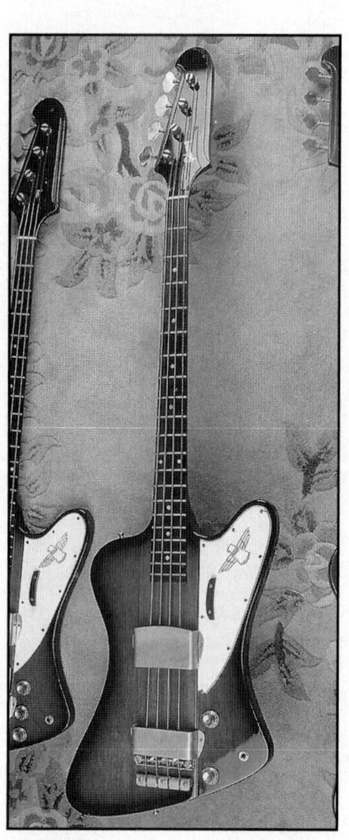

Gibson Thunderbird II

MODEL YEAR	FEATURES	EXC. COND. LOW	HIGH

Electric Bass EB-1

1953-1958. Introduced as Gibson Electric Bass in '53, but was called the EB-1 by Gibson in its last year of '58. Thus, the whole line is commonly called the EB-1 by collectors. Reissued in '69 as the EB-1 (see EB-1 listing). Brown.

1953-1958		$3,500	$4,500

Explorer Bass

1984-1987. Alder body, 3-piece maple neck, ebony board, dot inlays, 2 humbuckers, various colors.

1984-1987		$800	$900

Flying V Bass

1982 only. Solidbody, Flying V body.

1982	Blue stain or Ebony	$800	$1,400
1982	Silverburst	$1,800	$2,400

Gibson IV Bass

1986-1988. Mahogany body and neck, double cut, 2 pickups, black chrome hardware, red or natural.

1986-1988		$400	$450

Gibson V Bass

1986-1988. Double cut 5-string, 2 pickups.

1986-1988		$550	$750

Grabber Bass (G-1)

1974-1982. Double cut solidbody, 1 pickup, bolt maple neck, maple board, various colors.

1974-1982		$575	$700

Grabber III Bass (G-3)

1975-1982. Double cut solidbody, 3 pickups, bolt maple neck, maple board, nickel-plated hardware, various colors.

1975-1982		$600	$750

Les Paul Bass

1970-1971. Single cut solidbody, 2 pickups, walnut finish. Renamed Les Paul Triumph Bass '71-'79.

1970-1971		$1,300	$1,50

Les Paul Signature Bass

1973-1979. Double cutaway, semi-hollowbody, one pickup. Sunburst or Gold (Gold only by '76).

1973-1979		$1,800	$2,300

Les Paul Special LPB-1 Bass

1991-1998. Two pickups, ebony 'board, active electronics, also available as 5-string.

1991-1998		$500	$600

Les Paul Triumph Bass

1971-1979. Renamed from Les Paul Bass.

1971-1979	Various colors	$900	$1,100
1973-1974	White optional color	$1,100	$1,250

Q-80 Bass

1986-1988. Victory Series body shape, 2 pickups, bolt neck, black chrome hardware. Renamed Q-90 in '88.

1986-1988		$400	$500

Q-90 Bass

1988-1992. Renamed from Q-80. Mahogany body, 2 active humbuckers, maple neck, ebony board.

1988-1992		$400	$500

RD Artist Bass

1977-1982. Double cut solid maple body, laminated neck, 2 pickups, active electronics, string-through-body, block inlays, various colors.

1977-1982		$700	$850

RD Artist Custom Bass

1977-1982. Custom option with bound top, low production.

1977-1982	Sunburst, mild figure	$800	$1,000

RD Standard Bass

1977-1979. Double cutaway, solid maple body, laminated neck, two pickups, regular electronics, string-through-body, dot inlays. Various colors.

1977-1979		$650	$800

Ripper Bass

1974-1982. Introduced as L-9 S Bass in '73. Double cut solidbody, glued neck, 2 pickups, string-through-body.

1974-1982	Various colors	$600	$700
1975-1981	Various colors, fretless	$600	$750

Thunderbird II Bass

1963-1969. Reverse solidbody until '65, non-reverse solidbody '65-'69, one pickup, custom colors available. Reintroduced with reverse body for '83-'84.

1963	Sunburst, reverse body	$3,500	$5,000
1964	Pelham Blue Metallic, reverse body	$4,000	$5,000
1964	Sunburst, reverse body	$3,500	$4,500
1965	Inverness Green, non-reverse body	$3,000	$4,500
1965	Sunburst, reverse body	$2,800	$4,300
1966	Sunburst, non-reverse body	$1,800	$2,800
1967	Sunburst, non-reverse body	$1,700	$2,700
1968	Cardinal Red, non-reverse body	$2,700	$3,800
1968	Sunburst, non-reverse body	$1,700	$2,600
1969	Sunburst, non-reverse body	$1,700	$2,500

Thunderbird IV Bass

1963-1969. Reverse solidbody until '64, non-reverse solidbody '65-'69, two pickups, custom colors available. Reintroduced with reverse body for '86-present (see Thunderbird IV Bass Reissue).

1963	Sunburst, reverse body	$4,500	$6,000
1964	Frost Blue, reverse body	$6,000	$7,000
1964	Pelham Blue Metallic, reverse body	$6,000	$7,000

MODEL YEAR	FEATURES	EXC. COND. LOW	HIGH
1964	Sunburst, reverse body	$4,500	$5,500
1965	Cardinal Red, non-reverse body	$4,500	$5,500
1965	Inverness Green, non-reverse body	$4,500	$6,000
1965	Sunburst, reverse body	$4,300	$5,300
1966	Sunburst, non-reverse body	$2,800	$3,300
1966	White, non-reverse body	$3,800	$4,800
1967	Sunburst, non-reverse body	$2,500	$3,000
1968	Sunburst, non-reverse body	$2,400	$2,900
1969	Sunburst, non-reverse	$2,200	$2,800

Thunderbird IV Bass (reissue)

1987-present. Has reverse body and two pickups. Sunburst.

1980s		$1,000	$1,200
1990s		$800	$1,050

Thunderbird 76 Bass

1976 only. Reverse solidbody, 2 pickups, rosewood board, various colors.

1976		$1,900	$2,600

Thunderbird 79 Bass

1979 only. Reverse solidbody, 2 pickups.

1979	Sunburst	$1,500	$1,800

Victory Artist Bass

1981-1985. Double cut solidbody, 2 humbuckers and active electronics.

1981-1985		$450	$550

Victory Custom Bass

1982-1984. Double cut solidbody, 2 humbuckers, passive electronics, limited production.

1982-1984		$450	$550

Victory Standard Bass

1981-1986. Double cut solidbody, 1 humbucker, active electronics, various colors.

1981-1986		$400	$500

Gold Tone

1993-present. Wayne and Robyn Rogers build their intermediate grade, production/custom acoustic basses in Titusville, Florida. They also offer lap steels, mandolins, banjos and banjitars.

Goya

1955-1996. Originally imports from Sweden, brand later used on Japanese and Korean imports. See Guitar section for more company info.

Electric Solidbody Basses

Various models.

1960s		$250	$350

Graf, Oskar

1970-present. Luthier Oskar Graf builds his premium grade, production/custom upright solidbody and acoustic basses, flat-top, classical, and flamenco guitars, and lutes in Clarendon, Ontario.

Greco

1960s-present. Early models were vague copy guitars, but the '70s models were more exact copies. See Guitar section for more company info.

Beatle Bass Copy

1970s		$300	$400

Gretsch

1883-present. Gretsch came late to the electric bass game, introducing their first models in the early '60s. See Guitar section for more company info. Currently Gretsch offers intermediate and professional grade, production, solidbody, hollow body, and acoustic/electric basses.

'68 Model 6072 Bass (double cutaway)

Reissue of the '68 double-cut hollowbody, 2 pickups, sunburst, gold hardware.

1998		$1,000	$1,100

Bikini Doubleneck

1961-1962. Solidbody electric. Separate six-string and bass-neck body units that slid into one of three body "butterflies"–one for the six-string only (6023), one for bass only (6024), one for doubleneck (six and bass-6025). Components could be purchased separately. Prices here are for both necks and all three bodies.

1961		$1,500	$1,700

Broadkaster Bass (7605/7606)

1975-1979. Double cut solidbody, 1 pickup, bolt-on maple neck. Natural (7605) or Sunburst (7606) finish.

1975-1979		$550	$650

Committee Bass (7629)

1977-1980. Double cut walnut and maple soldibody, neck-through, 1 pickup, natural.

1977-1980		$350	$550

Model 6070 Bass (double cutaway)

1968-1971. Country Gentleman thinline archtop double cut body, fake F-holes, 1 pickup, gold hardware.

1968-1971		$800	$1,000

Model 6071 Bass (single cutaway)

1968 only. Single cut hollowbody, fake F-holes, 1 pickup, padded back, red mahogany.

1968		$700	$900

Model 6072 Bass (double cutaway)

1968-1971. Two pickup version of Model 6070 Bass.

1968-1971		$900	$1,300

Model 6073 Bass (single cutaway)

1968-1971. Two pickup version of Model 6071 Bass, red mahogany.

1968		$800	$1,000

TK 300 Bass (7626/7627)

1976-1981. Double cut solidbody, 1 pickup, Autumn Red Stain or natural.

1976-1981		$450	$600

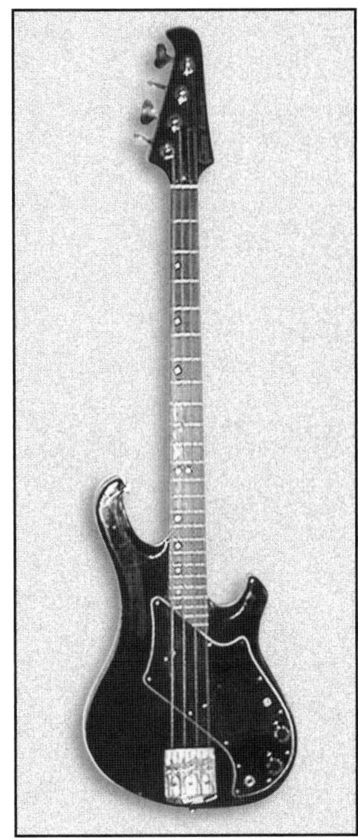

Gibson Victory

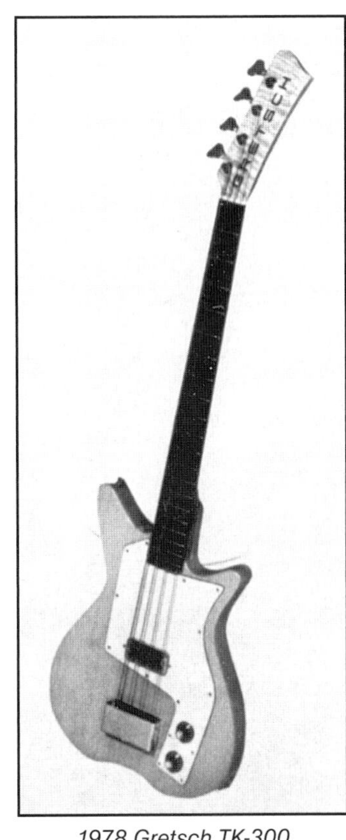

1978 Gretsch TK-300

BASSES

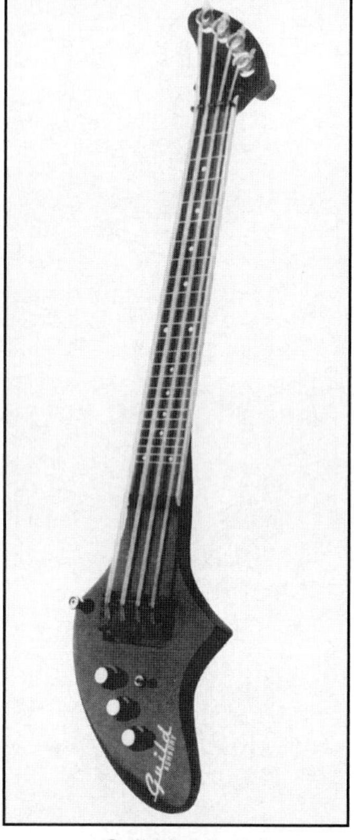
Guild Ashbory

1967 Guild Starfire Bass

MODEL YEAR	FEATURES	EXC. COND. LOW	HIGH

Guild

1952-present. Guild added electric basses in the mid-'60s. See Guitar section for more company info.

Ashbory Bass

1986-1988. 18" scale, total length 30", fretless, silicone rubber strings, active electronics, low-impedance circuitry.

1987		$350	$500

B-4 E Bass

1993-1999. Acoustic/electric, flat-top, single cut, mahogany sides with arched mahogany back, multi-bound, gold hardware until '95, chrome after.

1993-1999		$800	$900

B-30 E Bass

1987-1999. Single cut flat-top acoustic/electric, mahogany sides with arched mahogany back, multi-bound, fretless optional.

1987-1999		$1,100	$1,200

B-50 Acoustic Bass

1975-1987. Acoustic flat-top, mahogany sides with arched mahogany back, spruce top, multi-bound. Renamed B-30 in '87.

1976-1987		$850	$1,250

B-301 Bass

1976-1981. Double cut mahogany solidbody, 1 pickup, chrome-plated hardware, various colors.

1976-1981		$450	$600

B-301 A Bass

1977-1981. Same as B-301 Bass, but with ash body.

1977-1981		$500	$600

B-302 Bass

1976-1981. Double cut mahogany solidbody, 2 pickups, chrome-plated hardware.

1976-1981		$500	$600

B-302 AF Bass

1977-1981. Same as B-302, but with ash body and fretless board.

1977-1981		$500	$600

Jet Star Bass

1964-1970 (limited production '68-'70). Offset double cut solidbody, short treble horn, 1 pickup, two-on-a-side tuners '64-'66 and four in-line tuners '66-'70.

1964-1970		$700	$800

JS I Bass

1970-1976. Single pickup version of JS II.

1970-1976		$400	$700

JS II Bass

1970-1976. Double cut solidbody, 2 pickups, mini-switch, selector switch. Renamed JS Bass 2 in '73 with carved oak leaf design available.

1970-1976		$500	$800

M-85 I BluesBird Bass

1972-1973. Archtop, single cut, 1 humbucker, Chesterfield headstock inlay, mahogany.

1972-1973		$550	$700

M-85 II BluesBird Bass

1972-1976. Archtop, single cut, 2 humbuckers, Chesterfield headstock inlay, cherry mahogany.

1972-1976		$800	$1,000

MB-801 Bass

1981-1982. Double-cut solidbody, 1 pickup, dot inlays.

1981-1982		$400	$600

SB-601 Pilot Bass

1983-1988. Offset double cut solidbody, bolt neck, 1 pickup, poplar body.

1983-1988		$450	$600

SB-602 Pilot Bass (P-602)

1983-1993. Same as SB-601 Pilot Bass, but with 2 pickups. Listed as P-602 in last few years of run.

1983-1993		$500	$700

SB-602 Pilot V (5-String) Bass

1983-1988. Five-string version.

1983-1988		$500	$700

Starfire Bass

1965-1975. Semi-hollow thinbody, double cut, 1 pickup, mahogany neck, chrome-plated hardware, cherry or sunburst.

1965-1969		$800	$1,000
1970-1975		$600	$800

X-701 Bass

1982-1984. Body with four sharp horns with extra long bass horn, 1 pickup, various metallic finishes.

1982-1984		$700	$800

X-702 Bass

1982-1984. Two pickup version of X-701.

1982-1984		$800	$900

Guyatone

1933-present. Large Japanese maker. Also produced instrument under the Marco Polo, Winston, Kingston, Kent, LaFayette, and Bradford brandnames. See Guitar section for more company info.

Electric Solidbody Basses

Various models.

1960s		$250	$400

Hagstrom

1921-1983. This Swedish guitar company offered a variety of guitar and bass models. See Guitar section for more company info.

8-String Bass

1967-1969. Double cut solidbody, 2 pickups, various colors.

1967-1969		$850	$1,000

F-300 Bass

1965-1966. Cherry.

1965-1966		$300	$400

F-400 Bass (Hag II)

1965-1966. Sunburst.

1966		$375	$475

MODEL YEAR	FEATURES	EXC. COND. LOW	HIGH

Model 1 Bass

1965-1966, 1971-1973. Double cut solidbody, 2 pickups.

1965-1966		$300	$400

Swede 2000 Bass (with synth)

1977. Circuitry on this Swede bass connected to the Ampeg Patch 2000 pedal so bass would work with various synths.

1977		$400	$700

Swede Bass

1971-1976. Single cut solidbody, block inlays, cherry.

1971-1976		$600	$750

Hamer

1975-present. Founded in Arlington Heights, Illinois, by Paul Hamer and Jol Dantzig, Hamer was purchased by Kaman in '88. See Guitar section for more company info. Currently Hamer offers intermediate and professional grade, production/custom, acoustic and electric basses.

12-String Short-Scale Bass

1978-1996. Four sets of three strings - a fundamental and two tuned an octave higher. Maple and mahogany solidbody, 30.5" scale.

1970s		$1,000	$1,500

Blitz Bass

1982-1990. Explorer-style solidbody, two pickups, bolt-on neck.

1982-1988		$450	$600
1989-1990		$400	$550

Chaparral Bass

1986-1995, 2000-present. Solidbody, two pickups, glued-in neck, (later basses have bolt-on neck).

1986-1995		$550	$700

Chaparral 5-String Bass

1987-1995. Five-string version. Later basses have five-on-a-side reverse peghead.

1987-1995		$600	$750

Chaparral Max Bass

1986-1995. Same as Chaparral Bass, but with figured maple body, glued neck and boomerang inlays.

1986-1995		$400	$550

CruiseBass

1982-1990, 1995-1999. J-style solidbody, two pickups, glued neck ('82-'90) or bolt neck ('95-'99). Also available as a 5-string.

1982-1990		$500	$700

CruiseBass 5

1982-1989. Five-string version, various colors.

1982-1989		$500	$700

FBIV Bass

1985-1987. Reverse Firebird shape, 1 P-Bass Slammer and 1 J-Bass Slammer pickups, mahogany body, rosewood board, dot inlays, roller bridge.

1985-1987		$500	$750

Standard Bass

1975-1984. Explorer-style bound body with two humbuckers.

1970s		$750	$900
1980s		$450	$700

Harmony

1892-1974. Harmony once was one of the biggest instrument makers in the world, making guitars and basses under their own brand and for others. See Guitar section for more company info.

H-22 Bass

Introduced in 1970. Single cutaway.

1970s	Sunburst	$300	$500

Rocket Bass

1960s-1970s. First models single cut, later models double cut, similar to Rocket guitar.

1960s	Sunburst	$400	$500

Hartke

Hartke offered a line of wood and aluminum-necked basses from 2000 to 2003.

Heartfield

1989-1994. Distributed by Fender, imported from Japan. See Guitar section for more company info.

DR-4 Bass

1989-1994. Double cut solidbody, graphite reinforced neck, 2 single-coil pickups, 4-string (available in 5- and 6-strings).

1989-1994		$350	$550

Heit Deluxe

Ca. 1967-1970. Imported from Japan. Many were made by Teisco.

Höfner

1887-present. Höfner basses, which are made in Germany, were made famous by one Paul McCartney. Currently Höfner offers professional grade, production, basses. See Guitar section for more company info.

'63 Model 500/1 Beatle Bass

1990s	Lefty	$1,300	$1,350

JB-59 Upright Jazz Bass

Electric solidbody, 3/4-size, solid mahogany, pickup, preamp.

1982		$900	$1,100

Model 500/1

1956-present. Semi-acoustic, bound body in violin shape, glued neck, 2 pickups, sunburst. Currently listed as the 500/1 Cavern '61 Electric Bass Guitar.

1963		$2,000	$3,000
1964		$2,000	$2,900
1965		$2,000	$2,400
1965	Lefty	$2,000	$3,000
1966-1968		$1,500	$1,800
1969		$1,400	$1,700
1970-1971		$1,300	$1,600

Hamer Chaparrel 5-string Bass

1988 Hamer CruiseBass

BASSES

1963 Höfner 500/1

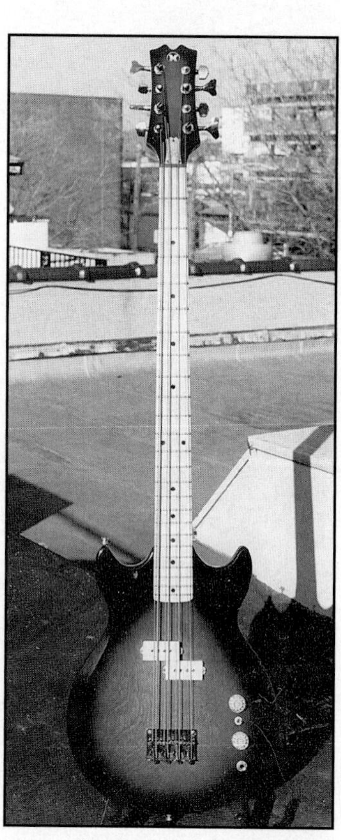
Ibanez Black Eagle

MODEL YEAR	FEATURES	EXC. COND. LOW	HIGH
1971	Lefty	$1,400	$1,800
1973		$1,200	$1,500
1975		$1,100	$1,300
1977-1979		$1,000	$1,200

Model 500/2 Bass

1965-1970. Similar to the 500/1, but with "Club" body Hofner made for England's Selmer. Sunburst. Club Bass has been reissued.

1965-1970		$1,400	$1,700

Model 500/5 Bass

1959-1979s. Single cut body with Beatle Bass-style pickups, sunburst.

1960s		$1,800	$2,000

Model 5000/1 Super Beatle Bass (G500/1)

1969-present. Bound ebony board, gold-plated hardware, natural finish. The version with active circuit is called G500/1 Super Beatle. Reissued in '94

1971-1972		$1,400	$1,600

President Bass

Single cut archtop, 2 pickups, sunburst.

1961-1965		$1,500	$2,000
1968-1969		$1,100	$1,300
197-1972		$1,000	$1,200

Slap-Bass Plus

1989. Pickup built into the bridge plus humbucker pickup.

1989		$325	$375

Slap-Bass Standard

Pickup built into the bridge.

1980s		$300	$350

Hohner

1857-present. Hohner has been offering guitar and basses at least since the early '70s. Currently Hohner offers intermediate and professional grade, production, solidbody basses. See Guitar section for more company info.

B-Bass

1990-present. Solid maple neck-thru-body, 4-string, rosewood board, 2 pickups, DB-Bridge with fine tuners.

1990s		$250	$400

B2AFL Bass

1990-1994. Headless, 2 humbuckers, active circuitry, fretless.

1990-1994		$250	$300

HAB-1 Acoustic/Electric Bass

1990-1993. Rounded triangular soundhole, medium-size dreadnought, single cutaway.

1990-1993		$250	$400

Jack Bass

1989-1994. Headless, offset body, 2 pickups, active tone circuitry.

1989-1994		$300	$400

JJ Bass

Late 1980s-1991. Sunburst finished solid maple body, 2 pickups, active tone circuitry.

1980s		$250	$350

MODEL YEAR	FEATURES	EXC. COND. LOW	HIGH

Hondo

1969-1987, 1991-present. Hondo (named after a small town near San Antonio, Texas) instruments originally imported by International Music Corporation. See Guitar section for more company info.

Electric Solidbody Basses

Various models.

1970s		$100	$250
1980s		$100	$250
1990s		$100	$250

Longhorn Copy Bass

1970s. Copy of Danelectro Longhorn Bass, one split pickup.

1970s		$450	$550

Ibanez

1932-present. Ibanez instruments were first imported into the U.S. in the early '60s. Currently Ibanez offers intermediate and professional grade, production, solidbody basses. See Guitar section for more company info.

Axstar 50 AXB Bass

1986-1987. Headless solidbody, one-piece maple neck, rosewood 'board, 2 humbuckers.

1986-1987		$275	$325

Axstar 60 AXB Bass

1986-1987. As 50, but with 2 low impedance pickups.

1986-1987		$400	$450

Axstar 65 AXB Bass

1986-1987. 5-string version of the 60 AXB.

1986-1987		$350	$450

Axstar 1000 AXB Bass

1986-1987. Headless alder solidbody, one-piece maple neck-thru-body, ebony 'board, 2 low impedance pickups.

1986-1987		$375	$425

BTB500 Bass

1999-2000. Offset double cut ash solidbody, 2 pickups, extra long bass horn, dot markers.

1999-2000		$500	$600

Destroyer X Series Bass

1983-1986. Explorer-style body, P and J-style pickups, dot markers, X Series notation on headstock, bolt neck, black.

1983-1986		$375	$425

MC800 Bass

1978-1980. Solidbody, laminated neck.

1978-1980		$350	$450

MC900 Bass

1978-1980. Solidbody, laminated neck, onboard three-band EQ.

1978-1980		$400	$500

Model 2030 Bass

1970-1973. First copy era bass modeled after the Jazz Bass.

1972		$325	$375

MODEL YEAR	FEATURES	EXC. COND. LOW	HIGH

Newport Bass

1974-1975. Copy of a Mapleglo Rickenbacker 4001 Bass.

1975	Mapleglo (Blond)	$800	$850

PL 5050 Bass

ca. 1985-ca. 1988. Part of the Pro Line Series.

1980s		$200	$350

Roadstar II Bass

1982-1987. Solidbody basses, includes several variations.

1982-1987		$250	$350

Rocket Roll Bass

1974-1976. Korina solidbody, Flying V-shape. Natural.

1970s		$800	$1,000

SB-900 Bass

1990-1993. Ultra slim solidbody.

1990-1993		$300	$375

SR-500 Bass

1993-1996. Offset double cut with typical long extended bass horn, P and J-style active pickups, bolt neck.

1993-1996		$350	$450

SR-505 5-String Bass

1993 only. Five strings, dot markers.

1993		$450	$550

Imperial

Ca.1963-ca.1970. Imported by the Imperial Accordion Company of Chicago, Illinois. Early guitars made in Italy. By ca. '66 Japanese-made.

Electric Solidbody Basses

1960s. Various models.

1960s		$150	$250

Hollowbody Bass

1960s. Hollowbody with sharp double cutaways.

1960s		$250	$275

J. T. Hargreaves

1995-present. Luthier Jay Hargreaves builds his premium grade, production/custom, acoustic basses, classical, and steel-string guitars in Seattle, Washington.

Jackson

1980-present. Founded by Grover Jackson, who owned Charvel. See Guitar section for more company info. Currently Jackson offers intermediate, professional, and premium grade, production, solidbody basses. They also offer guitars.

Concert Custom Bass (U.S.-made)

1984-1995.

1984-1990		$550	$650
1991-1995		$450	$550

Concert EX 4-String (import)

1992-1995.

1990s		$250	$350

Concert V 5-String (import)

1992-1995.

1990s		$450	$550

MODEL YEAR	FEATURES	EXC. COND. LOW	HIGH

Concert XL 4-String (import)

1992-1995.

1990s		$350	$450

Piezo Bass

1986. Four piezoelectric bridge pickups, neck-through, offset double cut, EQ, shark tooth inlays. Student model has rosewood board, no binding. Custom Model has ebony board and neck and headstock binding.

1986		$350	$450

Jerry Jones

1981-present. Intermediate grade, production, semi-hollow body electric basses from luthier Jerry Jones, and built in Nashville, Tennessee. They also build guitars and sitars.

Longhorn Bass 6

1988-present. Reproduction of the Danelectro longhorn design, six strings, two lipstick-tube pickups, 30" scale, 24-fret poplar neck.

1988-1999		$500	$600

Johnson

Mid-1990s-present. Budget and intermediate grade, production, solidbody and acoustic basses imported by Music Link, Brisbane, California. Johnson also offers acoustic, classical, acoustic/electric, and solidbody guitars, amps, mandolins, ukuleles and effects.

Juzek

Violin maker John Juzek was originally located in Prague, Czeckoslovakia, but moved to West Germany due to World War II. Prague instruments considered by most to be more valuable. Many German instruments were mass produced with laminate construction and some equate these German basses with the Kay laminate basses of the same era. Juzek still makes instruments.

Master Art Series 3/4 Bass

Upright bass.

1964		$7,000	$8,000

Prague 3/4 Bass

Upright bass, carved top.

1920		$6,000	$7,000

Kalamazoo

1933-1942, 1965-1970. Kalamazoo was a brandname Gibson used on one of their budget lines. They used the name on electric basses from '65 to '67.

Electric Basses

1960s	Bolt-on neck	$250	$400

Kapa

Ca. 1962-1970. Kapa was founded by Kope Veneman in Maryland. See Guitar section for more company info.

Ibanez SR-500

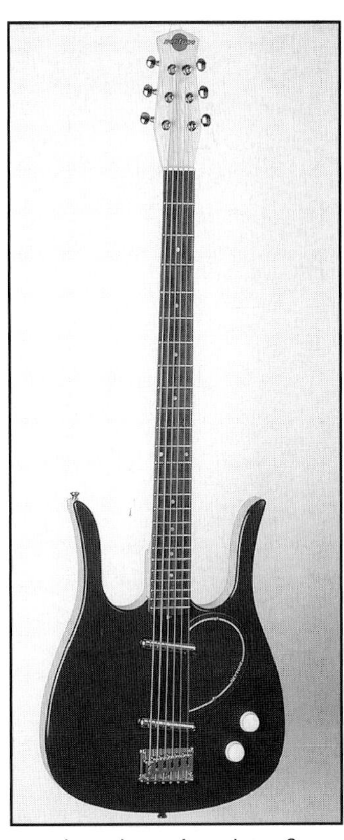

Jerry Jones Longhorn 6

1955 Kay K160

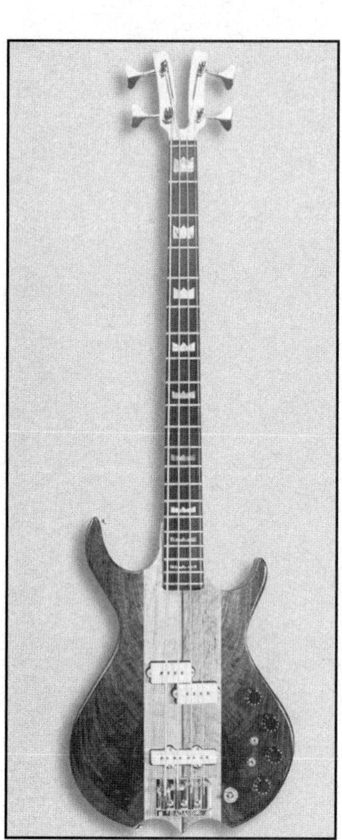
1979 Kramer DMZ 6000B

MODEL YEAR	FEATURES	EXC. COND. LOW	HIGH

Minstrel Bass

1968-1970. Teardrop shape, thinline.

1968-1970	$250	$400

Kawai

1927-present. Japanese instrument manufacturer Kawai started offering guitars under other brandnames around '56. There were few imports carrying the Kawai brand until the late-'70s; best known for high quality basses. Kawai recently quit offering guitars and basses. See Guitar section for more company info.

Electric Solidbody Basses

1960s	$150	$300

F2B Bass

1987-1999. Laminated body, active, neck-through, gold-plated tuners, various options.

1980s	$500	$600

KRB 55 Bass

1987-mid 1990s. Maple neck, rosewood board, 3+1 tuner format.

1980s	$300	$500

KRB 105 Bass

1987-mid 1990s. Carbon-graphite neck, 34" scale.

1980s	$400	$600

KRB 120 Bass

1987-mid 1990s. Carbon-graphite neck, 34" scale, active circuitry.

1980s	$400	$600

Kay

Ca. 1931-present. Kay was once one of the biggest manufacturers around. They introduced upright acoustic laminate basses and 3/4 viols in '38 and electric basses in '54. See Guitar section for more company info or or Guitar Stories Volume II, by Michael Wright, for a complete history of Kay with detailed model listings.

C1 Concert String Bass

1938-1967. Standard (3/4) size student bass, laminated construction, spruce top, figured maple back and sides, shaded Light Brown.

1940s	$1,500	$1,900
1960s	$1,300	$1,700

K-5935 Bass

1966-1968. Renumbered from 5930. Plain style, double cutaway, solidbody.

1966-1968	$300	$500

M-1 (Maestro) String Bass

1952-late-1960s. Standard (3/4) size bass, laminated construction, spruce top and curly maple back and sides. Model M-3 is the Junior (1/4) size bass. Model M-1 B has a Blond finish. Other models include the S-51 B Chubby Jackson Five-String Bass and the S-9 Swingmaster.

1960s	$1,500	$1,900

M-5 (Maestro) String Bass

1957-late-1960s. Five strings.

1960s	$1,700	$2,100

Kay (Asian-American Mgf. Co.)

1980-present. Tony Blair, president of Asian-American Mfg. Co., purchased the Kay nameplate in 1980, with a market focus on first-time buyers.

335 Copy Bass

1990s. Copy of 335 dot neck, Cherry.

1990s	$400	$450

Ken Smith

See listing under "Smith."

Kent

Ca. 1962-1969. Imported from Japan by Buegeleisen and Jacobson of New York, NY. Manufactures unknown but many early instruments by Guyatone and Teisco.

Electric Solidbody Basses

1962-1969. Import models include 628 Newport, 634 Basin Street, 629, and 635.

1960s	$100	$200

Semi-Hollow Electric EB-2 Copy Bass

1960s. Offset soft cutaway EB-2 copy, single pickup, two control knobs.

1960s	$200	$300

Kingston

Ca. 1958-1967. Imported from Japan by Westheimer Importing Corp. of Chicago, IL. Early examples by Guyatone and Teisco.

Electric Solidbody Basses

Various models.

1960s	$100	$150

Klein Acoustic Guitars

1972-present. Luthiers Steve Klein and Steven Kauffman build their production/custom, premium and presentation grade acoustic basses and flat-tops in Sonoma, California.

Klein Electric Guitars

1988-present. Steve Klein added electrics to his line in 1988. In 1995, he sold the electric part of his business to Lorenzo German, who continues to produce professional and premium grade, production/custom, solidbody guitars and basses in Linden, California.

Knutson Luthiery

1981-present. Professional and premium grade, custom, electric upright basses built by luthier John Knutson in Forestville, California. He also builds archtops, flat-tops, and acoustic and electric mandolins.

Kramer

1976-1990, 1997-present. The first guitars and basses featured aluminum necks with wooden inserts on back. Around '80 Kramer started to switch to more economical wood necks and alu-

MODEL YEAR	FEATURES	EXC. COND. LOW	HIGH

minum necks were last produced in '85. Gibson acquired the brandname in '97 and currently offers budget grade, production, solidbody basses. They also offer guitars. See Guitar section for details on import series and import serialization.

250-B Special Bass

1977-1979. Offset double cut, aluminum neck with Ebonol board, zero fret, 1 single-coil, natural.

1977		$500	$600

450-B Bass

Late-'70s-early-'80s. Aluminum neck, burled walnut body, 2 humbuckers, natural walnut.

1977		$650	$700

650-B Artist Bass

1977-1980. Double cut, bird's-eye maple/burled walnut, aluminum neck, zero fret, mother-of-pearl crowns, 2 humbuckers.

1978		$550	$600

BKL Bass

8 strings, 2 DiMarzio pickups, 2 octaves.

1980		$500	$600

DMZ 4000 Bass

1978-1982. Bolt aluminum neck, slot headstock, double cut solidbody, active EQ and dual-coil humbucking pickup, dot inlay.

1978		$500	$600
1982	Bill Wyman-type	$500	$900

DMZ 4001 Bass

1979-1980. Aluminum neck, slot headstock, double cut solidbody, 1 dual-coil humbucker pickup, dot inlay.

1979		$400	$500

DMZ 5000 Bass

1979-1980. Double cut solidbody, aluminum neck, slotted headstock, 2 pickups, crown inlays.

1979-1980		$400	$500

DMZ 6000B Bass

1979-1980. Double cut, aluminum neck with slotted headstock, 2 pickups, crown inlays.

1979-1980		$400	$500

Duke Custom/Standard Bass

1981-1983. Headless, aluminum neck, 1 humbucker.

1981-1983		$250	$400

Duke Special Bass

1982-1985. Headless, aluminum neck, 2 JBX pickups.

1982-1985		$250	$400

Ferrington KFB-1/KFB-2 Acoustic Bass

1987-1990. Acoustic/electric, bridge-mounted active pickup, tone and volume control, various colors. KFB-1 has binding and diamond dot inlays; the KFB-2 has no binding and dot inlays. Danny Ferrington continued to offer the KFB-1 after Kramer closed in '90.

1987-1990		$450	$550

Ferrington Signature Acoustic Bass

1990. Acoustic/electric, bridge-mounted active pickup, 4-band EQ, glued neck, various colors.

1990		$550	$650

MODEL YEAR	FEATURES	EXC. COND. LOW	HIGH

Forum I Bass

1988-1990. U.S.-made double cut, through-neck, arched top, active EMG or passive Seymour Duncan pickups.

1988-1990		$300	$350

Gene Simmons Axe Bass

1980-1981. Axe-shaped bass, slot headstock.

1980-1981		$1,300	$1,800

Pacer Bass

1982-1984. Basic double cutaway.

1982-1984		$400	$500

Ripley Five-String Bass

1985-1987. Offset double cut, 5 strings, stereo, pan pots for each string, front and back pickups for each string, active circuitry.

1985-1987		$450	$550

Stagemaster Custom Bass

1981-1985, 1987-1990. First version had an aluminum neck (wood optional). Later version was neck-through-body, bound neck, either active or passive pickups.

1987-1990		$350	$550

XL 8 Bass

1980-1981. Solidbody 8-string, 2 pickups, tuners mounted on both headstock and body.

1980-1981		$650	$750

XL 24 Bass

1980-1981. Solidbody 4-string with one or two pickups.

1980-1981		$250	$350

ZX-70 Aerostar Series (import)

1986-1989. Offset double cut solidbody, 1 pickup.

1986-1989		$200	$300

Kubicki

1973-present. Professional and premium grade, production/custom, solidbody basses built by luthier Phil Kubicki in Santa Barbara, California. Kubicki began building acoustic guitars when he was 15. In 1964 at age 19, he went to work with Roger Rossmeisl at Fender Musical Instrument's research and development department for acoustic guitars. Nine years later he moved to Santa Barbara, California, and established Philip Kubicki Technology, which is best known for its line of Factor basses and also builds acoustic guitars, custom electric guitars, bodies and necks, and mini-guitars and does custom work, repairs and restorations.

Ex Factor 4 Bass

1985-present. Solidbody, maple body, bolt-on maple neck, two pickups, active electronics.

1990		$800	$900

Factor 4 Bass

1985-present. Solidbody, maple body, bolt-on maple neck, fretless available, 4 strings, 2 pickups, active electronics.

1989		$800	$900

Factor 5-String Bass

1985-ca.1990. Five string version.

1986		$800	$900

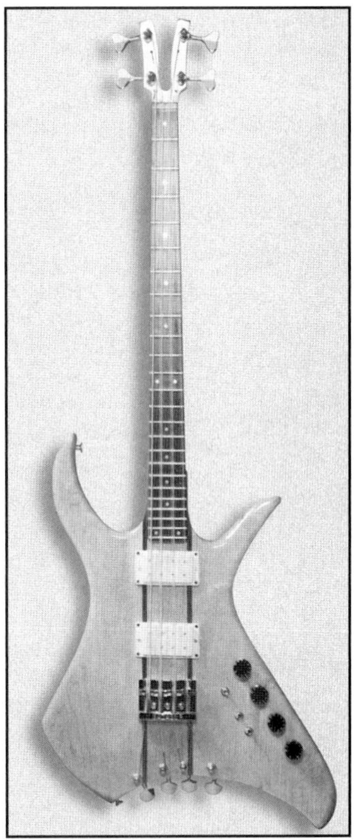

1980 Kramer XL-8

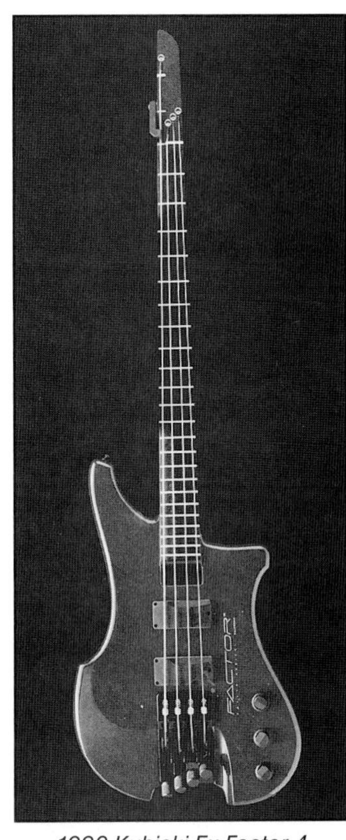

1990 Kubicki Ex Factor 4

Lakland 4-94

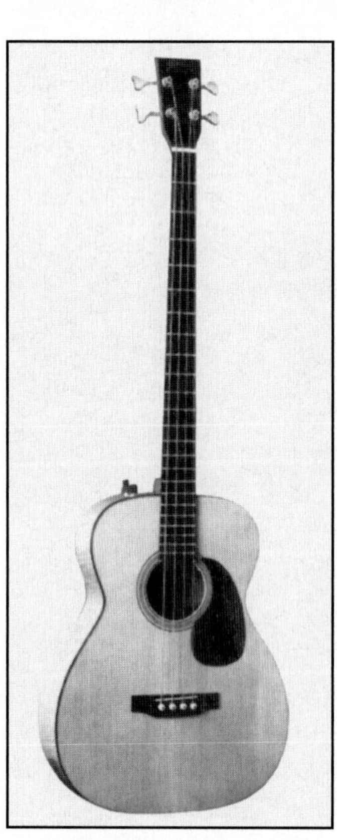

Martin B-40

MODEL YEAR	FEATURES	EXC. COND. LOW	HIGH

Kustom

1968-present. Founded by Bud Ross in Chanute, Kansas, and best known for the tuck-and-roll amps, Kustom also offered guitars and basses from '68 to '69. See Amp section for more company info.

Electric Hollowbody Basses

1968-1969. Various colors.

1968-1969		$650	$850

La Baye

1967. Short-lived brand out of Green Bay, Wisconsin and built by the Holman-Woodell factory in Neodesha, Kansas. See Guitar section for more company info.

Model 2x4 II Bass

1967. Very low production, dual pickups, long-scale, small rectangle solidbody, sometimes referred to as the Bass II.

1967		$1,100	$1,400

Model 2x4: Mini-Bass

1967. Short-scale, one pickup, small rectangle solidbody.

1967		$700	$800

Lafayette

Ca. 1963-1967. Sold through Lafayette Electronics catalogs. See Guitar section for more info.

Lakland

1994-present. Professional and premium grade, production/custom, solid and hollowbody basses from luthier Dan Lakin in Chicago, Illinois. Lakland basses are built in the U.S. and overseas.

4 - 63 Classic Bass

1990s. Offset double cut, alder body with large bass horn, bolt neck, various colors.

1990s		$1,700	$1,900

4 - 63 Deluxe Bass

1990s. Offset double cut, figured maple top on ash body with large bass horn, bolt neck, various colors.

1990s		$1,900	$2,100

4 - 63 Standard Bass

1990s. Offset double cut, swamp ash body with large bass horn, bolt neck, various colors.

1990s		$1,700	$1,900

4 - 94 Classic Bass

1990s. Offset double cut, alder body with large bass horn, bolt neck, various colors.

1990s		$1,700	$1,900

4 - 94 Deluxe Bass

1990s. Offset double cut, figured maple top on ash body with large bass horn, bolt neck, various colors.

1990s		$1,900	$2,100

4 - 94 Standard Bass

1990s. Offset double cut, swamp ash body with large bass horn, bolt neck, various colors.

1990s		$1,600	$1,800

Larrivee

1968-present. Founded by Jean Larrivee in Toronto and currently located in Vancouver, British Columbia. Has built solidbody electric guitars but now concentrates on acoustics. See Guitar section for more company info.

RB-2 Carved Top Bass

Carved Top Series. Sunburst or translucent finishes.

1980s		$900	$1,000

RB-2-5 CM Carved Top Bass

Carved Top Series. Sunburst or translucent finishes.

1980s		$700	$900

RB-2-6 CM Carved Top Bass

Carved Top Series. Sunburst or translucent finishes.

1980s		$700	$900

Lyle

Ca. 1969-1980. Japanese instruments imported by distributor L.D. Heater in Portland, Oregon.

Electric Solidbody Basses

Various models.

1970s		$150	$250

Marco Polo

1960- ca.1964. One of the first inexpensive Japanese brands to be imported into the U.S.

Solidbody Basses

Various models.

1960s		$100	$200

Marling

Ca. 1975. Budget line instruments marketed by EKO of Recanati, Italy; probably made by them, although possibly imported.

Electric Solidbody Basses

Models include the E.495 (copy of LP), E.485 (copy of Tele), and the E.465 (Manta-style).

1970s		$100	$150

Martin

1833-present. In 1978, Martin re-entered the electric market and introduced their solidbody EB-18 and EB-28 Basses. In the '80s they offered Stinger brand basses. By the late '80s, they started offering acoustic basses. Currently they offer professional grade, production, acoustic basses. See Guitar section for more company info.

B-40 Acoustic Bass

1989-1996. Jumbo-size, spruce top and Indian rosewood back and sides, mahogany neck, ebony fingerboard, built-in pickup and volume and tone controls. The B-40B had a pickup.

1989-1996	B-40B with pickup	$1,400	$1,700
1989-1996	without pickup	$1,200	$1,500

MODEL YEAR	FEATURES	EXC. COND. LOW	HIGH

B-65 Acoustic Bass

1989-1993. Jumbo-size, spruce top, maple back and sides, mahogany neck, ebony fingerboard with 23 frets, built-in pickup and volume and tone controls, Natural.

1989-1993		$1,200	$1,500

EB-18 Bass

1979-1982. Electric solidbody, neck-through, one pickup, Natural.

1979-1982		$450	$750

EB-28 Bass

1980-1982. Electric solidbody.

1980-1982		$550	$850

SBL-10 Bass

Stinger brand solidbody, maple neck, one split and one bar pickup.

1980s		$150	$350

Marvel

1950s-mid-1960s. Brandname used for budget instruments marketed by Peter Sorkin Company in New York, New York.

Electric Solidbody Basses

Various models.

1950s	Various models	$100	$200

Messenger

1967-1968. Messengers featured a neck-thru metal alloy neck. See Guitar section for more company info.

Bass

1967-1968. Metal alloy neck. Messenger mainly made guitars - they offered a bass, but it is unlikely many were built.

1967		$1,500	$2,000

Microfrets

1967-1975. Manufactured in Frederick, Maryland, Microfrets sported innovative designs and features.

Husky Bass

1971-1974/75. Double cut, 2 pickups, two-on-a-side tuners.

1970-1975		$500	$600

Signature Bass

1969-1975. Double cut, 2 pickups, two-on-a-side tuners.

1969		$600	$700
1970-1973		$550	$650
1974-1975		$500	$600

Stage II Bass

1969-1975. Double cut, 2 pickups, two-on-a-side tuners.

1969-1975		$600	$700

Mike Lull Custom Guitars

1995-present. Professional and premium grade, production/custom, guitars and basses built by luthier Mike Lull in Bellevue, Washington.

Modulus

1978-present. Founded by aerospace engineer Geoff Gould, Modulus currently offers professional and premium grade, production/custom, solidbody basses built in California. They also build guitars.

Bassstar SP-24 Active Bass

1981-ca. 1990. EMG Jazz Bass pickups, active bass and treble circuits.

1980s		$1,000	$1,400

Quantum-4/SP/SPi Bass

1986-present. 4-string, 35" scale, bolt-on graphite neck, 2 pickups. The original Quantum 4 (1982) was neck-thru.

1980s		$1,100	$1,400

Quantum-5/SPX/SPi Bass

1987-present. 5-string, 35" scale, bolt-on graphite neck, 2 pickups. The original Quantum 5 (1982) was neck-thru.

1980s		$1,200	$1,500

Quantum-5/TBX Bass

1982-1996. Neck-through-body version of the 5-string Quantum, 2 pickups.

1980s		$1,700	$1,900

Quantum-6/SPi Bass

1989-present. 6-string, 35" scale, bolt-on graphite neck, 2 pickups. The original Quantum 6 (1982) was neck-thru.

1989		$1,300	$1,600

Moon

1979-present. Imported from Japan, Moon offers a line of guitars and basses.

Moonstone

1972-present. Premium grade, production/custom, acoustic and electric basses built by luthier Steve Helgeson in Eureka, California. They also build guitars.

Explorer Bass

1980-1983. Figured wood body, Explorer-style neck-through-body.

1980s		$1,300	$1,500

Morales

Ca.1967-1968. Made in Japan by Zen-On and not heavily imported into the U.S.

Electric Solidbody Basses

Various models.

1967		$100	$250

Mosrite

Semie Moseley's Mosrite went through many ups and downs during its history. See Guitar section for more company info.

Brut Bass

Late-1960s. Assymetrical body with small cutaway on upper treble bout.

1968		$900	$1,000

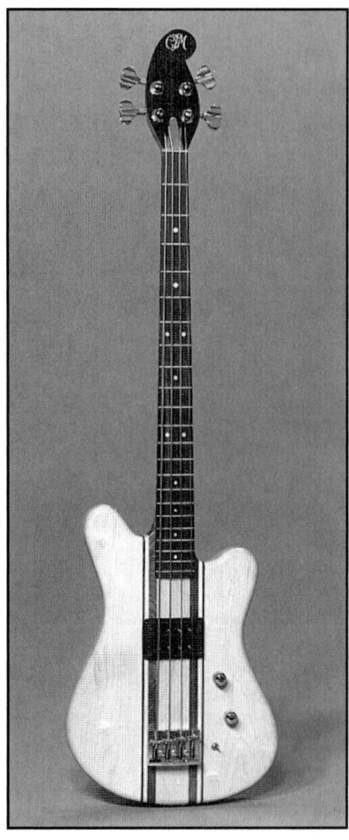

Martin EB-18

Modulus FB-4 Flea bass

BASSES

BASSES

Mosrite Ventures Bass

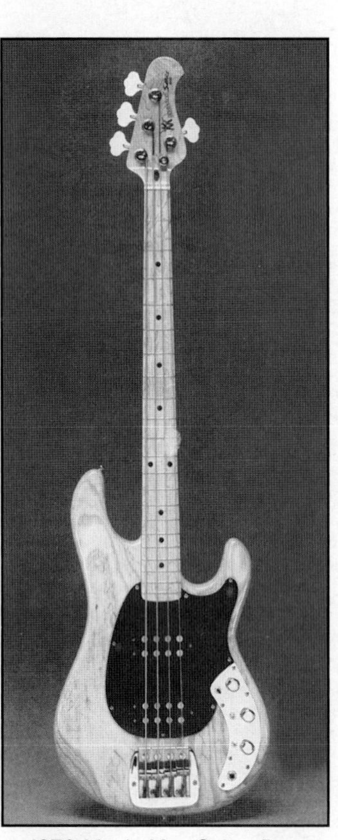
1979 Music Man Sabre Bass

MODEL YEAR	FEATURES	EXC. COND. LOW	HIGH

Celebrity Bass

1965-1969. ES-335-style semi-thick double cutaway body with F-holes, two pickups.

1965-1968	Sunburst or red	$600	$900
1966	Custom color	$800	$1,500
1969	Sunburst or red	$500	$850

Joe Maphis Bass

1966-1969. Ventures-style body, hollow without F-holes, 2 pickups.

1966-1969	Natural	$1,000	$1,400

V-II Bass

1973-1974. Ventures-style, 2 humbuckers.

1973-1974	Sunburst	$700	$1,000

Ventures Bass

Two pickups.

1965	Blue or red	$1,500	$2,100
1965	Sunburst	$1,600	$2,000
1966	Sunburst	$1,400	$2,000
1967-1968	Sunburst, red sparkle, or blue metallic	$1,300	$1,800
1969	Sunburst	$1,200	$1,700
1970-1972	Sunburst	$800	$1,100

MTD

1994-present. Intermediate, professional, and premium grade, production/custom, electric basses built by luthier Michael Tobias (who founded Tobias Basses in '77) in Kingston, New York.

Music Man

1972-present. Music Man was founded by a couple of ex-Fender employees and is presently owned by Ernie Ball. See Guitar section for more company info. Currently Music Man offers intermediate and professional grade, production, electric basses. They also build guitars.

Cutlass I Bass

1982-1987. Ash body, graphite neck, string-through-body.

1982-1987		$1,100	$1,500

Cutlass II Bass

1982-1987.

1982-1987		$1,400	$1,600

Sabre Bass

1978-ca.1991. Double cut solidbody, 3-and-1 tuning keys, 2 humbuckers, onboard preamp, natural.

1978-1979		$800	$1,000
1980-1991		$600	$900

Stingray Bass

1976-present. Offset double cut solidbody, 1 pickup, 3-and-1 tuners, string-through until '80, various colors.

1976-1979		$1,600	$2,200
1980-1989		$1,100	$1,800
1990-1999		$900	$1,000

Stingray 5-String Bass

1987-present. Active electronics, bird's-eye maple bolt neck, 1 humbucker, 3-band EQ.

1992		$800	$1,000

Musicvox

1996-present. Intermediate grade, production, Korean-made retro-vibe guitars and basses from Matt Eichen of Cherry Hill, New Jersey.

National

Ca. 1927-present. National offered electric basses in the '60s when Valco owned the brandname. See Guitar section for more company info.

N-850 Bass

1967-1968. Semi-hollow double cutaway (similar to EB-2-style), art deco F-holes, dual pickups, block markers, bout control knobs.

1967		$800	$900

Val-Pro 85 Bass

1961-1962. Res-O-Glas body shaped like the U.S. map, two pickups, Snow White. Renamed National 85 in 1963.

1961-1962		$600	$900

Noble

Ca. 1950-ca. 1969. Distributed by Don Noble and Company of Chicago. Made by other companies. See Guitar section for more company info.

Electric Solidbody Basses

Various models.

1950s		$150	$300

Norma

Ca.1965-1970. Imported from Japan by Chicago's Strum and Drum.

Electric Solidbody Basses

Various models.

1960s		$150	$250

Northworthy

1987-present. Professional and premium grade, production/custom, basses, flat-tops, electric guitars, and mandolin-family instruments built by luthier Alan Marshall in Ashbourne, Derbyshire, England.

Novax

1989-present. Luthier Ralph Novak builds his fanned-fret professional and premium grade, production/custom, solidbody and acoustic guitars and basses in San Leandro, California.

O'Hagan

1979-1983. Designed by Jerol O'Hagan in St. Louis Park, Minnesota. See Guitar section for more company info.

Electric Solidbody Basses

1979-1983. Models include the Shark Bass, NightWatch Bass, NightWatch Regular Bass, and the Twenty Two Bass.

1980s		$300	$600

MODEL YEAR	FEATURES	EXC. COND. LOW	HIGH

Old Kraftsman

1930s-1960s. Brandname used by the Spiegel Company.

Electric Solidbody Basses

Various models.

1950s	$150	$300

Ovation

1966-present. Ovation offered electric solidbody basses early on and added acoustic basses in the '90s. See Guitar section for more company info. Currently Ovation offers intermediate and professional grade, production, acoustic/electric basses.

Celebrity Bass

1990-1993. Deep bowl back, cutaway, acoustic/electric.

1990-1993	$300	$450

Magnum I Bass

1974-1980. Odd-shaped mahogany solidbody, 2 pickups, mono/stereo output, mute. Originally available in sunburst, red or natural.

1974-1980	$500	$700

Magnum II Bass

1974-1980. Same as Magnum I, but with battery-powered preamp and three-band equalizer.

1974-1980	$500	$700

Typhoon II Bass

1968-1971. Semi-hollowbody, 2 pickups, red or sunburst.

1968-1971	$500	$700

PANaramic

1960s. Imported from Italy.

Electric Bass

1960s. Double cut solidbody, 2 pickups, dot markers, brandname on headstock.

1960s	$300	$400

Parker

1992-present. Parker currently offers premium grade, production/custom, solidbody electric basses.

Paul Reed Smith

1985-present. PRS added basses in '86, but by '92 had dropped the models. In 2000 PRS started again offering professional and premium grade, production, solidbody electric basses. Bird inlays can add $100 or more to the values of PRS basses listed here.

Bass-4

1986-1992. Set neck, 3 single-coils, hum-cancelling coil, active circuitry, Brazilian rosewood board.

1986-1987	$1,500	$1,800
1988-1992	$1,400	$1,700

Bass-5

1986-1992. 5-string, set-neck, rosewood 'board, 3 single-coil pickups, active electronics. Options include custom colors, bird inlays, fretless 'board.

1986-1987	$1,500	$1,800
1988-1992	$1,400	$1,700

CE Bass 4

1990-1991. Solidbody, maple bolt neck, alder body, rosewood 'board, 4-string.

1990-1991	$900	$1,100

CE Bass 5

1990-1991. 5-string solidbody, maple bolt neck, alder body, rosewood 'board.

1990-1991	$1,000	$1,300

Curly Bass-4

1986-1992. Double-cut solidbody, curly maple top, set maple neck, Brazilian rosewood board (ebony on fretless), 3 single-coil and 1 hum-cancelling pickups, various grades of maple tops, moon inlays.

1986-1987	$1,800	$2,200
1988-1992	$1,700	$2,100

Curly Bass-5

1986-1992. 5-string version of Curly Bass-4.

1986-1987	$2,000	$2,400
1988-1992	$1,900	$2,300

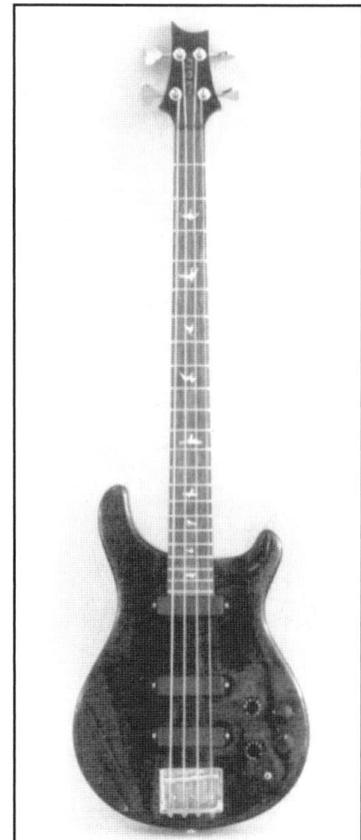

PRS Curly Bass 4

Peavey

1965-present. Hartley Peavey's first products were guitar amps and he added guitars to the mix in '78. Headquartered in Meridan, Mississippi, Peavey currently offers intermediate and professional grade, production/custom, electric basses.

Axcelerator Bass

1994-1998. J-bass styling with longer thinner horns, 2 humbuckers, stacked control knobs, bolt neck, dot markers, various colors.

1994-1998	$350	$450

Dyna-Bass

1987-1993. Double cut solidbody, active elctronics, 3-band EQ, rosewood board.

1987-1993	$300	$400

Dyna-Bass Limited

1987-1990. Neck-through-body, ebony board, flamed maple neck/body, purple heart strips, mother-of-pearl inlays.

1987-1990	$375	$475

Forum Bass

1994-1995. Double cut solidbody, rosewood board, dot inlays, 2 humbuckers.

1994-1995	$250	$325

Forum Plus Bass

1994. Same as Forum Bass, but with added active electronics.

1994	$275	$350

Foundation Bass

1984-2002. Double cut solidbody, 2 pickups, maple neck.

1980s	$275	$375

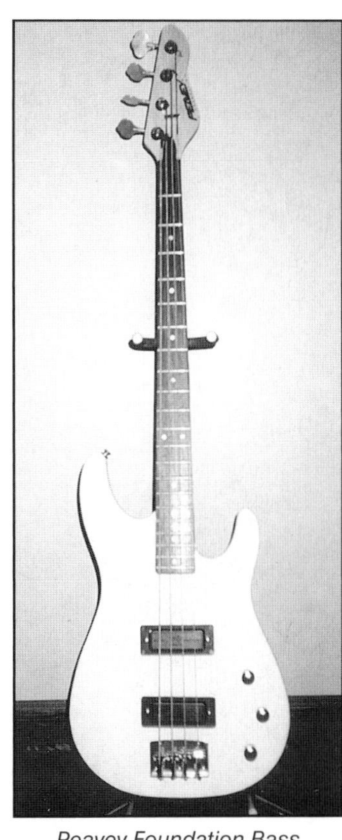

Peavey Foundation Bass

BASSES

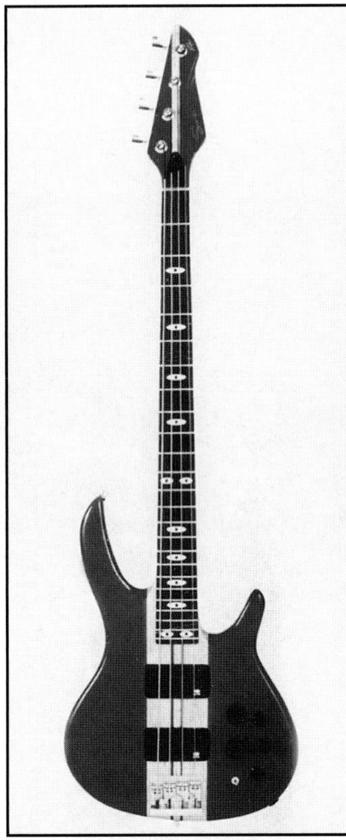
Peavey Rudy Sarzo bass

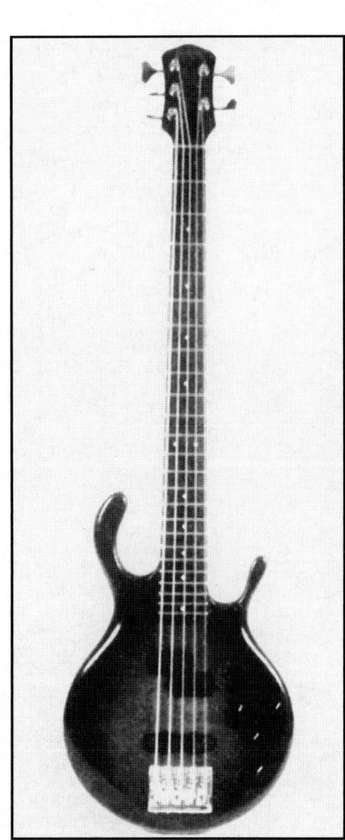
Pedulla MVP-5

MODEL YEAR	FEATURES	EXC. COND. LOW	HIGH

Foundation S Active Bass

1987-1991. Similar to Foundation S Bass with added active circuitry, provides low-impedance output.

1987-1991		$275	$400

Foundation S Bass

1986-1991. Two split-coils, maple body, rosewood board, black hardware, black headstock.

1986-1991		$200	$300

Fury Bass

1986-1999. Double cut solidbody, rosewood board, 1 split-coil humbucker.

1986-1999		$150	$250

Fury Custom Bass

1986-1993. Like Fury Bass but with black hardware and narrow neck.

1986-1993		$250	$350

Patriot Bass

1984-1988. General J-bass styling with larger thinner horns, 1 single-coil, maple neck.

1984-1988		$150	$200

Patriot Custom Bass

1986-1988. One single-coil, rosewood neck, matching headstock.

1986-1988		$250	$300

RJ-4 Bass

1989-1991. Randy Jackson Signature model, neck-through-body, 2 split-coil active pickups, ebony board, mother-of-pearl markers.

1989-1991		$400	$500

Rudy Sarzo Signature Bass

1988-1993. Double cut solidbody, active EQ, ebony fingerboard, 2 pickups.

1988-1993		$400	$600

T-20FL Bass

1980s. Fretless solidbody, 1 pickup.

1982		$250	$350

T-40 Bass

1978-ca.1988. Double cut solidbody, 2 pickups.

1978-1988		$250	$350

T-40FL Bass

1980s. Fretless, 2 pickups.

1980s		$250	$350

TL-Five Bass

1988-1998. 5-string, neck-through-body, gold hardware, active humbuckers, EQ, Eastern flamed maple neck and body.

1980s		$500	$700

TL-Six Bass

1989-1998. 6-string version of TL-5, various colors.

1989		$750	$800

Pedulla

1975-present. Founded by Michael Pedulla. Professional and premium grade, production/custom, electric basses made in Rockland, Massachusetts. Pedulla offers various upscale options which affect valuation so each instrument should be evaluated on a case-by-case basis. Unless specifically noted, the following listings have standard to mid-level features. High-end options are specifically noted; if not, these options will have a relatively higher value than those shown here.

Buzz-4/Buzz-5 Bass

1984-present. Double cut, neck-through solidbody, fretless, long-scale, maple neck and body wings, 2 pickups, preamp, some with other active electronics, various colors. 4- and 5-string versions.

1984-1989		$1,200	$1,400
1990-1999		$1,200	$1,400

Interceptor Bass

1980s. Double cut, maple/walnut laminated neck-through.

1980s		$1,000	$1,300

MVP Bass

1984-present. Fretted version of Buzz Bass.

1980s	Flame top	$1,100	$1,500
1980s	Standard top	$1,000	$1,300

MVP-5 Bass

1984-present. 5-string version of MVP Bass.

1980s		$1,000	$1,300

MVP-6 Bass

1984-present. 6-string version of MVP Bass.

1980s		$1,100	$1,400

Orsini Wurlitzer 4-String Bass

Mid-1970s. Body style similar to late-1950s Gibson double cut slab body SG Special, neck-through, 2 pickups. Sold by Boston's Wurlitzer music store chain.

1975	Natural	$900	$1,500

Quilt Ltd. Bass

Neck-through-body with curly maple centerstrip, quilted maple body wings, 2 Bartolini pickups, available in fretted or fretless 4- and 5-string models.

1980s		$1,100	$1,500

Rapture 4-String/5-String Series Bass

1995-present. Solidbody with extra long thin bass horn and extra short treble horn, various colors.

1995-1999		$800	$1,300

Series II Bass

Bolt neck, rosewood board, mother-of-pearl dot inlays, Bartolini pickups.

1980s		$600	$900

Thunderbass 4-String/5-String Series Bass

1993-present. Solidbody with extra long thin bass horn and extra short treble horn.

1993-1999	Standard features	$1,500	$1,800
1993-1999	AAA top	$2,000	$2,200

Phantom Guitar Works

1992-present. Intermediate grade, production/custom, classic Phantom, Teardrop and Mandoguitar shaped solid and hollowbody guitars and basses assembled in Clatskanie, Oregon.

Premier

1938-1975, 1990-present. Originally American-made instruments, but by the '60s imported parts

MODEL YEAR	FEATURES	EXC. COND. LOW	HIGH

were being used. See Guitar section for more company info.

Bantam Bass

1950-1970. Small body, single cut, short-scale archtop electric, torch headstock inlay. Sunburst.

1960s		$400	$600

Electric Solidbody Basses

Various models.

1960s		$200	$350

Renaissance

1978-1980. Plexiglass solidbody electric guitars and basses made in Malvern, Pennsylvania.

Plexiglas Bass

1978-1980. Plexiglas bodies and active electronics, models include the DPB bass (double cut, one pickup, '78-'79), SPB (single cut, two pickups, '78-'79), T-100B ("Bich-style," one pickup, '80), S-100B (double cut, one pickup, '80), and the S-200B (double cut, two pickups, '80).

1978-1980		$400	$650

Renaissance Guitars

1994-present. Professional grade, custom, semi-acoustic flat-top and nylon-string guitars and basses and solidbody guitars and basses built by luthier Rick Turner in Santa Cruz, California.

Reverend

1996-present. Intermediate grade, production, guitars and basses built in Warren, Michigan, by luthier Joe Naylor, who also founded Naylor Amps. They also build amps and effects.

Rick Turner

1979-1981, 1990-present. Rick Turner has a long career as a luthier, electronics designer and innovator. He also makes the Renaissance line of guitars in his shop in Santa Cruz, California.

Electric Bass

Mahogany.

1980		$600	$750

Rickenbacker

1931-present. Rickenbacker introduced their first electric bass in '57 and has always been a strong player in the bass market. Rickenbacker currently offers professional grade, production/custom, electric basses. They also offer guitars. See Guitar section for more company info.

Blackstar Bass

1988-1997. Ebony-black maple board, black finish, pin-dot position markers, black knobs, chrome and black hardware, custom silver raised-letter nameplate.

1980s		$500	$700

Model 2001 Bass

Black.

1970s		$500	$800

Model 2030 Hamburg Bass

1984-1997. Double rounded cutaway, 2 pickups, active electronics.

1980s		$500	$700

Model 3000 Bass

1975-1984. Double rounded cutaway, 30" scale, 1 pickup, brown sunburst.

1975-1984		$500	$800

Model 3001 Bass

1975-1984. Same as Model 3000 but with longer 33-1/2" scale, wine red.

1975-1984		$600	$750

Model 4000 Bass

1957-1985. Cresting wave body and headstock, 1 horseshoe pickup (changed to regular pickup in '64), neck-through-body.

1957	Horseshoe pickup	$3,800	$4,500
1959	Autumnglo	$3,800	$4,500
1960	Fireglo	$3,800	$4,500
1960	Mapleglo	$4,000	$5,000
1961	Fireglo	$3,600	$4,300
1962	Black	$3,400	$4,200
1963	Black	$3,200	$4,300
1965	Fireglo	$2,500	$3,000
1968	Black	$1,600	$2,000
1970-1979	Various colors	$1,000	$1,500
1980-1985	Various colors	$900	$1,300

Model 4001 Bass

1961-1987. Fancy version of 4000 Bass with 1 horseshoe magnet pickup (changed to regular pickup in '64) and 1 bar magnet pickup, triangle inlays, and bound neck.

1961-1963	Fireglo, horseshoe pickup	$3,800	$5,000
1963	Mapleglo, horseshoe pickup	$4,000	$5,500
1964	Fireglo, horseshoe pickup	$3,600	$5,000
1965	Mapleglo, regular pickup	$2,800	$3,800
1967	Fireglo	$2,300	$3,300
1968	Mapleglo	$2,600	$3,600
1969	Mapleglo	$2,400	$3,400
1970	Mapleglo	$1,900	$2,900
1970	Wine Red	$1,700	$2,200
1971	All colors	$1,500	$2,000
1972	All colors	$1,400	$1,900
1973	All colors	$1,300	$1,700
1974	All colors	$1,200	$1,600
1975-1977	All colors	$1,100	$1,400
1978-1979	All colors	$1,000	$1,300
1980-1983	All colors	$800	$1,100
1984-1987	All colors	$700	$900

Model 4001 V63 Bass

1984-2000. Vintage 1963 reissue of Model 4001, horseshoe-magnet pickup.

1985-1995	Mapleglo	$1,000	$1,200

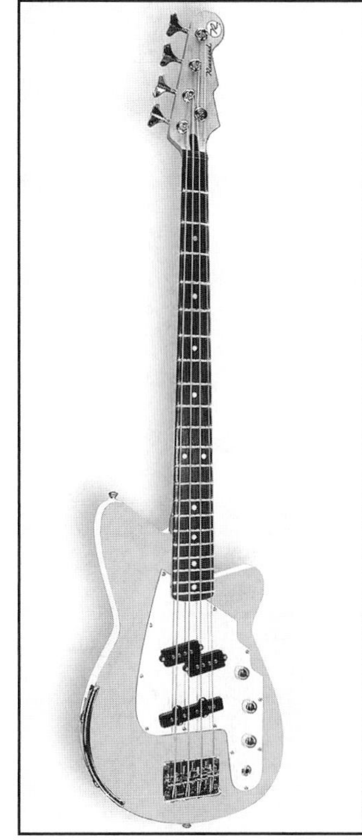

Reverend Rumblefish P/J

1970s Rickenbacker 4001

BASSES

BASSES

1979 Rickenbacker 4005

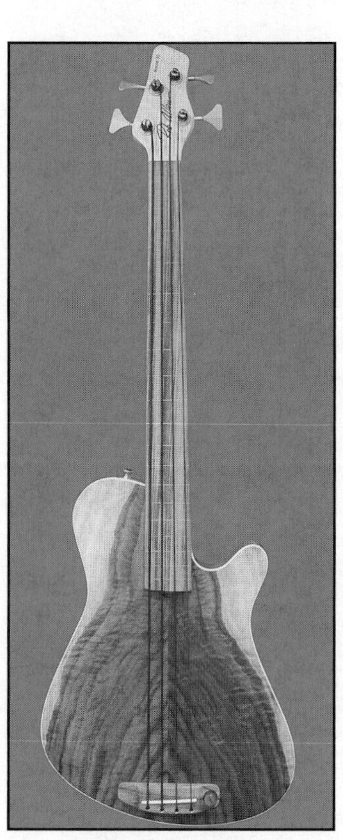
Rob Allen Mouse

MODEL YEAR	FEATURES	EXC. COND. LOW	HIGH

Model 4001-S Bass

1964-1985. Same as Model 4000, but with 2 pickups.

1980-1985		$900	$1,300

Model 4003 Bass

1979-1998. Similar to Model 4001, split pickguard, deluxe features.

1979-1989		$900	$1,200
1990-1998		$800	$1,100

Model 4003-S Tuxedo Bass

1980-1997. Non-deluxe feature version of Model 4003. White body with black guard and hardware.

1980s		$1,000	$1,200

Model 4003-S/5 Bass

1987-1997. Model 4003-S with 5 strings, 2 pickups.

1980s	Fireglo	$1,100	$1,300

Model 4005 Bass

1965-1984. Double cut hollowbody, 2 pickups, R tailpiece, cresting wave headstock.

1966	Fireglo	$3,500	$3,900
1967	Mapleglo	$3,500	$3,900
1968	Black	$3,100	$3,500
1970	Fireglo	$2,600	$2,900
1972	Mapleglo	$2,100	$2,300
1976	Fireglo	$1,900	$2,100
1979	Black	$1,500	$1,700

Model 4005 WB Bass

1966-1983. Model 4005 with white-bound body

1966	Mapleglo	$4,000	$5,200
1967	Burgundy	$4,000	$4,900
1967	Fireglo	$4,000	$4,900
1967	Mapleglo	$4,000	$4,900

Model 4005-6 Bass

1965-1977. Model 4005 with 6 strings.

1966	Mapleglo	$3,800	$5,000
1967	Fireglo	$3,500	$4,700

Model 4008 Bass

1975-1983. Eight strings, cresting wave body and headstock.

1980s		$800	$1,100

Model 4080 Doubleneck Bass

1974-1985. Bolt necks with 6 and 4 strings.

1970s	Mapleglo	$1,800	$2,600

Rob Allen

1997-present. Professional grade, production/custom, lightweight basses made by luthier Robert Allen in Santa Barbara, California.

Robin

1982-present. Founded by David Wintz and located in Houston, Texas, Robin builds professional and premium grade, production/custom, guitars. They also make Metropolitan (since 1996) and Alamo (since 2000) brandname guitars.

Freedom Bass

Double cut, EQ controls. Available in blond, metallic red, black, and sunburst.

1980s		$400	$500

Freedom Bass I Passive

Offset double cut ash solidbody, bolt maple neck, rosewood board, 1 humbucker, two-on-a-side tuners.

1980s		$400	$550

Medley Bass

Reverse headstock, deep cutaways, 1 bridge-position humbucker and 2 single-coils.

1980s		$400	$500

Ranger Bass

1991-present. Vintage style body with P-style and J-style pickup configuration, dot markers.

1991-1999		$750	$850

Rock Bass

2002-present. Chinese-made, intermediate and professional grade, production, bolt-neck solidbody basses from the makers of Warwick basses.

S.D. Curlee

1975-1982. S.D. Curlee instruments were made in Illinois; S.D. Curlee International instruments were made in Japan. See Guitar section for more company info.

Electric Solidbody Basses

1975-1981.

1970s		$250	$400

Samick

1956-present. They also build guitars, mandolins, and banjos. Samick began moderate imports of their Korean-made instruments by '78, importing significant numbers by the '90s. The Samick line was completely redesigned in 2001. Currently Samick offers budget, intermediate, and professional grade, production, acoustic and electric basses. They also offer guitars, ukes, mandolins and banjos.

Artist 4 Bass

1992-2000. Offset double cut, 1 pickup.

1990s		$250	$350

Artist 5 Bass

1992-2000. 5-string, offset double cut, 1 pickup.

1990s		$250	$350

Student Model Bass

Variety of copy and original designs.

1990s		$100	$200

Schecter

1976-present. Founded by David Schecter, who started a repair-modification business selling a wide variety of guitar components, such as necks and bodies. Currently Schecter offers intermediate and professional grade, production/custom, electric basses made in the U.S. and overseas. They also offer acoustic, semi-hollowbody, and solidbody guitars.

Bass

1980s		$300	$500

BASSES

MODEL YEAR	FEATURES	EXC. COND. LOW	HIGH

Shifflett

Luthier Charles Shifflett builds his premium grade, production/custom, acoustic basses in High River, Alberta. He also builds flat-top, classical, flamenco, resophonic, and harp guitars, and banjos.

Silvertone

1941- ca.1970, present. Brandname used by Sears. Instruments were U.S.-made and imported. See Guitar section for more company info. Currently Samick offers a line of amps under the Silvertone brand.

Bass VI

One lipstick pickup.

1960s	$500	$600

Smith

1978-present. Professional and premium grade, production/custom, electric basses built by luthier Ken Smith in Perkasie, Pennsylvania. Earlier models had "Ken Smith" on headstock, recent models hav a large "S" logo.

B.T. Custom VI Bass

1985-present. 6 strings, double cut, neck-through-body.

1995	$1,600	$1,700

Burner Custom 4 Bass

1989-2000. Double cut figured maple body, bolt neck. Burner models were called the BSR 'B' (Burner) for '98-2000.

1990s	$800	$900

Burner Deluxe 4 Bass

1989-2000. Double cut swamp ash body, bolt neck.

1990s	$700	$800

Burner Standard 4 Bass

1989-2000. Double cut alder body, bolt neck.

1990s	$650	$750

Spector/Stuart Spector Design

1975-1990 (Spector), 1991-1998 (SSD), 1998-present (Spector SSD). Stuart Spector's first bass was the NS and the company quickly grew to the point where Kramer acquired it in '85. After Kramer went out of business in '90, Spector started building basses with the SSD logo (Stuart Spector Design). In '98 he recovered the Spector trademark. Currently Spector offers imtermediate, professional, and premium grade, production/custom, basses made in the U.S., the Czech Republic, Korea, and China.

Bob 4 Bass

1996-1999. Offset deep double cut, swamp ash or alder body, bolt neck, various colors, SSD logo on headstock.

1990s	$800	$900

Bob 5 Bass

1996-1999. 5-string version.

1990s	$900	$1,000

NS-1 Bass

1977-1980. Offset, double cut solidbody, neck-through, 1 pickup, gold hardware.

1977-1979	$1,000	$1,300
1980-1982	$900	$1,100

NS-2 Bass

1979-present. Offset, double cut solidbody, neck-through, 2 pickups, gold hardware.

1980s	$1,000	$1,200

St. Moritz

1960s. Japanese imports, generally shorter-scale, beginner basses.

Electric Solidbody Basses

Various models.

1960s	$100	$300

Standel

1952-1974, 1997-present. Amp builder Bob Crooks offered instruments under his Standel brandname three different times during the '60s. See Guitar section for production details. See Amp section for more company info.

Custom Solidbody 501 Bass

1967-1968. Solidbody, single pickup, various colors.

1967	$500	$700

Custom Deluxe Solidbody 401 Bass

1967-1968. Custom with higher appointments, various colors.

1967	$800	$1,100

Custom Thinbody 502 Bass

1967-1968. Thin solidbody, dual pickups, various colors.

1967	$700	$800

Custom Deluxe Thinbody 402 Bass

1967-1968. Custom with higher appointments, various colors.

1967	$900	$1,200

Steinberger

1979-present. Founded by Ned Steinberger, after designing a headless model in '79. Purchased by Gibson in '87. See Guitar section for more company info. Currently Steinberger offers budget and intermediate grade, production, electric basses. They also offer guitars.

Q-4 Bass

1990-1991. Composite neck, Double Bass system, headless with traditional-style maple body, low-impedance pickups.

1990-1991	$650	$800

Q-5 Bass

1990-1991. 5-string version of Q-4.

1990-1991	$750	$900

XL-2 Bass

1984-1993. Rectangular composite body, 4-string, headless, 2 pickups.

1984-1989	$650	$1,000
1990-1993	$600	$900

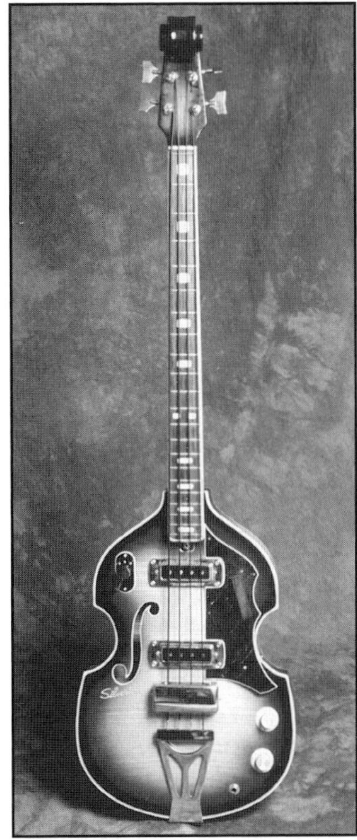

1960s Silvertone bass

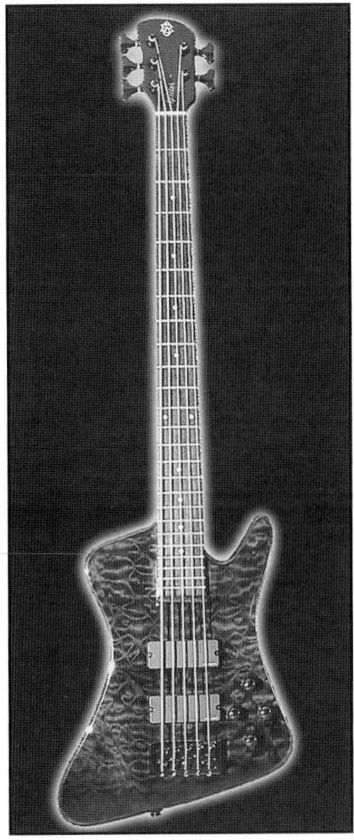

Spector Rex 5

Steinberger XL-2

1968 Teisco EB-200

MODEL YEAR	FEATURES	EXC. COND. LOW	HIGH

XL-2GR Bass

1985-1990. Headless, Roland GR synthesizer controller.

1980s		$750	$950

XM-2 Bass

1986-1992. Headless, double cut maple body, 4-string, 2 low-impedance pickups, optional fretted, lined fretless or unlined fretless. Black, red or white.

1990s		$775	$825

Stinger

See Martin listing.

Supro

1935-1968. Supro was a budget brand for the National Dobro Company. Supro offered only two bass models in the '60s. See Guitar section for more company info.

Pocket Bass

1960-1968. Double cut, standard neck pickup and bridge mounted pickup, semi-hollow, short-scale, black.

1960s		$400	$700

Tacoma

1995-present. Professional grade, production, acoustic basses produced in Tacoma, Washington. They also build acoustic guitars and mandolins.

Taylor

1974-present. Professional and premium grade, production, acoustic basses built in El Cajon, California. See Guitar section for more company info.

AB1 Bass

1996-present. Acoustic/electric, Sitka spruce top, Imbuia walnut back and sides, designed for 'loose' woody sound.

2000		$1,300	$1,400

AB2 Bass

1996-present. Acoustic/electric, all Imbuia walnut body.

2000		$1,300	$1,400

AB3 Bass

1998-present. Acoustic/electric, Sitka spruce top, maple back and sides.

2000		$1,400	$1,500

Teisco

1946-1974, 1994-present. The Japanese Teisco line started offering basses in '60. See Guitar section for more company info.

EB-100 Bass

1968-1969. One pickup, White pickguard.

1968	Blue	$100	$200

EP-200 B Bass

1968-1969. Semi-hollowbody.

1966		$150	$250

MODEL YEAR	FEATURES	EXC. COND. LOW	HIGH

Tele-Star

1965-ca.1972. Imported from Japan by Tele-Star Musical Instrument Corporation of New York. Primarily made by Kawai, many inspired by Burns designs, some in cool sparkle finishes.

Electric Solidbody Basses

Various models.

1960s		$100	$200

Tobias

1977-present. Founded by Mike Tobias in Orlando, FL. Moved to San Francisco for '80-'81, then to Costa Mesa, eventually ending up in Hollywood. In '90, he sold the company to Gibson which moved it to Burbank. In '92, the company was moved to Nashville. Mike left the company in '92 and started a new business in '94 called MTD where he continues to make electric and acoustic basses. In '99, production of Tobias basses was moved overseas. In late '03, Gibson started again offering U.S.-made Tobias instruments; they are made in Conway, Arkansas, in the former Baldwin grand piano facility. Currently Tobias offers imported and U.S.-made, intermediate and professional grade, production, acoustic and electric basses.

Basic B-4 Bass

1984-1999. 30", 32", or 34" scale, neck-through-body in alder, koa or walnut, 5-piece laminated neck.

1980s		$1,500	$2,500

Classic C-4 Bass

1978-1999. 1 or 2 pickups, active or passive electronics, two-octave rosewood board. Available in short-, medium-, and long-scale models.

1980s		$1,800	$3,000

Classic C-5 Bass

1985-1999. 30", 32" or 34" scale, alder, koa or walnut body, bookmatched top, ebony or phenolic board, hardwood neck.

1980s		$1,800	$3,000

Classic C-6 Bass

ca. 1986-1999. Flamed maple and padauk neck, alder body, padauk top, ebony board, active electronics, 32" or 34" scale.

1980s		$2,000	$3,200

Growler GR-5 Bass

1996-1999. 5-string, offset double cut, bolt neck, various colors.

1996-1999		$800	$900

Killer Bee KB-5 Bass

1991-1999. Offset double cut, swamp ash or lacewood body, various colors.

1990s		$1,400	$1,700

Model T Bass

1989-1991. Line of 4- and 5-string basses, 3-piece maple neck-through-body, maple body halves, active treble and bass controls. Fretless available.

1989		$1,100	$1,300

BASSES

MODEL YEAR	FEATURES	EXC. COND. LOW	HIGH

Signature S-4 Bass

1978-1999. Available in 4-, 5-, and 6-string models, chrome-plated milled brass bridge.

1987		$2,000	$2,300

Standard ST-4 Bass

1992-1995. Japanese-made, 5-piece maple neck-thru, swamp ash body wings.

1990s		$1,000	$1,200

Toby Deluxe TD-4 Bass

1994-1996. Offset double cut, bolt neck, various colors.

1990s	Various colors	$600	$700

Toby Deluxe TD-5 Bass

1994-1996. 5-string, offset double cut, bolt neck, various colors.

1990s	Various colors	$600	$700

Tokai

1947-present. Tokai started making guitars around '70 and by the end of that decade they were being imported into the U.S. See Guitar section for more company info.

Vintage Bass Copies

1970s-1980s. Tokai offered near copies of classic U.S. basses.

1970s		$400	$500

Tonemaster

1960s. Import from Italy by U.S. distributor with typical '60s Italian Sparkle plastic finish and push-button controls, bolt-on neck.

Electric Bass

Sparkle finish.

1960s		$500	$600

Travis Bean

1974-1979, 1999. The unique Travis Bean line included a couple of bass models. Travis Bean produced some new instruments in '99. See Guitar section for more company details.

TB-2000 Bass

Aluminum neck with T-slotted headstock. Longer horned, double cutaway body, two pickups, four controls, dot markers, various colors.

1970s		$1,400	$1,800

Univox

1964-1978. Univox started out as an amp line and added guitars and basses around '69. Guitars were imported from Japan by the Merson Musical Supply Company, later Unicord, Westbury, NY. Generally mid-level copies of American designs. See Guitar section for more company info.

'Lectra Bass (model 1970F)

Violin bass, walnut.

1970s		$250	$350

Bicentennial Carved P-Bass (Aria)

1976. Carved Eagle in body, matches Univox Bicentennial Carved Strat (see that listing), Brown stain, maple board.

1976		$600	$800

Hi Flyer Bass

Mosrite Ventures Bass copy, two pickups, rosewood board.

1970s		$350	$450

Precisely Bass

Copy of Fender P-Bass.

1970s		$200	$300

Stereo Bass

Rickenbacker 4001 Bass copy, model U1975B.

1970s		$350	$450

Vaccaro

1997-present. Founded by Henry Vaccaro, Sr., one of the founders of Kramer Guitars. Intermediate and professional grade, production/custom, aluminum-necked guitars and basses designed by Vaccaro, former Kramer designer Phil Petillo, and Henry Vaccaro, Jr., and made in Asbury Park, New Jersey.

Vantage

1977-present. Imported from Japan until 1990. Currently imported from Korea and offering intermediate grade, production, electric basses.

Model 895B Bass (Alembic-style 4-string)

1970s-1980s. Double cut, high quality wood, neck-through-body.

1970s		$400	$450

Veillette

1991-present. Luthier Joe Veillette (of Veillette-Citron fame) builds his professional and premium grade, production/custom, electric basses in Woodstock, New York. He also builds guitars, baritone guitars, and mandolins.

Veillette-Citron

1975-1983. Founded by Joe Veillette and Harvey Citron who met at the NY College School of Architecture in the late '60s. Joe took a guitar building course from Michael Gurian and by the Summer of '76, he and Harvey started producing neck-thru solidbody guitars and basses. Veillette and Citron both are back building instruments.

Standard Bass

Maple.

1975		$1,100	$1,300
1978	Tiger-striped maple	$1,200	$1,400
1979		$1,100	$1,300

Ventura

1970s. Import classic bass copies distributed by C. Bruno (Kaman).

EB-2 Copy Bass

1970s		$300	$400

Univox Hi Flyer

1981 Veilette-Citron Standard

1960s Vox Mark IV

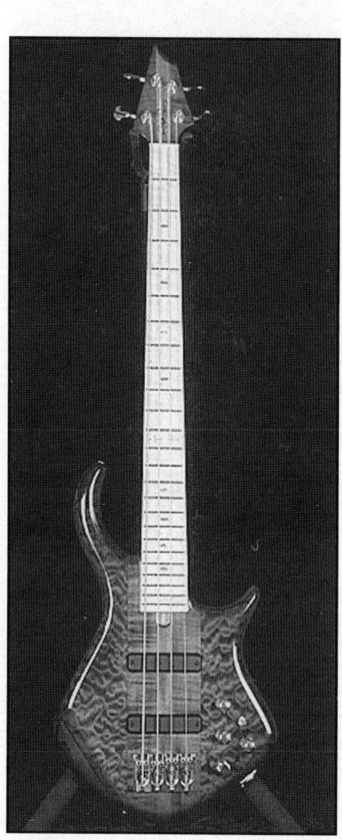

Warrior Studio

MODEL YEAR	FEATURES	EXC. COND. LOW	HIGH

Vox

1957-1972, 1982-present. The first Vox products were amplifiers brought to market in '58 by Tom Jennings and Dick Denny. By '61 they had added instruments to the line. Guitars and basses bearing the Vox name were offered from 1961-'72, '82-'88, and for '98-2001. See Guitar section for more company info.

Apollo IV Bass

1967-1969. Single cut hollowbody, bolt-on maple neck, 1 pickup, onboard fuzz, booster, sunburst.

1967-1969	$650	$750

Astro IV Bass

1967-1969. Bass, 2 pickups, sunburst.

1967-1969	$800	$900

Clubman Bass

1961-1966. Double cut 2 pickup solidbody.

1960s	$300	$400

Constellation IV Bass

1967-1968. Teardrop-shaped body, 2 pickups, 1 F-hole, 1 set of controls, treble, bass and distortion boosters.

1967-1968	$600	$800

Cougar Bass

1963-1967. Double-cut 335-style body, 2 F-holes, 2 pickups, 2 sets of controls, sunburst.

1960s	$600	$700

Delta IV Bass

1967-1968. 5-sided body, 2 pickups, 1 volume and 2 tone controls, distortion, treble and bass boosters.

1960s	$650	$850

Mark IV Bass

1963-1969. Teardrop-shaped body, 2 pickups, 1 set of controls.

1960s	$800	$900

Panther Bass

1967-1968. Double cut solidbody, 1 slanted pickup, rosewood board.

1960s	$400	$600

Phantom IV Bass

1963-1969. 5-sided body, 2 pickups, 1 set of controls.

1960s	$900	$1,200

Saturn IV Bass

1967-1968. Single cut, 2 F-holes, 1 set of controls, 1 pickup.

1960s	$500	$700

Sidewinder IV Bass (V272)

1967-1968. Double-cut 335-style body, 2 F-holes, 2 pickups, 1 set of controls, treble, bass, and distortion boosters.

1960s	$600	$800

Stinger Bass

1968. Teardrop-shaped, boat oar headstock.

1960s	$600	$800

Wyman Bass

1966. Teardrop-shaped body, 2 pickups, 1 F-hole, 1 set of controls, sunburst.

1960s	$700	$900

Wandre (Davoli)

Ca. 1956/57-1969. Italian-made guitars and basses. See Guitar section for more company info.

Warrior

1995-present. Professional and premium grade, production/custom, solidbody basses built by luthier J.D. Lewis in Roseville, Georgia. Warrior also builds acoustic and solidbody electric guitars.

Jack Bruce Signature Bass

1993	$1,700	$1,900

Warwick

1982-present. Professional and premium grade, production/custom, electric and acoustic basses made in Markneukirchen, Germany; founded by Hans Peter Wilfer, whose father started Framus guitars.

Streamer I-5 Bass

1984-present. Five strings, Gold hardware, active electronics.

1992	$1,500	$1,900

Thumb Bass

1980s-present. Walnut, neck-through, double cutaway, solidbody, two pickups.

1985	$1,300	$1,700

Washburn

1974-present. Intermediate and professional grade, production, acoustic and electric basses. Washburn instruments were mostly imports early on, U.S. production later, currently a combination of both. Washburn also offers guitars, mandolins, and amps. See Guitar section for more company info.

AB20 Bass

1989-1999. Acoustic/electric, single sharp cutaway, flat, laminated top, mini-slat diagonal cover soundhole, dot markers.

1989-1999	$350	$500

AB40 Bass

1989-1994. Acoustic/electric, arched solid spruce top, three-band EQ.

1989-1994	$350	$500

B-80 Bass

1988-1990. Extended cutaway, neck-through-body, active electronics, flamed or quilted maple tops.

1988	$350	$500

B-100 Bass

1988-1992. Extended cutaway, neck-through-body, active electronics, flamed or quilted maple tops.

1988-1992	$350	$500

MODEL YEAR	FEATURES	EXC. COND. LOW	HIGH

Bantam B62 Doubleneck Bass

1985. Squared-body, headless doubleneck bass with 1 fretted neck, 1 fretless.

1985	$300	$500

Force ABT Bass

1987-1989. Offset double cut sculptured body, active electronics, P-J pickups.

1987-1989	$300	$400

MB-4 Bass

1992-1994. Offset double cut, bolt neck, various colors.

1992-1994	$300	$400

Series 1000 Status Bass

1988-1989. Headless, solid brass hardware, carbonite board, active electronics.

1988	$300	$400

Watkins

1957-present. Watkins Electric Music (WEM) was founded by Charlie Watkins. Their first commercial product was the Watkins Dominator (wedge Gibson stereo amp shape) in '57. They made the Rapier line of guitars and basses from the beginning. Watkins offered guitars and basses up to 1982.

Rapier Bass

Two pickups, British-made.

1960s	$400	$500

Wechter

1984-present. Intermediate and professional grade, production/custom flat-top, 12-string, and nylon string guitars and acoustic basses from luthier Abe Wechter in Paw Paw, Michigan. Until 1994 Abe built guitars on a custom basis. In 1995, he set up a manufacturing facility in Paw Paw to produce his new line.

Westbury-Unicord

1978-1981. Japanese imports by Unicord.

Electric Solidbody Basses

Various models.

1980s	$150	$250

Westone

1970s-1980s. Imported from Japan by St. Louis Music. See Guitar section for more company info.

Electric Solidbody Basses

Various models.

1980s	$150	$250

Winston

Ca. 1963-1967. Imported by Buegeleisen & Jacobson of New York.

Electric Solidbody Basses

1960s	$100	$200

Wurlitzer

1970s. Private branded by Pedula for the Wurlitzer music store chain. Manufacturer and retailer were both based in Massachusetts. Refer to Pedulla listing.

Yamaha

1946-present. Yamaha began producing solidbody instruments in '66. Currently Yamaha offers budget, intermediate, prfessional and premium grade, production, electric basses. They also build guitars. See Guitar section for more company info.

Attitude Custom Bass

1990-1994. Part of the Sheehan Series.

1990s	$600	$800

BB-300 Bass

1983-1992. 1 pickup, bolt-on maple neck, rosewood board.

1980s	$250	$500

BB-350F Bass

1987-1996. Fretless bolt neck, split single-coil pickups.

1980s	$250	$500

BB-400 Bass

1983-1992. Soldibody, bolt neck, 2 pickups.

1980s	$250	$500

BB-1600 Bass

1984-1992. Offset double cut solidbody, 2 pickups, gold hardware, oval markers.

1980s	$250	$500

BB-3000A Bass

1988-1992. Solidbody, thru-body neck, 2 active pickups.

1980s	$300	$600

BB-5000A Bass

1988-1992. 5-string, neck-through, active pickups, gold hardware.

1980s	$400	$500

BX-1 Bass

1985-1992. Headless solidbody, 2 humbuckers, coil-tap switch.

1980s	$350	$450

RBX 5 Bass

1987-1992. 5-string, bolt maple neck, basswood body.

1980s	$350	$400

RBX 200F Bass

1987-1992. Fretless, active electronics, 1 split single-coil pickup.

1980s	$200	$300

SB-30 Bass

1972-1973. Bolt neck, single cut.

1972-1973	$300	$500

SB-30S Bass

1972-1973. Bolt neck, single cut.

1972-1973	$300	$500

SB-50 Bass

1972-1973. Bolt neck, single cut.

1972-1973	$300	$500

SB-55 Bass

1972-1976. Long bass horn, Fender-like bass body.

1972-1976	$300	$500

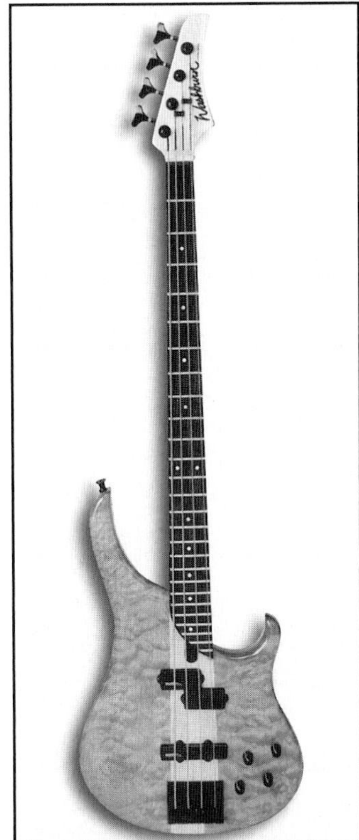

Washburn B-100

1983 Yamaha BB-2000

BASSES

Zeta Prism 4

Zon Bass

MODEL YEAR	FEATURES	EXC. COND. LOW	HIGH

SB-70 Bass

1972-1973. Bolt neck, single cut.

1972-1973		$300	$500

SB-75 Bass

1972-1976. Long bass horn, Fender-like bass body.

1972-1976		$300	$500

Zemaitis

1960-1999. Tony Zemaitis began selling his guitars in '60 and he retired in '99. He emphasized simple lightweight construction and his instruments are known for hand engraved metal fronts. Each hand-built custom guitar was a unique instrument. Approximately ten custom guitars were built each year.

Electric Bass

1980s	1/2 metal & spruce	$14,500	$16,000
1980s	Metal-front 4-string	$14,500	$17,000

Zen-On

1946-ca.1968. Japanese-made. By '67 using the Morales brandname. Not heavily imported into the U.S., if at all (see Morales).

Electric Solidbody Basses

Various models.

1950s		$100	$200

Zeta

1982-present. Professional and premium grade, production/custom, acoustic and electric basses and upright basses, with MIDI options, made in Oakland, California.

Crossover 4 (Model XB-304) Bass

1990s-present. Sleek offset body design, bolt-on neck, playable as strap-on or upright.

1999		$1,500	$1,700

MODEL YEAR	FEATURES	EXC. COND. LOW	HIGH

Jazz Standard Uprite Bass

1990s-present. Hourglass-shaped body, bass-violsize version of sleek electric violin, active electronics.

1999		$2,400	$2,600

Zim-Gar

1960s. Japanese imports from Gar-Zim Musical Instrument Corporation of Brooklyn, NY.

Electric Solidbody Basses

Various models.

1960s		$100	$175

Zolla

1979-present. Professional grade, production/custom, electric basses built by luthier Bill Zolla in San Diego, California. Zolla also builds guitars, necks and bodies.

BZ-1 Bass

1988-present. Offset double cut solidbody, 2 pickups, offered in 4-, 5-, and 6-string versions.

1980s		$400	$600

Zon

1981-present. Luthier Joe Zon builds his professional and premium grade, production/custom, solidbody basses in Redwood City, California. Zon started the brand in Buffalo, New York and relocated to Redwood City in '87.

Legacy Elite VI Bass

1989-present. 6-string, 34" scale carbon-fiber neck, Bartolini pickups, ZP-2 active electronics.

1989		$1,000	$1,200

Scepter Bass

1984-1993. Offset body shape, 24 frets, one pickup, tremolo.

1985		$900	$1,100

JMP
OFF
STANDBY
ON
ON
INDICATOR
PRESENCE
BASS
MIDDLE
TREBLE
VOLUME I
VOLUME II
INPUTS

Amps

1977 Acoustic 125

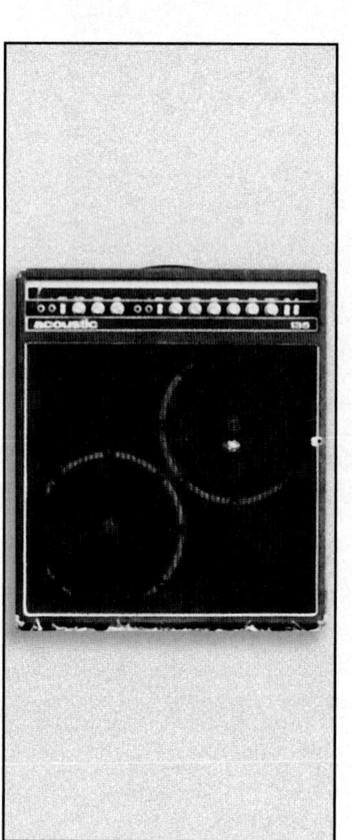
1977 Acoustic 135

MODEL YEAR	FEATURES	EXC. COND. LOW	HIGH

Acoustic

Ca. 1965-ca. 1987, present. The Acoustic Control Corp., of Los Angeles, CA was mostly known for solidstate amplifiers. Heads and cabinets were sold separately with their own model numbers, but were also combined (amp sets) and marketed under a different model number (for example, the 153 amp set was the 150b head with a 2x15" cabinet). The brandname was revived by Samick a few years ago.

114 Amp

Ca. 1977-mid- 1980s. Solidstate, 50 watts, 2x10", reverb, master volume.

1978-1984		$200	$350

115 Amp

1977-1978. Solidstate, 1x12", 50 watts, reverb, master volume.

1977-1978		$225	$375

116 Bass Amp

1978-mid-1980s. Solidstate, 75 watts, 1x15", power boost switch.

1978-1984		$250	$375

120 Amp Head

1980s. Solidstate head, 125 watts.

1981		$200	$275

124 Amp

1977-mid-1980s. Solidstate, 4x10", five-band EQ, 100 watts, master volume.

1977-1984		$250	$400

125 Amp

1977-mid-1980s. Solidstate, 2x12", five-band EQ, 100 watts, master volume.

1977-1984		$250	$400

126 Bass Amp

1977-mid-1980s. Solidstate, 100 watts, 1x15", five-band EQ.

1977-1984		$250	$400

134 Amp

1972-1976. Solidstate, 100-125 watts, 4x10" combo.

1972-1976	125 watts	$275	$425

135 Amp

1972-1976. Solidstate, 125 watts, 2x12" combo, reverb, tremolo.

1972-1976		$275	$425

136 Amp

1972-1976. Solidstate, 125 watts, 1x15" combo.

1972-1976		$275	$425

140 Bass Head

1972-1976. Solidstate, 125 watts, two channels.

1972-1976		$175	$275

150 Amp Head

1960s-1976. Popular selling model, generally many available in the used marked. Solidstate, 110 watts until '72, 125 watts after.

1968-1976		$175	$275

150b Bass Head

1960s-1971. Bass amp version of 150 head.

1968-1971		$150	$250

MODEL YEAR	FEATURES	EXC. COND. LOW	HIGH

153 Bass Amp Set

1960s-1971. 150b head (bass version of 150) with 2x15" 466 cabinet, 110 watts.

1968-1971		$375	$450

165 Amp

1979-mid-1980s. All tube combo, switchable to 60 or 100 watts, Brown Tolex.

1979-1984		$250	$400

220 Bass Head

1977-1980s. Solidstate, five-band EQ, either 125 or 160 watts, later models 170 or 200 watts, black Tolex.

1977-1984	170 or 200 watts	$200	$300

230 Amp Head

1977-1980s. Solidstate head, 125/160 watts, five-band EQ.

1977-1984		$225	$325

260 Amp Head

1960s-1971. Solidstate, 275 watt, stereo/mono.

1968-1971		$250	$350

320 Bass Head

1977-1980s. Solidstate, five-band EQ, 160/300 watts. two switchable channels. Black Tolex.

1977-1984	225 watts head into 4 ohms	$300	$375
1977-1984	300 watts head onto 2 ohms	$325	$400

360 Bass Head

1960s-1971. One of Acoustic's most popular models, 200 watts. By '72, the 360 is listed as a "preamp only."

1968-1971		$400	$500

370 Bass Head

1972-1977. Solidstate bass head, 365 watts early on, 275 later.

1972-1977	275 or 365 watts	$325	$500

402 Cabinet

1977-1980s. 2x15" bass cab, Black Tolex, Black grille.

1977-1984		$200	$250

450 Amp Head

1974-1976. 170 watts, five-bank EQ, normal and bright inputs.

1974-1976		$200	$300

455 Amp Set

1974-1976. 170 watt 450 head with 4x12" cabinet. Black.

1970s	Black	$450	$550

470 Amp Head

1974-1977. 170 watt, dual channel.

1974-1977		$300	$400

G20-110 Amp

1981-mid-1980s. Solidstate, 20 watts, 1x10". The G series was a lower-priced combo line.

1981-1985		$100	$200

G20-120 Amp

1981-mid-1980s. Solidstate, 20 watts, 1x12".

1981-1985		$125	$225

MODEL YEAR	FEATURES	EXC. COND. LOW	HIGH

G60-112 Amp
1981-mid-1980s. Solidstate, 60 watts, 1x12".

1981-1985 $150 $250

G60-212 Amp
1981-mid-1980s. Solidstate, 60 watts, 2x12".

1981-1985 $175 $275

G60T-112 Amp
1981-1987. Tube, 60 watts, 1x12".

1981-1985 $300 $375

Tube 60 Amp
1986-1987. Combo, 60 watts, 1x12", spring reverb, bright switch, master volume control, effects loop.

1986-1987 $300 $375

ADA
1977-2002. ADA is an acronym for Analog/Digital Associates. The company was located in Berkeley, California, and introduced its Flanger and Final Phase in 1977. The company later moved to Oakland and made amplifiers, high-tech signal processors, and a reissue of its original Flanger.

B-500 B Bass Power Biamp
1989-1995. Five hundred watts, in bi-amp mode the two outputs drive cabinets of four to 16 ohms.

1989-1995 $375 $420

Aguilar
U.S.-made tube and solidstate amp heads, cabinets, and pre-amps from New York, New York.

Aiken Amplification
2000-present. Tube amps, combos, and cabinets built by Randall Aiken in Buford, Georgia.

Airline
Ca. 1958-1968. Brandname for Montgomery Ward. Built by Kay, Harmony, and Valco.

Large Tube Amps
1960s Various models $275 $400

Small Tube Amps
1960s Various models $175 $300

Alamo
1947-1982. Founded by Charles Eilenberg, Milton Fink, and Southern Music, San Antonio, TX and distributed by Bruno and Sons. Alamo started producing amps in '49. The amps were all-tube until '73; solidstate preamp and tube output from '73 to ca. '80; all solidstate for ca. '80 to '82. See Guitar section for more company info or Guitar Stories Volume II, by Michael Wright, for a complete history of Alamo with detailed model listings.

Birch "A" Combo Amps
1949-1962. Birch wood cabinets with A-shaped grill cutout, two to five tubes. Models include the Embassy Amp 3, Jet Amp 4, Challenger Amp 2, Amp 5, and the Montclair.

1949-1962 $175 $275

MODEL YEAR	FEATURES	EXC. COND. LOW	HIGH

Bass Tube Amps
1960-1972. Leatherette covered, all tube, 20 to 35 watts, 15" speakers, combo or piggyback. Some with Lansing speaker option. Models include the Paragon Special, Paragon Bass, Piggyback Band, Piggyback Bass, Fury Bass, and Paragon Bass (piggyback).

1960-1972 $200 $300

Small Tube Amps
1960-1972. Leatherette covered, all tube, three to ten watts, 6" to 10" speakers, some with tremolo. Models include the Jet, Embassy, Challenger, Capri, Fiesta, Dart, and Special.

1960-1972 $200 $300

Mid-power Tube Amps
1960-1970. Leatherette covered, all tube, 15 to 30 watts, 12" or 15" speakers, some with tremolo and reverb. Some with Lansing speaker option. Models include Montclair, Paragon, Paragon Band, Titan, and Futura.

1960-1970 $250 $350

Twin Speaker and Piggyback Tube Amps
1962-1972. Leatherette covered, all tube, up to 45 watts, 8", 10", 12" or 15" speaker configurations, some with tremolo and reverb. Some with Lansing speaker option. Models include the Electra Twin Ten, Century Twin Ten, Futuramic Twin Eight, Galaxie Twin Twelve, Galaxie Twin TwelvePiggyback, Piggyback Super Band, Alamo Pro Reverb Piggyback, Futura, Galaxie Twin Ten, Twin-Ten, and Band Piggyback.

1962-1972 $300 $400

Bass Solidstate Preamp-Tube Output Amps
1973-ca.1979. Solidstate preamp section with tube output section, 35 or 40 watts, 15" speakers, combo or piggyback. Models include the Paragon Bass, Paragon Bass Piggyback, Paragon Country Western Bass, Paragon Super Bass, and the Fury Bass.

1973-1979 $150 $250

Small Solidstate Preamp-Tube Output Amps
1973-ca.1979. Solidstate preamp section with tube output section, three to 12 watts, 5" to 12" speaker, some with reverb. Models include the Challenger, Capri, Special, Embassy, Dart, and Jet.

1973-1979 $100 $200

Mid-powered Solidstate Preamp-Tube Output Amps
1973-ca.1979. Solidstate preamp section with tube output section, 25 watts, 12" speaker, with reverb and tremolo. Models include the Montclair.

1973-1979 $150 $225

Twin & Combo Solidstate Preamp-Tube Output Amps
1973-ca.1979. Solidstate preamp section with tube output section, 20 or 70 watts, 10", 12" and 15" speaker configurations, some with reverb and tremolo. Models include the 70 watt Paragon Super Reverb piggybacks, the 45 watt Futura 2x12, and the 20 watt Twin-Ten.

1973-1979 $150 $225

'60s Alamo Jet

1962 Alamo 2566 Century Twin Ten

AMPS

Alessandro Redbone Special

1960s Ampeg GV-22

MODEL YEAR	FEATURES	EXC. COND. LOW	HIGH

Solidstate Amps

ca. 1980-1982. All solidstate.

1980-1982		$75	$150

Alessandro

1998-present. Founded by George Alessandro in 1994 as the Hound Dog Corporation. In 1998 the company name was changed to Alessandro. The Redbone ('94) and the Bloodhound ('96) were the only models bearing the Hound Dog mark. Serial numbers are consecutive regardless of model (the earliest 20-30 did not have serial numbers). In '98 the company converted to exotic/high-end components and the name changed to Alessandro High-End Products.

Bloodhound Amp Head

1996-1998. Stained wood amp cabinet, 55 watts with El-34 power tubes, 12AX7 preamp tubes.

1996-1998		$1,400	$1,600

Redbone Amp Head

1994-1998. Stained hardwood amp cabinet, 55 watts with EL-34 power tubes, octal preamp tubes.

1994-1998		$1,700	$1,900

Allen Amplification

1998-present. David Allen's company, located in Richwood, Kentucky, produces tube combo amps, heads and cabinets. He also offers the amps in kit form and produces replacement and upgrade transformers and a tube overdrive pedal.

Aloha

Late-1940s. Electric lap steel and amp Hawaiian outfits for Dallas-based Aloha.

Ampeg

Ampeg is primarily known for their bass amps. In the eastern Uunited States, Ampeg was Fender's greatest challenger in the '60s and '70s bass amplifier market. St. Louis Music currently offers a line of Ampeg guitars and amps. See the Guitar section for more company history.

Amp Covering Dates

Wood veneer	1946-1949
Smooth Brown	1949-1952
Dot Tweed	1952-1954
Tweed	1954-1955
Rough Gray	1957-1958
Rough Tan	1957-1958
Cream	1957-1958
Light Blue	1958
Navy Blue	1958-1962
Blue check	1962-1967
Black pebble	1967
Smooth Black	1967-1980
Rough Black	1967-1985

AC12 Amp

1970 only. 20 watts, 1x12", accordion amp that was a market failure and dropped after one year.

1970		$300	$400

MODEL YEAR	FEATURES	EXC. COND. LOW	HIGH

AP3550 Amp

1992-1993. 350 watts or 200 watts rackmount solidstate head, black metal.

1992-1993	350 watts	$225	$275

B-2 Bass Amp

1994-present. Solidstate, 200 watts, 1x15" combo or 4x8" combo, Black vinyl, Black grille, large A logo.

1994-2000	1x15"	$500	$600

B-3 Amp

1995-2001. Solidstate head, 150 watts, 1x15".

1995-2001		$400	$450

B-12 N Portaflex Amp

1961-1965. 25 watts, 2x12", two 6L6 power tubes.

1961-1965		$800	$1,000

B-12 XT Portaflex Amp

1965-1969. Tube, 50 watts, 2x12", reverb, vibrato, two 7027A power tubes.

1965-1969		$700	$900

B-15 N (NB, NC, NF) Portaflex Amp

1960-1970. Introduced as B-15 using two 6L6 power tubes, B-15 N in 1961, B-15 NB in 1962, B-15 NC with rectifier tube in 1964, B-15 NF with fixed-bias two 6L6 power tubes and 30 watts in 1967, 1x15".

1960-1965		$850	$1,050
1966-1970		$750	$950

B-15 NC Portaflex Amp (2nd version)

1967-1968. A different version than the 1964 to 1967 version. 50 watts, two 7027A power tubes, column 2x15" cabinet.

1967-1968		$750	$950

B-15 R Portaflex Amp (reissue)

1990s. Reissue of 1965 Portaflex 1x15". Blue check.

1990s		$750	$850

B-15 S Portaflex Amp

1971-1977. 60 watts, two 7027A power tubes, 1x12".

1971-1977		$750	$950

B-18 N Portaflex Amp

1964-1969. Bass, 50 watts, 1x18".

1964-1965		$850	$1,000
1966-1969		$800	$950

B-25 Amp

1969 only. 55 watts, two 7027A power tubes, 2x15", no reverb, guitar amp.

1969		$700	$900

B-25B Bass Amp

1969-1980. Bass amp, 55 watts, two 7027A power tubes, 2x15" bass speakers.

1969		$700	$900

B-50R Rocket Bass Amp (reissue)

1996-present. Fifty watts, 1x12" combo, vintage-style Blue check cover.

1996-1999		$250	$300

B-100R Rocket Bass Amp (reissue)

1996-present. Solidstate, 100 watts, 1x15" combo bass amp, vintage-style Blue check cover.

1996-1999		$300	$350

MODEL YEAR	FEATURES	EXC. COND. LOW	HIGH

B-3158B Bass Amp

1990s. Solidstate, 100 watts, 1x15", Black vinyl, Black grille, large A logo.

1990s		$500	$575

BT-15 Amp

1966-1968. Ampeg introduced solidstate amps in '66, the same year as Fender. Solidstate, 50 watts, 1x15", generally used as a bass amp. The BT-15D has two 1x15" cabinets. The BT-15C is a 2x15" column portaflex cabinet.

1966-1968		$300	$350

BT-18 Amp

1966-1968. Ampeg introduced solidstate amps in 1966, the same year as Fender. Solidstate, 50 watts, 1x18", generally used as a bass amp. The BT-18D has two 1x15" cabinets. The BT-15C is a 2x18" column portaflex cabinet.

1966-1968		$250	$300

ET 1 Echo Twin Amp

1961-1964. Tube, 30 watts, 1x12", stereo reverb.

1961-1964		$600	$700

ET 2 Super Echo Twin Amp

1962-1964. Tube, 2x12", 30 watts, stereo reverb.

1962-1964		$650	$750

G-12 Gemini I Amp

1964-1971. Tube, 1x12", 22 watts, reverb.

1964-1971		$500	$600

G-15 Gemini II Amp

1965-1968. Tube, 30 watts, 1x15", reverb.

1965-1968		$500	$600

G-110 Amp

1978-1980. Solidstate, 20 watts, 1x10", reverb, tremolo.

1978-1980		$250	$350

G-115 Amp

1979-1980. Solidstate, 175 watts, 1x15" JBL, reverb and tremolo, designed for steel guitar.

1979-1980		$300	$400

G-212 Amp

1973-1980. Solidstate, 120 watts, 2x12".

1973-1980		$350	$450

GS-12 Rocket 2 Amp

1965-1968. This name replaced the Reverberocket 2 (II), 15 watts, 1x12".

1965-1968		$400	$500

GS-12-R Reverberocket 2 Amp

1965-1969. Tube, 1x12", 18 watts, reverb. Called the Reverberocket II in 1968 and 1969, then Rocket II in 1969.

1965-1969		$400	$500

GS-15-R Gemini VI Amp

1966-1967. 30 watts, 1x15", single channel, considered to be "the accordion version" of the Gemini II.

1966-1967		$450	$550

GT-10 Amp

1971-1980. Solidstate, 15 watts, 1x10", basic practice amp with reverb.

1971-1980		$250	$350

GV-22 Gemini 22 Amp

1969-1972. Tube, 30 watts, 2x12".

1969-1972		$450	$550

J-12 A Jet Amp

1964		$400	$500

J-12 D Jet Amp

Jet Amp with solidstate rectifier.

1964-1966		$400	$500

J-12 Jet Amp

1958-1972 (no 1964-66 models). Twenty watts, 1x12".

1958-1963		$400	$500
1967-1972	Model reappears	$350	$450

J-12 T Jet Amp

1964-1965		$400	$500

M-12 Mercury Amp

1957-1965. Fifteen watts, two channels, Rocket 1x12".

1957-1959		$600	$700
1960-1965		$550	$650

M-15 Big M Amp

1959-1965. 20 watts, 2x6L6 power, 1x15".

1959		$600	$700
1960-1965		$550	$650

R-12 Rocket Amp

1957-1963. 12 watts, 1x12", one channel.

1957-1963		$500	$600

R-12-B Rocket Amp

1964. 12 watts, 1x12", follow-up to the R-12 Rocket.

1964		$500	$600

R-12-R Reverberocket Amp

1961-1965.

1961-1965		$400	$500

R-12-R Reverberocket Amp (reissue)

1996-present. 50 watts, two EL34 power tubes, 1x12" (R-212R is 2x12").

1996-1999		$350	$375

R-12-R-B Reverberocket Amp

1964 variant. 7591A power tubes replace R-12-R 6V6 power tubes.

1964		$400	$500

R-12-R-T Reverberocket Amp

1965 variant. 7591A or 7868 power tubes.

1965		$400	$500

R-212-R Reverberocket Combo 50 Amp (reissue)

1996-present. 50 watts, 2x12", all tube reissue, vintage-style blue ckeck cover, vintage-style grille.

1996-1999		$325	$375

SB-12 Portaflex Amp

1965-1971. 22 watts, 1x12", designed for use with Ampeg's Baby Bass, black.

1965-1971		$600	$700

SBT Amp

1969-1971. 120 watts, 1x15", bass version of SST Amp.

1969-1971		$700	$800

SE-412 Cabinet

Four 12" speakers.

1996-1999		$300	$350

1959 Ampeg J-12 Jet

1965 Ampeg R-12-R-T Reverberocket

AMPS

Ampeg SVT

Ampeg SVT 350

MODEL YEAR	FEATURES	EXC. COND. LOW	HIGH

SJ-12-R/SJ-12-RT Super Jet Amp

1996-present. 50 watts, tube, 1x12", SJ-12-RT has tremolo added.

1996-1999		$300	$350

SS-35 Amp

1987-1992. Solidstate, 35 watts, 1x12", Black vinyl, Black grille, large A logo.

1990		$150	$200

SS-70 Amp

1987-1990. Solidstate, 70 watts, 1x12".

1990		$300	$350

SS-70 C Amp

1987-1992. Solidstate, 70 watts, 2x10", chorus, Black vinyl, Black grille, large A logo.

1990		$300	$350

SVT Bass Amp Set

1969-1985. 300 watt head with matching two 8x10" cabs.

1976	Amp and cab	$2,100	$2,300

SVT Bass Cabinets

1969-1985. Two 8x10" cabs only.

1970s		$800	$900

SVT Bass Head Amp

1969-1985. 300 watt head only.

1969-1972		$1,200	$1,400
1973-1979		$1,100	$1,300
1980-1985		$900	$1,100

SVT-II Pro Bass Head Amp

1992-present. Three hundred watts, rack-mountable, all tube circuit similar to original SVT, Black metal.

1992-1999		$850	$1,150

SVT-III Pro Bass Head Amp

1993-present. Tube preamp section and MOS-FET power section, 350 watts, rack-mountable, black metal.

1993-1999		$600	$800

SVT-4 Pro Bass Head Amp

1997-present. Hybrid rack-mountable, all tube preamp, MOS-FET power section yielding, 1600 watts.

1997-1999		$900	$1,000

SVT 100T Bass Combo Amp

1990-1992. Solidstate, ultra-compact bass combo, 100 watts, 2x8".

1990-1992		$400	$450

SVT 200T Head Amp

1987 only. Solidstate, 200 watts to eight ohms or 320 watts to four ohms.

1987		$375	$475

SVT 350 Head Amp

1995-present. Solidstate head, 350 watts, graphic EQ.

1990s		$375	$475

SVT 400 Amp

1987-1997. Solidstate, 400 watts per side, rack-mountable head with advanced (in 1987) technology.

1990s		$375	$475

V-2 Amp Set

1971-1980. Sixty-watt head with 4x12" cab, Black Tolex.

1971-1980		$700	$850

V-2 Head Amp

1971-1980. 60 watt tube head.

1971-1980		$300	$450

V-4 4x12" Cab

1970s. Single 4x12" cabinet only.

1970-1980		$350	$400

V-4 Amp Stack

1970-1980. One hundred watts, with two 4x12" cabs.

1970-1980	Head and cabs	$950	$1,050
1970-1980	Head only	$450	$600

V-4-B Bass Head Amp

1972-1980. Bass version of V-4 without reverb.

1972-1980		$450	$600

V-7-SC Amp

1981-1985. Tube, 100 watts, 1x12", master volume, channel switching, reverb.

1981-1985		$450	$600

VH-70 Amp

1991-1992. 70 watts, 1x12" combo with channel switching.

1991-1992		$300	$350

VH-140C Amp

1992-1995. Varying Harmonics (VH) with Chorus (C), two 70-watt channel stereo, 2x12".

1992-1995		$350	$425

VH-150 Head Amp

1991-1992. 150 watts, channel-switchable, reverb.

1991-1992		$325	$375

VL-502 Amp

1991-1995. 50 watts, channel-switchable, all tube.

1991-1995		$300	$400

VL-1001 Head Amp

1991-1993. 100 watts, non-switchable channels, all tube.

1991-1993		$300	$350

VL-1002 Head Amp

1991-1995. 100 watts, channel-switchable, all tube.

1991-1995		$350	$450

VT-22 Amp

1970-1980. 100 watt combo version of V-4, 2x12".

1970-1980		$500	$650

VT-40 Amp

1971-1980. 60 watt combo, 4x10".

1971-1980		$500	$650

VT-60 Combo Amp

1989-1991. Tube, 6L6 power, 60 watts, 1x12".

1989-1991		$400	$550

VT-60 Head Amp

1989-1991. Tube head only, 6L6 power, 60 watts.

1989-1991		$350	$500

VT-120 Combo Amp

1989-1992. Tube, 6L6 power, 120 watts, 1x12", also offered as head only.

1989-1992		$500	$650

MODEL YEAR	FEATURES	EXC. COND. LOW	HIGH

VT-120 Head Amp

1989-1992. 120 watts, 6L6 tube head.

1989-1992		$450	$600

Ashdown Amplification

1999-present. Founded in England by Mark Gooday after he spent several years with Trace Elliot, Ashdown offers intermediate and professional grade, production, amps, combos, and cabinets.

Auralux

2000-present. Founded by Mitchell Omori and David Salzmann, Auralux builds effects and tube amps in Highland Park, Illinois.

Bad Cat Amplifier Company

2000-present. The company was founded in Corona, California by James and Debbie Heidrich with Mark Sampson as the chief designer and engineer. Bad Cat offers class A combo amps, heads, cabinets and effects.

Baldwin

1965-1970. Piano maker Baldwin started offering amplifiers in '65. The amps were solidstate with "organ-like" pastel-colored pushbutton switches.

Exterminator Amp

1965-1970. Solidstate, 100 watts, 2x15"/2x12"/2x7", four feet vertical combo cabinet, reverb and tremolo, Supersound switch and slide controls.

1965-1970		$600	$700

Model B1 Bass Amp

1965-1970. Solidstate, 45 watts, 1x15"/1x12", two channels.

1965-1970		$300	$350

Model B2 Bass Amp

1965-1970. Solidstate, 35 watts, 1x15", two channels.

1965-1970		$275	$325

Model C1 Custom (Professional) Amp

1965-1970. Solidstate, 45 watts, 2x12", reverb and tremolo, Supersound switch and slide controls.

1965-1970		$350	$400

Model C2 Custom Amp

1965-1970. Solidstate, 40 watts, 2x12", reverb and tremolo.

1960s		$300	$350

Barcus-Berry

1964-present. Pickup maker Barcus-Berry offered a line of amps from '75 to '79.

Blue Tone Amplifiers

2002-present. Founded by Alex Cooper in Worcestershire, England, Blue Tone offers amps employing their "virtual valve technology."

MODEL YEAR	FEATURES	EXC. COND. LOW	HIGH

Bogner

1988-present. Tube combos, amp heads, and speaker cabinets from builder Reinhold Bogner of North Hollywood, California.

Bruno (Tony)

1995-present. Tube combos, amp heads, and speaker cabinets from builder Tony Bruno of Cairo, New York.

Underground 30 Combo Amp

1995-present. Thirty-five watts, 1x12", no reverb.

1995-1999		$1,100	$1,250

Budda

1995-present. Amps, combos, and cabinets from San Rafael, California. They also produce effects pedals.

Callaham

1989-present. Tube amp heads and solidbody electric guitars built by Bill Callaham made in Winchester, Virginia.

Carr Amplifiers

1998-present. Steve Carr started producing amps in his Chapel Hill, North Carolina amp repair business in '98. The company is now located in a converted '50s chicken hatchery outside of Chapel Hill and makes tube combo amps, heads, and cabinets.

Carvin

1946-present. Carvin added small tubes amps to their product line in '47 and today offers a variety of models. See Guitar section for more company info.

Amp

1950s. Tweed, 4x10".

1950s		$325	$450

Pro-Bass II Amp Head

1986-ca.1989. Available in 100- and 300-watt models, preamp, noise gate, EQ, effects loop.

1986	100 watts	$225	$275

VT-112 Amp

Tube, 1x12", seven-band equalizer.

1978		$200	$275

X-60 Amp

1984-ca.1989. Sixty-watt combo, reverb, 1x12".

1984		$250	$300

XB-112 Amp

Thirty watts, 1x12".

1981		$300	$375

XV-112E Amp

One hundred watts, 1x12" ElectroVoice speaker.

1981		$350	$450

XV-212 Amp

One hundred watts, 2x12".

1981		$350	$450

Bad Cat Hot Cat 15

Carr Mercury

Danelectro Commando

Danelectro Model 78 Maestro

MODEL YEAR	FEATURES	EXC. COND. LOW	HIGH

Clark Amplification

Hand-wired, tweed-era replica amplifiers from builder Mike Clark, of Cayce, South Carolina.

Tyger Amp (non-reverb)

2000-present. Classic tweed Fender 5E7 Bandmaster circuit, 3x10", 35 watts.

2000	Tweed	$1,000	$1,100

Tyger Amp (reverb)

2000-present. Tyger Amp with optional three-knob reverb, and three-position power attenuator.

2000	Tweed	$1,200	$1,300

Crate

1979-present. Complete line of mostly solidstate amplifiers distributed by St. Louis Music.

Solidstate Amps

Various student to mid-level amps, up to 150 watts.

1970s		$100	$175
1980s		$100	$175

Vintage Club 50 Amp

Mid-1990s. Fifty watts, 3x10", tube amp, vintage-looking White cover, Brown grille.

1990s	White	$300	$400

Cruise Audio Systems

1999-present. Founded by Mark Altekruse, Cruise offers amps, combos, and cabinets built in Cuyahoga Falls, Ohio

Da Vinci

Late-1950s-early-1960s. Another one of several private brands (for example, Unique, Twilighter, Titano, etc.) that Magnatone made for teaching studios and accordian companies.

Model 250 Amp

1958-1962. Similar to Magnatone Model 250 with about 20 watts and 1x12".

1958-1962		$400	$500

Danelectro

1946-1969, 1997-present. Founded in Red Bank, New Jersey, by Nathan I. "Nate" or "Nat" Daniel. His first amps were made for Montgomery Ward in 1947, and in 1948 he began supplying Silvertone Amps for Sears. His own amps were distributed by Targ and Dinner as Danelectro and S.S. Maxwell brands. See Guitar section for more company info.

Cadet Amp

Six watts, 1x6".

1955-1959		$250	$300
1960-1963		$150	$250

Centurion Model 275 Amp

Two 6V6 power tubes for approximately 15-18 watts, 1x12", Gray cover.

1959-1960		$250	$350

DM-10 Amp

Five watts, 1x6".

1960s		$125	$200

MODEL YEAR	FEATURES	EXC. COND. LOW	HIGH

DM-25 Amp

Thirty-five watts, 1x12".

1960s		$275	$325

Model 217 Twin 15 Amp

1960s. Combo amp, 100 watts, 2x15" Jensen C15P speakers, Black cover, White-Silver grille, two channels with tremolo.

1962		$375	$475

Model 68 Amp

1950s. Twenty watts, 1x12", light Tweed-fabric cover, light grille, leather handle, script Danelectro plexi-plate logo.

1950s		$250	$350

Model 98 Twin 12 Amp (Series D)

1954-ca.1957. Blond tweed-style cover, brown control panel, 2x12", vibrato speed and strength, rounded front Series D.

1954-1957		$500	$700

Viscount Model 142 Amp

Late-1950s. Combo amp, lower watts, 1x12", light cover, Brown grille, vibrato.

1959		$250	$350

Dean Markley

The string and pickup manufacturer added a line of amps in the early '80s. The current line continues to have emphasis on smaller solidstate amps.

K-15 Combo Amp

1980s. Recently reintroduced. Solidstate, 10 watts, 1x6", dark cover, dark grille, script Dean Markley logo bottom left on grille.

1986		$75	$85

K-20 Amp

1980s. Solidstate, 10 to 20 watts, 1x8", master volume, overdrive switch, line output and headphone jack.

1986		$75	$85

K-50 Amp

1980s. Twenty-five watts, 1x10", master volume, reverb, headphone jack, line in/out.

1986		$100	$125

K-75 Amp

1980s. Thirty-five watts, 1x12", master volume, reverb, headphone jack, line in/out.

1986		$125	$150

Demeter

1980-present. James Demeter founded the company as Innovative Audio and renamed it Demeter Amplification in '90. Located in Van Nuys, California. First products were direct boxes. By '85, amps were added. Currently they build amp heads, combos, and cabinets. They also have pro audio gear and guitar effects.

Diaz

Early 1980s-2002. Cesar Diaz restored amps for many of rock's biggest names, often working with them to develop desired tones. Along the

MODEL YEAR	FEATURES	EXC. COND. LOW	HIGH

way he produced his own line of high-end custom amps and effects. Diaz died in 2002.

Dickerson

1937-1947. Dickerson was founded by the Dickerson brothers in 1937, primarily for electric lap steels and small amps. Instruments were also private branded for Cleveland's Oahu company, and for the Gourley brand. By '47, the company changed ownership and was renamed Magna Electronics (Magnatone).

Oasis Amp

1940s-1950s. Blue pearloid cover, 1x10", low wattage. Dickerson silk-screen logo on grille with Hawaiian background.

1940s	Blue pearloid	$150	$250

Dr. Z Amps

1988-present. Mike Zaite started producing his Dr. Z line of amps in the basement of the Music Manor in Maple Heights, Ohio. The company is now located in its own larger facility in the same city. Dr. Z offers combo amps, heads and cabinets.

Duca Tone

The Duca Tone brand was distributed by Lo Duca Brothers, Milwaukee, Wisconsin, which also distributed EKO guitars in the U.S.

Tube Amp

Twelve watts, 1x12".

1950s		$400	$450

Dumble

1963-present. Made by Howard Alexander Dumble, an early custom-order amp maker from California. Initial efforts were a few Mosrite amps for Semie Moseley. First shop was in 1968 in Santa Cruz.

Overdrive Special Amp and Cabinet

One hundred watts, 1x12", based on Fender design, known for durability, cabinets vary.

1970s	Black	$11,000	$13,000
1980s	Black	$11,000	$13,000
1990s	Black	$11,000	$13,000

Earth Sound Research

Earth Sound was a product of ISC Audio of Huntington, New York, and offered a range of amps, cabinets and PA gear.

2000 G Half-Stack Amp

1970s. One hundred watts plus cab.

1972		$450	$550

Amps

Various lower to mid-level amplifiers KT and MV Series.

1970s	Various models	$300	$400

Eden

1976-present. Started as a custom builder, Eden now offers a full line of amps, combos, and cabinets for the bassist. The brand is a division of U.S. Music Corp.

Egnater

1980-present. Tube amps, combos, preamps and cabinets built in Michigan by Bruce Egnater.

EKO

1959-1985. In '67 EKO added amps to their product line, offering three piggyback and four combo amps, all with dark covering, dark grille, and the EKO logo. The amp line may have lasted into the early '70s.

Electro-Harmonix

1968-1981, 1996-present. Electro-Harmonix offered a few amps to go with its line of effects. See Effects section for more company info.

Freedom Brothers Amp

Introduced in 1977. Small AC/DC amp with two 5-1/2" speakers. E-H has reissued the similar Freedom amp.

1977		$135	$165

Mike Matthews Dirt Road Special Amp

Twenty-five watts, 1x12" Celestion, built-in Small Stone phase shifter.

1977		$300	$400

Elk

Late-1960s. Japanese-made by Elk Gakki Co., Ltd. Many were copies of American designs.

Custom EL 150L Amp

Late-1960s. Piggy-back set, all-tube with head styled after very early Marshall and cab styled after large vertical Fender cab.

1968		$375	$425

Guitar Man EB 105 (Super Reverb) Amp

Late-1960s. All-tube, reverb, copy of Blackface Super Reverb.

1968		$300	$325

Twin Amp 60/Twin Amp 50 EB202

Late-1960s. All-tube, reverb, copy of Blackface Dual Showman set (head plus horizontal cab) but named Twin.

1968		$375	$425

Viking 100 VK 100 Amp

Late-1960s. Piggy-back set, head styled after very early Marshall and cab styled after very large vertical Fender cab.

1968		$375	$425

Emery Sound

1997-present. Founded by Curt Emery in El Cerrito, California, Emery Sound specializes in custom-made low wattage tube amps.

Dr. Z Maz 18

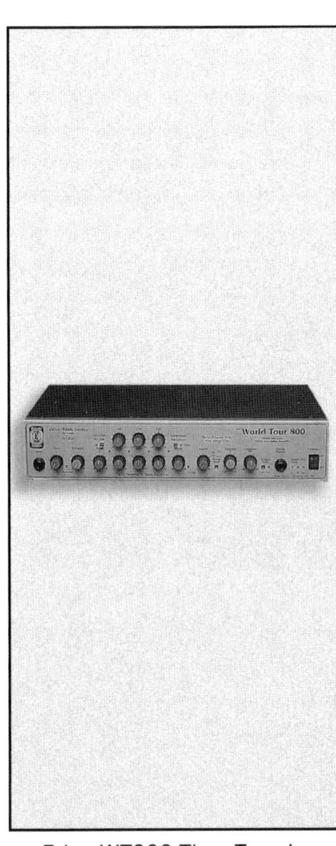

Eden WT800 Time Traveler

AMPS

Epiphone Electar Zephyr

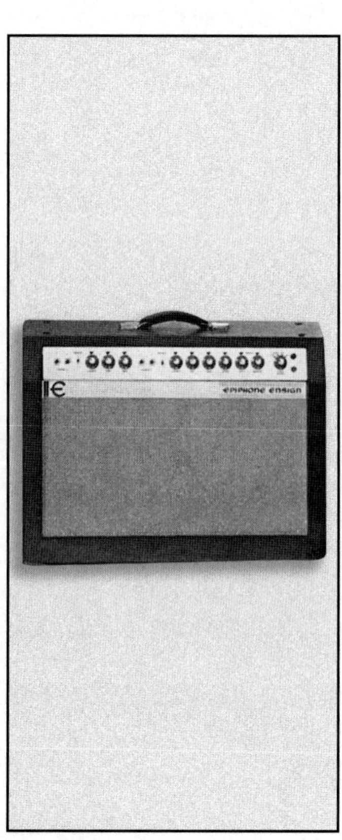

1966 Epiphone EA-14 RVT Ensign

MODEL YEAR	FEATURES	EXC. COND. LOW	HIGH

Epiphone

1928-present. Epiphone offered amps into the mid-'60s. They reintroduced an amp line around '90. See Guitar section for more company info.

The price ranges listed for excellent condition, all original amps though tubes may be replaced without affecting value. Many amps have missing or broken logos. The prices listed are for amps with fully intact logos. A broken or missing logo changes the amp's status from excellent collector quality to player quality and can diminish the value of an amp. Amps with a changed handle, power cord, and especially a broken logo should be taken on a case-by-case basis.

E-60 Amp

1972-1975. Solidstate model offered similarly to Gibson G-Series, three watts, 1x10", volume and tone knobs.

1972-1975 $75 $100

E-60 T Amp

1972-1975. E-60 with tremolo, volume, tone, and tremolo knobs.

1972-1975 $60 $80

E-1051 Amp

1970s. Tube practice amp, 1x10".

1970s $150 $175

E-30B Amp

1972-1975. Solidstate model offered similarly to Gibson G-Series (not GA-Series), 30 watts, 2x10", four knobs.

1972-1975 $150 $200

EA-12 RVT Futura Amp

1962-1967. Low- to mid-power, 4x8", 1960s Gray Tolex, light grille.

1962-1967 $650 $750

EA-14 RVT Ensign Amp

1965-1967. Gray Tolex with Silver-Gray grille, 50 watts, 2x12", split C logo.

1965-1967 Gray Tolex $450 $550

EA-16 RVT Regent Amp

1966-1967. Twenty-five watts, 1x12", Gray vinyl, Gray grille, tremolo, reverb.

1966-1967 $400 $500

EA-26 RVT Electra Amp

1965-1967. Gray Tolex, reverb, tremolo, footswitch, 1x12".

1965-1967 $300 $400

EA-28 RVT Zephyr Amp

1961-1965. Fourteen or twenty watts, 1x15", Gray Tolex, light grille, split C logo on panel, tremolo and reverb, script Epiphone logo lower right grille.

1961-1965 $300 $500

EA-32 RVT Comet Amp

One 10" speaker.

1965-1967 $300 $400

EA-33 RVT Galaxie Amp

1963-1965. Gray Tolex with Gray grille, 1x10".

1963-1965 $350 $450

EA-35 Devon Amp

1961-1963. One 10" speaker.

1961-1963 $300 $350

EA-50 Peacemaker Amp

1961-1967. One 8" speaker.

1961-1967 $200 $250

EA-300 RVT Embassy Amp

1965-1967. Ninety watts, 2x12", Gray vinyl, Gray grille, tremolo, reverb.

1965-1967 $550 $650

EA-500 Panorama/EA-400 Panorama II Amp

1964-1967. Sixty-five watts, 1x15" or 2x10", Gray vinyl, Gray grille, amp head and large cabinet with casters, tremolo, no reverb.

1964-1967 $300 $600

EA-600 RVT Maxima Amp

1966-1967. Solidstate Epiphone version of Gibson GSS-100, Gray vinyl, Gray grille, two 2x10" cabs and hi-fi stereo-style amp head.

1966-1967 $500 $550

Electar Zephyr Amp

Maple cabinet, 'E' logo on front, 1x12" silver frame speaker.

1940s $500 $800

Fender

1946-present. Leo Fender established Fender's Radio Service in '38 in Fullerton, California (which eventually became the Fender Electric Instrument Company in '46). His early manufacturing focus was on P.A. systems and he attempted to improve the inferior offerings of the day. He also private-branded a few Fender tube radios. Western Swing and Hawaiian music were popular at the time and Fender wanted to supply those musicians with superior products. Fender contributed many groundbreaking instruments, but Leo's primary passion was amplifiers, and of all his important contributions to musicians, none exceed those he made to the electric tube amplifier.

Fender Tweed amp circuits are highly valued because they 'defined' the tones of Rock and Roll. It has often been said, "It seemed like everybody was playing a Fender amp." Fender amps known as Blackface models remained basically the same until mid-1967. Some Silverface circuits remained the same as the Blackface circuits, while others were changed in the name of "reliability." Fender amps ruled the business until things changed in the late-'60s when powerful arena amps were introduced by Marshall.

Price guide values are for all original, excellent condition amps. Small differences in an amp's condition can generate larger differences in selling prices. Non-original speakers will significantly reduce a pre-'68 amp's value. Reconed speakers will reduce the value, but a reconed speaker is preferable to a replacement speaker. Multi-speaker amps generally have matching speaker codes. Different

MODEL YEAR	FEATURES	EXC. COND. LOW	HIGH

speaker codes require explanation. Fender leather handles are often broken and replaced. A replacement handle drops the value of an amp. Tweed was not the best covering, being prone to stains and damage. Grille cloths should have no tears. A single tear can drop the value of an amp. Each Tweed amp should be evaluated on a case-by-case basis, and it is not unusual for a Tweed amp to have a wide range of values. Alnico speaker replacement is more significant than ceramic speaker replacement. Fender converted to ceramic about '62. Speaker replacement is of less concern in post-'70 Fender amps.

The speaker code found on the frame of an original speaker will identify the manufacturer, and the week and year that the speaker was assembled. The speaker code is typically six (sometimes seven) digits. The first three digits represent the Electronics Industries Association (E.I.A.) source code which identifies the manufacturer. For example, a speaker code 220402 indicates a Jensen speaker (220), made in '54 (4) during the second week (02) of that year. This sample speaker also has another code stamped on the frame. ST654 P15N C4964 indicates the model of the speaker, in this case it is a P15N 15" speaker. The sample speaker also had a code stamped on the speaker cone, 4965 1, which indicates the cone number. All of these codes help identify the originality of the speaker. The value ranges provided in the Guide are for amps with the original speaker and original speaker cone.

Most Fender speakers from the '50s will be Jensens (code 220). By the late-'50s other suppliers were used. Their supplier's codes are as follows: Oxford (code 465), C.T.S. (code 137), Utah (code 328). JBL speakers were first used in the late-'50s Vibrasonic, and then in the Showman series, but JBL did not normally have a E.I.A. source code. An amp's speaker code should be reconciled with other dating info when the amp's original status is being verified. Professional vintage guitar dealers will have already done this verification prior to offering an amp for sale.

See Guitar section for more company info.

75 Combo Amp

1980-1983. Tube, 75 watts, 1x15".

1980-1983		$400	$450

85 Combo Amp

1988-1992. Solidstate, 85 watts, 1x10", Black cover, Silver grille.

1988-1992		$250	$300

Acoustasonic Jr. Amp

1998-2000. Acoustic technology, 2x40 watts, 2x8" and Piezo horn. Brown Tolex and Wheat grille.

1998		$300	$350

Acoustasonic SFX Amp

1998-present. SFX technology, 32 stereo digital present effects, 2x10 watts, 1x10" and 1x8", and Piezo horn. Brown Tolex and Wheat grille.

1998-2002		$375	$425

Bandmaster Amp

1953-1974. Wide-panel 1x15" combo 1953-1954, narrow-panel 3x10" combo 1955-1960, Tolex 1960, Brownface with 1x12" piggy back speaker cabinet 1961, 2x12" 1962, Blackface 1962-1967, Silverface 1968-1974.

1953-1954	Tweed, 1x15"	$3,000	$4,000
1955-1960	Tweed, 3x10"	$4,000	$5,000
1960	Brown Tolex, 3x10"	$4,000	$5,000
1961	Rough White and Oxblood, 1x12"	$1,400	$2,000
1961-1962	Rough White and Oxblood, 2x12"	$1,400	$1,600
1963-1964	Smooth White and Gold, 2x12"	$1,300	$1,600
1964-1967	Black Tolex, 2x12"	$1,000	$1,200
19681969	Silverface, 2x12"	$850	$950
1970-1974	Silverface, 2x12"	$550	$650

Bandmaster Cabinet

1961-1975. Two 12" speakers.

1960s	Silverface vertical cabinet	$400	$450

Bandmaster Head Amp

1961-1975. Non-reverb model.

1961-1962	Rough White Tolex	$750	$950
1963-1964	Smooth White Tolex	$750	$950
1964-1967	Blackface, Black Tolex	$650	$750
1967-1969	Silverface	$450	$500
1970-1971	Silverface, Black Tolex	$350	$450

Bandmaster Reverb Amp

1968-1981. Cabinet for 2x12", 45 watts, Silverface.

1968-1972		$1,000	$1,200
1973-1981		$800	$1,000

Bandmaster Reverb Head Amp

1968-1981. Reverb, 45 watts.

1969-1972		$650	$750
1973-1981		$550	$650

Bantam Bass Amp

1970-1972. Fifty watts, large unusual (prone to malfunction) 1x10" Yahama speaker.

1971-1972		$450	$550

Bassman Amp

1952-1971. Tweed TV front combo, 1x15" in '52, wide-panel '53-'54, narrow-panel and 4x10" '54-'60, Tolex, brownface with 1x12" in piggyback cabinet '61, 2x12" cabinet '61-'62, Blackface '63-'67, Silverface '67-'71, 2x15" cabinet '68-'71. Renamed the Bassman 50 in '72.

1952	TV front, 1x15"	$3,000	$4,000
1953-1954	Wide panel, 1x15"	$3,000	$4,000
1955-1957	Tweed, 4x10", two inputs	$4,000	$5,000
1957-1960	Tweed, 4x10", four inputs	$4,200	$5,200
1961	White and Oxblood, 1x12"	$1,800	$2,200
1961-1962	White and Oxblood 2x12"	$1,500	$1,900

1964 Fender Bandmaster head

Late-'50s Fender Bassman

AMPS

1960 Fender Champ

1986 Fender Champ 12

MODEL YEAR	FEATURES	EXC. COND. LOW	HIGH
1963-1964	White and Gold, 2x12"	$1,400	$1,900
1964-1967	Black Tolex, 2x12"	$1,000	$1,200
1968-1969	Silverface, 2x15"	$700	$800
1970-1971	Silverface, 2x15"	$650	$750

Bassman Head Amp

1961-1962	Rough White Tolex	$900	$1,100
1963-1964	Smooth White Tolex	$900	$1,100
1964-1967	Blackface, Black Tolex	$700	$800
1967-1969	Silverface, Black Tolex	$450	$500
1970-1971	Silverface, Black Tolex	$350	$450

Bassman Blackface Cab

1964-early-1967. Blackface, 2x12" small horizontal cab, replaced in 1967 with larger vertical cab.

1964-1967		$300	$400

Bassman '59 Reissue Amp

1990-present. Tube, 45 watts, 4x10", Tweed covering.

1990		$600	$750

Bassman 10 Amp

1972-1982. 4x10" combo, silver face and 50 watts for '72-'80, black face and 70 watts after.

1972-1980	50 watts	$400	$600
1981-1982	70 watts	$400	$600

Bassman 20 Amp

1982-1985. Tubes, 20 watts, 1x15".

1982-1985		$300	$350

Bassman 50 Amp

1972-1976. Fifty watts, 2x12".

1972-1976		$400	$600

Bassman 70 Amp

1977-1979. 70 watts, 2x15".

1977-1979		$400	$600

Bassman 100 Amp

1972-1979. Tube, 100 watts, 4x12".

1972-1979		$400	$600

Bassman 135 Amp

1979-1983. Tube, 135 watts, 4x10".

1980		$400	$600

Bassman 400 Combo Amp

2000-present. Solidstate, 350 watts with 2x10" plus horn, combo, black cover, black metal grille.

2002		$600	$700

Blues De Ville Amp

1993-1997. All tube Tweed Series, 60 watts, 4x10" (optional 2x12" in 1995), reverb, high-gain channel, Tweed covered (Blond Tolex optional 1995 only).

1990s	Blond Tolex, 4x10"	$500	$550
1990s	Tweed, 2x12"	$450	$525
1990s	Tweed, 4x10"	$450	$525

Blues Deluxe Amp

1993-1998. All tube Tweed Series, 40 watts, two 5881 output tubes, normal footswitchable channel, reverb, 1x12", Tweed covering (Blond Tolex optional 1995 only).

1990s	Blond	$400	$450
1990s	Tweed	$350	$400

Blues Junior Amp

1995-present. All tube Tweed Series, 15 watts, 1x10", spring reverb, Tweed cover in 1995, Black Tolex with Silver grille 1996 on.

1990s		$250	$325

Bronco Amp

1968-1974, 1993-2001. One 8" speaker, all tube, 5 watts until '72, 6 watts for '72-'74. '90s issue is 15 watts, solidstate, tweed covering (Blond Tolex was optional for '95 only).

1968-1974		$275	$375

Bullet Amp

1994-present. Solid state, 15 watts, 1x8", with or without reverb.

1990s	With reverb	$100	$125
1990s	Without reverb	$75	$100

Capricorn Amp

1970-1972. Solidstate, 105 watts, 3x12".

1970-1972		$200	$300

Champ Amp

1953-1982. Renamed from the Champion 600. Tweed until 1964, Black tolex after, three watts in 1953, four watts 1954-1964, five watts 1965-1971, six watts 1972-1982, 1x6" until 1957, 1x8" after.

1953-1954	Wide panel, 1x6"	$500	$750
1955-1956	Narrow panel, Tweed, 1x6"	$500	$750
1956-1964	Narrow panel, Tweed, 1x8"	$800	$1,000
1964	Old cab, Black, 1x8"	$700	$900
1964-1967	New cab, Black Tolex, 1x8"	$350	$450
1968-1972	Silverface, 1x8"	$250	$350
1973-1982	Silverface, 1x8"	$200	$325

Champ II Amp

1982-1985. Eighteen watts, 1x10".

1982-1985		$300	$400

Champ 12 Amp

1986-1992. Tube, 12 watts, overdrive, reverb, 1x12".

1986-1992	Black	$225	$325
1986-1992	Red, White, Gray or Snakeskin	$300	$350

Champion 600 Amp

1949-1953. Replaces the Champion 800 in 1948. Three watts, 1x6", two-tone Tolex, TV front. Replaced by the Champ in 1953.

1949-1953		$500	$750

Concert Amp

1960-1965, 1992-1995. Introduced with 40 watts and 4x10", Brown Tolex until 1963, Blackface 1963-1965. In 1962 White Tolex was ordered by Webbs Music (CA) instead of the standard Brown Tolex. A wide range is noted for this "rare" White Tolex model, and each amp should be valued on a case-by-case basis. In 1960, the very first Brown Tolex had a Pink tint but the Brown-Pink was only on the first year amps. Reissued in 1992 with 60 watts and a 1x12".

1960	Brown (Pink) Tolex	$1,400	$1,800
1961-1963	Brown Tolex	$1,400	$1,700

MODEL YEAR	FEATURES	EXC. COND. LOW	HIGH
1962	White Tolex (Webb Music)	$1,800	$3,800
1963-1965	Blackface	$1,100	$1,500

Concert 112 Amp

1982-1985. Tube, 60 watts, 1x12".

1982-1985		$600	$675

Concert 210 Amp

1982-1985. Tube, 60 watts, 2x10".

1982-1985		$625	$700

Concert 410 Amp

1982-1985. Tube, 60 watts, 4x10".

1982-1985		$675	$750

Cyber Twin Combo Amp

2000-present.

2000-2003		$750	$850

Deluxe Amp

1948-1981. Name changed from Model 26 (1946-1948). Ten watts (15 watts by 1954 and 20 watts by 1963), 1x12", TV front with Tweed 1948-1953, wide-panel 1953-1955, narrow-panel 1955-1960, Brown Tolex with Brownface 1961-1963, Black Tolex with Blackface 1963-1966.

1948-1952	Tweed, TV front	$1,300	$1,800
1953-1954	Wide panel	$1,300	$1,800
1955-1956	Narrow panel, smaller cab	$1,500	$2,000
1956-1960	Narrow panel, slightly larger cab	$1,500	$2,200
1961-1963	Brown Tolex	$1,300	$1,500
1964-1966	Black Tolex	$800	$1,000

Deluxe 85 Amp

1988-1993. Solidstate, 65 watts, 1x12", Black Tolex with Silver grille, Red Knob Series.

1988-1993		$225	$325

Deluxe 112 Amp

1992-1995. Solidstate, 65 watts, 1x12", Black Tolex with Silver grille.

1992-1995		$225	$325

Deluxe 112 Plus Amp

1995-2000. Ninety watts, 1x12", channel switching.

1995-2000		$250	$350

Deluxe Reverb Amp

1963-1981. Blackface 1963-1967, Silverface 1968-1980. Mid-1980 the Blackface with Silver grille option was introduced and lasted through 1982. Deluxe Reverb discontinued in 1981 in favor of Deluxe Reverb II. Blackface reissued in 1993 as Deluxe Reverb '65 Reissue.

1963-1967	Blackface	$1,500	$2,000
1968-1972	Silverface	$900	$1,000
1973-1980	Silverface	$700	$900
1980-1981	Blackface	$700	$900

Deluxe Reverb '65 Reissue Amp

1993-present. Blackface reissue of Deluxe Reverb, 22 watts, 1x12".

1993-1999	Black Tolex	$550	$700
1993-1999	Blond (limited production)	$600	$750

Deluxe Reverb II Amp

1982-1986. Updated Deluxe Reverb with 2x6V6 power tubes, all tube preamp section, black Tolex, Blackface, 20 watts, 1x12".

1982-1983		$600	$675

Dual Professional Amp

1994-2002. Custom Shop amp, all tube, point-to-point wiring, 100 watts, 2x12" Celestion Vintage 30s, fat switch, reverb, tremolo, white Tolex, Oxblood grille.

1994-2002		$1,400	$1,600

Dual Showman Amp

1962-1969. Called the Double Showman for the first year. White Tolex (Black available from 1964), 2x15", 85 watts. Reintroduced 1987-1994 as solidstate, 100 watts, optional speaker cabs.

1962	Rough Blond and Oxblood	$1,900	$2,500
1963	Smooth Blond and Wheat	$1,600	$2,300
1964-1967	Black Tolex, horizontal cab	$1,500	$1,900
1968	Blackface, large vertical cab	$1,000	$1,400
1968-1969	Silverface	$750	$900

Dual Showman Head Amp

1962-1969. Dual Showman head with output transformer for 2x15" (versus single Showman's 1x15" output ohms), Blackface '62-'67, the late-'67 model logo stipulated "Dual Showman" while the '62-early-'67 head merely stated Showman (could be a single Showman or Dual Showman), '68-'69 Silverface.

1962-1963	Blond	$1,100	$1,400
1964-1968	"Dual Showman" Blackface	$1,000	$1,200
1968-1969	Silverface	$550	$650

Dual Showman Reverb Amp

1968-1981. Black Tolex with Silver grille, Silverface, 100 watts, 2x15".

1968-1972		$1,100	$1,400
1973-1981		$900	$1,200

Dual Showman Reverb Head Amp

1968-1981. Amp only.

1969-1972	Includes TFL 5000 series	$750	$850
1973-1981		$650	$750

Frontman 15B Amp

2000-present. 15 watts, 1x8" combo bass amp.

1990s		$50	$65

H.O.T. Amp

1990-1996. Solidstate, 25 watts, 1x10", Gray carpet cover (Black by 1992), Black grille.

1990-1996		$75	$95

Harvard Amp (tube)

1956-1961. Tweed, 10 watts, 1x10", two knobs volume and roll-off tone, some were issued with 1x8". Reintroduced as a solidstate model in 1980.

1956-1961		$1,000	$1,300

Fender Concert II 112

1955 Fender Deluxe

AMPS

'70s Fender Musicmaster Bass

1957 Fender Princeton Amp

MODEL YEAR	FEATURES	EXC. COND. LOW	HIGH

Harvard Amp (solidstate)

1980-1983. Reintroduced from tube model. Black Tolex with Blackface, 20 watts, 1x10".

1980-1983		$100	$150

Harvard Reverb Amp

1981-1982. Solidstate, 20 watts, 1x10", reverb, replaced by Harvard Reverb II in 1983.

1981-1982		$175	$225

Harvard Reverb II Amp

1983-1985. Solidstate, Black Tolex with Blackface, 20 watts, 1x10", reverb.

1983-1985		$175	$225

Hot Rod De Ville 212 Amp

1997-present. Updated Blues De Ville. Tube, 60 watts, black Tolex, 2x12".

1997-2000		$500	$550

Hot Rod De Ville 410 Amp

1997-present. Updated Blues De Ville. Tube, 60 watts, black Tolex, 4x10".

1997-2000		$500	$550

Hot Rod Deluxe Amp

1996-present. Updated Blues Deluxe. Tube, 40 watts, Black Tolex (Tweed optional by 1998), 1x12".

1996-2000		$400	$500

J.A.M. Amp

1990-1996. Solidstate, 25 watts, 1x12", four preprogrammed sounds, Gray carpet cover (Black by 1992).

1990-1996		$75	$115

Libra Amp

1970-1972. Solidstate, 105 watts, 4x12" JBL speakers, Black Tolex.

1970-1972		$300	$400

London 185 Amp

1988-1992. Solidstate, 160 watts, black Tolex.

1988-1992	Head only	$200	$250

London Reverb 112 Amp

1983-1986. Solidstate, 100 watts, black Tolex, 1x12".

1983-1986		$250	$350

London Reverb 210 Amp

1983-1986. Solidstate, 100 watts, black Tolex, 2x10".

1983-1986		$275	$375

M-80 Amp

1989-1994. Solidstate, 90 watts, 1x12".

1989-1994		$200	$300

M-80 Bass Amp

1991-1994. Solidstate, bass and keyboard amp, 160 watts, 1x15".

1991-1994		$200	$275

M-80 Chorus Amp

1990-1994. Solidstate, stereo chorus, two 65-watt channels, 2x12".

1990-1994		$200	$275

Model 26 Amp

1946-1947. Tube, 10 watts, 1x10", hardwood cabinet. Sometimes called Deluxe Model 26, renamed Deluxe in 1948.

1946-1947		$2,000	$3,000

Montreux Amp

1983-1985. Solidstate, 100 watts, 1x12", Black Tolex with Silver grille.

1983-1985		$250	$350

Musicmaster Bass Amp

1970-1983. Tube, 12 watts, 1x12", Black Tolex.

1970-1972	Silverface	$250	$350
1973-1980	Silverface	$250	$300
1981-1983	Blackface	$250	$300

PA-100 Amp

One hundred watts.

1970		$300	$500

Performer 650 Amp

1993-1995. Solidstate hybrid amp with single tube, 70 watts, 1x12".

1993-1995		$225	$325

Performer 1000 Amp

1993-1995. Solidstate hybrid amp with a single tube, 100 watts, 1x12".

1993-1995		$250	$325

Princeton Amp

1948-1979. Tube, 4.5 watts (12 watts by 1961), 1x8" (1x10" by 1961), Tweed 1948-1961, Brown 1961-1963, Black with Blackface 1963-1969, Silverface 1969-1979.

1948-1953	Tweed, TV front	$800	$1,100
1953-1954	Tweed, wide panel	$800	$1,100
1955-1961	Tweed, narrow panel	$900	$1,200
1961-1963	Brown Tolex	$575	$775
1963-1967	Blackface	$550	$750
1968-1972	Silverface	$375	$475
1973-1979	Silverface	$350	$450

Princeton Chorus Amp

1988-1996. Solidstate, 2x10", two channels at 25 watts each, Black Tolex. Replaced by Princeton Stereo Chorus in 1996..

1988-1996		$275	$325

Princeton Reverb Amp

1964-1981. Tube, black Tolex, Blackface until 1967, Silverface after.

1964-1967	Blackface	$900	$1,200
1968-1972	Silverface	$700	$800
1973-1979	Silverface	$600	$700
1980-1981	Blackface	$600	$700

Princeton Reverb II Amp

1982-1985. Tube amp, 20 watts, 1x12", black Tolex, silver grille, distortion feature.

1982-1985		$500	$575

Princeton 112 Amp

1993-1995. Solidstate, 40 watts, 1x12", Black Tolex.

1993-1995		$150	$200

Pro Amp

1947-1965. Called Professional 1946-1948. Fifteen watts (26 watts by 1954 and 25 watts by 1960), 1x15", Tweed TV front 1948-1953, wide-panel 1953-1954, narrow-panel 1955-1960, Brown Tolex and Brownface 1960-1963, Black and Blackface 1963-1965.

1947-1953	Tweed, TV front	$2,000	$3,000
1953-1954	Wide panel	$2,000	$3,000

MODEL YEAR	FEATURES	EXC. COND. LOW	HIGH
1955	Narrow panel (old chasis)	$2,000	$3,000
1955-1959	Narrow panel (new chasis intro'd.)	$2,500	$3,500
1960-1962	Brown Tolex	$1,700	$2,000
1963-1965	Black Tolex	$1,500	$1,600

Pro 185 Amp
1989-1991. Solidstate, 160 watts, 2x12", Black Tolex.

1989-1991		$200	$325

Pro Junior Amp
1994-present. All tube Tweed Series, two EL84 tubes, 15 watts, 1x10" Alnico Blue speaker, Tweed until 1995, Black Tolex 1996 on..

1994-1999		$275	$300

Pro Reverb Amp
1965-1982. Tube, Black Tolex, 40 watts (45 watts by 1972, 70 watts by 1981), 2x12", Blackface 1965-1969 and 1981-1983, Silverface 1969-1981.

1965-1967	Blackface	$1,500	$2,000
1968-1972	Silverface	$900	$1,000
1973-1980	Silverface	$650	$900
1981-1982	Blackface	$650	$900

Pro Reverb Amp (reissue Pro Series)
Early-2000s. Fifty watts, 1x12", two modern designed channels - clean and high gain.

2002		$750	$850

Pro Reverb Amp (solidstate)
1967-1969. Fender's first attempt at solidstate design, the attempt was unsuccessful and many of these models will overheat and are known to be unreliable. Fifty watts, 2x12", upright vertical comb cabinet.

1967-1969		$300	$350

Prosonic Amp
1996-2001. Custom Shop combo, 60 watts, two channels, three-way rectifier switch, 2x10" Celestion or separate cab with 4x12", tube reverb, black, red or green.

1996-1999		$700	$800

Prosonic Head Amp
1996-2001. Amp head only version.

1996-1999		$500	$650

Quad Reverb Amp
1971-1978. Black Tolex, Silverface, 4x12", tube, 100 watts.

1971-1978		$500	$675

R.A.D. Amp
1990-1996. Solidstate, 20 watts, 1x8", Gray carpet cover until 1992, Black after.

1990-1996		$50	$65

R.A.D. Bass Amp
1992-1994. Twenty-five watts, 1x10", renamed BXR 25 in 1994.

1992-1994		$50	$65

Satellite SFX Amp
Introduced in late-1990s. SFX extension cab adding a variety of digital effects, 1x12", Black Tolex, Light Silver grille.

2000		$225	$250

Scorpio Amp
1970-1972. Solidstate, 56 watts, 2x12", Black Tolex.

1970-1972		$250	$300

Showman 12 Amp
1960-1966. Piggyback cabinet with 1x12", 85 watts, Blond Tolex (changed to Black in 1964), Maroon grille 1961-1963 (Gold grille 1963-1964, Silver grille 1964-1967).

1960-1962	Rough Blond and Oxblood	$1,900	$2,500
1963-1964	Smooth Blond and Gold	$1,600	$2,300
1964-1966	Black	$1,400	$1,800

Showman 15 Amp
1960-1968. Piggyback cabinet with 1x15", 85 watts, Blond Tolex (changed to Black in 1964), Maroon grille 1961-1963 (Gold grille 1963-1964, Silver grille 1964-1967).

1960-1962	Rough Blond and Oxblood	$1,900	$2,500
1963-1964	Smooth Blond and Gold	$1,600	$2,300
1964-1967	Blackface	$1,400	$1,800
1967-1968	Silverface	$750	$900

Showman 112 Amp
1983-1987. Solidstate, two channels, 200 watts, reverb, four button footswitch, five-band EQ, effects loop, 1x12".

1983-1987		$275	$425

Showman 115 Amp
1983-1987. Solidstate, 1x15", two channels, reverb, EQ, effects loop, 200 watts, Black Tolex.

1983-1987		$300	$450

Showman 210 Amp
1983-1987. Solidstate, two channels, reverb, EQ, effects loop, 2x10", 200 watts, Black Tolex.

1983-1987		$300	$450

Showman 212 Amp
1983-1987. Solidstate, two channels, reverb, EQ, effects loop, 2x12", 200 watts, Black Tolex.

1983-1987		$325	$475

Sidekick 10 Amp
1983-1985. Small solidstate Japanese or Mexican import, 10 watts, 1x8".

1983-1985		$40	$70

Sidekick Reverb 20 Amp
1983-1985. Small solidstate Japanese or Mexican import, 20 watts, reverb, 1x10".

1983-1985		$60	$90

Sidekick Reverb 30 Amp
1983-1985. Small solidstate Japanese or Mexican import, 30 watts, 1x12", reverb.

1983-1985		$90	$120

Sidekick Reverb 65 Amp
1986-1988. Small solidstate Japanese or Mexican import, 65 watts, 1x12".

1986-1988		$100	$140

Fender Pro Junior

1980s Fender Showman Amp

AMPS

1959 Fender Super Amp

1969 Fender Super Reverb

MODEL YEAR	FEATURES	EXC. COND. LOW	HIGH

Squire SKX 15 Amp

1990-1992. Solidstate, 15 watts, 1x8".

1990-1992		$35	$65

Squire SKX 15R Amp

1990-1992. Solidstate, 15 watts, 1x8", reverb.

1990-1992		$70	$90

Stage Lead/Stage Lead II Amp

1983-1985. Solidstate, 100 watts, 1x12", reverb, channel switching, Black Tolex. Stage Lead II has 2x12".

1983-1985	1x12"	$225	$300
1983-1985	2x12"	$250	$325

Studio Lead Amp

1983-1986. Solidstate, 50 watts, 1x12", Black Tolex.

1983-1986		$225	$300

Super Amp

1947-1963, 1992-1997. Introduced as Dual Professional in 1946, renamed Super '47. Two 10" speakers, 20 watts (30 watts by '60 with 45 watts in '62), Tweed TV front '47-'53, wide-panel '53-'54, narrow-panel '55-'60, brown Tolex '60-'64. Reintroduced '92-'97 with 4x10", 60 watts, black

1947-1952	Tweed, V front	$3,000	$3,500
1953-1954	Tweed, wide panel	$2,200	$3,200
1955	Tweed, narrow panel, 6L6 tubes	$2,500	$3,500
1956-1957	Tweed, narrow panel, 5E4.6V6 tubes	$2,400	$3,200
1957-1960	Tweed, narrow panel, 6L6 tubes	$2,600	$3,600
1960	Pink/Brown metal knobs	$1,900	$2,100
1960	Pink/Brown reverse knobs	$2,400	$3,400
1961-1962	Brown, Oxblood then Tan, 6G4 tubes	$1,700	$2,400

Super (4x10") Amp

1992-1997. 60 watts, 4x10", black Tolex, silver grille, blackface control panel.

1992-1997		$550	$600

Super 60 Amp

1989-1993. Red knob series, 1x12", 60 watts, earlier versions with Red knobs, later models with Black knobs.

1989-1993		$250	$400

Super 112 Amp

1990-1993. Red knob series, 1x12", 60 watts, earlier versions with Red Knobs, later models with Black knobs, originally designed to replace the Super60 but the Super 60 remained until 1993.

1990-1993		$250	$400

Super 210 Amp

1990-1993. Red knob series, 2x10", 60 watts, earlier versions with Red knobs, later models with Black knobs.

1990-1993		$300	$450

MODEL YEAR	FEATURES	EXC. COND. LOW	HIGH

Super Champ Amp

1982-1985. Black Tolex, 18 watts, Blackface, 1x10".

1982-1985		$500	$600

Super Reverb Amp

1963-1982. 4x10" speakers, Blackface until '67 and '80-'82, Silverface '68-'80.

1963-1967	Blackface	$1,800	$2,000
1967-1972	Silverface	$1,000	$1,200
1973-1980	Silverface, no MV	$650	$900
1981-1982	Blackface	$650	$900

Super Reverb '65 Reissue Amp

2000s. Forty watts, all tube, 4x10", Vintage Reissue Series, Blackface cosmetics.

2000s		$800	$900

Super Six Reverb Amp

1970-1979. Large combo amp based on the Twin Reverb chassis, 100 watts, 6x10", Black Tolex.

1970-1979		$700	$800

Super Twin (non-reverb) Amp

1975-1976. One hundred eighty watts (using 6x6L6 power tubes), 2x12", distinctive dark grille.

1975-1976		$450	$550

Super Twin Reverb Amp

1976-1980. One hundred eighty watts (using 6x6L6 power tubes, 2x12", distinctive dark grille.

1976-1980		$550	$650

Taurus Amp

1970-1972. Solidstate, 42 watts, 2x10" JBL, Black Tolex, Silver grille, JBL badge.

1970-1972		$250	$300

Tonemaster Head Amp

1993-2002. Custom Shop, hand-wired high-gain head, 100 watts, two channels, effects loop.

1993-1999		$700	$800

Tonemaster 212 Cabinet

1993-2002. Custom Shop extension cabinet for Tonemaster head, blond Tolex, Oxblood grille, 2x12" Celestion Vintage 30.

1993-1999		$300	$400

Tonemaster 412 Cabinet

1993-2002. Custom Shop extension cabinet for Tonemaster head, blond Tolex, 4x12" Celestion Vintage 30.

1993-1999		$500	$550

Tonemaster Set Amp

1993-2002. Custom Shop, hand-wired head with Tonemaster 2x12" or 4x12" cabinet.

1993-1999	Blond and Oxblood	$1,300	$1,400
1993-1999	Custom color Red	$1,400	$1,500

Tremolux Amp

1955-1966. Tube, Tweed, 1x12" 1955-1960, White Tolex with piggyback 1x10" cabinet 1961-1962, 2x10" 1962-1964, Black Tolex 1964-1966.

1955-1960	Tweed, 1x12", narrow panel	$1,200	$2,000
1961	Rough White and Oxblood, 1x10"	$1,400	$2,000
1961-1962	Rough White and Oxblood, 2x10"	$1,400	$1,600

MODEL YEAR	FEATURES	EXC. COND. LOW	HIGH
1963-1964	Smooth White and Gold, 2x10"	$1,300	$1,600
1964-1966	Black Tolex, 2x10"	$1,000	$1,200

Twin Amp

1952-1963, 1996-present. Tube, 2x12"; 15 watts, tweed wide-panel '52-'55; narrow-panel '55-'60; 50 watts '55-'57; 80 watts '58; brown Tolex '60; white Tolex '61-'63. Reintroduced in '96 with black Tolex, spring reverb and output control for 100 watts or 25 watts.

1953-1954	Tweed, wide-panel	$3,600	$4,600
1955-1957	Tweed, 50 watts	$4,000	$5,000
1958-1959	Tweed, 80 watts	$5,500	$6,500
1960	Brown Tolex, 80 watts	$5,250	$6,250
1960-1962	Rough White and Oxblood	$4,800	$6,000
1963	Smooth White and Gold	$4,300	$5,500

Twin "The Twin"/"Evil Twin" Amp

1987-1992. One hundred watts, 2x12", Red knobs, most Black Tolex, but White, Red and Snakeskin covers offered.

1987-1992		$550	$650

Twin '65 Reissue Amp

Introduced 1991/1992. Reissue of 1965 Twin Reverb, high or low output, 2x12".

1992-2002		$800	$900
1994		$800	$800
1995		$765	$765

Twin Reverb Amp

1963-1982. Black Tolex, 85 watts (changed to 135 watts in '81), 2x12", Blackface '63-'67 and '81-'82, Silverface '68-'80. Reverb reintroduced as Twin in '96.

1963-1967	Blackface	$1,800	$2,200
1968-1972	Silverface, no master vol.	$1,000	$1,200
1973-1975	Silverface, master volume	$800	$1,000
1976-1980	Silverface, push/pull	$700	$900
1981-1982	Blackface	$700	$900

Twin Reverb '65 Reissue Amp

1992-present. Reissue of 1965 Twin Reverb, Black Tolex, 2x12", 85 watts.

1990s	High or low output	$800	$900

Twin Reverb Amp (solidstate)

1966-1969. One hundred watts, 2x12", Black Tolex. Early Fender solidstate amps are generally considered unreliable.

1966-1969		$350	$500

Twin Reverb II Amp

1983-1985. Black Tolex, 2x12", 105 watts, channel switching, effects loop, Blackface panel, Silver grille.

1983-1985		$650	$950

Ultimate Stereo Chorus DSP Amp

Solidstate, 2x65 watts, 2x12", 32 built-in effect variations, Blackface cosmetics.

1999		$350	$400

MODEL YEAR	FEATURES	EXC. COND. LOW	HIGH

Ultra Chorus Amp

Introduced in 1993. Solidstate, 2x65 watts, 2x12", standard control panel with chorus.

1990s		$300	$350

Vibrasonic Amp

1959-1963. First amp to receive the new Brown Tolex and JBL, 1x15", 25 watts.

1959-1963		$1,800	$2,200
1961	Brown Tolex	$1,400	$1,800
1962	Brown Tolex	$1,400	$1,800

Vibrasonic Custom Amp

1995-1997. Custom Shop designed for steel guitar and guitar, Blackface, 1x15", 100 watts.

1995-1997	Blackface	$750	$850

Vibro-Champ Amp

1964-1982. Black Tolex, four watts, (five watts 1969-1971, six watts 1972-1980), 1x8", Blackface 1964-1968, Silverface 1969-1980.

1964-1967	Blackface	$500	$600
1968-1972	Silverface	$300	$400
1973-1981	Silverface	$275	$375
1982	Blackface	$275	$375

Vibro-King 212 Cabinet

1993-present. Custom Shop extension cabinet, blond Tolex, 2x12" Celestion GK80.

1993-1999		$400	$500

Vibro-King Amp

1993-present. Custom Shop combo, Blond Tolex, 60 watts, 3x10", vintage reverb, tremolo, single channel, all tube.

1993-1999		$1,200	$1,500

Vibrolux Amp

1956-1965. Narrow-panel, 10 watts, Tweed with 1x10" 1956-1961, Brown Tolex and Brownface with 1x12" and 30 watts 1961-1963, Black Tolex and Blackface 1964-1965.

1956-1961	Tweed, 1x10"	$1,200	$1,500
1961-1962	Brown Tolex, 1x12", 2x6L6	$1,500	$1,700
1963-1965	Black Tolex, 1x12"	$1,600	$1,800

Vibrolux Reverb Amp

1964-1982. Black Tolex, 2x10", Blackface and 35 watts 1964-1969, Silverface and 40 watts 1970-1979. Reissued in 1996 with Blackface and 40 watts.

1964-1967	Blackface	$1,900	$2,300
1968-1972	Silverface	$1,100	$1,350
1973-1980	Silverface	$900	$1,100
1981-1982	Blackface	$900	$1,100

Vibrolux Reverb (reissue) Amp

1996-present. Forty watts, 2x10", all tube, Black or Blond Tolex.

1996-1999	Blond and Tan	$750	$900
1996-2003	Black and Silver	$700	$850

Vibrolux Reverb Amp (solidstate)

1967-1970. Fender-CBS solidstate, Black Tolex, 35 watts, 2x10".

1960s		$300	$350

1964 Fender Twin Reverb Amp

Fender '65 Twin Reverb reissue

1963 Fender Vibroverb Amp

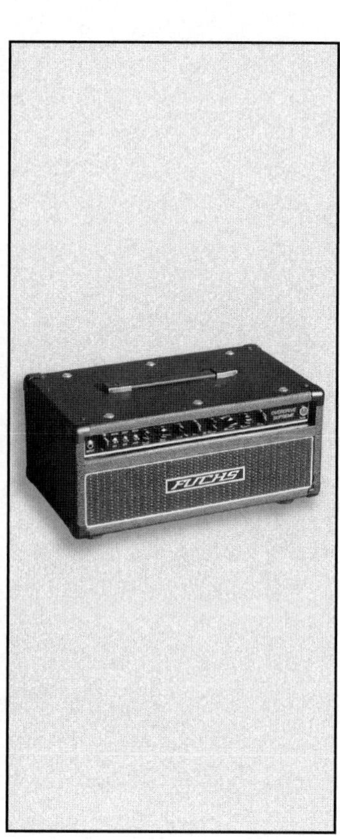

Fuchs OD Supreme

MODEL YEAR	FEATURES	EXC. COND. LOW	HIGH

Vibrosonic Reverb Amp

1972-1981. Black Tolex, 100 watts, 1x15", Silverface.

1972-1981		$700	$800
1973	Silverface	$700	$800
1978	Silverface	$600	$700

Vibroverb Amp

1963-1965. Brown Tolex with 35 watts, 2x10" and Brownface 1963, Black Tolex with 1x15" and Blackface 1964-1965.

1963	Brown Tolex, 2x10"	$4,000	$5,000
1964-1965	Black Tolex, 1x15"	$2,200	$3,000

Vibroverb '63 Reissue Amp

1990-1995. Reissue of 1963 Vibroverb, 40 watts, 2x10", reverb, vibrato, Brown Tolex.

1990s		$700	$750

Yale Reverb Amp

1982-1985. Solidstate, Black Tolex, 50 watts, 1x12", Silverface.

1982-1985		$225	$275

Flot-A-Tone

Ca. 1946-early 1960s. Flot-A-Tone was located in Milwaukee, Wisconsin, and made a variety of tube guitar and acordion amps.

Large Amp

Four speakers.

1960s		$500	$800

Small Amp

One eight inch speaker.

1962		$300	$400

Fuchs Audio Technology

2000-present. Andy Fuchs started the company, located in Bloomfield, New Jersey, in '99 to rebuild and modify tube amps. In 2000 he started production of his own brand of amps, offering combos and heads from 10 to 150 watts. They also custom build audiophile and studio tube electronics.

Gallien Krueger

1969-present. Gallien-Krueger has offered a variety of bass and guitar amps, combos and cabinets and is located in San Jose, California.

212GS Amp

1986-ca.1989. One hundred forty-watt mono or 70-watt stereo, 2x12", Black carpet.

1986-1989		$200	$300

250ML Amp

Small practice amp, 2x4-1/2", chorus and echo.

1986-1989		$175	$300

2100CEL Digital Stereo Guitar Combo Amp

1989-1991. Two hundred watts (100 per channel), 2x8", EQ, compression, chorus and reverb.

1989-1991		$300	$400

MODEL YEAR	FEATURES	EXC. COND. LOW	HIGH

Garnet

Mid 1960s-1989. In the mid '60's, "Gar" Gillies started the Garnet Amplifier Company with his two sons, Russell and Garnet, after he started making PA systems in his Canadian radio and TV repair shop. The first PA from the new company was for Chad Allen & the Expressions (later known as The Guess Who). A wide variety of tube amps were offered and all were designed by Gar, Sr. The company also produced the all-tube effects The Herzog, H-zog, and two stand alone reverb units designed by Gar in the late '60s and early '70s. The company closed in '89, due to financial reasons caused largely by a too rapid expansion. Gar still repairs and designs custom amps.

Genesis

Genesis was a 1980s line of student amps from Gibson.

B40 Amp

1984-late-1980s. Bass combo with 40 watts.

1984-1989		$125	$175

G10 Amp

1984-late-1980s. Combo amp with 10 watts.

1984-1989		$75	$125

G25 Amp

1984-late-1980s. Combo amp with 25 watts.

1984-1989		$100	$150

G40R Amp

1984-late-1980s. Combo amp with 40 watts, reverb.

1984-1989		$150	$200

George Dennis

1991-present. Founded by George Burgerstein, original products were a line of effects pedals. In '96 they added a line of tube amps. The company is located in Prague, Czech Republic, and the products are distributed in the U.S. by Midco International.

Gerhart

2000-present. Production/custom, amps and cabinets from builder Gary Gerhart of West Hills, California. He also offers an amp in kit form.

Germino

2002-present. Tube amps, combos and cabinets built by Greg Germino in Graham, North Carolina.

Gibson

1880s (1902)-present. Gibson has offered a variety of amps since the mid-'30s to the present under the Gibson brandname and others. See the Guitar section for more company info.

The price ranges listed are for excellent condition, all original amps though tubes may be replaced with affecting value. Many Gibson amps

MODEL YEAR	FEATURES	EXC. COND. LOW	HIGH

have missing or broken logos. The prices listed are for amps with fully intact logos. A broken or missing logo changes the amp's status from excellent collector-quality to player quality and can diminish the value of the amp. Amps with a changed handle, power cord, and especially a broken logo should be taken on a case-by-case basis.

Atlas IV Amp

1963-1967. Piggyback head and cab, introduced with trapezoid shape, changed to rectangular cabs in 1965-1966 with Black cover, simple circuit with four knobs, no reverb or tremolo, mid-power with 2x6L6, 1x15".

1963-1965	Brown	$300	$600
1966-1967	Black	$300	$600

Atlas IV L Amp

1967. Atlas with Lansing speakers, offered only in 1967, Black cover.

1967		$300	$600

Atlas Medalist Amp

1964-1967. Combo version with 1x15".

1964-1967		$300	$600

BR-1 Amp

1945-1949. Fifteen watts, 1x12" field-coil speaker, Brown leatherette cover, rectangular metal grille with large G.

1945-1949		$350	$450

BR-3 Amp

1946-1947. Twelve watts, 1x12" Utah field-coil speaker (most BR models used Jensen speakers).

1946-1947		$300	$400

BR-4 Amp

1946-1947. Fourteen watts, 1x12" Utah field-coil speaker (most BR models used Jensen speakers).

1946-1947		$350	$450

BR-6 Amp

1946-1956. Ten to twelve watts, 1x10", Brown leatherette, speaker opening split by cross panel with G logo, bottom mounted chassis with single on-off volume pointer knob.

1946-1947	Verticle cab	$300	$400
1948-1956	Horizontal cab	$200	$300

BR-9 Amp

1948-1953. Cream leatherette, 10 watts, 1x8". Originally sold with the BR-9 lap steel. Renamed GA-9 in 1954.

1948-1953		$200	$300

EH-100 Amp

1936-1941. Electric-Hawaiian companion amp, 1x10"

1936-1941		$400	$500

EH-125 Amp

1941-1942. One 12" speaker, rounded shoulder cab, Brown cover in 1941 and Dark Green in 1942, leather handle.

1941	Brown	$425	$525
1942	Dark Green	$425	$525

MODEL YEAR	FEATURES	EXC. COND. LOW	HIGH

EH-150 Amp

1935-1941. Electric-Hawaiian companion amp, 1x12".

1935	13 3/4" sq. cab	$500	$600
1936-1937	14 3/4" sq. cab	$500	$600
1937-1942	15 3/8" round cab	$500	$600

EH-185 Amp

1939-1942. One 12" speaker, Tweed cover with Black and Orange vertical stripes, round speaker opening with higher oblong opening, marketed as companion amp to the EH-185 Lap Steel.

1939-1942		$550	$650

G-10 Amp

1972-1975. Solidstate, 10 watts, 1x10", no trem or reverb.

1972		$75	$125

G-20 Amp

1972-1975. Solidstate with trem, 1x10", 10 watts.

1972		$125	$175

G-30 Amp

1972. Solidstate without trem or reverb, 1x12", 15 watts.

1972		$150	$200

G-35 Amp

1975. Solidstate, 30 watts, 1x12".

1975		$175	$250

G-40 Amp

1972. Solidstate with trem and reverb, 1x12", 20 watts.

1972		$200	$300

G-50 Amp

1972. Solidstate with trem and reverb, 1x12", 40 watts.

1972		$225	$325

G-60 Amp

1972. Solidstate with trem and reverb, 1x15", 60 watts.

1972		$225	$325

G-70 Amp

1972. Solidstate with trem and reverb, 2x12", 60 watts.

1972		$250	$350

G-80 Amp

1972. Solidstate with trem and reverb, 4x10", 60 watts.

1972		$250	$350

GA-5 Les Paul Jr. Amp

1954-1957. Tan fabric cover (Mottled Brown by 1947), seven inch oval speaker, four watts. Renamed Skylark in 1958.

1954-1957		$200	$300

GA-5 Skylark Amp

1957-1967. Gold cover (brown by '63 and black by '66), 1x8" (1x10" from '64 on), 4.5 watts (10 watts from '64 on), tremolo. Often sold with the Skylark Lap Steel.

1957-1962	Gold, 4.5 watts, 1x8"	$200	$275
1963	Brown, 4.5 watts, 1x8"	$200	$250

1960s Gibson Atlas

'55 Gibson GA-5 Les Paul Junior

AMPS

1965 Gibson GA-19RVT Falcon

1962 Gibson GA-20T Ranger

MODEL YEAR	FEATURES	EXC. COND. LOW	HIGH
1964	Brown, 10 watts, 1x10"	$200	$250
1965-1967	Black, 10 watts, 1x10"	$200	$250

GA-5 T Skylark Amp

1960-1967. Tremolo, 4.5 watts, gold covering and 1x8" until '63, brown '63-'64, black and 1x10" after.

1961-1962	Gold, 4.5 watts, 1x8"	$250	$300
1963	Brown, 4.5 watts, 1x8"	$250	$300
1964	Brown, 10 watts, 1x10"	$250	$300
1965-1967	Black, 10 watts, 1x10"	$250	$300

GA-6 Amp

1956-1959. Replaced the BR-6, 8 to 12 watts, 1x12", 'Gibson 6' above the grill. Renamed GA-6 Lancer in '60.

1956-1959		$300	$400

GA-6 Lancer Amp

1960-1962. Renamed from GA-6, 1x12", tweed cover, three knobs.

1960-1962		$450	$550

GA-8 Discoverer Amp

1962-1964. Renamed from GA-8 Gibsonette. Gold fabric cover, 1x12", 10 watts.

1962-1964		$275	$400

GA-8T Discoverer Amp

1960-1967. Gold fabric cover, 1x10", nine watts (Tan cover, 1x12" and 15 watts by 1963), tremolo.

1960-1962	9 watts, 1x10"	$300	$450
1963-1967	15 watts, 1x12"	$300	$450

GA-8 Gibsonette Amp

1952-1962. Tan fabric cover (Gold by 1958), 1x10", eight watts (nine watts by 1958). Name changed to GA-8 Discoverer in 1962.

1952-1962		$275	$400

GA-9 Amp

1954-1961. Renamed from BR-9. Tan fabric cover, eight watts, 1x10". Often sold with the BR-9 Lap Steel.

1954-1961		$250	$350

GA-14 Titan Amp

1959-1961. About 15 watts using 2x6V6 power tubes, 1x10", Tweed cover.

1959-1961		$400	$500

GA-15 RV (Custom Shop) Amp

2002. Custom Shop built, 15 watts, 1x12", quilted maple cabinet in Natural finish, companion amp to Custom Shop L-5C or Super 400 set.

2002		$1,900	$2,100

GA-15 RV Goldtone Amp

Fifteen watts, Class A, 1x12", spring reverb.

1999-2002		$400	$500

GA-15 RVT Explorer amp

1965-1967. Tube, 1x10", tremolo, reverb, Black vinyl.

1965-1967		$300	$350

GA-17 RVT Scout Amp

1963-1965. Low power, 1x12", reverb and tremolo.

1963-1964	Brown	$300	$475
1965	Black	$275	$450

GA-18 Explorer Amp

1959. Tube, 14 watts, 1x10". Replaced in 1960 by the GA-18T Explorer.

1959		$400	$500

GA-18T Explorer Amp

1959-1964. Tweed, 14 watts, 1x10", tremolo.

1959-1962		$500	$600
1963-1964		$300	$400

GA-19 RVT Falcon Amp

1961-1966. One of Gibson's highest sales volume amplifiers. Initially Tweed covered, followed by smooth Brown, textured Brown, and Black. Each amp has a different tone. One 12" Jensen with deep-sounding reverb and tremolo.

1961-1962	Tweed	$600	$700
1963	Smooth Brown	$400	$450
1964	Textured Brown	$350	$425
1965	Black	$350	$425

GA-20 RVT Minuteman Amp

1965-1967. Black, 14 watts, 1x12", tube, reverb, tremolo.

1965-1967		$350	$500

GA-20 T Amp

1956-1962. Tube, 16 watts, tremolo, 1x12". Renamed Ranger in 1960.

1956-1958	Two-tone	$650	$750
1959-1962	Tweed	$650	$750

GA-20/GA-20 Crest Amp

1950-1962. Brown leatherette (two-tone by 1955 and Tweed by 1960), tube, 12 watts early, 14 watts later, 1x12". Renamed Crest in 1960.

1950-1954	Brown, 14 watts	$600	$700
1955-1958	Two-Tone, 14 watts	$600	$700
1959-1962	Tweed/Crest, 14 watts	$600	$700

GA-25 Amp

1947-1948. Brown, 1x12" and 1x8", 15 watts. Replaced by GA-30 in 1948.

1947-1948		$400	$500

GA-25 RVT Hawk Amp

1963-1967. Reverb, tremolo, 1x15".

1963	Smooth Brown	$400	$500
1964	Rough Brown	$300	$500
1965-1967	Black	$300	$500

GA-30 Amp

1948-1961. Brown until 1954, two-tone after, Tweed in 1960, 1x12" and 1x8", 14 watts. Renamed Invader in 1960.

1948-1954	Brown	$500	$700
1955-1958	Two-tone	$500	$700
1959	Tweed	$500	$700

GA-30 RV Invader Amp

1961-1962. Tweed, 1x12" and 1x8", 14-16 watts, reverb but no trem.

1961-1962		$700	$900

GA-30 RVT Invader Amp

1962-1964. Updated model with reverb and tremolo, dual speakers 1x12" and 1x8", first issue in Tweed.

1962	Tweed	$700	$900

MODEL YEAR	FEATURES	EXC. COND. LOW	HIGH
1963	Smooth Brown	$450	$600
1964	Rough Brown	$450	$600

GA-35 RVT Lancer Amp

1966-1967. Black, 1x12", tremolo, reverb.

1966-1967		$400	$500

GA-40 Les Paul Amp

1952-1960. Introduced in conjunction with the Les Paul Model guitar. 1x12" Jensen speaker, 14 watts on early models and 16 watts later, recessed leather handle using spring mounting (the handle is easily broken and an unsimilar replacement handle is more common than not).

Two-tone leatherette covering, '50s checkerboard grille ('52-early-'55), Les Paul script logo on front of the amp ('52-'55), plastic grille insert with 'LP' monogram, Gold Gibson logo above grille. Cosmetics changed dramatically in early/mid-'55. Renamed GA-40 T Les Paul in '60.

1952-1955	Brown two-tone, LP grille	$900	$1,200
1955-1956	Mottled Gray two-tone	$900	$1,200
1957-1959	Two-tone	$900	$1,200
1959-1960	Tweed	$800	$1,000

GA-40 T Les Paul Amp

1960-1965. Renamed from GA-40 Les Paul, 1x12", 16 watts, tremolo. Renamed Mariner in 1965-1967.

1961	Tweed	$800	$900
1962-1963	Smooth Brown	$600	$650
1964-1965	Rough Brown	$400	$500

GA-45 RVT Saturn Amp

1965-1967. Two 10" speakers, mid power, tremolo, reverb.

1965-1967		$450	$550

GA-50 T Amp

1948-1955. Brown leatherette, 25 watts, 1x12" and 1x8", tremolo.

1948-1955		$900	$1,100

GA-55 RVT Ranger Amp

1965-1967. Black cover, 4x10", tremolo, reverb.

1965-1967		$550	$650

GA-55/GA-55 V Amp

1954-1958. With or without vibrato, 2x12", 20 watts.

1954-1958	GA-55 V with vibrato	$1,500	$1,700
1954-1958	GA-55 without vibrato	$1,200	$1,500

GA-70 Country and Western Amp

1955-1958. Twenty-five watts, 1x15", two-tone, long-horn cattle western logo on front, advertised to have extra bright sound (to compete with Fender).

1955-1958		$1,100	$1,400

GA-75 Amp

1950-1955. Mottled Brown leatherette, 1x15", 25 watts.

1950-1955		$900	$1,100

GA-77 Amp

1954-1960. Brown Tolex, 1x15" JBL, 25 watts, two 6L6 power tubes, near top-of-the-line for the mid-1950s.

1954-1958	Two-tone	$1,000	$1,200
1959-1960	Tweed	$1,000	$1,200

GA-77 RET Amp

1964-1967. Two 10" speakers, reverb, echo, tremolo.

1964-1967		$500	$600

GA-79 RV Amp

1961-1962. Stereo-reverb, 2x10", 30 watts.

1961	Tweed	$1,700	$2,400
1962	Gray tolex	$1,500	$2,200

GA-79 RVT Multi-Stereo Amp

1961-1967. Introduced as GA-79 RVT, Multi-Stereo was added to name in 1961. Stereo-reverb and tremolo, 2x10", Tweed (Black and Brown also available), 30 watts.

1961-1962	Gray	$1,500	$2,200
1963-1964	Textured Brown	$1,500	$2,200
1965-1967	Black	$1,300	$1,800

GA-80 T Vari-Tone Amp

1959-1961. Twenty-five watts, 1x15", two channels, described as "6-in-1 amplifier with improved tremolo", six Vari-Tone pushbottons which give "six distinctively separate sounds", seven tubes, Tweed cover.

1959-1961		$1,000	$1,300

GA-83 S Stereo-Vibe Amp

1959-1961. Interesting stereo amp with front baffle mounted 1x12" and 4x8" side-mounted speakers (2 on each side), 35 watts, Gibson logo on upper right corner of the grille, Tweed cover, Brown grill (late '50s Fender-style), three pointer knobs and three round knobs, four inputs.

1959-1961		$1,500	$2,200

GA-85 Bass Reflex Amp

1957-1958. Removable head, 25 watts, 1x12", very limited production.

1957-1958		$600	$800

GA-90 High Fidelity Amp

1953-1960. Twenty-five watts, 6x8", two channels, advertised for guitar, bass, or accordion, or hi-fi.

1953-1960		$1,000	$1,300

GA-95 RVT Apollo Amp

1965-1967. Ninety watts, 2x12", Black vinyl, Black grille, tremolo, reverb.

1965-1967		$550	$650

GA-100 Bass Amp

1960-1963. Tweed, 35 watts, 1x12" cabinet, tripod was available for separate head.

1960-1963		$600	$700

GA-200 Rhythm King Amp

1957-1962. Introduced as GA-200, renamed Rhythm King in 1960, two-channel version of GA-400. Bass amp, 60 watts, 2x12".

1957-1959	Two-tone	$1,000	$1,400
1959-1962	Tweed	$1,000	$1,400

1959 Gibson GA-40 Les Paul Amp

1959 Gibson GA-55 RVT Ranger

Gibson Thor

1950s Gretsch Model 6169 Electromatic Twin

AMPS

MODEL YEAR	FEATURES	EXC. COND. LOW	HIGH

GA-400 Super 400 Amp

1957-1962. Sixty watts, 2x12", three channels, same size as GA-200 cab, one more tube than GA-200.

1957-1959	Two-tone	$1,100	$1,500
1959-1962	Tweed	$1,100	$1,500

GSS-50 Amp

1966-1967. Solidstate, 50 watts, 2x10" combo, reverb and tremolo, Black vinyl cover, Silver grille, no grille logo.

1966-1967		$400	$450

GSS-100 Amp

1966-1967. Solidstate, 100 watts, two 24"x12" 2x10" sealed cabs, Black vinyl cover, Silver grille, eight Black knobs and three Red knobs, slanted raised Gibson logo. Speakers prone to distortion.

1966-1967		$500	$550

Medalist 2/12 Amp

Late-1960s-1970. Vertical cab, 2x12", reverb and temolo.

1970		$350	$425

Medalist 4/10 Amp

Late-1960s-1970. Vertical cab, 4x10", reverb and tremolo.

1970		$350	$425

Mercury I Amp

1963-1965. Piggyback trapezoid-shaped head with 2x12" trapezoid cabinet, tremolo, Brown. There was also a Mercury II Amp from 1965-1967.

1963-1965		$300	$500

Mercury II Amp

1963-1967. Piggyback, initially trapezoid cabs then changed to rectangular with 1x15" and 1x10", tremolo.

1963-1964	Brown trapezoid cabs	$300	$500
1965-1967	Black rectangular cabs	$300	$500

Plus-50 Amp

1966-1967. Fifty watts, add-or/powered extension amplifier, usable with another master amplifier. Similar to GSS-100 cabinet of the same era, 2x10" cab, Black vinyl cover, Silver grille, slant Gibson logo.

1966		$400	$500

Super Thor Bass Amp

Early-1970s. Solidstate, part of the new G-Series (not GA-Series), 65 watts, 2x15", Black Tolex, Black grille, upright vertical cab with front control, single channel.

1971-1972		$275	$375

Thor Bass Amp

Early-1970s. Solidstate, part of the new G-Series (not GA-Series), 50 watts, 2x10", Black Tolex, Black grille, upright vertical cab with front controls, single channel.

1971-1972		$250	$300

Titan I Amp

1963-1965. Piggyback trapezoid-shaped head and 2x12" trapezoid-shaped cabinet, tremolo.

1963-1965		$250	$500

Titan III Amp

1963-1967. Piggyback trapezoid-shaped head and 1x15" + 2x10" trapezoid-shaped cabinet, tremolo.

1963-1964	Brown	$300	$600
1965-1967	Black	$300	$600

Titan V Amp

1963-1967. Piggyback trapezoid-shaped tube head and 2x15" trapezoid-shaped cabinet, tremolo.

1963-1964	Brown	$300	$600
1965-1967	Black	$300	$600

Titan Medalist Amp

1964-1967. Combo version of Titan Series with 1x15" and 1x10", tremolo only, no reverb, Black.

1964-1967		$300	$600

Ginelle

Rick Emery builds his tube combo amps in Somerdale, New Jersey.

Gorilla

1980s-present. Small solidstate entry-level amps, distributed by Pignose, Las Vegas.

Compact Practice Student Amp

1980s-present. Solidstate, 10 to 30 watts, compact design.

1980s		$35	$55
1990s		$35	$55
2000s		$40	$60

Goya

1955-1996. Goya was mainly known for acoustics, but offered a few amps in the '60s. The brand was purchased by Avnet/Guild in 1966 and by Martin in the late '70s. See Guitar section for more company info.

Amps

1960s	Various models	$150	$200

Gretsch

1883-present. Gretsch offered amps from the '50s into the '70s. Initially private branded for Gretsch by Valco (look for the Valco oval or rectangular serialized label on the back). Early-'50s amps were covered in the requisite tweed, but evolved into the Gretsch charcoal gray covering. The mid-'50s to early-'60s amps were part of the Electromatic group of amps. The mid-'50s to '62 amps often sported wrap-around and slanted grilles. In '62, the more traditional box style was introduced. In '66, the large amps went piggyback. Baldwin-Gretsch began to phase out amps effective '65, but solidstate amps continued being offered for a period of time. See Guitar section for more company info.

Model 6149 De Luxe Reverb Unit

1963-1967. Similar to Gibson's GA-1 introduced around the same time, 17 watts, 1x10".

1965		$275	$375

Model 6150 Compact Amp

Early-1950s-1960s. Early amps in Tweed, 1960s amps in Gray covering, no tremolo, single volume knob, no treble or bass knob, 1x8".

1950s	Tweed	$225	$325
1960s	Gray	$225	$325

MODEL YEAR	FEATURES	EXC. COND. LOW	HIGH

Model 6150T Compact Amp

Early-1960s-mid-1960s. Gray covering, tremolo, 1x8".

1960s	Gray	$275	$375

Model 6151 Electromatic Standard Amp

Late-1940s-late-1950s. Five or six watts, 1x10", Blue with Silver strip early-1950s, Gray fabic covering mid-1950s, wraparound grille 1955 and after.

1949	Brown leatherette	$250	$350
1959		$425	$500

Model 6152 Compact Tremolo Reverb Amp

Ca.1964-late-1960s. Five watts, 11x6" elliptical speaker.

1960s		$425	$500

Model 6154 Super-Bass Amp

Early-1960s-late-1960s. Gray covering, 2x12", 70 watts, tube.

1963	Gray	$425	$500

Model 6156 Playboy Amp

Early-1950s-1966. Tube amp, 17 watts, 1x10" until 1961 when converted to 1x12", Tweed, then Gray, then finally Black covered.

1950s	Tweed	$350	$550
1960-1962	Tweed, 1x10" or 1x12"	$325	$525
1963-1966	Black or Gray, 1x12"	$250	$350

Model 6157 Super Bass Amp (piggyback)

Mid-late-1960s. Thirty-five watts, 2x15" cabinet, single channel (competitors offered dual channel amps).

1960s		$425	$500

Model 6159 Super Bass Amp (combo)

Mid-late-1960s. Thirty-five watts, 2x12" cabinet, dual channel, Black covering.

1960s	Black	$425	$500

Model 6160 Chet Atkins Country Gentleman Amp

Early-late-1960s. Combo tube amp, 35 watts, 2x12" cabinet, two channels.

1960s		$450	$550

Model 6161 Dual Twin Amp

Ca.1962-late-1960s. Nineteen watts (later 17 watts), 2x10" with five inch tweeter, tremolo.

1960s		$450	$600

Model 6161 Electromatic Twin Amp

Ca.1953-ca.1960. Gray Silverflake covering, two 11x6" speakers, 14 watts, tremolo, wraparound grille 1955 and after.

1950s		$450	$600

Model 6162 Dual Twin with Reverb Amp

Ca.1964-late-1960s. Seventeen watts, 2x10", reverb, tremolo. Vertical combo amp style introduced in 1968.

1964-1967	Horizontal combo style	$350	$450
1968-1969	Vertical combo style	$250	$350

Model 6163 Chet Atkins Amp (piggyback)

Mid-late-1960s. Seventy watts, 2x12", Black covering.

1960s	Black	$350	$450

Model 6164 Variety Amp

Early-mid-1960s. Thirty-five watts, tube, 2x12".

1960s		$350	$450

Model 6165 Variety Plus Amp

Early-mid-1960s. Tube amp, 35 watts, 2x12", separate controls for both channels.

1960s		$400	$500

Model 6166 Fury Amp

Early-mid-1960s. Tube amp, 70 watts, 2x12", separate controls for both channels.

1960s		$400	$500

Model 6169 Electromatic Twin Western Finish Amp

Ca.1953-ca.1960. Western finish, 14 watts, two 11x6" speakers, tremolo, wraparound grill 1955 and after.

1950s	Western finish	$1,000	$1,900

Model 6170 Pro Bass Amp

1966-late-1960s. Twenty-five or 35 watts, depending on model, 1x15", vertical cabinet style (vs. box cabinet).

1966-1968		$250	$350

Model 7517 Rogue Amp

1970s. Solidstate, 40 watts, 2x12", tall vertical cabinet, front control panel.

1970s		$200	$250

1964 Gretsch 6164 Variety

Groove Tubes

1979-present. Started by Aspen Pittman in his garage in Sylmar, California, Groove Tubes is now located in San Fernando. GT manufactures and distributes a full line of tubes. In '86 they added amp production and in '91 tube microphones. Aspen is also the author of the "Tube Amp Book."

Guild

1952-present. Guild offered amps from the '60s into the '80s. See Guitar section for more company info.

Model Four Amp

Early-1980s. Six watts.

1980s		$100	$175

Model Five Amp

Early-1980s. Ten watts, 6.25" speaker.

1980s		$100	$175

Model Six Amp

Early 1980s. Same as Model Five but with reverb.

1980s		$100	$175

Model Seven Amp

Early-1980s. Small amp for guitar, bass and keyboard, 12 watts.

1980s		$100	$175

Thunderbird Amp

1960s		$300	$400

Thunderstar Bass Amp

Fifty watts, bass head or combo.

1966-1968		$450	$650

Groove Tubes Soul-O Single

AMPS

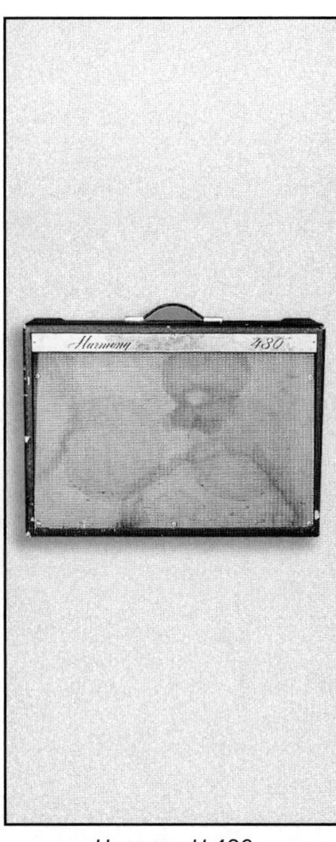

Harmony H-430

Hartke B120

MODEL YEAR	FEATURES	EXC. COND. LOW	HIGH

Harmony

1892-1974. Harmony was once one of the biggest producers of guitars, and offered amps as well. See Guitar section for more company info.

Model H-303A Amp

1960s. Valco-made, like Supro, black covering, silver grille, large Harmony logo upper left front, 1x8", blue bottom-mounted control panel with one chicken head control knob.

1960s	$225	$300

Model H-305A Amp

1960s. Valco-made, like Supro, Black covering, Harmony Silver front panel.

1960s	$250	$350

Model H-415 Amp

1960s. Valco-made, like Supro, Black covering, Harmony Silver front panel, 20 watts, 2x10".

1960s	$300	$400

Model H-420 Amp

1960s. Valco-made, like Supro Thunderbolt, Black covering, Harmony Silver front panel, 20 watts, all tube combo, 1x12".

1960s	$300	$400

Small Solidstate Amps

Dark covering, dark grille.

1970s	$75	$125

Small Tube Amps

1950s	$150	$250

Harry Joyce

1993-2000. Hand-wired British tube amps, combos, and cabinets from builder Harry Joyce. Joyce was contracted to build Hiwatt amps in England during the '60s and '70s. He passed away on January 11, 2002.

Hartke

1984-present. Made in the United States. Founded by Larry Hartke, specializing in bass amps. Since the mid-'80s, Hartke has been distributed by Samson Technologies. Hartke also offered basses in the past.

2000 Bass Head Amp

1992-present. 200 watts, tube preamp, solidstate power section, tube/solidstate switchable.

1990s	$150	$200

3500 Bass Head Amp

1992-present. Solidstate, 350 watts, 10-band graphic equalizer, rack-mount.

1990s	$225	$275
2000s	$300	$350

4.5 XL Cab

1994-present. XL Series, 4x10" and 5" driver rated at 400 watts, larger ported cab.

2000s	$400	$475

B 30 Bass Combo Amp

1999-present. Compact practice amp, 30 watts, 1x10".

1999-2000	$100	$125

HA 1415 Bass Combo Amp

1994-present. Solidstate, 140 watts, 1x15".

1990s	$200	$250

Transporter 115TP Cab

1993-present. 1x15" speaker cabinet, rated at 150 watts.

1990s	$200	$225

XL115B Cab

1994-present. XL Series, 1x15" rated at 180 watts, larger cab.

1990s	$225	$250

Haynes

Haynes guitar amps were built by the Amplifier Corporation of America (ACA) of Westbury, New York. ACA also made an early distortion device powered by batteries. Unicord purchased the company in around 1964, and used the factory to produce its Univox line of amps, most likely discontinuing the Haynes brand at the same time.

Jazz King II Amp

1960s. Solidstate, stereo console-style, 2x12", Haynes logo upper right side.

1960s	$200	$300

Hilgen

1960s. Mid-level amplifiers from Hilgen Manufacturing, Hillside, New Jersey. Dark Tolex covering and swiggle-lined light color grille cloth. Examples have been found with original Jensen speakers.

Model T-2512 Star Amp

1960s. Twenty-five watts, 1x12" combo, tremolo.

1960s	$175	$325

Model T-2513 Galaxie Amp

1960s. Twenty-five watts, 1x12" piggyback cabinet, tremolo.

1960s	$175	$325

HiWatt

Bulldog SA112 Amp

1980s, 1994-present. Fifty watts, combo, 1x12".

1980s	$600	$1,000

Bulldog SA112FL Amp

1980s. One hundred watts, combo, 1x12".

1980s	$600	$1,000

Lead 20 (SG-20) Amp Head

1980s. Tube amp head, 30 watts, Black cover, rectangular HiWatt plate logo.

1980s	$600	$1,000

Lead 50R (combo) Amp

1980s. Combo tube amp, 50 watts, 1x12", reverb, dark cover, dark grille, HiWatt rectangular plate logo.

1980s	$600	$1,000

Model DR-103 Amp Head

1970-late-1980s, 1995-present. Tube head, 100 watts. Some people feel that HiWatt amps are relatively difficult to maintain, therefore a wider range of values.

1970-1977	$900	$1,500
1978-1988	$700	$1,200

MODEL YEAR	FEATURES	EXC. COND. LOW	HIGH

Model DR-504 Amp Head

1970-late-1980s, 1995-1999. Tube head amp, 50 watts.

1970-1977		$800	$1,300
1978-1987		$600	$1,100

PW-50 Tube Amp

1989-1993. Stereo tube amp, 50 watts per channel.

1989-1993		$500	$1,000

S50L Amp Head

1989-1993. Lead guitar head, 50 watts, gain, master volume, EQ.

1989-1993		$400	$800

SE 4122 4x12 Speaker Cabinet

1971- mid-1980s. Salt and Pepper grille cloth, 4x12" Fane speakers, 300 watts.

1970s		$600	$900

Hoffman

1993-present. Tube amps, combos, reverb units, and cabinets built by Doug Hoffman from 1993 to '99, in Sarasota, Florida. Hoffman no longer builds amps, concentrating on selling tube amp building supplies, and since 2001 has been located in Pisgah Forest, North Carolina.

Hohner

1857-present. Matthias Hohner, a clockmaker in Trossingen, Germany, founded Hohner in 1857, making harmonicas. Hohner has been offering guitars and amps at least since the early '70s.

Panther P-12 Amp

Twelve watts, master volume and gain controls, footswitching, equalization.

1987		$75	$100

Panther P-20 Amp

Twenty watts, master volume and gain controls, footswitching, equalization.

1987		$80	$140

Panther P-25R Amp

Twenty-five watts, master volume and gain controls, footswitching, equalization.

1987		$100	$150

Panther PBK-20 Amp

Twenty-five watts for bass/keyboard, master volume and gain controls, equalization.

1987		$135	$155

Sound Producer BA 130 Bass Amp

Dual channels, EQ, master volume, bass, middle, and treble controls for each channel.

1986		$100	$150

Sound Producer SP 35 Amp

Master volume, normal and overdrive, bright switch and reverb, line output, headphone jack.

1986		$75	$125

Sound Producer SP 55 Amp

Master volume, normal and overdrive, bright switch, reverb, headphone jack.

1986		$100	$150

Sound Producer SP 75 Amp

Master volume, normal and overdrive, bright switch, reverb, line output, headphone jack.

1986		$130	$180

Holland

1992-present. Tube combo amps from builder Mike Holland, originally in Virginia Beach, Virginia, and since 2000 in Brentwood, Tennessee. In 2000, Holland took Lane Zastrow as a partner, forming L&M Amplifiers, which owns the Holland brand.

Holmes

1970-late 1980s. Founded by Harrison Holmes. Holmes amplifiers were manufactured in Mississippi and their product line included guitar and bass amps, PA systems, and mixing boards. In the early '80s, Harrsion Holmes sold the company to On-Site Music which called the firm The Holmes Corp.

Products manufactured by Harrison have an all-caps HOLMES logo and the serial number plate says "The Holmes Company."

Performer PB-115 Bass Amp

Sixty watts, 1x15", Black Tolex.

1982		$125	$200

Pro Compact 210S Amp

Sixty watts, 2x10", two channels, active EQ, Black Tolex.

1982		$125	$200

Pro Compact 212S Amp

Sixty watts, 2x12", two channels, active EQ, master volume knob, Black Tolex.

1982		$125	$175

Rebel RB-112 Bass Amp

Thirty-five watts, 1x12", Black Tolex

1982		$100	$175

Hondo

1969-1987, 1991-present. Imported. 1990s Models ranged from the H20 Practice Amp to the H160SRC with 160 watts (peak) and 2x10" speakers. See Guitar section for more company info.

Amps

1970s	Various models	$50	$125
1980s	Various models	$50	$125
1990s	Various models	$50	$125

Hound Dog

1994-1998. Founded by George Alessandro as the Hound Dog Corporation. Name was changed to Alessandro in 1998 (see that brand for more info).

Hughes & Kettner

Hughes & Kettner offers a line of guitar and bass combos, heads, cabinets and tube effects, all made in Germany.

Holland Lil' Jimi

Hughes & Kettner ATS-60

AMPS

1962 Kay 703

1963 Kay Vanguard 704

MODEL YEAR	FEATURES	EXC. COND. LOW	HIGH

ATS MkII 112 Combo Amp

1990-1993. MOS-FET power amp, two-stage tube channel, transistorized clean channel, compressor, EQ, reverb. Available with 1x12", 2x12", or 4x12" cabinets (GL 112, GL 212, or GL 412).

1990-1993		$300	$350

Fortress Bass Preamp

1990-1994. Built-in compressor, EQ, tube preamp section.

1990-1994		$150	$200

Idol

Late-1960s. Made in Japan. Dark tolex cover, dark grille, Hobby Series with large Idol logo on front.

Model 007 Amp

1968		$35	$45

Hobby 10 Amp

1968		$80	$90

Hobby 20 Amp

1968		$125	$150

Hobby 45 Amp

1968		$175	$200

Hobby 100 Amp

1968		$200	$250

Imperial

Ca.1963-ca.1970. The Imperial Accordion Company of Chicago, Illinois offered one or two imported small amps in the '60s.

Jackson

1980-present. The Jackson-Charvel Company offered amps and cabinets in the late '80s and the '90s.

4x12" Cabinet

1990s. Red cone Jackson speakers in slant cabinet with see-through metal grille.

1990s		$350	$500

JG-2 Head Amp

Tube head, 50 watts, two-stage preamp, midrange boost, presence, effects loop, EL-34 tubes.

1988		$300	$450

JG-3 Head Amp

Tube head, 100 watts, two-stage preamp, midrange boost, presence, effects loop, EL-34 tubes.

1988		$350	$500

Johnson

Mid-1990s-present. Budget line of amps imported by Music Link, Brisbane, California. Johnson also offers acoustic, classical, acoustic/electric, and solidbody guitars, basses, mandolins and effects.

Johnson Amplification

1997-present. Modeling amps and effects designed by John Johnson, of Sandy, Utah. The company is part of Harman International. In 2002, they quit building amps, but continue the effects line.

JoMama

1994-present. Tube amps and combos under the JoMama and Kelemen brands built by Joe Kelemen in Santa Fe, New Mexico.

Kalamazoo

1933-1942, 1965-1970. Kalamazoo was a brandname Gibson used on one of their budget lines. They used the name on amps from '65 to '67.

Model 1 Amp

1965-1967. No tremolo, 1x10", front control panel, Dark Gray vinyl cover.

1965-1967		$75	$125

Model 2 Amp

1965-1967. Same as Model 1 with tremolo, Black.

1965-1967		$100	$150

Reverb 12 Amp

1965-1967. Black vinyl cover, 1x12", reverb, tremolo.

1965-1967		$200	$250

Kay

Ca. 1931-present. Kay offered amps throughout their history up to around '68 when the brandname changed hands. See company information in the Guitar section or *Guitar Stories Volume II*, by Michael Wright, for a complete history of Kay with detailed model listings.

K506 Vibrato 12" Amp

1960s. Twelve watts, 1x12", swirl grille, metal handle.

1962		$150	$250

K507 Twin Ten Special Amp

1960s. Twenty watts, 2x10", swirl grille, metal handle.

1962		$200	$300

Small Tube Amps

1940s	Wood cabinet	$175	$375
1950s	Various models	$75	$150
1960s	Models K503, K504, K505	$75	$150

Kay (Asian-American Mfg. Co)

1980-present. Tony Blair, president of Asian-American Mfg. Co., purchased the Kay brandname in '80, with a market focus on first-time buyers.

Kelemen

1994-present. Tube amps and combos under the JoMama and Kelemen brands built by Joe Kelemen in Santa Fe, New Mexico.

Kendrick

1989-present. Founded by Gerald Weber in Austin, Texas and currently located in Kempner, Texas. Mainly known for their handmade tube amps, Kendrick also offers guitars, speakers, and

AMPS

MODEL YEAR	FEATURES	EXC. COND. LOW	HIGH

effects. At the end of '03 Weber quit building amps, but still offers guitars. Gerald writes monthly columns for *Vintage Guitar* magazine and has authored books and videos on tube amps.

2210 Amp

1990s. Fender tweed Super copy, 2x10".

1999 $1,100 $2,100

4212 Amp

1990s. Fender tweed Twin copy, 2x12".

1999 $1,200 $2,200

Baby Hughey Combo Amp

1990s. Low production, 2x12" with reverb and built-in features.

1999 $1,500 $2,500

Black Gold BG-35 Amp

1996-2003. 35 watts, 1x12" or 2x10".

1990s $850 $1,200

Black Gold Stereo BG-15 Amp

1997-2003. Class A, 2x15 watt output to separate output transformer and speaker.

1990s $750 $1,050

Model 4000 Special Amp Head

1990-1991. Solidstate rectifiers with four 6L6GC output tubes, switchable to 120 or 60 watts, black tolex, only 25 made.

1991 $750 $950

Texas Crude Gusher Amp

1994-2003. Fifty watts, 2x12" or 4x10" combo.

1994 $1,200 $2,200

The Gusher Combo Amp

1990s. Small production, 1x15" JBL and 2x10" in combo amp.

1999 $1,300 $2,300

Kent

Ca. 1962-1969. Imported budget line of guitars and amps. See Guitar section for more company info.

Model 1475 Amp

Three tubes, Brown.

1966 $40 $50

Model 2198 Amp

Three tubes, Brown.

1966 $50 $60

Model 5999 Amp

Three tubes, Brown.

1966 $60 $70

Model 6104 Piggyback Amp

Twelve watts, Brown.

1966 $100 $125

Kingston

1958-1967. Economy solidstate amps imported by Westheimer Importing, Chicago, IL.

Cat P-1 Amp

Mid-1960s. Solidstate economy amp, three watts, very small speaker, dark vinyl, dark grille, Cat Series. The original retail selling price in the mid-1960s was $25.99.

1960s $25 $45

MODEL YEAR	FEATURES	EXC. COND. LOW	HIGH

Cat P-2 Amp

Mid-1960s. Solidstate economy amp, five watts, very small speaker, dark vinyl, dark grille, Cat Series.

1960s $30 $50

Cat P-3 Amp

Mid-1960s. Solidstate economy amp, eight amps, 1x8", dark vinyl, dark grille, Cat Series.

1960s $35 $55

Cat P-8 T Amp

Mid-1960s. Solidstate economy amp, 20 watts, 1x8", tremolo, dark vinyl, dark grille, Cat Series.

1960s $35 $55

Cougar BA-21 Bass Amp (piggyback)

Mid-1960s. Solidstate economy piggback amp, 60 watts, 2x12" cab, dark vinyl, Light Silver grille, Cat Series.

1960s $50 $150

Cougar PB-5 Bass Amp (combo)

Mid-1960s. Solidstate economy combo amp, 15 watts, 1x8", dark vinyl cover, dark grille.

1960s $35 $55

Lion 2000 Amp (piggyback)

Mid-1960s. Solidstate economy piggyback amp, 90 watts, 2x12" cab, dark tuck-and-roll-type cover, dark grille.

1960s $75 $175

Lion 3000 Amp (piggyback)

Mid-1960s. Solidstate economy piggyback amp, 250 watts, 4x12" cab, dark tuck-and-roll-type cover, dark grille.

1960s $100 $200

Lion AP-281 R Amp (piggyback)

Mid-1960s. Solidstate economy piggyback amp, 30 watts, 2x8" cab, dark vinyl cover, Light Silver grille.

1960s $50 $90

Lion AP-281 R10 Amp (piggyback)

Mid-1960s. Solidstate economy piggyback amp, 30 watts, 2x10" cab, dark vinyl cover, Light Silver grille.

1960s $50 $150

Kitchen-Marshall

Private branded for Kitchen Music by Marshall in 1965-1966. Primarily P.A. units with block logos. Limited production.

JTM 45 MKII 45-Watt Head Amp

1965-1966. Private branded for Kitchen Music, JTM 45 Marshall with Kitchen logo plate, 45 watts.

1966 $5,000 $6,000

Slant 4x12 1960 Cab

1966. Slant front 4x12" 1960-style cabinet with Gray bluesbreaker grille, very limited production privated branded for Kitchen Music.

1966 Black on Green vinyl $4,000 $5,000

KJL

1995-present. Founded by Kenny Lannes, MSEE, a professor of Electrical Engineering at the University of New Orleans. KLJ makes tube combo amps, heads and an ABY box.

Kendrick Texas Crude

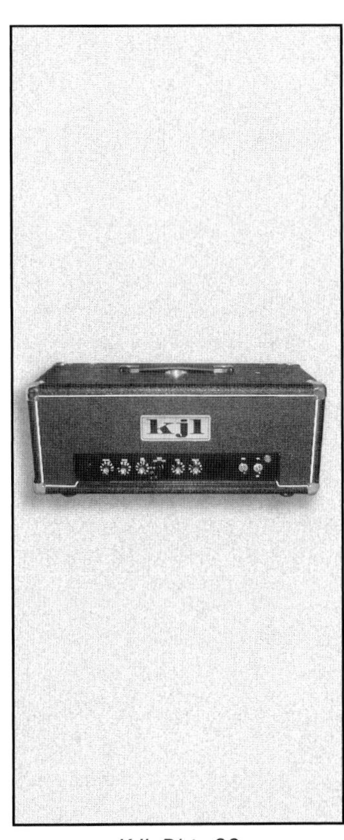

KJL Dirty 30

AMPS

Kustom K-25 Combo

Kustom Commander

MODEL YEAR	FEATURES	EXC. COND. LOW	HIGH

Kustom

1965-present. Founded by Bud Ross in Chanute, Kansas. Ross offered tuck-and-roll amps as early as '58, but began using the Kustom brandname in '65. From '69 to '75 Ross gradually sold interest in the company (in the late '70s, Ross introduced the line of Ross effects stomp boxes). The brand changed hands a few times, and by the mid-'80s it was no longer used. In 1989 Kustom was in bankruptcy court and was purchased by Hanser Holdings Incorporated of Cincinnati, Ohio (Davitt & Hanser). From 1989 to 1996 Hanser Holding experimented with different design and manufacturing locations in an attempt to re-establish the proprietary legacy. Prices are for excellent condition amps with no tears in the tuck-and-roll cover and no grille tears. A tear in the tuck-and-roll will reduce the value, sometimes significantly.

100 Combo Amp

Fifty watts, 2x10" or 1x15", tremolo.

1966-1970	Black	$300	$500
1966-1970	Color options	$400	$700

100 Head Amp

Late-1960s-mid-1970s. Solidstate head, 50 watts, Black tuck-and-roll standard.

1970	Black	$200	$250
1970	Color options	$350	$450

100 Head and Cab Set

Late 1960s-mid-1970s. Solidstate head, 50 watts, with matching 1x15" cab, Black tuck-and-roll standard, but several Sparkle colors.

1960s	Color options	$400	$700

200 Amp and Cab

One hundred watts, reverb, tremolo, with 2x15" or 3x12" cabinet.

1966-1970	Black	$300	$500
1966-1970	Charcoal Sparkle	$400	$700
1966-1970	Gold Sparkle	$600	$900
1966-1970	Red Sparkle	$500	$800
1966-1970	Teal/Cascade Sparkle	$500	$800
1966-1970	White/Silver Sparkle	$500	$800

200 Head Amp

Late-1960s-mid-1970s. Solidstate head, 100 watts, Black tuck-and-roll standard.

1970	Black	$250	$300
1970	Color options	$400	$500

400 Amp and Cab

Late-1960s-early-1970s. Four hundred designation on front panel, two vertical cabs, or four smaller cabs, tuck-and-roll covering.

1970s	Black	$400	$550
1970s	Color options	$550	$850

Challenger Amp

One 12" speaker.

1960s	Blue Sparkle	$400	$500

Hustler Amp

Solidstate combo amp, 4x10", Super Reverb-style, tremolo.

1970	Black	$400	$500
1970	Color options	$500	$650

K25/K25 C-2 Combo Amp

1960s. Small combo tuck-and-roll, 1x12", solidstate, reverb, Black control panel.

1960s	Black	$300	$350
1960s	Color options	$400	$500

KBA-20 Combo Amp

Late-1980s-early-1990s. Compact solidstate bass amp with built-in limiter, 20 watts, 1x8".

1989-1990		$40	$75

KBA-40 Combo Amp

Late-1980s-early-1990s. Compact solidstate bass combo amp with built-in limiter, 40 watts, 1x12".

1989-1990		$50	$100

KBA-80 Combo Amp

Late-1980s-early-1990s. Solidstate bass amp with built-in limiter, 80 watts, 1x15".

1989-1990		$75	$125

KBA-160 Combo Amp

Late-1980s-early-1990s. Solidstate bass amp with built-in limiter, 160 watts, 1x15".

1989-1990		$100	$150

KLA-15 Combo Amp

Late-1980s-early-1990s. Compact solidstate amp with built-in footswitchable overdrive, 15 watts, 1x8".

1989-1990		$50	$100

KLA-20 Amp

Mid-1980s-late-1980s. One 10", MOS-FET, gain, EQ, reverb, headphone jack.

1986		$75	$125

KLA-25 Combo Amp

Late-1980s-early-1990s. Compact solidstate amp with built-in footswitchable overdrive and reverb, 25 watts, 1x10".

1989-1990		$75	$125

KLA-50 Combo Amp

Late-1980s-early-1990s. Compact solidstate amp with built-in footswitchable overdrive and reverb, 50 watts, 1x12".

1989-1990		$100	$150

KLA-75 Amp

Mid-1980s-late-1980s. Seventy-five watts, dual channels with independent tone and level controls, reverb, footswitching.

1987		$125	$175

KLA-100 Combo Amp

Late-1980s-early-1990s. Solidstate amp with reverb, 100-watt dual channel, 1x12".

1989-1990		$150	$200

KLA-185 Combo Amp

Late-1980s-early-1990s. Solidstate amp with reverb, 185-watt dual channel, 1x12".

1989-1990		$175	$225

MODEL YEAR	FEATURES	EXC. COND. LOW	HIGH

Lab Series

1977-1980s. Five models of Lab Series amps, ranging in price from $600 to $3,700, were introduced at the '77 NAMM show by Norlin (then owner of Gibson). Two more were added later. The '80s models were Lab Series 2 amps and had a Gibson logo on the upper-left front.

B120 Amp

Ca.1984. Bass combo, 120 watts, two channels, 1x15".

1984		$150	$250

G120 R-10 Amp

Ca.1984. Combo, 120 watts, three-band EQ, channel switching, reverb, 4x10".

1984		$300	$400

G120 R-12 Amp

Ca.1984. Combo, 120 watts, three-band EQ, channel switching, reverb, 2x12".

1984		$225	$325

L2 Head Amp

1977-1983. Head, 100 watts, Black covering.

1977-1983	Black	$200	$300

L3 Amp

1977-ca.1983. Combo, 60 watts.

1977-1983		$275	$375

L5 Amp

1977-ca.1983. Solidstate, 100 watts, 2x12".

1977-1983		$450	$550

L7 Amp

1977-1983. Solidstate, 100 watts, 4x10".

1977-1983		$450	$550

L11 Amp

1978-1983. Head only, 200 watts.

1977-1983		$200	$300

Lafayette

Ca. 1963-1967. Japanese-made guitars and amps sold through the Lafayette Electronics catalogs.

Small Tube Amp

Japanese-made tube, 1x12", art deco design.

1960s	Gray Speckle	$150	$225

Laney

1968-present. Founded by Lyndon Laney and Bob Thomas in Birmingham, England. Laney offered tube amps exclusively into the '80s. A wide range of solidstate and tube amps are currently being offered.

EA-120 Amp

1990s. One hundred twenty watts, 2x10", dark vinyl cover.

1998		$300	$375

GC-30 Amp

1990s. Compact combo amp, 30 watts, dark vinyl cover, reverb, dark see-through grille.

1990s		$175	$225

GS-412 4x12" Cab

1980s-1990s. Straight-front cab, 4x12" rated at 150 watts, Black vinyl cover.

1990s		$250	$400

LC-15 Amp

1990s. Compact practice amp, 15 watts.

1997		$150	$175

MY-50 Amp

All tube, 50 watts, master volume, four-stage cascaded preamp, active boosts for treble, middle and bass.

1986		$200	$250

MY-100 Amp

All tube, 100 watts, master volume, four-stage cascaded preamp, active boosts for treble, middle and bass.

1986		$300	$425

Quarter Stack Amp

All tube, 2x12", self-contained, sealed back, footswitchable reverb and overdrive, effects loop, active tone controls with push/pull switches.

1986		$300	$425

Legend

1978-1984. From Legend Musical Instruments of East Syracuse, NY, these amps featured cool wood cabinets. They offered heads, combos with a 1x12" or 2x12" configuration, and cabinets with 1x12", 2x12" or 4x12".

A-30 Amp

Natural wood cabinet, Mesa-Boogie compact amp appearance.

1980s		$300	$425

Rock & Roll 50 Combo Amp

Mesa-Boogie-style wood compact combo, either 1x12" or 2x12" configuration, tube preamp section and solidstate power supply.

1978-1979	2x12" option	$200	$300

Leslie

Most often seen with Hammond organs, the cool Leslie rotating speakers have been adopted by many guitarists. Many guitar effects have tried to duplicate their sound. And they are still making them.

16 Rotating Speaker Cab

1960s-1970s. One ten inch or 1x12" rotating speaker (requires an amp head), Black vinyl cover, Silver grille, Leslie 60 logo on grille.

1960s	Black, 1 cabinet	$250	$350
1970s	Black, 1 cabinet	$250	$350

60 M Rotating Speaker Cabs

1960s-1970s. Two by one by 10" rotating speaker cabs with 45-watt amp, Black vinyl cover, Light Silver grille, Leslie logo upper left on grille.

1960s	2 cabinets	$550	$600

118 Amp

One 12" Altec speaker.

1968		$250	$350

Line 6

1996-present. Founded by Marcus Ryle and Michel Doidic and specializing in digital signal processing in both effects and amps.

Laney VC30-212

Line 6 Duoverb

AMPS

1958 Maestro

Magnatone Model 3802

MODEL YEAR	FEATURES	EXC. COND. LOW	HIGH

Little Lanilei

1997-present. Small amps made by Songworks Systems & Products of San Juan Capistrano, California. They also build a reverb unit and a rotary effect.

Louis Electric Amplifier Co.

1993-present. Founded by Louis Rosano in Bergenfield, New Jersey. Louis produces custom-built tweeds and various combo amps from 35 to 80 watts.

Maestro

Maestro amps are associated with Gibson and were included in the Gibson catalogs. For example, in the '62-'63 Orange cover Gibson catalog, tweed Maestro amps were displayed in their own section. Tweed Maestro amps are very similar to Gibson Tweed amps. Maestro amps were often associated with accordions in the early-'60s but the amps featured standard guitar inputs. Gibson also used the Maestro name on a line of effects.

The price ranges listed are for excellent condition, all original amps though tubes may be replaced without affecting value. Many amps have missing or broken logos. The prices listed are for amps with fully intact logos. A broken or missing logo changes the amp's status from excellent collector quality to player quality and may diminish the value of the amp. Amps with a changed handle, power cord, and especially a broken logo, should be taken on a case-by-case basis.

Amp models include in 1958 the Super Maestro and Maestro, in 1960 Stereo Maestro Accordion GA-87, Super Maestro Accordion GA-46 T, Standard Accordion GA-45 T, Viscount Accordion GA-16 T, in 1962 Reverb-Echo GA-1 RT, Reverb-Echo GA-2 RT, 30 Stereo Accordion Amp, Stereo Accordion GA-78 RV.

GA-1 RT Reverb-Echo Amp

1961. Tweed, 1x8".

1961	$350	$450

GA-2 RT Deluxe Reverb-Echo Amp

1961. Deluxe more powerful version of GA-1 RT, 1x12", Tweed.

1961	$700	$800

GA-15 RV/Bell 15 RV Amp

1961. Fifteen watts, 1x12", Gray Sparkle.

1961	$450	$600

GA-16 T Viscount Amp

1961. Fourteen watts, 1x10", Gray Sparkle. Gibson also had a GA-16 Viscount amp from 1959-1960.

1961	$350	$500

GA-45 Maestro Amp

1955-1960. Sixteen watts, 4x8", Two-tone.

1955-1960	$650	$750

MODEL YEAR	FEATURES	EXC. COND. LOW	HIGH

GA-45 RV Standard Amp

1961. Sixteen watts, 4x8", reverb.

1961	$700	$900

GA-45 T Standard Accordion Amp

1961. Sixteen watts, 4x8", tremolo.

1961	$650	$750

GA-46 T Super Maestro Accordion and Bass Amp

1957-1961. Based on the Gibson GA-200 and advertised to be "designed especially for amplified accordions." Sixty watts, 2x12", vibrato, Two-tone cover, large Maestro Super logo on top center of grille.

1957-1960	$900	$1,300

GA-78 Amp

1960-1961. Wedge stereo cab, 2x10".

1960-1961	$1,200	$1,700

Magnatone

Ca. 1937-1971. Magnatone made a huge variety of amps sold under their own name and under brands like Dickerson, Oahu (see separate listings), and Bronson. They also private branded amps for several accordion companies or accordion teaching studios. Brandnames used for them include DA VINCI, PAC - AMP, PANaramic, TITANO, TONEMASTER, TWILIGHTER, and UNIQUE (see separate listings for those brands). See Guitar section for more company info.

Model 108 Varsity Amp

1948-1954. Gray pearloid cover, small student amp or lap steel companion amp.

1948-1954	$200	$300

Model 110 Melodier Amp

1953-1954. 12 watts, 1x10", brown leatherette cover, light grille.

1953-1954	$250	$350

Model 111 Student Amp

1955-1959. 2 to 3 watts, 1x8", brown leatherette, brown grille.

1955-1959	$175	$225

Model 112/113 Troubadour Amp

1955-1959. 18 watts, 1x12", brown leatherette, brown grille, slant back rear control panel.

1955-1959	$300	$400

Model 120B Cougar Bass Amp

1967-1968. Initial Magnatone entry into the solidstate market, superseded by Brute Series in 1968. One hundred twenty watts, 2x12" solidstate bass piggyback amp, naugahyde vinyl cover with polyester rosewood side panels.

1967-1968	$200	$275

Model 120R Sting Ray Reverb Bass Amp

1967-1968. Initial Magnatone entry into the solidstate market, superseded by Brute Series in 1968. One hundred fifty watts, 4x10" solidstate combo amp, naugahyde vinyl cover with polyester rosewood side panels.

1967-1968	$200	$275

MODEL YEAR	FEATURES	EXC. COND. LOW	HIGH

Model 130V Custom Amp

1969-1971. Solidstate 1x12" combo amp.

1969-1971 $175 $200

Model 150R Firestar Reverb Amp

1967-1968. Initial Magnatone entry into the solidstate market, superseded by Brute Series in 1968. One hundred twenty watts, 2x12" solidstate combo amp, naugahyde vinyl cover with polyester rosewood side panels.

1967-1968 $200 $250

Model 180 Triplex Amp

Mid-to-late-1950s. Mid-level power using 2x6L6 power tubes, with 1x15" and 1x8" dual speakers.

1958 $300 $400

Model 210 Deluxe Student Amp

1958-1960. 5 watts, 1x8", vibrato, brown leatherette with V logo lower right front on grille.

1959-1960 $200 $250

Model 213 Troubadour Amp

1957-1958. 10 watts, 1x12", vibrato, brown leatherette cover, V logo lower right of grille.

1957-1958 $400 $500

Model 240 SV Magna-Chordion Amp

1967-1968. Initial Magnatone entry into the solidstate market, superseded by Brute Series in 1968. Two hundred forty watts, 2x12" solidstate stereo accordion or organ amp, naugahyde vinyl cover with polyester rosewood side panels, standard input jacks suitable for guitar, reverb and vibrato, lateral combo cab, rear mounted controls.

1967-1968 $200 $250

Model 250 Professional Amp

1958-1960. 20 watts, 1x12", vibrato, brown leatherette with V logo lower right front of grille.

1959-1960 $450 $550

Model 260 Amp

1957-1958. 35 watts, 2x12", brown leatherette, vibrato, V logo lower right front corner of grille.

1957-1958 $800 $1,000

Model 262 Jupiter/Custom Pro Amp

1961-1963. 35 watts, 2x12", vibrato, brown leatherette.

1961-1963 $550 $650

Model 280/Custom 280 Amp

1957-1958. 50 watts, brown leatherette covering, brown-yellow tweed grille, 2x12" plus 2x5" speakers, double V logo.

1957-1958 $800 $1,100

Model 280A Amp

1958-1960. 50 watts, brown leatherette covering, brown-yellow tweed grille, 2x12" plus 2x5" speakers, V logo lower right front.

1958-1960 $750 $950

Model 410 Diana Amp

1961-1963. 5 watts, 1x12", advertised as a 'studio' low power professional amp, brown leatherette cover, vibrato.

1961-1963 $250 $350

MODEL YEAR	FEATURES	EXC. COND. LOW	HIGH

Model 413 Centaur Amp

1961-1963. 18 watts, 1x12", brown leatherette cover, vibrato.

1961-1963 $400 $500

Model 415 Clio Bass Amp

1961-1963. 25 watts, 4x8", bass or accordion amp, brown leatherette cover.

1961-1963 $400 $500

Model 432 Amp

Mid-1960s. Compact student model, wavey-squiggle art deco-style grille, Black cover, vibrato and reverb.

1965 $250 $350

Model 435 Athene Bass Amp

1961-1963. 55 watts, 4x10", piggyback head and cab, brown leatherette.

1961-1963 $550 $750

Model 440 Mercury Amp

1961-1963. 18 watts, 1x12", vibrato, brown leatherette.

1961-1963 $500 $600

Model 450 Juno/Twin Hi-Fi Amp

1961-1963. 25 watts, 1x12" and 1 oval 5"x7" speakers, reverb, vibrato, brown leatherette.

1961-1963 $600 $800

Model 460 Victory Amp

1961-1963. 35 watts, 2x12" and two oval 5"x7" speakers, early-'60s next to the top of the line, reverb and vibrato, brown leatherette.

1961-1963 $650 $850

Model 480 Venus Amp

1961-1963. 50 watts, 2x12" and two oval 5"x7" speakers, early-'60s top of the line, reverb and stereo vibrato, brown leatherette.

1961-1963 $700 $900

Model M6 Amp

1964 (not seen in 1965 catalog). 25 watts, 1x12", black molded plastic 'suitcase' amp.

1964 $300 $400

Model M7 Bass Amp

1964-1966. 38 watts, 1x15" bass amp, black molded plastic 'suitcase' amp.

1964-1966 $300 $400

Model M8 Amp

1964-1966. 27 watts, 1x12", reverb and tremolo, black molded plastic 'suitcase' amp.

1964 $400 $700

Model M9 Amp

1964-1966. 38 watts, 1x15", tremolo, no reverb, black molded plastic 'suitcase' amp.

1964 $300 $600

Model M10 Amp

1964-1966. 38t watts, 1x15", tremolo, transistorized reverb section, black molded plastic 'suitcase' amp.

1964-1966 $400 $700

Model M12 Amp

1964-1966. 80 watts, 1x15" or 2x12", mid-1960s top of the line bass amp, black molded plastic 'suitcase' amp.

1965 $400 $650

1958 Magnatone Model 111

'50s Magnatone Troubadour

Magnatone Custom 280

Magnatone Custom 450

MODEL YEAR	FEATURES	EXC. COND. LOW	HIGH

Model M14 Amp

1964-1966. Stereo, 75 watts, 2x12" plus two tweeters, stereo vibrato, no reverb, black molded plastic 'suitcase' amp.

1964-1966	$600	$700

Model M15 Amp

1964-1966. Stereo 75 watts, 2x12" plus two tweeters, stereo vibrato, transistorized reverb, black molded plastic 'suitcase' amp.

1964-1966	$650	$750

Model M27 Bad Boy Bass Amp

1968-1971. 150 watts, 1x15" and 1x15" passive speaker, reverb, vibrato, solidstate, vertical profile bass amp, part of Brute Series.

1968-1971	$250	$300

Model M30 Fang Amp

1968-1971. 150 watts, 1x15", additional 1x15" passive and one exponential horn, solidstate, vibrato, reverb, vertical profile amp.

1968-1971	$250	$300

Model M32 Big Henry Bass Amp

1968-1971. 300 watts, 2x15" solidstate vertical profile bass amp.

1968-1971	$250	$300

Model M35 The Killer Amp

1968-1971. 300 watts, 2x15" and two horns, solidstate, vibrato, vertical profile amp.

1968-1971	$250	$300

Model M192 Troubadour Amp

1947-mid-1950s. About 30 watts, 1x12", White linen-style cover, metal handle, art deco baffle, vertical profile cab.

1940s	$250	$300

Model M194 Lyric Amp

1947-mid-1950s. One 12" speaker, old-style Tweed vertical cab typical of 1940s.

1940s	$250	$300

Model M195 Melodier Amp

1951-1954. Vertical cab with 1x10" speaker, pearloid with flowing grille slats.

1951-1954	$200	$300

Model M196 Amp

1947-mid-1950s. 5 to 10 watts, 1x12", scroll grille design, snakeskin leatherette cover.

1940s	$250	$300

Model M199 Student Amp

1950s. About 6 to 10 watts, 1x8", snakeskin leatherette cover, metal handle, slant grille design.

1950s	$200	$300

Model MP-1 (Magna Power I) Amp

1966-1967. 30 watts, 1x12", dark vinyl, light grille, Magnatone-Estey logo on upper right of grille.

1966-1967	$300	$350

Model PS150 Amp

1968-1971. Powered slave speaker cabinets, 150 watts, 2x15" linkable cabinets.

1968-1971	$150	$200

Model PS300 Amp

1968-1971. Powered slave speaker cabinets, 300 watts, 2x15" (one passive) linkable cabinets.

1968-1971	$150	$200

Small Pearloid Amp

1947-1955. Pearloid (MOTO) covered low and mid power amps generally associated with pearloid lap steel sets.

1947-1955	$200	$300

Starlet Amp

1951-1952. Student model, 1x8", pearloid covering.

1951-1952	$200	$300

Starlite Model 401 Amp

Magnatone produced the mid-'60s Starlite amplifier line for the budget minded musician. Each Starlite model prominently notes the Magnatone name. The grilles show art deco wavy circles. Magnatone 1960-'63 standard amps offer models starting with 12" speakers. Starlight models offer 10" and below. Model 401 has 15 watts, 1x8" and three tubes.

1964	$150	$200

Starlite Model 411 Amp

Mid-1960s. 15 watts, 1x8", five tubes, tremolo (not advertised as vibrato), art deco wavy grille.

1964	$175	$225

Starlite Model 441A Bass Amp

Early-mid-1960s. Lower power with less than 25 watts, 1x15", tube amp.

1964	$300	$350

Starlite Model Custom 421 Amp

Early-mid-1960s. Tube amp, 25 watts, 1x10".

1964	$250	$350

Starlite Model Custom 431 Amp

Early-mid-1960s. Tube amp, 30 watts, 1x10", vibrato and reverb.

1964	$350	$400

Marlboro Sound Works

1970-1980s. Economy amps imported by Musical Instruments Corp., Syosset, New York. Initially, Marlboro targeted the economy compact amp market, but quickly added larger amps and PAs.

GA-2 Amp

1970s. Economy solidstate, three watts, 1x8", dark vinyl cover, dark grille, square plate logo.

1970s	$10	$25

GA-3 Amp

1970s. Economy solidstate, three watts, 1x8", tremolo, dark vinyl cover, dark grille, square plate logo.

1970s	$15	$30

GA-20B Amp

1970s. Economy solidstate bass/keyboard amp, 25 watts, 1x12", dark vinyl cover, dark grille, square plate logo.

1970s	$25	$75

MODEL YEAR	FEATURES	EXC. COND. LOW	HIGH

GA-20R Amp

1970s. Economy solidstate, 25 watts, 1x12", tremolo and reverb, dark vinyl cover, dark grille, square plastic logo.

1970s	$25	$75

GA-40R Amp

1970s. Economy solidstate, 30 watts, 1x12", tremolo and reverb, dark vinyl cover, dark grille, square plate logo.

1970s	$50	$100

Model 520B Amp

1970s. Economy solidstate, 25 watts, 1x15", bass/keyboard amp, dark vinyl cover, dark grille, square plate logo.

1970s	$50	$100

Model 560A Amp

1970s. Economy solidstate, 45 watts, 2x10", dark vinyl cover, dark grille, square plate logo.

1970s	$50	$100

Model 760A Amp

1970s. Economy solidstate guitar/bass/keyboard combo amp, 60 watts, 1x15", dark vinyl cover, dark grille, square plate logo.

1970s	$50	$100

Model 1200R Head Amp

1970s. Economy, 60 watts, single channel head with reverb.

1970s	$50	$100

Model 1500B Bass Head Amp

1970s. Economy, 60 watts, single channel head.

1970s	$50	$100

Model 2000 Bass Amp Set

1970s. Economy, one 1500B 60-watt head and one LS12FH 1x12" with Piezo horn cab.

1970s	$50	$100

Marshall

1962-present. Drummer Jim Marshall started building bass speaker and PA cabinets in his garage in 1960. He opened a retail drum shop for his students and others and soon added guitars and amps. When Ken Bran joined the business as service manager in '62, the two decided to build their own amps. By '63 they had expanded the shop to house a small manufacturing space and by late that year they were offering the amps to other retailers. Marshall also made amps under the Park, CMI, Narb, Big M, and Kitchen-Marshall brand names. Marshall continues to be involved in the company.

Mark I, II, III and IVs are generally '60s and '70s and also are generally part of a larger series (for example JTM), or have a model number that is a more specific identifier. Describing an amp only as Mark II can be misleading. The most important identifier is the Model Number, which Marshall often called the Stock Number. To help avoid confusion VG has added the Model number as often as possible. In addition, when appropriate, VG has included the wattage, number of channels, master or no-master info in the title. This should help the reader more quickly find a specific amp. Check the model's description for such things as two inputs or four inputs, because this will help with identification. Vintage Marshall amps do not always have the Model/Stock number on the front or back panel, so the additional identifiers should help. The JMP logo on the front is common and really does not help with specific identification. For example, a JMP Mark II Super Lead 100 Watt description is less helpful than the actual model/stock number. Unfortunately, many people are not familiar with specific model/stock numbers. *VG* has tried to include as much information in the title as space will allow.

Marshall amps are sorted as follows:

AVT Series - new line for Marshall
JCM 800 Series - primarily '80s
JCM 900 Series - primarily '90s
JTM Series
Micro Stack Group
Model Number/Stock Number (no specific series, basically the '60s, '70s) - including Artist and Valvestate models (Valvestate refers to specific Model numbers in 8000 Series)
Silver Jubilee Series

AVT 20 Combo Amp

2000-present. Solidstate, 20 watts, tube preamp, 1x10". Advanced Valvestate Technology (AVT) models have black covering and grille, and gold panel.

2000s	$200	$250

AVT 50 Combo Amp

2000-present. Solidstate, 50 watts, 1x12".

2000s	$300	$375

AVT 100 Combo Amp

2001-present. Solidstate, 100 watts, tube preamp, 1x12".

2000s	$500	$550

AVT 150 Combo Amp

2001-present. Solidstate, 100 watts, 1x12", additional features over AVT 100.

2000s	$600	$650

AVT 275 Combo Amp

2000-present. Solidstate DFX stereo, 75 watts per side, 2x12".

2000s	$700	$750

AVT 412/412A Cab

2000-present. Slant half-stack 4x12" cab, 200 watt load.

2000s	$300	$400

AVT 412B Cab

2000-present. Straight-front half-stack 4x12" cab, 200-watt load.

2000s	$275	$375

Club and Country Model 4140 Amp

1978-1982. Tubes, 100 watts, 4x12" combo, Rose-Morris era, designed for the country music market, hence the name, Brown vinyl cover, straw grille.

1978-1982	$650	$900

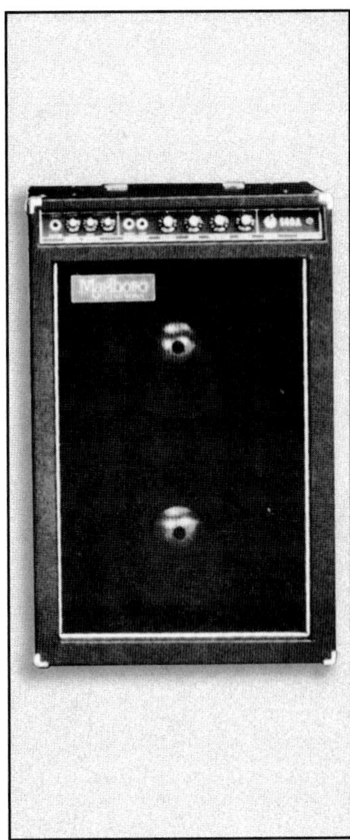

Marlboro 560A

Marshall AVT-20

AMPS

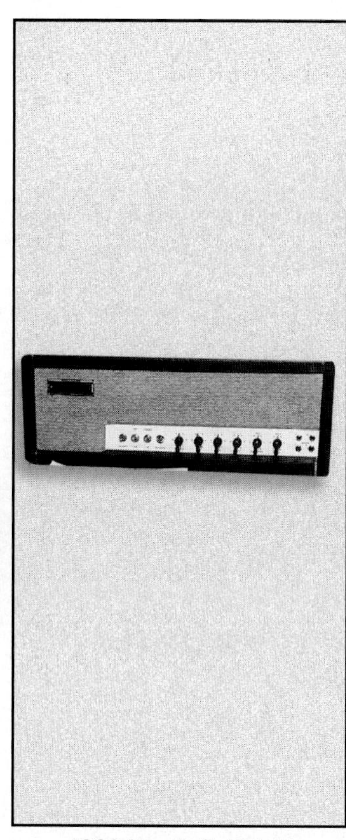

1962 Marshall JTM 45

Marshall 4101

MODEL YEAR	FEATURES	EXC. COND. LOW	HIGH

Club and Country Model 4145 Amp

1978-1982. Tubes, 100 watts, 4x10" combo, Rose-Morris era, designed for the country music market, hence the name, Brown vinyl, straw grille.

1978-1982		$650	$900

Club and Country Model 4150 Bass Amp

1978-1982. Tubes, 100 watts, 4x10" bass combo, Rose-Morris era, designed for the country music market, hence the name, Brown vinyl cover, straw grille.

1978-1982		$600	$800

JCM 800 Model 1959 Amp Head

1981-1991. Lead head amp, 100 watts.

1981-1991		$700	$800

JCM 800 Model 1987 Amp Head

1981-1991. Lead head amp, 50 watts.

1981-1991		$600	$700

JCM 800 Model 2000 Amp Head

Introduced in 1981, lead head amp, 200 watts.

1980s		$700	$800

JCM 800 Model 2001 Amp Head

Introduced in 1981, bass head amp, 300 watts.

1980s		$700	$800

JCM 800 Model 2203 Amp Head

1981-1990. Lead head amp, 100 watts, master volume. JCM 800 Lead Series noted on front panel, replaced by Model 2210. Reissued in 2003.

1981-1990		$700	$800

JCM 800 Model 2204 Amp Head

1981-1990. 50 watts, one channel, two inputs, master volume, front panel says JCM 800 Lead Series.

1981-1990		$700	$800

JCM 800 Model 2204S Amp Head

1986-1987. Shorty head, 50 watts, 4x10" cab, brown grillecloth.

1986-1987		$700	$800

JCM 800 Model 2205 Amp Head

1983-1990. 50 watts, split channel (one clean and one distortion), switchable, both channels with reverb, front panel reads JCM 800 Lead Series.

1983		$700	$800

JCM 800 Model 2210 Amp Head

1983-1990. 100 watts.

1983-1990		$700	$800

JCM 800 Model 4010 Combo Amp

1980-1990. 50 watts, 1x12", reverb, single channel master volume.

1980-1990		$600	$700

JCM 800 Model 4103 Combo Amp

1980-1990. Lead combo amp, 50 watts, 2x12".

1980-1990		$700	$800

JCM 800 Model 4104 Amp

1980-1990. All tube lead combo amp, 50 watts, 2x12".

1980-1990	Black	$700	$800
1980-1990	White option	$900	$1,000

JCM 800 Model 4210 Combo Amp

1982-1990. 50 watts, 1x12" tube combo, split-channel, single input, master volume.

1982-1990		$600	$700

JCM 800 Model 4211 Combo Amp

1983-1990. Lead combo amp, 100 watts, 2x12".

1983-1990		$700	$800

JCM 800 Model 5005 Combo Amp

1983-1990. Solidstate combo amp, 12 watts, master volume, 1x10".

1983-1990		$250	$350

JCM 800 Model 5010 Combo Amp

1983-1990. Solidstate combo amp, 30 watts, master volume, 1x12".

1983-1990		$300	$350

JCM 800 Model 5150 Combo Amp

1987-1991. Combo amp, 150 watts, specially designed 12" Celestion speaker, split channel design, separate clean and distortion channels, presence and effects-mix master controls.

1987-1991		$450	$500

JCM 800 Model 5213 Combo Amp

1986-1991. MOS-FET solidstate combo, 2x12", channel-switching, effects loop, direct output, remote footswitch.

1986-1991		$325	$375

JCM 800 Model 5215 Combo Amp

1986-1991. MOS-FET solidstate, 1x15", Accutronics reverb, effects loop.

1986-1991		$400	$450

JCM 900 2100 Mark III Amp Head

1990-1993. FX loop, 100/50-watt selectable lead head.

1990-1993		$500	$600

JCM 900 2100 SL-X Amp Head

1993-1998. Updated Model 2100 with added ECC83 preamp tube for more gain, JCM 900 SL-X on panel, 100/50 watts selectable.

1993		$550	$650

JCM 900 2500 (SL-X) Amp Head

1990-2000. 50/25 head amp, black. SL-X added in '93.

1990-2000		$500	$600

JCM 900 4100 Amp Head

1990-2000. 100/50 switchable head, JCM 900 on front panel, black with black front.

1990-2000		$600	$700

JCM 900 4102 Combo Amp

1990-2000. Combo amp, 100/50 watts switchable, 2x12".

1990-2000		$700	$800

JCM 900 4500 Amp Head

1990-2000. All tube, two channels, 50/25 watts, EL34 powered, reverb, effects loop, compensated recording out, master volume, Black.

1990-2000		$600	$700

JCM 900 4501 Dual Reverb Combo Amp

1990-2000. 50/25 switchable, 1x12".

1990-2000		$700	$800

JCM 900 4502 Combo Amp

1990-2000. 50/25 switchable, 2x12".

1990-2000		$750	$850

MODEL YEAR	FEATURES	EXC. COND. LOW	HIGH

JCM 2000 TSL 100 Amp

1998-present. TSL means Triple Super Lead, three channels.

1998-2003		$600	$700

JTM 45 Amp Head

1962-1964. Amp head, 45 watts. The original Marshall amp. Became the Model 1987 45-watt for 1965-1966.

1962-1964		$6,000	$12,000

JTM 45 Amp (Model 1987) Amp Head Reissue

1989-1999. Black/Green Tolex.

1988-1999		$650	$750

JTM 45 MK IV Model 1961 4x10 Combo Amp

1965-1966. 45 watts, 4x10", tremolo, JTM 45 MK IV on panel, Bluesbreaker association.

1965-1966		$6,000	$10,000

JTM 45 MK IV Model 1962 2x12 Combo Amp

1965-1966. 45 watts, 2x12", tremolo, JTM 45 MK IV on panel, Bluesbreaker association.

1965-1966		$9,000	$12,000

JTM 45 Model 1987 Mark II Lead Amp Head

1965-1966. Replaced JTM 45 Amp (1962-1964), but was subsequently replaced by the Model 1987 50-watt Head during 1966.

1965-1966		$4,500	$6,000

JTM 45 Offset Limited Edition Amp Set Reissue

Introduced in 2000. Limited run of 300 units, old style cosmetics, head and offset 2x12" cab, dark vinyl cover, Light Gray grille, rectangular logo plate on front of amp and cab, Limited Edition plate on rear of cab, serial number xxx of 300.

2000		$3,700	$4,700

JTM 50 MK IV Model 1961 4x10 Amp

1965-1972. 50 watts, 4x10", Bluesbreaker association, tremolo, JTM 50 MK IV on front panel to 1968, plain front panel without model description 1968-1972.

1966-1967		$6,000	$9,000
1968		$5,000	$7,000
1969		$4,000	$6,000
1970		$3,000	$4,000
1971-1972		$2,500	$3,500

JTM 50 MK IV Model 1962 2x12 Amp

1966-1972. 50 watts, 2x12", tremolo, Bluesbreaker association, JTM 50 MK IV on front panel to 1968, plain front panel without model description 1968-1972.

1966-1967		$7,000	$10,000
1968	Plain panel	$6,000	$9,000
1969	Plain panel	$5,000	$7,000
1970	Plain panel	$3,500	$4,500
1971-1972	Plain panel	$3,000	$4,000

JTM 50 Amp (Model 1962) Bluesbreaker Reissue

1989-present. 50 watts, 2x12", Model 1962 reissue Bluesbreaker.

1989-1999		$750	$850

MODEL YEAR	FEATURES	EXC. COND. LOW	HIGH

JTM 50 Model 1963 PA Amp Head

1965-1966. MK II PA head, block logo.

1965		$2,400	$2,800

JTM 310 Amp

1995-1997. Tube combo, reverb, 30 watts, 2x10", effects loops, 5881 output sections, footswitchable high-gain modes.

1995-1997		$550	$650

JTM 612 Combo Amp

1995-1997. Tube combo amp, 60 watts, 1x12", EQ, reverb, effects loop.

1995		$550	$650

Micro Stack 3005 Amp

Solidstate head, 15 watts with two 1x10" stackable cabs (one A - slant and one B - straight). Standard model is black, but was also offered in white, green, red, or silver. A Silver Jubilee version has Jubilee 25/50 logo.

1989	Black	$300	$400
1989	Green, Red, White	$400	$450
1989	Silver Jubilee/Silver	$450	$550
1990	Black	$300	$400

Mini-Stack 3210 MOS-FET Amp Head with 2x4x10"

1984-1991. Model 3210 MOS-FET head with two 4x10" cabs, designed as affordable stack.

1984-1991		$300	$400

Model 1930 Popular Combo Amp

1972-1973. Combo Amp, 10 watts, 1x12", tremolo.

1972-1973		$2,000	$3,000

Model 1935A 4x12" Bass Cab

1990s. Four 12" speakers cab.

1990s		$325	$375

Model 1936 2x12" Cab

1981-present. Two 12" speakers, extension straight-front cab, Black.

1990s		$275	$325

Model 1958 18-Watt Lead Amp

1966-1968. 18 watts, 2x10" combo, Bluesbreaker cosmetics, slant logo 1966 and '67, straight logo '68.

1966-1967	Non-reverb model	$5,500	$8,500
1968	Non-reverb model	$4,500	$6,000

Model 1958 20-Watt Lead Amp

1968-1972. 20 watts, 2x10" combo, tremolo.

1968		$4,500	$6,000
1969		$3,500	$4,500
1970		$3,000	$4,000
1971-1972		$2,500	$3,500

Model 1959 Super Lead Amp

1966-1981. Two channels, 100 watts, four inputs, no master volume. Plexiglas control panels until mid-1969, aluminum after. See Model T1959 for tremolo version. Early custom color versions are rare and more valuable.

1966-1969	Black, plexi	$4,000	$5,500
1967-1969	Custom color, plexi	$5,000	$8,000

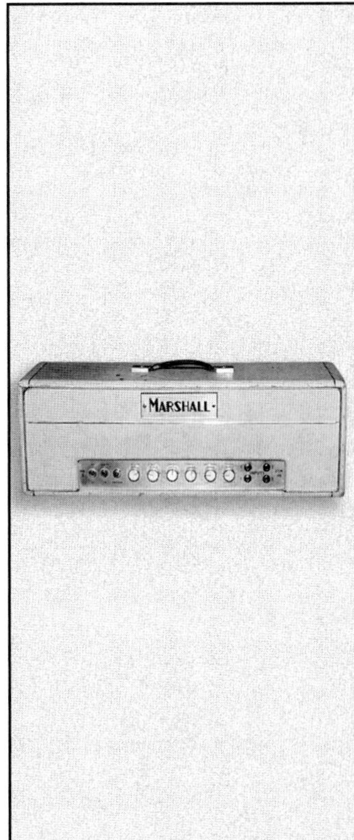

Marshall JTM 45 Mk II Lead

Marshall 3005 (plexi)

AMPS

Marshall 1959 SLP reissue

Marshall 1960A slant cab

MODEL YEAR	FEATURES	EXC. COND. LOW	HIGH
1969-1970	Black, aluminum panel	$2,500	$3,500
1969-1970	Custom color, aluminum panel	$3,000	$5,000
1971-1972	Hand-wired, small box	$1,500	$1,800
1973-1979	Printed C.B., large box	$900	$1,300
1980-1981	Black	$800	$1,100

Model T1959 Super Lead (Trem) Amp Head

1966-1973. Head amp, 100 watts, plexi until mid-1969, aluminum after. Tremolo version of the Model 1959 Amp.

MODEL YEAR	FEATURES	EXC. COND. LOW	HIGH
1966-1969	Black, plexi	$4,100	$5,600
1969-1970	Black, aluminum	$2,600	$3,600
1971-1972	Hand-wired, small box	$1,600	$1,900

Model 1959 Super Lead Matching Full Stack Set

1966-1981 option. Head with 100 watts and matching color slant and straight front 4x12" cabinets.

MODEL YEAR	FEATURES	EXC. COND. LOW	HIGH
1966-1968	Black	$8,000	$10,000

Model 1959 Super Lead Matching Set

1966-1981 option. Head with 100 watts and matching color 4x12" cabinet. Plexiglass control panels made from 1965 to mid-1969, followed by aluminum panel. Matching set requires that the head and cab are the exact matching set that came out of the factory as a set. A mismatched set that is of similar color but not built as a set is not applicable for this pricing. As is the case with all vintage amps, the speakers must be the factory original (untouched) speakers.

MODEL YEAR	FEATURES	EXC. COND. LOW	HIGH
1967-1969	Custom color, plexi	$10,000	$14,000
1969	Custom color, aluminum panel	$5,000	$8,000

Model 1959 SLP Reissue Amp Head

1992-present. SLP refers to Super Lead Plexi.

MODEL YEAR	FEATURES	EXC. COND. LOW	HIGH
1993	Black vinyl	$900	$1,100
1993	Purple vinyl	$1,200	$1,400
1997	White limited edition	$1,100	$1,300

Model 1959 SLP Reissue Amp Set

1992-present. 100 watt Super Lead head and matching 4x12" slant cab.

MODEL YEAR	FEATURES	EXC. COND. LOW	HIGH
1990s	Purple vinyl	$2,200	$2,500

Model 1960 4x12 Slant Speaker Cabinet

1964-1979. The original Marshall 4x12" cab designed for compact size with four 12" speakers. This first issue in 1964/1965 was a 60-watt cab, from 1965-1970 75 watts, from 1970-1979 100 watts. After 1979, models numbers contained an alpha suffix. Suffix A implies slant-angle front, suffix B implies straight-front cabinet, often the bottom cabinet of a two cabinet stack.

MODEL YEAR	FEATURES	EXC. COND. LOW	HIGH
1966-1968	Custom colors	$4,000	$5,000
1969	Black, basketweave	$1,800	$2,500
1970-1971	Black, basketweave	$1,600	$2,000
1971	Custom colors	$2,400	$2,800
1972	Black, basketweave	$1,200	$1,400
1973-1975	Black, checkerboard	$800	$1,000
1973-1975	Custom colors	$2,200	$2,600
1976-1979	Black	$600	$800

Model 1960A 4x12 Slant Speaker Cabinet

1979-1983 (260-watts), 1984-1986 (280-watts), 1986-1990 (300-watts).

MODEL YEAR	FEATURES	EXC. COND. LOW	HIGH
1979-1983	260 watts	$600	$800
1984-1986	280 watts, JCM 800 era	$600	$800
1986-1990	300 watts, JCM 800 era	$600	$800

Model 1960A JCM 900 4x12 Slant Speaker Cabinet

1990-present. JCM 900 Series updated to 300 watts, stereo-mono switching.

MODEL YEAR	FEATURES	EXC. COND. LOW	HIGH
1990-2000		$450	$650

Model 1960AV 4x12 Slant Speaker Cabinet

1990-present. JCM 900 updated, stereo/mono switching.

MODEL YEAR	FEATURES	EXC. COND. LOW	HIGH
1990-2000	Black vinyl, grille	$550	$650
1990s	Red vinyl, Tan grille	$700	$800

Model 1960AX 4x12 Slant Speaker Cabinet

1990-present. Cab for Model 1987X and 1959X reissue heads.

MODEL YEAR	FEATURES	EXC. COND. LOW	HIGH
1990-1999		$550	$650

Model 1960B 4x12 Straight Front Cabinet

1965-1970 (75 watts), 1970-1979 (100 watts), 1979-1983 (260 watts), 1983-1986 (280 watts), 1986-1990 (300 watts).

MODEL YEAR	FEATURES	EXC. COND. LOW	HIGH
1973-1979	Checkboard grille	$800	$1,000
1979-1983	Checkboard grille	$600	$800
1983-1986		$500	$700

Model 1960B JCM 900 4x12 Straight Front Cabinet

1990-present. JCM 900 updated cabinet, stereo/mono switching, 300 watts.

MODEL YEAR	FEATURES	EXC. COND. LOW	HIGH
1990-1999		$450	$650

Model 1960BX 4x12 Straight Front Cabinet

1990-present. Cab for Model 1987X and 1959X reissue heads.

MODEL YEAR	FEATURES	EXC. COND. LOW	HIGH
1990s		$400	$600

Model 1960TV 4x12 Slant Cabinet

1990-present. Extra tall for JTM 45, mono, 100 watts.

MODEL YEAR	FEATURES	EXC. COND. LOW	HIGH
1990s		$550	$650

Model 1964 Lead/Bass 50-Watt Amp Head

1973-1976. Head with 50 watts, designed for lead or bass.

MODEL YEAR	FEATURES	EXC. COND. LOW	HIGH
1973-1976		$900	$1,300

Model 1967 Pig 200-Watt Amp Head

1967-early-1968 only. Head with 200 watts. The control panel was short and stubby and nicknamed the "Pig", the 200-watt circuit was dissimilar (and unpopular) to the 50-watt and 100-watt circuits.

MODEL YEAR	FEATURES	EXC. COND. LOW	HIGH
1967-1968		$1,600	$2,000

MODEL YEAR	FEATURES	EXC. COND. LOW	HIGH

Model 1967 Major 200-Watt Amp Head

1968-1974. 200 watts, the original Marshall 200 'Pig' was not popular and revised into the 200 'Major'. The new Major 200 was similar to the other large amps and included two channels, four inputs, but a larger amp cab.

1968		$1,700	$2,100
1969		$1,600	$2,000
1970		$1,400	$1,900
1971-1974		$1,300	$1,800

Model 1968 100-Watt Super PA Amp Head

1968-1975. P.A. head with 100 watts, two sets of four inputs (identifies P.A. configuration), often used for guitar.

1966-1969	Plexi panel	$2,300	$2,700
1969-1972	Aluminum panel	$1,300	$1,800

Model 1973 JMP Lead & Bass 20 Amp

1973 only. Front panel: JMP, back panel: Lead & Bass 20, 20 watts, 1x12" straight front checkered grille cab, head and cab Black vinyl.

1973		$1,400	$1,600

Model 1987 50-Watt Amp Head

1966-1981. Head amp, 50 watts, plexiglas panel until mid-1969, aluminum panel after.

1966-1969	Black, plexi	$3,000	$4,500
1967-1969	Custom color, plexi	$4,000	$7,000
1969-1970	Black, aluminum panel	$2,000	$3,000
1971-1972	Hand-wired, small box	$1,000	$1,400
1973-1979	Printed C.B., large box	$800	$1,200
1980-1981		$700	$1,000

Model 1987 50-Watt Matching Set

Head and matching 4x12" cab, plexiglas control panels from 1965 to mid-1969, aluminum panel after.

1966-1969	Custom color, plexi	$8,000	$12,000
1969	Custom color, aluminum	$4,500	$6,800

Model 1992 Super Bass Amp Head

1966-1981. 100 watts, plexi panel until mid-1969 when replaced by aluminum front panel, two channels, four inputs.

1966-1969	Black, plexi	$3,000	$4,500
1966-1969	Custom color, plexi	$4,000	$7,000
1969-1970	Black, aluminum panel	$1,800	$2,800
1971-1972	Hand-wired	$1,000	$1,500
1973-1979	Printed C.B.	$800	$1,300
1980-1981		$700	$1,100

Model 2040 Artist 50-Watt Combo Amp

1971-1978. 50 watts, 2x12" Artist/Artiste combo model with a 'different' (less popular?) circuit.

1971-1978		$1,500	$1,700

Model 2041 Artist Head and Cab Set

1971-1978. 50 watts, 2x12" half stack Artist/Artiste cab with a 'different' (less popular?) circuit.

1971-1978		$1,500	$1,700

Model 2060 Mercury Combo Amp

1972-1973. Combo amp, 5 watts, 1x12", available in red or orange covering.

1972-1973	Red	$600	$700

Model 2061 20-Watt Lead/Bass Amp Head

1968-1973. Lead/bass head, 20 watts, plexi until 1969, aluminum after.

1968-1969	Black, plexi	$2,000	$3,000
1969	Black, aluminum	$1,200	$1,500

Model 2103 100-Watt 1-Channel Master Combo Amp

1975-1981. One channel, two inputs, 100 watts, 2x12", first master volume design, combo version of 2203 head.

1975-1981		$1,100	$1,500

Model 2104 50-Watt 1-Channel Master Combo Amp

1975-1981. One channel, two inputs, 50 watts, 2x12", first master volume design, combo version of 2204 head.

1975-1981		$1,000	$1,400

Model 2144 Master Reverb Combo Amp

1978 only. Master volume similar to 2104 but with reverb and boost, 50 watts, 2x12".

1978		$1,100	$1,500

Model 2159 100-Watt 2-Channel Combo Amp

1977-1981. 100 watts, two channels, four inputs, 2x12" combo version of Model 1959 Super Lead head.

1977-1981		$800	$1,200

Model 2203 Lead Amp Head

1975-1981. Head amp, 100 watts, two inputs, first master volume model design, often seen with Mark II logo.

1975-1981		$800	$1,000

Model 2203 Lead/1960B Cab Half Stack

1975-1981. 100 watts, one channel, two inputs, first master model design, with matching 1960B straight front 4x12" cab.

1975-1981	Red custom color	$1,800	$2,000

Model 2204 50-Watt Amp Head

1975-1981. Head amp, 50 watts with master volume.

1975-1981		$750	$850

Model 3203 Artist Amp Head

1986-1991. Tube head version of earlier 1984 Model 3210 MOS-FET, designed as affordable alternative, 30 watts, standard short cab, two inputs separated by three control knobs, Artist 3203 logo on front panel, Black.

1986-1991		$300	$400

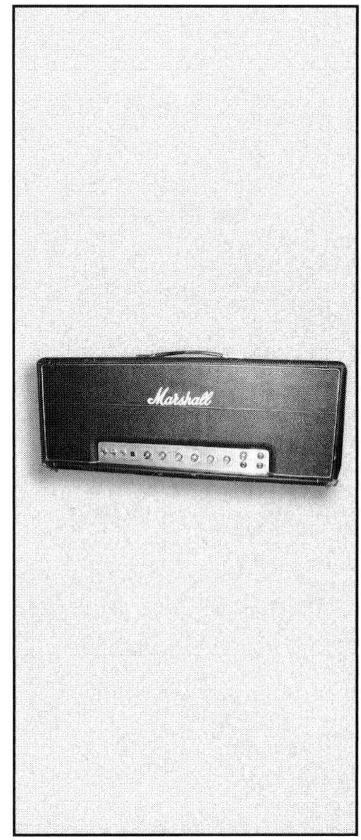

1972 Marshall 1967 Major

Marshall 3203 Artist

AMPS

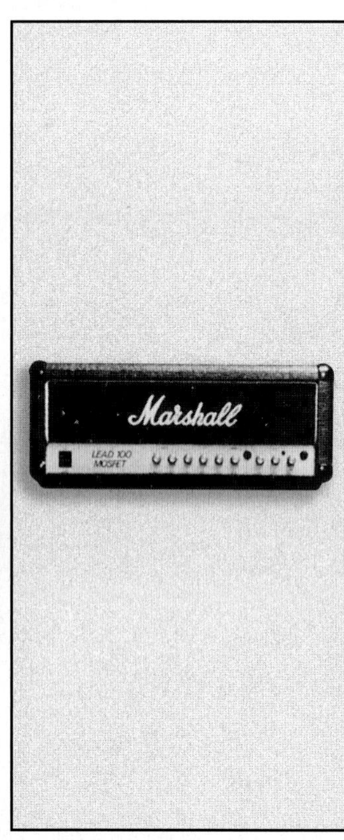

1985 Marshall 3210 head

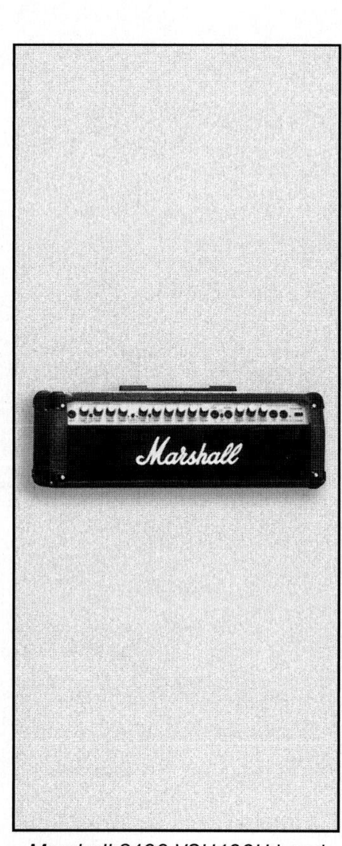

Marshall 8100 VSH100H head

AMPS

MODEL YEAR	FEATURES	EXC. COND. LOW	HIGH

Model 3210 MOS-FET Amp Head

1984-1991. MOS-FET solidstate head, refer Mini-Stack listing for 3210 with 4x10" stacked cabinets. Early-1980s front panel: Lead 100 MOS-FET.

1984-1991 $200 $300

Model 3310 100-Watt Lead Amp

1988-1991. Solidstate, 100 watts, lead head with channel switching and reverb.

1988-1991 $500 $600

Model 4001 Studio 15 Amp

1985-1992. 15 watts using 6V6 (only model to do this up to this time), 1x12" Celestion Vintage 30 speakers.

1985-1992 $500 $600

Model 5002 Combo Amp

1984-1991. Solidstate combo amp, 20 watts, 1x10", master volume.

1984-1991 $200 $250

Model 5005 combo Amp

1984-1991. Solidstate, 12 watts, 1x10", practice amp with master volume, head phones and line-out.

1984-1991 $150 $200

Model 5302 Keyboard Amp

1984-1988. Solidstate, 20 watts, 1x10", marketed for keyboard application.

1984 $150 $200

Model 5502 Bass Amp

1984-ca.1992. Solidstate bass combo amp, 20 watts, 1x10" Celestion.

1984 $175 $225

Model 6100 30th Anniversary Amp Head

1992-1995. All tube, three channels, 100 watts, EQ, gain, contour, full and half power modes, Blue vinyl covering, front panel: 6100 LM Anniversary Series. Listed as JCM 900 6100 in 1995.

1992-1995 $1,100 $1,200

Model 6100 30th Anniversary Amp Set

1992-1995. Matching head with 100/50/25 watts and 4x12" cabinet (matching colors), first year was Blue Tolex.

1992-1995 Blue/Purple $1,600 $2,000

Model 6101 LE Combo Amp

1992-1995. 1x12", 100/50/25 switchable watts, blue/purple cover, limited edition.

1992-1995 $1,200 $1,300

Model 8008 Valvestate Rackmount Amp

1991-2001. Valvestate solidstate rackmount power amp with dual 40-watt channels.

1990s $175 $275

Model 8010 Valvestate VS15 Combo Amp

1991-1997. Valvestate solidstate, 10 watts, 1x8", compact size, Black vinyl, Black grille.

1990s $150 $200

Model 8040 Valvestate 40V Combo Amp

1991-1997. Valvestate solidstate with tube preamp, 40 watts, 1x12", compact size, Black vinyl, Black grille.

1990s $300 $400

Model 8080 Valvestate 80V Combo Amp

1994-1997. Valvestate solidstate with tube 12AX7 preamp, 80 watts, 1x12", compact size, Black vinyl, Black grille.

1990s $300 $400

Model 8100 100-Watt Valvestate VS100H Amp Head

1991-2001. Valvestate solidstate head, 100 watts.

1990s $300 $400

Model 8200 200-Watt Valvestate Amp Head

1991-1998. Valvestate solidstate reverb head, two 100-watt channels.

1990s $350 $450

Model 8240 Valvestate Stereo Chorus Amp

1992-1996. Valvestate, 80 watts (2x40 watts stereo), 2x12" combo, reverb, chorus.

1992-1996 $400 $500

Model 8280 2x80-Watt Valvestate Combo Amp

1991-1996. Valvestate solidstate, 2x80 watts, 2x12".

1990s $450 $550

MS-2/MS-2R Amp

1990s. One watt, battery operated, miniature piggyback amp and cab, MS-2R in Red.

1990s $20 $30

MS-4 Amp

1990s. Similar to MS-2 but with additional mini-cab, black vinyl.

1990s $30 $50

Silver Jubilee Model 2550 50/25 (Tall) Amp Head

1987-1989. 50/25 switchable tall box head for full Jubilee stack.

1987-1989 Black $800 $900

Silver Jubilee Model 2553 (short) 2556A (mini)

1987-1989. Short box, 100/50 watt, 2x2x12".

1987-1989 $1,900 $2,100

Silver Jubilee Model 2553 50/25 (Short) Amp Head

1987-1989. 50/25 switchable small box head for mini-short stack.

1987-1989 $500 $700

Silver Jubilee Model 2554 1x12 Combo Amp

1987-1989. 50/25 watts, 1x12" combo using 2550 chasis.

1987-1989 $1,100 $1,300

Silver Jubilee Model 2555 Amp with Full Stack

1987-1989. Silver vinyl covering, chrome control panel, 100/50 watts with two 2551A 4x12" cabinets.

1987-1989 $2,300 $2,500

Silver Jubilee Model 2555 Amp with Half Stack

1987-1989. 100/50 watts, 1x4x12".

1987-1989 $1,700 $1,800

MODEL YEAR	FEATURES	EXC. COND. LOW	HIGH

Silver Jubilee Model 2556 4x12 Cab

1987-1989. Cab with 4x12" speakers in three brand name options.

1987-1989		$700	$800

Silver Jubilee Model 2556A/AV 2x12 Cab

1987-1989. Cab with 2x12" speakers with 3 brand name options.

1987-1989		$500	$600

Silver Jubilee Model 2558 2x12 Combo Amp

1987-1989. 50/25 watts, 2x12" combo using 2550 chasis.

1987-1989		$1,200	$1,400

Martin

Martin has dabbled in amps a few times, under both the Martin and Stinger brand names. See the Guitar section for more company info.

Matchless

1989-1999, 2001-present. Founded by Mark Sampson and Rick Perrotta in California. Circuits based on Vox AC-30 with special attention to transformers. A new Matchless company was reorganized in 2001 by Phil Jamison, former head of production for the original company.

1x12 Speaker Cabinet

1990s.

1990s		$500	$750

1x15 Bass Speaker Cabinet

1990s.

1990s		$500	$600

2x10 2x12 Speaker Cabinet

1990s.

1990s		$900	$1,200

2x10 Speaker Cabinet

1990s.

1990s		$600	$700

2x12 Speaker Cabinet

1990s.

1990s		$700	$900

4x10 Bass Speaker Cabinet

1990s.

1990s		$550	$700

4x10 Speaker Cabinet

1990s.

1990s		$700	$900

4x12 Speaker Cabinet

1990s.

1990s		$800	$1,200

Brave 40 112 Amp

1990s. Forty watts class A, 1x12", footswitchable between high and low inputs.

1990s		$1,500	$1,800

Brave 40 212 Amp

1990s. Forty watts class A, 2x12", footswitchable between high and low inputs.

1990s		$1,700	$2,200

MODEL YEAR	FEATURES	EXC. COND. LOW	HIGH

Chief Amp Head

1995-1999. One hundred watts class A, head.

1995-1999		$2,600	$3,000

Chief 212 Amp

1995-1999. One hundred watts class A, 2x12", reverb.

1995-1999		$3,000	$3,300

Chief 410 Amp

1995-1999. One hundred watts class A, 4x10", reverb.

1995-1999		$3,000	$3,500

Chieftan Amp Head

1995-1999. Forty watts class A head.

1995-1999		$2,200	$2,500

Chieftan 112 Amp

1995-1999. Forty watts class A, 1x12", reverb.

1995-1999		$2,600	$3,000

Chieftan 210 Amp

1995-1999. Forty watts class A, 2x10", reverb.

1995-1999		$2,900	$3,300

Chieftan 212 Amp

1995-1999. Forty watts class A, 2x12", reverb.

1995-1999		$3,000	$3,500

Chieftan 410 Amp

1995-1999. Forty watts class A, 4x10", reverb.

1995-1999		$3,000	$3,500

Clipper 15 112 Amp

1990s. Fifteen watts, single channel, 1x12".

1990s		$1,000	$1,400

Clipper 15 210 Amp

1990s. Fifteen watts, single channel, 2x10".

1990s		$1,000	$1,400

Clubman 35 Amp Head

1991-1999. Thirty-five watts class A head.

1991-1999		$2,000	$2,500

DC-30 Exotic Wood Cabinet Option

1991-1999. Thirty watts, 2x12", with or without reverb, limited production.

1991-1999	Non-reverb	$5,600	$6,000
1991-1999	With reverb	$6,100	$6,500

DC-30 Standard Cabinet

1991-1999. Thirty watts, 2x12", with or without reverb.

1991-1999	Non-reverb	$3,300	$3,500
1991-1999	With reverb	$3,800	$4,000

HC-30 Amp Head

1991-1999. The first model offered by Matchless, 30 watts class A head.

1991-1999		$2,600	$3,000

Hurricane 112 Amp

1990s. Fifteen watts class A, 1x12".

1990s		$1,400	$1,600

Hurricane 210 Amp

1990s. Fifteen watts class A, 2x10".

1990s		$1,400	$1,600

Hurricane Amp Head

1990s. Fifteen watts class A head.

1990s		$1,200	$1,400

Matchless Chief 410

Matchless Spitfire 112

AMPS

1997 Matchless Thunderchief

Maven Peal Zeetz 0.5>50

MODEL YEAR	FEATURES	EXC. COND. LOW	HIGH
JJ-30 112 John Jorgensen Amp			
1990s. Thirty watts, DC-30 chasis with reverb and tremolo, 1x12" Celestion 30, offered in White, Blue, Gray Sparkle Tolex or Black.			
1990s		$4,000	$5,500
Lightning 15 Amp Head			
1990s. Fifteen watts class A head.			
1990s		$1,300	$1,700
Lightning 15 112 Amp			
1990s. Fifteen watts class A, 1x12".			
1990s	Non-reverb	$1,600	$1,800
1990s	With reverb	$2,100	$2,300
Lightning 15 210 Amp			
1990s. Fifteen watts class A, 2x10".			
1990s	Non-reverb	$1,800	$2,300
1990s	With reverb	$2,300	$2,800
Lightning 15 212 Amp			
1990s. Fifteen watts class A, 2x12".			
1990s	Non-reverb	$1,800	$2,300
1990s	With reverb	$2,300	$2,800
SC-30 Exotic Wood Cabinet Option			
1991-1999. Thirty watts class A, 1x12", limited production.			
1991-1999	Non-reverb	$5,400	$5,700
1991-1999	With reverb	$5,900	$6,200
SC-30 Standard Cabinet			
1991-1999. Thirty watts class A, 1x12".			
1991-1999	Non-reverb	$2,900	$3,200
1991-1999	With reverb	$3,400	$3,700
Skyliner Reverb 15 112 Amp			
1990s. Fifteen watts, 1x12".			
1990s		$1,100	$1,500
Skyliner Reverb 15 210 Amp			
1990s. Fifteen watts, 2x10".			
1990s		$1,100	$1,500
Spitfire 15 Amp Head			
1990s. Fifteen watts, head.			
1990s		$1,200	$1,400
Spitfire 15 112 Amp			
1990s. Fifteen watts, 1x12".			
1990s		$1,400	$1,600
Spitfire 15 210 Amp			
1990s. Fifteen watts, 2x10".			
1990s		$1,600	$1,800
Starliner 40 212 Amp			
1990s. Forty watts, 2x12".			
1990s		$1,800	$2,200
Superchief 120 Amp Head			
1990s. One hundred twenty watts class A head.			
1990s		$2,300	$2,800
TC-30 Exotic Wood Cabinet Option			
1991-1999. Thirty watts, 2x10" class A, limited production.			
1991-1999	Non-reverb	$5,600	$6,000
1991-1999	With reverb	$6,100	$6,500
TC-30 Standard Cabinet			
1991-1999. Thirty watts, 2x10" class A, low production numbers makes value approximate with DC-30.			
1991-1999	Non-reverb	$3,100	$3,500
1991-1999	With reverb	$3,600	$4,000

MODEL YEAR	FEATURES	EXC. COND. LOW	HIGH
Thunderchief Bass Amp Head			
1990s. Two hundred watts class A bass head.			
1990s		$1,200	$2,000
Thunderman 100 Bass Combo Amp			
1990s. One hundred watts, 1x15" in portaflex-style flip-top cab.			
1990s		$1,500	$2,200
Tornado 15 112 Amp			
1994-1995. Compact, 15 watts, 1x12", two-tone covering, simple controls—volume, tone, tremolo speed, tremolo depth.			
1994-1995		$1,100	$1,300

Matchless (reorganized 2001)

2001-present. Phil Jamison, former head of production for the original Matchless company, reorganized Matchless in 2001. The first products offered were the new C-30 series, Clubman Head, Chieftan series, and Lightning series.

Maven Peal

November 1999-present. Founded by David Zimmerman and located in Plainfield, Vermont, the name stands for "expert sound." Serial number format is by amp wattage and sequential build; for example, 15-watt amp 15-001, 30-watt 30-001, and 50-watt 50-001with the 001 indicating the first amp built. S = Silver Series, no alpha = Gold Series.

Mega Amplifiers

Solidstate and tube amps from Guitar Jones, Inc. of Pomona, California.

Merlin

Rack-mount bass head built in Germany by Musician Sound Design and distributed by Godlyke Distributing in the U.S.

Mesa-Boogie

1971-present. Founded by Randall Smith in San Francisco. Circuits styled on high-gain Fender-based chassis designs, ushering in the compact high-gain amp market. The following serial number information and specs courtesy of Mesa Engineering.

MODEL YEAR	FEATURES	EXC. COND. LOW	HIGH
.50 Caliber Amp Head			
Jan. 1987-Dec. 1988. Serial number series: SS3,100-SS11,499. Mesa Engineering calls it Caliber .50. Tube head amp, 50 watts, five-band EQ, effects loop. Called the .50 Caliber Plus in 1992 and 1993.			
1987-1988		$500	$600
.50 Caliber+ Combo Amp			
Dec. 1988-Oct. 1993. Serial number series FP11,550-FP29,080. Fifty watts, 1x12" combo amp.			
1988-1993		$550	$650

MODEL YEAR	FEATURES	EXC. COND. LOW	HIGH

20/20 Amp

June 1995-present. Serial number series: TT-01. Twenty to 22 watts per channel.

1995-2001		$425	$475

50/50 (Fifty/Fifty) Amp

May 1989-present. Serial number series: FF001- One hundred watts total power, 50 watts per channel, front panel reads 'Fifty/Fifty', contains four 6L6 power tubes.

1989-1995		$450	$550

395 Amp

Feb. 1991-April 1992. S2,572 to S3,237.

1991-1992		$400	$600

500 Amp

June 1991-April 1992. S2,552- .

1991-1992		$400	$600

Bass 400 Amp

Aug. 1989-Aug. 1990. Serial number series: B001-B1200. About 500 watts using 12 5881 power tubes, replaced by 400+.

1989-1990		$700	$900

Bass 400+ Amp Head

Aug. 1990-present. Serial number series: B1200-update change to seven-band EQ at serial number B1677, uses 12 5881 power tubes to give about 500 watts.

1990		$700	$900

Blue Angel Amp

June 1994-present. Serial number series BA01-. Lower power, 1x12" combo.

1990s		$700	$800

Buster Bass Amp Head

Dec. 1997-Jan. 2001. Serial number series: BS-1 - 999, 200 watts via six 6L6 power tubes (similar to Ampeg SVT).

1997-2001		$600	$700

Coliseum 300 Amp

Oct. 1997-2002. Serial number series: COL-01 to COL-132, 200 watts per channel using 12 6L6 power tubes, rackmount.

1997-2002		$650	$800

D-180 Amp Head

July 1982-Dec. 1985. Serial number series D001-D681. All tube head amp, 200 watts, preamp, switchable.

1982-1985		$650	$700

DC-5 Amp

Oct. 1993-Jan. 1999. Fifty-watt head, 1x12" combo. Serial numbers: DC1024-DC31,941.

1993-1999		$650	$850

DC-10 Amp Head

May 1996-Jan. 1999. Serial number series: DCX-001 to DCX-999. Dirty/Clean (DC) 60 or 100 watts (6L6s).

1996-1999		$750	$850

Formula Preamp

July 1998-2002. Serial number series: F-01, used 15 12AX7 tubes, three channels.

1998-2002		$525	$575

MODEL YEAR	FEATURES	EXC. COND. LOW	HIGH

Heartbreaker Amp

June 1996-2001. Serial number series: HRT-01 - 60 watts to 100 watts switchable, 2x12" combo, designed to switch-out 6L6s, EL34s or the lower powered 6V6s in the power section, switchable solidstate or tube rectifier.

1996-2001		$1,200	$1,300

M-180 Amp

April 1982-Jan. 1986. Serial number series M001-M275.

1982-1986		$500	$800

Mark I Combo (Model A) Amp

1971-1978. The original Boogie amp, not called the Mark I until the Mark II was issued. Sixty or 100 watts, 1x12", Model A serial number series: 1-2999, very early serial numbers 1-299 had 1x15".

1971-1978		$850	$950

Mark I Reissue Amp

Nov. 1989-present. Serial number series: H001-. One hundred watts, 1x12", reissue features include figured maple cab and wicker grille.

2000-2001		$650	$850

Mark II Combo Amp

1978-1980. Late 1978 1x12", serial number sequence: 3000-5574. Effective Aug. 1980 1x15", serial number sequence: 300-559 until Mark II B replaced.

1978-1980	1x12"	$900	$1,200
1978-1980	1x15"	$900	$1,200

Mark II B Combo Amp

1980-1983. Effective Aug. 1980 1x12" models, serial number sequence 5575-110000. May 1983 1x15" models, serial number series 560-11000. The 300 series serial number series K1-K336.

1981-1983	1x12"	$900	$1,200
1981-1983	1x15"	$900	$1,200

Mark II C+ Head Amp

1983-1985. Sixty watts, head.

1983-1985		$900	$1,200

Mark II C/Mark II C+ Amp

May 1983-March 1985. Serial number series 11001-14999 for 60 watts, 1x15", offered with optional White Tolex cover. 300 series serial numbers after C+ are in the series K337-K422.

1983-1985		$900	$1,200
1983-1985	White Tolex	$1,000	$1,300

Mark III Amp Head

1985-1999. One hundred watts, Black vinyl.

1985-1990		$700	$850

Mark III Combo Amp

Mar. 1985-Feb. 1999. Serial number series: 15,000-28,384. 300 series serialization K500- . Graphic equalizer only Mark III since August 1990, 100 watts, 1x12" combo. Custom cover or exotic hardward cab will bring more than standard vinyl cover cab.

1985-1990	Black	$900	$1,200
1985-1990	Custom color	$1,000	$1,300
1985-1991	Custom hardward cab	$1,200	$1,400

1980 Mesa/Boogie Mark II

Mesa/Boogie Mark II B

AMPS

Mesa/Boogie Nomad 55

1984 Mesa/Boogie Son of Boogie

MODEL YEAR	FEATURES	EXC. COND. LOW	HIGH

Mark III 1x12 Cab

Late 1980s-early 1990s. Typically sized 1x12" extension cab with open half back, Black vinyl, Black grille, not strictly for Mark III, usable for any Boogie with matching output specs, rated for 90 watts.

1988-1990s Black $200 $300

Mark III 4x12 Cab

Late-1980s-early-1990s. Half stack 4x12" slant cab with open half back or straight-front cab, not strictly for Mark III, usable for any Boogie with matching output specs, often loaded with Celestion Vintage 30s, small weave grille (not see-through crossing strips).

1988-1990s Slant cab $550 $650
1988-1990s Straight-front cab $550 $650

Mark IV Head and Half Stack Amp Set

1991-2000. Mark IV head and matching 4x12" slant half stack cab.

1991-2000 $1,300 $1,500

Mark IV/Mark IV B Combo Amp

May 1990-1994. Model IV B Feb. 1995 to present, serial number series IV001. Clean rhythm, crunch rhythm and lead modes, 40 watts, EQ, three-spring reverb, dual effects loops, digital footswitching.

1991-1999 $1,200 $1,400

Maverick Amp Head

1994-present. Thirty-five watts, Dual Rectifier head, White/Blond vinyl cover.

1994-2000 White/Blond $600 $800

Maverick Combo Amp

1997-present. Dual channels, four EL84s, 35 watts, 1x12" or 2x12" combo amp, 5AR4 tube rectifier, Cream vinyl covering. Serial number identification MAV. Also available as head.

1997-2000 1x12" $850 $950
1997-2000 2x12" $950 $1,050

Maverick Half Stack Amp Set

April 1994-present. Serial number series: MAV001- . Thirty-five watts, Dual Rectifier head and half stack cab set.

1990s $1,200 $1,300

Nomad 45 Combo Amp

July 1999-present. Serial number series: NM45-01. Forty-five watts, 1x12 or 2x12" combo, dark vinyl cover, dark grille.

1999-2001 $750 $800

Nomad 55 Combo Amp

July 1999-present. Serial number series: NM55-01. Fifty-five watts, 1x12" or 2x12" combo.

1999-2001 1x12" $1,050 $1,150
1999-2001 2x12" $1,150 $1,250

Nomad 100 Amp Head

July 1999-present. One hundred watts, Black cover, Black grille.

1999-2001 $950 $1,150

Nomad 100 Combo Amp

July 1999-present. One hundred watts, 1x12" or 2x12" combo, Black cover, Black grille.

1999-2001 1x12: $1,250 $1,350
1999-2001 2x12" $1,350 $1,450

Quad Preamp

Sept. 1987-1992. Serial number series: Q001-Q2,857. Optional Quad with FU2-A footswitch Aug. 1990-Jan. 1992, serial number series: Q2,002 to Q2,857.

1987-1992 Without footswitch $550 $600
1990-1992 With FU2-A footswitch $750 $800

Recto Verb Combo Amp

Dec. 1998-present. Serial number series R50- . Fifty watts, 1x12", Black vinyl cover, Black grille.

1998-2001 $1,000 $1,150

Recto Verb I Amp Head

Dec. 1998-2001. Serial number series: R50- . Fifty watts, head with two 6L6 power tubes, upgraded April 2001 to II Series.

1998-2001 $850 $950

Road Ready 1x15 Cabinet

1990s. One 15" speaker, cabinet built with anvil-style road case with metal grille and castes, heavy duty.

1990s $400 $500

Road Ready 2x12 Cabinet

1990s. Two 12" speakers, cabinet built into anvil-style road case with metal grille and casters, heavy duty.

1990s $500 $550

Rocket 440 Amp

March 1999-Aug. 2000. Serial number series: R440-R44-1159. Forty-five watts, 4x10".

1999-2000 $700 $800

Satellite/Satellite 60 Amp

Aug. 1990-1999. Serial number series: ST001-ST841. Uses either 6L6s for 100 watts or EL-34s for 60 watts, dark vinyl, dark grille.

1990-1999 $450 $600

Solo 50 Rectifier Series II

April 2001 upgrade. Serial number series: S50-1,709. Upgrades preamp section, head with 50 watts.

2001 $650 $750

Son Of Boogie Amp

May 1982-Dec. 1985. Serial number series: S100-S2390. Sixty watts, 1x12", considered the first reissue of the original Mark I.

1982-1985 $400 $500

Stereo 290 (Simul 2: Ninety) Amp

June 1992-present. Serial number series: R0001- . Dual 90-watt stereo channels, rackmount.

1992-1999 $750 $950

Stereo 295 Amp

March 1987-May 1991. Serial number series: S001-S2673. Dual 95-watt class A/B stereo channels, rackmount. Selectable 30 watts Class A (EL-34) power tubes) power.

1987-1991 $500 $600

Strategy 400 Amp

March 1987-May 1991. Serial number series: S001-S2627. Four hundred to 500 watts, power amplifier with 12 6L6 power tubes.

1987-1991 $650 $850

MODEL YEAR	FEATURES	EXC. COND. LOW	HIGH

Studio .22 Amp

Nov. 1985-1988. Serial numbers: SS000-SS11499. Black vinyl, Black grille, 22 watts, 1x12".

1985-1988 $450 $550

Studio .22+ Amp

Dec. 1988-Aug. 1993. Serial number series: FP11,500-FP28,582. Twenty-two watts, 1x12", Black vinyl cover, Black grille.

1988-1993 $450 $550

Studio Caliber DC-2 Amp

April 1994-Jan. 1999. Serial number series: DC2-01-DC2-4247 (formerly called DC-2). Twenty watts, 1x12" combo, dark vinyl, dark grille.

1994-1999 $450 $550

Studio Preamp

Aug. 1988-Dec. 1993. Serial number series: SP000-SP7890. Tube preamp, EQ, reverb, effects loop.

1988-1993 $350 $450

Subway Reverb Rocket Amp

Jun. 1998-Aug. 2001. Serial number series: RR1000-RR2461. Twenty watts, 1x10".

1998-2001 $600 $650

Subway Rocket (no reverb) Amp

Jan. 1996-July 1998. Serial number series: SR001-SR2825. No reverb, 20 watts, 1x10".

1996-1998 $500 $550

Subway/Subway Blues Amp

Sept. 1994-Aug. 2000. Serial number series: SB001-SB2,515. Twenty watts, 1x10".

1994-2000 $450 $500

Trem-O-Verb Dual Rectifier 4x12 Cab

Late-1980s-early-1990s. Half stack 4x12" slant cab with open half back, or straight-front cab, not strictly for this model, useable for any Boogie with matching output specs, often loaded with Celestion Vintage 30s, small weave grille (not see-through crossing strips).

1988-1990s Slant cab $550 $650

1988-1990s Straight-front cab $550 $650

Trem-O-Verb Dual Rectifier Amp Head

June 1993-Jan. 2001. One hundred-watt head version.

1992-2001 $1,000 $1,200

1992-2001 Rackmount version $1,000 $1,200

Trem-O-Verb Dual Rectifier Combo Amp

June 1993-Jan. 2001. Serial number series R- to about R-21210. One hundred watts, 2x12" Celestion Vintage 30.

1993-2000 $1,400 $1,500

Trem-O-Verb Dual Rectifier Half Stack Amp

June 1993-Jan. 2001. One hundred watts, head with matching 4x12" slant cab.

2001 $1,500 $1,800

Triaxis Preamp

Oct. 1991-present. Serial number series: T0001-Five 12AX7 tube preamp, rackmount.

1991-2000 $900 $1,100

MODEL YEAR	FEATURES	EXC. COND. LOW	HIGH

Walk About M-Pulse Bass Amp Head

Sept. 2001-present. Serial number series WK-01-Lightweight and portable at 13 pounds, 2x12AX7 + 300 MOS-FET.

2001 $450 $550

Mission Amps

1996-present. Bruce Collins' Mission Amps, located in Arvada, Colorado, produces a line of custom-made combo amps, heads, and cabinets.

Mojave Amp Works

2002-present. Tube amp heads and speaker cabinets by Victor Mason in Apple Valley, California.

Montgomery Ward

Amps for this large retailer were sometimes branded as Montgomery Ward, but usually as Airline (see that listing).

Model 8439 Amp

1950s. One 12" speaker, around 12 watts.

1954 $150 $250

Morley

Late 1960s-present. The effects company offered an amp in the late '70s. See Effects section for more company info.

Bigfoot Amp

1979-ca.1981. Looks like Morley's '70s effects pedals. Produced 25 watts and pedal controlled volume. Amp only, speakers were sold separately.

1979-81 $150 $250

Mountain

Mountain builds a 9-volt amp in a wood cabinet. Originally built in California, then Nevada; currently being made in Vancouver, Canada.

Multivox

Ca.1946-ca.1984. Multivox was started as a subsidiary of Premier to manufacture amps, and later, effects.

New York 1st AVE Amp

1982. Fifteen watts, 1x8".

1982 $100 $125

New York 6th AVE Amp

1982. Sixty watts, 1x12".

1982 $125 $175

Music Man

1972-present. Music Man made amps from '73 to '83. The number preceding the amp model indicates the speaker configuration. The last number in model name usually referred to the watts. RD indicated "Reverb Distortion." RP indicated "Reverb Phase." Many models were available in head-only versions and as combos with various speaker combinations. See Guitar section for more company info.

Mesa/Boogie Son of Boogie combo

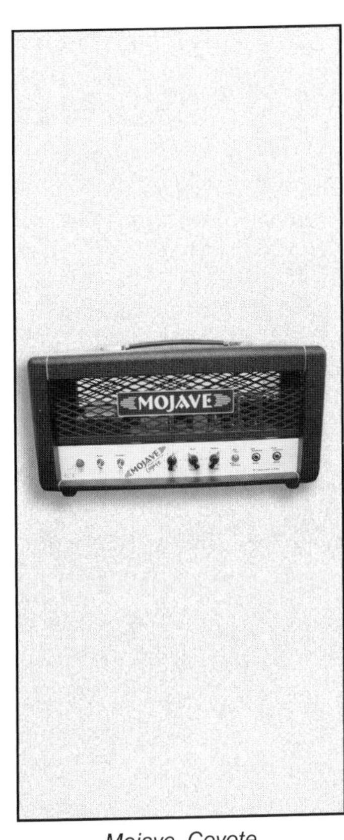

Mojave Coyote

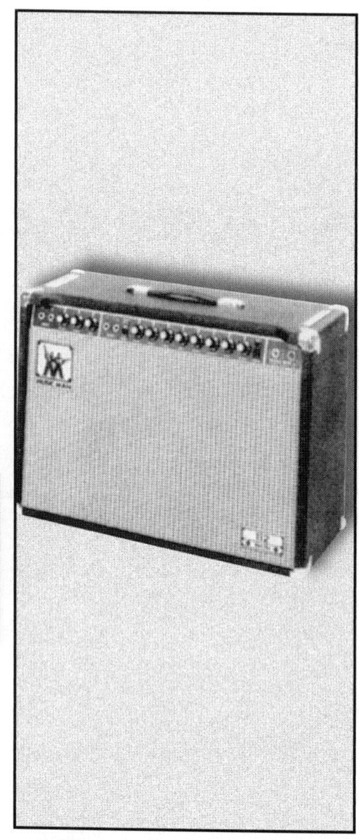

Music Man 115 Sixty Five

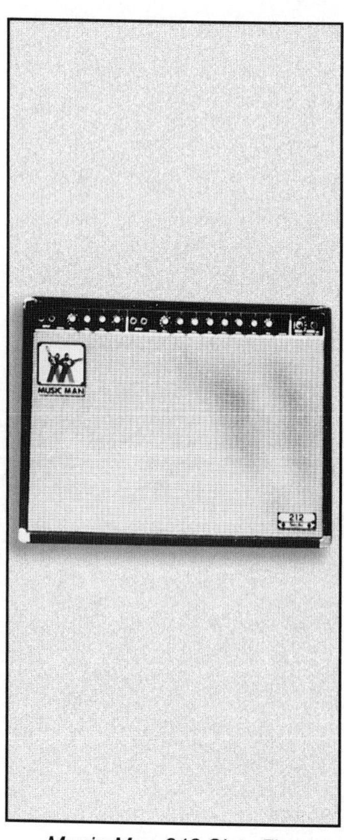

Music Man 212 Sixty Five

MODEL YEAR	FEATURES	EXC. COND. LOW	HIGH

110 RD Fifty Amp

1980-1983. Fifty watts, 1x10", reverb, distortion.

1980-1983		$400	$550

112 RD Fifty Amp

1980-1983. Fifty watts, 1x12", reverb, distortion.

1980-1983		$450	$600

112 RD Sixty Five Amp

1978-1983. Sixty-five watts, 1x12", reverb, distortion.

1978-1983		$450	$600

112 RD One Hundred Amp

1978-1983. One hundred watts, 1x12", reverb, distortion.

1978-1983		$450	$600

112 RP Sixty Five Amp

1978-1983. Sixty-five watts, 1x12", reverb, built-in phaser.

1978-1983		$450	$550

112 RP One Hundred Amp

1978-1983. Combo amp, 100 watts, 1x12", reverb, built-in phaser.

1978-1983		$450	$600

112 Sixty Five Amp

1973-1981. Combo amp, 65 watts, 1x12", reverb, tremolo.

1973-1981		$450	$550

115 Sixty Five Amp

1973-1981. Combo amp, 65 watts, 1x15", reverb, tremolo.

1973-1981		$450	$550

210 HD130 Amp

1973-1981. Combo amp, 130 watts, 2x10", reverb, tremolo.

1973-1981		$550	$600

210 Sixty Five Amp

1973-1981. Sixty-five watts, 2x10", reverb, tremolo.

1973-1981		$550	$600

212 HD130 Amp

1973-1981. One hundred thirty watts, 2x12", reverb, tremolo.

1973-1981		$600	$700

212 Sixty Five Amp

1973-1981. Sixty-five watts, 2x12", reverb, tremolo.

1973-1981		$600	$700

410 Sixty Five Amp

1973-1981. Sixty-five watts, 4x10", reverb, tremolo.

1973-1981		$600	$650

410 Seventy Five Amp

1982-1983. Seventy-five watts, 4x10", reverb, tremolo.

1982-1983		$600	$650

HD-130 Amp

1973-1981. Head amp, 130 watts, reverb, tremolo.

1973-1981		$400	$500

RD Fifty Amp

1980-1983. Head amp, 50 watts, reverb, distortion.

1980-1983		$350	$450

Sixty Five Amp

1973-1981. Head amp, 65 watts, reverb, tremolo.

1973-1981		$350	$450

MODEL YEAR FEATURES EXC. COND. LOW HIGH

National

Ca. 1927-present. National/Valco amps date back to the late-'30s. National introduced a modern group of amps about the same time they introduced their new Res-O-Glas "space-age" guitar models in '62. In '64, the amp line was partially redesigned and renamed. By '68, the Res-O-Glas models were gone and National introduced many large vertical and horizontal piggyback models which lasted until National's assets were assigned during bankruptcy in '69. The National name went to Chicago importer Strum N' Drum who then advertised "National is back and better than ever." Initially, Strum N' Drum had one amp, the National GA 950 P Tremolo/Reverb piggyback. See Guitar section for more company info.

Glenwood 90 Amp (Model N6490TR)

1964-1967. Thirty-five watts, 2x12", tremolo (not listed as vibrato) and reverb.

1964-1967		$500	$650

Glenwood Vibrato Amp (Model N6499VR)

1964-1967. Seventy watts, 2x12", vibrato and reverb.

1964-1967		$550	$700

Model 100 Amp

Tube amp, 40 watts, 1x12".

1940		$250	$400

Model GA 950-P Tremolo/Reverb Piggyback Amp

1970s. Strum N' Drum/National model, solidstate, 50 watts, two channel 2x12" and 1x7" in 32" tall vertical cabinet, black.

1970s		$150	$250

Model N6800 - N6899 Piggyback Amps

1968-1969. National introduced a new line of tube amps in 1968 and most of them were piggybacks. The N6895 was sized like a Fender piggyback Tremolux, the N6875 and N6878 bass amps were sized like a 1968 Fender large cab piggyback with a 26" tall vertical cab, the N6898 and N6899 were the large piggyback guitar amps. These amps feature the standard Jensen speakers or the upgrade JBL speakers, the largest model was the N6800 for P.A. or guitar, which sported three 70-watt channels and two column speakers using a bass 2x12" + 1x3" horn cab and a voice-guitar 4x10" + 1x3" horn cab.

1968-1969	Various tube models	$175	$375

Model N6816 Amp (Model 16)

1968-1969. Valco-made tube amp, 6 watts, 1x10" Jensen speaker, 17" vertical cab, tremolo, no reverb, Black vinyl cover and Coppertone grille, "National" spelled out on front panel.

1968-1969		$125	$150

Model N6820 Thunderball Bass Amp

1968-1969. Valco-made tube amp, about 35 watts, 1x15" Jensen speaker, 19" vertical cab, Black vinyl cover and Coppertone grille, "National" spelled out on front panel.

1968-1969		$150	$175

MODEL YEAR	FEATURES	EXC. COND. LOW	HIGH

Model N6822 Amp (Model 22)

1968-1969. Valco-made, six watts tube (four tubes) amp, 1x12" Jensen speaker, 19" vertical cab, tremolo and reverb, Black vinyl cover and Coppertone grille, "National" spelled out on front panel.

1968-1969	$150	$175

Westwood 16 Amp (Model N6416T)

1964-1967. Five watts using one 6V6 power, two 12AX7 preamp, one 5Y3GT rectifier, tremolo, 2x8", dark vinyl cover, Silver grille.

1964-1967	$250	$300

Naylor Engineering

1994-present. Joe Naylor and Kyle Kurtz founded the company in East Pointe, Michigan, in the early '90s, selling J.F. Naylor speakers. In '94 they started producing amps. In '96, Naylor sold his interest in the business to Kurtz and left to form Reverend Guitars. In '99 David King bought the company and moved it to Los Angeles, then to Dallas. Currently Naylor builds tube amps, combos, speakers, and cabinets.

Nemesis

From the makers of Eden amps, Nemesis is a line of made-in-the-U.S., FET powered bass combos and extension cabinets. The brand is a division of U.S. Music Corp.

NC-200P Combo Amp

1990s. Compact transporter-style cabinet with 200 watts, solidstate, 4x10", Black cover, Black grille.

1997	$500	$600

Norma

1965-1970. Economy solidstate line imported and distributed by Strum N' Drum, Wheeling (Chicago), IL. As noted in the National section, Strum N' Drum acquired the National brand name in the '70s. Low values reflect the market's low demand for an import solidstate amp.

GA-93 Amp

1969-1970. Economy solidstate, six watts, 1x6", Dark Brown vinyl cover, Dark Brown grille.

1969-1970	$50	$75

GA-97 T Amp

1969-1970. Economy solidstate, 13 watts, 1x8", Dark Brown vinyl cover, dark grille, tremolo.

1969-1970	$55	$85

GA-725 B Amp

1969-1970. Economy solidstate bass amp, 38 watts, 1x10" bass speaker, Dark Brown vinyl cover, sparkle grille.

1969-1970	$55	$85

GA-918 T Amp

1969-1970. Economy solidstate, 24 watts, 1x12", Dark Brown vinyl cover, dark grille, tremolo and reverb.

1969-1970	$65	$95

MODEL YEAR	FEATURES	EXC. COND. LOW	HIGH

GA-930 P (piggyback) Amp

1969-1970. Economy solidstate, 40 watts, 2x12", piggyback, dark vinyl cover, dark grille.

1969-1970	$75	$125

GA-6240 Amp

1969-1970. Economy solidstate portable, 50 watts, dark vinyl cover, medium light grille.

1969-1970	$75	$125

GAP-2 Amp

1969-1970. Economy solidstate, three watts, 1x4", Dark Brown vinyl cover, Light Brown grille.

1969-1970	$50	$75

Oahu

The Oahu Publishing Company and Honolulu Conservatory, based in Cleveland, started with acoustic Hawaiian and Spanish guitars, selling large quantities in the 1930s. As electric models became popular, Oahu responded with guitar/amp sets. See Guitar section for more company info. The brandname has been revived on a line of U.S.-made tube amps.

Tonemaster 230K Amp

All tube combo, 20 watts, 1x12".

1960s	$200	$225

Tunemaster Amp

Twenty watts, 1x12" Jensen speaker.

1949	$200	$225

Oliver

Ca.1966-late-1970s. Oliver Sound Company, Westbury, New York, founded by former Ampeg engineer, Jess Oliver, after he left Ampeg in '65. Tube amp designs were based upon Oliver's work at Ampeg. The Oliver Powerflex Amp is the best-known design, and featured an elevator platform that would lift the amp head out of the speaker cabinet.

Model G-150R Combo Amp

Two 6L6 power tubes, reverb, tremolo, Black Tolex with Black grille, Silver control panel, 40 watts, 1x15".

1970s	$500	$600

Model P-500 Combo Amp

All tube combo with 15" motorized amp chassis that rises out of tall lateral speaker cabinet as amp warms up.

1960s	$600	$700

Orbital Power Projector Amp

Late-1960s-early-1970s. Rotating speaker cabinet with horn, Leslie-like voice.

1970s	$600	$700

Sam Ash Oliver Amp

Late-1960s-early-1970s. Private branded for Sam Ash Music, about 30 watts using the extinct 2x7027A power tubes, Sam Ash script logo on front grille.

1960s	$175	$225

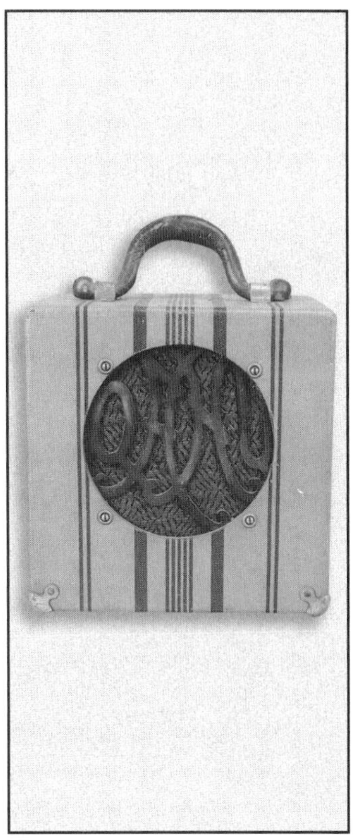

Oahu Tonemaster

'70s Oliver 6200R Uniflex

AMPS

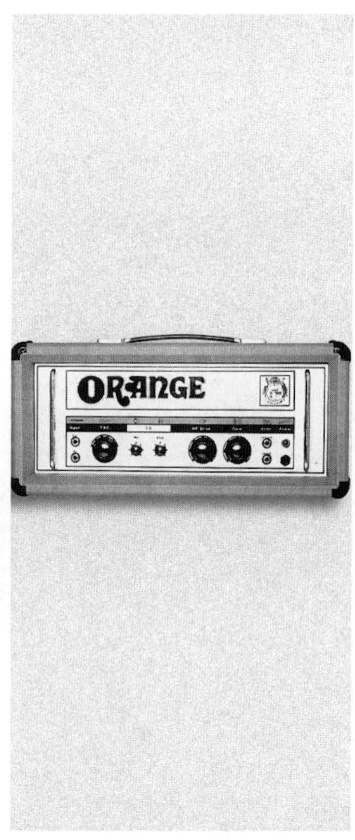

Orange Model 112

Park G10

MODEL YEAR	FEATURES	EXC. COND. LOW	HIGH

Orange

1969-1981, 1995-present. Orange amps and PAs were made in England by Cliff Cooper and Matthew Mathias. The Orange-colored amps were well-built and were used by many notable guitarists. Since '95, Cliff Cooper is once again making Orange amplifiers in England, with the exception of the small Crush Practice Combo amps, which are made in Korea.

Model OR-80 Combo Amp

1970s. About 60 watts, 2x12" combo.

1970s		$1,500	$1,700

Model OR 80-Watt Amp w/4x12 Bottom.

1970s. Eighty watts, 4x12" straight-front cab with Orange crest on grille, Orange vinyl and Light Orange grille.

1970s		$1,800	$2,000

Model OR-112 Graphic Overdrive Amp Head

One hundred twenty watts.

1978		$1,000	$1,200

Model OR-120 Graphic Head Amp and Half Stack

1970s. One hundred twenty watts, 4x12" straight front cab with Orange crest on grille, Orange vinyl and Light Orange grille.

1970s		$2,000	$2,200

Model OR-200 212 Twin Amp

1970s. One hundred twenty amps, 2x12" combo, Orange vinyl, dark grille, Orange crest on grille, reverb and vibrato, master volume.

1970s		$1,600	$1,800

Orpheum

Late-1950s-1960s. Student to medium level amps from New York's Maurice Lipsky Music.

Small/Mid-Size Amps

Late-1950s-1960s. Two 6V6 power tubes, U.S.-made, Jensen P12R 12" speaker, light cover with Gray Swirl grille.

1959		$175	$225

Ovation

1966-present. Kaman made few amps under the Ovation name. They offered a variety of amps under the KMD brandname from '85 to around '94. See Guitar section for more compnay info.

Little Dude Amp

1969-ca. 1971. 100 watt solidstate combo with 1x15" and horn, matching slave unit could also be had.

1970s		$200	$300

Overbuilt Amps

1999-present. Tube amps and combos built by Richard Seccombe in West Hills, California.

PAC-AMP (Magnatone)

Late-1950s-early-1960s. Private branded by Magnatone, often for accordion studios.

Model 280-A Amp

1961-1963. About 50 watts, 2x12" + 2x5", Brown leatherette, Light Brown grille, stereo vibrato, PAC-AMP nameplate logo.

1961-1963		$650	$850

PANaramic (Magnatone)

1961-1963. Private branded equivalent of '61-'63 Magnatone Brown leatherette series, large PANaramic logo combining PAN in capital letters and aramic in small alpha script. Many Magnatone private brands were associated with accordion companies or accordian teaching studios. The PANaramic amp was associated with the PANaramic accordion.

Model 260/262-style Amp

1961-1963. Thirty-five watts, 2x12", Gray vinyl and light grille, vibrato, large PANaramic logo.

1961-1963		$650	$850

Model 413-style Amp

1961-1963. Eighteen watts, 1x12", Black leatherette cover, Light Silver grille, vibrato, large PANaramic logo.

1961-1963		$400	$500

Model 440/460-style Amp

1961-1963. Twenty watts, 1x12", reverb and vibrato, reverb not generally included in an early-1960s 1x12" Magnatone amp, dark vinyl, dark cross-threaded grille, large PANaramic logo.

1961-1963		$500	$600

Park

1965-1982, 1992-2000. Park amps were made by Marshall from '65 to '82. In the '90s, Marshall revived the name for use on small solidstate amps imported from the Far East.

Model 75 Amp Head

Head amp, 50 watts, two KT88s, small-box plexi (later aluminum), Black Tolex.

1967	Plexi	$2,800	$4,300
1968	Plexi	$2,500	$4,000
1969	Plexi	$2,400	$3,900
1969-1971	Aluminum panel	$2,000	$3,000

Model 1206 50-Watt Amp Head

1981-1982. Fifty watts, based upon JCM 800 50-watt made at the same time period.

1981-1982		$600	$700

Model 1213 100-Watt Reverb Combo Amp

1970s. One hundred watts, 2x12", reverb, dark vinyl, light grille, Park logo on front with elongated P.

1970s		$1,100	$1,500

Model 1228 50-Watt Lead Head Amp

1970s. Fifty watts, based upon Marshall 50-watt made at the same time period.

1970s		$800	$1,400

MODEL YEAR	FEATURES	EXC. COND. LOW	HIGH

Paul Reed Smith

1985-present. In the late '80s, PRS offered two amp models. Only 350 amp units shipped. Includes HG-70 Head and HG-212 Combo. HG stands for Harmonic Generator, effectively a non-tube, solidstate amp.

HG-70 Amp Head

1989-1990. Seventy watts, reverb, effects loop, noise gate. Options include 150-watt circuitry and 4x12" straight and slant cabinets, Gray-Black.

1989		$400	$500

HG-212 Amp

1989-1990. Combo, 70 watts, 2x12", reverb, effects loop, noise gate. Options include 150-watt circuitry and 4x12" straight and slant cabinets,Gray-Black.

1989		$500	$600

Peavey

1965-present. Hartley Peavey's first products were guitar amps. He added guitars to the mix in '78. Headquartered in Meridan, Mississippi, Peavey has offered a huge variety of guitars, amps, and PAs over the years.

5150 212 Combo Amp

1995-present. Combo version of 5150 head, 60 watts, 2x12", large 5150 logo on front panel, small Peavey logo on lower right of grille.

1995		$600	$650
1996		$550	$650

5150 EVH Head and Cab Amp Set

1995-present. Half stack 5150 head and 4x12" cab, large 5150 logo on front of amp.

1995-1999	Cab only	$375	$400
1995-1999	Head and cab	$850	$900
1995-1999	Head only	$475	$500

Alphabass Amp

1988-1990. Rackmount all tube, 160 watts, EQ, includes 2x15" Black Widow or 2x12" Scorpion cabinet.

1988		$350	$450

Artist Amp

120 watts, 1x12", bright and normal channels, EQ, reverb, master volume.

1975		$300	$350

Artist 110 Amp

TransTubes, 10 watts.

1995		$100	$130

Artist VT Amp

1990s. Combo amp, 120 watts, 1x12".

1990s		$250	$300

Audition 30 Amp

1990s. Thirty watts, 1x12" combo amp, channel switching.

1990s		$125	$150

Audition Chorus Amp

Two 10-watt channels, 2x6", channel switching, post gain and normal gain controls.

1987		$100	$150

Audition Plus Amp

1980s. Solidstate, 20 watts, 1x10" compact practice amp, standard Peavey Black Tolex, Black grille and slant logo.

1980s	Black Tolex	$75	$100

Backstage Amp

1977-mid-1980s. Master gain control, 18 watts, 1x10", three-band EQ.

1977		$100	$150

Backstage 30 Amp

30 watts, 1x10".

1984		$100	$150

Backstage 110 Amp

Repackaged and revoiced in 1988, 65 watts, 1x10", Peavey SuperSat preamp circuitry, new power sections.

1988		$100	$150

Backstage Chorus 208 Amp

1990s. 150 watts, 2x8", reverb, channel switching.

1990s		$150	$225

Backstage Plus Amp

1980s. 35 watts, 1x10" combo, reverb, saturation effect.

1980s		$100	$150

Bandit 75 Amp

Redesigned and renamed Bandit 112 in 1988. Channel switching, 75 watts, 1x12", four-band EQ, reverb, post-effects loop, Superstat.

1987		$175	$250

Bandit 112 Amp

1988-2001. 80 watts, 1x12", active EQ circuit for lead channel, active controls.

1988		$175	$250

Basic 40 Amp

40 watts, 1x12".

1986		$125	$150

Basic 60 Amp

1988-1995. Solidstate combo amp, 60 watts, 1x12", four-band EQ, gain controls.

1988	Black	$175	$225

Bass Head Series 400

Solidstate, Black

1970	Black	$150	$200

Blazer 158 Amp

1995-present. 15 watts, 1x8", clean and distortion, now called the TransTube Blazer III.

1995-2000	Black Tolex	$85	$115

Bluesman Amp

1992. Tweed, 1x12" or 1x15".

1992	1x12"	$350	$400
1992	1x15"	$400	$450

Bravo 112 Amp

1988-1994. All tube reverb, 25 watts, 1x12", three-band EQ, two independent input channels.

1988		$200	$325

Classic 20 Amp

Small tube amp with 2xEL-84 power tubes, 1x10", Tweed cover.

1990s		$200	$250

Peavey Bandit 65

1977 Peavey Backstage 30

AMPS

Peavey Classic 50/212

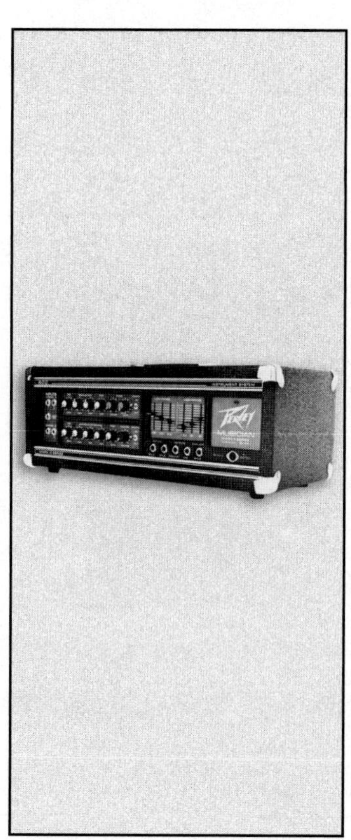

Peavey Musician (head)

MODEL YEAR	FEATURES	EXC. COND. LOW	HIGH

Classic 30 Amp

1994-present. Tweed, 30 watts, 1x12", EL84 tubes.

1994		$250	$300
1995		$250	$300

Classic 50/212 Amp

1990-present. Combo, 2x12", EL84 tubes, reverb, high-gain section.

1992		$450	$525

Classic 50/410 Amp

1990-present. Combo amp, 4x10", EL84 power, reverb, footswitchable high-gain mode.

1990s	Cab only	$275	$300
1994		$450	$525

Classic 120 Amp

1988-ca.1990. Tube, 120 watts.

1988		$375	$425

Classic Chorus 130 Amp

Combo amp, 2x12", channel switching, two 65-watt power amps, reverb, built-in chorus and effects loops.

1988		$200	$300

DECA/750 Amp

1989-ca.1990. Digital, two channels, 350 watts per channel, distortion, reverb, exciter, pitch shift, multi-EQ.

1989		$275	$325

Decade Amp

1970s. Practice amp, 10 watts, 1x8", runs on 12 volt or AC.

1970s		$65	$85

Delta Blues Amp

1995-present. 30 watts, tube combo, 4xEL84 tubes, 1x15", tremolo, large-panel-style cab, blond tweed.

1998		$500	$525

Deuce Amp

1975-1980s. 120 watts, tube amp, 2x12" or 4x10".

1975-1980		$300	$350

Deuce Head Amp

1975-1980s. Tube head, 120 watts.

1975-1980		$200	$225

Encore 65 Amp

1990s. Compact solidstate amp, 1x12", reverb, channel switching.

1990s		$175	$250

Envoy 110 Amp

1988-2001. Solidstate, 40 watts, 1x10", patent-applied-for circuitry, TransTubes.

1988		$125	$175

Heritage VTX Amp

1980s. 130 watts, four 6L6s, solidstate preamp, 2x12" combo.

1980s		$200	$250

Jazz Classic Amp

Solidstate, 210 watts, 1x15", electronic channel switching, six-spring reverb.

1985		$250	$350

KB-100 Amp

Keyboard amp, 1x15".

1988		$225	$325

MODEL YEAR	FEATURES	EXC. COND. LOW	HIGH

LTD Amp

1975-1980s. Solidstate, 200 watts, 1x12" Altec or 1x15" JBL.

1975		$225	$300

MegaBass Amp

Rackmount preamp/power amp, 200 watts per twp channels, solidstate, EQ, effects loop, chorus.

1986		$300	$400

Minx 110 Bass Amp

1988-present. Solidstate, 35 watts RMS, 1x10" heavy duty speaker.

1988		$100	$150

Musician Amp Head

Tube head, 200 watts.

1975		$200	$250

Pacer Amp

1977-1980s. Master volume, 45 watts, 1x12", three-band EQ.

1977		$150	$175

ProBass 1000 Amp

Rackmount, effects loops, preamp, EQ, crossover, headphone output.

1986		$200	$275

Rage/Rage 158 Amp

1980s-1990s. Compact practice amp, 15 watts, 1x8".

1987		$75	$125

Reno 400 Amp

Solidstate, 200 watts, 1x15" with horn, four-band EQ.

1983		$225	$300

Renown 112 Amp

1989-1994. Crunch and lead SuperSat, 160 watts, 1x12", master volume, digital reverb, EQ.

1989		$250	$350

Renown 212 Amp

1989-1994. Crunch and lead SuperSat, 160 watts, 2x12", master volume, digital reverb, EQ.

1989		$400	$300

Renown 400 Amp

Combo, 200 watts, 2x12", channel switching, Hammond reverb, pre- and post-gain controls.

1985		$300	$400

Session 500 Amp

1980s. 250 watts, 1x15", standard Black with metal panels appearance.

1986		$400	$500

Special 112 Amp

160 watts, 1x12", channel-switching, effects loops, EQ. In 1988, available in wedge-shaped enclosures slanted back 30 degrees.

1988		$200	$250

Studio Pro 112 Amp

Repackaged and revoiced in 1988. Solidstate, 65 watts, 1x12", Peavey SuperSat preamp circuitry, new power sections

1988		$150	$200

TKO-115 Bass Amp

1985		$250	$350

MODEL YEAR	FEATURES	EXC. COND. LOW	HIGH

TKO-75 Bass Amp

1987-1995. Solidstate, 75 watts, 1x15", EQ, compression and pre-/post-gain controls.

1987-1995	$225	$275

TNT-150 Bass Amp

Solidstate, 150 watts, 1x15", EQ, compression, chorus. In 1988, available in wedge-shaped enclosures slanted 30 degrees.

1980s	$300	$400

Triumph 60 Amp

Tube head, effects loop, reverb, 60 watts, 1x12", multi-stage gain.

1987	$200	$250

Triumph 120 Amp

Tube, 120 watts, 1x12", three gain blocks in preamp, low-level post-effects loop, built-in reverb.

1989-1990	$250	$300

Vegas 400 Amp

1980s. 210 watts, 1x15", reverb, compression feature, parametric equalizer.

1980s	$500	$700

Penn

1994-present. Tube amps, combos, and cabinets built by Billy Penn, originally in Colts Neck, New Jersey, currently in Long Branch, New Jersey.

Pignose

1972-present. Made in the U.S. Pignose Industries was started by people associated with the band Chicago, including guitarist Terry Kath, with help from designers Wayne Kimball and Richard Erlund.

30/60 Amp

1978-ca.1987. Solidstate, 30 watts, 1x10", master volume.

1978-1987	$125	$175

60R Studio Reverb Amp

Solidstate, 30 watts.

1980	$150	$200

7-100 Practice Amp

1972-present. The "original Pignose," 7"x5"x3" battery-powered portable amplifier, 1x5".

1972-1999	$50	$70

Polytone

1960s-present. Made in North Hollywood, California, Polytone offers compact combo amps, heads, and cabinets and a pickup system for acoustic bass.

Brute IV Amp

1994-present. 110 watts, 1x15", EQ, reverb, overdrive.

1990s	$275	$375

RMS Pro Series Bass Amp

Rackmount, 240 watts, two power amps, two preamps, crossover for bi-amping.

1985	$375	$450

MODEL YEAR	FEATURES	EXC. COND. LOW	HIGH

Premier

Ca.1938-ca.1975. Produced by Peter Sorkin Music Company in Manhattan. First radio-sized amplifiers introduced by '38. After World War II, established Multivox subsidiary to manufacture amplifiers ca. '46. By mid-'50s at least, the amps featured lyre grilles. Dark brown/light tan amp covering by '60. By '64 amps covered in brown woodgrain and light tan. Multivox amps were made until around '84.

B-160 Club Bass Amp

1960s. Fifteen to twenty amps, 1x12" Jensen speaker, 1960s two-tone Brown styling, 6v6 tubes.

1963-1968	$350	$400

Model 50 Combo Amp

1940s-1960s. Four to five watts, 1x8" similar to Fender Champ circuit with more of a vertical cab.

1957	$325	$375

Model 76 Combo Amp

1950s. Suitcase latchable cabinet that opens out into two wedges, Premier 76 logo on amp control panel, two-tone Brown, lyre grille, 1x12".

1950s	$450	$550

Model 88N Combo Amp

1950s-early-1960s. Rectangular suitcase cabiinet, two-tone Tan and Brown, Premier and lyre logo, 25 watts, 1x12".

1950s	$450	$550
1960s	$450	$550

Model 100R Amp

Combo amp, 1x12", reverb and tremolo.

1968	$400	$500

Twin 8 Amp

1960s. 20 watts, 2x8", tremolo, reverb.

1964-1966	$500	$600

Twin 12 T-12R Amp

Late-1950. Early reverb amp with tremolo, 2x12", rectangular cabinet typical of twin 12 amps (Dano and Fender), brown cover.

1957	$500	$700

Quantum

1980s. Economy amps distributed by DME, Indianapolis, Indiana.

Q Terminator Economy Amps

1980s. Economy solidstate amps ranging from 12 to 25 watts and 1x6" to 1x12".

1980s	$75	$125

Randall

1960s-present. Randall Instruments was originally out of California and is now a division of Washburn. They have offered a range of combo amps, heads and cabinets over the years.

Commander II Bass Amp

Solidstate, 100 watts, 2x12", reverb, tremolo.

1980-1985	$225	$300

Commander-HG Amp

Two footswitch selectable channels, 2x12".

1984	$250	$325

1988 Peavey Special 112

Randall RG-200 ES

AMPS

AMPS

Reeves

Reverend Hellhound

MODEL YEAR	FEATURES	EXC. COND. LOW	HIGH

DAC-15 Preamp

Fifteen watts, 1x8", EQ, preamp, master volume, Clipper distortion controls.

1986	$75	$125

R112C Extension Cab

1980s. Open back extension cabinet 1x12", in and out, Black Tolex, Black grille.

1980s	$200	$225

RB-125 Bass Combo Amp

One 15" speaker.

1989	$275	$325

RC-280 Amp

Stereo chorus, 100 watts per channel, 2x12", bright, sustain/boost, effects loop.

1989	$175	$300

RG-15X Amp

1990s. Compact practice amp, 15 watts, 1x8", Black Tolex, Black grille.

1990s	$100	$125

RG-100 HT Amp

Solidstate, 120 watts, FET preamp circuitry, reverb, two channels, rack-mount, effects loop.

1986	$250	$300

RG-300 Amp Head

1980s. RG-300 logo on front, Black Tolex, Black grille.

1980s	$250	$300

RG-2000 Bass Bi-Amp

One hundred fifty watts into four ohms/low-frequency 370 watts, EQ, compressor, effects loops.

1990	$225	$300

RGP-1000 Preamp

Stereo chorus preamp, presence, reverb, effects loops, channel-switching.

1989	$150	$225

RGT-100 Amp

Late-1980s. Tube amp, 1x12", Gray Tolex combo with Black metal grille.

1988	$225	$275

Sustainer 140 Amp

Introduced in 1978 as part of new Professional Series, single-channel version of Switchmaster 150, 1x12" combo.

1979	$200	$275

Switchmaster 150 Amp

Introduced in 1978. Pre-set channel switching (thus the name) from totally independent foot switchable channels, dark cover, dark grille, 120 watts, 1x12" combo.

1978	$225	$300

Red Bear

1994-1997. Tube amps designed by Sergei Novikov and built in St. Petersburg, Russia. Red Bear amps were distributed in the U.S. under a joint project between Gibson and Novik, Ltd. Novik stills builds amps under other brandnames.

MK 60 Lead Tube Amp

1990s. Amp with 4x12" half stack, Red Bear logo on amp and cab.

1992	$750	$850

Reeves Amplification

2002-present. Started by Bill Jansen, Reeves builds tube amps, combos, and cabinets based on the classic British designs of Dan Reeves.

Reverend

1996-present. Joe Naylor started building amps under the Naylor brand in '94. In '96 he left Naylor to build guitars under the Reverend brand. In 2001, Reverend started offering tube amps, combos, and cabinets built in Warren, Michigan, that Naylor co-designed with Dennis Kager.

Rickenbacker

1931-present. Rickenbacker made amps from the beginning of the company up to the late '80s. Rickenbacker had many different models, from the small early models that were usually sold as a guitar/amp set, to the large, vey cool, Transonic. See Guitar section for more company info.

Electro-Student Amp

Late-1940s. Typical late-'40s vertical combo cabinet, 1x12" speaker, lower power using 5 tubes, bottom mounted chassis, dark gray leatherette cover.

1948-1949	$225	$250

Model M-8 Amp

Gray, 1x8".

1950s	$300	$350
1960s	$275	$325

Professional Model 200-A Amp

1938	$250	$350

RB30 Amp

1986. Bass combo amp, 30 watts, tilted control panel, 1x12".

1986	$100	$150

RB60 Amp

1986. Bass combo amp, 60 watts, tilted control panel, 1x15".

1986	$200	$250

RB120 Amp

1986. Bass combo amp, 120 watts, tilted control panel, 1x15".

1986	$200	$275

Supersonic Model B-16

Four 10" speakers, Gray cover.

1964	$600	$800

TR14 Amp

Solidstate, 1x10", reverb, distortion.

1982	$100	$125

TR75G Amp

1978-ca.1982. Seventy-five watts, 2x12", two channels.

1978-1982	$125	$175

TR75SG Amp

1978-ca.1983. One 10" and one 15" speakers.

1978-1982	$175	$250

MODEL YEAR | FEATURES | EXC. COND. LOW | HIGH

TR100G Amp

1978-ca.1982. Solidstate, 100 watts with 4x12", two channels.

1978 $175 $275

Transonic Amp

1967-1970. Trapezoid shape, 2x12", head and cabinet, Rick-O-Select.

1967-1970 $800 $1,200

Rivera

1985-present. Amp designer and builder Paul Rivera modded and designed amps for other companies before starting his own line in California. He offers heads, combos, and cabinets.

Clubster 40 Amp

2000s. Forty watts, 1x12" combo, Burgundy Tolex, light grille.

2000-2001 $700 $950

Fandango R-55 212 Combo Amp

Fifty watts, 2x12" tube amp.

1990s $1,200 $1,400

Knuckle Head 55 Amp

1990s. Fifty-five watts, head amp.

1990s $550 $750

Los Lobottom Amp

1997-present. Three hundred watts, 12" subwoofer, 1x12".

1997-1999 $500 $700

M-60 112 Combo Amp

1992-present. Sixty watts, 1x12".

1990s $600 $800

M-100 212 Combo Amp

1990s. One hundred watts, 2x12" combo.

1990s $700 $900

M-100 Head Amp

1990s. One hundred watts, head amp.

1990s $600 $800

Quiana R-55 112 Combo Amp

Combo amp, 55 watts, 1x12".

1990s $900 $1,200

R-30 112 Combo Amp

1990s. Thirty watts, 1x12", compact cab, Black Tolex cover, Gray-Black grille.

1990s $500 $700

R-100 212 Combo Amp

One hundred watts, 2x12".

1990s $700 $900

Supreme R-55 112 Combo Amp

Tube amp, 55 watts, 1x12".

1990s $1,000 $1,200

TBR-1 Amp

1986-1990s. First Rivera production model, rackmount, 60 watts.

1990s $600 $800

Roccaforte Amps

1993-present Tube amps, combos, and cabinets built by Doug Roccaforte in San Clemente, California.

MODEL YEAR | FEATURES | EXC. COND. LOW | HIGH

Rodgers

1993-present. Custom tube amps and cabinets built by Larry Rodgers in Naples, Florida.

Roland

Japan's Roland Corporation's products include amplifiers and keyboards and, under the Boss brand, effects.

AC-100 Amp

1995-present. Acoustic amp, 50 watts, 1x12" and 2x5", chorus, reverb, EQ, effects loop.

1995 $200 $250

Bolt 60 Amp

Solidstate/tube, 1x12".

1984 $200 $250

Cube 20 Amp

1978-1980s. Portable, 1x8", normal and overdrive channels, headphone jack.

1978 $150 $200

Cube 40 Amp

1978-1980s. Portable, 1x10", normal and overdrive channels, headphone jack, effects send and receive and lines in/out.

1978 $100 $200

Cube 60 Amp

1978-1980s. Normal and overdrive channels.

1979 $250 $300

Cube 60B Bass Amp

1978-1980s. One speaker, normal and overdrive channels, headphone jack.

1979 $200 $300

Cube 100 Amp

Late-1970s-early-1980s. Solidstate, 100 watts, 1x12", Orange cover, large Cube-100 logo on back chassis, rear-mounted controls.

1980s $250 $350

JC-50 Jazz Chorus Amp

1980s. Fifty watts, 1x12".

1980s $250 $350

JC-55 Jazz Chorus Amp

Stereo amp, 25 watts per side, 2x8", stereo chorus, preamp section has treble, middle and bass controls and distortion circuit and reverb.

1986 $250 $350

JC-77 Jazz Chorus Amp

1990s. One hundred twenty watts, 2x12".

1990s $300 $400

JC-120 Jazz Chorus Amp

Two channels, 120 watts, 2x12", chorus, vibrato.

1987-1990 $350 $450

Spirit 30 Amp

1980s. Compact practice amp, 30 watts, 1x12", Orange Spirit 30 logo on front panel, Black Tolex, light grille.

1980s $100 $200

Sam Ash

1960s-1970s. Sam Ash Music was founded by a young Sam Ash (formerly Ashkynase - an Austro-Hungarian name) in 1924. Ash's first store

1996 Roland BC-60

Roland Spirit 10A

MODEL YEAR	FEATURES	EXC. COND. LOW	HIGH

was in Brooklyn and by '66 there were about four Ash stores. During this time Ash Music private branded their own amp line which was built by Jess Oliver of Oliver Amps and based upon Oliver's Ampeg designs.

Sam Ash Oliver Amp Head

Late-1960s-early-1970s. Private branded for Sam Ash Music, about 30 watts using the extinct 2x7027A power tubes, Sam Ash script logo on front grille.

1960s $200 $300

Selmer

Savage

Tube amps and combos built by Savage Audio in Burnsville, Minnesota.

Selmer

1960s. The Selmer UK distributor offered mid- to high-level amps.

Mark 2 Treble and Bass Head Amp

1960s. About 30 watts (2xEL34s), requires power line transformer for U.S. use, large Selmer logo on grille.

1960s $500 $700

Seymour Duncan

Pickup maker Seymour Duncan, located in Santa Barbara, California, offered a line of amps from around '84 to '95.

84-40 Amp

Tube combo amp, 40 watts, two switchable channels, 1x12" or 2x10", gain boost.

1980s 1x12" $350 $425

Bass 300 x 2 Amp

Solidstate, two channels (300 watts or 600 watts), EQ, contour boost switches, effects loop, electronic speaker protection circuitry.

1986 $300 $400

Bass 400 Amp

Solidstate, 400 watts, EQ section, contour boost, post-preamp balanced line output, effects loop, electronic speaker protection circuitry.

1986 $300 $350

Convertible 100 Amp

Solidstate, 60 watts, effects loop, Accutronics spring reverb, EQ.

1986 $350 $425

Convertible 2000 Amp

Solidstate, 100 watts, holds five interchangeable modules, 1x12", two switchable channels.

1984 $650 $775
1990 $650 $775

KTG-2965 Stereo Amp

1989-1993. Part of the King Tone Generator Series. Dual channels with 75 watts per channel.

1989 $200 $225

Silvertone Model 1482

Sho-Bud

Distributed by Kustom/Gretsch in the 1980s. Models include D-15 Model 7838, S-15 Model 7836, Twin Tube Model 7834, and Twin Trans Model 7832.

MODEL YEAR	FEATURES	EXC. COND. LOW	HIGH

D-15 Model 7838 Amp

Solidstate, 100 watts. D-15 is dual channels, S-15 is single channel, both with 1x15" JBL speaker.

1980s $200 $300

Siegmund Guitars & Amplifiers

1993-present. Chris Siegmund founded the company in Seattle, moving it to Austin, Texas for '95-'97, and is currently located in Los Angeles. Siegmund offers handmade tube amps and preamp pedals.

Silvertone

1941-ca. 1970, present. Brandname used by Sears. All Silvertone amps were supplied by American companies up to around '66. See Guitar section for more company info.

Model 100 Amp

Mid-late-1960s. Solidstate, piggyback amp and 2x12" cabinet with Gold-label Jensen speakers.

1960s $300 $400

Model 150 Amp

Mid-late-1960s. Solidstate, piggyback amp and 6x10" cabinet with Gold-label Jensen speakers.

1960s $450 $500

Model 1331 Amp

Ca.1954-ca.1957. Danelectro-made, luggage Tweed, rounded front, a whole series made this style.

1955 Tweed $250 $350

Model 1336 (early Twin Twelve) Amp

Ca.1954-ca.1957. Danelectro-made twin-twelve, luggage tweed, rounded front.

1954-1957 $500 $700

Model 1340 (Student Model) Amp

Early-1950s. Small student model, Tan cover, Brown grille with Silvertone logo, Brown sides.

1951 $150 $175

Model 1346 (Twin Twelve) Amp

Ca.1958-ca.1961. Danelectro-made with Brown control panel, 2x12", 4x6L6 power, vibrato, leather handle, Silvertone logo on front bottom of cabinet, Tan smooth leatherette cover, two separate speaker baffle openings.

1958-1961 $500 $700

Model 1391 Amp

1950s. Blond-Tan Tweed-cloth cover, Brown grille, single small speaker, leather handle.

1950s $150 $225

Model 1392 Amp

1950s. Student amp with tremolo, five control knobs, Brown cover and Brown grille.

1950s $125 $175

Model 1432 Amp

Late-1950s. One 12" speaker, low- to mid-power with 2x6L6, late-'50s overhanging top style cabinet.

1959 $150 $200

MODEL YEAR	FEATURES	EXC. COND. LOW	HIGH

Model 1433 Combo Amp

Late-1950s. Tube amp, mid-level 2x6L6 power, 1x15", Gray cover cabinet with pronounced overhanging top, light colored grille.

1959		$500	$550

Model 1451 Amp

Late-1950s. Three-four watts, three tubes, 1x6" or 1x8" speaker, Brown Sparkle cover, Wheat grille, by Danelectro.

1959	1x6"	$125	$150

Model 1457 Amp-In-Case (case only)

1960s. The amp-in-case with the electric Silvertone guitar, this is the higher powered model with tremolo and higher quality speaker.

1965	Amp only (no guitar)	$100	$150

Model 1459 Amp

1960s. Four watts, 1x6" or 1x8".

1960s		$100	$125

Model 1463 Bass 35 Amp

1960s. Solidstate, 2x12", piggyback.

1960s		$250	$300

Model 1465 Head Amp

Mid-1960s. Rectangular amp head, solidstate, 50 watts, Spotted Gray cover, used with Twin 12 bottom.

1960s		$200	$300

Model 1471 Amp

One 8" speaker.

1960s		$125	$175

Model 1472 Amp

1960s. 15-18 watts, 2x6V6 tubes provide mid-level power, 1x12", front controls mounted vertically on front right side, dark cover with silver grille, large stationary handle, tremolo.

1962-1963		$150	$200

Model 1474 Amp

1960s. Mid-power, mid-level, dual speakers, tube combo amp, Gray Tolex, Gray grille.

1960s		$400	$500

Model 1481 Amp

1960s. Low power, student amp, 1x6", Gray cover, light grille, two controls.

1960s		$125	$150

Model 1482 Amp

1960s. Lower power, 1x12" combo, Gray Tolex, Silver grille, control panel mounted on right side vertically, tremolo.

1960s		$175	$250

Model 1483 Piggyback Amp

1960s. Mid-power, 1x15" piggyback tube amp, Gray Tolex and Gray grille.

1960s		$400	$575

Model 1484 Twin Twelve Amp

1960s. Medium power, 2x12" piggyback tube amp, classic Silvertone colors–Gray cover with light grille.

1966		$450	$600

SMF (Sonic Machine Factory)

2002-present. Tube amps and cabinets designed by Mark Sampson (Matchless, Bad Cat) and Rick Hamel (SIB effects) and built in California.

Smicz Amplification

Tube combos and extenstion cabinets built by Bob Smicz in Bristol, Connecticut.

Soldano

1987-present. Made in Seattle by amp builder Mike Soldano, the company offers a range of all-tube combo amps, heads and cabinets.

Astroverb 16 Combo Amp

1990s. Combo amp, 20 watts, 1x12", reverb.

1998	Snakeskin cover	$600	$650

Atomic 212 Amp

1990s	.	$450	$650

Decatone Amp

Late-1990s-2000s. Combo amp with rear mounted controls.

1999	No footswitch	$1,700	$1,800
1999	With Decatrol footswitch	$2,100	$2,300

Lucky 13 Combo Amp

1990s. One hundred watts, 2x12" combo.

1990s		$950	$1,050

SLO-100 Super Lead Overdrive 100-Watt Amp

1987-present. First production model, super lead overdrive, 100 watts.

1990s	Snakeskin cover	$1,300	$1,500

Songworks Systems

See listing under Little Lanilei.

Sonny Jr.

1996-present. Harmonica amplifiers built by harmonica player Sonny Jr. in conjunction with Cotton Amps in Tolland, Ct.

Sound City

Made in England from the late-'60s to the late-'70s, the tube Sound City amps were Marshall-looking heads and separate cabinets. They were imported, for a time, into the U.S. by Gretsch.

50-Watt Head Amp

Late-1960s-late-1970s. Head amp, labeled 50 Plus or 50 R.

1960s		$400	$500
1970s		$400	$500

120-Watt Head Amp

Early-late-1970s. The 120-watt head replaced the late-1960s 100-watt model.

1970s		$500	$550

Concord Combo Amp

Eighty watts, 2x12" Fane speakers, Cream, basketweave grille.

1968	Cream	$450	$500

L-80 Cabinet

1970s. Four by ten inch cabinet.

1970s		$300	$350

X-60 Cabinet

1970s. Two 12" speaker cabinet.

1970s		$350	$400

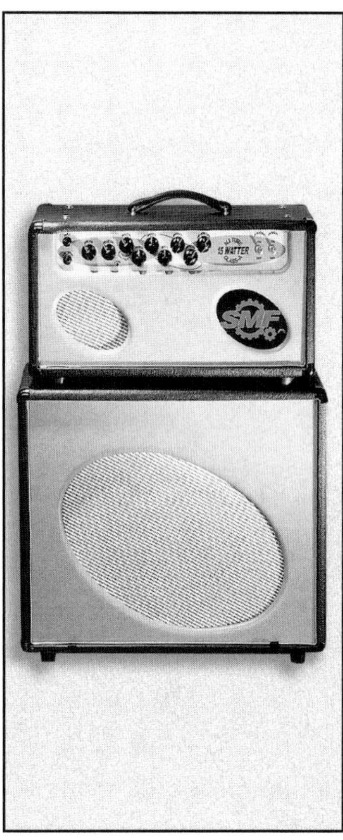

SMF 15 Watter (stack)

Soldano Lucky 13

AMPS

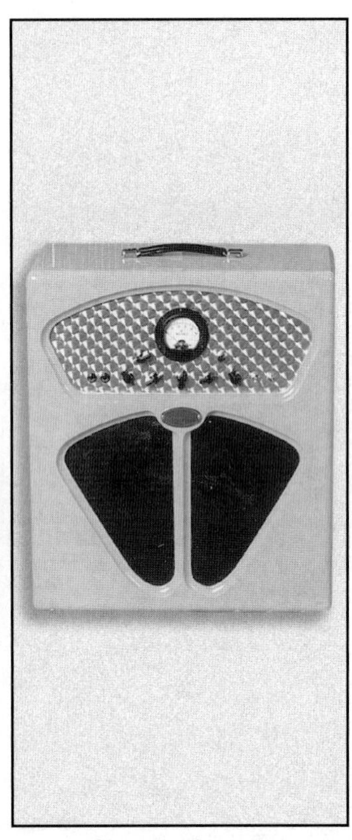

Speester Custom

Standel Custom

MODEL YEAR	FEATURES	EXC. COND. LOW	HIGH

Sound Electronics

Sound Electronics Corporation introduced a line of amplifiers in '65 that were manufactured in Long Island. Six models were initially offered, all with tube preamps and solidstate power sections. Their catalog did not list power wattages but did list features and speaker configurations. The initial models had dark vinyl-style covers and sparkling silver grille cloth. The amps were combos with the large models having vertical cabinets, silver script 'Sound' logo on upper left of grille (same placement as Fender blackface amps). The larger models used JBL D120F and D130F speakers. Stand alone extension speakers were also available.

Various Model Amps

Mid-1960s. Includes X-101, X-101R, X-202 Bass/Organ, X-404 Bass and Organ, X-505R amps, hi-fi chassis often using 7868 power tubes.

1965	$250	$350

Sovtek

1992-present. Sovtek amps are products of Mike Matthews of Electro-Harmonix fame and his New Sensor Corporation. The guitar and bass amps and cabinets are made in Russia.

Mig 50 Head Amp

1994-present. Tube head, 50 watts.

1990s	$300	$350

Mig 60 Head Amp

1994-2001. Tube head, 60 watts, point-to-point wiring.

1990s	$350	$400

Mig 100 Head Amp

1990s. One hundred watts, tube head.

1990s	$400	$450

Mig 100B Head Amp

1996-present. Bass tube head, 100 watts.

1990s	$350	$400

Speedster

1995-2000. Tube combos designed by Bishop Cochran with looks inspired by dashboards of classic autos, and made in Gig Harbor, Washington.

Standel

1952-1974, 1997-present. Bob Crooks started custom building amps part time in '52, going into fulltime standard model production in '58 in Temple City, CA. In '61 Standel started distributing guitars under their own brand and others (see Guitar section for more instrument details). By late '63 or '64, Standel had introduced solidstate amps, two years before Fender and Ampeg introduced their solidstate models. In '67 Standel moved to a new, larger facility in El Monte, California. In '73 Chicago Musical Instruments (CMI), which owned Gibson at the time, bought the company and built amps in El Monte until '74. In '97 the Standel name was revived (see next listing).

A-30 B Artist 30 Bass Amp

1964-early-1970s. Artist Series, the original Standel solidstate series, 80 watts, 2x15".

1964-1969	$300	$500

A-30 G Artist 30 Guitar Amp

1964-early-1970s. Artist Series, the original Standel solidstate series, 80 watts, 2x15".

1964-1969	$350	$550
1970s	$350	$550

A-48 G Artist 48 Guitar Amp

1964-early-1970s. Artist Series, the original Standel solidstate series, 80 watts, 4x12".

1964-1969	$450	$700
1970s	$450	$700

A-60 B Artist 60 Bass Amp

1964-early-1970s. Artist Series, the original Standel solidstate series, 160 watts, 4x15".

1964-1969	$400	$650
1970s	$400	$650

A-60 G Artist 60 Guitar Amp

1964-early-1970s. Artist Series, the original Standel solidstate series, 160 watts, 4x15".

1964-1969	$450	$700
1970s	$450	$700

A-96 G Artist 96 Guitar Amp

1964-early-1970s. Artist Series, the original Standel solidstate series, 160 watts, 8x12".

1964-1969	$500	$900
1970s	$500	$900

Model 10L8/15L12/25L15

1953-1958. Early custom made tube amps made by Bob Crooks in his garage, padded naugahyde cabinet with varying options and colors. There are a limited number of these amps, and brand knowledge is also limited, therefore there is a wide value range. Legend has it that the early Standel amps made Leo Fender re-think and introduce even more powerful amps.

1953-1958	$1,000	$2,000

S-10 Studio 10 Amp

Late-1960s-1970s. Studio Slim Line Series, solidstate, 30 watts, 1x10", dark vinyl, dark grille.

1970s	$300	$400

S-50 Studio 50 Amp

Late-1963 or early-1964-late-1960s. Sixty watts, Gray Tolex, Gray grille, piggyback, not listed in 1969 Standel catalog.

1964	$450	$700

Standel (new Standel est. 1997)

1997-present. Founded by Danny McKinney who, with the help of original Standel founder Bob Crooks and Frank Garlock (PR man for first Standel), set about reissuing some of the early models.

MODEL YEAR	FEATURES	EXC. COND. LOW	HIGH

Starlite

Starlite was a budget brand made and sold by Magnatone. See Magnatone for listings.

Stinger

Budget line imported by Martin.

Sunn

1965-present. Started in Oregon by brothers Conrad and Norm Sundhold (Norm was the bass player for the Kingsman). Sunn introduced powerful amps and extra heavy duty bottoms and was soon popular with many major rock acts. Norm sold his interest to Conrad in the late-'60s. Conrad later sold the company to the Hartzell Corporation of Minnesota. Fender Musical Instruments acquired the brand in '84 shortly after parting ways with CBS and resurrected the brand a few years later.

200S/215B Amp & Cab Set

Late-1960s. Sixty watts, 2x6550 power tubes, large verticle cab with 2x15" speakers.

1969 $600 $800

Alpha 115 Amp

1980s. MOS-FET preamp section, 1x15", clean and overdrive.

1980s $150 $200

Alpha 212 R Amp

1980s. MOS-FET preamp section, 2x12", reverb.

1980s $150 $200

Concert 215S Bass Amp Set

1970s. Solidstate head, 200 watts, Model 215S tall vertical cabinet with 2x12" Sunn label speakers, dark vinyl cover, Silver Sparkle grille.

1970s $300 $400

Concert Bass Head Amp

1970s. Solidstate, 200 watts.

1970s $150 $200

Concert Lead 610S Amp Set

1970s. Solidstate, 200 watts, 6x10" piggyback, reverb and built-in distortion.

1970s $350 $400

Model T Head Amp

Early-1970s.

1970s $500 $700

Model T Head Amp and Cab

1990s. Head has 100 watts, 4x12" cab, reissue model.

1990s $800 $900

Model T Head Amp Reissue

1990s. Reissue of 1960s Model T, see through amp grille displays tubes, dark vinyl cover.

1990s $500 $600

SB-200 Amp

Introduced in 1985. Two hundred watts, 1x15", four-band equalizer, master volume, compressor.

1985 $225 $300

Sceptre Head Amp

1968-1970s. Head amp, 60 watts, 6550 power tubes, tremolo, reverb.

1972 $200 $250

Solarus Amp

1967-1970s. Tube amp (EL-34s), 40 watts (upgraded to 60 watts in 1969), 2x12", reverb, tremolo.

1970s $350 $500

Sonoro Head Amp

Early-1970s. Sixty watts, 2x6550 power tubes.

1970s $400 $500

SPL 7250 Amp

Dual channels, 250 watts per channel, forced air cooling, switch-selectable peak compressor with LEDs.

1989 $225 $300

Supertone

1914-1941. Supertone was a brandname used by Sears for their musical instruments. In the '40s Sears started using the Silvertone name on those products. Amps were made by other companies. See Guitar section for more company info.

Amp

1930s $100 $200

Supro

1935-1968. Supro was a budget brand of the National Dobro Company, made by Valco in Chicago. See Guitar section for more company details.

Bantam 1611S Amp

1961-1964. Four watts, three tubes, 1x 8" Jensen, petite, Spanish Ivory fabric cover, Gold weave saran wrap grille.

1961-1964 $225 $275

Combo 1696T Amp

1961-1964. Twenty-four watts, six tubes, 1x15" Jensen, Rhino-Hide covering in Black and White, light grille, tremolo.

1961-1964 $300 $350

Comet 1610B Amp

1957-1959. Grey Rhino Hide, 1x10".

1957-1959 $225 $275

Dual-Tone S6424T Amp

1964-1965. Seventeen watts, six tubes, 1x12" Jensen, restyled in 1964, tremolo, Trinidad Blue vinyl fabric cover, light color grille.

1964-1965 $350 $375

Royal Reverb 1650TR Amp

1963-1964. Seventeen watts, 15 tubes, 2x10" Jensens, catalog says "authentic tremolo and magic-reverberation."

1963-1964 $425 $475

Super 1606S Amp

1961-1964. Four point five watts, three tubes, 1x8", Black and White fabric cover, light saran wrap grille.

1966-1964 $250 $300

Thunderbolt S6420(B) Bass Amp

1964-1967. Thirty-five watts, 1x15" Jensen, introduced in the 1964 catalog as a "no frills - no fancy extra circuits" amp.

1964-1967 $400 $500

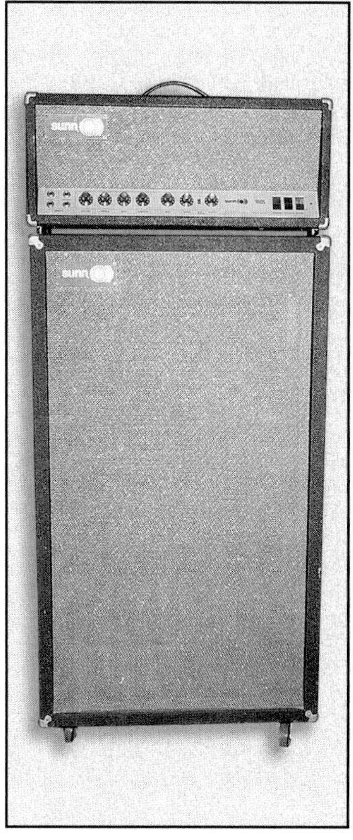

1969 Sunn 100S

1966 Supro Thunderbolt

AMPS

1964 Supro Tremo-Verb

Teisco Checkmate 17

MODEL YEAR	FEATURES	EXC. COND. LOW	HIGH

Thunderbolt S6920 Amp

1967-1968. Redesign circuit replaced S6420B.

1967-1968		$300	$400

Tremo-Verb S6422 TR Amp

1964-1965. Lower power using four 12AX7 tubes, one 5Y3GT tube, one 6V6 tube (six tubes), 1x10", tremolo and reverb.

1964-1965		$400	$450

Trojan Tremolo 1616T/S6416T Amp

1961-1966. Five watts, four tubes, 1x11"x6" oval (generally Rolla) speaker, 1961-1964 Black and White fabric cover and saran wrap grille, 1964-1966 new larger cab with vinyl cover and light grille.

1961-1966		$250	$300

Vibra-Verb S6498VR Amp

1964-1965. "Supro's finest amplifier", two 35-watt channels, 1x15" and 1x10" Jensens, vibrato and reverb.

1964-1965		$525	$625

SWR Sound

1984-present. Founded by Steve W. Rabe in 1984, with an initial product focus on bass amplifiers. Fender Musical Instruments Corp. acquired SWR in June, 2003.

Baby Blue Studio Reverence Bass System

Combo, all tube preamp, 150 watts solidstate power amp, 2x8", one 5" cone tweeter, gain, master volume, EQ, effects-blend.

1989		$400	$500

Basic Black Amp

1990s. Solidstate, 100 watts, 1x12", Basic Black block logo on front, Black Tolex, Black metal grille.

1990s		$450	$500

Goliath Junior Amp

High-end driver, 2x10", 300 watts, can function as a high-fidelity monitor or as part of a bi-amp system.

1988		$400	$500

Goliath Junior III Cab

1990s. Two 10" speakers, Black Tolex, Black metal grille.

1990s		$400	$450

Studio 200 Bass Amp

1990s.

1990s		$400	$450

Working Man 15 Bass Amp

1990s. Combo amp with 1x15", Black Tolex, Black metal grille.

1990s		$450	$500

Takt

Late-1960s. Made in Japan, tube and solidstate models.

GA Series Amps

1968. GA-9 (two inputs and five controls, three tubes), GA-10, GA-11, GA-12, GA-14, GA-15.

1968	GA-14/GA-15	$40	$50
1968	GA-9 through GA-12	$25	$35

MODEL YEAR	FEATURES	EXC. COND. LOW	HIGH

Teisco

1946-1974, 1994-present. Japanese brand first imported into the U.S. around '63. Teisco offered both tube and solidstate amps. See Guitar section for more company info.

Checkmate 50 Amp

Late-1950s-early-1960s. Fifty watts using two 6L6 power tubes, 2x12" open back cab, reverb and tremolo, piggyback, similar looking to Silvertone Twin 12 piggyback of the same era, Gray Tolex cover, Light Gray grille, Teisco slant logo on cab.

1960s		$400	$450

Checkmate CM-15 Amp

Late-1960s. Tubes, 15 watts.

1968		$75	$100

Checkmate CM-20 Amp

Late-1960s. Tubes, 20 watts.

1968		$100	$125

Checkmate CM-25 Amp

Late-1960s. Tubes, 25 watts.

1968		$125	$150

Checkmate CM-60 Amp

Late-1960s. Tubes, 60 watts, piggyback amp and cab with wheels.

1968		$200	$250

Checkmate CM-100 Amp

Late-1960s. Tubes, 4x6L6 power, 100 watts, piggyback with Vox-style trolley stand.

1968		$300	$400

King 1800 Amp

Late-1960s. Tubes, 180 watts, piggyback with two cabinets, large Teisco logo on cabinets, King logo on lower right side of one cabinet.

1968		$400	$500

Teisco 8 Amp

Late-1960s. Five watts

1968		$25	$50

Teisco 10 Amp

Late-1960s. Five watts.

1968		$25	$50

Teisco 88 Amp

Late-1960s. Eight watts.

1968		$50	$75

THD

1987-present. Tube amps and cabinets made in Seattle, Washington.

Titano (Magnatone)

1961-1963. Private branded by Magnatone, often for an accordion company or accordion studio, uses standard guitar input jacks.

Model 262 R Custom Amp

1961-1963. Thirty-five watts, 2x12" + 2x5", reverb and vibrato make this one of the top of the line models, Black vinyl, Light Silver grille.

1961-1963		$800	$1,000

MODEL YEAR	FEATURES	EXC. COND. LOW	HIGH

Model 415 Bass Amp

1961-1963. Twenty-five watts, 4x8", bass or accordion amp, Black cover, darkish grille.

1961-1963	$400	$500

Tone King

1993-present. Tube amps, combos, and cabinets built by Mark Bartel in Baltimore, Maryland. The company started in New York and moved to Baltimore in '94.

Tonemaster (Magnatone)

Late-1950s-early-1960s. Magnatone amps private branded for Imperial Accordion Company. Prominent block-style capital "TONEMASTER" logo on front panel, generally something nearly equal to Magnatone equivalent. This is just one of many private branded Magnatones. Covers range from Brown to Black leatherette and Brown to Light Silver grilles.

Model 214 (V logo) Amp

1959-1960. Ten watts, 1x12", vibrato, Brown leatherette, V logo lower right corner front, large TONEMASTER logo.

1959-1960	$350	$450

Model 260 Amp

1961-1963. About 30 watts, 2x12", vibrato, Brown leatherette and Brown grille, large TONEMASTER logo on front.

1961-1963	$550	$650

Model 380 Amp

1961-1963. Fifty watts, 2x12" and two oval 5"x7" speakers, vibrato, no reverb.

1961-1963	$650	$800

Top Hat Amplification

1994-present. Mostly Class A guitar amps built by Brian Garhard in Anaheim, California. They also make a overdrive pedal.

Ambassador 100 TH-A100 Head Amp

Jan. 1999-present. 100 watts, class AB, four 6L6 tubes, reverb, dark green vinyl cover, white chicken-head knobs.

1999-2003	$1,100	$1,300

Ambassador T-35C 212 Amp

1999-present. 35 watts, 2x12" combo, reverb, master volume, blond cover, tweed-style fabric grille.

1999-2003	$1,100	$1,300

Club Deluxe Amp

1998-present. 20 watts, 6V6 power tubes, 1x12".

2000s	$800	$900

Club Royale TC-R2 Amp

Jan. 1999-present. 20 watts, class A using EL84s, 2x12".

1999-2003	$900	$1,000

Emplexador 50 TH-E50 Head Amp

Jan. 1997-present. 50 watts, class AB vint/high-gain head.

1997-2003	$1,000	$1,200

King Royale Amp

1996-present. 35 watts, class A using 4xEL84s, 2x12".

2000s	$1,200	$1,400

Portly Cadet TC-PC Amp

Jan. 1999-present. 5 watts, 6V6 power, 1x8", dark gray, light gray grille.

1999-2003	$450	$500

Prince Royale TC-PR Amp

Jan. 2000-2002. 5 watts using EL84 power, 1x8", deep red, light grille.

2000-2003	$500	$550

Super Deluxe TC-SD2 Amp

Jan. 2000-present. 30 watts, class A, 7591 power tubes, 2x12".

2000-2003	$1,000	$1,200

Torres Engineering

Founded by Dan Torres and building tube amps, combos, cabinets and amp kits in San Mateo, California. Dan authored the book *Inside Tube Amps.*

Trace Elliot

1978-present. Founded in a small music shop in Essex, England. Currently owned by Gibson.

TA35CR Acoustic Guitar Amp

1990s. Compact lateral-style cab with 2x5", 35 watts, with reverb and chorus, dark vinyl cover, dark grille.

1990s	$250	$350

TA100R Acoustic Guitar Amp

1990s. Compact lateral-style cab with 4x5", 100 watts, with reverb, dark vinyl cover, dark grille.

1990s	$500	$600

Vellocette Amp

Late-1990s. Class A, 1x10", Green cover, round sound speaker hole, from the make of the early-2000s Gibson amps.

1997	$250	$350

Trainwreck

1983-present. Founded by Ken Fischer. Limited production, custom-made amps that are generally grouped by model. Models include the Rocket, Liverpool and Express, plus variations on those themes. Each amp's value should be evaluated on a case-by-case basis.

Traynor

1963-present. Started by Pete Traynor and Jack Long in Canada and made by Yorkville Sound.

Guitar Mate Reverb YGM3 Amp

1969-1979. 25 watts, 1x12", tube amp, Black Tolex, Gray grille.

1970s	$350	$450

Mark II Bass Master Amp

1970s.

1970s	$400	$500

'97 Top Hat Club Royale T-20 CR

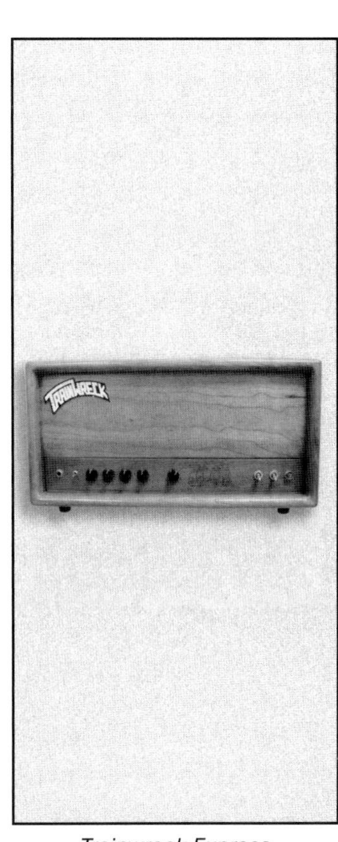

Trainwreck Express

AMPS

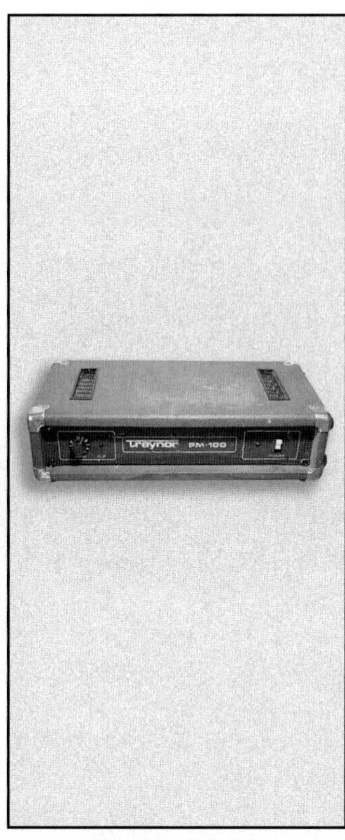

Traynor PM-100

Univox U130B

MODEL YEAR	FEATURES	EXC. COND. LOW	HIGH

Mark III (YGL-3) Amp

1971-1979. All tube, 80 watts, 2x12" combo, reverb, tremolo.

1970s	$350	$450

YBA3 Custom Special Bass Amp Set

1967-1972. Tube head with 130 watts and 8x10" large vertical matching cab, dark vinyl cover, light grille.

1968	$600	$700

True Tone

1960s. Guitars and amps retailed by Western Auto, manufactured by Chicago guitar makers like Kay.

Hi-Fi 4 (K503 Hot-Line Special) Amp

1960s. Four watts from three tubes, Gray cabinet, Gray grille, metal handle, similar to K503.

1964	$100	$150

Vibrato 704 Amp

1960s. Solidstate, ten watts, 1x8", White sides and Gray back, Gray grille.

1964	$125	$175

Vibrato 706 Amp

1960s. Solidstate, 15 watts, 1x15", White sides and Gray back, Brown grille.

1964	$150	$200

Tube Works

Originally out of Denver, now a division of Genz Benz Enclosures of Scottsdale, Arizona. Tube Works' first products were tube guitar effects. They have added tube/solidstate amps, cabinets, and DI boxes to the product mix.

Twilighter (Magnatone)

Late-1950s-early-1960s. Magnatone amps private branded for LoDuca Brothers. Prominent block-style capital "TWILIGHTER" logo on front panel, generally something nearly equal to Magnatone equivalent. This is just one of many private branded Magnatones. Covers range from brown to black leatherette, and brown to light silver grilles.

Model 213 Amp

1961-1963. About 20 watts, 1x12", vibrato, Brown leatherette and Brown grille, prominent TWILIGHTER logo on front.

1961-1963	$400	$500

Model 260R Amp

1961-1963. About 18 to 25 watts, 1x12", vibrato, Brown leatherette cover, large TWILIGHTER logo.

1961-1963	$500	$600

Model 280A Amp

Late-1950s-early-1960s. About 35 watts, 2x12", vibrato, Brown leatherette cover, large TWILIGHTER logo.

1961-1963	$550	$650

MODEL YEAR	FEATURES	EXC. COND. LOW	HIGH

Two-Rock

1999-present. Established by Joe Mloganoski and Bill Krinard in Cotati, California. Tube 25, 50, or 100 watt heads. Cabinets with Fane Alnicos speakers.

Emerald Pro Head Amp

2000s. Fifty-watt switchable head.

2000s	$2,100	$2,300

UltraSound

A division of UJC Electronics, UltraSound builds acoustically transparent amps, designed by Greg Farres for the acoustic guitarist, in Adel, Iowa.

Unique (Magnatone)

1961-1963. Private branded, typically for an accordion company or accordion studio, uses standard guitar input jacks.

Model 26R Amp

1961-1963. Based on Magnatone 260 Series amp, 35 watts, 2x12" but with reverb, Black vinyl-style cover with distinctive Black diamond-check pattern running through the top and sides.

1961-1963	$600	$800

Model 460 Amp

1961-1963. Thirty-five watts, 2x12" and oval 5"x7" speakers, reverb and vibrato make it one of the top models, Black vinyl, Black grille.

1961-1963	$800	$1,000

Univox

1964-ca.1978. From '64 to early-'68, these were American-made tube amps with Jensen speakers. By '68, they were using Japanese components in American cabinets, still with Jensen speakers. Electronics were combination of tube and transistors during this time; this type lasted until the mid-'70s.

Around '71, Univox introduced a line of all solidstate amps, as well. See Guitar section for more company info.

Bass Model U130B Amp

1976-1978. One hundred thirty watts, 1x15".

1976	$200	$300

Lead Model Tube Amp

1960s. Tube amp, 2x10".

1965-1969	$350	$450

Lead Model U130L Amp

1976-1978. Solidstate.

1976	$150	$200

Valco

Valco, from Chicago, was a big player in the guitar and amplifier business. Their products were private branded for other companies like National, Supro, Airline, Oahu, and Gretsch.

Vesta Fire

1980s. Japanese imports by Shiino Musical Instruments Corp.; later by Midco International. Mainly known for effects pedals.

MODEL YEAR	FEATURES	EXC. COND. LOW	HIGH

J-I Preamp

1980s		$50	$100

J-II Preamp

1980s		$50	$100

PT-I Power Amp

1980s		$100	$150

PT-II Power Amp

1980s		$150	$200

VHT

1989-present. Founded by Steven M. Fryette, Burbank, California's VHT builds amps, combos, and cabinets.

Fifty-Twelve Amp

Late-1990s. Fifty watts, all tube preamp section, 1x12".

1990s		$750	$850

Victor

Late-1960s. Made in Japan.

MA-25 Amp

Late-1960s. Student model, light cover, dark grille, solidstate, six controls, two inputs, script Victor logo.

1968		$75	$100

Victoria

1994-present. Tube amps, combos, and reverb units built by Mark Baier in Naperville, Illinois.

Double Deluxe Amp

1994-present. Thirty-five watts, 2x12".

1994-1999		$1,400	$1,500

Model 518 Amp

1994-present. Tweed, 1x8".

2000s		$700	$800

Model 20112 Amp

1994-1999. Twenty watts, 1x12", Tweed.

1994-1999		$950	$1,000

Model 35210 Amp

1994-1999. Thirty-five watts, 2x10", Tweed.

1994-1999		$1,400	$1,500

Model 35310-T Amp

1994-present. 35 watts, 3x10".

1994-1999		$1,500	$1,600
2000s		$1,500	$1,600

Model 45410-T Amp

1994-present. 45 watts, 4x10" combo.

1994-1999	Tweed	$1,500	$1,600

Model 50212-T Amp

2000s. New low power offering.

2000s		$1,600	$1,700

Model 80212 Amp

1994-1999. One hundred watts, 2x12", Tweed.

1994-1999		$1,600	$1,700

Voltmaster

Trapezoid-shaped combo amps and reverb units made in Plano, Texas, in the late '90s.

Vox

1957-1972, 1982-present. Tom Jennings and Dick Denney combined forces in '57 to produce the first Vox product, the 15-watt AC-15 amplifier. The short period between '63-'65 is considered to be the Vox heyday. Vox produced tube amps in England and also the U.S. from '64 to the early part of '66.

English-made tube amps were standardized between '60 and '65. U.S.-made Vox amps in '66 were solidstate. In the mid-'60s, similar model names were sometimes used for tube and solidstate amps. Vox products are currently distributed in the U.S. by Korg USA.

A Vox amp stand is correctly called a "trolley" and those amps that originally came with a trolley are priced accordingly, that is the price below includes the original trolley, and an amp without the trolley will be worth less than the amount shown. Smaller amps were not originally equipped with a trolley.

AC-4 Amp

1958-1965. Made in England, early Vox tube design, 3.5 watts, 1x8", tremolo.

1958-1965		$1,300	$1,600

AC-10 Amp

1960-1965. Made in England, 12 watts, 1x10", tremolo, this tube version not made in U.S. (1964-1965).

1960-1965		$1,500	$2,400

AC-10 Twin Amp

1960-1965. Made in England, also made in U.S. 1964-1965, 12 watts (two EL84s), 2x10".

1960-1965		$1,500	$2,400

AC-15 Twin Amp

1958-1965. Tube, 2x12", 18 watts.

1958-1965	Black Tolex	$3,000	$4,000
1960-1963	Custom colors	$3,500	$4,500

AC-15 Twin Amp Reissue

1990s. Fifteen watts, 1x12".

1990s		$900	$950

AC-30 Super Twin Head Amp

1960-1965. Made in England, 30-watt head.

1960-1963	Custom color	$2,000	$2,800
1960-1965	With footswitch	$1,500	$2,000

AC-30 Twin/AC-30 Twin Top Boost Amp

1960-1965. Made in England, 30-watt head, 36 watts 2x12", Top Boost includes additional treble and bass. Custom colors available in 1960-1963.

1960-1963	Custom colors	$3,500	$4,500
1960-1965		$2,300	$3,500

AC-30 Collector Model

1991. Limited production. 'Collector' brass model plate on back panel, high-grade solid mahogany cabinet, reverb.

1991	Mahogany cabinet	$1,900	$2,100

AC-30 Reissue

1980s		$900	$1,200
1990s		$900	$1,200
1990s	Blond custom color	$1,500	$1,700

Victoria Victorilux

1963 Vox AC-2

AMPS

Vox AC-50 Super Twin

Vox Pathfinder

MODEL YEAR	FEATURES	EXC. COND. LOW	HIGH

AC-50 Head Amp

1960-1965. Made in England, 50-watt head, U.S. production 1964-1965 tube version is Westminster Bass, U.S. post-1966 is solidstate.

1960-1965		$1,000	$1,300

Berkeley II V108 (tube) Amp

1964-1966. U.S.-made tube amp. Revised 1966-1969 to U.S.-made solidstate model V1081, 18 watts, 2x10" piggyback.

1964-1966		$1,000	$1,200

Berkeley II V1081 (solidstate) Amp

1966-1969. U.S.-made solidstate model V1081, 35 watts, 2x10" piggyback, includes trolley stand.

1966-1969		$700	$750

Berkeley III (solidstate) Amp

1966-1969. Berkeley III logo on top panel of amp.

1966-1969		$700	$750

Buckingham Amp

1966-1969. Solidstate, 70 watts, 2x12" piggyback, includes trolley stand.

1966-1969		$800	$850

Cambridge 30 Reverb Twin 210 Amp

1990s. Thirty watts hybrid circuit, 2x10" with reverb.

1990s		$300	$400

Cambridge Reverb (tube) V103 Amp

1964-1966. U.S-made tube version, 18 watts, 1x10", a Pacemaker with reverb, superceded by solidstate Model V1031 by 1967.

1964-1966		$800	$1,000

Cambridge Reverb (solidstate) V1031 Amp

1966-1969. Solidstate, 35 watts, 1x10", model V1031 replaced tube version V103.

1966-1969		$500	$600

Churchill PA Head Amp

Late-1960s. PA head with multiple inputs.

1960s		$400	$450

Climax V-125/V-125 Lead Combo Amp

1970-1991. Solidstate, 125 watts, 2x12" combo, five-band EQ, master volume.

1970-1991		$500	$650

Defiant Amp

1966-1969. Made in England, 50 watts, 2x12" + Midax horn cabinet.

1966-1969		$1,300	$1,500

Escort Amp

AC/DC, portable.

1972		$300	$400

Essex Bass V1042 Amp

1965-1969. U.S.-made solidstate, 35 watts, 2x12".

1965-1969		$700	$800

Foundation Bass Amp

1966-1969. Solidstate, 50 watts, 1x18", made in England only.

1966-1969		$500	$550

Kensington Bass V1241 Amp

1965-1969. U.S.-made solidstate bass amp, 22 watts, 1x15", G-tuner.

1965-1969		$450	$500

MODEL YEAR	FEATURES	EXC. COND. LOW	HIGH

Pacemaker (tube) V102 Amp

1964-1965. U.S.-made tube amp, 18 watts, 1x10", replaced by solidstate Pacemaker model V1021.

1964-1965		$700	$800

Pacemaker (solidstate) V1021 Amp

1966-1969. U.S.-made solidstate amp, 35 watts, 1x10", replaced Pacemaker model V102.

1967-1969		$350	$400

Pathfinder (tube) V101 Amp

1964-1965. U.S.-made tube amp, four watts, 1x18", 1966-1969 became U.S.-made solidstate V1011.

1964-1965		$500	$700

Pathfinder (solidstate) V1011 Amp

1966-1969. U.S.-made solidstate, 25 watts peak power, 1x8".

1966-1969		$250	$350

Pathfinder 10 Amp Reissue

2000s. Compact practice amp with 1960s cosmetics, 10 watts, 6 1/2" speaker.

2000s		$70	$90

Royal Guardsman V1131/V1132 Amp

1966-1969. U.S.-made solidstate, 50 watts piggyback, 2x12" + one horn, the model below the Super Beatle V1141/V1142.

1966-1969		$800	$900

Scorpion (solidstate) Amp

1968. Solidstate, 60 watts, 4x10" Vox Oxford speaker.

1968		$500	$600

Super Beatle V1141/V1142 Amp

1966-1967. U.S.-made 120 watt solidstate, 4x12" + two horns, with distortion pedal (V1141), or without (V1142).

1966-1967		$1,600	$1,900

Viscount V1151/V1152 Amp

1966-1969. U.S.-made solidstate, 70 watts, 2x12" combo.

1966-1969		$700	$800

Westminster V118 Bass Amp

1966-1969. Solidstate, 120 watts, 1x18".

1966-1969		$600	$750

Wabash

1950s. Private branded amps distributed by the David Wexler company.

Model 1158 Amp

Danelectro-made, 1x15", two 6L6 power tubes.

1955	Tweed	$200	$300

Washburn

1974-present. Imported guitar and bass amps from Washburn, which also offers guitars, mandolins, and basses. See Guitar section for more company info.

Watkins

1957-present. Watkins Electric Music (WEM) was founded by Charlie Watkins. Their first commercial product was the Watkins Dominator (wedge Gibson stereo amp shape) in 1957, followed by the Copicat Echo in 1958.

MODEL YEAR	FEATURES	EXC. COND. LOW	HIGH

Dominator V-Front Amp

Late-1950s-1960s. Eighteen watts, 2x10", wedge cabinet similar to Gibson GA-79 stereo amp, tortoise and Light Beige cab, light grille. Requires 220V step-up transformer.

1959-1962		$1,300	$1,500

Yamaha

1946-present. Japan-based Yamaha started offering amps in the '60s.

Budokan HY-10G II Amp

1987-1992. Portable, 10 watts, distortion control, EQ.

1980s		$50	$100

G100-112 Amp

1983-1992. One hundred watts, 1x12" combo, Black cover, striped grille, large Yahama logo upper left corner of grille.

1980s		$200	$250

G100-212 Amp

1983-1992. One hundred watts, 2x12" combo, Black cover, striped grille, large Yahama logo upper left corner of grille.

1980s		$250	$300

JX30B Amp

1983-1992. Bass amp, 30 watts.

1980s		$150	$200

TA-20 Amp

1968-1972. Upright wedge shape with controls facing upwards, solidstate.

1968-1972		$100	$150

TA-25 Amp

1968-1972. Upright wedge shape with controls facing upwards, 40 watts, 1x12", solidstate, Black or Red cover.

1968-1972		$100	$150

TA-30 Amp

1968-1972. Upright wedge shape, solidstate.

1968-1972		$150	$200

TA-50 Amp

1971-1972. Solidstate combo, 80 watts, 2x12", includes built-in cart with wheels, black cover.

1971-1972		$200	$250

TA-60 Amp

1968-1972. Upright wedge shape, solidstate, most expensive of wedge-shape amps.

1968-1972		$225	$275

VR4000 Amp

1988-1992. 50-watt, Stereo, two channels, EQ, stereo chorus, reverb and dual effects loops.

1980s		$250	$300

MODEL YEAR	FEATURES	EXC. COND. LOW	HIGH

VR6000 Amp

1988-1992. 100 watt, Stereo, 2 independent channels which can also be combined, parametric EQ, chorus, reverb and dual effects loops.

1980s		$350	$400

VX-15 Amp

1983-1992. 10 watts.

1980s		$100	$150

YBA-65 Bass Amp

1972-1976. Solidstate combo, 60 watts, 1x15".

1972-1976		$125	$175

YTA-25 Amp

1972-1976. Solidstate combo, 25 watts, 1x12".

1972-1976		$100	$150

YTA-45 Amp

1972-1976. Solidstate combo, 45 watts, 1x12".

1972-1976		$125	$175

YTA-95 Amp

1972-1976. Solidstate combo, 90 watts, 1x12".

1972-1976		$150	$200

YTA-100 Amp

1972-1976. Solidstate piggyback, 100 watts, 2x12".

1972-1976		$200	$250

YTA-110 Amp

1972-1976. Solidstate piggyback, 100 watts, 2x12" in extra large cab.

1972-1976		$200	$250

YTA-200 Amp

1972-1976. Solidstate piggyback, 200 watts, 4x12".

1972-1976		$225	$275

YTA-300 Amp

1972-1976. Solidstate piggyback, 200 watts, dual cabs with 2x12" and 4x12".

1972-1976		$325	$375

YTA-400 Amp

1972-1976. Solidstate piggyback, 200 watts, dual cabs 2x4x12".

1972-1976		$350	$400

Zapp

Ca. 1978-early 1980s. Zapp amps were distributed by Red Tree Music, Inc., of Mamaroneck, New York.

Z-10 Amp

1978. Small student amp, eight watts.

1979		$40	$60

Z-50 Amp

1978. Small student amp, 10 watts, reverb, tremelo.

1978		$50	$75

Vox Super Beatle

Watkins Dominator

AMPS

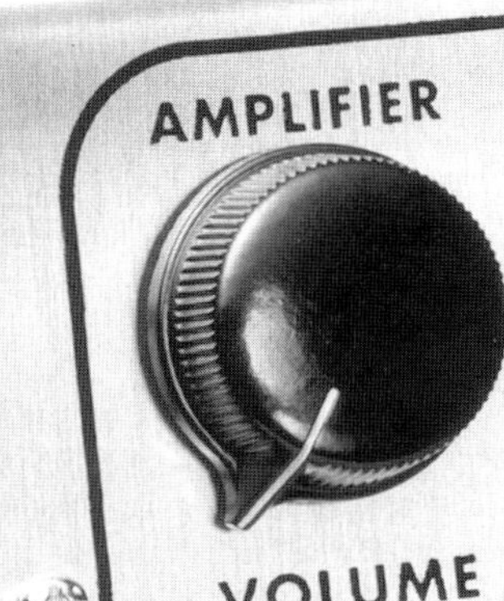

AMPLIFIER
INPUT
VOLUME
TONE
SUSTAIN
BIG MUFF
MADE IN NYC, USA

Effects

ADA Flanger

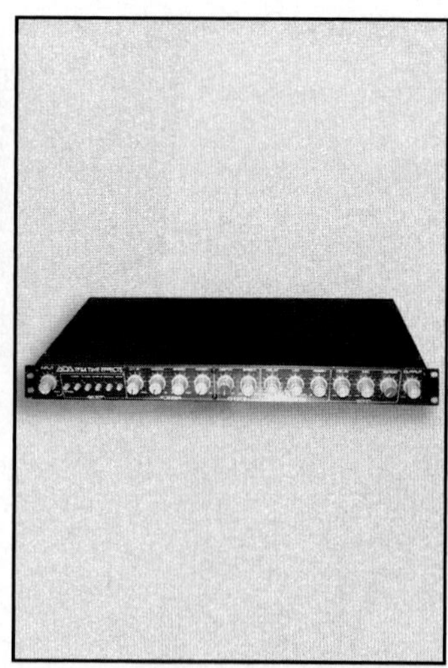

ADA TFX4 Time Effects

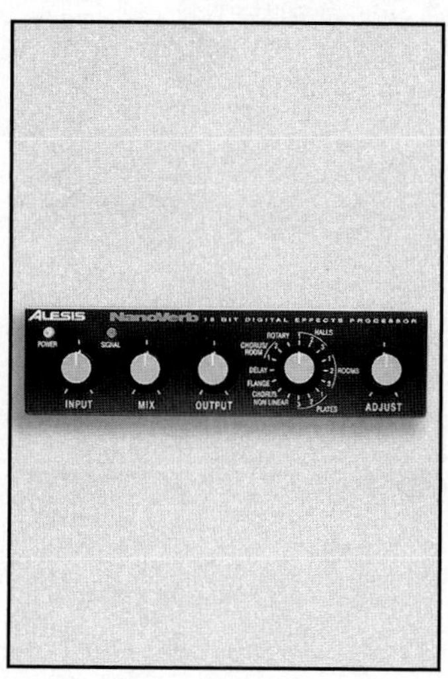

Alesis Nanoverb

MODEL YEAR	FEATURES	EXC. COND. LOW	HIGH

Ace-Tone

Late-1960s-early-1970s. Ace Electronic Industry (aka Ace-Tone) was a part of Sakata Shokaie Limited of Osaka, Japan. Ace-Tone was the precedessor to Roland and Boss.

Fuzz Master FM-1

Distortion and overdrive.

1968 $100 $125

Wah Master WM-1

Filter wah.

1969 $100 $125

Acoustyx

1977-1982. Made by the Highland Corporation of Vermont.

Image Synthesizer IS-1

1977-1982.

1977-1982 $40 $60

Phase Five

1978-ca.1982. Used six 'C' cell batteries!

1977-1982 $40 $60

ADA

1977-2002. ADA is an acronym for Analog/Digital Associates. The company was located in Berkeley, California, and introduced its Flanger and Final Phase in 1977. The company later moved to Oakland and made amplifiers, high-tech signal processors, and a reissue of its original Flanger.

Final Phase

1977-1979. Reissued in 1997.

1977-1979 $300 $400

Flanger

1977-1983. Reissued in 1996.

1977-1979 With control pedal $350 $400

1977-1979 Without control pedal $300 $350

1980-1983 $200 $300

Flanger Reissue

1996-2002.

1990s $75 $100

MP-1

1987-1995. Tube preamp with chorus and effects loop, MIDI.

1987-1995 Without optional foot controller $125 $175

MP-2

Ca.1988-1995. Tube preamp with chorus, nine-band EQ and effects loop, MIDI.

1988-1995 $150 $200

Pitchtraq

1987. Programmable pitch transposer including octave shifts.

1987 $200 $250

Stereo Tapped Delay STD-1

Introduced in 1981.

1980s $100 $150

TFX4 Time Effects

Introduced in 1982, includes flanger, chorus, doubler, echo.

1980s $100 $150

MODEL YEAR	FEATURES	EXC. COND. LOW	HIGH

Aguilar

The New York, New York amp builder also offers a line of tube and solidstate pre-amps.

Alamo

1947-1982. Founded by Charles Eilenberg, Milton Fink, and Southern Music, San Antonio, TX. Distributed by Bruno & Sons. Mainly known for guitars and amps, Alamo did offer a reverb unit. See Guitar section for more company info or *Guitar Stories Volume II*, by Michael Wright, for a complete history of Alamo with detailed model listings.

Reverb Unit

1965-ca. 1979. Has a Hammond reverb system, balance and intensity controls. By 1973 the unit had three controls - mixer, contour, and intensity.

1965 $175 $275

Alesis

1992-present. Initial offerings included digital processors and reverb.

Effects Processors

1992-present. Various digital processors for reverb, echo, etc.

1990s $125 $350

Allen Amplification

1998-present. David Allen's company, located in Richwood, Kentucky, mainly produces amps, but they also offer a tube overdrive pedal.

Altair Corp.

1977-1980s. Company was located in Ann Arbor, Michigan.

Power Attenuator PW-5

1977-1980. Goes between amp and speaker to dampen volume.

1977-1980 $100 $130

Amdek

Mid-1980s. Amdek offered many electronic products over the years, including drum machines and guitar effects. Many of these were sold in kit form so quality of construction can vary.

Delay Machine DMK-200

1983. Variable delay times.

1983 $75 $125

Octaver OCK-100

1983. Produces tone one or two octaves below the note played.

1983 $75 $125

Ampeg

Ampeg entered the effects market in the late-'60s. Their offerings in the early-'60s were really amplifier-outboard reverb units similar to the ones offered by Gibson (GA-1). Ampeg offered a line of imported effects in '82-'83, known as the A-series (A-1 through A-9). See Guitar section for more company info.

MODEL YEAR	FEATURES	EXC. COND. LOW	HIGH

Analog Delay A-8
1982-1983. Made in Japan.

1982-1983		$40	$60

Chorus A-6
1982-1983. Made in Japan.

1982-1983		$35	$45

Compressor A-2
1982-1983. Made in Japan.

1982-1983		$35	$45

Distortion A-1
1982-1983. Made in Japan.

1982-1983		$30	$40

Echo Jet (EJ-12) Reverb
1963-1965. Outboard, alligator clip reverb unit with 12" speaker, 12 watts, technically a reverb unit. When used as a stand-alone amp, the reverb is off. Named EJ-12A in 1965.

1963-1965		$275	$325

Echo Satellite (ES-1)
1961-1963. Outboard reverb unit with amplifier and speaker alligator clip.

1961-1963		$250	$300

Flanger A-5
1982-1983. Made in Japan.

1982-1983		$40	$50

Multi-Octaver A-7
1982-1983. Made in Japan.

1982-1983		$50	$70

Over Drive A-3
1982-1983. Made in Japan.

1982-1983		$30	$40

Parametric Equalizer A-9
1982-1983. Made in Japan.

1982-1983		$30	$40

Phaser A-4
1982-1983. Made in Japan.

1982-1983		$50	$60

Phazzer
1975-1977.

1970s		$50	$70

Scrambler Fuzz
1969-1971. Distortion pedal.

1969-1971		$90	$150

Analog Man

1994-present. Founded by Mike Piera in '94 with full-time production by 2000. Located in Bethel, Connecticut, producing Chorus, Compressor, Fuzz, and Boost pedals by 2003.

Apollo

Imported by St. Louis Music in the 1970s. Includes Fuzz Treble Boost Box, Crier Wa-Wa, Deluxe Fuzz.

Crier Wa-Wa
1970s.

1970s		$65	$90

Fuzz
1970s. Includes the Fuzz Treble Boost Box and the Deluxe Fuzz.

1970s		$75	$110

Arbiter

Ivor Arbiter and Arbiter Music, London, began making the circular Fuzz Face stompbox in '66. Other products included the Fuzz Wah and Fuzz Wah Face. In '68 the company went public as Arbiter and Western, later transitioning to Dallas-Arbiter. Refer to Dallas-Arbiter for listings.

Aria

Aria provided a line of effects in the mid-1980s. See the Guitar section for more company info.

Analog Delay AD-10
1983-1985. Dual-stage stereo.

1983-1985		$60	$70

Chorus ACH-1
1986-1987. Stereo.

1980s		$30	$40

Chorus CH-5
1985-1987.

1980s		$30	$40

Chorus CH-10
1983-1985. Dual-stage stereo.

1980s		$30	$40

Compressor CO-10
1983-1985.

1980s		$30	$40

Digital Delay ADD-100
1984-1986. Delay, flanging, chorus, doubling, hold.

1980s		$50	$70

Digital Delay DD-X10
1985-1987.

1980s		$50	$70

Distortion DT-5
1985-1987.

1980s		$40	$60

Distortion DT-10
1983-1985. Dual-stage.

1980s		$40	$70

Flanger AFL-1
1986. Stereo.

1980s		$40	$60

Flanger FL-5
1985-1987.

1980s		$40	$60

Flanger FL-10
1983-1985. Dual-stage stereo.

1980s		$40	$60

Metal Pedal MP-5
1985-1987.

1980s		$30	$50

Noise Gate NG-10
1983-1985.

1980s		$20	$40

Ampeg Chorus

Aria Chorus CH-10

Aria Jet Phaser RE-202

EFFECTS

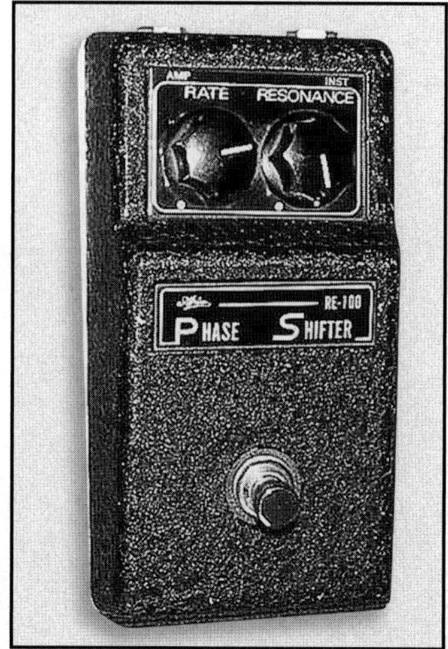

Arion Phase Shifter RE-100

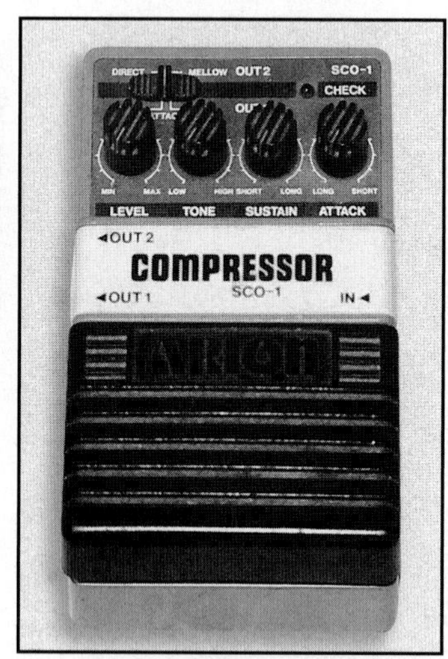

Arion Compressor SCO-1

Austone Fuzz Nutz

MODEL YEAR	FEATURES	EXC. COND. LOW	HIGH

Over Drive OD-10

1983-1985. Dual-stage.

1980s		$35	$50

Parametric Equalizer EQ-10

1983-1985.

1980s		$40	$50

Phase Shifter PS-10

1983-1984. Dual-stage.

1980s		$40	$60

Programmable Effects Pedal APE-1

1984-1986. Compression, distortion, delay, chorus.

1980s		$50	$60

Arion

1984-present. Imports distributed by Matthews and Ryan of Brooklyn, NY.

Compressor SCO-1

1985-present. Stereo. The "-1" was dropped on later models.

1980s		$30	$40

Distortion SDI-1

1984-2002. Stereo. The "-1" was dropped on later models.

1980s		$25	$35

Hot Watt II

1984-present. Headphone amp.

1980s		$30	$40

Metal Master SMM-1

1984-present. Stereo. The "-1" was dropped on later models.

1980s		$15	$30

Over Drive SOD-1

1984-2002. Stereo. The "-1" was dropped on later models.

1980s		$25	$40

Parametric EQ SPE-1

1985-late-1980s?. Stereo.

1980s		$20	$30

Stereo Chorus SCH-1

1984-present. The "-1" was dropped on later models.

1980s		$30	$40

Stereo Delay SAD-1

1984-present. Analog delay.

1980s		$40	$50

Stereo Flanger SFL-1

1984-present. The "-1" was dropped on later models.

1980s		$30	$40

Stereo Phaser SPH-1

1984-present. The "-1" was dropped on later models.

1980s		$30	$40

Tube Mania

1987-early-1990s.

1980s		$30	$40

Astrotone

Late 1960s. By Universal Amp, which also made the Sam Ash Fuzzz

Fuzz

Ca.1967. By Universal Amp.

1960s		$150	$250

ATD

Mid-1960s-early 1980s. Made by the All-Test Devices corporation of Long Beach, NY. In the mid-'60s, Richard Minz and an associate started making effects part-time, selling them through Manny's Music in New York. They formed All-Test and started making Maestro effects and transducer pickups for CMI, which owned Gibson at the time. By '75, All-Test was marketing effects under their own brandname. All-Test is still around making products for other industries, but by the early to mid-'80s they were no longer making products for the guitar.

PB-1 Power Booster

1976-ca.1980.

1979		$40	$60

Volume Pedal EV-1

1979-ca.1980.

1979		$25	$35

Wah-Wah/Volume Pedal WV-1

1979-ca.1981.

1979		$35	$60

Audio Matrix

1980s. The company was located in Escondido, California.

Mini Boogee B81

1981. Four-stage, all-tube preamp, overdrive, distortion.

1980s		$90	$140

Audioworks

1980s. Company was located in Niles, Illinois.

F.E.T. Distortion

1982.

1980s		$25	$60

Auralux

2000-present. Founded by Mitchell Omori and David Salzmann, Auralux builds effects and tube amps in Highland Park, Illinois.

Austone Electronics

1997-present. Founded by Jon Bessent and Randy Larkin, Austone offers of range of stomp boxes, all made in Austin, Texas.

Overdrive and Fuzz Pedals

1997-present. Various overdrive and fuzz boxes.

1997		$100	$175

MODEL YEAR | FEATURES | EXC. COND. LOW | HIGH

Automagic

1998-present. Hand-made wah pedals made in Germany by Musician Sound Design and distributed in the U.S. by Godlyke Distributing.

Avalanche

Brianizer

Late-1980s. Leslie effect, dual rotor, adjustable speed and rates.

1980s $60 $90

B & M

1970s. Private brand made by Sola/Colorsound.

Fuzz Unit

1970s. Long thin Orange case, volume, sustain, tone knobs, on-off stomp switch.

1970s $200 $250

Bad Cat Amplifier Company

2000-present. Founded in Corona, California by James and Debbie Heidrich with Mark Sampson as the chief designer and engineer. Bad Cat offers class A combo amps, heads, cabinets and effects.

Bartolini

The pickup manufacturer offered a few effects in the mid-1980s.

Tube-It

1982-ca.1988. Marshall tube amplification simulator with bass, treble, sustain controls..

1980s Red case $65 $90

Basic Systems' Side Effects

1980s. Company was located in Tulsa, Oklahoma.

Audio Delay

1986-ca.1987. Variable delay speeds.

1986-1987 $60 $90

Triple Fuzz

1986-ca.1987. Selectable distortion types.

1986-1987 $40 $60

BBE

1985-present. BBE, located in California, currently manufactures rack-mount effects and also owns G&L Guitars.

601 Stinger

1985-ca. 1989.

1980s $50 $70

Bell

Vibrato

1970s $100 $150

Bigsby

Bigsby has been making volume and tone pedals since the '50s. They currently offer a volume pedal. See Guitar section for more company info.

Foot Volume and Tone Control

1950s $100 $150

Binson

1960s. Italian-made.

Echorec

1960s. Echo, delay unit, used a magnetic disk instead of tape. Guild later offered the "Guild Echorec by Binson" which is a different stripped-down version.

1961 Tube model $350 $700

Bixonic

1995-present. Originally distributed by SoundBarrier Music, Bixonic is currently distributed by Godlyke, Inc.

Expandora EXP-2000

1995-2000. Analog distortion, round silver case.

1990s $150 $200

Blackbox Music Electronics

2000-present. Founded by Loren Stafford and located in Minneapolis, Minnesota, Blackbox offers a line of effects for guitar and bass.

Bon, Mfg

Bon was located in Escondido, California.

Tube Driver 204

1979-ca.1981.

1979-1981 $75 $150

Boss

1976-present. Japan's Roland Corporation first launched effect pedals in 1974. A year or two later the subsidiary company, Boss, debuted its own line. They were marketed concurrently at first but gradually Boss became reserved for effects and drum machines while the Roland name was used on amplifiers and keyboards. Boss still offers a wide line of pedals.

Acoustic Simulator AC-2

1997-present. Four modes that emulate various acoustic tones.

1997-1999 $50 $60

Auto Wah AW-2

1991-1999.

1991-1999 $40 $50

Bass Chorus CE-2B

1987-1995.

1987-1995 $40 $50

Bass Equalizer GE-7B

1987-1995. Seven-band, name changed to GEB-7 in 1995.

1987-1995 $40 $50

Bad Cat 2 Tone

BBE 601 Stinger

Blackbox Oxygen

Boss Super Chorus CH-1

Boss Distortion DS-1

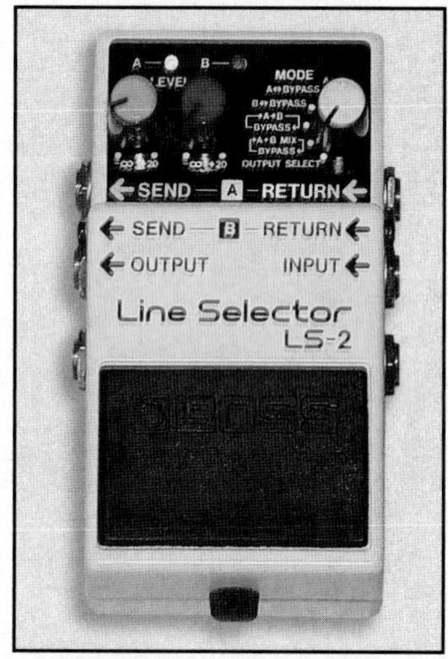

Boss Line Selector LS-2

MODEL YEAR	FEATURES	EXC. COND. LOW	HIGH
Bass Flanger BF-2B			
1987-1994.			
1987-1994		$40	$50
Bass Limiter LM-2B			
1990-1994.			
1990-1994		$30	$40
Bass Overdrive ODB-3			
1994-present.			
1994-1999		$45	$55
Blues Driver BD-2			
1995-present.			
1995-1999		$40	$50
Chorus Ensemble CE-1			
1976-1984. Vibrato and chorus.			
1976-1984	With vibrato	$150	$250
Chorus Ensemble CE-2			
1979-1982		$50	$60
Chorus Ensemble CE-3			
1982-1992		$30	$40
Chorus Ensemble CE-5			
1991-present.			
2000s		$60	$50
Compressor Sustainer CS-1			
1978-1982.			
1978-1982		$80	$100
Compressor Sustainer CS-2			
1981-1986.			
1981-1986		$75	$90
Compressor Sustainer CS-3			
1986-present.			
1986-1999		$40	$55
Delay DM-2			
1981-1984. Analog.			
1981-1984		$165	$185
Delay DM-3			
1984-1988.			
1984-1988		$150	$160
Digital Delay DD-2			
1983-1986.			
1983-1986		$80	$150
Digital Delay DD-3			
1986-present. Up to 800 ms of delay.			
1986-1989		$80	$150
1990s		$80	$125
Digital Delay DD-5			
1995-present. Up to two seconds of delay.			
1995-1999		$80	$125
Digital Dimension C DC-2			
1985-1989. Two chorus effects and tremolo.			
1985-1989		$110	$150
Digital Metalizer MZ-2			
1987-1992.			
1987-1992		$75	$90
Digital Reverb RV-2			
1987-1990.			
1987-1990		$110	$150
Digital Sampler/Delay DSD-2			
1985-1986.			
1985-1986		$100	$150

MODEL YEAR	FEATURES	EXC. COND. LOW	HIGH
Digital Space-D DC-3/Digital Dimension DC-3			
1988-1993. Originally called the Digital Space-D, later changed to Digital Dimension. Chorus with EQ.			
1988-1993		$130	$160
Digital Stereo Reverb RV-70			
1990s. Rack mount, MIDI control, reverb/delay, 199 presets.			
1990s		$130	$160
Distortion DS-1			
1978-1989.			
1978-1989		$40	$60
Dr. Rhythm DR-55			
1981-present. Drum machine.			
1981-1989		$150	$200
Dual Over Drive SD-2			
1993-1998.			
1993-1998		$45	$55
Dynamic Filter FT-2			
1986-1988. Auto wah.			
1986-1988		$70	$100
Enhancer EH-2			
1990-1998.			
1990-1998		$30	$40
Flanger BF-1			
1977-1980.			
1977-1980		$50	$75
Flanger BF-2			
1980-present.			
1980-1989		$50	$75
1990-1999		$40	$60
Foot Wah FW-3			
1992-1996.			
1992-1996		$40	$50
Graphic Equalizer GE-6			
1978-1981. Six bands.			
1978-1981		$45	$65
Graphic Equalizer GE-7			
1981-present. Seven bands.			
1982-1989		$50	$80
1990-1999		$45	$75
Harmonist HR-2			
1994-1999. Pitch shifter.			
1994-1999		$90	$120
Heavy Metal HM-2			
1983-1991. Distortion.			
1983-1991		$35	$45
Hyper Fuzz FZ-2			
1993-1997.			
1993-1997		$40	$50
Hyper Metal HM-3			
1993-1998.			
1993-1998		$35	$45
Limiter LM-2			
1987-1992.			
1987-1992		$30	$40
Line Selector LS-2			
1991-present. Select between two effects loops.			
1991-1999	With adapter	$65	$85

MODEL YEAR	FEATURES	EXC. COND. LOW	HIGH

Metal Zone MT-2
1991-present. Distortion and three-band EQ.
1991-1999 $40 $60

Multi Effects ME-5
1990s $100 $130

Multi Effects ME-6
1992-1997.
1992-1997 $100 $130

Multi Effects ME-8
1996-1997.
1996-1997 $100 $130

Multi Effects ME-30
1990s $100 $130

Noise Gate NF-1
1979-1988.
1979-1988 $50 $60

Noise Suppressor NS-2
1987-present.
1987-1999 $50 $60

Octaver OC-2/Octave OC-2
1982-present. Originally called the Octaver.
1982-1999 $50 $60

Overdrive OD-1
1977-1985.
1977-1979 $100 $175
1980-1985 $80 $150

Overdrive OD-3
1997-present.
1997-1999 $35 $45

Parametric Equalizer PQ-4
1991-1997.
1991-1997 $40 $70

Phaser PH-1
1977-1981.
1977-1981 $65 $75

Phaser PH-1R
1982-1985. Resonance control added to PH-1.
1982-1985 $60 $70

Pitch Shifter/Delay PS-2
1987-1993.
1987-1993 $70 $85

Reverb Box RX-100
1981-mid-1980s.
1981-1985 $60 $80

Reverb/Delay RV-2
1980s $70 $110

Reverb/Delay RV-3
1994-present.
1994-1999 $70 $110

Rocker Distortion PD-1
1980-mid-1980s. Variable pedal using magnetic field.
1980-1985 $50 $70

Rocker Volume PV-1
1981-mid-1980s.
1980-1985 $40 $60

Rocker Wah PW-1
1980-mid-1980s. Magnetic field variable pedal.
1980-1985 $50 $79

MODEL YEAR	FEATURES	EXC. COND. LOW	HIGH

Slow Gear SG-1
1979-1982. Reverse simulator.
1979-1982 $200 $250

Slow Gear SG-2
1980s. "Violin" volume swell effect.
1980s $60 $90

Spectrum SP-1
1977-1981. Single band parametric EQ.
1977-1981 $150 $200

Super Chorus CH-1
1989-present.
1989-1999 $40 $50

Super Distortion & Feedbacker DF-2
1984-1994. Also labeled as the Super Feedbacker & Distortion.
1984-1994 $70 $80

Super Over Drive SD-1
1981-present.
1981-1989 $40 $50
1990-1999 $30 $40

Super Phaser PH-2
1984-2001.
1984-1989 $45 $55
1990-1999 $40 $50

Super Shifter PS-5
1999-present. Pitch shifter.
2000s $100 $110

Touch Wah TW-1/T Wah TW-1
1978-1987. Auto wah. Early models were labeled as Touch Wah.
1978-1987 $75 $100

Tremolo TR-2
1997-present.
1997-1999 $60 $75

Tremolo/Pan PN-2
1990-1995.
1990-1995 $140 $150

Turbo Distortion DS-2
1987-present.
1987-1999 $40 $60

Turbo Overdrive OD-2
1985-1994. Called OD-2R after 1994, due to added remote on/off jack.
1985-1994 $60 $80

Vibrato VB-2
1982-1986. True pitch-changing vibrato, warm analog tone, 'rise time' control allows for slow attach, four knobs. Aqua-Blue case.
1982-1986 $200 $300

Volume FV-50H
1987-present. High impedance, stereo volume pedal with inputs and outputs.
1987-1999 $45 $55

Volume FV-50L
1987-present. Low impedance, stereo volume pedal with inputs and outputs.
1987-1999 $30 $40

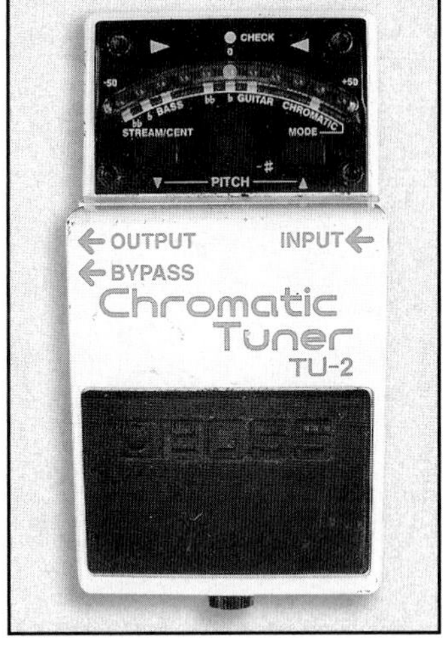

Boss Chromatic Tuner TU-2

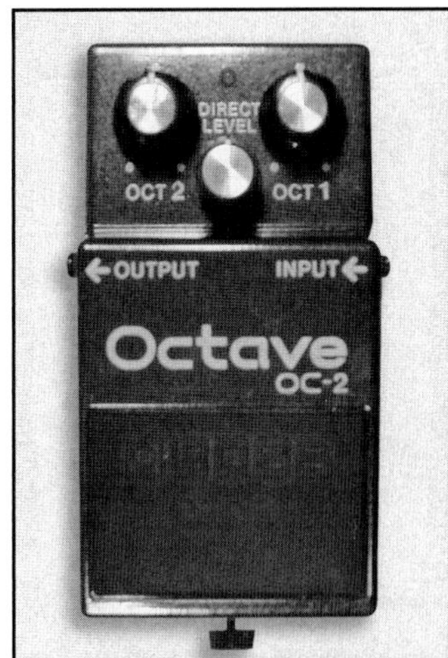

Boss Octave OC-2

Boss Phase Shifter PH-3

Carl Martin Two Faze

Carl Martin Hot Drive N Boost

Colorsound Sustain Module

MODEL YEAR	FEATURES	EXC. COND. LOW	HIGH

Volume Pedal FV-100
Late-1980s-1991. Guitar volume pedal.

1988-1991		$35	$45

Budda
1995-present. Wahs and distortion pedals from San Rafael, California. They mainly produce amp heads, combos, and cabinets.

Carl Martin
1993-present. Line of effects from Søren Jongberg and East Sound Research of Denmark.

Carrotron
Late-1970s-mid-1980s. Carrotron was out of California and offered a line of effects.

Noise Fader C900B1
1980-1982.

1980-1982		$40	$50

Preamp C821B
1981-ca.1982.

1981-1982		$55	$65

Carvin
2002-present. Carvin introduced its line of Ground Effects in 2002 and discontinued them in 2003.

Castle Instruments
Castle was located in New Jersey.

Phaser III
1980-1982. Offered mode switching for various levels of phase.

1980-1982		$75	$175

Chandler
1984-present. Located in California, Chandler Musical Instruments offers instruments, pickups, and pickguards, as well as effects.

Digital Echo
1992-2000. Rackmount, one second delay, stereo.

1992-2000		$375	$475

Tube Driver
1986-1991. Uses a 12AX7 tube.

1980s	Large Box	$140	$170
1980s	Rackmount	$100	$140
1990s	Rackmount	$100	$140

Chapman
From Emmett Chapman, maker of the Stick.

Patch of Shades
1981-Late-1980s. Wah, with pressure sensitive pad instead of pedal.

1980s		$40	$60

Clark

SS-600 Fuzz

1960s		$125	$150

Colorsound
1965-present. Colorsound effects were produced by England's Sola Sound, which in '65 was founded by former Vox associate Larry Macari. The first product was a fuzzbox called the Tone Bender, designed by Gary Hurst and sold at Macari's Musical Exchange stores. The first readily available fuzz in Britain, it was an instant success. In the late-'60s, wah and fuzz-wah pedals were added, and by the end of the '70s, Colorsound offered 18 different effects, an amp, and accessories. Few early Colorsound products were imported into the U.S., so today they're scarce. Except for the Wah-Wah pedal, Colorsound's production stopped by the early '80s, but in '96 most of their early line was reissued by Dick Denny of Vox fame. Denny died in 2001. The brand is now owned by Mutronics who offers a rack mount combination of four classic Colorsound effects.

Flanger

1970s		$90	$100

Fuzzphase

1970s		$140	$160

Octivider

1970s		$125	$150

Overdriver
Introduced in 1972, controls for drive, treble and bass.

1970s		$150	$175

Supa Tonebender Fuzz

1970s		$175	$200

Supaphase

1970s		$150	$175

Supasustain

1960s		$100	$125

Tonebender Jumbo (Sola Sound)

1979		$150	$200

Tremolo

1970s		$150	$175

Wah Fuzz Straight
1970s. Aqua-Blue case, Wah-Fuzz-Straight in capital block letters on end of wah pedal.

1970s		$150	$175

Wah Wah
1970s. Dark Gray case, Wah-Wah in capital block letters on end of wah pedal.

1975		$175	$200

Wah Wah Reissue
1990s. Red case, large Colorsound letter logo and small Wah Wah lettering on end of pedal.

1990s		$100	$120

Companion
1970s. Private branded by Shinei of Japan.

Wah pedal

1970s		$100	$150

Crybaby
See listing under Vox for early models, and see Dunlop for recent versions.

EFFECTS

Dallas Arbiter

Dallas Arbiter, Ltd., was based in London and it appeared in the late-1960s as a division of a Dallas group of companies headed by Ivor Arbiter. They also manufactured Sound City amplifiers and made Vox amps from '72 to '78. The Fuzz Face is still available from Jim Dunlop.

Fuzz Face

Introduced in 1966. The current reissue of the Dallas Arbiter Fuzz Face is distributed by Jim Dunlop USA.

MODEL YEAR	FEATURES	EXC. COND. LOW	HIGH
1968	Red	$300	$500
1969	Red	$300	$500
1970	Red	$250	$350
1970-1976	Blue	$250	$400
1977-1980	Blue	$150	$300
1981	Grey, reissue	$100	$150
1990s	Red, reissue	$55	$65
2000s	Red, reissue	$55	$65

Fuzz Wah Face

MODEL YEAR	FEATURES	EXC. COND. LOW	HIGH
1970s	Black	$150	$200
1990s	Reissue copy	$55	$65

Sustain

MODEL YEAR	FEATURES	EXC. COND. LOW	HIGH
1970s		$100	$225

Treble & Bass Face

MODEL YEAR	FEATURES	EXC. COND. LOW	HIGH
1960s		$175	$275

Trem Face

Ca.1970-ca.1975. Reissued in 1980s. Round Red case, depth and speed control knobs, Dallas-Arbiter England logo plate.

MODEL YEAR	FEATURES	EXC. COND. LOW	HIGH
1970-1975	Red	$225	$275

Wah Baby

1970s. Gray Speckle case, Wah Baby logo caps and small letters on end of pedal.

MODEL YEAR	FEATURES	EXC. COND. LOW	HIGH
1970s		$200	$250

Dan Armstrong

In 1976, Musitronics, based in Rosemont, New Jersey, introduced six inexpensive plug-in effects designed by Dan Armstrong. Perhaps under the influence of John D. MacDonald's Travis McGee novels, each effect name incorporated a color, like Purple Peaker. Shipping box labeled Dan Armstrong by Musitronics. They disappeared a few years later but were reissued by WD Products in the 1990s.

Blue Clipper

1976-1981. Fuzz, Blue-Green case.

MODEL YEAR	FEATURES	EXC. COND. LOW	HIGH
1976-1981		$75	$85

Green Ringer

1976-1981. Ring Modulator/Fuzz, Green case.

MODEL YEAR	FEATURES	EXC. COND. LOW	HIGH
1970s		$75	$85

Orange Squeezer

1976-81.

MODEL YEAR	FEATURES	EXC. COND. LOW	HIGH
1976-1981		$80	$90

Purple Peaker

1976-1981. Frequency Booster, Light Purple case.

MODEL YEAR	FEATURES	EXC. COND. LOW	HIGH
1976-1981		$75	$85

Red Ranger

1976-1981. Bass/Treble Booster, Light Red case.

MODEL YEAR	FEATURES	EXC. COND. LOW	HIGH
1976-1981		$75	$85

Yellow Humper

1976-1981. Yellow case.

MODEL YEAR	FEATURES	EXC. COND. LOW	HIGH
1976-1981		$75	$85

Danelectro

The Danelectro brand name was revived in 1996 with a line of effects pedals. In 1998 the company started to reissue guitars as well.

Cool Cat Chorus

1996-present.

MODEL YEAR	FEATURES	EXC. COND. LOW	HIGH
1990s		$25	$30

Daddy-O Overdrive

1996-present.

MODEL YEAR	FEATURES	EXC. COND. LOW	HIGH
1990s		$25	$30

Dan Echo

1998-present.

MODEL YEAR	FEATURES	EXC. COND. LOW	HIGH
1990s		$35	$45

Fab Tone Distortion

1996-present.

MODEL YEAR	FEATURES	EXC. COND. LOW	HIGH
1990s		$35	$45

Reverb Unit

MODEL YEAR	FEATURES	EXC. COND. LOW	HIGH
1965		$150	$200

Davoli

1970s. Italian import.

TRD

1970s. Solidstate tremolo, reverb, distortion unit.

MODEL YEAR	FEATURES	EXC. COND. LOW	HIGH
1970s		$175	$225

Dean Markley

The string and pickup manufacturer offered a line of effects from the '70s to the early-'90s.

Overlord Classic Tube Overdrive

1988-1991. Uses a 12AX7A tube, AC powered.

MODEL YEAR	FEATURES	EXC. COND. LOW	HIGH
1980s		$55	$80

Overlord III Classic Overdrive

1990-1991. Battery powered version of Overlord pedal.

MODEL YEAR	FEATURES	EXC. COND. LOW	HIGH
1990s		$45	$70

Voice Box 50 (watt model)

1976-1979.

MODEL YEAR	FEATURES	EXC. COND. LOW	HIGH
1970s		$70	$120

Voice Box 100 (watt model)

1976-1979, 1982-ca.1985.

MODEL YEAR	FEATURES	EXC. COND. LOW	HIGH
1970s		$70	$120

Voice Box 200 (watt model)

1976-1979.

MODEL YEAR	FEATURES	EXC. COND. LOW	HIGH
1970s		$70	$120

DeArmond

In 1947, DeArmond may have introduced the first actual signal-processing effect pedal, the Tremolo Control. They made a variety of effects into the 1970s, but only one caught on - their classic volume pedal. DeArmond is primarily noted for pickups.

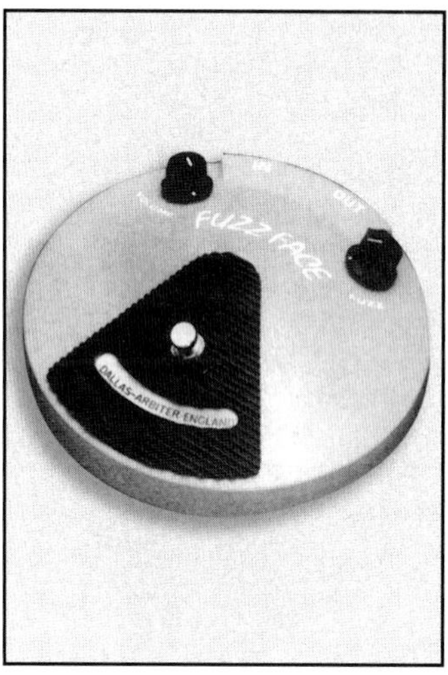

Dallas Arbiter Fuzz Face

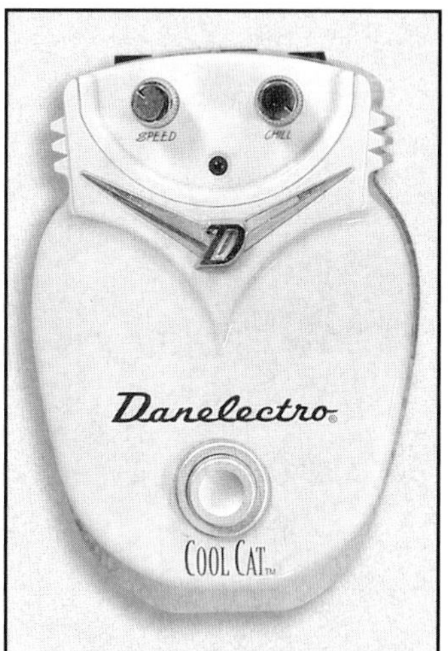

Danelectro Cool Cat

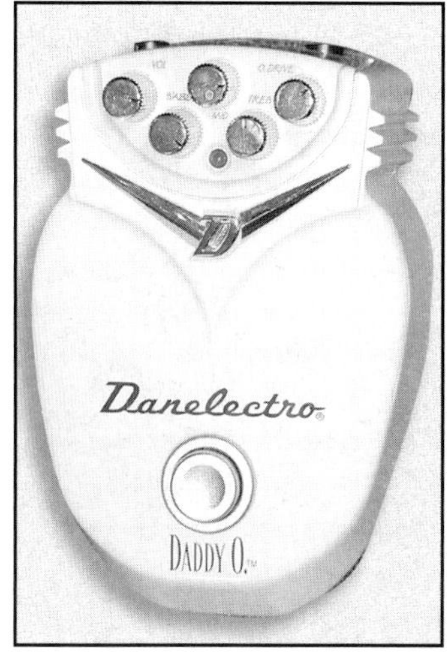

Danelectro Daddy-O

EFFECTS

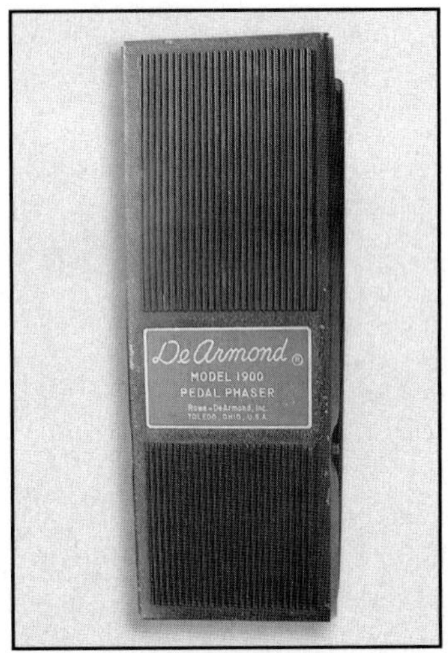

DeArmond Pedal Phaser 1900

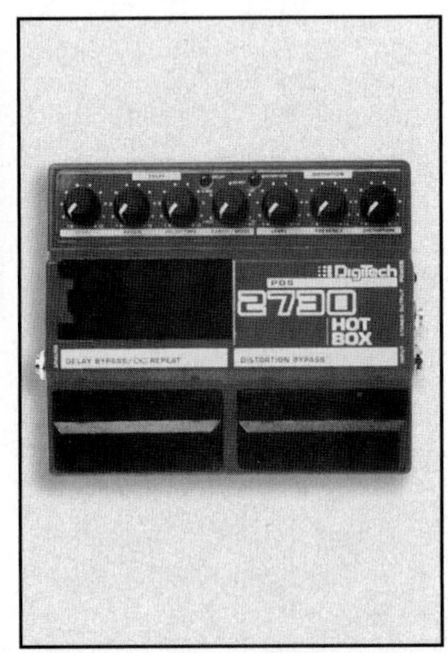

Digitech PDS 2730 Hot Box

Digitech Reverberator XP-400

MODEL YEAR	FEATURES	EXC. COND. LOW	HIGH

Pedal Phaser Model 1900

1974-ca.1979.

1970s $40 $50

Square Wave Distortion Generator

1977-ca.1979.

1970s $100 $140

Thunderbolt B166

1977-ca.1979. Five octave wah.

1970s $45 $55

Tone/Volume Pedal 610

1978-ca.1979.

1970s $40 $50

Tornado Phase Shifter

1977-ca.1979.

1970s $65 $90

Tremolo Control Model 60B

The Model 60 Tremolo Control dates from 1947 to the early-1950s. Model 60A dates from mid- to late-1950s. Model 60B, early-1960s.

1961 $65 $100

Twister 1930

1980. Phase shifter.

1980 $75 $115

Volume Pedal 1602

1978-ca.1980s.

1970s $30 $50

Volume Pedal 1630

1978-1980s. Optoelectric.

1970s $40 $50

Volume Pedal Model 602

1960s.

1960s $30 $70

Weeper Wah Model 1802

1970s $100 $125

DeltaLab Research

Early-1980s. DeltaLab was located in Chelmsford, MA.

Acousticomputer DL-2

1980s. Delay.

1980s $65 $90

Delay Control Pedal DLB-1

1980s. Controls other DeltaLab pedals, chrome, Morley-looking pedal.

1980s $30 $40

Time Line DL-4

1980s. Delay.

1980s $50 $80

Demeter

1980-present. Located in Van Nuys, California, James Demeter and company build amp heads, combos, cabinets, pro audio gear and guitar effects.

Diaz

Early 1980s-2002. Line of effects from the "amp doctor" Cesar Diaz. Diaz died in 2002.

MODEL YEAR	FEATURES	EXC. COND. LOW	HIGH

DigiTech

The DigiTech/DOD company is in Utah and the effects are made in the U.S.A. The DigiTech name started as a line under the DOD brand in the early '80s; later spinning off into it's own brand name. They also produce vocal products and studio processors and are now part of Harman International Industries.

Digital Delay PDS 1000

1985-ca.1989. One second delay.

1985-1989 $75 $100

Digital Delay PDS 2000

1985-1991. Two second delay.

1985-1991 $90 $125

Digital Stereo Chorus/Flanger PDS 1700

1986-1991.

1986-1991 $90 $120

Double Play PDS 2700

1989-1991. Delay and chorus

1989-1991 $90 $120

Guitar Effects Processor RP 1

1980s $80 $100

Guitar Effects Processor RP 3

1980s $80 $100

Guitar Effects Processor RP 6

1980s $80 $100

Guitar Effects Processor RP 14D

Floor unit with expression pedal, one 12AX7 tube, 100 programs, integrated amp modeling.

2000 $275 $325

Guitar Effects Processor RP 200

1990s $85 $105

Hot Box PDS 2730

1989-1991. Delay and distortion

1989-1991 $80 $100

Modulator Pedal XP 200

Floor unit with 61 present, including chorus, flanger, etc.

2000 $90 $100

Multi Play PDS 20/20

1987-1991. Multi-function digital delay.

1987-1991 $125 $150

Multi-Effects Processor RP 100

2000 $80 $100

Pedalverb Digital Reverb Pedal PDS 3000

1987-1991.

1987-1991 $100 $120

Programmable Distortion PDS 1550

1986-1991.

1986-1991 $30 $60

Programmable Distortion PDS 1650

1989-1991.

1989-1991 $30 $60

Rock Box PDS 2715

1989-1991. Chorus and distortion.

1989-1991 $30 $60

Sampler PDS 2000

1990s $70 $90

MODEL YEAR	FEATURES	EXC. COND. LOW	HIGH

Two Second Digital Delay PDS 1002
1987-1991.
1987-1991 $75 $100

Whammy Pedal WP I
1990-1993. Original issue WP I, Red case.
1990-1993 $300 $375

Whammy Pedal WP II
1994-1997. Can switch between two presets.
1990s $150 $200

Whammy Pedal WP IV
2000s. New version of classic WH-1 with some added features and updates.
2000s $120 $140

DiMarzio

The pickup maker offered a couple of effects in the late-1980s to the mid-1990s.

Metal Pedal
1987-1989.
1987-1989 $50 $60

Very Metal Fuzz
Ca.1989-1995. Distortion/overdrive pedal.
1989-1995 $55 $65

DOD

DOD Electronics started in Salt Lake City in 1974. Today, they're a major effect manufacturer with dozens of pedals made in the U.S.A. They also market effects under the name DigiTech. They are now part of Harman International Industries.

6 Band Equalizer EQ601
1977-1982.
1977-1982 $40 $60

AB Box 270
1978-1982.
1978-1982 $20 $30

American Metal FX56
1985-1991.
1985-1991 $25 $35

Analog Delay 680
1979-?
1979-1982 $85 $100

Attacker FX54
1992-1994. Distortion and compressor.
1992-1994 $30 $40

Bass Compressor FX82
1987-ca.1989.
1987-1989 $40 $50

Bass EQ FX42B
1987-1996.
1987-1996 $30 $40

Bass Grunge FX92
1995-1996.
1995-1996 $40 $50

Bass Overdrive FX91
1998-present.
1998-1999 $40 $50

Bass Stereo Chorus Flanger FX72
1987-1997.
1987-1997 $40 $50

Bass Stereo Chorus FX62
1987-1996.
1987-1996 $40 $50

Bi-FET Preamp FX10
1982-1996.
1982-1996 $20 $30

Buzz Box FX33
1994-1996. Grunge distortion.
1994-1996 $50 $60

Chorus 690
1980-ca.1982. Dual speed chorus.
1980-1982 $80 $100

Classic Fuzz FX52
1990-1997.
1990-1997 $25 $35

Classic Tube FX53
1990-1997.
1990-1997 $35 $45

Compressor 280
1978-ca.1982.
1978-1982 $35 $45

Compressor FX80
1982-1985.
1982-1985 $30 $40

Compressor Sustainer FX80B
1986-1996.
1986-1996 $30 $40

Death Metal FX86
1994-present. Distortion.
1994-1999 $20 $30

Delay FX90
1984-ca.1987.
1984-1987 $40 $60

Digital Delay DFX9
1989-ca.1990.
1989-1990 $30 $40

Digital Delay Sampler DFX94
1995-1997.
1995-1997 $40 $70

Distortion FX55
1982-1986.
1982-1986 $20 $30

Edge Pedal FX87
1988-1989.
1988-1989 $20 $30

Envelope Filter 440
1981-ca.1982. Reissued in 1995.
1981-1982 $60 $70

Envelope Filter FX25
1982-1997. Replaced by FX25B.
1982-1987 $30 $40

Envelope Filter FX25B
1981-1987
1982-1987 $30 $40

Equalizer FX40
1982-1986.
1982-1986 $30 $40

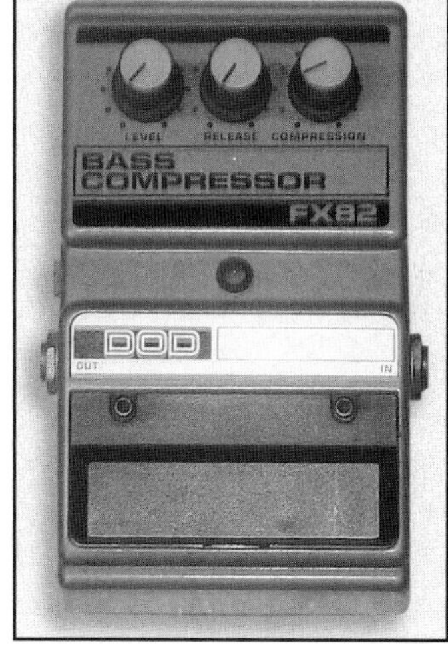

DOD Bass Compressor FX82

DOD Bass Stereo Flanger FX72

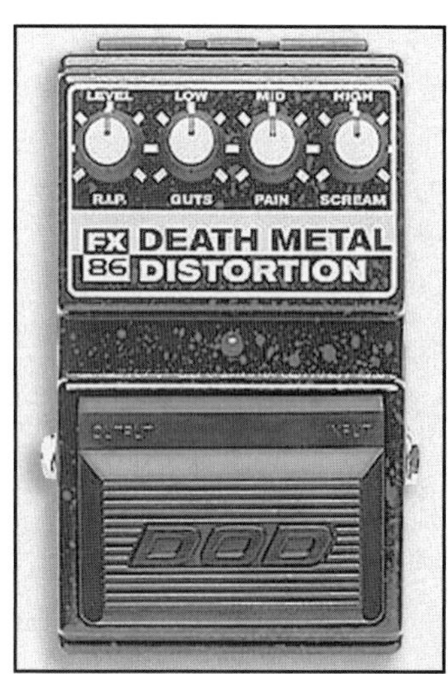

DOD Death Metal FX86

EFFECTS

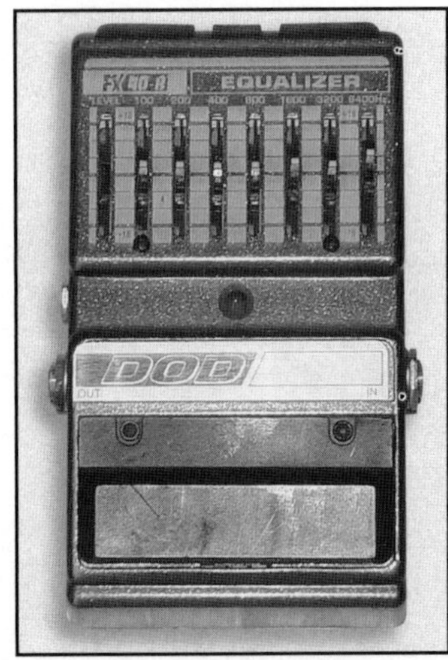

DOD Equalizer FX40B

DOD Milk Box FX84

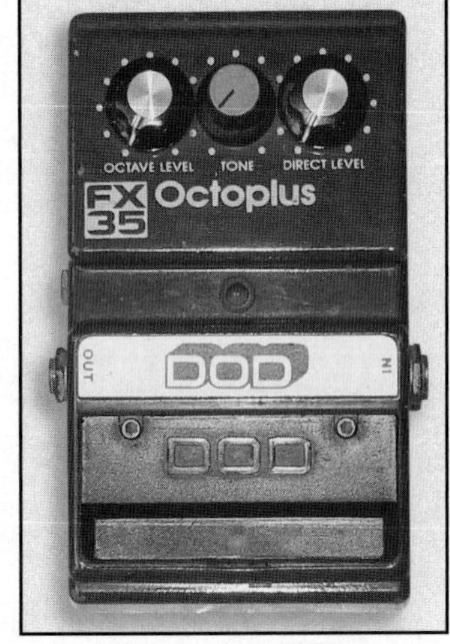

DOD Octoplus FX35

MODEL YEAR	FEATURES	EXC. COND. LOW	HIGH
Equalizer FX40B			
1987-present. Eight bands for bass.			
1987-1999		$30	$40
Fet Preamp 210			
1981-ca.1982.			
1981-1982		$30	$40
Flanger 670			
1981-1982.			
1981-1982		$65	$85
Gate Loop FX30			
1980s		$25	$35
Graphic Equalizer EQ-610			
1980-ca.1982. Ten bands.			
1980-1982		$40	$50
Graphic Equalizer EQ-660			
1980-ca.1982. Six bands.			
1980-1982		$30	$40
Grunge FX69			
1993-present. Distortion.			
1993-1999		$30	$40
Hard Rock Distortion FX57			
1987-1994. With built-in delay.			
1987-1994		$30	$40
Harmonic Enhancer FX85			
1986-ca. 1989.			
1986-1989		$30	$40
I. T. FX100			
1997. Intergrated Tube distortion, produces harmonics.			
1997		$45	$55
Juice Box FX51			
1996-1997.			
1996-1997		$30	$40
Master Switch 225			
1988-ca.1989. A/B switch and loop selector.			
1988-1989		$25	$35
Meat Box FX32			
1994-1996.			
1994-1996		$30	$40
Metal Maniac FX58			
1990-1996.			
1990-1996		$30	$40
Metal Triple Play Guitar Effects System TR3M			
1994.			
1994		$30	$40
Metal X FX70			
1993-1996.			
1993-1996		$30	$40
Milk Box FX84			
1994-present.			
1994-1999		$35	$45
Mini-Chorus 460			
1981-ca.1982.			
1981-1982		$50	$70
Mixer 240			
1978-ca.1982.			
1978-1982		$20	$30

MODEL YEAR	FEATURES	EXC. COND. LOW	HIGH
Momentary Footswitch			
Introduced in 1987, temporally engages other boxes.			
1980s		$20	$30
Noise Gate 230			
1978-1982.			
1970s		$25	$35
Noise Gate FX30			
1982-ca.1987.			
1980s		$25	$35
Octoplus FX35			
1987-1996. Octaves.			
1980s		$30	$40
Overdrive Plus FX50B			
1986-1997.			
1980s		$30	$40
Overdrive Preamp 250			
1978-1982. Reissued in 1995.			
1978-1982		$75	$100
Overdrive Preamp 250 (reissue)			
1995-1999.			
1995-1999		$35	$45
Overdrive Preamp FX50			
1982-1985.			
1982-1985		$30	$40
Performer Compressor Limiter 525			
1981-1984.			
1981-1984		$50	$60
Performer Delay 585			
1982-1985.			
1982-1985		$50	$60
Performer Distortion 555			
1981-1984.			
1981-1984		$30	$40
Performer Flanger 575			
1981-1985.			
1981-1985		$30	$40
Performer Phasor 595			
1981-1984.			
1981-1984		$30	$40
Performer Stereo Chorus 565			
1981-1985.			
1981-1985	FET switching	$50	$60
Performer Wah Filter 545			
1981-1984.			
1981-1984		$35	$45
Phasor 201			
1981-ca.1982. Rreissued in 1995.			
1981-1982		$60	$100
Phasor 401			
1978-1981.			
1978-1981		$60	$100
Phasor 490			
1980-ca.1982.			
1980-1982		$60	$100
Phasor FX20			
1982-1985.			
1982-1985		$30	$40

MODEL YEAR	FEATURES	EXC. COND. LOW	HIGH

Psychoacoustic Processor FX87

1988-1989.

1988-1989 $30 $40

Punkifier FX76

1997.

1997 $40 $50

Resistance Mixer 240

1978-ca.1982.

1978-1982 $25 $35

Silencer FX27

1988-ca.1989. Noise reducer.

1988-1989 $30 $40

Stereo Chorus FX60

1982-1986.

1982-1986 $30 $40

Stereo Chorus FX65

1986-1996.

1986-1996 $35 $45

Stereo Flanger FX70

1982-ca.1985.

1982-1985 $30 $40

Stereo Flanger FX75

1986-1987.

1986-1987 $30 $40

Stereo Flanger FX75B

1987-1997.

1987-1997 $30 $40

Stereo Phasor FX20B

1986-1999.

1986-1999 $30 $40

Stereo Turbo Chorus FX67

1988-1991.

1988-1991 $30 $40

Super American Metal FX56B

1992-1996.

1992-1996 $30 $40

Super Stereo Chorus FX68

1992-1996.

1992-1996 $30 $40

Supra Distortion FX55B

1986-present.

1986-1999 $20 $30

Wah-Volume FX-17 (pedal)

1987-2000.

1987-2000 $35 $45

Dredge-Tone

Located in Berkeley, California, Dredge-Tone offers effects and electronic kits.

Dunlop

Jim Dunlop, USA offers the Crybaby, MXR (see MXR), Rockman, High Gain, Heil Sound (see Heil), Tremolo, Jimi Hendrix, Rotovibe and Uni-Vibe brand name effects.

Crybaby Bass

1985-present. Bass wah.

1985-1989 $50 $60

1990-1999 $50 $60

MODEL YEAR	FEATURES	EXC. COND. LOW	HIGH

Crybaby Wah Pedal 535

1995-present. Multi-range pedal with an external boost control.

1995-1999 $70 $80

Crybaby Wah-Wah GCB-95

1982-present. Dunlop began manufacturing the Crybaby in 1982.

1982-1989 $45 $55

1990-1999 $35 $40

High Gain Volume + Boost Pedal

1983-1996.

1983-1996 $30 $40

High Gain Volume Pedal

1983-present.

1983-1999 $35 $45

Jimi Hendrix Fuzz (Round)

1987-1993.

1987-1993 $40 $60

Rotovibe JH-4S Standard

1989-1998. Standard is finished in bright Red enamel with chrome top.

1989-1998 $90 $100

Tremolo Volume Plus TVP-1

1995-1998. Pedal.

1995-1998 $100 $120

Uni-Vibe UV-1

1995-present. Rotating speaker effect.

1995-1999 $150 $200

2000-2003 $190 $210

Dynacord

1950-present. Dynacord is a German company that makes audio and pro sound amps, as well as other electronic equipment and is now owned by TELEX/EVI Audio (an U.S. company), which also owns the Electro-Voice brandname. In the '60s they offered tape echo machines. In '94 a line of multi-effects processors were introduced under the Electro-Voice/Dynacord name, but by the following year they were just listed as Electro-Voice.

EchoCord

Tape echo unit, introduced in 1959.

1960 $225 $275

Ecco Fonic

The Ecco Fonic was distributed by Fender in 1958-1959.

Echo Unit

1958-1959. Reverb unit.

1958-1959 With Brown case $250 $300

Echoplex

The Echoplex tape echo units were first sold under the Maestro brand name. After Maestro dropped the Echoplex, it was marketed under the Market Electronics name from the late-1970s-early-1980s. In the later 1980s, Market Electronics was dropped from the ads and they were marketed under the Echoplex brand name. Both the

DOD Flanger FX75

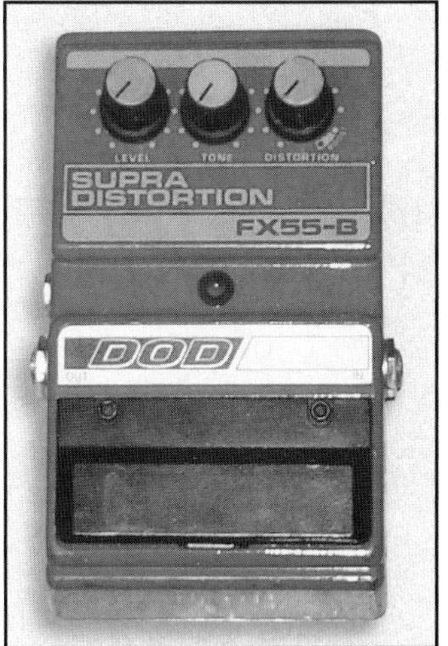

DOD Supra Distortion FX55B

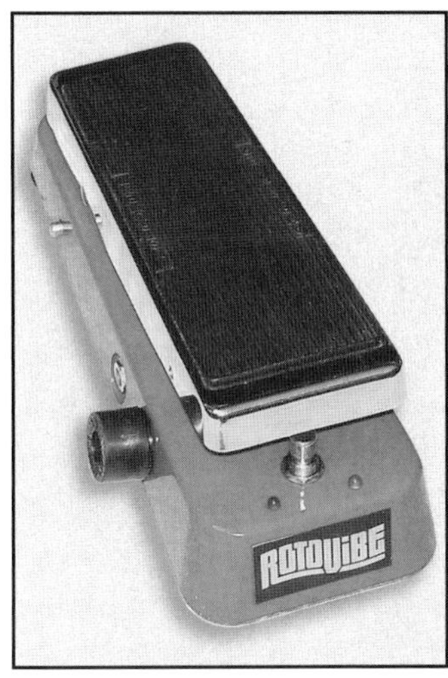

Dunlop Rotovibe JH-45

Electra Stereo Chorus 504CH

E-H Bassballs

E-H Big Muff Pi reissue

MODEL YEAR	FEATURES	EXC. COND. LOW	HIGH

Market and Exhoplex brands are listed here; for earlier models see Maestro.

Echoplex EP3

1984-ca. 1988. Solidstate version.

1984-1988		$250	$350

Echoplex EP4

1984-1991. Solidstate version.

1984-1991		$250	$350

Echoplex EP6T

1980-ca.1988. All-tube reissue of the EP2.

1980-1988		$350	$450

EFX

1980s. Brand name of the Los Angeles-based EFX Center; they also offered a direct box and a powered pedal box/board.

Switch Box B287

1984. Dual effects loop selector.

1984		$20	$25

Electra

1971-1984. A guitar brand name imported by St. Louis Music, Electra offered a line of effects in the late '70s. See Guitar section for more company info.

Chorus 504CH

ca.1975-ca.1980.

1975-1980		$45	$65

Compressor 502C

1975-1980.

1975-1980		$35	$45

Distortion 500D

ca.1976-ca.1980.

1975-1980		$60	$80

Fuzz Wah

ca.1975-ca.1980.

1975-1980		$90	$120

Pedal Drive 515AC

ca.1976-ca.1980. Overdrive.

1975-1980		$30	$40

Phaser Model 501P

ca.1976-ca.1980.

1975-1980		$40	$50

Phaser Model 875

1975-ca.1980.

1975-1980		$40	$50

Roto Phase I

1975-ca.1980. Small pocket phaser.

1975-1980		$50	$70

Roto Phase II

1975-ca.1980. Pedal phasor.

1975-1980		$60	$80

Electro-Harmonix

1968-1981, 1996-present. New York City's Electro-Harmonix was founded in '68 by Mike Matthews. The company initially produced small plug-in boosters such as the LPB-1. In '70, they unveiled the awe-inspiring Big Muff Pi fuzz. Dozens of innovative pedals followed. After years of disputes, the nonunion E-H factory became the target of union organizers. A '81 union campaign, combining picketing and harrying of E-H employees, brought production to a halt. Matthews' financier then cut his funding, and in early '82, E.H. filed for bankruptcy. Later that year, Matthews was able to reopen and continue through '84. In '96, he again began producing reissues of many of his classic designs as well as new designs.

MODEL YEAR	FEATURES	EXC. COND. LOW	HIGH

10 Band Graphic Equalizer

1977-1981. Includes footswitch.

1977-1981		$50	$70

16-Second Digital Delay

Early-1980s.

1980s	With foot controller	$600	$800
1980s	Without foot controller	$450	$650

3 Phase Liner

1981.

1981		$40	$50

5X Junction Mixer

1977-1981.

1977-1981		$25	$35

Attack Equalizer

1975-1981. Active EQ, a.k.a. "Knock Out."

1975-1981		$100	$200

Attack/Decay

1980-1981. Tape reverse simulator.

1980-1981		$175	$225

Bad Stone Phase Shifter

1975-1981.

1970s	Three knobs	$175	$250
1970s	Two knobs, color switch	$150	$225

Bass Micro-Synthesizer

1981-1984. Reissued in '99.

1981-1984		$275	$375

Bass Micro-Synthesizer (reissue)

1999-present.

1999		$150	$175

Bassballs

1978-1984. Bass envelope filter/distortion. Reissued in '98.

1978-1984		$175	$250

Big Muff Pi

1971-1984. Sustain, floor unit. Issued in three different looks, as described below. Reissued in 1996.

1970s	Earlier Black graphics, knobs in triangle	$200	$250
1970s	Later Red/Black graphics, 1/2" letters	$130	$150
1980s	Red/Black graphics, logo in 1" letters	$100	$125

Big Muff Pi (reissue)

1996-present. Originally made in Russia, but currently both Russian- and U.S.-made versions are available.

1996-1999	Russian-made	$30	$35

MODEL YEAR	FEATURES	EXC. COND. LOW	HIGH

Black Finger Compressor Sustainer
1977. Three knobs in triangle pattern. Reissued in 2003.

1977		$130	$150

Clap Track
1980-1984. Drum effect.

1980-1984		$30	$50

Clone Theory
1977-1981. Chorus effect.

1977-1981		$125	$155

Crash Pad
1980-1984. Percussion synth.

1980-1984		$30	$50

Crying Tone Pedal
1976-1978. Wah-wah.

1976-1978		$170	$200

Deluxe Big Muff Pi
1978-1981. Sustain, AC version of Big Muff Pi, includes a complete Soul Preacher unit.

1978-1981		$150	$175

Deluxe Electric Mistress Flanger
1977-1983. AC. Reissued in 1996.

1970s		$150	$250
1980s		$125	$175

Deluxe Memory Man
1977-1983. Echo and delay, featured four knobs 1977-1978, from 1979-1983 it has five knobs and added vibrato and chorus. Reissued in 1996.

1977-1978	Four knobs	$200	$275
1979-1983	Five knobs	$200	$275

Deluxe Octave Multiplexer
1977-1981.

1977-1981		$150	$200

Digital Delay
1981-84. With digital chorus.

1981-1984		$200	$250

Digital Rhythm Matrix DRM-15
1981-1984.

1981-1984		$150	$250

Digital Rhythm Matrix DRM-16
1979-1983.

1979-1983		$150	$250

Digital Rhythm Matrix DRM-32
1981-1984.

1981-1984		$150	$250

Doctor Q Envelope Follower
1976-1983. For bass or guitar. Reissued in '01.

1976-1983		$100	$150
2001-2003	Reissue	$25	$30

Domino Theory
1981. Sound sensitive light tube.

1981		$75	$125

Echo 600
1981.

1981		$125	$175

Echoflanger
1977-1982. Flange, slapback, chorus, filter.

1977-1982		$200	$250

Electric Mistress Flanger
1976-1984.

1976-1984		$75	$150

Electronic Metronome
1978-1980.

1978-1980		$20	$25

Frequency Analyzer
1977-1984. Ring modulator. Reissued in '01.

1977-1984		$200	$250

Full Double Tracking Effect
1978-1981. Doubling, slapback.

1978-1981		$75	$125

Fuzz Wah
Introduced around 1974.

1970s		$150	$200

Golden Throat
1977-1984.

1977-1984		$125	$200

Golden Throat Deluxe
1977-1979. Deluxe has a built-in monitor amp.

1977-1979		$125	$200

Golden Throat II
1978-1981.

1978-1981		$75	$150

Guitar Synthesizer
1981. Sold for $1,495 in May 1981.

1981		$250	$300

Hog's Foot Bass Booster
1977-1980.

1977-1978		$60	$80

Holy Grail
1977-1980.

2000s	With adapter	$75	$85

Hot Foot
1977-1978. Rocker pedal turns knob of other E-H effects.

1977-1980		$50	$60

Hot Tubes
1978-1984. Overdrive. Reissued in 2001.

1978-1984		$70	$100
2000s	Reissue	$60	$70

Linear Power Booster LPB-1
1968-1983.

1976-1979		$55	$65
1980-1983		$30	$40

Linear Power Booster LPB-2
Ca.1968-1983.

1968-1983		$65	$75

Little Big Muff Pi
1976-1980. Sustain, one knob floor unit.

1976-1980		$120	$130

Low Frequency Compressor
1977. For bass.

1977		$150	$175

Memory Man
1976-1984. Analog delay. Reissued in '01.

1976-1979		$200	$225
1980-1984		$100	$150

E-H Electric Mistress

E-H Black Finger

E-H Hot Foot

EFFECTS

E-H Screaming Tree

E-H Q-Tron

E-H Wiggler

MODEL YEAR	FEATURES	EXC. COND. LOW	HIGH
Micro Synthesizer			
1978-1984. Mini keyboard phaser. Reissued in '98.			
1978-1979		$200	$250
1980-1984		$200	$250
Micro Synthesizer (reissue)			
1998-present.			
1998-2002		$150	$175
Mini-Mixer			
1978-1981. Mini mic mixer. Reissued in '01.			
1978-1981		$25	$35
MiniSynthesizer			
1981-1983. Mini keyboard with phaser.			
1981-1983		$275	$375
MiniSynthesizer With Echo			
1981.			
1981		$325	$475
Mole Bass Booster			
1968-1978.			
1968-1969		$50	$75
1970-1978		$30	$40
Muff Fuzz Crying Tone			
1977-1978. Fuzz, wah.			
1977-1978		$100	$200
Octave Multiplexer Floor Unit			
1976-1980.			
1976-1980		$150	$200
Octave Multiplexer Pedal			
1976-1977. Reissued in '01.			
1976-1977		$150	$200
Panic Button			
1981. Siren sounds for drum.			
1981		$20	$30
Poly Chorus			
1981. Same as Echoflanger. Reissued in '99.			
1981		$175	$200
Poly Chorus (reissue)			
1999-present. Stereo.			
1999-2002		$125	$150
Polyphase			
1979-1981. With envelope.			
1979-1981		$125	$150
Pulse Modulator			
Ca.1968 -ca.1972. Triple tremolo.			
1968-1969		$200	$275
1970-1972		$150	$200
Q-Tron			
1997-present. Envelope controlled filter.			
1997-1999		$100	$150
Q-Tron +			
2000s		$125	$150
Queen Triggered Wah			
1976-1978. Wah/Envelope Filter.			
1976-1978		$100	$125
Random Tone Generator RTG			
1981.			
1981		$30	$40
Rhythm 12 (rhythm machine)			
1978.			
1978		$100	$125

MODEL YEAR	FEATURES	EXC. COND. LOW	HIGH
Rolling Thunder			
1980-1981. Percussion synth.			
1980-1981		$30	$40
Screaming Bird Treble Booster			
Ca.1968-1980. In-line unit.			
1968-1980		$50	$60
Screaming Tree Treble Booster			
1977-1981. Floor unit.			
1977-1981		$70	$80
Sequencer Drum			
1981. Drum effect.			
1981		$35	$45
Slapback Echo			
1977-1978. Stereo.			
1977-1978		$100	$125
Small Clone EH4600			
1983-1984. Analog chorus with depth and rate controls, purple face plate with white logo. Reissued in '99.			
1983-1984		$150	$200
Small Clone EH46000 (reissue)			
2000s		$50	$55
Small Stone Phase Shifter			
1975-1984. Reissued in 1996.			
1975-1979		$75	$125
1980-1984		$55	$75
Soul Preacher			
1977-1983. Compressor sustainer.			
1977-1983		$100	$150
Space Drum			
1980-1981. Percussion synth.			
1980-1981		$100	$150
Switch Blade			
1977-1983. A-B Box.			
1977-1983		$35	$45
Talking Pedal			
1977-1978. Creates vowel sounds.			
1977-1978		$225	$275
The Silencer			
1976-1981. Noise elimination.			
1976-1981		$50	$75
The Wiggler			
2000-present. All-tube modulator.			
2000s		$140	$150
The Worm			
2000-present. Wah/Phaser.			
2000s		$60	$70
Tube Zipper			
2001-present. Tube (two 12AX7EHs) envelope follower.			
2000-2003		$200	$225
Vocoder			
1978-1981. Modulates voice with instrument.			
1978-1981	Rackmount	$300	$500
Volume Pedal			
1978-1981.			
1978-1981		$40	$60
Y-Triggered Filter			
1976-1977.			
1976-1977		$100	$125

MODEL YEAR	FEATURES	EXC. COND. LOW	HIGH

Zipper Envelope Follower

1976-1978. The Tube Zipper was introduced in 2001.

1976-1978		$150	$200

Epiphone

Epiphone pedals are labeled "G.A.S Guitar Audio System" and were offered in the late-1980s-early-1990s.

Chorus EP-CH-70

1988-1989.

1988-1989		$30	$40

Compressor EP-CO-20

1988-1991.

1980s		$30	$40

Delay EP-DE-80

1988-1989. Twenty to 400 ms of delay.

1988-1989		$35	$45

Distortion EP-DI-10

1988-1991.

1980s		$30	$40

Flanger EP-FL-60

1988-1991.

1980s		$30	$40

Overdrive EP-OD-30

1988-1991.

1980s		$30	$40

Ernie Ball

Ernie Ball owned a music store in Tarzana, California, when he noticed the demand for a better selection of strings. The demand for his Slinky strings grew to the point where, in '67, he sold the store to concentrate on strings. He went on to produce the Earthwood brand of guitars and basses from '72-'85. In '84, Ball purchased the Music Man company.

Volume Pedal

1977-present.

1970s		$30	$50
1980s		$40	$60
1990s		$50	$70

EXR

The EXR Corporation was located in Brighton, Michigan.

Projector

1983-ca.1984. "Psychoacoustic enhancer pedal."

1983-1984		$60	$70

Projector SP III

1983-ca.1984. Volume pedal/sound boost.

1983-1984		$60	$70

Farfisa

The organ company offered effects in the 1960s.

Model VIP 345 Organ

Mid-1960s. Portable organ with Syntheslalom used in the rock and roll venue.

1960s		$500	$550

MODEL YEAR	FEATURES	EXC. COND. LOW	HIGH

Repeater

1969		$75	$85

Wah/Volume

1969		$85	$95

Fender

Although Fender has flirted with effects since the 1950s (the volume/volume-tone pedal and the EccoFonic), it concentrated mainly on guitars and amps. Fender effects ranged from the subline to the ridiculous, from the rube Reverb to the Dimension IV. The Reverb is the only Fender effect currently produced.

'63 Reverb

1994-present. Reissue of the 1960s three-knob, tube, spring reverb unit. Brown Tolex with Wheat grille, a few in Blond with Oxblood.

1990s	Brown Tolex	$300	$325
1990s	White (limited run)	$350	$375

Blender Fuzz

1968-1977. Battery operated fuzz and sustain.

1968-1969		$225	$275
1970-1977		$175	$225

Contempo Organ

1967-1968. Portable organ, all solidstate, 61 keys including a 17-key bass section, catalog shows with Red cover material.

1967-1968		$300	$500

Dimension IV

1968-1970. Multi-effects unit using an oil-filled drum.

1968		$175	$200

Echo-Reverb

1966-1970. Solidstate, echo-reverb effect produced by rotating metal disk, Black Tolex, Silver grille.

1966-1970		$200	$300

Electronic Echo Chamber

1962-1968. Solidstate tape echo, up to 400 ms of delay, rectangle box with two controls 1962-1967, slanted front 1967-1968.

1964		$250	$350

Fuzz-Wah

1968-1984. Has "Fuzz" and "Wah" switches on sides of pedal 1968-1973, has three switches above the pedal 1974-1984.

1960s	Switches on side	$150	$200
1970s	Switches above	$125	$175

Phaser

1975-1977. AC powered.

1975-1977		$100	$150

Reverb Unit

1961-1966, 1975-1978. Fender used a wide variety of Tolex coverings in the early-1960s. The coverings matched their amp coverings. Initially, Fender used rough Blond Tolex, then rough Brown Tolex, followed by smooth White or Black Tolex.

1961	Blond Tolex, Oxblood grille	$1,200	$1,500
1961	Brown Tolex	$800	$1,100

Fender Blender

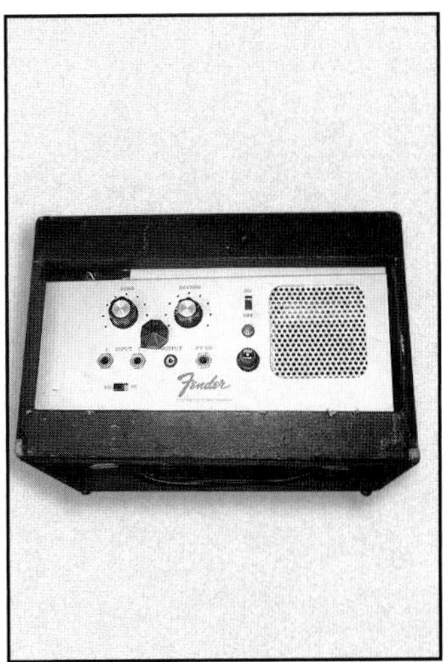
Fender Electronic Echo Chamber

Fender Fuzz Wah

EFFECTS

Foxx Tone Machine

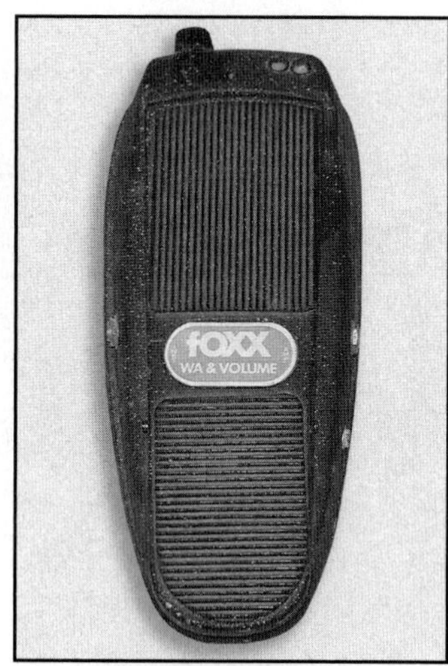

Foxx Wa & Volume

Frantone Peachfuzz

EFFECTS

MODEL YEAR	FEATURES	EXC. COND. LOW	HIGH
1962	Blond Tolex, Oxblood grille	$1,200	$1,500
1962	Brown Tolex, Wheat grille	$800	$1,100
1963	Brown Tolex	$700	$1,000
1963	Rough Blond Tolex	$1,100	$1,400
1963	Smooth White Tolex	$1,000	$1,400
1964	Black Tolex	$700	$1,000
1964	Brown Tolex	$700	$1,000
1964	Smooth White Tolex	$1,000	$1,400
1965	Black Tolex	$600	$800
1966	Black Tolex	$600	$800
1966	Solidstate, flat cabinet	$150	$250
1975-1978	Tube reverb reinstated	$500	$600

Tone and Volume Foot Pedal

1954-1984.

1960s		$125	$150

Vibratone

1967-1972. Leslie-type speaker cabinet made specifically for the guitar, two-speed motor.

1960s		$800	$1,000

FlexiSound

FlexiSound products were made in Lancaster, PA.

F. S. Clipper

1975-ca.1976. Distortion, plugged directly into guitar jack.

1975-1976		$45	$55

The Beefer

1975. Power booster, plugged directly into guitar jack.

1975		$30	$40

Flip

Line of tube effects by Guyatone and distributed in the U.S. by Godlyke Distributing.

FM Acoustics

Made in Switzerland.

E-1 Pedal

1975. Volume, distortion, filter pedal.

1975		$50	$70

Foxx

Foxx pedals are readily identifiable by their felt-like "fur" covering. They slunk onto the scene in 1971 and were extinct by 1978. Made by Hollywood's Ridinger Associates, their most notable product was the Tone Machine fuzz. Foxx-made pedals also have appeared under various brand names such as G and G, Guild, Yamaha and Sears Roebuck, generally without fur.

Clean Machine

1974-1978.

1974-1978		$175	$200

MODEL YEAR	FEATURES	EXC. COND. LOW	HIGH

Down Machine

1971-1977. Bass wah.

1971-1977		$175	$200

Foot Phaser

1975-1977.

1975-1977		$100	$150

Fuzz and Wa and Volume

1974-1978.

1974-1978		$150	$200

Guitar Synthesizer I

1975.

1975		$250	$300

O.D. Machine

1972-ca.1975.

1972-1975		$100	$150

Phase III

1975-1978.

1975-1978		$75	$100

Tone Machine

1971-1978. Fuzz with "Octave."

1971-1978		$250	$300

Wa and Volume

1971-1978.

1971-1978		$140	$160

Wa Machine

1971-ca.1978.

1971-1978		$125	$150

Framptone

2000-present. Founded by Peter Frampton, Framptone offers hand-made guitar effects.

Frantone

1994-present. Effects and accessories hand-built in New York City.

Fulltone

1991-present. Fulltone effects are based on some of the classic effects of the past. Fulltone was started in Los Angeles by Michael Fuller who says the company was born out of his love for Jimi Hendrix and fine vintage pedals.

Deja Vibe

1991-present. UniVibe-type pedal, later models have a Vintage/Modern switch. Stereo version also available.

1991-1999	Mono	$175	$225

Deja Vibe II

1997-present. Like Deja Vibe but with built-in speed control. Stereo version also available.

19971999	Mono	$200	$250

Octafuzz

1996-present. Copy of the Tycobrahe Octavia.

1996-1999		$100	$130

Furman Sound

1993-present. Located in Petaluma, California, Furman makes audio and video signal processors and AC power conditioning products for music and other markets.

MODEL YEAR	FEATURES	EXC. COND. LOW	HIGH

PQ3 Parametric EQ

1998-present. Rackmount preamp and equalizer.

1998-1999		$100	$150

PQ6 Parametric Stereo

1990s		$125	$175

RV1 Reverb Rackmount

1990s		$100	$150

George Dennis

1991-present. Founded by George Burgerstein, original products were a line of effects pedals. In '96 they added a line of tube amps. The company in located in Prague, Czech Republic, and the products are distributed in the U.S. by Midco International.

Gibson

See Maestro listing as most Gibson effects were offered under that brand name.

Godbout

Sold a variety of effects do-it-yourself kits in the 1970s. Difficult to value because quality depends on skills of builder.

Effects Kits

1970s		$15	$30

Goodrich Sound

Late-1970s. Goodrich was located in Grand Haven, Michigan.

Match Box 33670 Line Boost

Early-1980s. Small rectangular in and out box with control knob.

1980s		$40	$50

Volume Pedal 6122

1979-ca.1980. Uses a potentiometer.

1970s		$45	$55

Volume Pedal 6400ST

1979-ca.1980. Uses a potentiometer.

1970s		$40	$50

Volume Pedal 6402

1979-ca.1980. Uses photocell.

1970s		$40	$50

Gretsch

Gretsch has offered a limited line of effects from time to time. See Guitar section for more company info.

Controfuzz

Mid-1970s. Distortion.

1970s		$150	$170

Expandafuzz

Mid-1970s. Distortion.

1970s		$130	$150

Reverb Unit Model 6144 Preamp Reverb

1963-1967. Approximately 17 watts, preamp functionality, no speaker.

1963-1967		$150	$250

Tremofect

Mid-1970s. Tremolo effect.

1970s		$150	$250

MODEL YEAR	FEATURES	EXC. COND. LOW	HIGH

Guild

Primarily known for guitars, Guild marketed effects made by Electro-Harmonix, Foxx, WEM and Applied, in the 1960s and 1970s.

Copicat

1960s-1979. Echo

1970s		$250	$350

Foxey Lady Fuzz

Distortion, sustain.

1969-1975	Two knobs, made by E-H	$150	$250
1976-1977	3 knobs in row, same as Big Muff	$75	$150

Fuzz Wah FW-3

1975-ca.1979. Distortion, volume, wah. Made by Foxx.

1970s		$140	$160

HH Echo Unit

1976-ca.1979.

1970s		$150	$200

VW-1

1975-ca.1979. Volume, wah. Made by Foxx.

1970s		$150	$200

Guyatone

1998-present. Imported stomp boxes and tape echo units distributed by Godlyke Distributing.

Heathkit

1960s. Unassembled kits sold at retail.

TA-28 Distortion Booster

1960s. Fuzz assembly kit, heavy 1960s super fuzz, case-by-case quality depending on the builder.

1960s		$120	$140

Heavy Metal Products

Mid-1970s. From Alto Loma, California, products for the heavy metal guitarist.

Raunchbox Fuzz

1975-1976.

1975-1976		$60	$75

Switchbox

1975-1976. A/B box.

1975-1976		$15	$25

Heet Sound Products

1974-present. The E Bow concept goes back to '69, but a hand-held model wasn't available until '74. Made in Los Angeles.

E Bow

1977-1979, 1985-1987, 1994-present. The Energy Bow. Hand-held electro-magnetic string driver.

1970s		$45	$55

E Bow for Pedal Steels

1979. Hand-held electro-magnetic string driver.

1979		$25	$35

Heil Sound

1960-present. Founded by Bob Heil, Marissa, Illinois. Created the "talk box" technology as

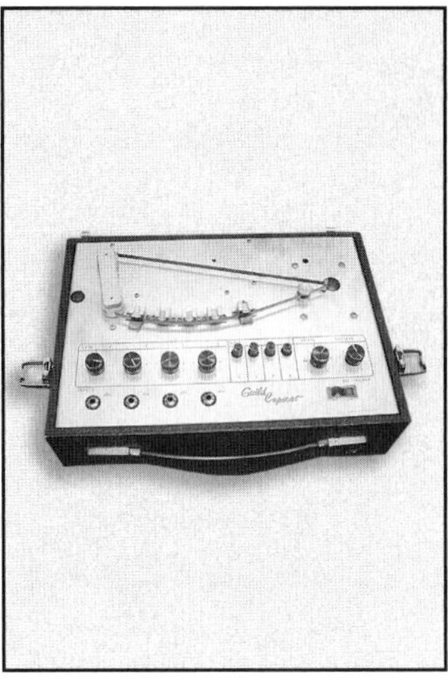

Guild Copicat

Guild Tweedy Bird MM500

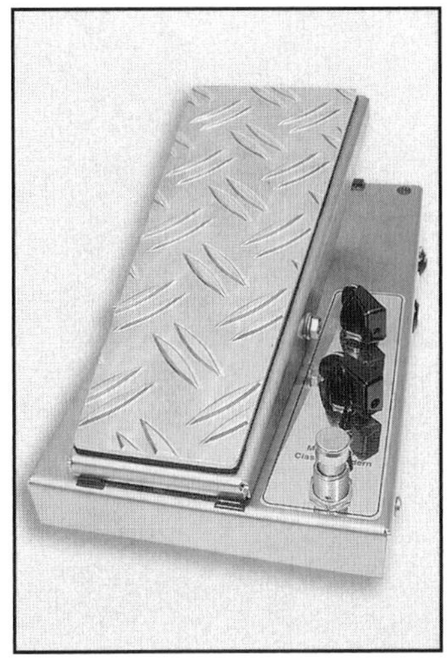

Guyatone Silver Machine

EFFECTS

Hohner Tri-Dirty Booster

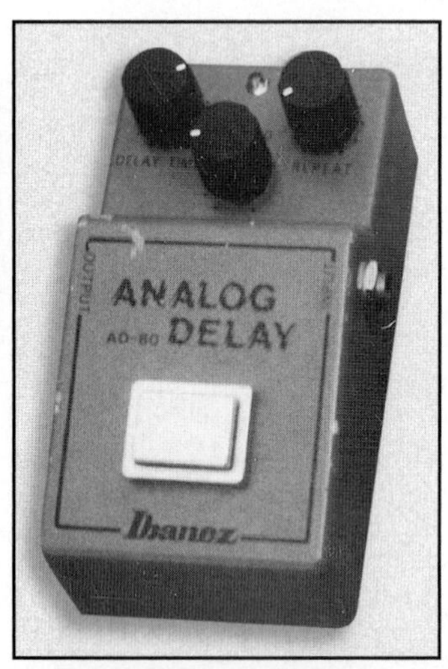

Ibanez Analog Delay AD-80

Ibanez Bass Compressor BP-10

MODEL YEAR	FEATURES	EXC. COND. LOW	HIGH

popularized by Peter Frampton. In the '60s and '70s Heil was dedicated to innovative products for the music industry. In the late-'70s, innovative creations were more in the Amateur Radio market, and by the '90s the focus was on the home theater market. By the 2000s, the Heil Sound brand name was offered by Jim Dunlop USA.

Talk Box

1976-ca.1980. Reissued in 1989.

1970s	$80	$100
1980s	$70	$80
1990s	$60	$70
2000s	$60	$70

High Gain

See listing under Dunlop.

Hohner

Hohner offered effects in the late-1970s.

Dirty Booster

1977-ca.1978. Distortion.

1977-1978 $45 $55

Dirty Wah Wah'er

1977-ca.1978. Adds distortion.

1977-1978 $55 $65

Fuzz Wah

1970s. Morley-like volume pedal with volume knob and fuzz knob, switch for soft or hard fuzz, Gray box with Black foot pedal.

1970s $55 $65

Multi-Exciter

1977-ca.1978. Volume, wah, surf, tornado, siren.

1977-1978 $50 $60

Tape Echo

1970s $200 $250

Tri-Booster

1977-ca.1978. Distortion, sustain.

1977-1978 $50 $60

Vari-Phaser

1977-ca.1978.

1977-1978 $25 $35

Vol-Kicker Volume Pedal

1977-ca.1978.

1977-1978 $25 $35

Wah-Wah'er

1977-ca.1978. Wah, volume.

1977-1978 $40 $50

HomeBrew Electronics

2001 - Present. Stomp box effects handmade by Joel Weaver in Glendale, Arizona.

Ibanez

Ibanez effects were introduced ca. 1974, as Ibanez guitars were carving a niche in the market. They were manufactured by Japan's Maxon Electronics. Although results were mixed at first, a more uniform and modern product line, including the now legenday Tube Screamer, built Ibanez's reputation for quality. They still produce a wide line of effects.

MODEL YEAR	FEATURES	EXC. COND. LOW	HIGH

60s Fuzz (Soundtank)

1989-1999. Fuzz with level, tone and distortion controls, Black plastic case, Green label.

1989-1999 $25 $30

7th Heaven SH7 (Tone-Lok)

1999-2000s. Lo, high, drive and level controls, Grey-Silver case, Blue-Green SH7 label.

2000s $30 $35

Acoustic Effects PT-4

2000s. Acoustic guitar enhancement floor unit with compressor/limiter, tone shaper, stereo chorus, digital reverb, with power supply.

2002 $90 $100

Analog Delay AD9

1982-1985. Three control analog delay, Hot Pink metal case.

1982-1985 $130 $150

Analog Delay AD99

1995-1999. Analog Delay reissue, three control knobs and on/off switch, reissue winged-hand logo.

1995-1999 $90 $100

Analog Delay AD-80

1980-1982.

1980-1982 $175 $200

Analog Delay AD-100 (Table Unit)

1980s. Stand-alone table/studio unit (not rack mount) with power cord.

1980 $190 $200

Analog Delay 202 (Rack Mount)

1980s. Rack mount with delay, doubling, flanger, stereo chorus, dual inputs with tone and level.

1980 $150 $160

Auto Filter AF9

1982-ca.1985. Replaces AF201 model.

1982-1985 $150 $175

Auto Filter AF201

1981-1982. Two min-max sliders, three mode toggle switches, Orange metal case.

1981-1982 $150 $175

Auto Wah AW5 (SoundTank)

1991-1999. Plastic case SoundTank series.

1989-1999 $30 $40

Auto Wah AW7

1999-2000s. Silver case.

1999-2000 $25 $30

Bass Compressor BP10

1986-1993.

1980s $60 $70

Bi-Mode Chorus BC-9

1984-1985. Dual channel (Bi channel) for two independent speed and width settings.

1984-1985 $70 $90

Chorus CS-505

1980s. Speed and depth controls, Gray-Blue case, stereo or mono input, battery or external power option.

1980s $65 $85

Chorus Flanger CF7 (Tone-Lok)

1999-2000s. Speed, depth, delay, regeneration controls, mode and crazy switches, Pink CF7 label.

2000s $35 $40

EFFECTS

MODEL YEAR	FEATURES	EXC. COND. LOW	HIGH

Classic Flange FL99

1995-1999. Analog reissue 99 Series flange, Silver metal case with winged-hand artwork, four controls and two on-off footswitch buttons.

1995-1999		$65	$75

Classic Phase PH99

1995-1999. Analog reissue 99 Series phase, Silver metal case with winged-hand artwork, speed, depth, feedback, and effect level controls and intense and bypass on-off footswitch buttons.

1995-1999		$65	$75

Compressor CP10

1987-1993.

1980s		$40	$60

Compressor CP-830

1976-1979.

1970s		$70	$80

Compressor II CP-835

1980-1982.

1980-1982		$70	$90

Compressor Limiter CP9

1982-1985.

1980s		$70	$90

Delay Champ CD10

1986-1989. Red case, three-knobs.

1986-1989		$80	$100

Delay Echo DE-7

1999-2000s. Digital delay and analog echo combines digital and analog tones.

1999-2000		$45	$55

Delay Harmonizer DM-1000

1980s. Rack mount delay harmonizer with chorus, nine control knobs.

1980s		$175	$225

Delay III DDL20 Digital Delay

1986-1989. Filtering, doubling, slap back, echo S, echo M, echo L, Seafoam Green coloring on pedal.

1986-1989		$65	$85

Delay PDD1 (DPC Series)

1987-1988. Programmable Digital Delay (PDD) with display screen.

1987-1988		$80	$100

Digital Chorus DSC10

1986-1989. Three control knobs and slider selection toggle.

1986-1989		$50	$60

Digital Delay DL5 (SoundTank)

1992-1999. Plastic case SoundTank series.

1992-1999		$35	$45

Digital Delay DL10

1986-1989. Digital Delay made in Japan, Blue case, three Green control knobs, stompbox.

1986-1989		$80	$90

Distortion DS7

2000s. Drive, tone, and level controls, Gray case, DS7 Green label logo.

2000s		$40	$50

Distortion Charger DS10

1986-1989.

1986-1989		$55	$65

Echo Machine EM5 (SoundTank)

1989-1999.

1989-1999		$40	$60

Fat Cat Distortion FC10

1986-1989. Three-knob pedal with distortion, tone, and level controls, made in Japan.

1986-1989		$45	$65

Flanger FFL5 (Master Series)

1984-1985. Speed, regeneration, width, D-time controls, battery or adapter option.

1984-1985		$30	$40

Flanger FL5 (SoundTank)

1991-1999. Plastic case SoundTank series.

1991-1999		$25	$35

Flanger FL9

1982-1984. Yellow case.

1982-1984		$45	$60

Flanger FL-301

1979-1982. Mini flanger, three knobs, called the FL-301 DX in late '81-'82.

1979-1982		$65	$110

Flanger FL-305

1976-1979. Five knobs.

1976-1979		$75	$125

Flying Pan FP-777

1976-1979. Auto pan/phase shifter, four control knobs, phase on/off button, pan on/off button, Silver metal case with Blue trim and Flying Pan winged-hand logo.

1976-1979		$425	$500

Fuzz FZ7 (Tone-Lok)

1999-2000s. Drive, tone and level controls, Gray-Silver case, blue-green FZ7 label.

2000s		$45	$55

Graphic Bass EQ BE10

1986-1993. Latered labeled as the BEQ10.

1986-1989		$50	$70

Graphic EQ GE9

1982-1985. Six EQ sliders plus one overall volume slider, Turquoise Blue case.

1982-1985		$50	$70

Graphic EQ GE10

1986-1993. Eight sliders.

1986-1993		$50	$70

Graphic Equalizer GE-601 (808 Series)

1980-1982. Seven-slider EQ in Aqua Blue metal case.

1980-1982		$75	$85

Guitar Multi-Processor PT5

1994-1997. Floor unit, programmable with 25 presets and 25 user presets, effects include distortion, chorus, flanger, etc.

1994-1997	Green case	$75	$95

LA Metal LM7

1986-1989. Silver case.

1986-1989		$35	$60

Ibanez Classic Phase PH-99

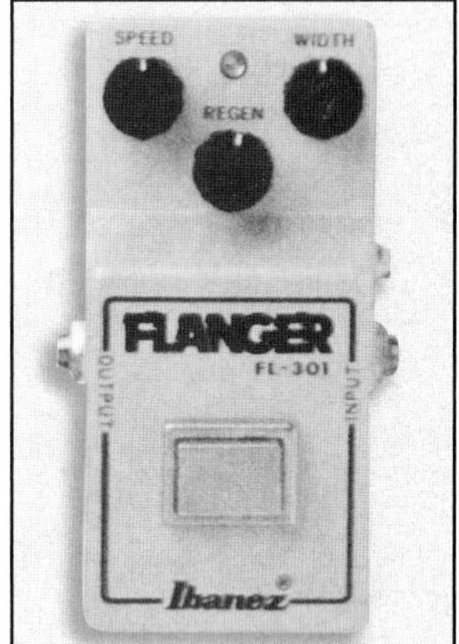

Ibanez Flanger FL-301

Ibanez LA Metal LM7

EFFECTS

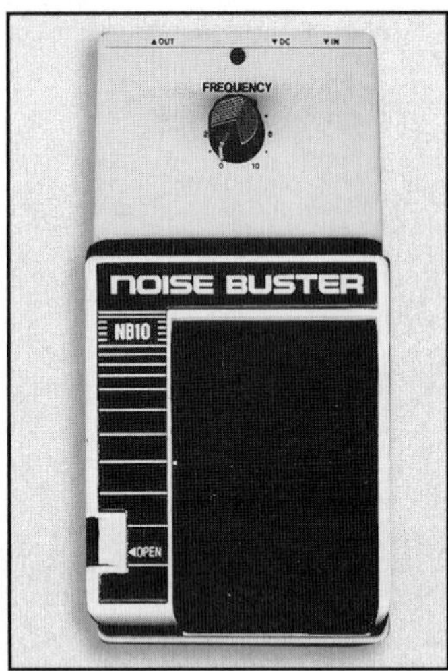

Ibanez Noise Buster NB10

Ibanez Phase Tone PT-909

Ibanez Super Metal SM-9

MODEL YEAR	FEATURES	EXC. COND. LOW	HIGH

LoFi LF7 (Tone-Lok)
1999-2000s. Four control knobs, Light Gray case, Red LF7 label.
2000s $20 $30

Metal Charger MS10
1986-1989. Distortion, level, attack, punch and edge control knobs, green case.
1986-1989 $50 $60

Metal Screamer MSL
1984-1985. Three control knobs.
1984-1985 $50 $60

Modern Fusion MF-5 (SoundTank)
1990s. Level, tone and distortion control knobs, battery or optional adapter.
1990s $45 $55

Modulation Delay DM500
1982-1984. Rack mount.
1982-1984 $50 $75

Modulation Delay DM1000
1982-1984. Rack mount with delay, reverb, modulation.
1982-1984 $85 $110

Mostortion MT10
Late-1980s-early-1990s. Mos-FET circuit distortion pedal, five control knobs, Green case.
1989-1991 $40 $50

Multi-Effect UE-300 (floor unit)
1980s. Floor unit, four footswitches for super metal, digital delay, digital stereo chorus, and master power, three delay modes.
1980s $100 $325

Multi-effect UE-300B (floor unit)
1983-1984. Floor unit for bass.
1983-1984 $100 $325

Multi-Effect UE-400 (rackmount)
1983-1985. Rackmount with foot switch.
1980s $125 $350

Multi-Effect UE-405 (rackmount)
1980s. Rackmount with analog delay, parametric EQ, compressor/limiter, stereo chorus and loop.
1980s $150 $350

Noise Buster NB10
1986-1989. Single frequency knob to eliminate 60-cycle hum and other outside signals, metal case.
1986-1989 $65 $75

Overdrive OD-850
1974-1979.
1974-1979 $200 $300

Overdrive II OD-855
1974-1979. Small stomp-box with distortion knob, tone knob, and level knob, Yellow/Green case, large Overdrive II logo.
1974-1979 $200 $300

Pan Delay DPL10
1986-1989. Royal Blue case, three Green control knobs, small stomp box, large Pan Delay logo.
1986-1989 $90 $100

Parametric EQ PQ9
1982-1985.
1980s $90 $100

Parametric EQ PQ401
1979-1982. Three sliders and dial-in knob, Light Aqua Blue case.
1979-1982 $100 $150

Phase Tone II PT-707
1976-1980. Blue box, one knob, script logo for first two years.
1970s $100 $125

Phase Tone PT-909
1979-1982. Blue box, three knobs, early models with flat case (logo at bottom or later in the middle) or later wedge case.
1979-1982 $100 $130

Phase Tone PT-999
1976-1978. Script logo, one knob, round footswitch, becomes PT-909.
1976-1978 $110 $140

Phase Tone PT-1000
1974-1981. Morley-style pedal phase, Light Blue case, early model of Phase Tone.
1974-1981 $150 $200

Phaser PH5
1991-1999. Plastic case SoundTank series.
1991-1999 $20 $30

Phaser PH7 (Tone-Lok)
1999-2000s. Tone-Lok Series phaser with Silver case, speed, depth, feedback and level controls, Purple PH7 label.
1999-2003 $35 $45

Phaser PT9
1982-1985. Three control knobs, Red case.
1982-1985 $50 $75

Powerlead PL5 (SoundTank)
1989-1999. SoundTank series, metal case '89-'91, plastic case '91-'99.
1989-1991 1st issue metal case $25 $45
1991-1999 2nd later issue plastic case $15 $20

Renometer
1976-1979. Five-band equalizer with preamp.
1976-1979 $80 $90

Rotary Chorus RC99
1995-1999. Black or Silver cases available, requires power pack and does not use a battery.
1995-1999 Black case $55 $85

Session Man SS10
1988-1990. Distortion, chorus.
1988-1990 $60 $70

Session Man II SS20
1988-1990. Four control knobs + toggle, Light Pink-Purple case.
1988-1990 $60 $70

Slam Punk SP5 (SoundTank)
1991-1999. Plastic case SoundTank series.
1990s $35 $45

MODEL YEAR	FEATURES	EXC. COND. LOW	HIGH

Smash Box SM7 (Tone-Lok)

1999-2000s.

2000s		$30	$40

Sonic Distortion SD9

1982-1984.

1982-1984		$70	$80

Standard Fuzz (No. 59)

1974-1979. Two buttons (fuzz on/off and tone change).

1974-1979		$150	$200

Stereo Box ST-800

1976-1977. One input, two outputs for panning, small Yellow case.

1976-1977	Yellow case	$150	$200

Stereo Chorus CS9

1982-1984.

1980s		$60	$75

Stereo Chorus CSL

1985-1986.

1985-1986		$55	$65

Super Chorus CS5 (SoundTank)

1991-1999. Plastic case SoundTank series.

1991-1999		$20	$30

Super Metal SM-9

1984-1985. Distortion.

1984-1985		$75	$100

Super Stereo Chorus SC-10

1986-1993.

1980s		$40	$50

Super Tube Screamer ST9

1982-1984. Four dial-in knobs, Light Green metal case.

1982-1984		$200	$300

Super Tube STL

1985-1986.

1985-1986		$65	$75

Swell Flanger SF10

1986-1989. Speed, regeneration, width and time controls, Yellow case.

1986-1989		$45	$55

Trashmetal TM5 (SoundTank)

1989-present. Tone and distortion pedal, three editions (1st edition, 2nd edition metal case, 2nd edition plastic case).

1989-1999		$15	$20

Tremolo Pedal TL-5

1980s		$30	$40

Tube King TK999

1994-1995. Has a 12AX7 tube and three-band equalizer.

1994-1995	Includes power pack	$125	$200

Tube King TK999US

1996-2000. Has a 12AX7 tube and three-band equalizer, does not have the noise switch of original TK999. Made in the U.S.

1996-2000	Includes power pack	$125	$200

Tube Screamer TS5

1991-1999. Plastic case SoundTank series.

1990s		$20	$30

Tube Screamer TS7

1999-present. Part of the Tone-Lok series, Gray-Blue case, three control knobs.

1999		$30	$40

Tube Screamer TS9

1982-1984. Reissued in 1993.

1982-1984		$100	$200

Tube Screamer TS9 Reissue

1993-present. Reissue of the '80s TS9.

1990s		$70	$90

Turbo Tube Screamer TS9DX

2000s. Tube Screamer circuit with added three settings for low-end.

2000s		$75	$85

Tube Screamer Classic TS10

1986-1993.

1986-1993		$80	$100

Tube Screamer TS-808

1980-1982.

1980s		$350	$400

Twin Cam Chorus TC10

1986-1989. Four control knobs, Light Blue case.

1986-1989		$40	$60

Virtual Amp VA3 (floor unit)

1990s. Digital effects processor.

1990s		$50	$70

VL10

1986-1997. Stereo volume pedal.

1980s		$40	$50

Wah Fuzz Standard (Model 58)

1974-1981. Fuzz tone change toggle, fuzz on toggle, fuzz depth control, balance control, wah volume pedal with circular friction pads on footpedal.

1974-1981		$127	$200

Wah WH10

1989-1999.

1989-1999		$50	$60

Intersound

Made by Intersound, Inc. of Boulder, Colorado.

Reverb-Equalizer R100F

1977-1979. Reverb and four-band EQ, fader.

1977-1979		$60	$70

Jacques

One-of-a-kind handmade stomp boxes and production models made in France. Production models are distributed in the U.S. by Godlyke Distributing.

Jan-Mar Industries

Jan-Mar was located in Hillsdale, New Jersey.

The Talker

1976. Thirty watts.

1976		$55	$65

The Talker Pro

1976. Seventy-five watts.

1976		$70	$80

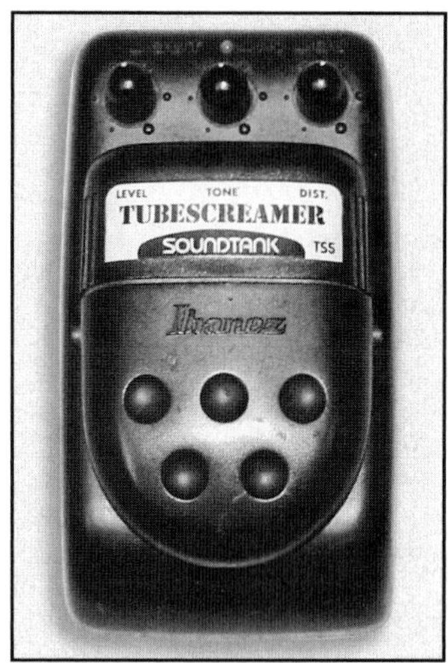

Ibanez Tube Screamer TS5

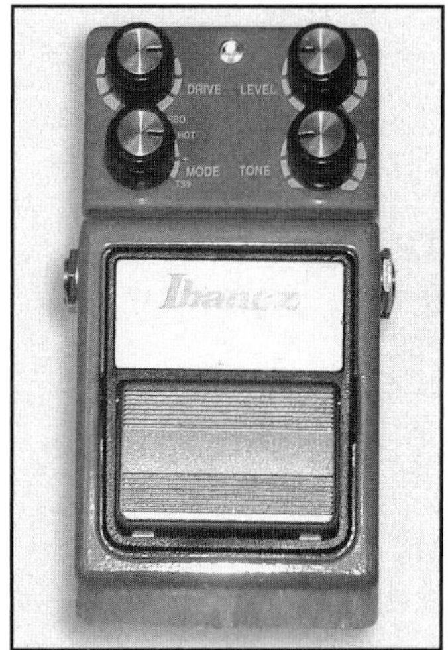

Ibanez Turbo Tube Screamer TS9DX

Jacques Fuse Blower

EFFECTS

Kendrick Model 1000 Reverb

Kendrick Power Glide

Klon Centaur

EFFECTS

MODEL YEAR	FEATURES	EXC. COND. LOW	HIGH

Jax

1960s. Imports.

Fuzz Master

1960s		$65	$75

Vibrachorus

Variant of Univibe by Shinei.

1969		$700	$900

Wah-Wah

1960s		$65	$75

Jet Sounds LTD

Hoze Talk Box

1977.

1977		$80	$90

JHD Audio

Super Cube

1970s. Sustain coupler with reverb.

1970s		$50	$60

Jimi Hendrix

See listing under Dunlop.

John Hornby Skewes & Co.

Mid-1960s-present. Large English distributor of musical products which has also made their own brands, or self-branded products from others, over the years.

Johnson

Mid-1990s-present. Budget line of effects imported by Music Link, Brisbane, California. Johnson also offers acoustic, classical, acoustic/electric, and solidbody guitars, amps, mandolins, ukuleles and basses.

Johnson Amplification

1997-present. Modeling amps and effects designed by John Johnson, of Sandy, Utah. The company is part of Harman International. In 2002, they quite building amps, but continue the effects line.

Jordan

Late-1960s effects.

Boss Tone Fuzz

Late-1960s. Plugged into guitar's output jack.

1968		$90	$100

Compressor J-700

1960s		$70	$90

Creator Volume Sustainer

1960s		$150	$170

Gig Wa-Wa Volume

1960s		$100	$140

Phaser

Black case, Yellow knobs.

1960s	Black case	$120	$140

MODEL YEAR	FEATURES	EXC. COND. LOW	HIGH

Kay

1931-present. Kay was once one of the largest instrument producers in the world, offering just about everything for the guitarist. See the Guitar section for more company info or *Guitar Stories Volume II*, by Michael Wright, for a complete history of Kay with detailed model listings.

Graphic Equalizer GE-5000

1978-ca.1979.

1978-1979		$30	$40

Rhythmer

1970s		$30	$40

Tremolo

1970s		$30	$40

Kendrick

1989-present. Texas' Kendrick offers guitars, amps, and effects. See Guitar section for more company info.

ABC Amp Switcher

1990s.

1990s		$100	$130

Buffalo Pfuz

1990s.

1990s		$60	$90

Model 1000 Reverb

1991-present. Vintage style, three knobs: dwell, tone, and mix, Brown cover, Wheat grille with art deco shape.

1990s		$350	$400

Power Glide Attenuator

1998-present. Allows you to cut the output before it hits the amp's speakers, rackmount, metal cab.

1990s		$175	$200

Kern Engineering

Located in Kenosha, Wisconsin, Kern offers pre-amps and wah pedals.

Klon

1994-present. Originally located in Brookline, MA and now located in Cambridge, MA, Klon was started by Bill Finnegan after working with two circuit design partners on the Centaur Professional Overdrive.

KMD (Kaman)

1986-ca. 1990. Distributed by Kaman (Ovation, Hamer, etc.) in the mid-1980s.

Analog Delay

1986-ca.1990.

1980s		$60	$90

Distortion

1987-ca.1990.

1980s		$35	$45

Flanger

1987-ca.1990.

1980s		$20	$35

MODEL YEAR	FEATURES	EXC. COND. LOW	HIGH

Overdrive

1986-ca.1990.

1980s $25 $40

Phaser

1987-ca.1990.

1980s $35 $45

Stereo Chorus

1987-ca.1990.

1980s $20 $35

Korg

The Korg effects listed below are modular effects. The PME-40X Professional Modular Effects System holds four of them and allows the user to select several variations of effects. The modular effects cannot be used alone. This system was sold for a few years starting in 1983.

KAD-301 Analog Delay

1983-ca. 1986. Modular effect.

1980s $50 $60

KCH-301 Stereo Chorus

1983-ca. 1986. Modular effect.

1980s $20 $25

KCO-101 Compressor

1983-ca. 1986. Modular effect.

1980s $40 $50

KDI-101 Distortion

1983-ca. 1986. Modular effect.

1980s $40 $50

KDL-301 Dynamic Echo

1983-ca. 1986. Modular effect.

1980s $80 $100

KFL-401 Stereo Flanger

1983-ca. 1986. Modular effect.

1980s $40 $45

KGE-201 Graphic EQ

1983-ca. 1986. Modular effect.

1980s $20 $25

KNG-101 Noise Gate

1983-ca. 1986. Modular effect.

1980s $20 $25

KOD-101 Over Drive

1983-ca. 1986. Modular effect.

1980s $40 $50

KPH-401 Phaser

1983-ca. 1986. Modular effect.

1980s $40 $50

OCT-1 Octaver

1980s. Octave pedal with direct level control knob and effect level control knob, stomp switch, dark case.

1980s $55 $75

PEQ-1 Parametric EQ

1980s. Dial-in equalizer with gain knob, bandwidth knob, and frequency knob, Black case.

1980s $40 $45

PME-40X Professional Modular Effects System

1983-ca. 1986. Board that holds up to four of the above modular effects.

1980s $100 $125

MODEL YEAR	FEATURES	EXC. COND. LOW	HIGH

Laney

1968-present. Founded by Lyndon Laney and Bob Thomas in Birmingham, England. Mainly known for amps.

Reverberation Unit

1968-1969. Sleek reverb unit, plexi-style front panel, Black vinyl cover.

1969 Black $250 $300

Line 6

1996-present. Founded by Marcus Ryle and Michel Doidic who were product line designers prior to forming their own design company. A sixth company telephone line was added to their product design business to handle their own product line, thus Line 6. Line 6 specializes in digital signal processing. All prices include Line 6 power pack if applicable.

AM-4 Amp Modeler

Includes power pack, box and manual, Yellow case.

1996-2002 $175 $200

DL-4 Delay Modeler

Includes power pack, box and manual, Green case.

1996-2002 $175 $200

DM-4 Distortion Modeler

Includes power pack, box and manual, Red case.

1996-2002 $175 $200

FM-4 Filter Modeler

Includes power pack, box and manual, Purple case.

2000-2002 $175 $200

MM-4 Modulation Modeler

Includes power pack, box and manual, Aqua Blue case.

2000-2002 $175 $200

POD 2.0

2000s. Amp modeler.

2000s $160 $200

Little Lanilei

1997-present. Best known for their small handmade amps, Songworks Systems & Products of San Juan Capistrano, California, also offers effects bearing the Little Lanilei name.

Loco Box

Loco Box was a brand name of effects distributed by Aria Pro II for a short period starting in 1982. It appears that Aria switched the effects to their own brand name in 1983.

Analog Delay AD-01

1982-1983.

1982-1983 $30 $40

Chorus CH-01

1982-1983.

1982-1983 $50 $60

Korg Tube Works Tube Driver

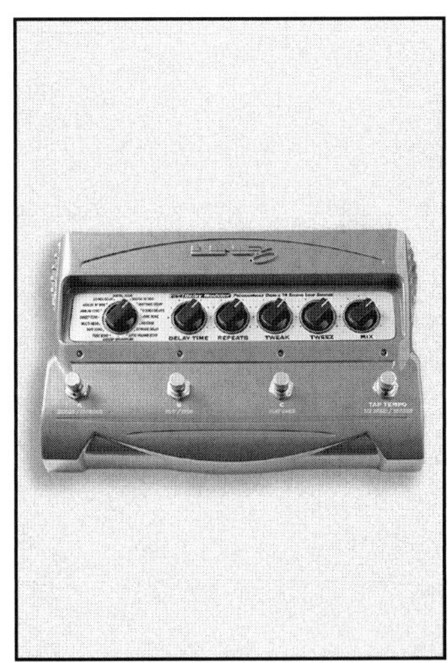
Line 6 Delay Modeler

Loco Box Graphic EQ GE-06

EFFECTS

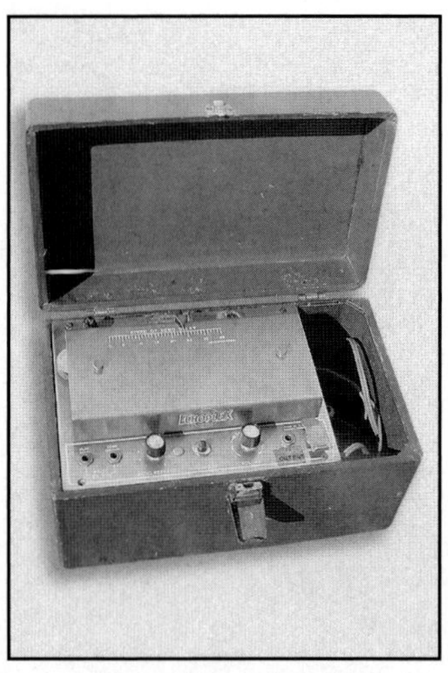

Maestro Echoplex EP-1

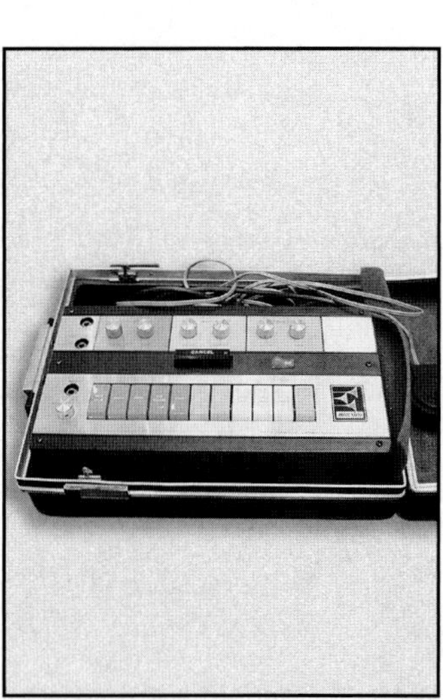

Maestro Rhythm and Sound G-2

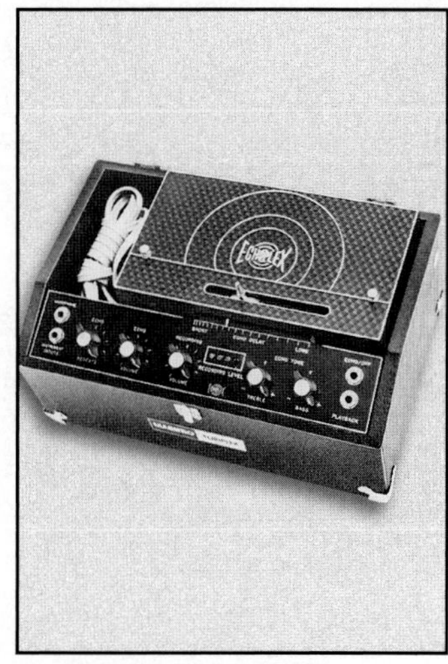

Mestro Echoplex IV (EP-4)

MODEL YEAR	FEATURES	EXC. COND. LOW	HIGH

Compressor CM-01

1982-1983.

1982-1983		$30	$40

Distortion DS-01

1982-1983.

1982-1983		$35	$45

Flanger FL-01

1982-1983.

1982-1983		$30	$40

Graphic Equalizer GE-06

1982-1983.

1982-1983		$25	$35

Overdrive OD-01

1982-1983.

1982-1983		$35	$45

Phaser PH-01

1982-1983.

1982-1983		$40	$50

Lovetone

1995-present. Hand-made analog effects from Oxfordshire, England.

Ludwig

Phase II Guitar Synth

1970-1971. Oversized synth, mushroom-shaped footswitches.

1970-1971	Vertical silver case	$300	$400

M.B. Electronics

Made in San Francisco, California.

Ultra-Metal UM-10

1985. Distortion.

1985		$30	$40

Maestro

Maestro was a Gibson subsidiary; the name appeared on '50s accordian amplifiers. The first Maestro effects were the Echoplex tape echo and the FZ-1 Fuzz-Tone, introduced in the early-'60s. Maestro products were manufactured by various entities such as Market Electronics, All-Test Devices, Lowrey and Moog Electronics. In the late-'60s and early-'70s, they unleashed a plethora of pedals; some were beautiful, others had "great personality." The last Maestro effects were the Silver and Black MFZ series of the late-'70s.

Bass Brassmaster BB-1

1971-ca.1974. Added brass to your bass.

1971-1974		$250	$450

Boomerang

CA.1969-ca.1972. Wah pedal made by All-Test Devices.

1969-1972		$125	$175

Boomerang BG-2

1972-ca.1976. Wah pedal made by All-Test Devices.

1972-1976		$100	$150

MODEL YEAR	FEATURES	EXC. COND. LOW	HIGH

Echoplex (EP-1)

1962/63-mid-1960s. Original model, Smaller box, tube, separate controls for echo volume and instrument volume, made by Market Electronics. Though not labeled as such, it is often referred to as the EP-1 by collectors.

1960s	Earlier smal Green box	$900	$1,000

Echoplex EP-2

Mid-1960s-ca. 1970. Larger box than original, tube, single echo/instrument volume control, made by Market Electronics. Around 1970, the EP-2 added a Sound-On-Sound feature.

1960s	Larger Green box	$900	$1,000

Echoplex EP-3

Ca.1970-1977. Solidstate, made by Market Electronics, Black box.

1970-1977		$350	$400

Echoplex IV (EP-4)

1977-1978. Solidstate. Last version introduced by Maestro. See brand names Market Electronics and Echoplex for later models.

1977-1978		$350	$400

Echoplex Sireko ES-1

ca.1971-mid-1970s. A budget version of the Echoplex, solidstate. Made by Market.

1971-1975		$250	$300

Envelope Modifier ME-1

1971-ca.1976. Tape reverse/string simulator. Made by All-test.

1972-1976		$175	$225

Filter Sample and Hold FSH-1

1975-ca.1976.

1975-1976		$400	$450

Full Range Boost FRB-1

1971-ca.1975. Frequency boost with fuzz. Made by All-test.

1971-1975		$125	$150

Fuzz MFZ-1

1976-1979. Made by Moog.

1976-1979		$125	$150

Fuzz Phazzer FP-1

1971-1974.

1971-1974		$150	$200

Fuzz Tone FZ-1

Mid-1960s. Brown, uses two AA batteries.

1960s		$150	$200

Fuzz Tone FZ-1A

Late-1960s. Brown, uses one AA battery.

1960s		$150	$200

Fuzz Tone FZ-1B

Late-1960s- early-1970s. Black, uses nine-volt battery.

1970s		$150	$175

Fuzztain MFZT-1

1976-1978. Fuzz, sustain. Made by Moog.

1976-1978		$175	$225

Mini-Phase Shifter MPS-2

1976.

1976		$100	$125

MODEL YEAR	FEATURES	EXC. COND. LOW	HIGH

Octave Box OB-1

1971-ca.1975. Made by All-Test Devices.

1971-1975		$175	$250

Phase Shifter PS-1

1971-1975. With or without three-button footswitch. Made by Oberheim.

1971-1975	With footswitch	$200	$250
1971-1975	Without footswitch	$125	$175

Phase Shifter PS-1A

1976.

1976		$150	$200

Phase Shifter PS-1B

1970s.

1970s		$125	$150

Phaser MP-1

1976-1978. Made by Moog.

1976-1978		$100	$125

Rhythm and Sound G-2

Ca.1969-1970s. Multi-effect unit.

1969-1975		$350	$400

Ring Modulator RM-1

1971-1975.

1971-1975	With control pedal	$600	$700
1971-1975	Without control pedal	$500	$600

Rover Rotating Speaker

1971-ca.1973. Rotating Leslie effect that mounted on a large tripod.

1971-1973		$700	$900

Stage Phaser MPP-1

1976-1978. Had slow, fast and variable settings. Made by Moog.

1976-1978		$150	$200

Super Fuzz FZ-1S

1971-ca.1975. Made by All-Test Devices.

1971-1975		$200	$250

Sustainer SS-2

1971-ca.1975. Made by All-Test Devices.

1971-1975		$75	$175

Theramin TH-1

1971-mid-1970s. Device with two antenna, made "horror film" sound effects. A reissue "Theremin" is available from Theremaniacs in Milwaukee, WI.

1971-1975		$700	$1,000

Magnatone

1937-1970s. Magnatone built very competitive amps from '57 to '66. In the early-'60s, they offered the RVB-1 Reverb Unit. The majority of Magnatone amps pre-'66 did not have on-board reverb. See Guitar section for more company info.

Model RVB-1 Reverb Unit

1961-1966. Reverb unit that works between the guitar and amp, typical Brown leatherette cover, square box-type cabinet. From 1964-1966, battery operated, solidstate version of RVB-1, low flat cabinet.

1961-1963		$250	$400
1964-1966	Battery and solidstate	$150	$300

MODEL YEAR	FEATURES	EXC. COND. LOW	HIGH

Mannys Music

Issued by the New York-based retailer.

Fuzz

1960s		$200	$300

Market Electronics

Market, from Ohio, made the famous Echoplex line. See Maestro section for earlier models and Echoplex section for later versions.

Marshall

The fuzz and wah boom of the 1960s led many established manufacturers to introduce variations on the theme. Marshall was no exception, but its pedals never neared the popularity of their amps. They made another foray into stomp boxes in 1989 with the Gov'nor distortion, and currently produce several distortion/overdrive units.

Blues Breaker (effect)

1992-1999. Replaced by Blues Breaker II in 2000.

1992-1999		$70	$80

Blues Breaker II Overdrive

2000-present. Overdrive pedal, four knobs.

2000s	Silver	$55	$65

Drive Master

1992-1999.

1992-1999		$70	$80

Guv'nor

1989-1991. Distortion. Gov'nor Plus introduced in 2000.

1989-1991		$100	$125

Power Brake

1990s		$200	$225

Shred Master

1992-1999.

1992-1999		$70	$90

Supa Fuzz

1967		$200	$300

Supa Wah

1969		$200	$300

Matchless

1989-1999, 2001-present. Matchless amplifiers offered effects in the '90s.

AB Box

1990s. Split box for C-30 series amps (DC 30, SC 30, etc.)

1990s		$200	$300

Coolbox

1990s. Tube preamp pedal.

1990s		$300	$350

Dirtbox

1990s. Tube-driven overdrive pedal.

1990s		$250	$350

Echo Box

1990s. Limited production because of malfunctioning design which included cassette tape.

1990s		$200	$300

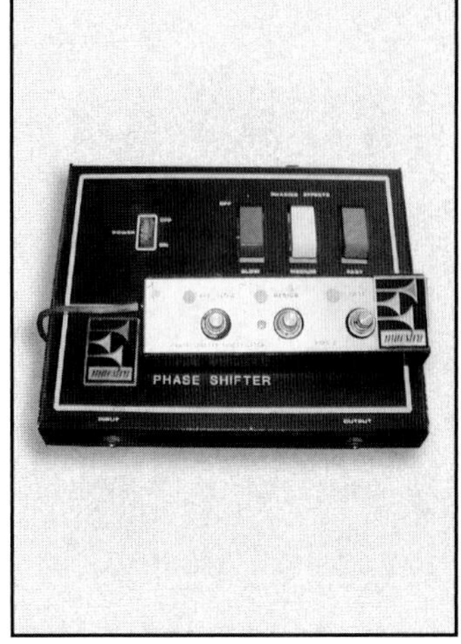

Maestro Phase Shifter PS1-A

Marshall Jackhammer JH-1

Matchless Coolbox

EFFECTS

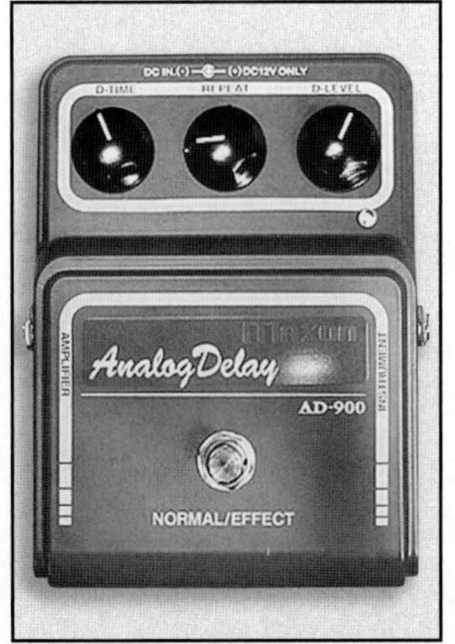

Maxon AD-900 Analog Delay

Moonrock

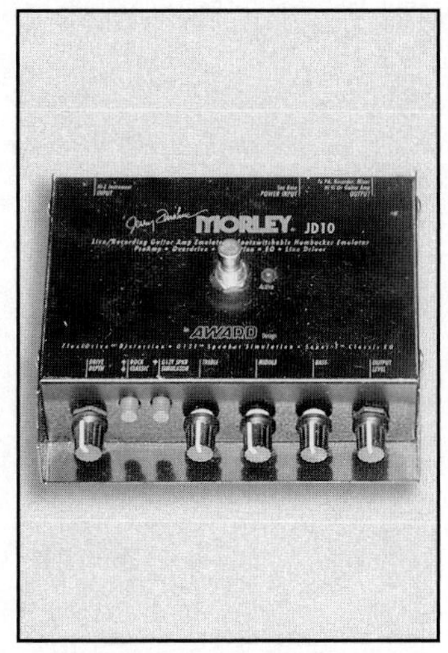

Morley Jerry Donahue JD-10

EFFECTS

MODEL YEAR	FEATURES	EXC. COND. LOW	HIGH

Hotbox
1990s. Higher-end tube-driven preamp pedal.

1990s		$350	$400

Hotbox II
1990s. Higher-end tube-driven preamp pedal with more than the Hotbox I.

1990s		$350	$400

Mix Box
1990s. Four-input tube mixer pedal.

1990s		$300	$400

Reverb RV-1
1990s. Five control knobs, reverb tank in relatively large rectangular cab.

1990s	Various colors	$900	$1,300

Split Box
1990s. Tube AB box.

1990s	Standard AB	$250	$350

Tube Vibrato
1990s.

1990s		$300	$400

Maxon

1970s-present. Currently offering retro 1970s era stomp boxes distributed in the U.S. by Godlyke distributing. Maxon was the original manufacturer of the Ibanez line of effects.

AD-900 Analog Delay
2001-present.

2001-2003		$250	$300

OD-820 Overdrive Pro
2001-present.

2001-2003		$150	$180

Mesa-Boogie

1971-present. Founded by Randall Smith in San Francisco, Mesa added pre-amps in the mid '90s.

V-Twin Preamp
Dec. 1993-present. Serial number series: V011- . One hundred watts, all tube preamp, floor unit, Silver case.

1993-1999		$200	$275

Mica

Tone Fuzz
Silver case, Black knobs.

1970s	Silver case	$200	$225

Tone Surf Wah Siren
1970s. Wah pedal.

1970s		$140	$160

Wailer Fuzz

1970		$60	$70

Moonrock

2002-present. Fuzz/distortion unit built by Glenn Wylie and distributed by Tonefrenzy.

Morley

Late-1960s-present. Founded by brothers Raymond and Marvin Lubow, Morley has produced a wide variety of pedals and effects over the years, changing with the trends. In 1989, the brothers sold the company to Accutronics (later changed to Sound Enhancements, Inc.) of Cary, Illinois.

ABY Switch Box
1981-ca.1985. Box.

1981-1985		$20	$25

Auto Wah PWA
1976-ca.1985.

1976-1985		$30	$40

Black Gold Stereo Volume BSV
1985-1991.

1985-1991		$30	$40

Black Gold Stereo Volume Pan BSP
1985-1989.

1985-1989		$35	$45

Black Gold Volume BVO
1985-1991.

1985-1991		$25	$35

Black Gold Wah BWA
1985-1991.

1985-1991		$40	$50

Black Gold Wah Volume BWV
1985-1989.

1985-1989		$40	$50

Chrystal Chorus

1980s		$30	$35

Deluxe Distortion DDB
1981-1991. Box, no pedal.

1980s		$45	$65

Deluxe Flanger FLB
1981-1991. Box, no pedal.

1981-1991		$60	$70

Deluxe Phaser DFB
1981-1991. Box, no pedal.

1981-1991		$45	$65

Distortion One DIB
1981-1991. Box, no pedal.

1981-1991		$40	$50

Echo Chorus Vibrato ECV
1982-ca.1985.

1982-1985		$90	$100

Echo/Volume EVO-1
1974-ca.1982.

1974-1982		$60	$70

Electro-Pik-a-Wah PKW
1979-ca.1982.

1979-1982		$60	$70

Emerald Echo

1990s		$50	$60

Jerry Donahue JD-10
Multi-effect, distortion, overdrive.

1990s		$85	$95

Power Wah PWA
1990s. Wah with boost.

1990s		$45	$55

Power Wah PWO
Ca.1969-1984.

1969-1984		$65	$75

MODEL YEAR	FEATURES	EXC. COND. LOW	HIGH

Power Wah/Boost PWB

Introduced in 1973, doubles as a volume pedal.

1970s		$80	$90

Power Wah/Fuzz PWF

ca.1969-ca.1984.

1969-1984		$140	$150

Pro Compressor PCB

1978-1984. Stomp box without pedal, compress-sustain knob and output knob.

1980s		$50	$60

Pro Flanger PFL

1978-1984.

1978-1984		$125	$135

Pro Phaser PFA

1975-1984.

1975-1984		$70	$80

Rotating Sound Power Wah Model RWV

1974-1982.

1974-1982		$275	$325

Select-Effect Pedal SEL

Lets you control up to five other pedals.

1980s		$25	$30

Slimline Echo Volume 600

1983-1985. Twenty to 600 ms delay.

1983-1985		$50	$60

Slimline Echo Volume SLEV

1983-1985. Twenty to 300 ms delay.

1983-1985		$55	$65

Slimline Variable Taper Stereo Volume SLSV

1982-1986.

1982-1986		$90	$100

Slimline Variable Taper Volume SLVO

1982-1986.

1982-1986		$30	$50

Slimline Wah SLWA

1982-1986. Battery operated electro-optical.

1982-1986		$60	$80

Slimline Wah Volume SLWV

1982-ca.1986. Battery operated electro-optical.

1982-1986		$60	$80

Stereo Chorus Flanger CFL

1980s	Footswitch	$50	$60

Stereo Volume CSV

Box, no pedal.

1980s		$35	$45

Volume Compressor VCO

1979-1984.

1979-1984		$35	$45

Volume Phaser PFV

1977-1984. With volume pedal.

1977-1984		$130	$150

Volume VOL

1975-ca.1984.

1975-1979		$35	$45
1980-1984		$30	$40

Volume XVO

1985-1988.

1985-1988		$30	$40

Volume/Boost VBO

1974-1984.

1974-1984		$40	$50

Wah Pedal PWA

1994		$35	$55

Wah Volume CWV

1987-1991. Box, no pedal.

1987-1991		$70	$80

Wah Volume XWV

1985-ca.1989.

1985-1989		$70	$80

Wah/Volume WVO

1977-ca.1984.

1977-1984		$90	$110

Mosrite

Semie Moseley's Mosrite company dipped into effects in the '60s. See the Guitar section for more company info.

Fuzzrite

1966		$150	$175

Mu-tron

1972-ca. 1981. Made by Musitronics (founded by Aaron Newman), Rosemont, New Jersey, these rugged and unique-sounding effects were a high point of the 1970s. The Mu-Tron III appeared in '72 and more products followed, about 10 in all. Musitronics also made the U.S. models of the Dan Armstrong effects. In '78 ARP synthesizers bought Musitronics and sold Mutron products to around '81. A reissue of the Mu-Tron III was made available in '95 by NYC Music Products and distributed by Matthews and Ryan Musical Products.

Bi-Phase

1975-ca.1981. Add $50-$75 for Opti-Pot Pedal.

1975-1981	With 2-button footswitch	$550	$650

Flanger

1977-ca.1981.

1977-1981		$250	$400

III Envelope Filter

1972-ca.1981. Envelope Filter.

1972-1981		$250	$400

Micro V

Ca.1975-ca.1977. Envelope Filter.

1970s		$150	$200

Octave Divider

1977-ca.1981.

1977-1981		$225	$300

Phasor

Ca.1974-ca.1976. Two knobs.

1974-1976		$150	$200

Phasor II

1976-ca.1981. Three knobs.

1976-1981		$150	$200

Volume-Wah C-200

1970s		$150	$200

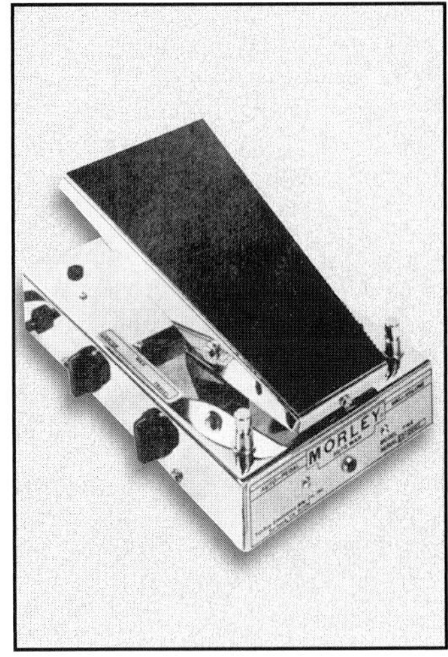

Morley Power Wah PWA

Morley Swivel Tone

Morley Volume/Boost VBO

EFFECTS

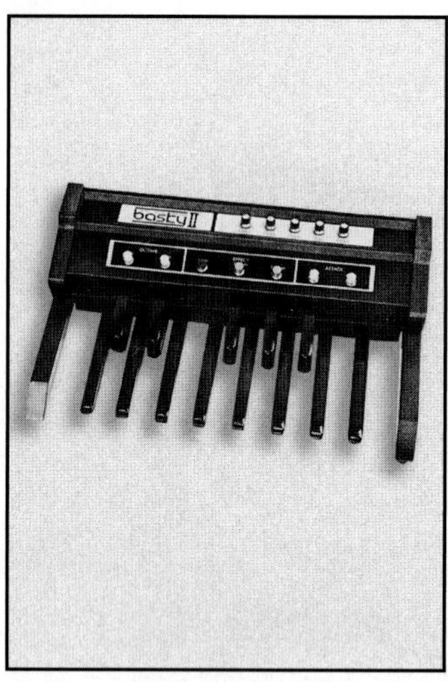

Multivox Basky II

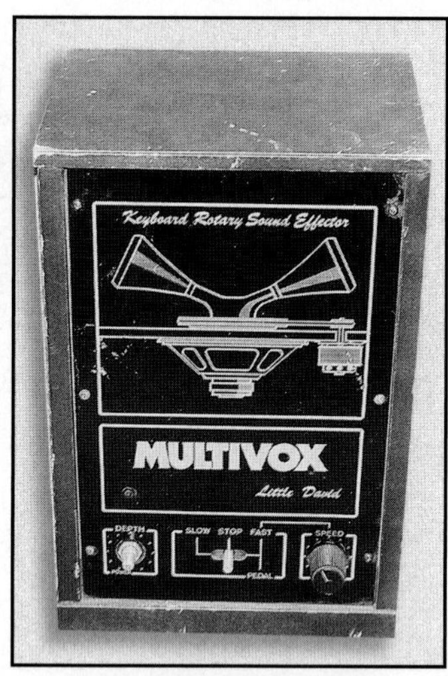

Multivox Little David

MXR Analog Delay

MODEL YEAR	FEATURES	EXC. COND. LOW	HIGH

Multivox

New York-based Multivox offered a variety of effects in the '70s and '80s.

Big Jam 6-Band EQ

1980-ca.1983.

1980-1983		$30	$40

Big Jam Analog Echo/Reverb

1980-ca.1983.

1980-1983		$90	$100

Big Jam Bi-Phase 2

1980-ca.1983.

1980-1983		$40	$50

Big Jam Chorus

1980-1983		$35	$45

Big Jam Compressor

1980-ca.1983.

1980-1983		$30	$40

Big Jam Delay

1982-ca.1983.

1982-1983		$50	$60

Big Jam Distortion

1980-ca.1983.

1980-1983		$60	$70

Big Jam Flanger

1980-ca.1983.

1980-1983		$40	$50

Big Jam Jazz Flanger

1980-ca.1983.

1980-1983		$40	$50

Big Jam Noise Gate

1981-ca.1983.

1981-1983		$25	$30

Big Jam Octave Box

1980-ca.1983.

1980-1983		$30	$40

Big Jam Parametric EQ

1982-ca.1983.

1982-1983		$30	$35

Big Jam Phaser

1980-ca.1983.

1980-1983		$30	$40

Big Jam Space Driver

1981-ca.1983. FET electronic switching, distortion, compression.

1981-1983		$50	$60

Big Jam Spit-Wah

1980-ca.1983.

1980-1983		$30	$40

Big Jam Volume Pedal

1982-ca.1983.

1982-1983		$25	$30

Full Rotor MX-2

1978-ca.1982. Leslie effect.

1978-1982		$200	$300

Little David LD-2

Rotary sound effector.

1970s	With pedal	$350	$400
1970s	Without pedal	$275	$325

Multi Echo MX-201

Tape echo unit, reverb.

1970s		$150	$200

Multi Echo MX-312

Tape echo unit, reverb.

1970s		$200	$250

Rhythm Ace FR6M

Twenty-seven basic rhythms.

1970s		$50	$70

MXR

1972-present. MXR Innovations launched its line of pedals in '72. Around '77, the Rochester, New York, company changed lettering on the effects from script to block, and added new models. MXR survived into the mid-'80s. In '87, production was picked up by Jim Dunlop. Original issues of block logo boxes can be differentiated from reissues as the reissues have an LED above the switch and the finish is slightly rough; the originals are smooth.

6 Band Equalizer

1975-1982.

1975-1979		$60	$90
1980-1982		$50	$75

6 Band Equalizer M-109 (reissue)

1987-present. Reissued by Jim Dunlop.

1987-1999		$40	$45

10 Band Graphic Equalizer

1975-1981.

1975-1981	With AC power cord	$70	$100

Analog Delay

1976-1981.

1976-1981	Green case, power cord	$200	$225

Blue Box

1972-ca.1978. Octave pedal, M-103.

1970s	Earlier script logo	$200	$250
1970s	Later block logo	$150	$200

Blue Box (reissue)

1995-present. Reissued by Jim Dunlop. Produces an octave above or two octaves below.

1995-1999		$45	$50

Commande Overdrive

1981-1983. The Commande series featured plastic housings and electronic switching.

1981-1983		$35	$40

Commande Phaser

1981-1983.

1981-1983		$90	$100

Commande Preamp

1981-1983.

1981-1983		$35	$40

Commande Stereo Chorus

1981-1983.

1981-1983		$50	$60

Commande Stereo Flanger

1982-1983.

1982-1983		$60	$70

MODEL YEAR	FEATURES	EXC. COND. LOW	HIGH
Commande Sustain			
1981-1983.			
1981-1983		$50	$60
Commande Time Delay			
1981-1983.			
1981-1983		$60	$70
Distortion +			
1972-1982.			
1970s	Earlier script logo	$175	$225
1970s	Later block logo	$75	$100
1980s	Block logo	$70	$90
Distortion + (Series 2000)			
1983-1985.			
1983-1985		$50	$60
Distortion + M-104 (reissue)			
1987-present. Reissued by Jim Dunlop.			
1980s		$45	$55
1990s		$35	$45
Distortion II			
1981-1983.			
1981-1983	With AC power cord	$130	$140
Dyna Comp			
1972-1982. Compressor.			
1970s	Earlier script logo, battery	$150	$175
1970s	Later block logo, battery	$120	$140
1980s	Block logo, battery	$80	$90
Dyna Comp (Series 2000)			
1980s		$55	$65
Dyna Comp M-102 (reissue)			
1987-present. Reissued by Jim Dunlop.			
1987-1999		$40	$50
Envelope Filter			
1976-1983.			
1976-1983		$120	$130
Flanger			
1976-1983. Analog. Reissued by Dunlop in 2000s.			
1976-1979	With AC power cord	$120	$130
1980-1983	With AC power cord	$90	$100
2000s	Dunlop MXR reissue	$70	$80
Flanger/Doubler			
1979	Rackmount	$130	$140
Limiter			
1980-1982. AC, four knobs.			
1980-1982	AC power cord	$90	$100
Loop Selector			
1980-1982. A/B switch for two effects loops.			
1980-1982		$40	$50
Micro Amp			
1978-1983. Variable booster.			
1978-1983		$80	$100
Micro Chorus			
1980-1983.			
1980-1983		$105	$125
Micro Flanger			
1981-1982.			
1981-1982		$80	$100
Noise Gate Line Driver			
1974-1983.			
1970s	Script logo	$55	$65
1980s	Block logo	$50	$60
Omni			
1980s		$300	$400
Phase 100			
1974-1982.			
1970s	Earlier script logo	$160	$180
1970s	Later block logo, battery	$120	$140
Phase 45			
Ca.1976-1982.			
1970s	Script logo, battery	$75	$85
1980s	Block logo, battery	$60	$70
Phase 90			
1972-1982.			
1970s	Earlier script logo	$140	$165
1970s	Later block logo	$135	$155
1980s	Block logo	$120	$140
Phase 90 M-101 (reissue)			
1987-present. Reissued by Jim Dunlop.			
1987-1989	Block logo	$50	$60
1990-1999	Block logo	$40	$50
Phaser (Series 2000)			
1982-1985. Series 2000 introduced cost cutting die-cast cases.			
1982-1985		$50	$60
Pitch Transposer			
1980s		$350	$400
Power Converter			
1980s		$40	$60
Smart Gate			
2000s. Dunlop MXR noise-gate, single control, battery powered.			
2003	Battery	$65	$75
Stereo Chorus			
1978-1985.			
1978-1979	With AC power cord	$165	$185
1980-1985	With AC power cord	$150	$160
Stereo Chorus (Series 2000)			
1983-1985. 2000 Series introduced cost cutting die-cast cases.			
1983-1985		$50	$55
Stereo Flanger (Series 2000)			
1983-1985. 2000 Series introduced cost cutting die-cast cases.			
1983-1985	Black with Blue lettering	$60	$70
Super Comp			
2000s. Dunlop MXR, three knobs, battery powered.			
2003	Battery power	$45	$55

Nobels

1997-present. Offered by Musicorp. German-designed effects.

MODEL YEAR	FEATURES	EXC. COND. LOW	HIGH
ODR-1			
1997-present. Overdrive.			
1997-2002		$70	$75

MXR Distortion +

MXR Phase 90

MXR Phase 100

EFFECTS

Olson Reverberation Amplifier RA-844

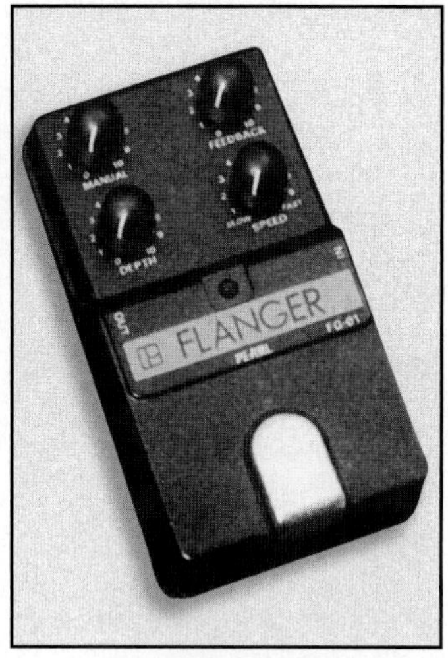

Pearl Flanger FG-01

Peavey Companded Chorus CMC-1

MODEL YEAR — FEATURES — EXC. COND. LOW — HIGH

TR-X Tremolo

1997-present. Tremolo effect using modern technology.

1997-1999 $40 $50

Nomad

Fuzz Wah

1960s. Import from Japan, similar looking to Morley pedal with depth and volume controls and fuzz switch, Silver metal case and Black foot pedal.

1960s $80 $90

Olson

Olson Electronics was in Akron, Ohio.

Reverberation Amplifier RA-844

1967. Solidstate, battery-operated, reveb unit, depth and volume controls, made in Japan.

1967 $100 $125

PAIA

1967-present. Founded by John Paia Simonton in Edmond, Oklahama, specializing in synthesizer and effects kits. PAIA did make a few complete products but they are better known for the various electronic kit projects they sold. Values on kit projects are difficult as it depends on the skills of the person who built it.

Roctave Divider 5760

Kit to build analog octave divider.

1970s $60 $70

Pax

1970s. Import Maestro copies.

Fuzz Tone Copy

1970s $130 $140

Octave Box Copy

1970s $120 $130

Pearl

Pearl, located in Nashville and better known for drums, offered a line of guitar effects in the 1980s.

Analog Delay AD-08

1983-1985. Four knobs.

1983-1985 $70 $80

Analog Delay AD-33

1982-1984. Six knobs.

1982-1984 $90 $100

Chorus CH-02

1981-1984. Four knobs.

1981-1984 $90 $120

Chorus Ensemble CE-22

1982-1984. Stereo chorus with dual-program sound choice toggling between chorus and vibrato, six knobs are labeled input, chorus rate, chorus rate, vibrato depth, vibrato speed and vibrato delay.

1982-1984 $90 $120

Compressor CO-04

1981-1984.

1981-1984 $50 $60

Distortion DS-06

1982-1986.

1982-1986 $45 $55

Flanger FG-01

1981-1986. Clock pulse generator, ultra-low frequency oscillator.

1981-1986 $70 $80

Graphic EQ GE-09

1983-1985.

1983-1985 $35 $45

Octaver OC-07

1982-1986.

1982-1986 $70 $80

Overdrive OD-05

1981-1986.

1981-1986 $70 $80

Parametric EQ PE-10

1983-1984.

1983-1984 $40 $50

Phaser PH-03

1981-1984. Four knobs.

1981-1984 $70 $80

Phaser PH-44

1982-1984. Six knobs.

1982-1984 $90 $100

Stereo Chorus CH-22

1980s Blue case $70 $80

Thriller TH-20

Exciter.

1980s Black case, four knobs $180 $200

Peavey

1965-present. Peavey made stomp boxes from 1987 to around 1990. They offered rackmount gear after that. See Guitar section for more company info.

Accelerator Overdrive AOD-2

1980s $30 $40

Biampable Bass Chorus BAC-2

1980s $30 $40

Companded Chorus CMC-1

1980s $25 $35

Compressor/Sustainer CSR-2

1980s $35 $45

Digital Delay DDL-3

1980s $30 $40

Digital Stereo Reverb SRP-16

1980s $50 $60

Dual Clock Stereo Chorus DSC-4

1980s $30 $40

Hotfoot Distortion HFD-2

1980s $25 $35

Pharaoh Amplifiers

1998-present. Builder Matt Farrow builds his effects in Raleigh, North Carolina.

MODEL YEAR	FEATURES	EXC. COND. LOW	HIGH

Premier

Ca. 1938-ca. 1975, 1990-present. Premier offered a reverb unit in the '60s. See Guitar section for more company info.

Reverb Unit

1961-late-1960s. Two-tone Brown, tube, footswitch.

1960s	Brown two-tone	$150	$300

Prescription Electronics

1994-present. Located in Portland, Oregon, Prescription offers a variety of hand-made effects.

Yardbox

1994-present. Patterned after the original Sola Sound Tonebender.

1994-1999		$80	$90

Pro-Sound

The effects listed here date from 1987, and were, most likely, around for a short time.

Chorus CR-1

1980s		$20	$30

Delay DL-1

Analog.

1980s		$35	$45

Distortion DS-1

1980s		$20	$30

Octaver OT-1

1980s		$30	$40

Power and Master Switch PMS-1

1980s		$15	$25

Super Overdrive SD-1

1980s		$20	$30

ProCo

1974-present. Located in Kalamazoo, Michigan and founded by Charlie Wicks, ProCo produces a range of cables and audio products, as well as effects.

Rat

1979-1987. Fuzztone, large box until 1984. The second version was one-third smaller than original box. The small box version became the Rat 2. The current Vintage Rat is a reissue of the original large box.

1979-1984	Large box	$100	$150
1984-1987	Compact box	$50	$60

Rat 2

1987-present.

1987-1999		$45	$55
2000s		$45	$55

Turbo Rat

1989-present. Fuzztone with higher output gain.

1989-2003		$45	$55

Vintage Rat

1992-present. Reissue of early-1980s Rat.

1992-1999		$40	$50

Rapco

The Jackson, Missouri based cable company offers a line of switch, connection and D.I. Boxes.

MODEL YEAR	FEATURES	EXC. COND. LOW	HIGH

The Connection AB-100

1988-present. A/B box

1988-1999		$20	$25

Real McCoy Custom

1993-present. Wahs and effects by Geoffrey Teese. His first wah was advertised as "the Real McCoy, by Teese." He now offers his custom wah pedals under the Real McCoy Custom brand. He also used the Teese brand on a line of stomp boxes, starting in '96. The Teese stomp boxes are no longer being made.

Reverend

1996-present. Guitars, amps and effects by luthier Joe Naylor, who also founded Naylor Amps, and built in Warren, Michigan.

Rockman

See listings under Scholz Research and Dunlop.

Rocktek

1986-present. Imports formerly distributed by Matthews and Ryan of Brooklyn, New York; currently handled by D'Andrea USA.

6 Band EQ GER-01

1987-present.

1986-1999		$10	$15

Bass EQ BER-01

1986-present.

1986-1999		$10	$15

Chorus CHR-01

1986-present.

1986-1999		$10	$15

Compressor COR-01

1986-present.

1980s		$10	$15

Delay ADR-02

1986-present.

1986-1999		$15	$20

Distortion DIR-01

1986-present.

1986-1999		$10	$15

Flanger FLR-01

1986-present.

1986-1999		$10	$15

Metal Worker MWR-01

1986-present.

1986-1999		$10	$15

Overdrive ODR-01

1986-present.

1986-1999		$10	$15

Phaser PHR-01

1986-present. Black case with white letters on green background logo.

1986-1999		$10	$15

Super Delay ADR-01

1986-present.

1986-1999		$10	$15

Premier Reverb unit

ProCo Vintage Rat

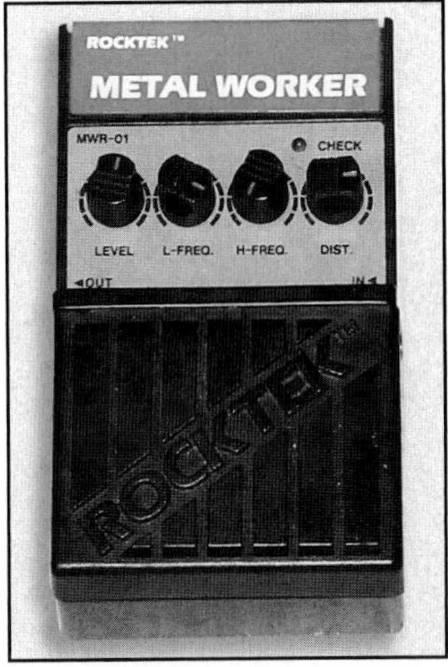

Rocktek Metal Worker MWR-01

EFFECTS

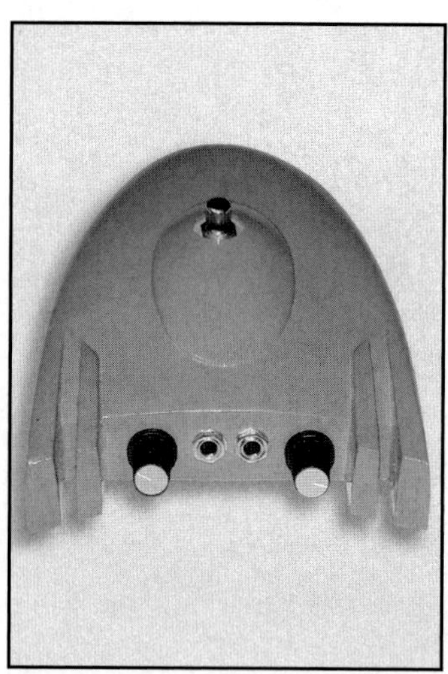

Roger Mayer Rocket Axis Fuzz

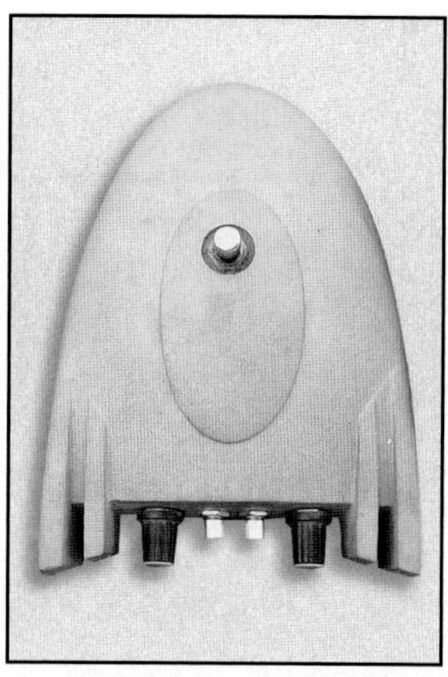

Roger Mayer Octavia

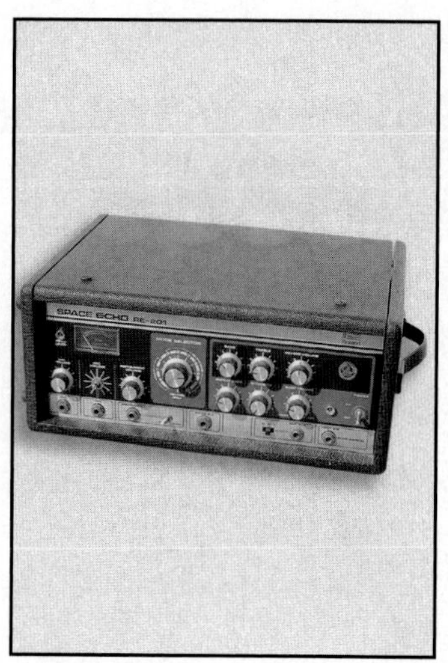

Roland Space Echo RE-201

MODEL YEAR	FEATURES	EXC. COND. LOW	HIGH

Vibrator Tremolo VIB

Ca. 1990-present.

1990-1999		$10	$15

Rocktron

1980s-present. Rocktron is a division of GHS Strings and offers a line of amps, controllers, stomp boxes, and preamps.

Austin Gold Overdrive

2000s. Light overdrive enhancement without changing guitar-amp tone, Gold case.

2000	Battery power	$30	$35

Banshee Talk Box

2000s. Includes power supply.

2000s	With power supply	$100	$110

Hush

2000s. Noise reduction, Blue case.

2000s	Battery power	$30	$35

Rampage Distortion

2000s. Sustain, high-gain and distortion, White case.

2000s	Battery power	$30	$35

Surf Tremolo

2000s.

2000s		$80	$90

Tsunami Chorus

2000s. Battery or optional AC adapter.

2000	Battery power	$40	$50
2000	With power supply	$55	$65

Vertigo Vibe

2000s. Rotating Leslie speaker effect.

2000	Battery power	$50	$55
2000	With power supply	$65	$70

XDC

1980s. Rackmount stereo preamp, distortion.

1980s		$90	$140

Roger Mayer Electronics

1964-present. Roger Mayer started making guitar effects in England in 1964 for guitarists like Jimmy Page and Jeff Beck. He moved to the U.S. in 1969 to start a company making studio gear and effects. He returned to England in 1989.

Axis Fuzz

1987-present.

1987-1999		$100	$150

Classic Fuzz

1987-present. The Fuzz Face.

1987-1999		$160	$190

Metal Fuzz

1987-1994.

1987-1994		$90	$120

Mongoose Fuzz

1987-present.

1987-1999		$140	$150

Octavia

1979-present. Famous rocket-shaped box.

1979-1999		$150	$175

MODEL YEAR	FEATURES	EXC. COND. LOW	HIGH

VooDoo-1

Ca.1990-present.

1990s		$150	$175

Roland

Japan's Roland Corporation first launched effect pedals in 1974; a year or two later the subsidiary company, Boss, debuted its own line. They were marketed concurrently at first, but gradually Boss became reserved for effects and drum machines while the Roland name was used on amplifiers and keyboards.

Bee Baa AF-100

1975-ca.1980. Fuzz and treble boost.

1975-1980		$250	$300

Bee Gee AF-60

1975-ca.1980. Sustain, distortion.

1975-1980		$70	$90

Double Beat AD-50

1975-ca.1980. Fuzz wah.

1975-1980		$150	$200

Expression Pedal EV-5

1970s		$40	$45

Guitar Synth Pedal GR-33 and Pickup GK-2A

2000-present. Requires optional GK-2A pickup.

2000-2003		$450	$500

Human Rhythm Composer R-8

1980s. Drum machine, key pad entry.

1980s		$150	$250

Jet Phaser AP-7

1975-ca.1978. Phase and distortion.

1975-1978		$200	$250

Phase II AP-2

1975-ca.1980. Brown case.

1975-1980		$150	$200

Phase Five AP-5

1975-ca.1978.

1975-1978		$175	$225

Space Echo RE-101

1974-ca.1980. Tape echo and reverb.

1974-1980		$350	$500

Space Echo RE-201

1974-ca.1980. Tape echo and reverb.

1974-1980		$350	$500

Space Echo RE-301

1977-ca.1980. Tape echo and reverb.

1977-1980		$350	$500

Space Echo RE-501

Tape echo and reverb.

1970s		$400	$600

Vocoder SVC-350

Late-1970s-1980s. Vocal synthesis (vocoder) for voice or guitar, rackmount version of VP-330.

1980		$550	$600

Vocoder VP-330 Plus

Late-1970s-1980s. Analog vocal synthesis (vocoder) for voice or guitar, includes 2 1/2 octaves keyboard.

1978-1982		$700	$800

MODEL YEAR	FEATURES	EXC. COND. LOW	HIGH

Wah Beat AW-10

1975-ca.1980.

1975-1980		$75	$100

Ross

Founded by Bud Ross, who also established Kustom, in Chanute, Kansas, in the 1970s. Ross produced primarily amplifiers. In about 1978, they introduced a line of U.S.-made effects. Later production switched to the Orient.

10 Band Graphic Equalizer

1970s		$40	$75

Compressor

1970s		$185	$225

Distortion

1978-ca.1980. Brown, made in U.S.A.

1979-1980		$50	$75

Flanger

1977-ca.1980. Red, made in U.S.A.

1977-1980		$90	$100

Phase Distortion R1

Purple, made in U.S.A.

1979		$100	$110

Phaser

1978-ca.1980. Orange, made in U.S.A.

1978-1980		$75	$100

Stereo Delay

1978-ca.1980. Made in U.S.A.

1978-1980		$110	$130

Rotovibe

See listing under Dunlop.

S. Hawk

Hawk I Fuzz

1975		$90	$100

LTD

1975	Silver case, slider	$90	$100

Sam Ash

1960s-1970s. Sam Ash Music was founded by a young Sam Ash (formerly Askynase - an Austro-Hungarian name) in '24. Ash's first store was in Brooklyn, and was relocated to a better part of Brooklyn in '44. By '66, there were about four Ash stores. During this time, Ash Music private branded their own amps and effects.

Fuzzz Boxx

Ca.1967. Red, made by Universal Amplifier Company.

1967		$150	$250

Volume Wah

Italian-made.

1970s		$150	$175

Scholz Research

Started by Tom Scholz of the band Boston in the early 1980s. In 1996, Jim Dunlop picked up the Rockman line (see Dunlop).

MODEL YEAR	FEATURES	EXC. COND. LOW	HIGH

Power Soak

1980s		$60	$80

Rockman

1980s		$45	$55

Rockman X100

Professional studio processor.

1980s		$65	$75

Soloist

Personal guitar processor.

1980s		$40	$50

Seamoon

Seamoon made effects from 1973 until 1977, when Dave Tarnowski bought up the remaining inventory and started Analog Digital Associates (ADA).

Fresh Fuzz

1975-1977. Recently reissued by ADA.

1975-1977		$100	$150

Funk Machine

1974-1977. Envelope Filter. Recently reissued by ADA.

1974-1977		$150	$200

Studio Phase

1975-1977. Phase shifter.

1975-1977		$60	$80

Sekova

Mid-1960s-mid-1970s. Entry level instruments imported by the U.S. Musical Merchandise Corporation of New York.

Fuzz

1960s		$90	$125

Shinei

Japanese imports. Shinei also made effects for Univox and probably others.

Fuzz wah

1970s		$100	$120

Resly (repeat time) Machine

Black case, three speeds.

1970s		$300	$400

Sho Bud

Volume Pedal

1965		$90	$110

SIB

Effects pedals from Rick Hamel, who helped design SMF amps.

Siegmund Guitars & Amplifiers

1993-present. Chris Siegmund founded the company in Seattle, moving it to Austin, TX for '95-'97, and is currently located in Los Angeles. Siegmund offers handmade tube amps and preamp pedals.

Ross Distortion

Scholz Acoustic Guit Pedal

SIB Fatdrive

EFFECTS

Snarling Dogs
Bawl Buster Bass Wah

Snarling Dogs
Black Dog SDP-2

Tech 21 Comptortion

MODEL YEAR	FEATURES	EXC. COND. LOW	HIGH

Snarling Dogs

1997-present. Started by Charlie Stringer of Stringer Industries, Warren, New Jersey in 1997. Stringer died in May 1999. The brand is now carried by D'Andrea USA.

Whine-O Wah

1997-present. Three classic wah sounds in die-cast pedal.

1997-2002 $45 $55

Sobbat

1995-present. Line of effects from Kinko Music Company of Kyoto, Japan.

Sola/Colorsound

1965-present. Sola was founded by London's Macari's Musical Exchange in '65. Sola made effects for Vox, Marshall, Park, and B & M and later under their own Colorsound brand. Refer to Colorsound for listings and more company info.

Stinger

Stinger effects were distributed by the Martin Guitar Company from 1989 to 1990.

CH-70 Stereo Chorus

1989 $25 $55

CO-20 Compressor

1989 $25 $55

DD-90 Digital Delay

1989 $25 $55

DE-80 Analog Delay

1989 $30 $60

DI-10 Distortion

1989 $35 $70

FL-60 Flanger

1989 $25 $55

OD-30 Overdrive

1989 $25 $55

TS-5 Tube Stack

1989 $35 $60

Supro

1935-1968. Supro offered a few reverb units in the '60s. See Guitar section for more company info.

500 R Standard Reverb Unit

1962-1963. Outboard reverb unit.

1962-1963 $200 $300

Auxiliary Reverb S6405(R)

1964-1968. Reverb unit, offered in Rhino Hide ('64-'68) or black and grey Tolex ('66-'67).

1960s $200 $300

Sweet Sound

1994-present. Line of effects from Bob Sweet, originally made in Trenton, Michigan, currently in Coral Springs, Florida.

Systech (Systems & Technology in Music, Inc)

Systech was located in Kalamazoo, Michigan.

Envelope and Repeater

1975-late-1970s.

1975-1979 $80 $100

Envelope Follower

1975-late-1970s.

1975-1979 $80 $100

Flanger

1975-late-1970s.

1975-1979 $80 $100

Harmonic Energizer

1975-late-1970s.

1975-1979 $125 $225

Overdrive Model 1300

1975-late-1970s.

1975-1979 $80 $100

Phase Shifter Model 1200

1975-late-1970s.

1975-1979 $80 $100

T-Rex

2003-present. Made in Denmark and imported by European Musical Imports.

T.C. Electronics

1976-present. Brothers Kim and John Rishøj founded TC Electronic in Risskov, Denmark, and made guitar effects pedals for several years before moving into rack-mounted gear. Currently they offer a wide range of pro audio gear.

Booster + Distortion

1980s $300 $400

Dual Parametric Equalizer

1980s $250 $350

Stereo Chorus/Flanger

Introduced in 1982, and reissued in '91.

1980s $150 $200

Sustain + Equalizer

1980s $200 $300

Tech 21

1989-present. Tech 21 offers a variety of products out of New York City.

Sansamp

1989-present. Offers a variety of tube amp tones.

1989-1999 $100 $125

XXL Pedal

1995-2000. Distortion, fuzz.

1995-2000 $50 $60

Teese

Geoffrey Teese's first wah was advertised as "the Real McCoy, by Teese." He now offers his custom wah pedals under the Real McCoy Custom brand. The Teese brand name was used on his line of stomp boxes, starting in '96. The Teese stomp boxes are no longer being made.

MODEL YEAR	FEATURES	EXC. COND. LOW	HIGH

Thomas Organ

The Thomas Organ Company was heavily involved with Vox from '64 to '72, importing their instruments into the U.S. and designing and assembling products, including the wah-wah pedal. Both Thomas Organ and JMI, Vox's European distributor, wanted to offer the new effect. The problem was solved by labeling the Thomas Organ wah the Crybaby. The Crybaby is now offered by Dunlop. Refer to Vox listing for Crybaby Stereo Fuzz Wah, Crybaby Wah, and Wah Wah.

Top Gear

Rotator

Leslie effect.

1970s		$75	$125

Top Hat Amplification

1994-present. The Anaheim, California, based amp builder also offers effects.

Tremolo

See listing under Dunlop.

Tube Works

Originally out of Denver, now a division of Genz Benz Enclosures of Scottsdale, Arizona, they also offer tube/solidstate amps, cabinets, and DI boxes.

Real Tube

Ca. 1987-present. Overdrive with 12AX7A tube.

1987-1999		$80	$100

Tube Driver

1989-present. With tube.

1989-1999	With tube	$90	$100

Tycobrahe

The Tycobrahe story was over almost before it began. Doing business in 1976-1977, they produced only three pedals and a direct box, one the fabled Octavia. The company, located in Hermosa Beach, California, made high-quality, original devices, but they didn't catch on. Now, they are very collectible.

Octavia

1976-1977. Octave doubler.

1976-1977		$300	$500

Parapedal

1976-1977. Wah.

1976-1977		$300	$500

Pedalflanger

1976-1977. Blue pedal-controlled flanger.

1976-1977		$300	$500

Uni-Vibe

See listing under Dunlop.

MODEL YEAR	FEATURES	EXC. COND. LOW	HIGH

Univox

Univox was a brand name owned by Merson (later Unicord), of Westbury, New York. It marketed guitars and amps, and added effects in the late-1960s. Most Univox effects were made by Shinei, of Japan. They vanished in about 1981.

EC-100 Echo

Tape, sound-on-sound.

1970s		$100	$150

EC-80 A Echo

Early-1970s-ca.1977. Tape echo, sometimes shown as "The Brat Echo Chamber."

1970s		$90	$140

Echo-Tech EM-200

Disc recording echo unit.

1970s		$125	$175

Micro 41 FCM41 4 channel mixer

1970s		$40	$50

Micro Fazer

1970s		$45	$90

Noise-Clamp EX110

1970s		$40	$50

Phaser PHZ1

AC powered.

1970s		$50	$80

Pro Verb

1970s. Reverb (spring) unit, Black Tolex, slider controls for two inputs, one output plus remote output.

1970s	Black Tolex	$90	$100

Square Wave SQ150

Introduced in 1976, distortion.

1970s	Orange case	$90	$100

Superfuzz

1971	Gray box, normal bypass switch	$200	$300
1973	Unicord, various colors, large Blue bypass	$200	$300

Uni-Fuzz

1960s. Fuzz tone in Blue case, two Black knobs and slider switch.

1960s	Blue case	$250	$350

Uni-Tron 5

A.k.a. Funky Filter, envelope filter.

1975		$100	$150

Uni-Vibe

Introduced around 1969, with rotating speaker simulation, with pedal.

1960s		$800	$900
1970s		$600	$800

Uni-Wah Wah/Volume

1970s		$80	$120

Unicomp

Compression limiter.

1970s		$40	$90

Unidrive

1970s		$90	$200

Tycobrahe Parapedal

Univox Univibe

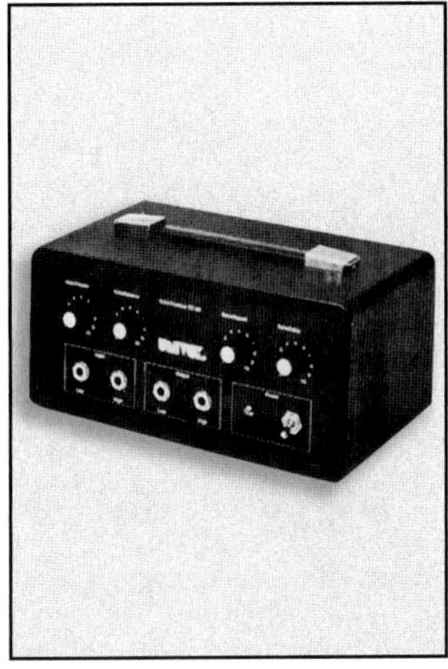

Univox EC-80 Echo Chamber

Vox Clyde McCoy Wah

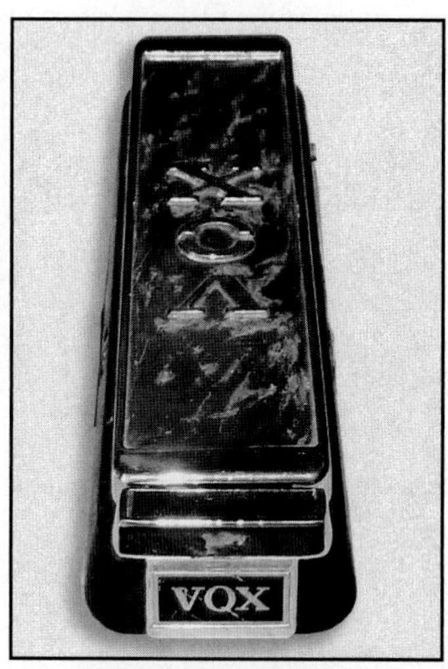

Vox Fuzz Wah

Vox King Wah

MODEL YEAR	FEATURES	EXC. COND. LOW	HIGH

Vesta Fire

Ca.1981-ca.1988. Brand name of Japan's Shiino Musical Instrument Corp.

Digital Chorus/Flanger FLCH

1980s		$35	$45

Distortion DST

1980s		$35	$45

Flanger

1980s		$35	$45

Noise Gate

1980s		$25	$35

Stereo Chorus SCH

Foot pedal.

1980s		$25	$35

VooDoo Lab

1994-present. Line of effects offered by Digital Music Corp. of California.

Analog Chorus

1994-1999.

1994-1999		$100	$130

Bosstone

1994-1999. Based on 1960s Jordan Electronics Fuzz.

1994-1999		$65	$75

Micro Vibe

1994-1999. Uni-Vibe swirl effect.

1994-1999		$95	$100

Overdrive

1994-2000. Based on '70s overdrive.

1994-2000		$50	$55

Super Fuzz

1994-1999.

1994-1999		$70	$75

Tremolo

1994-present. Vintage trem.

1994-1999		$80	$90

Vox

1957-present. Vox offered a variety of guitars, amps, organs and effects. Circa '66, they released the Tone Bender, one of the classic fuzzboxes of all time. A year or so later, they delivered their greatest contribution to the effects world, the first wah-wah pedal. The American arm of Vox (then under Thomas Oragan) succumbed in '72. In the U.K., the company was on-again/off-again. See the Guitar section for more company info.

Clyde McCoy Wah-Wah Pedal

Introduced in 1967, reissued in 2001.

1967	Clyde's picture on bottom cover	$500	$650
1968	No picture on bottom plate	$400	$550

Crybaby Wah

Introduced in 1968. The Thomas Organ Company was heavily involved with Vox from '64 to '72, importing their instruments into the U.S. and designing and assembling products. One product developed in conjunction with Vox was the wah-wah pedal. Both Thomas Organ and JMI, Vox's European distributor, wanted to offer the new effect. The problem was solved by labeling the Thomas Organ wah the Crybaby. The original wahs were built by Jen in Italy, but Thomas later made them in their Chicago and Sepulveda, CA plants. Thomas Organ retained the marketing rights to Vox until '79, but was not very active with the brand after '72. The Crybaby brand is now offered by Dunlop.

1960s	Jen-made	$175	$225
1970	Sepulveda-made	$100	$120

Double Sound

Jen-made, Double Sound model name on bottom of pedal, double sound derived from fuzz and wah ability.

1970s		$150	$250

King Wah

Chrome top, Italian-made.

1970s		$75	$100

Stereo Fuzz Wah

1970s		$125	$150

Tone Bender V-828

1966-1970s. Fuzz box. Reissued as the V-829 in '94.

1966	Gray	$275	$350
1969	Black	$225	$300

V-807 Echo-Reverb Unit

Solidstate, disc echo.

1967		$200	$300

V-837 Echo Deluxe Tape Echo

Solidstate, multiple heads.

1967		$200	$300

V-846 Wah

1969-1970s. Chrome top, Italian-made.

1969	Transitional Clyde McCoy	$350	$500
1970s		$200	$300

V-847 Wah

1992-present. Reissue of the original V-846 Wah.

1990s		$60	$80

Volume Pedal

Late 1960s. Reissued as the V850.

1963		$55	$75

Washburn

Washburn offered a line of effects from around 1983 to ca. 1989. See Guitar section for more company info.

Analog Delay AX:9

1980s		$25	$35

Flanger FX:4

1980s		$30	$40

Phaser

1980s		$35	$45

Stack in a Box SX:3

Tube-like distortion.

1980s		$25	$35

MODEL YEAR	FEATURES	EXC. COND. LOW	HIGH

Watkins/WEM

1957-present. Watkins Electric Music (WEM) was founded by Charlie Watkins. Their first commercial product was the Watkins Dominator (wedge Gibson stereo amp shape) in 1957, followed by the Copicat Echo in 1958.

Copicat Tape Echo

1958-1970s. The Copicat has been reissued by Watkins.

1960s	Tube	$500	$600
1968	Solidstate	$200	$400

Way Huge Electronics

1995-1998. Way Huge offered a variety of stomp boxes, made in Sherman Oaks, California.

WD Music

Since 1978, WD Music has offered a wide line of aftermarket products for guitar players. Many effects were copies of original Dan Armstrong color series (refer to Dan Armstrong listing). Large WD logo on Armstrong copies with Strat-pickguard logo on top of pedal.

Blue Clipper

1992-present. Fuzz.

1990s		$30	$40

Orange Squeezer

1992-present. Signal compressor.

1990s	Light Orange case	$40	$45

Purple Peaker

1992-present. Mini EQ.

1990s		$40	$45

Westbury

1978-ca. 1983. Brandname imported by Unicord. See Guitar section for more company info.

Tube Overdrive

1978-1983. 12AX7.

1978-1983		$100	$150

Whirlwind

1980s. Whirlwind called Rochester, New York home.

Commander

Boost and effects loop selector.

1980s		$60	$80

Xotic Effects

2001-present. Hand-wired effects made in the U.S. and distributed by Prosound Communications.

Yamaha

Yamaha offers effects as part of their musical instrument line. See Guitar section for more company info.

Analog Delay E1005

1980s. Free standing, double space rackmount-sized, short to long range delays.

1980s	Gray case	$150	$160

Yubro

Yubro, of Bellaire, Texas, offered a line of nine effects in the mid- to late-'80s.

Analog Delay AD-800

Three hundred ms.

1980s		$60	$80

Stereo Chorus CH-600

1980s		$30	$40

Zoom

Effects line from Samson Technologies Corp of Syosset, New York.

503 Amp Simulator

1990s.

1990s		$25	$45

504 Acoustic Pedal

1997-2000. Compact multi-effects pedal, 24 effects, tuner, replaced by II version.

1990s		$25	$45

505 Guitar Pedal

1995-2000. Compact multi-effects pedal, 24 effects, tuner, replaced by II version.

1990s		$30	$50

506 Bass Pedal

1997-2000. Compact multi-effects bass pedal, 24 effects, tuner, replaced by II version.

1990s	Black box, Orange panel	$30	$50

507 Reverb

1990s		$25	$45

1010 Player

1996-1999. Compact multi-effects pedal board, 16 distortions, 25 effects.

1990s		$40	$80

Xotic AC Booster

Xotic RC Booster

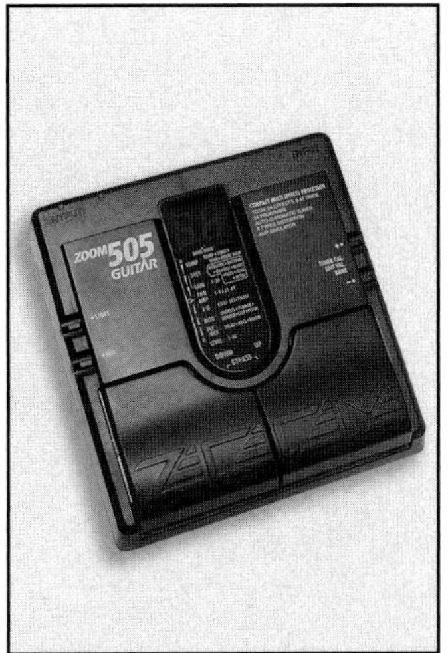

Zoom 505 Guitar Pedal

Steels & Lap Steels

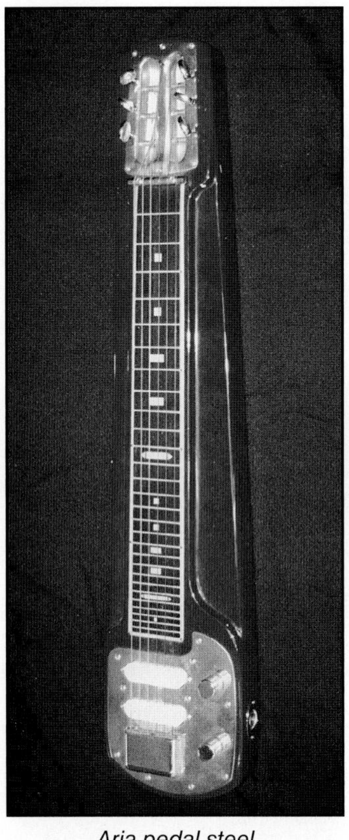
Aria pedal steel

1947 Dickerson-made Leilani

MODEL YEAR	FEATURES	EXC. COND. LOW	HIGH

Airline

Ca.1958-1968. Brand name for Montgomery Ward. Built by Kay, Harmony and Valco.

Lap Steel

1960s	Rec-O-Glas/plastic	$500	$550
1960s	Wood	$150	$250

Rocket 6-String Steel

Black and White, three legs, Valco-made.

1964		$300	$375

Student 6 Steel

1950	Black	$125	$175

Alamo

1947-1982. Founded by Charles Eilenberg, Milton Fink, and Southern Music, San Antonio, TX. Distributed by Bruno & Sons. Alamo's first musical instruments were lap steel and amp combos. The early models were sold with small birch amplifiers. See Guitar section for more company info or *Guitar Stories Volume II*, by Michael Wright, for a complete history of Alamo with detailed model listings.

Hawaiian Lap Steels

1947-ca. 1967. Models include the 1950s Challenger and Futuramic Dual Eight, the 1950s and early-1960s Embassy (pear-shape) and Jet (triangular), the early-1960s Futuramic Eight and Futuramic Six, and the late-1960s Embassy (triangular Jet).

1950s		$100	$200

Alkire

1939-1950s. Founded by Eddie Alkire, musician and teacher. Instruments may have been built by another company.

E-Harp 10-String Steel

1939-1950s. Similar to Epiphone lap steel with Epi-style logo, offered in lap steel or console.

1940s		$700	$1,000
1950s		$700	$1,000

Alvarez

Ca. 1966-present. Imported by St. Louis Music from mid-1960s.

Model 5010 Koa D Steel-String

Koa.

1960s		$250	$350

Aria

1960-present. Japan's Aria offered steels and lap steels in the '60s. See Guitar section for more company info.

Bigsby

1947-1965. All handmade by Paul Arthur Bigsby, in Downey, California. Bigsby was a pioneer in developing pedal steels and they were generally special order or custom made and not mass produced. Instruments should be valued on a case-by-case basis. Models include the Single Neck pedal steel, Double 8 pedal steel, 8/10 Doubleneck pedal steel, Triple 8 pedal steel (all ca. 1947-'65), and the 1957-'58 Magnatone G-70 lap steel. See Guitar section for more company info.

Triple 8-String Neck Steel

1947-1965. Bigsby steels were generally special order or custom-made and not mass produced. Instruments should be valued on a case-by-case basis.

1950s	Natural	$2,500	$5,000

Bronson

George Bronson was a steel guitar instructor in the Detroit area from the 1930s to the early '50s and sold instruments under his own brand. Most instruments and amps were made by Rickenbacker, Dickerson or Valco.

Melody King Model 52 Lap Steel

Brown Bakelite body with five gold cavity covers on the top, made by Rickenbacker.

1950s		$600	$800

Carvin

1946-present. Founded by Lowell C. Kiesel who produced lapsteels under the Kiesel brandname for 1947-'50. In late '49, he renamed the instrument line Carvin after sons Carson and Galvin. Until 1977, they offered lap, console, and pedal steels with up to four necks.

Double 6 Steel With Legs

1960		$500	$600

Double 8 Steel With Legs

1960	Sunburst	$600	$700

Electric Hawaiian Lap Steel

1950s		$200	$300

Single 8 With Legs

Large block position markers, one pickup, two knobs. Blond finish.

1965		$400	$500

Cromwell

1935-1939. Budget model brand built by Gibson and distributed by various mail-order businesses.

Lap Steel

Charlie Christian bar pickup.

1939	Sunburst	$300	$350

Danelectro

1946-1969, 1997-present. Known mainly for guitars and amps, Danelectro did offer a few lap steels in the mid-'50s. See Guitar section for more company info.

Lap Steels

1950s		$250	$300

Dickerson

1937-1948. Founded by the Dickerson brothers in 1937, primarily for electric lap steels and small amps. Besides their own brand, Dickerson made instruments for Cleveland's Oahu Company, Varsity, Southern California Music,

MODEL YEAR	FEATURES	EXC. COND. LOW	HIGH

Bronson, Roland Ball and Gourley. The lap steels were often sold with matching amps, both covered in pearloid Mother-of-Toilet-Seat (MOTS). By 1948, the company changed ownership and was renamed Magna Electronics (Magnatone).

Lap Steel with matching amp

1950s. Gray Pearloid with matching amp.

1950s		$400	$600

Dobro

1929-1942, ca.1954-present. Dobro offered lap steels from 1933 to '42. See Guitar section for more company info.

Hawaiian Lap Steel

1930s		$300	$350

Lap Steel Guitar and Amp Set

1930s-1940s. Typical pearloid covered student six-string lap steel and small matching amp (with three tubes and single control knob).

1940	White pearloid	$375	$425

Dwight

1950s. Private branded instruments by National - Supro.

Lap Steel

1950s. Pearloid, six strings.

1950s	Gray pearloid	$300	$350

Emmons

1970s-present. Owned by Lashley, Inc. of Burlington, North Carolina.

Lashley LeGrande III Steel

2001. Double-neck, eight pedals, four knee levers, 25th Anniversary.

2001		$2,600	$2,800

S-10 Pedal Steel

Single ten-string neck pedal steel.

1970s		$800	$1,000

English Electronics

1960s. Norman English had a teaching studio in Lansing, Michigan, where he gave guitar and steel lessons. He had his own private-branded instruments made by Valco in Chicago.

Tonemaster Lap Steel

Cream Pearloid, six strings, three legs, Valco-made.

1960s		$200	$300

Epiphone

1928-present. The then Epiphone Banjo Company was established in 1928. Best known for its guitars, the company offered steels from 1935 to 1958 when Gibson purchased the brand. See Guitar section for more company info.

Century Lap Steel

1939-1957. Rocket-shaped maple body, one pickup, metal fingerboard, six, seven or eight strings. Black finish.

1940s		$375	$425

Console Triple-Neck Steel

1950-1958. Three necks. Sunburst or Natural finish.

1954		$600	$800

Electar Century Lap Steel

1930s	Black	$350	$450

Electar Kent Hawaiian Lap Steel

1949-1953. Guitar-shaped maple body, six strings, lower-end of Epiphone Hawaiian line. Electar script logo below bottom of fretboard.

1949		$300	$350

Electar Model M Lap Steel

1936-1939. Hawaiian setup, stair-step body, art deco, six, seven or eight strings.

1938	Black	$350	$400

Electar Zenith Lap Steel

Six-string neck.

1943	Black	$350	$450

Electar Zephyr Lap Steel

1939-1957. Maple body, metal fingerboard, six, seven or eight strings.

1930s	Black, art deco	$500	$600
1940s	Black and White, 8 strings	$450	$600
1942	Six strings	$450	$600
1950s	Black, 7 strings	$400	$550

Skylark Steel

1962	Natural korina	$700	$850

Solo Console Steel

1939-1954. Maple with White mahogany laminated body, Black binding, Black metal fingerboard, six, seven or eight strings.

1951		$400	$450

Fender

1946-present. Fender offered lap and pedal steels from 1946 to 1980. See Guitar section for more company info.

400 Pedal Steel

1958-1976. One eight-string neck with four to 10 pedals.

1960s	Blond	$650	$950

800 Pedal Steel

1964-1976. One 10-string neck, six to 10 pedals.

1964-1976	Sunburst	$600	$750

1000 Pedal Steel

1957-1976. Two eight-string necks and eight or 10 pedals.

1957-1976	Natural, 8 pedals	$750	$1,200
1957-1976	Sunburst, 10 pedals	$750	$1,200
1957-1976	Sunburst, 8 pedals	$750	$1,200

2000 Pedal Steel

1964-1976. Two 10-string necks, 10 or 11 pedals. Sunburst.

1964-1976	10 pedals	$750	$1,200

Artist Dual 10 Pedal Steel

1976-1981. Two 10-string necks, eight pedals, four knee levers. Black or Mahogany.

1976-1981		$650	$850

Epiphone Electar Model M

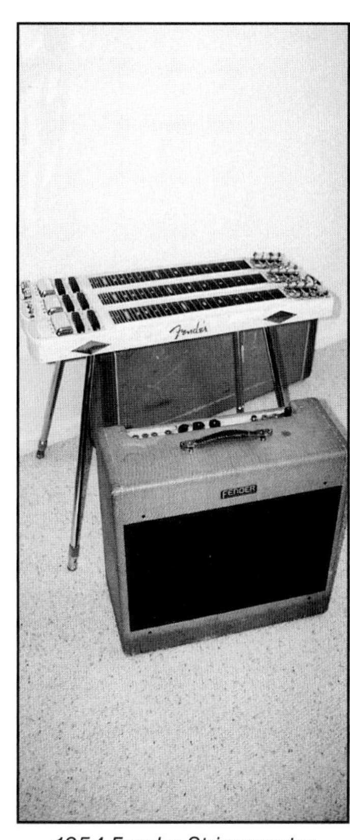

1954 Fender Stringmaster

STEELS & LAPS

Fender Dual 8 Professional

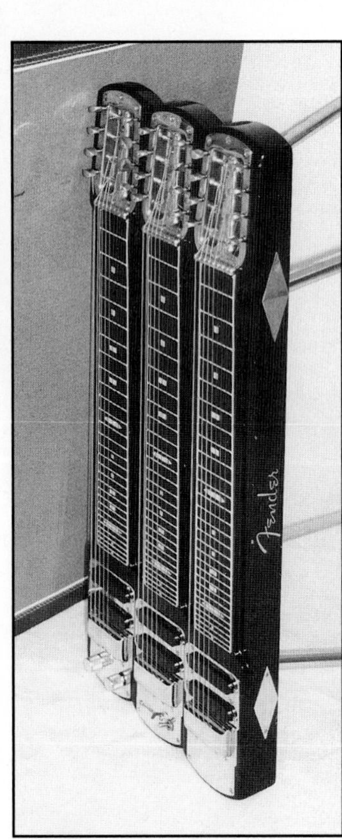

1961 Fender Stringmaster

MODEL YEAR	FEATURES	EXC. COND. LOW	HIGH
Champ Lap Steel			
1955-1980. Replaced Champion Lap Steel.			
1955-1959	Tan	$700	$750
1960-1969	Tan	$650	$700
1970-1980	Tan	$500	$600
Champion Lap Steel			
1949-1955. Covered in what collectors call Mother of Toilet Seat (M.O.T.S.) finish, also known as Pearloid. Replaced by Champ Lap Steel.			
1949-1955	Tan	$700	$750
1949-1955	White Pearloid	$700	$750
1949-1955	Yellow Pearloid	$700	$750
Deluxe 6/Stringmaster Single Steel			
1950-1981. Renamed from the Deluxe, six strings, three legs.			
1950-1959	Blond or Walnut	$700	$900
1960-1969	Blond or Walnut	$700	$900
1970-1981	Black or White	$500	$800
Deluxe 8/Stringmaster Single Steel			
1950-1981. Renamed from the Deluxe, eight strings, three legs.			
1950-1959	Blond or Walnut	$700	$900
1960-1969	Blond or Walnut	$700	$900
1970-1981	Black or White	$500	$800
Deluxe Steel			
1949-1950. Strings-through-pickup, Roman numeral markers. Became the Deluxe 6 or Deluxe 8 Lap Steel in 1950.			
1946	Wax	$800	$900
1947-1950	Blond or Walnut	$800	$900
Dual 6 Professional Steel			
1950-1981. Two six-string necks, three legs optional. Blond or Walnut.			
1952-1981		$700	$900
Dual 8 Professional Steel			
1946-1957. Two eight-string necks, three legs optional. Blond or Walnut.			
1946-1957		$750	$950
K & F Steel			
1945-1946. Made by Doc Kauffman and Leo Fender, strings-through-pickup.			
1945-1946	Black	$1,400	$1,500
Organ Button Steel			
1946-1947.			
1946-1947	Wax	$800	$950
1947	Wax	$750	$950
Princeton Steel			
1946-1948. Strings-through-pickup, Roman numeral markers.			
1946-1948	Wax	$600	$700
Stringmaster Steel (two-neck)			
1953-1981. The Stringmaster came in three versions, having two, three or four eight-string necks (six-string necks optional).			
1953-1959	Blond	$1,000	$1,400
1953-1959	Walnut	$800	$1,000
1960-1969	Blond	$1,000	$1,200
1960-1969	Walnut	$800	$1,000
1970-1981	Blond or Walnut	$700	$900
Stringmaster Steel (three-neck)			
1953-1981. The Stringmaster came in three versions, having two, three or four eight-string necks (six-string necks optional).			
1953-1959	Blond	$1,300	$2,000
1953-1959	Walnut	$1,000	$1,500
1960-1969	Blond	$1,200	$1,700
1960-1969	Walnut	$900	$1,200
1970-1981	Blond	$900	$1,300
1970-1981	Walnut	$800	$900
Stringmaster Steel (four-neck)			
1953-1968. The Stringmaster came in three versions, having two, three or four eight-string necks (six-string necks optional).			
1953-1959	Blond	$1,400	$2,100
1953-1959	Walnut	$1,100	$1,600
1960-1968	Blond	$1,300	$1,600
1960-1968	Walnut	$1,000	$1,300
Studio Deluxe Lap Steel			
1956-1981. One pickup, three legs.			
1956-1981	Blond	$600	$700

Framus

1946-1977, 1996-present. Founded by Fred Wilfer, Erlangen, Germany in 1946. Relocated to Bubenreuth in 1954, and to Pretzfeld in 1967. Imported into the U.S. by Philadelphia Music Company in the 1960s.

Brand revived in 1996, and distributed in the US by Dana B. Goods. See Guitar section for more company info.

MODEL YEAR	FEATURES	EXC. COND. LOW	HIGH
Deluxe Table Steel 0/7			
1973	White	$250	$350
Student Hawaiian Model 0/4			
1973	Red	$150	$200

G.L. Stiles

1960-1994. Gilbert Lee Stiles made a variety of instruments, mainly in the Miami area. See Guitar section for more company info.

MODEL YEAR	FEATURES	EXC. COND. LOW	HIGH
Doubleneck Pedal Steel			
1970s		$500	$600

Gibson

1902-present. Gibson offered steels from 1935-1968. See Guitar section for more company info.

MODEL YEAR	FEATURES	EXC. COND. LOW	HIGH
BR-4 Lap Steel			
1947. Guitar-shaped of solid mahogany, round neck, one pickup, varied binding.			
1947	Sunburst	$375	$425
BR-6 Lap Steel			
1947-1960. Guitar-shaped solid mahogany body, square neck (round by 1948).			
1950s		$375	$425
BR-9 Lap Steel			
1947-1959. Solidbody, one pickup, Tan.			
1947-1949	Non-adj. Poles	$300	$350
1950-1959	Adj. Poles	$400	$450
1950-1959	Matching Steel and Amp	$600	$700

MODEL YEAR	FEATURES	EXC. COND. LOW	HIGH

Century 6 Lap Steel

1948-1968. Solid maple body, six strings, one pickup, silver fingerboard.

1950s		$450	$550

Century 10 Lap Steel

1948-1955. Solid maple body, 10 strings, one pickup, silver fingerboard.

1950s	Black	$450	$550

Console Grand Steel

1938-1942, 1948-1967. Hollowbody, two necks, triple-bound body, standard seven and eight-string combination until 1942, double eight-string necks standard for 1948 and after.

1938-1942	Sunburst	$950	$1,100
1948-1959	Sunburst	$950	$1,100

Console Steel (C-530)

1956-1966. Replaced Consolette during 1956-1957, two eight-string necks, four legs optional.

1955-1966	With legs	$800	$950

Consolette Table Steel

1952-1957. Rectangular body of Korina, two eight-string necks, four legs. Replaced by maple-body Console after 1956.

1950s	Natural Korina	$950	$1,100

EH-100 Lap Steel

1936-1949. Hollow guitar-shaped body, bound top, six or seven strings.

1936-1939		$550	$650
1940s-1941		$350	$450

EH-125 Lap Steel

1939-1942. Hollow guitar-shaped mahogany body, single-bound tody, metal fingerboard.

1939-1942	Sunburst	$650	$750

EH-150 Doubleneck Electric Hawaiian Steel

1937-1939. Doubleneck EH-150 with seven- and eight-string necks.

1937-1939		$2,150	$2,650

EH-150 Lap Steel

1936-1943. Hollow guitar-shaped body, six to ten strings available, bound body.

1936	1st offering metal body	$2,200	$2,800
1937-1939	Sunburst	$850	$950
1940-1943	Sunburst	$750	$850

EH-150 Lap Steel Matching Set (guitar and amp)

1936-1942. Both electric Hawaiian steel guitar and amp named EH-150, with matching tweed guitar case.

1936-1939	Guitar with Christian pickup	$1,600	$1,800
1940-1942		$1,300	$1,500

EH-185 Lap Steel

1939-1942. Hollow guitar-shaped curly maple body, triple-bound body, six, seven, eight or ten strings.

1939-1942	Sunburst, lap steel and amp	$1,600	$1,900
1939-1942	Sunburst, lap steel only	$900	$1,300

EH-500 Skylark Lap Steel

1956-1968. Solid korina body, eight-string available by 1958.

1956-1968	Natural, 6 strings	$750	$900

EH-620 Steel

1955-1967. Eight strings, six pedals.

1960s	Natural	$550	$750

EH-630 Electraharp Steel

1941-1967. Eight strings, eight pedals (four in 1949-'67). Called just EH-630 from '56-'67.

1941-1956	Sunburst	$650	$900

EH-820 Steel

1960-1966. Two necks, eight pedals, Vari-Tone selector.

1960s	Cherry	$650	$950

Royaltone Lap Steel

1950-1952. Symmetrical wavy body, volume and tone knobs on treble side of pickup, Gibson silk-screen logo, Brown pickup bridge cover.

1950-1952	Natural	$700	$800

Ultratone Lap Steel

1946-1959. Solid maple body, plastic fingerboard, six strings.

1940s	White	$700	$900
1950s	Dark Blue or Seal Brown	$650	$850

1951 Gibson Royaltone

Gold Tone

1993-present. Wayne and Robyn Rogers build their intermediate grade, production/custom lap steels in Titusville, Florida. They also offer acoustic basses, mandolins, banjos and banjitars.

Gourley

See Dickerson listing.

Gretsch

1883-present. Gretsch offered a variety of steels from 1940-1963. Gretsch actually only made one model; the rest were built by Valco. See Guitar section for more company info. Currently they offer one lap steel.

Electromatic Console (6158) Twin Neck Steel

1949-1955. Two six-string necks with six-on-a-side tuners, Electromatic script logo on end cover plates, three knobs, metal control panels and knobs, pearloid covered.

1949-1955		$650	$850

Electromatic Standard (6156) Lap Steel

1950-1955.

1950-1955	Brown Pearloid	$350	$450

Electromatic Student (6152) Lap Steel

1949-1955. Square bottom, pearloid cover.

1949-1955	Brown Pearloid	$350	$450

Jet Mainliner (6147) Steel

1955-1963. Single-neck version of Jet Twin.

1955-1963		$450	$550

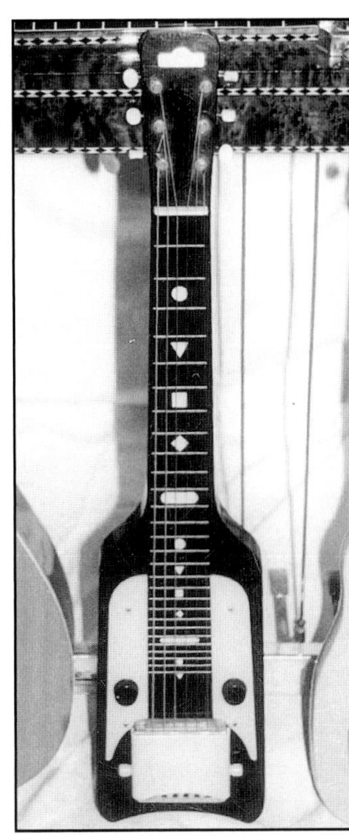

1950s Gretsch Electromatic

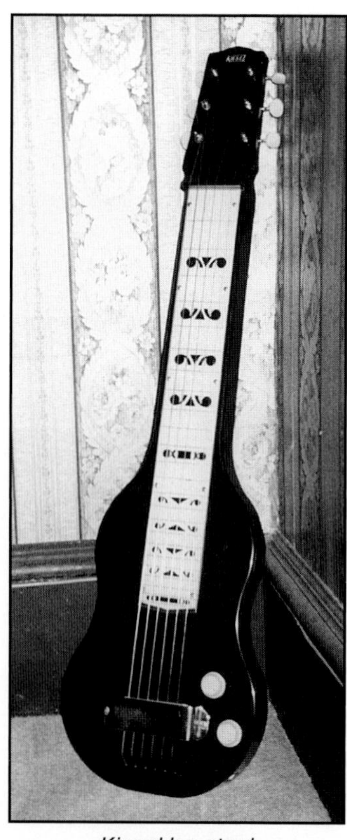
Kiesel lap steel

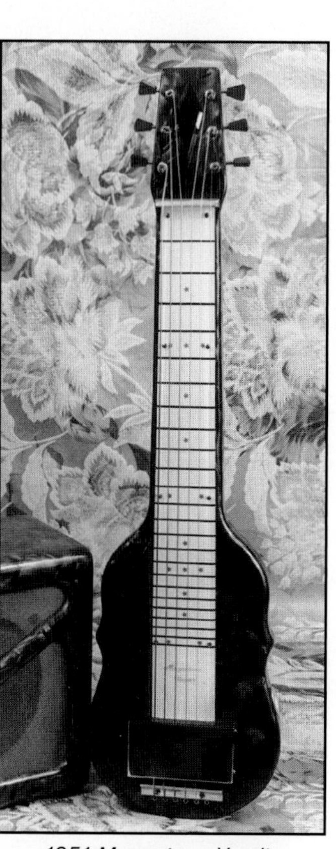
1951 Magnatone Varsity

MODEL YEAR — FEATURES — EXC. COND. LOW — HIGH

Jet Twin Console (6148) Steel

1955-1963. Valco-made, two six-string necks, six-on-a-side tuners. Jet Black.

1955-1963 Black $650 $850

Guyatone

1933-present. Large Japanese maker. Brands also include Marco Polo, Winston, Kingston, Kent, LaFayette and Bradford. They offered lap steels under various brands from the '30s to the '60s. See Guitar section for more company info.

Lap Steels

1960s $200 $300

Table Steels

Three legs, two pickups.

1960s $300 $350

Harmony

1882-1975. Founded by Wilhelm Schultz in 1892, and purchased by Sears in 1916. The company evolved into the largest producer of stringed instruments in the U.S. in the 1930s. They offered electric lap steels by '36. See Guitar section for more company info.

Lap Steels

1950s Various models $250 $300
1960s Painted body $250 $300
1960s Pearloid body $300 $400

Roy Smeck Steel

1950s-1960s. Single neck six-string steel, Roy Smeck logo, three legs, dark finish.

1950s $400 $500

Table Steel

1960s-1970s. Single neck with black and white plexiglass fingerboard, three legs.

1960s $300 $400
1970s $275 $375

K & F (Kaufman & Fender)

See listing under Fender.

Kalamazoo

1933-1942, 1946-1947, 1965-1970. Budget brand produced by Gibson in Kalamazoo, Michigan. They offered lap steels in the '30s and '40s.

Lap Steels

1938-1942, 1946-1947.

1938-1942 Sunburst $250 $350
1946-1947 Sunburst $250 $350

Kay

Ca. 1931-present. Huge Chicago manufacturer Kay offered steels from '36 to '60 under their own brand and others. See Guitar section for more company info or *Guitar Stories Volume II*, by Michael Wright, for a complete history of Kay with detailed model listings.

K-24 Deluxe Steel

1950s Honey Sunburst $250 $400
1960s $250 $400

MODEL YEAR — FEATURES — EXC. COND. LOW — HIGH

Lap Steel

1940s. Kay crest logo.

1940s Blond $250 $400

Lap Steel with matching amp

1940s Dark mahogany $400 $500
1950s Green $400 $500

Kiesel

1946-1949. Founded by Lowell Kiesel as L.C. Kiesel Co., Los Angeles, but renamed Carvin in 1949. Kiesel logo on the headstock.

Bakelite Lap Steel

1946. Small guitar-shaped bakelite body, single pickup, two knobs, diamond markers.

1946 $300 $400

Maestro

A budget brand made by Gibson.

Lap Steel

Pearloid, one pickup, six strings.

1940s $250 $300
1950s $225 $275

Magnatone

Ca. 1937-1971. Magnatone offered lap steels from '37 to '58. Besides their own brand name, they also produced models under the Dickerson, Oahu, Gourley, and Natural Music Guild brands. See Guitar section for more company info.

Lap Steel and Amp MOTS Set

Late-1940s-mid-1950s. Matching pearloid acetate covered lap steel and small amp.

1948-1955 $550 $650

Lyric Doubleneck Lap Steel

Ca.1951-1958. Model G-1745-D-W, eight strings per neck, hardwood body.

1950s $400 $550

Maestro Tripleneck Steel

Ca.1951-1958. Model G-2495-W-W, maple and walnut, eight strings per neck, legs.

1950s $500 $700

Pearloid (MOTS) Lap Steels

1950s. These were often sold with a matching amp; price here is for lap steel only.

1950s $250 $400

Marvel

1950-mid 1960s. Budget brand marketed by the Peter Sorkin Company of New York. See Guitar section for more company info.

Electric Hawaiian Lap Steel

1950s $125 $175

May Bell

See listing under Slingerland.

McKinney

Lap Steel

1950s White Pearloid $150 $300

MODEL YEAR	FEATURES	EXC. COND. LOW	HIGH

Melobar

1970-present. Designed by Walt Smith, of Smith Family Music, Melobar instruments are designed for slide and feature a guitar body with a tilted neck, allowing the guitarist to play lap steel standing up. The instrument was developed and first made in Ed and Rudy Dopyera's Dobro factory. Most were available in 6-, 8-, or 10-string versions. Ted Smith took over operations from his father. Ted retired in late 2002.

10-String Electric Steel

1970s. Double cutaway guitar-shaped body, portable Melobar-style. Similar model currently offered as the Skreemr.

1970s		$800	$900

Skreemr Electric Steel

Early 1990s-present. The classic Melobar in a V (Skreemr SK2000) or doublecut (Skreemr) version. Available in 6-, 8- and 10-string versions.

1990s	6-string version	$500	$600

V-10 Power-Slide Guitar

1982-early 1990s. Solidbody, Flying V-style body, tilted neck, ten strings (six- or eight-string models were available). Similar model now called the Skreemr SK2000.

1981		$700	$900

X-10 Power-Slide Guitar

1981-early 1990s. Solidbody, Explorer-style body, tilted neck, ten strings (six- or eight-string models were available). Called the Power-Slide One in early literature.

1981		$700	$900

National

Ca. 1927-present. Founded in Los Angeles as the National String Instrument Corporation in 1927 by John Dopyera, George Beauchamp, Ted Kleinmeyer and Paul Barth. The brand has gone through many ownership changes over the years. National offered lap steels from '35 to '68. See Guitar section for more company info.

Chicagaon Lap Steel

1948-1961. Gray pearloid, metal hand rest.

1948-1961		$325	$400

Console (Dual 8) Steel

1939-1942. Two eight-string necks, parallelogram markers. Black top with White sides.

1939-1942		$950	$1,050

Dynamic Lap Steel

1942-1968. New Yorker-style body, six strings, three detachable screw-in legs added by 1956.

1942-1968	Various colors	$300	$600

Electric Hawaiian Lap Steel

1935-1937. Cast aluminum round body, one pickup, square neck, six or seven strings.

1935-1937	6 strings	$600	$750
1935-1937	7 strings	$650	$800

Grand Console Steel

1947-1968. Two eight-string necks, "Totem Pole" fingerboard markers.

1947-1968		$500	$700

New Yorker Lap Steel

1939-1967. Introduced as Electric Hawaiian model in 1935. Square end body with stair-step sides, seven or eight strings. Black and White finish.

1939-1949		$450	$600
1950-1959		$350	$450
1960-1967		$300	$400

Princess Lap Steel

1942-1947. Strings-through-pickup, parallelogram markers, White pearloid.

1942-1947		$450	$550

Rocket One Ten Lap Steel

1955-1958. Rocket-shaped, White finish.

1955-1958		$450	$550

Trailblazer Steel

1948-1950. Square end, numbered markers. Black.

1948-1950		$300	$400

Triplex Chord Changer Lap Steel

1949-1958. Maple and walnut body, two knobs. Natural.

1950s		$300	$400

Oahu

1926-1985. The Oahu Publishing Company and Honolulu Conservatory, based in Cleveland, published a hughly popular guitar study course. They sold instruments to go with the lessons, starting with acoustic Hawaiian and Spanish guitars, selling large quantities in the '30s. As electric models became popular, Oahu responded with guitar-amp sets. Lap steel and matching amp sets were generally the same color; for example, yellow guitar and yellow amp, or white pearloid guitar and white amp. These sets were originally sold to students who would take private or group lessons. The instruments were made by Oahu, Valco, Harmony, Dickerson, and Rickenbacker and were offered into the '50s and '60s. See Guitar section for more company info.

Hawaiian Lap Steel

1930s	Sunburst	$200	$300
1940s	Pearloid, Supro-made	$200	$300
1950s	Pearloid or painted	$200	$300

Lap Steel/Amp Set

1930s	Pearloid, small rectangular amp	$350	$550
1930s	Sunburst, mahogany	$350	$550
1950s	White Valco Amp, 1x10"	$300	$500
1950s	Yellow Valco amp	$300	$500

Lolana Dual 6 Lap Steel

1950-1951. Gold hardware, two six-string necks.

1950-1951		$400	$500

National New Yorker

STEELS & LAPS

1951 Oahu Lolana Dual 6

Rickenbacker seven-string

Rickenbacker Model B-6

MODEL YEAR	FEATURES	EXC. COND. LOW	HIGH

Recording King

Ca. 1930-1943. Brand used by Montgomery Ward for instruments made by Gibson, Regal, Kay, and Gretsch.

Electric Hawaiian Lap Steel

1930s		$350	$450

Roy Smeck Model AB104 Steel

1938-1941. Pear-shaped body, one pickup.

1940s		$350	$450

Regal

Ca. 1884-1954. Regal offered their own brand and made instruments for distributors and mass-merchandisers. The company sold out to Harmony in 1954. See Guitar section for more company info.

Acoustic Lap Steel

1970		$200	$250

Electric Hawaiian Lap Steel

1940s		$150	$250

Octophone Steel

1930		$300	$500

Reso-phonic Steel

1930s. Dobro-style resonator and spider assembly, round neck, adjustable nut.

1930s		$800	$1,100

Rickenbacker

1931-present. Rickenbacker produced steels from 1932 to 1970. See Guitar section for more company info.

Acadamy Lap Steel

1946-1947. Bakelite student model, horseshoe pickup. Replaced by Ace.

1946-1947		$250	$350

Ace Lap Steel

1948-1953. Bakelite body, one pickup.

1948-1953		$250	$350

DC-16 Steel

1950-1952. Metal, double eight-string necks.

1950-1952		$550	$700

Electro Doubleneck Steel

1940-1953. Two Bakelite eight-string necks.

1940-1953		$800	$1,300

Electro Tripleneck Steel

1940-1953		$1,000	$1,400

Model 59 Lap Steel

1937-1943. Sheet steel body, one pickup.

1937-1943		$550	$750

Model 100 Lap Steel

1956-1970. Wood body, six strings, block markers, light or Silver Gray finish.

1950s		$350	$450

Model A-22 "Frying Pan" Steel

1932-1950, 1954-1958. "Frying Pan" Electro Hawaiian Guitar. Cast aluminum body, one pickup, slotted peghead.

1932-1936		$1,300	$1,500

Model B Steel

1935-1955. Bakelite body and neck, one pickup, string-through-body, decorative metal plates, six strings.

1940s	Black	$650	$750

Model BD Steel

1949-1970. Bakelite body, six strings, deluxe version of Model B. Black.

1950s		$700	$800

Model CW-6 Steel

1957-1961. Wood body, grille cloth on front, six strings, three legs. Renamed JB (Jerry Byrd) model in 1961.

1960	Walnut	$500	$650

Model DW Steel

1955-1961. Wood body, double six- or eight-string necks, optional three legs.

1950s	Two eight-string necks	$550	$700

Model G Lap Steel

Ca.1948-1957. Chrome-plated ornate version of Silver Hawaiian, Gold hardware and trim, six or eight strings.

1950s		$550	$700

Model S/NS (New Style) Steel

1946-early-1950s. Sheet steel body, one pickup, also available as a doubleneck.

1946-1949	Gray Sparkle	$550	$700
1946-1949	Gray, metal body	$550	$700
1946-1949	Grayburst	$550	$700

Model SD Steel

1949-1953. Deluxe NS, sheet steel body, six, seven or eight strings. Copper Crinkle Finish.

1949-1953		$550	$700

Silver Hawaiian Lap Steel

1937-1943. Chrome-plated sheet steel body, one horseshoe pickup, six strings.

1930s		$700	$800

Roland Ball

See Dickerson listing.

Sho-Bud

1972-1979. Distributed by Gretsch. Colors include Jet Black, Blue stain, Ebony stain, Walnut stain, Natural, Red Rosewood stain, and Green stain.

Maverick Pedal Steel

Introduced in the early '70s, burl elm cover, three pedals.

1972		$450	$500

Pro I

Three pedals, Natural.

1978		$650	$800

Pro II

Bird's-eye maple, double ten-string necks, Natural.

1978		$850	$950

Pro III

1978	Red Rosewood	$850	$950

MODEL YEAR	FEATURES	EXC. COND. LOW	HIGH

Super Pro

Doubleneck 10 strings, eight floor pedals, six knee levers, Jet Black.

1978		$1,200	$1,600

Silvertone

1940-1970. Brand name for instruments sold by Sears. See Guitar section for more company info.

Six-String Lap Steels

1950s		$175	$250
1960s		$150	$225

Slingerland

1916-present. Offered by Slingerland Banjos and Drums. They also sold the May Bell brand. Instruments were made by others and sold by Slingerland in the '30s and '40s. See Guitar section for more company info.

May Bell Lap Steel

1930s. Guitar-shaped lap steel with May Bell logo. This brand also had 1930s Hawaiian and Spanish guitars.

1930s	Black	$200	$450

Supertone

1914-1941. Brand name for Sears which was replaced by Silvertone. Instruments made by Harmony and others. See Guitar section for more company info.

Electric Hawaiian Lap Steel

1930s		$250	$300

Supro

1935-1968. Budget brand of the National Dobro Company. See Guitar section for more company info.

Clipper Lap Steel

1941-1943. One pickup, bound rosewood fingerboard, dot inlay. Brown pearloid.

1941-1943		$250	$350

Comet Lap Steel

1947-1966. One pickup, attached cord, painted-on fingerboard, pearloid.

1947-1949	Gray pearloid	$250	$350
1950-1966	White pearloid	$250	$350

Comet Steel (with legs)

1950s-1960s. Three-leg six-string steel version of the lap steel, two knobs, Supro logo on cover plate, single pickup.

1960s	Black and White	$500	$600

Console 8 Steel

1958-1960. Eight strings, three legs. Black and White.

1958-1960		$500	$600

Jet Airliner Steel

1962-1964. One pickup, totem pole markings, six or eight strings, pearloid, National-made.

1962-1964	Red	$250	$350

MODEL YEAR	FEATURES	EXC. COND. LOW	HIGH

Professional Steel

Light Brown pearloid.

1950s		$300	$400

Special Steel

1955-1962. Pearloid lap steel, student model, large script "Special" logo near pickup on early models. Red until 1957, White after.

1955-1957	Red pearloid	$300	$350
1957-1962	White pearloid	$300	$350

Spectator Steel

1952-1954. Wood body, one pickup, painted-on fingerboard. Natural.

1952-1954		$200	$275

Student De Luxe Lap Steel

1952-1955. One pickup, pearloid, large script "Student De Luxe" logo located near pickup. Replaced by Special in 1955.

1952-1955	Black and White pearloid	$300	$350
1952-1955	Natural wood	$225	$275
1952-1955	Red pearloid, art deco inserts	$300	$350
1952-1955	White paint	$225	$275

Supreme Lap Steel

1947-1960. One pickup, painted-on fingerboard. Brown pearloid until ca.1955, then Red until ca.1958, Tulip Yellow after that.

1940s	Brown pearloid	$250	$350
1950s	Yellow pearloid	$250	$350

Twin Lap Steel

1948-1955. Two six-string necks, pearloid covering. Renamed Console Steel in 1955.

1950		$400	$450

Teisco

1946-1974. The Japanese guitar-maker offered many steel models from '55 to around '67. Models offered during '55 to '61 include the EG-7L, -K, -R, -NT, -Z, -A, -S, -P, -8L, -NW, and -M. Models offered during '61 to '67 include the EG-TW, -O, -U, -L, -6N, -8N, -DB, -DB2, -DT, Harp-8, H-39, H-905, TRH-1, and the H-850. See the Guitar section for more company info.

Hawaiian Lap Steels

1950s		$125	$250

Timtone Custom Guitars

Luthier Tim Diebert builds custom lap steel guitars in Grand Forks, British Columbia. He also builds solidbody, chambered-body, and acoustic guitars.

True Tone

1960s. Brand name sold by Western Auto (hey, everybody was in the guitar biz back then). Probably made by Kay or Harmony.

Lap Steel

1950s. Guitar-shaped, single cutaway, single pickup.

1960s		$200	$300

1950s Supro DeLuxe

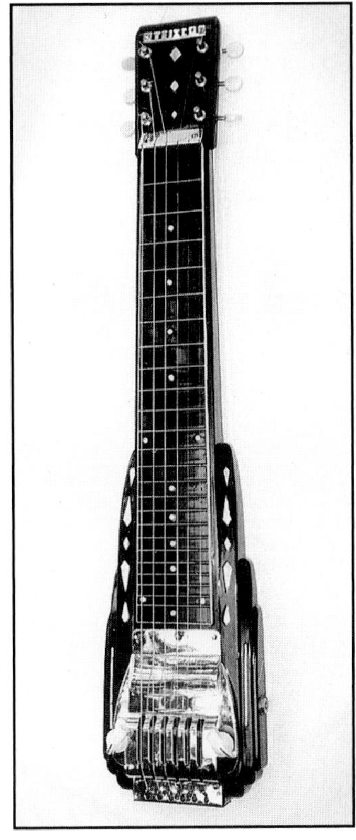

Teisco

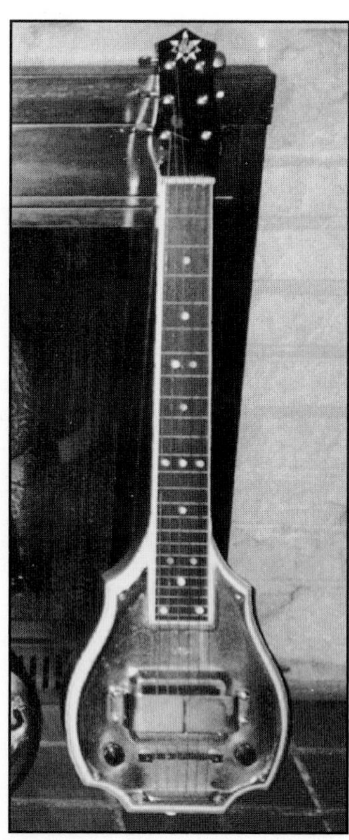

1930s Vega

MODEL YEAR	FEATURES	EXC. COND. LOW	HIGH

Varsity

See Dickerson listing.

Vega

1903-present. The original Boston-based company was purchased by C.F. Martin in 1970. In 1980, the Vega trademark was sold to a Korean company. The company was one of the first to enter the electric market by offering products in 1936 and offered lap steels into the early '60s.

DG-DB Steel

Two necks, eight strings.

1951		$500	$600

Odell Lap Steel

White pearloid.

1950s		$250	$450

Other Lap Steels

1930s		$250	$450
1940s	Art deco-style	$250	$450

Wabash

Brand name of Larry Wexler and Company of Chicago.

Lap Steel (Hawaiian Scene tailpiece)

Twelve frets. Natural.

1950		$200	$300

White

1955-1960. The White brand, named after plant manager Forrest White, was established by Fender to provide steel and small amp sets to teaching studios that were not Fender-authorized dealers. A standard guitar was planned, but never produced.

6 String Steel

1955-1956. White finish, block markers, two knobs, three legs. The 6 String Steel was usually sold with the matching White Amp Model 80. Possibly only one batch of these was made by Fender in October/November '55.

1955-1956		$600	$800

Mandolins

1920 Lyon & Healey Style A

Breedlove Olympic

MODEL YEAR	FEATURES	EXC. COND. LOW	HIGH

Airline

Ca. 1958-1968. Brandname for Montgomery Ward. Instruments were built by Kay, Harmony and Valco.

Electric Mandolin (Kay K390)

Early-1960s. In 1962 the K390 was advertised as the "Kay Professional Electric Mandolin." Venetian shape with sunburst spruce top, curly maple back and sides, tube-style pickup, white 'guard, rope-style celluloid binding.

1962		$350	$500

Mandolin (lower end)

1960s. Acoustic, plainer features.

1960s		$200	$400

Allen

1982-present. Premium grade, production resonators, steel-string flat-tops, and mandolins built by Luthier Randy Allen, Colfax, CA.

Alvarez

C.1966-present. An import brandname for St. Louis Music, Alvarez currently offers intermediate grade, production, mandolins.

Model A Mandolins

Classic F-style mandolin features, round soundhole or F-holes. Models include the A700 and A910.

1970s		$300	$600

American Conservatory (Lyon & Healy)

Late-1800s-early-1900s. Mainly catalog sales of guitars and mandolins from the Chicago maker. Marketed as a less expensive alternative to the Lyon & Healy Washburn product line.

Mandolin Style G2603

Early-1900s. Bowl back-style, 28 rosewood ribs (generally more ribs and use of rosewood ribs versus mahogany indicates higher quality), color corded soundhole and edge inlay, inlaid tortoise shell celluloid guard plate underneath strings and below the soundhole, bent top, butterfly headstock inlay.

1917		$300	$350

Mandolin Style G2604

Early-1900s. Bowl back-style, 42 rosewood ribs (generally more ribs incidated higher quality), extra fancy color corded soundhole and edge inlay around, extra fancy inlaid tortoise shell celluloid guard plate underneath strings and below the soundhole, bent top, butterfly headstock inlay.

1917		$450	$500

Andersen Stringed Instruments

1978-present. Luthier Steve Andersen builds premium and presentation grade, production/custom flat-tops, archtops, and mandolins in Seattle, Washington.

Applause

1994-present. Kaman Music's entry-level Ovation-styled import brand added mandolins in 1994. Applause currently offers intermediate grade, production, mandolins.

MAE148 Mandolin

1994-present. Acoustic/electric import.

1990s	Black	$225	$275

Aria/Aria Pro II

1976-present. Japan based Aria/Aria Pro II added mandolins to their line in '76, which were produced in Japan and Korea. Currently they offer intermediate grade, production, acoustic and electric mandolins.

AM200/BS Style A Mandolin

1994-present. Beginner-grade import, pear-shaped body, Sunburst.

1990s		$175	$275

AM300/BS Style F Mandolin

1990s. F-style, Sunburst.

1990s		$350	$425

PM750 Style F Mandolin

Mid-1970s. F-style Loar copy, Sunburst.

1976		$400	$500

Bacon & Day

Established in 1921 by David Day and Paul Bacon, primarily known for fine quality tenor and plectrum banjos in the 1920s and 1930s.

Mandolin Banjo "Orchestra"

1920s. Mandolin neck and banjo body with open back, headstock with Bacon logo.

1920s		$350	$450

Senorita Banjo Mandolin

1930s		$400	$550

Bishline

1985-present. Luthier Robert Bishline builds custom-made flat-tops, resonators, mandolins, and banjos in Tulsa, Oklahoma.

Bohmann

1878-ca.1926. Established by Czechoslavakian-born Joseph Bohmann in Chicago. See Guitar section for more company info.

Fancy Bowl Mandolin

Spruce top, marquetry trimmed, inlay, pearl.

1890		$400	$550

Brandt

Early 1900s. John Brandt started making mandolin-family instruments in Chicago around 1898.

Mandola

1900s. Spruce top, rosewood body, scroll headstock, pearl and abalone fretboard binding.

1900		$1,200	$1,400

Presentation Mandolin

Spruce top, tortoise shell-bound.

1900s		$700	$900

MANDOLINS

MODEL YEAR	FEATURES	EXC. COND. LOW	HIGH

Breedlove

1990-present. Founded by Larry Breedlove and Steve Henderson. Professional and premium grade, production/custom, mandolins made in Tumalo, Oregon. They also produce guitars.

K-5 Mandolin

Asymmetric carved top, maple body.

1990s		$1,600	$1,700

Olympic Mandolin

Solid spruce top, teardrop-shaped, oval soundhole, highly flamed maple back, Sunburst.

1990s		$1,200	$1,300

Bruno and Sons

1834-present. Established in 1834 by Charles Bruno, primarily as a distributor, Bruno and Sons marketed a variety of brandnames, including their own; currently part of Kaman. In the '60s or '70s, a Japanese-made solidbody electric mandolin was sold under the Bruno name.

Banjo Mandolin

Open back, 10" model.

1920s		$300	$350

Bowl Back Mandolin

1890s-1920s. Brazilian rosewood, spruce, rosewood ribs.

1920s		$400	$500

Calace

1825-present. Nicola Calace started The Calace "Liuteria" lute-making workshop in 1825 on the island of Procida, which is near Naples. The business is now in Naples and still in the family.

Lyre/Harp-Style Mandolin

Late-1800s-early-1900s. Lyre/harp-style, eight strings, round soundhole, slightly bent top. Condition is important for these older instruments and the price noted is for a fully functional, original or pro-restored example.

1900		$500	$1,500

Carvin

1946-present. Carvin offered solidbody electric mandolins from around 1956 to the late '60s, when they switched to a traditional pear-shaped electric/acoustic. See guitar section for more company info.

MB Mandolins

1956-1968. Solidbody, one pickup. Single cutaway Les Paul shape until '64, double cutaway Jazzmaster/Strat shape after. Models include the #1-MB and the #2-MB, with different pickups.

1950s		$500	$600

Conrad

Ca. 1968-1977. Imported from Japan by David Wexler and Company, Chicago, Illinois. Mid- to better-quality copy guitars, mandolins and banjos.

Crestwood

1970s. Copy models imported by La Playa Distributing Company of Detroit.

Mandolin

Includes models 3039 (electric A-style), 3041 (bowl back-style, flower pickguard), 3043 (bowl back-style, plain pickguard), 71820 (A-style), and 71821 (F-style).

1970s		$100	$300

Cromwell

1935-1939. Private branded instruments made by Gibson at their Parsons Street factory in Kalamazoo. Distributed by a variety of mail order companies such as Continental, Grossman, and Richter & Phillips. Gibson private branded during the depression to keep their staff busy, and to enter the low-to-mid priced market.

GM-4 Mandolin

1935-1939. Style A with F-holes, solid wood arched top, mahogany back and sides, block capital letter Cromwell headstock logo, dot markers, elevated pickguard. Sunburst.

1935-1939		$700	$800

D'Angelico

1932-1949. Handcrafted by John D'Angelico. Models include Excel, Teardrop, and Scroll. Appointments can vary from standard to higher-end so each mandolin should be evaluated on a case-by-case basis.

Mandolin

1932-1949. Various models and appointments.

1932-1949	High-end appointments	$19,000	$21,000
1932-1949	Plain, non-elevated pickguard	$6,000	$8,000

D'Aquisto

1965-1995. James D'Aquisto apprenticed under D'Angelico. He started his own production in 1965.

Mandolin

1970s. Various models and appointments.

1970s	Only 3 made	$22,000	$25,000

Ditson

Mandolins made for the Oliver Ditson Company of Boston, an instrument dealer and music publisher. Turn of the century and early-1900s models were bowl back-style with the Ditson label. The 1920s Ditson Style A flat back mandolins were made by Martin.

Style 1 Standard Mandolin

Size three small body, plain styling.

1922		$1,100	$1,200

Style A Mandolin

1920s. Style A flat back made by Martin, mahogany sides and back, plain ornamentation.

1920s		$700	$850

Carvin 1-MB

D'Angelico

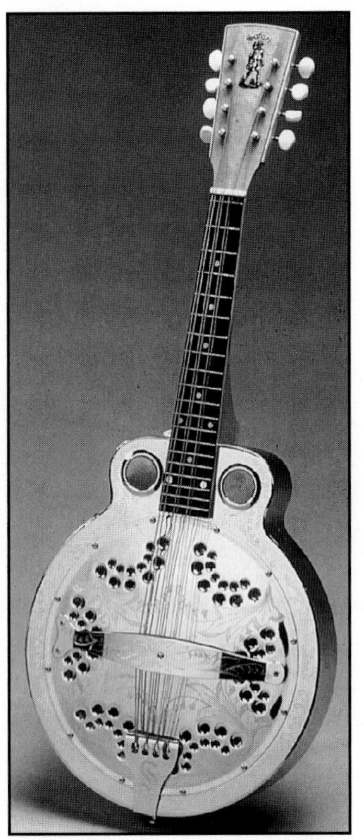

1970 Dopyera resonator mando

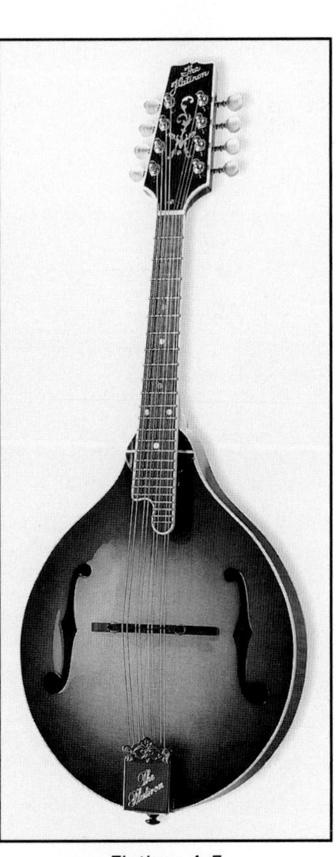

Flatiron A-5

MODEL YEAR	FEATURES	EXC. COND. LOW	HIGH

Victory Bowl Back Mandolin

1890s. Brazilian rib bowl back-style with fancy inlays.

1890s		$650	$750

Dobro

1929-1942, 1954-present. Dobro offered mandolins throughout their early era and from the '60s to the mid-'90s. See Guitar section for more company information.

Mandolin (wood body)

Resonator on wood body.

1930s		$900	$1,100
1968		$700	$900

Model 65 Mandolin

Wood body, sandblasted design.

1929		$800	$1,200

EKO

1961-1985. The Italian-made EKOs were imported by LoDuca Brothers of Milwaukee.

Baritone Mandolin

1960s. Baritone mandolin with ornate inlays.

1960s		$300	$400

Octave Mandolin

1960s. Octave mandolin with ornate inlays.

1960s		$250	$350

Epiphone

1928-present. Epiphone has offered several mandolin-family models over the years. Those from the '30s to the '60s were U.S.-made, the later models imported.

Adelphi Mandolin

1932-1948. A-style body, maple back and sides, F-holes, single-bound top and back.

1940s		$550	$700

Strand Mandolin

1932-1958. Walnut back and sides, F-holes, multi-bound, Sunburst.

1944		$600	$750

Venetian Electric Mandolin

1961-1970. Gibson-made, pear-shaped body, four pole P-90 'dog-ear' mounted pickup, volume and tone knobs, dot markers. Sunburst finish.

1961-1964		$1,300	$1,500
1965-1970		$1,100	$1,300

Zephyr Mandolin

1939-1958. A-style, electric, F-holes, maple body, one pickup, slotted block inlay.

1951		$600	$700

Esquire

1930s. Student level instruments with painted Esquire logo and painted wood grain.

Mandolins

1930s. Laminate A-style wood body, sunburst.

1930s		$200	$225

MODEL YEAR	FEATURES	EXC. COND. LOW	HIGH

Euphonon

1934-1944. Euphonon was a brandname of the Larson Brothers of Chicago. The brand was introduced so Larson could compete in the guitar market with the new larger body 14-fret guitar models. Production also included mandolins, and most models were A-style, with teardrop body and flat backs.

Mandolin

1934-1944. Various models and appointments, each mandolin should be evaluated on a case-by-case basis.

1934-1944		$3,500	$10,000

Evergreen Mountain

1979-present. Professional grade, custom, mandolins, flat-tops, tenor guitars, and acoustic basses built by luthier Jerry Nolte in Cove, Oregon. He also built over a hundred dulcimers in the 1970s.

Fairbanks (A.J.)

1875-ca.1920s. Primarily known for banjos, Fairbanks also offered mandolins.

Mandolin

1890-1910. Typical late-1890s bent top-style mandolin, with decorated top and rope-style binding.

1900s	Naural	$200	$300

Fender

1946-present. Fender offered an electric mandolin for 20 years. See Guitar section for more company information.

Mandolin

1956-1976. Electric solidbody, often referred to as the Mandocaster by collectors.

1956-1957	Blond	$2,400	$2,600
1958-1959	Sunburst	$2,100	$2,300
1960-1961	Sunburst	$1,900	$2,100
1962-1963	Sunburst	$1,800	$2,000
1964-1965	Sunburst	$1,700	$1,900
1966-1970	Sunburst	$1,500	$1,600
1971-1976	Sunburst	$1,400	$1,500

Fine Resophonic

1988-present. Professional grade, production/custom, wood and metal-bodied resophonic mandolins, guitars (including reso-electrics), and ukuleles built by luthiers Mike Lewis and Pierre Avocat in Vitry Sur Seine, France.

Flatiron

1977-present. Gibson purchased Flatiron in 1987. Production was in Bozeman, Montana until the end of 1996, when Gibson closed the Flatiron mandolin workshop and moved mandolin assembly to Nashville. Currently Flatirons are available on a special order basis.

MANDOLINS

MODEL YEAR	FEATURES	EXC. COND. LOW	HIGH

A-5 Artist Mandolin

Teardrop shape, F-holes, flamed maple body and neck, carved spruce top, bound ebony board, gold hardware, fern headstock inlay.

1980s	Sunburst	$1,300	$1,700

A-5 Mandolin

Teardrop shape, F-holes, flamed maple body and neck, carved spruce top, unbound ebony board, nickel hardware fleur-de-lis headstock inlay.

1980s	Sunburst	$1,300	$1,700

Cadet Mandolin

Flat top, oval body, spruce top, maple body, rosewood board, nickel hardware.

1990s	Black	$350	$500

F-5 Artist Mandolin

F-style body, F-holes, flamed maple body and neck, carved spruce top, x-braced, bound ebony board, gold hardware, fern headstock inlay.

1980s	Sunburst	$2,850	$3,000
1990s	Sunburst	$2,850	$3,000

Festival A Mandolin

Teardrop shape, carved spruce top, maple body, ebony board, F-holes.

1990s		$900	$1,300
2000s	Gibson Nashville assembly	$1,200	$1,400

Festival F Mandolin

F-style body, F-holes, maple body and neck, carved spruce top, tone bar bracing, ebony board, nickel hardware, fern headstock inlay, top binding.

1990s		$1,500	$1,800
2000s	Gibson Nashville assembly	$1,700	$2,000

Model 1 Mandolin

Oval shape, spruce top, maple body, rosewood board.

1980s	Natural	$350	$500

Model 2-K Mandolin

Oval body, flamed koa back and sides, spruce top, ebony fingerboard.

1980s	Natural	$500	$650

Model 2-M Mandolin

1980s. Round teardrop body, flat top and back.

1980s		$350	$500

Model 3 Octave Mandolin

Oval shape, bird's-eye maple (MB) or curly maple (MC) body, spruce top, ebony board, longer scale.

1980s	Natural bird's-eye	$650	$900

Performer F Mandolin

F-style body, F-holes, maple body and neck, carved spruce top, tone bar bracing, ebony board, nickel hardware, fern headstock inlay, top, back and headstock binding.

1990s		$1,500	$1,800

Fletcher Brock Stringed Instruments

1992-present. Custom flat-tops, archtops, and mandolin-family instruments made by luthier Fletcher Brock in Ketchum, Idaho.

Fylde

1973-present. Luthier Roger Bucknall builds his intermediate and professional, production/custom mandolins and mandolas in Penrith, Cumbria, United Kingdom. He also builds acoustic guitars and basses, bouzoukis, and citterns.

G.L. Stiles

1960-1994. Built by Gilbert Lee Stiles in Florida. He also built acoustics, soldibodies, basses, steels, and banjos.

Mandolin

1960s		$400	$600

Gibson

1880s-present. Incorporated 1902 as the Gibson Mandolin-Guitar Manufacturing Company. Orville Gibson created the violin-based mandolin body-style that replaced the bowl back-type. Currently Gibson offers professional, premium and presentation grade, production/custom, mandolins.

Special Designations:

Snakehead headstock: 1922-1927 with production possible for a few months plus or minus.

Lloyd Loar era: Mid-1922-late 1924 with production possible for a few months plus or minus.

A Mandolin

1902-1933. Oval soundhole, snakehead headstock 1922-1927, Loar era mid-1922-late-1924.

1910-1918	Orange Top	$1,500	$1,600
1918-1921	Brown	$1,700	$1,900
1922-1924	Loar era	$2,700	$2,800

A Jr. Mandolin

1920-1927. The Junior was the entry level mandolin for Gibson, but like most entry level Gibsons (re: Les Paul Junior), they were an excellent product. Oval soundhole, dot markers, plain tuner buttons. Becomes A-0 in 1927.

1920s	Sheraton Brown	$1,200	$1,400

A-0 Mandolin

1927-1933. Replaces A Jr., oval soundhole, dot inlay. Brown finish.

1927-1933		$1,300	$1,500

A-00 Mandolin

1933-1943. Oval soundhole, dot inlay, carved bound top.

1933-1943	Sunburst	$1,400	$1,700

A-1 Mandolin

1902-1918, 1922-1927, 1933-1943. Snakehead headstock 1923-1927.

1902-1918	Orange	$1,300	$1,600
1922-1924	Loar era	$3,000	$3,200
1925-1927	Black	$1,500	$1,800
1933-1943	Sunburst, F-holes	$1,500	$1,800

Flatiron Festival

1917 Gibson A-1

MANDOLINS

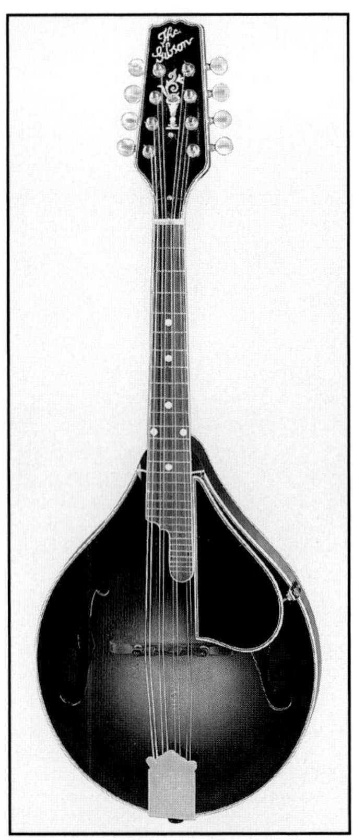

Gibson A-5

1906 Gibson F-4

MODEL YEAR	FEATURES	EXC. COND. LOW	HIGH

A-2/A-2Z Mandolin

1902-1908, 1918-1922. A-2Z 1922-1927. Renamed A-2 1927-1928. Snakehead headstock 1923-1927. Lloyd Loar era mid-1922-late-1924.

Year	Features	Low	High
1902-1908	Orange	$1,300	$1,800
1918-1921	Brown	$1,500	$2,000
1922-1924	Loar Era	$3,000	$4,000
1925-1928		$1,700	$2,200

A-3 Mandolin

1902-1922. Oval soundhole, single-bound body, dot inlay.

Year	Features	Low	High
1902-1922	Various colors	$1,300	$2,000

A-4 Mandolin

1902-1935. Oval soundhole, single-bound body, dot inlay, snakehead 1923-1927.

Year	Features	Low	High
1902-1917	Various colors	$1,900	$2,400
1918-1921	Dark mahogany	$2,000	$2,500
1922-1924	Loar era	$4,000	$5,000
1925-1935	Various colors	$2,500	$3,000

A-5 Mandolin

1957-1979. Oval soundhole, maple back and sides, dot inlay, scroll headstock. Sunburst.

Year	Features	Low	High
1957-1964		$1,800	$2,300
1965-1969		$1,700	$2,200
1970-1979		$1,500	$2,000

A-5 G Mandolin

1988-1996. Less ornate version of the A-5 L, abalone fleur-de-lis headstock inlay.

Year	Features	Low	High
1988-1996		$1,300	$1,500

A-5 L Mandolin

1988-present. A-5-style body, raised fingerboard, flowerpot headstock inlay, curly maple and spruce.

Year	Features	Low	High
1988-1999	Sunburst	$2,100	$2,400

A-12 Mandolin

1970-1979. F-holes, long neck, dot inlay, fleur-de-lis inlay. Sunburst.

Year	Features	Low	High
1970-1979		$1,500	$1,900

A-40 Mandolin

1948-1970. F-holes, bound top, dot inlay. Natural or Sunburst.

Year	Features	Low	High
1948-1949		$1,100	$1,400
1950-1964		$1,000	$1,300
1965-1970		$900	$1,100

A-50 Mandolin

1933-1971. A-style oval bound body, F-holes. Sunburst.

Year	Features	Low	High
1933-1941	Larger 11.25" body	$1,200	$1,400
1942-1965	Smaller 10" body	$1,100	$1,200
1966-1971		$900	$1,000

A-C Century Mandolin

1935-1937. Flat back, bound body, oval soundhole.

Year	Features	Low	High
1935-1937	Sunburst	$2,600	$3,200

Army and Navy Special Style DY/Army-Navy Mandolin

1918-1922. Lower-end, flat top and back, round soundhole, no logo, round label with model name. Reintroduced as Army-Navy (AN Custom) 1988-1996.

Year	Features	Low	High
1918-1922	Brown stain	$900	$1,000

Bill Monroe Model F Mandolin

1995. Limited run of 200.

Year	Features	Low	High
1995	Sunburst	$8,000	$10,000

C-1 Mandolin

1932. Flat top, mahogany back and sides, oval soundhole, painted on pickguard, a 1932 version of the Army and Navy Special. This model was private branded for Kel Kroydon in the early-1930s.

Year	Features	Low	High
1932	Natural	$1,000	$1,100

EM-100/EM-125 Mandolin

1938-1943. Initially called EM-100, renamed EM-125 in 1941-1943. Style A (pear-shape) archtop body, single blade pickup, two knobs on either side of bridge, dot markers, tortoise pickguard. Sunburst.

Year	Features	Low	High
1938-1940	EM-100	$1,700	$1,900
1941-1943	EM-125	$1,600	$1,800

EM-150 Mandolin

1936-1971. Electric, A-00 body, one Charlie Christian pickup early on, one P-90 later, bound body. Sunburst.

Year	Features	Low	High
1936-1940	Charlie Christian pickup	$1,800	$2,400
1941-1949	Rectangular pickup	$1,500	$1,700
1949-1965	P-90 pickup	$1,400	$1,600
1966-1971	P-90 pickup	$1,200	$1,400

EM-200/Florentine Mandolin

1954-1971. Electric solidbody, one pickup, gold-plated hardware, 2 control knobs, dot markers. Sunburst. Called the EM-200 in 1960 and 1961.

Year	Features	Low	High
1954-1960	Florentine	$2,200	$2,400
1960-1961	Renamed EM-200	$2,000	$2,200
1962-1971	Florentine	$2,000	$2,200

F-2 Mandolin

1902-1934. Oval soundhole, pearl inlay, star and crescent inlay on peghead.

Year	Features	Low	High
1902-1909	3-point	$2,500	$3,500
1910-1917	2-point	$2,800	$3,800
1918-1921	2-point	$3,000	$4,000
1922-1924	Loar era	$4,500	$6,500
1925-1934		$3,200	$4,500

F-3 Mandolin

1902-1908. Three-point body, oval soundhole, scroll peghead, pearl inlayed pickguard, limited production model. Black top with Red back and sides.

Year	Features	Low	High
1902-1908		$3,700	$4,400

F-4 Mandolin

1902-1943. Oval soundhole, rope pattern binding. Various colors.

Year	Features	Low	High
1902-1909	3-point	$3,800	$4,500
1910-1917	2-point	$4,000	$4,700
1918-1921	2-point	$4,200	$5,500
1922-1924	Loar era	$6,000	$8,000
1925-1943		$4,500	$5,500

F-5 Mandolin

1922-1943; 1949-1980. F-holes, triple-bound body and pickguard. The 1920s Lloyd Loar era F-5s are extremely valuable. Reintroduced in 1949 with single-bound body, redesigned in 1970.

Year	Features	Low	High
1922-1924	Loar era	$90,000	$100,000

MODEL YEAR	FEATURES	EXC. COND. LOW	HIGH
1925-1928	Fern, Master-built	$45,000	$55,000
1928-1929	Fern, not Master-built	$42,500	$50,000
1930	Fern peghead inlay	$40,000	$45,000
1931	Fern peghead inlay	$38,000	$43,000
1932	Fern peghead inlay	$36,000	$41,000
1933	Fern peghead inlay	$34,000	$39,000
1934	Fern peghead inlay	$32,000	$37,000
1935	Fern peghead inlay	$31,000	$36,000
1936-1940	Fern peghead inlay	$30,000	$35,000
1940-1943	Fleur-de-lis peghead inlay	$28,000	$30,000
1949	Flower pot, mahogany neck	$7,000	$8,000
1950	Flower pot, maple neck	$6,000	$7,000
1951-1956	Flower pot peghead inlay	$5,000	$6,000
1957-1959	Flower pot peghead inlay	$4,500	$5,500
1960-1965		$4,000	$5,500
1966-1969		$4,000	$5,000
1971-1980		$3,000	$4,000

F-5 Bella Voce Mandolin

1989. Custom Shop master-built model, high-end materials and construction, engraved tailpiece with "Bella Voce F-5". Sunburst.

1989		$8,400	$8,600

F-5 L Mandolin

1978-present. Reissue of Loar F-5, gold hardware, fern headstock inlay (flowerpot inlay with silver hardware also offered for '88-'91). Sunburst.

1978-1999		$4,000	$5,000

F-5 V Mandolin

Varnish Cremona Brown Sunburst finish.

1995		$6,600	$6,800

F-7 Mandolin

1934-1940. F-holes, single-bound body, neck and pickguard, fleur-de-lis peghead inlay. Sunburst.

1934-1937		$7,000	$8,000

F-10 Mandolin

1934-1936. Slight upgrade of the 1934 F-7 with extended fingerboard and upgraded inlay. Black finish.

1934-1936		$7,000	$8,000

F-12 Mandolin

1934-1937, 1948-1980. F-holes, bound body and neck, scroll inlay, raised fingerboard until 1937, fingerboard flush with top 1948-on. Sunburst.

1934-1937		$6,000	$7,500
1948-1959		$3,400	$3,600
1960-1969		$2,500	$3,200
1970-1980		$1,500	$3,000

H-1 Mandola

1902-1936. Has same features as A-1 mandolin, but without snakehead headstock.

MODEL YEAR	FEATURES	EXC. COND. LOW	HIGH
1902-1908	Orange	$1,600	$1,900
1918-1921	Brown	$1,700	$2,000
1922-1924	Loar era	$3,000	$3,500
1925-1928		$1,900	$2,200

H-1 E Mandola

Late-1930s. Limited number built, electric with built-in adjustable bar pickup. Sunburst.

1938		$3,500	$3,700

H-2 Mandola

1902-1922. Has same features as A-4 mandolin.

1902-1922	Various colors	$2,100	$2,300

H-4 Mandola

1910-1940. Same features as F-4 mandolin.

1910-1921		$3,500	$4,000
1922-1924	Loar era	$7,000	$8,000
1925-1940		$3,800	$4,400

H-5 Mandola

1923-1929 (available by special order 1929-1936). Same features as the high-end F-5 Mandolin. This is a very specialized market and instruments should be evaluated on a case-by-case basis.

1923-1924	Loar ear	$29,000	$31,000
1925-1928	Fern, Master-built	$15,000	$16,000
1928-1929	Fern, not Master-built	$13,000	$14,000

K-1 Mandocello

1902-1943. Same features as H-1 mandola, off & on production, special order available.

1902-1908	Orange	$1,800	$2,300
1918-1921	Brown	$2,000	$2,500
1922-1924	Loar era	$3,200	$4,000

K-2 Mandocello

1902-1922. Same features as A-4 mandolin.

1902-1922	Black or Red mahogany	$2,500	$3,500

K-4 Mandocello

1912-1929 (offered as special order post-1929). Same features as F-4 mandolin. Sunburst.

1912-1921		$5,000	$6,000
1922-1924	Loar era	$8,000	$10,000
1925-1929		$6,000	$7,000

MB-1 Mandolin Banjo

1922-1923, 1925-1937.

1920s		$850	$1,000

MB-2 Mandolin Banjo

1920-1923, 1926-1937.

1920s		$900	$1,100

MB-3 Mandolin Banjo

1923-1939.

1920s		$950	$1,200

MB-4 Mandolin Banjo

1923-1932. Fleur-de-lis inlay.

1920s		$1,000	$1,300

Style J Mando Bass

1912-1930 (special order post-1930). A-style body, four strings, round soundhole, bound top, dot inlay.

1912-1930		$3,000	$3,500

1927 Gibson F-5

1915 Gibson H-2 mandola

MANDOLINS

Gilchrist Model 5

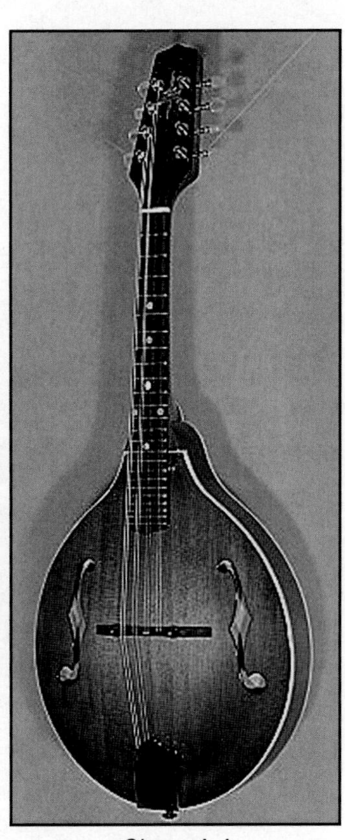
Givens A-4

MODEL YEAR	FEATURES	EXC. COND. LOW	HIGH

Style TL-1Tenor Lute Mandolin
1924-1926. A-style, four strings, F-holes, dot inlay. Natural top with Brown back and sides.

1924-1926		$1,500	$1,700

Gilchrist
1978-present. Premium and prestation grade, custom, mandolins made by luthier Steve Gilchrist of Warrnambool, Australia. Custom ordered but were also initially distributed through Gruhn Guitars, Nashville, TN and then exclusively by Carmel Music Company. Designs are based upon Gibson mandolins built between 1910 and 1925.

Model 5 Mandolin
1978-present. Based on the Gibson 1922-1924 Loar-era F-5 mandolin, Gilchrist slant logo, spruce top, flamed maple back, sides, and neck, ebony board, multiple binding. Sunburst.

1978-2000	Sunburst	$12,000	$17,000

Givens
1962-1992. Luthier R. L. (Bob) Givens handcrafted about 800 mandolins and another 700 in a production shop. Price ranges established with assistance from Greg Boyd.

A Mandolin
1962-1975. Early production A-style.

1962-1975		$2,000	$2,700

A-3 Mandolin
Mid-1970s-mid-1980s. Distinguished by use of decal (the only model with Givens decal).

1975-1988		$2,000	$2,500

A-4 Mandolin
1988-1993. No fingerboard binding, simple "block-like multiple-line RL Givens" inlay, nicer maple.

1988-1993		$1,700	$2,200

A-5 Mandolin
1988-1993. Bound fingerboard, pearl headstock inlay.

1988-1993		$1,500	$2,000

A-6 (Torch) Mandolin
1988-1992. Torch inlay (the only model with this), Gold hardware, snow flake markers.

1988-1992		$2,500	$3,500

A-6 Custom Mandolin
1991-1992. Elaborate customized A-6 model.

1991-1992		$3,600	$4,200

F-5 (Fern) Mandolin
1973-1985. Givens' own version with fern ornamentation.

1973-1985		$3,500	$4,500

F-5 (Loar) Mandolin
1962-1972. Givens' own version based upon the Loar model F-5.

1962-1972		$3,500	$4,500

F-5 (Torch) Mandolin
1988-1992. Givens F-5 with torch inlay (the only F model with this).

1988-1992		$6,000	$8,000

MODEL YEAR	FEATURES	EXC. COND. LOW	HIGH

F-5 (Wheat Straw) Mandolin
1986-1988. Givens F-5-style with Wheat Straw ornamentation.

1986-1988		$5,000	$6,200

Gold Tone
1993-present. Wayne and Robyn Rogers build their intermediate grade, production/custom mandolins in Titusville, Florida. They also offer lap steels, acoustic basses, banjos and banjitars.

Goya
Mid-1950s-1996. Import brand, originally from Sweden, by late '70s from Japan, then from Korea. See Guitar section for more company info.

Mandolin

1960s		$200	$300

Gretsch
1883-present. Gretsch started offering mandolins by the early 1900s. See Guitar section for more company info. Currently Gretsch does not offer mandolins.

New Yorker Mandolin
Late 1940s-late 1950s. Teardrop shape, F-holes, arched top and back, spruce top, maple back, sides, and neck, rosewood board.

1950s		$400	$500

GTR
1974-1978. GTR (for George Gruhn, Tut Taylor, Randy Wood) was the original name for Gruhn Guitars in Nashville (it was changed in 1976). GTR imported mandolins and banjos from Japan. An A-style (similar to a current Gibson A-5 L) and an F-style (similar to mid- to late-1920s F-5 with fern pattern) were offered. The instruments were made at the Moridaira factory in Matsumoto, Japan by factory foreman Sadamasa Tokaida. Quality was relatively high but quantities were limited.

F-Style Mandolin
1974-1978. F-5 Fern copy with slant GTR logo on headstock, handmade in Japan.

1970s	Sunburst	$2,000	$2,500

Harmony
1982-1975. Founded by Wilhelm Schultz in 1892, and purchased by Sears in 1916. The company evolved into one of the largest producers of stringed instruments in the U.S. in the 1930s. See Guitar section for more company info.

Baroque H425 Mandolin
F-style arched body, close grained spruce top. Sunburst.

1970		$200	$275

Lute H331 Mandolin
1960s-1970s. A-style, flat top and back, student level.

1960s	Sunburst	$150	$175

MODEL YEAR	FEATURES	EXC. COND. LOW	HIGH

Monterey H410 Mandolin

A-style arched body. Sunburst.

1950s		$150	$250
1970s		$150	$200

Heiden Stringed Instruments

1974-present. Luthier Michael Heiden builds his premium grade, production/custom flat-top guitars and mandolins in Chilliwack, British Columbia.

Heritage

1985-present. Started by former Gibson employees in Gibson's Kalamazoo plant, Heritage offered mandolins for a number of years.

H-5 Mandolin

1986-1990s. F-style scroll body, F-holes.

1989		$2,500	$3,500

Hofner

1887-present. Old World company since 1887, offering a wide variety of products, including mandolins, particularly during the guiter boom of the 1960s.

A-Style Mandolin

1960s. Pear-shaped A-style with cat's-eye F-holes, block-style markers, engraved headstock, "Genuine Hofner Original" and "Made in Germany" on back of headstock.

1968-1969	Transparent Brown	$400	$450

Hondo

1969-1987, 1991-present. Hondo offered mandolins from around 1974 to 1987. Imported by IMC of Fort Worth, Texas.

Mandolin

1974-1987. Hondo offered F-style, A-style, and bowl back mandolin models.

1970s		$100	$150

Howe-Orme

1893-early-1900s. Edward Howe patented a guitar-shaped mandolin on November 14, 1893.

Mandola

1893-early-1900s. Guitar body-style with narrow waist, not the common mandolin F or S-style body, pressed (not carved) spruce top, mahogany back and sides, flat top guitar-type trapeze bridge, decalomania near bridge.

1887	Natural	$1,100	$1,700

Ibanez

1932-present. Ibanez offered mandolins from around 1977 to the early 1980s. See Guitar section for more company info.

Model 514 Mandolin

1977-early 1980s. Arched back, spruce, rosewood, dot inlays.

1970s	Sunburst	$300	$400

Model 521 A Mandolin

1977-early 1980s. A-style, carved top, Sunburst, F-holes, gold hardware.

1980		$250	$350

Model 524 Mandolin

1977-early 1980s. F-5 copy, solid wood carved top and solid wood back.

1970s	Sunburst	$500	$1,000

Imperial

1890-1922. Imperial mandolins were made by the William A. Cole Company of Boston.

Bowl Back Mandolin

1890s		$250	$350

J.R. Zeidler Guitars

1977-present. Luthier John Zeidler builds his mandolins in Wallingford, Pennsylvania. He also builds flat-top, 12-string, and archtop guitars.

John Le Voi Guitars

1970-present. Production/custom, gypsy jazz guitars, flat-tops, archtops, and mandolin family instruments built by luthier John Le Voi in Lincolnshire, United Kingdom.

Johnson

Mid-1990s-present. Budget and intermediate grade, production, mandolins imported by Music Link, Brisbane, California. Johnson also offers acoustic, classical, acoustic/electric, and solidbody guitars, amps, ukuleles and effects.

F Model Mandolin

Late 1990s-present. F-style, scroll, spruce top, maple back and sides, bound rosewood board.

1999	Sunburst	$375	$425

Kalamazoo

1933-1942, 1946-1947, 1965-1970. Budget brand produced by Gibson in Kalamazoo, Michigan. They offered mandolins until '42.

KM-11 Mandolin

1935-1941. Gibson-made, A-style, flat top and back, round soundhole, dot inlay.

1930s	Sunburst	$700	$900

KM-21 Mandolin

1936-1940. Gibson-made, A-style, F-holes, arched bound spruce top and mahogany back.

1930s	Sunburst	$800	$1,000

Kay

1931-present. Located in Chicago, the Kay company made an incredible amount of instruments under a variety of brandnames, including the Kay name. From the beginning, Kay offered several types of electric and acoustic mandolins. In 1969, the factory closed, marking the end of American-made Kays. The brand name survives today on imported instruments. See the Guitar section for more company info or *Guitar Stories Volume II*,

Hondo mandolin

Kay Concert mandolin

MANDOLINS

1950s Kay K73

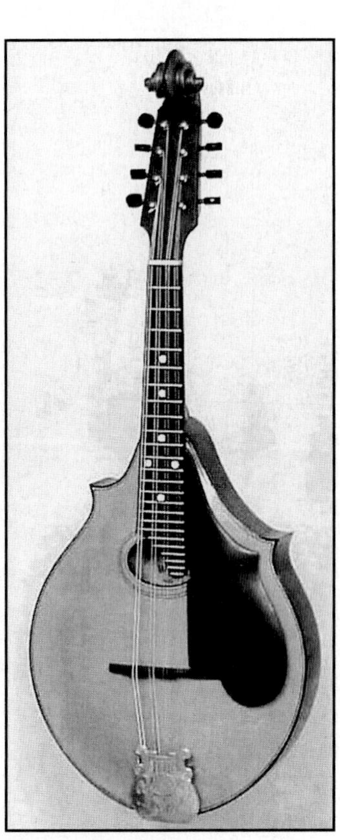

1920 Lyon & Healy Style A

MODEL YEAR	FEATURES	EXC. COND. LOW	HIGH

by Michael Wright, for a complete history of Kay with detailed model listings.

K390/K395 Professional Electric Mandolin

1960-1968. Modified Venetian-style archtop, single pickup, F-hole, spruce top, curly maple back and sides. Sunburst finish. Renamed K395 in 1966.

1960s		$400	$500

K494/K495 Electric Mandolin

1960-1968. A-style archtop, single metal-covered (no poles) pickup, volume and tone control knobs, the K494 was originally about 60% of the price of the K390 model (see above) in 1965. Renamed K495 in 1966.

1960s	Sunburst	$300	$400

K68/K465 Concert Mandolin

1952-1968. Pear shape, close-grain spruce top, genuine mahogany back and sides. Renamed the K465 in 1966. Kay also offered a venetian-style mandolin called the K68 in 1937-1942.

1952-1968	Natural	$250	$300

K73 Mandolin

1939-1952. Solid spruce top, maple back and sides, A-style body, F-holes, Cherry Sunburst.

1950s		$250	$300

Kay Kraft

1931-1937. First brand name of the newly formed Kay Company. Brand replaced by Kay in 1937. See Kay and Kay Kraft in the Guitar section for more info.

Mandolin

1931-1937. Kay Kraft offered Venetian and tear-drop-shaped mandolins.

1930s		$250	$350

Kel Kroyden (by Gibson)

1930-1933. Private branded budget level made by Gibson.

KK-20 (Style C-1) Mandolin

1930-1933. Flat-top, near oval-shaped body, oval soundhole, Natural finish, dark finish mahogany back and sides.

1930-1933		$700	$900

Kent

Ca. 1962-1969. Japanese-made instruments. Kent offered teardrop, A style, and bowlback acoustic mandolins up to '68.

Acoustic Mandolin

1961-1968. Kent offered teardrop, A style, and bowlback acoustic mandolins up to '68.

1960s		$100	$150

Electric Mandolin

1964-1969. Available from '64-'66 was a solidbody electric (in left- and right-hand models) and from '67-'69 an electric hollowbody venetian-style with F-holes (they called it violin-shaped).

1960s		$125	$175

Kentucky (Saga M.I.)

1977-present. Brand name of Saga Musical Instruments currently offering budget, intermediate, and professional grade, production, A- and F-style mandolins.

Kingston

Ca. 1958-1967. Japanese imports. See Guitar section for more company info.

Acoustic Mandolin

1960s		$100	$125

EM1 Electric Mandolin

1964-1967. Double cutaway solidbody electric, 15.75" scale, one pickup.

1960s		$125	$200

Knutson Luthiery

1981-present. Professional and premium grade, custom, acoustic and electric mandolins built by luthier John Knutson in Forestville, California. He also builds archtops, flat-tops and electric upright basses.

La Scala

Ca. 1920s-1930s. La Scala was another brand of the Oscar Schmidt Company of New Jersery, and was used on guitars, banjos, and mandolins.

Lakeside (Lyon & Healy)

Late-1800s-early-1900s. Mainly catalog sales of guitars and mandolins from the Chicago maker. Marketed as a less expensive alternative to the Lyon & Healy Washburn product line.

Style G2016 12-String Mandolin

Early-1900s. Twelve-string, 18 mahogany ribs with white inlay between, celluloid guard plate, advertised as "an inexpensive instrument, possessing a good tone, correct scale, and durable construction."

1917		$300	$350

Larson Brothers (Chicago)

1900-1944. Made by luthiers Carl and August Larson and marketed under a variety of names including Stetson, Maurer, and Prairie State.

Bowl Back Mandolin

1900s. Neopolitan-style (bowl back) with 36 Brazilian rosewood ribs, spruce top, engraved rosewood pickguard, fancy abalone trim and headstock inlay.

1900		$500	$600

Lion

Mandolins

1900s		$300	$400

Lyon & Healy

1964-ca. 1945. Lyon & Healy was a large musical instrument builder and marketer, and produced under many different brandnames.

MODEL YEAR	FEATURES	EXC. COND. LOW	HIGH

Style A Mandocello

Scroll peghead, symmetrical two-point body. Natural.

1910s		$5,000	$9,000
1920s		$5,000	$9,000

Style A Professional Mandolin

Violin scroll peghead. Natural.

1918		$3,400	$4,200

Style B Mandolin

Maple back and sides, two-point body. Natural.

1920		$1,800	$2,200

Style C Mandolin

1920s. Like Style A teardrop Gibson body style, oval soundhole, carved spruce top, carved maple back. Natural.

1920s		$1,800	$2,200

Maccaferri

1923-1990. Mario Maccaferri made a variety of instruments over his career. He produced award-winning models in Italy and France until he fled to the U.S. due to W.W. II. He applied the new plastic to a highly successful line of instruments after the war. A mandolin was about the only stringed instument they didn't offer in plastic. His Europe-era instruments are very rare.

Mandolins/Mandolas made by Maccaferri (1928-ca. 1931): No. 1 Mandolone, No. 2 Mandoloncello, No. 3 Mandola Baritono, No. 4 Mandola Tenore, No. 5 Mandola Soprano, No. 6 Mandolino, No. 7 Quartino. See Guitar section for more company info or *Guitar Stories Volume II*, by Michael Wright, for a complete history of Maccaferri with detailed model listings.

Martin

1986-present. Martin got into the mandolin market in 1896 starting with the typical bowl back designs. By 1914, Gibson's hot selling, innovative, violin-based mandolin pushed Martin into a flat back, bent top hybrid design. By 1929, Martin offered a carved top and carved back mandolin. Most models were discontinued in 1941, partially because of World War II. Currently Martin offers only a Backpacker mandolin.

Style 0 Mandolin

1905-1925. Bowl back-style, 18 rosewood ribs, solid peghead.

1915		$900	$1,000

Style 00 Mandolin

1908-1925. Bowl back-style, nine rosewood ribs (14 ribs by 1924), solid peghead.

1908-1925		$600	$900

Style 000 Mandolin

1914 only. Bowl back, solid peghead, dot inlay, nine mahogany ribs.

1914		$500	$800

MODEL YEAR	FEATURES	EXC. COND. LOW	HIGH

Style 1 Mandolin

1898-1924. Bowl back, German silver tuners, 18 ribs.

1910s		$1,000	$1,100

Style 2-15 Mandolin

1936-1964. Carved spruce top, maple back and sides, F-hole, single-bound back, solid headstock.

1936-1964		$1,100	$1,200

Style 2-20 Mandolin

1936-1941. Carved spruce triple-bound top and bound maple back and sides, F-hole, dot inlay.

1936-1942		$2,000	$2,200

Style 2-30 Mandolin

1937-1941. Carved spruce top and maple back and sides, multi-bound, F-holes, diamond and square inlays.

1937-1941		$3,000	$3,500

Style 5 Mandolin

1898-1920. Bowl back, vine inlay, abalone top trim.

1898-1899		$2,100	$2,500
1900-1920		$2,000	$2,500

Style 6 Mandolin

1898-1921. Bowl back, top bound with ivory and abalone, vine or snowflake inlay.

1919	Snowflake inlay	$2,500	$2,800

Style A Mandolin

1914-1995. Flat back, oval soundhole, dot inlay, solid headstock.

1920s		$1,000	$1,200
1930s		$1,000	$1,200
1940s		$900	$1,100
1950s		$800	$1,000
1960s		$800	$1,000
1970s		$700	$900
1980s		$700	$900

Style AK Mandolin

1920-1937. Koa wood version of Style A, flat back.

1920-1937		$1,000	$1,300

Style B Mandolin

1914-1946, 1981-1987. Flat back with bent top, spruce top and rosewood back and sides, herringbone back stripe, multi-bound.

1910s		$1,000	$1,400
1920s		$1,000	$1,400

Style BB Mandola

1917-1921, 1932-1939. Brazilian rosewood, herringbone trim, features like Style B mandolin. This is the only Mandola offered.

1917-1921		$1,400	$1,700

Style E Mandolin

1915-1937. Flat back, rosewood back and sides, bent spruce top, Style 45 snowflake fretboard inlay and other high-end appointments. Highest model cataloged.

1915-1919		$4,000	$5,000
1920-1937		$3,500	$4,500

Martin Style B

1926 Martin Style E

MANDOLINS

Monteleone Grand Artist

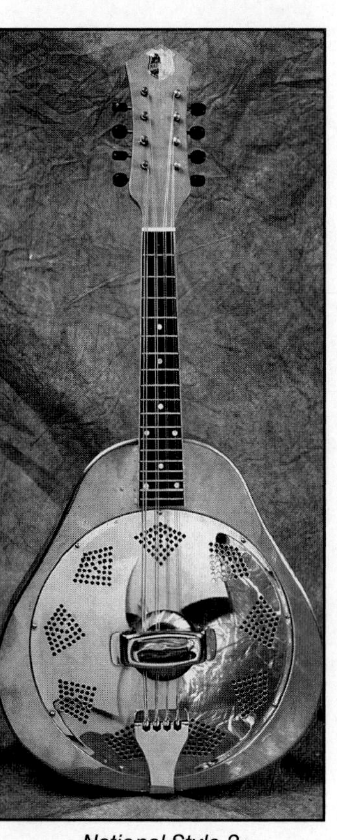

National Style 2

Maurer

Maurer Mandolins from the 1930s include Style 30 Flat Model, Style 40, Octave Mandola Style 45, Mandocello Style 50, and Mandola Tenor.

Mandolin

Brazilian rosewood, bird's-eye maple, bowl back.

MODEL YEAR	FEATURES	EXC. COND. LOW	HIGH
1930		$1,000	$1,200

Mayflower

1904-1920s. Small builder associated with several distributors.

Bowl Back Mandolin

1901-1920s. Mid-level bowl back-style with 19 rosewood ribs and mid-level appointments.

MODEL YEAR	FEATURES	EXC. COND. LOW	HIGH
1900s		$600	$900

Menzenhauer & Schmidt

1894-1904. Founded by Frederick Menzenhauer and Oscar Schmidt International. Menzenhauer created the guitar-zither in the U.S. He had several patents including one issued in September 1899 for a mandolin-guitar-zither. Control of operations quickly went to Oscar Schmidt.

12-String Mandolin

1890s. Bowl back mandolin with three strings per course that were tuned in octaves. Designed during an experimental era for mandolin-related instrumetns, 13 rosewood ribs, spruce top, inlays.

MODEL YEAR	FEATURES	EXC. COND. LOW	HIGH
1890s		$200	$250

Michael Lewis Instruments

1992-present. Luthier Michael Lewis builds his premium grade, custom, mandolins in Grass Valley, California. He also builds premium and presentation grade archtop guitars.

Mid-Missouri

1995-present. Intermediate grade, production, acoustic and electric mandloins and mandolas built by luthier Michael Dulak in Columbia, Missouri.

M Series Mandolin

1995-1999. Teardrop A style body, solid Engleman spruce top, solid maple, mahogany or rosewood back and sides. Includes M-1, M-2 and M-4.

MODEL YEAR	FEATURES	EXC. COND. LOW	HIGH
1995-1999		$300	$500

Monteleone

1971-present. Primarily a guitar maker, luthier John Monteleone also builds presentation grade, custom, mandolins in West Islip, New York.

10-String Cittern/Mandocello

1980s. Carved spruce top, oval soundhole, sword-excalibur headstock inlay optional.

MODEL YEAR	FEATURES	EXC. COND. LOW	HIGH
1986	"Excalibur" inlay option	$8,000	$10,000
1989	Amber Brown	$7,000	$9,000

Grand Artist Style F Mandolin

1990s. Style F body, spruce top, curly maple back and sides, dot markers.

MODEL YEAR	FEATURES	EXC. COND. LOW	HIGH
1990s	Sunburst	$12,000	$14,000

Style B Mandolin

1980s. Long A body style with long F-holes, flamed curly maple back and sides, elongated fretboard over body.

MODEL YEAR	FEATURES	EXC. COND. LOW	HIGH
1988	Sunburst	$9,000	$10,000

Morales

Ca.1967-1968. Japanese-made, not heavily imported into the U.S.

Electric Mandolin

1967-1968.

MODEL YEAR	FEATURES	EXC. COND. LOW	HIGH
1967		$200	$300

Mozzani

Late-1800s-early-1900s. Founder Luigi Mozzani was an Italian (Bologna) master luthier and renowned composer and musician. There are original Mozzani-built mandolins and also factory-built instruments made later at various workshops.

Mandolin

Factory-built bowl back model.

MODEL YEAR	FEATURES	EXC. COND. LOW	HIGH
1920s		$300	$400

Original Bowl Back Mandolin

Late-1800s-early-1900s. Handcrafted by Luigi Mozzani, about 24 ribs, soundhole ornamentation, snowflake-like markers.

MODEL YEAR	FEATURES	EXC. COND. LOW	HIGH
1904		$1,300	$1,500

National

Ca.1927-present. The National brandname has gone through many ownership changes. National offered resonator mandolins from around 1927 to '41. Currently, National does not offer a mandolin. See Guitar section for more company info.

Style O Mandolin

1931-early-1940s. Metal body with Hawaiian scenes, single-cone resonator.

MODEL YEAR	FEATURES	EXC. COND. LOW	HIGH
1930s	Hawaiian scene	$2,000	$3,000

Style 1 Mandolin

1928-1936. Plain metal body, tri-cone resonator.

MODEL YEAR	FEATURES	EXC. COND. LOW	HIGH
1928-1936		$2,800	$3,200

Style 2 Mandolin

1928-1936. Metal body with rose engraving, tri-cone resonator.

MODEL YEAR	FEATURES	EXC. COND. LOW	HIGH
1928-1936		$3,500	$4,000

Style 3 Mandolin

MODEL YEAR	FEATURES	EXC. COND. LOW	HIGH
1930s		$4,000	$5,000

Style 97 Mandolin

1936-1940. Metal body, tri-cone resonator.

MODEL YEAR	FEATURES	EXC. COND. LOW	HIGH
1936-1940		$3,500	$4,000

Triolian Mandolin

1928-1940. Metal body with palm trees, single-cone resonator.

MODEL YEAR	FEATURES	EXC. COND. LOW	HIGH
1928-1940		$1,500	$2,500

MODEL YEAR	FEATURES	EXC. COND. LOW	HIGH

Northworthy

1987-present. Professional and premium grade, production/custom, flat-tops, electric guitars, basses, and mandolin-family instruments built by luthier Alan Marshall in Ashbourne, Derbyshire, England.

Nugget

1970s-present. Luthier Mike Kemnitzer builds his premium grade mandolins in Central Lake, Michigan.

Nyberg Instruments

1993-present. Professional grade, custom, flat-top and Maccaferri-style guitars, mandolas, bouzoukis, and citterns built by luthier Lawrence Nyberg in Hornby Island, British Columbia.

Old Kraftsman

1930s-1960s. Brand name used by the Siegel Company on instruments made by Kay and others (even Gibson). Quality was mixed, but some better-grade instruments were offered.

Mandolin

1950s		$300	$400

Orpheum

Founded in the very late-1890s. An old brand name often associated with banjos, 1930s branded guitars sold by Bruno and Sons. 1950s branded guitars and mandolins sold by Maurice Lipsky Music, New York, NY.

Electric Mandolin Model 730 E

1950s. Private branded for Maurice Lipsky. Cataloged as a student model designed for ensemble playing. A-style body, single neck bar pickup, two side-mounted knobs, spruce top, maple back and sides, dot markers. Sunburst.

1953		$450	$600

Oscar Schmidt

1886-present. The Oscar Schmidt Company, Jersey City, NJ was founded in the late-1800s. The company offered a variety of fretted stringed instruments. Guitar models included Sovereign and Stella. Oscar Schmidt was also involved with zithers and eventually became very well known for autoharps.

Products were often low to low-mid level instruments. In 1979, Washburn acquired the brand name, currently using it on electric and acoustic guitars, mandolins, banjos, and the famous Oscar Schmidt autoharp. Currently, Schmidt offers budget and intermediate grade, production, mandolins.

Mandolin Harp Style B

1890s. More zither-autoharp than mandolin, flat autoharp body with soundhole.

1890s		$100	$125

Sovereign Mandolin

1920s. Bowl back, bent top, rope-style binding, mahogany ribs, dot inlay, plain headstock.

1920s	Natural	$250	$300

Ovation

1966-present. Founded by Charles H. Kaman in Bloomfield, Connecticut. Known for innovative fiberglass-backed bowl back acoustic and acoustic/electric guitars. Ovation added mandolins in '94 and currently offers intermediate and professional grade, production, mandolins.

Celebrity Mandolin

1994-present. Single cutaway, small typically Ovation body, with typical Ovation headstock.

1990s	Red Sunburst	$400	$475

P. W. Crump Company

1975-present. Luthier Phil Crump builds his custom mandolin-family instruments and flat-tops in Arcata, California.

Phoenix

1990-present. Premium grade, production/custom, mandolins built by luthier Rolfe Gerhardt (formerly builder of Unicorn Mandolins in the '70s) in South Thomaston, Maine. Gerhard's Phoenix company specializes in a two-point Style A (double cutaway) body style.

Bluegrass (double-point) Mandolin

1990-present. Double-point shallow body voiced for bluegrass music, adirondack spruce top, figured maple body.

2000	Sunburst	$1,700	$1,900

Premier

Ca.1938-ca.1975, 1990s-present. Brand produced by Peter Sorkin Music Company in New York City. Around 1957 the company acquired Strad-O-Lin and many of their mandolins were offered under that brand name. By '75, the Premier brand went into hiatus. The Premier brand name currently appears on Asian-made solidbody guitars and basses. See more company information in the Guitar section.

Recording King

1929-1943. Montgomery Ward house brand. Suppliers include Gibson, Kay, Regal, and Gretsch.

Mandolin (Gibson-made)

1929-1940. A-style body.

1930s	Sunburst	$350	$550

Regal

Ca.1884-1954. Large Chicago-based manufacturer which made their own brand name and others for distributors and mass merchandisers. Absorbed by the Harmony Company in 1955. See Guitar section for more company info.

Nugget Deluxe Two Point

Regal Fancy Scroll

MANDOLINS

Rigel G-5

Rigel G-110

Mandolin

MODEL YEAR	FEATURES	EXC. COND. LOW	HIGH
1920s	Flat-top A-style	$300	$400
1930s	Sunburst, standard model	$300	$400
1930s	Ultra grand deluxe model	$800	$1,000

Octophone Mandolin

1920s. Octave mandolin, long body with double points, round soundhole.

MODEL YEAR	FEATURES	EXC. COND. LOW	HIGH
1920s		$800	$1,000

Resonator Mandolin

MODEL YEAR	FEATURES	EXC. COND. LOW	HIGH
1950s		$300	$400

Rigel

1990-present. Professional and premium grade, production/custom mandolins and mandolas built by luthier Pete Langdell in Hyde Park, Vermont.

A-Plus Oval Mandolin

1990s. A-style body, oval soundhole, dot markers.

MODEL YEAR	FEATURES	EXC. COND. LOW	HIGH
1998	Sunburst	$900	$1,000

Roberts

1980s. Built by luthier Jay Roberts of California.

Tiny Moore Jazz 5 Mandolin

1980s. Based on Bigsby design of the early-1950s as used by Tiny Moore, five-string electric.

MODEL YEAR	FEATURES	EXC. COND. LOW	HIGH
1985	Sunburst	$1,700	$1,800

S. S. Stewart

Late-1800s-early-1900s. S. S. Stewart of Philadelphia was primarily known for banjos. Legend has it that Stewart was one of the first to demonstrate the mass productioin assembly of stringed instruments.

Mandolin Banjo

Early-1900s. Mandolin neck and a very small open back banjo body, 'star' inlay in headstock.

MODEL YEAR	FEATURES	EXC. COND. LOW	HIGH
1900s		$350	$400

Sawchyn

1972-present. Intermediate and professional grade, production/custom, mandolins built by luthier Peter Sawchyn in Regina, Saskatchewan. He also builds flat-top and flamenco guitars.

Silvertone

1941-ca.1970. Brand name used by Sears on their musical instruments. See Guitar section for more company info.

Mandolin

Arched top and back.

MODEL YEAR	FEATURES	EXC. COND. LOW	HIGH
1940s	Sunburst	$200	$300
1950s	Sunburst	$200	$300

Smart Musical Instruments

1986-present. Luthier A. Lawrence Smart builds his premium and presentation grade, custom, mandolin family instruments and flat-top guitars in McCall, Idaho.

Stahl

William C. Stahl instruments were "made" (per their literature they were not manufactured) in Milwaukee, Wisconsin, in the early-1900s. Models included Style 4 (22 ribs) to Style 12 Presentation Artist Special. The more expensive models were generally 44-rib construction.

Bowl Back Mandolin (deluxe professional model)

Rosewood, 40 ribs.

MODEL YEAR	FEATURES	EXC. COND. LOW	HIGH
1910s		$750	$950

Bowl Back Mandolin (mid-level)

Pearl floral design on pickguard, 32 ribs.

MODEL YEAR	FEATURES	EXC. COND. LOW	HIGH
1910s		$400	$600

Stathopoulo

1903-1916. Original design instruments, some patented, by Epiphone company founder A. Stathopoulo.

A Style Mandolin

1903-1916. A-style with higher-end appointments, bent-style spruce top, figured maple back and sides.

MODEL YEAR	FEATURES	EXC. COND. LOW	HIGH
1912		$850	$1,250

Stefan Sobell Musical Instruments

1982-present. Premium grade, production/custom, flattop, 12-string, and archtop guitars, mandolins, citterns and bouzoukis built by luthier Stefan Sobell in Hetham, Northumberland, England.

Stella

Founded in 1879, Stella was a brand name of the Oscar Schmidt Company and produced all types of stringed instruments. The company was an early contributor to innovative mandolin designs and participated in the 1900-1930 mandolin boom. Pre-World War II Stella instruments were low-mid to mid-level instruments. 1950s and '60s Stella instruments were student grade, low-end instruments. In '39, Harmony purchased the Stella name. See the Guitar section for more company info.

Banjo-Mandolin

1920s. One of several innovative designs that attempted to create a new market. Eight-string mandolin neck with a banjo body. Stella logo normally impressed on the banjo rim or the side of the neck.

MODEL YEAR	FEATURES	EXC. COND. LOW	HIGH
1920s		$150	$200

Bowl Back Mandolin

1920s. Typical bowl back, bent top-style mandolin with models decalomania, about 10 (wide) maple ribs, dot markers.

MODEL YEAR	FEATURES	EXC. COND. LOW	HIGH
1920s		$100	$175

MODEL YEAR	FEATURES	EXC. COND. LOW	HIGH

Pear-Shape Mandolin

1940s-1960s. Harmony-made lower-end mandolins. Pear-shaped (Style A) flat back, oval soundhole.

1940s	Natural	$200	$250
1950s		$200	$250
1960s	Sunburst	$200	$250

Strad-O-Lin

Ca.1920s-ca.1960s. The Strad-O-Lin company was operated by the Hominic brothers in New York, primarily making mandolins for wholesalers. In the late '50s, Multivox/Premier bought the company and used the name on mandolins and guitars.

Baldwin Electric Mandolin

1950s. A style, single pickup, tone and volume knobs, spruce top, maple back and sides, Baldwin logo on headstock.

1950s	Natural	$300	$350

Junior A Mandolin

1950s. A style, Stradolin Jr. logo on headstock, dot markers.

1950s	Sunburst	$300	$350

Superior

1987-present. Intermediate grade, production/custom mandolin-family instruments and Hawaiian, flamenco and classical guitars made in Mexico for George Katechis Montalvo of Berkeley Musical Instrument Exchange.

Supertone

1914-1941. Brand name used by Sears before they switched to Silvertone. Instruments made by other companies. See Guitar section for more company info.

Mandolin

Spruce top, mahogany back and sides, some with decalomania vine pattern on top.

1920s		$250	$350
1930s	Decalomania vine pattern	$250	$350

Supro

1935-1968. Budget line from the National Dobro Company. See Guitar section for more company info.

T30 Electric Mandolin

1950s		$300	$400

Tacoma

1995-present. Intermediate, professional and premium grade, production, all-solid wood mandolins made in Tacoma, Washington. Tacoma also builds acoustic guitars and basses.

M-1 Mandolin

1990s-present. Solid spruce top, mahogany back and sides, typical Tacoma body-style with upper bass bout soundhole.

2000	Natural	$375	$400

M-2 Mandolin

1990s-2002. Solid spruce top, solid rosewood back and sides, typical Tacoma body-style with upper bass bout soundhole.

2000	Natural	$500	$600

Timeless Instruments

1980-present. Luthier David Freeman builds his intermediate grade, mandolins in Tugaske, Saskatchewan. He also builds flattop, 12-string, nylon-string, and resonator guitars and dulcimers.

Unicorn

1970s-late 1980s. Luthier Rolfe Gerhardt (currently luthier for Phoenix Mandolins) founded Unicorn in the mid-1970s. Gerhardt built 149 mandolins before selling Unicorn to Save Sjnko in 1980. Sinko closed Unicorn in the late-1980s.

F-5 Style Mandolin

1976-1980	Sunburst	$800	$1,000

Vega

1903-present. The original Boston-based company was purchased by C.F. Martin in 1970. In 1980, the Vega trademark was sold to a Korean company. Vega means "star" and a star logo is often seen on the original Vega instruments.

Lansing Special Bowl Mandolin

Spruce top, abalone, vine inlay.

1900s		$500	$700

Little Wonder Mandolin Banjo

Maple neck, resonator.

1920s		$400	$600

Mando Bass Mandolin

1910s-1920s. Large upright bass-sized instrument with bass tuners, body-style similar to dual-point A-style, scroll headstock.

1920s		$2,500	$3,500

Style 202 Lute Mandolin

Early-1900s. Basic A-style with small horns, Natural spruce top, mahogany sides and cylinder back, dot markers.

1910s		$700	$900

Style A Mandolin

1910s		$500	$600

Style K Mandolin Banjo

1910s		$400	$600
1920s		$400	$600
1930s		$400	$600

Style L Banjo Mandolin

1910s. Open back banjo body and mandolin 8-string neck.

1910s		$900	$1,000

Super Deluxe Mandolin

1939	Sunburst	$700	$750

Tubaphone Style X Mandolin Banjo

1923		$700	$750

1920s Supertone

Tacoma M-1

Washburn Style 115 bowlback

Weber Bitteroot

MODEL YEAR	FEATURES	EXC. COND. LOW	HIGH

Vinaccia

Italian-made by Pasquale Vinaccia, luthier.

Bowl Back Mandolin

High-end appointments and pickguard, 30 rosewood ribs.

1904		$2,600	$2,800

Ward

Depression era private brand by Gibson's Kalamazoo factory.

Style A Mandolin

1930s. Style A body with round soundhole and flat top and back, dot markers, mahogany back and sides, silkscreened Ward logo.

1935	Sunburst	$350	$400

Washburn (Lyon & Healy)

1880s-1949. Made by Lyon and Healy. See Guitar section for more company info.

Bowl Back Mandolin

Lyon and Healy sold a wide variety of bowl back mandolins. Brazilian ribs with fancy inlays and bindings.

1890s	Fancy inlays and bindings	$500	$1,000
1900s	Fancy inlays and bindings	$500	$1,000
1900s	Plain appointments	$300	$500
1910s	Standard appointments	$300	$500

Style A Mandolin

Brazilian rosewood.

1920s		$800	$1,000

Style E Mandolin

1915-1923. Brazilian rosewood.

1915-1923		$900	$1,100

Washburn (Post 1974)

1974-present. Currently, Washburn offers imported intermediate and professional grade, production, mandolins. See Guitar section for more company info.

M-3 SWSB Mandolin

Gibson F-5-style, import.

1980s	Sunburst	$400	$600

M-4S Mandolin

F-5-style.

1982		$400	$600

MODEL YEAR	FEATURES	EXC. COND. LOW	HIGH

Weber

1996-present. In 1996, Gibson moved the manufacturing of Flatiron mandolins from Bozeman, Montana, to Nashville. Many former Flatiron employees, including Bruce Weber, formed Sound To Earth, Ltd., to build Weber instruments in Belgrade, Montana. Currently, they offer intermediate, professional, and premium grade, production/custom, mandolins, mandolas, and mandocellos.

Style F Yellowstone Mandolin

1996-present. Style F mandolin built with solid spruce top and flamed maple back and sides.

1998	Sunburst	$1,800	$2,000

Weymann

1864-1940s. H.A. Weymann & Sons was a musical instrument distributor located in Philadelphia. They also built their own instruments.

Keystone State Banjo Mandolin

Maple rim and back, ebony fretboard.

1910s		$300	$500

Model 20 Mando-Lute

1920s. Lute-style body, spruce top, flamed maple sides and back, rope binding, deluxe rosette.

1920s	Natural	$550	$750

Model 40 Mandolin Banjo

1910s-1920s. Mandolin neck on a open banjo body with a larger sized 10" head.

1920s		$450	$650

Wurlitzer

The old Wurlitzer company would have been considered a mega-store by today's standards. They sold a wide variety of instruments, gave music lessons, and operated manufacturing facilities.

Mandolin

Koa.

1920		$550	$700

Mandolin Banjo

1900s. Mandolin neck on open back banjo body, plain-style.

1900s		$150	$200

Ukuleles

Aloha

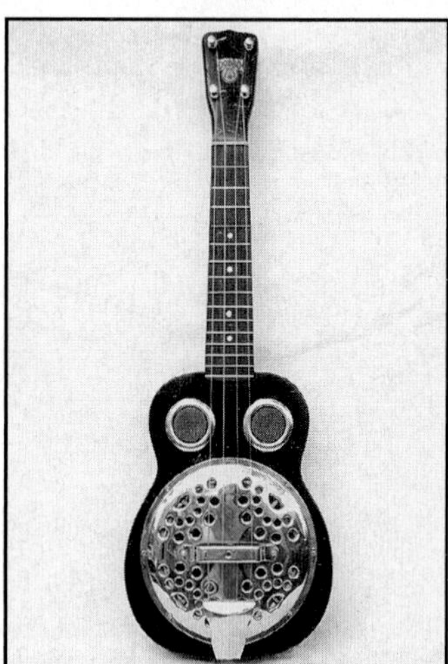
Dobro resonator

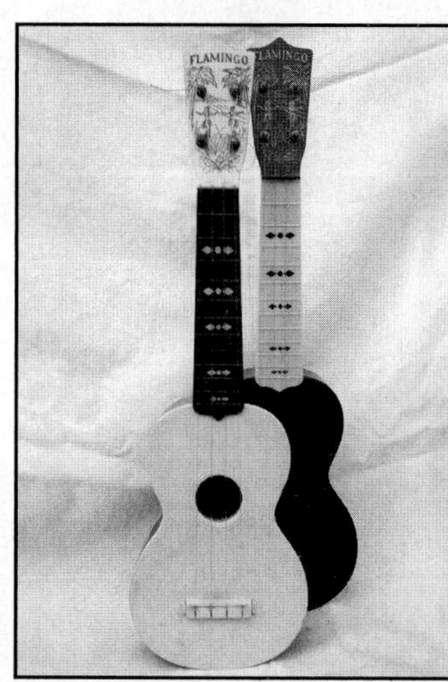

Flamingo

MODEL YEAR	FEATURES	EXC. COND. LOW	HIGH

Until recently, if a passing interest in the ukulele sent you off to your local retail music store to bring one home, you were pretty much destined to go home empty-handed. Without any fanfare – and while you were out chasing guitars, amps, and mandolins – the poor uke had dropped like a rock out of the merchandising programs of its former manufacturers. For several decades not a single uke of any kind was being regularly produced anywhere on mainland soil.

Your remaining purchasing options consisted of either low-quality Asian imports (virtually unplayable and little more than stage props, really, suitable for hula girl trick-or-treating, Polynesian-themed window displays, and high school productions of *South Pacific*), or a genuine Hawaiian-made Kamaka (finely crafted of native woods, still highly prized throughout the islands, and infrequently shipped this-a-way). You would also likely have been advised to hit your local flea market, swap meet, or online auction, where forlorn-looking, underpriced ukes were fouling ground tarps, fold-up card tables, and grainy digital photos. You might well have followed up on Mr. Retailer's lead, too, and picked up an old uke, just to strum around with, or even two or three (or, if you were like me, two or three hundred).

The word didn't take very long, however, to travel from Mr. Retailer to Mr. Music Industry Executive that not only were mopes like us (armed with a little disposable income) beating the bushes for the old ukes (and driving vintage prices way up in the process), but also that a current crop of young folkies and not-so-folkies were actually incorporating the ukulele in their recorded music for the first time since Tiny Tim. And faster than you could say "jumping on the bandwagon," those crafty entrepreneurial manufacturers were cranking the wheels of industry to fill store shelves with ukes.

And so it goes that today you can walk into almost any retail music store in downtown Anywhere, USA, to see shiny new ukuleles in a variety of sizes, materials, and decorative options, and priced to move without delay. Not so ironically, that plain, scuffed-up vintage Martin uke that you bought for hundreds of dollars at a time when just finding one at all seemed like the work of a Neanderthal hunter/gatherer, isn't worth nearly so much as it should be now that Martin is back in the uke biz. It's true, new ukes by National, Maui Music, Larivee, and nearly a dozen other makers are giving vintage ones a run for their money.

Still, new is new, and old is old. And just as a modern reissue guitar isn't quite the same as the guitar it's modeled after, for my money, you can never match the character, the patina, or the tone of a vintage uke.

R.J.Klimpert
klimpert@earthlink.net

Aero Uke

Most likely produced by the Stromberg-Voisenet Company, the precursor of Kay, the Aero Uke is an instrument unto itself. With its spruce-capped body resembling an airplane wing and a neck and headstock that approximate a plane's fuselage, this clever 1920's offering cashed in on the Lindbergh craze, and must have been a big hit at parties.

Aero Uke

Airplane body.

c.1927	Black deco on wing	$1,300	$1,700
c.1927	Gold deco on wing	$1,600	$2,000

Aloha

The variety of features exhibited by Aloha ukuleles leads the observer to believe ukes bearing this headstock decal were made by many different manufacturers. Many were undoubtedly Island-made, with all koa bodies and some with fancy rope binding. Some of these have a more traditional look and are stamped "Akai" inside the soundhole, while others, strongly resembling mainland C.F. Martins in design, typically sport a decal of the Sam F. Chang curio shop on the reverse of the headstock.

Soprano ukulele

Koa body, plain.

c.1950		$250	$350

Akai soprano ukulele

Koa construction.

c.1930		$250	$350

Bear Creek Guitars

1995-present. Luthier Bill Hardin worked for OMI Dobro and Santa Cruz Guitar before introducing his own line of Wessenborn-style guitars and ukuleles, made in Kula, Hawaii.

Bruno

This New York distributor almost certainly subcontracted all of its ukulele production to other manufacturers, and as a result Bruno ukuleles vary widely in design, construction, and ornamentation.

Soprano ukulele

Koa.

c.1920	Rope soundhole	$250	$300
c.1930	Rope bound body	$300	$350

DeCava Guitars

1983-present. Ukuleles built by luthier Jim DeCava in Stratford, Connecticut. He also builds guitars, banjos, and mandolins.

Del Vecchio Dimonaco

With a basic configuration loosely based on the earlier work of Dobro and National, this Brazilian company produced a full line of resonator instruments, all constructed of native Brazilian rosewood, from the 1950s onward.

MODEL YEAR	FEATURES	EXC. COND. LOW	HIGH

Resonator ukulele

Brazilian rosewood.

c.1950		$500	$550
c.1980		$500	$550

Ditson

While many of the ukes commissioned by this East Coast music publisher and chain store were actually manufactured by C.F. Martin, they were by no means the sole supplier. The Martin-made instruments often bear a Martin brand as well as a Ditson one, or, barring that, at least demonstrate an overall similarity to the rest of the ukes in the regular Martin line.

Soprano ukulele

c.1922	Same appointments as Martin Style O	$700	$800
c.1922	Same appointments as Martin Style 1 M	$800	$900
c.1922	Same appointments as Martin Style 2 M	$1,000	$1,200
c.1922	Same appointments as Martin Style 3 M	$2,000	$2,500
c.1922	Same appointments as Martin Style 1 K	$1,000	$1,500
c.1922	Same appointments as Martin Style 2 K	$1,200	$2,000
c.1922	Same appointments as Martin Style 3 K	$2,000	$3,000
c.1922	Same appointments as Martin Style 5 K	$4,500	$6,000

Dobro

The ukulele version of the popular resonator instruments produced first in California, later in Chicago, the Dobro uke was offered in two sizes (soprano and tenor), two styles (f-holes and screen holes), and two colors (brown and black). Models with Dobro headstock decals are often outwardly indistinguishable from others bearing either a Regal badge or no logo at all, but a peek inside often reveals the presence of a sound well in the belly of the former, making them more desirable.

Resonator ukulele

Wood body.

c. 1930	F-holes, Regal-made	$700	$1,100
c. 1930	Screen holes	$700	$1,100

Favilla

This small New York City family-owned factory produced primarily guitars, but managed to offer some surprisingly high quality ukes, the best of which rivaled Martin and Gibson for craftsmanship and tone.

MODEL YEAR	FEATURES	EXC. COND. LOW	HIGH

Baritone ukulele

Plain mahogany body

c.1950		$150	$350

Soprano ukulele

c.1950	Plain mahogany body	$300	$350
c.1950	Mahogany body, triple bound	$350	$375
c.1950	Teardrop-shaped, birch body	$300	$325
c.1950	Teardrop-shaped, stained blue	$325	$375

Fin-der

The sales pitch for this short-lived plastic ukulele was apparently the ease of learning, since the included instructional brochure helped you to "find" your chords with the added help of color-coded nylon strings.

Diamond head

Styrene plastic.

c.1950	In original box	$100	$150

Fine Resophonic

1988-present. Wood and metal-bodied resophonic ukuleles built by luthiers Mike Lewis and Pierre Avocat in Vitry Sur Seine, France. They also build guitars and mandolins.

Flamingo

If swanky designs hot-stamped into the surface of these '50s swirly injection molded ukes didn't grab you, certainly the built-in functional pitch pipe across the the top of the headstock would.

Soprano ukulele

c.1955	Brown top with white fingerboard	$100	$150
c.1955	White top with brown fingerboard	$100	$150

Gibson

A relative late-comer to the uke market, Gibson didn't get a line off of the ground until 1927, fully nine years after Martin. Even then they only produced three soprano styles and one tenor version. Nonetheless, Gibson ukuleles exhibit more unintentional variety than any other major maker, with enough construction, inlay, binding, and cosmetic variations to keep collectors buzzing for years to come. In general, the earliest examples feature a "The Gibson" logo in script, later shortened to just "Gibson." Post-war examples adopted the more square-ish logo of the rest of the Gibson line, and, at some point in the late '50s, began sporting ink-stamped serial numbers on the back of the headstock

TU 1 tenor ukulele

c.1930	Mahogany body	$600	$800

Dobro Resonater

Favilla

Gibson UKE-2

UKULELES

Gibson UKE 3

Gretsch

1920s Harmony Roy Smeck Vita

MODEL YEAR	FEATURES	EXC. COND. LOW	HIGH
UKE 1 soprano ukulele			
c.1927	Plain mahogany body	$400	$600
c.1951	Plain body, red SG guitar-like finish	$400	$700
UKE 2 soprano ukulele			
Mahogany body			
c.1934	Triple-bound	$500	$700
c.1950	Single-bound	$400	$500
UKE 3 soprano ukulele			
Dark finish, diamonds and squares inlay.			
c.1933		$800	$2,000

Gretsch

The first (and most desirable) ukuleles by this New York manufacturer were actually stamped with the name "Gretsch American." Subsequent pieces, largely inexpensive lamination-bodied catalog offerings, are distinguished by small round "Gretsch" headstock decals.

MODEL YEAR	FEATURES	EXC. COND. LOW	HIGH
Plain soprano ukulele			
Natural mahogany body, no binding.			
c.1950		$100	$200
Round ukulele			
Round body, blue to green sunburst.			
c.1940		$100	$200
Soprano ukulele			
c.1940	Koa wood body, fancy fingerboard inlay	$600	$750
c.1940	Mahogany body, fancy fingerboard inlay	$500	$750
c.1940	Unbound body, engraved rose in peghead	$750	$900
c.1950	Darker finish, bordered in dark binding	$250	$350

Guild

By rights this fine East Coast shop should have produced a full line of ukes to complement its impressive flat and carved-top guitar offerings. Alas a lone baritone model was all that they ever came up with.

MODEL YEAR	FEATURES	EXC. COND. LOW	HIGH
B-11 Baritone ukulele			
Mahogany body, rosewood fingerboard.			
c.1960		$300	$400

Harmony

Chicago-based Harmony surely produced more ukuleles during the '60s than all other makers put together. Their extensive line ran the gamut from artist-endorsed models, to ukes in unusual shapes and materials, to fanciful creations adorned with eye-catching decals and silk screening. Earliest examples have a small paper label on the back of the headstock, and a brand inside the body. This is replaced by several versions of decal applied to the front of the headstock, first gold and black, later green, white, and black.

MODEL YEAR	FEATURES	EXC. COND. LOW	HIGH
Baritone ukulele			
Bound mahogany body.			
c.1960		$200	$250
Concert Ukulele			
Mahogany body, bound, concert-sized.			
c.1935		$200	$250
Johnny Marvin Tenor			
"Airplane" bridge.			
c.1930	Sunburst mahogany	$350	$500
c.1930	Flamed koa	$500	$800
Roy Smeck Concert			
Concert-sized, sunburst spruce top.			
c.1935		$300	$400
Roy Smeck Ukulele			
Mahogany.			
c.1955	Wooden fingerboard	$300	$400
c.1955	Plastic fingerboard	$100	$150
Roy Smeck Vita Uke			
Pear-shaped body, seal-shaped f-holes.			
c.1926		$450	$700
Ukulele			
Unbound.			
c.1930	Koa wood body	$200	$250
c.1935	Plain mahogany body	$250	$350
Tiple			
Ten steel strings, multicolored binding.			
c.1935		$500	$750

Hohner

Hohner currently offers tenor, baritone, standard, pineapple, and concert ukes.

Johnson

Mid-1990s-present. Ukuleles imported by Music Link, Brisbane, California. Johnson also offers guitars, amps, mandolins and effects.

K & S

1992-1998. Ukes distributed by George Katechis and Marc Silber and handmade in Paracho, Mexico. They also offered guitars. In '98, Silber started marketing the ukes under the Marc Silber Guitar Company brand and Katechis continued to offer instruments under the Casa Montalvo brand.

Kamaka

Part of the "second wave" of Island ukulele builders (after Nunes, Dias, and Santos), Kamaka distinguished itself first with ukes of extremely high quality, then with one of the most enduring non-guitar-derived designs, the Pineapple Uke, patented in 1928. Kamaka has been in continuous production for nearly a hundred years, offering Hawaiian-made products from native woods in virtually every size and ornamentation.

MODEL YEAR	FEATURES	EXC. COND. LOW	HIGH
Concert uke			
Koa body, extended rosewood fingerboard.			
c.1975		$250	$500

UKULELES

MODEL YEAR	FEATURES	EXC. COND. LOW	HIGH

Lili'u uke
Concert-sized koa body.

c.1965	Eight strings	$450	$600
c.1985	Six strings	$450	$500

Pineapple Uke

c.1925	Pineapple art painted onto top or back	$1,300	$1,500
c.1930	Monkeypod wood, plain, unbound	$600	$950
c.1930	Rope bound top only, koawood body	$800	$1,000
c.1935	Rope bound soundhole only	$700	$900
c.1960	Koa body, unbound, two "K"s logo	$500	$600
c.1970	Koa body, extended rosewood fingerboard	$350	$650

Tenor uke
Koa body, extended rosewood fingerboard.

c.1955		$300	$650

Kent
Student quality ukes of laminated construction were offered by this Japanese concern throughout the '60s.

Baritone ukulele
Mahogany body, bound top, bound back.

c.1960		$150	$200

Knutsen
Christopher Knutsen was the inventor and patent-holder of flat-topped harp instruments featuring an integral sound chamber on the bass side of the body. Kooky metal hardware brackets were also standard.

Harp ukulele
Koa body, large "horn" chamber.

c. 1915	Bound	$2,000	$3,500
c. 1915	Unbound	$1,500	$2,500

Harp taro patch
Koa body, as above but 8 strings, unbound.

c. 1915		$3,000	$4,000

Kumalae
Like Kamaka, another of the "second wave" of Hawaiian uke makers, Jonah Kumalae's company won the prestigious Gold Award at the Pan Pacific Exhibition in 1915, and the headstock decals and paper labels aren't about to let you forget it, either. Many assume that these all date from exactly that year, when in fact Kumalaes were offered in several sizes and degrees of ornamentation - all from native Koa wood - right up through at least the late '30s.

Soprano ukulele

c.1919	Figured koa body, bound body and fingerboard	$600	$800
c.1920	Koa body, rope bound body	$500	$700
c.1927	Figured koa body, bound body and fingerboard, fiddle-shaped peghead	$800	$1,400
c.1930	Koa body, unbound body	$400	$600
c.1933	Koa body, rope bound soundhole only	$400	$600

Tenor ukulele
Koa body, unbound body.

c.1930		$600	$800

Le Domino
These striking ukuleles turned the popularity of domino playing into a clever visual motif, displaying not only tumbling dominos on the bellies and around the soundholes of the ukes, but fingerboard markers represented in decal domino denominations (3, 5, 7, 10, 12, etc.). The ukes were, in fact, produced by at least two different companies, Stewart or Regal, but you can scarcely tell them apart.

Concert ukulele
Concert size, black-finished, white bound, domino decals.

c.1932		$800	$1,000

Soprano ukulele
Domino decals

c.1930	Black-finished, white bound	$400	$550
c.1940	Natural finished, unbound	$150	$250

Leonardo Nunes
Leonardo was the son of Manuel, the self professed "Inventor of the Ukulele." Whether the actual first or not, the old man was certainly on the ship that brought the inventor to the islands in 1879. Instead of joining up and making it Manuel & Son, Leonardo set out on his own to produce ukes that are virtually indistinguishable from his pop's. All constructed entirely of koa, some exhibit considerable figure and rope binding finery, making them highly desirable to collectors.

Soprano ukulele
Koa body.

c.1919	Figured body, bound body and fingerboard	$750	$1,100
c.1920	Rope bound body	$650	$1,000
c.1927	Bound body, finger-board, and head	$750	$1,600
c.1930	Unbound body	$450	$600
c.1933	Rope bound soundhole only	$550	$650

Kamaka Tenor

Kumalae

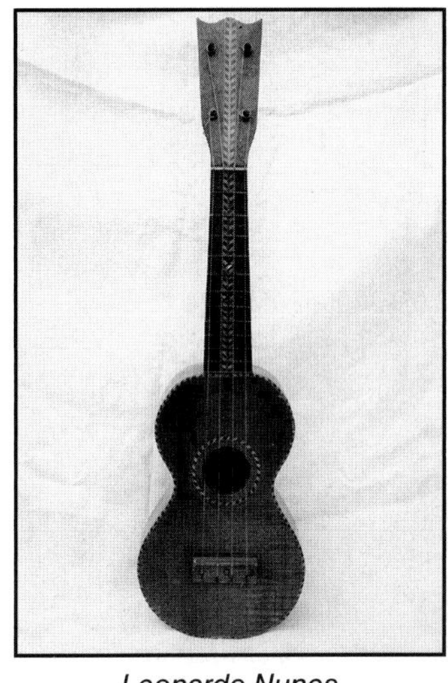
Leonardo Nunes

1920s Lyon & Healey Leland

1950s Maccaferri Islander

Martin 1K Taro Patch

MODEL YEAR	FEATURES	EXC. COND. LOW	HIGH
Taro Patch fiddle			
Koa body, unbound body.			
c.1930		$1,600	$2,000
Tenor ukulele			
Koa body, unbound body.			
c.1930		$800	$1,100

Lyon & Healy

During different periods several different makers constructed ukes bearing this stamp - often with a "Washburn" tag as well. After initial production by Lyon & Healy, manufacture apparently bounced between Regal, Stewart, and Tonk Brothers all within a span of only a few years. To add to the confusion, ukes surface from time to time bearing no maker's mark that can be reasonably attributed to Lyon & Healy. Suffice it to say that the best of these ukes, those displaying the highest degrees of quality and ornamentation, rival Gibson and Martin for collectability and tone.

MODEL YEAR	FEATURES	EXC. COND. LOW	HIGH
"Bell-shaped" uke			
Mahogany body.			
c.1927		$1,000	$1,500
Camp Uke			
Round "nissa" wood body, black binding.			
c.1935		$100	$200
Concert ukulele			
Mahogany body, bound body.			
c.1930		$1,300	$1,750
Shrine Uke			
Triangular body, green binding.			
c.1930	Mahogany body	$750	$1,000
c.1933	Koa body	$1,200	$1,500
Soprano ukulele			
c.1927	Koa body, bound top, pearl rosette	$1,600	$2,000
c.1930	Plain mahogany body, unbound	$350	$500
c.1932	Mahogany body, bound top, bound back	$450	$700
c.1934	Koa body, bound top, bound back	$650	$850
c.1935	Koa body, pearl bound top and back	$4,000	$5,000
Tenor ukulele			
Mahogany body, bound body.			
c.1933		$1,500	$2,200

Maccaferri

Manufacturing genius Mario Maccaferri created a line of stringed instruments revolutionary for their complete plastic construction. The ukuleles were by far the greatest success, and each one bore the tiny Maccaferri coat of arms on its tiny headstock. See *Guitar Stories Volume II*, by Michael Wright, for a complete history of Maccaferri with detailed model listings.

MODEL YEAR	FEATURES	EXC. COND. LOW	HIGH
Baritone ukulele			
Polystyrene cutaway body.			
c.1959		$100	$200
Islander ukulele			
Polytyrene plastic body, crest in peghead.			
c.1953		$100	$150
Playtune ukulele			
Polystyrene body.			
c.1956		$100	$150
TV Pal ukulele			
Polystyrene body.			
c.1955		$100	$150
TV Pal Deluxe ukulele			
Extended fingerboard.			
c.1960		$100	$150

Manuel Nunes

The self professed father of the ukulele was at least one of the first to produce them in any quantity. Beginning after 1879, when he and the boat load of Portuguese settlers landed in Hawaii, until at least the 1930s, Manuel and his son Leonardo (see Leonardo Nunes section) produced some of the most beautiful and superbly crafted ukes offered by any Island maker.

MODEL YEAR	FEATURES	EXC. COND. LOW	HIGH
Soprano ukulele			
Koa body.			
c.1919	Figured body, bound body, fingerboard	$1,000	$1,250
c.1920	Rope bound body	$800	$1,000
c.1927	Bound body, fingerboard, and head	$900	$1,500
c.1930	Unbound body	$600	$700
c.1933	Rope bound soundhole only	$600	$700
Taro Patch fiddle			
Koa body, unbound top, unbound back.			
c.1930		$1,500	$2,000
Tenor ukulele			
Koa body, unbound top, unbound back.			
c.1930		$900	$1,000

Marc Silber Guitar Company

1998-present. Mexican-made ukes from designer Marc Silber of Berkley, California. He also offers guitars.

Martin

Martin knew that they wanted in on the uke craze, and played around with some prototypes as early as 1907 or so, but didn't get around to actually issuing any until 1916. The first of these were characterized by rather more primitive craftsmanship (by stringent Martin standards), bar frets, and an impressed logo in the back of the headstock. By '20, koa became available as an option, and by the early '30s, regular frets and the familiar Martin headstock decal had prevailed. Martin single-handedly created the standard by

MODEL YEAR	FEATURES	EXC. COND. LOW	HIGH

which all mainland ukes are measured. Martin currently offers a soprano size uke.

Style 0 ukulele

Mahogany body, unbound body.

c.1920	Wood pegs	$400	$550
c.1953	Patent pegs	$400	$600

Style 1 ukulele

Mahogany body.

c.1940	Rosewood bound top only	$450	$750
c.1950	Tortoise bound top only	$450	$750
c.1960	Tortoise bound top only	$450	$725
c.1967	Tortoise bound top only	$450	$700

Style 1C Concert uke

Concert-sized mahogany body, bound top.

c.1950		$1,000	$1,300

Style 1C K Concert uke

Concert-sized koa body, bound top.

c.1950		$1,800	$2,000

Style 1K ukulele

Koa body, rosewood bound top.

c.1922	Wood pegs	$1,500	$1,600
c.1939	Patent pegs	$1,500	$1,700

Style 1T Tenor uke

Tenor-sized mahogany body, bound top only.

c.1940		$1,100	$1,500

Style 1 Taro Patch

Mahogany body, 8 strings, rosewood bound.

c.1933		$1,350	$1,700

Style 1K Taro Patch

Koa body Style 1.

c.1940		$1,750	$1,900

Style 2 ukulele

Mahogany bound body.

c.1922	Ivoroid-bound	$900	$1,100
c.1935	Ivoroid-bound	$900	$1,100
c.1961		$900	$1,000

Style 2K ukulele

Figured koa body, bound body.

c.1923	Wood pegs	$1,700	$2,400
c.1939	Patent pegs	$1,800	$2,500

Style 2 Taro Patch

Mahogany body, 8 strings, ivoroid bound.

c.1931		$1,550	$1,700

Style 2K Taro Patch

Koa body Style 2.

c.1937		$2,000	$2,500

Style 3 ukulele

Mahogany body.

c.1925	Kite headstock inlay	$1,500	$1,700
c.1940	B/W lines in ebony fingerboard	$1,500	$1,700
c.1950	Extended finger-board, dots	$1,500	$1,700

Style 3K ukulele

Figured koa body.

c.1924	Bow-tie fingerboard inlay	$3,500	$4,000
c.1932	B/W lines, diamonds, squares	$3,500	$4,000
c.1940	B/W lines, dot inlay	$3,500	$4,300

Style 3C K ukulele

Concert size 3K.

c.1930		$5,500	$9,000

Style 3 Taro Patch

Mahogany body, 8 strings, multiple bound.

c.1941		$2,600	$3,000

Style 3K Taro Patch

Koa body Style 3.

c.1929		$3,600	$4,000

Style 5K ukulele

Highly figured koa body, all pearl trimmed.

c.1926		$6,000	$8,000

Style 5M ukulele

Mahogany body style 5, 1941 only.

1941		$10,000	$12,000

Style 51 Baritone ukulele

Mahogany body, bound body.

c.1966		$950	$1,500

Style T 15 Tiple

Mahogany body, 10 metal strings, unbound.

c.1971		$500	$700

Style T 17 Tiple

Mahogany body, unbound.

c.1950		$750	$1,100

Style T 28 Tiple

Rosewood body, bound body.

c.1969		$1,500	$1,900

Mirabella

Custom ukuleles built by luthier Cristian Mirabella in Babylon, New York. He also builds guitars and mandolins.

National

To capitalize on the success of their "amplifying" guitars, the Dopyera brothers introduced mental-bodied ukuleles and mandolins as well, though rather large and ungainly by today's standards. Their switch to a smaller body shape produced an elegant and sweet-sounding resonator uke that became much soughtafter. Currently National offers a couple of uke models.

Style 1 ukulele

Nickel body.

c.1928	Tenor size, 6 in. resonator	$2,500	$4,000
c.1933	Soprano size	$2,500	$4,000

Style 2 ukulele

Nickel body, engraved roses.

c.1928	Tenor size	$4,000	$6,000
c.1931	Soprano size	$4,000	$6,000

Martin 2K Tenor

Martin 2M Concert

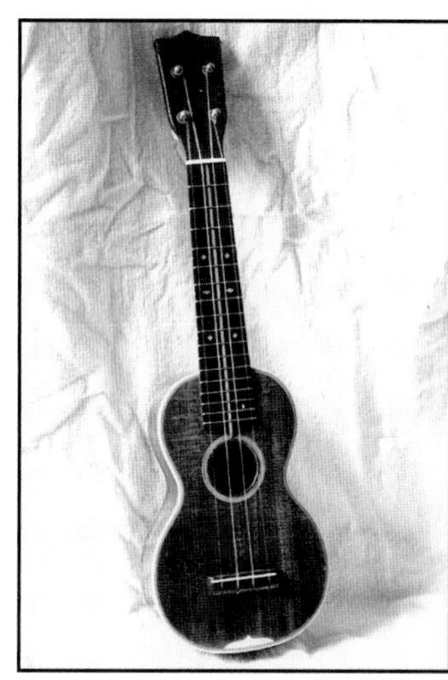

Martin Style 3K

Regal Archtop Uke

Regal Jungle Uke

Regal Wendell Hall Red Head

MODEL YEAR	FEATURES	EXC. COND. LOW	HIGH

Style 3 ukulele

Nickel body, lilies of the valley.

c.1929	Tenor size	$4,000	$7,000
c.1933	Soprano	$5,000	$8,000

Style O ukulele

Metal body, soprano size, sanblasted. scenes.

c.1931		$2,000	$2,850

Triolian ukulele

c.1928	Sunburst painted body, tenor	$1,400	$1,850
c.1930	Sunburst painted body, soprano	$1,600	$2,200
c.1934	Wood-grained metal body, soprano	$1,200	$1,550

Oscar Schmidt

The same New Jersey manufacturer responsible for Leadbelly's 12 string guitar offered ukes as well during that same period.

Soprano ukulele

Spruce top, bound mahogany body.

c.1930		$200	$250

Pegasus Guitars and Ukuleles

1977-present. Ukulele family instruments built by luthier Bob Gleason in Kurtistown, Hawaii, who also builds steel-string guitars.

Polk-a-lay-lee

These inexplicably shaped oddities were produced by Petersen Products of Chicago circa the mid-1960s, and common wisdom has it that their intent was to be offered as giveaways for the Polk Brothers, a local appliance chain. This may be how they ended up, although the gargantuan original packaging makes no reference to any such promotion. The box does call out what the optional colors were.

Many have noted the striking similarity to the similarly named wares of the Swaggerty company (see Swaggerty) of California, who also offered brightly colored plywood-bodied ukes in comical shapes and sizes, but who was copying whom has yet to be determined.

Ukulele

Long "boat oar" body, uke scale.

c.1965	Brown	$150	$250
c.1965	Natural	$150	$250
c.1965	Red body	$150	$250
c.1965	Black	$150	$250

Regal

Like the other large Chicago makers, Harmony, Kay, and Lyon & Healy, the good Regal ukes are very, very good, and the cheap ukes are very, *very* cheap. Unlike its pals, however, Regal seems to have produced more ukuleles in imaginative themes, striking color schemes, and in more degrees of fancy trim.

MODEL YEAR	FEATURES	EXC. COND. LOW	HIGH

Resonator ukulele

Black body, f holes, see Dobro uke.

c.1934		$1,200	$1,500

Soprano ukulele

c.1930	Figured mahogany body, multiple bound top	$450	$650
c.1930	Koa body, multi-colored rope bound top	$250	$300
c.1931	Birch body, brown sunburst finish	$150	$250
c.1935	Spruce top mahogany body, inlays	$350	$650
c.1940	Mahogany body, extended fingerboard	$200	$300
c.1945	Painted birch body, "victory" themes	$400	$550

Tiple

c.1930	Birch body stained dark, black binding	$350	$450
c.1935	Spruce top, mahogany body, fancy binding	$450	$550

Wendell Hall Red Head

Koa body, celebrity decal on headstock.

c.1935		$400	$600

Sammo

Flashy internal paper labels trumpet that these ukes, mandolins and guitars were products of the "Osborne Mfg. Co. Masonic Temple, Chicago-Ill" and what the heck any of that means is still open to speculation. Still, the high quality and often opulent degree of ornamentation that the instruments exhibit, coupled with even the vaguest implication that they were made by guys wearing fezzes and/or men who ride around in tiny cars at parades is all the reason I need to buy every one I see.

Soprano ukulele

c.1925	Figured maple body, 5-ply body binding	$250	$350
c.1925	Unbound koa body, fancy headstock shape	$250	$350

Silvertone

Silvertone was the house brand of Sears after WWII, and most (if not all) of their ukes were manufactured by Harmony.

Soprano ukulele

Mahogany body, Harmony-made.

c.1950	Sunburst	$100	$150
c.1950	Unbound	$100	$150
c.1955	Bound	$100	$150
c.1960	Green	$100	$150

MODEL YEAR	FEATURES	EXC. COND. LOW	HIGH

Slingerland

Banjo ukuleles bearing this brand (see Slingerland Banjo uke section) were certainly made by this popular drum company. Slingerland standard ukuleles, on the other hand, bear an uncanny resemblance to the work of the Oscar Schmidt company.

Soprano ukulele

Koa body, top and soundhole rope bound.

c.1920		$250	$300

Specimen Products

1984-present. Luthier Ian Schneller builds his ukuleles in Chicago, Illinois. He also builds guitars, basses, tube amps and speaker cabinets.

S.S. Stewart

Not much is known about the ukuleles of this Philadelphia firm, except that they were most certainly sub-contracted from another maker.

Soprano ukulele

Mahogany bound body.

c.1927		$250	$350

Sterling

A minute reference on the headstock decal to a "T.B. Co." must mean that Sterling somehow fit into the mind-numbing Tonk Bros./Lyon & Healy/Regal/S.S.Stewart manufacturing puzzle. Nonetheless the brand must have been reserved for the cream of the crop, and Sterling ukes tend to be of the drop-dead-gorgeous variety.

Soprano ukulele

Flamed Koa, multiple fancy binding all over.

c.1935		$900	$1,500

Stetson

Popular misconception - and wishful thinking - has it that all instruments labeled with the Stetson brand were the work of the Larson Brothers of Chicago. Some guitars and a few mandolins may be genuine Larson product, but the ukes surely were fashioned elsewhere.

Soprano ukulele

Mahogany body, single bound body.

c.1930		$180	$225

Supertone

Supertone was the name attached to Sears' musical instruments before a name change to Silvertone (see above) occurred around the time of WWII. These, too, were all Harmony made.

Soprano ukulele

Harmony-made.

c.1930	Mahogany, unbound	$150	$200
c.1935	Koa, rope bound	$250	$350
c.1940	Mahogany, bound	$150	$200
c.1943	Koa, unbound	$150	$250

Swaggerty

Little is known of this west coast company, except that their line of unusually shaped four stringed novelty instruments oddly mirrors those made by Petersen Products in Chicago at the same time (see Polk-a-lay-lee). The two companies even seem to have shared plastic parts, such as fingerboards and tuners. Go figure.

Surf-a-lay-lee

Plywood body, long "horn, green, orange or yellow."

c. 1965		$150	$250

Tabu

The "Tabu" brand on either the back of a ukulele's headstock or inside its soundhole was never an indication of its original maker. Rather, it was intended to assure the purchaser that the uke was, indeed of bona fide Hawaiian origin. So rampant was the practice of mainland makers claiming Island manufacture of their wares, that in the late 'teens Hawaii launched a campaign to set the record straight. The Tabu mark actually was used to mark the ukes of several different makers.

Soprano ukulele

Figured koa body.

c.1915	Rope bound	$600	$750
c.1915	Unbound	$450	$600

Vega

Famous for their banjos, the Vega name was applied to a sole baritone uke, tied with the endorsement of Arthur Godfrey.

Arthur Godfrey Baritone

Unbound mahogany body.

c.1955		$250	$350

Washburn

See Lyon & Healy.

Weissenborn

The mainland maker famous for their hollow-necked Hawaiian guitars was responsible for several uke offerings over the course of its 20-or-so-year run. Like their six-stringed big brothers, they were the closest to Island design and detail to come from the mainland.

Soprano ukulele

Figured koawood body.

c.1920	Rope bound	$800	$1,400
c.1920	Unbound	$650	$950

Weyman

Renowned for fine tenor banjos, Weyman offered a full line of soprano ukes of varying degrees of decoration, quite certainly none of which were made under the same roof as the banjos.

Soprano ukulele

c.1925	Mahogany, unbound	$300	$500
c.1930	Koa, fancy pearl vine fingerboard inlay	$1,200	$1,500

Supertone Cheerleader

Sammo

Weissenborn

Gibson BU 3

Ludwig Banjo Uke

MODEL YEAR	FEATURES	EXC. COND. LOW	HIGH

Banjo Ukuleles

Bacon

This Connecticut banjo maker just couldn't resist the temptation to extend their line with uke versions of their popular banjos. As with Gibson, Ludwig, Slingerland, and Weyman, the banjo ukuleles tended to mimic the already proven construction techniques and decorative motifs of their regular banjo counterparts. In materials, inlay, finish, and hardware, most banjo ukes share many more similarities with full sized banjos than differences. The banjo ukes were simply included as smaller sized variations, much as concert, tenor, and later, baritone options fleshed out standard ukulele lines.

Banjo ukulele

Walnut rim, fancy fingerboard inlays.

c.1927		$900	$1,200

Silver Bell banjo ukulele

Engraved pearloid fingerboard & headstock.

c.1927		$1,500	$2,000

Gibson

BU 1 banjo ukulele

Small 6" head, flat panel resonator.

c.1928		$400	$500

BU 2 banjo ukulele

8" head, dot inlay.

c.1930		$500	$650

BU 3 banjo ukulele

8" head, diamond and square inlay.

c.1935		$800	$1,200

BU 4 banjo ukulele

8" head, resonator and flange.

c.1932		$1,000	$1,500

BU 5 banjo ukulele

8" head, resonator and flange, gold parts.

c.1937		$1,500	$2,000

Le Domino

Banjo ukulele

Resonator, decorated as Le Domino uke.

c.1933		$200	$500

Ludwig

Wendell Hall Professional

Walnut resonator, nickel-plated flange.

c.1930		$1,100	$1,500

Regal

Banjo ukulele

Mahogany rim, resonator, fancy rope bound.

c.1933		$350	$550

Richter

Allegedly, this Chicago company bought the already-made guitars, ukes, and mandolins of other manufacturers, painted and decorated them to their liking and resold them.

Banjo ukulele

2 f-holes in back.

c.1930	Chrome plated body	$200	$300
c.1930	Painted body and neck	$200	$300

Slingerland

May Bell banjo ukulele

Walnut resonator with multicolored rope.

c.1935		$350	$450

Weyman

Banjo ukulele

Maple rim, open back, ebony fingerboard.

c.1926		$650	$800

Bibliography

'50's Cool: Kay Guitars, by Jay Scott, 1992, Seventh String Press, Inc.

Acoustic Guitars and Other Fretted Instruments, A Photographic History, by George Gruhn and Walter Carter, 1993, GPI Books.

American Guitars, An Illustrated History, by Tom Wheeler, 1992, Harper Collins.

Ampeg - The Story Behind The Sound, by Gregg Hopkins and Bill Moore, 1999, Hal Leonard publishing.

Amps! The Other Half of Rock 'n' Roll, by Ritchie Fliegler, 1993, Hal Leonard publishing.

Art as an Investment and the Underperformance of Masterpieces: Evidence from 1875-2000, by Jiangping Mei, Ph.D. and Michael Moses, Ph.D., 2001, Abstract, New York University.

The Bass Book, A Complete Illustrated History of Bass Guitars, by Tony Bacon and Barry Moorhouse, 1995, Miller Freeman Books.

The Boss Book, 2001, Hal Leonard Publishing.

The Burns Book, by Paul Day, 1990, PP Publishing and The Bold Strummer.

Classic Guitars U.S.A., by Willie G. Moseley, 1992, Centerstream.

The Complete History of Rickenbacker Guitars, by Richard R. Smith, 1987, Centerstream.

Consumer Demand and the Social Construction of Industry, Working Paper #22, by Thomas Ford Brown, Ph.D, John Hopkins University.

A Desktop Reference of Hip Vintage Guitar Amps, by Gerald Weber, 1994, Kendrick Books.

Economics: An Analysis of Unintended Consequences - Volume One Microeconomics, by Robert E. Schenk, Ph. D., 1988 Ingrid Germayne, Publisher, Rensselaer, IN.

Electric Guitars and Basses, A Photographic History, by George Gruhn and Walter Carter, 1994, GPI Books.

Elektro-Gitarren Made in Germany, by Norbert Schnepel and Helmuth Lemme (German, with English translation), 1987, Musik-Verlag Schnepel-Lemme oHG.

Epiphone: The Complete History, by Walter Carter, 1995, Hal Leonard publishing.

Epiphone: The House of Stathopoulo, by Jim Fisch & L.B. Fred, 1996, Amsco Publications.

The Fender Amp Book, by John Morrish, 1995, Balafon Books and GPI Books.

Fender Amps: The First Fifty Years, by John Teagle and John Sprung, 1995, Hal Leonard Publishing.

The Fender Bass, by Klaus Blasquiz, 1990, Mediapresse.

The Fender Bass, An Illustrated History, by J.W. Black and Albert Molinaro, 2001, Hal Leonard Publishing.

The Fender Book, by Tony Bacon and Paul Day, 1992, Balafon and GPI Books.

Fender: The Sound Heard 'Round the World, by Richard R. Smith, 1995, Garfish Publishing.

The Fender Stratocaster, by Andre Duchossoir, 1988, Mediapresse.

The Fender Telecaster, by Andre Duchossoir, 1991, Hal Leonard Publishing.

G&L: Leo's Legacy, by Paul Bechtoldt, 1994, Woof Associates.

Gibson Electrics, The Classic Years, by A. R. Duchossoir, 1994, Hal Leonard Publishing.

Gibson's Fabulous Flat-Top Guitars, by Eldon Whitford, David Vinopal, and Dan Erlewine, 1994, GPI Books.

Gibson Guitars: 100 Years of An American Icon, by Walter Carter, 1994, W. Quay Hays.

The Gibson Les Paul Book, A Complete History of Les Paul Guitars, by Tony Bacon and Paul Day, 1993 Balafon Books and GPI Books.

The Gibson Super 400, Art of the Fine Guitar, by Thomas A. Van Hoose, 1991, GPI Books.

Gibson Shipping Totals 1948-1979, 1992, J.T.G.

The Gretsch Book, by Tony Bacon & Paul Day, 1996, Balafon Books and GPI Books.

Gruhn's Guide to Vintage Guitars, 2nd Edition, by George Gruhn and Walter Carter, 1999, Miller Freeman Books.

The Guild Guitar Book: The Company and the Instruments 1952-1977, by Hans Moust, 1995, GuitArchives Publications.

Guitar Identification: Fender-Gibson-Gretsch-Martin, by Andre Duchossoir, 1983, Hal Leonard Publishing Corporation.

Guitar People, by Willie G. Moseley, 1997, Vintage Guitar Books.

Guitar Player magazine, various issues, Miller Freeman.

Guitar Stories, Vol. I, by Michael Wright, 1994, Vintage Guitar Books.

Guitar Stories, Vol. II, by Michael Wright, 2000, Vintage Guitar Books.

Guitar World magazine, various issues, Harris Publications.

The Guitars of the Fred Gretsch Company, by Jay Scott, 1992, Centerstream.

Guitars From Neptune, A Definitive Journey Into Danelectro-Mania, by Paul Bechtoldt, 1995, Backporch Publications.

Guitar Graphics, Vol. 1 (Japanese), 1994, Rittor Music Mooks.

The Guru's Guitar Guide, by Tony Bacon and Paul Day, 1990, Track Record and The Bold Strummer.

The History and Artistry of National Resonator Instruments, by Bob Brozman, 1993, Centerstream.

The History of Marshall, by Michael Doyle, 1993, Hal Leonard Publishing.

The History of the Ovation Guitar, by Walter Carter, 1996, Hal Leonard publishing.

The Martin Book, by Walter Carter, 1995, Balafon Books and GPI Books.

Martin Guitars, A History, by Mike Longworth, 1988, 4 Maples Press.

Martin Guitars: An Illustrated Celebration of America's Premier Guitarmaker, by Jim Washburn & Richard Johnston, 1997, Rodale Press, Inc.

The Official Vintage Guitar Magazine Price Guide, all editions.

The PRS Guitar Book, by Dave Burrluck, 1999, Outline Press, London.

Rickenbacker, by Richard R. Smith, 1987, Centerstream Publishing

The Rickenbacker Book, by Tony Bacon & Paul Day, 1994, Balafon Books and GFI Books.

Stellas & Stratocasters, by Willie G. Moseley, 1994, Vintage Guitar Books.

Stompbox, by Art Thompson, 1997, Miller Freeman Books.

The Tube Amp Book, 4th Edition, by Aspen Pittman, 1993, Groove Tubes.

The Ultimate Guitar Book, by Tony Bacon and Paul Day, 1991, Alfred A. Knopf.

Vintage Guitar magazine, various issues, Vintage Guitar, Inc.

VG Classics magazine, various issues, Vintage Guitar, Inc.

The Vox Story, A Complete History of the Legend, by David Peterson and Dick Denney, 1993, The Bold Strummer, Ltd.

Washburn: Over One Hundred Years of Fine Stringed Instruments, by John Teagle, 1996, Amsco Publications.

Various manufacturer catalogs, literature, and web sites.

Dealer Directory
A Geographical Guide

CANADA

Folkway Music
Contact: Mark Stutman
163 Suffolk Street West
Guelph, Ontario N1H2N7
Phone: 519-763-5524
e-mail: info@folkwaymusic.com
web: www.folkwaymusic.com

The Twelfth Fret Inc.
Contact: Grant MacNeill and David Wren
2132 Danforth Avenue
Toronto, Ont., Canada M4C 1J9
Phone: 416-423-2132
Fax: 416-423-0012
e-mail: sales@12fret.com
web: www.12fret.com

ENGLAND

Ampaholics
Contact: Paul GT
P.O. Box 542
Surrey, GU1 12F, England
Phone: +44-1483-825102
Fax: +44-1483-825102
web: www.ampaholics.org.uk

Watford Valves & Speakers
Contact: Derek Rocco
Bricket Wood, Street Albans.
Herts. England AL2 3TS
Phone: 44-1923-893270
Fax: 44-1923-679207
e-mail: sales@watfordvalves.com
web: www.watfordvalves.com

GERMANY

Guitar and Coffee Shop GvR
Wilhelmstr. 9 D68723
Plankstadt, Germany
Phone: +49-06202-126811
Fax: +49-06202-127032
e-mail: guitar-coffee-shop@t-online.de
web: www.guitar-coffee-shop.com

ITALY

Real Vintage
Contact: Nino Fazio
via Manzoni, 13
98057 Milazzo ME, Italy
Phone: +39-090-40646
e-mail: realvintage@realvintage.it
web: www.realvintage.it

UNITED STATES

Arizona

Antique Electronic Supply
Contact: Brian Campanella
6221 South Maple Avenue
Tempe, AZ 85283
Phone: 480-820-5411
Fax: 800-706-6789
e-mail: info@tubesandmore.com
web: www.tubesandmore.com

CE Distribution
Contact: Noreen Cravener
6221 South Maple Avenue
Tempe, AZ 85283
Phone: 480-755-4712
Fax: 480-820-4643
e-mail: info@cedist.com
web: www.cedist.com

Willies Music
Contact: Willie
P.O. Box 1090
Dewey, AZ 86327
Phone: 928-632-0528
Fax: 928-632-9052
Cell: 928-713-3956
e-mail: willieduck@yahoo.com

Arkansas

Blue Moon Music, Inc.
Contact: Les Haynie
1904 North College
Fayetteville, AR 72703
Phone: 501-521-8163
e-mail: blumnmus@aol.com
web: bluemoonmusic.com

Blue Moon Music, Inc.
Contact: Les Haynie
1706 South East Walton Blvd., Suite A
Bentonville, AR 72712
Phone: 479-271-2455
e-mail: blumnmus@aol.com
web: bluemoonmusic.com

California

AA-Ibanez/Gibson Guitar Collector
All 1970's - '80s Japanese Relics - Archtops/Semi-hollows/Solids
Phone: 310-672-2432
e-mail: bluesfingers@earthlink.net

Aantone's Music
Contact: Antone
36601 Newark Boulevard #11
Newark, CA 94560
Phone: 510-795-9170
Fax: 510-795-9170
e-mail: aantones@pacbell.net
web: www.aantones.com

Bad Cat Amps
Contact: James Heidrich
PMB #406, 2621 Green River Road
Corona, CA 92882
Phone: 909-808-8651
Fax: 909-279-6383
e-mail: badcatamps@earthlink.net
web: www.badcatamps.com

Bill Lawrence Pickups
Contact: Bill or Becky Lawrence
1785 Pomona Road, Unit D
Corona, CA 92880
Phone: 909-737-5853
Fax: 909-737-7834
e-mail: becky@billlawrence.com
web: billlawrence.com

Buffalo Bros. Guitars
Contact: Bob or Tim Page
2270-C Camino Vida Roble
Carlsbad, CA 92009
Phone: 760-431-9542
Fax: 760-431-9532
e-mail: BuffaloBros@aol.com
web: www.buffalobrosguitars.com

Chandler Musical Instruments
Contact: Paul
Phone: 530-899-1503
web: www.chandlerguitars.com
www.pickguards.us

Demeter Amplification
Contact: James Demeter
15730 Stagg Street
Van Nuys, CA 91406
Phone: 818-994-7658
Fax: 818-994-0647
e-mail: info@demeteramps.com
web: www.demeteramps.com

Eric Schoenberg Guitars
Contact: Eric
106 Main Street
Tiburon, CA 94920
Phone: 415-789-0846
e-mail: eric@om28. com
web: www.om28.com

Freedom Guitar, Inc.
Contact: Dewey L. Bowen
6334 El Cajon Boulevard
San Diego, CA 92115
Phone: 800-831-5569
Fax: 619-265-1414
e-mail: info@freedomguitar.com
web: www.freedomguitar.com

Guitar Center (CA)
7425 Sunset Boulevard
Hollywood, CA 90046
Phone: 323-874-2302
323-874-1060
Fax: 323-969-9783
web: www.vintageguitars.net

Guitar Heaven (CA)
Contact: Frank Benna
1892 Contra Costa Boulevard
Pleasant Hill, CA 94523
Phone: 925-687-5750
e-mail: guitarheaven@juno.com
web: www.guitarheaven.com

Koz-ax's
Contact: Jeff
Phone: 909-397-0991
e-mail: jeff@kozaxs.com
web: www.kozaxs.com

Neal's Music
Contact: Neal and Cathy Shelton
16458 Bolsa Chica Road PMB133
Huntington Beach, CA 92647
Phone: 714-901-5393
Fax: 714-901-5383
e-mail: nealmuzic@aol.com
web: www.nealsmusic.com

Players Vintage Instsruments
P.O. Box 445

Inverness, CA 94937-0445
Phone: 415-669-1107
Fax: 415-669-1102
e-mail: info@vintageinstruments.com
web: www.vintageinstruments.com
Sales by Internet/Phone/Appointment

Soest Guitar Shop
Contact: Steve Soest
760 North Main Street Suite D
Orange, CA 92668
Phone: 714-538-0272
Fax: 714-532-4763
e-mail: soestguitar@earthlink.net
web: www.soestguitar.com

Virtual Vintage Guitars
Contact: Jason C. Allen
Phone: 949-635-9797
e-mail: sales@virtualvintageguitars.com
web: www.virtualvintageguitars.com

Virtuoso Polish and Cleaner
The Virtuoso Group, Inc.
P.O. Box 9775
Canoga Park, CA 91309-0775
Phone: 818-992-4733
e-mail: sales@virtuosopolish.com
web: www.virtuosopolish.com

Wild West Guitars
Contact: Bo Harrison
1546 7th Street
Riverside, CA 92507
Phone: 909-369-7888 x205
Fax: 909-369-7371
e-mail: sales@wildwestguitars.com
web: www.wildwestguitars.com

Wings Guitar Products, Inc.
Contact: Art Wiggs
5622 Comanche Court
San Jose, CA 95123
Phone: 408-225-2162
Fax: 408-225-5147

Connecticut

Acousticmusic.org/Serious Strings
Contact: Brian Wolfe
1238 Boston Post Road
Guilford, CT 06437
Phone: 203-458-2525
e-mail: brian@seriousstrings.com
web: www.acousticmusic.org

Analog Man Guitar Effects
Contact: Mike Piera
36 Tamarack Avenue #343
Danbury, CT 06811
Phone: 203-778-6658
e-mail: AnalogMike@aol.com
web: www.analogman.com

Guitar Hanger
Contact: Rick Tedesco
61 Candlewood Lake Road
Brookfield, CT 06804
Phone: 203-740-8889
Fax: 203-730-8327
e-mail: sales@guitarhanger.com
web: www.guitarhanger.com

Florida

Andy's Guitars
Contact: Andy
1208 North Monroe Street
Tallahassee, FL 32303
Phone: 850-224-9944
Fax: 850-224-5381
e-mail: info@andysguitars.com
web: www.andysguitars.com

Crescent City Music
Contact: Allen Glenn
111 North Summit Street
Crescent City, FL 32112
Phone/Fax: 386-698-2873
Phone: 386-698-2874
e-mail: ccmusic@crescentcitymusic.biz
web: www.crescentcitymusic.biz

Dixie Guitar Trader
Contact: Tom Williams
5068 North Dixie Highway
Ft. Lauderdale, FL 33334
Phone: 954-772-6900
e-mail: dixieguitar@aol.com

Guitar Avenue LLC
Contact: Gary Winterflood
1733 Kewka Avenue
New Port Richey, FL 34655-6731
e-mail: guitarav@tampa.rr.com
web: www.guitaravenue.com

Guitar Broker
Contact: Craig Brody
Phone: 954-385-8488
Fax: 954-349-1943
e-mail: vintage@guitarbroker.com
web: www.guitarbroker.com

Kummer's Vintage Instruments
Contact: Timm Kummer
Phone: 954-752-6063
e-mail: prewar99@aol.com
web: www.kummersvintage.com

Legends Music, Inc.
Contact: Kent Sonenberg
4340 West Hillsborough Avenue
Tampa, FL 33614
Phone: 813-348-0688
fax: 813-348-0689
e-mail: sales@legendsmusic.com
web: www.legendsmusic.com

Music Magic
Contact: Robert Graupera
1135 West 68th Street
Hialeah, FL 33014
Phone: 305-556-6656
Fax: 305-556-0834
e-mail: UsedGuitar@aol.com
web: www.magicguitars.com

Georgia

Atlanta Vintage Guitars
Contact: Frank Moates
561 Windy Hill Road
Smyrna, GA 30080
Phone: 770-433-1891
Fax: 770-433-1858
e-mail: avg@mindspring.com
web: www.atlantavintageguitars.com

Dreamcatcher Guitars
Contact: Eddie Mathis
26 Webb Street Suite. 1
Roswell, GA 30075
Phone: 877-241-2359
Fax: 770-587-9962
e-mail: guitars@gtrs4u.com
web: www.dreamcatcherguitars.com

Hawaii

Coconut Grove Music
Contact: Fred Oshiro
418 Kuulei Road
Kailua, HI 96734
Phone: 808-262-9977
Fax: 808-263-7052
e-mail: cgmusic@lava.net
web: www.coconutgrovemusic.com

Illinois

Chicago Music Exchange
Contact: Scott Silver
3270 North Clark Street
Chicago, IL 60657
Phone: 773-477-0830
Fax: 773-477-0427
e-mail: sales@chicagomusicexchange.com
web: www.chicagomusicexchange.com

Guitar Works Ltd
Contact: Steve or Terry
709 Main Street
Evanston, IL 60202
Phone: 847-475-0855
Fax: 847-475-0715
e-mail: guitarworksltd@aol.com
web: www.guitarworksltd.com

Make 'n Music
Contact: Greg
250 North Artesian
Chicago, IL 60612
Phone: 312-455-1970
e-mail: makenmusic@earthlink.net

Music Gallery
Contact: Frank
2558 Greenbay Road
Highland Park, IL 60035
Phone: 847-432-6350 / 847-432-8883
e-mail: MusicGlry@aol.com
web: www.musicgalleryinc.com

RWK Guitars
P.O. Box 1068
Highland Park, IL 60035
Phone: 800-454-7078
e-mail: Bob@RWKGuitars.com
web: www.RWKGuitars.com

Indiana

The Music Shoppe
Contact: John Beeson
1427 South 25th Street
Terre Haute, IN 47803
Phone: 812-232-4095
Fax: 812-238-1901
e-mail: themusicshoppe@abcs.com
web: www.abcs.com/themusicshoppe

WeberVST
Contact: T.A. Weber
329 E Firmin Street
Kokomo, IN 46902
Phone: 765-452-1249
Fax: 765-236-0270
web: www.webervst.com

www.weberspeakers.com

Kansas

E.M. Shorts Guitars
Contact: Jon Ray
2525 East Douglas Avenue
Wichita, KS 67211
Phone: 800-835-3006
Fax: 316-684-6858
e-mail: wbic@wichitaband.com
web: www.wichitaband.com

Overland Express Guitars
Contact: David Schaefer
10739 West 109th Street
Overland Park, KS 66210
Phone: 913-469-4034
Fax: 913-469-9672
e-mail: dave@overlandexpress.com
web: www.overlandexpress.com

Kentucky

Guitar Emporium
1610 Bardstown Road
Louisville, KY 40205
Phone 502-459-4153
Fax: 502-454-3661
e-mail:
guitar-emporium@mind
spring.com
web: www.guitar-emporium.com

Willcutt Guitars
419 Rosemont Garden
Lexington, KY 40503
Phone: 859-276-3519
e-mail: info@willcuttguitars.com
web: www.willcuttguitars.com

Louisianna

International Vintage Guitars
Contact: Steve Staples
1011 Magazine Street
New Orleans, LA 70130
Phone: 504-524-4557
Fax: 504-524-4665
e-mail: guitars@comm.net
web: www.webcorral.com

Maryland

First World Guitar Congress
Contact: Dr. Helene Breazeale
8000 York Road
Admin Bldg 423
Baltimore, MD 21252-0001
Phone: 410-704-2451
Fax: 410-704-4012
e-mail: hbreazeale@towson.edu
web: www.towson.edu/world
musiccongresses

Garrett Park Guitars, Inc.
Contact: Rick Hogue or Dylan Steele
150 East Jennifer Road 150-0
Annapolis, MD 21401
Phone: 401-573-0500
Fax: 401-573-0502
e-mail: gpguitars@toad.net
web: www.gpguitars.com

Guitar Exchange
Contact: Bruce Sandler
740 Frederick Road
Baltimore, MD 21228
Phone: 410-747-0122
Fax: 410-747-0525

Nationwide Guitars
Contact: Bruce Rickard
P.O. Box 2334
Columbia, MD 21045
Phone: 410-997-7440
Fax: 410-997-7440
e-mail: bigredjr@comcast.net

Southworth Guitars
Contact: Gil Southworth
7845 Old Georgetown Road
Bethesda, MD 20814
Phone: 301-718-1667
Fax: 301-718-0391
e-mail: southworthguitar@aol.com
web: www.southworth
guitars.com

Massachusetts

Bay State Vintage Guitars
Contact: Craig D. Jones
295 Huntington Avenue, Room 304
Boston, MA 02115
Phone: 617-267-6077

Cold Springs Electrical Works
Contact: Norm Moren
332 Rock Rimmon Road
Belchertown, MA 01007
Phone: 413-323-8869
e-mail: norm@coldsprings
electricalworks.com
web: www.coldsprings
electricalworks.com

The Guitar Shelter
Contact: Ken Kirklewski
270 Main Street, Unit 4
Buzzards Bay, MA 02532-3257
Phone: 508-743-0663
Fax: 508-743-9400
e-mail: gtrshelter@aol.com
web: www.guitarshelter.com

Lucchesi Vintage Instruments
Contact: Frank Lucchesi
518 Pleasant Street
Holyoke, MA 01040
Phone: 413-532-8819
Fax: 413-532-9504
e-mail: LoukZ2@aol.com

The Perfect Note
Contact: Bob Ogulnick
Wales, MA 01057
Phone: 413-267-3392
Fax: 413-267-3392

RC Guitars
Contact: Corey Buckingham or Justin Kolack
378 Highland Avenue
Somerville, MA 02144
Phone: 617-623-7100
888-964-7100
e-mail: rcg@rockcityguitar.com

Michigan

Elderly Instruments
Contact: Stan Werbin
1100 North Washington
P.O. Box 14210 -VGF
Lansing, MI 48901
Phone: 517-372-7890
Fax: 517-372-5155
e-mail: elderly@elderly.com
web: www.elderly.com

Huber & Breese Music
33540 Groesbeck Highway
Fraser, MI 48026
Phone: 586-294-3950
Fax: 586-294-7616
e-mail: handbmusic@aol.com
web: www.huberbreese.com

Rockin' Daddy's
Contact: Randy Volin
P.O. Box 210368
Auburn Hills, MI 48321
Fax: 248-420-8499
e-mail: gtrs@rockindaddys.com
web: www.rockindaddys.com

Minnesota

Schaefer Guitars
Contact: Ed Schaefer
4221 West 4th Street
Duluth, MN 55807
Phone: 218-624-7231
e-mail: sguitars@airmail.net
web: www.schaeferguitars.com

Solidbodyguitar.com
Contact: Bruce Barnes
2566 Highway 10
Mounds View, MN 55112
Phone: 763-783-0080
Fax: 763-783-0090
e-mail: solidbodyguitar@
quest.net
web: www.solidbodyguitar.com

Willie's American Guitars
254 Cleveland Avenue South
St. Paul, MN 55105
Phone: 651-699-1913
Fax: 651-690-1766
e-mail: willies@ix.netcom.com
web: www.williesguitars.com

Missouri

Fly By Night Music
Contact: Dave Crocker
103 South Washington
Neosho, MO 64850-1816
Phone: 417-451-5110
Show number: 800-356-3347
e-mail: crocker@joplin.com
web: www.texasguitarshows.com

Grubville Guitars
Contact: Glen Meyers
P.O. Box 14
Grubville, MO 63041
Phone: 636-274-4738
Fax: 636-285-9833
e-mail: glencogg@aol.com
web: grubvilleguitars.com

Hazard Ware Inc./ Killer Vintage
Contact: Dave
P.O. Box 190561
St. Louis, MO 63119
Phone: 314-647-7795
800-646-7795
Fax: 314-781-3240
web: www.killervintage.com

Nashville Guitar Show
P.O. Box 271
Kirksville, MO 63501
Phone: 660-665-7172
Fax: 660-665-7450
e-mail: spbgma@kvmo.net

Nevada

AJ's Music In Las Vegas
Contact: Peter Trauth
2764 North Green Valley Parkway
Henderson, NV 89014
Phone: 702-436-9300

Fax: 702-436-9302
e-mail: pete@ajsmusic.com
web: www.ajsmusic.com

Cowtown Guitars
2797 South Maryland Parkway, Suite. 14
Las Vegas, NV 89109
Phone: 888-682-3002
Fax: 702-866-2520
web: www.cowtownguitars.com

New Hampshire

Guitar Gallery of New England
Contact: David Stearns
5 Route 101A #4
Amhearst, NH 03031
Phone: 603-672-9224
e-mail: info@guitargallery.com
web: guitargallery.com

Retro Music
Contact: Jeff Firestone
38 Washington Street
Keene, NH 03431
Phone: 603-357-9732
Fax: 603-358-5185
e-mail: retromusic@webryders.com
web: www.retroguitar.com

New Jersey

Dr. Bob's Guitar & Stringed Instrument Repair
Contact: Robert "Dr. Bob" Pinaire
By Appointment Only
Princeton, NJ Area
Phone: 609-921-1407 or 888-921-2461
Fax: 609-434-1643
e-mail: swtsongman@aol.com
web: www.DrBobsMusic.com

Fuchs Audio Technology
Contact: Andy Fuchs
73 Collins Avenue
Bloomfield, NJ 07003-4504
Phone: 973-893-0225
e-mail: sales@fuchsaudiotechnology.com
web: fuchsaudiotechnology.com

Golden Age Fretted Instruments
Contact: John Paul Reynolds
720 Monroe Street, Suite E209
Hoboken, NJ 07030-6350
Phone: 201-798-1300
Fax: 908-301-0770
e-mail: info@goldenageguitars.com
web: www.goldenageguitars.com

Hi Test Guitars
341 Westwind Court
Norwood, NJ 07648
Phone/Fax: 201-750-2445
By appointment Mon.-Sat. 11-6 EDT

Hoboken Vintage Guitars
Contact: Jim Pasch
164 1st Street
Hoboken, NJ 07030-3544
Phone: 201-222-8977
Fax: 201-222-9127
e-mail: hoboken@extend.net
web: www.hobokenvintage.com

Lark Street Music
479 Cedar Lane
Teaneck, NJ 07666
Phone: 201-287-1959
e-mail: Larkstreet@aol.com
web: www.larkstreet.com

New Jersey Guitar & Bass Center
Contact: Jay Jacus
995 Amboy Avenue
Edison, NJ 08837
Phone: 732-225-4444
Fax: 732-225-4404
e-mail: NJGtrBass@aol.com
web: www.members.aol.com/NJGtrBass

New York

Bernunzio Vintage Guitars
Contact: John Bernunzio
875 East Avenue
Rochester, NY 14607
Phone: 585-473-6140
Fax: 585-442-1142
e-mail: info@bernunzio.com
web: www.bernunzio.com

Diamond Strings
Contact: Bruce Diamond
572 East River Road
Rochester, NY 14623
Phone: 585-424-3369
Fax: 585-475-1818
e-mail: dstrings@rochester.rr.com
web: diamondstrings.com

Gothic City Guitars
Contact: Charles Dellavalle
P.O. Box 123
Staten Island, NY 10310
Phone: 718-273-1691
web: www.GothicCityGuitars.com

Imperial Guitar and Soundworks
Contact: Bill Imperial
99 Route 17K
Newburgh, NY 12550
Phone: 845-567-0111/845-567-0404
e-mail: igs55@aol.com
web: www.imperialguitar.com

Keyboard Instrument Rentals
Buy & Sell Vintage Effects & Pedals
1697 Broadway Suite 504
New York, NY 10019
Phone: 212-245-0820
Fax: 212-245-8858
e-mail: keyboardrentals@aol.com

Laurence Wexer Ltd.
Contact: Larry
251 East 32nd Street #11F
New York, NY 10016
Phone: 212-532-2994
e-mail: info@wexerguitars.com

Ludlow Guitars
Contact: Robert
164 Ludlow Street
New York, NY 10002
Phone: 212-353-1775
Fax: 212-353-1749
web: www.ludlowguitars.com

Mandolin Brothers, Ltd.
629 Forest Avenue
Staten Island, NY 10310
Phone: 718-981-3226/8585
Fax: 718-816-4416
e-mail: mandolin@mandoweb.com
web: www.mandoweb.com

Manny's Music
Contact: Matt DeSilva and Richard Friedman
156 West 48th Street
New York, NY 10036
Phone: 212-819-0576
Fax: 212-391-9250
e-mail: guitarparts1@aol.com

Michael's Music
Contact: Michael Barnett
29 West Sunrise Highway
Freeport, NY 11520
Phone: 5163-379-4111
Fax: 516-379-3058
e-mail: info@michaelsmusic.com
web: www.michaelsmusic.com

Mirabella Guitars & Restorations
Contact: Cris Mirabella
P.O. Box 482
Babylon, NY 11702
Phone: 631-842-3819
Fax: 631-842-3827
e-mail: mirguitars@aol.com
web: www.mirabellaguitars.com

Music Services
Contact: Gary Blankenburg
2008 Wantagh Avenue
Wantagh, NY 11793
Phone: 516-826-2525
e-mail: vcoolg@aol.com
web: www.verycoolguitars.com

Rudy's Music
Contact: Rudy
169 West 48th Street
New York, NY 10036
Phone: 212-391-1699
e-mail: info@rudysmusic.com
web: www.rudysmusic.com

Rumble Seat Music
Contact: Eliot Michael
121 West State St.
Ithica, NY 14850
Phone: 607-277-9236
Fax: 607-277-4593
e-mail: rumble@rumbleseatmusic.com
web: www.rumbleseatmusic.com

Sam Ash Music
Contact: David Davidson
385 Old Country Rd.
Carle Place, NY 11514
Phone: 516-333-8700
Fax: 516-333-8767
e-mail: stratguy98@aol.com
web: www.samashmusic.com

Top Shelf Music
Contact: Scott Freilich
1232 Hertell Ave.
Buffalo, NY 14216
Phone: 716-876-6544
Fax: 716-876-7343
e-mail: shelftop@aol.com
web: www.topshelfmusic.com

Toys From The Attic
Contact: John or Mario

203 Mamaroneck Avenue
White Plains, NY 10601
Phone: 914-421-0069
Fax: 914-328-3852
e-mail: info@tfta.com
web: www.tfta.com

North Carolina

Bee-3 Vintage
Contact: Gary Burnette
25 Arbor Lane
Ashville, NC 28805
Phone: 828-298-2197
email: bee3vintage@hotmail.com
web: www.bee3vintage.com

Carr Amplifiers
Contact: Steve
433 West Salisbury St.
Pittsboro, NC 27312
Phone: 919-545-0747
Fax: 919-545-0739
e-mail: info@carramps.com
web: www.carramps.com

Coleman Music
Contact: Chip Coleman
1021 South Main Street
China Grove, NC 28023
Phone: 704-857-5705
Fax: 704-857-5709
e-mail: sales@colemanmusic.com
web: www.colemanmusic.com

Maverick Music
Contact: Phil Winfield
1100 Kirkview Lane, Suite. 201
Charlotte, NC 28213
Phone: 704-599-3700
Fax: 704-599-3712
e-mail: sales@maverick-music.com
web: www.maverick-music.com

Ohio

Dr. Z Amplification
www.drzamps.com

Fretware Guitars
Contact: Dave Hussung
400 South Main
Franklin, OH 45005
Phone: 937-743-1151
Fax: 937-743-9987
e-mail: guitar@erinet.com
web: www.fretware.cc

Gary's Classic Guitars
Contact: Gary Dick
Cincinnati, OH
Phone: 513-891-0555
Fax: 513-891-9444
e-mail: garysclssc@aol.com
web: www.garysguitars.com

Mike's Music
Contact: Mike Reeder
2615 Vine Street
Cincinnati, OH 45219
Phone: 513-281-4900
Fax: 513-281-4968
web: www.mikesmusicohio.com

String King Products
Contact: John Mosconi
P.O. Box 9083
Akron, OH 44305
Phone: 330-798-1055

Oklahoma

Strings West
Contact: Larry Briggs
P.O. Box 999
20 E. Main Street
Sperry, OK 74073
Phone: 800-525-7273
Fax: 918-288-2888
e-mail: larryb@stringswest.com
web: www.stringswest.com

Oregon

Exceptional Guitars
Contact: Alan R. Buchalter
e-mail: info@exceptionalguitars.com
web: www.exceptionalguitars.com

Kalapuya Music & Trading Co.
Contact: Tim Floro
6791/2 Main Street
Lebanon, OR 97355
Phone: 541-451-3957

McKenzie River Music
455 West 11th
Eugene, OR 97401
Phone: 541-343-9482
Fax: 541-465-9060
web: www.McKenzieRiverMusic.com

Pennsylvania

Alessandro (HoundDog Corp.)
Contact: George Alessandro
933 Robin Lane, P.O. Box 253
Huntington Valley, PA 19006
Phone: 215-355-6424
Fax: 215-355-6424
e-mail: hounddogcorp@msn.com
web: www.alessandro-products.com

Guitar-Villa – Retro Music
Contact: John Slog
216A Nazareth Pike
Bethlehem, PA 18020
Phone: 610-746-9200
Fax: 610-746-9135
e-mail: gvilla@guitar-villa.com
web: www.guitar-villa.com

Guitar-Villa – Retro Music
Contact: John Slog
30 S. Westend Boulevard.
Quakertown, PA 18951
Phone: 215-536-5800
e-mail: gvilla@guitar-villa.com
web: www.guitar-villa.com

JH Guitars
Contact: Jim Heflybower
Pennsylvania
Phone: 610-363-9204
Fax: 610-363-8689
e-mail: JHGuitars@webtv.net
web: www. jhguitars.com

Personalized Covers
Contact: Bob Mansure
Lansdowne, PA 19050
Phone: 800-54-COVERS
800-542-6837
e-mail: bmansure@aol.com
web: www.personalizedcovers.com

Vintage Instruments & Frederick W. Oster Fine Violins
Contact: Fred W. Oster
1529 Pine Street
Philadelphia, PA 19102
Phone: 215-545-1100
Fax: 215-735-3634
web: www.vintage-instruments.com

Tennessee

Chambers Guitars
Contact: Joe
3205 West End Avenue
Nashville, TN 37209
Phone: 615-279-9540
web: www.ChambersGuitars.com

George L's
P.O. Box 238
Madison, TN 37115
Phone: 615-868-6976
Fax: 615-868-4637
web: www.georgels.com

Gruhn Guitars
Contact: George Gruhn
400 Broadway
Nashville, TN 37203
Phone: 615-256-2033
Fax: 615-255-2021
e-mail: gruhn@gruhn.com
web: www.gruhn.com

Guitar Heaven
Contact: Mark Murphy
5211 Hickory Hollow Parkway # 107
Antioch, TN 37013
Phone: 615-717-1470
e-mail: gtrheaven@aol.com
web: www.gtrheaven.com

Kangaroo Amp Covers
Contact: Steve Purcell
P.O. Box 120593
Nashville, TN 37212
Phone: 800-431-5537
615-361-5537
e-mail: info@kangarooampcovers.com
web: www.kangarooampcovers.com

Music Room Guitars
Contact: Brad Gibson
5103 Kingston Pike
Knoxville, TN 37919
Phone: 865-584-0041
Toll Free: 877-584-0099
e-mail: mrgknox@aol.com

Nashville Guitar Show
Contact: Chuck Stearman
P.O. Box 271
Kirksville, MO 63501
Phone: 660-665-7172
Fax: 660-665-7450
e-mail: spbgma@kvmo.net

StringDeals.com
(a division of Guitar Heaven)
Contact: Mark Murphy
5211 Hickory Hollow Parkway #107
Antioch, TN 37013
Phone: 615-717-0600
e-mail: sales@stringdeals.com
web: stringdeals.com

Texas

Allparts
13027 Brittmoore Park Drive
Houston, TX 77041
Phone: 713-466-6414
e-mail: allpartgtr@aol.com
web: www.allparts.com

Eugene's Guitars Plus
Contact: Eugene Robertson
2010 South Buckner Boulevard
Dallas, TX 75217-1823
Phone: 214-391-8677
e-mail: pluspawnguitars@yahoo.com
web: www.texasguitarshows.com

Hill Country Guitars
Contact: Kevin Drew Davis
106 Wimberley Square
Wimberley, TX 78676-5020
Phone: 512-847-8677
web: www.hillcountryguitars.com

Kendrick Amplifiers
Route. 2 P.O. Box 871
Kempner, TX 76539
Phone: 512-932-3130
Fax: 512-932-3135
e-mail: kendrick@kendrick-amplifiers.com
web: kendrick-amplifiers.com

Southpaw Guitars
Contact: Jimmy
5813 Bellaire Boulevard
Houston, TX 77081
Phone: 713-667-5791
Fax: 713-667-4091
e-mail: southpawguitars@sbcglobal.net
web: www.southpawguitars.com

Texas Amigos Guitar Shows
Arlington Guitar Show (The 4 Amigos)
Contact: John or Ruth Brinkmann
Phone: 800-329-2324
Fax: 817-473-1089
web: www.texasguitarshows.com

Chicago/Austin Guitar Show
Contact: Dave Crocker
Phone: 800-356-3347
Fax: 817-473-1089
e-mail: crocker@joplin.com
web: www.texasguitarshows.com

California World Guitar Shows
Contact: Larry Briggs
Phone: 800-525-7273
Fax: 918-288-2888
e-mail: larryb@stringswest.com
web: www.texasguitarshows.com

Van Hoose Vintage Instruments
Contact: Thomas Van Hoose
2722 Raintree Drive
Carrollton, TX 75006
Phone: (days) 972-250-2919 or (eves) 972-418-4863
Fax: 972-250-3644
e-mail: tv0109@flash.net
web: www.vanhoosevintage.com

Waco Vintage Instruments
Contact: John Brinkman
1275 North Main Street, Ste #4
Mansfield, TX 76063
Phone: 817-473-9144
Guitar Show Phone: 888-473-6059

Utah

Intermountain Guitar and Banjo
Contact: Leonard or Kennard
712 East 100 South
Salt Lake City, UT 84102
Phone: 801-322-4682
Fax: 801-355-4023
e-mail: guitarandbanjo@earthlink.com
web: www.guitarandbanjo.net

Virginia

Authentic Guitars
Contact: Michael Hansen
12715-Q Warwick Blvd.
Newport News, VA 23606
Phone: 757-595-4663
web: www.AuthenticGuitars.com

Authentic Guitars - 2nd Store
Contact: Michael Hansen
5251-42 John Tyler Highway
Williamsburg, VA 23185
Phone: 757-259-9711
web: www.AuthenticGuitars.com

Callaham Vintage Guitars & Amps
Contact: Bill Callaham
114 Tudor Drive
Winchester, VA 22603
Phone: 540-955-0294 - Shop
e-mail:callaham@callahamguitars.com
web: www.callahamguitars.com

Legato Guitars
Contact: Bill Fender
107 South West Street, Suite 101
Alexandria, VA 22314
By Appointment Only
e-mail: bfender@legatoguitars.com
web: www.legatoguitars.com

Vintage Sound
Contact: Bill Holter
P.O. Box 11711
Alexandria, VA 22312
Phone: 703-914-2126
Fax: 703-914-1044
e-mail: bhvsound@vintagesound.com
web: www.vintagesound.com
Guitars - Amps - Effects

Washington

Emerald City Guitars
Contact: Jay Boone
83 South Washington in Pioneer Square
Seattle, WA 98104
Phone: 206-382-0231
e-mail: jayboone@emeraldcityguitars.com

Guitarville
Contact: Tommy Steinley
19258 15th Avenue North East
Seattle, WA 98155-2315
Phone: 206-363-8188
Fax: 206-363-0478
e-mail: gv@guitarville.com
web: www.guitarville.com

Jet City Guitars LLC
Contact: Allen Kaatz
6920 Roosevelt Way North East, PMB 135
Seattle, WA 98115
Phone: 206-361-1365
e-mail: contact@jetcityguitars.com
web: www.jetcityguitars.com

Wisconsin

Bizarre Guitars
Contact: Brian Goff
2501 Waunona Way
Madison, WI 53713
Phone: 608-222-8225
e-mail: bdgoff@terracom.net
web: www.bizarreguitars.com

Dave's Guitar Shop
Contact: Dave Rogers
1227 South 3rd Street
La Crosse, WI 54601
Phone: 608-785-7704
Fax: 608-785-7703
e-mail: davesgtr@aol.com
web: www.davesguitar.com

Index

Page numbers indicate guitar listing unless otherwise noted

Page numbers indicate guitar listing unless otherwise noted

Page numbers indicate guitar listing unless otherwise noted

Page numbers indicate guitar listing unless otherwise noted

Page numbers indicate guitar listing unless otherwise noted